Making the Irish American

Making the Irish American

*History and Heritage of the Irish
in the United States*

EDITED BY

J. J. Lee and Marion R. Casey

Copublished with Glucksman Ireland House,
New York University

Developed in Association with the Philip Lief Group, Inc.

New York University Press

NEW YORK AND LONDON

This book has been brought to publication with the generous assistance of the
Irish Institute of New York, Inc., and the estate of Jean Downey.

NEW YORK UNIVERSITY PRESS
New York and London
www.nyupress.org

FRONTISPIECE: In 1921 Margaret Gorman of Washington, D.C., became the first "Miss America" to be crowned at the now famous Atlantic City beauty pageant. The name Gorman, a variation of the Gaelic surname O'Gorman, was principally associated by 1890 with Ireland's counties Antrim, Dublin, and Tipperary. Yet just how aware Miss Gorman, subsequently Mrs. Cahill, was of her Irish ancestry remains unknown. Pictured here literally dressed as Miss America to preside over the 1922 competition, Margaret Gorman represents the complexities of making the Irish American. (Bettmann/CORBIS)

Library of Congress Cataloging-in-Publication Data
Making the Irish American : history and heritage of the Irish in the
United States / J.J. Lee & Marion R. Casey, editors.
p.   cm. — (Ireland House series)
Includes bibliographical references and index.
ISBN-13: 978-0-8147-5218-0 (pbk. : alk. paper)
ISBN-10: 0-8147-5218-7 (pbk. : alk. paper)
ISBN-13: 978-0-8147-5208-1 (cloth : alk. paper)
ISBN-10: 0-8147-5208-X (cloth : alk. paper)
1. Irish Americans—History.   I. Lee, Joseph, 1942– .
II. Casey, Marion R., 1962– . III. Series.
E184.I6M23 2006
973'.049162—dc22   2005024658

In memory of Richard J. Purcell (1887–1950)

Dedication

You will have noticed our dedication of this volume to the memory of Richard Purcell. Most readers will probably wonder who he was, and they are entitled to do so: his name is almost entirely forgotten, even among specialists. It points to some progress in the subject that for all our consciousness of the work still to be done, today's leading practitioners will be remembered, unlike Purcell who, as far as we can ascertain, plowed a lonely pioneering furrow. We don't know nearly as much about him ourselves as we would wish. But we are clear that his name deserves to be honored.

That Purcell is so forgotten reflects on the slow development of a sense of esprit de corps among the historians of Irish America. It is out of that sense of pietas that every self-respecting scholarly community—and, above all, historians—should have for those who helped clear the land, hacked away the undergrowth, began cutting out many of the familiar paths we now take for granted that we dedicate this book to his memory.

Purcell was the first Irish-American historian to try to put the study of Irish America on the scholarly map as a valid subject of inquiry. If he was not quite a voice crying in the wilderness, it was a thankless task, and as far as one can tell, he had no professional need to do so. His reputation was established by the publication in 1918 of his prize-winning 1917 Yale doctorate on *Connecticut in Transition, 1775–1818*, deemed worthy of republication in 1963 as "a classic."[1]

With a "successful" career beckoning within the mainstream of the profession, Purcell was already a recognized scholar, part of the academic establishment associated with the flagship journal, the *American Historical Review*, and holding a history chair at Catholic University in Washington, D.C. Then he moved, by what must have been deliberate choice, from the highly respectable subject of the American Revolution to the unfashionable—and to many of his colleagues, probably even inconceivable—topic of Irish America. At just about the time when the handful of pioneers like Arthur Schlesinger Sr., Marcus Lee Hansen, and George M. Stephenson were making their initial probes, Purcell was pondering the potential of Irish immigration as a research subject. Among the first to appreciate the importance of exploring closely the circumstances of the country of origin, he went to Ireland on a Guggenheim Fellowship in 1926, when he could no doubt have chosen to graze on more salubrious scholarly pastures, and he immersed himself in Irish material. Irish scholarship on emigration was itself so backward at the time that he had to dig out basics for himself, as his painstaking notes testify, some of them preserved in the archives of Catholic University of America and referenced for the first time by Kerby Miller.

Except when interrupted by work for the government during the Second World

War, Purcell kept up a stream of publications, including numerous articles on the nineteenth-century immigrant experience, and no fewer than 175 entries, the biggest number by any contributor, in the *Dictionary of American Biography,* as well as supervising numerous dissertations. It was indispensable, intensive, but unspectacular and largely overlooked work, written almost all the time under pressure and against deadlines; he was making the bricks for the building rather than producing a big book of the type that he could doubtless have written had he chosen more mainstream topics for which the spadework had already been done. It was not the type of career choice fashionable in American academe then or now.[2]

Purcell made mistakes in detail in his work, as David Doyle, one of the few later scholars to even acknowledge his existence, has detected—although, one might add, which of us doesn't?—and one will not be able to provide a full portrait of his scholarly strengths and weaknesses without further exploration. But his story seems to veer close to that of being a prophet without honor among his own people when he could have followed less stony paths. Evidence begins to accumulate, too, that he was far-seeing beyond his published work. Referring to the preface of a Catholic University master's thesis of circa 1934, "The Pioneer Women of Kansas 1854 to 1864" by Ruth Considine (the grandchild of Irish immigrants to Kansas), her niece records, "Her choice of subject was the result of a lecture presented by Doctor Richard J. Purcell, one of her history professors, who commented that if we knew more about the women of history we would know more about history."[3]

That was not a sentiment that was exactly the flavor of the time in the historical profession. That Purcell is almost totally forgotten reflects just how fragile the foundations still were at the time of his death in 1950 for the study of the Irish-American experience. It is also why we have felt it right to dedicate this book to his memory, however much of that memory remains to be recovered. It can hardly be deemed premature recognition.

NOTES

1. Richard J. Purcell, *Connecticut in Transition, 1775–1818* (Washington, D.C.: American Historical Association, 1918).

2. J. J. Lee, "Millennial Reflections on Irish-American History," *Radharc: Chronicles of Glucksman Ireland House, New York University* 1 (2000), 62. See Barbara Braun, *Richard J. Purcell, 1887–1950: A Bio-Bibliography* (Washington, D.C., 1955).

3. Mary Ann Sachse Brown, "Aunt Ruth's Pioneer Woman," the Kansas Collection, available at http://www.kancoll.org/articles/ruthcons.htm.

Contents

List of Illustrations		*xiii*
Preface		*xv*
Acknowledgments		*xvii*

1   Introduction: Interpreting Irish America   1
    J. J. Lee

The Irish Background

2   Modern Ireland: An Introductory Survey   63
    Eileen Reilly

Foundations

3   Scots Irish or Scotch-Irish   151
    David Noel Doyle

4   The Irish in North America, 1776–1845   171
    David Noel Doyle

5   The Remaking of Irish-America, 1845–1880   213
    David Noel Doyle

Conflicts of Identity

6   Ulster Presbyterians and the "Two Traditions" in Ireland
    and America   255
    Kerby A. Miller

7   Religious Rivalry and the Making of Irish-American Identity   271
    Irene Whelan

8   Address to the Ulster-Irish Society of New York, 1939   286
    Henry Noble MacCracken

9   American-Irish Nationalism   289
    Kevin Kenny

10 Refractive History: Memory and the Founders of the
    Emigrant Savings Bank   302
    Marion R. Casey

11   Ubiquitous Bridget: Irish Immigrant Women in Domestic Service
in America, 1840–1930   332
Margaret Lynch-Brennan

12   Labor and Labor Organizations   354
Kevin Kenny

13   Race, Violence, and Anti-Irish Sentiment in the Nineteenth Century   364
Kevin Kenny

Popular Expressions of Identity

14   Irish-American Popular Music   381
Mick Moloney

15   The Irish and Vaudeville   406
Robert W. Snyder

16   Irish Traditional Music in the United States   411
Rebecca S. Miller

17   Before *Riverdance*: A Brief History of Irish Step Dancing in America   417
Marion R. Casey

18   Irish-American Festivals   426
Mick Moloney

19   Irish Americans in Sports: The Nineteenth Century   443
Ralph Wilcox

20   Irish Americans in Sports: The Twentieth Century   457
Larry McCarthy

Reflections

21   The Irish (1963, 1970)   475
Daniel Patrick Moynihan

22   Once We Were Kings (1999)   526
Pete Hamill

23   Democracy in Action (1988)   535
Calvin Trillin

24   Irish America, 1940–2000   548
Linda Dowling Almeida

25   Twentieth-Century American Catholicism and Irish Americans   574
Thomas J. Shelley

26   The Fireman on the Stairs: Communal Loyalties in the
Making of Irish America   609
Timothy J. Meagher

27 The Tradition of Irish-American Writers: The Twentieth Century   649
        Daniel J. Casey and Robert E. Rhodes

28 Looking for Jimmy (1999)   663
        Peter Quinn

29 The Future of Irish America (2000)   680
        Peter Quinn

        Appendix: The Irish in the U.S. Census: An Explanatory Note   687
        Contributors   693
        Permissions   697
        Index   699

Illustrations

Margaret Gorman, Miss America, 1922   *frontispiece*

"A Letter from Pat in America," 1902   19

Satirical cartoon by Frederick Opper for *Puck*, 1894   26

Muckross Abbey, Killarney, County Kerry, circa 1920s   34

Irish on board the S.S. *St. Louis*, 1930s   42

Map, Ireland, 1922 to the Present   62

Poster, *The Rebel, A Drama of the Irish Rebellion*, 1900   79

Souvenir print, "Ireland for the Irish," circa 1835–1845   87

Souvenir print, "The Fenian Banner," 1866   97

Charles Stewart Parnell, circa 1880–1900   102

Limerick children by the Treaty Stone, 1903   108

Market Day, Cork City, 1905   112

Dublin Quay during the Easter Rising, 1916   118

Éamon de Valera, February 1920   123

Membership certificate, Hibernian Society of Charleston, circa 1820s   181

By-laws, Hibernian Benevolent Association of Troy, New York, 1834   196

"Irish Emigrants Leaving Their Home for America," 1866   222

Boston recruiting poster for the Irish Brigade, circa 1860s   227

Hibernian Hall, Charleston, South Carolina, 1865   229

"The Herald of Relief from America," 1880   239

Henry Eaton's headstone, Maryland, 1943   259

Lithograph, "Jamie and the Bishop," 1844   277

Advertisement, Fenian brand shirt collars, circa 1866   291

The Cuba Five, 1871   293

Flyer, "The Republic of Ireland Appeals to You," 1919   296

Gregory Dillon, circa 1851   307

Henry Hoguet, circa 1880   311

Minutes, Emigrant Industrial Savings Bank, 20 April 1850   317

Passport for Mary Anne (Molly) Ryan, 1932   335

Hannah Collins, 1898   339

Nora McCarthy and Mary Hayes, circa 1900   342

Hall Farm employee record for Sarah Byrne Green, circa 1944   344

Factory boys, Lowell, Massachusetts, 1911   361

Cartoon, "Champion of the Fenians," 1876   366

Postcard, "The Color-Bearers, St. Patrick's Day," 1905   374

Songster, *Squatter's Sovereignty*, 1882   390

Sheet music, "If They'd Only Move Old Ireland over Here," 1913 — 394
Sheet music, "Arrah Wanna," 1906, and "Santiago Flynn," 1908 — 396
Flyer for the McNulty Family Irish Showboat, 1937 — 400
Record album cover, *Ireland in America: Irish Dance Music,* circa 1966 — 414
James T. McKenna, circa 1914 — 421
The Green Fields of America, 1999 — 422
Advertisement for the Memorial Day Weekend Irish Festival at
   Gaelic Park, Chicago, 2000 — 431
Advertisement for the Irish Weekend at the Pines, South Fallsburg,
   New York, 1994 — 436
James J. Corbett, 1897 — 445
Hugh Duffy, 1895 — 448
Gaelic Society of New York's Football and Hurling Team, 1892 — 454
Connie Mack, 1930 — 460
Cigarette card, James P. Sullivan, circa 1910 — 466
Advertisement for Spalding, featuring Martin Sheridan, 1910 — 468
John F. Kennedy with John Fitzgerald and Joe Kennedy, circa 1940s — 505
President John F. Kennedy in Wexford, 1963 — 527
Judge James J. Comerford with Mayor Ed Koch, circa 1980s — 537
Emigrants departing Queenstown, County Cork, circa 1910 — 549
St. Patrick's Day parade, New York City, 1951 — 553
American Roses depart for Ireland, 1960 — 555
Presidents Mary Robinson and Bill Clinton, 1993 — 560
Archbishop John Ireland, circa 1910 — 577
Mass at Camp Cass, Virginia, 1861 — 579
Faculty, University of Notre Dame, Indiana, 1914 — 594–595
Fundraisers for the Kiltegan Fathers, Philadelphia, 1966 — 600
Membership certificate, Ancient Order of Hibernians, 1894 — 614
Lithograph, "St. Patrick's Day in America," 1872 — 621
American women picketing for the Irish Republic, 1920 — 624
Parade sidelines, New York City, 17 March 2002 — 639
Finley Peter Dunne, n.d. — 651
"Lunchtime atop a Skyscraper," 1932 — 662
Cartoon, "The Ignorant Vote—Honors Are Easy," 1876 — 666
John Francis Fitzgerald, 1906 — 668
Gene Tunney, circa 1926 — 675
Sheet music, "Pretty Kitty Kelly," 1920 — 681
Map, Distribution of the Irish in America, 1890 — 690

Preface

J. J. Lee and Marion R. Casey

The study of Irish America has blossomed in recent decades. Editors of a volume of this type are like chefs wondering how to choose a tasting menu from a wide range of possible dishes in order to both provide solid fare and whet the appetite for more, blending the familiar with the unfamiliar, as well as adding some new ingredients in what they hope is an appetizing mix. The objective is to present perspectives on Irish America through writing and illustrations which we feel deserve higher profile. As it is also essential that the Irish background be properly appreciated, but as very few books on Irish America include an authoritative survey of the appropriate type, Dr. Eileen Reilly's chapter is especially designed to present an informed and concentrated survey of modern Irish history.

It would be presumptuous of us to seek to replace or displace the standard accounts. No student of Irish America can afford, for instance, to overlook Kerby Miller's 1985 *Emigrants and Exiles*, whose wealth of material, range of reference, power of expression, and clarity of interpretive thrust ensure it classic status, however much debate has swirled around its central theses. As interested readers must be expected to engage with *Emigrants and Exiles* themselves, and as it must be digested whole to savor the full flavor of it, reprinting extracts could do only inadequate justice to a work epic in conception, execution, and scale. Lawrence J. McCaffrey's thirty years or more of intimate engagement with the Irish-American experience has ripened into his richly reflective *Irish Catholic Diaspora in America*, published in 1997. Readers seeking a lucid recent overview will find Kevin Kenny's textbook, *The American Irish*, published in 2000, an effective digest that processes the vast mass of material published in the decades since William V. Shannon's *The American Irish* in 1963. As these works are widely available, we seek to complement rather than compete with them.

The most ambitious contribution to the study of Irish America ever completed, *The Encyclopedia of the Irish in America*, edited by Michael Glazier and published by the University of Notre Dame Press in 1999, contains a host of entries that go far beyond our sampling approach—and as editors of a more modest venture we can only pause here to wryly salute Glazier's towering achievement in bringing 250 contributors to the starting line! It was tempting to seek to reprint several of the entries, but as that volume should be available in every self-respecting library, we have confined ourselves to reprinting only one essay, that by David Doyle on the Scotch-Irish.

Doyle is the leading Irish authority on Irish-American history, and this essay comple-ments his two major (but in America largely inaccessible) chapters on immigration in the century after 1776, from the monumental *New History of Ireland,* by treating with exemplary fairness a topic that remains particularly vulnerable to ideological inter-pretations ranging from the enthusiastic to the envenomed.

In general, and although there is no editorial rule that cannot be broken, we've tried to include classic contributions that either are now out of print or may consti-tute only one essay on the Irish in books dealing with other immigrant peoples, like the late Senator Daniel Patrick Moynihan's chapter in *Beyond the Melting Pot;* or from books on Ireland that do not deal mainly with Irish America, like Doyle's chapters in *A New History of Ireland;* or articles published originally in magazines, which may have been overlooked by many readers but which convey the acute perceptions of leading writers and thinkers, like the evocative essays by Pete Hamill, Calvin Trillin, and Peter Quinn.

As our purpose is to bridge the gap, without sacrificing the rigor of the argument, between the general reader and the student, we have taken particular care with our recommendations for further reading. On the one hand, we want readers to have advice on how to follow up matters of particular interest, but without inundating them with endless bibliographical lists. We try to achieve this by including brief lists for further reading after the relevant chapters and by keeping the number of titles in the final bibliography short and to the point. On the other hand, several chapters are copiously documented, and specialists already familiar with the subject matter will naturally wish to consult the footnotes from the outset, to satisfy themselves as to the appropriateness of the sources used.

In 1963 Moynihan identified three developments contributing to "a decline of Irish identity in America—the decline of immigration, the fading of Irish nationalism, and the relative absence of Irish cultural influence from abroad on the majority of Ameri-can Irish." It warns of the hazards of prophecy by even the most penetrating intel-lects that all three predictions would come to be partly reversed over the next forty years. While the history of these decades can be placed in only the most provisional perspective, a period that saw the eruption of another round of troubles, much to Moynihan's own mortification, revolving around conflicting identities in Northern Ireland, a surge in immigration in the 1980s, even if now subsided again, and a virtual cultural invasion from Ireland—in poetry, theatre, film, music, and dance (popularly associated with the phenomenon of *Riverdance*)—exerted more cultural influence not only on Irish America but also on America generally than anyone could have anticipated forty years ago.

The identity of Irish America is of course changing, as indeed are the identities of, and relations between, America and Ireland themselves. But we all live in a rapidly changing world, where there are many possible futures. It is appropriate that the last word should be left to Peter Quinn, hazarding a look into the future from a fasci-nating perspective that combines the experience of a child of the Bronx with the imagination of a great historical novelist and the insights of a profound historical intelligence.

Acknowledgments

Our appreciation goes to Dean Carol Mandel, Steve Maikowski, Despina Papazoglou Gimbel, and Eric Zinner of New York University Press for their fortitude and faith.

Once again, Kevin Morrissey has shown both foresight and practicality in the need to underwrite historical scholarship; *go raibh mile maith agat* to him and the members of the Irish Institute of New York.

For permission to reprint material we thank Pete Hamill, Patricia Harty and *Irish America* magazine, Peter Quinn, Calvin Trillin and Lescher and Lescher, Ltd., MIT Press, Oxford University Press, and University of Notre Dame Press.

We are grateful to Linda Dowling Almeida, Kevin Kenny, Margaret Lynch-Brennan, Larry McCarthy, Rebecca Miller, Mick Moloney, Eileen Reilly, Thomas Shelley, Robert Snyder, and Irene Whelan for undertaking research and revisions to meet a daunting publication schedule.

For illustrations we are especially indebted to Mick Moloney; the Library of Congress; and the Archives of Irish America, Bobst Library, New York University. We are also grateful for the generosity of Patricia Trainor O'Malley, Donald F. Arnold Jr., Donald A. Kelly, and the Park-McCullough House Association.

At Glucksman Ireland House we have drawn heavily on the support of Eileen Reilly and Scott Spencer, supported by Sam Anderson, Mike Donovan, Ryan Grim, Mary Krinock, and Kit Nicholls. It was ultimately the combination of the personal and managerial skills of Anne Solari that held this enterprise together, both by her painstaking attention to numerous details and, not least, by managing its distracted editors.

On the home front, Anne Lee, Joan Casey, and David Boldt Smith provided much appreciated balance. Finally, we acknowledge Hannah Dineen Smith, who heard all about this project while in utero and whose sunny little personality helped us both see it through to completion.

Chapter 1

Introduction
Interpreting Irish America[1]

J. J. Lee

Ireland has had one of the most extraordinary histories in the world. Winston Churchill would bear unlikely witness in exhorting the House of Commons on 15 December 1921 to accept the Anglo-Irish Treaty by asking them:

> Whence does this mysterious power of Ireland come? It is a small, poor, sparsely popu-lated island, lapped about by British sea power, accessible on every side, without iron or coal. How is it that she sways our councils, shakes our parties and infects us with her bit-terness, convulses our passions and deranges our actions? How is it that she has forced generation after generation to stop the whole traffic of the British Empire in order to debate her domestic affairs?[2]

Churchill's own answer was that "Ireland is not a daughter race. She is a parent na-tion." This was, of course, a heavily coded message. Although Churchill himself pur-ported to be talking about the Irish in the British Empire, what he meant even more was that it was in the interests of England's relations with America for it to make some concessions to Irish demands for independence. His listeners in the House of Commons knew perfectly well he meant that those for whom she was mainly "the parent nation" were the American Irish and that they were playing a crucial role in the struggle for independence. Eighty years later Peter Quinn could still observe that "Ire-land remains a canvas on which many of the broad brush strokes of the modern world's formation—imperialism, colonialism, nationalism, revolution, emigration, democratization, et al.—can be fruitfully studied and examined."[3]

This Irish background is crucial to an understanding of the historical role of the American Irish, however much that role may be adapting to the changing circum-stances of the present. Indeed, a popular version of the Irish story in America casts it as a saga, with refugees from the Great Famine of the 1840s flung on America's shores, clawing their way up against powerful enemies to scale the heights they have since reached in politics, law, media, business, and culture—and this by a people who were for so long axiomatically dismissed by those who fancied themselves their "betters" as incapable of mastering any of the higher arts of life. It found its incarnation in the Kennedy story, summarized by Doris Kearns Goodwin: "My father was the son of Irish immigrants. His accounts of his heritage and his family's struggle to establish a place for themselves in a strange, harsh and promising land, had illuminated my childhood musings and fueled my young ambition." She discovered as she progressed that

> the story of the Fitzgeralds and the Kennedys—despite its unique magnitude—was both symbol and substance of one of the most important themes of the second century of American life: the progress of the great wave of nineteenth-century immigration, the struggle of newcomers to force open the doors of American life so zealously guarded by those who had first settled the land. That story—in an undefinable sense, both real and metaphorical—culminated with the inauguration of John Fitzgerald Kennedy."[4]

From Famine to the White House was an even more exotic symbol of a country open to talent than was Lincoln's rise from the log cabin; it was a symbolic confirmation of the American Dream, of the "anybody can make it in America" image, admittedly with a certain time lag in this case, an image President John F. Kennedy himself was eager to endorse during his visit to Ireland in June 1963. But while genuinely inspiring, this story also has its darker, more somber, shades. It is both more complex and more nuanced than the popular version allows, and the manner in which its history has come to be written is itself an integral part of that story. How a people come to know themselves—how, in particular, a cadre of scholars emerges that seeks to probe how they came to be who they are—is itself, however distant from day-to-day concerns it may appear to be, a key issue in the formation of their sense of identity.

The Struggle to Understand: The Pioneers

The publication of the *Harvard Encyclopedia of American Ethnic Groups* in 1980 marked the end of a phase in American immigrant historiography. It was the reaping of a harvest that had been ripening over several decades. The two contributions to the volume, by Patrick Blessing on the Irish and by Maldwyn Jones on the Scotch-Irish, both excellent summaries of the existing state of knowledge, provide a measuring rod against which to gauge the degree of progress recorded in the attempts to understand the Irish experience in America at that time. Both contributors confronted the challenge that scholarly reflection on the Irish experience had been slow to develop.

Art Mitchell has observed that "there was no serious work about the general subject of the Irish in this country" until 1956, when Carl Wittke "produced the first academically respectable history of the Irish in America."[5] Carl Wittke is hardly a name to make the rafters ring with instant recognition in Irish America. But Irish America should be grateful to him. The son of an immigrant German mechanic, who taught at Ohio State, Oberlin, and Case Western Reserve Universities, he gave generous attention to the Irish in his prolific writing on the American immigrant experience, particularly in his 1939 textbook *We Who Built America*. The fact that he published *The Irish in America* sixteen years later, because he could find nothing remotely adequate in the existing literature as late as the 1950s, itself indicates how much remained to be done.[6]

The Irish, it is true, were not quite as relatively backward as this would suggest at first glance. But the few attempts that predate Wittke—like Thomas D'Arcy McGee's *History of the Irish Settlers in North America* (1850), John Francis Maguire's *The Irish in*

America (1868), and Edward O'Meagher Condon's *The Irish Race in America* (1887)—were written prior to the professionalization of history as a discipline. And scholarly American writing about immigration in general has been remarkably slow to develop. Most historians came from old-stock British backgrounds, belonged to comfortable classes, usually attended universities where few immigrant faces were to be seen except as servants, and for practical purposes lived in a different country from the bulk of the immigrants. It was not until the 1920s that even a small section of the mainstream historical profession began to think of immigrants as an integral part of American history.

Up until then, and in many cases long afterward, immigrant peoples in general indulged mainly in filiopietism, a polite term for ancestor worship. Dismissively though the term was normally used, this was a quite natural response to the lack of recognition that many immigrant groups felt. They sought to compensate for their sense of neglect by extolling the exploits, real or imagined, of any of their number who could be claimed to have made a "contribution" to America, and particularly to the American Revolution. Excavation of ancestors could reach archaeological intensity at times.

The problem in the Irish case was that because of the Catholic/Protestant divide, by the late nineteenth century there were two Irish filiopietisms, Irish Catholic and Scotch-Irish, in far from harmonious relationship with one another. If relations between the two identities had been strained since at least the 1820s, they had worsened further by the end of the century. Consumed by fear that the contributions of the Scotch-Irish—"a people whose music, religious fundamentalism, individualism and suspicion of authority remain prominent elements in the culture of the American South"[7]—were being submerged beneath the torrent of Irish Catholic newcomers, the Scotch-Irish Society, established in 1889 and growing in political strength, was first in the field. While nominally neutral in the denominational stakes, its publications could not be accused of understating Scotch-Irish contributions to America. It was largely in reaction to the Scotch-Irish initiative that the American Irish Historical Society (AIHS) was established in 1897.

While also ostensibly nondenominational, the AIHS proceeded to produce a journal devoted to filiopietistic inquiry and responded to the taunts of Protestant critics about the essential paucity of Catholic Irish contributions to the American Revolution with counterclaims, inevitably exaggerated, about their own prominent role. They made this simpler for themselves by the convenient device of insisting that the Scotch-Irish were Irish, whereas the Scotch-Irish were equally adamant that they were not. The writings therefore tend to focus obsessively on those who marched with Washington's army, seeking to stake their filiopietistic claims especially by surname analysis. Although valuable material can be found in the publications of the two societies, it was generally deployed in a manner designed to serve the conflicting propagandistic purposes of the ethnic belligerents, and it must be rescued from its context to yield its full scholarly potential.[8]

R. J. Dickson, author of a standard work on Scotch-Irish emigration to America in the eighteenth century, felt that the indefatigable Michael J. O'Brien (who in the midst of a job in insurance worked tirelessly to dig out every possible, and some impossible, Irish contributors to Washington's victories) and Charles Hanna (author of a massive compilation on the Scotch-Irish in 1902) both treated the immigrant as "a pawn in a game he sought no part in," marching him in battle formation under flags of author-ial convenience.[9] In their defense it may be said they would not be the only ones to do that, however carefully their findings must be handled, and that at least they did leave posterity with something to engage with—a compass to the very sources of primary evidence that must inform our own endeavors—which is more than can be said of many of their contemporaries and critics.

The historiography of Irish Protestants and Catholics has many similarities. But we must be careful in talking about Irish Protestants. Here terminology becomes crucial. We say Irish Protestants, rather than Ulster Protestants, in that the history of the emi-gration of Protestants from Ireland in general, other than Scotch-Irish Presbyterians from Ulster, has been grossly neglected. Even the Scotch-Irish have written only spo-radically about themselves, while the possibly substantial numbers of adherents to the Anglican Church of Ireland who immigrated to America during the nineteenth century have written scarcely anything, and their history in America remains to be explored. This may be partly because they were able to fit into, or disappear into, established American Protestant society, rising without trace, so to speak, and being sufficiently affluent, educated, and religiously correct not to have to cluster in a way that would make them conspicuous to contemporaries. Therefore, they remained in large measure below, or rather above, the horizons of commentators who were so busy looking down at the Catholic Irish that it rarely occurred to them to look up at, or even across to, the Protestant ones, who thus came to have even less written about them than the "invisible" English.

Protestants from the rest of Ireland were not "Ulstermen," as that phrase came to be used in Scotch-Irish discourse. They therefore tend to fall out of sight due to the focus, with a few exceptions, of Catholic historians on Irish Catholics and Scotch-Irish historians on the Scotch-Irish. Recovering the story of those vanished Protestant Irish, insofar as it can be done, poses an intriguing challenge.

We must be sensitive to distinctions between the propagandistic use of terminol-ogy, to which we are all prone, and the actual historical record. That is one reason it is important to have a sound knowledge of the Irish background, presented in chapter 2 here in Eileen Reilly's compact and cogent survey. Saying that immigrants came from Ireland may tell us little about them unless we know what area they came from and the traditions they brought with them, which could vary in different places and at dif-ferent times. Hence, too, the delineation by David Doyle in chapter 3 of the precise Irish background of his Scotch-Irish immigrants. This is important because the im-pression is often given that the province of Ulster was always predominantly Protes-tant. "Protestant Ulster" is a standard phrase in the literature. True, the term "Ulster-man" came to be used by Ulster Protestants to refer exclusively to Protestants, even though the majority of the population of the province was Catholic until the 1860s. Much more a state of mind than an accurate description of the population of the province, however, "Ulsterman" was not a geographical description but an ideological designation that was brilliantly deployed by Ulster Protestants and their English sup-porters to subliminally blot out of their own consciousness, and as far as possible everyone else's, the existence of Catholics in Ulster.

How the Scotch-Irish of the eighteenth and early nineteenth centuries, and indeed other Irish Protestants, many of whom saw themselves, and were seen, as simply "Irish"—whatever "Irish" might mean at the time—ceased to think of themselves as Irish, and the extent to which this happened remains to be explored in depth. All of this points to the inclusion in this volume of the detailed exegesis on the Scotch-Irish by David Doyle, of the probing analyses by Kerby Miller and Irene Whelan in chapters 6 and 7, and the exuberant twentieth-century toast to the Ulster-Scots in chapter 8 by Henry Noble MacCracken. MacCracken was president of Vassar College from 1915 to 1946, a graduate of New York University with a doctorate from Harvard, and a former member of the English faculty at Yale and Smith, himself scion of a distinguished educational family: his father was a notable chancellor of New York University from 1891 to 1910, and his grandmother was a pioneer of women's higher education in Ohio. Of course, no man is on his oath in a dinner toast, and pedants may quibble over some of the oratorical flourishes, but MacCracken certainly conveyed the essence of a congenial self-image.

However exactly it happened, the break between Catholic and Protestant seems to have been deep and bitter by the time the filiopietistic societies were founded. The AIHS published more than the Scotch-Irish Society. Yet, its journal concentrates on extolling the role of the Irish in the American Revolution, sometimes on dubious grounds. The irony from a later vantage point is that the Catholic Irish had a greater story to tell than inflating their role in the Revolution, if only they realized it. The journal contains only fleeting references to the Great Famine or to the actual day-to-day lives of the immigrants since then. It has little on what made these immigrants truly distinctive.

Because history at that time was seen so much in terms of "Great Men," because so little attention was paid to the lives of ordinary men and women, the opportunity to write contemporary social history of an epic nature was ignored. The AIHS can hardly be blamed for this. They were fighting on ground of another's choosing and had to adopt the standards of mainstream culture. But there is also little evidence that the alternative had much attraction for them. The objective of the bulk of the affluent middle-class New York and Boston professional people who dominated the society was to proclaim their patriotism and respectability, which would allow them to ease their way into established American society. One hardly did that by adopting the approach of Finley Peter Dunne's Mr. Dooley over in Chicago, who had the bad grace to be inconveniently philosophizing with a heavy "brogue" in those same years.

Again, one must be careful about context. What the AIHS, as well as the Scotch-Irish Society, produced could have been described as "undaunted sentimentality." Although these words were used about filiopietistic history, but they weren't referring to the Irish; rather, they were used by a rising Jewish scholar to describe the state of Jewish writing about Jewish America, and not in the 1920s, but as late as the 1950s.[10] There was, in short, nothing unusual about Irish-American filiopietism. Denunciations of it from a dismissive latter-day vantage point fail to comprehend the America of the time. From a scholarly perspective, it wasn't right, but from a psychological perspective it was normal. And the Irish were as normal as anyone.

The differences at that time between the academic fortunes of immigrant history and of Celtic studies are striking.[11] For it was to Celtic studies rather than immigration studies, or Irish studies more generally, that universities turned, when they turned toward things Irish at all. Celtic studies was pioneered in Harvard, within the ambience of the English department, through the initiative of Fred Robinson, who was given permission by President Charles William Eliot to teach Celtic studies on returning in 1893 from a year of study at Freiburg in Germany under Rudolf Thurneysen, the great Celtic scholar with whom so many young acolytes in America and Ireland would study. The gifted Robinson would come to be widely venerated as the founding father of the subject in the United States, but courses were taught also, at various times in the first half of the twentieth century, in Catholic University in Washington, D.C., where the Ancient Order of Hibernians sponsored a Chair of Gaelic Studies in 1896; in Wisconsin at Madison; in Chicago, Northwestern, Columbia, New York, Fordham, Berkeley, Indiana, Temple, and some other universities. What is striking about most of these courses is that they depended on the enthusiasm of individuals and often disappeared with them. And these scholars did not generally consider it their function to teach Irish history, much less Irish-American history. There was no reason they should. Their reputation depended on their identification with a respected academic discipline: philology.

Celtic studies was ideologically very different from immigration studies. Philology enjoyed an enormous reputation under the aegis of German scholarship and thus could be securely established in English departments. Great credit is due to those scholars and administrators who promoted Celtic studies, and this initiative no doubt helped enhance the status of the Celtic dimension in American scholarship, long before anybody had a thought that "Celtic" would come to be so fashionable a brand name a century later. But Celtic studies belonged to a very different intellectual, and in some ways social, world than subjects closer to the immigrant bone. It had none of the potentially public impact of immigrant or even Irish studies. True, one of the most celebrated of all Celtic scholars, who would later grace the Harvard chair, John Kelleher, published over an extraordinary range, including contemporary events in Ireland and America.[12] But that was after the Second World War and was not what Celtic studies as a university subject was about. Kelleher's great distinction enabled him to couple the Celtic studies chair with another in Irish studies, allowing more latitude for comment on recent centuries.

It was understandable, indeed inescapable, that Celtic studies should have steered decisively clear of the Irish-American history promulgated at the time. Irish America was doubly disliked—as immigrant and as Catholic. Catholicism was still deeply suspect to many in the major universities, still suffused by assumptions of the inherent inferiority of Catholics, on intellectual, cultural, social, political, and religious grounds. Celtic was just about safe because philology was decently recondite, validated moreover by the laying on of revered Teutonic hands and uncontaminated by contact with the calloused paws of the Paddy in the street. The beauty of the Celts was that, allowing for harmless druidic reincarnations, they were safely dead, and the political beauty of Celtic was that it was long, long ago. This is not, of course, to detract from the outstanding contributions to the scholarship of Celtic studies in

America, extending well beyond Ireland to the wider Celtic world. But it does help explain the limited resonance it roused in Irish America.

The Struggle to Understand: From Filiopietists to Professors

Ironically, it was not from the perspective of either Celtic studies or the American Irish Historical Society, but through the interest in the Irish displayed by non-Irish historians—striving to understand the phenomenon of immigration in general and realizing they could not do so without exploring the role of the Irish—that the scholarly study of Irish America would be properly launched. In Harvard, Arthur M. Schlesinger Sr., less familiar as a public name than his illustrious son, Arthur M. Schlesinger Jr., but a major figure in American intellectual development, brought the subject of immigration into respectability for scholarly study with a seminal article in 1922.[13] The outstanding pioneer, the Norwegian-American historian Marcus Lee Hansen (born in 1892, died prematurely in 1938), gave the Irish their due in his posthumously published work, *The Atlantic Migration, 1607–1860*, edited by Schlesinger. He also gave encouragement to the rising young star, Oscar Handlin, who would become the leading authority of the next generation. After Hansen's death, Handlin became a Harvard professor and the doyen of American immigration historians, duly presiding as consulting editor over the *Harvard Encyclopedia of American Ethnic Groups*.

Handlin's Harvard doctorate, published in 1941 as *Boston's Immigrants, 1790–1865*, was inspired by his supervisor, none other than Arthur Schlesinger Sr., promoting the cause of immigration history, who suggested Boston as a suitable case for study. By happy chance, Handlin's first major work was therefore devoted heavily to the experience of Irish immigrants. Irish-American history was now catapulted to the forefront of American immigration study by virtue of the fact that the most exciting immigration historian of his generation had in effect devoted his first book to them—a book that moreover pioneered the history of the immigrant in the city and would serve as a model for others. Moses Rischin, who was beginning his career as a leading historian of Jewish America, noted that Robert Ernst (author in 1949 of *Immigrant Life in New York City, 1825–1863*) was "consciously pursuing the pioneer path blazed by Oscar Handlin" eight years earlier.[14] Florence Gibson, in her still valuable study of New York's Irish political attitudes, completed under Allan Nevins at Columbia and published in 1951, steered a rather different course; this was not to challenge Handlin and Ernst but to largely ignore them, her work being "confined . . . almost exclusively to the political side, not making any attempt to enter into the economic problems which beset the immigrant."[15]

Handlin's path provided a bleak enough vista of the immigrant experience. Handlin found the Boston Irish enjoying little economic or social improvement until after the Civil War—he would bring the study down to 1880 in an expanded edition published in 1959. The swarms of Catholic economic refugees fleeing from the Great Famine for several years after 1845 would have made matters very difficult, both for themselves and for others, even if they had not suffered discrimination from the deeply entrenched, and deeply horrified, Brahmin upper classes. If Handlin's Boston was in truth an unwelcoming place for Irish Catholic immigrants, the story hardly suffered by being told through the sympathetic eyes of the child of Ukrainian Jews who doubtless detected several parallels with his own growing up in the dreadful years of the Depression in Brooklyn.[16]

Important though the works of Handlin and Ernst were, these were the only two studies of their type available when Wittke found himself having to make bricks with very little straw as he tackled the challenge of a general history of Irish immigration in the 1950s. Of the contributions of that decade to come from within Irish America, only Thomas N. Brown's celebrated articles on "Nationalism and the Irish Peasant 1800–1848" and "The Origins and Character of Irish-American Nationalism" in the *Review of Politics,* in 1953 and 1956, portended a career in Irish-American history. Brown's incisive and imaginative analysis of the relationship between Irish nationalism and Irish-American identity still rewards reflection by students of nationalism in general, as well as of Irish America. Brown suggested that the embracing of Irish nationalism by a substantial section of Irish America served as a compensatory mechanism for their feeling of alienation in America, hoping that the achievement of independence by their homeland would elevate their status by enhancing respect for them in America.

For actual publication, 1963 would be a highly significant year, thanks to two works in particular. William V. Shannon's *The American Irish* was the first interpretive overview of their history. Although sometimes dismissed as journalistic, it was a notable achievement. Shannon was working outside the academic milieu that would have allowed the extra hours required for refining and revising. But his intelligence was superior to that of many an academic and his insights are still worth pursuing, providing a valuable guide to what one might call the instinctive feelings of those Irish Americans who actively identified with Ireland at the time. Nor did he lack an academic orientation. He had been taught by Handlin, whose influence on his "understanding of immigrant history" he acknowledged, together with that of Moses Rischin, "once my classmate in the Harvard Graduate School and my longtime friend."[17] His work was destined to find a far wider readership than that of another journalist, the Providence-based George Potter, whose book, *To the Golden Door: The Story of the Irish in Ireland and America*, published posthumously through the devotion of his widow in 1960, was a labor not only of love but also of enormous erudition; it continues to tantalize scholars who just wish he had had time to provide his references.

If Shannon's could still be deemed nearly forty years later "the most readable general history of Irish America,"[18] the second contribution of 1963, reprinted here as chapter 21, Daniel Patrick Moynihan's essay, "The Irish," in *Beyond the Melting Pot: The Negroes, Puerto Ricans, Jews, Italians, and Irish of New York City*, edited by Nathan Glazer and himself, was more programmatic. Banished from the mainstream of American thought for forty years, the ethnics were coming back in. In truth, they had never gone away. But academics had managed not to see him—much less her—even when they swarmed before their gaze. In what became the seminal volume on the role of ethnicity in America, Glazer and Moynihan in effect shouted that the emperor, in the sense of contemporary sociological theory and observation, had no clothes. They garbed their subject with such style that it has not been possible to look at it in the same manner since. For all the possible criticisms that can be made of it, it was a landmark volume in American, including Irish-American, intellectual history.[19]

Written in sparkling style, Moynihan's chapter (described by Andrew Greeley in 1972 as "the only attempt I know of by a social scientist to say anything meaningful about the American-Irish," adding for good measure, "there is little serious history and practically no sociology about the American Irish")[20] bubbled with ideas and insights. One could already sense in Moynihan a mind that would be among the most fertile and incisive in American public life for the rest of the century. But it would also be among the most controversial, and one can see from this essay how both conclusions could be reached. Its importance historiographically was twofold. First, by locating the Irish experience in comparative ethnic context it shifted perspective from contemplation of one's own navel. Second, by suggesting the Irish might not be wholly blameless for their own problems, it introduced a note of self-criticism that had rarely disturbed the vision of Irish-American navel gazers. Nor did his tone, more mordant than reverential, help soothe sensitive nerves frayed by his content.

At a serious substantive level, Moynihan's argument that the Irish did not know what to do with political power, once they had achieved control of so many City Halls by the late nineteenth century, through highly professional command of the techniques of acquisition, roused strong resistance on scholarly grounds from those like Lawrence J. McCaffrey who contended that they did in fact do much "to alleviate urban poverty and bring ethnics into the mainstream of American politics."[21] If they often sought to satisfy the new immigrants from southern and eastern Europe with baubles, with the symbols rather than the substance of power, after the turn of the century, that was still very different from trying to shut the door in their faces by keeping them out of America altogether, as anti-immigration activists would succeed in doing from the early 1920s.

It was appropriate from this perspective that, even as the book was published in 1963, the policy shift toward reversing the anti-immigration legislation of the 1920s should be initiated by the only Catholic Irish-American president, the fruits of whose initiative would not be harvested until after his death in the new immigration legislation of 1965. At just the moment when President John F. Kennedy had projected a new image for the Catholic Irish in general American affairs, Moynihan was urging a new approach toward understanding the Irish Catholic experience, not least among themselves. But behind the sardonic style, or so it seems to me, lay a deep desire that those who identified themselves as Irish should raise their game. Where the first edition, written mostly in 1960–1961, and published before the assassination of Kennedy, is noncommittal about the new president, the second edition, published in 1970, is highly revealing. The body of the text remains unchanged. But the mood abruptly alters as Moynihan substitutes for his original conclusion on his final page, utterly incongruously and therefore all the more strikingly, one of the most searing of all laments for the death of Kennedy. His clinical tone of intellectual distance, at times verging on Olympian hauteur, is suddenly saturated, even seven years after the event, with a sense of tragedy, of a future snatched away, transforming a detached intellectual disquisition into a rending of the garments for the dream turned to ashes.

It was a feeling that extended far beyond Catholic Irish America, or Ireland itself, where President Kennedy's state visit in June 1963 had been welcomed in the spirit of a joyous family reunion. It was shared by millions throughout the world, who lived in the hope that America was, after all, the city on a hill, however dimly the lights might flicker at times. The hope that Kennedy symbolized for many beyond America is memorably captured in Pete Hamill's passionate and evocative elegy, reprinted as chapter 22 here.

If with JFK's election "the symbolic exclusion was ended, and with it the psychological basis"[22] for the tendency to make overcompensatory claims because of decades of denigration, the Irish political culture that groomed him for the White House did not vanish overnight. It just became less visible. Calvin Trillin's *New Yorker* meditation, reprinted as chapter 23 here, on the ways of organizing the distribution of power and recognition in Irish New York, is based on a case study of the political anthropology of selecting the grand marshal of the St. Patrick's Day parade. It reinforces many of Moynihan's observations even while it traces the decline of the political culture portrayed by Moynihan, in what one might call a study in political still life that assumes the form—so exquisitely is it etched—of a work of art itself.

"Annus horribilis" though it was in historical terms with the death of Kennedy, 1963 was a promising one for the interpretation of the Irish-American experience. But the foundations laid by Shannon and Moynihan remained foundations. It is true that much of interest for students of Irish America appeared in other contexts during the 1960s, and that there were too few specialists in Irish America to fully reap the potential harvest. American immigration historiography went through a phase of near infatuation with "social mobility," leading to a formidable accumulation of information on mobility patterns in various towns and cities—many of them, like New York State's Buffalo, Troy, and Poughkeepsie, with Irish populations. The results of Stephen Thernstrom's Newburyport, Massachusetts, study in 1964 seemed to vindicate Handlin's gloomy assessment of the mobility performance of the Irish in nineteenth-century Boston on the basis of a more scientific, in the sense of being statistically based, reconstruction of social mobility in this small New England textile town.

Tom Brown's arguments of the 1950s about Irish nationalism found their classic expression a decade later in his *Irish-American Nationalism 1870–1890*, published in 1966. Brown's influence would permeate the thinking of an entire generation to the extent that his University of Massachusetts–based legacy would even surmount the Chicago suspicion of easterners bearing gifts when Larry McCaffrey dedicated his outstanding edited volume, *The Irish in Chicago,* to Brown in 1987. Except for *Irish-American Nationalism*, originally supervised by Handlin as a Harvard doctorate, the most challenging volumes were Earl Niehaus on the Irish in antebellum New Orleans and Edward Levine's less than enchanted appraisal in 1966 of Irish political styles based on his Chicago experience.[23]

The 1970s would be distinctly better. Significant work emerged from many of the biggest names that would fructify the field in the following decades, with Greeley,

McCaffrey, Dennis Clark, Jay P. Dolan, Charles Fanning, David N. Doyle, James P. Walsh, Daniel J. Casey, and Robert E. Rhodes all making their mark. Thernstrom consolidated his contribution with a 1973 study of poverty and progress in Boston 1880–1970, which followed on and seemed to confirm again the Handlin conclusions by establishing the continuing slow social mobility of the Irish. It did little to dispel the atmosphere of gloom surrounding the Irish experience, with of course all its subliminal, or not so subliminal, implications in the eyes of observers (friendly or not) of some inherent defects in the Irish Catholic character. The influence and staying power of this thesis is reflected in recent popular culture, for example *Monument Avenue*, Ted Demme's gritty 1998 film about Charlestown, and in Michael Patrick MacDonald's 1999 *All Souls*, a bleak memoir of South Boston.

From Boston to San Francisco

The bicentennial year, 1976, proved to be exceptionally fruitful. The Cumann Merriman conference in Ennis, Co. Clare, published under the editorship of Owen Dudley Edwards and David N. Doyle, included contributions from nearly every leading available scholar working on Irish America. The very title, *America and Ireland, 1776–1976: The American Identity and the Irish Connection,* indicates the ambitious range of its contents. It remains indispensable for any serious study of the subject. One of the prominent participants in Ennis, Lawrence J. McCaffrey, published his own invigorating study, *The Irish Diaspora in America*, that same year. From his base at Loyola University, Chicago, McCaffrey joined with Margaret Connors of Harvard and James P. Walsh of San Jose, a triumvirate spanning the country from the Atlantic to the Pacific —with Doyle, earlier a McCaffrey student from Ireland at Iowa State University, central to the selection process—to launch the Arno Press series of no fewer than forty-two volumes on the Irish-American experience, many of them dissertations hitherto hidden from the public eye. Indeed, Doyle's own volume in the series, his probing exploration of Irish-American attitudes toward American expansionism in the late nineteenth century, has acquired renewed topicality from recent shifts in American foreign policy.[24] All three ventures were notable for their attack on the "east coast" model of Irish-American experience, based ultimately on Handlin's 1941 *Boston's Immigrants.*

Handlin's image was that of an immigrant generation consumed by a sense of loss, even of desolation, suffering from a desperate feeling of loneliness in the seething urban American cauldron after their "uprooting" from the familiar fields of home. This image dominated understanding of the American immigrant experience for several years. It was reinforced by the Pulitzer Prize Handlin won in 1951 for *The Uprooted,* whose eloquent exposition of immigrant disorientation owed much to his image of the Boston Irish experience. But his model began to become problematic in the face of vigorous criticism from several scholars, most forcefully by Rudolph J. Vecoli, who felt the immigrant experience to have been a much more positive one, with satisfaction far outweighing dissatisfaction among the newcomers. The image of the uprooted was gradually transformed into that of the transplanted, the title of John

Bodnar's 1985 general survey, distancing the subject from the image of immigrants as victims and allowing them more agency in their own fate; rather than history being something that happened to them from outside, the emphasis was now more on what the immigrants did than on what had been done to them.[25]

The issues of satisfaction versus dissatisfaction, spilling over into the related if objectively different issue of success versus failure, began to loom large in the historiography of the Irish, too. Here, however, the debate acquired a regional cutting edge, as specialists on the midwest and west began to reject the hegemony of models and images based on Boston, or rather more vaguely, on the "east" in general. Boston, it was held, was just about the most unrepresentative possible city in America from an Irish perspective. The obstacles to social mobility were more formidable in the particularly unfriendly and unhelpful ambience of a slow-growing, socially rigid, intensely anti-Catholic milieu than in any other city. No generalization should be based on it, an objective of the Arno series being, in the words of McCaffrey, to insist on "the varieties of Irish-America—the impact of American regionalism on Irish values and attitudes."[26]

While the general proposition seems plausible, the terms of the discussion can sometimes be confusing, if not restrictive. McCaffrey, looking east from the midwest in 1976, would lump New York with Boston as part of a single "east coast" Irish-American identity.[27] Even as late as 1997 his splendid section on recommended reading in his *Irish Catholic Diaspora*, the revised version of his 1976 *Irish Diaspora,* was preoccupied with relative regional "success." Stephen Thernstrom's *Other Bostonians* (1973), for instance, demonstrates "that the New England Irish were exceptions to the general Irish American success story." JoEllen Vinyard's *Detroit* "makes a strong case that the Irish on the urban frontier, from Buffalo west, achieved more social mobility than those in the east." Cochran on St. Louis "concludes that midwestern Irish were more successful than those in the east." The contributors to Meagher's *From Paddy to Studs, 1880–1920* "conclude that Irish Americans made more progress in the West than in the East." Dennis Clark's *Hibernia America: The Irish and Regional Cultures,* suggests that "eastern ghettoization retarded both (success and assimilation)."[28] Yet even if all this were true—and some of the verdicts may be oversimplified—it seems to verge on the obsessive to reduce the range of issues analyzed in these volumes to this single topic, important though it may be.

McCaffrey, it seems safe to conclude, is no fan of the "east coast" perspective on the Irish experience. But perceptions can change depending on one's own location. For he would in turn find himself reproached in R. A. Burchell's *The Irish in San Francisco* for his own neglect of—guess where?—San Francisco.[29] "East" is a moveable location! And it was San Francisco, built virtually from the ground up from the gold rush of 1849, that as Jim Walsh persuasively argued at the bicentennial conference in 1976, emerged as the polar opposite of Boston, providing a much more hospitable environment for Irish economic and social performance.[30]

The contrast was so vivid that one can understand Burchell's shock at discovering that the San Francisco Irish were so optimistic and self-satisfied after the doom and gloom of Handlin's *Boston* and Ernst's *New York*.[31] It was only in post–Civil War Boston that Handlin had detected the hint of a break in the clouds, whereas the San Francisco Irish flourished under a sunny sky from the start, symbolized by their having their first Irish mayor as early as 1867, compared with New York's in 1880 and Boston's in 1884. Nowhere else in the United States, he insists, "presents a better case study of what happened to the immigrant in mid–nineteenth century America, when the traditional mold was broken and relations between native stock and immigrants were set free from the shackles of history, to take a new course."[32]

Burchell's argument, like McCaffrey's and Walsh's, shifts the focus from the immigrants to the obstacles posed and the opportunities proffered by the host society. It is less because the immigrants are different than because the cities are different that east and west appear different. The culture they brought with them recedes in importance; the culture they found advances in importance. But did they, in fact, remain so spectacularly different over time? A major problem is that there are very few city histories that stretch over several generations and allow sustained comparison of urban experiences, as distinct from incisions over a short period. Until that evidence becomes available, it probably behooves us to keep a fairly open mind. Even within the time frame of two or three generations after the Great Famine, it is not clear that the east should be dismissed so brusquely, while readily admitting that generalization for the country as a whole must take full account of midwest and west.

While Burchell might lump Handlin and Ernst together as equally merchants of gloom, Moses Rischin would draw a clear distinction between Boston and New York, observing in 1950 that "the broad chasm separating the Boston Brahmin from the Irish Catholic had no analogy in New York City. Characterized by a constant social flux and greater diversity among the elements of its population, ideological and cultural differences were more readily blurred and diluted."[33] This sounds uncommonly like Burchell on San Francisco! To William Shannon, introducing Dennis Clark's *Erin's Heirs: Irish Bonds of Community*, "everyone knows that Philadelphia is considerably different from Boston and New York and that the experience of the Philadelphia Irish took a notably different course."[34] It almost sounds as if Philadelphia is not in the east! If Shannon did lump New York and Boston together here, Tim Meagher, summing up contributions on several cities across the country a decade later, wondered how representative Boston was of even New England, "much less the entire East Coast."[35] Although Doyle, too, believes the east coast experience to have been "untypical of that of any composite Irish America," he insisted even before Meagher on the "very considerable differences" within the east coast area.[36] Despite the undoubted differences among cities, then, it may be time to revisit the entire issue to determine if it is possible to establish more systematic criteria for comparison.[37]

It is important in this respect for champions of various regional loyalties to step back and see matters in perspective. In 1880 nearly two-thirds of Irish-born in the country lived in east coast states. If San Francisco mushroomed from under 1,000 people in 1848 to 150,000 in 1870 and to 250,000, including suburbs, in 1880, this still left it far behind Chicago, much less New York.[38] In 1870, the number of Irish born in New York was more than the combined Irish-born populations of the next six biggest centers of Irish settlement: Philadelphia, Boston, Chicago, San Francisco, St. Louis, and Cincinnati. For that matter, it was just about the equal of London, Liverpool, Glasgow, and Manchester combined, the four biggest centers of Irish-born in Britain.

One should not claim that New York, anymore than anywhere else, was "representative" of America. But it is no denigration of anywhere else to say as a simple matter of fact that nineteenth- and twentieth-century Irish America without New York would have been a very different world, and by extension so would the Irish diaspora in general, as well as Ireland itself. Important though it is to identify internal distinctions, it is also important to keep in mind the big picture within which these distinctions occur. As late as 1996 what struck the editors of *The New York Irish* was the relative neglect of the subject compared with the study in depth of not only other ethnic groups in the city, but the Irish in other cities.[39]

Handlin himself did not claim Boston was representative of Irish America. It was his fate to have others generalize loosely from him for so long, simply because there was so little else to generalize from. And Boston, representative or not, was after all no mean city. Boston was important in its own right. It was important enough to inspire further work by Stephen Thernstrom, Handlin's successor at Harvard, as well as by Dennis P. Ryan and by Thomas H. O'Connor and his students, digging further into the same ground while also extending coverage down to the present.[40]

Indeed, the 1890 census recorded slightly more Irish-born in Boston than in Chicago, though Chicago's explosive growth saw the number of Irish-born just overtake Boston's in 1900, with 74,000 compared with 70,000, having risen spectacularly from only 6,000 in 1850. While Chicago could not compete with New York's Irish-born population figures, it had one writer no other city could claim: Finley Peter Dunne, who in the bitter years of the 1890s depression conceived in his protagonist Martin Dooley the most memorable philosopher of the people in the entire repertoire of Irish-American fiction. Those who want to delve into Mr. Dooley, or into human nature in general and Irish nature in particular, should dig deep, not just into Dooley but into Charles Fanning's exquisitely wrought meditations on Dunne and Dooley. Fanning ponders the aspirations and pretensions, foibles and follies, joys and sorrows of a community in transition, rising and dissolving simultaneously, as Bridgeport, one of the first Irish working-class neighborhoods in the city, came to be overrun by "foreigners" like Germans.[41] Fanning may be right to surmise that it was only in Chicago, or at least most plausibly in Chicago (of all those Irish settlements outside the suffocating genteel ambiance of the correctness of the eastern literary establishment), that the vernacular genius of Dunne could have flourished in the first instance, even if he soon "abdicated" to New York. Does Fanning's charged choice of verb still convey, at the distance of nearly a century, a hint of a sense of betrayal by Dunne of his Chicago roots?[42]

Irish and Scotch Irish—Again!

If the Merriman conference was notable for a reconsideration of the location question on the basis of James P. Walsh's presentation of the perspective from San Francisco, the volume of the proceedings, published in 1980, was also notable for an introduction by William Shannon, by now ambassador to Ireland under President Jimmy Carter, who reputedly appointed him partly on the strength of *The American Irish.*

What is particularly noticeable is the change in tone toward the Scotch-Irish. Whereas in 1963 Shannon had concentrated on the Catholic Irish on the grounds that the Scotch-Irish had no sense of affinity with, or sympathy for, Ireland—taking Woodrow Wilson's dismissive hauteur toward Irish claims for independence as his classic example—now he adopted a much more positive tone, observing that "originally, Catholic and Protestant immigrants from Ireland made little or no distinction among themselves along religious lines."[43] This presumably reflected the influence of the intervening outbreak of conflict in Northern Ireland, which increasingly impressed on policymakers in both the Irish Republic and the United States that some sort of alternative to an image of perpetual animosity should be sought.

It was an arduous quest. The memories by this stage were scarcely ecumenical. The filiopietistic instincts articulated through the Scotch-Irish Society and the American Irish Historical Society at the turn of the century were still strong. Although Shannon's phraseology suggested a desperate snatching at a golden age of retrospective harmony, there had begun to be a growing objective realization, which would become much more extensive subsequently, that relations had not always been as hostile as seemed the natural order in Northern Ireland or in the filiopietistic American rivalries. The existing literature, however, did not provide convenient exits from the impasse.

The then–most recent substantial narrative study on the Scotch-Irish, James Leyburn's *Scotch-Irish: A Social History*, had appeared in 1962. A sociology professor, an authority on Haiti, Leyburn's approach was based on the contention that "after the Revolution the Scotch-Irish were no longer a separate national stock but were Americans; thus little attention is paid to immigrants of Scottish ancestry from Ulster after the colonies became the United States."[44] This wasn't very helpful in the search for sweetness and light. After all, it is hard to kiss and make up if the estranged partner has vanished, or even mutated—and even harder if they had no recollection of ever having been a partner in the first place!

A slender volume edited in 1969 by Rodney Green, of Queen's University Belfast, on the Scotch-Irish in America was reissued in a very different political climate twenty-three years later. It included a perceptive introduction by Steve Ickringill carrying the story forward. A contribution by Maldwyn Jones established that Scotch-Irish immigration did continue into the nineteenth century,[45] adding to the substantial immigration from Ireland in the decades immediately before the Great Famine, although with the rapidly growing Catholic emigration it was declining sharply as a proportion of the total.

The Famine and Its Legacy

Let us be careful, then, not to blaspheme Providence by calling this God's famine.
—Bishop John Hughes of New York, 1847

Green's volume made a significant contribution to understanding pre-famine Scotch-Irish immigration. But an obvious omission from Green was the lack of any systematic attempt to address the implications of the Great Famine for relations between Catholic and Protestant—not least Catholic and Protestant from Ulster—in the United States. It can be argued, of course, that the actual Famine immigration, from 1846 to 1855, amounted to only about one-quarter of the total number of Irish immigrants and that as many—about 1.5 million—came before the Famine, to say nothing of the three million between 1855 and 1930. David Doyle has shown, too, in his major contributions in the *New History of Ireland,* reprinted as chapters 4 and 5 here, how many of the political and ecclesiastical institutions identified with the Famine immigrants were actually in place before they arrived.

Nevertheless it is the Famine immigration that not only continues to dominate the public imagination but also determines many of the professional judgments about the impact of the Irish on America. It was the Famine and its consequences that ensured, as Bill Williams puts it:

> Irish Catholics were in many respects the first "ethnic" group in America . . . the first immigrant group to arrive in extremely large numbers, to gain high visibility by clustering in cities, to retain a strong identification with the old homeland, and to appear sufficiently "different" in religion and culture so that acceptance by native-born Americans was not automatic, and assimilation was, therefore, prolonged. For their part the Irish immigrants in America came to realize that they shared a uniquely (tragic) experience and, in the face of Yankee hostility, a common destiny. Unlike other immigrants from Great Britain, the Irish had to succeed as a people, not just as individuals. They would have to construct an image of themselves as Irish *and* as Americans that would gain acceptance in the broad mainstream of American culture.[46]

Apart from the slip about them being from Great Britain—which would have disturbed many Britons as much as themselves—this graphically captures the challenge confronting the Catholic Irish, above all the Famine Irish, and the importance for American history in general of the manner in which they confronted that challenge. In doing so, their political skills would become legendary, culminating in the election of John F. Kennedy to the White House in 1960—even if it is worth pondering that, for all their mastery of the darker arts of municipal politics, for all the numbers of mayors of the great cities that they would produce, only one president would emerge from Irish Catholic ranks. But that itself may be to underrate the achievement. The bitter anti-Catholicism of much of Protestant America made a Catholic president impossible before 1960. Al Smith found to his immense political and personal cost in 1928 just how bitter the backlash against his Catholicism could be, even if his command of Catholic doctrine was reflected in his exasperated question, "What the hell is an encyclical?"

Smith may well have lost to Herbert Hoover in that boom year anyway. But much of the campaign against him was cast in terms of anti-Catholic fundamentalism. Indeed, it might be argued that no Catholic candidate other than John F. Kennedy could have carried the election in 1960. We now know how concerned his father was that the anti-Catholic vote that had helped destroy Al Smith would once again surface and that he minutely studied the campaign against Smith. In many respects 1960 could have been a rerun of 1928, except for the skill with which Kennedy defused the religious issue. That he *could* do so reflected how much had changed; that he *had* to do so reflected how much had to be changed.

Relations between Protestants and Catholics form a central theme in American history. By the later nineteenth century, according to the standard work of John Higham, the doyen of American historians of anti-immigration thought, "few Americans hated the Catholic Irish more than did the Protestant Irish."[47] But even if this were then true, it had not always been so, or at least apparently not to the same extent. The current consensus appears to be that relations between the two religions deteriorated sharply in the twenty or thirty years before the Famine. It may be that the image of irenic relations between Catholics and Protestants in the late eighteenth century, if anything, was reinforced by the arrival of distinguished political refugees like United Irish rebels Thomas Addis Emmet, William James McNeven, and William Sampson, who preached and practiced nonsectarianism. This image lends a more benign glow to the issue of denominational relations even before their deterioration came to be symbolized by the first Orange-Green riots in New York in 1824. In any case, relations between Catholics, mostly Irish, and Protestants, including, but by no means confined to Irish, were clearly worsening well before the Famine brought a huge surge in the number of Catholic immigrants.

If a community is to be defined on the basis of a common collective memory, there was little enough of that left by 1846 between Irish Protestants in general, Scotch-Irish in particular, and Catholic Irish in Ireland or America. Insofar as their memory involved relations with one another, it was a memory of almost continually strained relations in both countries over the previous generation. When Daniel O'Connell finally achieved Catholic Emancipation in 1829, many Protestants interpreted it as the beginning of the end of Protestant ascendancy, now that Catholics would gradually be able to make their three-fold superiority in numbers tell. Protestant immigrants from Ireland, and not only Scotch-Irish ones at this stage, were likely to provide support for any measures designed to keep Catholics in their place. The evangelical revival, gathering momentum among many Protestants in America, Britain, and Ireland itself, at this juncture, formed one mechanism by which this could be accomplished.

The injection of even sharper religious antipathies into public attitudes partly helps explain why Famine memories would become so divisive—why they would feature centrally in the Catholic sense of identity and scarcely at all in the Protestant. Collective memories decisively diverged, insofar as they had not done so already. Why should this be so, given the numbers of pre-Famine immigrants we mentioned earlier? Why should they have been flooded out of memory, so to speak, by the Famine inundation? Part of the answer derives from a closer examination of the implications of the figures.

Probably about three-quarter of a million Protestants, perhaps somewhat more, and probably more than half of them Scotch-Irish Presbyterians, immigrated from Ireland in the century and a half before 1846. This would average out—although the migration tended to occur in spurts—at about five or six thousand a year. A rather smaller number of Catholics appear to have emigrated over the same period, far fewer at first (the colonies were generally highly discriminatory against Catholics) but overtaking the number of Protestants by about 1830 at the latest. The immediate pre-Famine immigration had already become predominantly Catholic, even before the heavily Catholic Famine influx exceeded in a single decade the entire Protestant immigration of the previous century and a half.

Not only did the annual numbers dwarf the earlier inflow, but also the settlement of the immigrants in the cities gave them an instant profile far more pronounced than that of previous arrivals, especially Protestants who had either disappeared into the backcountry or who could be incorporated within the existing value system almost as easily as the "invisible immigrants" from England itself.[48] If the publicity for the Famine arrivals was far from uniformly positive—although much of America's response to the colossal challenge was remarkably constructive—it certainly made an impact on public perceptions.[49]

What proportion of emigrants were witnesses of famine, whether they came out during the Great Famine itself or later? Early childhood memories burn themselves into adult consciousness to varying degrees. A twenty-five-year-old leaving in 1860 would have been fifteen in 1850, old enough to have seen sights he or she would never forget. Many born shortly before 1845 will have lost a parent, grandparent, or sibling during the Famine. But many children born down to about 1880, if not later, were likely to have had at least a mother, and perhaps a father, who had survived the Famine to tell the tale. The likelihood of having heard of the death of a kinsman or kinswoman was high. Emigrants born in 1830 who left Ireland in 1851 or 1852, the years of peak emigration, would have experienced five or six famine years in their impressionable late teen and early adult years; if these children lived to be seventy, they could have kept direct famine memories alive until 1900. Their children, born between about 1855 and 1870, and who in turn lived to be seventy, could have retold the stories as late as 1940. None of these scenarios can be definitive, but they do provide a chronological framework for the exploration of memory.[50]

For that matter, many of the pre-Famine immigrants, most of whom would have arrived in the United States after 1830, would have heard of the horrors from relatives still in Ireland, apart altogether from the vivid reporting in the American press. Many would presumably have sent remittances back, partly to bring over other family members, who would have given eyewitness accounts to the earlier immigrants, many of whom would still have felt a close relationship with the afflicted communities. The majority of immigrants of the two pre-Famine decades may have regarded the Great Famine as something happening in a far away country. But it was definitely not one of which they knew little.

We cannot know how much explicit recall occurred in individual families over the years, but many children growing up down to the end of the century, or even surviving well into the twentieth century, may have heard firsthand accounts from survivors, inside or outside the family. Between them, those with direct memories of the Famine, or who could have heard of it from their parents or grandparents, are likely to have constituted the large majority of immigrants well into the twentieth century.

In light of all this, it is understandable that Kerby Miller can describe Tom Brick, who was born in 1881 and immigrated in 1902, and whose early life in Kerry and the American midwest Miller reconstructs with exemplary scholarship, as living "in the

The Keystone View Company of Meadsville, Pennsylvania, clearly targeted Irish-American consumers with this 1902 stereograph card. Its thatched cottage plays on their nostalgia for home at the same time that its title, "A Letter from Pat in America," focuses on the proverbial American letter that was eagerly awaited in Ireland, especially if it contained a remittance. (Library of Congress, Prints and Photographs Division, LC-USZ62-123754)

Famine's shadow," even though he didn't die until 1979.[51] It seems reasonable, too, to suppose that there were others like Elizabeth Gurley Flynn (1890–1964), the celebrated labor activist, who "carried memories of the Great Hunger through her Irish grandfather's stories."[52] That grandfather came from Mayo and her grandmother came from Galway, two neighboring western counties among those worst affected by the Famine. Indeed, an increasing proportion of immigrants as the century progressed came from those western areas where memories are likely to have remained most vivid.

Not all those who could bear witness did so. Memory operates in a variety of ways. There were bound to be survivors who would not speak of their famine experience. Silence has been observed in some survivors of all traumatic experiences. Some sought to banish the memories, fleeing from even any shadow that invaded their minds. Their children may never have heard a word fall from their lips. But if they were growing up with other Irish children, as they so often were, and then mixing with Irish workers, and patronizing Irish saloons, is it really conceivable that they never heard a solitary reference to it outside their homes?

How did the Irish, in Ireland or America, make sense of the Famine? The instinctive appeal of all peoples under pressure was to Providence in the first instance. Some Great Famine victims did attribute their plight to the will of God, as a divine chastisement for their sins. Some evangelical Protestants fully concurred, interpreting it as divine retribution for Catholic defiance of God's will.

Much of the interpretation of the Famine in the British official mind was also to present it as the will of God—in this case, not so much a sign of displeasure at Catholics as a sign of Providence's plans for economic progress, which, of course, some may have thought could come to much the same thing. The most eloquent Irish nationalist contribution to the analysis of causation sought to secularize the source of the disaster: John Mitchel famously dismissed the appeal to the supernatural with the caustic comment that "the Almighty indeed sent the potato blight, but the English created the Famine."[53] But it wasn't only Mitchel, and many other Irish nationalists, who rejected the attribution of responsibility to a grand divine plan, whether out of Old Testament wrath or, alternatively, to stamp the seal of approval on the idea of economic "progress" as part of the Divinity's long-term planning for His creatures.

Bishop John Hughes of New York, the most prominent Catholic spokesman in America, born in Tyrone in 1797, whose exposition of human rights in famine conditions remains striking even today, took his stand on the principle that the right to life took precedence over all other natural rights—indeed, even over supernatural ones—in his graphic image of the starving man having the right to seize the bread from the altar. The occasion for Hughes's public declamation was an invitation from the General Irish Relief Committee of the City of New York to deliver a public lecture at the Broadway Tabernacle in March 1847. This was no insignificant affair but a major public event, the *Tribune* greeting the occasion as "one of the intellectual waymarks of the season. There is hardly another man among us so eminently fitted by origin, education, sympathy, intellect, observation and experience to shed such light upon the causes and intensity of Ireland's unexampled miseries as will compel the most reckless or selfish to pause, to shudder, and deplore."[54]

Hughes's long exposition is fascinating for several reasons. His solution rests squarely on his interpretation of morality and his attribution of the Famine to human rather than divine agency:

> The sacredness of the rights of property must be maintained at all sacrifices, unless we would have society to dissolve itself into its original elements; still the rights of life are dearer and higher than those of property; and in a general famine like the present, there is no law of Heaven, nor of nature, that forbids a starving man to seize on bread wherever he can find it, even though it should be the loaves of proposition on the altar of God's temple. But, I would say to those who maintain the sacred and inviolable rights of property, if they would have the claim respected, to be careful also and scrupulous in recognizing the rights of humanity. In a crisis like that which is now passing, the Irish may submit to die rather than violate the rights of property; but on such a calamity, should it ever happen, which God forbid, the Scotch will not submit; the English will not

submit; the French should not submit; and depend upon it, the Americans will not submit. Let us be careful, then, not to blaspheme Providence by calling this God's famine. Society, the great civil corporation which we call the State, is bound so long as it has the power to do so, to guard the lives of its members against being sacrificed by famine from within, as much against their being slaughtered by the enemy from without. But the vice which is inherent in our system of social and political economy is so subtle that it eludes all pursuit, that you cannot find or trace it to any responsible source. The man, indeed, over whose dead body the coroner holds the inquest, has been murdered, but no one has killed him. There is no external wound; there is no symptom of internal disease. Society guarded him against all outward violence; it merely encircled him around in order to keep up what is termed the regular current of trade, and then political economy, with an invisible hand, applied the air-pump to the narrow limit within which he was confined, and exhausted the atmosphere of his physical life. Who did it? No one did it, and yet it has been done.[55]

A different tone could be heard from some members of Congress during attempts to vote American government aid for Ireland at just this juncture, which despite apparently substantial sympathy failed, perhaps partly because President James Polk had made clear he would veto any such bill—itself suggesting he thought there was a chance it might pass—on the grounds that it would be unconstitutional.[56] However academic in the circumstances, the arguments on both sides make interesting reading in light of "human rights" interventionist proposals today, with Senator John Niles of Connecticut opposing the proposal for relief on the grounds that it would be "disrespectful" toward England by implying inadequacy on its part.[57]

Despite the senator's optimism, the Great Famine did not, and will not, go away. This obliges us to remain alert to the extraordinary experience of the Famine generation. The first great wave of mass immigration to the United States consisted of refugees from a famine that seems to have killed a higher proportion of the Irish national population than any other natural catastrophe anywhere over the past three centuries; this means that the Famine must be considered a building block in the making of America. Many more of those who joined the post-Famine emigration over the following century had their fates at least heavily influenced by the impact of the Famine on Irish society over the long term. In that sense, although chronologically post-famine, for the surge of immigrants unloosed by the Famine ended in 1855, nevertheless they too are children, or grandchildren, of the Famine experience in an Ireland significantly shaped, physically and psychologically, by the impact of the disaster.

Memories of the Famine were revived by news of evictions of tenant farmers from their holdings by landlords. Though the number of evictions declined sharply after the flood of the Famine years, the fear of eviction continued to stalk the Irish countryside, intensifying once more with the agricultural slump of the late 1870s. It is instructive to note how large it looms in Tom Brick's memory well into the twentieth century, and long after the landlord class had been bought out. The circumstances of the late-nineteenth-century eviction recorded by Brick were far less desperate than those during the Famine. Nevertheless, two impressions emerge strikingly from his account. First, the entire neighborhood rallied around the evicted family and relished their subsequent subterfuges in outwitting the landlord. Second, although this was an objectively better off family, in no way threatened by starvation, this was an identity conflict as much as an economic one, a "them versus us" confrontation. Eviction violated a sense of fairness, of the proper moral order of things, as well as involving purely material considerations. It belonged to the class of moral economy, as well as monetary economy.[58]

This sense of violated justice encompassed hatred of landlordism and was intimately intertwined with hatred of British rule, then stoked by searing memories of the Famine and widespread desire for revenge. It was no accident that "Revenge for Skibbereen," the ballad derived from the harrowing accounts of the Famine death scenes in Skibbereen, Co. Cork, in 1847, was so popular in America.[59] Injustice fueled the substantial and crucial financial support Irish Americans provided for Fenianism (the Irish independence movement actually founded in New York in 1858), for the Irish Land League founded in 1879 to resist and finally destroy the power of the English-supported landlord class in Ireland, for the Irish Volunteer force that led to the Easter Rising in 1916, and for the Irish Republican Army that would fight the War of Independence between 1919 and 1921 that led to a substantial degree of self-government in the Anglo-Irish Treaty of December 1921. It was no accident that the president of the Irish Republic and of the Sinn Fein movement, Éamon de Valera, should spend from June 1919 to December 1920 in America raising funds for the struggle and seeking to influence American politics in favor of the Irish cause. However convoluted the relations between different varieties of Irish nationalism that Kevin Kenny delineates in chapter 9, the memory of the Famine became the focal point around which crystallized Irish America's search for historical understanding of why they found themselves where they were.[60]

The Famine was therefore central to the type of country America became, for the Irish who poured in left their distinctive mark on politics, on religion, and on the labor movement, to mention only the three most obvious examples. As this impact was most prominent in north and central east coast states, it is not surprising that Famine memorials have been erected recently, or that Famine curricula have come to be devised for teaching within human rights courses in some public school systems. The New York American Irish Teachers Association helped promote the 1997 New York State bill, using a curriculum constructed under the inspirational direction of Professor Maureen Murphy of Hofstra University, herself the editor of a fascinating eyewitness account of the Famine by Asenath Nicholson.[61]

Whatever chance there still was of Catholics and Protestants from Ireland being able to identify with the common name of Irishman after the 1840s, and that had shrunk under the twin pressures of the evangelical revival and Catholic Emancipation in Ireland, the Famine effectively buried it at a mass level for long to come. Although poor Protestants suffered from the Famine, it became part of the self-image of many Protestants at the cutting edge of the evangelical crusade that the Famine was a peculiarly Catholic affliction, targets of a grand providential plan. If the Famine was designed in the strategic thinking of the Divinity to rid Him of these devotees of the anti-Christ, how could Protestants die from famine unless they were already half-Catholics? This perspective made it logically impossible for real Protestants to die from famine. Despite the fact, too, that several Church of Ireland clergymen ministered valiantly to the Famine victims, some dying themselves from contagion, the landlords engaged in seizing the opportunity for mass evictions of tenants were predominantly Protestant, as were the bulk of government officials responsible for administering relief, which could bring gratitude for their labors but also resentment at perceived harshness in the implementation of often heartless relief regulations. Despite, then, the heroic work of some individual Protestants, the Famine intensified the already growing sense of difference between Catholic and Protestant in Ireland, a difference widening almost to a chasm in the conditions of religious conflict in many places in the United States.

From "Coffin Ship" to City Hall

One of the mysteries of world history is how the most impoverished of European immigrants should adapt so effectively in so many respects not only to urban living but also to life in the biggest and most dynamic cities of all. "Adapt" in the sense that within two generations of arriving, or in some cases even less than that, they were to a quite disproportionate degree actually governing these cities.[62] In principle they ought to have been suffering disorientation from all types of anomie. Some were, at least as far as the medical and criminal statistics record behavior influenced by this experience. While these statistics require further analysis—there are huge interpretive problems with them—it would be surprising if they did not, to at least some extent, partly reflect psychological difficulties of adjustment to new lifestyles.[63] But that makes the political success of the immigrants all the more striking. How did so improbable a transformation occur, and occur so quickly? The arrivals were not of course victims of coffin ships, in the sense that by definition they survived, and for that matter the majority of ships were not coffin ships in the literal sense. But conditions on board were hideous during the Famine years—immigrants of later generations could actually enjoy the voyage, "sailing in style"—and the Famine Irish might seem to have come off the ships little better than a repulsive rabble.[64] What turned them into such effective players on the political stage?

If it is striking that San Francisco elected its first Irish mayor in 1867, whereas New York had to wait until 1880 and Boston until 1884, is it not even more striking that we should assume that 1884, much less 1880, was somehow slow or delayed? Certainly, Irish immigrants had played a far from inactive role in the politics of the late eighteenth and early nineteenth centuries, but they were not generally as impoverished as the Famine immigrants.[65] If immigrant involvement in politics had become increasingly common in the immediate pre-Famine decades, the bulk of Famine immigrants came in far more wretched circumstances. Did not their patent poverty, their ragged raucousness, make them seem more like deadweight than a new political class? If their numbers were ominous, could they ever punch their weight, or were they not more likely to reinforce the reputation of their countrymen already here, notoriously fractious, renowned for the faction fights that pitted county against county, conspicuously deaf to "the common name of Irishman," as Kevin Kenny's account of their internecine labor disputes in chapter 12 reminds us? Driven by internal rivalries, it might seem they brought as little political as economic capital with them. The skeptical observers would soon learn, however, that no immigrants so impoverished would ever bring as much political experience, and political craft, to America. When blended with the political experience acquired by the pre-Famine immigrants in the intense struggles over religious and school issues, they would make a formidable addition to the political power of the Irish in New York.

The irony was that the county, often held to be a bastion of faction, became the basis of immigrant social organization. The county proved to be the stepping stone toward, rather than an obstacle to, cooperation on the basis of a common sense of nationality. Many other factors contributed, but it is a misconception in much of the historiography to think of local organizations as inevitably obstructing the emergence of a sense of common Irish identity. Rather, counties, not unlike parishes within the Church, were building blocks for the greater glory of the whole. However intense the internal and external rivalries, they were driven by a sense of common objective for the grander purpose which they served. County loyalty and a sense of Irish nationality were far more likely to be mutually reinforcing than mutually exclusive.[66]

This may have been partly because although immigrants from the same county, or even parish, did cluster in their American settlements as was normal for all immigrants, they were also thrown cheek by jowl for the first time with men and women from other counties. Immigrants met far more non-countymen and women than could ever be the case in Ireland. Intermarriage, meaning intercounty marriage, became familiar on a significant scale for the first time, even if intracounty marriage remained more frequent.[67] To cite only the most obvious example, the best known Irish American of the century, the heavyweight boxing champion, John L. Sullivan, could never have been born to the same parents in Ireland, because Athlone and Tralee were so far apart that they would never have met.

One cannot claim that immigrants only began to be "nationalized" when they arrived. That had begun already in Ireland; since 1825, under the guiding genius of Daniel O'Connell, who emerged as the greatest popular leader of the age, the masses had been mobilized in pursuit of Catholic Emancipation, and repeal of the Act of Union with Britain. But the seed sown in Ireland ripened more quickly in the kinder political climate of the United States, which should count the legacy of O'Connell among its potent political influences for long after the Famine. Of course, the seed did not fall on unbroken ground. In America, too, the need for the Catholic Church to defend itself against the hostility, or even the aggression, of the dominant Protestantism of the time helped hone popular political skills. Catholic immigrants who had become politicized during O'Connell's campaigns in Ireland found themselves on familiar territory in America. The emergence of the Catholic Church out of the overwhelmingly Protestant country of the eighteenth century was a highly political affair. Famine immigrants could mesh easily into the political culture of American Catholicism of the time. The big difference with Ireland was that America was relatively far more democratic and therefore provided far more opportunity for effective political action. For all their capacity for internal dissension, sometimes virulent, what really distinguished Irish immigrants was their ability to organize and cooperate.[68] America offered them both occasion and opportunity to do so.

The creation of a common sense of national identity builds on both positive and negative influences. The Famine, following on O'Connell's campaigns, provided a powerful common memory. The Catholic Church provided spiritual, and often enough material, solace. It probably derived enhanced status, among both Americans in general and the Irish in particular, from the Civil War, which contributed toward tightening, or even forging, bonds between the fighting men and the Church, given the social and religious role of chaplains as links with their families and the role of nuns, many themselves born in Ireland, as nursing sisters.[69]

A common enemy, particularly one already familiar from home, provides an enormous incentive to pull together. And the hostility and derision they met from the anti-Catholic, anti-immigration Know-Nothing movement, in particular, recycled over later generations by the American Protestant Association in the 1890s and by the Ku Klux Klan in the 1920s, provided just the incentive to present a united front. Apart from African Americans, who endured a unique horror, they were the most frequent Americans to be regularly mocked as subhominid, as apes and monkeys, in the pages of "respectable" intellectual periodicals. Negative stereotype almost compels "contribution" history and ideology—the besetting sin of filiopietism. But it is the instinctive way of overcoming denigration—to insist that one's contributions are just as important as those of one's tormentors—that inevitably results in exaggerated claims, which, in turn, can be mocked by their detractors. For example, *Puck*'s depiction of the St. Patrick's Day parade from 1894 presented the stalwart sons of Erin with monkey faces.[70] The memory would linger on and fester, even as the enemy had retreated, to affect the perspectives of the descendants—perhaps to be wiped away, or at least completely repressed—only when the irrefutable conspicuous material success of later generations silenced the sneers directed at their "inherent inferiority."

Fueled by these impulses, they would show remarkable ability to pull together, to mobilize their numbers in the only place on earth then that gave effective voice to numbers. At the same time, and essential to the coherence of the entire Irish-American urban political system, their myriad of political activists would show remarkable patience in waiting their turn for their rewards, a central theme of both Moynihan and Trillin in their chapters in this volume.

The manner in which a community looks after its poor (in the days before a welfare state) says much about the idea of that community—indeed, about its very existence. While welfare organizations stretched back to at least the charitable Irish Society of Boston in 1737, with the Friendly Brothers and Friendly Sons of St. Patrick being established in New York and Philadelphia in 1767 and 1771, respectively, it was the St. Vincent de Paul Society that formed the backbone of philanthropic endeavor throughout Catholic Irish America after the Famine. However often presented by hostile witnesses, even sometimes justifiably, as mean spirited, the St. Vincent de Paul Society served an indispensable purpose. One might ask what realistic alternative did its critics propose?

Among the most active philanthropists in New York were the directors of the Emigrant Savings Bank, established in 1850, with close connections to the Catholic

Frederick Opper's 1894 anti-Irish illustration for *Puck* was prompted by the American Protective Association's petition to New York City Mayor George B. McClellan demanding that the March 17th tradition of flying a green flag on municipal buildings, including City Hall, be abolished. McClellan replied that the Irish were a noble class and deserved much credit "and if Americans did try to down the flag it was a dishonorable kind of patriotism." (Courtesy of John T. Ridge)

Church. The extraordinary savings surge on which so many immigrants embarked almost immediately on arrival in New York City—depositing savings, however humble the amounts, on a regular basis for years—and which was presumably replicated wherever comparable institutions were available, may have reflected something of the search for security among people who had seen the price of insecurity paid through eviction and death. In fact, they quite possibly oversaved, stinting themselves in order to help bring other family members out through remittances and to build up some protection against what they saw as a callous and unpredictable world. How else could they see it?

The Emigrant Savings Bank flourished on this deposit and remittance trade, its board members counting among the economic leaders of the Irish community in New York, enjoying high public esteem, as Marion Casey shows in her original and meticulous reconstruction in chapter 10, which also serves to remind us of the vagaries of "memory" history. If the directors did well out of the bank, they generally did well for the bank, too. But a bank on this scale served a public, as well as a purely private purpose—as a bonding agent in its own right, an "Irish" institution, almost all its business dealing with matters Irish, linking the emigrants with home and with one another, creating something akin to a stakeholder sense of a common institutional base among its thousands of depositors. As in any case, savings bank deposits at this stage could be invested only in public bonds or in real estate, they had no choice but to be intimately involved with the political process. And although a private bank, their close connections with the Commissioners of Emigration involved them, in a proactive manner, in a highly politicized business, carving out space for the Catholic Irish in a world of non-Catholic, or even anti-Catholic, charity.

The parish was a bonding unit for Irish Catholics, with the church—often the most impressive construction they could consider their own, built from their own dollars and cents—the psychological and the physical focal point of their communal identity. What the parish did not provide, in the Irish case, in contrast to other immigrant Catholic experiences, was a sense of a distinctive identity through language. The Irish appear to have been the main Catholic immigrants whose own pastors advocated language abandonment both at home and abroad. This was partly in pursuit of the ideal of an Americanization, which had already adopted English as the national language, of which the Irish clergy were enthusiastic agents.[71] Indeed, the Irish ecclesiastical officer class often sought to impose English on other immigrants in America, to the extent of sometimes provoking intense resistance from European Catholics who sought to retain their own languages. Part of the tension between Irish bishops and other Catholics derived from Irish ecclesiastical pressure on the others to abandon their languages, although it was also an Irish bishop who first allowed the establishment of "national parishes" in Chicago. As late as 1912 there were among the 1,600 national parishes in America (based mainly on language, as distinct from the normal territorial parishes) 346 German, 336 Polish, and 211 Italian churches.[72]

The Irish were the only major English-speaking immigrants apart from inhabitants of Britain. All other European immigrants arrived without knowledge of English. Yet the social mobility of their first generations appears to have been broadly similar to that of the Irish at comparable stages, however uncertain such general statements must be in our present state of knowledge. Immigrants in general naturally acquired English gradually after arriving. But many immigrants preserved a vigorous linguistic community for more than one generation. Jewish immigrants promoted several widely read newspapers, as well as a lively literature in Yiddish, even if it would decline as the twentieth-century progressed.

It is natural to assume that the knowledge of English with which all Irish Protestant, and most Irish Catholic immigrants arrived—even if perhaps over a quarter of the Famine immigrants had Irish as their first language—must have been a major asset in the social mobility stakes. That would appear to be simple common sense. The problem is that it is actually very difficult to establish firm correlations between language and social mobility. The most obvious comparison would appear to be that of the Irish who arrived between 1845 and 1860 and the almost equal number of Germans. If language were a decisive variable, one would expect Irish social mobility to have been significantly higher than that of the Germans. The most recent study to refer to the issue, however, does not find this to have been the case, to the author's puzzlement.[73] One possibility is that other advantages the Germans had—particularly higher skills and more capital—helped compensate for their disadvantage on the language side, if disadvantage it was, and that they would have risen relatively more rapidly had they brought a knowledge of English with them. But like so much else in our present state of knowledge, or rather ignorance, that remains a hypothesis.

The mechanics and psychology of language acquisition, language loss, language abandonment, and language denial are among the most fascinating of all human experiences, which still require much research in the case of Ireland itself and the Irish abroad. This is a difficult and complex subject, with both concepts and evidence still grossly underdeveloped. One must therefore be acutely conscious of the danger of generalization on the basis of prejudice, stereotype, and unexamined assumptions, and we must couch our conclusions in the most tentative terms.

This does not necessarily mean that Irish mobility was not influenced by language. But the situation seems more complex than a simple equation between knowledge of English and automatically higher social mobility. What seems safer to surmise in our present state of uncertainty is that their knowledge of English influenced the Irish routes of mobility as well as, if not more than, the rates. It clearly gave them a practical advantage, as well as a psychological one, in areas of public employment. Knowledge of English facilitated municipal employment, in politics, in the police, in anything requiring literacy in English, as well as in the Church and trade unions, even if many skilled unions long conducted affairs in German.[74] It may have helped direct their thoughts toward politics in the first place in that the Irish newspapers, which played a central bonding role in fostering the idea of an Irish community—for they purported to represent Irish national and not simply local interests and issues—were published in English.

One can speculate at length, but inconclusively, about the implications of language shift in Ireland before the majority of immigrants arrived in America. The wider question is whether the routes so many of them adopted would impede their mobility over a longer period. Moynihan surmised that "instead of profiting by their success in the all-but despised roles of ward heeler and policemen, the Irish seem to have been trapped by it," invoking Eugene O'Neill to add, "as with the elder Tyrone, they seem almost to have ruined their talent by playing one role over and over again until 'they could do little else.'"[75]

Melodramatic though this sounds, could there be any truth in it? "The economic rewards in America over the past century," Moynihan insisted, "have gone to entrepreneurs, not to fonctionnaires,"[76] believing the Irish to have become trapped in a political and bureaucratic rut. But did their relative success in occupations for which knowledge of English was an immediate asset in fact inhibit the development of an entrepreneurial attitude among Irish Catholics? Even if so—and a majority of Irish men, and a much bigger majority of women, did not work in the public sector, although this does not mean they did not aspire to the security of public sector employment for their children—how can this be weighed against the desperate desire for security among the Famine generation in particular, as reflected in the saving habits of many of them? The entire issue is a subject for large-scale research without rigid a priori assumptions.

Perhaps the boldest surmise in our present state of knowledge is that had Irish Catholics arrived in the normal way, without a knowledge of English, they too would have achieved social mobility, but perhaps in a different way and at a different pace (though whether faster or slower is at present uncertain) from the way in which it actually happened.[77]

If the language issue is a complex and speculative one, the importance of music as a bonding mechanism, to say nothing of its wider social and cultural role, has recently become much clearer as the subject has attracted greatly increased research interest. Music was a language that spoke to Irish immigrants across county, class, gender, and distance—both songs and tunes of home and songs that related to incidents and episodes in their American experience—in a manner with which they instantly associated, creating a communal cultural well from which immigrants from all over Ireland could drink deeply. Much of this music entered wider American popular culture, so that in giving voice to their sense of Irish identity, their music actually helped them bond more firmly with many other Americans, too. As in other spheres, they became more American by becoming initially more, rather than less, Irish.

Although after Finley Peter Dunne had departed to New York, before 1900 Chicago could still boast Captain Francis O'Neill, the indefatigable founder-collector of Irish music. Dancing was widely and spontaneously popular, as Tom Brick, a step dancer of renown, realized on finding himself much in demand in the midwest.[78] The great fairs in New York and Chicago in 1897 prominently featured Irish dance, duly organized on a county basis.[79] Music has remained so central to Irish America, and Irish music has won so many adherents outside the Irish community, that chapters 14 to 18, by Marion Casey, Rebecca Miller, Mick Moloney, and Rob Snyder, are devoted to the rich variety of Irish musical experience from several different perspectives. Their range allows one to appreciate the vitality and significance of the subject.

Some of the most enduring songs themselves evoked another mass bonding experience, at least in the northern states, for they recalled the experience of the Civil War. While the exploits of Meagher's Brigade and the Fighting 69th are well known, important, too, was the fact that many of the 150,000 Irish, who are said to have served in the Union army, at times mixed with Irish soldiers from other areas whom they would otherwise have never met. And the songs crossed the country, premised on both the Irish and the American national sentiments of their audiences, it being the good fortune of the majority of the Irish-born that circumstances permitted their two loyalties to be mutually reinforcing during the formative post-Famine period.

If sport was often war by another name, from the boxing ring to the playing fields —the Fighting Irish was not an accidental soubriquet for Notre Dame football[80]—it served as a bonding agent in Irish-American consciousness for many, as Ralph Wilcox and Larry McCarthy well illustrate in chapters 19 and 20, while it also came to serve as a conduit into a strong sense of popular American consciousness.

Men and Women

One of the most distinctive of all bonding features of the post-Famine immigrant experience was the balanced gender ratio. This was crucial in permitting the Irish to sustain themselves as a distinctive community as long as they wished, although not everywhere all the time, because the ratio did not necessarily remain in balance everywhere. Irish immigration was unusual in European terms in that the number of males and females, taking one decade with another, remained broadly in balance for most of the period, certainly since the Famine. This derived largely from circumstances in Ireland, arising in substantial measure from a combination of slow economic growth that created few jobs and the inheritance patterns that emerged mainly after the Famine. These factors effectively left only one son and one daughter per farm family with inheritance or marriage prospects, compelling most of the remainder to emigrate to find jobs and husbands or wives.

The first scholar, to my knowledge, to note the unusual gender balance was D. A. E. Harkness in the 1931 volume on international migration commissioned by the National Bureau of Economic Research.[81] The implications were first explored in a series of Thomas Davis lectures on emigration, broadcast on Radio Eireann between September 1972 and January 1973. In that series the distinguished Irish sociology and economics professors, Damian Hannan and James Meenan, as well as myself, referred to the significance of the gender ratio.

As publication of summaries of the lectures remained confined to the *Irish Press*, the *Irish Times*, and the *RTE (Radio Telefís Eireann) Guide*, however, they remained unknown to the wider academic public.[82] While there would be some subsequent Irish references to the topic, it would be a decade or more before the work of Hasia Diner and Janet Nolan in the United States put the subject firmly on the academic map in the 1980s, followed by the synoptic survey by Miller, Doyle, and Patricia Kelleher.[83] Nevertheless the subject is one of such potential that much still remains to be discovered about the relative roles of men and women in shaping the contours of the entire immigrant experience.

The Irish immigrant woman as the subject of thorough scholarly inquiry was long neglected because the two types of historians most eager to explore her history— labor historians and exponents of women's history—were more interested in limited aspects of the behavior of Irish women than in their full lives as actually lived.[84]

Labor historians produced important studies of Irish workers, summarized here in Kevin Kenny's chapter 12. But they tended to be attracted by visible clusters of labor in factories and on building sites, canals and railways, all conducive to high-profile conflict situations, or to attempts at large-scale labor organization. Labor history tended to focus disproportionately on conflicts between capital and labor, which involved mainly male workers. That about half of all Irish female immigrants became domestic servants tended to make them even more invisible to labor historians of this persuasion. There was doubtless frequent tension between middle-class women as mistresses of working-class women, but these occurred behind closed doors and drawn curtains, unless they were recounted to a later public through such sources as Boston's Mayor James Michael Curley's autobiography, regaling the reader with his description of the unscheduled abrupt parting of the ways of his mother, a servant, from her employer. These did not provide the source material of major public conflict.

If labor historians were mainly interested in women as paid workers, historians of women were ironically also mainly interested in them as paid workers. They accepted, at least for practical purposes, the male concept of work as work outside the home, or at least outside one's own home. Housework qualified as work, of course, if domestic servants did it. If it was merely wives and mothers who did it, however, housework was not work. By male definition in the first instance, a working wife was a wife who earned money outside the home. She was not, by ideological definition, working while at home. As most Irish female immigrants spent most of their adult lives as wives and mothers and in the first couple of generations could not normally afford to hire domestic servants, this left them beneath the historical radar.

It is precisely in the context of family that they feature most prominently, in a matter of fact way, in Finley Peter Dunne's *Mr. Dooley*. While it is the irrepressible Molly Donohue who catches Mr. Dooley's eye—she who scandalized the street by being the first, among other civilization-enriching contributions, to ride a bicycle in bloomers and but for whom, in Mr. Dooley's sympathetic estimation, half the life would be gone out of Bridgeport[85]—the women who lagged behind her were people, too. Many of them, in fact, were quite formidable personalities in their own right. Dooley's depictions of marital relations rarely convey any sense of the woman being other than the equal, if not indeed the manager, of the man. For example, he recounts the ploy of Honoriah Nolan to get Danny Duggan to propose; he depicts the disposition of Mrs. Malachi Duggan, who was singularly lacking any sense of deference toward her husband; and he shows the despondency of the hapless Hogan in the face of his wife's determination to christen their children according to her notions of rising social respectability. Hogan became another to succumb helplessly, in Charles Fanning's felicitous phrase, to "the disappearance of the old rough-and-tumble in favor of the more insidious scramble for genteel status."[86]

In any group of rising social aspirations and pretensions, wives were likely to wield disproportionate influence in normal circumstances, as Dan Mulligan recognized in resigning himself to spending his life trundling in the slipstream of the social ambitions of his wife in Edward Harrigan's *Cordelia's Aspirations* of 1883. That does not necessarily mean they choose to jettison, in gadarene fashion, traditional names in favor of "fashionable" ones among their social betters whom they craved to emulate or impress. Naming can nonetheless provide a clue to the mindsets of mothers, perhaps in "the abandonment of the name Bridget by the second generation of Irish Americans," that Ruth-Ann Harris has detected, because in her view of its too intimate identification with domestic service, at just the moment when the mothers were determined to move beyond it.[87]

Women, then, are often neglected on several scores—as workers in the home, their own homes or those of others; as mothers; as wives providing psychological support for their husbands and children (generally at least equally neglected in the historiography, it must be said); as influences on their children's choice of job paths, where they had any choice; as grandmothers, often giving mothers some relief in taking care of children; as widows, almost wholly neglected in research; as consumers, making a significant impact on the economy through their purchasing decisions, both for themselves and their families, à la Cordelia, where they were crucial to the functioning of the retail market; and often, indeed, as managers of the family finances, including savings.[88] All these roles remain to be further explored.

Accepting that the exposure of about half of Irish-born girls to domestic service gave them an opportunity of observing the domestic habits of their social superiors, how much depended on how superior their superiors were? How far would the informal education of a domestic in a distinctly better off household differ from one in which the woman of the house was only a step above the servant? Did domestics think of treating their own children like their employer treated hers? For that matter, how did the other half of women, those who did not go into domestic service, approach all these issues? The more rewarding are studies of domestic servants (like Margaret Lynch-Brennan's chapter 11 in this volume), the more questions they stimulate.

In the 1972–1973 Thomas Davis Lectures, and again in *Dreamers of Dreams* (1984), I surmised that the settlement patterns of Irish males may have been influenced by the job prospects for females. Girls traveled for the most part as individuals, needed work quickly after arriving, and qualified for little but domestic service—all pointing inexorably to urban employment.[89] It seems likely that the location of the females could have exerted a magnetic influence on decisions by young males as to where to try their fortune.

Irish Catholic culture (despite concerns occasionally expressed by clergy and the provision of welfare services at ports or railway stations to assist unaccompanied girls) was far less restrictive of the independent activity of young women than was the case in several other immigrant European cultures. Irish Catholic culture exalted their "honor" in a manner that imposed a code of sexual restraint that "repressed" Irish males, so that females were not felt to require the constant vigilance deemed necessary in cultures where such repression was not as central to male behavior. This was also true of Irish Protestant culture, so that Catholics and Protestants had far more in common on this score than their doctrinal disputes might lead the unwary to surmise. Girls were allowed to emigrate on their own and to venture into outside society on their own. Female (and male) repression in this respect (or civilized self-restraint, as it was seen in the Irish Catholic and Irish Protestant culture of the time) fashioned assumptions about the degree of sexual self-control that was unimaginable in cultures that sanctioned more sexually active behavior. Hence, this was one reason that Irish immigrant culture regarded domestic service as a viable, even desirable, occupation for young, single females, and it was perhaps one reason for Irish girls to accept positions in domestic service to a much greater extent than did females in several other immigrant cultures.

It would still be interesting to have this hypothesis explored further to see how far female settlement patterns influenced the overall location of Irish immigrants. "Go West, Young Man" was the famous injunction of Horace Greeley. But what about Young Woman? Would more young men have gone if the young women had been willing to go at the time? Some young men did, but most young men did not. Although the shortage of Irish girls did not prevent young men from seeking their fortunes in the Californian Gold Rush, or other west coast ventures, the absolute numbers involved were very small, compared with those who remained in the east. The venture could be represented as an intended temporary sojourn way out west, and the fate of individuals depended heavily on circumstances.

Worth investigating, too, would be the relationships between the gender ratio and the practice of religion. In Ireland women were probably the main carriers of the intensified religious devotion in roughly the century after the Famine, the phenomenon christened by Emmet Larkin as "the Devotional Revolution" in his seminal contributions to the understanding of Irish Catholicism.[90] There seems a high probability that the same was true in Irish America. It is clear, too, that many nuns were formidable personalities who brooked no nonsense from God or man. It is good to see the current exploration of the massive contribution of nuns in coping with the challenges of destitution and orphanage. The role of women in general, and of nuns in particular—not only in philanthropy but also in education—has only gradually come to be recognized, thanks mainly to contributions by several female historians of Catholic background. These include Ellen Skerrett, Suellen Hoy, Margaret MacCurtain, Janet Nolan, Maureen Fitzgerald, and Deirdre Mageean, who appear to be more sensitive than male historians in general, or non-Catholic female historians, to this dimension of female entrepreneurial and managerial activity, both within and without the Church.

It has been widely asserted that Irish-American women married relatively late, and relatively rarely, allegedly reflecting their desire for independence from the horrors of "patriarchy." Unless the recent explosive findings of Marc Foley and Timothy Guinnane to the contrary (based for the first time on statistical rather than anecdotal evidence) can be overturned, much of this type of reasoning will require revision, with serious potential consequences for interpretations based on the assumption of relatively rare and relatively late marriage by American standards—which I must admit to having to some extent shared myself.[91]

The image of real nineteenth- and early-twentieth-century Irish-American women that emerges from serious research into the values, attitudes, and behavior of actual women—mostly working class, mostly wives and mothers—as distinct from, and sometimes in contrast to, views about them expressed mainly by outside observers, is of people with a sense of their own dignity and their own rights as understood in the context of their own culture.[92] Just such a picture emerges from Margaret Mulrooney's model analysis of the women of the Dupont factory, making her work a significant contribution.[93] It may well be—suspicious though one must be of stereotype—that the image of Irish women, "long symbols of strong-willed women in American popular culture," has a certain basis in reality.[94] It is also clear, however, that despite the advances made in the study of the subject, much remains to be learned about all aspects of women's lives, and especially marriage, motherhood, and widowhood, in circumstances and value systems very different from those of today. Of course, it also remains to be learned about the lives of men and boys in corresponding male roles, which are almost wholly unresearched.

What is crucial in all this is to hear the voices of the principals themselves, insofar as the sources allow, as emerges vividly in Margaret Lynch-Brennan's chapter, bringing to life the personalities and perspectives of some real-life domestic servants, re-creating the reality of their actual experience.

What we ideally need next—but the source material becomes even more elusive—is the behavior of the daughters and granddaughters of the domestic servants, if and

Elizabeth Mulvey, a second-generation Irish-American teacher from the Bronx, New York, took this snapshot of friends at Muckross Abbey in Killarney, County Kerry, during the 1920s. Such tourist excursions to the land of their parents' birth was novel at the time but strongly encouraged by the new Irish Free State government, which marketed Ireland as the first stop on any European Grand Tour. (Archives of Irish America, New York University, Gift of Kathleen Bergin Mulvey)

when they in turn became employers of servants in their own right. Once they climbed the pole of social status, did they replicate the attitudes their mothers or grandmothers endured? Did their memories extend to where they came from, or did they seek to imitate their American employers of earlier generations?

Lives lived away from the limelight of conflict will never provide the dramatic material for blockbuster films like Martin Scorsese's *Gangs of New York* (2002). Sharply criticized from a scholarly perspective for the liberties it took with historical reality, *Gangs of New York* culminates with the Draft Riots of 1863. What is really interesting in these riots, from a gender perspective, is the participation of at least some Irish women, apparently as equals, reflecting their sense of solidarity with, maybe even sense of authority in, their communities.

Race and Class

Interpretations of the New York City Draft Riots still vary widely, though the horrors, if not the actual scale, of the atrocities perpetrated by some Irish on blacks are clear enough. The riots raise numerous issues about the interplay of race and class in the attitudes and behavior of many working-class Irish in various cities. The subject is itself prone to spawn stereotypes, however, many themselves tinged with racist assumptions, and one can only echo Bayor and Meagher in stressing that, in light of research by Graham Hodges and John Kuo Wei Tchen on relations involving Irish, American blacks, and Chinese in New York City, that study of racial cooperation deserves much closer analysis, less spectacular though it be than those that focus on conflict.[95]

In rejecting the premise of Noel Ignatiev's *How the Irish Became White*, Peter Quinn (who provided so graphic a portrait of post-Famine and early Civil War New York and confronted the Draft Riots in all their horror in his great historical novel, *Banished Children of Eve*)[96] insists in chapter 29 that the issue is a false one. A better historical question, in Quinn's view, is "how the Irish stayed Irish" at a time when the great divide for the vast majority was religion and when the Catholic Irish had the wrong religion from the dominant perspective. "If the question of Irish acceptance were simply a passage from one color to another," Quinn pungently observes, "the Christian, English-speaking, white Irish should have rapidly blended into America's Anglo-Saxon woodwork."[97] The question of race in the thinking and behavior of Irish America is an important and intriguing one, as Kevin Kenny well illustrates in chapter 13. Race and class, as Kerby Miller has likewise insisted, remain stubbornly interrelated in the wider Irish-American experience.[98]

David Doyle has established the disproportionate role of the Irish in the leadership of trade unions about the turn of the century,[99] and David Montgomery has drawn attention to the manner in which, in the industrial unions especially, the Irish American leadership had to earn the confidence of ethnically diverse memberships.[100] On a regular basis, Irish men, mostly working class, came into contact with the millions of immigrants who came pouring in after 1880 far more than with White Anglo-Saxon

Protestant (WASP) Americans. How did they relate to the newcomers, and how did the newcomers in turn relate to the Irish, or form their images of Irish Americans?

Relations on a regular basis, at grassroots level, between different immigrant ethnicities remain relatively neglected in American historiography. Irish men played a central role in all of this, if only because they were the quintessential urban immigrants to whom most immigrant newcomers, overwhelmingly based in cities, would have had to relate.[101] Irish women, on the other hand, at least of the first generation, are much more likely to have had wider contact, at least as domestic servants, with those who regarded themselves as pure Americans. Insofar as their daughters went into teaching, of course, as Janet Nolan has emphasized, they will have played a potentially formative role in the education of immigrant children from the early twentieth century, presumably bringing an intriguing mixture of values to their task. Much more work like Jay Dolan's on Irish and German Catholics in nineteenth-century New York, or Ronald Bayor's on ethnic relations in New York in the 1930s, is badly needed.[102] It is an eloquent, if sadly silent, tribute to Dolan and Bayor that so few have been able to fill their shoes and walk in their footsteps.[103]

Into the Twentieth Century

Kevin Kenny has suggested that "the twentieth century will be the next growth area in the study of Irish America."[104] He is doubtless right, much though understanding of the earlier centuries remains to be deepened.

But when was the twentieth century? As the timing of immigration was mainly driven by economic factors, the establishment of the Irish Free State in 1922 made little difference to emigration patterns, and as the American quotas imposed on immigration from Ireland during the 1920s were never filled, they did not impede Irish inflows. Rather, it was the onset of the Great Depression that brought the greatest change.[105] A date that should loom much larger in the consciousness of Irish-American historiography is 1931, for in effect it marks the end of the immigration flow that had lasted since before the Famine. With no jobs in America, immigration declined to a trickle until after the Second World War. When it then resumed, it was at a much lower rate than before, a full-employment England having emerged in the meantime as a jobs market big enough to cater to virtually the entire Irish outflow.

Illegal immigration did flourish in the 1980s as Ireland stagnated and the English economy experienced sluggish growth. But once the Irish economy surged to levels of unprecedented growth and job creation in the booming Ireland of the 1990s—thanks in large measure to heavy American investment in the computer and pharmaceutical sectors—the flows turned around, with Ireland itself becoming a net immigration society.

That does not mean the immigrant experience since 1945 does not have its own significance. It raised issues about intergenerational relationships in particular that had rarely impinged to the same extent previously, as the judiciously modulated contribution in this volume by the leading authority on postwar immigration, Linda Dowling Almeida, makes very clear in chapter 24.

Despite the arrival of these new immigrants, study of the twentieth century will, as Kenny notes, be increasingly a study of generations long removed from Ireland. That will require deep reflection on methodology. Some historians are enthusiastic advocates of the concept of "the multigenerational ethnic community."[106] But how far can the techniques of inquiry into Irish-born generations be simply transferred to later generations?

More than forty million Americans claimed some Irish ancestry in the 1980 census. But the numbers fell to just over thirty million by the 2000 census, when in principle they should have continued to multiply. If this partly reflected changed criteria of enumeration, it suggests how fragile, even fickle, the numbers may be, how elusive is their real meaning.[107] More important than the actual numbers is the question of what they mean to Irish descendants. How many of those returning the census schedules simply respond to the ancestry question mechanically, jotting down the answer without giving a second thought to it, and without it meaning anything further to them? Numbers alone mean little, or else the German ethnic returns, more numerous than the Irish, would by definition feature far more prominently on the ethnic spectrum and loom much larger in public consciousness.

The real question is how many consider their recorded ancestry a significant part of their sense of who they are. And insofar as they do, what exactly is their sense of the Irish dimension in their identity? What does the "multigenerational ethnic community" mean in this context? A skeptic might say there are only three things wrong with it: mutigenerational, ethnic, and community! Does it mean that fifth- or sixth-generation Irish Americans descended from Famine immigrants, or tenth-generation Scotch-Irish (in the case of descendants of immigrants of 1720) must think of themselves, and behave, as if they were Irish born? That would be nonsense. There may be individuals of those generations who find inspiration in the idea of an Irish ancestry. They are perfectly entitled to do so, but they are also perfectly entitled not to. Immigration historians have no mandate to corral humans into ethnic pens.

It may be, of course, that the descendents are unconsciously influenced by their ancestry to behave in a certain "ethnic" manner. But that implies that the historian knows just what qualities to attribute to ethnicity: if it is dangerous for the first generation, it must become increasingly arbitrary as generations pass. For historians to claim they can recognize ethnic traits even in generations after immigration, and perhaps after generations of intermarriage, must inevitably lead to primitive stereotypes substituting for the complexity of historical reality. Tim Meagher's splendid account of Worcester a century ago shows how much more complex are the issues that arise in the study of even the second generation, much less later ones, compared with the first.[108] Among the questions stimulated by Reginald Byron's ethnographic research on present-day Albany is why the fifth or sixth generations have such a faint sense of origins; thus invoking the census returns on ancestry, as if all generations can be counted as equal within the enveloping embrace of the "multigenerational ethnic community," strains credence.[109]

In real life, although individuals of later generations, like Tom Hayden, may come to revel in a heritage which earlier generations had sought to conceal,[110] it is likely that except for those who work systematically to sustain it, consciousness of an Irish dimension of their lives will be confined mainly to the immigrant generation itself, and perhaps to the second and third generations, and even many of those will have begun to melt into the American mainstream. That mainstream will of course in turn be influenced by the impact of the immigrants, as the nature of the mainstream itself mutates under their influence. But that is very different from claiming that an Irish identity lives on in its full, undiluted strength, with every later generation equally ethnically conscious as the first.

What then is Irish America? One must distinguish sharply between the ancestral association and the active identification. The idea of forty million hearts, or even thirty million, beating as one, begs basic questions. The essential one is how many of them allow their lives to be influenced by the fact. Only when that can be determined —and no scholarly estimates exist of the number—can any serious conclusions be deduced from census returns. For that matter, as many of the respondents cited several ancestries, thanks to intermarriage, even the most enthusiastic Hibernizer can often claim no more than a leg of the descendants that will be forever green (or maybe orange, given that more than half who claim Irish descent turn out to be Protestant). And that could be shriveled yet further by more intermarriage. Until we have actually sorted out what we are talking about, one is tempted to suggest there should be a moratorium on the use of the census returns for these purposes.[111]

The returns did however corroborate findings by Andrew Greeley's National Opinion Research Center from the 1970s that the majority of those recording Irish ancestry were Protestant, which caused confusion—and, in some cases, consternation— among those who assumed the overwhelming majority would be Catholic. No really definitive explanation—definitive in the sense of being based on evidence that satisfies scholarly standards—has yet been proposed, although various explanations have been proffered. One is that, given that the bulk of immigrants from Ireland from roughly 1720 to 1820 had been Protestant, they had a head start in the propagation stakes and therefore would have far more descendants per head, even if there was always a substantial majority of Catholics among Irish-born since before the Famine.[112]

It wasn't just the numbers in themselves but the willingness of so many Protestants to acknowledge any Irish ancestry that surprised some observers. This, too, led to a variety of surmises. Some believed Protestants had felt Irish all along but for some reason did not write as extensively about themselves as the Catholic Irish did. Others felt that after the religious and political antipathies that increasingly emerged with the Catholic influx from the 1820s, and especially from the Famine, Protestants repudiated an Irish association. They were, they claimed, from Ireland, but not of it. Others feel that they remained aware of an Irish ancestry but detested the idea of identification with the socially and economically inferior Catholics, preferring to keep their distance until the emergence of President Kennedy cast Catholics in a more attractive light. There may be much merit in one or more of these views, but as of now they remain hypotheses, not conclusions, until the necessary research is conducted to test them.

If the scholarly history of the Protestant Irish and of the Scotch-Irish, despite the substantial amount actually written about them in religious and regional terms,[113] remains to be more capaciously conceptualized, David Doyle's contribution to the

Encyclopedia of the Irish in America (reprinted as chapter 3 here) provides the most learned and sensitive overview of the current state of knowledge on the Scotch-Irish. Among its many qualities is a sense of how much we do *not* know; Doyle refuses to pluck at isolated bits of evidence as decisive in favor of some propaganda position of the present. That would be an impressive achievement at any time, and all the more so in view of the passions roused by the ethno-religious conflict in Northern Ireland in recent decades, which some fear even now threaten to subordinate scholarship once more to propaganda. But it does mean that scholarly standards can be preserved only by refusing to sacrifice learning to simplistic assertions and by a willingness to engage with the complexity of situations that propagandists would love to reduce to black and white, to "them" and "us."

If serious scholarship on the Scotch-Irish in America is still at too early a stage to hazard more than tentative generalization, one must welcome some excellent recent work, including Patrick Griffin's *The People with No Name*,[114] and the prodigious labors of Kerby Miller, equally sensitive to all religious persuasions, whether in his 1985 *Emigrants and Exiles* or more recently, in conjunction with David Doyle, Bruce Boling, and Arnold Schrier, in the immaculately edited collection of letters, *Irish Immigrants in the Land of Canaan: Letters and Memoirs from Colonial and Revolutionary America, 1675–1815*,[115] whose riches will be mined for long to come. *Canaan* resonates with a sense of the sheer diversity of eighteenth-century Irish experience and mutations in the meaning of Irishness. So does Miller's extraordinary series of articles, striving to build an edifice of understanding, brick by brick, by reconstructing, with exemplary attention to detail, the life stories of individual immigrants. While everything Miller writes has to be savored in the original to capture the full flavor, and his numerous articles should certainly be collected in a separate volume or volumes, his essay in this book distills his present thinking at its most incisive, pared to the bone, but backed by the authority of his unrivaled range of archival reference.[116]

In the circumstances, all that anyone with the slightest respect for evidence can do is echo David Doyle's conclusion in chapter 3 that "it would be foolhardy to attempt a synthesis in the absence of even a rudimentary literature."[117]

"Success," "Failure," and Stereotype

If the number of Protestants revealed by Greeley's research and subsequently recorded in the census caused surprise, so did another of Greeley's findings. If Catholics hadn't dreamed there were so many Protestants to claim some Irish ancestry, Protestants could be forgiven for being perplexed by the finding that Irish Catholics, axiomatically economically backward, appeared to be, on average, better educated and earning more than themselves, blatantly enjoying the rewards of supposedly Protestant virtues. They themselves, and indeed virtually all other Protestant America, now appeared to be lagging behind by the criteria that were deemed to constitute "success" in the American value system. There was an apparently simple explanation, however: it all depended on location. Irish Protestants did just as well as Irish Catholics in the same places. There just happened to be far more of them in the wrong place—the south—where they fell below the educational and income levels of their more "successful" brethren to the north and west. That does leave one with the question as to why they stayed where they were, and how people once celebrated for their internal mobility apparently could not be moved for love or money.

Or at least not for money. Because that was what "success" had come to be defined as, and by, in the late twentieth century, if not long before. Their critics would say this is where the Irish recorded by Greeley have sold their birthright, even if the mess of pottage is very substantial indeed. But is it impossible to, in effect, satisfy the two masters—the pocket and the soul? Or must a man—and increasingly woman—lose his or her immortal soul to gain the whole world? Both Finley Peter Dunne and J. T. Farrell were acutely conscious of the dilemma, which is why Mr. Dooley, Studs Lonigan, and Danny O'Neill remain such vitally contemporary figures. It is indicative of the depth of the issues, which have always been with us, and always will be, that one turns instinctively to writers for insight. Writers, as artists, can guide us to the aortic core of the issues. They can see into the heart. As Fanning phrases it: "The Dooley pieces embody the peculiar mixture of fulfillment and frustration that went along with being Irish in America at that time."[118]

What writers cannot tell us is the balance between all the impulses they discern. That is for quantifiers to do, and then the evidence has to be inferred—and for that we need historians. Believe it or not, we historians are of divided views. All we can suggest, like writers, is that the picture is more nuanced than either black or white interpretations suggest. But we do not know, any more than artists know, what the proportions are between gaining the world and losing souls, although those of us who allow our primal identity to guide our wishes might hope that the Irish would be the ones to cut that Gordian knot.

It is only proper to acknowledge that the use of fiction for historical illumination, which began to be studied in the 1970s, with notable works by Charles Fanning and by Daniel Casey and Robert Rhodes,[119] is even more central to the study of the recent past, where it is so often the fiction writer who puts his or her finger on the pulse of an age, while the historian is still wondering how to formulate the questions. Notable novels by writers of the stature of William Kennedy and Alice McDermott, which have penetrated the experience of Irish-American generational relations in the later twentieth century, as Daniel Casey and Robert Rhodes skillfully illustrate in chapter 27,[120] will provide indispensable sources of inspiration when its social history comes to be written in depth.

It is Kerby Miller who has most stimulatingly linked the argument about "success" to the issue of Irish values, in this case specifically Gaelic, Catholic values. In his view, many, though by no means all, first-generation immigrants suffered intensely from a sense of alienation because their version of Gaelic Catholic culture, with its emphasis on the importance of thinking for one's family and community rather than for oneself, left them peculiarly unprepared to flourish in the cutthroat competitiveness of mid-nineteenth-century America. Miller relies heavily on emigrants' letters to document the loneliness and alienation from which he believes those of that disposition suffered.

Larry McCaffrey takes issue with the entire argument. He rejects letters as an adequate source, arguing they are unrepresentative, and even if alienation did occur in individual cases, it was only a temporary condition. McCaffrey suggests letters home are likely to be dripping with nostalgia. Others argue that, on the contrary, they are likely to exaggerate the degree of success and to conceal failure and frustration. They can doubtless do both. How does the historian decide where the balance lies? And what about the non-writers? Are they failing to write because they have no good news, or because they are doing so well they have forgotten Ireland? The likelihood is much of both, and the problem again is how representative are both categories.

Miller has argued that turn-of-the-century Irish America constituted "a remarkably heterogeneous and deeply ambivalent society."[121] Generational differences were significant and, because generations existed cheek by jowl, there is likely to have been a good deal of disparity between attitudes and ambitions. As the 1900 census recorded 1,615,459 Irish-born and 3,375,546 American-born with at least one Irish parent, a wide range of responses to loneliness or success could coexist. That is why, in dealing with intergenerational experience, the judgment of historians is particularly important. This issue is still open. Or, rather, it is open with one qualification. It has been argued that as relatively few immigrants returned to Ireland, compared with return migration to several other European countries, they must have been "successful." Return migration, however, is not a decisive confirmation of their "success" in America— although, of course, there can be wide differences between external and internal concepts of success. In contrast to the much higher rate of returnees from several other countries, the Irish came to be permanent residents, not as temporary sojourners to make enough money to return home. The Irish economy did not provide opportunity for economic success. They had nothing to go back to—until very recently. For them, there was no alternative. One cannot therefore infer anything about their "success" abroad, by the criteria of the host societies, from return rates.

There is a bittersweet tone to some of McCaffrey's eloquent elegies on the "success" of Irish Americans, as he sees it:[122] "Their psychological and physical passage from rural Ireland to urban America; their effort to surmount the burdens of their history, their poverty, their ignorance, and the hostility of the host society; and their successful quest for power and respectability were the paradigm of the American ethnic experience." That "success" now is marked by the degree of "absorption into the middle-class mainstream," of disappearing into "suburban melting pots," which he believes effectively means the end of Irish America. "Success" is thus, in the ultimate irony, measured by the degree of extinction.[123]

Andrew Greeley, in turn, vigorously disputes the disappearance of ethnic identity in the suburbs.[124] Finding out what actually happens in the suburbs is one of the prime challenges for current scholarship. The contributions by Robert Snyder and Marion Casey in *The New York Irish*[125] suggest potentially quite complex relationships rather than a linear decline in a sense of ethnic identity, at least in New York. Casey, for example, demonstrates that geographical change reflected horizontal rather than vertical social mobility, a conclusion that raises many more questions about the standard assumption that outward movement means upward movement.

Irish passengers on board the S.S. *St. Louis* in the 1930s, a transatlantic passenger ship built in 1929 for the Hamburg-America Line operating between Hamburg, Southampton, and New York. (Archives of Irish America, New York University, Gift of Dorothy Hayden Cudahy)

David Montgomery argues that "the success ethic inspired but one segment of Irish-American society," juxtaposing it against the solidarity ethic of another segment.[126] It may have been more complicated, a mixture of the two, with many being pulled in both directions, responding differently in different circumstances. The very issue of buying into the American idea of success was itself in part a struggle for the idea of America. Who determined what counted as "success" in the American value system? There can be all sorts of variations within any of these types, as Tim Meagher brings out in his sustained meditation in chapter 26 on the meaning of solidarity, incarnated in the evocative figure of the fireman on the stairs, since 9/11 forever burned into our memories and psyches.

The "success" debate has the merit of forcing us to think about the danger of stereotype. No one has done more than Andrew Greeley to undermine stereotypes about the Irish—many of them Irish held. He begins *The Irish Americans: the Rise to Money and Power* with seven popular stereotypes about the Irish—meaning Irish Catholics —"which everyone knows to be true." He then proceeds to demolish them all.[127]

What we find time and again is that "evidence" about Irish America consists of no more than stereotype, based on assumed but unscholarly comparison. That, of course, is the way most of us think most of the time. But that does not make the conclusions any more valid. It is difficult for all of us to resist generalizing wildly about ethnic groups, saving ourselves the need for thought by substituting stereotype for evidence. In this manner individuals belonging to particular groups can be stripped of their individuality as men, or women, or children and shriveled to ciphers. The coming of the movies gave stereotype a new and even more lethal boost, however amiable some, if only some, of the Irish images portrayed.[128]

What do the stereotypes say about the preachers and wielders of the stereotypes? Why do they need stereotypes for their own psychological security and sense of superiority or purity? If the Irish suffered from stereotype, as they did, how often did they, in turn, perpetrate it? Among the many reasons Mr. Dooley is remarkable is because of the way he employs a framework of stereotype familiar to his readers to undermine stereotypes, much though he appears to rely on the idea, by investing his characters with an individuality and a humanity that defies, indeed mocks at, stereotype.[129]

The Struggle to Understand: Successes and Failures

It would be nice to think that historiography has made striking advances in the past generation. David Doyle was already sanguine in 1980 about the preeminence of scholarly standards among historians of Irish America,[130] a view apparently confirmed by the appearance that year of the excellent contributions to the *Harvard Encyclopedia of American Ethnic Groups* by Patrick Blessing and by Maldwyn Jones. Certainly, many of the major themes that we are urged to pursue today were already on the table at that stage.[131]

A decade later, however, Donald Akenson was using language that could be read to imply that Irish-American historians, or at least the Catholics among them, were likely to be either fools or charlatans, if not both.[132] Although Maldwyn Jones felt in 1969 that "the study of the Scotch-Irish emigration has now reached maturity,"[133] it is not entirely clear what "maturity" meant. It seems to be high time for a scholarly scrutiny of all the issues involved.

Even as progress was being reported a generation ago, murmurings of discontent could be heard. By 1960, the state of the once resplendent American Irish Historical Society provoked Daniel Patrick Moynihan, in his sardonic but deadly serious style, to a disenchanted view of its standing at that stage: "Its *Journal* . . . has long ceased publication . . . the Society continues to occupy a great tomb of a mansion on Fifth Avenue, with a fine library that few seem interested in using, and splendid meeting rooms where no one evidently wants to meet."[134] This may have been unfair, and he would rescind the verdict a decade later.[135] One can happily record that if the original journal has not been revived, the successor journal, the *Recorder*, flourishes, albeit as more literary than historical. While revising his verdict on the AIHS, however, Moynihan simultaneously explained the lack of Irish studies programs in his own City College of New York, at a time when ethnic programs of this type were beginning to proliferate, partly on the grounds that Irish Americans "did not develop an intellectual tradition strong enough to command the interest of themselves, and certainly not of others."[136]

This hardly took adequate account of the time and energy invested by the devoted founders of the American Conference for Irish Studies from the late 1950s to the promotion of Irish studies. A seed was sown by Professor Robin Dudley Edwards of University College Dublin—whose son Owen would contribute to illuminating not just the Irish-American but the American experience—under the guidance of a cluster of Irish Americans whose interest in the first instance was more in Irish than in Irish-American studies. After growth and mutation, the American Conference for Irish Studies led to a flowering of Irish studies and prepared the ground for much more work on Irish America.[137] It was at this juncture, too, that Eoin McKiernan, a trojan worker for Irish culture in America, founded (in 1962) the Irish American Cultural Institute at the College of St. Thomas in Minneapolis and (in 1966) the journal *Eire-Ireland*, which are now handsomely established but were visionary ventures at the time.[138]

Knowledge of the Irish background was obviously important for the understanding of Irish America, even if it was no substitute for it. While the relationship between Irish studies and Irish-American studies was rather tenuous, they were drawing on broadly the same sense of cultural identity. What was good for one was likely to be good for the other in due course, sometimes even directly, as when some authorities on Ireland, like McCaffrey and James S. Donnelly Jr., would come to make impressive contributions to Irish-American history.

Moses Rischin's withering critique of American Jewish history in 1954 implied that, if anything, it lagged behind Irish-American history. At that stage it had no equivalent of Handlin's *Boston* or Ernst's *New York*. Yet by 1976, Rischin, described by Tom Brown as "the patron of Irish-American Studies,"[139] could greet the appearance of the Arno Series as virtual manna, observing that "the American Irish have become one of the most conspicuously well-integrated ethnic groups in American society. Yet the complex history of this highly visible group, intimately and transparently associated and counterpointed with Anglo-America, is remarkably little known."[140] How could Rischin make this judgment? Was he casually dismissing so much good earlier work? Or was it because, for all the growing accumulation of local detail, coverage was still so spotty? Dennis Clark, beginning his own series of studies of his beloved Philadelphia three years earlier, had anticipated the Rischin perspective in relation to his own case, lamenting that "the Irish community in the city has hardly been adverted to by professional historians."[141] Over the intervening two decades since 1954 Irish-American studies had apparently slipped down the relative scale of immigrant historiography.

One argument frequently heard was put pungently by Clark himself:

> Ironically, the Catholic universities and colleges, frequently built with Irish money, and led by those with Irish background, were rarely disposed to advance Irish studies. American Catholics were so conservative at the level of higher education that they retained curricula with a classical orientation long after such studies faded elsewhere. Latinity, philosophy and theology dominated, and limited resources permitted little experimentation. The cultural diversity of the ethnic Catholics was seen as a pastoral problem by church leaders who controlled the colleges and as a regrettable anachronism by clerics

who taught in colleges and by bourgeois Catholics who patronized them. Only in the 1950s did this attitude begin grudgingly to change. The simplistic universalism of the American clergy in Catholic institutions effectively forestalled any vigorous ethnic scholarship, except in some cases in which immigrant religious orders created small ethnically identified colleges. Religious triumphalism of a self-assured Latinized Catholicism left little room for propagators of subcultural preservation.[142]

There is doubtless some truth in this. But much writing about the Catholic Church is influenced by, in some cases even distorted by, strong prejudices, whether positive or negative, which make it difficult to arrive at proper historical judgments. It is only recently that a later generation has begun to build on the highly promising initiative of Professor Paddy Corish of Maynooth in striving to produce a properly historically grounded study of the Irish Catholic Church worldwide, which in the American case resulted in 1970 in two valuable, if relatively brief, overviews by Fr. Thomas McAvoy on the *Irish Clergyman* and by Tom Brown on *The Irish Layman*.[143] Even then McAvoy could begin his bibliography with the observation that "printed materials dealing specifically with Irish clergymen in the United States are quite scarce."[144] Nonetheless, a great deal of material on the immigrant experience is contained in the studies of institutions and individuals, churches, convents, colleges, and cardinals, which needs to be recycled and reinterpreted from the perspective of immigration history.[145]

It may therefore be inaccurate to say that not much work was done. Rather, it may have been that a good deal was done but not from a specifically immigrant perspective. But then we must remember, too, how slowly the American historical profession came to realize the significance of immigration as a major field of study for understanding American society. Why should church historians be held to a higher standard than the mainstream standards of their age? The difference perhaps is that so much of the work of Catholic historians in particular was dealing with material absolutely central to immigration history, whereas the bulk of the material used by the historical profession in general was not so potentially rewarding for the immigration historian. It would take the work of scholars of the caliber of Jay Dolan, John Tracy Ellis, Gerald Fogarty, Philip Gleason, Randall Miller, and Thomas Shelley to provide a harvest for the student of immigration, as Shelley's wide-ranging synoptic survey demonstrates in his analysis in chapter 25 of the centrality of immigration to the fortunes of the Church. If Irene Whelan in chapter 7 evoked the atmosphere of festering conflict between Protestant and Catholic in the nineteenth century, this looms less large in Shelley's contribution on the twentieth century—although, of course, centuries are arbitrary demarcations—which instead reflects the more insidious type of challenge posed to the Church from secularization and recently reinforced by the widely perceived inadequacy of its own handling of clerical sexual abuse cases. Ironically and tragically this is just the type of defensive, evasive, furtive bureaucratic response one might expect from secular institutions devoid of faith.

To see Irish America in its full roundness one needs to know far more about the experience of Irish immigrants in other countries and of other immigrants in America. A major contribution to Irish-American self-knowledge is still likely to come from this direction, and it requires scholars of ethnicity to learn from scholars of religion who have experience, above all through the Cushwa Center at Notre Dame (founded under the direction of Jay Dolan in 1975) of studying the variety of ethnicities that are enveloped beneath the Catholic umbrella. Needless to say, the study of religious experience can also benefit from comparative perspective, for religions no less than ethnicities can become inward looking. Immigration from Ireland, taken in its entirety, precisely because it included different religions and different ethnicities, can provide a bracing intellectual and emotional challenge for scholarship. One may need not less but more synergy between writing on religion—Protestant as well as Catholic—and the history of Irish America. Robert Dunne, for instance, has argued strongly that Catholic literary culture in the nineteenth century, at any rate, can only be properly understood when "seen in terms of a dialogue with Protestant mainstream rhetoric."[146] One is entitled to one's views on religion. One is not entitled to the view that religion is not central to understanding the history of Irish Americans of all persuasions.

In contemplating the massive list of publications in the bibliographies compiled by Seamus Metress, Patrick Blessing, and Ann Shea and Marion Casey, one becomes aware of the inaccuracy, even unfairness, in claiming that so little work has been done.[147] Why then does it feel as if so much remains to be done? Is it in part that because the Catholic Irish were on the defensive for so long, much of it is defensive writing—a species of war history—with all its inevitable defects? Is it in part simply because there is so much ground to be covered—in numbers and in distance over time and over place? The Irish immigration was huge, after all, and it spread widely.

And there were relatively few laborers in the vineyard. It could take a lifetime to dig as deeply as David Emmons did in his absorbing excavations of the Irish in Butte, Montana, and several years to provide overviews—for even part of the period—like David Gleeson's on the Irish in the south in general, or like Graham Davis on some Irish in Texas in particular.[148] Or might it be that far more work has been done that lies buried in theses or that has received only minimal recognition because of the lack of the institutional mechanisms for ensuring publicity? Who would have believed the Arno Press series could have amounted to forty-two volumes if they had not been in large part dredged out of doctoral dissertations? How many more may have been completed—perhaps, indeed, in those Catholic institutions so berated for their failure to encourage research of this type—but never became more widely known? If that is indeed the case, it is ironic that a people who make their political reputation on the basis of their organizational skills should have been so relatively slow to apply similar skills to enhancing their scholarly standing.

For that matter, focusing on problems may be to almost casually undervalue the scale of the existing achievement. Today, when American historians are strongly urged to become less inward looking and less provincial and to seek to locate the American experience in the context of "Atlantic history" or "Pacific history" or "transnational history" or "global history," it is instructive to see Kerby Miller describing (as early as 1985) *Emigrants and Exiles* as "an essay in trans-Atlantic history."[149] Of course it is that: an outstanding example of the genre, appearing at a time when that was beginning to be preached but little practiced.

In 1987, the Cushwa Center at Notre Dame sponsored a major conference entitled

"Ireland and the United States: The Transatlantic Connection, 1800–1980." Earlier still, much of the Edwards-Doyle bicentennial volume was cast in the transatlantic mold. Despite the remarkable work of such scholars as David Quinn, Nicholas Canny, and Hugh Kearney in recent decades, despite the axiomatically "Atlantic" dimension of the United Irish movement, despite the reference to the Atlantic in the very title of Patrick Griffin's recent work, *The People with No Name: Ireland's Ulster Scots, America's Scots Irish, and the Creation of a British Atlantic World, 1689–1764*,[150] it may be wondered if the historical profession in America is even now fully aware of the role of Ireland in Atlantic history, or in global diaspora history. In a wide-ranging article published in 2002 in the *Journal of American History* Kevin Kenny sought to impress on the profession the relevance of the Irish diasporic experience for understanding general American history.[151]

The history of the Irish diaspora encompasses not only Britain and Canada, as well as the United States, but Australia and New Zealand, with instructive experiences recorded in South Africa and Argentina also, to say nothing of continental Europe in earlier centuries.[152] In fact, many Irish immigration historians have been pioneering a variety of American history as well as of Irish history—almost, it seems at times, unbeknownst to the historical profession in America. Specialized but important examples of it are the interpretive studies of Irish-born priests and nuns active in America for nearly two centuries.[153] What difference, if any, for instance, did the thousands of priests and nuns sent from Ireland over the past two centuries make to the nature of American Catholicism?[154]

It may indeed be that so many historians of Irish America simply took all this for granted that it didn't cross their minds to stress the matter. However controversial, Miller's emphasis on the "Gaelic, Catholic" Irish inheritance has stimulated a lively debate that once again indicates how important it is to have a thorough knowledge of the country of origin. Fortunately, Miller, Doyle, Boling, and Schrier have all hung in there, insofar as their institutional circumstances permitted, with *Irish Immigrants in the Land of Canaan* now a monument to their dedication and scholarship in the field of "Atlantic" history.

Nevertheless, when all this has been duly put on the scales, as it must be, and despite the quality of the best work, it remains true that Irish America emerged relatively slowly as an object of systematic scholarly inquiry. If it is natural to ask how it faltered after so promising a start, this is to ask the wrong question. For the "promise" of the start was highly deceptive. It depended on the almost accidental commitment of non-Irish scholars whose early subject matter included chance encounters with the Irish, but who were already moving mainly in other directions. Behind the patina of the work on early and mid-nineteenth-century Boston and New York, the study of Irish America, or of Irish immigration in the context of American immigration more generally, had in the postwar decades no institutional base, no presiding scholars able to mobilize sufficient institutional weight to give the field a sense of direction.

American academic production is heavily market driven. The general market for immigration and ethnic scholars was still a sluggish one in the 1950s unless it was sponsored by a particular institution. Arnold Schrier, for instance, whose *Ireland and the American Emigration* was published in 1958 and remains a pioneering study of enduring value, found there was little demand for knowledge about Ireland in the U.S. university system of the time. Instead he taught mainly Russian history, his interest in Irish immigration history having to take a secondary role for much of the period.

So what is the market? Who determines the nature of academic markets? Roland Blenner-Hassett concluded his survey of Celtic studies in 1954 with a lament about the indifference of the vast majority of immigrants to the subject:

> Most regrettable is the apathy displayed toward Celtic studies by the great majority of people of Celtic origins in the United States. One might reasonably suppose that, in view of their numerical strength and prominence they have achieved in all walks of life, Americans of Celtic origin would display a far more active and generous interest than they have thus far in the cultures and lands of their forbears.[155]

If that was the case with a subject which, for all its intrinsic interest and importance, might nevertheless be felt by many of its potential patrons to keep itself somewhat detached from the rest of the culture of "the great majority of people of Celtic origins," it would be another generation before that began to be displayed, and in one outstanding case the Celt was a Jew. Who would have guessed that the number of students taking courses in Irish studies, including Irish-American studies, at New York University would have risen from sixty-five to over seven hundred in the ten years between 1993 and 2003, if Lewis Glucksman and Loretta Brennan Glucksman hadn't had the imagination and courage to endow an Irish studies program in a university with no sustained historical or institutional connection with things Irish?

How many other institutions where a proven demand now exists for Irish studies would be still waiting to establish them if they had not been established in the first place? Would Notre Dame or Boston College have such flourishing programs if Don Keough or Brian Burns had not been prepared to take a risk? The market in this respect is far from an objective concept. It is called into existence in response to the imagination and daring of visionary philanthropists if properly supported by universities. For that matter, it can be called into existence by universities themselves, if they are prepared to encourage, or just allow, dedicated scholars to follow their inspiration, as in the case of Charles Fanning's program in Carbondale, Illinois.[156]

It is worth remembering, too, that on the supply side, Irish-American studies not only originally achieved recognition in large measure from the interest of non-Irish scholars but also in more recent years has been fortunate to attract contributions from scholars, whether with or without Irish connections, like Hasia Diner, Tom Archdeacon, Maldwyn Jones, Ronald Bayor, Matthew Frye Jacobsen, and David Roediger, already independently established in general ethnic and immigration studies. And even some of those who have devoted their entire research lives to the subject came into it by complete accident, not least Kerby Miller himself.[157]

When the splendid general volume *The New York Irish* appeared in 1996—now the envy of many another city, in England as well as America, with students of the Irish in England lamenting they have nothing comparable for London—it was only because the Irish Institute of New York and the vision of Paul O'Dwyer made it possible for the enterprise to be organized. O'Dwyer was deeply impressed by Jewish scholarly achievement, and he built on the momentum generated by the devoted grassroots work of the New York Irish History Roundtable, founded in 1985 (thanks not least to the vision and energy of Professor William D. Griffin, himself a pioneer of popularizing Irish-American history). O'Dwyer, and his compatriot Kevin Morrissey, had the imagination and dedication to commit resources to recruit high-quality editors and commission numerous contributors, many from outside Irish-American circles. Moreover, this occurred at a time when Irish America was basking in the glow of its unprecedented success, second only to the phenomenal Jewish record in the *Fortune 500*.

If substantial resources (on the Jewish model for Israel) were happily channeled through the American Ireland Fund into worthy causes in Ireland, remarkably little of the Jewish model toward internal philanthropy could be found in Irish America. Although individuals associated with American Irish organizations like Joe Gannon, William Shannon, and Bill Vincent were strongly supportive as early as the 1960s and 1970s, it is sad to think of the momentum that might have been achieved with more imagination, dedication, and investment on that model that would have done credit to Irish-American scholarship, to Irish America itself, and, indeed, to American scholarship in general.[158] It was not to be, or at least not yet.

The Future of the Past?

Who knows what the future may hold? Irish America is changing rapidly. But then so is America. So is Ireland. But change is the law of life. It may mean death. But it need not. From some perspectives Irish America has been a long time a-dying. John Kelleher penned a dyspeptic obituary for the Irish connection as early as 1961.[159] Moynihan concluded the 1970 edition of his essay with an obituary not only for Kennedy but for an entire political tradition:

> It was the Last Hurrah. He, the youngest and newest, served in a final moment of ascendancy. On the day he died, the President of the United States, the Speaker of the House of Representatives, the Majority Leader of the United States Senate, the Chairman of the National Committee, were all Irish, all Catholic, all Democrat. It will not come again.[160]

Nor did it. Nevertheless, it was not quite the Last Hurrah. The Northern Ireland conflict would call forth the Four Horsemen in due course: Moynihan himself, the elected Democratic senator for New York in 1972; Edward Kennedy; Tip O'Neill; and Hugh Carey.[161] But only Senator Kennedy remains, and it seems clear that their era will not come again, either. It is this type of assumption that lies behind the initiative, for instance, of Trina Vargo, a former advisor to Senator Kennedy, in launching the Mitchell scholarships, named in honor of Senator George Mitchell, who played so central a role in brokering the Good Friday Agreement in Northern Ireland in 1998. The Mitchell scholarships seek to bring some of the brightest and best, on the model of the Rhodes scholars, to Irish universities, with a view to fostering consciously a type of link that can no longer be taken for granted, and to develop that link to embrace all traditions on the island, with Northern Irish universities involved no less than those in the Irish Republic.

This does not mean that the political influence of Irish America is coming to an end. For apart from the continuing role of individual politicians, huge political influence is wielded by business in which the Irish now count among the big hitters of that world. Men like Bill Flynn, Don Keough, Chuck Feeney, and Tom Moran are widely recognized for their influence on the Clinton administration's activist approach toward Northern Ireland.[162]

Their rise in big business is arguably the single most striking feature of the story of Irish America since the Second World War, and particularly in the last generation. It is not, of course, the only story in Irish America, whose experience encompasses many stories—some involving continuing influence in the labor movement, some still traumatic. Brian Hanley's finely judged analysis of NORAID (Irish Northern Aid, an American-based group), which strongly supported the republican movement in Northern Ireland, explains how it "promoted an Irish ethnic identity based on a history of nativist discrimination against, and class division among, Irish Americans."[163] The NORAID story, as told by Hanley, is a fascinating one, far more complex than surface media appearances suggest. But it is mainly a replaying of an old story, for all the variations on the theme, and it is the rise of Irish Americans to prominence in the business world that constitutes the new story that will loom large in the history of this period. Until that history can be written, much can be learned from surveys of leading personalities like those in Niall O'Dowd's and Patricia Harty's handsomely produced magazine, *Irish America*. The listing of the one hundred leading Irish-American business people in the January 2000 issue, for instance, provides fascinating glimpses into a still largely private world.

There is nothing infallible or final about such listings. But one can form impressions from them. The most notable single one is the role of education in their backgrounds. About 90 percent have university degrees. About 50 percent have taken graduate courses, including quite a number with Harvard MBAs or similar business qualifications. The basic degrees were acquired at a wide range of colleges across the country, with Catholic colleges particularly prominent. Whatever the institutional background, their educational qualifications are well above the American average, including quite possibly the business average.

It is no longer news that the Catholic Irish rank among the best educated of all American ethnic groups. Even if, like myself, one is not a huge devotee of league tables of this sort, given that they require so much deconstructing, nevertheless they can certainly puncture complacent assumptions, in every direction, and their implications have to be incorporated into wider analysis. That the Catholic Irish were such big beneficiaries of the GI Bill of 1944, which provided extensive educational support for veterans after that and subsequent wars, probably reflects the quality of their secondary education, which laid the foundations for their subsequent success at higher levels.

Two other factors stand out in appraising the profiles. The counties with the biggest number of ancestral representatives are, in order, Cork, Mayo, Kerry, and Clare, followed jointly by Galway and Dublin. The west of Ireland is clearly asserting itself in the present generation. "Mayo—God help us" used be a familiar phrase a century or even half a century ago. Maybe the Good Lord has done His bit, but it seems clear from this that Mayo is well able to help itself nowadays, certainly in a propitious American environment.

A second factor that emerges, and which may be closely linked to education, is the role in management in which the Irish seem to particularly flourish. They are widely seen as good communicators and effective managers of people—in other words, natural politicians. Politics is central to any activity involving human contact, of course —not necessarily the politics of party but the politics of people. In an age revolving ever more around services rather than old-style industrial production, which means the primacy of people rather than machines, this is an invaluable natural asset to have.

Many of those profiled in Patricia Harty's "Top 100" list do indeed claim that it is their people skills that particularly distinguish the Irish style. That is true as far as it goes. But when one probes further, what is striking is how many of these top one hundred are employed in strategic planning. Strategic planning can cover a multitude of activities, some of them a far cry from either strategy or planning. Nevertheless it must be indicative of something. It seems to me to signal an increasing blend of people and planning skills, skills that fuse intuitive insight with the discipline of trained thinking.

Imagination is a powerful weapon in its own right, and the Irish can reasonably claim, all stereotypes aside, to have had their fair share of it. Imagination and discipline together constitute a formidable combination. It may be this combination that is turning Irish Americans into exceptionally successful businessmen and women, and that they will now long remain so, as long as they do not lose the Irish dimension of their identity.

Peter Quinn, in bringing this volume to a conclusion in chapters 28 and 29, pondering past, present, and future in meditations of lyrical beauty, takes us literally and metaphorically across the face of Irish America. It is appropriate that his very final piece, "The Future of Irish America," was originally delivered on the occasion of the first Ernie O'Malley Lecture in 1999, sponsored by Ernie's son, Cormac O'Malley, under the auspices of Glucksman Ireland House at New York University, specifically to promote the study of Irish America. The pleasure derived from the felicity of Quinn's style can divert attention from the deep learning and hard-headed, though never cold-blooded, realism that undergirds everything he writes. When as acute and artistic a sensitivity as Quinn's stresses that the United States is a "spin" society, where you are not seen if your voice is not heard, then you know it is time to raise the decibel level.[164] Irish America has plenty to give voice to. One purpose of this volume will be achieved if it reminds us of the richness of tone and variety of range of that voice, however gruff at times, in the belief that it has something worth saying not only to Irish America but also to America itself, to Ireland and perhaps even, for those with eyes to see, to the wider world.

NOTES

1. This chapter could not have been written but for the generosity of Marion Casey with ideas, insights, and material and with her time in giving it so close a reading. It is only on her

insistence that she is not cited as co-author. She cannot, of course, be held responsible for any misuse I may have made of her inspiration. I should also stress that the text is not intended to duplicate or summarize any of the other contributions or to provide comprehensive bibliographical coverage. It is in the nature of a meditation on the subject, indicative rather than comprehensive.

2. This Churchill quotation and those in the following paragraph are from Robert Rhodes James, ed., *Winston S. Churchill: His Complete Speeches, 1897–1963*, Vol. 3 (New York: Chelsea House Publishers, 1974), 3155.

3. Peter Quinn, "How the Irish Stayed Irish," *America*, 16 March 1996, 15.

4. Doris Kearns Goodwin, preface to *The Fitzgeralds and the Kennedys* (New York: Simon and Schuster, 1987), xiii.

5. Art Mitchell, "Historians of Irish America," in *Encyclopedia of the Irish in America*, ed. Michael Glazier (South Bend, IN: Notre Dame University Press, 1999), 388.

6. On Wittke, see Harvey Wish, "Carl Wittke, Historian," in *In the Trek of the Immigrants: Essays Presented to Carl Wittke*, ed. O. Fritiof Ander (Rock Island, IL: Augustana College Library, 1964), 3–16, and O. Fritiof Ander, *Four Historians of Immigration* (Rock Island, IL: Augustana College Library, 1964), 17–32.

7. Quinn, "How the Irish Stayed Irish," 15.

8. Kenneth J. Moynihan, "History as a Weapon for Social Advancement: Group History as Told by Jewish, Irish, and Black Americans, 1892–1950" (Ph.D. diss., Clark University, 1973); Meaghan Dwyer, "'To Make Better Known the Irish Chapter in American History': The Objectives of the American Irish Historical Society, 1897–1941" (seminar paper, Glucksman Ireland House, New York University, December 15, 1999).

9. R. J. Dickson, *Ulster Emigration to Colonial America, 1718–1775* (London: Routledge and Kegan Paul, 1966), x.

10. Jeffrey S. Gurock, "Introduction: An Inventory of Promises: Moses Rischin and American Jewish Historiography, 1954–1994," in *An Inventory of Promises: Essays on American Jewish History in Honor of Moses Rischin*, ed. Jeffrey S. Gurock and Marc Lee Raphael (Brooklyn: Carlson, 1995), vii–xiv; quotation from p. vii.

11. The basic information in this section is drawn from Roland Blenner-Hassett, "A Brief History of Celtic Studies in North America," *PMLA: Publications of the Modern Language Association of America* 69, no. 4 (September 1954): 2–21. I'm grateful to Sean Ó Coileáin, professor of Irish at University College Cork, for both drawing this article to my attention and providing me with a copy of it.

12. William F. Adams, *Ireland and Irish Emigration to the New World from 1815 to the Famine* (New Haven, CT: Yale University Press, 1932).

13. Arthur M. Schlesinger Sr., "The Influence of Immigration on American History," in *New Viewpoints on American History* (New York: Macmillan, 1922), 1–22.

14. Moses Rischin, review of *Immigrant Life in New York City, 1825–1863* by Robert Ernst, *American Journal of Sociology* 56, no. 1 (July 1950): 116.

15. Florence E. Gibson, introduction to *The Attitudes of the New York Irish toward State and National Affairs, 1848–1892* (New York: Columbia University Press, 1951), n.p.

16. See Alan O'Day, "The Irish Diaspora," in *The Making of Modern Irish History: Revisionism and the Revisionist Controversy*, ed. George W. Boyce and Alan O'Day (New York: Routledge, 1996), 201.

17. William V. Shannon, acknowledgements in *The American Irish: A Political and Social Portrait* (New York: Macmillan, 1963), n.p.

18. Jay Dolan, review of *The American Irish: A History* by Kevin Kenny, *New York Irish History* 14 (2000): 51.

19. Dennis Clark, *Erin's Heirs: Irish Bonds of Community* (Lexington: University Press of Kentucky, 1991), 128; Harold J. Abramson, *Ethnic Diversity in Catholic America* (New York: Wiley, 1973), 8–9.

20. Andrew Greeley, *That Most Distressful Nation: The Taming of the American Irish* (Chicago: Quadrangle Books, 1972), 50.

21. Lawrence J. McCaffrey, *The Irish Catholic Diaspora in America* (Washington, DC: Catholic University Press, 1997), 217; Lawrence J. McCaffrey, "Irish-American Politics: Power with or without Purpose?" in *The Irish in America: Emigration, Assimilation and Impact*, ed. P. J. Drudy (New York: Cambridge University Press, 1985), 169–190. For an ambitious, challenging interpretation, including Canada as well as the United States, see David N. Doyle, "Irish Elites in North America and Liberal Democracy, 1820–1920," *Radharc: Chronicles of Glucksman Ireland House, New York University* 3 (2002): 29–54.

22. Owen Dudley Edwards, "Conclusion: Some Counterthemes," in *America and Ireland, 1776–1976: The American Identity and the Irish Connection*, ed. David N. Doyle and Owen Dudley Edwards (Westport, CT: Greenwood Press, 1980), 307.

23. Earl F. Niehaus, *The Irish in New Orleans, 1800–1860* (Baton Rouge: Louisiana State University Press, 1965); Edward M. Levine, *The Irish and Irish Politicians: A Study of Cultural and Social Alienation* (South Bend, IN: Notre Dame University Press, 1966).

24. David N. Doyle, *Irish Americans, Native Rights, and National Empires* (New York: Arno Press, 1976).

25. Rudolph J. Vecoli, "Contadini in Chicago: A Critique of 'The Uprooted,'" *Journal of American History* 51 (1964): 404–417; John E. Bodnar, *The Transplanted: A History of Immigration in Urban America* (Bloomington: Indiana University Press, 1985).

26. Lawrence J. McCaffrey, introduction, Arno Press Collection Prospectus for *The Irish-Americans* (New York: Arno Press, 1976), 4.

27. McCaffrey, introduction to *The Irish-Americans*, 4.

28. All quotations from McCaffrey, *The Irish Catholic Diaspora in America*, 212–213.

29. Robert Arthur Burchell, *The Irish in San Francisco, 1848–80* (Berkeley: University of California Press, 1980), 188.

30. James P. Walsh, "The Irish in the New America: Way Out West," in *America and Ireland 1776–1996*, ed. O. D. Edwards and David N. Doyle (Westport, CT: Greenwood Press, 1980), 165–176.

31. Burchell, *The Irish in San Francisco*, 188.

32. Ibid., 3.

33. Rischin, review of *Immigrant Life in New York City*, 116.

34. William V. Shannon, foreword to *Erin's Heirs: Irish Bonds of Community*, by Dennis Clark (Lexington: University Press of Kentucky, 1991), ix.

35. Timothy J. Meagher, conclusion in *From Paddy to Studs: Irish-American Communities in the Turn of the Century Era, 1880–1920* (Westport, CT: Greenwood Press, 1986), 183.

36. David Noel Doyle, "The Regional Bibliography of Irish America, 1800–1930: A Review and an Addendum," *Irish Historical Studies* 23, no. 91 (May 1983): 255.

37. See the judicious conclusions of Ronald H. Bayor and Timothy J. Meagher, eds., *The New York Irish* (Baltimore: John Hopkins University Press, 1996), 534–537.

38. Burchell, *The Irish in San Francisco*, 3.

39. Bayor and Meagher, *The New York Irish*, 7–8.

40. James M. O'Toole and David Quigley, eds., *Boston's Histories: Essays in Honor of Thomas H. O'Connor* (Chicago: Northwestern University Press, 2004).

41. See, in particular, Charles Fanning, ed., new introduction to *Mr. Dooley and the Chicago Irish: The Autobiography of a Nineteenth-Century Ethnic Group*, revised edition, by Finley Peter Dunne (Washington, DC: Catholic University of America Press, 1987), and his chapter, Fanning, "The Literary Dimension," in Lawrence J. McCaffrey, ed., *The Irish in Chicago* (Urbana: University of Illinois Press, 1987), 98–145.

42. Fanning, "The Literary Dimension," 98–145.

43. William V. Shannon, introduction to *America and Ireland, 1776–1976: The American Identity and the Irish Connection*, ed. David N. Doyle and Owen Dudley Edwards (Westport, CT: Greenwood Press, 1980), xiii.

44. James Leyburn, foreword to *The Scotch-Irish: A Social History* (Chapel Hill: University of North Carolina Press, 1962), vi.

45. Maldwyn A. Jones, "Ulster Emigration, 1783–1815," in *Essays in Scotch-Irish History*, ed. E. R. R. Green (Belfast: Ulster Historical Foundation, 1991), 46–47; see also David N. Doyle, *Ireland, Irishmen and Revolutionary America, 1760–1820* (Dublin: Mercier Press, 1981), and "Scots Irish or Scotch Irish," chapter 3 in this volume; Maurice J. Bric, "Patterns of Irish Emigration to America, 1783–1800," *Eire-Ireland* 36, no. 1–2 (Spring/Summer 1997): 10–28.

46. William H. A. Williams, *"'Twas Only an Irishman's Dream": The Image of Ireland and the Irish in American Popular Song Lyrics, 1800–1920* (Urbana and Chicago: University of Illinois Press, 1996), 1.

47. John Higham, *Strangers in the Land: Patterns of American Nativism, 1860–1925* (New York: Atheneum, 1978), 61.

48. Charlotte Erickson, *Invisible Immigrants: The Adaptation of English and Scottish Immigrants in Nineteenth-Century America* (Leicester, UK: Leicester University Press, 1972).

49. See J. Matthew Gallman, *Receiving Erin's Children: Philadelphia, Liverpool, and the Irish Famine Migration, 1845–1855* (Chapel Hill: University of North Carolina Press, 2000).

50. The classic survey is James S. Donnelly, "Constructing the Memory of the Famine, 1850–1900," in *The Great Irish Potato Famine*, ed. James S. Donnelly (Stroud, UK: Sutton, 2001), 209–245.

51. Kerby Miller and Bruce D. Boling with Liam Kennedy, "The Famine's Scars: William Murphy's Ulster and American Odyssey," in *New Directions in Irish-American History*, ed. Kevin Kenny (Madison: University of Wisconsin Press, 2003), 36–60.

52. Hasia R. Diner, *Hungering for America: Italian, Irish and Jewish Foodways in the Age of Migration* (Cambridge, MA: Harvard University Press, 2001), 113.

53. John Mitchel, *The Last Conquest of Ireland (Perhaps)* (Dublin: Irishman Office, 1861).

54. *Tribune* quote from 1847 reproduced in Marion R. Casey, "New York and the Irish Famine," *Irish Echo*, March 15–21, 1995, 35.

55. Bishop John Hughes, "A Lecture on the Antecedent Causes of the Irish Famine in 1847: Delivered under the Auspices of the General Committee for the Relief of the Suffering Poor of Ireland, at the Broadway Tabernacle, March 20, 1847" (New York: Edward Dunigan, 1847), n.p. For the effect of this lecture in Ireland, see Donnelly, "Constructing the Memory of the Famine, 1850–1900," 214, 233.

56. Timothy J. Sarbaugh, "The Spirit of Manifest Destiny: The American Government and Famine Ireland, 1845–1849," in *Fleeing the Famine: North America and Irish Refugees, 1845–1851*, ed. Margaret M. Mulrooney (Westport, CT: Praeger, 2003), 49–52.

57. Sarbaugh, "The Spirit of Manifest Destiny," 50.

58. Kerby A. Miller, "In the Famine's Shadow," *Eire-Ireland* 36, no. 1 (2001): 116–117.

59. Kerby A. Miller, "'Revenge for Skibbereen': Irish Emigration and the Meaning of the Great Famine," in *The Great Famine and the Irish Diaspora*, ed. Arthur Gribben and Ruth-Ann M. Harris (Amherst: University of Massachusetts Press, 1999), 180–195.

60. Mick Mulcrone, "The Famine and Collective Memory: The Role of the Irish-American Press in the Early Twentieth Century," in *The Great Famine and the Irish Diaspora*, ed. Arthur Gribben and Ruth-Ann M. Harris (Amherst: University of Massachusetts Press, 1999), 219–238.

61. Tom Archdeacon, "The Irish Famine in American School Curricula," *Eire-Ireland* 37 (2002): 130–152.

62. The standard study of the even bigger subject of the general urbanization of the immigrant is David N. Doyle, "The Irish as Urban Pioneers in the United States, 1850–1870," *Journal of American Ethnic History* 10, no. 1–2 (Fall 1990): 36–59.

63. The medical history of immigration remains badly underdeveloped, but its potential can be sensed from Alan M. Kraut, "Illness and Medical Care among the Irish Immigrants in Antebellum New York," in *The New York Irish*, ed. Ronald H. Bayor and Timothy J. Meagher (Baltimore: Johns Hopkins University Press, 1996), 153–168.

64. Robert J. Scally has written about both in Breandán Ó Conaire, ed., *The Famine Lectures: Léachtaí an Ghorta* (Boyle, Roscommon: Comhdháil an Chraoibhín, 1995–97), 276, and Scally, "Liverpool Ships and Irish Emigrants in the Age of Sail," *Journal of Social History* 17, no. 1 (Fall 1993): 5–30.

65. Maurice Bric, "The Irish and the Evolution of the 'New Politics' in America," in *The Irish in America: Emigration, Assimilation, and Impact*, ed. P. J. Drudy (New York: Cambridge University Press, 1985), 143–168; David A. Wilson, *United Irishmen, United States: Immigrant Radicals in the Early Republic* (Ithaca: Cornell University Press, 1998).

66. Much work remains to be done on county societies everywhere, comparable to John T. Ridge's pioneering, "Irish County Societies in New York, 1880–1914," in *The New York Irish*, ed. Ronald H. Bayor and Timothy J. Meagher (Baltimore: Johns Hopkins University Press, 1996), 275–300.

67. See Cormac Ó Gráda, *Black '47 and Beyond: The Great Irish Famine in History, Economy and Memory* (Princeton: Princeton University Press, 1999), 114ff.

68. See the illuminating study by Dale Light Jr., "The Role of the Irish-American Organizations in Assimilation and Impact," in *The Irish in America: Emigration, Assimilation and Impact*, ed. P. J. Drudy (New York: Cambridge University Press, 1985), 111–141.

69. Randall M. Miller, "Catholic Religion, Irish Ethnicity and the Civil War," in *Religion and the American Civil War*, ed. Randall M. Miller, Harry S. Stout, and Charles Reagan Wilson (New York: Oxford University Press, 1998), 261–296.

70. John T. Ridge, *The St. Patrick's Day Parade in New York* (New York: St. Patrick Day's Parade Committee, 1988), illustrations, [187].

71. Marion R. Casey, "The Limits of Equality, 1789–1836," in *Race and Ethnicity in America: A Concise History*, ed. Ronald H. Bayor (New York: Columbia University Press, 2003), 47, 54–55.

72. James S. Pula, "Ethnic Relations: The Poles and the Irish," in *Encyclopedia of the Irish in America*, ed. Michael Glazier (South Bend, IN: Notre Dame University Press, 1999), 291.

73. Joseph P. Ferrie, *Yankees Now: Immigrants in the Antebellum United States, 1840–1860* (New York: Oxford University Press, 1999), 120–122.

74. David Montgomery, "The Irish and the American Labor Movement," in *America and Ireland, 1776–1976: The American Identity and the Irish Connection*, ed. David N. Doyle and Owen Dudley Edwards (Westport, CT: Greenwood Press, 1980), 210.

75. Daniel Patrick Moynihan, "The Irish," in *Beyond the Melting Pot*, ed. Daniel Patrick Moynihan and Michael Glazier (Cambridge, MA: MIT Press, 1963), 256.

76. Moynihan, "The Irish," 260.

77. Works that deal directly with the actual fortunes of the Irish language among immigrants include T. W. Ihde, ed., *The Irish Language in the United States* (Westport, CT: Bergin and Garvey, 1994); Una Ní Bhroiméil, *The Gaelic Revival and America, 1870–1915* (Dublin: Four Courts, 2003); K. E. Nilsen, "The Irish Language in New York City, 1850–1900," in *The New York Irish*, ed. Ronald H. Bayor and Timothy J. Meagher (Baltimore: Johns Hopkins University Press, 1996), 252–274.

78. Miller, "In the Famine's Shadow," 122.

79. Diner, *Hungering for America*, 129.

80. Murray Sperber, "Notre Dame Football—'The Fighting Irish,'" in *The Encyclopedia of the Irish in America*, ed. Michael Glazier (South Bend, IN: Notre Dame University Press, 1999), 704–707; see also Jerrold Casway, "Review of *Ed Delahanty in the Emerald Age of Baseball* by James Silas Rogers," *Irish Literary Supplement* (Fall 2004): 10.

81. D. A. E. Harkness, "Irish Emigration," in *International Migrations*, ed. Walter F. Willcox (New York: National Bureau of Economic Research, 1931; repr., New York: Gordon and Breach Science Publishers, 1969), 2:275–277. Page references are to 1969 edition.

82. See, for instance, *Irish Press*, September 4, 1972; *Irish Times*, October 2 and 9, 1972, and January 15, 1973.

83. Hasia Diner, *Erin's Daughters in America: Irish Immigrant Women in the Nineteenth Century* (Baltimore: Johns Hopkins University Press, 1983); Janet Nolan, *Ourselves Alone: Women's Emigration from Ireland, 1885–1920* (Lexington: University Press of Kentucky, 1989); Kerby A. Miller with David N. Doyle and Patricia Kelleher, "'For Love and Liberty': Irish Women, Migration and Domesticity in Ireland and America, 1815–1920," in *The Irish World Wide: History, Heritage, Identity*, vol. 4, *Irish Women and Irish Migration*, ed. Patrick O'Sullivan (London: Leicester University Press, 1995), 41–65.

84. For relevant reflections on the historiography of women, see Donna Gabaccia, "Immigrant Women: Nowhere at Home?" *Journal of American Ethnic History* 10, no. 4 (Summer 1991): 61–87.

85. All quotes and discussions in this paragraph from Finley Peter Dunne, *Mr. Dooley and the Chicago Irish: The Autobiography of a Nineteenth-Century Ethnic Group*, revised edition, ed. Charles Fanning (Washington, DC: Catholic University of America Press, 1987), 139ff, 91, 86ff, 73–74, 137ff.

86. Charles Fanning, "The Literary Dimension," in *The Irish in Chicago*, ed. Lawrence J. McCaffrey (Urbana and Chicago: University of Illinois Press, 1987), 109.

87. Ruth-Ann M. Harris, "'Come All You Courageously': Irish Women in America Write Home," *Eire-Ireland* 36, no. 1 (2001): 183.

88. On women and saving, see ibid., 175.

89. J. J. Lee, introduction to *Dreamers of Dreams*, ed. Donal O'Donovan (Bray: Kilbride Books, 1984), x–xi.

90. Emmet J. Larkin, "The Devotional Revolution in Ireland, 1850–75," *American Historical Review* 77, no. 3 (June 1972): 625–652.

91. Marc C. Foley and Timothy W. Guinnane, "Did Irish Marriage Patterns Survive the Emigrant Voyage? Irish-American Nuptiality, 1880–1920," *Irish Economic and Social History* 26 (1999): 15–34.

92. For a good example, see Colleen McDannell, "Going to the Ladies' Fair: Irish Catholics in New York City, 1870–1900," in *The New York Irish*, ed. Ronald H. Bayor and Timothy J. Meagher (Baltimore: Johns Hopkins University Press, 1996), 234–251.

93. Maureen M. Mulrooney, *Black Powder, White Lace: The Dupont Irish and Cultural Identity in Nineteenth-Century America* (Hanover: University of New Hampshire, published by University Press of New England, 2002).

94. Bayor and Meagher, introduction to *The New York Irish*, 7.

95. Bayor and Meagher, conclusion to *The New York Irish*, 542. Also in *The New York Irish* both: Graham Hodges, "'Desirable Companions and Lovers': Irish and African Americans in the Sixth Ward, 1830–1870," 107–124, and John Kuo Wei Tchen, "Quimbo Appo's Fear of Fenians: Chinese-Irish-Anglo Relations in New York City," 125–152.

96. Noel Ignatiev, *How the Irish Became White* (New York: Routledge, 1995); Peter Quinn, *Banished Children of Eve* (New York: Penguin, 1995).

97. Peter Quinn, "How the Irish Stayed Irish," *America,* March 16, 1996, 24.

98. Kerby Miller, "Class, Culture, and Immigrant Group Identity in the United States: The Case of Irish-American Ethnicity," in *Immigration Reconsidered: History, Sociology, and Politics,* ed. Virginia Yans-McLaughlin (New York: Oxford University Press, 1999), 96–129.

99. David Noel Doyle, "The Irish and American Labour, 1880–1920," *Saothar: Journal of the Irish Labour History Society* 1 (May 1975): 42–53.

100. David Montgomery, "The Irish and the American Labor Movement," in *America and Ireland, 1776–1976: The American Identity and the Irish Connection,* ed. David N. Doyle and Owen Dudley Edwards (Westport, CT: Greenwood Press, 1980), 207; Eric Foner, "Class Ethnicity, and Radicalism in the Gilded Age: The Land League in Irish America," *Politics and Ideology in the Age of the Civil War* (New York: Oxford University Press, 1980), 150–200.

101. See John R. McKivigan and Thomas J. Robertson, "The Irish American Worker in Transition, 1877–1914: New York as a Test Case" in *The New York Irish,* ed. Ronald H. Bayor and Timothy J. Meagher (Baltimore: Johns Hopkins University Press, 1996), 301–320.

102. Jay Dolan, *The Immigrant Church: New York's Irish and German Catholics, 1815–1865* (Baltimore: Johns Hopkins University Press, 1975); Ronald Bayor, *Neighbors in Conflict: The Irish, Germans, Jews, and Italians of New York City, 1929–1941* (Urbana: University of Illinois Press, 1988).

103. Bayor and Meagher rightly emphasize the need to study inter-ethnic relations in their conclusion to *The New York Irish,* 542. See also David Noel Doyle, "Review Article: Small Differences? The Study of the Irish in the United States and Britain," *Irish Historical Studies* 29, no. 113 (May 1994): 116.

104. Kevin Kenny, introduction to *New Directions in Irish-American History* (Madison: University of Wisconsin Press, 2003), 245.

105. J. J. Lee, "Emigration, 1922–1998," in *Encyclopedia of the Irish in America*, ed. Michael Glazier (South Bend, IN: Notre Dame University Press, 1999), 263–266.

106. Donald H. Akenson, "No Petty People: Pakeha History and the Historiography of the Irish Diaspora," in *A Distant Shore: Irish Migration and New Zealand Settlement*, ed. Lyndon Fraser (Dunedin: University of Otago Press, 2000), 18.

107. For a nuanced discussion of the whole issue of responses to the census question, see Mary Waters, *Ethnic Options: Choosing Ethnic Identities in America* (Berkeley: University of California Pres, 1990).

108. Timothy J. Meagher, *Inventing Irish America* (South Bend, IN: Notre Dame University Press, 2001).

109. Reginald Byron, *Irish America* (New York: Oxford University Press, 1999).

110. Tom Hayden, *Irish on the Inside: In Search of the Soul of Irish America* (New York: Verso, 2001).

111. Michael Hout and Joshua R. Goldstein, "How 4.5 million Irish Immigrants Became 40 Million Irish Americans: Demographic and Subjective Aspects of the Ethnic Composition of White Americans," *American Sociological Review* 59 (February 1994): 64–82.

112. Donald H. Akenson, *The Irish Diaspora: A Primer* (Toronto: P. D. Meany, 1993), 223–224.

113. David Noel Doyle, "Review Article: Small Differences? The Study of the Irish in the United States and Britain," *Irish Historical Studies* 29, no. 113 (May 1994): 117–118.

114. On identity of Scotch-Irish in particular, see Patrick Griffin, *The People with No Name: Ireland's Ulster Scots, America's Scots Irish, and the Creation of a British Atlantic World, 1689–1764* (Princeton: Princeton University Press, 2001), 4–8, 177–179.

115. Kerby A. Miller, Arnold Schrier, Bruce D. Boling, and David N. Doyle, eds., *Irish Immigrants in the Land of Canaan: Letters and Memoirs from Colonial and Revolutionary America, 1675–1815* (Oxford: Oxford University Press, 2003).

116. Other immediately pertinent essays by Kerby Miller include "'Scotch-Irish' Myths and 'Irish' Identities in Eighteenth- and Nineteenth-Century America," in *New Perspectives on the Irish Diaspora*, ed. Charles Fanning (Carbondale: Southern Illinois University Press, 1998), 75–92; "'Scotch-Irish,' 'Black Irish' and 'Real Irish': Emigrants and Identities in the Old South," in *The Irish Diaspora*, ed. Andy Bielenberg (Harlow: Pearson, 2000), 139–157.

117. David N. Doyle, "Scots Irish or Scotch-Irish," in *Encyclopedia of the Irish in America*, ed. Michael Glazier (South Bend, IN: Notre Dame University Press, 1999), reprinted here as chapter 3.

118. Fanning, "The Literary Dimension," 108.

119. Fanning, New introduction to *Mr. Dooley and the Chicago Irish*; Daniel J. Casey and Robert E. Rhodes, *Irish-American Fiction: Essays in Criticism* (New York: AMS Press, 1979).

120. McCaffrey, *The Irish Catholic Diaspora in America*, 222–223, has an admirably succinct commentary.

121. Kerby Miller, "Assimilation and Alienation: Irish Emigrants' Responses to Industrial America, 1871–1921," in *The Irish in America: Emigration, Assimilation and Impact*, ed. P. J. Drudy (New York: Cambridge University Press, 1985), 87.

122. McCaffrey, *The Irish Catholic Diaspora in America*, 10

123. Lawrence J. McCaffrey, "The Irish Dimension," *The Irish in Chicago* (Urbana: University of Illinois Press, 1987), 1; McCaffrey, *The Irish Diaspora in America*, 116.

124. Andrew M. Greeley, *The Irish Americans: The Rise to Money and Power* (New York: Time Books, 1981), 8–9, 204–205.

125. Marion R. Casey, "'From the East Side to the Seaside': Irish Americans on the Move in New York City," 395–438; Robert W. Snyder, "The Neighborhood Changed: The Irish of Washington Heights and Inwood since 1945," 439–60—both in *The New York Irish*, ed. Ronald H. Bayor and Timothy J. Meagher (Baltimore: Johns Hopkins University Press, 1996).

126. David Montgomery, "The Irish and the American Labor Movement," in *America and Ireland, 1776–1976: The American Identity and the Irish Connection*, ed. David N. Doyle and Owen Dudley Edwards (Westport, CT: Greenwood Press, 1980), 217.

127. Greeley, *The Irish Americans*, 1–2.

128. Joseph M. Curran, *Hibernian Green on the Silver Screen: The Irish and American Movies* (New York: Warner Books, 1989).

129. For particularly interesting reflections on the issue of stereotype, see Dale R. Knobel, *Paddy and the Republic: Ethnicity and Nationality in Antebellum America* (Middletown, CT: Wesleyan University Press, 1986), and Knobel, *America for the Americans: The Nativist Movement in the United States* (New York: Twayne Publishers, 1996); Stephen Watt, "Irish American

Drama of the 1850s: National Identity, 'Otherness,' and Assimilation," in *Fleeing the Famine: North America and Irish Refugees, 1845–1851*, ed. Margaret M. Mulrooney (Westport, CT: Praeger, 2003), 97–109; and more generally, L. Perry Curtis, *Apes and Angels: The Irishman in Victorian Caricature* (Washington, DC: Smithsonian Institute Press, 1996).

130. David N. Doyle, "Conclusion: Some Further Themes," in *America and Ireland, 1776–1976: The American Identity and the Irish Connection*, ed. David N. Doyle and Owen Dudley Edwards (Westport, CT: Greenwood Press, 1980), 317.

131. Owen Dudley Edwards, "Conclusion: Some Counterthemes," in *America and Ireland, 1776–1976: The American Identity and the Irish Connection*, ed. David N. Doyle and Owen Dudley Edwards (Westport, CT: Greenwood Press, 1980), 310–313.

132. Donald H. Akenson, "The Irish in North America: Catholic or Protestant?" *Irish Review* 11 (Winter 1991/1992): 17–22.

133. Maldwyn A. Jones, "Ulster Emigration, 1783–1815," in *Essays in Scotch-Irish History*, ed. E. R. R. Green (Belfast: Ulster Historical Foundation, 1969), 46–47.

134. Moynihan, "The Irish," 253.

135. Daniel Patrick Moynihan, foreword to *The Most Distressful Nation*, ed. Andrew Greeley (Chicago: Quadrangle Books, 1972), xiv.

136. Ibid., xvii. It is a pleasure to record that the City University of New York is today making up lost ground in promoting rich teaching on Ireland and Irish America.

137. Lawrence J. McCaffrey, "American Conference for Irish Studies: A Co-Founder's Memoir," in *Encyclopedia of the Irish in America*, ed. Michael Glazier (South Bend, IN: Notre Dame University Press, 1999), 12–14.

138. "Eoin KcKiernan," in *Encyclopedia of the Irish in America*, ed. Michael Glazier (South Bend, IN: Notre Dame University Press, 1999), 594–595; "A Memorial Tribute to Dr. Eoin McKiernan, 1915–2004," *Dúchas: A Publication of the Irish American Cultural Institute* (November 2004): 6–7.

139. Thomas N. Brown, *Irish-American Nationalism, 1870–1890* (New York; Lippincott, 1966), xi.

140. Moses Rischin, comment, Arno Press Collection Prospectus for *The Irish-Americans* (New York: Arno Press, 1976), 3.

141. Dennis Clark, preface to *The Irish in Philadelphia: Ten Generations of Urban Experience* (Philadelphia: Temple University Press, 1973), xiv.

142. Clark, *Erin's Heirs: Irish Bonds of Community*, 126.

143. Patrick J. Corish, ed., *A History of Irish Catholicism*, vol. 6, bk. 2 (Dublin: Gill and Macmillan, 1970).

144. Thomas McAvoy, *The United States of America: The Irish Clergyman* (New York: Gill and Macmillan, 1970), 98.

145. For a wide-ranging survey of issues in Catholic higher education, see Philip Gleason, "A Half-Century of Change in Catholic Higher Education," *U.S. Catholic Historian* 19, no. 1 (Winter 2001): 1–20.

146. Robert Dunne, *Antebellum Irish Immigration and Emerging Ideologies of "America": A Protestant Backlash* (Lewiston, NY: Edwin Mellen Press, 2002), 116.

147. Seamus Metress et al., *The Irish-American Experience: A Guide to the Literature* (Washington, DC: University Press of America, 1981); Patrick J. Blessing, *The Irish in America: A Guide to the Literature and the Manuscript Collections* (Washington DC: Catholic University of America Press, 1992); Ann M. Shea and Marion R. Casey, *The Irish Experience in New York City: A Select Bibliography* (New York: New York Irish History Roundtable, 1995).

148. David Emmons, *The Butte Irish: Class and Ethnicity in an American Mining Town,*

1875–1925 (Urbana: University of Illinois Press, 1989); David Gleeson, *The Irish in the South, 1815–1877* (Chapel Hill: University of North Carolina Press, 2001); Graham Davis, *Land! Irish Pioneers in Mexican and Revolutionary Texas* (College Station: Texas A&M University Press, 2002).

149. Kerby Miller, *Emigrants and Exiles: Ireland and the Irish Exodus to North America* (New York: Oxford University Press, 1985), 3.

150. Griffin, *The People with No Name.*

151. See Kevin Kenny, "Diaspora and Comparison: The Global Irish as a Case Study," *Journal of American History* 90, no. 1 (June 2002): 134–162; also, Donald M. MacRaild, "Crossing Migrant Frontiers: Comparative Reflections on Irish Migrants in Britain and the United States during the Nineteenth Century," in *The Great Famine and Beyond: Irish Migrants in Britain in the Nineteenth and Twentieth Centuries,* ed. Donald M. MacRaild (Dublin: Irish Academic Press, 1999), 40–70.

152. For an impressively wide-ranging survey of recent work, see David N. Doyle, "Cohesion and Diversity in the Irish Diaspora," *Irish Historical Studies* 21, no. 123 (1999): 411–434.

153. Suellen Hoy and Margaret MacCurtain, *From Dublin to New Orleans: Nora and Alice's Journey to America, 1889* (Cork: Attic Press, 1995).

154. William L. Smith, "Priests from Ireland," in *Encyclopedia of the Irish in America,* ed. Michael Glazier (South Bend, IN: Notre Dame University Press, 1999), 790.

155. Blenner-Hassett, "A Brief History of Celtic Studies in North America," 20.

156. Elizabeth Brymer, "Charles Fanning," in *Encyclopedia of the Irish in America,* ed. Michael Glazier (South Bend, IN: Notre Dame University Press, 1999), 309–310.

157. Kerby Miller, interview by J. J. Lee, Glucksman Ireland House, New York University, New York City, March 27, 2003.

158. Kerby Miller, Bruce Boling, and David Noel Doyle, taped interview by J. J. Lee, Glucksman Ireland House, New York University, March 27, 2003.

159. John V. Kelleher, "Irishness in America," *Atlantic Monthly* (July 1961): 38–40.

160. Moynihan, "The Irish," 287.

161. Andrew J. Wilson, *Irish America and the Ulster Conflict: 1968–1995* (Belfast: Blackstaff Press, 1995).

162. Conor O'Clery, *Daring Diplomacy: Clinton's Secret Search for Peace in Ireland* (Boulder, CO: Roberts Rinehart, 1997); see more generally, Tim Pat Coogan, *Wherever Green Is Worn: The Story of the Irish Diaspora* (London: Hutchinson, 2000).

163. Brian Hanley, "The Politics of NORAID" (abstract), *Irish Political Studies* 19, no. 1 (Summer 2004): 1.

164. Peter Quinn, "Introduction: An Interpretation of Silences," *Eire-Ireland* 32, no. 1 (Spring 1997): xxxii, 1, 18.

The Irish Background

Map of Ireland, 1922 to the Present

Chapter 2

Modern Ireland
An Introductory Survey

Eileen Reilly

This survey is intended to introduce the primary themes and events of the past five centuries to those who are just becoming acquainted with the history of Ireland. It necessarily compresses the historical experience in the interest of concision, but it aims to be a lucid primer for those who will, hopefully, pursue their specific interests further. The select list of titles at the conclusion of this essay provides an initial bibliography to that end.

The Earls of Kildare

Although Ireland had been nominally conquered by Norman barons in the name of Henry II of England in the twelfth century, it had never been subjugated. Individual Norman barons such as John de Courcy and Hugh de Lacy carved out important spheres of power in northeast Ulster and the Leinster midlands, while the de Burgos and FitzGeralds were prominent in the temporary conquest of Connaught in the early thirteenth century, but there was no systematic attempt at complete conquest. The Normans intermarried with the Gaelic Irish, introduced a centralized administration, built towns that led to the growth of trade, encouraged the activities of new religious orders such as the Dominicans and Franciscans, and were responsible for the building of the great cathedrals such as St. Patrick's in Dublin and St. Canice's in Kilkenny.

From the middle of the thirteenth century onward, the Gaelic Irish began to reassert themselves against the newcomers, and by the end of the fifteenth century, the descendants of the Normans were settled predominantly in the east, the midlands, and the southeast. Their area of influence, the fortified hinterland around Dublin that waxed and waned in size and importance, was known as the English Pale. Control of the Pale and maintaining the authority of the English crown in the lordship of Ireland was the responsibility of the leading families of Norman descent, known as the Anglo-Irish or the Old English, the most prominent of which were the FitzGeralds, earls of Kildare.

Henry VIII, who became king of England in 1509, was the second Tudor monarch. His father, Henry VII, claimed the throne in 1485 in the aftermath of a series of dynastic conflicts known collectively as the Wars of the Roses. Concerned with consolidating his position in England, Henry VII paid little sustained attention to the lordship of Ireland except when events there concerned the security of his throne. For the most part, he was content to leave the governance of the island in the traditional hands of his lord deputy. Henry VIII (1509–1547) continued this policy during the early years of his reign when he was preoccupied by foreign policy and continental wars.

Garrett Mór FitzGerald occupied the position of lord deputy from 1496 to 1513, when he was succeeded by his son, Garrett Óg, who held it unchallenged until 1520 and was reappointed in 1524 when various replacements proved unsatisfactory. He continued as lord deputy until his death in 1534. The FitzGeralds were a powerful dynasty. They controlled large estates within the Pale but also exerted authority outside it. Over time they had forged important alliances with leading Gaelic families such as the O'Neills of Tyrone. They commanded allegiance from Anglo-Irish families and support from Gaelic clans. In return, they guaranteed protection. For the Anglo-Irish families, the FitzGeralds provided security from aggressive and costly raids by the Gaelic Irish who bordered the Pale. For the Gaelic Irish, an alliance with the FitzGeralds discouraged ambitious attacks from enemies.

The FitzGeralds' position of great power and influence encouraged rivals, most notably the Butlers, earls of Ormond. This Anglo-Irish family had designs on the position of lord deputy and doggedly pursued their goal of discrediting the FitzGeralds, chiefly with accusations of degeneracy. As the power brokers of early-sixteenth-century Ireland, the FitzGeralds spoke the Gaelic language, intermarried with important Gaelic families, and adopted some of their social and cultural customs. This left them vulnerable to the charge that they had abandoned their English civility and were neglecting the interests of the crown in favor of their own power and prestige. This was true in some respects. On the one hand, it was necessary for the FitzGeralds to communicate and interact with the Gaelic families in order to maintain control and exert influence. On the other hand, they used their power chiefly for their own aggrandizement and made it very clear on several occasions that they could implement their threat of making Ireland ungovernable if removed from office, as was the case during the 1520s, when Henry VIII returned power to Garrett Óg after experimenting with replacements. The FitzGeralds had successfully exhibited their indispensability, but, ironically, this success strengthened Henry VIII's resolve to change the nature of Ireland's government.

Desire for significant change in the government of the lordship of Ireland was linked to wider changes taking place in England. In the early 1530s, Henry VIII's chief administrator, Thomas Cromwell, was orchestrating far-reaching political and religious change on Henry's behalf. Henry's frustrated desire for a papal annulment of his first marriage led to legislation enacted in the English parliament that declared him to be the supreme head of the Church of England and dissolved his first marriage, allowing him to marry Anne Boleyn. Simultaneously, Cromwell was introducing significant changes in central and local government (including the political union of Wales and England), some of the effects of which were felt in closer royal attention to Ireland and a desire to extend royal dominion. The chief casualties of this change in the traditional Irish policy of English monarchs were the FitzGeralds.

Garrett Óg was called to London in 1534 to answer accusations of treason brought against him by his enemies in Ireland. He left his son, Thomas, Lord Offaly, in charge in his absence. On his arrival in London, he was immediately charged with using royal artillery for his own personal use and was confined in the Tower of London. Thomas, popularly known as "Silken Thomas" because of his fondness for fine clothes, responded to his father's arrest with defiant rebellion, one that was met with a ruthless response by the forces of the crown. The consequence of this action was the effective destruction of the earls of Kildare. Garrett Óg died in the Tower of London. Thomas and his male relatives (with the exception of a young half-brother hidden by his aunt) were executed. In one fell swoop the powerful House of Kildare was destroyed, and with it the traditional power of the Anglo-Irish lords. From 1534 onward, the Tudor monarchs of England appointed English lord deputies to carry out their new Irish policies. These policies revolved around two main issues. The first was extending and consolidating power in Ireland. The second was religion.

Plantation

In 1541, the Irish parliament declared Henry VIII king of Ireland. The change in Ireland's status from a medieval lordship to a kingdom reflected the evolving change in royal attitudes to Ireland. However, extending royal authority in Ireland required an expensive military campaign to subdue both the Gaelic chiefs and those Anglo-Irish lords who had long been accustomed to latitude in their spheres of influence. Desire and accomplishment are not necessarily found together. Henry VIII certainly exhibited the desire to increase his authority in Ireland, but accomplishment by military means was expensive. Instead, he considered an alternative method—peaceful submission whereby Gaelic *taoisigh* (chiefs) and Anglo-Irish nobles recognized the king as sovereign, surrendered their lands and Gaelic titles to the king, and applied for a land grant and a peerage. English titles were conferred in lieu of renounced Gaelic titles; the recipients promised to uphold English law and customs, pay rent to the crown, and render military service. In some cases this seemed to be a viable procedure, but at the heart of the policy were the English laws of land tenure and succession that clashed with the traditional Gaelic system. Under the latter, sons and daughters could inherit land, but their tenure of it depended on kinship obligations, for land was the property of the clan. The head of a *tuath* (clan) was elected by eligible members of the clan, and position and title were not strictly hereditary. The land tenure system in England was based on the principle that the king was the absolute owner of all land, which others held according to royal grants and leases, and succession emphasized primogeniture. Thus Henry's policy of "surrender and regrant" met with resistance and, inevitably, conflict. With the failure of this approach, Henry's successors (Edward VI, 1547–1553; Mary I, 1553–1558; and Elizabeth I, 1558–1603) emphasized finite military campaigns, confiscation, and plantation of

English settlers, although Elizabeth, as financially canny as her father, placed great hopes in negotiation.

The first plantation was carried out during the reign of Mary I. The counties of Leix and Offaly had been confiscated by the crown after a rebellion by the Gaelic O'Connors and O'Mores in the mid 1540s. The counties were renamed King's and Queen's Counties and were settled with planters whose duty was to uphold English law and custom in the face of Gaelic aggression and encroachment. Resistance and rebellion by the Gaelic Irish or Anglo-Irish resulted in confiscation followed by plantation, as with the earl of Desmond's lands in Munster in the 1580s. In more extensive and fiercely resisted plantations in Munster and Connaught during the Elizabethan period, protecting and extending the Protestant religion in Ireland became an important theoretical aspect of planter duty. In practice, however, the Protestant Reformation had little impact on Ireland for a variety of reasons, which included the geographical isolation of large parts of Ireland especially in the west and north of the island, the linguistic gap between English-speaking clergymen and the predominately Gaelic-speaking population, and, overall, the somewhat surprising lack of zeal employed. The Old English (the term most commonly used in the late sixteenth century to describe those descendants of earlier settlers) were for the most part committed Catholics, and there was a certain reluctance to force religious change on such an influential group. Therefore, although the practice of Catholicism was discouraged and penalized, conversion was not undertaken in any systematic way. Yet with the Tudor plantations of the late sixteenth century, and more especially those carried out by the Stuart monarchs in the seventeenth century, a significant new Protestant element was added to the Irish population.

By the end of Elizabeth's reign, great progress had been made in the authority of the crown in Ireland and, thus, the defense of England in the face of European enemies. Elizabeth ruled the whole island upon the defeat of Hugh O'Neill's army, despite his Spanish allies, in 1603 at the battle of Kinsale. O'Neill had pursued an ambitious war for many years against Elizabeth's authority, stressing his sovereignty in Ulster and using his Catholicism as a call to arms for those continental powers who opposed the "heretic queen." His defeat marked the end of the powerful Gaelic lords and, in political terms at least, the end of Gaelic Ireland. The power of the Old English lords, so shrewdly wielded and protected by the FitzGeralds in the early sixteenth century, had been drastically curtailed. By the beginning of the seventeenth century, those same families were anxiously trying to maintain their reduced influence and wealth, given the rising prominence and power of the new Protestant planters in Ireland. This trend continued throughout the next century, uniting the once distinct Gaelic and Old English groups in a common cause of Catholic resistance to Protestant power and privilege.

Religion and Power

The seventeenth century in Ireland, as in Europe, was one of religious and political conflict. The Stuart monarchs, who succeeded the Tudors as rulers of England and

Ireland, in addition to their own Scottish crown, continued the policy of plantation. The settlement of Ulster, carried out by James I (1603–1625), was the most comprehensive and successful of all. With the defeat of Hugh O'Neill in 1603 and his flight to Europe in 1607 with his ally Hugh O'Donnell and their extended families, Ulster was substantially planted with Anglican English and Presbyterian Scots settlers at the expense of those native inhabitants who had previously occupied the land. Those new settlers who were granted land in Ulster were charged with responsibility for its defense against the return of the native or the hybridization of the newcomer. The Irish Society and its shareholders, the City of London guild-companies, were granted a charter by the crown in 1613, giving them responsibility for fortifying and colonizing the region west of the Bann River, which was renamed Londonderry. The new settlers arrived in significant numbers from England and lowland Scotland, in contrast to earlier Tudor plantation schemes. By 1630 about 6,500 British males had settled on confiscated lands. They undertook the task of planting Ulster with eagerness and fortitude, building towns and villages, clearing the land, practicing arable farming, and establishing market centers. Despite this auspicious beginning and substantial change, there were not enough new settlers to completely modify the territory. As with earlier and later plantation attempts, the Gaelic Irish, theoretically expelled from the land, were necessary to work it as tenants and laborers.

Yet the Gaelic Irish were only one of the Catholic groups that made up the Irish population. The fortunes of the Old English had declined dramatically in the sixteenth century as a result of Tudor centralization and the Protestant Reformation. Despite their persistent reduction in power, they were still an influential and wealthy group in the first part of the seventeenth century. This advantage was fleeting, however. Charles I (1625–1649), embroiled in expensive foreign wars and in conflict with his English parliament, used the predicament of the Catholic Old English, whose loyalty as subjects was open to question because of their religious allegiance to Rome, to obtain grants of money in exchange for promises to secure their lands and positions. Charles I never kept his royal promises to the Old English, but by the time this was apparent to them, it was too late. Every aspect of their status was beset because of their Catholicism. The increase in the numbers of Protestants in Ireland, largely as a result of the Ulster plantation, led to a Protestant-dominated Irish parliament in Dublin, and its continued ascendancy depended on the continued decline of the Old English. Two societies were developing along religious lines: the dispossessed and threatened Catholics and the thriving yet vulnerable Protestants.

1641

External factors may have an unexpected yet decisive influence on the course of events. Such a moment for Ireland was during the late 1630s and early 1640s when the pace of events in England and Scotland, centering on the hostility between an ambitious king and an equally ambitious parliament, approached a civil crisis.

In 1641, a small coterie of Gaelic and Old English notables plotted to take advantage of the discord between king and parliament by seizing control of Dublin Castle, the center of English government in Ireland, and to simultaneously capture Ulster in a series of military maneuvers, mimicking a successful revolt in Scotland. The plot failed, and the risings in Ulster degenerated into a series of vicious attacks on Protestants by enraged and bitter Catholics. As many as four thousand Protestants were killed, many by torture, and thousands more were attacked and driven out of their homes and farms. While there were certainly atrocities committed, what happened in Ulster almost instantly transformed itself into a myth of massacre. Protestants fleeing Ulster sought shelter and protection in garrison towns, in Dublin, and in England. Their accounts of what had taken place led to demands for immediate and harsh revenge against Irish Catholics.

Vengeance, however, had to await the outcome of the civil war in England. The division between Parliamentarians and Royalists in Scotland and England had its echo in Ireland. Having placed their political future in the hands of the monarchy over the past decades, most Irish Catholics supported the Royalist cause in the faint hope of an end to the aggressively Protestant policies of the English and Irish parliaments if Charles I was successful, and the certainty of serious retribution if he was not. Yet this Catholic Confederation of Old English and Gaelic Irish, which declared that Irish Catholics composed the Irish nation and adopted *Pro Deo, pro rege, pro patria* (For God, king, and country) as its motto, was rent by internal mistrust and dissension, and was, in turn, viewed with suspicion by the Royalist army in Ireland, led by the Protestant earl of Ormond.

The Irish parliament built up a Protestant army. A Puritan Scots army under the leadership of Robert Munro arrived in Ulster in 1642 to protect Protestant settlers there and do battle with Catholic insurgents. They recaptured important garrison towns and successfully held the province for the duration of the conflict. The Scots were anti-Royalist with regard to Charles I but were also suspicious of the Parliamentarians.

Thus there were four armies in Ireland during a period of seven years, which eyed one another warily but partook of little direct fighting (with the exception of a serious battle at Benburb in June 1646 when the Confederate army under the leadership of Owen Roe O'Neill defeated Munro's Scots army) while awaiting the outcome of events in England. In 1649, the defeated Charles I was tried and executed. The parliament then turned its attention to Ireland and the question of vengeance for 1641. Chaos reigned as armies disintegrated and participants changed sides in hopes of survival.

Oliver Cromwell

Oliver Cromwell, the leader of the Parliamentary army, arrived in Ireland in 1649 with twenty thousand men and two aims. The first and most immediate objective was to punish the papist Irish for their atrocities against Ulster Protestants. The second was to make his own contribution to the project that had begun with the Tudors: the stable settlement of Ireland in a manner satisfactory to England and Protestantism. For Cromwell, this involved the elimination of Catholicism by force and by conversion, coupled with a more ambitious plantation scheme. Cromwell's refusal to distinguish between Gaelic and Old English Catholics in his harsh military campaigns at Drogheda, Wexford, and Clonmel, and his determination to have satisfaction for the events of 1641 consolidated two previously distinct groups in Irish society into a more homogeneous association whose division from the other section of Irish society, the Protestants, was becoming wider and more acrid. His settlement scheme provided for extensive escheatment of Catholic land, the transplantation to and confinement of the Catholic Irish west of the Shannon River in the comparatively poor province of Connaught, and the replacement of those Catholics with Protestant settlers in the other three provinces. Confiscated estates were used to pay Cromwellian soldiers and those who had invested in this latest conquest, referred to as "Adventurers."

This caused serious problems. Apart from overestimating the amount of land available for redistribution, many soldiers and Adventurers who received land grants were uninterested in settling as farmers in Ireland and quickly sold at low prices. Those with the means to purchase this land were Protestant settlers who had been in Ireland since the late sixteenth and early seventeenth centuries. They took advantage of the opportunity and added large amounts of land to their existing estates. So although the confiscation of Catholic land was substantial, it did not result in the new population of Protestant planters of all classes that Cromwell had envisioned. Certainly there were new settlers, but the general pattern was of a limited number of very large Protestant landowners who needed tenants and laborers to work their estates. This resulted, as had happened in Ulster earlier in the century, in the dispossessed, embittered Catholic Irish returning to fulfill these roles. Cromwell's evangelical schemes to convert the papist Irish to Protestantism also failed, despite energetic beginnings, due to divisions within Protestantism itself and the inability of most of the Protestant clergy to speak Gaelic.

The Glorious Revolution

English political change directed the course of events in Ireland until the end of the seventeenth century. The first change was the decision in 1660 to restore the Stuart monarchy upon the death of Cromwell. With the restoration of Charles II (1660–1685) as the new king of England, Ireland, and Scotland, many of those who had remained loyal to his family since the civil war recovered lost lands.

The Irish situation was more complicated. Charles was unwilling and unable to undo the Cromwellian land settlement. He could not antagonize his current Protestant supporters by showing leniency toward Irish Catholics, and the land settlement stayed essentially as it was. When Charles's brother, James, became king in 1685, Catholics were hopeful of more positive change. James II was the first Catholic monarch of England since the brief reign of Mary I more than a century previously. Irish Catholics expected the restoration of property and influence under this new monarch, and they were not disappointed with the initial signs of change. Richard Talbot, duke of Tyrconnell and the new lord lieutenant of Ireland, instantly set about putting Catholics in influential public offices, the parliament, and the army. This naturally alarmed Irish and English Protestants. If Catholics were experiencing reversals of fortune, then it would be at the expense of Protestant gains.

James's tactless pro-Catholic policies caused consternation in England but parliament, unwilling to take drastic action against another king so soon, comforted itself with the thought that the middle-aged James II was mortal, and his heir, his daughter Mary, was Protestant. This slim consolation disappeared when James, against all expectations, fathered a male heir in 1688. In response, the English parliament offered the throne to Mary and her husband, the Dutch Prince William of Orange.

James II fled for France when he received the news that William had landed in England. The coup was bloodless thus far, but King Louis XIV of France, at war with William's forces on the continent, encouraged James II to fight. The now largely Catholic army in Ireland, allied with the French troops sent by Louis XIV with James II at its head, prepared to do battle with William's supporters, until William himself arrived with an army to take up the challenge. Irish Protestants feared a repetition of the bloody events of 1641 and swiftly sought shelter in garrison towns such as Enniskillen and Londonderry; the latter refused to surrender to James's army and victoriously withstood a prolonged and bitter siege in 1689.

The first and very decisive victory went to William. After engaging with the Jacobite army, his force crossed the Boyne River in July 1690 and marched toward Dublin. James's army strategically retreated southward, while James himself fled once more to France. His supporters in Ireland withstood William's forces at Limerick, but despite giving valiant battle at Athlone and Aughrim in 1691, they were defeated. Catholic hopes were again dashed. Land was once more confiscated, and most of the Catholic officers in the Jacobite army availed themselves of William's offer of exile rather than ignominy in their own land. For more than a century these émigrés and their descendants fought in the great armies of Europe, especially that of France.

Yet the promises of religious toleration for Irish Catholics embodied in the 1691 Treaty of Limerick were quickly abandoned. Legislation enacted by the English parliament ensured that a Catholic would never again sit on the English throne. The Protestant position in Ireland was secured by military victory and buttressed by penal legislation designed to remove any vestiges of Catholic influence that remained and provide against another resurgence of Catholic power.

Penal Laws

The beginning of the eighteenth century was dominated by Irish Protestants' need to protect their ascendancy as a minority among a large Catholic population. This anxiety, despite recent victory, was given form in the penal code (formally, Penal Laws), a collection of laws passed by the exclusively Protestant Irish parliament with the approval of the English parliament, which were designed to maintain the ascendant position of Irish Protestants and guard against a Catholic recovery. Restrictive laws based on religion were not unusual in Europe, but Ireland presented the example of a political and social code that discriminated against the majority rather than the minority. The penal laws effectively prohibited those who were not Anglican Protestants—namely, Catholics, and to a lesser extent "Dissenters" (Presbyterians, Methodists, and Quakers)—from participating in political life.

There were provisions specific to Catholics that restricted their ownership or tenure of land, which was the foundation of political power and influence. Catholics could not vote or be elected to parliament, join the army or navy, practice law, or seek education abroad, the latter an attempt to dam the influence of European Catholicism. There were restrictions on owning or displaying the symbols of rank—namely, the right to bear arms and be suitably mounted. Priests remaining in Ireland after warnings to leave had been issued could be hanged if caught. Catholic worship was forbidden and forced underground. A few Catholics did manage to retain ownership of some land, but on their death the land was divided among all the male heirs, resulting in the effective breakup of farms. If one heir converted to Protestantism, he inherited everything.

The penal code was enacted over a number of years in the early part of the eighteenth century. The provisions were severe, but there is some disagreement among historians over when and how they were enforced. The consensus is that the implementation of most of these laws was sporadic in the first half of the century and unusual from mid-century onward. Catholicism kept a low profile but remained strong. By 1730, almost every diocese had a bishop and priests again, even if their activities were furtive. New urban churches were discreetly built, although worship outdoors and in private houses continued in rural areas. Early in the eighteenth century, priests and scholars operated mobile schools known as "hedge-schools" as they were often held in the open. By the 1730s, proper Catholic schools were more widespread and were systematically organized by the clergy. Recent research has revealed a healthy and thriving urban Catholic middle class engaged predominantly in commercial activity, as they were effectively excluded from agrarian and political activity.

By the 1750s, a Catholic group of gentlemen who had retained some vestiges of property and influence allied with members of this Catholic middle class and began diplomatically to articulate gentle arguments for reform and the restoration of their political rights. They emphatically refuted accusations of conspiracy against Protestants, emphasized their loyalty to Britain and the crown, and asserted that their religious duty did not interfere in any way with their allegiance to the state and monarch. This rhetoric did not bear immediate fruit. Irish Protestants were still very easily alarmed by the notion of incorporating Catholics into the political nation, and their objections were strong enough to prevent any immediate changes from occurring. As King William's Protestant successors, the German Hanoverians, became more secure on the throne, and as the likelihood of a serious Stuart attempt to seize back the throne faded throughout the eighteenth century, the penal laws were essentially allowed to lapse, especially after 1745, and were beginning to be actively repealed after 1778.

Patriots and Patronage

As with its model and counterpart in England, the Irish parliament had evolved from medieval assemblies of the great men of the lordship meeting at the king's summons and carrying out a range of administrative functions, to a body that had judicial, consultative, and legislative features. The Irish parliament formally dates from the thirteenth century, but at first it was a regional parliament that excluded the Gaelic Irish completely. They became members in the mid-sixteenth century, but only those who had received English titles as part of Henry VIII's "surrender and regrant" policy.

As the power of the English monarch and government expanded throughout the island in the sixteenth century, the geographical area represented in the parliament correspondingly developed from the initially restricted area of the Pale. A creation of the English crown, the Irish parliament was expected to follow English policy. As early as the fourteenth century, however, the members of the Irish parliament, the powerful Anglo-Irish lords, expressed signs of divergent thought and action. The crown's response was to assume firmer control of the Irish legislative body and to restrict its power and activities, culminating in Poyning's Law (1494). This law stated that all past legislation of the English parliament was applicable to Ireland and that all meetings and proposed legislation of the Irish parliament had to be approved by the English monarch. The effect of the law was to remove control of the Irish parliament from the Anglo-Irish lords and to place it in the hands of the crown. As power successively passed from the monarch to the parliament in England, especially throughout the seventeenth century, the English parliament came to control the Irish parliament.

Like the earlier Anglo-Irish lords who were the progeny of Norman settlers, eighteenth-century Irish Protestants, the descendants of sixteenth- and seventeenth-century planters, exclusively made up the membership of the Irish parliament. They were ambivalent toward the new entity of Great Britain formed by the political union of Scotland with England and Wales in 1707. Linked by heritage and family, dependent on the security that Britain offered to a minority population amid a majority of Catholics, and linked by a common monarch, Irish Protestants were also resentful of the control exerted by the British parliament over their political activities. Secure as the ruling elite of the island, girded by past victory and the penal code, Irish Protestants such as William Molyneaux and Jonathan Swift began to articulate a rhetoric of political independence that ironically owed much to earlier arguments put forward by the Old English Catholics in the seventeenth century. Political theories were advanced that argued that the Irish parliament had the sole right to legislate for Ireland based on the fact that Ireland was not a kingdom dependent on the kingdom of England but was a "sister kingdom" equal to England. Molyneaux also argued that Ireland was not a colony because it had a legislative assembly and courts of justice. These arguments would later influence the developing political rhetoric of American colonists.

Members of the Irish parliament took up this theme to express their resentment at legislation passed in the British parliament that, according to Poyning's Law, was binding on Ireland. Much of this legislation restricted aspects of Irish commercial activity, such as the woolen industry, to reduce competition against British products. Another area of conflict was the debate over whether the Irish House of Lords or the British House of Lords was the supreme judicial body in Irish matters. This debate resulted in the British parliament passing the Declaratory Act of 1720 (also known as the "Sixth of George I"), which firmly stated that it was the superior legislative body. Rather than decreasing support for what was being called "Protestant Patriotism" this measure intensified the claims of the "Protestant nation" to parliamentary autonomy in matters relating to Ireland. Irish Protestants regarded themselves as constituting a specific Irish nation. By this they meant a narrowly defined exclusive political nation loyal to the crown. As Catholics and Dissenters were excluded from political activity and influence, it followed that they could not be part of the political nation. By mid-century, influenced by the propaganda of Charles Lucas, the Patriots had further developed their ideology of the Protestant nation of Ireland, which unsurprisingly continued to emphasize the constitutive rights of the parliament but also concentrated on campaigning for low taxation, supporting investment in the Irish economy, and containing the pervasive Catholic hazard.

Despite the stirring Patriot rhetoric regarding the political autonomy of the Irish parliament, the reality of eighteenth-century politics was one of factionalism and patronage, or what is termed the "undertaker" system. Factions were based on a broad political outlook and family connections. Each faction competed for access to patronage, which was distributed by officials representing the British crown and government in Ireland, the most senior of whom was the viceroy or lord lieutenant. Patronage usually came in the form of pensions or lucrative places in the government, the civil service, and the army. The strategic disposal of patronage by influential members of the Irish parliament who undertook to manage the factions guaranteed strong support for the policies of the British government. From a modern perspective this seems a bluntly corrupt form of political activity, but it was the accepted way the machinery of government operated in both parliaments. Yet the practice of essentially selling votes in support of British governmental policies for political and personal gain sat uneasily with Patriot claims of Irish parliamentary sovereignty.

Secret Societies

Since the early eighteenth century there had been significant migration of Ulster Presbyterians to America. The reasons were economic, political, and religious. Rents for land and taxes were already high; the population had almost doubled over the century and thus had increased competition for jobs and land; the linen industry, which was mostly confined to Ulster, provided at best precarious employment; legislation passed by the British parliament had effectively destroyed the woolen industry; and the penal code had instituted religious and civil disabilities against both Presbyterians and Catholics. Throughout Ireland, economic tensions had erupted into widespread peasant violence from the 1760s onward. Secret societies, disguised and predominantly nocturnal, protested agrarian grievances such as the move to enclose common land, as well as economic and religious grievances such as the mandatory tax (the tithe) levied from all to support the Anglican Church of Ireland; these societies destroyed property and attacked, tortured, and sometimes murdered the tithe-proctors or tax collectors.

The most notorious of these peasant groups were the Whiteboys of Munster and Leinster, so known because they wore white smocks. The Whiteboys represented Catholic peasants and indulged in some sectarian violence against Protestant farmers and landlords, but their grievances were mainly economic and thus their violence centered on the destruction of property. In response to the violence, the parliament in Dublin passed a series of laws that rendered participation in such activities a capital offense. Despite the best efforts of the forces of law and order to suppress the White-boys and others, these secret agrarian societies survived and influenced the rise of the Catholic Defender movement that allied with the radical United Irishmen in rebellion at the end of the century. Secret agrarian societies were active well into the nineteenth century; they continued to protest agrarian economic conditions and the tithe with attacks on property and individuals, giving rise to the so-called Tithe War in the 1820s and 1830s, and they furnished the methodological foundation of the Land League in the 1880s.

Ulster had its own peasant secret societies—the Hearts of Oak (or Oakboys) and the Hearts of Steel (or Steelboys). These groups represented Presbyterian tenants and small farmers who protested the oppressive actions of landlords in levying labor and prohibitive fines for renewing farm leases by attacking and destroying property. They were also resentful of the relatively few Catholics who were able and willing to pay exorbitant rent for land. In contrast to the Whiteboys in the south, the secret societies of Ulster were relatively short-lived. One explanation offered for this difference is emigration.

Ulster was generally more prosperous than the rest of the country, and many Pres-byterians there were slightly less impecunious than most Catholics and thus could afford to emigrate. For those who could not afford the price of passage, an option was to sign on as an indentured servant on American ships making the return journey after having delivered their cargoes of flaxseed. As with later patterns of Irish emigra-tion, once begun, the process was self-sustaining. Ulster Presbyterians settled in New England, Pennsylvania, Delaware, and South Carolina. Newcomers in a tolerant envi-ronment with cheap land and without political restrictions, they began to prosper, and as they did, they encouraged the transplantation of communal groups. There are conflicting estimates of the number of people who emigrated, as rates varied accord-ing to fluctuating economic conditions in Ireland, but between 1700 and 1776 over 200,000 Presbyterians left Ulster for colonial America. There was also a considerable rate of Catholic emigration during the same period, estimated at around one hundred thousand individuals. Colonists of Ulster origin played important roles in the politi-cal life of their new home. They brought with them a developed sense of political phi-losophy, which is credited as an important influence on the developing defiance of America toward the British crown and government; America, in turn, later influenced the development of radical politics in Ulster.

Grattan's Parliament

The American War of Independence had a profound effect on Ireland. There were obvious parallels in that both Ireland and the American colonies had limited repre-sentative assemblies within an imperial framework. Americans had listened to the developing political rhetoric and ideology of the Protestant Patriots, many of whom in turn identified with the frustrated position of the colonists and even admired their revolutionary stand against Britain. The Irish parliament, controlled by the undertakers and the system of patronage, officially supported the British government in its American policy. While individual members of the Irish parliament firmly disapproved of disloyalty to the crown, others secretly applauded American independence of action. Irish Catholics were rigidly in support of government policy based on their hopes that in showing staunch loyalty to crown and government, they might make a stronger case for full repeal of the penal code. American sympathy was strongest in Ulster, based on the links forged by half a century of migration between the two, to the point where the lord lieutenant described Ulster Presbyterians as being in their hearts American. Yet in the initial stages of the war, there were clear signs of support for America among many Irish Protestants outside parliament who resented the trade restrictions imposed by Westminster and who desired reform of the parliament in Dublin in order to render it more representative.

However, when France and Spain entered the war on the American side in 1778–1779, Irish Protestant opinion was firmly inspired toward defending Ireland and Britain against any threat of invasion from ancient Catholic enemies. The formation of the Irish Volunteers in 1778 was thus originally undertaken in the spirit of Protestant defense. Companies were raised locally by subscription, and before long they were uniformed and armed. Real danger of invasion remained remote, and the Volunteers became a forum for political debate. Influenced by events in America, they eventually adopted the principles of Protestant patriotism in supporting the demand for the restoration of full legislative sovereignty to the Irish parliament. The support of an estimated forty thousand armed Protestants in the Volunteers renewed the energy of the Patriot movement in the parliament. Led by Henry Grattan, an astute and effective orator, the Patriots demanded that the British parliament acknowledge the autonomy of the Irish parliament, which passed a Declaration of Independence in 1782.

The British government's recent American experiences, coupled with the implied military threat of the Volunteers, resulted in their acceptance of the Irish parliament's Declaration of Independence and their subsequent repeal of the Declaratory Act of 1720 and Poyning's Law. An ostensible victory enthusiastically celebrated by the Patriots soon proved a fantasy. The nominally independent Irish parliament under the British crown remained independent in name only, because the undertaker system based on the power of crown patronage continued to shape the conduct of political business. From 1782 onward, an era traditionally referred to as "Grattan's Parliament," the technically sovereign legislative body was easily manipulated by the extension of patronage. Britain had consolidated its practical power over the Irish parliament by appearing to accede to its demands. Unless the parliament itself was reformed to eliminate the power of factions and the allure of patronage, the independent Irish parliament would remain a corrupt toothless institution.

Unanimity on the future of the parliament was short-lived. There was much dissension about what parliamentary reform should entail. Grattan and others argued that the Irish parliament had to become more representative and dependent on the will of the electorate, thus destroying the traditional power of the factions and the undertakers. This raised the issue of representation in general, and specifically the troublesome question of whether all Catholics should continue to be excluded from politics. Catholics naturally reiterated their traditional argument that they were loyal subjects of the crown and therefore deserved to exercise the same political rights as Protestants. Some Protestants agreed that Catholics should be tentatively incorporated into the political nation, but the majority were wary of such a radical move. While significant changes in political terms appeared a distant prospect, there were at least optimistic signs of Protestant willingness to support an alleviation of the penal code. A more tolerant attitude in matters of religion had spread throughout Europe in the eighteenth century, and this had an impact on some Protestant attitudes toward Catholics and Dissenters. Added to a more liberal outlook was a stronger sense of security among Irish Protestants, given their political dominance, their economic strength, the military potential of the Volunteers, and the willing conformity of Catholics to monarchy and state during the century.

Yet shrewd political calculation also informed Protestant readiness to consider repealing some of the Penal Laws. Since the 1760s Catholics had directed their arguments regarding the restoration of political rights and the inequity of penal legislation toward the British government rather than the Irish parliament. Some Irish Protestants feared that a strategic British policy of conciliating Irish Catholics by granting substantial reform would undermine the foundations of their political hegemony and allow Britain to further consolidate its power over Ireland. They reasoned that introducing minor abatements in specific penal laws themselves would promote some controlled progress toward the eventual incorporation of Catholics into the political life of the nation and also prevent any threatening alliance of Catholic and British interests.

Catholic Relief Act

The first significant step in formally dismantling the penal code came with the Catholic Relief Act of 1778. This measure focused specifically on land. Catholics were permitted to take long-term leases and to inherit and bequeath land, in addition to taking an Oath of Allegiance that enabled them to express their fidelity to the crown without trespassing upon their spiritual obligation to the pope. A further measure in 1782 increased their rights regarding property, education, and the position of the clergy. In the following decade, Catholic seminaries were founded; the restrictions on intermarriage were relaxed; the rights to practice law, bear arms, and join the military were returned; and most important, after 1793 Catholics could vote, subject to strict property qualifications. The main restrictions that remained were their exclusion from the judiciary, the higher offices of government, and parliament. Edmund Burke, in his letter to Sir Hercules Langrishe, published in 1792, saw these as crucial developments toward national unity, but while there was evidence of changing attitudes toward Catholics, and while pressure from the Catholic middle class was an important factor, the prime motivation informing these later concessions was to protect Protestant ascendancy interests in the face of pressure from Britain, further demands for radical political reform from Protestants and Catholics, and impending political crisis.

The United Irishmen

That crisis had been brewing since the 1770s but was profoundly intensified by the French Revolution in 1789, which led directly to the establishment of a new political organization. The Society of United Irishmen was founded in Belfast in October 1791 and emerged to represent the political views of mainly Presbyterian and Anglican political radicals who demanded significant reform of the Irish parliament. The views of a young Protestant barrister, Theobald Wolfe Tone, which had been published in 1791 as *An Argument on Behalf of the Catholics of Ireland*, declared that sweeping parliamentary reform was the only solution to the increasing influence of Britain in Irish affairs and that such change could be delivered only if Protestants and Catholics united in a political movement that would campaign to extend the franchise and make parliament more representative.

Originally, the Society of United Irishmen was a political movement whose methods centered on pacifist pressure and debate. The organization sought to galvanize public opinion with the publication of reform proposals which, in addition to parliamentary reform and Catholic political inclusion, called for the abolition of the hated tithe, the extension of education, and the expansion of trade. The United Irishmen were also very effective distributors of literary propaganda that emphasized the principles of liberty, equality, and fraternity—with specific reference to America and France—and encouraged national unity, irrespective of religious creed.

Operating in a parallel, if more limited, fashion was the Catholic Committee, a pressure group that had evolved since the first tentative calls for repeal of the penal laws and the restoration of political rights in the 1760s. Strengthened by the 1778 Catholic Relief Act and the further concessions that removed the core of the penal code, by the early 1790s the Catholic Committee was energetically campaigning for the abolition of the remaining political restrictions. As war loomed between Britain and the brashly expansionist new French Republic, the British government was naturally eager to conciliate Catholic Irish opinion—to abolish the "bank of discontent," as Edmund Burke termed it—in an effort to preclude any dangerous revolutionary sympathy or political alliance with France. It was predominantly British pressure on the Irish parliament that resulted in the Relief Act of 1793 when Catholics were admitted to the franchise on the same terms as Protestants.

Concession was allied to repression as Britain and France went to war. Mindful of the implied threat of the Protestant Volunteer movement wielded by the Irish parliament in the 1770s and 1780s, the British government suppressed the movement and raised a controlled Irish militia composed of Catholics and Protestants to provide for the defense of Ireland as regular army troops went to war. Conventions and political assemblies were banned, and the Society of United Irishmen was suppressed in 1794. Domestically, there were still significant levels of agrarian violence, the result of continued economic distress as the population, specifically among the lower levels of society, continued to expand at an alarming rate. By 1791, the population of the country had almost doubled from approximately 2.3 million early in the century to 4.4 million. The increased competition for land resulted in higher rents, which in turn led to agrarian violence that had a distinctly sectarian character in Ulster. The Orange

Order, a political society committed to recalling the "glorious and immortal" memory of William's victory over James II in 1690, was formed in 1795 after a battle between the Peep O'Day Boys and the Defenders. Employing sectarian intimidation and violence, the Peep O'Day Boys articulated Ulster Presbyterian and Protestant fears of being ousted by aggressive, land-hungry Catholics who were willing to live remarkably meagerly in order to pay higher rents. Common tactics included physical beatings and burning property. Ulster Catholics responded by forming the Defenders. Clashes between the two were often bloody and fatal. The Orange Order attracted Protestants from all ranks, who were alarmed at both recent and potential concessions to Catholics. Further violent clashes led to several thousand Catholics fleeing the province. Convinced that the Orange Order was tacitly endorsed by influential members of the Irish parliament, Catholics joined the Defenders in significant numbers, and the movement spread outside Ulster.

Forced underground by the government, the United Irishmen had developed into a more radical political movement that embraced revolutionary republicanism. Theobald Wolfe Tone and others had earlier recognized the potential strength of Catholic discontent. Although the middle-class Catholic Committee was content to continue petitioning the government for political concessions, the leadership of the United Irishmen believed that Catholics could be effectively channeled in a political direction, merging peasants with smoldering local and sectarian grievances with a radical Protestant movement that wanted a republican revolution based on a suprasectarian national identity.

Wolfe Tone traveled to France in 1796 where he effectively argued the case for a supportive expeditionary force to aid the proposed rebellion. The revolutionary nature of the United Irish movement now recruiting the Catholic peasantry caused great anxiety within the government, which responded with coercion and repression. An Insurrection Act was passed, giving increased powers to local magistrates to arrest and sentence those suspected of disaffection. A mainly Protestant yeomanry force was established under the leadership of prominent local landowners to ruthlessly suppress any signs of rebellious intent; by 1798 it numbered nearly forty thousand.

Discipline was often poor, and the atrocious activities of certain corps of militia and yeomen are notorious in this period of Irish history. They enthusiastically burned peasant homes and Catholic churches; they publicly flogged, half-hanged, and mutilated peasants suspected of membership of the United Irishmen or of rebellious intrigue. Pitch-capping, the placing of a paper cap filled with hot tar over a suspect's head and ripping it off, was a common method of extracting confessions and information. While the yeomanry was a predominantly Protestant force and the government militia was mainly Catholic, both forces commonly engaged in these activities. Paradoxically, yet not surprisingly, the common result of such methods was to increase membership of the United Irishmen and the Defenders and support for rebellion.

Wolfe Tone's skillful efforts in France resulted in an expeditionary force of forty-three ships with fifteen thousand troops under the command of General Lazar Hoche, which set sail for Ireland in December 1796. Violent storms dispersed the fleet, and the few ships that reached the southern Irish coast could not land and had to turn back

The centenary/centennial of Ireland's 1798 Rebellion was commemorated in many ways in Irish America, including through popular theatrical interpretations. Andrew Mack, singer and comedian, starred in James B. Fagan's *The Rebel, A Drama of the Irish Rebellion*, as depicted in this 1900 poster by the Strobridge Lithograph Company of Cincinnati and New York. (Library of Congress, Prints and Photographs Division, POS-TH-1900.R42, no. 4 [C size])

for France. There, Wolfe Tone renewed his efforts to convince the French to send another expedition. This French invasion attempt at the invitation of the United Irishmen was extremely alarming for the government, which now resolved to comprehensively suppress the revolutionary movement. Martial law was proclaimed in troubled parts of the country, most notably in Ulster. The undaunted United Irishmen continued their preparations for rebellion. Strongest in Ulster, they organized, recruited, drilled, and armed themselves with muskets and pikes (shafted weapons with bayonet-like blades, easily made by local blacksmiths). The efforts of the government and military to smother the revolutionary plot often fanned the flames of rebellion, but one notable success in government strategy was the employment of informers to infiltrate the leadership of the United Irishmen.

In March 1798, two months before the projected date of the rebellion, most of the leaders were arrested, with the temporary exception of Lord Edward FitzGerald. FitzGerald, a descendant of the sixteenth-century earls of Kildare, had fought as an officer with the British army during the American Revolution. He flirted with revolutionary thought from the early 1790s onward but did not join the United Irishmen until 1796. He was popularly perceived as a dashing romantic revolutionary, and his numerous dramatic escapes from the authorities fueled this image. He was finally caught in May 1798 and died of wounds received during his arrest.

A few days later, when a badly coordinated sporadic rebellion spluttered into existence, the remnants of the leadership of the United Irishmen attempted to exert some authority over localized insurrections. The rebellion occurred in isolated pockets—Wexford and Waterford in southeast Leinster, Antrim and Down in Ulster, and, belatedly, Mayo in the west. The rebellion in Wexford began on May 26 and initially scored some swift and telling victories over the local militia and yeomanry. Led by the Catholic priest Father John Murphy and the Protestant United Irishman Beauchamp Bagenal Harvey, the rebels captured Wexford town and Enniscorthy. Buoyed by success, their numbers increased. With much of the county under their control, they tried to occupy New Ross in a bloody battle that they narrowly lost to government forces after a full day of furious fighting. With this rebel loss, Protestant prisoners of both genders and of all ages, hemmed into a barn at Scullabogue, were burned to death. The capture and execution of Protestant prisoners had also taken place in the rebel camp at Oulart Hill. Government forces were equally bloodthirsty in their treatment of captured rebels. The rebellion in Wexford was characterized by sectarian division, with little evidence of the secular emphasis of the United Irishmen. Despite the involvement of some radical Protestants in the Wexford rebellion, the rebels were predominantly Catholic peasants and regarded Protestants of all classes and varieties as their natural oppressors and enemies. Here, the insurrection fractured along clear religious divides based on ancient and local grievances.

The limited Ulster insurrection led by Henry Joy McCracken, one of the founders of the society, was mostly Presbyterian in composition. The successful arms seizures the previous year, the arrest of the leadership, the growing strength of the Orange Order, and the vicious sectarianism in Wexford led to the defection of many from the movement. At the head of approximately four thousand men, McCracken failed in his attempt to capture the town of Antrim. Within ten days, the Ulster rebellion had been suppressed by the forces of the government, who tried and executed the leaders while shrewdly pardoning most of the rank and file who surrendered their arms.

Further pressure exerted by Wolfe Tone in France led to a minor and belated French expedition of three ships and one thousand men led by General Jean Joseph Humbert. The expedition arrived in Mayo in August 1798 and, together with peasant support, inflicted an extraordinary defeat on the forces of the government at Castlebar but then was quickly defeated itself. Connaught was the weakest area of the United Irish organization, and the rebellion in other parts of the country had already been suppressed by the time the French arrived. The peasants who joined with the French were unarmed and unprepared, and they were slaughtered when the militia finally caught up with them in Longford. The French were captured and eventually exchanged for British prisoners of war. Another small French expedition of about three thousand troops had sailed for the northern coast where Wolfe Tone hoped to land and link up with Humbert's men, perhaps inspiring the remnants of the United Irish movement and their Defender allies to a last stand. The British navy intercepted the small fleet and captured Wolfe Tone. Tried by court-martial, he was sentenced to hang but committed suicide in prison when his request to be shot was denied.

Whereas the ideology of the United Irishmen had emphasized national identity above division of creed, the irony of the rebellion in its incarnation was that it was principally a conflict of Irishmen against Irishmen, militia and yeomanry against rebels, and Catholics against Protestants, with an estimated thirty thousand deaths. As with other revolutionary projects in Irish history, the bitter reality of the conflict is much less significant than the legacy of the event. The United Irishmen had failed utterly in their project of combining Catholic and Protestant in the cause of national independence, but the tradition of revolutionary republicanism they inaugurated survived and deeply influenced the course of events in the century to come.

Act of Union

Traditionally, the 1801 Act of Union that ended the existence of the Irish parliament and incorporated Ireland into the political structure of Great Britain has been seen as an inevitable coda to the rebellion. Yet the proposal for a constitutional union between Ireland and Britain was not new. The Irish parliament had briefly toyed with the idea when the union of Scotland and England took place in 1707 but then pursued a course of rhetorical independence. The British parliament had unsuccessfully raised the matter on several occasions during the eighteenth century as the Irish parliament had become more irascible, especially during the 1780s. The rebellion confirmed strong support for such a union in the British parliament, and the prime minister, William Pitt, embarked on a course of persuading the Protestant members of the Irish parliament of the advantages that would accrue to them if they voted for a bill that would dissolve their separate legislature.

The key term in all the language associated with pro-union argument was *survival*. Great emphasis was placed on the recent insurrection and the dependence of Protestants on British military aid in a perilous situation. A constitutional union would place Irish Protestants within a larger Protestant political unit and thus potentially remove their fears of the repercussions of incorporating Catholics into political life. Pitt also argued that a political union would remove commercial restrictions and encourage capital investment, hence transforming the Irish economy.

The Irish parliament was deeply divided on the issue. The Patriot element, still led by Henry Grattan, vehemently opposed the proposal, insisting that Ireland was a separate political nation, symbolized by its parliament. Abolishing it would undo the Irish political nation. However, the experience of the rebellion had been a dreadful shock to the Protestant ascendancy. Visions of the sectarian violence in Wexford haunted them, and many members of parliament began to seriously consider the advantages of the union as outlined by Pitt. When the first vote was taken in the Irish parliament in 1799, the proposal for union was rejected by a majority of five. In terms of public opinion, members of the Orange Order viewed the proposal for political union as a compromise of Irish Protestant power and adamantly opposed it. Most Protestants were fearful that union would weaken both their elite position as the ruling class and the Irish economy. Catholics were generally in favor of the union, as they were given to understand that removal of the restrictions on their sitting in parliament would form part of the legislation. In addition, they had little sentimental attachment to the institution. The British government embarked on a serious campaign toward obtaining a parliamentary majority in favor of the proposal. While weighty political and economic arguments were employed, the chief strengths of the government's position were the traditional and recently revived Protestant fear of Catholics and the system of political patronage that had long allowed the British parliament to manipulate the Irish parliament.

As was customary, titles, places, promotions, and pensions were widely distributed in exchange for votes, and when the next vote took place in January 1800, despite an impassioned speech from Grattan representing a significant section of Protestant opinion, an amendment proposing to maintain an independent Irish parliament was defeated by 138 votes to 96. By August, the legislation that ended the existence of the Irish parliament was signed into law and took effect in January 1801. Ireland was politically merged with Great Britain. Irish representation in the British House of Commons was fixed at 100 members out of a total of 658, while 32 Irish peers sat in the House of Lords. The British monarchy continued to be represented in Ireland by a lord lieutenant, and the policies of the British government were carried out by the chief secretary for Ireland.

Catholic Emancipation

Although the removal of the final political restrictions against Catholics was part of the original proposals for the political union, Catholic Emancipation (as it was commonly termed) was not part of the final legislation, even though Pitt had virtually guaranteed that it would follow almost immediately after the union had been established. Most of the Penal Laws had been repealed before the 1798 rebellion. Catholics could again lease and own land, publicly worship, join the professions, and vote at parliamentary elections subject to a property qualification, but they could still not sit in parliament or occupy senior judicial, military, and political positions. Pitt was quite sincere in his commitment to reform for Catholics and in his intent to include it with the union legislation, but he faced significant opposition from public opinion, from his cabinet, and, more important, from his monarch, George III, who believed that legislation to include Catholics in the political life of the nation violated his coronation oath, which emphasized the monarch's duty to preserve the Protestant settlement of the kingdom. Given the king's adamant opposition, Pitt had little choice but to abandon any further attempt to achieve Catholic Emancipation for the foreseeable future.

For Catholics it was a long and disagreeable interlude. Pressure from the relatively small number of influential Catholic merchants, professionals, and landowners was ineffectual. Attempts by members of parliament in Westminster to raise the issue for discussion consistently failed. It was not until 1823 that a serious campaign was launched, with the formation of the Catholic Association by a successful and charismatic Catholic barrister named Daniel O'Connell. O'Connell resolved that this campaign would be inclusive of all Catholics. His first departure from older campaigns was to involve the clergy as the organizational skeleton of a movement that aimed to include every Irish Catholic, from the majority who were peasants, laborers, and tenant farmers to those of the merchant class and the professions. To achieve this mass membership, O'Connell shrewdly introduced a "Catholic rent," a subscription of one penny per month. Given the enormous population of Ireland in the early nineteenth century, the majority of whom were Catholic, the income of the association was significant, but the most important result was psychological. For the vast majority of the members, Catholic Emancipation was a vague political concept that would not confer any immediate or significant benefit on them. Yet these people translated the significance of the campaign they were about to embark on into simply and compellingly a popular *Catholic* campaign. Given the experience of penal legislation in the previous century, Catholics were eager to identify with a political movement that aimed to change their position, however specific and limited that change might be.

O'Connell liberally employed aggressive language in his numerous addresses to mass meetings of Catholics throughout the countryside. It was a deliberate gesture designed to arouse the confidence of his listeners long used to an inferior position in society, but it was also directed at the British government, which obligingly responded by attempting to prosecute him for incitement to insurrection and then by suppressing the Catholic Association in 1825. O'Connell promptly reestablished it as the New Catholic Association and continued as before. An opportunity to push the issue presented itself in 1826 with a general election to the British parliament. The Catholic Association called on all Catholic voters (those who rented or owned property worth more than forty shillings per year, the so-called forty-shilling freeholders) to ignore the favored candidates of their landlords and vote only for candidates who committed themselves to supporting Emancipation. Four counties were selected for special concentration, and four pro-Emancipation candidates were successfully elected. The secret ballot was not incorporated into elections until 1870; thus this was a significant achievement in that the majority of voters were strong tenant farmers who took grave risks in openly and publicly defying their landlords' political choices.

In 1828, a by-election was scheduled for Clare, as the member representing it in the British parliament had been appointed to a ministerial position and was thus obliged to stand for reelection. The member in question was a popular Protestant landlord, Vesey FitzGerald, who was sympathetic toward O'Connell's campaign but could not commit himself to supporting it in parliament. O'Connell, as a Catholic, could not sit in parliament, but there was no specific restriction against contesting an election. The Catholic Association, under the relentless direction of the clergy, marshaled all eligible Catholic voters to travel to Ennis and cast their vote for O'Connell. He was elected by 2,057 votes to 982.

This success forced the British government to react. Led by the hero of the Napoleonic Wars, the Irish-born Duke of Wellington, and strongly influenced by Robert Peel, the home secretary, the government considered its options. While not in favor of Emancipation, neither was it intractable. Despite colorful speeches, O'Connell had always abided by his publicly articulated pacifist views, but the potential for serious violence—indeed, a popular revolution such as those breaking out in Europe—had to be considered. With the removal of monarchical opposition, a considerable body of support in the House of Commons, and, most important, the potential for revolution, the British government conceded the repeal of the final remnants of the penal code in 1829. With the exception of the positions of lord lieutenant of Ireland, lord chancellor of Ireland, and lord chancellor of England, Catholics could sit in parliament; become government ministers; and aspire to the highest offices in the judiciary, army, and navy.

The campaign for Catholic Emancipation is a significant development in Irish history, not so much for its immediate political gains as for its successful mobilization and politicization of Irish Catholics, including the clergy. They had campaigned as a disciplined group without violence and had achieved their aim. Psychologically, this was an enormous boost to Catholic confidence. Yet the many gains resulting from the measure have to be considered in tandem with another piece of legislation that raised the property qualification for the vote from forty shillings to ten pounds. The backbone of O'Connell's electoral campaign found themselves disenfranchised.

Robert Emmet

Violence had not ceased in Ireland after the 1798 rebellion had been suppressed, although it was agrarian rather than political in character. The exception to this was the doomed attempt by Robert Emmet to resurrect the United Irishmen and launch another republican rebellion. A Trinity College student and younger brother of United Irish leader Thomas Addis Emmet, Robert had been peripherally included in the counsels of the United Irishmen as they prepared for revolution in the 1790s. In the immediate aftermath of the rebellion, he undertook the task of reorganizing the movement and planning for another strike. He traveled to Paris and attempted to convince the French, who were still at war with Britain, to launch an invasion force, but cessation of hostilities between the two from 1802 to 1803 seemed to render this moot. His attempts to revive the movement in Ireland met with a listless response. Upon his release from prison in 1802 Thomas Addis Emmet emigrated to America, where he built a successful legal career.

Robert considered following the same path given the apparently dormant nature of the republican cause, but in 1803, with a renewal of the war between Britain and

France, Emmet set about organizing his own rebellion. His general aim was to seize Dublin Castle, the center of British administration in Ireland, and consequently inspire a popular rebellion. This utopian approach belied Emmet's impressive munitions operation in Dublin, along with the strong if limited support of the Kildare, Wicklow, and Dublin United Irishmen.

The first disaster of the enterprise was the accidental explosion of one of the munitions depots, which drew the attention of the authorities to the plot (although they lacked sufficient information to arrest Emmet). The second disaster was the breakdown in communications that resulted in the failure of the Wicklow men to arrive in time for the rebellion. The third fiasco was the attempt to seize the castle. Emmet at the head of about one hundred men soon found himself in the middle of a riotous mob that surrounded the coach of the lord chief justice of Ireland, Lord Kilwarden, and who brutally murdered him and his son-in-law with pikes. Further violent rioting continued, and thirty people were killed. Emmet, distraught at the disintegration of his revolution into a bloody brawl, went into hiding but was arrested shortly afterward, then tried and sentenced to death.

Emmet's revolution was a catastrophe, but his lasting contribution to Irish republicanism lies in his famous speech from the dock in which he outlined his political philosophy. In a phrase that fired Irish republican imaginations in the decades to follow, he requested that his epitaph remained unwritten until Ireland had taken "her place among the nations of the earth."

Nineteenth-Century Society

The agrarian violence of the secret societies flourished in the early nineteenth century, particularly after the end of the Napoleonic Wars in 1815 resulted in a sharp economic depression that seriously affected agricultural prices. Tenants fell into rent arrears, and evictions increased. Sharp resentment of the tithe, the religious tax payable to the Anglican Church, continued to particularly inform Catholic peasant violence. In Leinster and Munster, the Rockites, Whiteboys, and Ribbonmen registered their anger with widespread destruction of property and personal attacks on tithe-proctors and landlords during the 1820s and 1830s.

The demographic increase of the eighteenth century continued in the early nineteenth century. Estimated at 4.4 million in 1791, the population rose to 6.8 million by 1821 and to 8.2 million by 1841. The majority of this population depended on agriculture to survive. It was among the lowest and poorest levels of society that the population increased most rapidly. These people eked out a precarious subsistence existence on small plots of land that were subdivided among children and that supported the crops and livestock that paid the rent and fed the family. As a cheap, abundant, and nutritious crop, the potato had long formed the staple element of Irish peasant diets. Other crops and livestock went toward paying the high rents on land and the tithe in combinations of cash and kind, as in many areas of rural Ireland a money economy was limited.

The increasing dependence of the Irish peasantry on the potato was viewed by many contemporaries as a potential disaster. Hunger was a familiar element of life. The potato crop had partially failed several times in the past century, with widespread distress and death in 1720 and especially during 1739–1741. A tentative estimate of a quarter-million deaths during the latter failure explains the Irish-language reference *Bliadhain an Air,* or the Year of the Slaughter. Crop failures in 1817 and 1822 resulted in widespread hunger, which was partially alleviated by relief committees and schemes of public works that provided employment.

Emigration remained at high levels during the first three decades of the century. Although statistics are unreliable, historians estimate that between 1 and 1.5 million people left Ireland between 1815 and 1845 for England, Canada, and the United States. As in the emigration of Ulster Presbyterians to America in the eighteenth century, those who emigrated were those who had some money, and, once settled, they helped members of the family to follow by sending passage money. To emigrate with a family cost the equivalent of a laborer's wages for a year. For the majority of peasants in the lower levels of society, emigration was out of the question unless a landlord, eager to clear his estate, offered assisted-emigration schemes.

In the upper middle class of rural society, more substantial tenant farmers weathered the economic depressions and occasional crop failures with better success. During the 1830s they prospered, as agricultural prices temporarily recovered. These people could afford to invest capital, expand holdings, and provide for their children without subdividing their land. Their children were educated and took up careers in the church and professions. Dowries for suitable marriages could be provided. More modestly situated farmers, removed from the subsistence lifestyle of the landless laborer, lived meagerly and struggled to provide opportunities for children without resorting to subdivision or emigration.

Repeal of the Union

Daniel O'Connell built on the popularity and political power that followed his successful emancipation campaign with one aimed at repealing the political union between Ireland and Britain. The union had failed to deliver the political and economic benefits that had been anticipated. Ireland had limited representation and occupied limited attention in an expanding imperial parliament. Once the boom in the demand for agricultural produce, and thus high prices, disappeared with the end of the Napoleonic Wars in 1815, depression rather than expansion had characterized the economy. The Irish manufacturing industry, with the exception of the linen industry in Ulster, had declined.

As a barrister, O'Connell was convinced of some validity in the argument that Henry Grattan had articulated against the union. The first element of the case was the traditional point that the Irish parliament was independent of the British parliament; the second was that the parliament was the symbol of an independent nation linked to Britain only by a shared monarchy; the third was that the decision of the members

"Ireland for the Irish," the slogan of Daniel O'Connell's Repeal Association, was declared on this souvenir print published in London circa 1835–1845 and circulated in the United States. O'Connell (1775–1847) politicized Irish Catholics in the 1829 achievement of Catholic Emancipation and aspired to follow that success with repeal of the Act of Union. A distinguished barrister, master orator, adroit performer, and skillful tactician, O'Connell was a progressive politician whose example and methods deeply influenced nationalist generations to follow. (Library of Congress, Prints and Photographs Division, LC-USZ62-123389)

of the Irish parliament of 1800 to abolish that legislature was invalid, given the extensive employment of patronage to secure their cooperation. O'Connell knew that an Irish legislature would now be dominated by Catholics because of their demographic strength and the removal of political barriers. He did not call for separatism in his campaign for repeal; rather, he emphasized the restoration of an Irish parliament that would be linked to Britain through the monarchy.

Nor did he believe in social radicalism. O'Connell held deeply conservative views about the privileges of property owners. He supported the prevailing economic policy of the day, laissez-faire, which discouraged government interference in economic matters. He condemned the violence of the agrarian secret societies. He disapproved of the embryonic trade union movement in Britain. He was deeply loyal to the monarchy and believed that Ireland would benefit from continued association with the expanding British Empire while conducting its own domestic affairs.

The repeal campaign was launched in the early 1830s but failed to make any significant headway. For some time, the sheer exuberance that attended the success of the emancipation campaign and O'Connell's immense personal popularity carried the movement, but there were important distinctions between a campaign to remove specific restrictions of political rights and one that sought to alter the British political structure. While many influential Protestants had been sympathetic to and active in the emancipation campaign as a matter of principle, they had come to view the political union as the bulwark against Catholic political and social ambitions that threatened to consume the remains of their influence.

It is one of the ironies of Irish history that most Protestants were initially deeply suspicious of the proposal for political union while Catholics had supported it. Within three decades, Irish Protestants believed that political union with Britain, and membership of a larger Protestant polity, was their only defense against an evolving Catholic nation in which their influence would be negligible. Similarly, Catholics who had supported the union in the expectation of the restoration of full political rights and an end to the power of the Irish Protestants now identified it as the root of many evils. In particular, the union was blamed for poor economic conditions and consequent distress. With O'Connell's encouragement, Catholics began to think in terms of breaking the union and restoring an Irish parliament.

The British government was implacably opposed to discussion of repeal, and for most of the 1830s O'Connell made little progress in this direction. He worked with commitment in Westminster in supporting measures to restore law and order in Ireland, given the increased activity of the secret societies. He supported government proposals to establish primary schools with a decided agenda of Anglicization, to deal with issues of poverty, to solve the tithe question, and to introduce minor parliamentary reform, while evading attempts to suppress the repeal campaign. A renewed effort was launched in 1840 with the founding of the Repeal Association and an attempt to repeat the successful tactics of the emancipation campaign. Mass meetings were held all over the country, and just as before, the vast majority of O'Connell's supporters were the peasants who interpreted repeal of the union as the panacea for all their daily struggles.

O'Connell, having tried parliamentary persuasion with little success, believed that a repeated demonstration of the strength of desire, and the implied threat that such enormous gatherings signaled, would convince the government to acquiesce once more to his demand. The government was determined not to yield and called his bluff when, despite the risk of popular violence, they banned his mass meeting at Tara in 1843. O'Connell complied with the ban, and the movement lost what impetus it had gathered.

Young Ireland

One of the somewhat indirect products of the repeal movement was a cultural and political nationalist group called Young Ireland. Significantly influenced by prevailing ideals of romantic nationalism in Europe, this group of educated young men from both Protestant and Catholic backgrounds had supported O'Connell's repeal campaign through the columns of their weekly newspaper, the *Nation*. Drawing from the ideology of the United Irishmen, Young Ireland expressed support for a concept of inclusive Irish national identity. Thomas Davis, James Clarence Mangan, and Charles Gavan Duffy used literature, history, and mythology to fashion a pluralist Irish identity. In political terms, while some members of the group supported a constitutional approach, others like John Mitchel formulated a more separatist point of view that looked back to the radical republicanism of the United Irishmen. Another member, James Fintan Lalor, presciently expressed the revolutionary notion that Irish peasants should become owners of their land and that any campaign for independence would fail to harness the support of the people if it did not link the land issue to politics. As the political views within the group became more radical, they broke from O'Connell's Repeal Association. The death of Thomas Davis removed an important influence, and between 1845 and 1848 the prevailing ideology was one of rebellion. Because the country was in the throes of the Great Hunger, the prospects of a handful of idealistic individuals launching a popular revolution were bleak. After a minor skirmish in 1848, most of the members fled or were deported.

Again, the pathetic nature of the actual skirmish was less important than the legacy of the Young Ireland movement for later nationalists. They had taken up the inheritance of the United Irish movement and attempted to breathe new life into it. Despite the failure of their attempt at rebellion, they had preserved a practice of protest in arms. In literary terms, the work of Davis in particular, in trying to carve an inclusive national identity from a fractured and bitter historical experience, would influence later cultural nationalists who believed, as he did, that cultural unity took precedence over political sovereignty.

The Great Hunger

On the eve of the era known as *An Gorta Mór,* or the Great Hunger, the Irish population exceeded eight million, the result of a demographic boom that had begun in the mid–eighteenth century but had already started naturally to subside by the 1830s. The majority of these people were directly dependent on agriculture for their livelihood and on the potato for their survival. Nearly half of all farms in Ireland were less than five acres in size. The partial failure of the potato crop was frequent enough to give rise to some speculation about the nature of a complete failure and predictions of disaster on a grand scale. The government's reform policies in the 1830s had established a system of primary education, set up public works to build roads, and—in 1838, mirroring the English Poor Law—introduced workhouses throughout the country, but they failed to foresee the overwhelming nature of the catastrophe that was about to strike. Despite the tremors caused by fourteen partial potato failures between 1816 and 1842, and despite the forebodings of many commentators, no one anticipated the appearance of a new fungal disease that would repeatedly destroy the crop for five successive years.

Phytophthora infestans was first observed on the east coast of the United States in 1843 and is generally believed to have originated in South America. It was reported in Europe in the autumn of 1845. There were serious crop failures throughout Europe, most notably in the Scottish Highlands and the Netherlands. Thriving in damp conditions, the "blight" spread rapidly throughout the Irish countryside from September onward, although early eyewitness reports suggest it did so in an erratic pattern. It destroyed 40 percent of the potato crop. The British government initially reacted quickly. Prime Minister Sir Robert Peel appointed a commission to study the new disease and make recommendations for dealing with it. He also acted with political courage and rapidity in organizing relief measures. His first step was to contravene prevailing economic principles by buying significant amounts of American maize for controlled sale in Ireland in order to prevent the inflation of food prices. More familiar reactions included the establishment of relief commissions to finance and organize public works (funded equally by the government and property owners at a total cost of one million pounds) to provide employment for approximately 150,000 people, enabling them to buy food.

For some time, Peel had been convinced of the wisdom of repealing the protective tariffs imposed on imported grain, known as the corn laws. These laws were designed to guarantee a minimum market price for domestic grain by making imported grain more expensive and less competitive. Yet Peel and others had questioned the benefits of protectionism for the British economy and advocated free trade. The failure of the Irish potato crop in 1845 convinced him that repeal of the corn laws must be undertaken to facilitate the further importation of cheap American grain if it proved immediately necessary, but he also considered the long-term policy of encouraging the permanent substitution of the potato with maize in Ireland. Peel succeeded in convincing the British parliament to repeal the corn laws, but at the cost of his Conservative Party government, which split and was replaced by the Liberal Party under the leadership of Lord John Russell in 1846.

Historians conclude that while distress and suffering were widespread among the poorest classes of society during 1845–1846, few people actually died of hunger. Public works, private charity, the availability of maize, and disposable resources enabled cottiers and laborers to survive, although they fell farther into rent arrears. The prevailing attitude, reflecting the pattern of limited sporadic failure in the past, was that the potato crop which had been planted for the following harvest (using a portion of the crop that had escaped the blight) would flourish.

One of the most puzzling realities of the famine era for a modern reader is that even though the potato crop was destroyed, other crops and livestock continued to be exported from the country in 1845–1846, although the poor were beginning to feel the pinch of serious hunger. Prohibiting food exports would have contravened the essence of the popular laissez-faire economic philosophy, which held that government interference in the economy was erroneous. In any case, the class of substantial farmers who produced the surplus crops and livestock for the export market, and who did not depend on the potato for survival, would have resisted any attempt at prohibiting exports.

Peel decided that further government interference in the economy was unmerited. His administration had proved equal to the initial task of organizing relief works, which had mitigated distress during previous potato crop failures. The complete failure of the potato crop in the autumn of 1846 was not foreseen, and by that time a Liberal Party government led by Russell had replaced Peel's Conservative Party administration.

While Peel was not adverse to taking political risks in pursuit of what he believed was necessary, including bending the rules of laissez-faire, his successors in government (most notably the permanent head of the treasury, Charles Trevelyan, and the chancellor of the exchequer, Sir Charles Wood) were more rigid in their devotion to economic nonintervention. When the second and almost complete crop failure occurred in 1846, the government at first refused to consider supplying food for sale, insisting that this activity properly lay within the sphere of private enterprise. Food prices soared. Politicians also emphasized that it was the duty of property owners to take entire fiscal responsibility for the poverty in their own area. "Irish property must support Irish poverty" was a political maxim. Thus the impossible burden of completely financing sufficient public works to meet the needs of a larger number of people was firmly placed on landowners.

While there were certainly extremely wealthy landlords whose Irish estates provided them with large incomes, many landlords were in financial trouble themselves. The agricultural depression of the previous decades had resulted in tenants falling into serious arrears of rent. While some landlords responded with evictions, others accepted the genuine difficulties of tenants who paid what they could. The cost of the workhouses had to be subsidized by landowners; the more tenants were evicted, the bigger the numbers in workhouses. It was often less of a financial liability to accept what little rent could be paid than resort to evictions. Many a landlord found himself with an actual income that bore little resemblance to his rent rolls. Most estates had carried large debts for generations—heirs borrowed on their future prospects, marriage settlements for sisters and daughters had to be provided, and large houses had to be maintained. The added burden of having to finance relief works without any incoming rent, however meager, broke many landlords completely.

The winter of 1846–1847 was one of the harshest in memory. People who had been hungry but survived the previous winter were beginning to starve by the end of 1846. Although guarded exports of grain continued, they were one-third lower than usual. Imports of maize and rice into Ireland grew to twice the rate of grain exports, but these imports arrived in quantity only after the winter, which had witnessed many deaths from hunger. Desperate people sought employment by breaking stones on the relief works, but this financially fragile system was completely unable to cope with the demands of a quarter-million people in November and half a million in December 1846.

For those who had succeeded in obtaining such employment, their wages were completely inadequate, given the rise in food prices. Crime increased as survival became more precarious. The winter and spring of "Black '47" were bitterly cold. People congregated in towns and especially around the workhouses, which were crammed to capacity. Disease began to spread rapidly, most notably typhus and relapsing fever, but fatal bacillary dysentery was also widespread. Those who had the means emigrated with all possible speed. By the end of 1847, two hundred thousand people had left; some using their own resources, some because landlords assisted with the costs, others because of money sent to them for their passage from family members who had left in prior decades. These remittances totaled half a million pounds by 1849 and a further million pounds by 1851.

The Irish Society of Friends (Quakers) imported food supplies from America, established soup kitchens in 1846, and provided grants for the purchase of boilers to set up further soup kitchens. Their tours of the country and their written reports detailing their observations and experiences were crucial in shaping public opinion and fund-raising in Britain and abroad. The Quakers were noted for their philanthropy and nonproselytism. While "souperism," or the exchange of food for religious conversion, rarely occurred, those conversion societies and individuals who pursued this agenda initiated a popular myth about these years that eclipsed the impartial aid of genuinely altruistic organizations.

The British Relief Association founded in 1847 was made up of businessmen and merchants who raised an estimated £470,000. Contributions came from all over the world: £14,000 came from Calcutta in 1846, £3,000 arrived from Bombay, Jamaica sent £2,000, and the Choctaw tribe in Oklahoma sent $710 in 1849. America contributed $1 million from private donations in 1846, and special relief commissions were established to continue fund-raising during 1847. New York raised $170,000, Philadelphia sent $50,000, Boston collected $45,000, New Orleans and Albany each raised $25,000, New Jersey sent $35,000, and Baltimore sent $40,000. With the approval of Congress, American warships were used to carry shipments of food.

While public opinion expressed great sympathy and a desire to help, and while some members of the government risked political careers in vainly drawing up proposals for new state-subsidized relief schemes, the prevailing attitude toward any serious government intervention was still negative. In a manner reminiscent of the fable of the ant and the grasshopper, Charles Trevelyan worked with great commitment in dealing with the bureaucratic burdens created by the crisis, but he was personally convinced that Irish irresponsibility, fecundity, and improvidence had created the potential for this disaster in which he could see the hand of God at work in eliminating the "cancer of dependency" and the overpopulation of the island.

The situation was so grave by the spring of 1847 that the government conceded it had to temporarily abandon both its cherished economic policy and public works and then provide direct relief in the form of free food. Even given the desperate situation in Ireland, this was a radical decision in the context of its time. Attitudes toward poverty dictated that direct charity merely begot further dependents, and many people genuinely worried that if the indigent in Ireland were given a taste of such charity, the problem would be exacerbated in the long run by the creation of a population of paupers.

Government-subsidized soup kitchens were established to feed the starving a daily meal. Yet there were significant and widespread delays in setting them up, even though the public works division had already been shut down. Therefore, in parts of the country, there were fatal delays throughout the late spring when no relief was available. By the late summer of 1847, these outdoor kitchens were distributing one meal to more than three million people per day. An amendment to the Irish Poor Law in June allowed for continued relief to be given outside workhouses to those who had absolutely no other resources. Relief would be denied to anyone who leased or rented more than a quarter-acre of land. Again, the burden of financing this increased relief fell on Irish property owners, but the quarter-acre clause allowed some landlords to clear their estates with greater rapidity. The number of evictions soared.

Direct government relief was regarded as a short-term response to the crisis. In the expectation of a healthy crop or perhaps in sheer disbelief that it could fail completely again, the government decided to close its soup kitchens by the end of September 1847. The very small autumn crop of potatoes was again the victim of blight but was not completely destroyed. A cautious optimism arose that with three consistent crop failures surely the worst had passed, yet food was still very scarce and what was available was prohibitively expensive. The relief works had ended, the soup kitchens were closed, and those clamoring outside the workhouses for food could not be appeased. Thousands of people were dying every week from the combined effects of malnutrition and disease, which were exacerbated by thousands flocking into and around the workhouses. In 1848, the crop failed almost completely again, and in this year the appearance of cholera, which raged until the summer of 1849, claimed thousands of those weakened by prolonged hunger. Between 1849 and 1850, over 400,000 emigrated. In 1851, the total was just under 250,000.

Charity subscriptions from private sources had peaked and declined. In the summer of 1849, the financially and physically exhausted Quakers shut down their soup kitchens and called on the government to intervene. But the government held firm to its policy of laissez-faire. As far as official responses were concerned, the need for direct relief had ended in the autumn of 1847, and it was the responsibility of landlords and property owners to deal with the consequences of the continued crop failures. The small 1849 crop showed signs of improvement, the 1850 crop recovered further, and in the following years the effect of the blight on the crop declined, although it was not until later in the century that bluestone (or copper sulfate) was used to control the disease.

The census of 1851 revealed a population of about 6.5 million. There is some disparity among scholars about excess mortality during the years 1845–1850, but most agree that the number is over one million. Those most vulnerable, the youngest and the oldest, died in large numbers. The landless laborer and the small tenant farmer were most adversely affected. More than £8 million had been raised in Ireland by increased property taxes and private borrowing by landlords to deal with the costs of public works and workhouse relief. The British government spent just over £8 million on relief measures; half of this was in the form of loans to be repaid by Irish property owners over time in increased taxes. Given the inability of property owners to meet these financial commitments, and the fact that numerous bankrupt estates were sold from 1849 onward when legal restrictions regarding inheritance had been removed, the government canceled the debt in 1853.

While Robert Peel's early response to what was initially perceived as another partial and limited failure of the potato crop was swift and effective, the actions of the Liberal Party government that took office in 1846 proved ultimately deficient. An inflexible economic philosophy and an implacable belief in harsh providentialism dictated government policy from 1846 onward, even when it became strikingly clear that this was a departure from the sporadic and partial potato failure. Yet, at a moment of extreme crisis when the government temporarily bowed to the desperation of the starving in setting up the soup kitchens, it became clear that with sufficient intervention of this kind by the state, the death toll could have been reduced.

After the Famine

Important differences marked the post-Famine era. Historians have long argued about whether the traumatic experiences of the 1840s initiated or accelerated these changes. The rate of population growth had slowed in the 1830s, but after the chilling fatalities of the 1840s and continually high levels of emigration until the late twentieth century (over four million people left Ireland between 1851 and 1911), the Irish population continued to decline. This was also partly the result of changing practices with regard to land and marriage.

In the earlier part of the century, the widespread practice of subdivision of land among the children of tenants and small farmers had facilitated marriage at a young age and, consequently, large families. With high levels of mortality among these vulnerable tenant classes during the famine years, and with increased emigration added to numerous evictions that had cleared the land of its dense population, landlords and strong farmers emphasized consolidation and, where possible, expansion of landholdings. From then on, the accepted practice among tenants and farmers of all classes was for one heir to inherit the intact holding, usually not until the death of both parents. This postponed inheritance implied celibacy until marriage at much later ages and, consequently, smaller families. Siblings who had no prospect of inheriting land and few other employment options faced the choice of emigration or remaining as an unpaid and unwed laborer on the family farm.

The British army and the Catholic Church were two popular career options for young men. Women for whom marriage dowries were not available faced spinsterhood, emigration, or the convent, although the latter usually demanded a financial settlement similar to a marriage dowry. In 1850, there were approximately fifteen hundred nuns in Irish convents. By 1900, there were eight thousand. With the consolidation of land into larger farms after the famine years, livestock farming became more popular and profitable, especially as the continued expansion of the railways in Ireland in the 1850s and 1860s made transport to British markets easier.

The physical landscape changed after 1850 with the consolidation of land and the marked absence of those whose small, self-contained rural villages (or *clachans*) were

eerie crumbling monuments to their lives and deaths. Mass grave sites dotted an op-
pressively silent countryside. People felt that they were living among ghosts, an emotion that continued into the next century. Social customs and traditions were
neglected. The Irish language, strongest among those who had suffered most severely,
entered a period of decline that was intensified by continued emigration, a state education system that was hostile to it, and a growing popular attitude that characterized
the language as backward. In many parts of the country, within the space of one generation between 1840 and 1870, English replaced Irish as the people's first language.

In the decades after the Famine, the Catholic Church experienced a renewal, or
what some scholars have called a "devotional revolution." The substantial increase in
vocations, for which there were compelling economic explanations, and attendance
at religious services have often been characterized as a reaction to a devastating experience that many interpreted as an act of divine wrath. An increase in Church personnel and authoritarian power was certainly due in part to the determined efforts of
Archbishop (Cardinal from 1866) Paul Cullen, who had been sent from Rome in 1849
to lead the meandering Irish Catholic Church back into line with papal policy. Reform had been a priority since well before the famine, as pilgrimages to holy wells,
energetic and earthy wakes following death, a prevalent belief in magic, and ancient
celebrations of seasonal change such as *Lughnasa* were intertwined with orthodox
Catholicism, particularly among rural peasants.

Yet the grim puritanism and continence of Catholicism in the second half of the
century was due neither to the reforming zeal of Paul Cullen nor to a population
appeasing a wrathful deity who had sent the famine to punish them. It emerged as the
response of a society intent on survival, which required celibacy, discipline, and material resources, subordinating the aspirations of the individual to the well-being of the
family. Consolidation of land inherited by one male heir, the emphasis on limited
strategic marriages, the diffusion of surplus offspring by means of emigration and
vocation, and the societal taboo on unsanctioned sexuality fed the repressive character of late nineteenth- and twentieth-century Irish Catholicism.

Puritanical religious revival was not confined to Catholicism. Protestant evangelicalism with an energetic attempt at proselytism had flourished in the early nineteenth
century as Presbyterianism became more fundamental in the aftermath of the 1798
rebellion. Protestantism, predominantly concentrated in Ulster, responded in the
1850s to the Famine with another bout of enthusiastic evangelicalism that was articulated in street preaching that denounced popery. Mid-nineteenth-century American
revivalism had a tremendous influence on Presbyterianism, especially among the
urban working class in 1859, but the overall effect of religious revival in Ulster was to
emphasize the common Protestant ground between Presbyterians and members of
the Church of Ireland in reaction to ultramontane Catholicism. The Orange Order,
which had languished since the beginning of the century, was revived to rally Ulster
Protestantism, provoking in response the establishment of the Catholic Ancient Order
of Hibernians, both of which formed extensive and effective political networks in the
coming decades.

The political implications of the Famine were profound, although they did not
fully emerge for some time. Many of those who had lost family members, who had

been evicted, or who had emigrated burned with a bitterness directed principally at Great Britain. John Mitchel's assessment of the Famine as a deliberate attempt at genocide by the government found a receptive audience, especially among emigrants who willingly supported and financed organizations that sought to sever the political connection with Britain during the coming decades. Political activity in the 1850s was mainly confined to unsuccessful attempts at organizing tenant leagues to campaign for agrarian reform; in addition, there was a loose and short-lived coalition of Irish Members of Parliament (MPs) in the British House of Commons whose aim was to act as a pressure group for reform of Irish issues. The Catholic Church under the leadership of Cullen favored the political union with Britain and sought to obtain concessions in the area of education by emphasizing its support of the political status quo. Many contemporaries characterized the 1850s as a decade of political stagnation, but by its close a new Irish republican movement emerged that embodied the ghost of revolutions past and articulated once again the call to arms.

The Fenians

The Irish Republican Brotherhood (IRB) was established in Dublin in 1858 and drew extensively from the republicanism of Wolfe Tone and the literary bequest of Young Ireland, along with the agrarian radicalism of James Fintan Lalor. The leaders of this latest incarnation of revolutionary nationalism were James Stephens and John O'Mahony, both veterans of the Young Ireland skirmish in 1848 who had fled to France and New York in its aftermath. The secret oath-bound organization, borrowing from its American branch established by O'Mahony in New York, quickly became known as the Fenian Brotherhood, a name that reflected the influence of the Young Irelanders among others in popularizing Irish mythology. The name "Fenian" was an anglicized version of the Gaelic word *Fianna,* which referred to an ancient band of warriors.

Reflecting Stephens's sojourn in Paris, the Fenians were organized in a secret cell structure that aimed at thwarting infiltration by informers. Recruits swore allegiance to the Irish Republic, but the traditional interpretation of the Fenians as a disciplined popular force intent on rebellion has been modified by research that argues that for some it was predominantly a middle-class organization with notable literary, social, and recreational functions. The opposition of the hierarchy of the Catholic Church to the Fenian movement has been well documented. Paranoid about revolutionaries, committed to government support in return for concessions, and upholding the papal censure of oath-bound societies, Paul Cullen condemned the movement and combined with other constitutionally minded individuals to launch the ineffective National Association whose mild program requested denominational education, modest land reform, and the disestablishment or removal of the privileged position of the Church of Ireland.

Stephens's efforts to build up a substantial armed force relied heavily on funding and support from Irish Americans in the Fenian Brotherhood led by O'Mahony. While there was significant popular support among the Irish in Britain where cells

Published by firms in New York City and Hartford, Connecticut, this 1866 lithograph incorporates portraits of Irish political and cultural nationalists with the poem "The Fenian Banner." (Library of Congress, Prints and Photographs Division, LC-USZ62-38607)

were established, and while the organization spread rapidly in the major east coast cities of the United States, the American Civil War postponed any plans for a rebellion in Ireland. Although this was a disagreeable delay in some respects, there were also certain experiences to be gained from the conflict. Thousands of emigrant Irishmen were recruited as soldiers for both armies, from which seasoned military officers and men could be drawn for a future rebellion in Ireland. Hopes were high of escalated tension between the American government and Great Britain, resulting in a war that the Fenians could profit from by launching a simultaneous rebellion in Ireland or by allying themselves with the federal army. While the latter hope proved futile, the end of the Civil War resulted in a few hundred experienced officers and soldiers traveling from America to Ireland in the expectation of an imminent rebellion.

The authorities in Dublin Castle were aware of the conspiracy. After accumulating sufficient evidence, they moved against the Fenians late in 1865, suppressing their newspaper and arresting most of the significant leaders who were summarily tried and convicted of treason. Stephens was captured but escaped the country in 1866. Long sentences of penal servitude were imposed on the rest, but the numerous trials also allowed the effective employment of oratorical propaganda that fueled the romantic legacy of the movement. In America, the movement split into two factions. One group, led by William R. Roberts, advocated an ambitious if quixotic invasion of Canada in order to provoke a conflict between America and Britain. The other faction, headed by O'Mahony, was still determined to launch a rebellion in Ireland. The arrival of Stephens in New York did not heal the rift but precipitated further hostility after his appropriation of O'Mahony's position. The Roberts faction obstinately attempted their invasion three times—in 1866, 1870, and 1871—before they finally decided it was a futile strategy.

While the Fenians fractured in America, those in Ireland were preparing to make at least a gesture toward rebellion. In March 1867 during a snowstorm, ill-prepared and badly armed groups of Fenians attempted a rising in Dublin, Tipperary, Cork, and a few other areas around the country in which police barracks were attacked and twelve people died. The insurrection fizzled out almost as quickly and as ingloriously as its predecessor in 1848. Those arrested were dealt with quite leniently by the government, which imposed sentences of life imprisonment for leading rebels and lighter prison terms for the rest. A government amnesty released many within a few years.

Little sustained popular attention was paid to the attempted rising, but the execution of three Fenians accused of murdering a policeman in Manchester while trying to rescue a colleague resulted in an immediate wave of sympathy and sentiment directed at those now described as martyrs in the nationalist cause. Once again, a plot for a definitive and glorious revolution in Ireland had fallen far short of the mark despite years of planning. Yet Fenianism did not cease with the failure of 1867. It regrouped over the following decades while maintaining a low profile and proved very adept at infiltrating all aspects of nationalist organization—constitutional, literary, and agrarian—while biding its time for a resurrection of the revolutionary enterprise.

The Irish Question

William Ewart Gladstone, the Liberal Party's prime minister of Britain, believed that support for Fenianism was a symptom of Irish grievances that could be solved by legislative means. Gladstone, though sometimes popularly portrayed as a champion of Irish interests, was firmly committed to the political union and sought to strengthen that union by dealing with two of the chief subjects of instability: religion and land. Both of these lay at the heart of surviving Protestant influence in Ireland. The Church of Ireland was the established church, which meant that although the fiercely resented tithe had been merged into general property taxes in the 1830s, the Protestant religion was still heavily subsidized by the government while representing only one-fifth of the population. The Liberal Party was in principle opposed to state support for religion and introduced a Disestablishment Act in 1869 that removed such support from the Church of Ireland, as well as grants to the Catholic seminary at Maynooth. Although the Church of Ireland was a wealthy and influential body, it was predictable that with its protected status removed it would diminish over time to reflect the small percentage of the population that adhered to it. Irish Protestants were alarmed at this move, which they interpreted as the first step of British abandonment.

Gladstone's second measure of reform, the Land Act of 1870, was a cautious response to the continued demand for reform of land tenure conditions by farmers and tenants. In particular, they demanded fair rents and fixity or security of tenure. The measure legalized the "Ulster Custom" where it existed—a tradition strongest in the north—whereby tenants were allowed to sell their leases and were not evicted as long as they paid their rent. In the rest of the country, tenants who were evicted for any reason, except for nonpayment of rent, were entitled to compensation for disturbance. While in many ways this legislation was limited and certainly did not satisfy tenants' ambitions, it is significant in that the government for the first time officially interfered with the absolute rights of property and recognized that tenants had valid claims to compensation and protection.

Despite his positive efforts, Gladstone had succeeded in alienating most groups in Ireland. Protestants resented his disestablishment of their church and his government's meddling with property rights, and they suspected his ultimate intentions regarding the union. The Tenant League, formed in 1869, was disappointed with the limitations of the Land Act. Supporters of amnesty for the Fenian prisoners were discontented with the limited releases approved. Representing a section of Irish Protestant opinion that resented the power of the Westminster parliament to dictate policy for Ireland, especially when policy threatened their interests, Isaac Butt, a Protestant barrister and MP, launched the Home Government Association in 1870. An eccentric mix of conservative Protestant landowners, tenant rights advocates, constitutional nationalists, and several secret Fenians, the association's aim was the establishment of a domestic Irish legislature. "Home Rulers," as they quickly became known, contested by-elections with some success in the early 1870s and capitalized on these steps with the return of fifty-nine MPs after the 1874 general election.

The Catholic Church was initially suspicious of the Protestant character of the association, and Paul Cullen unsuccessfully attempted to form a rival group to express Catholic support for the union. His policy of loyalty to the British government in the expectation of state subsidies for an exclusively Catholic university received a rude setback when Gladstone introduced proposals for a University Bill in 1873 that were highly unsatisfactory to the Catholic Church. The hierarchy began to view the Home Government Association in a new light, and several bishops joined it. Irish constitutional nationalists, the mostly Catholic progeny of O'Connellism, were attracted to the Home Government Association and joined in substantial numbers. Their membership changed the balance of composition: a strongly conservative and Protestant character was steadily eclipsed by the solid presence of the Catholic hierarchy and constitutional nationalists. Many of the original Protestant members who flirted uncertainly with an attempt to resurrect the spirit of eighteenth-century Patriotism fled from a movement that, despite Butt's continued leadership, was increasingly representative of Catholic nationalism with Fenianism prowling in its shadows.

The New Departure

The reorganized Fenian movement in America led by John Devoy, now known as Clan na Gael (Family of the Gael), had adopted a new policy. Devoy observed with interest the burgeoning Home Rule movement and paid close attention to a cabal within Butt's ranks that ruthlessly used the practice of obstruction—filibustering or the strict employment of the procedures of parliamentary debate—to frustrate the business of legislating in order to focus attention on a grievance. Joseph Biggar, an MP from Belfast and a member of the Irish Republican Brotherhood, initiated the practice among a select number of Irish MPs in order to draw attention to the current Conservative Party government's studied neglect of Irish issues. On one memorable occasion they kept up a continuous relay debate for twenty hours.

While Butt and many of the Home Rule MPs disapproved of such an ungentlemanly subversion of the parliament, Biggar was joined by a Protestant landlord from County Wicklow, Charles Stewart Parnell. This behavior attracted the attention of extreme nationalists like Devoy who saw the potential of an alliance of Fenian interests with those of the parliamentarians and agrarian reformers. Other Fenians, especially those in Ireland, disagreed and remained adamant that the best policy was to resist dabbling in land reform or parliamentary politics and concentrate on building up a secret force that could take advantage of potential British vulnerability, such as when the country would be involved in the next major European war. Devoy, secure in his leadership of the lucrative and influential Clan na Gael, ignored their objections and pursued an alliance with Parnell, whom he believed would emerge as the leader of the parliamentary party.

James Fintan Lalor had emphasized the importance of land reform several decades earlier, prophesying that it would be the issue of land that would propel a successful campaign for national independence. In the late 1870s, depressed agricultural prices, an industrial depression in Britain, and bad weather and consequently poor harvests revived the clamor for further land reform. In 1878, John Devoy and Michael Davitt approached Parnell with their proposal for a "new departure" that would ally Fenian, agrarian, and Home Rule interests. While there are conflicting accounts of this secret discussion, the result was Parnell's inclusion in a new program that allowed him access to the considerable organizational and financial support of Clan na Gael in America and involved him in Davitt's new movement for agrarian reform, the Irish National Land League. In return, it was accepted that Parnell would become leader of the Irish Parliamentary Party and work to advance the cause of land reform and nationalism. Devoy believed that Parnell was committed to going farther than Home Rule and would advocate a separatist revolution if necessary, but Davitt recalled that Parnell had refused to commit himself.

The Land League

Parnell was elected president of the Land League, a movement that organized the tenant farmers to resist high rents and evictions during the current crisis, demanded protective legislative reform, and, ultimately, established peasant proprietorship. In 1880, in a two-month tour around America to highlight the severe agrarian crisis in Ireland, Parnell raised $200,000 for relief of the food shortages that threatened Connaught. Private charity and government grants added to the financial aid available, which enabled people to buy maize in order to supplement a very poor potato crop. An unexpected general election recalled Parnell to Ireland to campaign for his seat in parliament. The election restored Gladstone's Liberal Party to power, and the Irish Parliamentary Party, led by William Shaw since Butt's death in 1879, won sixty-one seats. Parnell was shortly afterward chosen as the new party leader.

The Land League campaign increased in intensity during 1880–1881. Meetings attended by thousands were held throughout the country, and tenants were advised to defend themselves. While the leadership of the movement, especially Parnell, were careful that their language did not directly incite violence and thus invite official suppression and imprisonment, tenants told to keep a firm grip on their land interpreted it to include "by any means necessary." The traditional methods of the agrarian secret societies, largely dormant since the famine, reemerged as landlords and their property became the targets of violence. A very effective practice of ostracization, with roots in Gaelic society, isolated landlords and their families from supplies, service, and society. Popularly called boycotting, after Mayo landowner Captain Charles Boycott had experienced it, this weapon was also used against any tenant who rented a farm from which another had been evicted or against those accused of helping victims of a boycott. Agrarian crime rose as evictions increased. Cattle were maimed, hay and turf supplies were burned, crude threatening letters warned landlords of their imminent demise unless they repaired their ways, and murder was attempted and committed. Those landlords who escaped direct personal violence faced serious financial difficulties as a result of intimidation, ostracism, and property destruction.

The government responded to the escalating violence with a Coercion Act in January 1881, which allowed for the arrest and imprisonment of suspects without trial. Gladstone followed this with another Land Act in April, which gave Irish tenants the "3Fs" they had demanded: fair rent to be established by an independent commission; fixity of tenure if rents were paid on time; and free sale, the ability independently to sell a lease for profit. This was a significant achievement in agrarian reform and essentially granted the Land League's immediate demands, but many still were unhappy with its complicated provisions that did not offer any protection to tenants who were in rent arrears—namely, one-third of all tenants and two-thirds of those who lived in Connaught.

Parnell was in a delicate position. The legislation offered significant advances in land reform and from his perspective fulfilled the terms of his compact with Davitt and Devoy as far as agrarian issues were concerned. The act was welcomed by stronger farmers and businessmen, who together composed the majority of the Irish electorate,

Charles Stewart Parnell (1846–1891) a Protestant landlord of Irish and American lineage (his mother, Delia Tudor Stewart, was of a prominent Boston family) was an ostensibly unlikely leader in the movement for agrarian reform and Home Rule. Parnell spent ten weeks in 1880 touring the United States to raise funds for the Irish National Land League, during which time he addressed Congress and hinted at the potential of American diplomatic pressure as a force for change in Ireland. His political ascendancy and alliance with Prime Minister Gladstone augured a fundamental change in Anglo-Irish relations, but personal scandal led to his political ruin. (Library of Congress, Prints and Photographs Division, LC-USZ62-123392)

and was approved of by the Catholic Church. But smaller tenants were unhappy, as were many members of the League leadership. The majority of Fenians were hostile to the measure because satisfied farmers did not make for successful revolutionaries. Given the political quicksand in which he could easily find himself, his solution was to remain noncommittal. Home Rule MPs in Westminster abstained from voting on it while simultaneously criticizing it in public and trying to ensure its survival behind the scenes.

When it became law, Parnell convinced moderates in the Land League to test its provisions, while he made a series of deliberately violent speeches that had the required effect of landing him in Kilmainham prison, thus appeasing extremist elements in the League who had suspected his commitment to their cause. From there he endorsed a "No Rent Manifesto" and encouraged tenants to boycott the commission established to decide fair rents. The government promptly suppressed the Land League, and the violence of secret societies such as the Moonlighters escalated.

By 1882, the government was ready to negotiate. Gladstone agreed to amend the Land Act to help tenants in arrears to take advantage of its provisions, while Parnell agreed to convince the league to accept this and to use his influence to end the agrarian violence. Successive governments, particularly Conservative Party administrations, passed further land reform measures in the hope that popular support for Home Rule would decrease as land reform increased. The successful Ashbourne Land Purchase Act of 1885 provided attractive loans to enable tenants to purchase their farms, while further measures such as Balfour's Land Act of 1891 and the Wyndham Land Act of 1903 increased the financial support that was available to tenants for purchasing their farms.

The central political significance of the land issue lay in its popular support. Parnell had taken a calculated yet successful gamble in involving himself with the Land League. He had recognized the potential of what Lalor had pointed out in the 1840s: the land issue was the engine that would pull political self-determination in its wake if the two could be harnessed. With the settlement of the major demands of the Land League in 1882, Parnell began to build a tightly disciplined and effective political party in Westminster, diligently supported by a committed grassroots organization of those who had benefited from land reform, with which he intended to achieve Home Rule.

Home Rule

A significant percentage of the Liberal Party, including Gladstone, had begun to accept that some measure of self-determination was necessary for stability in Ireland. When Gladstone's views became public, the Conservative Party declared its opposition to Home Rule and its support for the union. Some members of his own party vehemently disagreed with his change in policy and formed a splinter group, taking the name Liberal Unionists. Undaunted once he had made his decision to introduce Home Rule, Gladstone rallied the remnants of his party together and, allied with Parnell's party, drew up a bill that was presented to parliament in 1886. This proposed establishing an Irish legislature in Dublin that would control domestic affairs, while imperial matters remained the preserve of Westminster where Irish MPs would no longer sit. An intense debate ensued, culminating in rejection of the bill by a majority combination of Liberal Unionists, Conservatives, and Irish Unionists, who collectively believed that Home Rule would be the first step toward complete separation, a precedent that would be disastrous for Protestantism and for the future of the British Empire.

Irish Unionism

There were two distinct types of Irish unionism. The first was generally referred to as southern unionism and was composed of a small number of influential upper-class individuals, most notably Protestant landlords but also wealthy businessmen and professionals, who had founded the Irish Loyal and Patriotic Union in 1885 to oppose any attempt to interfere with the political union. The second unionist group was more numerous, cohesive, and ultimately effective. Ulster unionism reflected the numerical strength of Protestants in the north of Ireland where they composed more than 50 percent of the population and were distributed among all classes. Whereas southern unionism sought to protect the increasingly fragile position of the descendants of the Protestant ascendancy, given their slender numbers and declining influence in society, Ulster unionism was more aggressively hostile to Catholicism.

In particular, Ulster unionists feared that an Irish parliament would be ultimately dominated by the authoritarian Catholic Church and thus that "Home Rule would be Rome Rule." Additionally, unionists in Ulster emphasized that Belfast and its hinterland had prospered in the nineteenth century with the strong linen and shipbuilding industries, and they feared the economic repercussions of Home Rule. Ulster unionists formed the Anti-Repeal Union and joined with their southern counterparts in 1886 to form a Unionist Party whose MPs in Westminster would combat proposals for an Irish parliament. In terms of their share of Irish representation in the British parliament, they won only 18 seats out of a total of 103 in the 1885 general election. Parnell's Irish Parliamentary Party held the balance of Irish seats. Yet the unionists had powerful allies in the Conservative Party and in the Liberal Unionist Party, which together formed an effective bulwark against the passage of Home Rule in the House of Commons in 1886 and again in the House of Lords in 1893.

Continued Land Reform

During the late 1880s, agricultural depression produced another crisis. Evictions and emigration rose sharply, accompanied by traditional agrarian violence. The Land League reconstituted itself as the National League and embarked on the Plan of Campaign, another battle on behalf of tenant farmers. Parnell, unwilling to risk his alliance with Gladstone and immersed in his complicated private life, remained aloof from the campaign, which encouraged tenants to stage rent strikes if landlords rejected reasonable proposals for rent reductions. Boycotting was again employed to intimidate those tempted to lease farms from which others had been evicted. The popularity of the campaign alarmed Parnell, who feared that his Liberal Party allies would abandon Home Rule given the unrest in Ireland.

The Conservative Party government, which had replaced Gladstone's administration after the defeat of the 1886 Home Rule Bill, appointed Arthur Balfour as chief secretary for Ireland. He introduced a Coercion Act to suppress lawlessness but also proposed a Land Act that was passed in 1887; it revised rents and satisfied some of the immediate grievances. Balfour continued his work on land reform until the early

1890s. He was responsible for drawing up legislation, which the Conservative government passed in 1891, making attractive loans available to tenants to purchase their farms. A Congested Districts Board was established to consolidate farms along the western coast by buying and redistributing land, to encourage education in agricultural methods and production, and to promote local industries. By 1923 when it was dissolved, this body had spent more than £11 million in buying, apportioning, and improving two million acres of land, encouraging craft industry, and improving infrastructure.

The Fall of Parnell

Parnell's private life became public in 1889 and consumed his political career, split the Irish Parliamentary Party, and almost destroyed the prospects of achieving Home Rule. While Gladstone and Parnell were planning their tactics for the next attempt at passing a Home Rule Bill whenever the Liberal Party returned to power, Parnell was named a co-respondent in a divorce case. Katherine O'Shea, estranged wife of William O'Shea, had been involved with Parnell since 1880 and had been living with him since 1886. Her husband, well aware of the love affair, had chosen to ignore it while he awaited the spoils of a significant inheritance due to Katherine from her aunt. When the aunt died, her will bequeathed the money directly to Katherine, with provisions that made it impossible for O'Shea to benefit. In the aftermath of this disappointment, he initiated divorce proceedings which Parnell initially welcomed in his desire to marry Katherine, a marriage that took place in 1891.

The revelation of this long-term affair, although known to many of Parnell's colleagues, resulted in an uproar in Britain and Ireland. Gladstone made his continued support of Home Rule conditional on Parnell's resignation as party leader. The Catholic Church, long suspicious of Parnell as a political leader, roundly condemned him as an adulterer. Irish public opinion split in a bitter divide that mirrored that of the Parliamentary Party that had the responsibility of choosing between the leader and the policy. They chose the latter by a majority of twenty. Parnell was advised by his supporters in the party to retire temporarily, but he refused and campaigned at by-elections in Ireland where his candidates were consistently defeated. In September he fell gravely ill, and he died of pneumonia in October 1891. His death failed to heal the divide within the party, which lost its parliamentary effectiveness for years by choosing to continue bickering, but it transformed the man into a mythic nationalist victim who quickly joined the ranks of those who had preceded him. Fickle public opinion, which had been harsh in its condemnation of him in life, loved him in death. His ghost assumed the persona of an uncrowned king who had been deliberately destroyed by his petty enemies.

The Gaelic Revival

While many contemporaries, most effectively W. B. Yeats, characterized the closing decade of the nineteenth century as apolitical, the temporary eclipse of the fractured

Irish Parliamentary Party merely threw into relief economic, cultural, and political developments that had been brewing for some time. "Revival" was the shibboleth of the next two decades. As the achievement of an Irish parliament seemed unlikely in the near future, with the retirement of Gladstone after the Lords' rejection of the 1893 Home Rule Bill, the factionalism of the Irish Parliamentary Party, and the strength of unionist opposition, increased emphasis was placed on self-reliance, the de-anglicization of Irish life, and achievement in cultural, economic, and political spheres.

Sport was the first area of cultural revival with the founding of the Gaelic Athletic Association (GAA) in 1884 to halt the replacement of traditional Irish games with, in Archbishop Croke's view, "alien" sports such as cricket, tennis, soccer, and rugby. Founded in Tipperary by Michael Cusack, Archbishop Croke, and Maurice Davin, the GAA formalized and encouraged the playing of native games such as hurling and Gaelic football. Immensely popular and well organized throughout rural Ireland (with the exception of strong unionist areas), the GAA emphasized its exclusive nationalism by barring from membership and participation those who played "foreign" games.

Entrenched within the leadership of the movement was the Irish Republican Brotherhood (IRB). The Fenians had maintained a superficially dormant existence for many years while awaiting another opportunity for revolution. The GAA—with its superb organization from the local to the national level; its emphasis on male team sports, training, and fitness; and its nationalist character—provided the perfect cover for the careful rejuvenation of IRB membership and morale. The Catholic Church was also part of the power structure of the GAA. Organization at the local club level necessarily involved the parish priest, whose approval was essential for the survival of any organization within his sphere of considerable influence.

Emphasis on linguistic identity is a hallmark of nationalism. Two approaches to language and literature emerged in Ireland toward the close of the century. The theme of de-anglicizing Ireland, first articulated by Archbishop Croke, who deplored a native tendency to imitate English "effeminate follies," provided the motif for other cultural projects. Conradh na Gaelige (the Gaelic League) was established by Douglas Hyde, Eoin MacNeill, and Fr. Eugene O'Growney in 1893 to resuscitate the rapidly declining Irish language (spoken by fewer than 14 percent of the population in 1901) and to promote the writing and publication of literature in Irish. Hyde, a native speaker of the language, collected and published popular collections of stories and poetry in Irish and English during the late 1880s. Slow to spread at first, there were more than six hundred branches of the League by 1908, which taught the language using O'Growney's textbook, encouraged traditional music and dance, organized *feiseanna* (festivals), and published a newspaper (*An Claidheamh Soluis,* The Sword of Light) that promoted Gaelic literature. It successfully campaigned to introduce the language into the educational curriculum at all levels, was responsible for making St. Patrick's Day a national holiday, encouraged sobriety, and worked with other organizations in fostering native industry and business.

While the league originally aimed to avoid divisive issues such as politics and religion in an attempt to encourage pluralist membership, the bond between language and nationalism, as well as the increasing power of the Catholic Church in the organizational structure, discouraged Protestant membership. Douglas Hyde, from a Church of Ireland background, recognized the necessity of Catholic clerical involvement if the League was to prosper, but disturbing examples of clerical power in League matters quickly alienated those Protestants who had initially been enthusiastic members, while confirming the forebodings of those who had remained aloof. Never as popular as the GAA, the Gaelic League was a profoundly influential cultural organization which, despite Hyde's insistence that it was nonpolitical, was the nationalist nursery for a new generation of political activists who came of age within a decade.

Building on the work of eighteenth- and nineteenth-century scholars in preserving, translating, and annotating manuscripts in the Irish language, writers such as Samuel Ferguson and Standish O'Grady published popular versions of mythic tales in English, admitting many to a hitherto undiscovered world of Gaelic literature and mythology. The creation of a distinct Irish literature in the English language was the goal of a movement that came to be known as the Anglo-Irish literary revival. Energized by W. B. Yeats and Lady Augusta Gregory, this movement sought to revive the power of Gaelic literature by publishing it in English and, using that early literature and mythology as a wellspring, to create a new national literature of the highest quality. Deeply influenced by European developments, the Irish Literary Theatre was founded in 1899 by Yeats, Gregory, and Edward Martyn. Its emphasis on poetic drama enacted by English players (in the absence of a professional Irish acting company) was of limited appeal, with the sole exception of *Cathleen ní Houlihan* in 1902, a popular allegorical treatment of Ireland as an old woman awaiting rejuvenation from the death of male patriots who fight for the restoration of her stolen "four green fields."

Partnership with an amateur group of Irish actors headed by William and Frank Fay led to the formation of the Abbey Theatre in 1904. The dramas produced in this theatre by Yeats, Gregory, and John Millington Synge in the first decade of this century represent the crowning achievement of the movement in literary terms, but the hostile and violent reaction of Irish (and Irish American) audiences to Synge's plays, most notably *The Playboy of the Western World* in 1907, with its perceived slurs on Irish nationalism and womanhood, revealed the uneasy relationship between literary endeavors and nationalist priorities.

Some of those priorities were ably articulated in the pages of *The Leader* by D. P. Moran, who advocated a philosophy of Irish-Ireland that supported the revival of the language and called for the rejuvenation of industry. He believed that economic self-reliance and cultural nationalism were more important than parliamentary politics, which he regarded as innately corrupt. Deprecating the slavish imitation of British trends that Archbishop Croke had earlier criticized, a tendency that Moran scathingly termed "West Britonism," Moran was also heartily critical of the Protestant personnel of the Anglo-Irish literary revival, insisting that the essence of cultural nationalism was Gaelic and Catholic.

Sinn Féin (Ourselves) was a name suggested by Mary Butler when Arthur Griffith described to her his concept of Irish self-reliance in economic, political, and cultural terms. Griffith was a Dubliner by birth and a printer by trade who returned from South Africa in 1898 to edit the *United Irishman*, a newspaper with limited circulation

This generation of Limerick children, pictured at the Treaty Stone in 1903, included many who, like Frank McCourt's mother, Angela, would try their luck in the United States during the 1920s. McCourt's 1996 memoir, *Angela's Ashes,* opens with her experiences in Depression-era Brooklyn. (Library of Congress, Prints and Photographs Division, LC-USZ62-68061)

but considerable force in expressing new directions in nationalist thought. Sinn Féin was formed in 1907 under Griffith's leadership, from a number of movements that had emerged around the turn of the century to represent nationalist feminism, to assert opposition to the British role in the Boer War and to the royal visit of King Edward VII to Ireland in 1903, and to promote republicanism in Ulster.

Although a coalition of moderate and militant elements, Sinn Féin's program of pacifism, economic self-reliance, and political abstention from Westminster was developed by Griffith. His study of the constitutional arrangement between Austria and Hungary (two separate kingdoms with a shared monarchy) convinced him that this modern model could be profitably applied to Ireland, arguing that it was in essence a return to what the Protestant Patriots had aimed at in 1782. Given Griffith's espousal of both nonviolence and political abstention from the imperial parliament, the new movement had limited appeal for either constitutional nationalists who still strongly supported the recently reunited Irish Parliamentary Party, or for militant nationalists such as the Fenians who were committed to revolution. Its role was to change utterly after 1916, largely due to a confused insistence by the government that Sinn Féin had been responsible for the rebellion, but for the first decade of its life it had a peripheral existence.

Nationalism and Radicalism

While the potential for revolution did not loom large on the horizon in the first decade of this century, the IRB, albeit limited in numbers, was found in every nationalist organization and was especially active in organizing events commemorating the centenary of the 1798 rebellion and in supporting the South African Boers in their war against Britain between 1899 and 1902. The gradual revival of the IRB from 1898 onward was largely due to the emergence of a new generation of revolutionaries, most notably Belfast men Denis McCullough and Bulmer Hobson, and Seán MacDiarmada from Leitrim. McCullough and Hobson established the Dungannon Clubs in 1905, which were separatist organizations that publicly debated nationalist issues and campaigned against Irish recruitment to the British army, and were one of the movements that combined to form Sinn Féin in 1907. MacDiarmada traveled all over the country in his overt role as an organizer for Sinn Féin, but he also covertly rebuilt IRB ranks and established networks of committed republicans.

Bulmer Hobson and Countess Constance Markievicz founded Na Fianna Éireann (Warriors of Ireland), a nationalist youth movement for boys that functioned as a crèche for IRB recruits. Countess Markievicz, a member of an established Sligo gentry family who had married a Polish count, was the most radical female republican of her time. She was involved with the militantly nationalist feminist movement Inghinidhe na hÉireann (Daughters of Ireland), founded by Maud Gonne in 1900 (it merged with Sinn Féin in 1907). In future years she became deeply involved in the labor movement, took part in the 1916 rebellion for which she received a death sentence (commuted to a prison term), and was the first woman ever elected to the British House of Commons in 1918.

One of the most important personalities in this IRB revival came from America. In 1907 John Devoy, leader of Clan na Gael, sent Thomas Clarke (a veteran of the 1880s dynamiting campaign in England for which he served fifteen years in prison) to Ireland to restructure the Brotherhood and to prepare to take advantage of any decent opportunity for revolution. Given the successive crises in European diplomacy and the intricate tangles of alliances and secret treaties, there was every likelihood of a major war erupting in the near future. British involvement in such a European war was virtually guaranteed, and this was the opportunity that the IRB were determined to seize. From his tobacconist's and newsagent's shop in Dublin's North Great Britain Street, Clarke reorganized the supreme council of the IRB and supported the replacement of older members with fresh blood, so that by 1912 the leadership of the movement in Ireland had passed into the hands of a new generation. While active membership in Ireland was fewer than two thousand men, Clarke and MacDiarmada preferred to bide their time in recruiting. Instead, they encouraged the placement of small numbers of IRB men in key leadership positions of other organizations such as the Gaelic League, the GAA, and Sinn Féin, rather than risking infiltration by informers that would likely attend a wholesale recruitment campaign.

Militant nationalism was not the sole radical development of the decade, nor was the IRB the only group dreaming of revolution. Dublin in the early years of the twentieth century was a slum city, one that is brilliantly evoked in the dramas of Sean O'Casey. Thousands of families lived in single-room tenement apartments without heat or sanitation. Dublin's rates of infant and adult mortality were the highest in Britain and among the highest in Europe, while disease and malnutrition were rife. In a city dependent on trade rather than industry, skilled employment was limited. Male unemployment was estimated to be around 20 percent; female unemployment was much higher, and prostitution was prevalent.

The labor movement was slow to develop in Ireland for a number of reasons. The predominance of the national question and strong confessional allegiances that were hostile to socialism precluded the development of parties based on class division, as was the case in Britain and much of Europe. Political activity was dominated by nationalism and unionism. A conservative and largely rural society, with the exception of northeast Ulster, Ireland had not experienced significant industrialization, and trade unions, affiliated with British unions, tended to represent small groups of craftsmen. James Connolly, the son of Irish emigrants who had settled in Edinburgh, arrived in Ireland in 1896 to organize socialist clubs and to articulate his developing philosophy that socialism and nationalism were symbiotic with the formation of an Irish Socialist Republican Party. Having made little progress in spreading socialist ideology in Ireland and barely earning enough to provide for his family, in 1903 he left for America, where he worked as an organizer and writer for the Industrial Workers of the World, embraced syndicalism, and founded the Irish Socialist Federation in New York.

While Connolly's socialism had met with an unenthusiastic response from the Irish proletariat, James Larkin founded the first unskilled Irish union, the Irish Transport and General Worker's Union (ITGWU), in 1909. Born in Liverpool, Larkin was also of Irish descent. He arrived in Ireland in 1907 as a British union organizer, in which role he orchestrated a short-lived but significant strike of dockworkers in Belfast. Connolly returned to Ireland in 1910 to lead the new Socialist Party of Ireland and to organize the ITGWU in Ulster, having developed his philosophy in *Labour in Irish History* (1910), which interpreted early Gaelic society as "primitive communism," thus providing a historical and nativist precedent for an Irish socialist state. He argued that the nationalist struggle was in essence a social struggle and asserted that political independence had to precede the full development of Irish socialism.

The ITGWU spread rapidly in Dublin but also in cities such as Cork and Belfast, with an estimated membership of ten thousand by 1913. A series of strikes in 1911 and 1912, with roots in a general trade depression in Britain, culminated in a lockout of Dublin ITGWU members from work in 1913 when the representative of the Employers' Federation, William Martin Murphy, a strong supporter of the Irish Parliamentary Party and the owner of the *Irish Independent* newspaper and the Dublin Tramway Company, convinced his fellow employers to refuse to hire members of the union. In response Larkin called a strike, and workers who were members of the ITGWU were subsequently locked out of their jobs. The struggle was bitter and demonstrated impressive solidarity among the workers, given the infancy of the labor movement, but hunger and desperation at the onset of winter, as well as the influential disapproval of the Catholic Church, resulted in a victory for the employers as the men slowly returned to work.

The following year, Larkin departed for a lecture tour in America where he spoke against Britain at Irish American and German American events and was involved in the founding convention of the American Communist Party, for which he served a three-year prison sentence. Upon his release in 1923 he returned to find the Irish labor movement besieged by intense political divisions, not only between nationalists and unionists but also between advanced republicans and moderate nationalists. Connolly took over the leadership of the ITGWU in 1914 and developed the Irish Citizen Army (a small socialist militia founded to protect the striking workers from attacks by the Dublin Metropolitan Police) toward a revolutionary role. But the labor movement after 1913, along with other initiatives such as the suffrage campaign and industrial committees, occupied a distinctly subservient position in Irish politics as the issue of Home Rule came to the fore once again.

Constructive Unionism

The Irish Parliamentary Party had called a truce in its post-Parnellite bickering and combined its factions under the leadership of John Redmond in 1900, but with successive Conservative Party governments in power from 1895 until 1905, the prospects for again raising the subject of Home Rule were not encouraging. Allied with the unionists, the conservatives were implacably opposed to a separate parliament for Ireland. They believed, as Gladstone once did, that the movement to modify the union by achieving Home Rule could be halted by social amelioration. "Killing Home Rule by kindness" was the epithet employed to describe an evolving constructive unionist policy that was committed to dealing with land ownership, local government, and social issues. The land acts that Arthur Balfour introduced in 1887 and 1891, supporting and extending the concept of peasant proprietorship, were based on a belief that ownership of land would reduce agrarian discontent and activity while satisfying the immediate and long-term interests of a significant section of the population that were among the strongest supporters of the Irish Parliamentary Party. Many Irish unionists, particularly landlords in the south, were keen to support this government initiative and make the union work in economic and social terms.

Returning from a decade of ranching in Wyoming, Horace Plunkett, a Meath landlord and a Liberal Unionist MP from 1892 to 1900, worked to address economic and educational issues with the organization of an Irish agricultural cooperative movement in 1889 and the Irish Agricultural Organization Society in 1894. Pressure on the government resulted in the establishment in 1898 of an Irish Department of Agriculture and Technical Instruction under Plunkett's direction. Plunkett emphasized economic initiative and self-sufficiency, and while his political attitudes differed

The vendor's harvest day market in the city of Cork, Ireland, 1905. (Library of Congress, Prints and Photographs Division, LC-USZ62-68068)

markedly from D. P. Moran's, for example, self-reliance in all areas of Irish life was encouraged in the Gaelic League, the Irish-Ireland movement, the literary revival, the arts and crafts movement, and Sinn Féin.

Arguably the most important piece of legislation introduced by the Conservative Party government was the Local Government Act in 1898. This essentially transferred power in local matters from the old grand juries, traditionally controlled by landlords, to new democratically elected councils voted in by an increased electorate, which for the first time included female voters. These councils were responsible for collecting and expending local property taxes on the maintenance of roads and the provision of public services. The effects of this legislation were not quite what the government had envisioned. Instead of satiating political aspirations, the revision of local government intensified the desire for Home Rule and support for the Irish Parliamentary Party as nationalists quickly came to dominate the new councils outside northeast Ulster.

Constructive unionism was at once a product of European conservative ideology, which had recognized that adaptability was the only meaningful way of preserving an old order in the face of new forces, and a specific British response to the Irish question. While the Conservative Party government was ready and able to introduce traditional coercive measures in response to a breakdown of law and order, they combined this with conciliation, producing legislation of great benefit to Ireland. Yet, as a policy it failed in its attempt to kill the desire for Home Rule which, with the return of the Liberal Party to government in 1905, was once more within the bounds of possibility.

While the Irish Parliamentary Party renewed its alliance with the Liberals after the 1905 election, the latter were not dependent on their support and were reluctant to commit to another campaign for Home Rule. They advocated the complete postponement of the Home Rule issue for five years while they experimented with the concept of gradual devolved powers such as the establishment of an Irish Council that would exercise limited jurisdiction in specific areas of Irish life. This proposal was ultimately rejected by Irish nationalists, but the Liberal-Irish Parliamentary Party alliance continued and important legislation was passed: a Labourer's Act (1906) to provide housing; the Old Age Pensions Act (1908) for those over age seventy; the Irish University Act (1908), which gave university status to Queen's College, Belfast, and established the National University of Ireland; and another Land Act (1909), which amended some of the financial aspects of the 1903 Wyndham Land Act and gave the Congested Districts Board increased powers of appropriation.

Reform of the House of Lords

Escalating tension between the British House of Commons and the House of Lords, over the power of the latter to exercise a veto on legislation passed by the Commons, was brought to a head in 1909. The House of Lords was traditionally a strong and effective ally of Conservatism and Unionism, with the result that, if the Lords so inclined, the Liberals were unable to pass much legislation without significant amendment or continued rejection. In 1909, the Liberal Party government passed a number of resolutions asserting the right of the Commons as the representative body of the legislature to have the final say on legislation, but the crisis climaxed when David Lloyd George, the chancellor of the exchequer, introduced a stiff budget that the Lords rejected. Parliament was dissolved, and a general election followed, which gave the balance of power between the Liberal Party (allied to the relatively new Labour Party) and the Conservatives (allied with the Unionists) to the Irish Parliamentary Party. If Redmond agreed to support the Liberals, then they would be able to form a government. In return for that support, the Liberals would have to commit once more to championing Home Rule.

The death of King Edward VII in 1910 and the succession of King George V led to a vain attempt by the political parties to avoid a constitutional crisis with regard to the Lords, but a second general election in less than a year produced a similar result. The Liberals and the Conservatives allied with Unionists each won exactly the same number of seats, while Labour captured forty-two. Again the Irish Parliamentary Party held the balance of power, and the Liberal Party leader, Henry Asquith, agreed to commit his government to Home Rule. Threatened with the creation of numerous new peers, the House of Lords rather than be flooded with the nouveau riche and other *parvenus*, agreed to an amendment of its veto power. Thenceforth legislation passed by the Commons could be delayed no more than two years before becoming law. Although this was a considerable constitutional change in British parliamentary history, the significance of the Parliament Act of 1911 for Ireland was that it made the passing of the next Home Rule Bill inevitable if Asquith's Liberal Party, committed to introducing the legislation, remained in government.

The Third Home Rule Bill

In April 1912, Asquith introduced the Government of Ireland Bill to the House of Commons. It proposed the establishment of a bicameral parliament in Dublin to be made up of an elected lower house of 164 members, and a senate of 40 members elected on a property franchise. This parliament would exercise devolved power in domestic issues while Westminster reserved power in anticipated areas such as the monarchy, foreign affairs, and defense (including the police force) but also in matters such as customs, taxes, social policy, and land issues. The representative of the monarchy, the lord-lieutenant, would serve as the leader of an executive council made up of ministers in charge of various Irish departments and would retain a veto power over legislation. Forty-two Irish MPs would continue to sit in Westminster to enable representation at the imperial table, a role that many eagerly anticipated.

Despite the rhetoric employed during election campaigns, Irish constitutional nationalism did not embrace separatism but, rather, regarded the empire in terms of its potential for Ireland. After all, Irishmen had played a crucial part in the establishment of the British Empire, especially in the ranks of the army, the navy, and the civil service. Redmond looked forward to the benefits for Ireland that a voice in imperial affairs could provide, as well as to his own role as a statesman of the empire.

A very modest form of devolved power, this proposed legislation did not address the objections and forebodings of the substantial unionist community in Ireland except for a general prohibition against the Irish parliament enacting discriminatory legislation. Welcomed by the Irish Parliamentary Party as the victorious outcome of a long battle, Irish nationalists somewhat precipitately celebrated this limited yet idealized form of self-government, while Irish unionists prepared to resist it by any means necessary. Unionists had not remained idle after the previous Home Rule crisis of 1893. They had recognized that while a Conservative Party government had remained in power, the threat against the union was held in hiatus, but if a sufficiently powerful Liberal-Irish Parliamentary Party alliance emerged in the future, that threat would reappear.

Since 1907 the Ulster Unionist Council and the Irish Unionist Alliance had coordinated their efforts through the establishment of a Committee of Unionist Associations. Led from 1910 by Edward Carson, a distinguished Dublin-born barrister, the Unionist Party in Westminster cooperated closely with the Conservatives, but on the removal of the Lords' veto power in 1911, they realized that extraparliamentary activities would be necessary in their fight against Home Rule. Unionism had always been concentrated in northeast Ulster. As its southern counterpart grew weaker, a result of the general decline in the economic and political position of its leading personnel who were predominantly landlords, Ulster unionism, led by James Craig MP intensified.

In 1910, the Orange Order had directed its members to prepare to exercise their duties in voting in that year's general election to return the Unionist Party in strength to combat the predicted deadly blow at the Union. In the event that constitutional measures were inadequate, members were warned to prepare for a struggle. The anti–Home Rule campaign was formally launched in Ulster in 1911 when the Ulster Unionist Council, after a rally at which an estimated one hundred thousand people attended, decided to resist Home Rule. Meetings were held all over the province, and just before Asquith introduced the bill for the first time in Westminster, a demonstration was held in Belfast at which the Church of Ireland primate, the moderator of the Presbyterian Church, and many members of the Conservative Party were in attendance. A male Solemn League and Covenant and a female Declaration endorsing the former were signed by nearly half a million people of Ulster birth in September 1912. These documents were a declaration of unionist intent to uphold religious and civil liberties in resisting Home Rule by any means necessary. By the beginning of 1913, as the Home Rule Bill passed its final reading in the House of Commons, the Ulster Unionist Council established volunteers into a military body, the Ulster Volunteer Force (UVF), which at once began to arm and drill in preparation for the coming conflict.

As the government procrastinated over its response to Ulster defiance, Irish nationalists consistently underestimated the resolve of the unionists, characterizing the public demonstrations and declarations as mere bluff. The foundation of the UVF with ninety thousand members shook that complacency. If unionists claimed a right to resist Home Rule by force, why should nationalists not have the right to establish their own force to demand its implementation? The Irish National Volunteers were established under the leadership of Eoin MacNeill, who had publicly called for such a development. Eight of the thirteen founding members were IRB men. The Volunteers stressed that their role was the defense of Home Rule and thus sought an alliance with the Irish Parliamentary Party, which accounted for the rapid rate of recruitment estimated at nearly two hundred thousand members in less than a year. Redmond, recognizing the dangers of allowing this movement to develop independently of the political party, successfully demanded control of the Volunteers in the summer of 1914.

The secret cabal of IRB men on the executive committee was unperturbed at what they regarded as a temporary expedient. Following the example of the UVF, although with less volume and success, the Irish National Volunteers armed themselves by gunrunning. A female auxiliary corps, Cumann na mBan (Women's League), was established to support the Volunteers. Composed of middle-class professionals, working-class women, and those of independent means, it was politically radical but was thwarted by its subservient relationship to the Volunteers. On the eve of war in Europe, two paramilitary groups were preparing for conflict over the issue of self-government, while the government vacillated in deciding on a course of action.

The Great War

The outbreak of the First World War had the immediate effect of defusing the impending domestic crisis by transferring it to the front. The implementation of the Home Rule Bill was suspended for the duration of the war. Edward Carson pledged that Ulster unionists would shed their blood for crown and empire, a sanguine demonstration of loyalty that unionists were confident would guarantee their political future. The 36th (Ulster) Division was formed in October 1914 and was composed of more than thirty thousand members of the UVF. It was decimated at the battles of the Somme in July 1916, suffering thirty-two thousand casualties by the end of the war, a blood sacrifice that Frank McGuinness explores in his extraordinary play, *Observe the Sons of Ulster Marching towards the Somme*. John Redmond, conscious of an opportunity to prove Ireland's imperial credentials, and anticipating that nationalist support for the war effort would guarantee the implementation of Home Rule, likewise pledged the Irish National Volunteers to the war effort; the majority of members supported this decision. Almost thirty thousand men joined the 10th and 16th Divisions to fight for Home Rule, but a minority of between three and ten thousand men rejected his call to fight, insisting that it was not an Irish conflict. This splinter group retained the name Irish Volunteers, while those who supported Redmond called themselves the National Volunteers. Cumann na mBan supported the Irish Volunteers. Between nationalists and unionists, Catholics and Protestants, it is estimated that more than two hundred thousand Irishmen fought in the war, of whom nearly fifty thousand died. Yet within nationalist consciousness, the contribution of Irishmen to the Great War was eclipsed by the rebellion of 1916.

The Easter Rising

The IRB had responded to the war with a decision to stage an armed rebellion. Clarke and MacDiarmada led a committee to plan the insurrection and secured the cooperation of James Connolly and his small Citizen Army. Other members of the committee included Patrick Pearse, Thomas MacDonagh, Éamonn Ceannt, and Joseph Plunkett. All were leading members of the Irish Volunteers: Pearse as director of organization, MacDonagh as director of training, Ceannt as director of communications, and Plunkett as director of military operations. Pearse and Ceannt joined the IRB in 1913; both MacDonagh and Plunkett were recruited in 1915. All poets, Pearse, MacDonagh, and Plunkett were the products of the cultural nationalist movement, especially the Gaelic League. Pearse was the editor of *An Claidheamh Soluis* from 1903 until 1909, after which he concentrated on the development of St. Enda's, his bilingual school for boys in Dublin. Originally a supporter of Home Rule, his address at a Wolfe Tone commemoration ceremony in 1913, and most notably his oration in 1915 at the funeral of Fenian Jeremiah O'Donovan Rossa (whose body had been shipped from New York for burial), when he declared that "Ireland unfree shall never be at peace," confirmed his commitment to insurrection. His avocation of blood sacrifice has been well documented by Irish historians who have recently placed him in the context of heightened

European militarism and comparative unionist rhetoric. Stating that from the graves of patriots spring living nations, Pearse believed that the Irish nation required a "cleansing and sanctifying" blood sacrifice to rejuvenate the national spirit in the fight for independence, a theme he explored in poetry and drama employing imagery from both Irish mythology and Catholicism.

While Eoin MacNeill ostensibly led the Irish Volunteers, whom he regarded as a pressure group rather than a military force, he was unaware of the IRB plot taking shape within the organization. Much of the initiative for the rebellion came from John Devoy and Clan na Gael in America who had approached Count Bernstorff, the German ambassador to the United States, in 1914 to apprise him of their intention to organize a rebellion and to request military aid. Sir Roger Casement, a British diplomat with a distinguished record of human rights activity and a recent convert to advanced Irish nationalism, was smuggled to Germany from New York to negotiate for official recognition and military aid and to raise a brigade of Irishmen from among the Allied prisoners of war.

The IRB planned to form the central core of the rebellion, which would remain completely secret until the last moment, when strategically placed members of the Brotherhood in the Volunteer movement would command the ranks to follow them into conflict. The Volunteers campaigned energetically against the war effort and recruitment to the British army, as did Arthur Griffith's pacifist party, Sinn Féin, and it is from this parallel labor that the misconception arose that resulted in the Irish Volunteers becoming labeled as "Sinn Féin Volunteers" in weekly and monthly police reports. Fear of conscription was widespread, and as the war dragged on, the IRB was hopeful of popular support for an insurrection. But the intense secrecy it nurtured as its only weapon against government informers was ultimately counterproductive. Casement eventually succeeded in procuring and shipping a consignment of dated arms and mismatched ammunition from Germany, but faulty communications (which had to be routed through Clan na Gael in New York) led to confusion over the date of arrival. The ignorance of the local population on the eve of the rebellion as to what the German ship the *Aud* (disguised as a Norwegian trawler) was patiently waiting for in Tralee Bay led to her eventual interception by the British navy. Casement himself was arrested shortly afterward, having been brought to Ireland by German submarine. Transferred to London, he was later tried for treason and executed.

The rebellion was scheduled for Easter Sunday, April 23, 1916, but the belated realization by Eoin MacNeill of what was afoot, and his attempts to halt it by countermanding a public notice of Volunteer exercises (the insurrection signal), resulted in widespread confusion. IRB commanders throughout the countryside lacked clear information, although messengers were hastily dispatched from Dublin to inform them that the supreme council had decided to go ahead with the rebellion the following day. Government authorities in Dublin Castle had heard rumors of a rising, but with no confirmation from informers within the Volunteer movement, believed that with the capture of Casement the threat had been neutralized.

On Easter Monday, just before noon, to the initial amusement and subsequent bewilderment of the pedestrians strolling about the city on that civic holiday, about fifteen hundred Volunteers and members of the Citizen Army, led by the IRB, seized a

The American newspapers gave a lot of coverage to Ireland's Easter Rising in 1916. This Wide World photograph from the *New York World-Telegram and Sun* shows British troops marching Irish prisoners west along Bachelors Walk on the north side of the Liffey River in the aftermath of the rebellion. (Library of Congress, Prints and Photographs Division, LC-USZ62-115086)

number of buildings in Dublin (the majority of which had little apparent strategic value compared to Trinity College and Dublin Castle, which were ignored). They declared the establishment of the Irish Republic and held their positions for five days, during which a British gunboat shelled the city center from Dublin Bay. Cumann na mBan played an active role in first aid and delivering dispatches. Forced to capitulate to prevent further civilian deaths (of 450 fatalities, most were civilians), Pearse took responsibility for issuing the order to surrender that was delivered to the various outposts by Cumann na mBan member Elizabeth Farrell.

The government declared martial law and appointed General Sir John Maxwell as military governor. Public responses varied. There was widespread confusion and rumors based on lack of information. People wondered about the identity of the rebels and the purpose of their actions while Irishmen were dying at the front for the sake of self-government. Some were convinced that it was inspired by socialism. Others, including John Redmond, characterized the insurrection as a German plot, an interpretation that found fertile ground in the minds of the public.

The severity of the government's response to treason during wartime was predictable, yet shortsighted. Maxwell supervised the arrest of thousands of suspected "Sinn Féiners" (a term increasingly used as a catchphrase for advanced nationalists), nearly two thousand of whom were immediately deported without trial to internment camps and prisons in Britain. One hundred and seventy rebels were secretly court-martialed in Dublin. Ninety death sentences were pronounced, although seventy-five of these were commuted to life imprisonment. These included Éamon de Valera, born in New York to an Irish mother, and (to her indignation if also relief) Countess Constance Markievicz, because of her gender. Fifteen executions were carried out by degrees between May 3rd and May 12th. The names of the seven who signed the Proclamation of the Republic—Clarke, MacDiarmada, Connolly, Pearse, Plunkett, MacDonagh, and Ceannt—became familiar as bafflement slowly gave way to anger at the indiscriminatory nature of arrests and distress at the protracted executions.

The Rise of Sinn Féin

The leadership of the Irish Parliamentary Party rapidly anticipated the consequences of a serious swing in public opinion and advised the British government that Home Rule must be implemented immediately in order to prevent political polarization. Contingent upon compromise between constitutional nationalists, who were fast losing their traditional support to advanced nationalism as the rebels became martyrs, and Carson, who insisted on permanent exclusion for six counties of Ulster from Home Rule, the negotiations conducted by Lloyd George quickly broke down. Partition was not a new proposal. It had been raised in the summer of 1912 when a Liberal Party MP suggested that Home Rule should not apply to the four Protestant-dominated counties of northeast Ulster: Antrim, Armagh, Down, and Londonderry. Carson countered six months later, as the legislation moved inexorably toward law, with a proposal that all nine Ulster counties should be permanently excluded from the measure.

By the summer of 1914, the Irish Parliamentary Party had conceded the concept of temporary partition with a suggested scheme of opting out of Home Rule on a county basis, which they anticipated would result in several Ulster counties with strong nationalist populations, such as Donegal, Cavan, Fermanagh, Tyrone, and Monaghan, deciding to accept Home Rule. The Unionist Party still insisted on the permanent exclusion of the province, although in principle they were prepared to surrender the counties of Cavan, Donegal, and Monaghan. Permanent exclusion of the remaining six counties was their final offer before the matter was suspended for the duration of the war.

By the end of the war and the next general election in 1918, the Irish Parliamentary Party had irrevocably lost its political mandate, as a significantly increased electorate due to the extension of the franchise voted for the program of advanced nationalism represented by Sinn Féin, which had been modified as a political party to campaign for recognition of the Republic. Griffith's party had originally supported the moderate political goal of dual monarchy but had also contained within its composition several militant elements. That inherent separatism came to the fore in the aftermath of 1916, aided by the fact that Sinn Féin was mistakenly associated by the government and in the popular mind with the rebellion. Sinn Féin provided an organizational umbrella for many aspects of moderate and advanced nationalism—monarchists, disenchanted parliamentarians, militant republicans, feminists, and socialists—as well as addressing issues of popular import, such as the fear of conscription and agrarian crime.

The only surviving male commandant of the rebellion was Éamon de Valera who, while imprisoned, emerged as the leading republican voice. His agenda emphasized securing international recognition of the Republic at the peace conferences following the end of the war. In particular, he was confident that America, just entering the war, would endorse Ireland's claim to be an independent nation and pressure Great Britain into acknowledging it. While conceding the power of the Irish-American political voice, given that America and Britain were allies in warfare, and that both Clan na Gael and Sinn Féin had engaged in pro-German activities, the chances of achieving American recognition for the Irish Republic were bleak.

De Valera was born in New York in 1882 but was raised from the age of three by his mother's family in Limerick. An enthusiastic member of the Gaelic League and a teacher by profession, he joined the Irish Volunteers in 1913. Upon his release from prison in the summer of 1917, due to a second government amnesty for Irish prisoners designed to create a more favorable climate for political negotiation, de Valera stood successfully as a Sinn Féin candidate in a Clare by-election. Supported by the Volunteer movement in whose uniform he campaigned, his was the third victory over the Irish Parliamentary Party within a year for abstentionist Sinn Féin candidates. Personally a devout Catholic, de Valera's electoral rhetoric stressed the essential relationship of religion and patriotism, smoothing over the traditional hostility the church had expressed for republicanism. A détente between the political movement and the church was evident in the aftermath of the 1916 rebellion, when periodicals and newspapers produced hagiographical treatments of the executed rebels as Catholic martyrs, while the members of Cumann na mBan under the presidency of Countess Markievicz organized commemorative ceremonies. De Valera skillfully reassured most of the hierarchy of the essential conservatism of the Sinn Féin movement, although Cardinal Michael Logue spoke openly about the immorality of utopian rebellion.

In October 1917 at the Sinn Féin *Ard Fheis* (national convention), de Valera skillfully trumped Griffith in securing leadership of the party and was the sole architect of a formula designed to smooth over the uneasy alliance of the various factions. Sinn Féin's agreed mission was to secure international recognition for an independent Irish Republic. Once that was achieved, the Irish people would participate in a referendum to decide the future form of government. Abstention from Westminster, appeals to the postwar peace talks, and passive pressure were the methods endorsed by the delegates in pursuit of this aim. Alternative methods of achieving their aims were not overtly addressed, but the threat of force remained an option, given the close relationship with the Irish Volunteers who, at their own national convention on the day following the Sinn Féin Ard Fheis, also elected de Valera as their president. While another rebellion was not anticipated, the Volunteer executive reserved the power to declare war if the issue of conscription was forced.

Several key members of Sinn Féin occupied powerful positions in the Volunteers, and vice versa. Cathal Brugha, who like so many had progressed from the GAA and the Gaelic League into the Volunteers in 1913, was elected its chief of staff. Supporting the goals and methods that Sinn Féin had agreed upon, the role of the Volunteers as envisioned by de Valera and Brugha was to act as political lever rather than as militant army. De Valera recognized both the potential and the limitations of armed resistance. The Volunteers could not inflict a formal military defeat on the British army, but they could be strategically employed in combination with political action to convince the government to recognize the demands of Irish nationalists.

The IRB pursued a different path, placing little faith in a modus operandi that excluded revolution. The more clandestine recovery of the Brotherhood paralleled the renovation of the Volunteers and Sinn Féin. In 1909, Michael Collins joined the IRB in London, where he worked as a civil servant. He returned to Ireland early in 1916 to take part in the rebellion. Interned in the aftermath with hundreds of others in a Welsh prison camp, Collins set about quietly reorganizing the Brotherhood and recruiting fellow prisoners, some of whom had no radical political background while others were members of Sinn Féin and the Volunteers. Released toward the end of 1916 as part of the first government amnesty, Collins quickly joined the supreme council of the IRB. The established policy of secret infiltration was continued, as IRB members sought significant positions in both Sinn Féin and the Volunteers. Collins occupied Pearse's former position as director of organization and orchestrated the appointment of members of the Brotherhood to most of the executive positions. In 1917, with the death of Thomas Ashe, the president of the supreme council, as a result of forced feeding while on a prison hunger strike, Collins became the leader of the IRB. The political and military wings of nationalism were out of sync, despite de Valera's presidency of both the political party and the Volunteers. He pursued a program of conservative republicanism conducted through political pressure, while Collins, committed to further insurrection, controlled the IRB and covertly gained control of the Volunteers.

The political negotiations initiated by Lloyd George, which had resulted in de Valera's release from prison in the summer of 1917, dragged on until April 1918. Chaired by Horace Plunkett and attended by one hundred delegates, this convention was an exercise in futility. Sinn Féin boycotted it, while Ulster unionists retained their antipathy to Home Rule and reiterated their demand for exclusion. Southern unionists, conscious of the splendid isolation of their northern counterparts, belatedly accepted that their future lay in cooperation with Redmond's party and agreed to participate in a domestic parliament, but it remained a concession in principle only as Home Rule became increasingly passé among Irish nationalists. The death of John Redmond in March 1918 and the government's decision to implement conscription in Ireland confirmed the demise of constitutional nationalism. The convention was doomed to irrelevance as it refused to recognize the new political priorities, but the difficult political issues with which it sincerely wrestled continued to defy resolution in the following decades.

The conscription crisis solidified Sinn Féin's usurpation of nationalist politics. Despite dwindling rates of recruitment, Ireland had been excluded from conscription, which had been in force in Britain since 1915. With the German offensive on the western front in the spring of 1918, the government moved to apply conscription in

Ireland with a vague and pointless gesture in the direction of implementing Home Rule to sweeten the pill. This was met by a successful anti-conscription campaign led by Sinn Féin, the Irish Volunteers, and Cumann na mBan, with the cooperation of the Irish Parliamentary Party, which withdrew from Westminster in protest, and the influential participation of the Catholic Church. The government hastily responded with the discovery of a "German plot," a clumsy and transparent claim of evidence that Sinn Féin was plotting another rising. De Valera, Griffith, and seventy-three others were imprisoned, while Sinn Féin and the Gaelic League were suppressed. In the general election to Westminster held in December 1918, abstentionist Sinn Féin won seventy-three seats, many of them uncontested, while the Irish Parliamentary Party in a humiliating and terminal performance won six. Ulster Unionists returned to Westminster with twenty-six seats.

Those Sinn Féin members who had won seats and were not in prison, met in Dublin in January 1919 as Dáil Éireann (parliament of Ireland) and proceeded to adopt a provisional constitution, ratifying the declaration of the Irish Republic in 1916. This assembly issued a vain appeal for recognition to the nations at the peace conference in Paris to which it sent delegates. De Valera escaped from prison with Collins's help in February. Before furtively making his way to America where he intended to campaign for funds and political recognition, he attended the second meeting of the Dáil in April and was elected Príomh Aire (prime minister). He appointed Arthur Griffith as minister of home affairs and Cathal Brugha as minister of defense. Finance was Michael Collins's political portfolio, while Countess Markievicz became minister of labour and Eoin MacNeill was in charge of industry.

The infrequent and hasty meetings of the Dáil, many of whose members were busy evading arrest, were initially ignored by the Conservative Party–dominated coalition government led by Lloyd George, which was preoccupied with demobilization and peace negotiations. However, the 1914 Home Rule Act, which had been suspended for the duration of the war, was now due to come into effect once a decision had been made about Ulster. Against a background of escalating insurrection in Ireland orchestrated by Collins's IRB-dominated Volunteers, Dáil Éireann was proclaimed an illegal assembly in the late summer of 1919. In the absence of any nationalist voice at Westminster, a cabinet committee chaired by Walter Long, a former leader of the Unionist Party, recommended the implementation of legislation to establish two Irish parliaments. Although it was successful in achieving exclusion from a Dublin parliament, the Unionist Party found itself in the ironic position of accepting the principle of self-government after having campaigned so arduously to avoid it.

Partition

However reluctant some were to accept self-government, the benefits of a devolved state with a Protestant majority within Great Britain proved attractive to those who mistrusted the long-term commitment of the British government to protect their political future. Ulster unionists prevailed in their desire for a six-county zone, athough

Éamon de Valera (1882–1975) dominated Irish politics in the twentieth century. Born in New York City and raised in Ireland by his mother's family, he escaped execution and prison in the aftermath of the 1916 Rising. He spent eighteen months in the United States between 1919 and 1920 raising funds for the independence struggle and seeking to influence American politics in favor of an Irish Republic, picking up an honorary degree from Catholic University of America on February 26, 1920. He rebounded from political darkness in the aftermath of the civil war to found a new political party and to legislatively modify Anglo-Irish relations. He served successive terms as Taoiseach and as president of the Republic of Ireland. (Library of Congress, Prints and Photographs Division, LC-USZ62-123528)

this was naturally unpopular with those unionists who lived in the three excluded counties on the periphery of the province. The argument for six counties was based on compromise: the full nine counties of the province would result in a very slim unionist majority (given the strong nationalist character of Cavan, Donegal and Monaghan), while the four counties that formed the core of unionism were too small an area to justify a regional parliament. While both Fermanagh and Tyrone contained nationalist majorities, they would be contained by the unionist strength of Antrim, Armagh, Down, and Londonderry. The Government of Ireland Act, which became law in 1920, established two parliaments and also a Council of Ireland that was designed to draw its membership from and promote cooperation between the two regional parliaments, providing a bridge that would evolve eventually into a single parliament, thereby ending partition of the island. As before, Westminster reserved power over foreign affairs, external trade, and finance, and each region was to elect a small number of representatives to sit in the imperial parliament. Each parliament was to consist of a senate of twenty-six members and a lower house of fifty-two members elected by proportional representation to ensure a role for the respective minorities.

The inaugural election to the Northern Irish parliament took place in May 1921 with the return of forty unionists, six Sinn Féin representatives, and six nationalists to the lower house. Sinn Féin continued its policy of abstention, and the constitutional nationalist representatives followed suit, thus leaving the unionist members led by Prime Minister Sir James Craig in control of proceedings. The border dividing Northern Ireland from the rest of the country was drawn along county lines, excluding areas with strong unionist populations while including nationalist communities. The partition of Ireland, for so long a reality in perspective and practice, was thus formally accomplished in 1920.

The War of Independence

While this legislation also provided for a matching parliament in Dublin, the concept of a limited measure of Home Rule was obsolete in the south, given the developments in Irish nationalism since 1916 and the current state of guerrilla warfare initiated by the Irish Volunteers the previous year. On the very day that the Dáil first met in January 1919, the inaugural event of a protracted and patchy conflict between militant republicans and the forces of the government took place when two policemen were killed in a Volunteer ambush. Increasingly known as the Irish Republican Army (IRA), given that the Dáil had ratified the republic, they conducted guerrilla-style arms raids and attacks on the police force throughout 1919 and 1920, but the frequency and effectiveness of action depended on the initiative of local commanders.

Strongest in Munster and in the midland counties of Longford and Westmeath, the conflict intensified sharply during 1920 as the government responded by deploying police reinforcements. An auxiliary division of the Royal Irish Constabulary (RIC) was created, drawing on demobilized officers from the British army, while a second force made up of former soldiers were quickly dubbed the "Black and Tans" in reference to their khaki and dark-green uniforms. Reprisal and retaliation were committed in an escalating pattern of violence and terror, which until the end of 1920 the British government refused to legitimize as a war by sending in the army. By July 1921, 405 policemen and 160 soldiers had been killed by the IRA, while there were 750 fatalities among civilians and the IRA.

Ignoring the political provisions of the Government of Ireland Act, Sinn Féin, with the help of Cumann na mBan, proceeded to usurp judicial, governmental, and administrative functions. It established its own system of courts, police, departments, commissions, and local government to which nationalists adhered. In Dublin, Collins established a group known as the "squad" to eliminate detectives (or "G-men") from Dublin Castle who threatened his formidable intelligence system.

The first "bloody Sunday" of Irish history occurred in November 1920 when Collins's squad killed thirteen British intelligence agents who had replaced the defunct detective division. In reprisal, the Auxiliaries opened fire that afternoon upon a crowd at a Gaelic football match in Dublin's Croke Park. Twelve people died. Attacks by the "flying columns" of the IRA, using guerrilla tactics borrowed from the Boers, met with brutal reprisals upon local communities by the Black and Tans and Auxiliaries. Desperately short of arms and ammunition, the estimated five thousand active members of the IRA had the advantage of being able to strike rapidly and disappear, sheltered by a supportive population. The police reinforcements responded by burning towns and villages. The IRA operated largely without reference to the Dáil, which only nominally exercised control over the military wing of republicanism, although several of its leaders, such as Michael Collins, were elected representatives. Martial law was declared at the end of 1920.

De Valera had left for America in June 1919, where he aimed to raise funds and to use the Irish-American political organizations to exert pressure on an unsympathetic President Woodrow Wilson to recognize the Irish Republic. Although he was successful in his first goal, he was ineffective in the political sphere, apart from rousing propaganda delivered on his comprehensive tour. Wilson was indifferent to the Irish claim, disliked Clan na Gael for its pro-German activities during the war, and was preoccupied by ill health and the League of Nations. Clan na Gael's political effectiveness was debatable, given its antipathy to Wilson and internal power struggles as Joseph McGarrity clashed with Devoy's heir apparent, Judge Daniel Cohalan. Cohalan strove to use the considerable fund-raising efforts of the Friends of Irish Freedom, the popular front of Irish-American nationalism founded in 1916, to wage a battle against the League of Nations, but McGarrity believed that the Irish Victory Fund should go toward the struggle in Ireland. A compromise was reluctantly reached, by which a quarter of a million dollars was earmarked for supporting the political struggle in Ireland, and the Irish Victory Fund's activities temporarily ceased in order to facilitate a bond drive in aid of the republic. Bonds were issued for purchase on an ascending scale from $10 to $10,000. Some $600,000 were was raised in New York City, where the first bond was purchased by the Gaelic League, and by the time de Valera returned to Ireland toward the end of 1920, $10 million had been collected.

Sinn Féin participated in the elections held in May 1921 as a result of the Government of Ireland Act to reiterate its mandate. The 124 Sinn Féin candidates were returned unopposed to form the second Dáil Éireann, which sat from August 1921 to June 1922. With partition an accomplished fact, and as fatalities increased and martial law failed to break the IRA, Lloyd George, ever mindful of negative public opinion, recognized that his government would have to negotiate with Sinn Féin. The conciliatory tenor of King George V's speech as he opened the Belfast parliament that summer allowed Lloyd George to invite de Valera to exploratory talks. A truce was in effect from July 1921 as de Valera went to London to consider political solutions. But a united republic was an impossible objective.

While expressing support for the concept of unity, Lloyd George offered dominion status (self-government within the empire) for the twenty-six counties, stressing that Northern Ireland's constitutional status would remain unaffected except with the consent of its parliament. This was superficially rejected by de Valera, who nonetheless realized that partition was a political fact and that conceding a republic was at present unfeasible from an imperial perspective. The channels of communication remained open throughout the following months as a lengthy and detailed correspondence between Lloyd George and de Valera concluded with an invitation to negotiations in London to discuss Irish national aspirations and their relationship to the British Empire.

Choosing a delegation proved difficult. For reasons that are still debated by historians and biographers, de Valera insisted on remaining in Dublin. Some scholars attribute this to his realization that the delegation would fail to achieve a republic and his determination not to be the fated messenger. Others argue that jealousy of Collins's popularity and legendary exploits prompted de Valera to set him up as the scapegoat. His own convoluted explanation of why he refused to lead the delegation lay in his position as president of the republic (a title he evolved from his position as prime minister of the Dáil). As such, he cast himself as the symbol of the republic and declared that participation in negotiation would compromise that position, a fairly feeble argument given his previous talks with Lloyd George. He also persuaded his cabinet colleagues that by staying in Dublin he would give the delegation a practical fallback position by having to consult with him at each stage of negotiation.

The Anglo-Irish Treaty

Arthur Griffith headed the delegation of plenipotentiaries that included a suspicious and reluctant Michael Collins. Robert Barton, Eamon Duggan, and George Gavan Duffy—chosen for their economic, legal, and constitutional qualifications—completed the negotiating team. The experienced and savvy British delegation was led by Lloyd George and included Winston Churchill, Austen Chamberlain, and Lord Birkenhead. De Valera had developed a concept that he called "external association," whereby Ireland would be associated with the British Empire but would not be a member of it. This was rejected by Lloyd George, who correctly interpreted it as the essence of republicanism with a new title. External association would remove Ireland from direct allegiance to the crown and establish political sovereignty, a formula de Valera hoped would satisfy the aspirations of those sworn to defend the republic, and which he persuaded the delegation to reintroduce despite Lloyd George's emphatic rejection.

Two months of negotiation produced a dramatic moment when Lloyd George, threatening immediate and terrible war within three days, urged the Irish delegates to sign a treaty that established a twenty-six-county Irish Free State within the empire, granted fiscal autonomy, and provided for a boundary commission to examine the border between Northern Ireland and the proposed Free State. Although the agreement was applicable to all of Ireland, thus recognizing the concept of essential unity, provision was made for the six counties of Northern Ireland to opt out, which they promptly did. The provision in the Government of Ireland Act for a Council of Ireland was also included in the agreement. The British government reserved access to specified naval facilities. Religious freedom was to be guaranteed. Faced with a choice between the treaty with its restrictions on political sovereignty and the resumption of a war that Collins knew the IRA could not win, the delegates signed the articles of agreement with misgivings on December 6, 1921.

Bitter divisions during cabinet meetings while negotiations were ongoing provided the overture for the reception of the treaty. On December 3, de Valera had rejected the draft treaty and sent his frustrated negotiators back to vainly present external association again. At the next cabinet meeting on December 8, when the delegates presented the signed articles of agreement, de Valera, Cathal Brugha, and Austin Stack voted to reject, while Griffith, Collins, Barton, and W. T. Cosgrave voted to accept. A secret meeting of the IRA executive endorsed their leader's belief that it was the best deal available and one that could be built on to eventually achieve the united republic.

The Dáil, which met on December 14 and 19, was characterized by rancorous debate. Extremists simply rejected the agreement because it did not provide for a united republic, while others, led by de Valera, sought to reject it in favor of yet again presenting external association. Troubled principally by the oath of allegiance to the crown, they argued that Irish independence of political action would be seriously restricted. Griffith and Collins emphasized that the concept of external association had been categorically and repeatedly rejected by the British government, which was prepared to declare all-out war if the treaty was rejected. Griffith stressed the benefits: British troops would evacuate the twenty-six-county Free State, which would exercise fiscal and political sovereignty symbolized by its own flag and army. He argued that the Boundary Commission would significantly revise the border between the two states, while economic considerations and the Council of Ireland would lead to mutual cooperation and eventual unity. Membership of the empire, which was clearly evolving toward equality and independence, was an asset rather than a disadvantage. Collins, in particular, was passionate in his defense of a measure that he defined as a stepping-stone to the republic and in his vain appeal for unity among nationalists.

On January 7, 1922, the Dáil voted in favor of accepting the treaty by sixty-four votes to fifty-seven, to which de Valera responded by resigning and withdrawing his supporters. Griffith was elected as prime minister of the Dáil, while Collins continued as minister of finance and Richard Mulcahy took over from Brugha as minister of defense. Under the terms of the treaty, ratified by the British parliament in March, a provisional government was established from the remaining members of the second Dáil. Collins was elected chairman of this interim body, which was responsible for overseeing the transition of power and drafting a constitution reflecting the articles of agreement. Meanwhile, Griffith's government continued to operate until elections and the ratification of a written constitution enabled the end of dual government.

Civil War

In the deliberate interim between the establishment of the provisional government and the summer elections, the factions polarized. Public opinion was generally in favor of a measure that would end the violence, remove the hated Black and Tans, and establish an Irish government. While Collins had convinced the IRA executive to accept the treaty, the ranks split on the issue. Many agreed with Collins's pragmatism and long-term perspective, but others were passionate in their rejection of what they regarded as the betrayal of those who had fought and died for the republic. Those who were pro-treaty formed the new army of the Free State, while the "Irregulars" refused to recognize the government and, in April 1922, seized and occupied the Four Courts in the heart of Dublin. Cumann na mBan also split with most of its members rejecting the treaty. De Valera formed an anti-treaty party, Cumann na Poblachta (Republican Party), but he mistrusted and was mistrusted by the military extremists whose actions made the slide toward hostilities seem inevitable. Attempts by Collins and de Valera to find stable ground for political compromise failed, as Winston Churchill rejected the first draft of the new constitution in which Collins had subtly worked the essence of external association in the hope of defusing republican hostility to the treaty.

On June 16, 1922, the elections returned a majority of pro-treaty candidates: fifty-eight from pro-treaty Sinn Féin, seventeen Labour candidates, seven independents, four southern unionists representing Dublin University seats, and seven from the recently established Farmers' Party. Thirty-five anti-treaty Sinn Féin candidates were elected. Thus 93 out of 128 new Teachtaí Dála (Dáil deputies) supported the agreement. Arthur Griffith was elected president of the Executive Council in the new Free State government. The new constitution of Saorstát Éireann (Irish Free State) established a lower house, which retained the name Dáil Éireann, to be henceforth elected by proportional representation based on universal suffrage. An upper house, Seanad Éireann (Senate of Ireland), was made up of thirty candidates elected by the Dáil and thirty nominated by the president of the Executive Council to represent the interests of the Protestant minority. W. B. Yeats served as a senator from 1922 to 1928, while Douglas Hyde became a senator in 1925.

On June 22, 1922, Field Marshal Sir Henry Wilson, a native of Longford, security adviser to the Northern Irish government, and Unionist Party MP for North Down, was assassinated by two IRA men in London. Although the origins of the order to kill Wilson remain uncertain, the British government reacted to his death with an ultimatum to the Free State government to deal with the anti-treaty faction led by Rory O'Connor that had repudiated civil authority and seized the Four Courts the previous April. Spurred finally and obviously reluctantly to action by the kidnapping of J. J. O'Connell, the deputy chief of staff of the Free State army, Collins as commander in chief ordered an attack, which within a week ruined the building that housed irreplaceable historical manuscripts and thus ended the republican occupation. One of the fatalities was Cathal Brugha.

With the defeat of his party and position in the recent election, and with the military action of the new government, de Valera and his followers formally aligned themselves with the republican militants. Declaring the Free State and its institutions illegitimate, republicans established an ineffective underground government headed by de Valera and prepared for civil war that ensued throughout the twenty-six counties, although the heart of resistance lay in Munster. Badly armed, limited in numbers, employing familiar guerrilla tactics, and lacking the civilian support that had buoyed IRA efforts during the War of Independence, the Irregulars were no match for the superior manpower and resources of the Free State army. By August, republicans had been routed by Collins's troops throughout Munster. Although pockets of IRA resistance remained during the following months, and the order to cease hostilities did not come until May 1923, the outcome of the conflict was obvious by the end of that summer.

Yet the fledgling Free State government endured other crises that summer. On August 12, 1922, Arthur Griffith suddenly died from a cerebral hemorrhage. Michael Collins was killed ten days later during an ambush by Irregulars at Béal na mBláth in west Cork. Their successors in government—W. T. Cosgrave as prime minister, Kevin O'Higgins as minister for justice and external affairs, and Richard Mulcahy as commander in chief of the armed forces—implemented draconian emergency powers to suppress republican dissent. Army tribunals were empowered to dispense punishments such as internment, imprisonment, and execution for offenses against the government, including the unlawful possession of firearms. Erskine Childers, a former Dáil minister who had used his yacht to smuggle guns for the Irish Volunteers in 1914, was executed for possession of a pistol that had been a gift from Michael Collins. In December 1922, Sean Hales, TD (*Teachta Dála,* Irish for Dáil Deputy), brother of prominent republican Tom Hales, was shot by the IRA. The government responded by executing leading republican prisoners, including Rory O'Connor and Liam Mellows. Between November 1922 and April 1923, the government executed seventy-seven prisoners. In all, the civil war counted for approximately twelve hundred deaths. More than eleven thousand republicans, including four hundred members of Cumann na mBan, were interned, although most of them were released over the following year. The IRA did not surrender its arms in May 1923 but, rather, declared a cessation of hostilities. Republicans continued to regard the Free State government as an illegitimate body and remained committed to the goal of subverting an executive and legislature founded on what they regarded as the betrayal of the treaty.

Northern Ireland

Sir James Craig and the unionists of Northern Ireland had successfully resisted attempts by Lloyd George to pressure them into political concessions during the treaty negotiations, arguing that the Government of Ireland Act was from their perspective a final settlement. Yet the treaty was greeted with dismay by unionists, as the essential unity of Ireland had been recognized in an article that applied the agreement to the entire country with provision for the six counties to opt out and the establishment of a Boundary Commission to examine the border between the two states. Political and sectarian violence was rife in the new state. IRA activities increased against the army and police force as thousands of Catholics were driven from their homes. High unemployment levels, fear of socialism, and sectarian tension resulted in the mass expulsion of more than five thousand Catholics and nearly two thousand suspect Protestants from the Belfast shipyards in the summer of 1920. Riots, arson, and murder left one hundred people dead in Belfast in 1921. Between 1920 and 1922, political and sectarian violence in Northern Ireland accounted for 428 deaths and 1,766 wounded.

Augmenting the thirteen units of the British army and the new police force, the Royal Ulster Constabulary (RUC), the Ulster Special Constabulary was established in September 1920, with the consent of the British government. Three classes of constables (A, full-time paid members; B, part-time paid auxiliaries; and C, volunteer reservists) were created, composed mainly of former UVF members. An entirely Protestant force, which frequently engaged in sectarian violence against Catholics, it was effective in containing IRA activity, while Craig's government introduced a Civil Authorities (Special Powers) Act in 1922 that enabled internment without trial, prohibited assembly, and enforced a strict curfew. The possession of firearms was punishable by flogging, while the minister of home affairs had unspecified discretionary powers in preserving law and order. While one-third of the places in the new RUC were initially reserved for the nationalist minority of the state, nationalists repeated their abstention from parliament with a boycott of the new police force, which as a result was dominated by unionists.

The refusal by nationalists to recognize the legitimacy of the state or to participate in any of its evolving institutions was met with concerted sectarian discrimination by a government that viewed them as essentially disloyal and subversive. Although nationalists comprised about one-third of Northern Ireland's population, the government's statements regarding inclusion and equality were shallow. Instead, priority was given to establishing a Protestant state for a Protestant people. This, in turn, contributed to the increasing alienation of nationalists from the state. The vicious sectarian and political cycles showed no signs of change under new management. As civil war dominated life in the twenty-six counties, the government of the six counties concentrated on consolidating the institutions and powers of their state and suppressing the IRA, which in Northern Ireland set aside the split over the treaty in its campaign against British and unionist forces.

The Boundary Commission finally met toward the end of 1924. It was composed of Eoin MacNeill, representing the Free State; Justice Richard Feetham of the South African Supreme Court, representing the British government; and Belfast lawyer Joseph R. Fisher, who represented Northern Ireland but was appointed by the British government, as the Northern Irish government refused to cooperate with what it viewed as an attack on its territory. Feetham interpreted the specific clause of the treaty relating to the functions of the commission to exclude alteration of the entire boundary. Rather, he examined the economic and geographic considerations that might lead to a limited alteration of the border. After a year of deliberation, he recommended that part of South Armagh and slivers of Fermanagh be transferred to the Free State but that the strongly nationalist area of south Down remain part of Northern Ireland, while a section of east Donegal be transferred from the Free State to Northern Ireland. In terms of people, the Free State would gain about twenty-seven thousand

Catholics but surrender over four thousand Protestants and twenty-seven hundred Catholics.

When these conclusions were leaked to an English newspaper, public opinion in the Free State was outraged by the limitations of the gains, the continued exclusion of nationalist areas, and, worst of all, the surrendering of territory and Catholics to Northern Ireland. Eoin MacNeill resigned. W. T. Cosgrave hurriedly met with James Craig and English Prime Minister Stanley Baldwin in London. The outcome of the meeting was the suppression of the commission's recommendations. This left the border unchanged, transferred the moot Council of Ireland's powers to the Northern Irish government, and thus ended potential cross-border cooperation and canceled the Free State's obligation to contribute to the British national debt. Envisioned as a measure to undermine partition, the Boundary Commission bolstered it.

Sinn Féin maintained its abstentionist position as IRA activity decreased after 1925, but for Northern Irish constitutional nationalists the failure of the Boundary Commission was a bitter experience that alerted them to the permanence of partition and to the need for a nationalist voice in parliament. In 1926, a former Irish Parliamentary Party MP, Joseph Devlin, led five nationalists into the Belfast parliament and was shortly joined by five more who reconsidered their abstentionist positions in 1927. But this Nationalist Party was not strong enough to offer effective opposition to the government, and it further declined as changes in the electoral system were implemented. The Government of Ireland Act had provided for a proportional representation system of voting in order to represent minority interests, but the passive resistance of Sinn Féin—which stood for election yet refused to participate in government—led to the abolition of proportional representation in local government in 1922 and parliamentary elections in 1929. Electoral boundaries were modified (gerrymandered) in favor of unionism, and by 1924 unionists controlled all but two local government councils.

The switch to the British electoral system strengthened unionist representation in their own parliament while eliminating the electoral prospects of independents and smaller parties. Unionists consistently held ten to twelve of the thirteen seats reserved for Northern Ireland in Westminster. In Lord Craigavon's (Craig became a viscount in 1927) view, one was either a unionist or a subversive, and with the abolition of proportional representation, a unionist monopoly of political power was confirmed. By 1932, Devlin's Nationalist Party had again withdrawn from participation in parliament, convinced that the policy of the government was to pursue sectarianism.

Relations between Catholics and Protestants, nationalists and unionists continued to worsen over the following decades as unionist dominance over every aspect of life became more deeply entrenched. Nationalists were perceived as the enemies of the state, and discrimination in employment and allocation of housing was thus justifiable in terms of proven loyalty versus subversion. Unemployment rose as agriculture and the shipbuilding and linen industries declined, with an average of 19 percent of the labor force unemployed from 1923 until 1930 and approximately 27 percent during the 1930s. Health conditions were poor, and the availability of public housing fell far short of demand. Despite such economic difficulties, the sectarian division of society and politics in Northern Ireland prevented the development of the Labour Party, which never won more than three or four seats in parliament, mistrusted as it was by nationalists and unionists alike.

Seasonal sectarian violence between the two communities continued unabated, peaking in the summer months when the Orange Order triumphantly celebrated past and present victories over Catholics in a series of provocative marches. An attack on an Orange march in 1931 resulted in a wave of violent reprisals, while in July 1935 rioting in Belfast resulted in nine deaths and hundreds were driven from their homes. The British government, although ultimately in control of the devolved government in its new parliament building at Stormont, chose to abdicate its responsibilities toward the nationalist minority of the state over the following decades by adopting the official position that domestic problems required domestic solutions.

The Free State

In 1923, the pro-treaty element of Sinn Féin, which had been elected to the third Dáil the previous summer, reconstituted themselves as Cumann na nGaedheal (Irish Party) under the leadership of Griffith's successor, W. T. Cosgrave. Contesting its first election in August 1923, Cosgrave's new party won sixty-three seats and was supported in government by representatives of the Farmers' Party. Those elected as independents, including some southern unionists and former Home Rulers, were somewhat critical of Cumann na nGaedheal but supportive of the treaty and constitution on which the government was based. The Labour Party, despite a strong showing in the 1922 election, failed to capitalize upon that success, capturing only fourteen seats in 1923. The explanation for its decline lay in ideological disputes and internal splits that coincided with the return of Jim Larkin from the United States and his subsequent clashes with union leaders. Added to factionalism, economic depression led to high unemployment and decreases in social benefits and wages, which the trade unions were unable to prevent.

The main opposition to Cumann na nGaedheal remained outside the Dáil as those thirty-five anti-treaty Sinn Féin TDs elected in 1922 refused to take their seats in a government that they regarded as illegitimate. With the formation of Cumann na nGaedheal, Sinn Féin, now in its third incarnation, solely represented anti-treaty republicans led by de Valera who contested the 1923 election, winning forty-four seats. They continued their policy of nonparticipation as Cumann na nGaedheal formed a one-party government with no formal opposition in the Dáil, but de Valera was quick to realize that principled opposition outside the legislature was a limited policy. In November 1925, suspicious of his political intentions, the IRA withdrew support. At its Ard Fheis in March 1926, Sinn Féin rejected de Valera's proposal to enter the Dáil if the oath of allegiance to the monarchy were removed. Followed by approximately 50 percent of the Sinn Féin TDs and local party branches, de Valera founded a new republican party, Fianna Fáil (Warriors of Ireland), which campaigned against the oath of allegiance to the crown and supported a program of economic and social development.

Cumann na nGaedheal had faced the important task of state building with fortitude if with limited imagination, reorganizing the civil service, government departments, the legal system, and local government with efficiency but departing only slightly from the British models they had inherited. A new unarmed police force, Garda Síochána (Guardians of the Peace), was established in 1922. The reduction of the army, which had swollen during the civil war, was a priority that Kevin O'Higgins briskly accomplished in 1924, despite the serious opposition of senior officers and the resentment of those being demobilized.

The economy was a more intractable problem. Agriculture, the backbone of the economy, suffered serious recession as a result of the postwar slump in prices and the loss of British markets. Cosgrave's government committed itself to completing the transfer of land ownership to those who farmed it. Under the direction of Patrick Hogan as minister for agriculture, the 1923 Land Act established compulsory purchase of land from the few remaining landlords in the twenty-six counties, thus further depleting the small southern Protestant population, which decreased by 3 percent in the first decade of the Free State's existence. By the 1930s, Protestants accounted for just over 7 percent of the population. Agricultural production standards were targeted, and by 1929 the value of agricultural exports had significantly improved. Industry was limited in the Free State, and the government did little to encourage its development, although some protective tariffs were imposed on goods. Unemployment was high at about 17 percent, while an estimated one hundred thousand people emigrated in 1924 and 1925. The one achievement in the industrial sphere was the adoption of an electrification scheme and the establishment of the state-sponsored Electricity Supply Board.

Culturally, as the new state strove to assert its separate identity, great emphasis was placed on reviving the Irish language, which had continued to decline despite the initiative of the Gaelic League. The constitution specified that Irish was the national language, and the government committed itself to making the language a compulsory subject in secondary education. Financial incentives were offered for teacher training and for teaching all subjects through the language. Examinations were weighted in favor of candidates who answered in Irish. Steps were taken to make Irish compulsory for positions in the police, the army, and the civil service, and for university matriculation. Although the few remaining areas of the country where people spoke Irish as their first language, the Gaeltacht, were subsidized by the government, the number of native speakers halved in the first seventeen years of the Free State and continued to decline throughout the rest of the century.

Insularity was a hallmark of the conservative Free State as it emphasized its Gaelic and Catholic identity and strove to exclude foreign and modern influences including radio, newspapers, films, books, and music. The compulsory element of the language revival was an indication of official thinking that led to the establishment of film censorship in 1925 and a Censorship Board in 1929 to protect Irish society from immoral literature, pornography, and birth control information. Works by George Bernard Shaw, Ernest Hemingway, and Sean O'Casey were among those banned, while the Catholic Church happily cooperated in denouncing dance halls and jazz music. While the constitution specified freedom of religious allegiance, it was inevitable that the character of the Free State was shaped by Catholicism. Divorce was at first officially obstructed and then prohibited in 1937, while the importation and sale of contraception was illegal from 1935 onward. Educational and social welfare matters largely remained the church's prerogative. The 1908 papal decree *Ne Temere*, which had confirmed Protestant fears about the aggressive nature of Catholicism in its stipulation that children of mixed marriages had to be reared as Catholics, was fully enforced by the church in the new Free State, whatever lip service had been paid to minority interests.

In external affairs, the Cumann na nGaedheal government took advantage of the changing nature of the evolving commonwealth. Kevin O'Higgins and Desmond Fitz-Gerald worked effectively behind the scenes at the 1926 Imperial Conference, which declared that each dominion was an equal and autonomous community within the empire, while the outcome of the 1930 conference resulted in the landmark Statute of Westminster, which withdrew the right of the imperial parliament to legislate for the dominions without their consent and provided for the repeal of legislation affecting the dominions that had previously been passed by Westminster. The implications of this legislation for the Free State were tremendous, giving it the freedom to alter the provisions of the treaty, a power that de Valera was to exercise with great effect in the following decade. An ambassador to the United States was appointed in 1928, and in 1930 the Free State won a seat on the League of Nations Council that it had joined in 1923.

Fianna Fáil contested its first election in 1927 and won forty-four seats, compared with Cumann na nGaedheal's significantly reduced tally of forty-seven seats. Labour had temporarily gained back significant ground with twenty-two seats, while the independents and the Farmers' Party captured twenty-three seats between them. Sinn Féin and independent Republicans won a mere seven seats. If Fianna Fáil took its place in the Dáil it could threaten Cumann na nGaedheal's ability to form a government, but in order to enter the legislature de Valera and his elected colleagues would have to take the oath of allegiance to the monarchy. The assassination of Kevin O'Higgins by the IRA a few days later led to a Public Safety Act, which again imposed the death penalty for illegal possession of arms and gave the government wide powers of arrest and detention in its campaign to suppress the unlawful IRA. Accompanying this legislation was an Electoral Amendment Bill, which introduced a prerequisite pledge to take the oath of allegiance for any candidate seeking election. Fianna Fáil responded to Cosgrave's throwing down of the gauntlet by declaring that the oath was merely an "empty formula" and, arriving at the Dáil to take their seats, signed the book containing the oath, which allowed de Valera to claim that he was simply signing his name as a technicality and not taking an oath of allegiance to the crown.

Cosgrave rapidly called another election. This resulted in the formation of a government by Cumann na nGaedheal that combined its sixty-two seats with the Farmers' and independents' total of eighteen seats. Fianna Fáil increased its share to fifty-seven seats, mostly at the expense of Labour, which declined again to thirteen TDs. Sinn Féin did not even contest the election. De Valera's party energetically opposed Cosgrave's administration throughout the following five years, while quietly disassociating itself from its past links with the IRA and successfully wooing the support of the Catholic Church. Fianna Fáil replaced a jaded Cumann na nGaedheal as the dominant party in the 1932 general election when it captured seventy-two seats compared to the latter's fifty-seven and formed a government with the support of the seven Labour Party TDs who had been returned to office.

Dismantling the Treaty

As the new president of the Executive Council, de Valera immediately tackled the task of dismantling the treaty by initiating the abolition of the oath of allegiance, undermining the position of governor general, and withholding the annuities still owed to the British government from numerous land purchase loans advanced to Irish farmers over the previous forty years. Britain responded by imposing heavy duties on Irish agricultural exports to recoup the annual payment of £3 million, and this was countered by the Irish government imposing similar tariffs on British exports, most notably iron, cement, coal, and steel. The economic conflict that ensued over the next six years severely affected Irish agricultural exports, which had already fallen in 1929 due to decreased demands in the British market and the general economic depression. From an annual value of £49 million in 1929 they fell to £18 million in 1934.

Farmers suffered but generally supported de Valera's stance in the ultimately disappointed expectation that the annuities they had to pay each year would be abolished. De Valera halved the amounts they had to pay but continued to collect the fee. The mutually damaging conflict was brought to a close in 1938 when the Irish government undertook to pay a final settlement of £10 million while, to the consternation of many of his colleagues, British Prime Minister Neville Chamberlain improvidently agreed to surrender British control of the ports and facilities reserved for its use in the twenty-six counties. An enormous political coup for de Valera, this agreement enabled his dogged pursuit of a policy of neutrality for the Free State during the imminent war.

The Army Comrades Association (ACA) was formed in 1932 by former soldiers of the Free State army. It rapidly assumed a political position when its leader T. F. O'Higgins (brother of the late Kevin O'Higgins), declared that the organization would oppose communism and defend free speech. As Cumann na nGaedheal meetings were popular targets for IRA attacks, the ACA assumed a protective role that led to violent clashes with republicans. A new political party simultaneously emerged in the Dáil led by James Dillon. Incorporating the Farmers' Party, the new National Centre Party proposed a settlement of the economic conflict with Britain and sought to bridge the gap of the civil war conflict that lay at the heart of Irish politics. De Valera astutely responded with a snap election early in 1933, which increased his party's strength to seventy-seven seats, while Cumann na nGaedheal fell farther to forty-eight seats and the National Centre Party won only eleven seats.

As Fianna Fáil increased in strength, the opposition parties sought out each other and strengthened their links to the ACA (now led by ex-Garda commissioner Eoin O'Duffy), which, following the example of Mussolini's black-clad supporters, had recently adopted a uniform of blue shirts and the straight-arm salute. In essence, however, the ACA, popularly known as the Blueshirts, remained a rural-dominated conservative movement. It called for an end to the British model of party politics in favor of a vocational model, recently advocated by Pope Pius XI, whereby TDs would represent certain groups such as farmers or business interests. Attempted government suppression of the movement led to the combination of Cumann na nGaedheal, the National Centre Party, and the Blueshirts in the formation of a new party, Fine Gael (Irish Tribe). Led briefly by O'Duffy (who subsequently departed to fight in the Spanish Civil War, having been ousted from his position as a result of his reckless and violent speeches), and under the subsequent leadership of W. T. Cosgrave, Fine Gael endorsed traditional party politics and effectively reorganized itself to become the main opposition party in the Dáil.

The tacit indulgence of the IRA by de Valera, and vice versa, proved temporary as militant republicans were consistently disappointed with his political performance. The paced and selective dismantling of the treaty provisions, however progressive from a political perspective, was not enough for those who had anticipated an immediate assertion of the republic and an attack on partition. De Valera spent considerable energy and resources in cajoling republicans into Fianna Fáil through pension and compensation schemes, but his attempts to persuade the IRA to give up its arms were futile. Following several murders, the government banned the IRA in 1936 and used military tribunals to imprison its leaders. Driven underground, the movement split into numerous factions, one of which pursued a bombing campaign in Britain during 1938 and 1939. Membership declined from an estimated thirty thousand in the Free State in 1932 to a few hundred individuals with no effective leadership by the middle of the following decade.

Seizing upon the abdication crisis in Britain in 1936, the result of Edward VIII's determination to marry Wallis Simpson, de Valera legislatively removed all reference to the crown in the Free State constitution and proceeded in 1937 to introduce a new constitution that incorporated his scheme of external association with the Commonwealth. The name of the state was changed to Éire (Ireland), and even though the word "Republic" was not used in this document, de Valera achieved a republic in all but name. The new constitution denied Northern Ireland's constitutional status by claiming that the national territory comprised the entire island, although jurisdiction would be limited to the twenty-six counties pending reintegration of the national territory. An elected president became the head of state, an office that combined ceremonial functions with guardianship of the constitution. The office of president of the Executive Council was replaced by that of a prime minister called Taoiseach (chief), who would lead a cabinet of government ministers. The Dáil and the general electoral system remained unchanged, but the Seanad was remodeled so that of its sixty members, eleven would be nominated by the Taoiseach, six elected by university graduates, and the remaining forty-three elected on a vocational basis by members of government and local government.

Human and civil rights were guaranteed subject to public order and morality, which allowed the government considerable discretionary powers. Irish remained the first language of the state, while English was recognized as its second language. Religious freedom was guaranteed, but the document's language was permeated by Christian references, and the "special position" of the Catholic Church was officially recognized. The integrity of the family was emphasized, leading to an article that defined the premier role of females as wives and mothers whose position in the home was morally supported by the state. This led to a marriage ban in public service employment that was not finally removed until 1973. Divorce was prohibited, as was the remarriage of persons divorced elsewhere. Contraception had been made illegal two years previously, while abortion was so abhorrent that it was not even mentioned, although an amendment was added in 1983 to protect the life of the unborn. On July 1, 1937, the new constitution was approved by a slim majority of the electorate, and Fianna Fáil was returned to power with de Valera as Taoiseach. Endorsed by all parties, Douglas Hyde became the first president of Éire.

The Emergency

During the first years of political sovereignty within the empire, foreign affairs had revolved around the evolving commonwealth and the League of Nations. De Valera, who served as president of the Council of the League of Nations in 1932 and as president of the Assembly of the League in 1938, anticipated the approaching war and determined that Éire would remain neutral. The surrender of British control over specified ports and facilities in 1938 made this policy possible, and when the war began in September 1939, Éire declared its neutrality and a state of emergency was implemented by the Dáil that allowed the government powers to impose strict censorship and to take action against threats to the state. One such threat was the remnants of the IRA, which the new Offenses Against the State Act was designed to counter with its extensive powers of internship and the introduction of the death penalty for treason. German attempts to initiate contact with the IRA to discuss anti-British activity revealed the IRA's inherent disorganization and weakness, which were compounded by the government's swift action in interning known militants. The army and its reserves were expanded to a quarter of a million men, while a coastal patrol watched for signs of attack.

Supported by the electorate, de Valera was resolute in maintaining neutrality despite considerable pressure from Prime Minister Winston Churchill and President Franklin D. Roosevelt to join the Allied cause. Concessions for Allied flights over Irish air space and antisubmarine patrols in Irish waters were agreed on, but applications for port facilities at Berehaven in Cork for the essential Atlantic convoys were denied, which led Churchill to threaten invasion. The availability of Northern Ireland's ports eased the pressure on the convoys, although it added some two hundred miles to their hazardous journey. In the absence of those facilities, it is doubtful that Irish neutrality would have survived British need.

In essence, the Irish government's policy was one of benevolent neutrality whereby discreet and unofficial cooperation was given to Allied forces, such as turning a blind eye toward Allied pilots who inadvertently landed in Éire and allowing them to cross the border into Northern Ireland, while any Germans found in southern Ireland were interned for the duration of the war. Reflecting poor economic conditions in the twenty-six counties, as well as popular disapproval of German aggression, fifty thousand Irishmen joined the British army while several thousand male and female Irish emigrants to Britain provided labor for war production and, despite domestic rationing, Irish farmers supplied price-controlled food for the British market. The twenty-six counties suffered from general shortages of food, fuel, and other essentials, and once from a misdirected German bombing raid that hit Dublin in May 1941, but the most significant result of the war was the affirmation of political sovereignty and national identity that the policy of neutrality had enabled.

The political landscape changed in the postwar period with the emergence of smaller parties expressing discontent with economic and political conditions as Fine Gael and the Labour Party continued to lose ground. Clann na Talmhan (Agricultural Party), which called for reform of land division and general farming conditions, drew support away from Fine Gael and Fianna Fáil with the election of fourteen deputies in 1943, but ultimately it proved a transitory party. More significant was the establishment in 1946 of Clann na Poblachta (Republican Party), led by ex-IRA chief of staff Sean MacBride, the son of former revolutionaries Maud Gonne and John MacBride, the latter who had been executed for his part in the 1916 rebellion.

Composed of IRA members who had realized the futility of a military campaign and radicals who sought social and economic reform, this new party threatened Fianna Fáil's claim to represent republican interests. In the 1948 general election, a coalition of Fine Gael, Labour, Clann na Talmhan, and Clann na Poblachta succeeded in ousting de Valera from power for the first time in sixteen years. This interparty government, led by John A. Costello and based on an uneasy coalition of different agendas, was short-lived, but it accomplished the unanticipated declaration of a republic, and in its controversial fall, illuminated the power of the Catholic Church. The decision to change the name and constitutional status of the state was announced by the Taoiseach while on a Canadian visit in 1948 and was a surprise to the Irish public. But reflecting Sean MacBride's position as minister of external affairs, this move had been decided upon by the cabinet the previous summer. With the repeal of the External Relations Act severing Éire's relationship with the commonwealth, the Republic of Ireland was finally realized at Easter 1949.

Republic of Ireland

The young minister for health, Dr. Noel Browne, successfully tackled the severe problem of tuberculosis, which accounted for approximately four thousand deaths per year, by spending £30 million in building and staffing sanatoriums throughout the countryside. Free treatment was provided to those suffering from the disease, and within ten years the fatality rates had been reduced by two-thirds and continued to fall until the disease was eliminated. Less successful was his innovative Mother and Child Scheme, which aimed to provide free medical care for mothers and children under sixteen. The medical profession opposed free health care (worried that it would undermine their practices), but it was the powerful opposition of the Catholic

Church that killed the plan and provoked the fall of the government. The church insisted that the provision of health care was the parents' prerogative and worried that state intervention would evolve into state control and thus lead to policies that the church opposed, such as birth control and abortion. Browne's refusal to compromise on the legislation led to demands for his resignation by his party leader, Sean MacBride.

Browne's departure was repeated by some of his party colleagues, and with the withdrawal of their support, the coalition government collapsed, resulting in a general election that enabled Fianna Fáil to assume power once again. Clann na Poblachta never recovered from the experience. Apart from a second short experience of inter-party government under Costello between 1954 and 1957 (during which time the Republic of Ireland joined the United Nations), Fianna Fáil held power for the next twenty-two years. De Valera was eventually convinced to retire from leadership of the party at the age of seventy-seven when he succeeded Sean T. O'Kelly as president, allowing the younger and dynamic Sean Lemass to succeed him as Taoiseach in 1959. De Valera served as president of the republic from 1959 until 1973. He died in 1975 at the age of ninety-two.

Throughout the 1960s, Lemass concentrated on the sluggish economy that he had inherited from de Valera. Job creation in industry after the war was offset by the substantial decreases in agricultural employment. The republic was still heavily dependent on British markets, and emigration rose to late-nineteenth-century levels. Between 1936 and 1946, some 187,000 people left the twenty-six counties; during the following decade, 316,000 emigrated, followed by more than 200,000 between 1956 and 1961. The population of the state according to the 1961 census was only 2.8 million. Implementing the recommendations of the 1958 Whitaker Report, successive programs for economic expansion were implemented that aimed at joining the European Economic Community (EEC), stimulating private industrial investment, and encouraging foreign capital into the state with attractive financial incentives for multinational companies establishing a base. These plans were aided by a general improvement in economic conditions, which resulted in an average annual growth of 4 percent during the early 1960s. In 1965, an Anglo-Irish free trade agreement stimulated further development and made economic cooperation with Northern Ireland possible. Some 350 foreign companies were attracted into the twenty-six counties during the 1960s, while emigration slowed down and the population increased for the first time in more than a century. The Republic of Ireland became a member of the EEC in 1973, which enabled it to direct a higher percentage of its exports outside the British market.

Important developments were evident in Irish society. Free secondary education was introduced in 1967 by Donogh O'Malley, with a dramatic increase in the number of pupils who went on to the post-primary grades, while the number of university students also rose as financial aid increased. From the mid-1960s, the number of women in the workforce (only 34 percent of those employed were female in 1961) rose, as did the number of female graduates from universities and colleges. The prohibition on employing married female teachers, which was the result of the constitutional emphasis on a woman's place being in the home as wife and mother, was abandoned in 1957, although married women were prevented from working in the civil service until 1973. The Married Women's Status Act was passed in 1957 to take the first step toward equalizing the position of female spouses. For the first time in the history of the state, married women could hold property in their own name, enter into contracts, and initiate legal proceedings. The Guardianship of Infants Act in 1964 gave mothers and fathers an equal role in decisions about their children's upbringing (previously, fathers exercised sole rights in the rearing of children). The 1965 Succession Act legally entitled widows to a share of their deceased spouse's estate, whereas previously they could be completely disinherited. Welfare provisions such as children's allowances, work insurance, and pensions improved.

Radio Telefís Éireann (RTE), the national television service, was established in 1961. Censorship declined from 1966 onward as the republic abandoned its parochial shell. The Second Vatican Council slightly eased the puritanism of Catholicism, and a referendum held in 1972 removed the "special position" of the Catholic Church from the constitution, although divorce and contraception remained prohibited. In 1979, legislation was passed that permitted married couples to purchase birth control with a prescription. It was not until 1993 that contraception was made freely available and homosexual activity was decriminalized. An amendment protecting the life of the unborn was added to the constitution in 1983, and subsequent attempts to remove it have failed, although public opinion accepts the fact that Irish women travel to Britain for abortions. In 1992, a constitutional crisis occurred when the High Court interpreted the constitution to prevent a minor, pregnant as the result of rape, from traveling outside the country to terminate the pregnancy. The Supreme Court overturned this decision, and in 1993 the right to travel, and to avail oneself of information about abortion services, was approved in a referendum. In 1986, a proposal to permit limited divorce was rejected by the electorate, but in 1995 a second referendum resulted in the repeal of the relevant article in the constitution, allowing for a moderate form of divorce.

Economic recession from 1974 until the late 1980s saw unemployment and emigration soar again. Fine Gael under the leadership of Garret FitzGerald, in coalition with the Labour Party, provided an alternative to Fianna Fáil, which had suffered from the implication of two government ministers in republican gunrunning schemes in 1970. Yet by 1977, Fianna Fáil had recovered power with the largest majority in its history, winning eighty-four seats to the combined sixty-four of the other parties. Led by Charles Haughey from 1979, Fianna Fáil announced its determination to work toward a solution of the conflict in Northern Ireland, building upon Sean Lemass's pragmatic overtures that had been engulfed by the disintegration of the northern state into social and political anarchy in the late 1960s. With the Anglo-Irish Agreement of 1985, and the ongoing "peace process" of the 1990s, successive Irish governments have been cooperating with successive British governments in developing political initiatives aimed at ending the civil and political conflict in the six counties.

The role of the European Economic Community (now the European Union) has been vital in the Republic's economic development. Financial aid has improved the state's infrastructure, while the Common Agricultural Policy has benefited Irish farming. In May 1987, the Irish electorate approved the implementation of the Single European Act and followed this by endorsing the 1992 Maastricht Treaty that provided for closer integration in economic, judicial, and security issues. Ireland's vibrant economy, recently christened the Celtic Tiger, experienced the highest rates of growth in Europe in the 1990s. Emigration declined to its lowest levels in the history of the state, as did unemployment. Ireland has modernized rapidly in the past decade, transforming its image from a minor and peripheral member of the European Union. It is now regarded as an economic success; its population is young, well educated, confident, and affluent; and it no longer experiences the depletion of emigration. Recently, the *Economist* named the Republic of Ireland as the best place to live according to a quality-of-life assessment, because it combines desirable factors such as high growth and low unemployment with the preservation of stable family and community life. Yet, the modernization of Ireland has led many to question the future of traditional values and culture.

Northern Ireland

Northern Ireland was exempt from conscription during the Second World War but participated fully in the Allied war effort for which it had been preparing since 1937, a role that paid dividends in the postwar period. Northern Irish ports offered protection for the Atlantic convoys excluded from Éire's ports and upon which the survival of the Allied campaign depended. Londonderry provided the site for an important American naval base, while Canadian naval forces were transferred there from Iceland. Thousands of American troops arrived in 1942 and 1943 as Northern Ireland became the Allied forces' main training site for the Normandy invasion. The shipbuilding industry was temporarily rejuvenated, while the rapid development of the limited aircraft industry and the building of airfields provided much needed employment and transformed the six-county state into a virtual aircraft carrier. One hundred and fifty ships were produced in Belfast during the war years, while fifteen hundred aircraft and five hundred tanks were also produced. Agricultural production was increased threefold to meet mainland war needs as compulsory tillage raised the production of crops and livestock numbers rose dramatically.

As an important center of war production, Belfast was targeted by German bombers, suffering four air raids in 1941 that killed hundreds of civilians. Early in April, six bombers destroyed a crucial Harland and Wolff factory and killed thirteen people. One week later, 150 bombers hit Belfast again, destroying residential areas, churches, hospitals, a linen mill, and a railway station, as well as inflicting further damage to sections of Harland and Wolff and killing approximately 745 people. Two further attacks occurred early in May, with a loss of more than 150 lives and extensive damage to crucial sites of aircraft production. One hundred thousand people were rendered homeless by the attacks, causing temporary problems in providing food and shelter. The war resulted in economic prosperity for Northern Ireland as heavy industry was revived and agricultural production intensified, but the political and sectarian divisions remained.

Craigavon had died in the early stages of the war and was first replaced by J. M.

Andrews and then by Sir Basil Brooke (afterward Viscount Brookeborough) as prime minister. Constitutional nationalists remained an ineffective force, while the Northern Ireland Labour Party alienated what nationalist support it might have had by supporting the British connection. Unionists were keenly aware of the valuable contribution that Northern Ireland had made to the Allied war effort, in stark contrast to Éire, and were determined to capitalize upon Britain's acknowledgment of their role.

The 1945 general election in Britain produced a Labour government that the unionists were initially wary of as a dubious ally, but their suspicions were put aside in pursuit of the advantages of the modern welfare state that Prime Minister Clement Attlee introduced to Great Britain in the postwar period. A series of financial agreements reached between 1946 and 1951 resolved the financial limitations that had hampered the Northern Irish government since 1920. Britain agreed to subsidize the cost of implementing new welfare measures in Northern Ireland, which benefited from a new system of national insurance incorporating unemployment benefits, family allowances, pensions, free health care, funds for public housing, and free primary and secondary education in a remodeled system that also provided grants for building new schools and financial support for university education, regardless of social and religious background.

Taoiseach John A. Costello's announcement of Éire's decision to leave the commonwealth and declare itself a republic in 1949 alarmed the Northern Irish government, which imagined that an attack on partition would follow. Brookeborough called a general election, which eliminated Labour Party representation in Stormont and reaffirmed unionist power. A recently founded conservative and largely rural nationalist organization, the Anti-Partition League, aimed at achieving a parliamentary presence to work toward ending the division of the island, failed to get any of its candidates elected. Legislation introduced in Westminster to recognize the changed status of the twenty-six counties reasserted the status of Northern Ireland, declaring that in no event would Northern Ireland cease to be part of the United Kingdom without the consent of the parliament of Northern Ireland. While the Republic's hopes of undermining partition were dashed by the passing of this Ireland Act, the unionist government of Northern Ireland was comforted by this legislative guarantee of its state's political status and by the official visit of Princess Elizabeth and her husband, the Duke of Edinburgh, to Belfast.

With the security of the Ireland Act, and particularly after the replacement of de Valera by Sean Lemass as Taoiseach, certain limited measures of cross-border cooperation became possible and practical from an economic perspective. Land-drainage plans, the establishment of a hydroelectric station, and management of railway services offered civil servants and government ministers from both states opportunities for constructive and mutually beneficial interaction, but little of substance changed in internal politics, despite an improving economy that was benefiting from the welfare state and the attraction of new industries. Unemployment and emigration among Catholics remained high, as Sinn Féin with its endorsement of armed resistance won only two seats in the 1955 elections and the IRA struggled to reorganize. It conducted a futile border campaign between 1956 and 1962, which cost nineteen lives and considerable property damage but was eventually abandoned as a result of internal factions and security measures employed by both governments, combined with a lack of popular support.

Former minister of finance, Captain Terence O'Neill, who succeeded Brookeborough as prime minister in 1963, was determined to tackle unemployment, which was four times higher than in mainland Britain, and the forces of hatred and violence that had long paralyzed Northern Ireland's development. Genuine in his desire for reform, reconciliation, and an end to economic and social discrimination, O'Neill's policy proved much too radical for his unionist colleagues in government, and he was also mistrusted by extreme nationalists. A false dawn of good feeling was symbolized by his visits to Catholic schools and his much vaunted economic plans that aimed at attracting foreign investment, financing industrial centers, and improving road transport. A new ministry of development and an advisory Economic Council were established, and a number of multinational companies, including Imperial Chemical Industries (ICI), Grundig, and Michelin, set up bases in Northern Ireland, but the postwar decline of long-established industries such as shipbuilding and linen manufacture with significant job losses continued. Some scholars have dismissed O'Neill's economic initiatives as superficial and badly planned, but twenty-nine thousand jobs were created, although taking into consideration job losses, a net gain of only five thousand was achieved by the end of the decade.

A new pragmatic willingness on the part of the republic to recognize the existence of Northern Ireland was becoming more apparent under the leadership of Sean Lemass. O'Neill's first meeting with Lemass in Belfast early in 1965 to discuss economic matters was arranged without seeking the approval of his cabinet, but after some initial sulking they followed public opinion in welcoming practical economic cooperation. O'Neill took an official visit to Dublin the following month. The Nationalist Party in Northern Ireland, led by Eddie McAteer, welcomed these positive developments, and in February 1965 the nine elected nationalist representatives accepted the role of official opposition in Stormont. In the general election the following November, voters endorsed O'Neill's modernizing economic and integrative policies by voting for his party in higher numbers than in any election since 1921, yet serious opposition to O'Neill was forming within the Unionist Party.

Disturbed by his liberalism and conciliatory attitude to Catholics, and the implications for unionist employment and control of government if nationalists were brought in from the cold, members of his party looked toward Minister of Commerce Brian Faulkner as a more suitable leader. Condemnation of O'Neill and his policies also came from outside Stormont, as the strident voice of Presbyterian fundamentalism, the Reverend Ian Paisley, accused him of betraying the British and Protestant heritage of the state. A member of the Orange Order, Paisley established the Free Presbyterian Church of Ulster in 1951 and entered the political arena in 1956 as a leading member of the extremist group, Ulster Protestant Action, which aimed at maintaining Protestant dominance in all aspects of Northern Irish life. His combination of fundamentalism and fiery political rhetoric proved popular with Protestants worried about the threat to their political and social hegemony if O'Neill pursued his integrationist policies. In 1966, Paisley founded the Protestant Unionist Party and chaired the Ulster Constitution Defence Committee, which supervised the revival of the UVF to prepare for the protection of Protestant Ulster.

Despite O'Neill's intentions of improving the position of Catholics and modernizing Northern Ireland, little of practical significance was actually achieved. Products of the postwar reform of the education system, a new generation of university-educated Catholics grew impatient with empty promises and organized a movement to demand equality of treatment as British citizens. Founded in 1966, the Northern Ireland Civil Rights Association (NICRA) demanded human and civil rights; reform of the police force; reform of the electoral system, the franchise, and the electoral boundaries; reform of housing and employment practices; and repeal of the Special Powers Act.

Taking its cue from the civil rights movement in the United States, the leaders of the NICRA organized nonviolent marches that were quickly characterized by clashes with an aggressive RUC and were broadcast all over the world, as the power of television focused international attention on the state. With prominent and effective spokespersons in Bernadette Devlin and John Hume, the NICRA was composed of disparate elements representing socialist interests (Young Socialist Movement), students from Queen's University, militant activists (People's Democracy), and local interest groups (Derry Citizens' Action Committee). This combination of elements held together for the time being, but an inherent split between the pacifist position represented by John Hume and the urge to physically resist the violence of the state articulated by Bernadette Devlin was inevitable. Popularly viewed as a republican plot by leading unionists, the NICRA marches were regarded as legitimate targets for police action and inspired counterdemonstrations by Paisley's followers. On October 5, 1968, a banned civil rights march in Derry degenerated into vicious rioting by demonstrators and members of the RUC.

A belated reform package unveiled by O'Neill in cooperation with British Prime Minister Harold Wilson promised reform in public housing allocation, local government elections, and the repeal of the Special Powers Act. This was welcomed by the moderate members of the civil rights movement but was rejected by the more militant elements and inspired ominous opposition from within unionist ranks. Brian Faulkner resigned from the government, and members of the Unionist Party publicly criticized O'Neill who responded with a general election that split the party between those who supported him and those who opposed his continued leadership. The Nationalist Party was eclipsed by the new Social Democratic Labour Party (SDLP), which succeeded in electing civil rights activists John Hume and Ivan Cooper to the parliament, while Bernadette Devlin of the People's Democracy movement was elected the following month as a Westminster MP.

O'Neill resigned in April 1969, and his seat in the following by-election was ominously won by Ian Paisley, while James Chichester-Clark emerged as the new prime minister. To the anger of unionists, the British government initiated experimental "direct rule by proxy," whereby they supervised the conduct of the Stormont government. Riots continued between marchers and police in Londonderry and Belfast throughout the summer of 1969 as civil rights marches were banned but traditional

Orange Order marches proceeded. The disintegration of law and order in the region prompted the British government to send in ten thousand soldiers to act as a buffer between the police and the Catholic community, which also suffered from attacks at the hands of Protestant extremists such as the "B Specials" and the Ulster Defence Association.

Regenerated by the anxiety and anger of the nationalist community, both Sinn Féin and the IRA divided into factions. The traditional militant wing of the IRA, split from an element that had turned toward socialism, became the superior faction rechristened as the Provisional IRA, or "Provos." Under the leadership of Seán MacStiofáin, and financed by sympathizers in the Republic and in the United States, the Provos energetically proceeded to recruit and rearm. Sinn Féin also split into official and provisional factions, with the former pursuing parliamentary politics in the Republic (as the Workers' Party from 1977), while the latter, true to its abstentionist heritage, supported the military campaign of the Provisional IRA.

Chichester-Clark resigned in March 1971 when his demand for more British troops was refused by British Prime Minister Edward Heath. He was replaced by Brian Faulkner, who persuaded the British government to counteract IRA activity with the reintroduction of internment without trial. In a disastrously counterproductive policy, more than three hundred Catholics were arrested at dawn on August 9, 1971, and subjected to harsh interrogation; 240 of them were interned without trial. Protestants remained exempt from government strategies to combat terrorist activity. The nationalist community was enraged. IRA recruitment rapidly increased, violence escalated, and nationalist politicians withdrew from Stormont and local government. A banned civil rights march in Derry in January 1972 resulted in the deaths of fourteen people shot by British paratroopers on a day known as Bloody Sunday, the subject of an official inquiry established by British Prime Minister Tony Blair in April 1998. The British embassy in Dublin was set on fire by furious protestors, while Westminster suspended the Northern Irish government and imposed direct rule in 1972. More than four hundred people died as a result of political and sectarian violence between 1969 and 1972.

Direct rule was regarded as a temporary measure that would be succeeded by the reintroduction of devolved government based on power-sharing between the unionist and nationalist communities in Northern Ireland. The Sunningdale Agreement reached in November 1973 among William Whitelaw (representing the British government), the Official Unionist Party, the SDLP, and the Alliance Party proposed the establishment of a power-sharing executive composed of unionists and nationalists, but attempts to implement it crumbled amid republican and unionist opposition.

Paramilitary terrorism has dominated life in Northern Ireland over the past three decades as both republican and unionist forces expressed their opposing aspirations in retaliatory acts of violence that have claimed and maimed thousands of lives. The IRA targeted Northern Ireland and mainland Britain with a series of bombings and assassinations in their campaign against what they characterized as forces of occupation. Protestant paramilitary forces such as the Ulster Defence Association and the Ulster Freedom Fighters targeted known republicans, and Catholics in general, in retaliation for IRA activity. In the aftermath of the 1981 hunger strikes by incarcerated IRA members seeking political prisoner status, which resulted in ten deaths before the tactic was abandoned, the British and Irish governments agreed to cooperate in the search for a political solution to the obstinate problems that Northern Ireland presented.

The vested interest of the Republic of Ireland in its neighboring state had been recognized in the early 1970s but was given political force in the Anglo-Irish Agreement signed by Prime Minister Margaret Thatcher and Taoiseach Garret FitzGerald in 1985. Endorsed by the SDLP, this agreement provided the foundation for the subsequent peace process in establishing meaningful intergovernmental cooperation in security and judicial matters. Predictably, both republicans and unionists were unhappy with the agreement: the former because the Republic had acknowledged that Northern Ireland was part of Great Britain, and the latter because a "foreign" government was given a voice in Northern Irish affairs. Yet their opposition proved ineffectual, and despite continued violence and fiery extremist rhetoric from both sides, political initiatives have been gaining ground in the six counties.

In the late 1980s, Sinn Féin recognized that its policy of political abstention deserved some thought. The Official Unionist Party also recognized that ending the political stalemate and vicious circle of sectarian and political violence in which the region was trapped required new approaches. By the early 1990s, formal talks were established based on three strands: internal Northern Irish arrangements, North-South arrangements, and Anglo-Irish relationships. Meanwhile, the SDLP and Sinn Féin, led by John Hume and Gerry Adams, respectively, engaged in talks over the future of nationalist endeavors, as Prime Minister John Major and Taoiseach Albert Reynolds announced the Downing Street Declaration at the end of 1993. This agreement repeated that Great Britain had no "selfish strategic or economic interest in Northern Ireland" but that both governments would work toward a peaceful resolution of the conflict based on consent. Political parties that renounced paramilitary violence would be included in talks about the future of the state.

Diplomatically encouraged by the United States under the leadership of President Bill Clinton, delicate and lengthy negotiations, accompanied by fragile paramilitary cease-fires, produced an agreement, endorsed by the political parties in Northern Ireland (with the exception of Ian Paisley's Democratic Unionist Party) and approved of by the Northern Irish people and the citizens of the Republic. Chaired with great skill and patience by American Senator George Mitchell, two years of negotiations resulted in the 1998 Good Friday Agreement that follows the three-strand model and is based on the principle of consent. Constitutional change may come about only with the consent of the majority of the people, but in the event that change is favored, it is the responsibility of both governments to implement it. The people of Northern Ireland can identify themselves as British, Irish, or both, with the right to hold dual citizenship.

Approved in May 1998 by 95 percent of those who voted in the Republic and by 71 percent of Northern Irish voters, the Good Friday Agreement resulted in the repeal of the Government of Ireland Act and the removal of the Republic's territorial and jurisdictional claims pending the establishment of an assembly and executive. A legislative assembly elected by proportional representation was established, with positions in the executive allocated according to party strength. Elections in the summer of 1998 produced an assembly made up of multiple parties, led by David Trimble of the Ulster Unionist Party as first minister, with Seamus Mallon of the SDLP as his deputy. Since then, the issue of decommissioning arms has proven a major obstacle in implementing the agreement, and the assembly had been prorogued. In the interim, political support has shifted from the moderate center parties—the SDLP representing nationalists, and the Ulster Unionist Party representing Unionists—toward the more radical parties: the Democratic Unionist Party and Sinn Féin. Unionists fear the sincerity of the republican commitment to peace, while republicans are frustrated with unionist obduracy. Yet, despite the often exasperating pace of political progress, there is the potential for Northern Ireland to evolve beyond its polarized past, to become peaceful and prosperous, and to be at ease with itself, with Great Britain, and with the Republic of Ireland.

SUGGESTED READING

S. J. Connolly, *The Oxford Companion to Irish History* (Oxford: Oxford University Press, 1999).

R. F. Foster, *Modern Ireland, 1600–1972* (London: Allen Lane, 1988).

K. T. Hoppen, *Ireland since 1800: Conflict and Conformity* (New York: Longman, 1989, 1999).

Alvin Jackson, *Ireland, 1798–1998: Politics and War* (Oxford: Blackwell, 1999).

J. J. Lee, *Ireland, 1912–1985: Politics and Society* (New York: Cambridge University Press, 1989).

Kerby A. Miller, *Emigrants and Exiles: Ireland and the Irish Exodus to North America* (New York: Oxford University Press, 1985).

Cormac Ó Gráda, *Ireland: A New Economic History, 1780–1939* (Oxford: Clarendon Press, 1994).

Cormac Ó Gráda, *Black '47 and Beyond: The Great Irish Famine in History, Economy and Memory* (Princeton: Princeton University Press, 1999).

Foundations

Chapter 3

Scots Irish or Scotch-Irish

David Noel Doyle

From 1700 to 1820, between a quarter of a million and half a million immigrants came from Ireland to America. They accounted for 30 percent of all European immigrants in that period (and 50 percent between 1776 and 1820). They constituted the largest single nationality group from Europe, and the largest up to 1800 from any single political jurisdiction anywhere, the Kingdom of Ireland.

Irish immigrants were themselves ethnically and radically subdivided. The largest element between the mid-1740s and mid-1790s consisted of Protestants from the north of Ireland, or Ulster. These were themselves ethnically and religiously subdivided, with most of them being of Scottish origin and Presbyterian faith. This emigration was unrepresentative of the population of the region as a whole, which was only a third Presbyterian and roughly 45 percent native Irish and Catholic in 1715, with the balance (a fifth) being English and Anglican (Episcopalian) with some Baptists and Quakers. In the period 1720–1835, disproportionate Presbyterian migration altered that ratio to one-quarter Presbyterian and over one-half Catholic, with a larger change in west Ulster. Migration from Ulster to America always included Anglican, Catholic, and Quaker elements. Perhaps from the mid-1790s, certainly after 1812, Presbyterians no longer were the majority, if a plurality, until the mid-1830s, and a very sizable element thereafter.

Terms and Usages

Thus in strict usage, Scots Irish or Scotch-Irish refers only to this Ulster Presbyterian *plurality* of the overall *Irish* migration, 1700–1820, and to the *majority* element within overall *Ulster* migration in the same years. Ulster today consists of Northern Ireland together with the surrounding counties of the Irish Republic: Cavan, Monaghan, and Donegal; there was also some Presbyterian settlement (later depleted) in contiguous counties of Louth, Leitrim, and Sligo. In educated American usage between 1870 and 1925, however, the term was also used to refer to any Protestants in or from this area (and their descendants), regardless of ethnic origin. Confusion resulted when many later were described as Scotch-Irish, even southern Irish Presbyterians (such as Dublin-born George Bryan, the anti-slavery governor of revolutionary Pennsylvania).

Although the term Scotch-Irish wasn't unknown, it was rarely used in the eighteenth century itself, either in Ireland or colonial America, but the reality of Ulster

Presbyterians and their subculture was then well recognized in both countries. Indeed, the majority of the descendants of the migration, especially in the southern United States today, refer to themselves as of Irish descent for this reason. "Scotch-Irish" became a more common term from the 1850s as the Know-Nothing party and other prejudices caused Protestants of Irish origin to set themselves apart from an Irish-America redefined as Catholic. That was the consensus of most Americans according to the demographics and character of emigration from Ireland since the 1820s, and by the post-Famine remaking of Irish society in America's cities and mining and industrial areas. The old claim of Irish nationalists and others (such as Woodrow Wilson and Theodore Roosevelt, both historians) that the term refers to a "mixed race" has no meaning. Nor has the claim that the Scots Irish were basically part of one pan-Gaelic people any force, even if a quarter of first-wave settlement, those from west Galloway, Argyll, and elsewhere, spoke Scots Gaelic and, in turn, recruited Irish speakers to their first congregations.

This was not an age of cultural nationalism. Evidence suggests that isolated groups of Irish were absorbed where early Scots settlement was dominant, as in north Down (as one might expect on a frontier). Intermarriage was not uncommon, following the earliest migration, which largely male. And the reverse happened among isolated Scots settlers. Later there were some conversions, notably where a few Irish-speaking ministers were active. More usually as religious antagonism and land rivalry sharpened from the 1630s, and as further migration and population growth made it fully feasible, endogamy within the Scots community became the norm, except where there was marked overlap with English settlement. It was monitored in the oversight of relationships by kirk sessions and kinship group; and it expressed the solidity of subcultural preference, at least into the early nineteenth century.

In Europe today, these Irish Presbyterians of largely Scottish origin live almost wholly in Northern Ireland. This polity now allows all its citizens a dual identity, British and Irish. In the eighteenth century, the Scots Irish at home had in effect a triple identity: Scottish in religion, local dialect, and specific culture; Irish by birth, polity, and local associations; and British by ultimate political allegiance and aspects of their wider culture (educated speech, legal and commercial procedures, etc.). Their national and ethnic identities were scarcely fixed, and they themselves were divided about these, as was politically evident between 1775 and 1783 in America, and between 1775 and 1815 in Ireland itself. Their sense of affinity with Scotland was as strong as their sense of descent from it was weak: in Ulster, genealogies in the mid-eighteenth century were invariably traced since settlement in Ireland. This was an age of localities. Terms of wider identification are not common in the letters and papers of the time, and self-description as Scots Irish was very rare. Yet their collective behavior requires some such term. Similar problems are well understood by scholars of most of Europe's national and subcultural populations before about 1850.

Noncontemporary literary and political overemphasis on the variable British dimension of this people came much later in the 1850s. It has had four consequences for scholarship. It displaced mixed Irish elements by combined British ones (English, Welsh, Scottish, and Scots Irish) as the preponderant fact of all in-migration in the formative eighteenth century. (Irish and Scots Irish persons had been together only about 2.5 percent to less than 5 percent of all immigrants in the first formative century, 1609–1699). This reinforced now outmoded and restrictive characterizations of American nationality (as preferentially white, Protestant, and of pre-Revolutionary and British origins). Second, it was used to differentiate later immigrants from Ireland, about 1825–1932, on a similar basis, to give advantage to those of presumed greater affinity with such a national norm. As a stereotype, it thus screened out the modernizing aspect of most Irish immigrants (literacy, small commercial skills, market experience, English language, social discipline) by downplaying these in all but northern Protestant newcomers. Third, and ironically, the Scots Irish tradition became part of the sustaining ideology of Northern Ireland within the United Kingdom between 1922 and 1985, as a polity preferentially British, Protestant, and of colonial origin. The irony stems from the complex nature of past Scots Irish culture, its long erosion and its homogenization toward an Ulster standard between 1780 and 1900, and its always being a minority strain even within Ulster. (Ulster's leading Unionist historian, J. C. Beckett, always opposed use of the term and tradition as inaccurate and noninclusive.)

Further, Irish nationalists, largely Catholic, in effect denied *any* Scots Irish identity, as a fourth result of exclusive Scots Irish/British linkages. Seeking recognition and advancement in America, they reacted against the restrictive implication of the term, as a buttress to white Protestant definitions of the society, and they perhaps resented the supposed ease with which new Irish Protestant immigrants (as well as older stock) could rank within it. (The actual and comparative performance of Presbyterian and Catholic immigrants in industrial America from the 1830s remains unstudied.) Predictably enough, nationalists in Ireland, seeking national autonomy or independence, feared any recognition of Irish Protestant subcultures as an obstacle to their goals. Very few of them in Ireland, outside Ulster and Dublin, had any direct knowledge of Ulster Presbyterians. In the diaspora, experience in cities like Philadelphia, Toronto, and even New York did not always redress this ignorance, but sometimes added a prejudicial edge to it. The result was a general failure to grasp the real character of Ulster Presbyterian society, and of its own Scots Irish diaspora. The simple view that these were ordinary Irish led to false claims about the Ulster Presbyterians' patriotic traditions, both American (1775–1783) and Irish (1798). This led to exaggerations of the Irish nationalism of Ulster Scots and its force within Ulster itself.

Simple identification also led to false expectations of familiarity with a largely evangelical America in the years about 1820–1880s, as T. C. Grattan recognized in the 1840s. Since the Scots Irish were apparently accepted, the mass of the Irish claimed the same on arrival. The failure to grant the distinctiveness of the Scots Irish thus helped lead many Irish to a false understanding of the otherness of America in those years. This complicated problems of assimilation, even though it sharpened eventual realism about their self-dependence. (This was by contrast with Canada, where a gingerly Irish Catholic respect for the dominant position of Anglicans and Presbyterians in their own nationality group had different results.)

With the acceptance from 1985 of the complex and mutual character of Northern Ireland, agreed by its peoples in 1998, these prejudices should give way to a wider appreciation of the distinctive Scots Irish past, just as the fuller democratization of

American culture in our century (anticipated between 1795 and 1835) has long led the United States Irish of different traditions to cooperate politically and socially.

Background: Settlement, Religion, and Economy, 1605–1715

The Scots Irish originated in a sequence of colonization projects from Britain to Ireland, designed to ensure the island's political dependence on England. In southern Ireland (Munster and Leinster) these built on a medieval pattern of English immigration, descendants of which, the Old English, were distanced from the Tudor and Stuart monarchies by their retention of Catholicism. Hence, new projects were begun to create a Protestant and politically reliable colonization. The last major barrier to English authority, the Gaelic lordships of Ulster, were overthrown between 1595 and 1603. Within a month of the submission of Hugh O'Neill, Earl of Tyrone, and his allies, Elizabeth I died and was succeeded by her Stuart cousin, James VI of Scotland, who also became James I of England.

Long at odds, different in culture and languages, and differentially developed, England and Scotland now had a single monarch, while retaining distinct laws, parliaments, politics, administrations, church life, and schools. The Reformation was dominant and Calvinist in both countries by 1603, but in Scotland, the reform had tended to Presbyterianism and the denial of bishoprics. The Stuarts sought to retain bishops there, and were successful even before 1637, and sought much less successfully to modify Calvinist theology. (Most Protestants in Ireland upheld this theology, as in 1615, creating common ground between Scots and English settlers. Isolated groups of Scots, as in Fermanagh, were well integrated into the Church of Ireland before Presbyterian structures spread from the 1640s.)

James I at first accepted the conditions of the native Ulster surrender. Yet he was obliged to foster the interests of English and Scottish factions and administrators, and to help the Crown's many officers and veterans ("servitors") in Ireland. There was also the legal problem of how to transform loose native lordships into English-style landownership without increasing the real power of the defeated. Pressures on the Ulster nobility and their lands mounted. Their leaders fled to the continent in 1607 and their lands were declared forfeit. The future of most of Ulster lay now in the hands of a Scottish king with English power, in a sense, the first British king. The result was a state blueprint for the "plantation" of six of Ulster's nine counties. (Antrim and Down were already partly planted with Lowland Scots, at the edge since the 1570s, more fully since 1605; Monaghan was omitted.) Scotland is visible from the east Ulster coast only several hours away by sea.

Thus, the settlement of Scots Lowlanders in Ireland was subordinate to renewed English colonization. A Scots king in England favored such joint colonization, which would give flesh to the juncture of his two kingships. He realized that the "ruder" Scots might prove better intermediaries with Irish culture. There was a problem: the Lowlanders were strongly Protestant but estranged from non-Calvinist culture and post-Calvinist change in England. Implanted in a newly conquered region without major "Old English" tradition, they were less inclined to temporize politically with

Irish-born Catholics (notably the English-speaking ones of eastern Irish towns and manors, whom London found often useful to conciliate). These Scots came chiefly from the modern Strathclyde and Galloway, directly opposite east Ulster, then from Ayrshire, Renfrew, Wigtonshire, Bute, and parts of Argyll. Economically this was a rural and partly commercial society, less developed than that of England. They came to a land not radically dissimilar to their own, so that practically the Scots settlers had greater affinities with the lifestyles of the Ulster Irish than did many English there or elsewhere. This made them suitable colonists in the area, and they gradually displaced their English fellow settlers in areas such as rural Londonderry and towns like Coleraine. There was even a precedent, in the Gaelic-speaking older Highland Scots settlements of north Antrim, which had merged with the Lordship of the Isles (the Scottish Hebrides) by Randall MacDonnell. Symptomatically, these Catholic Scots were called Irish after the plantation began, and later joined forces militarily with the Stuart cause in Scotland (led by Montrose) to oppose their Presbyterian rivals there in 1645 as they did in Ulster itself.

Under the plantation schemes, six counties were divided into tracts and estates called precincts, usually of 1,000 acres. These were granted to Scots and English "undertakers" to settle with at least ten British families as key tenants, and to do so around a central settlement (with church and fortified dwelling). Much of Colerain County (renamed Londonderry) was given to London companies on similar terms. In turn, the undertakers' or companies' chief tenants would settle further British families of small holders and craftsmen. Limited Irish settlement was later accepted from 1628.

Church lands, up to one-sixth of all Ulster, some skeletally settled from the 1570s by ex-soldiers, were given to the Episcopalian bishops (or purchased from them) for less restrictive settlement, as were tracts granted to "servitors" (equivalent to the veterans' land grants of eighteenth-century America). Native Irish remained on both of these with (or in place of) newcomers, under newly domiciled gentry (not always the owner). Between 1609 and 1641, some estates were regranted to select native gentry, most of whom were later dispossessed. On much of all these lands, Scots were settled in varied numbers. The post-1605 settlement of south Antrim and north Down also filled out rapidly (notably into the "route" of northwest Antrim). Further colonization spread with formal plantation.

The core Scots area took shape by 1630, more clearly by 1659: a coastal and riverbank crescent from 15 to 30 miles deep, stretching from northeast Donegal through County Londonderry to the first settlements in southeast Antrim and northeast Down [Robinson, maps 7 and 8, pp. 94, 98]. This zone remained accessible to Scottish ports. It was the most viable *en bloc* colonization in modern Ireland. After the initial waves of plantation 1605–1620, further less formal immigration and internal migration (from Antrim and Down) strengthened it, notably between 1630 and 1641 and again in the 1680s and the 1690s–c. 1710. There were also inland enclaves, in mid-Cavan, mid-Armagh, and south Tyrone, more subject to native Irish and to English acculturation and erosion over time.

By contrast, the second-wave English settlement came between 1654 and the 1670s, and was thereafter minimal. Even from the 1620s, the English settlers remigrated and concentrated where fellow settlers, market access, good land, security, more wooded landscapes, and favorable leases encouraged them: within the inland mid-Ulster belt, from the Lagan valley across the rich soils south and west of Lough Neagh, thence to the Lough Erne area. Thus, a broad regional segregation set Scots and English apart, despite heavy initial overlap. Landlords excepted, surprisingly little is known about this English zone, which has led American historians in the past to take its emigrants as Scots Irish, but this was not so. Even the two dialects did not begin to influence one another much until the nineteenth century.

Despite its repute as the most stringent of the many varieties of seventeenth-century Calvinist puritanism in the British empire, Scots Presbyterianism took shape slowly and with mixed characteristics. The rigors of clergy and elders did not always affect folkways in either the Lowlands or in Ulster. Unlike in England, there was no real persecution of Catholics as such in Scotland before the crisis of the 1640s, although in Ireland the Scots were on the defensive, and attitudes were sharper from the start. Stuart pressures for adoption of the (Episcopalian) Book of Common Prayer resulted in the National Covenant in Scotland in reaction (1637), and two short "bishops' wars" against the Crown. Ulster Scots were divided between those who would also adopt this covenant and those who would let things be.

Two events dramatically changed these positions. The Dublin administration attempted to force compliance with the King's religious control by enforcing oaths of acceptance. Then the native Irish rose in revolt in October 1641, and the Ulster Scots now believed the security of their religious culture and of their new farms and towns were inextricably linked, a view strengthened by the arrival of a Scottish Army in 1642, many of its soldiers veterans of the wars for the covenant. With encouragement from the Ulster Scots, presbyteries were first formally organized, although long hampered by insufficient ministers and few churches (kirks). The role of lay conveners and elders was thus often stronger than in Scotland, and worship was more communal and informal. Fragmentation of authority in Ireland ensued as England's Civil Wars followed and deepened this Irish revolt. Royalist, Scots Presbyterian, pro-Parliamentary, and Irish Confederate forces played their distinct Irish interests but also acted as auxiliaries to the main parties in both England and Scotland.

That the Irish Confederation was explicitly Catholic, and that the revolt opened with some atrocities (although Scots settlers were less commonly the victims than English) gave a sharp edge to the convergence of Presbyterian recommitment and fear for homes, farms, and estates. For another century or more, the Ulster Scots were torn between the demands of Presbyterian distinctiveness, in a state officially Episcopalian, and the need for security against Irish Catholics by reliance upon that same state. They could never unanimously support a single policy line, but they were now much more consciously an Irish Presbyterian people. Their initial harassment at the hands of victorious Parliamentarians, and even more by the restored Charles II, confirmed this identity. But the succession of the Catholic Stuart, James II, whose Irish forces briefly controlled the island, before his defeat at Londonderry and the Boyne (1689–1690), likewise confirmed their dependence on a British-run Irish polity.

On the other side, despite contemporary allegations, administrators in Dublin could never systematically persecute, much less dispossess, this bulwark people of the state's Protestant establishment, rooted as they were in the province of strongest native resentments. But the state did discourage attempted Ulster Scots settlement beyond their traditional zones (e.g., southward to Drogheda, Belturbet, and Longford) and disliked attempts by the Synod of Ulster to provide ministers to southern towns. Times of real state pressure were rare: in 1637–1641, 1648–1653, 1661–1663, 1704–1714, and usually during wartime insecurity. By contrast, Charles II inaugurated a grant to Presbyterian ministers in 1672, sustained even when his forces were harrying their more radical co-religionists in Scotland.

Full toleration was effectively accorded mainline Presbyterians by 1690, to match the recognition of the same faith as the official Church of Scotland in their fatherland. The church then established the Synod of Ulster, which presided over ten presbyteries, including Down, Antrim, Route (north Antrim), Belfast, Laggan (east Donegal), and Tyrone. The ten later accredited many ministers to America. The presbyteries also tried to exert ministerial guidance over early lay initiative, sent future ministers to Scotland for training, and attempted the fuller Christianization of their often uncatechized and undisciplined people. This history means that growth and distribution of mainline Presbyterian churches offers only a broad outline of the Scots Irish increase in Ulster to 1690 and is deceptive thereafter: from thirteen congregations between 1611 and 1640 to seventy by 1660, and to one hundred and four by 1690, with only forty-four additions thereafter to 1720 and only six more by 1740. Thus, too, "there is no absolute identification between settlement and culture" [Gailey].

Progress for Presbyterians was hampered by their exclusion from higher civic, state, and military office after 1704. As with Catholics, virtual exclusion from the landowning class by the 1720s was perhaps more demeaning and would of itself have ensured much of this civic incapacity in an age when most such offices went to the gentry and nobility. But as with Catholics also, an exaggerated account of such things became itself part of the survival, cohesion, and group memory of the Scots Irish. Protestants pledged to native Catholic exclusion, their relationship with the ruling Anglo-Irish was one of convenience and irritation, not one of affection or of radical estrangement. All of this has much to do with the psychodynamics of Scots Irish migration to America, and the traditions brought over with it. Little is known of the actual relations of the Scots Irish and ordinary English settlers in Ulster. The full Union of Scotland and England in 1707 made a socially composite Presbyterianism part of the legal establishment across the Irish Sea. By contrast, socially, politically, and legally, the Scots Irish now became the largest bloc of Protestant dissent in the British Isles, a whole community (unlike the varied social fragments elsewhere). This explains the élan and ease with which they would later fit into the American drive for republican polities and religious disestablishment in a broadly Calvinist framework.

Contrary to later self-praise by Victorian businessmen in Belfast or Pittsburgh, the original Scots Irish were initially no models of the Weber thesis as to the mutual support of Calvinism and industrious innovation. Contrary to their critics, neither were they, as such, progenitors of the indolent backwoods subsistence of the Ozarks and remoter Appalachian valleys of the years before the automobile. Contrary also to quasiofficial ideology in Northern Ireland from the 1870s to the 1950s, they had not been the sudden source of modernization in Ulster after 1610 or its sole stem after 1720. Nor had they represented a sharp break with supposedly rudimentary native

Irish lifestyles. They themselves changed markedly over time. Their development in Ulster was shaped by varied Scots backgrounds (regional and social); by the patterns, locations, and density of their settlement; and by preexistent Gaelic Irish economic activity. Local Irish and British market and communications networks, technical innovations and their diffusion, immigrant English example, commercial legislation in London and Dublin, and, perhaps above all, the local structure of landownership all prompted Scots changes within Ulster. Adaptability and borrowing capacity went together.

Ulster was markedly underpopulated in 1605. Immigration itself was a key to growth. This was well understood at the time. Early population figures are incomplete (indeed, this remains true of Irish surveys as late as 1821). That so many counts were made, if often only of heads of households, showed that officials were zealous not merely for plantation and taxes but also for development. The slow, phased subordination and concentration of the native Irish within Ulster's tenancies owed as much to economic situations as to political calculation. Productivity required population, and settlers themselves came slowly and preferred to come to fruitful fields and pastures. The myth that the Scots Irish were thus natural frontiersmen, used to pioneering wilderness from scratch, is nonsense. Migrants returning to America, and even their adult offspring, expressed shock at what total wilderness entailed. It is not known how many persons of Irish, Scotch, and English stock there were at any time, since English and Scots were usually aggregated. Religious statistics (as in 1732 or 1766) offer only a rough retrospect and guide, and the poor generally, and native Irish particularly, were undercounted. By the 1630s, there were over 14,000 British adult males in Ulster, perhaps two-thirds Scottish, and 20,000 by 1659. Native Irish were probably twice those figures. A total Ulster population of less than 250,000 in 1659 was 15 percent of Ireland's apparent total. By 1706, Ulster population had doubled and was then 25 percent of Ireland's. Thereafter it stagnated at around 600,000 for the next forty years. The years to about 1706 were also years of net in-migration; those from the later 1720s of probably net out-migration. Later again, after 1753, Ulster would enter a period of sustained economic and population growth. Before that, however, there was no neat relationship between the two, yet apart from war years (1641–1653 and 1689–1691) the rise in Ulster's population did indicate real growth to about 1705.

Most Scots came from a countryside undergoing improvement, at least from the 1630s. Famines and even dearths, common before, were almost unknown after the 1650s, although a major one between 1695 and 1699 prompted further flight to Ireland. In the better Lowlands, tenants (even lesser ones) were borrowing against rising assets of stock and better housing. Gentry were often indebted to them. Larger landowners encouraged the efficient; fostered farm consolidation; and patronized the rise of crafts and skills both among those displaced to villages, towns, and estates and among those settled as cottars in the vicinity of farms (and unlike Irish cottiers, these supplied service skills and functions to tenant farmers). As in Ireland, if less markedly so, this pattern was modified by considerations of wider family. Tenants with favorable long leases and larger holdings, tacksmen, were often kin of the granting gentry (lairds), if not of the lord and landowner. On the other hand, laborers had lower wages and higher food costs than counterparts in Ireland. But such changes were far from universal and less marked in the secondary areas of settler recruitment to Ulster (the borders and uplands above England) than in the sea-fronting counties which were its primary origin. Indeed, some less innovative tenants, laborers, and smallholders may have fled to Ulster (as later their grandsons fled to the American backcountry) to escape commercial pressures rather than to exploit them. Others indeed would have come with working knowledge of such changes. Native Ulster, by contrast, had affinities with the more traditional, but not noncommercial, parts of Scotland. Kin-rights were much stronger to favorable lands. Ulster, too, had a partially monetary economy, based largely upon cattle raising and on cultivation of oats, rye, and barley, pursuits common in Scotland. There was also native, if small-scale, linen and woolen output, first imitated and then improved by newcomers. The old, open fields system of tillage in the Lowlands, jointly plowed and periodically redistributed, paralleled that of native Ulster. It was called "run-rig" in Scotland and "rundale" in Ireland. The attested readiness of native Ulstermen to pay double rents and to add additional dues of produce "in kind," in order to stay on farmlands newly owned by British undertakers and servitors, shows the resilience of native economy. By contrast, a similar poverty was endured by lesser ranks in both societies, including one-room thatched cabins, without chimneys, shared with calves (and a cow or two during storms or frosts).

Scots and English in the six forfeited counties settled according to the existent patterns of the old society. Estates were divided or sectioned into *ballyboes* or townlands. These were various-sized units of productivity geared to the cattle-grazing capacity required by two or more families of some status, i.e., acreage for twenty cows or more, with some tillage land for oats. As the Scots increased, they tenanted the better land within the ballyboes, adding to the overall numbers of tenants (for the Irish often remained). They then slowly squeezed the Irish onto marginal lands. Both used the same markets, mills, and towns; the plantation towns all developed both Scotch and Irish streets and quarters. Thus, a pattern of ethnic mini-segregation accompanied by the 1660s the wider map of regional segregation. Despite politico-religious rivalry, this pattern actually testified to the wealth of the province, rising at a pace probably stimulated by mutual competition. Yet this was a stumbling growth. Hundreds of markets and villages established in the first years of plantation (1610–1630), failed to flourish (a sequence later common to new settlements in America). This was especially true of inland centers. As the Scots became dominant in the English ports of Londonderry, Coleraine, and Carrickfergus and partly turned their trade toward Scotland, and as the port of Belfast emerged to connect largely English mid-Ulster with Liverpool, Chester, and London, the economy of the entire province quickened. The restrictive English Navigation and Cattle Acts reshaped Irish commerce as a whole from the 1660s. The former before 1707 did not include trade with Scotland, but rather gave a new impetus to it, although the Scots did bar Irish live cattle from 1672. How far the more varied and finished businesses, skills, and farm techniques of the English settlers transformed those of the Scots (as was the hope of the Crown) awaits proper study of these English.

The landlord structure was a key element in first encouraging Scottish emigration, and then (in quick succession) shutting it off and directing discontented Scots Irish to America beginning about 1717. For a century before that Scots lords normally imposed short leases to tie their tenants to prompt efficient production, while the less able were forced off, and subdivision of land, especially subletting, was strongly discouraged. In contrast, Ulster tenures were designed to attract and retain rural population, not discriminate between types of producers. Scots landlordism was "hands-on" and closely involved with discipline, innovation, and output. Until after 1700 in Ulster, the undertakers and servitors owed a basic Crown rent and were usually of a different faith and ethnicity (English or at least Scots Episcopalian), and usually lived away from their estates. To pay their own dues, and earn the costs of their status, they used tenants and nonfarming stewards and bailiffs to get it from them. These found that only life tenures, or even three lives, could entice Scots to come, farm, and stay. Even native Irish were granted similar tenures although at higher rents. Only with political security after 1690, and a base settler population achieved, could Ulster landlords begin to move, albeit slowly, toward a Scottish or mainline English pattern of landlordism. By then, however, tenant customs were very strongly entrenched, including patterns of subletting that brought profits to intermediate farmers and others. Subletting also underpinned ethnic mini-segregation (even between Scots and English, as on the Rawdon estates in Down). It also facilitated social bonding among layers of the Scots Irish. This bonding grew with the rising stress on customary and kin duties among them, and with their efforts to avoid, negotiate, and curb the costs of the interplay of Irish boundary systems and customs. It was also aided by remembered Scots rights and laws and by English efforts to recast landholding and obligation through their own law systems (directly or as modified in Dublin). Because the top layers of tenants in Ulster were in effect "tacksmen," they could sublet safely. Because the economy was less developed, the cottier subtenants needed parcels of farmland; they could not rely on sale of their skills, unlike cottars in Scotland. Futile top-down attempts to change all this with the threat or possibility of hard times prompted the first real emigration to America, not of the capable and innovative but rather of tenants used to perhaps the most relaxed landlord regimen in the British Isles, and fearing its loss. Indeed, Scots Irish tenants threatened emigration as a lever against "modernizing" owners through the eighteenth century.

Eighteenth-Century Ulster and Its Emigration

Economy and culture quickened from about 1695 and "took off" from the 1740s, if unevenly, and variously, by district. Where an emigrant came from, and at what date, tells most about the outlook and skills he brought, not the mere fact of his being Scots Irish. Francis Makemie's early injunction to the first settlers in America to promote towns and trade was understood by contemporaries. Thus while inheriting the formative experiences and folk memories of the years 1610–1700, most Scots Irish emigrants came from a changing Ireland, that of the eighteenth century. Even their religious culture reflected this as many congregations recruited "New Light" ministers, influenced by the "Common Sense" fusion of theology and rationality taught in Glasgow; these did not subscribe to the benchmark of their ancestors, the Westminster Confession. This was a century of social and economic acceleration, most marked after 1745. From

1700 to 1775, Irish exports increased in value almost five times, with cattle and their products among these tripling in worth. Hemp, flax, and linen multiplied almost thirty times in value, until they accounted for 52 percent of the earnings of all Irish exports. Most of the production of linen was now north of a line from Drogheda to Sligo, and largely in east and mid-Ulster.

Since Ulster's population roughly doubled in these years, on paper it enjoyed an impressive rise in per capita income. It was protected from the worst ravages of the famine of 1740–1741, which elsewhere caused proportionately more deaths than did the great nineteenth-century Famine of 1845–1851. There were marked gains in living standards, and dwellings and holdings were improved. Numbers of taxable homes increased faster than population, suggesting a shift from untaxed impoverished cabins by some. Business in Ulster's ports expanded, and Londonderry, Belfast, Coleraine, and Newry traded regularly with Philadelphia and other North American towns, which offered markets for finished linens, while sending back the flax seed most preferable to Ulster's smallholders. These links offered the base for an organized emigrant trade. Ironically, because ships' captains could make enough from the flax and linen trade, they were not pressured (as were captains sailing from Dublin, Cork, or Rotterdam) to fill up outgoing vessels with indentured servants. Instead, independent passengers, often families realizing the market value of their "interest" in their farms (the land of which was owned by landlords), went out as free, paying passengers. These were recruited both in the ports and in the inland market towns of the linen districts. Yet the main migration from Ireland from the 1680s to 1717 was from southern ports. Only after 1717 did Ulster surpass an established Leinster/Munster outflow, which it never fully displaced. The main movement of Irish emigrants to America apparently came in waves: in 1717/18–1720, 1725–1729, 1740–1741, 1754–1755, 1766–1767, and 1770–1775. These movements were related to crises of living costs. Probably (as later with nineteenth-century Irish patterns generally) contemporaries noticed only such periodic bulges, exaggerated these, and missed a continuous low-level flow. The flow was also mixed. Half of the servants from west Ulster indentured in Philadelphia in 1745–1746 were neither of Scottish nor English stock. Among free migrants, Scots Irish predominated.

Numbers are irrecoverable, despite heroic efforts by scholars such as R. J. Dickson, M. Wokeck, and G. Kirkham. Even for later emigrations, Robert Swierenga, Cormac Ó Gráda, and others have shown the unreliability of most figures (by nationality and volume) for emigrants to the United States as late as the 1860s, forty years after mandatory reportage of arrivals there. By contrast, very few eighteenth-century port records survive listing arrivals. The method of multiplying the tonnage of incoming vessels by a passenger-per-ton vessels multiplier (usually 1 or 1.5 per ton) begs many questions, not least of which is the great difference between pack-them-in ships with indentured servants and cargo vessels with a few cabin and deck passengers. Ship tonnages were routinely exaggerated in Ireland to attract business. Moreover, wherever scholars drill new holes into uncharted areas of surviving eighteenth-century documentation (customs records, advertisements for sailings, lists of incoming arrivals) new patterns emerge (as for 1700–1725 and 1783–1800). Arrivals to minor ports such as Kittery (now in Maine), Savannah, or Annapolis, even early New York, often, if not usually, went unrecorded, as did sailings from lesser Ulster ports, such as Ramelton, Portrush, Kilkeel, and even Newry. Remigration from Portpatrick, Glasgow, Dublin and elsewhere is unstudied. Unlike Belfast, Londonderry, the main port sending out emigrants, lacked a newspaper advertising sailings for much of the eighteenth century. Indeed, the hunt for specificity in these matters may still have something of the ring of the ethnic point scoring of the decades 1905–1930, when a quasi-racist ranking of population groups in 1790 was used as a basis for entitlements to twentieth-century immigration quotas. In short, quasiracism fueled the search for quasinumbers.

As to proportional rankings between the ethnic groups leaving Ulster in those years, uncertain evidence provides almost little guide. Literary evidence, Irish reports indicating areas of recruitment, return letters, American genealogical and church records from colonial times, and (more reliably, though still contestable) census tract nomenclature studies all point to the Scots Irish and Presbyterian character of the emigrant majority from the province. But actual numbers remain elusive. One can only report that this knowledge is not broadly inconsistent with traditional and recent estimates. These range from a careful estimate of 108,600 Irish immigrants altogether (1700–1775), of whom probably two-thirds sailed from northern ports, if the pattern of the Delaware ports holds generally true. They rise to "probably 200,000" [Leyburn] or "at least 250,000" (1680s–1775) Ulster Scots alone [Doyle]. These are now discounted. From 1776 to 1809, a further 149,500 Irish immigrants are estimated [Fogelman]. Claims that "perhaps 100,000" of these were from Ulster [M. A. Jones] do not match other evidence that an increasing portion were from southern Ireland, or from among the non-Scottish, Catholic, and Anglican populations of Ulster [Bric].

Overall, then, a reliable minimum of 150,000 Scots Irish came to America between the 1680s and 1810, possibly more, arguably many more. The Scots Irish were from 6 percent to 15 percent of the white heads of household in 1790, with 10.5 percent the best estimate [Purvis]. They provided most of the [only] 15,000 full membership of the main Presbyterian church in 1800. These indications suggest that the lower emigration figures are more likely. But much depends on how many with Scottish surnames in 1790 are assessed as properly Scots Irish. This may not be relevant if (as in east Ulster the previous century) there was a trend for the Scots Irish to absorb other Scottish, north of England, and Irish elements. Demographic reconstitution from parish and kirk records in Ulster may eventually give more certainly in all this.

As Ulster was improving, why did they go? Land values and hence rents rose even more dramatically than overall output. Thus, both rising and thwarted, expectations played joint parts. Tithes, county and parish taxes, market charges, and a host of legal and professional dues, even semifeudal payments in kind, depreciated the gains of effort and belittled civic pride. Unstable linen prices cheated the calculations of honest debtors. Although religiously and ethnically fragmented in the later 17th century, Ulster had then offered Presbyterians security in their "column" of society. In the eighteenth century, they were subject to the rigors of market pressures as to the interplay of earnings, rents, and other costs. Catholics and plebeian Anglicans bid higher rents as leases fell due. While outlets in trade and artisanship in the rising towns existed, the upper ranks of rural society were largely closed to non-Anglicans, as were those of government by the Test Act of 1704, left unchanged by the Toleration Act of

1719. Even fairly prosperous farmers faced the problem of providing for their numerous offspring. They encouraged the migration of all but two or three family members, or sometimes anticipated this loss by choosing to migrate themselves when with young families. The alternative was to see the probable downward mobility of at least some of one's offspring.

Reports from relatives and neighbors who had gone to America were almost wholly laudatory about land quality and availability, livelihood, living costs, status, and general contentment. Only the familiarity, kin, and sociability of a more crowded Ulster were missed. Men harassed by debt and worry were less inclined to cherish such things than those looking back to them. If modern economic historians celebrate Ulster's textile-driven prosperity, social and cultural historians are less sure. The new changes were labor intensive. Women worked in the fields, kitchen gardens, and hen-runs and over the spinning wheel, as well as doing the household tasks of cottage and family. Therefore, women were often keen to go. Men of an older rural culture given to easier rhythms (the transition was regional not chronological in Ulster), and used to much visiting, drinking, hunting, and "cayleying" [in evening gatherings], found attractive the backcountry style in the colonies. Later eighteenth-century emigrants were often more commercially minded, sometimes even avoiding their kin in the Appalachian valleys and Carolinas' piedmont district who embodied an earlier eighteenth-century outlook, now marginalized in Ulster. In short, some went to avoid the burdens of change; others to apply the lessons of change to broader opportunities; still others because they simply wished wider fields. Almost all, however, went to reestablish the Ulster priorities of family, kin, and community in more secure circumstance, not to cut loose as frontier individualists. Some even took servants with them, or later purchased the time of imported indentured ones, whether Scots Irish or native Ulster Catholics. Perhaps they believed that the Ulster way of life was more fully portable than later proved the case.

Toward an Ulster America, 1720–1790

Late colonial America was proportionately more Irish than the United States in 1850 or 1900, if the Irish-born and their American offspring are any measure. Because these people were usually rural and often aggregated, they inclined to that partial retention of culture over generations that is usually associated with Pennsylvania's colonial Germans. Yet from the start, what they had was a mutating lifestyle, mediated through inherited patterns of kin, kirk, spoken language, and song, as well as some farm practices, that had not been fixed in Ulster either. Thus, the new way of life in America accentuated a preexistent adaptability. Partial isolation had the same effect that only strong concentrations could attain in the late nineteenth century, that of a viable collective inheritance. It also meant that such transmission was quite compatible with wide-ranging practical alterations in semi-frontier and post-frontier conditions. While some aspects of material culture were imported, others were adopted from colonial neighbors, and others newly prompted by fresh exigencies. Borrowings included the V-notched log cabin of the Swedes and Finns of the Delaware valley and the winter foddering techniques and wagon styles from the Germans of Pennsylvania. Such acculturation varied by region. Valid re-creations of the experience exist at Staunton, Virginia, and in the Ulster American Folk Park at Omagh in Northern Ireland.

The newcomers to America did *not* choose the wilderness as such. The Scots Irish reputation as frontiersmen came with the behavior of their post-Revolutionary descendants. The immigrants largely sought and settled available lands proximate to inhabited and developed areas. This is evident in their first settlements in Delaware and eastern Maryland (from 1683), northern New England (from 1718), in the Jerseys (from the 1690s), and the lower Hudson valley. More numerous were those going to southeastern Pennsylvania (from 1717/1718), which then enjoyed a century-long inflow. The counties along the lower Delaware became the hub of a diffusion northward in its valley (1728–1730) and that of the lower Susquehanna (1710–1731), and thence north and west to the Cumberland valley (1725–1755). Another flow turned south between the Blue Ridge/Catoctin and Appalachian mountains into western Maryland (1727) and the Shenandoah valley (1730–1741). The preemption of coastal and tidewater lands in the South, and the direction of this intermountain valley system southwestward directed the flow into western Virginia, then beyond it southward into the rolling piedmont country of the inland Carolinas (1740/1745), where it met a direct colonization from Ulster coming in from the coast (since 1736).

By the 1750s the eddies of the migration reached a similar direct inflow into backcountry Georgia via Savannah. Entrepreneurial encouragement and official sponsorship was active in many of these movements (e.g., James Logan, William Gooch, William Beverley, Benjamin Borden, James Patton, Arthur Dobbs, and Matthew Rea). The now 700-mile crescent was linked back to Philadelphia by the Great Wagon road, which had spread with the colonists. If some backcountry settlers regressed socially and culturally, those in the main, road-served, valleys were market-dependent, varying from multiple-market initiatives (Pennsylvania) to mixing farm production for home use with commodity-led enterprise (Virginia Valley). In North Carolina, butter casks were produced, as flax and potatoes were in Pennsylvania, to lend Ulster notes to the output of livestock and grain. A partly commercialized farming/trade nexus thus promoted reconstruction of familial and kin networks and prompted the rise of families of the "better sort." These often remained Presbyterian and were the backbone of that faith's spread in the South; whereas, less prosperous and the simply more isolated groupings later became Baptist or Methodist. Probably the reunification of Presbyterianism in 1758 had left many desirous of a simpler, more accessible and enthusiastic Calvinism for which the New Side already had set a precedent. The hostile evidence of Charles Woodmason, prejudiced by his Anglo-Irish and pro-episcopal outlook, is debatable (and belied by his own work on behalf of the Regulators in 1767–1771), if accounts of later Ulster newcomers to the backcountry confirm some of his strictures.

A trading class, with associated teachers and lawyers, serviced this population from York and Lancaster in Pennsylvania down through Staunton and Rockbridge in Virginia and on to towns like Camden in the Carolinas. Its members often came from families similarly engaged in Ulster, where crafts, merchandising, and the professions ran in families, and among the sons of farmers apprenticed to them. Ulster Quakers (if rarely of Scots background) joined this flow. The so-called backcountry was thus developed by greater or lesser levels of activity, depending on the nearness of such a service grid, which was extended even by newcomers well beyond 1800 (as at Asheville, North Carolina). The entire region wanted sound, just, representative, and orderly government, ethnically and socially (but not racially) inclusive, if stronger farmers and traders sought to be its preferred personnel. The distinct Regulator movements of North Carolina (1768–1771) and South Carolina (1767–1769), the Paxton uprising (1763), and even the later Whisky Insurrection (1794) have to be understood in that context, as does the drive for greater western representation in those colonies before the Revolution. The relative political peace in the Virginia valley confirms this, since government and administration there had such early characteristics. Far from seeking to escape from relations with the seaboard elites, the Scots Irish sought an interaction of mutual advantage. Likewise, their relations with German Protestant and Anglo-American stock seem to have been proper and friendly, if distant. With Indians, of course, it was a much more negative relation. Slavery characterized but few families, was often thought un-Christian, and spread widely in the upcountry only after 1815, although some prominent Shenandoah and Carolinas low-country Scots Irish were slaveholders even in the settler generation.

During and After the American Revolution

In this era, 1763–1800, the Scots Irish properly hold a place in "world history" as a key component in the first of the great modern revolutions. Whether one emphasizes the strictly Scots Irish inheritance prompting this role, or stresses that American circumstances and ambitions fueled and defined it, their place in the Revolutionary era is secure. Filiopietistic celebration of their anti-imperial patriotism, and post–F. J. Turner beliefs that their frontier activism was formative of democratic habits have now passed. Modern studies of eighteenth-century political cultures and ideas have sustained a close and appropriate relation between these middle-brow, enterprising, and rights-seeking localists of strong, if secularizing, Calvinist bent, and the mind-sets and politics of the revolutionary mainstream everywhere (except in the seaboard plantation areas, with their distinctive cultures and motivations). In the middle colonies, especially in Pennsylvania, New Jersey, and Delaware, they furnished committed blocs to pre-independence agitation, to the War of Independence, and to the radical and moderate politics of revolutionary change. In Maryland, Virginia, and the Carolinas, most (not all) supported both the war and associated political change, if slower of original commitment. Only in New York was there less decision and more confusion (as also among that colony's Presbyterians generally). This was partly a response to long-term British occupation, to economic interests in empire, and to the inchoate nature of politics in the Hudson valley, recently seigneurial, as also to Calvinist fragmentation.

Pennsylvania was central. The key link on the north-south axis of the colonies, it was at least one-fifth of Scots Irish derivation. Yet Philadelphia, home to the two Continental Congresses and first capital of the Confederacy and then the United States, had only a smallish Scots Irish element before the Revolution (skeletal to judge by church mortality records but more from indications from among the town's "lower sort"). By the end of the century, it had become their major center in America. This change epitomizes the story. During the Revolutionary era, the Scots Irish came from the colony's political margins to the center of state events. Before the 1760s, they were powerless, and their settlements (then largely mid-Pennsylvanian) were very under-represented in government. Even liberal newcomers like Benjamin Franklin had felt more at home with the secular, Quaker, and interdenominational cultures of the long-settled southeastern counties. Ulster's immigrants were also badly fractured by the split between New Side and Old Side Presbyterianism (1745–1758). Although there were Ulster-born leaders on both sides, most incoming clergy from Ulster, whether New Light or Old Light, stuck with the Old Side in America (which emphasized an educated ministry and ordered worship) against the experiments, revivals, and sub-jectivism of the New Side. Reunion in 1758 created the largest mid-colonial denomi-nation, and a vital link to New England Congregationalism when London pressed for an Anglican episcopate for the colonies in 1763.

Meantime, plainer frontier farmers had become aware of Quaker disdain for their security: The Paxton boys murdered Christian Indians and marched on Philadelphia to make their point, just as the Quakers became aware of their own isolation from influence in London. Convergent attempts at imperial regulation as the Seven Years War ended, with new taxation, currency, and settlement policies, enabled the Ulster Presbyterians to fuse frontier, religious, and American interests together against both Quakers locally and the British imperially, buttressed by a strong connection to New England (1763–1768). Thus, a nationalist "Presbyterian Party" emerged. Yet since most nonimportation and other agitations took place in port cities, not until the 1770s did the inland Scots Irish move to the forefront of events.

They did this by joining with radical seaport elements. Encouraged by the Conti-nental Congress, they displaced the Quaker assembly, and through a network of com-mittees, established first a constitutional convention and then a radical constitution with a unicameral assembly, general male suffrage, and a unique "council of censors" to guard the experiment. Wartime had brought a sense of crisis. A Calvinist coalition, including German, Dutch, and other elements, as well as urban radicals of English descent, sought to impose tests of loyalty (to the new nation and the state's constitu-tion) by oaths which thereby restricted the political community and deprived Quak-ers and Anglicans of civic and political rights. When the British invaded and occupied Philadelphia and its environs (Sept. 1777–June 1778), the Scots Irish sought to defend the state militarily, both by local militias and through the Continental Army. George Washington himself seems to have avoided tilting to any one party among Irish Penn-sylvanians, despite the preponderance of the Scots Irish, whose localism he probably mistrusted. Realism, ambition, and the needs of the nation as a whole caused more conservative and educated Scots Irish, such as Thomas McKean, George Read, Joseph

Read, and Charles Thompson, to lead and moderate the state's revolutionary coalition. McKean, Read, John McKinly, and William Paterson were also instrumental in securing the allegiance of both nearby Delaware and New Jersey to the American cause by adopting more cautious courses than were used in Pennsylvania. Despite massive documentation on specific services (by scholars from 1880 to 1940), the Scots Irish military contribution in the mid-colonial campaigns has not been proportionately quantified nor properly assessed. If visibly greater in western campaigns (under John Armstrong, James Potter, and others), probably the greater numbers fought at Brandywine, Germantown, and their environs, mixed with all the then-ethnicities of a rising nationality. That one of them, James McHenry, later became secretary of War under John Adams was a sign of the Scots Irish contemporary recognition, even though his political career was later made in Maryland. The Pennsylvania Line of the Continental Army, called by some "the Line of Ireland," was preponderantly Scots Irish, though not wholly so (nor indeed wholly Irish). The bugbear of American Tories and British officers, it was credited by members of the Continental Congress with saving it on occasion, and thus America's independence, as reported in the circle of the Marquis de Chastellux.

In Virginia, political enfranchisement and representation of the Scots Irish of the Shenandoah and its environs, and the acceptance of kirk sessions to fill the local functions of Anglican vestries elsewhere, inclined the Presbyterians to support the tidewater patriot planters wholeheartedly. They were also linked by remigration, trade, and culture with their patriot kin in Pennsylvania. In the Carolinas, matters were more complex. The Scots Irish on the uplands were remote from the seaboard. Deprived of representation, governance, and law adequate to their social order, yet periodically exploited by outsider circuit justices, they had fought "Regulations" (in South Carolina against their own frontier lawless men; in North Carolina against coastal injustices). Mostly second and third generation, they included some more recent immigrants from Ireland (via Charleston). Then largely without slaves (which changed in the 1820s), they had little in common with the propertied and patrician bias of seaboard patriot politics. While this meant a certain hesitancy as to wartime solidarity, any doubts disintegrated with the British invasion of the backcountry by Gen. Charles Cornwallis, who miscalculated their temper. If, as in Pennsylvania in 1777, some Scots Irish joined Loyalist militias, in the Carolinas, too, the active majority fought as American forces: notably in the battles of the Waxhaws, Camden, King's Mountain, Cowpens, and Guildford Couthouse (May 1780–March 1781). They thus helped secure British exhaustion and withdrawal.

The Revolutionary War precipitated the Scots Irish to full civic participation and political action everywhere except New England. Residual prejudice against them disappeared. Their goal was to enter the American mainstream, and falling barriers now ensured this. Their experience that minority rights were jeopardized by ethnic majorities, power concentrations, or religious establishments, whether based in London, Dublin, Philadelphia, or Charleston, placed most of them on the radical-to-moderate side. Their special fear of any convergence of such forces biased them strongly in favor of states rights and even more of local administrations as the best bulwark of their freedom. Doctrines thus later linked to slaveholders were for them independently rooted. The foundations were there for their later association with the party of Jefferson and later of Jackson. Their belief in minority rights and states rights found outlet in the planter champions of regional autonomy, slavery, and the common man. Their stance on democracy itself was ambiguous before the 1800s. Their belief in open access to skills, property, and hence to office holding had not yet eliminated the notion (taught by Francis Alison to a generation of their leaders) that there was a natural order in society and polity, duly weighted to men of probity and substance. This anti-egalitarianism, when taken with their localism, helps account for the shifts and divisions of their positions between 1776 and 1790.

Thus, in the middle states, the strains between backcountrymen and those elevated by America's independence were considerable. Many of the latter were also absorbed into the Masonic networks that were then fashionable. Yet immigrant United Irishmen of the 1790s, committed to a doctrinal (though not practical) egalitarianism and to a centralist (not localist) idea of revolutionary authority, found the Americanized Scots Irish of every sort difficult to fathom: wedded to a practical, but not doctrinal, equality of opportunity and to an anticentralist view of power. Moreover, the Scots Irish majority remained broadly Christian (with their deist minority respecting this) unlike many newcomers who were often assertively secular. There was some political excitement in Philadelphia and New York among newcomers and poorer urban Scots Irish in the 1790s. The Federalists disliked all the Irish (and did not distinguish among them), and the nascent Jeffersonian opposition sought to harvest any Irish support. This story is much retold to create an early American pedigree for both Irish-American nationalism and for later Irish participation in popular and reform politics within America. Most immigrants of the 1780s–1790s, however, were apolitical, politics having failed them in Ireland. The Scots Irish, so recently established but out of power from 1790 to 1800, preferred this, so as not to disturb their own status gains. They were happy to see any malcontent Scots Irish (whether among newcomers, United Irishmen, or once-Whiskey insurrectionists) made politically safe within the Jeffersonian coalition that triumphed in 1800. In the next year, the "Plan of Union" between Presbyterian and Congregational churches confirmed this advancing assimilation, while in Kentucky and Tennessee the revival meetings of James McGready and others confirmed the drift of second- and third-generation Ulster Americans in the South toward the revivalist churches.

The social rise in the middle and south Atlantic states was matched by another result of the postrevolutionary era. The Scots Irish, by *now* frontiersmen proper, flooded westward from the 1770s in three major movements. Streams of Scots Irish crossed the Alleghenies into western (and northern) Pennsylvania. From there groups entered the Ohio country (as the Indians were cleared), often initially as land grantees under bounty laws for military service. Others entered Kentucky and Tennessee via the Cumberland Gap, while yet others filled up the far western intermountain portions of North Carolina and western and southwestern Virginia. Movements into Alabama and Mississippi came after 1800, as did a full dispersal into the Great Lakes basin. If American-born Scots Irish were largely involved, all these movements drew settlers (often cousins) direct from Ulster. Otherwise, how *Scots Irish* a story it was will be long debated, probably at least as authentically as the main *Irish-American* story is Irish in the years 1880–1920. Acculturation in the older rural distribution or source areas had been limited by partial isolation and by much endogamy or intra-marriage (often to cousins) within the older communities.

The study of the cultural continuity, fresh immigration, and, from the 1830s, final total assimilation of the Scots Irish (and hence of their differentiation from a newer Irish America) has not been subject to the same scrutiny as the story before 1800. Until it has, it would be foolhardy to attempt a synthesis in the absence of even a rudimentary literature. There are sufficient indications to suggest that it may finally prove as substantive a subject as that of the colonial era. Indeed, it raises key questions about the fate of ethnicity in American life. Between 1775 and 1820, the Scots Irish (with others) pioneered the parameters, rights, laws, politics, and institutions of cultural diversity in the United States, on which the incoming Irish would now rely. Simultaneously, these Ulster Americans were also pioneering the abandonment of such enclaves for a full assimilation and (except in unconscious retentions) a full acculturation. Both modes of being *e pluribus unum* became central to the history of the country thereafter.

SELECTED BIBLIOGRAPHY

Bric, Maurice J. "The American Society of United Irishmen," *Irish Journal of American Studies,* 7 (1977): 163–77.

Dickson, David *New Foundations: Ireland, 1660–1800* (Dublin, 1987), esp. 96–127.

Doyle, David N. *Ireland, Irishmen and Revolutionary America, 1760–1820* (Dublin: Mercier, 1981).

Fogelman, Aaron S. "Migrations to the Thirteen British North American Colonies: New Estimates," *Journal of Interdisciplinary History* 22 (1992): 691–709.

Gailey, Alvin. "The Scots Element in North Irish Popular Culture," *Ethnologia Europaea,* 8:1 (1975): 2–22.

Jones, Maldwyn A. "The Scotch-Irish in British America," in B. Bailyn and P. D. Morgan, eds, *Strangers within the Realm* (Chapel Hill: University of North Carolina Press, 1991).

Leyburn, James G. *The Scotch-Irish: A Social History* (Chapel Hill: University of North Carolina Press, 1962).

Purvis, T. L. "The European Ancestry of the United States Population, 1790," *Journal of Presbyterian History,* 41 (1984): 85–101.

Robinson, Philip. *The Plantation of Ulster,* 2nd ed. (Belfast, 1994).

Wokeck, Marianne. *Trade in Strangers: The Beginnings of Mass Migration to North America* (University Park: Pennsylvania State University Press, 1999).

For full bibliography see *The Encyclopedia of the Irish in America,* ed. Michael Glazier (Notre Dame, IN: University of Notre Dame Press, 1999), p. 851.

SUGGESTED READING

H. Tyler Blethen and C. W. Wood Jr., eds., *Ulster and North America: Transatlantic Perspectives on the Scotch-Irish* (Tuscaloosa: University of Alabama Press, 1997).

R. J. Dickson, *Ulster Emigration to Colonial America, 1718–1775,* 2nd ed. (London: Routledge and Kegan Paul, 1966).

David Noel Doyle, *Ireland, Irishmen, and Revolutionary America, 1760–1820* (Dublin: Mercier, 1981).

Patrick Griffin, *The People with No Name: Ireland's Ulster Scots, America's Scots Irish, and the Creation of a British Atlantic World, 1689–1764* (Princeton: Princeton University Press, 2001).

E. R. R. Green, *Essays in Scotch-Irish History* (London: Routledge and Kegan Paul, 1969); 2nd ed. (Belfast: Ulster Historical Foundation, 1992).

Maldwyn A. Jones, "The Scotch-Irish in British America," in *Strangers within the Realm,* ed. B. Bailyn and P. D. Morgan (Chapel Hill: University of North Carolina Press, 1991).

James G. Leyburn, *The Scotch-Irish: A Social History* (Chapel Hill: University of North Carolina Press, 1962).

Kerby A. Miller, Arnold Schrier, Bruce D. Boling, and David Noel Doyle, *Irish Immigrants in the Land of Canaan: Letters and Memoirs from Colonial and Revolutionary America, 1675–1815* (New York: Oxford University Press, 2003).

Chapter 4

The Irish in North America, 1776–1845

David Noel Doyle

Since the 1770s, the major developments in Irish political and cultural history cannot be adequately portrayed without consideration of the role of great numbers of Irishmen in the New World. The Volunteers, the United Irishmen, and the movements for Catholic emancipation and repeal had their American dimensions: a stimulus in the first instance, a problematic resource in the latter three. The United States became a refuge for radicals in 1848 as well as in 1798, and Ontario became a frontier of opportunity for Orangeism after the suppressions of 1825 and 1836. Later, Fenianism, the Land League, and the Gaelic League are more certainly clearly dependent on Irish-American impetus and support, while Catholic growth after 1850, Home Rule politics, the literary revival, Sinn Fein, and the war of independence were at least partially financed and encouraged from the United States.

It is now possible to describe the principal Irish-American communities from 1840 to 1920 with some accuracy and attention to their regional variations, and thereby to illuminate the special strengths and difficulties of their tributary part in Irish development. For the seventy years before 1840, however, the evidence is more impressionistic: fewer sources survive, and the first censuses to record immigrants' country of birth with any accuracy came in 1842 (Ontario), 1845 (New York State), 1850 (United States), and 1871 (Canada)—although careful extrapolation from nomenclature has yielded results for the United States in 1790.

From an economic historian's viewpoint, to emphasize only the political and the cultural effects of emigrant feedback is to turn the story inside out, for even before the famine, Ireland contributed a third of all migration to the United States: between 1815 and 1845 certainly 420,000 and possibly as many as 500,000 people. Another contribution to the United States came through British North America: the Scotswoman Frances Wright reported in 1819 that servants "in the Atlantic cities where servants must generally be sought . . . are, for the most part, stragglers from the crowd of emigrants poured into the St Lawrence,"[1] although the cities involved, New York and Philadelphia, were themselves important entry points. Taking the perspective of a full century, it can be estimated from the statistical reports compiled by American, British, and Irish authorities, including extrapolations made for the years before 1834 and for 1846–55, when these series prove least complete, that between 1820 and 1920 from 4.3 to 4.9 million Irish emigrants went to the United States. (Moreover, a significant part of Connacht's mid-century population, in addition to recorded emigrants, disappears if births are compared with deaths and known migration figures, confirming the recognized failure of the authorities to catch all migration from the west, particularly that to North America via Scottish ports.) Thus Irish emigrants to the United States in that century numbered at least five million, or one-sixth of all European emigrants (about 29.8 million)—roundly fifteen times more than Ireland's share of Europe's population should warrant.[2] Although only a quarter or less of these had arrived in the United States by 1851, two-thirds of the 1,120,000 going direct to British North America in the period 1815–1920 had arrived by that year.

As stated, large numbers of the Canadian Irish later (often with little delay) reemigrated to the United States: 920,000 Irish arrivals to British North America between 1815 and 1861 produced a total of only 286,000 Irish-born in the Canadian censuses of 1861. Indeed the Irish-born and their offspring constituted probably the second largest ethnic ingredient, after French Canadians, in Canada's 1.97 million migrants to the United States from 1820 to 1920—a migration even less reliably chronicled by officials than the transatlantic one.[3] Also, Irish came from Australia to America: almost half of San Francisco's Irish-born in 1852 had come from there. Even more considerable were those of Irish birth or parentage who came to industrial America after training in the mills and mines of Lancashire, Staffordshire, south Wales, and central Scotland. These identified with Irish-American communities, especially in Massachusetts, Pennsylvania, and Illinois. Allowing for shortcomings in the basic official sources, such as failure to count returnees and reentrants—allowing too for those who died within their first six months after arrival, especially many in 1846–50—the immigrant base of Irish America, 1820–1920, cannot have been less than five million and may have been as many as five and a half million; more if Irish Canada is added. This is the stuff of true drama, as their return letters show.[4]

Unsurprisingly, this migration is widely interpreted as a demographic adjustment, which allowed Ireland's high levels of fertility to coexist with limited expansion in agriculture and a fairly sustained decline in industry. It also changed the ratio of Protestants to Catholics in Ireland: indeed, differential migration had probably been doing this from at least the 1770s, but the absence of reliable figures before 1861 makes the impact of the years 1770–1834, when Protestants clearly made up a majority of mass migration, difficult to assess.[5] More importantly and popularly, the emigration was an epic involving more active participants than any other conscious mass movement in Irish history, although strangely it has found neither Irish nor Irish-American literary figures equal to its scope—unlike the Scandinavian, Italian, German, and Jewish migrations—perhaps because it cut too deep. For it was an epic that emptied countrysides; separated families; scattered talent, vivacity, and ability;[6] spread Irish Christianity and its divisions; and introduced myriads of country people to the strains and opportunities of a vast commercialized society.

In American terms, the migration can be seen as a huge importation of manpower, skills, and consumers during the formative century 1770–1870—a transfer that was neither marginal nor indispensable but substantial, which declined proportionately as further Irish migrants were overshadowed by continental Europeans. The quality of the transfer is difficult to evaluate, as immigrants found when confronted by native Americans' complaints about the tax costs of imported poverty, but the youthfulness of the newcomers made its credit value unanswerable. From indentures of the 1740s and 1770s, from the ships' passenger lists of the Napoleonic period, and from the unpublished pre-famine American returns and the published post-famine British and Irish ones, the youthfulness of the emigrants is clear, and indeed increased as time went on. The proportion of emigrants aged fifteen to twenty-four rose from 37 percent in 1803–5 to 45 percent in 1847–8, and to 57 percent in 1881. Together with those aged twenty-five to thirty-four, the migration was rarely less than 65 percent and usually from 70 to 85 percent composed of those with the bulk of their productive years ahead of them and the costs of their rearing and education complete.[7] In pre-famine years, family migration was not uncommon, usually consisting of two or three members (presumably a young couple and a child), as during the first two years of the famine. Even then unaccompanied emigrants were a considerable percentage, and from 1848 onward they were a growing majority, as indeed they may have always been —if poorer remigration from British North America could be properly studied.[8]

There is little evidence of sustained large-scale unemployment among the emigrants (apart from seasonal joblessness among construction workers), except during the major recessions of 1818–21, 1837–43, 1873–7, 1883–5, and 1891–7, and during the labor gluts in special sectors, such as casual labor, in the famine and pre-famine years, 1847–55. Emigration from Ireland to the United States was sensitive to the downturns in opportunity; for example, it fell from 75,000 in 1873 to 12,000 in 1877, as earlier it had fallen from 30,000 in 1836 to 12,500 in 1838. This suggests a process of rational preparation and massive feedback of information from forerunners, which the surviving letters demonstrate but scarcely measure.[9] It underlines what should be evident: America absorbed virtually all the labor Ireland could send, 1847–55 excepted, and during recessions the majority of the Irish remained in employment. This contrasts with the long-term quasi-employment characteristic of Irish experience in Glasgow, Merseyside, and Salford, and especially in Dublin, Cork, and Galway. The emigrants' distribution confirms this: contrary to the anguished complaints of Irish visitors like Francis Wyse, Canon John O'Hanlon, and John Francis Maguire, among many others, there was no overconcentration in seaboard slums. Again, apart from a short period (1847–51), immigrants spread in almost exact proportion to the incidence of expanding economic opportunities; their preference, for example, for the northeastern and midwestern states reflected the development of transport, trade, commercial temperate farming, and manufacturing there.[10]

In short, the volume, periodic variation, and age-structure of the migration, and the ensuing employment and distribution patterns of those who went, show the coherence of the overall movement, which responded to the development of the host economy. Individual misfortunes and nationalist dismay should not obscure this, nor should the special features of the famine decade and its aftermath, which unquestionably furnished thousands of images of overwhelming wretchedness, be permitted to disguise the prosaic power of a mass migration that had begun before it, and would have continued, even accelerated, without it. Finally, in this calculus of effects, it is being established that, from at least 1875, Irish-American fertility patterns in states such as Massachusetts compensated for a decline in middle-class native American fertility, although by 1910–11 these differentials were more marked in rural areas and small towns than in the cities.[11] Here the behavior of the American Irish contrasted with that of the Irish in Britain.

American historians are again demonstrating the role of the Irish as a potent force in the creation of popular and representative politics and a variegated culture. As participants in the revolution, in state constitution making, voters, and small politicians during the years 1790–1816 (usually on the more radical side of the Jeffersonian Republicans) and as rebels against the newly respectable National Republicanism (and thereby supporting Jackson's new Democratic Republicans to 1836), the Irish helped to transform a politics of deference based on religious tests, closed candidate selection, restricted franchises, and unequal electoral districts. Then they divided: the Protestants and their descendants became first Whigs, then Republicans; the majority, the Catholic Irish, remained associated with the now less progressive, but yet assertively popular, Democratic Party, which they slowly forged into an instrument of immigrant-stock power in local and metropolitan government. As generally poorer immigrants—including Presbyterian, Anglican, and Catholic—they joined those Americans who opposed the merchant-responsive Protestant establishment, which exerted disproportionate power from about 1824 on standards of civil acceptability.

That such an establishment was informal and identified more often with the losing Whig cause than with the triumphant Democratic one did not incline the Irish to accept its pretensions, although both sides believed in the need for a virtuous republic; for a natural-law base for legislation, equity, and jurisprudence; and for the moral and patriotic foundation of education. Social barriers—disdain on one side, resentment on the other—rather than opposed ideas or simple class antagonisms, probably accounted for the Irish Catholics joining with the antiestablishment Jacksonians. The recent historiographical fashion for multiethnic pluralism can generate but a minor rainbow of special effects, apart from blacks, free or enslaved, for the years 1775–1890; but this rainbow everywhere refracts specific characteristics and dispositions among the Irish, as among the Germans, the major white minorities. These were primarily ethno-cultural and religious, linking classes in a shared politics.[12] The sharper class distinctions, however, developing with the simultaneous coming of the factory system and vast numbers of Catholic Irish, further influenced their status and subculture. Ironically, Catholic Irish could thus find outlets in a Protestant Irish tradition of seeking popular rights. In short, a truly postrevolutionary party had to promote outsiders and small men; the Catholic choice had been determined by a preexisting presbyterian logic.

From an Irish-American standpoint, the emigration and its early results were only the beginning of a protean history, not the least important parts of which were a tenacious sentiment of descent and a remarkable continuity of institutional association, based ultimately on huge and ever-reinforced numbers.[13] English and German emigration to the United States was as numerous and continuous as the Irish, from the days of indentured servants, through the mid-nineteenth-century arrivals of hundreds of thousands of skilled workers and farmers, to the early-twentieth-century mass migrations from the cities of northern England and the Rhineland to Chicago and Cleveland. But English and German migration was not linked to such unchanging emphasis on group identification as was the Irish. With the English, assimilation came easily and spelled rapid social mobility; with the Germans, assimilation meant the loss of their language, which was the core of their subculture in America. In both cases, therefore, strong group identity rarely survived the second generation and often did not survive the first. With the Irish, new arrivals interacted with the Americanized and the American-born in such a way that assimilation in manners, livelihood, and education neither opened all doors to social acceptance and career advancement nor snapped the links forged by churchgoing and pride of ancestry between the poor and the better-off or those men born in Ireland and those born in the United States. A common outlook and appearance, however imponderable, survived the loss of Irish accents and customs and even survived American birth: Governor George Clinton of New York (1739–1812) was known as the "Old Irishman," though born in the state of 1720s Longford immigrant parents.

There is perhaps no need to presume the continued existence of a complex subculture, based on insulation from the modernizing and individualizing host society, in order to explain Irish-American continuities. Some immigrants could indeed have agreed with their mid-century fellow countryman in New York City who confessed: "We are a primitive people wandering wildly in a strange land, the nineteenth century";[14] but young people adapted rapidly, for such comments can be balanced by many on the ease with which young Irish people became American in accent and outlook. In addition, the general identification with the Irish tradition, even among the American-born, extends beyond those most sensitive to the clash of cultures. This is especially true in the institutional continuity that was sustained by the successful: the Charitable Irish Society of Boston (1737), the Friendly Sons of St. Patrick of Philadelphia (1771), the Friendly Sons of St. Patrick (1784), and the Shamrock Society (c. 1812) of New York; the Hibernian Societies of Charleston (1803), Baltimore (1816), and New Orleans (1817); and the Erin Society of St. Louis (1819)—each may have deserved the tart comment of the New York *Freeman's Journal* on the Friendly Sons, that it was by 1863 "a sort of Irish 'What-is-it?'"[15] But they could function charitably as well as convivially, comprehensively as well as exclusively, and first institutionalized the message that one might be successful, monied, American, nonsectarian, even second- or third-generation, and yet organize as Irish without partisan political purpose. Legitimate Irishness was thus pioneered by the least alienated in America; much later did it become an instrument of either the uprooted or the upwardly mobile.[16]

Yet, in search of Irish-American consciousness, Irish-American historians exaggerate its importance. Millions can be identified as Irish in the census schedules, parish registers, press obituaries, and voter rolls. Often, however, such origins played little part in their subjects' immediate lives. The father of writer and diplomat Maurice Francis Egan, who came from Tipperary in the 1820s, though with romantic feelings about the old Irish brigade in France, withdrew from the Democrats over Copperheadism; opposed Irish-American nationalism and Irish separatism; distrusted his convert American wife's forceful Catholic spirituality; was enthusiastic above all about the development of machinery; and of his Irish home recollected only the picture "of a small running river half choked by water cresses."[17] Although he took an Irish-American weekly newspaper, he was not pleased when his son made his first career in the Catholic press. Such complicated personalities were doubtless more common and typical than an emphasis on strictly Irish-American or census documents might indicate.

This emphasizes the greatest problem of assessing Irish-Americans' influence on Ireland. They were not a country, a single caste, a general class, an establishment, a set of statistical certainties, or a predictable pattern of behavior: they were a populace scattered and distended by a vast geography—within states as well as throughout the union—frequently changing home and home town, immersed in a workaday world, and preoccupied with raising families. Waves of young newcomers washed afresh into them yearly, and seasoned men sought ever wider opportunities. Such changes eventually produced discernible shifts of collective character; from the rudimentary disorganization of the Pennsylvania frontier in the 1740s to the settled "Scotch-Irish" farmer communities of the revolution, and to the more eclectic but still largely Protestant and Protestant-led minority in a nationalist young nation (c. 1815); from the quiet, widely spread, Munster and south Ulster people, seeking assimilation in laboring, farming, and in the smaller cities (c. 1835), to the pathetic post-famine crowds of the eastern cities' tenements (c. 1855), and thence to the mature urban Irish-American society of 1880–1920, which mirrored the social patterns of the wider metropolis. Yet such shifts, so useful to scholarship, distort the continuing accumulations and dispersals and hide the multitudinous relations between the separate layers of experience: at the most simple, for example, they ignore the tendency of newcomers to seek their American relatives, regardless of their politics, culture, or place of birth.[18]

Amid such change, the precarious and transient quality of much Irish-American life seems natural, even within the skeletal continuities of clubs and societies. It is the sustained interest of small groups in overcoming this that is all the more remarkable, and particularly the determination of a few to direct the variable "Irishness" of their people beyond local concerns to the affairs of Ireland. Familiarity with the sources compels admiration for the sheer amount of work and journeying required. Neither the homesick patriotism of the unsuccessful nor the respectable ambitions of the resolutely American *and* Irish could alone have overcome the centrifugal fragmentation begun by the decision to leave Ireland and accelerated on arrival in America. Irish-America was an almost formless quantity that was the product of emigration, remigration, and the labor market, and purposeful Irish-American communities had to be made. Fortunately, the opportunities for work that America gave to newcomers, however unstable, helped organizers because they concentrated the Irish in towns, along canal and rail routes, and in manufacturing districts. Also, the resolve of churchmen to gather, identify, and minister to their flocks united for one purpose those whom others would unite for another purpose—indeed, clarified the very milieu in which contacts could be made.[19]

Nevertheless, the scale of the migration, the size of the Irish communities, the size of the Irish element in the American population, and the energies devoted to their organization contrast strangely with the scope of the return contribution to Irish development. Distance, difference, and inefficiency conspired to thwart many of the emigrants' efforts for their homeland, and to redirect them toward a mastery of American circumstances. Distance was probably most important, for the Atlantic passage took forty to forty-four days in the 1840s, at best thirty-five in the 1850s by sail, and ten or twelve days by steam thenceforward. Journeys between Liverpool and central or southwestern Ireland have to be added. In 1850 Iowa, Wisconsin, Chicago, and central Illinois were about two weeks by rail, steamboat, and canal from New York and Philadelphia; St Louis was eight days up river from New Orleans, and Pittsburgh and Cincinnati were a week from Philadelphia.[20] After the civil war, and the completion of the railway grid, although the west coast was twelve days, midwestern centers were only two or three days away from the eastern ports—one reason why Parnell and Davitt could enjoy more effective liaison with Irish-Americans than had O'Connell. Differences also sprang from separate situations, and in 1916–21, often separate nationality: successively men as diverse as Henry Flood, Edward Newenham, Archibald Hamilton Rowan, Daniel O'Connell, James Stephens, C. S. Parnell, James Larkin, and Eamon de Valera found themselves at odds with their American Irish sympathizers. The more informed Irish-Americans, by background and news, had a good grasp of Irish affairs, and in fact did not "see their way clearly" to simple solutions;[21] hence their poignant reliance on the dominant movement in contemporary Ireland. Irish leaders rarely had as good a grasp of the American situation but used Irish-Americans as a source of money and support, especially the more uncritical and excitable element, whom they thereby inevitably disappointed. Irishmen did, of course, have a better grasp of what was practicable at home than the more impatient in America, and even the best expatriates, from MacNeven in the 1820s to McGarrity in 1916–21, had been "out of things" for ten years or more.

Before and during the American revolution, Ulster-Americans were the predominant minority, apart from slaves, especially in the nine colonies south of New England, outnumbering other Irish, Scots, and Germans. As a cohesive group, strengthened by their struggles to control the Presbyterian church and to assert their right to representation in the colonial assemblies,[22] they largely dominated the radical patriot cause in Pennsylvania, Delaware, and the valley of Virginia in 1776. Elsewhere, less organized, more hesitant, and generally poorer, they mobilized in the revolution's defense following the British invasions of New York in 1776 and 1777, and of the Carolinas in 1780–81.[23] After the war, their power and status were enhanced by their military success and by the political liberality of the confederated states.

The period between the revolution and the election to the presidency in 1828 of Andrew Jackson (frontier-born son of south Antrim parents) was important, for it saw the formal emergence of an Irish-American community, with a discernible outlook, politics, and church life. By 1828 the slow fulfillment of the agenda of adult male equality and political participation, proclaimed in the Declaration of Independence, provided the context of this advance, as did the now rapid attainments of Ulster-Americans. Little is known of the social support of the new Irish leaders: all estimates of numbers, both of immigrants and of Irish stock, have been questioned, revised, and questioned again; even their significance has been questioned, because there was a widespread tendency among the Ulster-Americans to identify wholly with the new nation.[24] Nor can newcomers be precisely related to the large pre-revolutionary communities, although the natural links between the heavy migrations of the early 1770s and the later 1780s cannot be denied; for Ulster-Americans, the war of independence was only a punctuation mark in a cumulative process, as the civil war would be for Munstermen in the 1860s. After 1828 came an era of mass migration, strong native American reaction, a growing preponderance of Catholic immigrants, and a discernibly Catholic politics in the United States as in Ireland, so that ambiguities disappear over the next decade. At stake in America as in Ireland was the question; Whose traditions were to shape the chief elements of Irishness? Yet the changing answer was largely supplied in terms of the inertias of settlement.

Before 1828, with religious freedom guaranteed under the First Amendment (1791), and numbers limited, general assimilation and intra-Irish harmony were practicable, so that what became of Irishness was a tangential matter, not—as at home—the substance of conflict, power, and livelihood. Although the eirenic disposition of their lawyers, merchants, and politicians did not reflect the realities of Catholic and Protestant life, yet most immigrants looked up to those whose achievements made them both respectably American and self-respectingly Irish: especially the revolutionary survivors, Thomas McKean (1734–1817), governor of Pennsylvania 1799–1809, and George Clinton (1739–1812), governor of New York 1777–95 and 1801–4.[25] But the leadership of the newcomers fell to once radical immigrants, newly successful in America: the publisher Mathew Carey in Philadelphia; the former United Irishmen Thomas Addis Emmet, William Sampson, and William James MacNeven in New York; and others. Indeed, among these, George Cuming opposed the Clintonians in New York, and John Binns and James Reynolds led anti-McKean factions in Philadelphia, both struggles suggesting a breach between established American-born beneficiaries of the revolution and the newcomers, despite a common enthusiasm for Thomas Jefferson (although the back-country Ulster-Americans in Pennsylvania, led by Ulster-born veterans of 1776, also opposed McKean).[26] Yet it remains true that "what is striking about the group consciousness of this period ... is that immigrants from every part of Ireland shared a sense of fellow feeling,"[27] while a real Ulster-American continuity provided a context for loyalty to both new and old that transcended generational factions and the tensions between well-off and poor.

In 1790, from 14 to 17 percent of the white population of the United States were of identifiable Irish extraction: from 440,000 to 517,000 out of a population of 3.17 million whites. The majority, upward of 350,000, were of Scotch-Irish descent, with an unknown percentage actually Irish-born. The rest were of "native" Irish and some of Anglo-Irish origin. Scholars, though disagreeing about details, broadly agree that around 10 percent of early white Americans were Scotch-Irish, and 4 to 5 percent of partly "native" Irish stock.[28] Bulk migration, including many women, had enabled the former to reproduce themselves as a distinct people; regional concentration, rural isolation, common mores, and Presbyterian organization had ensured their coherence as a group for several generations, as had the prejudice and partial disfranchisement that they suffered before 1776. Afterward, only a minority remained Presbyterian (for many had been lost through frontier schisms and lack of ministers), although that church's organization kept pace with their distribution.[29] The total Scotch-Irish population of 1790 raises doubts about the standard figure of 300,000 pre-revolutionary Scotch-Irish immigrants, even of the approximate figure of 120,000 for 1753–75. Ships' tonnages were routinely exaggerated for purposes of advertising, and consequently passenger numbers have been inflated by historians.[30] High fertility in distinctive backcountry areas may account better for the Ulster-America of the 1770s and throw light on its enthusiastic Americanism, along with the tendency of its plainer members to leave the educated kirk.

The Catholic Irish almost wholly had come as indentured servants in fewer, more crowded, sailings, numbering at the very most not more than 100,000, including many Catholic servants from Ulster. They did not create a distinct community, for they were accompanied by few women, and Catholicism was proscribed almost everywhere outside Pennsylvania. In 1757 practicing Irish Catholics numbered less than 400 in southeastern Pennsylvania; in 1790 there were only 6,000 Catholics, largely German, in the same state.[31] Yet the population with Catholic Irish names then numbered as many as 43,000 in Pennsylvania and as many as 184,000 in the nation as a whole. This "hidden Ireland" confirms Michael J. O'Brien's classic defense of a pre-revolutionary Irish immigration apart from the Scotch-Irish;[32] but it was hidden precisely because it was intermarried and absorbed into the general population. Outside Philadelphia and a few Maryland counties, this Irish tradition was dissipated into little more than an anti-British bias favoring a new nationality, as both the revolutionary muster rolls and the cases of Matthew Lyon, Mathew Thornton, and General John Sullivan suggest[33]—a pattern analogous to Australia before the 1850s, except that the Ulster-Americans provided the main impetus to such "ex-servant" emotions in America.

Between 1782 and 1828 emigration was uneven, but its volume before 1803 startled observers and was put down to the new nation's prestige (its economic pull did not intensify until the 1820s). Maldwyn Jones argues that 100,000 emigrated from Ireland to the United States in the period 1783–1815.[34] Dublin Castle and opposition newspapers argued about the numbers, but reliable statistics are hard to come by. Robert Stephenson reported a heavy flow from Munster in 1784, "a circumstance not much known before the present time."[35] While the indentured servant trade declined gradually (a shipload of 300 from Cork in 1811 seemed unusual), American records confirm the overall increase in free migration in the 1790s. Fear of its scale, and consequent attempts to redirect the flow to British North America, caused Westminster in 1803, 1805, and 1816 to impose low passenger-per-ton ratios on American-bound vessels, while favoring the Canadian trade expressly in 1817.[36] This effectively doubled fares to the United States compared with Canada and deflected poorer migrants northward. Although Malthusian and political anxieties led to the repeal of the differentials in 1823 and 1827, new fares still favored British North America, so that a pattern persisted until 1838 whereby the better-off Ulster Presbyterians went to Philadelphia and the poorer Catholics to Quebec, St. John (New Brunswick), and later to New York.[37] British North America, however, was sought only as a transit base by the poor; apart from Newfoundland, government assistance was necessary for them to begin land settlement there.

Government policy contracted and redirected emigration after 1803; new policies encouraged its heavy resumption via Canada after 1816 and directly to the United States by 1826. The decay of the Irish economy and concurrent boom in North America after

1815, especially when the 1819–22 banking crisis ended, was the real stimulus. However, readiness to emigrate, most usual in those under thirty, seems to have accompanied the spread of English between 1780 and 1830 through much of Munster, the west midlands, and south Ulster.[38] These trends account for the characteristics of those leaving from 1815 to 1845. Emigrants from Ulster and north Leinster, who had under the 1803–5 acts consisted mainly of the more prosperous, now became more typical of the area's social and religious structure, except that the very poor did not go. Evidence from Cavan suggests an atypical level of literacy in the laborers' and small farmers' families whose sons emigrated.[39] The destruction of the weaving and spinning economy in south and west Ulster made subsistence more precarious as farmers hired fewer laborers in order to profit from cross-channel markets. But Cork and the southeast, gradually taking in Limerick and the south midlands, matched Ulster by the 1830s, with a similar outward flow of the better laborers and of distressed weavers, millers, artisans, and farmers, but especially of the sons of literate small farmers and cottiers. In pre-famine Ireland such people, whether from north or south, had some self-esteem and position.[40] Evidence from New York suggests that many attained a level of social mobility unusual by the standards of nineteenth-century Irish immigrants, most of whom came with little capital or useful skills.[41] In their first year, only the best connected and educated could avoid the stigma of being poor Irish (as New York City council complained of Newry arrivals in 1796). Contrasts between past and present status may well have accounted for the assertiveness of Irish communities after 1800 and explain why the rhetoric of equality attracted them.

These years also saw a basic shift in the American regions associated with the Irish. The 1790 census had confirmed the impressionistic geography of Ulster-American settlement and politics in the back country. Central and western Pennsylvania, western Maryland, the ridge-and-valley country of Virginia, and the Carolinas' piedmont and contiguous Georgia had populations that were half and more than half of Irish stock, giving those states, as a whole, Scots-Irish and largely post-Catholic Irish ingredients ranging from 15 percent to 25 percent.[42] They had spread west to the new states of Kentucky (admitted to the union in 1792) and Tennessee (admitted 1796), favorite resorts of would-be clerks and businessmen going out direct from Ulster to join American cousins. But between 1790 and 1820, the Irish element in Kentucky's population dropped from one-third to one-quarter.[43] The loss of control in the 1760s of American Presbyterianism by Irish Old Side ministers (whiggish and anti-revivalist) had hastened the tendency of Ulster-Americans to become Baptists and Methodists, as well as the erosion of the distinct regional community. The larger numbers of newer Presbyterian immigrants did not establish a church structure similar to that of the 1740s or to that of their Catholic contemporaries, nor did anti-Irish prejudice drive them together. Ironically, religious and political factionalism seem to have thrived as hallmarks of their now ready acceptance as Americans,[44] which has made their collective story difficult to establish.

The areas of Irish visibility shifted to the eastern cities and surrounding towns. Catholic parish life was established between 1775 and 1790; in New York, Boston, Albany, Alexandria, New Castle (Delaware), and Charleston; to the first diocese, Baltimore, erected in 1789, were added Boston, New York, Philadelphia, and Bardstown

A sunburst over the harp of Ireland tops the engraved immigration allegory on this 1820s blank membership form for the Incorporated Hibernian Society of South Carolina. The benevolent group—with clear ties to exiles from Ireland's 1798 Rebellion—was established in Charleston in 1801. South Carolina had the largest concentration of Irish-born residents in the American South in the late eighteenth century. (Library of Congress, Prints and Photographs Division, LC-USZ62-126785)

(Kentucky) in 1808. The paid clergy (not always happy choices) and bishops (usually better) were almost all Irish by birth or descent, reflecting a reality that Elizabeth Seton (canonized in 1975), whose father had given his life for fever-stricken Irish immigrants in 1801, candidly admitted meant a sharp fall into poverty and vulgarity when she became a Catholic in 1805.[45] Already by the 1770s one-quarter of Irish servants were indentured to urban masters; by 1815–18, the workforce of Du Pont's gunpowder works, south of Philadelphia, was an Ulster Catholic one.[46] In 1790 Mathew Carey founded an emigrant aid society in Philadelphia and Dr. Robert Hogan founded another in New York in 1814. Craftsmen, displaced in Ireland by rising costs before 1815 and unemployment thereafter, found a market for their strength if not their skills. The demand for diggers, hauliers, heavers, warehousemen, dockers, and carters grew as rapidly as the entrepôts of the new commerce.

If the "Old Irish" merchants kept up the amicable interdenominational Irishness of the 1780s in their various Hibernian societies, tensions among the poor led to riots: by poor Protestant Irish against established mercantile Catholics in Philadelphia in 1799; by poor Catholics against Orange parades in New York in 1824. These tensions broke up the St. Tammany Society of Philadelphia (which in 1783 had toasted Irish independence) when too many Catholics and Irish-speakers joined for comfort. Yet these two cities were exceptional, with the Irish constituting one-fifth of around 100,000 inhabitants in each by 1820. Elsewhere the Irish were as yet knots of people in small sea and river ports and market towns; or they were farmers and laborers in a vast countryside.

Hence the "American" quality of their life in these years and the mixed and liberal character of much of their organization and politics.

As America's buoyant economy gave livelihoods to the Irish, so too did the optimism of American popular politics give a stimulus to the dying Irish radicalism of the 1790s. The Federalists, architects of the constitution of 1787, and of its consolidation in the 1790s, mistrusted democracy and social equality, interpreted republicanism as the right of the propertied to representation; disliked the French revolution and the United Irishmen; favored Anglo-American understanding and trade; believed in national development under the joint guidance of business and government; and were homogenous, Protestant, and pre-revolutionary in origin. The Jeffersonian or Democratic Republicans favored extending the franchise, spoke of egalitarianism, stood for states' rights against federal power, sentimentalized French and Irish radicals, were anti-British, argued for decentralized economic growth, and believed that elites should be reborn continuously and without privilege from the people—broadly understood—whom all elites must serve. Ulster-Americans had either opposed the constitution before its ratification, like William Findley of Pennsylvania,[47] or later joined Jefferson in being disillusioned with the Federalist view of it, like Thomas McKean— the latter in spite of a sober anti-Jacobinism.

Naturally, Irish newcomers who were poor or radical, or both, favored the Jeffersonians, especially their extreme factions. This tendency was strengthened by four sets of grievances: restrictions on free speech and freedom of the press, impediments to free immigration and easy naturalization, the existence of religious tests and establishments, and the prevalence of restricted franchises and unequal electoral districts. Quite consistently, the "high" Federalists sought to restrain the right of opposition in times of diplomatic crisis, and one of the first victims of the consequent sedition law was the Wicklow-born congressman from Vermont, Matthew Lyon. Led by John Jay and Rufus King, they also sought to restrict the naturalization of foreigners, raising the residence requirement from James Madison's two years in 1790 to fourteen years in 1798 and linking this to their threatened deportation of United Irish radicals.[48] Federalist areas, such as New England, New York, and the Carolinas, made it more difficult to become naturalized, or to acquire citizenship—even to immigrate—than did states under Jeffersonian control. The Catholic Irish inherited this grievance from the presbyterians, and local regulations annoyed them until the 1850s.[49] Religious tests, linked to Federalist tradition, likewise irritated: the congregational establishment survived in Connecticut until 1818 and in Massachusetts until 1833; public office was restricted to protestants in New Hampshire until 1876, in North Carolina until 1835, and in New Jersey until 1844.[50] John Jay had secured an oath requiring the abjuration of foreign ecclesiastical authority as a condition of citizenship in New York in 1777 (repealed in 1806). By contrast, the four states of strongest Scotch-Irish presence,— Virginia, Maryland, Delaware, and Pennsylvania,—had abolished such disabilities during the revolution, apart from wartime anti-Anglican and anti-pacifist oaths in Pennsylvania. Ulster-Americans supported similar change in the Carolinas, Georgia, and New York, and liberal constitutions in the new states of Tennessee and Kentucky. From Virginia southward, they had joined Baptists, liberal Anglicans, and Deists in a continuation of the earlier post-revolutionary movement to ensure that Anglicanism was not restored as an established church. In all this, incoming Catholics adopted the Scotch-Irish ethos. Finally, the Jeffersonian movement for full male suffrage, the abolition of property qualifications for office, and equitable electoral districts (anticipated in Pennsylvania's wartime constitution) embodied semipermanent Ulster-American objectives (where these had not been achieved), and likewise attracted the immigrants.[51]

During the period of the first "Americanization" from 1800 to the mid-1820s, under successive Republican administrations, many of these grievances were removed, consolidating that party's appeal to the Irish. Local rivalries and minor appointments likewise secured their loyalty—a task made easier by their sentimental identification with American-born Irish Presbyterians such as Robert Smith (1757–1842) to whom high office could safely be given. Prominent exceptions, such as James McHenry, President John Adams's Ballymena-born secretary of war, and the Catholic merchant federalists of the ports, such as Thomas FitzSimons, could not stop the convergence of immigrants and Ulster-Americans in the Republican camp. (Nor could the belated sympathies for Ireland of younger and more pragmatic Federalists after 1800.) By 1824, the *National Gazette* listed seven Irish-Americans, of both stocks, one Irish-born, in the House of Representatives, all Republicans.[52] But by that time the respectability of the party under James Monroe and John Quincy Adams, and its inclination to resurrect a Federalist view of government and economy, was forcing most of the Irish toward its more populist faction led by Andrew Jackson, soon to emerge as the Democratic Party. Jackson was to carry four of the seven Irish-American congressmen of 1824 when he won the election in 1828. The history of the United Irish émigrés in politics, who became Jacksonians, has to be located in this tradition. Their great achievement was incorporating the discontents of new, largely Catholic, immigrants into the ordered politics of the Jeffersonian and later Democratic parties; in creating a common Irish consciousness that—despite factions—placed Ulster-American connections, achievements, and objectives at the service of their successors. The war of 1812 had offered an emotive outlet for this pan-Irish unity of purpose.[53]

Admittedly, even by 1820, with the foundation of the Orange Order in the United States, this unity had begun to decay into a partnership of tradition and convenience. William Sampson and Thomas Addis Emmet, indeed, took up Catholic emancipation, and branches of the Friends of Ireland, O'Connell's American auxiliary, flourished in several Ulster-American centers: Savannah, Huntsville, Natchez, and Charleston.[54] The Democratic Republicans championed O'Connell and defended the right of the Irish in America to organize in his support, a right the followers of John Quincy Adams tended to deny. Assisted by his Belfast-born cousin, Thomas Suffern, Jackson had the route to Irish hearts, though wiser heads—such as Mathew Carey, Robert Walsh of the *National Gazette,* and MacNeven from 1834—opposed his demagoguery. On the other hand, O'Connell rejected MacNeven's suggestion that he should use the Catholic Association to seek a federal solution to Anglo–Irish relations; his followers instead used the threat of the American Irish to warn Britain that if emancipation were delayed "the violent party would have triumphed over the moderate; the American would have gained over the British"[55]—a picture that exaggerated the weary aspirations of distant, now moderate, and fairly poor auxiliaries.

These episodes, nevertheless, presaged the beginning of a more distinctly Catholic "Irish-America," noticeable particularly in the composition of the Friends of Ireland, most of whose active twenty-four branches were in the port cities. They also suggested that residual Irish Protestant politics in America were by now artificial and somewhat manipulative. The journalists of the Protestant Irish supporters of Jefferson —William Duane, Thomas Branagan, John D. Burk, David McKeehan, and Joseph Charless—had, like their contemporaries Carey and Walsh, written consciously for American audiences.[56] With the appearance in New York of O'Connor's *Shamrock* in 1810 and the *Truth Teller* in 1825, as well as various newspapers in Philadelphia, all directed at Catholic and Irish readers, the creation of a distinctive Irish-American opinion was begun.[57] If it helped bishops to win their battles against American-born traders who sought uncanonical control over parish life as trustees of church property (the immigrants sometimes backing the churchmen),[58] this opinion also underlined the end of the earlier interdenominational informality and the beginning of an organized Irish-America. It was thus ironic that Andrew Jackson's accession (1829), partly a result of this older partnership, coincided with Catholic emancipation in Ireland, which was symptomatic of the passing of such a partnership on both sides of the Atlantic. Increasingly, the Catholics sought security in a new group-consciousness, realizing that the only reliable supporters of their difficult religious commitments and burdensome social predicament were themselves. Yet this realism was made possible only by the cultural diversity, religious freedom, and political rights pioneered for all Irishmen by Ulster-Americans and United Irishmen as prelude to their own happy assimilation into a republican society. Strangely, too, the paradox of getting Catholic emancipation by mass politics in a Europe where Catholicism was afraid of revolutionary democracy was not a problem in the United States. Indeed, the New York Irish, who in 1821 had welcomed the extension of the state franchise only slightly beyond "forty-shilling renters" but had to wait until 1837 for full rights in local elections, had a better grasp of the link between mass politics and religious rights than did those at home: thus they protested against the disfranchisement that accompanied emancipation in Ireland.[59]

Every distinctive aspect of Irish-America was discernible before the great famine. Elements present before 1828 had by 1845 been amplified in a growing and conscious society. Outside British North America, the fertile and ambiguous overlap with the Ulster tradition now largely disappeared. Irish and American historians and Victorian commentators have argued that the famine produced a uniquely Irish society overseas through the scale and character of the ensuing migration. They assumed that a flow along earlier lines would have been more naturally assimilated. The reality of the Irish in both the United States and British North America from 1829 to 1845 suggests otherwise.

Direct migration to the United States after 1829 fell below 10,000 only once, in 1838. If we accept reliable indications that just over half of Irish migrants bound for British North America later traveled south, then total emigration to the United States rose continuously from about 29,000 annually in 1830–40 to 50,000 annually in 1841–4.[60]

These years saw the real shift to mass migration, with no real evidence for W. B. Adams's belief that the turning point was around 1834–5. Instead, the increase in emigration during the American recession of 1837–43 reversed normal patterns and shows how the exodus from crisis-ridden Ireland, with a decade of momentum behind it, defied its usual sensitivity to U.S. business cycles. In 1843 the wholesale price index fell to 75, its lowest point in the nineteenth century, yet immigration increased to over 45,000 in 1844. (In 1819 a fall in the index to 125 had sharply curbed emigration, as would the depressions of the 1870s, 1890s, and 1930s.)

The mechanics of migration also changed during these years. The organized passenger business dated back to the 1750s in Ulster, Dublin, and Cork, proliferating in the 1770s. As late as 1830, it remained haphazard, with no scheduled services, with sailings delayed until complements were filled, and with rudimentary regard for the health and comfort of the travelers. A sharp decline in Irish–American trade after 1815 meant that return journeys from the States were often in ballast. From the 1820s, North American shippers concentrated their cotton, flaxseed, and even Canadian timber imports through Liverpool; low-volume return cargoes could be cheaply filled out with passengers, so that by 1834, 80 percent, and by 1845 92.6 percent, of Irish emigrants to the United States went from Liverpool.[61] Only the Derry–Philadelphia connection survived this vast redirection, apart from direct Irish–Canadian routes, used in 1842 by 80.6 percent of Quebec-bound emigrants, and in 1845 by 80 percent of *all* Canada-bound emigrants.[62] New York replaced Philadelphia as the terminus of most Liverpool sailings, with protean consequences, not least being the emergence of both Liverpool and New York as the dominant Irish centers in northern England and North America. New York, with a vigorous middle class and largely free of the strong Protestant Irish communities that characterized Philadelphia, became the virtual capital of the now less diversified American-Irish, while the two cities' links allowed easy remigration of industrially trained Irishmen from Lancashire to America's factory regions.

British policy increasingly favored emigration as a solution to Ireland's problems. Fear that she would "deluge Great Britain with poverty and wretchedness and gradually . . . equalise the state of the English and Irish peasantry" was strongly felt, since it was assumed that "two different rates of wages and two different conditions of the labouring classes cannot possibly coexist."[63] But such lessons from neither Malthus nor Ricardo could prompt general schemes of state-funded removal. Pilot schemes in 1823 and 1825, planned by Robert Wilmot Horton, under-secretary of state for war and the colonies, and implemented by Peter Robinson, brought 2,600 people from disturbed north Cork to Peterborough in Ontario. But the cost of £53,000 and unsatisfactory results won few friends in parliament, while as a venture of the "Protestant" party in Irish affairs it found no wide favor in Ireland. Parliamentary select committees of 1825 and 1826–7, which endorsed mass emigration, but on the laissez-faire principle, helped change restrictive passenger–tonnage ratios and led to official, if informal, promotion of a climate of emigration, including the establishment of a board of emigration in 1831 to collect information and encourage emigration to British possessions.[64] Worries about British livelihood, Irish stability, and the peopling of the empire suggested partial deregulation of the emigrant trade and its redirection to British North America, but the immediate and irreversible result was a greater flow to the United States.

Nationalist opinion reluctantly followed the government. In 1829, the Catholic Association petitioned against a revival of colonization by Horton, but in 1843 O'Connell joined others in establishing a Catholic Emigration Society.[65] Rejecting the view of Nassau William Senior and George Nicholls that emigration was a general panacea, they saw it now as a vital auxiliary relief; ironically, this had been the view of Malthus himself in 1816–17. Between 1831 and 1834, booklets urging emigration were published in Dublin and Westport. The poor inquiry foreshadowed the introduction of an Irish poor law, and many landlords came to prefer supporting the emigration of their poorer tenants, to supporting the tenants by a costly poor rate. James Grattan apart, they favored Horton's last appeal in 1829, and several now began private schemes, notably Lord Egremont's settlement of 1,800 Clare tenants in Canada before 1839. O'Connell helped such men incorporate a Canadian colonization company in 1835.[66]

Migration to the United Kingdom made many familiar with sea crossings. It is estimated that 254,000 went permanently to Britain in 1820–41 (probably an underestimate); in 1841 at least 57,651 went by steam packets, chiefly as migratory harvesters, and largely via Liverpool.[67] To move further afield was natural as opportunities became known. Likewise, the heavy recruitment of Irish into the British army and navy constituted another pool of potential emigrants: Irish fathers made no provision for demobilized soldiers, whose way thereafter was in the wider world. Again, Britain's public works, especially canals, begun many years before North America's, provided a mechanism whereby Irish countrymen could acquire marketable skills. Thus many of the blasters, artisans, contractors, and laborers who in 1825–6 built the Providence–Worcester canal were professional "canalers" of small farmer and artisan backgrounds in Cork, Tipperary, and southeast Ireland, trained in building English canals, often after service in the Napoleonic wars. Canal finishing involved brickwork and timberwork, which led many into brickmaking and laying, masonry work, lumbering, and carpentry. Tyrone Power's harrowing descriptions of those digging the canal from Lake Pontchartrain to New Basin near New Orleans in 1834 should not obscure the steps and skills by which youths of "middling" background used such works toward settlement and improved condition.[68]

Many of these projects got under way just as mass migration to North America began. A transport revolution laid the foundation of the continent's full-scale commercialization: "the annihilation of distance" as men called it. The Erie Canal, first envisaged by Christopher Colles of Kilkenny, trained on the Inistioge Canal, was begun in 1817 with American workers to link the Atlantic with the Great Lakes via the Hudson river, and finished in 1825 by huge Irish gangs. Their Irish bosses and subcontractors then bid for sections of the hundred or so other canals under construction by 1826. By the late 1820s, the 350-mile Erie Canal spread about 50,000 Irish-born men across upstate New York, with a middle class of brewers, salt-makers, and merchants in the canal ports of Buffalo, Rochester, Syracuse, and Albany.[69] Ex-canalers acquired land or permanent jobs along the 452-mile Wabash and Erie route as it was completed from Toledo (Ohio) to Evansville (Indiana) between 1832 and 1856, and along the Illinois and Michigan route from 1838 to 1848, with its nascent outport at Chicago.[70] Yet underpayment, the truck system, periodic layoffs, accident and disease, shanty housing, employers' abuse of whiskey rations, and permanent overstrain did produce a subculture of impoverished canalers who could never rise to such security. Others preferred road making. An "Irish brigade," 1,000 strong, worked the Pennsylvania sections (built 1811–18) of the vast national road linking Maryland and Illinois. Advantageous settlement resulted where canals and roads opened new or partly empty countryside, as in upper New York, Illinois, and mid-Pennsylvania, but when canals such as the Chesapeake and Ohio Canals (built 1828–50) crossed settled areas, tensions between canalers and settlers were high, and the former settled less frequently.

Unlike in Canada and the United Kingdom, railroad building also overlapped for a generation with canals in the United States: the Baltimore and Ohio, Memphis and Charleston, and Mohawk and Hudson lines, all begun 1828–9, provided further construction opportunities. These outlets lasted as line followed line into the 1890s. Here concurrent settlement awaited explicit company promotion as initiated by the Illinois Central Rail Road during the 1850s. Canada likewise built a competing series of canals to outflank the Erie system, to render the St. Lawrence navigable, and to facilitate imperial defense. The Welland, Lachine, and Rideau Canals (c. 1829–33) also depended upon Irish labor, as did a new system of government roads in Upper Canada. Indeed, it was here that the deliberate tying of land grants to construction work was pioneered—informally from the late 1820s, by legislation from 1841.

Yet public works, whether as means or as end, tended to concentrate immigrants in the United States and not in British North America, for, as the imperial emigration commissioners admitted, "Canada does not possess a tithe of the capital necessary for their employment."[71] Hence Ulster Anglicans with some means settled somewhat disproportionately in Upper Canada (Ontario), while rather more Presbyterians and Catholics tended southward.[72] This, rather than inducements to the former to build up an imperial interest on a Protestant basis, perhaps accounts for the patterns of chosen settlement. The several groups, nevertheless, interacted everywhere, not least on construction works. By the 1830s, the Irish conditions prompting mass movement of equal numbers of Ulstermen and Munstermen found expression in new tensions when they met in North America.

As many as 450,000 Ulster emigrants entered North America between 1800 and 1845. Between 1803 and 1819 they accounted for 65 percent and possibly 75 percent of the total Irish immigration, although after 1820 they fell to 60 percent of Canadian arrivals and 40 percent of American.[73] But total numbers were always increasing, and this new Ulster migration, which by 1845 was twice that of the entire eighteenth century, left many traces, most visibly in Ontario and Pennsylvania, although these were not microcosms of the whole. Emigrant letters, usually Presbyterian, reveal poor, earnest, ambitious youths moving from job to job to better themselves.[74] Yet Ulster emigrants can be found in the less skilled jobs, which did not require literacy: half the Ulster workers on Canada's Rideau canal in 1829 were illiterate, and many of the laborers of the Chesapeake and Ohio and the Wabash and Erie Canals were "Far Downs" (*Fear an Dúin* or *Fear aduain*, County Down man or stranger, the Munster term for northerners). After 1815 migration became more frequent in all areas and social groups in Ulster. By 1830, most emigrants would have had some schooling even from those counties, such as Cavan and Londonderry, which had relatively low levels of literacy before 1834. Likewise, the percentage of all emigrants who were artisans, textile workers, professional people, and farmers with capital and families fell. Such farmers alone fell from 44 percent of arrivals in the United States in 1819–20 (admitting that the poor were deterred in that year by financial crisis) to 15.8 percent in New York, 1820–45.[75] In short, the Ulster migration still influenced the whole Irish migration, though it no longer shaped it.

The Ulster migration had more to do with transferring the sharp rivalries of early-nineteenth-century Ireland to North America than the rising nationalism of Munster emigrants. Heavy numbers from Cavan, Monaghan, and Armagh, where Protestants and Catholics coexisted in large numbers in a contracting economy, sharpened craft competition in Philadelphia and competition for land in Ontario. However, the canal gang combats in 1834 and later in Ohio and Maryland show that regional factions were often non-religious: Munstermen anticipated scholarship by seeing Catholics from Longford (which had the highest pre-famine emigration rate) as Far Downs, products of the northern migration zone. More predictable distinctions appeared among the literate leadership: one-third of 1,116 known members of the Boston Repeal Association were from Ulster, chiefly from its Catholic south and west.[76] The Ancient Order of Hibernians, established in St. James's Church in New York in early 1836, was authorized by twelve signatories, all resident in Ulster, north Connacht, and north Leinster, and presumably Defenders. Among the Ulster Protestants, the Orange Order was established in New York (c.1820), the Gideonite Society (1829) and Orange Association (c.1830) in Philadelphia, and the Irish Protestant Association (c.1835) in Boston. As with the Hibernians, a constructive outlet for Ulster traditions lay in re-inforcing orthodoxy. After the Congregational–Presbyterian plan of union in 1800, a combination of New York's excited "new measures" and New England's liberal emphasis on human benevolence and will threatened the Westminster confession. Princeton University then reestablished Old School Presbyterianism with support from both ministers and kirk sessions from the so-called Pittsburgh–Philadelphia axis. Just as Irish Catholic immigrants helped their bishops against fractious trustees, so new Ulster immigrants, many influenced by Henry Cooke's revival, made possible a successful redefinition of orthodoxy against American experimentalism, though this split the church from 1837 (informally from 1828).[77]

Those with small capital might purchase farms in settled Scotch-Irish areas. In the woodlands of the Great Lakes basin, farms could be pioneered over several years for a minimum of $500, a sum within the reach of those who brought £20 to £50 or saved their first year's wages. Ulster Protestant group settlements developed here, as at Tyrone in upstate New York; Lima and Koshkonong in southern Wisconsin; and Allen County, Indiana, with some ranging outside this region, as those who pioneered Staggers Point in northeast Texas. But individual farm acquisition seems to have been more usual. The most concentrated settlement was on the northwest side of Lakes Ontario and Erie, amid the rolling postglacial topography of Upper Canada, with its rich woodland soils.

Nicholas Davin's later designation of "the Irish period" in Canadian history (1824–54)[78] was well based and threw much light on the belief of most Victorian Irishmen that the Irish could prosper in the empire and that their preference was for a "Canadian" (imperial) rather than "American" (republican) model for Anglo-Irish agreement. Here, too, strong intra-Irish differences invigorated, rather than paralyzed, their shared polity. From 120,000 to 134,000 Irish-born and their offspring lived in Ontario in 1842, over one-quarter of its population and twice as numerous as either the English, Scottish, or American elements. Two-thirds were Protestant, largely from Ulster. In 1851–61, three-quarters of the Irish-born were rural dwellers, both Catholic and Protestant, although later Catholic newcomers did settle disproportionately in towns. Settling in a common zone, twenty to sixty miles inland from the developed lakeshore area, the two groups took separate but contiguous blocks in each township, sometimes deliberately "lined out" as in Mono and Emily. In County Armagh, population densities varied from 383 to 453 per square mile from 1821 to 1851, but in Ontario similar community tensions persisted although there was plenty of land (the population density was only 30 per square mile). Ulster Protestants and southern Irish, however, used the same techniques of farming, but gradually learned Canadian innovations. Better initial land grants may explain the view of the former that they were better farmers, a view unshared by Davin and unsupported by the evidence.[79]

The Irish were prominent in politics, although their share of power was not commensurate with their numbers. They shared a common outlook and created a viable party by the 1820s (which survived and even linked the coming of separate Orange and Green organizations), in spite of being busy settling new farms, divided by religion, and grateful for their land. As earlier in the United States, this coalition had its roots in a common antagonism toward an established ruling party that was unresponsive, if not hostile, to their claims and controlled by the high-Tory "family compact." The opposition was inspired and organized by an immigrant Anglican Irish connection and their offspring, with roots in the Volunteer politics of Munster and in a whiggish Irish patriotism, not unsympathetic to Great Britain, that had opposed both union and rebellion at home. Its progenitor was Robert Baldwin, editor of the *Cork Volunteer Journal,* who came to Ontario in 1799 with his son, Dr. William Baldwin, effective founder of the group; others were William's Canadian-born son, Robert Baldwin; Robert Baldwin Sullivan, a nephew from Bandon; Cork-born Connell Baldwin, a Catholic, and cousin of William Baldwin and of Daniel O'Connell; and their immigrant kinsmen, Joseph and William Willcocks, who established the first opposition paper in 1807. By the 1820s this group took the view that only responsible government could prevent executive reaction from playing into the hands of the radical "American" party, a view similar to that of Robert Baldwin senior on Irish affairs in the 1790s.[80]

By contrast, Orangeism in Upper Canada, led by Wexford-born Ogle Gowan and other southern Irish protestants, grew rapidly in the Irish settlements, numbering 154 lodges with about 14,000 members by 1834. The need for society and mutual aid in the outback, the absence of old ties, and traditional religious and political motives encouraged its growth. Neither the first American settlers nor the family compact, much

less the liberal Irish reformers, had time for so divisive a loyalism. But the order, encouraged from London, helped Orangemen to get the better lands through official
connections, drew in Ulster settlers, and emboldened the "blazers" who "lined off"
Catholic districts.[81] Yet Ogle Gowan shared the Baldwins' antipathy to both the family
compact and the democratic radicals, and their desire for responsible government.
Together, their loose Orange and Green partnership temporarily abandoned reform
to outflank both extremes, and then joined to raise troops to quell the revolt of
William Lyon Mackenzie in 1837. As Lt.-Col. Charles Grey wrote to his father, Lord
Grey, "there was not a single instance of an Irishman being suspected. ... Protestant
and Catholic were equally loyal."[82] Perhaps these shifts reflect successful local drives
for power by the incoming Protestant Irish in a fluid society where both organized
self-advancement and a façade of tolerance were not inconsistent.[83]

Robert Baldwin converted Lord Durham to the idea of responsible government
during his term as governor-general, but Durham's proposal that French Lower Canada be united with Upper Canada (enacted in 1840)[84] changed Orange politics and divided the Irish. Gowan sought to exclude Quebec's Catholics from power and joined
the older Tories through the United Empire Association, until he accepted John Macdonald's need for conservative Francophone support and split the Orange Order.[85]
But most Irish, including many Ulster Presbyterians, believing in responsible government and the voluntary principle in education, also accepted Baldwin's Reform
Party's championing of Quebecois rights within the framework of the union. Indeed
Irish-born merchants in Montreal, such as Thomas Holmes and Francis Hincks, provided important links, since most non-Irish English-speakers in Quebec were Tory,
whereas through the nineteenth century most Quebec Irish identified with provincial rights. In 1847 Robert Baldwin, Hincks, and Louis Lafontaine won 57 seats in the
united assembly of the former provinces of Upper and Lower Canada, compared with
the Tories' 27; and effective responsible government, including Quebec influence,
came on their forming a government in February 1848. Hincks, noted for his broad
sympathies, succeeded Baldwin as chief minister in 1851 and held office until 1854. The
intra-Irish appeal of reform politics and their impact on Ireland await study, but the
clarity was blurred by the rival impulses in Orangeism, which in the early 1840s
sought the formation of a mounted police to disarm Irish canalers and an inquiry
into public contracts that benefited Irish Catholic businessmen.[86] Yet the character of
some newer immigrants, such as the Bytown (now Ottawa) timber workers under
Peter Aylen, who fought a "Shiners war" to gain local power, caused even the settled
Catholic Irish to distance themselves unheroically from their rowdier fellows.[87] As in
the United States, their place in reform politics partly depended on deferring to
Protestant leadership, and intra-Irish cooperation only partially survived the coming
of mass Catholic politics among O'Connellite immigrants and the Quebecois after
1840. In the more remote Maritime Provinces, less threatened by American or French-
Canadian interests, Irish-born editors and politicians, such as Lawrence O'Connor
Doyle and Edward Whelan, more safely organized the Irish in the reform interest
against the local family compacts and—like the Baldwins—combined this with support for repeal at home.[88] Enough of these traditions survived to entice Thomas
D'Arcy Magee north from the United States in 1857 and to keep most Canadian-Irish

out of Fenianism and assist the birth of confederation in 1867. Ontario did suggest, nevertheless, that even a modest Catholic use of representative politics could provoke a Tory realignment among some Ulster Protestants.

Indeed, even in Pennsylvania there were vertical combinations of Ulster immigrants. In mill villages south of Philadelphia, Samuel Riddle from Belfast and Bernard McCready employed large numbers of Protestant newcomers at Rockdale; while at Kellyville and Cobb's Crook, Dennis Kelly from Donegal built Catholic settlements around his mills.[89] Yet a common interest in securing protection for textiles united them all in favor of Henry Clay's American system (of which Mathew Carey was one of the theorists), and delayed and partly averted the intra-Irish conflicts that partisan rhetoric and new interests increasingly caused between Protestants and Catholics in New York as in Ontario. Whether these movements can be separated from the sharper distinctions in Ireland in the 1820s is questionable. In Canada Sir Richard Bonnycastle distinguished old settlers, including Catholics ("by no means the worst") from newcomers, "Orangemen . . . who defy the pope and are loyal to the backbone" and "repealers, sure of immediate wealth" who "kick up a deuce of a row; for two shillings and sixpence is paid for a day's labour, . . . a hopeless week's fortune in Ireland."[90] Suggestively, he linked the new tensions with economic, religious, and political changes. Renewal and revivalism were then transatlantic forces among both Catholics and Protestants. The elements that produced the self-conscious "Scotch-Irish" after the famine were already under way by 1840.

Apart from Ulster, Catholics came from two distinct regions before 1845. Between 5 and 22 percent of the 1801–21 birth cohorts emigrated or migrated from Sligo, Leitrim, Roscommon, Longford (with the highest percentage), and Louth. Likewise, 2.5 percent of the same generation emigrated from County Cork and surrounding areas, except Kerry. Most left between 1821 and 1841, not all for North America (though but few to other Irish counties).[91] All came from areas that strongly supported Daniel O'Connell and were troubled by agrarian disturbances. Canniness, organization, and a predisposition to regard livelihoods (however simplistically) as threatened by Protestant power made such people less amenable to gentlemanly "Old Irish" direction. Experience in North America confirmed their outlook; yet charting their movements is difficult, for only in Newfoundland were they numerous enough to shape politics. In 1811–16 and 1825–33 two waves of small farmers' sons, fishermen-farmers, and cottiers from Wexford, Waterford, and Tipperary intermarried with existing Irish settlers to produce by 1836 a Catholic population of 27,322, compared with 30,766 Protestants of largely English descent. From 1784 to 1893 the see of St. John's was held by Irish-born bishops; the Irish gained many seats on the governor's council and in the assembly after the 1832 reform. An attempt to upset the 1832 reform in 1842 by Lord Stanley prompted Daniel O'Connell to warn Bishop Michael Fleming of a bid "to transfer all power to the aristocracy or monopoly party."[92]

Almost three thousand miles southwest, in Matamoros in Mexico, an Irish merchant community was established by 1829, pointing to extensive, although thin, settlement along the gulf coast. From the 1750s, men from southeastern Ireland, often connected with continental trade or armed service, found their way to French Louisiana. Spanish control was consolidated after 1769 by Meath-born governor Alexander

O'Reilly, who favored established and new Irish families against the Voltairean creoles. Merchants such as John Fitzpatrick, Oliver Pollock, John Mullanphy, and the Forstalls built a network for the Irish who came to St. Louis and New Orleans after the United States's acquisition of Louisiana in 1803.[93] Four such Gulf merchants—John McGloin, James McMullen, James Power, and James Hewetson—received *empresario* (colonization) grants from Mexico in 1828 for two vast areas between the Neuces and San Antonio rivers. The first two brought Irish-Americans to their San Patricio colony; the latter two, between 1829 and 1834, brought Wexford settlers direct to their Refugio colony. These colonists supported Texan independence, fighting in the battles of Goliad and Coleto Creek. Climate and distance deterred many from following them, but like the Newfoundland Irish, they preserved in isolation the social and spiritual discipline of rural southeast Ireland.[94] Other knots of Irish in the gulf region were too scattered to cohere (the presence or absence of priests determining survival or disappearance). Paradoxically, the Old Irish merchants of New Orleans, St. Louis, Natchez, and Mobile, unusual in being largely Catholic, ensured that in a pseudo-aristocratic South Catholics lacked neither respect nor polished leadership, even as the plainer immigrants were ushering the church away from creole forms toward ordinary, even plebeian forms more suited to the American era.[95]

Irish cattle farming was skillfully transferred to the hot, dry bluestem prairies and mesquite savannahs of southern Texas and to the moist cool shores of eastern Newfoundland.[96] While most Irish went into cities and towns, more settled on the land than is usually supposed, entering as always the growth sectors of the American economy. In 1820, 72 percent of adult Americans were engaged in agriculture; by 1860, this had fallen to 59 percent, but actual numbers had tripled to 6.2 million.[97] It was a farmers' age, as the new transport networks linked expanding acreages and growing markets. Contemporary letters and settlement patterns show that many antebellum immigrants sought farms, if only after trying other things. Success came most often in developing zones, changing by decade: in central Pennsylvania and upstate New York in the 1820s and 1830s; in Illinois, Michigan, Iowa, and Wisconsin in the 1840s; and in Kansas, Nebraska, and Minnesota in 1855–75. In 1835 Tyrone Power noted that almost everywhere "the provident amongst the exiles … form an important portion of the freemen of the soil."[98] There were 50,000 Irish-born Catholics in the scattered parishes of the Albany area in 1845, and as many in the Buffalo area; both areas were erected into dioceses in 1847. In 1834, Bishop Francis Kenrick worried that only five places outside Philadelphia enjoyed permanent Catholic services; by 1845, five-sixths of his seventy-seven churches were outside the city (apart from those erected into the Pittsburgh diocese in 1843), in mill villages as well as rural townships. Some group farm colonies were set up, as in the Bombay, Java, and Hogansburg townships in New York after 1825–9.

As with Ulstermen, the settlement then shifted to the Great Lakes–Mississippi basin. In 1850 Irish settlers owned one-third of Dubuque County, Iowa, establishing townships such as the neighboring Garryowen. In 1850 there were but ten Irish paupers in the "canal belt" crossing Indiana diagonally, and 53 percent of 1,776 Irish-born household heads were farmers. In such areas, "the proportion of successful farmers among [the Irish] is as high as among the natives and English stock."[99] Wisconsin evidence confirms the view of Thomas Mooney that agriculture held the best that America then offered the Irish. In 1847–8 Rev. John O'Hanlon, chaplain to established farmer communities in Missouri, was worried at the ignorance, aimlessness, and dejection of the less prepared but noticed the success of others in wheat, maize, and stock production. To James Hack Tuke and Charles Casey, the efficient and well-liked Irish farmers did much to dispel the stigmas of prejudice.[100]

Deforestation rivaled public works in providing mobile manual work and a distribution grid for settlement. It took thirty-two days to clear one acre of forest. Over a hundred million acres were cleared between 1800 and 1850, and another 40 million acres in the 1850s, preceding the spread of farming from western New York to western Wisconsin. Many farmers employed woodsmen for land clearance, but timber companies used more. Well into the 1850s America built itself with timber and heated itself with wood. Irish lumbermen, many first trained in Canada, had a better entrée into local habits, society, and farm practices than did segregated canalers, and they followed the trade until they had enough to take a forest farm. Others went into timber milling or building. From Maine to Michigan, they provided much of the folk culture of American lumbering and helped to incline its politics—virulently Jacksonian— toward a melodrama of "sweats" against "wits."[101] Taken together, a much higher proportion than W. B. Adams's conjectured 10 percent of pre-famine immigrants worked on the land as farmers, laborers, jobbing or market-gardeners, dairymen, cattlemen, and lumbermen. Census takers' insistence on recording but one occupation per person (as in Ireland) obscured the full picture of the immigrant rural economy. Only in the South did several attempts to replace slaves with cheaper Irish labor fail: the Irish rejected the loss of status entailed.[102]

These patterns frustrate any attempt to see the American-Irish as a tight proletarian corollary to the rise of North American capitalism. Yet the shift from Ireland caught tens of thousands in an exploited, if fluid, dependence. Already the Irish were fragmented by place, task, and status, quite apart from religious differences, and many newcomers were at a disadvantage in a country of strenuous men on the make. The very successes of some sharpened the contrasts between them and the failures, and obscured, even among radical theorists, the engines of such relative debasement: past poverty and its habits, harsh and debasing early labor, low pay and loneliness, and the high cost of family maintenance. While pointing this out. Irish commentators conceded that most Americans judged men by success and not by nationality.[103] They did not pretend that foresight, industry, and initiative were tricks; they shared the century's respect for them, but instead argued that the poorer Irish should not be abused or underpaid simply for not having them. Indeed, precisely because the overall American view of the Irish was good, failure to concede their specific economic handicaps led to easy acquiescence in their condition, whereby after 1830 the majority seem "to toil without ceasing . . . , but a very limited proportion . . . ever reach to mediocrity, much less to affluence or station."[104] While the "respectable portion are more respected than the natives of any other country and amalgamate soonest with the Americans . . . , the lowest orders generally bear a bad character, particularly in New York."[105] Inundated with three-quarters of the Irish arriving after 1830, that city made such problems especially visible and presaged the post-famine years. Thomas Mooney believed it had 80,000 Irish in 1843 out of a population of 400,000. Philadelphia, though displaced as the first Irish city of America, also reflected such problems, though less sharply: in 1833 Mathew Carey believed that a quarter of its inhabitants were poor, and that these were largely Irish.[106]

In both cities the Irish unwittingly facilitated the shift from independent work-shops with well-paid craftsmen to large concentrations of employees in both out-work and factories. Those who examined this in the early 1840s urged their fellow countrymen to acquire skills that could not be degraded by technical change, but here native Americans were well established as cabinet-makers, ships' carpenters, machin-ists, metal workers, and quality tailors, leaving the Irish to mass employment in tex-tiles, construction, haulage, docking, and (in Massachusetts) shoe-making. Entrepre-neurs found that rationalized piece-work, by ignoring distinctions between masters and journeymen, led to success in the wider markets created by canals, roads, and the railways. In reply, workers created America's first large-scale labor movement, lead-ing to the world's first working men's parties, in New York City and Philadelphia in 1828–9. Their defeat revived earlier tactics of using city-wide unions to secure better wages and hours by strikes and to gain the ten-hour day by seeking pledges of support from local politicians. The first phase was almost wholly unconnected with the Irish, and the second included some leaders of Irish extraction (such as John Commerford, John Farrel, and Thomas Hogan) in organizing the inter-city National Trades Union in 1834, but usually the incoming Irish, unfamiliar with past patterns, and notably less interested in their own crafts as such, took what they could and accepted the new "boss" system as the norm. Farrel led the Irish weavers of Kensington to join Philadel-phia's General Trades' Union in 1835–6, but the recession of 1837–43 broke this early alliance and religious loyalties reasserted themselves, as feared by labor leaders.[107] The riots of 1844 were a serious setback for such attempts to unionize the Irish and to con-trol the paradox of the Irish weakening traditional labor even as they invigorated management and output. Afterward, union leaders drew in their horns, restricted the membership of their unions, and left the unskilled Irish to informal, and often vio-lent, activity.

Outside the trade unions, there was increasing organization before the 1840s. The Catholic population, now largely Irish, doubled from about 300,000 to 660,000 be-tween 1830 and 1840, and rose to about 1,100,000 by 1845.[108] New York city, which erected only four parishes between 1785 and 1829, added seven for the Irish between 1833 and 1845 (as well as four German and one French). Philadelphia's loss of primacy is shown by the fact that it erected none from 1834 to 1839, but six from 1839 to 1845. But such parochial provision lagged behind immigration. By contrast, dioceses were erected boldly, following the full pre-famine dispersal. To Charleston, Richmond, and Cincinnati (1820–21) were added St. Louis and New Orleans in 1826; Mobile in 1829; Detroit, Vincennes, Dubuque, Natchez, and Nashville in 1833–7; and Chicago, Mil-waukee, Little Rock, Pittsburgh, and Hartford in 1843.[109] Only Little Rock seems inex-plicable in terms of Irish settlement.

More than organization was involved. When in 1829 the first provincial council was convened at Baltimore, the dominant personalities were not Irish: for example, James Whitfield, archbishop of Baltimore, who presided, was English; apart from an Irish bishop in Philadelphia, the other sees were held by French, Italians, and Americans. Whitfield wished Rome to know of his opposition to "warm-headed" Irish colleagues, with "strong Irish predilections in favour of Irish bishops and Irish discipline for the U. States."[110] But within a few years the most populous sees had ignored his advice: the scholarly and prudent Dubliner Francis Kenrick was in effect bishop of Philadelphia from 1830 to 1851; the dynamic and imprudent Ulsterman John Hughes was coadjutor of New York from 1838 to 1842 and archbishop from 1842 to 1864; John Purcell became bishop of Cincinnati in 1833 (serving until 1883), his early years there being energetic and able; William Quarter, born in King's County, was first bishop of the Chicago diocese between 1843 and 1848; John England continued in Charleston until 1842, its three lone parishes signs that the Irish were flowing elsewhere; Michael O'Connor went to Pittsburgh as its first bishop in 1843. Thus by the famine the major centers of Irish presence and future growth were under Irish bishops long resident in America and familiar with its ways, yet at ease with their immigrant fellow countrymen.[111] It was a timely alteration.

These bishops, in turn, accelerated the creation of a distinct Irish-American culture that was urban and Catholic. The press supports this: early Irish journals had been chiefly political, but between 1836 and 1845 explicitly Catholic periodicals increased from six to fifteen, notably Patrick Donahoe's Boston *Pilot* (1838), the White brothers' New York *Freeman's Journal* (1840), and Bishop O'Connor's Pittsburgh *Catholic* (1844). Kenrick and Purcell put their brothers, who were priests, in charge of the Philadelphia *Catholic Herald* (founded 1833) and Cincinnati *Catholic Telegraph* (founded 1831). The journals were "calculated to explain our doctrines, protect our feelings, and increase our devotion,"[112] as the bishops wrote in 1833, the second object being extended to include O'Connellite nationalism and American aspirations after the narrowly religious papers had failed. At the same time, the Catholic school system was launched; twenty or so parish schools in New York City and Philadelphia reached at most a third of the children of Irish parents, with only 5,000 pupils or 8 percent of total school enrollments in New York in 1840—a low proportion, yet one not equaled again until 1880.[113] Irish-born bishops, zealous for press and schools, coordinated their efforts at five provincial councils between 1829 and 1843 to attain them. If not general, the response of a minority community was considerable, suggesting much common agreement on the need for specific, distinctive, and costly initiatives. Open opposition to such schools increased their Irish appeal after 1843–4 and clarified the adjustments necessary between Catholic, Protestant, and secular views of education.

Other indications of Irish solidarity emerged, but without the permanence of Catholic organization. In each city, humdrum Irish clubs, armed militias, mutual-aid groups, cultural societies, and emigrant assistance charities now paralleled the exclusive societies of the "Old Irish." Boston, New York, and New Orleans had units of Montgomery Guards in the 1830s, named after the County-Dublin-born hero of 1775; these cities created or revived Hibernian or Shamrock benevolent societies between 1839 and 1844 as the recession changed priorities; Boston's Hibernian Lyceum, Hartford's Hibernian Institute, and New York's Carroll Club served the bookish; the Irish in New York city also created provident and temperance societies. Indeed, the Boston Irish organized an Irish Temperance Society in 1836, two years before Fr. Mathew's in

AN ACT to incorporate the HIBERNIAN BE-
NEVOLENT ASSOCIATION of the city of
TROY.   [Passed March 7, 1834.]

The People of the State of New-York, represented
in Senate and Assembly, do enact as follows:

§ 1. There shall be established and located in the
city of Troy, a charitable society, by the name of the
HIBERNIAN BENEVOLENT ASSOCIATION, of the city of
Troy.

§ 2. Patrick Purcell, Patrick Brogan, John Hogan,
Patrick Keenan, Barney Reynolds, Samuel Russell, and
such other persons as are or may become members of
said Association, are hereby constituted a body corporate by the name aforesaid.

§ 3. The objects of this Association are charitable, and
to afford relief to its members in cases of sickness and
infirmity.

§ 4. The corporation shall have power to prescribe
rules and regulations for the admission of its members,
and their government, election of its officers, and their
duty, and expelling any of its members for not observing
its laws.

§ 5. The annual income of the real and personal estate which the said corporation may at any time hold,
shall not exceed two thousand dollars.

§ 6. The corporation shall possess the general powers, and be subject to the general restrictions and liabili-
ties prescribed in the third title of the eighteenth chapter
of the first part of the Revised Statutes.

§ 7. The Legislature may at any time modify, alter,
or repeal this act or any of its provisions.

STATE OF NEW-YORK, ⎱
    Secretary's Office, ⎰

I have compared the preceding with an original act of
the Legislature of this State, on file in this office, and do
certify that the same is a correct transcript therefrom,
and of the whole of said original.

                              ARCH'D CAMPBELL,
Albany, April 29, 1834.   *Dep. Secretary.*

Troy, Albany's industrial neighbor in upstate New York, successfully incorporated an Hibernian Benevolent Association in
1834. At the mouth of the Erie Canal and a cast-iron manufacturing giant in the early nineteenth century, Troy was a destination for the Irish—including those disembarking in Quebec—
who were attracted by employment in its factories from the
1820s. (Archives of Irish America, New York University)

Cork. Among all these, only the Irish Emigrant Aid Society, founded by Archbishop
Hughes in 1841, the Irish Emigrants' Society of 1844 (later the Emigrant Savings
Bank), and the Ancient Order of Hibernians of 1836 survived—all linked to church
circles in New York city. Much else failed, such as a movement for Catholic adult education. The young Thomas D'Arcy McGee, returning from Boston to Ireland in 1845,
concluded that much organization was born of a false sense of inferiority that fled
from improvement and failed because Irishmen were "too independent with each
other, and not sufficiently so with other classes."[114] Yet the extension of prejudice
drove immigrants with gifts of leadership and education to work with their fellow

Irishmen; whereas before 1835 visitors like Tyrone Power and Walter Myler assumed that prejudice existed against only the poorer Irish, afterward even suave sojourners such as Thomas Colley Grattan and Francis Wyse noted that all Irishmen now encountered some dislike.[115] As yet, the conditions to produce Irish organizations that were not linked to religion had not fully developed.

For churchmen, editors, and laymen saw the new country in a more optimistic light before 1840 than at any time until the 1890s. To Alexis de Tocqueville, Catholics were the most republican and democratic group in politics, but the most deferential in doctrine. Though fearing a certain Pelagian self-reliance in its culture, Francis Kenrick assumed this in his seven-volume application (1839–43) of Ligourian theology to American circumstance.[116] As a lower-class religious minority, Catholics had much to gain from republican institutions and the separation of church and state. To de Tocqueville, the religious principle moderated the race for comfort, and joined together men divided by an obsessive individuality. Roman Catholicism—certain, clear, and equal in its criteria of salvation—best performed these functions, for it was beyond the reach of pantheism and chaotic subjectivity, in a society of equals bent on self-improvement.[117] Less boldly, most Catholics experienced a natural connection between faith, everyday life, and politics, if few shared Bishop John England's enthusiasm for America as a field for evangelization.[118] Common and statute law, popular custom, and personal and property rights were largely congruent with Catholic ideas; jurists upheld a generalized Christianity as the civic religion of the republic, and a "common sense" natural law as the basis of constitutional and legal reasoning. Popular morality in the northern states respected feminine virtue and asserted family values to a degree that astounded continental Europeans and reassured the Irish, even if men's restless ambition did weaken the substance of social and family life. Waves of popular anti-Catholicism, still limited, broke as much on the decencies of American Protestants as on the example of the settled Irish: in 1836 Maria Monk's fabricated *Awful Disclosures* evoked an immediate and carefully researched rebuttal from William Stone, editor of New York's *Commercial Appeal* (though it did go on to sell 300,000 copies by 1860, becoming the "*Uncle Tom's Cabin* of Know Nothingism").[119]

If Charlestown's Ursuline convent was burned down in 1834 by New England working men, hundreds of other churches and schools were built without opposition, even with encouragement. Andrew Jackson, attuned to such currents, safely made Roger B. Taney (legal adviser to the Catholic hierarchy) attorney general in 1831, and Martin Van Buren promoted him to the chief-justiceship in 1837. Indeed, ordinary Irishmen tended to overlook the Protestant context of American law, custom, and behavior (as continental European visitors did not). They thus ascribed reaction against them to evangelical revival alone, failing to see the latter's intimate connections with American culture. Likewise, they overestimated the future convergence between American culture and Catholic beliefs: the Boston *Pilot* prophesied in 1843 that "catholicism will obtain an ascendancy over all the minds in the land," while the Cincinnati *Catholic Telegraph* asserted that by 1885 that city would be "a little Rome in the west."[120] Thus the very optimism of the 1830s fostered impolitic expectations, soon sharply reversed, and also emboldened Catholics to an extent that made the older mediating role of Irish Protestants awkward, though hardly superfluous.

The impact of American politics had similar effects. Grasped in an initial mood of cheerful—at times ructious—participation, party activities brought home the Irish presence to others, and by causing reaction played into the hands of those who wanted to win over various constituencies by anti-Irish rhetoric.[121] They also taught the Irish that—like it or not—their secular fortunes, too, were collective as well as individual. Irish-American nationalism presupposed these lessons; the expansion of church and community networks was aided by the rise of an Irish-American politics, with voting power used for local advantages. Party managers, especially Democrats, mobilized Irish Catholic voters more readily, if subordinately, when close elections and high turnouts (reaching 78 percent of those eligible by 1840) drove competing parties to secure every possible follower. To the attractions of the 1820s—franchise extension, abolition of religious tests, easy naturalization, the cult of the "Irish-American" Jackson—were added Working Men's Party reforms belatedly espoused by the Democrats: mechanics' lien laws, free public education, the ten-hour day on public works, and the abolition of imprisonment for debt; all important to poorer men.[122] The long resistance of the New England and the southern seaboard states to granting full civic rights for foreign-born, unpropertied, Catholic, and migratory males kept the earlier slights and issues alive, for the Irish were often all four. Moreover, the anti-elitist and anti-monopoly rhetoric of the Jacksonians, especially when aimed at the Second Bank of the United States, renewed such resentments, and had an appeal for newcomers, attracted by O'Connell's attacks at home on the Tory establishment and his efforts to break the power of the Bank of Ireland by establishing rival commercial, agricultural, and provincial banks.

The new-style electioneering—with mass meetings, barnstorming, canvassing, and demagoguery—appealed to immigrants who regarded politics as an outlet for participatory enthusiasm rather than as an object of systematic calculations (a Jacksonian spokesman believed the Irish correct but unattractive in their politics).[123] Local maneuverings suggest that many did understand the stakes and strengthened the drift to the Democrats. In upstate New York, transplanted New Englanders grasped successfully at the opportunities of the region, but Irish competition was close. The former embraced the "free grace" principle of revivalism, a general-access Calvinism, and the "fair field and no favor" economic ideal, turning first to political anti-Freemasonry (linked there with anti-Catholicism) and thence to the Whig Party. Ulster Protestant immigrants, and more slowly the settled Ulster-Americans of Ulster and Orange Counties, found this new politics congenial.[124] The countercoalition of poorer farmers, unrevived Protestants, old New Yorker families, private bankers, Freethinkers, lumbermen, and Irish Catholics formed logically enough. The Democrat Martin Van Buren opposed Irish enfranchisement in 1821, supported it in 1826, and won Catholic support as a result. In New York City, the old Irish merchant community and unrevived Protestants drew newcomers to the Democrats and gave various minor offices to Catholics by 1843, as well as the leading positions in the older Friendly Sons of St. Patrick. But in the city, too, anti-Catholicism was an ingredient in politics by 1835–6.[125] In short, a natural differentiation of communities in a helter-skelter world of rapid development produced a normal enough differentiation of voting patterns, and hence the emergence of a Catholic Irish-American politics.

The schools question accelerated this. Although the Democrats refused to support denominational schools, they benefited from the demand for them, being seen as more neutral than the rival Whigs, at least by the Irish. Catholics had two aims: to create parochial schools where they could and to make the public schools more acceptable by depriving them of specific Protestant management, content, and tone. Any neat Protestant–Catholic division (much less agreement) was precluded by the complexity of the jurisdictions involved, by the varied and changing values of their residents, by the prohibition of public aid to religious schools as such, and by the huge numbers of children of Irish Catholics attending public schools from poverty or preference. Catholics allied with less established Protestants to secure nondenominational schools (as indeed they did also in Ontario in the 1820s);[126] this was another factor drawing them to the Democrats. Whigs, and later Republicans, tended to be more sympathetic to the popular feeling that believed a broadly evangelical curriculum to be American without being a formal establishment of religion. Strangely, yet logically, the first major crisis came when New York's Whigs, wishing to redress their overreliance on such support, offered to create special public schools catering to minority convictions. Though sincere, Governor William Seward sought gains among the state's 120,000, largely Irish, Catholics. Archbishop John Hughes, in turn, sought funds from the State Assembly and the New York City Council for his parochial schools, since few Catholics could afford their fees, but both refused his request. Seward then replaced the city's Protestant Public Schools Society with an elective school board responsive to Catholics. The Democrats refused to back any aid schemes, yet held the Irish vote by patronage and tradition, while Hughes ran sufficient of his own candidates to irritate both parties. Affronted by these maneuvers, nativists organized their first major party and captured the city council in 1844, with strong immigrant Orange support.[127]

Seward and Hughes held that minority rights in a free republic ought to be given the fullest recognition, but failed to see that, for many Americans whose culture was inextricably bound to Protestantism, such objectivity could seem "a preconceived determination . . . to put down the whole protestant religion as being sectarian," as the nativist party manifesto put it.[128] Thereafter, the new school board did indeed veer toward the secular moralism of Horace Mann, doctrinaire secretary of the Massachusetts school board (1837–48), but politicians saw to it that teaching appointments reflected local realities, aiding over 80 percent of the city's children to attend common schools during the next half-century. Such intangible results persuaded the hierarchy of the need for parochial schools by their first plenary council in 1851 and caused them to make such provision mandatory in every parish by the third plenary council in 1884, although never obligatory for all Catholic children.[129]

In Philadelphia, where the schools issue was scarcely raised by Catholics, severe riots followed in the wake of New York's disputes. In 1834 Pennsylvania had abolished its education system, provided by a Protestant body, and replaced it with neutral public schools that attracted most Catholics, as Bishop Francis Kenrick's seminary rector, Dr. Edward Barron, wrote to Paul Cullen. Kenrick did not object to the common reading of the King James Bible in them, nor did he seek state aid, but on 12 November 1842 and 12 March 1844 he did request the city's school board to allow optional use of the Douai version of the Bible on request.[130] The American Protestant Association (to which most ministers belonged) and the local nativist party represented this as a full-scale threat to Bible education for American children. When they met on 3 May 1844 in Kensington, an Irish district, rioting broke out. During the next six days, nativists and Orangemen invaded the district, burning sixty Catholic Irish houses and two churches; twelve nativists died in an attack on the Hibernian volunteer firehouse. In July, rioting was renewed in the Southwark district, the St. Philip Neri's church was attacked, and at least thirteen were killed in clashes with state militia.

Although almost all the dead were native Americans, these incidents made a deep impression on Philadelphia's Irish parishes (the German ones had been unmolested). In New York, plans for mass agitation were called off when Archbishop Hughes warned that the city would be burned if a single church were attacked. Clearly, combustible men, rather than the progress of events, made Philadelphia the flash-point over schools. Heavy Irish immigration, bringing with it job rivalry and sectarian tension, too few police, the established pattern of anti-abolitionist violence (countenanced by the propertied in the 1830s), crude press and stage propaganda, the breakdown of trades unions, the strategies of nativists, exaggerated rumors from New York, and the failure of political leaders to cope—all explained the outbreaks.[131] They had the good effect, however, of discrediting nativism for a decade. In New York, the Whigs had contained the nativists by "ticket-fusion." In Philadelphia, nativism had mushroomed as the party of nationality, Protestant piety, temperance, craft-exclusiveness, and anti-Irishism, while the Whigs were split on how to conciliate these forces and retain such Irish support as they had. The general collapse of nativism now indicated how positive, if limited, were pre-famine American views of the Irish; these had to change before so narrow a movement could revive. But opposition in New York and the riot in Philadelphia dispelled optimisim and caused the Irish to regard political friendliness toward Catholic schools, or at least neutrality, as one yardstick of their own acceptance—more so than their children's attendance might suggest.

The extension of the repeal movement to America was the most direct and immediate re-creation of matters Irish in America in these years. From the 1780s to the 1820s, American Presbyterians supported Irish patriots and émigré radicals from motives of New World liberalism as well as Old World memory or descent. Between 1850 and 1921, such movements, even when, like Fenianism and Clan na Gael, they did not, originate in America, were led and supported by residents long Americanized and by the American-born Irish. By contrast, repeal had virtually no support from older Ulster-American communities and drew little impetus from long-established Catholic Americans. Instead, it began in 1840 among the Boston Irish, whose community was "as yet but infantine," employed generally "in manual labour . . . with the exception of those who keep little groceries, groggeries, boarding-houses, and the like"— yet "sensitively alive to the sufferings of their fellow countrymen."[132] This repeal view was confirmed by the British consul there, the Anglo-Irishman Thomas Colley Grattan: not "the historical names" (Emmet, O'Connor, and MacNeven), but "the oscure inhabitants of Boston . . . [with] such patronymics as McHugh, McGinniskin, and Murphy . . . and others of no note or position,"[133] created the movement on Monday 12 October 1840 in Boylston Hall, Boston, six months after its beginnings in Dublin.

Apart from Patrick Donahoe, editor of the *Pilot,* and his deputy, it was run by a fish-packer, a coal-dealer, and a hack-driver. The contrast with repeal's patrician leadership in Ireland may illuminate O'Connell's reserve about such auxiliaries. If at first the plainer Irish acted spontaneously, others came in by mid-December as the movement spread through the New England mill towns to Philadelphia and New York City. In the latter city, Tammany (the local Democratic organization) lent its hall, and Robert Emmet (Thomas Addis's son) presided until O'Connell criticized the men of 1798. The next year the Atlantic ports as far south as Baltimore, and the towns along the canals and rivers, formed branches.

The delegates to the first National Repeal Convention in Philadelphia (February 1842) included "a cross section of the substantial catholic Irish population … merchants, traders, shopkeepers, doctors, lawyers, journalists, and public works contractors,"[134] suggesting a natural cohesion and need for leadership by men of some means in the new Irish communities. Yet, incomprehensibly, they failed to set up a permanent organization. Support for repeal, educational freedom for Catholics, and the status of Irish-Americans were the chief concerns. So obvious an avenue to otherwise scattered voters could not be ignored: in September 1843, the second National Repeal Convention met in the Broadway Tabernacle, New York City, with President John Tyler's son, Robert, presiding—a somewhat complicating coup, for the Tylers were a power in search of a constituency. The father, the republic's first vice-president to succeed to the presidency (on the death of William Harrison in 1841) was an ex-Democrat, now deserted by the Whigs, and, like his son but unlike the Irish majority, he was pro-slavery and fiscally orthodox in his views. The Irish could not yet afford to ignore such support; for, as they realized, only outsiders for the 1844 presidential nominations such as John Tyler, R. M. Johnson, and Lewis Cass endorsed repeal;[135] insiders James Polk, Henry Clay, and George Dallas discreetly remained silent (though Dallas's patrons, the ex-president Andrew Jackson and the historian George Bancroft, did favor some settlement). The second convention harvested the enthusiasm of the "repeal year" but was shadowed by a growing realization that Peel would suppress the movement in Ireland. This gave an opening to those who wished to discuss physical force, but the five-man governing directory shrewdly interpreted physical force to mean monetary contribution, and Dr. Edmund Bailey O'Callaghan, historian of the state of New York, spoke eloquently on moral force from his experience as an exiled veteran of Louis Papineau's 1837–8 *émeute* in Lower Canada. With 405 delegates, large sums to spend, mass support, and much American sympathy, its wise leaders were attuned to O'Connell's mind and deserved better from him.

It was not the question of slavery as much as misinformation based on misunderstanding that separated O'Connell from these recent emigrants. He used the slavery question partly to distance himself from a movement he wrongly believed to be based on United Irish traditions. Thomas Mooney—mercurial and occasionally brilliant, O'Connell's self-appointed agent in America since early 1841, and his erstwhile banking rival—was an accurate observer of Irish-Americans' social exigencies but an unreliable reporter of their politics. He probably did more for repeal than his reputation suggests, certainly more than Thomas D'Arcy McGee, who arrived a year later to help in Boston. But Mooney split the New York movement and compromised the Boston society by placing guns on its table. Reporting meetings back to the *Nation* in Dublin, he exaggerated their radicalism, coyly decrying the danger of "ill-concerted insurrectionary attack" while urging the example of 1776, on his own account, if repeal were thwarted.[136] At Mullaghmast, on 1 October 1843, O'Connell revealed how closely his desire to conciliate Britain by denouncing American belligerence was linked to his use of anti-slavery:

> I denounce the slavery of the negro in America. I pronounce it an injustice against man, and a sin in its operation against the eternal God. ... Let that cry go to America. My friends, I want nothing for the Irish but their country, and I think the Irish are competent to obtain their own country for themselves. I like to have the sympathy of every good man everywhere, but I want not armed support or physical strength from any country. ... I want not the support of America; I have physical support about me to achieve any change; but you know well that it is not my plan.[137]

As he spoke, his followers distributed the latest repeal address of the pro-slavery Robert Tyler. In Britain, anti-slavery rhetoric was the then usual mode of reprobating America, given the friction between Britain and the United States in Texas, Oregon, and Maine; it was dear to the hearts of O'Connell's British allies, such as Lord Morpeth; it was conventional, because emancipation was already achieved in the British empire; and the transatlantic antislavery connection, notably the Quakers of New York and Dublin, kept up more pressure on O'Connell than did Irish-Americans.

O'Connell's abolitionism placed grave strains on America's repealers. At the first national meeting in 1842, his "Address of the people of Ireland to their countrymen and countrywomen in America," signed by 60,000 and just received made loyalty to him inconsistent with loyalty to the Democrats, who were determined to keep the issue out of federal politics. After some heat, they resolved to "avoid domestic American controversies."[138] Taking evidence of their anti-abolitionism to mean they were pro-slavery, O'Connell then in May 1843 threatened to disown Irish-American support. Only the prestige of the "repeal year" revived many of the split associations in America. Once again, the slavery question was excluded from the second convention in September 1843. When O'Connell returned to the matter, a few days after Clontarf, he showed a better grasp of their position: he asked that Irish-Americans should no longer defend slavery and should work to end the slave trade in Washington D.C., to repeal the rule prohibiting congressional debates on slavery, to promote voluntary manumission and the rights of free blacks, and to efface Irish racism.[139] His appeal was unquestionably sincere, yet its timing and motivation, at least partly for political uses, weakened its appeal. In 1840 James G. Birney (son of Ulster parents) received only 7,059 votes, or 0.3 percent of the total, as an anti-slavery presidential candidate. To weigh down the Irish in America with emancipationism, much less abolitionism, in 1841–3, would have been to jeopardize their acceptability in America; their small leverage was among the pro-slavery Democrats, and they rivaled abolitionists as targets of northern mob violence between 1835 and 1843. O'Connell scarcely grasped this; as a master politician he should have done.

Repeal helped fuel nativist reaction during these years. But it also caused leading Americans, from John Quincy Adams to Andrew Jackson, to argue that one might agitate for freedom in the Old World, despite the Monroe Docrine, stopping short of practical intervention[140]—a stand later applied to the European insurrections in 1848. Indeed, repeal arguments may have helped shape "American mission" ideology in the "Young America" movement of the time, especially that of its theorist John L. Sullivan. Repeal also brought the Irish question into American politics for the first time. For the Irish community, as Thomas Colley Grattan observed, it marked a movement for greater group esteem. In America, more than in Ireland, it inaugurated the appropriation of democracy (in the strict sense) by "obscure inhabitants."[141]

On the eve of the famine, the themes and structures of Irish-America were all in place. Already New York and Philadelphia knew overcrowding and division, although the Irish were dispersed wherever opportunity suggested: Thomas Mooney could point to established leaders in almost every northern and western town. The lessons of organization in a country where so much was achieved by voluntary cooperation were being learned by repealers, trade unionists, churchmen, educators, and businessmen—if more easily put into effect where people were congregated than (as was then more usual) where they were scattered. Very substantial contributions to education were made by Protestant immigrants, especially in Maryland, Virginia, Kentucky, and Tennessee, building on an eighteenth-century pattern begun by Francis Alison and others. John Oliver, Alexander McCaine, and Samuel Knox each founded academies in Baltimore by 1821, the last planning a free national system of education through to a federal university. In the west, adherents of a "family craft" approach divided from those favoring a "state craft" one, along lines of greater or lesser doctrinal commitment. Nonimmigrant Ulster-Americans continued their tradition of establishing colleges, academies, and reformed curricula for primary schools, which strongly emphasized "the evidence of Christianity," graded developments, and American material; William McGuffey was only the most influential. Incoming Irishmen could always find a township to give them the ill-paid and ill-regarded job of teaching literacy and numeracy to farm children in drafty, stove-warmed cabins. The Catholic contribution too had begun in more organized ways.[142]

The ambivalent attitudes of Americans toward Irishmen invited already an effort at self-explanation and self-improvement, which had a broadening effect. Americans were affable toward the Irishman's livelier aspects, simplifying him as warm, droll, friendly, brave, familiar, and impertinent, if rarely villainous, but dismissed him as lazy, passive, and insecure. Oddly, they did not notice his political and religious character, except during group conflict; perhaps he was not meant to be so complex, or perhaps historians exaggerate grand themes in the lives of ordinary people.[143] Employers thought highly of him; the wealthy distanced themselves from him; those of recent, unstable position slighted him; New Englanders disdained him—but most Americans from New York southward and westward took him as he was, more or less. Even evangelical sermons and novels sought a Gothic unfamiliarity of terrain for their anti-Roman themes, for the Irishman was too homely to furnish such overwrought imagination.[144] The very doubt, widely held and honored, that Catholicism could coexist with the psychology and institutions of free men, helped ensure that it would do so. Only armed nativism, grosser exploitation, and the cholera, which last devastated Irish settlements in 1832,[145] had no beneficial effects, other than to prepare the

Irish for their recurrence. The majority of Americans accepted it as natural that Irishmen should come among them, a vital preparation for the famine influx. The Ulster-American tradition had prepared the Irish to identify closely with the constitutions and people of the new land. Interdenominational amity, if damaged by politicized evangelicalism and electoral violence, still survived; survived even the launching of Orangeism in the 1820s, and its revival in New York as the Berean Order in 1844–5.

Hundreds of thousands of newer immigrants had found their feet by 1845. Family solidarity was already vital: in May and June 1844, 41 percent of Irish arrivals came to New York with passages prepaid. Knowledge of America was already diffused among them: only 5 percent of these 10,668 arrivals stayed in New York city.[146] The Irish Emigration Society—founded in 1841, although poorly financed by comparison with the repeal movement—did much useful work before merging its services with those of the state commissioners of emigration, established (partly at the prompting of the Irish Emigration Society and Archbishop John Hughes) in 1847 in time for the great migration.[147] The St. Vincent de Paul Society, with so vital a future in urban America in the absence of welfare systems, was nowhere established except in St. Louis (1845) and New York City (1846). Coming from Paris, it appealed only slowly to rural, family-conscious Irishmen, until they learned its urban potential; it was introduced by priests and laity of European education or background such as Bryan Mullanphy. Most important, the economy began a slow recovery in 1844, accelerating after 1849 with an inflow of British capital and the export of California gold to pay for the trade deficit. This started a railway boom; the recovery spread to Canada by 1850 and, apart from a short-lived panic in 1857–8, a long cycle of economic expansion continued effectively to the mid-1870s. Non-agricultural employment began to expand more rapidly than population, from 1.7 million jobs in 1840 to 4.3 million in 1860. Despite the real tragedy of the famine years, the capacity of the United States to absorb two million Irish immigrants, and the existence of a viable subculture in America to ground those that came in some real familiarity and spiritual comfort, ensured that the tragedy was far less horrific than otherwise might have been.

NOTES

1. Frances Wright, *Views of Society and Manners in America*, ed. Paul Barker (Cambridge, MA, 1963), p. 238.

2. Kerby A. Miller, *Emigrants and Exiles: Ireland and the Irish Exodus to North America* (Oxford and New York, 1985), pp. 193–9, 291–3, 346–53, 569–71; Cormac Ó Gráda, "A Note on Nineteenth-Century Irish Emigration Statistics," *Population Studies* 29 (1975), pp. 143–9; D. H. Akenson, *The Irish in Ontario* (Montreal, 1984), pp. 9–15, 28–32; *Historical Statistics of the United States to 1970* (Washington, DC, 1973), series C, pp. 89–92.

3. J. A. King, "Genealogy, History and Irish Immigration," *Canadian Journal of Irish Studies* 10, no. 1 (1984), pp. 41–50; Kathleen Neils Conzen, *Immigrant Milwaukee, 1836–1860* (Cambridge, MA, 1976), fig. 5, pp. 40, 41–2; D. H. Akenson, *Being Had: Historians, Evidence, and the Irish in North America* (Port Credit, Ont., 1985), pp. 52–9. The U.S. recorded land crossings from Canada only since 1893.

4. Patrick Blessing, "Irish Emigration to the United States, 1800–1920: An Overview," in P. J. Drudy (ed.), *The Irish in America* (Irish Studies 4) (Cambridge, 1985), table 2:1, p. 14; Akenson, *Irish in Ontario*, pp. 9–15, 28–32; Akenson, *Being Had*, pp. 52–4, 89.

5. Jacques Verrière, *La population de l'Irlande* (Paris, 1979), pp. 280, 392, table 3–21, p. 442; R. E. Kennedy Jr., *The Irish: Emigration, Marriage, and Fertility* (Berkeley, CA, 1975), pp. 15–18, 110–38, 173; William Forbes Adams, *Ireland and Irish Emigration to the New World from 1815 to the Famine* (Baltimore, 1980 [1932]), pp. 190–92.

6. Joel Mokyr, *Why Ireland Starved: A Quantitative and Analytical History of the Irish Economy, 1800–1850* (London, 1983), pp. 247–52.

7. Cormac Ó Gráda, "Across the Briny Ocean: Some Thoughts on Pre-famine Emigration to America" in T. M. Devine and David Dickson (ed.), *Ireland and Scotland, 1600–1850: Parallels and Contrasts in Economic and Social Development* (Edinburgh, 1983), table 1, p. 123; Mokyr, *Why Ireland Starved*, tables 8.1, p. 234, and 8.3, p. 242; Miller, *Emigrants and Exiles*, table 11, p. 581.

8. Ó Gráda, "Across the Briny Ocean," tables, 2, 3, and 6A, pp. 124–6; A. Gibbs Mitchell, "Irish Family Patterns: Nineteenth-Century Ireland, and Lowell, Massachusetts" (Ph.D. diss., Boston, 1976), tables 16–18, pp. 165–9.

9. Nicholas Nolan, "The Irish Emigration: A Study in Demography" (Ph.D. diss., National University Ireland [University College Dublin], 1935), pp. 196–8, 220ff; *Historical Statistics of the United States to 1970*, Series C-92 Correlated to Series N-111-17, U-187-9, and V-20-30.

10. Blessing, "Irish Emigration to the United States," pp. 21–3; Morton D. Winsberg, "Irish Settlement in the United States, 1850–1980," *Éire-Ireland* 20, no. 1 (spring 1985), pp. 7–14; David Ward, *Cities and Immigrants* (New York, 1971), pp. 3–83.

11. U.S. Senate, *Reports of the Immigration Commission*. Vol. 28: *Fecundity of Immigrant Women* (61 Congress, 2nd session, doc. no. 282) (Washington, 1911), pp. 733ff, especially tables 36 and 37, pp. 806–7, 808–9; Mitchell, "Irish Family Patterns," pp. 313–14; Hasia R. Diner, *Erin's Daughters in America* (Baltimore, 1983), p. 54 and p. 168, n. 17; Joellen M. Vinyard, *The Irish on the Urban Frontier: Nineteenth-Century Detroit* (New York, 1976), tables A-38, A-39, pp. 409–10.

12. Lee Benson, *The Concept of Jacksonian Democracy* (Princeton, 1961); Ronald Formisano, *The Birth of Mass Political Parties: Michigan, 1827–1861* (Princeton, 1971); Michael Holt, *Forging a Majority: Pittsburgh, 1848–1860* (New Haven, 1969); Paul Kleppner, *The Cross of Culture: A Social Analysis of Midwestern Politics, 1850–1900* (New York, 1970).

13. R. A. Burchell, "The Historiography of the American Irish," *Immigrants and Minorities*, 1 (1982), pp. 281–305; U.S. Bureau of the Census, *Statistical Abstract, 1981* (Washington, 1982), table 42, p. 35; Michael F. Funchion (ed.), *Irish American Voluntary Organizations* (Westport, CT, 1983).

14. Miller, *Emigrants and Exiles*, p. 326.

15. Funchion, *Irish American Voluntary Organisations*, pp. 69–74, 138–41, 141–5, 249–61; Robert Ernst, *Immigrant Life in New York City, 1825–1863* (New York, 1949), p. 32.

16. Cf. Miller, *Emigrants and Exiles*, pp. 328–9; Dale Light, "Irish-American Organisation" in P. J. Drudy (ed.), *The Irish in America* (Cambridge, 1985), pp. 120–35.

17. M. F. Egan, *Recollections of a Happy Life* (London, 1924), p. 56.

18. J. A. Dunlevy and H. A. Gemery, "British-Irish Settlement Patterns in the U.S.: The Role of Family and Friends," *Scottish Journal of Political Economy* 24 (1977), pp. 257–63.

19. Sheridan Gilley, "The Roman Catholic Church and the Nineteenth-Century Irish Diaspora," *Journal of Economic History* 35 (1984), pp. 188–207; Murray W. Nicholson, "The Role of Religion in Irish North American Studies," *Ethnic Forum* 4 (1984), pp. 64–77.

20. Miller, "Emigrants and Exiles" (Ph.D. thesis, University of California, Berkeley, 1976);

ch. 11, table 12, "Voyage length," pp. 677–80; Rev. John O'Hanlon, *The Irish Emigrant's Guide,* ed. E. J. Maguire (New York, 1976), pp. 79–91.

21. J. F. Maguire, *The Irish in America* (London, 1868; reprint, New York, 1969), p. 609.

22. Elizabeth I. Nybakken, "New Light on the Old Side: Irish Influences on Colonial Presbyterianism," *Journal of American History* 68 (1982), pp. 813–32; W. L. Bockelman and O. S. Ireland, "The Internal Revolution in Pennsylvania: An Ethno-Religious Interpretation," *Pennsylvania History* 41 (1974), pp. 125–59.

23. David Noel Doyle, *Ireland, Irishmen, and Revolutionary America, 1760–1820* (Dublin, 1981), pp. 109–37.

24. M. A. Jones, "The Scotch-Irish: Post-Revolutionary Migration" in Stephan Thernstrom (ed.), *Harvard Encyclopaedia of American Ethnic Groups* (Cambridge, MA, 1980), pp. 902–3; Miller, *Emigrants and Exiles,* pp. 169–97; Doyle, *Ireland, Irishmen,* pp. 186–7, 220–23.

25. John M. Coleman, *Thomas McKean* (Rockaway, NJ, 1975); L. K. Caldwell, "George Clinton—Democratic Administrator," *New York History* 32 (1951), pp. 134–56.

26. Doyle, *Ireland, Irishmen,* pp. 192–200, 214–18; Maurice J. Bric, "The Irish and the Evolution of the 'New Politics' in America" in P. J. Drudy (ed.), *The Irish in America* (Cambridge, 1985), pp. 149–61.

27. M. A. Jones, "Ulster Emigration, 1783–1815" in E. R. R. Green (ed.), *Essays in Scotch-Irish History* (London, 1969), p. 67.

28. Forrest McDonald and Ellen S. McDonald, "The Ethnic Origins of the American People, 1790," *William and Mary Quarterly,* 3rd ser., 38 (1980), pp. 179–99; [Thomas L. Purvis, Donald H. Akenson, and Forrest and Ellen McDonald], "The Population of the United States, 1790: A Symposium," *William and Mary Quarterly,* 3rd ser., 41 (1984), pp. 85–135; calculations from ibid., table 2, p. 98 (Purvis) and independently in Doyle, *Ireland, Irishmen,* pp. 71–6.

29. Nybakken, "New Light on the Old Side," pp. 829–34; L. J. Cappon, *Atlas of Early American History: The Revolutionary Era, 1760–1790* (Princeton, 1976), pp. 24, 36–9, 66, 71.

30. Contrast tonnages provided for the same vessels in R. J. Dickson, *Ulster Emigration to Colonial America, 1718–1775* (London, 1966), pp. 229–79, and Audrey Lockhart, *Emigration from Ireland to the North American Colonies, 1660–1775* (New York, 1976), pp. 175–208 (from advertisements), with those in John McCusker, "Ships Registered at the Port of Philadelphia before 1776," MS (1970) at the Historical Society of Pennsylvania, Philadelphia, based on first registrations there.

31. James F. Connelly (ed.), *The History of the Archdiocese of Philadelphia* (Philadelphia, 1976), pp. 35, 58.

32. M. J. O'Brien, *Irish Settlers in America: A Consolidation of Articles from the Journal of the American Irish Historical Society* (2 vols, Baltimore, 1979); McDonald and McDonald, "Ethnic Origins," p. 197; and Purvis et al., "Population of the U.S., 1790," table 2, p. 98; calculations mine.

33. Aleine Austin, *Matthew Lyon* (University Park, PA, 1980); Charles P. Whittemore, "John Sullivan: Luckless Irishman" in George A. Billias (ed.), *Washington's Generals* (New York, 1964), pp. 137–62.

34. Jones, "Ulster Emigration," p. 49.

35. Stephenson to Orde, 7 June 1784 (N.L.I., Bolton papers, MS 15827/3).

36. H. J. M. Johnston, *British Emigration Policy, 1815–1830* (Oxford, 1972), pp. 2, 25–6, 119. Oliver MacDonagh, *A Pattern of Government Growth, 1800–1860: The Passenger Acts and Their Enforcement* (London, 1961), 54–65.

37. Nolan, "Irish Emigration," pp. 119–24; Adams, *Irish Emigration to New World,* pp. 143–5, 156, 161; Ó Gráda, "Across the Briny Ocean," table 7, p. 127.

38. Cf. maps 1–5 in Garret Fitzgerald, "Estimates for Baronies of Minimum Level of Irish-Speaking Amongst Successive Decennial Cohorts, 1771–1781 to 1861–1871," *R.I.A. Proceedings* 84 (1984), sect. C, pp. 117–55, with those in S. H. Cousens, "The Regional Variations in Emigration from Ireland between 1821 and 1841," *Transactions and Papers of the Institute of British Geographers* 37 (1965), figs. 2–4, pp. 19–22.

39. Kevin O'Neill, *Family and Farm in Pre-Famine Ireland: The Parish of Killeshandra* (Madison, WI, 1985), pp. 121–2, 169–70.

40. Ó Gráda, "Across the Briny Ocean," pp. 120, 121–2, tables 3, 4, and 6B, pp. 125, 127; Joel Mokyr and Cormac Ó Gráda, "Emigration and Poverty in Pre-Famine Ireland," *Working Paper No. 1, Centre for Economic Research, U.C.D.* (Dublin, 1982), pp. 23–31, 39–40; Miller, *Emigrants and Exiles,* pp. 193–223.

41. Elizabeth M. O'Connell, "'The Best Poor Man's Country in the World': Irish Immigrants in New York in the Early Nineteenth Century," *Historian* [New York University] 8 (1977), pp. 37–47.

42. Purvis et al., "Population of the United States," table 2, p. 98; Doyle, *Ireland, Irishmen,* app. 1, p. 75.

43. Thomas L. Purvis, "The Ethnic Descent of Kentucky's Early Population," *Register of the Kentucky Historical Society,* 80 (1982), table 3, p. 263, and p. 266.

44. W. L. Fisk, "The Associate Reformed Church in the Old Northwest," *Journal of Presbyterian History* 46 (1968), pp. 157–74; W. W. McKinney, *Early Pittsburgh Presbyterianism, 1758–1839* (Pittsburgh, 1938).

45. Joseph I. Dirvin, *Mrs Seton: Foundress of the American Sisters of Charity* (new ed., New York, 1975), pp. 170–71; Theodore Roemer, *The Catholic Church in the United States* (St. Louis, 1950), pp. 79ff, 399–412.

46. Doyle, *Ireland, Irishmen,* pp. 96–7; Dennis Clark, *The Irish Relations* (Rutherford, NJ, 1982), pp. 47–8.

47. Callista Schramm, "William Findley in Pennsylvania Politics," *Western Pennsylvania Historical Magazine* 20 (1937), pp. 31–40; Robert G. Crist, *Robert Whitehill and the Struggle for Civil Rights* (Lemoyne, PA, 1958).

48. Bric, "The Irish and the Evolution of the 'New Politics,'" pp. 153–4, 156–7.

49. "Admission of Immigrants under State Laws, 1788–1882" in Edith Abbott, *Immigration: Select Documents and Case Records* (Chicago, 1924; reprint, New York, 1969), pp. 102–80; T. C. Grattan, *Civilized America* (2 vols, London, 1859), vol. 2, pp. 15–25.

50. F. X. Curran, *Catholics in Colonial Law* (Chicago, 1963), pp. 112, 115, 116, 120, 122, 124.

51. Kirk H. Porter, *A History of Suffrage in the United States* (Chicago, 1918; reprint, New York, 1971), pp. 20–46, 112–34.

52. Jeremiah O'Brien (Maine), George Casseday (New Jersey), Samuel McKean (Pennsylvania), Louis McLane (Delaware), Henry Connor (North Carolina), Henry Conway (Arkansas), and Patrick Farrelly (Pennsylvania): see *Biographical Directory of the American Congress, 1774–1961* (Washington, DC, 1961), pp. 672, 730, 732, 876, 1303, 1308, 1398–9.

53. "John Rhea" in *Dictionary of American Biography* [8, pt 1], Vol. 15, pp. 524–5; supporting areas were largely Scotch-Irish, see Marshall Smelser, *The Democratic Republicans, 1801–1815* (New York, 1968), map, p. 217.

54. Thomas F. Moriarty, "The Irish-American Response to Catholic Emancipation," *Catholic Historical Review* 44 (1980), pp. 356, 360, 364, 366, and n. 83, p. 371.

55. Ibid., quoting Wyse, *Catholic Association,* vol. 7, p. 320.

56. Joseph I. Shulim, *John Daly Burk, Irish Revolutionist* (Philadelphia, 1964); David Kaser, *Joseph Charless, Printer in the Western Country* (Philadelphia, 1963).

57. W. L. Joyce, *Editors and Ethnicity: A History of the Irish-American Press, 1848–1883* (New York, 1976), pp. 49–50.

58. Walter Cox, *A Short Sketch of the Present State of the Catholic Church in New York in a Letter to the Right Reverend Bishop Connolly* (New York, 1819), pp. 10–16; Patrick Carey, *People, Priests, and Prelates* (Notre Dame, IN, 1987), chs. 6 and 7.

59. Moriarty, "Irish-American Response to Catholic Emancipation," p. 369.

60. Adams, *Irish Emigration to New World*, pp. 197–200, app., pp. 413–15; Helen I. Cowan, *British Emigration to British North America* (rev. ed., Toronto, 1961), pp. 187, 190–91, 195–8, app. B, tables 2 and 4, pp. 289, 293; *Historical Statistics of the United States to 1970*, series C 89–92.

61. Adams, *Irish Emigration to New World*, p. 204; *Census Ireland, 1851*, pt. vi, *General Report, Appendix*, table 18, p. cii [2134], H.C. 1856, xxxi, 106.

62. Ibid., Cowan, "British Emigration," table 6, pp. 291–3; I have assumed that nine-tenths of Liverpool, and one-fifth of Glasgow–Greenock, embarkees were Irish.

63. Third report of the select committee on emigration from the United Kingdom, 1827, quoted in Adams, *Irish Emigration to New World*, p. 284.

64. Cormac Ó Gráda, "Poverty, Population and Agriculture, 1801–45," *A New History of Ireland*, vol. 5, *Ireland under the Union, I, 1801–70*, ed. W. E. Vaughan, (Oxford, 1989), p. 121. H. J. M. Johnston, *British Emigration Policy, 1815–1830* (Oxford, 1972), pp. 91–128; Cowan, *British Emigration*, pp. 87–93, 97–8; MacDonagh, *Pattern of Govt Growth*, pp. 66, 77, 79–80; Adams, *Irish Emigration to New World*, pp. 240–333.

65. *Nation*, 6 May 1843, p. 466; cf. Ó Gráda, "Poverty," pp. 586, 598.

66. Cowan, *British Emigration*, p. 127.

67. Lynn Hollen Lees, *Exiles of Erin* (Manchester, 1979), p. 36; Nolan, "Irish Emigration," pp. 77–8, 96–8, 110; Mokyr, *Why Ireland Starved*, p. 230.

68. [William Grattan] Tyrone Power, *Impressions of America during the Years 1833, 1834, and 1835* (2 vols, London, 1836), vol. 2, pp. 238–9.

69. Thomas Mooney, *Nine Years in America* (Dublin, 1850), pp. 98–105; George Potter, *To the Golden Door: The Story of the Irish in Ireland and America* (Boston and Toronto, 1960), pp. 184–7; W. E. Rowley, "The Irish Aristocracy of Albany, 1788–1878," *New York History*, 52 (1971), pp. 275–304.

70. Elfrieda Lang, "Irishmen in Northern Indiana before 1850," *Mid-America*, 36 (1954), pp. 190–98.

71. Colonial Land and Emigration Commission, 1850, quoted in Cowan, *British Emigration*, p. 199 (a retrospect).

72. Ó Gráda, "Across the Briny Ocean," table 7, p. 127; Akenson, *Irish in Ontario* pp. 23–6, 224–6, 263–7, 390–93; C. J. Houston and W. J. Smyth, *The Sash Canada Wore: A Historical Geography of the Orange Order in Canada* (Toronto, 1980), pp. 31–2, 93–6.

73. Ó Gráda, "Across the Briny Ocean," tables 5A and 5B, p. 126; Adams, *Irish Emigration to New World*, pp. 120–21, 420–25, calculated against total flows; see Ó Gráda, "Poverty," pp. 693, 700.

74. Miller, *Emigrants and Exiles*, pp. 263–8; P.R.O.N.I.: Brice Black letters, 1821–8 (T3633); Wray letters, 1817–22 (T1727); Cooke letters, 1824–30 (T3592); John McBride letters, 1819–27 (T2613); McClorg letters, 1819–37 (T1227).

75. Ó Gráda, "Across the Briny Ocean," table 3, p. 125.

76. Calculated from table 10 in Oscar Handlin, *Boston's Immigrants 1790–1880* (2nd rev. ed., New York, 1972), p. 247.

77. M. W. Armstrong and others, *The Presbyterian Enterprise* (Philadelphia, 1956), pp. 146–71.

78. Nicholas Flood Davin, *The Irishman in Canada* (Toronto, 1877; reprint, Shannon, 1970), pp. 582, 589.

79. Akenson, *Irish in Ontario,* pp. 14–28, 139–282; William J. Smyth, "The Irish in Mid-Nineteenth-Century Ontario," in *Ulster Folklife* 23 (1977), pp. 97–106; John Mannion, *Irish Settlements in Eastern Canada* (Toronto, 1974), pp. 15–18, 40–43, 74–86, 106–16, 159–74; Davin, *Irishman in Canada,* pp. 245, 309, 359–60. There were also 43,942 Irish-born in Lower Canada (Quebec) in 1844: see Patrick M. Redmond, *Irish Life in Rural Quebec: A History of Frampton* (Montreal, 1981).

80. H. H. Guest, "Upper Canada's First Political Party," *Ontario History* 54 (1963), pp. 296ff; Graeme Patterson, "Whiggery, Nationality, and the Upper Canadian Reform Tradition," *Canadian Historical Review* 56 (1975), pp. 25–44.

81. Houston and Smyth, *The Sash Canada Wore,* pp. 15–36, 86, 112–13, 127–31, 141.

82. Lt.-Col. Charles Grey to Earl Grey, 11 Aug. 1838 in William Ormsby (ed.), *Crisis in the Canadas, 1838–39: The Grey Journals and Letters* (Toronto, 1964), p. 98.

83. Akenson, *Irish in Ontario,* pp. 169–97.

84. 3 & 4 Vict., c. 35 (23 July 1840).

85. Houston and Smyth, *The Sash Canada Wore,* p. 147.

86. Davin, *Irishman in Canada,* pp. 491–3, 520–21.

87. Michael S. Cross, "'The Shiners' War: Social Violence in the Ottawa Valley in the 1830s," *Canadian Historical Review* 54 (1973), pp. 1–26; Ruth Bleasdale, "Class Conflict on the Canals of Upper Canada in the 1840s," *Labour/Le Travailleur* 7 (1981), pp. 9–39.

88. *Dictionary of Canadian Biography* (1861–70), pp. 224–7, 828–35; *Nation* (Dublin), 25 Feb. 1843, pp. 317–18.

89. A. F. C. Wallace, *Rockdale: The Growth of an American Village in the Early Industrial Revolution* (New York, 1980), pp. 37, 40, 43–4, 98–101; Dennis Clark, "Kellyville: Immigrant Enterprise," *Pennsylvania History* 39 (1972), pp. 40–49.

90. Quoted in Davin, *Irishman in Canada,* p. 401.

91. S. H. Cousens, "The Regional Variations in Emigration from Ireland between 1821 and 1841," *Transactions and Papers of the Institute of British Geographers* 37 (1965), figs. 2 and 3, pp. 19, 20.

92. O'Connell to Fleming, 2 June 1842 (*O'Connell Correspondence,* vol. 7, pp. 162–3); John F. Mannion (ed.), *The Peopling of Newfoundland* (St. John's, 1977), pp. 7–10; Arthur P. Monahan, "Canada" in Corish, *Irish Catholicism,* vol. 6, fasc. 3, pp. 2–8.

93. G. C. Din, "Spain's Immigration Policy in Louisiana," *Southwestern Historical Quarterly* 76 (1973), pp. 255–76; E. F. Niehaus, *The Irish in New Orleans, 1800–1860* (New York, 1976), pp. 3–22.

94. John B. Flannery, *The Irish Texans* (Austin, 1980), pp. 31–89.

95. Dennis Clark, "The South's Irish Catholics: A Case of Cultural Confinement" in R. M. Miller and J. L. Wakelyn (eds.), *Catholics in the Old South* (Macon, GA, 1983), pp. 195–210.

96. Ada L. K. Newton, "The Anglo-Irish [*recte* English-Speaking Irish] House of the Rio Grande," *Pioneer America* 5 (1973), pp. 33–8; Mannion, *Irish Settlements in Eastern Canada,* pp. 27–8, 63, 66–8, 73, 170.

97. *Historical Statistics of the United States to 1970,* series D 75–84, p. 134.

98. Power, *Impressions of America,* vol. 2, p. 348.

99. Joseph Schaefer, *Social History of American Agriculture* (New York, 1936), p. 212.

100. Merle Curti and others, *The Making of an American Community* (Stanford, 1969), pp. 93–4, 177, 182–7, 191, 196; Thomas Mooney, *Nine Years in America* (Dublin, 1850), pp. 19, 37, 40; J. H. Tuke, *A Visit to Connaught in the Autumn of 1847* (2nd ed., London, 1848), pp. 13, 43–4; Charles Casey, *Two Years on a Farm of Uncle Sam* (London, 1852), pp. 222–4, 241.

101. Michael Williams, "Clearing the United States Forests: The Pivotal Years," *Journal of*

Historical Geography 8 (1982), pp. 12–28; James A. King, *The Irish Lumberman-Farmer* (Lafayette, CA, 1982), pp. 65–8, 114–25; Lee Benson, *The Concept of Jacksonian Democracy* (Princeton, 1961), pp. 203–5.

102. U. B. Phillips, *Life and Labor in the Old South* (Boston, 1963), pp. 253–4; Sir Charles Lyell, *Travels in North America* (2 vols, London, 1845), vol. 7, p. 131.

103. Patrick O'Reilly, *Advice and Guide to Emigrants Going to the United States of America* (Dublin, 1834), pp. 12–14, 20–21, 44; Rev. John O'Hanlon, *The Irish Emigrant's Guide*, ed. E. J. Maguire (New York, 1976), pp. 216–24; Francis Wyse, *America* (3 vols, London, 1846), vol. 3, pp. 3, 26–32.

104. Wyse, *America*, vol. 3, p. 31.

105. Walter Myler, *Reminiscences of a Trans-Atlantic Traveller, 1831–2* (Dublin, 1835), pp. 20–21.

106. Mathew Carey, *Appeal to the Wealthy of the Land* (Philadelphia, 1833), p. 7.

107. David Montgomery, "The Shuttle and the Cross: Weavers and Artisans in the Kensington Riots of 1844," *Journal of Social History* 5 (1972), pp. 417–21.

108. Gerald Shaughnessy, *Has the Immigrant Kept the Faith?* (New York, 1925; reprint, 1969), p. 125; R. F. Hueston, *The Catholic Press and Nativism, 1840–1860* (New York, 1976), p. 34.

109. Theodore Roemer, *The Catholic Church in the United States* (St. Louis, 1950), pp. 151–2, 164–5, 182–5, 209–10.

110. Whitfield to Nicholas Wiseman (rector of English College, Rome), 6 June 1833 in Thomas T. McAvoy, *A History of the Catholic Church in the United States* (Notre Dame, 1969), p. 130.

111. E.g., Patrick O'Kelly, *Advice and Guide to Emigrants . . .* (Dublin, 1834), pp. 7, 37.

112. Peter Guilday (ed.), *The National Pastorals of the American Hierarchy, 1792–1919* (Washington, DC, 1923), p. 68.

113. Jay Dolan, *The Immigrant Church: New York's Irish and German Catholics, 1815–1865* (Baltimore, 1975), p. 105; Diane Ravitch, *The Great School Wars: New York City, 1805–1973* (New York, 1974), p. 405; James F. Connelly (ed.), *The History of the Archdiocese of Philadelphia* (Philadelphia, 1976), p. 171.

114. George Potter, *To the Golden Door* (Boston and Toronto, 1960), p. 434.

115. Myler, *Reminiscences of a Trans-Atlantic Traveller*, p. 21; Wyse, *America*, vol. 3, pp. 3–4, 33, 201; T. C. Grattan, *Civilized America* (2 vols, London, 1859), vol. 2, pp. 27–8.

116. Michael Moran, "The Writings of Francis Patrick Kenrick, Archbishop of Baltimore," *Records of the American Catholic Historical Society* 41 (1930), p. 245.

117. Alexis de Tocqueville, *Democracy in America*, ed. J. P. Mayer (New York, 1969), pp. 287–90, 445–51.

118. Patrick Carey, *An Immigrant Bishop* (Yonkers, 1982), p. 146.

119. Ray Allen Billington, *The Protestant Crusade, 1800–1860* (Chicago, 1964), pp. 99–107.

120. *Pilot*, 16 Sept. 1843, and *Catholic Telegraph*, 30 Dec. 1843, quoted in Hueston, *Catholic Press and Nativism*, pp. 38–9.

121. Blarney O'Democrat [pseud.], *The Irish-Office-Hunter-Oniad* (New York, 1838) [Library of Congress]; Grattan, *Civilized America*, vol. 2, pp. 7–8, 29–32; Francis J. Grund, *Aristocracy in America* [1839] (New York, 1959), pp. 50–51.

122. Lee Benson, *The Concept of Jacksonian Democracy* (Princeton, 1961), pp. 33–5; Edward Pessen, *Most Uncommon Jacksonians* (Albany, 1967), pp. 9–33.

123. Francis J. Grund, *The Americans* (2 vols, London, 1837), i, pp. 96–8.

124. Benson, *Concept of Jacksonian Democracy*, pp. 136–9, 167–8, 183, 185.

125. Myler, *Reminiscences*, pp. 88–9; Louis Dow Scisco, *Political Nativism in New York State* (New York, 1901; reprint, 1968), pp. 20–30.

126. Franklin A. Walker, *Catholic Education and Politics in Upper Canada* (Toronto, 1964).

127. Vincent Lannie, *Public Money and Parochial Education: Bishop Hughes, Governor Seward, and the New York School Controversy* (Cleveland, 1968); Ravitch, *Great School Wars* pp. 3–76; Scisco, *Political Nativism*, pp. 39–46; Hueston, *Catholic Press and Nativism*, pp. 52–66.

128. Scisco, *Political Nativism*, p. 41.

129. Harold Buetow, *Of Singular Benefit* (New York, 1970), pp. 146–54.

130. Hugh J. Nolan, "Francis Patrick Kenrick: First Coadjutor-Bishop" in James F. Connelly (ed.), *The History of the Archdiocese of Philadelphia* (Philadelphia, 1976), pp. 171–2, 174–5, and 177–86 *passim*; Vincent Lannie and Bernard Diethorn, "For the Honor and Glory of God: The Philadelphia Bible Riots of 1840 [*recte* 1844]," *History of Education Quarterly* 8 (1968), pp. 46, 55–7, 68–9, and 44–105 *passim*.

131. "A Protestant and Native Philadelphian" in *The Truth Unveiled . . . The Terrible Riots in Philadelphia on May 6th, 7th, and 8th, A.D. 1844* (Philadelphia, 1844); Michael Feldberg, *The Philadelphia Riots of 1844* (Westport, CT, 1975); Montgomery, "Shuttle and the Cross," pp. 411–46.

132. Thomas Mooney, *Nine Years in America* (Dublin, 1850), p. 118.

133. Grattan, *Civilized America*, vol. 2, p. 44.

134. Potter, *To the Golden Door*, pp. 396–8.

135. Wyse, *America*, vol. 3, pp. 40–41; "Letter from America IV," *Nation*, 22 Apr. 1843, p. 444.

136. "Letter from America IV," p. 444; and "Letter from America XVI," *Nation*, 14 Oct. 1843, p. 842; on Mooney, see G. L. Barrow, "Justice for Thomas Mooney," *Dublin Historical Record*, 24 (1970), pp. 173–88; Mooney, *Nine Years in America*.

137. *Nation*, 7 Oct. 1843, p. 829.

138. Potter, *To the Golden Door*, pp. 396–8.

139. *Nation*, 14 Oct. 1843, pp. 844–5.

140. Andrew Jackson to Thomas Mooney, 23 May 1842 in Wyse, *America*, vol. 3, pp. 45–7.

141. Grattan, *Civilized America*, vol. 2, pp. 3–11, 45.

142. Buetow, *Of Singular Benefit*, pp. 114ff, and the many articles on Irish pioneer educators listed in Barbara A. Braun, *Richard J. Purcell, 1887–1950: A Bio-Bibliography* (Washington, DC, 1955).

143. Dale T. Knobel, "A Vocabulary of Ethnic Perception: Content Analysis of the American Stage Irishman," *Journal of American Studies* 15 (1981), pp. 45–71.

144. Sir Charles Lyell, *A Second Visit to the United States* [1845–6] (2 vols, New York, 1849), vol. 2, p. 187; Grund, *The Americans*, vol. 1, pp. 90–96; Mooney, *Nine Years in America*, p. 88; Stephen G. Bolger, *The Irish Character in American Fiction, 1830–1860* (New York, 1976), pp. 122–51 and *passim*.

145. Charles E. Rosenberg, *The Cholera Years* (Chicago, 1962), pp. 24, 37, 55–7, 61–4.

146. Richard J. Purcell, "The Irish Emigrant Society of New York City," *Studies*, 27 (1938), p. 593.

147. Ibid., pp. 581–2, 594, 596; Oliver MacDonagh, "The Irish Famine Emigration to the United States," *Perspectives in American History*, 10 (1976), p. 394.

SUGGESTED READING

Patrick J. Blessing, "The Irish in America," in *The Encyclopedia of the Irish in America*, ed. Michael Glazier (Notre Dame, IN: University of Notre Dame Press, 1999), pp. 453–470.

David Noel Doyle, *Ireland, Irishmen, and Revolutionary America, 1760–1820* (Dublin: Mercier, 1981).

Kerby Miller, *Emigrants and Exiles: Ireland and the Irish Exodus to North America* (New York: Oxford University Press, 1985).

Kerby A. Miller, Arnold Schrier, Bruce D. Boling, and David N. Doyle, *Irish Immigrants in the Land of Canaan: Letters and Memoirs from Colonial and Revolutionary America, 1675–1815* (New York: Oxford University Press, 2003).

Thomas M. Truxes, *Irish-American Trade, 1660–1783* (New York: Cambridge University Press, 1989).

David A. Wilson, *United Irishmen, United States: Immigrant Radicals in the Early Republic* (Ithaca, NY: Cornell University Press, 1998).

Chapter 5

The Remaking of Irish America, 1845–1880

David Noel Doyle

Between 1845 and 1880 Irish-America was dramatically remade, then matured, and by 1921 was beginning to decline. The commonplace perception that it had always been an urban, industrial, and Catholic community (quite inaccurate as to its character before 1820, and only partially true before 1845) well describes it for a full century after that date. The decisive years of change were between 1845 and 1880; the following forty years saw a maturing of the patterns then established. Before 1845, diverse experiences in both the United States and in British North America had made for scattered, varied, and disunited communities: Irish Protestants and Catholics had mingled as farmers, traders, and artisans in varying proportions across a vast continent. Smallish numbers and Protestant preeminence had not only accelerated Americanization (or Canadianization) in terms of both acculturation and outright absorption, but also eased the direct contributions of the immigrants to still fluid host cultures.

Four major changes altered all this after 1845. First, the famine multiplied massively the numbers going to North America: "More people left Ireland in just eleven years than during the preceding two and one-half centuries," or 1.8 million between 1846 and 1855.[1] Declining demand for agricultural labor in Ireland, and the fall of Irish wages compared with those in America, inclined millions more to follow the great outflow between 1855 and 1921. Second, as many as nine-tenths of these famine and post-famine emigrants to the United States were Catholics, which, together with the vast numbers and a major new effort by churchmen in Ireland and North America to secure fuller levels of churchgoing than before, not merely cut the Protestant element in Irish-America, but (except in Canada) inclined the body of Irish Protestant migrants to dissociate themselves from their fellow countrymen. In the United States this trend was accelerated by a more sharply anti-Irish nativism,[2] which was now more strictly anti-Catholic, so that Irish Protestants were now no longer subjected to it, unlike those who had come to colonial America. Third, the triumph of Irish nationalist ideology, if in varying forms, among the Irish at home in this period, created an ethos of distinctiveness and techniques of group advancement that took renewed root, for other reasons, in the overseas communities. Fourth, this expanded migration was given new form and concentration by America's rapid industrialization from the early 1840s and its focus in certain regions.

It is striking that in British North America, where the transition from a mixed Protestant and Catholic migration was less marked, where industrialization was very limited, and where the hegemony of British traditions persisted (marginalizing Irish nationalism), "Irish-Canada" remained well into the 1880s what Irish-America had ceased to be after Andrew Jackson (president 1829–37): largely rural and agricultural, largely led by Protestants, and largely scattered. (The very inclusion of the Irish harp as a minor element in the flag of the dominion of Canada in 1867 appropriately reflected this.) By contrast, by the 1860s a new Irish-America, which was urban, industrial, and Catholic, had become intensely aware of itself, especially of its notable share in the armies and casualties of the civil war (only now passing from cliché to documentation).[3] Indeed, these new Irish-Americans were overwhelmingly more urban than were native Americans or Irish-Americans of colonial antecedents. They were found at all social levels of the burgeoning commercial as well as factory cities, which they humanized by networks of connections based on common local and regional origins in the old country. If churchmen instigated parish creation, they found myriads of natural cooperators among these newcomers.

The full period 1845–1921 thus has a natural unity. Continuous arrivals from Ireland counteracted dispersal and assimilation; those going to the United States greatly outnumbered those going to any other destination.[4] Thus the main story after 1845 plainly relates to the United States, where communities grew by continuous infusions from home, as well as by industrial concentration and the intergenerational loyalty between Irish-born and their American offspring. The Roman Catholic Church there became the most distinctively "Irish" institution outside Ireland. Such cohesion underpinned the role of the American Irish in funding and encouraging the Irish independence movement, especially in the 1880s and from 1910 to 1922, and in securing transatlantic attention for its objectives. This solidarity influenced the ethnic and religious simplifications surrounding the "Irish question" in the British Isles and also matters of minority rights and power in the United States. Whether either Irish independence or the full form of religious pluralism attained by metropolitan America by 1910 would have been attained, without such self-conscious organization around the symbols of national identity and Catholic belief, remains matter for doubt.

In America the Irish pioneered a distinctive new society: fluid, democratic, innovative, yet locally Catholic and competently industrial. They interacted as before with Anglo-Americans for most public and economic purposes, and aligned after the 1850s with German Catholics for religious and cultural ones. From 1880, they drew many other Europeans to themselves, providing both examples and leadership for the enclaves from which Italians and Poles, then many others, would gather the fruits of a modern mass society.

Some scholars have written as though the famine exodus and its continuation to 1914 gave Irish-America its distinctive characteristics.[5] Others have sought to emphasize the continuing consequences after 1845 of previous Protestant and mixed migrations, by reason both of their offspring and of continuing lesser Protestant flows from Ireland.[6] Protestant migrants did modify the remaking of Irish-America, and some indeed continued to identify with it despite the great change in its composition and traditions: the nationalists John Mitchel and George Pepper are prominent examples. These matters are shown best by contrast with Canada: scholars agree that the famine migration did not make for a distinctive Irish-Canada.[7] Canada was a different case, even apart from its chronology, whereby in much of the country the Irish preserved an older pattern after the famine, in an imperial framework, in which the Protestant Irish enjoyed both numerical supremacy and a preferential position. But what was the typical Irish-Canadian experience? Was it the religiously mixed (yet segregated) pre-famine rural settlements, or the post-famine industrial and laboring parishes of cities such as Hamilton, Kingston, Toronto, or even Montreal? Particularly in Ontario (and later in the western provinces) the Catholic Irish were discreetly and quietly subordinate to an Anglo-Canadian supremacy, of which Irish Protestants were favored clients. The history of all the Irish in Canada was indeed an "untold story," until a descendant, Brian Mulroney, became the dominion's prime minister in 1984. Their traditions were better remembered in isolated Catholic Irish "holylands" than among Catholic scholars or among the Anglo-Canadian Protestants of largely Irish descent. To present the nineteenth-century Ontario, therefore, as an ideal interplay of Irish identities and autonomies is wide of the mark. While Thomas D'Arcy McGee fled from New York in 1857, disenchanted with the poverty, urban captivity, and political manipulation of his countrymen there during the height of nativism, seeking a "pastoral utopia" in Canada's "tidy church-centred Irish Catholic farm communities," yet notably he was invited in as leader by the Irish of French, not English, Canada.[8] In 1873 a French churchman in New York reversed McGee's basic contrast: in Canada, "Irishmen are not at liberty to show the same feeling for their native country, and prove equally useful to her [as here] . . . they seem almost paralysed in their actions as Irish people."[9]

Although experience after 1845 varied greatly in the United States, the trend of change was clear. The urban and laboring Irish population, newly populous, more wholly Catholic, salved its trauma and poverty and maintained its self-esteem and cohesion by constructing a peculiar subculture around the familiarities of the neighborhood, the saloon, and the parish. Within these, Irishmen met, talked, and organized for the protection of their livelihood, the improvement of their social position, and the maintenance of their religious faith. The formal sides of these concerns saw the creation of trade unions and fraternal clubs, the support of the urban organizations ("machines") of the national Democratic Party, and the multiplication of Catholic churches, schools, and hospitals. Within these, in turn, Irish-American support for Irish independence grew inevitably from past experience, from present marginality, from the lessons of American republicanism, and from the respectability of the cult of nationalism, following in the wake of the war against Mexico and the Civil War.

Yet most of the originating cultural and institutional pattern of Irish-America had emerged before 1845, if only skeletally and only in the Atlantic port cities. It would have grown anyway without the famine, as the U.S. economy boomed between 1849 and 1857. On conservative estimates of an annual increase of 0.5 percent in the population of Ireland during the period 1846–60, and assuming a stable flow of emigration westward at average pre-famine rates, roughly one million would have settled compared with the actual two million who apparently did so. Then the Irish experience of Atlantic migration would have been closer to Scandinavian and rural British patterns, if more numerous, and the whole experience would be less melodramatized

by historians. Such counterfactual possibilities also show that not all famine emigrants were refugees from the tragedy. Many would have left home in any case: up to a
quarter of the 1846–50 flow, and perhaps half of that for 1851–60, would have emigrated. In short, the trends of demography and emigration, coupled with available
foundations laid in America by 1845, would have themselves assured the remaking of
Irish-America, if on a less imposing scale and with a less dramatic transition.

The decades 1861–80 are more straightforward. The United Kingdom commissioners of emigration reported 1,140,394 Irish bound for the United States, whose officials
in turn reported 872,649 arrivals.[10] Since such discrepancies had previously been
reversed (with better arrival than departure data), probably this under-reporting in
America was due partly to civil war disruptions and the desire of incoming young
Irishmen to avoid the draft. It was also due to a century-long pattern in which Irish
departees reported their ultimate planned destination, but stopped off to work at
intermediate points (usually in English and Scottish cities) on hearing of recession in
America, this time in 1865–6 and throughout the 1870s. Nevertheless, annual rates of
direct emigration to the United States settled at levels around or slightly above those
reached just before the famine—in the 1870s they were at 8.5 per thousand of population, the rate of 1842.

The effects of the famine bulge thus had already thinned out. The post-famine pull
of relatives, and the diffusion of the custom of maintaining a viable farm by sending
off most of its offspring to such kin-pools, were somewhat reduced by the diminished
domestic population on which they operated.[11] The full period 1845–80, nevertheless,
bears the clear impress of the famine itself. Most Irish-born in America in the thirty
years after 1850 would have clear memories associated with the famine. From 1880 to
1921, however, two new generations set the tone there—one born in the United States,
the other the product of later Victorian Ireland—both without such direct recollection. The fusion of constitutional nationalism and agrarian radicalism with fenianism
in the "new departure" of 1878 reflects a compromise between leaders molded in the
first era with the more pragmatic attitudes of these two rising generations. Although
the famine cannot be willed away, its effects were thus not unlimited.

Yet the effects of the famine were very important. It tested the narrow and conventional limits of government intervention in Britain, Ireland, and British North America, as well as the United States; it accelerated the tide of romantic humanitarianism
intolerant of widespread suffering; it instigated reforms, which in the United States
were chiefly municipal, from wide-ranging health and welfare reforms, to accelerated
provision of schools and prisons. Emigrant numbers were greatly boosted, although
abnormal death rates pursued the emigrants from Ireland, and shadowed their children and successors right into the 1920s. Already between 1840 and 1845 past ease of
assimilation had been disrupted by the press of incoming crowds. Between 1847 and
1854 the influx varied from three to six times the rate of the early 1840s; each year over
100,000 people were squeezed into or through America's still smallish ports. Probably
a minimum of 200,000 died within three years of arrival, although deaths on the incoming vessels have been much exaggerated. The destitution of many newcomers and
the anxiety of all, as they crowded available accommodation and employment, so
darkened public views of the Irish that their real character and their recent (and then

subsequent) progress were obscured. Political nativism was reborn, prejudicial stereo-types replaced friendliness, and hard treatment resulted, quite apart from hard labor.

The suffering of such large numbers also quickened charity: in many cities the first major Catholic hospitals, orphanages, and welfare funds were set up. The tide of the poor overwhelmed the young church and other voluntary agencies; public provision by municipalities had to be greatly expanded. There were extraordinary efforts, too, by men prominent in both Irish and non-Irish communities, to send aid direct to the starving in Ireland—from cities as distinct as New Orleans and Boston, and by men as varied as post-frontier politicians and Philadelphia gentlemen merchants. Choc-taws in Indian territory, the blacks of the North Liberties and Kensington (the Irish districts of greater Philadelphia), Shakers in Ohio, Jews in New York, military cadets at West Point, even the future Know-Nothing candidate Millard Fillmore gave money. In both the House of Representatives and Senate, however, the bills providing federal aid failed. (In any case President Polk believed that they were unconstitutional and planned to veto them.) Irish-Americans naturally raised the most money: $623,193 in New York City, Boston, Philadelphia, and Baltimore in the first two months of 1847 alone, against $143,540 raised by the general relief committees of the same four cities from November 1846 to early 1848. All this expressed the old conjoint pattern of lead-ership in pre-famine Irish communities in America, with deference both to general city and state leaderships and to their own leading merchants and lawyers; it also was a final flourish of immigrant Protestant Irish solidarity with the old country, charac-teristic of Irish-America since the American revolution. It seems that donor fatigue came more quickly to non–Irish Americans, however, than to the Irish, alerted by let-ter and church networks to continuing hardship well beyond 1847. Misery on one side, charity on the other, diminished the usual factionalism of Irish civic life in America and briefly replaced the recent tensions with its hosts. Yet now more emo-tionally "Irish," the communities were even less amenable to rapid Americanization than in the changing 1830s, even had native-stock Americans continued generally sympathetic. The great outpouring of compassion and aid by the latter for Ireland itself did not survive the wretched horde-like influx from Ireland. Boston in 1847 de-manded a bond of $1,000 from each sick passenger, which deflected many of the poor to New Brunswick and the St. Lawrence, in addition to those already bound for the British North American ports.

Although the organized nativists and their animus, numbers, and political pres-ence revived as the most wretched scenes receded, yet no one, not even the nativists, ever sought even partial exclusion of the Irish as such, nor sought to deny (as distinct from delay) their ultimate citizenship. Open ports and borders were perhaps Amer-ica's greatest generosity of the time, and in turn the famine immigration greatly re-inforced the humanitarian argument for an open immigration policy, with America as a haven for Europe's oppressed and miserable, which then ironically survived as long as mass immigration included substantial Irish and other north European com-ponents. The tendency of Irish-American scholars to emphasize the role of anti-Irish and anti-Catholic strains in U.S. culture, in catalyzing the emergence of the con-scious, defensive, and institutionalized Irish-America after 1850, tends to neglect this broader receptivity, even friendliness, and the role it played in allowing in the crowds whose numbers and dispositions were themselves sufficient cause to construct a sub-culture.

The famine trauma itself gave emigrants the need for an outlook in which continuing ill-fortune, whether providential or imposed, was a national fate to be nobly endured.[12] Famine, followed by a rough passage and migratory insecurity, was accompanied for many by culture shock, disease, poverty, hardship, and unemployment. American coldness, if not obloquy, hurt most. Finally the armies of the Civil War beckoned many with deadly finality. Thus the contexts nurturing a new fatalism were surely more extreme than those experienced in the hardened lives of pre-famine Irish country people.

Irish writers visiting America from 1850 to 1875 could only see the hard and meager lives of their fellow countrymen, and could not perceive the dynamics of America's exciting polity and economy. The emphasis of Victorian popular culture on the pain felt by those who left an empty nest proved as much goad as catharsis to their feelings: Stephen Foster (himself of Ulster-American descent) wrote from 1851 to 1863, and Thomas Moore remained the favorite lyric writer of all Americans. Thus even the migrants' change of country and often language did not save them from an emotionalized view of past associations.

The coming of a Young Irish élite of refugees after the rising of 1848 reinforced much of this. Disabused, romantic, assertive, and articulate, their highly charged sensibilities mixed with the chiaroscuro attitudes of their lowly fellow countrymen to incline both together away from any commonsense judgment that the worst was over by the mid-1850s. Both the journalism of the former and the ordinary letters of the latter confirm their common noble pessimism. Irish-Americans in the generation after 1850 were thus veined with a sadness that obscured their gifts, veiled their religious faith, and either shadowed or distanced their American-born children.

Ironically, the famine emigrants could hardly have come at a better time. By the treaty of Guadalupe Hidalgo (1848), the United States had newly added title to, or reconfirmed, possession of lands now one-third of its continental territory—over one million square miles. The country's rail network grew tenfold from 3,000 to 30,000 miles between 1840 and 1860, chiefly after 1850, multiplying construction jobs and quickening development of the northeastern industrial core, and its integration with the midwest's spreading wheat and maize fields. Although most factory workers up to the 1830s had been native Americans, not immigrants, by the 1850s most of them preferred life in trade, on farms, or as white-collar workers, leaving expanding industrial work to foreigners. Indeed, 3 million American-born left the Atlantic states for the interior by 1860, whereas very few then migrated the other way to compete with the incoming Irish. Manufacturing plants increased from 123,000 in 1849–50 to 140,000 in 1860, but their employment increased by a huge 50 percent as the scale of the larger, nationally oriented ones grew rapidly, although most remained small, averaging fewer than ten workers each. The per capita annual income in the northeastern states was $181 in 1860, which exceeded that of every other country except Australia, and indeed that of every other American region, except Texas and Louisiana.

Politics also broadly suited the Irish. The Democrats, who courted them, held federal power from 1845 to 1849, and from 1853 to 1861. The Mexican war, slavery, sectionalism, and competitive expansion distracted attention from the Irish, even when their arrival was agitated by the Know-Nothings as a counterissue. In short, had they entered a confined, united, and economically stagnant land, the brief flurries of nativism might well have proved more general, hostile, and enduring. Instead they came to a booming country, divided and distracted by vast questions linked to its growth. Rarely can almost 2 million newcomers anywhere have escaped becoming a matter of real and continuing obsession; yet in North America between 1845 and 1860 the Irish did so. Few enough of them realized all this at the time, and those that did, such as Thomas D'Arcy McGee, resented still the accompanying injustices. Most lived far from such broad perspectives, each in his or her own harassed, anxious place.

Who actually came, during the famine, in its aftermath, and thereafter?[13] A balanced view cannot rest on the images and self-images that sprang from the immediacy of disaster. The answers are vital to assessing the history of Irish-Americans. How can one explain their rapid diffusion and adaption, if they were the "wretched refuse of storm-tossed shores," the uprooted of Oscar Handlin's portrait,[14] or the Gaelic and post-Gaelic prisoners of a collectivism incapable of enterprise and individualism, who became the victims of an immature industrialism, as in Kerby Miller's portrait?[15] It is not surprising that Oliver MacDonagh accepted their initial immiseration and proletarianisation in America.[16] The Handlin or Miller pictures logically entail a sequence whereby they were at first the passive playthings of masterful forces they but gradually and dimly understood. Their proletarianisation was thus but the corollary of their ignorance, and the counterpart to the stewardship of the American-born élites who molded the country and forcefully remade the very circumstances and texture of Irish life within it. Such ideas tend to fuse with the view that on both sides of the Atlantic the Irish were also victims of a thoughtless fecundity.[17] The other side of the picture has received less emphasis: that the Irish were a versatile people availing themselves of fresh opportunity and diminishing prejudice to build an intelligent subcommunity open to all the ways of American life, and contributing considerably to its dynamism.[18] A close study of neither the emigrants' backgrounds nor their actual lives in America supports the pessimistic view of their fortunes, unless one concentrates on the misery of two groups: emigrants from Ireland's congested west coast, and tenement-dwelling, unskilled Irish newcomers in New England.

The characteristics of the migrants depended on where they came from. If the whole famine outflow came from places where previous migration was rare, then indeed Irish-America was remade even in its origins, especially if those coming after 1850 were relatives of the famine emigrants, and then the later mid-Victorian migration consisted of siblings, nieces, and nephews of these predecessors. The traditional view that Irish-America from 1850 to 1921 was the product of the famine would in that respect hold up. Yet study of depopulation and emigration rates by county, together with analysis of birth cohort depletion, support the broad conclusion that the famine brought first a new intensity of emigration from the "old" zones of south Ulster, north Connacht, and the midlands, from which emigration was long established,[19] and only then, in its aftermath, a shift in zones of relative intensity into the west and southwest. Initially, heavy transatlantic outmigration came from areas suffering high excess mortality and general destitution—if relatives outside Ireland could assist escape or even simply attract it. South Ulster, north Connacht, and the north midlands (Fermanagh, Monaghan, and Cavan; Sligo, Roscommon, Leitrim; Longford and Westmeath) all rank in the top half of county emigration rates before 1841, and all were in the upper half of county mortality rates during 1846–50. The first seven of these eight counties, plus contiguous Mayo, accounted for the top eight county emigration rates for the years 1846–51, with Westmeath also in the top half. Yet rates, as opposed to numbers, are deceptive: this region provided fewer than one-third of all emigrants between 1846 and 1855.[20] The real and distinguishing crowds now came from Munster (and nearby Galway).

For a new pattern that pointed to the future now intruded, although not without its own precedents. If a few anomalous counties at first suffered high famine mortality without commensurate recorded emigration, notably Cork and Clare in the southwest, and Galway and Mayo in the west, there is evidence that they too had sent away large numbers (if not proportions) of their people in the past and sent even more in 1846–50.[21] Thus they too were equipped with their own bridges out of disaster. Thereafter they indeed provided the most numerous flows abroad. Well over half a million people left County Cork from 1846 to 1921, and over a quarter of a million left from each of Counties Mayo and Galway.[22] Of older emigration zones, only County Antrim, the Scots-Irish heartland, kept pace in sheer numbers, with over 300,000 migrants in the same years. In this vital sense, maps of total county outflow are more useful than those of emigration rates now generally used.[23] In sum, there was a massive overlap between past emigration habits and famine consequences. The poorest might not have been able to escape immediately, but, through kin and neighbors, they too knew the way out and, as destitution and sickness receded, they took it.

The provinces of Munster and Connacht, from the famine (and until the 1930s), sent disproportionately more of their inhabitants to the United States than did Leinster or Ulster. America's appeal to Munster people, especially to those from Cork, was strong. So too was it to those Connacht people who could afford to get there. Some of Connacht's lost "cohort depletion" of the 1840s and 1850s (those born by 1841 or 1851 and unaccounted for in the migration or mortality statistics of 1851 and 1861) undoubtedly broke from the main flow to Britain to arrive in industrial Pennsylvania or on the construction sites of mid-Victorian Canada. Connacht's representatives in New York's Irish middle class seem an anomaly and originated in a pre-famine select flow from its better towns and families, notably from Sligo.

Thus, while the period 1846–55 increased Munster and Connacht elements within Irish-America, it diminished the shares of Leinster and Ulster, the politically important, commercially more advanced, and culturally more diverse provinces. Distribution throughout the United States seems to have been proportionate to these flows. Munster emigrants were everywhere boosted to preponderance by the famine, even if they took longer to establish social and business leadership. It is thus not by chance that the chief contemporary investigators of Irish-America between 1850 and 1880 were Munstermen, usually from Cork, notably the nationalist politicians J. F. Maguire and William Smith O'Brien, the priests Michael Buckley and Hugh Quigley, and the journalist Jeremiah O'Donovan (who should not be confused with Jeremiah O'Donovan Rossa). Probably 30 percent of all America's Irish immigrants in 1846–55 were from Munster.

Ulster was displaced, therefore, almost everywhere, by Munster as the most characteristic source of the Irish-born in North America. The exceptions are themselves revealing. New York City's mid-century middle-class Irish were heavily of Ulster background, and equally Protestant and Catholic, while Pennsylvania remained partly an Ulster stronghold, even if now Presbyterian farmers were less prominent than Catholic miners and mill workers.[24] Migration from Ulster from 1846 to 1855 was less than its population warranted by total Irish patterns. But Cavan, Monaghan, and Fermanagh did have high rates, as did the glens of Antrim. Large numbers emigrated from Tyrone, Donegal, and south Down, so that together the "outer Ulster" zones sent away from 330,000 to 350,000. It was in these areas that the famine struck most severely in Ulster.[25] One can safely assume that American indications of Ulster arrivals are of these people. Yet whether from northern or southern Ireland, in its regional composition the remade Irish-America was recruited from its own pre-famine foundations, if with a tilt in the originating axis within Ulster to its more Catholic zones, and along the axis toward inland Munster.[26]

All this helped set the Catholic character of Irish-America for the next three generations, which strengthened the drift to a more homogenous Irish-America, under way since the mid-1820s. Even excluding special calculations for Ulster, provincial figures show that 1.6 million or 85 percent of emigrants leaving Ireland in these years were Roman Catholic; and given the special migration patterns of the Protestants, this implies that nine out of ten migrants to the United States were likewise Catholic.[27] This produced a series of self-reinforcing tendencies among Irish-Americans, in the outlook of native Americans, and (not least) in the growing preference for Canada among Protestant emigrants. Irish-America now thought of itself as Catholic in essence; native Americans, to a greater or lesser degree, agreed with them; and the descendants of the earlier Presbyterian emigrants now distinctive abandoned their usual past identification of themselves as Irish for the distinctive and relatively novel (if not inaccurate) identification "Scotch-Irish". Indeed there was unconscious irony in the fact that most Irish-Americans, grasping the right to a dual national identity and culture as an immigrant people, denied that right to the Presbyterians of Ulster, aspects of whose culture were strongly retained and transmitted in the United States.

The nature of the migration's epicenter, its axis stretching from mid-Tyrone and Monaghan south to east Cork and Kilkenny, together with Connacht's outflow coming heavily into the pattern, meant that its Irish-speaking component was very considerable, although not a majority one. Some half a million people, perhaps 550,000, from Munster and Connacht, or two-thirds their outflow from 1846 to 1855, were then Irish-speaking. Barony analysis of depopulation in Ulster and north Leinster, as in Kilkenny, shows higher incidence in residually Irish-speaking areas than in English-speaking ones in the same years.[28] From 1856 to 1880 at least a half-million or more Irish-speakers left for America.[29] Most were bilingual, and over time the importance of their speaking Irish diminished, yet at mid-century both priests and politicians knew the value of Irish, and Protestant missionaries believed five-eighths of the Irish in New York City to be Irish-speakers.[30] From the 1870s the Irish language revival

The first stage of the long journey to America was leaving home. As depicted by *Frank Leslie's Illustrated Newspaper* in January 1866, the mail coach collects emigrants in Cahirciveen, County Kerry, no doubt headed for the port at Queenstown in County Cork. More than forty thousand left Kerry during the 1860s in what was, by then, a well-organized process. (Library of Congress, Prints and Photographs Division, LC-USZ62-2022)

movement took its initial force, and much of its finance, from America. (All this is not to confound the mid-Victorian migration with that of the later nineteenth century: unlike those after 1880, even Irish-speakers came more from Ireland's interior than from its western seaboard.)

This brings us back to the geographical, economic, and social background of the migrants. The east Munster and south Leinster region was well served by banks and trade networks, by roads and carriage services, and by schools. Population densities were hardly overwhelming, approximating those of northern France; land values were high.[31] Thackeray found the bookishness of its plain people unusual; Mgr Michael Buckley believed Cork people bought six of ten of all the books bought in Ireland, a fond if revealing judgment. The region had anticipated Pius IX's "devotional revolution": the pre-famine religious commitments of the area had long been properly institutionalized and catechized, despite residual folkloric survivals. This was more so of smallholders' families, which produced youthful emigration, than of laborers, too immiserated to go.[32] Most of the people were also strongly nationalist in politics, largely in the moderate framework advanced by Daniel O'Connell before 1845, but many also in the informal and sometimes violent conspiracies of men with more pressing grievances. Indeed, geographically, this was the most politicized region of the country until the late 1870s.[33] As emigrants, they were far from the hopeless, uprooted lemmings of the implicit imagery of Handlin or Freeman. They were not already without some prior knowledge of, and leverage on, the arts and skills of mid-Victorian modernity, before going to America, British North America, or Britain: this indeed explains why they moved so easily between the four countries. While their capacities were real, however, they did fall short of a measured grasp of the innovations, structures, and power in those countries. This helps explain the heroic superficiality, the courageous error, of the fenianism of so many of them after 1858; those who did better understand these things, by preparation or by observation, usually had the wit to stand back from such adventurism.

There were indeed the truly uprooted and bewildered. These came from the southwestern mountains and peninsulas, from parts of Clare and the more congested regions of Connacht. In the Atlantic seaboard areas, holdings were tiny, often still strips in common fields, English was little used, books and newspapers were little known, potato dependence almost absolute, population densities (in the habitable pockets) extraordinary, and real knowledge of the wider world—while not absent—mostly scraps gleaned from harvesting stays in Britain. Political consciousness was either dependent or inchoate.[34]

Outer Ulster was also distinctive. Population densities were very high, 300–350 per square mile in 1845, and normal holdings similar to Munster's, from five to twenty-five acres. But the canny marketing of skills, labor, and produce had partly withstood the decline of its chief base in domestic textiles, leaving a still monetized if precarious economy. Unlike Munster, outer Ulster had few proper towns; indeed, contrary to stereotype, only 9 percent of the province's people lived in centers of 2,500 or more, most in the factory and mill towns of northeastern, inner Ulster.[35] The anomaly in outer Ulster of a literate, market-oriented rural economy, without significant urbanization, was unique in Ireland, although not unknown in parts of western Pennsylvania, to which many had gone since the 1790s, and to which many continued to go from the 1830s to the early 1860s. If the newer migrants were now largely Catholic, they were sometimes more superstitious and less well catechized than those from Munster and Leinster, although by the later 1850s a striking improvement was clear across the province.[36] Yet they had the advantage of knowing both plain and poorer Protestants; unlike those from Munster, they did not normally associate Protestants with an oppressive and inherited social order. It is striking that such Ulster Catholics, in marked contrast with our own times, were rarely found among the nationalist ideologues of Irish-America between 1850 and 1900. The exceptions, such as John Mitchel, John McClenahan, and William Carroll, were Presbyterian townsmen.

Many small farmers fled all three of these distinctive regions, and more yet of their sons and daughters. They had much in common, despite what has just been said. Though few had capital and many were inured to hardship and privation, most had experience of money and markets, many of town life, almost all of labor and produce transactions, some of the law and the courts. Few came from the lowest, landless strata; few, by Irish rural standards, had been destitute. The tendency of most young immigrants to be described (or to describe themselves) from the late 1840s onward as laborers and servants, before departure, confounds the crucial distinction of the Irish countryside between those who were actually so as their parents had been also, and smallholders' offspring so denoted by reason of recent work with their own or others' families.[37] Most had a rudimentary education and were literate, adaptable, and (if Irish-speaking) bilingual.[38] Almost all, as noted, were Catholic, if they varied as to the seriousness of it. The men were politically inclined, if not politically skilled. Despite cliché, most were young and vigorous; few were heads of families. Convinced that Ireland had now failed them, they were determined on survival and improvement: "in certain respects well fitted for the life he was to enter," the emigrant was "from the moment of landing a special category of American, not a special category of Irish."[39] Such was true even of Irish-speakers. Men such as Brooklyn real-estate dealer Michael Logan (founder of *An Gaodhail*) and William Hughes of Detroit (later editor of the *Michigan Catholic*) made wholly English-speaking careers, no less than did the nationalist leaders Michael Doheny and John O'Mahony. Only in isolated pockets, such as the Schuylkill mining valleys, was Irish commonly used; and only in very remote ones, such as Beaver Island in Lake Michigan, or the Mirimichi basin in New Brunswick, was it commonly transmitted to the next generation.[40] All this confirms a broader Americanisation among both Irish- and English-speakers. "There are very few Irish people who do not pick up the American accent, and the American form of speech," granted that those who "studiously conceal that they are Irish . . . are units in thousands."[41]

Such change was oddly accelerated by the very provincialism of residual Irish identities. "The northerns look down on the southerns, and both dislike the Connacht-folk. The 'far downs' i.e., the northerns, are despised by the 'Corkeys,' while the latter are odious to the former in a similar degree."[42] For most, the evening balm of memory was thus of natal locality, not nationality, and scarcely threatened a workaday Americanism. Hence the vast provincial outflows from Ireland did not immediately constitute a common and vigorous Irish subculture in America to qualify the impact of the new society and polity. Instead Irish-America had to be actually made, partly by men with clear ideas of its possible potential forms, and partly more indirectly by the interplay of shared Irish traditions and the impact of America. Leaders were most effective when shaping the latter: churchmen in molding inchoate belief against the shock of the new country's impersonal secularity and aggressive evangelicalism, politicians and nationalists in turning community bonds and customs into instruments for group pride and urban improvement. So competing provincial biases did but limited damage, though they remained obstacles to a more unified Irish-America. Irish provincialism thus oddly speeded acculturation and even assimilation. But the character of the emigrant was evident less in how the past constrained him than in what he did in America.

The rapid urbanization of the Irish says most about their adaptability.[43] Certainly by 1850 they had already concentrated in the industrializing northern states touching the

Atlantic: here 748,000 of 962,000 of them lived—78 percent, as against 40 percent of all Americans. We lack evidence as to when this began, but so marked a pattern so close to 1847 suggests that it was no overnight product of the famine. By 1880, 1.2 million of 1.8 million Irish-born lived in the same states, or 67 percent.[44] William V. Shannon, following Carl Wittke's views of 1939, and those of many others, put it crisply: "The Irish were a rural people in Ireland and became a city people in the United States." By contrast, D. H. Akenson bluntly replies: "In 1870 even the Irish immigrants (much less the second or third generation) were not a city people." All three scholars are referring to this main migration.[45] Yet new research confirms the pattern of urbanization to be indeed fundamental, and even remarkable. For not only were the incoming Irish now urbanized almost *en bloc* in the United States (and considerably so in British America), they became among the most urbanized people in the world, notably more so than the Americans as a whole, and more so than almost all peoples in Europe, except in Britain and the Low Countries. They remained thus for half a century, until other major ethnic groups, and populations elsewhere, began to catch up.[46] While most notable in America's industrialized "core" area, as has long been argued,[47] the precise patterns were more distinctive than those of the core itself. Well over four-fifths of the specialized regional literature on the Irish in the United States deals with the Irish in towns and cities. It includes most of the earlier scientific literature on Irish-America, pioneered not by Irish-Americans seeking modernist credentials, but rather by America's founder scholars of urban history, such as Arthur Schlesinger Sr., Marcus Hansen, and Oscar Handlin.

In short, from the 1840s, building on precedents,[48] Irish-Americans became the people of the country's urban future, rather than of its then present of farms, commerce, and villages, much less of its almost wholly rural past. That the descendants of the previous migrants, for whom we lack data, may indeed have largely replicated native American (rather than newly immigrating Irish) patterns, and stayed or migrated within the countryside probably hastened the division between the "old" and the newer Irish-America, and further distanced the "Scotch-Irish" from others.

By 1870, just nine out of ten Irish-born, or 1.68 million out of 1.85 million, lived in the eighteen states of the nation's developed northern core.[49] This ran 500 miles from Portland in southern Maine to Baltimore in Maryland, and thence a thousand miles westward to southern Minnesota, and south to central Missouri at St. Louis. This vast area, roughly rhomboid in shape, was only one-fifth of the whole country, and as yet its industrial zones were confined to the east coast and the river valleys there, apart from a few outliers such as Pittsburgh and Cincinnati. But the region contained over three-quarters of the country's urban population, about two-thirds of all its people, and the great bulk of its manufacturing capacity. Elsewhere there were considerable numbers of Irish in only two states: fifty-four thousand in California and seventeen thousand in Louisiana. Whereas the American-born were well distributed throughout these twenty states in the core plus California and Louisiana, 70 percent (1.3 million) of the Irish lived in less than one-seventh of the twenty states' component counties (in but 146 out of 1,090 counties). These 146 counties were all urban and industrial, or occasionally mining, counties (or both).

The roots of such urban patterns go back to the later eighteenth century, but its reality owed most to the convergence of post-1840 mass migration with America's industrialization. Yet urban precedents in Ireland, the newer models of livelihood in Britain, and a distaste for wide-open spaces and their lack of community were contributory factors. The pattern in the core states was already established by 1850, pioneered by pre-famine arrivals, as was settlement in Louisiana. California, the sole post-famine addition to the pattern, owed its position to the coincidence of annexation, gold rush, and famine migration. From 1850 to 1870 concentration, as a proportion of all Irish in the United States, neither markedly increased nor diminished in the major industrial states of the core zone (New York, Pennsylvania, Massachusetts, and Ohio). It did increase, however, in New Jersey and Illinois, as these were absorbed into the manufacturing areas of the zone by the New York Central Railroad and its auxiliaries, a grid complete by 1860. Indeed, later nineteenth-century change was only toward even further concentration within the zone rather than dispersal away from it. After 1870, and especially after 1880, relative Irish densities in lower New England, New York, New Jersey, and Pennsylvania, began to rise again, for reasons similar to those of the 1840s: a renewed Irish outflow seeking former neighbors and kinfolk in cities enjoying further rounds of industrial growth, now based not only on steam, water power, iron, and coal but also on steel, oil, and chemicals. Even with the larger plants this new industrialism brought, most factories remained small. But the preference of male newcomers for mobile, often outdoor work, from the 1870s onward found men disproportionately taking railroad and construction jobs, and leaving much factory work to immigrant single women, a major change since the 1840s. Despite this, the years 1845–70 plainly laid out the pattern of the urban and industrial settlements of the Irish, a geography as distinct as that of the Scotch-Irish settlers a century before them, and for many of the same reasons: expanding and available livelihoods, kinship networks, familiarity of terrain, and the chance to re-create church and community. Both waves of Irish settled the available, unclosed America of their own times, and occasionally overlapped: James Crockett settled the still empty land of mid-Pennsylvania as a pioneer Presbyterian farmer in 1810 and was still alive when Catholic miners filled the region's new anthracite mining hamlets after 1845.

The urban-industrial counties of the core states contained grids of small cities, factory towns, and mill villages (called "villes" in Connecticut), and sometimes a large city, or mining center, or a railway junction. Such varied counties were not unknown to migrants who had lived in the Lagan valley, or remigrants who had worked in the Scots lowlands, northern England, or south Wales. Settlements, like workplaces, were small-scale. They were rarely far from each other before 1870. The Irish preferred counties geared to their own sense of distance, as they did towns of a certain intimacy. Finding these things, they dug in, even as America's industrialism distended geographically. This helps explain the irony that their concentration increased even as urban America spread. Industrial south New England was no larger than Munster and Leinster combined; New York City was only 88 miles from Philadelphia and 218 from Boston. By contrast, western distances chilled the newcomers: New York was 830 miles from Chicago and 1,300 from Omaha. The chief eastern factory districts were thus accessible to each other, even on foot for poorer job-seekers.

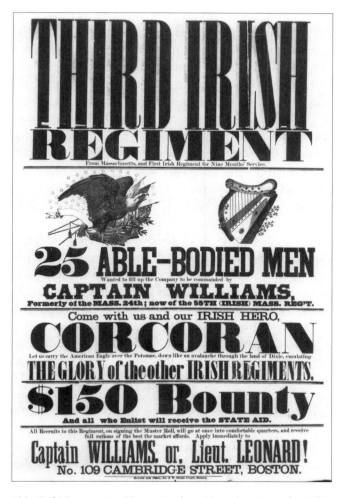

This Civil War–era recruiting poster from Massachusetts used a widely employed appeal to pride in Celtic valor as a means of attracting Boston Irish men to enlist in the Union Army. (Library of Congress, Prints and Photographs Division, LC-USZ62-40807)

This too explains why, within a broad continuity in the counties of the developed core region, there appear three changing stages of relative Irish settlement patterns as between their cities. First, an initial overconcentration in the largest cities, usually ports, to 1850. Second, a gradual dispersal from these through all the cities of the main eighteen-state core region and elsewhere, between 1850 and 1860. Third, after 1860, a slow abandonment of most interior and southern cities (except Chicago, Cleveland, Pittsburgh, and St Louis), a renewed identification with the country's leading fifteen cities, notably those of the Atlantic northeast, and a distinct web of lesser Irish centers in which their share of the inhabitants dwarfed these smaller cities' importance. These too were in the intimate, industrial northeast, notably Lowell, Worcester, and Cambridge. Despite a doubling of the number of American cities between 1870 and 1900, these latter trends held constant thereafter to the end of the century.[50]

Originally forced to become continent-wide pioneers by the famine crisis and the labor gluts created by it, chasing unskilled and semiskilled livelihoods wherever they offered (like the Mexican *braceros* of more recent times), eventually, given a choice, migrants sought locales that were congenial, familiar, and receptive: the heavily Irish working-class and Catholic subcultures of the northeastern factory cities or, alternatively, the cosmopolitan great cities, such as New York, Chicago, and San Francisco, each too large to permit imposition of a single cultural standard. Elsewhere, throughout the south and midwest, two major changes began to make the Irish uncomfortable in the local cities. First, even by 1860, both regions had ceased on balance to draw native-born Americans from the east coast states. Second, after 1870 these regions migrated their own children either further west or to the new cities (e.g., Tulsa, Rockford, Birmingham) or established ones (e.g., Milwaukee, Cincinnati, Atlanta), booming in their own zones. Both areas were now more local in tone.[51]

Thus the obvious thesis that the Irish avoided contracting opportunity cannot be sustained. Economically the more open midwestern region was growing. Indeed, while the relationship in the south between low wages for laboring and slow population growth and low in-migration does help account for virtual Irish abandonment of the zone by 1870, the midwest experienced high laboring wages, much foreign in-migration, and high population growth rates, and yet a dramatic fall-off in Irish new arrivals between 1850 and 1869. The comparison with New England and the Atlantic coast cannot explain it (except insofar as the laboring and other opportunities were there innumerable, though not markedly better paid).[52] For in the midwest there was no simple pattern of either increasing or declining opportunity, either for Irish newcomers or for long-term Irish residents. In Jacksonville, Illinois, the Irish were at the bottom of the social and occupational heap in 1880 as in 1850, whereas in Ripon, Wisconsin, they had markedly improved their situation. Midwestern pay levels and costs together were neither markedly better nor worse by the 1870s than in the east for incoming laborers and other workers granted initially favorable differences in the 1850s. True, for the highest levels of factory operatives, such as machinists, pay became somewhat higher in the east, as the market share of larger enterprises based there increased, but such positions were infrequently held by the Irish. On the railroads, which drew so many Irish, the real differentials of pay were between the various midwestern trunk systems in the mid-1870s, if differentials between laborers and skilled workers were sometimes less in the east. Perhaps a housing shortage directed the young Irish away from the midwest as they reached the stage of family formation. Above all, however, the real differences were in longer-term prospects for those who stayed around. The very "openness" of the midwest (and the mountain and Pacific states) itself posed a barrier against latecomers; in societies of so many recent "winners" the unsuccessful were more usually deemed to deserve their fate than in the more settled eastern states, as it was "the general temper of western society . . . to make its poorer members feel not only unfortunate but infamous."[53] It did not make it easier for Irish "losers," "on the other side of the tracks," that many of their Irish contemporaries, having migrated perhaps only a few years before them, were prosperously ensconced in good neighborhoods nearby.

Like a silent witness to ethnic resilience, Charleston's Greek-Revival Hibernian Hall on Meeting Street, built in 1840, including its harp motif iron gate, stands undamaged after the Union assault on South Carolina in 1865. It was designed by Thomas U. Walter of Philadelphia as the headquarters for the Hibernian Society of South Carolina and is a National Historic Landmark. (Library of Congress, Prints and Photographs Division, LC-B811-3439)

By contrast, in the south wages and conditions were fairly consistent, and lower than elsewhere. If provisions were as cheap as in the midwest, tenement rents were very high (after the civil war they were three times New England rates). Battered by yellow fever and malaria, despised even by free blacks, enclaves of Irish laborers diminished, lacking social mobility, or even secure niches, in the south's hierarchic, semitropical isolation. The exceptions networked the great railroads (once built)—a grid of opportunity, high wages, and promotion, unusually immune to southern patterns. Other Irish improved incrementally in the industrializing cities of the post-reconstruction south, especially if they brought acquired industrial skills.

Thus cultural and regional factors, the "personality" of individual cities, and even the attitudes of the Irish already there, played vital parts in redirecting Irish migration, doing so even from the south. Increasingly, the humbler Irish chose small factory cities, where low incomes and limited chances to rise were redeemed by Irish dominance and where working daughters (sons being more apt to roam) could supplement limited family budgets. Some more ambitious immigrants now chose those great cities mixed and fluid enough to allow blue-collar entry and white-collar upward mobility, even power, and (if desired) anonymity and secularity; others found in them a counterpointing familiarity and parish Catholicism to humanize the excitement of the large.

Catholicism of itself did not draw: western cities in the 1850s had consistently more Catholic Church provision relative to their populations than most eastern ones,[54] often funded by quite up-market "old" families who also had made an earlier start in the provision of Catholic secondary education. The new Irish clannishly preferred investment in their own social infrastructure: schools, churches, hospitals, orphanages, clubs. Orestes Brownson was not entirely the Catholic nativist that Irish editors held him when he noted: "The mass of our catholics think only of enjoying their religion for themselves."[55]

If the famine scattered the Irish as urban pioneers everywhere in the United States, and created their urban precedents in Canada, by the 1870s they were becoming less adventurous and settling for the predictable. They now more rarely went to non-eastern cities dominated by native Protestant,[56] or even German-American, populations, even those with a founding Catholic American element. Yet far from being demoralized "pioneers of the urban ghetto," many Irish early desired a secure social footing in prospering but open cities in which they were ghettoized neither by prejudice nor by their own parochial fears, but rather were able both to see themselves and their children improve their own livelihood and circumstances, and yet offer nephews and nieces from Ireland abundant, if more modest, beginnings. Only very rarely did they cling to a relatively declining city, though Albany offered one example. After 1880, there were major differences between the limited social mobility open to the Irish in New England factory towns, the greater chances open to them in New York and Pennsylvania (especially in both the cities with populations of over a million, and in towns in their interiors), and the relative equality of opportunity offered more widely in the midwest, so that their growing preference after 1860 against direct midwestern settlement might appear a mistaken gamble. Possibly the greater availability of skilled jobs in the east, as it grew and diversified so rapidly, meant that laborers and semiskilled Irishmen, for whom there were midwestern openings, sensed that the next rungs—if only for their sons—were eastward. Possibly that very availability absorbed the more venturesome anyway.

But, even more interestingly, it seems that the supplements to "family economy," which made the difference between poverty and comfort in Irish working families, were less available in the west. San Francisco in 1852 had only one job for an Irish girl or woman for every twenty-five jobs for Irish men, and even in 1880 but one to four. New York City had about two women's jobs for every three men's among the Irish in 1855.[57] The midwest was generally closer to the western than the eastern pattern: domestics in the midwest were usually native-born, German, or Scandinavian, and in the south, of course, black. By contrast, the heavy concentration of Irish in Rhode Island was due to the existence of large numbers of mill jobs, not merely for young women, but—unlike elsewhere in the north—even for children into the 1880s.[58] In short, it was not job opportunities so much as "family" survival patterns, born of necessity, that were involved. There are still unanswered questions about the Irish urban pattern of the mid-century and its long-term results, since adult job availability alone was not seemingly crucial after the 1850s. Certainly by 1870 their urban networks of 1900 were strikingly set already.[59]

America's cities were for many a sequence of temporary resting places; for others, death camps that soon turned escape into a graveyard; for others, a transfer from threadbare rural destitution to grinding tenement poverty, with the added burden of unremitting labor unknown in peasant society. Early death rates were appalling, if variable. While the great difference between rates in Philadelphia and those in lower Manhattan and in Broad Street and Fort Hill in Boston confirms the destructiveness of the worst slums, yet the persistence of high levels of mortality, after the severest poverty in America receded, raises questions, as do the lower levels among poor German Catholics in the Manhattan slums. Among Irish men, high rates were plainly related to hard physical labor, which lowered life expectancy well into the medically more competent early twentieth century. To the typhus, typhoid, and dysentery that spread through all the Irish settlements after 1845 but receded after 1849 were added a major cholera outbreak in the latter year, and, above all, the beginnings of mass endemic tuberculosis, which thereafter dogged the urban Irish beyond the 1920s. If slums made for the highest density of typhus, typhoid, and cholera deaths—partly sparing Philadelphia with its better housing for workers—dysentery was most common where (as in Boston or Lowell) civic sanitation was primitive. Tuberculosis, by contrast, followed the Irish disproportionately, almost regardless of their dwellings, just as it hit fewer immigrants from continental European cities, no matter how overcrowded their tenements. This was plainly a matter of previous exposure and the gradual genetic immunity acquired by continentals, in contrast with those from rural Ireland, where the disease had been rare or unknown. It multiplied in the moist, warm air of textile mills (falling off during lockouts and unemployment) and in apartments warmed by steam heat.

In the early and mid-1850s, death rates of the Irish-born in Boston were 142 percent of those of the native-born; but they were only 60 percent of native death rates in New York City, and 58 percent in Philadelphia. Thus Irish rates differed markedly by city: in 1855, Boston lost 37.7 per thousand of Irish birth, New York 21.1, and Philadelphia 12.2. Different circumstances of livelihood, housing, and sanitation were involved. Further, the Boston community was all but an overnight, famine-rooted one; those of the other cities were much older, so that in them the Irish made a high contribution to "native" deaths due to the high mortality of their offspring. This confuses direct contrast, as do the low death rates of established "old" Irish families.[60] The Irish were not unresponsive to the lessons taught. There was a persistent migration from the pest centers of the east coast upstate or inland. Most dramatically, an early diffusion throughout the cities of the south was rapidly scaled down, with few newcomers after the mid-1850s. There pandemic yellow fever and malaria added to the usual hazards, with extraordinary death rates from 1845 to 1860, peaking with a rate of about 200 per 1,000 in New Orleans in the epidemic year of 1853.[61]

High Irish death rates persisted in eastern cities, and indeed improvements after the 1850s were sometimes very slow: New York state in 1910 had a rate for Irish-born males of 25.9 compared with 13.8 for those of U.S. birth, and 12.9 for Italians (who had generally poorer living conditions). Even the American-born Irish reflected this. As late as 1920, the offspring of Irish mothers had mortality rates between one-third and one-half higher than those of native parentage in Chicago, as in Pennsylvania and New York State. A more balanced sample from various areas still showed a median differential of 42 percent. The children of the Irish suffered less in the 1920s than in the 1850s, but still unequally so: their infant mortality rate was 90.7 per 1,000 births compared with 75.8 for the infants of American-born mothers (though better than the 112.9 for those of Austrian-born mothers). The contrast of their higher adult mortality with those of poorer "new immigrants" from eastern and southern Europe (except in the matter of infant mortality), cannot be explained by housing, livelihood, or sanitation and raises still unanswered questions. Little wonder a leading Irish medical man in New York city correctly noted in 1918: "The Irish in America have by far the poorest resistance to diseases in general than [sic] all the immigrants from Europe," concluding America was a graveyard by contrast with home. Indeed, Irish life expectancy had for half a century been higher in Ireland's countryside than in America's cities (for men, but less so for women). Plainly, if mere economics do not explain the settlement patterns of the Irish in America, likewise the traditional measure, that holds life expectancy to be the arbiter and mirror of living standards, cannot explain (as the same doctor conceded) why nothing could hold the young from America.[62]

The key to their movement was the density of both life and prospects in the American city, which they learned before most native Americans. The United States was predominantly rural even in 1914, with its growing trend toward urbanization largely populated from Irish and other European countries; not dissimilar portions of the Irish at home lived in towns until that time (Table 1). And the earlier disproportionate urbanization of the Irish in the United States, together with continuing migration from Ireland, meant that the head start of the Irish element in the make-up of urban America was not lost throughout the nineteenth century. Indeed, by 1900 the offspring of Irish-born parents added between 100 percent and 200 percent to the Irish-born populations of most American cities. Total Irish elements in many of them (especially in the northeast) were thus not dissimilar to those between 1850 and 1870, despite the coming of millions of "new immigrants" from continental Europe. This dynamism of the Irish—in terms of livelihood, family formation, reproduction, and continuing in-migration—meant that, whether larger or smaller, American cities remained magnets of familiarity to newcomers. In Ireland, while towns represented impressive proportions of town-dwelling by the continental European standards of the time, they were after 1850 the residua of a people in decline, with the number of towns of between 2,500 and 100,000 inhabitants actually falling from 104 in 1841 to 87 in 1901. By contrast, America's towns and cities were the engines of a people in rapid growth. In 1840 there were but 129 places of those sizes (2,500 to 100,000), where in 1900 there were 2,654; in 1840, but three larger cities (of over 100,000), in 1900 another 61 (where Ireland still had but two large ones: Dublin and Belfast, the latter having surpassed Cork). The old commonplace that the cities of the Irish were in America acquires new meaning. In the case of County Cork, preeminent source of emigrants, it was indeed as though the very habit of urbanism itself underwent Atlantic migration.[63]

TABLE 1
Percentage of Population in Cities over 2,500

	1840/41	1870/71	1900/01	1920/26
Ireland	13	21	32	35
U.S.A.	10.7	25	40	51

Data computed from Vaughan and Fitzpatrick, *Irish Historical Statistics*, pp. 28–48;
U.S. Historical Statistics to 1970, ser. A 57–72.

Frequent participation in Ireland in town rituals and exchanges, at irregular fairs and more regular markets, habituated country folk to urban patterns (in Ireland fairs and markets were frequently in inverse proportion to formal urbanization, so that even those from the Atlantic west and outer Ulster thereby compensated for lack of formal experience of towns). Thus a people used to some urban living and excitement made the American city partly in their own image in its formative era, and then held on to it by demography, migration, and politics until the first world war. Moreover, the style and type of city in these years suited their jumbled, face-to-face custom of market and town relations. This crowded city—in which businesses, tenements, workshops, and small factories, stalls, shops, and carts all crowded brick-lined streets, in common neighborhoods—only later began to alter its character by segregating its districts both functionally and socially. One of these old, mixed, part-Irish streets (Polk Street, in San Francisco) has been remembered as "still little changed . . . still lit with gas, still bustling with a big-city-neighbourhood community life—modest, shoddy, and now so out of date."[64]

Livelihood was neither life nor community, but was indispensable to both. The Irish then, and their historians since, are divided as to whether the American city offered more, or less, than the Irish countryside in decline. D. W. Cahill, linguist, scientist, and priest, who came to America in 1859, conceded the new country's "exceptional poverty, its local distresses, its grinding destitutions" but held on balance that steady employment, high wages, and the chance of savings all made for the estimable "position, condition, and social life of the labouring classes in America." At home, Irish laborers rarely acquired farms or shops, or escaped the condition "of the half-starved slave of daily trade," so that the young and unmarried Irish were better off coming to the States. Others agreed, though Thomas Mooney saw that laboring was for those with no other skill, and to be abandoned quickly, except that the early marriage of new immigrants kept them "in the nasty labour which is alone open to friendless strangers" until they could put their daughters in service to improve their position. But Michael Kennedy, an immigrant for ten years, replied to Cahill from Troy (a heavily Irish iron and textiles town) that the Irish were "the hardest worked, the worst paid, the most abused, the oftenest insulted, and the least respected (by Americans) of any other [*sic*] people in this country."[65]

Kerby Miller gives the modern version of this:

Nearly all studies of the Irish in mid-century North America exhibit a deadening and depressing sameness. Irish emigrants were disproportionately concentrated in the lowest-paid, least-skilled, and most dangerous and insecure employment, with the highest rates of transience, residential density and segregation, inadequate housing and sanitation, commitals to prisons and charity institutions, and excess mortality. Upward occupational mobility was unusually slight.[66]

Such deadening sameness, punctuated only by misfortune and unemployment, would not have continued to draw millions from Ireland after 1855. True, the great body of male immigrants were increasingly drawn from among laborers at home (if one includes small farmers' sons calling themselves such);[67] and many would initially serve as general laborers after emigration. Had previous experience made many think favorably of laboring? Did American experience of it give grounds for hope? In Ireland seasonal agricultural labor, paying as little as 4d. daily in Munster in 1845, or temporary public works labor during the famine, could be much improved if one got a job among the 30,000–40,000 railroad laborers of the country's brief railroad boom of 1847; a remarkable 18d. daily was normal, and status was commensurate, quite unlike that of contemporary "railway navvies" in Britain. In America, laboring proved for some a lottery and for others a life sentence, sometimes mitigated by some job security and by family earnings. Comparison of the laboring communities from 1850 shows that they did not engross the majority of Irish working people anywhere; that the numbers and proportions so engaged differed widely; that there were great varieties of working condition among laborers; that their living conditions and housing also differed greatly; and that their chance to alter their condition, while low and uncertain, was not foreclosed.[68] Moreover, in the 1850s higher proportions of the Irish workforce were laborers in western, southern, and midwestern towns than in the east coast cities, though oddly laborers' wages were then higher in the east. Roughly between one-fifth and two-fifths of male immigrants were laborers in eastern cities between 1850 and 1870; inland and westward, up to one-half of them were (although their numbers were much smaller).[69] The sheer visibility of gangs of Irish laborers in construction, railroad-making, freightage, iron-making, and much else probably deflected attention from the majority of the Irish in blue-collar jobs. In 1855 New York city had 19,000 Irish laborers and porters in a city workforce of over 200,000 (of whom 85,000 were Irish-born). In 1850 Philadelphia had 8,000 in a male workforce of 100,000 (of whom 27,000 were Irish-born), and Boston had 7,000 in a workforce of 44,000 (of whom 15,000 were Irish-born). To the west, Buffalo had 600 laborers among 2,700 Irish heads-of-family.[70]

Such numbers should surely alter stereotypes. Extraordinary differences of condition separated $2.75-a-day rail-layers from 80c.-a-day laborers; or the well paid in San Francisco in the 1850s from those scrabbling for subsistence in Hartford or Providence during construction downturns in 1857 or 1877; or both from the migratory laborers who traveled seasonally to the American south in winter and worked in northern camps in summer; above all, great differences separated those in semipermanent employment from those fleeing from job to job. Once turned family men, Irish laborers sometimes accumulated property (houses and furniture) faster than other immigrants, and much faster than their analogues among native Americans. Boarding houses, trackside shanties, and casual work were, at best, traded for security of place and task.[71] If among native Americans laboring was increasingly linked to low-living social marginals and outcasts, the Irish saw it otherwise—as a youthful

TABLE 2
Laborers' Daily Wages, Ireland and the United States, 1850–70 (U.S. cents)

Year	Location	Occupation	Daily Wage (U.S. cents)
1850	Ireland	Farm, without board	12.5 <
		Dublin, builder's laborers	32–52
1850	U.S.A.	North Atlantic and Midwest: farm, with board	46
		General labor, national average	87
		N.Y. City, Erie Canal, Michigan: general labor	88 < 91
1870	Ireland	Farm labor, with board	17 < 61
		Farm labor, without board	24 < 97
		Urban and construction labor	48 < 62
1870	U.S.A.	North Atlantic and Midwest: farm, with board	95 < 145
		North Atlantic and Midwest: farm, without board	136 < 196
		North Atlantic and Midwest: general labor	106 < 168
		PA, NY, and MA: railroads, iron mills	140 < 156

SOURCES: Fergus D'Arcy, "Wages of labourers in the Dublin building industry," *Saothar*, 14 (1989), pp. 23, 24, 26; Lebergott, *Manpower . . . since 1800*, p. 299, table A-25, p. 541; U.S. Bureau of Statistics [Edward Young], *Labor in Europe and America* (Philadelphia, 1875), pp. 359–61, 739, 741, 743, 750, 758–9, 765, 785–6; Burchell, *San Francisco Irish*, table 13, p. 67; *Historical Statistics of the United States . . . to 1970*, pp. 163–5. For comparison with artisan differentials, see Table 3.

probation for more varied work or a more stable situation. Thomas Mooney in 1850 pointed out that common labor fetched 80c. or 3s. 4d. daily (four times the then Irish rate); that provisions were only a third of their Irish cost, although clothing, house rent, and fuel were closer to costs at home, and there was "a certainty of employment and the facility of acquiring houses and lands, and education for your children, a hundred to one greater" than in Ireland. Twenty-five years later, Mgr. Buckley reluctantly reached the same conclusions, a view then carefully supported by the touring representative of British and Irish agricultural labor, Peter O'Leary, in 1877.[72] While cruel exploitation was real enough, much of the laborers' hyperbole and aggression as to exploitation, disease, casual dismissal, and charges against their wages had to do with the failure of expected savings and of improving chances; but laboring in America still offered a real hope of improvement, denied at home. Indeed, wage data suggest this was more so for immigrant laborers than for artisans (Table 2). Yet they too suffered the not-unusual tendency of the Irishman eventually to reverse the normal pattern of self-betterment, and to lose both better-paid employment and better housing as age weakened his resistance to the effects of a lifetime's overwork.

Most Irish immigrants did not work as laborers.[73] In 1852, the New York *Irish American* ventured that "one-half (at least) of the mechanics" of the city were Irish.[74] The editor was somewhat exaggerating but was close enough for his pride to be pardonable. In 1855 the city had around 27,000 Irish-born skilled and semiskilled artisans, roughly 42 percent of all city workers in such categories, and around 51 percent of their own male workforce. Joined to a lesser middle-class and white-collar group of around 7,500 (from grocers, publicans, and hoteliers to officials, clerks, and policemen),[75] these artisans (and their providers of food, beer, and order) constituted the backbone of New York Irish society: modest, industrious, self-conscious, perhaps patriarchal, family men already or by intention. As yet, however, the real bourgeoisie of propertied merchants, lawyers, and manufacturers, if growing, was small and distant from their fellows. The pressure on them was to try to dissociate from their fellow countrymen, as Buckley recognized by 1871. For to non-Irish members of higher

TABLE 3
Daily Craft Wages in Ireland and America, 1850 and 1870 (U.S. $)

Year	Location	Carpenters	Masons	Bricklayers	Printers	Machinists	Tailors
1850	Ireland	1.20	1.04	1.20	1.25 <	< 1.08	.60 <
1850	U.S.A	1.50	1.50		1.40	1.30 <	1.60
1870/73	Ireland	1.32	1.32	1.32	1.75 <	1.80	1.22
1870	U.S.A.	2.88	3.00	3.16	3.30	2.67 <	2.48
1860	U.S.A.	1.52	1.78		1.64	1.64	

SOURCES: Fergus D'Arcy, "Wages of skilled workers in the Dublin building industry, 1667–1918" *Saothar,* 15 (1990), pp. 25–31; Maura Cronin, "Work and workers . . . 1800–1900" in O'Flanagan and Buttimer, *Cork,* pp. 730–31; Ernst, *Immigrant Life,* pp. 77–78; Wilentz, *Chants Democratic,* pp. 404, 405; Laurie and others, "Immigrants and Industry" in Hershberg (ed.), *Philadelphia,* pp. 104–5; Burchell, *Irish in San Francisco,* p. 67; Young, *Labor in Europe and America,* pp. 360–61, 745–8, 761–2, 795; *Historical Statistics of the United States to 1970,* pp. 163, 165. I have chosen maximum rates available in eastern U.S. cities, as in Ireland, but as a corrective the c. 1860 figures give Lebergott's calculations of real wages for the period from 1860 (effectively to 1880); apart from civil war and postwar fluctuations, he held these years to be ones of no real rise (*Manpower . . . since 1800,* pp. 154, 298–301).

society, distinctions between Irish laborers, artisans, and indeed the Irish generally did not matter: they were all "poor, ignorant, helpless, and degraded."

By Irish standards, nevertheless, money was to be made. How much, relative to living costs, was problematic. Irish craftsmen seemed to arrive with inflated expectations (Table 3). Their own sources spoke most commonly of higher wage levels and were less forthcoming on living costs.[76] Where they could, Irish artisans in New York dominated higher-paying skills, especially in construction, on its masonry, bricklaying, and stonecutting sides. It was their good fortune that New York was now (belatedly) following Philadelphia and Baltimore away from wooden building. The Irish were also the leading suppliers of the city's blacksmiths, plumbers, coopers, glassworkers, and brass and coppersmiths, as of its dressmakers.[77] They were not ousted from preeminence in these in half a century, fastening their hold as unions grew.[78] They were replaced as the chief source of tailors by Germans by 1855. Men not worried about mere survival sought security and sufficiency through craft routes familiar at home and through job-networking and protection. Income was much improved, not so much due to higher wage rates (of themselves almost canceled by higher living costs) but rather because craft work was in chronic short supply in Irish towns and usually abundant in New York.[79]

In cities other than New York half the younger Irish were artisans, construction and transport workers, and machine operatives, though smaller proportions of middle-aged men were such. By contrast, few young arrivals had white-collar positions, but over 10 percent of the immigrants over thirty years old had. Including New York City, Irish male household heads enjoyed a firmer economic footing and thus some more social information and leadership than one expects: overall, from one-third to three-fifths of Irish-born males were skilled or white-collar employees in five leading cities at mid-century.[80] Such gains were not sustained. The well-known simplification in the occupational profile of later Irish arrivals was not the only reason. The years from 1850 to 1880 were ones in which the convergence of further mechanization and workplace organization with mass immigration meant there was no effective gain in real wages, with immigrants in the 1850s constituting 91 percent of the labor force increase. Almost half these were Irish,[81] a heavy inflow that may explain why subsequently the proportions of Irish males in manufacturing trades fell significantly between 1850 and 1880, as in Philadelphia.[82]

The speed with which the refugees from famine sought to establish homes and families is remarkable, as is their dependence on the models of their immediate pre-famine predecessors. Such patterns have been best studied in communities away from the eastern seaboard, but migration inland was not necessary to begin them. In large coastal cities, the flight from tenements required the coming of streetcars, street railways, and large-scale Irish-controlled savings and loan societies to begin the process; in inland cities, cheap frame houses were available just off downtown itself from the start. Already from the 1850s to the 1870s the fringes of eastern cities saw similar developments, such as to midtown Manhattan, to the Flatbush area of Brooklyn, to Roxbury and Charlestown in Boston, and to outer Kensington, outer Moyamensing, and West Philadelphia in the latter city.[83] By 1855 Buffalo at the western end of New York's Erie Canal was funneling the grain of the midwest eastward and outranked Odessa as the world's leading grain port. A wave of largely married Irish worked their way slowly up the Hudson River and along the Erie in 1849–53 to offload the grain from lake boats and into canal barges. Not an Irishman survived there from the canal-building days of the 1820s.

Quickly the Irish entrenched themselves in Buffalo. Living there an average seven years, they were one-fifth of the city's 15,400 households. They clustered largely along the canal itself, four-fifths of them with an immediate Irish neighbor. They left the main downtown wards to the city's German Catholics, the largest group there. The youngest Irish, in their twenties, were least likely to be laborers: the consequence both of spreading literacy and the use of English in Ireland or (if brought over as children) of American upbringing; the older, often pre-famine immigrants, were more likely to be labourers. A quarter of working household heads had skilled or semiskilled jobs, proportions varying only slightly by length of residence. By the time they were aged thirty-five to fifty, most immigrants had established family homes, usually by renting, but commonly acquiring a cheap wooden house if the male could keep a semi-skilled or skilled job in the town more than seven years. This was more usual than job improvement. To sustain this, the Irish in Buffalo had a "niche" based on a system whereby each ethnic group "either dominated or was severely underrepresented in an occupation," a system unaffected by length of residence, and in place by 1855. Similar patterns characterized other western cities, if some had a larger Irish middle class.[84]

Home life made it all not just tolerable, but acceptable: "the Irish in general chose family life if they could."[85] The Irish at home responded to the pre-famine and post-famine livelihood crises by increasingly delaying, then even avoiding, family formation. Thus the young chose late marriage, emigration, or celibacy to protect a single stem-family succession, linked to a viable farm or small shop or craft. Abundant if straitened livelihoods in America allowed general family formation. As in the far west of Ireland, the commitment to young and fertile marriage persisted in the diaspora to the end of the nineteenth century (until migrants from a sadder and more calculating Ireland began to arrive from about 1890). All this gave a very different tone to Irish life in the United States as against Ireland between 1845 and 1921, and helps to explain the

compelling attraction of America to the young.[86] The course of life of most Irish immigrants was built toward and around marriage and child-bearing, not away from it
as increasingly was the case at home. This began as the famine receded. In Buffalo by
1855 as many as 85 percent of women would expect to marry, given established patterns (and even more of the men who stayed around or returned). Nine out of ten
married Irish-born spouses; in other cities, the pattern was almost the same. Effective
fertility rates were twice those of native New England–born women (as they were also
for the German Catholic majority there). But Irish families in Buffalo in 1850 were no
larger than native, averaging 2.1 children (as in San Francisco), suggesting even then
very high infant mortality as well as younger, incomplete families.

There was a general adaption of pre-famine Irish rural patterns to American circumstances: general, early, and fertile marriage, the family as an economic unit, the
desire to keep the young at home until they were twenty where possible, coupled with
the readiness to send them off early if necessary, and finally the search for money support and perhaps even a licit fertility control in the migratory work habits of established poorer fathers. Even the adjustments made to cut the growth rate were carried
to America: some delay on marriage age, and a celibacy rate of between 10 and 15
percent, especially among laborers, who had fewer children than skilled or white-
collar workers.[87] On the other hand, losses to infant mortality were perhaps greater
than those of rural Ireland before the famine (which were high); this must have given
poignancy to American experience, and sharpened the drive to better one's living
standards. By 1875–80 these losses seem indeed to have been partly reduced.

All this suggests the Irish after 1845 were hardly "pioneers of the ghetto" in its modern sense of communities of the chronically unemployed, the familially broken, and
the socially disorganized. Given the sixty-hour, six-day weeks then so common, the
Irish were in a sense overemployed, while often appallingly housed. Thus arose the
problems of their own Americanizing children, many of whom were in turn orphaned or "half-orphaned" (as was then said) by the high adult death rates. A great
deal of their response to their poverty, overwork, and threatened disorganization was
rooted in the harsh but important adaptions of rural Ireland, whose lessons were all
intensified by the great famine, and were a preparation for the relative indifference of
native American property-owners and employers throughout most of this period.[88]

The social conservatism of Catholic bishops in America from 1845 to 1880 partly
reflected their reading of the hopelessness of foreign and religious minorities' attempting to change the country's social order, and mirrored the greater conservatism
of the dominant Protestant churches. Yet these bishops were ready to see Irish immigrants and religious adapt to local conditions the patterns both of self-help and of
reliance on political intervention, learned first at home. Only where the "trade unionism" of the poor was secretive, oath-bound, illegal, and disposed to violence did bishops and middle-class Irish opinion (as in Ireland) condemn it, although generally the
church was quicker to distinguish between the necessity of such things and their less
acceptable expressions in alien urban America than it was in Ireland. As in Ireland,
one gets the impression of the various fragments, "the scattered debris" indeed of a
people, groping their way to survival, then to mutuality, amid their own "churning
motion" in the new cities.[89] The surprise is how much was achieved, and even at-

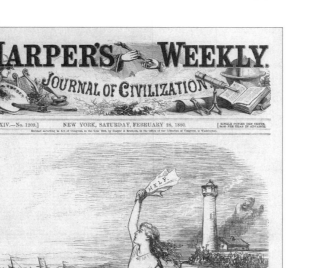

Irish-American relief was critical to staving off deaths from malnutrition when Ireland was revisited by famine in 1879–1880. In this unusually sympathetic depiction by Thomas Nast for a February 1880 cover of *Harper's Weekly,* Hibernia signals to American ships bringing supplies for her starving people. As a result of bleak economic conditions during the 1880s, emigration to America rose to its highest rates since the 1850s. (Library of Congress, Prints and Photographs Division, LC-USZ62-103220)

tempted, even before 1865, and how much more thereafter. Both ingenuity and cooperation made real contributions to alleviating the community's social problems.[90]

Irish experience of course had negative features. Neither in Ireland nor in the United States did it encourage dependence on government. As the organ of the Boston Irish put it in 1852, "It is a crime in Massachusetts to be poor. People are sentenced to our public institutions because they are destitute."[91] This drove the Irish into close-meshed reliance on their networks, on the Catholic church and its own institutions, but especially on their own families. Overworked and thus overburdened, such families bore much; and there was less margin for that helping of others that had carried so many in Ireland through the shortfall season each year when crops had been good. However, apart from meeting the noncompeting needs of others' pressing wants and of hospitality and work-sharing among friends, often the Irish "lower classes are unduly harsh and unfeeling towards each other in pecuniary matters" (as Daniel O'Connell admitted in 1825), and had been even more demonstrably so in matters of land.[92] This too carried over to hamper their urban cooperation, if also to prepare them for the harsh winds of Yankee individualism, short-term labor contracts, and the primacy of debt obligation. Their lately functioning "family economy" had been as close to monetary imperatives as to any supposed "moral economy of the poor"; for the Irish, sentiment and survival had been inextricable in families, and it proved true also in the United States throughout the nineteenth century.

In 1845 there were 1.1 million Catholics in the United States. By 1860 this had tripled to 3.1 million; in 1880 there were 6.3 million. Fewer than 4 percent of Americans in 1840, they were more than 12 percent by 1880. Irish immigration accounted for roughly half the increase between 1845 and 1860; the surviving offspring of Irish parents for maybe one-third of the balance. The increase was made more visible as it mirrored the northeastern distribution of the immigrants, and coincided with the growth of cities thrust to preeminence by the north's victory in the civil war and continuing industrialization. The early diocesan structure had reflected the dual southern and northern bases of independent America, with Baltimore as the effective leading see. But the populous new dioceses set up after 1840 reflected first the coming of the Irish and then that of the Germans. In about half of them the bishops were Irish-American or Irish for the rest of the century, often beyond that. Contrary to ethnic protest and rivalry after 1880, the Irish-born were consistently underrepresented at hierarchic levels, insofar as their numbers empowered church expansion, and indeed even the American-born Irish were never overrepresented before the 1890–1940 period. Apart from New York, created an arch-Episcopal see in 1850 (and anticipated or balanced by the creation of those of Oregon City, St. Louis, New Orleans, and Cincinnati), the other leading American cities and Irish-American centers, Philadelphia, Boston, and Chicago, waited a further quarter-century to achieve similar rank, along with such minor cities at that time as Santa Fe and Milwaukee. The Vatican was plainly moved neither by Irish demography nor by Irish politicking, but rather by an urge toward a balanced vision of America's prospects analogous to that of Henry Clay and Daniel Webster in secular matters, a vision it shared with most leading U.S. prelates, Irish or not.[93]

The Irish were usually portrayed as the core of the history of nineteenth-century American Catholicism by scholars working from the 1880s to the early 1960s. To be sure, they made a judicious distinction between U.S.-born, or long Americanized, bishops and clergy, and those more recently come from Ireland or enfolded by their fellow countrymen in the United States. From the scholarship of John Gilmary Shea to that of the students of Mgr. Peter Guilday and R. J. Purcell, the Americanized Irish were given credit for the skill with which they adapted the Irish Catholic inheritance to distinct American civic and religious circumstances—and the more narrowly Irish leadership was faulted for provoking reaction and hostility. Yet in both views the Irish contribution was seen as primary. Since the 1950s the role has been subject to an increasing change of emphasis, as the church has sought more distinctively American antecedents, and as ethnically diverse contemporary Catholics began to emphasize their forerunners' presence in the mosaic of the previous century. Then, too, a liberal (at times even modernist) establishment in the universities founded by the church has sought to distance itself from the Irish and their traditions: supposedly illiberal, authoritarian, provincial, and Roman among clergy, and tribal, ill-informed, unintellectual, familial, pragmatic, and devotionalist among ordinary emigrants. The counterview, once common, is still encountered among some clergy of Roman, German, or Polish training or background in the United States: that Irish Catholics were lax, undisciplined, and too secular, too uncritical of the dangers posed by America to the faith, and corrupt in their lay political leaderships. Indications that the mid-century Irish were less rigorously Catholic than their successors have been exaggerated in these contexts, although modern scholarship has reversed the more negative findings on these matters.[94] As early as 1855 the *New York Times,* then four years old and acceptable to the better-off Irish, could yet brand attempts to update, deepen, and discipline Catholic practice in Ireland as a plot to make its clergy "more Roman and less Irish" and ensure "Catholic Ireland would become a mere province or spiritual appendage of the Vatican."[95] Such artificial antitheses have dogged the understanding of nineteenth-century Irish Catholicism in America, as at home, among both its friends and its critics.

At least 2 million Irish-born and German-born Catholics in 1870 made up 45 percent of the country's 4.5 million Catholics, as they did 35 percent of its 5.6 million foreign-born overall. There were probably more. With their children, and adult offspring, they dominated the church. Even allowing that one-fifth of the Irish-born were not affiliated to parishes, whether as Protestants or by reason of choice or of unattached youth, the Irish-born component was at least twice that of the German (which had in fact considerably higher rates of non-affiliation).[96] Yet more interesting is the evidence of very different patterns of church identification, so often compounded by historians. Contrast of seating availability with Irish- and German-born adherents in 1870 for leading industrial counties suggests that the Irish provided best for themselves where the Catholic community was overwhelmingly their own (as in Scranton or Albany) and when additionally stimulated by a vigorous native Protestantism (as in New England cities). They were less fully active in the great cosmopolitan cities, where secularity, and a variety of rival cultures, met the disorientation and youthfulness of newcomers: notably in New York City and its satellites or Philadelphia; but also in poorer new industrial ones, especially where, as in Pittsburgh, many of them came from less well catechized roots. Where German or "old American" Catholics were preponderant, Irish minorities seem to have been sometimes encouraged (especially if more settled) but also sometimes put off. Oddly, there are no direct correlations between these patterns and the relative preponderance (or not) of an Irish-American clergy.[97] In short, the old story of majority Irish religiosity has been so oft told that such diversities have gone unexamined, as of course has the Protestantism of a signal minority, both of mid-century migrants and of converts from Catholicism, who were few.[98]

Irish visitors appreciated even by the 1860s the pressures toward a certain secularization operating in the United States; Irish churchmen were surprised at the levels of conviction and piety found equally in New York and County Cork. Plainly, while the ordinary (if not the more heroic) activities of churchmen were self-explanatory, the general commitment of the immigrants requires more perceptive study. As Oscar Handlin noted, the famine migrants, turned harassed operatives and servants, found vital explanation and solace in Christian mysteries. But this went further. Since a minority found in America the promise (if not always the reality) of a more this-wordly individualism, of an escape from the material deprivation, social obligations, and guilty anxieties of rural Irish society—and most emigrants were youthful in years and in their reading of such things—what drew the majority back to rebuilding their childhood convictions afresh, unsurrounded by censorious elders and the associations of the past? Was it the transplanting of the most carriageable and adaptable institution of their culture, as a refuge to the uprooted, a source of familiarity, an enclave of mutual trust, a point of reference drawing all the vague yearnings for the lost point of origin? Was it a reaction to the force of native prejudice, driving the Irish in on themselves, causing them to assert their worth in an incontestable framework, that of their souls' worth against the obloquy of Americans?

Yet American experiences nurtured shocks of recognition that gave life to the stale catechetical clichés of Irish childhoods. Neither Evangelicals, nor Know-Nothings, nor many Republicans believed that, given free schooling, free access to scripture, and the experience of a free society, the Irish would grow away from priestly tutelage. America gave the Irish access to an extraordinarily diverse book of life, uncoded by the rigid socio-religious polarities of home. One must assume that the lessons they learned were neither preconditioned nor those always intended by their hosts. Yet why find such wisdom almost exclusively in its Catholic reinforcement? It became shared and socialized in the dense life of the Irish parish, as Jay Dolan convincingly demonstrated, even as it was given deeper import by familiar liturgy and sacrament.[99] Yet it would be false to see it as solely a collective expression of the Irish against the world. Work needs to be done on the interactive nature of Irish-American Catholicism from the start. It is striking that the Irish were deeply impressed by the Catholicism of those not of their own nationality, especially when it was so often placed in their service. Examples include, in New York, the Cuban Felix Varela, the Haitian Pierre Toussaint, the Frenchman Alphonse Thébaud; in Philadelphia, the Czech bishop John Neumann; in Boston and in Ohio, the Frenchmen Jean de Cheverus and Jean Baptiste Lamy; even in remote Natchez, Bishops John Chanche and James Van de Velde, who both died serving the Irish; and everywhere numerous German clerics. It meant more in an age when such example was guaranteed by word of mouth in small "walking cities." Indeed, most of the orders of nuns either founded in, or transplanted to, America in these years, and drawing so many thousands of young Irish women, had continental European (or American) founders. The impact of native American Catholics and converts was equally strong and reinforcing: only a handful (such as Orestes Brownson and Isaac Hecker) seem to have disliked the Irish, and even their shared animus disguised lifelong contact with Irish acquaintances, publishers, penitents, associates, and confessors. While indeed the Irish seem to have preferred the parish to be mostly their own, as at home, the church as a whole came to them in a new form: as a witness of truth transcending their own pronounced provincialisms, reassuring them that their final convictions were no local idiom but a language of universal import, equal to the bewildering and exciting enormity of the American world. Before 1880, the Irish were as much debtors as creditors of the church in America, and in this era they seem to have accepted rather than resented this.

A continuous and unpredictable nightmare may destroy faith; but, among the Irish, successive traumas were set off against a continuing and youthful search for a promising normality. Their convictions and community carried them toward goals that many attained, with the promise of eternal redress where the balance often seemed set to subvert their modest efforts. "I feel a sort of anticipated consolation in reflecting that the religion which gave us comfort in our early days . . . enabled us to endure the stroke of affliction and endeared us to each other," wrote one. For the American-born Irish, reflection on their parents' very limitations could shape their key role as mediators between generations in the lay church. As John Gilmary Shea recalled of his father, an anti-Episcopal activist: "In my case we were negative poles and almost spontaneously I took the opposite. As soon as I saw those who went to their duties cling to the bishop it gave him a halo in my boyish fancy." For many, no such reaction to large dissent, but parental neglect, drunkenness, or disorder may have had a similar engrafting effect. And then there was the long-standing effect of native American good example, Protestant and Catholic: "A greater latitude and indifference on the score of religion is allowed to prevail amongst emigrants lately arrived . . . than amongst the Americans themselves. It is admitted by many Irish clergymen . . . that they [are] before our country people in their religious practice, particularly the catholics."[100] Yet these experiences were neither confining nor prescriptive. On the contrary, by contrast with German Catholicism, Irish immigrants enjoyed a comprehensive latitude in their secular pursuits: their clubs, benefit societies, saloons, militia companies, trade union activities, political alignments, and even the schooling of most of their children before the 1880s, had no formal church connection (though the informal press of numbers in Irish localities gave them a Catholic tone). Church societies drew only minorities of the devout. The deinstitutionalization of Catholicism, by contrast with that of Germany, was in Ireland the consequence of a long history of proscription and marginalization. Time would show it was not an ideal model for industrial America, and attempts to change it were well under way by the 1870s. But such informality gave the young incoming Irish a space in which to work out their own relations to America, while attaching themselves to a parish for essential religious continuity.

NOTES

1. Kerby Miller, *Emigrants and Exiles* (Oxford and New York, 1985), p. 291.

2. Nativism: an American political movement emphasizing "nationality, Protestant piety, temperance, craft-exclusiveness, and anti-Irishism" [See David Doyle, "The Irish in North America, 1776–1845," chapter 4 in this volume.]

3. David Power Conyngham, *The Irish Brigade and Its Campaigns,* ed. L. F. Kohl (New York, 1994); W. J. K. Beaudot and L. J. Herdegen (eds.), *An Irishman in the Iron Brigade: The Civil War Memoirs of James F. Sullivan* (New York, 1994); L. F. Kohl and M. C. Richard (eds.), *Irish Green and Union Blue: The Civil War Letters of Peter Welsh* (New York, 1993).

4. David Fitzpatrick, *Ireland under the Union, II, 1870–1921,* vol. 6 of *A New History of Ireland,* ed. W. E. Vaughan (Oxford: Claredon Press, 1996), 641, table 4.

5. This is true even of works giving attention to pre-famine elements: Carl Wittke, *The Irish in America* (Baton Rouge, LA, 1956), p. 23 and *passim;* Miller, *Emigrants and Exiles,* pp. 293–344, 492–555; Nicholas Nolan, "The Irish Emigration: a Study in Demography" (Ph.D. diss., National University Ireland [University College Dublin], 1935), pp. 135, 284–96; Oliver MacDonagh, "The Irish Famine Emigration to the United States," *Perspectives in American History* 10 (1976), pp. 430–46; Donald H. Akenson, *Being Had: Historians, Evidence, and the Irish in North America* (Port Credit, Ont., 1985), pp. 46–9.

6. David N. Doyle, "Afterward" in David N. Doyle and Owen Dudley Edwards, *America and Ireland, 1776–1976* (Westport, CT, and London, 1980), pp. 324–5; Ronald A. Wells, "Aspects of Northern Ireland Migration to America: Definitions and Directions," *Ethnic Forum* 4, no. 1 (1984), pp. 49–63; Christopher McGimpsey, "Internal Ethnic Friction: Orange and Green in Nineteenth-Century New York, 1868–1872," *Immigrants and Minorities,* 1 (1982), pp. 39–59; Akenson, *Being Had,* pp. 60–74; Miller, *Emigrants and Exiles,* pp. 348, 350, 352–3, 371, 378, 380.

7. Akenson, *Being Had,* pp. 77–102, quantifies more generally known facts; see Robert O'Driscoll and Lorna Reynolds, *Untold Story: The Irish in Canada* (2 vols, Toronto, 1988), vol. 1, pp. 30, 171–98, 203–11, 215–29; 253–8, 263–94, 309–35. Apart from urban factory districts, only New Brunswick possibly owed the body of its Irish population and traditions to the years of the famine and after (ibid., pp. 231–2), but cf. Donald McKay, *Flight from Famine: The Coming of the Irish to Canada* (Toronto, 1990), pp. 150–63; despite his title, McKay also stresses the pre-famine theme, even for New Brunswick.

8. Quoted in Thomas N. Brown, "The United States of America, the Irish Clergyman, and the Irish Layman" in *A History of Irish Catholicism,* ed. Patrick J. Corish, vol. 6 (Dublin: Gill and MacMillan, 1970), pp. 71–2.

9. A. J. Thébaud, *The Irish Race in the Past and the Present* (New York, 1873), p. 465; the author, born in Nantes in 1807, had been rector of Fordham College and served Irish-Americans in three states and in Canada.

10. Cormac Ó Gráda, "A Note on Nineteenth-Century Irish Emigration Statistics," in *Population Studies* 29 (1975), table 1, p. 144.

11. J. A. Dunlevy and H. A. Gemery, "British-Irish Settlement Patterns in the U.S.: The Role of Family and Friends," *Scottish Journal of Political Economy* 24 (1977), pp. 257–63.

12. Miller, *Emigrants and Exiles,* pp. 299 ff.

13. The first real effort to raise this was by MacDonagh, in "Irish Famine Emigration," pp. 357–91, 418–30; while mapping the outflow, he still generalizes it and assumes that departures meant equally proportionate arrivals, as was implied earlier in his "Irish Overseas Emigration during the Famine" in R. Dudley Edwards and T. Desmond Williams (ed.), *The Great Famine* (Dublin, 1956), pp. 320–26, 376, 380–81.

14. Oscar Handlin, *Boston's Immigrants* (Cambridge, MA, 1941; rev. ed., 1959). Most monographs on the nineteenth-century urban Irish followed this thesis before c.1970, notably Stephan Thernstrom, *Poverty and Progress: Social Mobility in a Nineteenth-Century City* (Cambridge, MA, and Oxford, 1964). This too was a study of an 1850s Massachusetts community, which must be balanced nationally. See following text.

15. Miller, *Emigrants and Exiles,* pp. 296–9, 303–4, 315–19, 325–8; Kerby Miller, Bruce Boling,

and David Doyle, "Emigrants and Exiles: Irish Cultures and Irish Emigration to North America, 1790–1922," *Irish Historical Studies* 22, no. 86 (Sept. 1980), pp. 97–125.

16. MacDonagh, "Irish Famine Emigration," pp. 360–64, 434–40.

17. Thus MacDonagh: "Two conclusions. . . . The first is the importance of emigration in cutting the Gordian knot of overpopulation. . . . [The Famine exodus] may be looked upon as a population movement unnaturally postponed" ("Irish Overseas Emigration," pp. 328, 331); and Handlin: "Fecundity was the only contribution of the Irish toward a solution of the community's social problems" (*Boston's Immigrants,* p. 117).

18. Notable are Dennis Clark, *The Irish in Philadelphia* (Philadelphia, 1973); his *Hibernia America* (Westport, CT, 1986); and his "The Irish in the American Economy: The Industrial Period" in P. J. Drudy (ed.), *The Irish in America: Emigration, Assimilation, Impact* (Cambridge, 1985), pp. 234–42; as earlier Wittke, *Irish in America,* pp. 23–113, 193–240.

19. David Fitzpatrick, "Emigration, 1871–1921," *Ireland under the Union, II, 1870–1921,* vol. 6 of *A New History of Ireland,* ed. W. E. Vaughan (Oxford: Clarendon Press, 1989), pp. 610–12.

20. S. H. Cousens, "The Regional Variation in Emigration from Ireland between 1821 and 1841," *Transactions and Papers of the Institute of British Geographers,* 37 (Dec. 1965), fig. 4, p. 22; Cousens, "The Regional Pattern of Emigration During the Great Irish Famine, 1846–51," ibid. 28 (1960), fig. 1, p. 121; David Fitzpatrick, "Emigration, 1801–70," *Ireland under the Union, I, 1801–70,* vol. 5 of *A New History of Ireland,* ed. W. E. Vaughan (Oxford: Clarendon Press, 1989), pp. 620, map 14; Joel Mokyr, *Why Ireland Starved* (London, 1982), p. 267. Roscommon apart, the discrepancies between Cousens and Fitzpatrick are less on this than the latter claims (Fitzpatrick, "Emigration, 1801–70," p. 571), and the general pattern has been confirmed by Mokyr (unpublished data, reported by James S. Donnelly, Jr. in "Excess Mortality and Emigration," *Ireland under the Union, I, 1801–70,* pp. 354–5.

21. The largest numbers of newcomers seeking knowledge of "missing friends" and relatives in the *Boston Pilot,* 1831–50, were (in rank order) from Cork, Tipperary, Limerick, Mayo, and Galway; see Ruth-Ann Harris and Donald M. Jacobs (ed.), *The Search for Missing Friends: Irish Immigrant Advertisements Placed in the Boston Pilot* (Boston, 1989), map A, p. xxxvi.

22. Standard figures are Cork, 575,000; Antrim, 325,000; Mayo, 258,000; Galway, 252,000; Kerry, 226,000; Tipperary, 224,000 (see MacDonagh, "Irish Famine Emigration," pp. 419–20, added to Miller, *Emigrants and Exiles,* pp. 570–71). But it must be stressed that "cohort depletion," constabulary reports, and ships' manifests all suggest that Galway and Mayo figures were much higher again for the years 1851–71, with the other counties somewhat higher. The headlong rush of 1846–51 would indicate this should be even more true of these years (for which we lack all these controls). Fitzpatrick, "Emigration, 1801–70," p. 608, table 1; Cormac Ó Gráda, "Some Aspects of Nineteenth-Century Irish Emigration" in L. M. Cullen and T. C. Smout (ed.), *Comparative Aspects of Scottish and Irish Economic and Social History* (Edinburgh, 1977), pp. 68–71. The discrepancies are too great to be reconciled, but at the maximum suggest total Galway and Mayo outflow could be increased up to one-third, that from Cork and Kerry up to one-fifth. Such numbers are consistent with the internal American evidence.

23. Contrast the maps of totals K. M. Davies, "Emigration, 1851–1911," *Maps, Genealogies, Lists: A Companion to Irish History,* vol. 9 of *A New History of Ireland,* ed T. W. Moody (Oxford: Oxford University Press, 1984), p. 69, map 77, with those of rates Fitzpatrick, "Emigration, 1801–70," p. 620, map 14, and in Cousens, "Regional variation . . . between 1821 and 1841," pp. 19, 20, 22, and "Regional pattern . . . 1846–51," p. 121.

24. Cormac Ó Gráda, "Across the Briny Ocean: Some Thoughts on Pre-Famine Emigration to America" in T. M. Devine and David Dickson (ed.), *Ireland and Scotland, 1600–1850* (Edinburgh, 1983), table 7, p. 127; Victor A. Walsh, "Across the 'Big Wather,' the Irish-Catholic

Community of Mid–Nineteenth Century Pittsburgh," *Western Pennsylvania Historical Magazine,* 66 (1983), table 1, p. 4; Harris and Jacobs, *Search for Missing Friends,* table 3, p. xx; Ruth-Ann Harris, "'On the Whole I'd Rather be Lost in Philadelphia': a Profile of Irish Migrants in Philadelphia, 1831–1851" (unpublished paper, 1988); Marion R. Casey, "A Quantitative Analysis of New York City's Irish and Irish-American Middle-Class Community in the Middle of the Nineteenth Century" (unpublished seminar paper, New York University, 1988), figs. 1 and 3, table 3, pp. 15, 17, 29.

25. See P. Mac Doinleibhe, "Glimpses of the Famine in Fermanagh," *Clogher Record* 4 (1962), pp. 187–9; Brian Ó Mórdha (ed.), "The Great Famine in Monaghan: A Coroner's Account," *Clogher Record* 4 (1960–61), pp. 29–41, 175–86; Mullagh Historical Committee, *Portrait of a Parish: Mullagh, Co. Cavan* (Cavan, 1988), pp. 52–61; Peadar Livingstone, *The Fermanagh Story* (Enniskillen, 1969), pp. 196–203; Wallace Clark, *Rathlin: Its Story* (2nd ed., Limavady, 1988), pp. 139–40; Ambrose Macaulay, *Patrick Dorrian: Bishop of Down and Connor, 1865–85* (Dublin, 1987), pp. 59–72; James Grant, "The Famine in Ulster" (Ph.D. diss., Queens University Belfast, 1986).

26. This balances Fitzpatrick's assertion that "the catastrophe of the famine thus generated an immediate and lasting transformation in the regional patterns of outward migration" ("Emigration, 1801–70," *Ireland under the Union, I, 1801–70,* p. 571).

27. Evidence from Detroit (1853) and Pittsburgh (1850) confirms this, the more convincingly since the early sample dates cover more mixed pre-famine immigration, and since the one was on the border with the new Ulster settlements of Ontario, the other was the effective capital of largely Ulster-American west Pennsylvania (J. E. Vinyard, *The Irish on the Urban Frontier: Detroit, 1850–1880* [New York, 1976], pp. 98–9; Walsh, "'Big Wather,'" p. 2 and n. 7).

28. For Ulster, collate *Census of Ireland, 1851,* H.C. 1852–3, xcii, 36, 61, 99, 150, 185, 224, 251, 285, 326, with ibid., *General Report,* H.C. 1856, pp. xiv, xxxi, 390, 404, 434, 448, 464, 475, 488, 500, 514. For Leinster, collate *Census of Ireland 1851,* H.C. 1852–3, pp. xci, 117, 185, 226, with ibid., *General Report,* H.C. 1856, pp. xxxi, 82, 117, 134; and T. Jones Hughes, "East Leinster in the Mid-Nineteenth Century" in *Irish Geography,* 3, no. 5 (1958), pp. 235–6, 239–40.

29. Miller, *Emigrants and Exiles,* p. 579, table 9.

30. John T. Ridge, "The Hidden Gaeltacht in Old New York" in *New York Irish History,* 6 (1991–2), p. 15.

31. Cf. "Densité de la population rurale, 1845" in René Rémond, *Atlas historique de la France contemporaine, 1800–1965* (Paris, 1966), p. 36, with the regional population maps in T. W. Freeman, *Pre-Famine Ireland* (Manchester, 1957), pp. 168, 177, 184, 212, 220, 226; W. J. Smyth, in Patrick O'Flanagan and C. G. Buttimer, *Cork: History and Society* (Dublin, 1993), pp. 657, 682–96.

32. Patrick J. Corish, *The Catholic Community in the Seventeenth and Eighteenth Centuries* (Dublin, 1981), pp. 101–9; Kevin Whelan, "The Catholic Church in County Tipperary, 1700–1900" in William Nolan and Thomas McGrath (ed.), *Tipperary: History and Society* (Dublin, 1985), pp. 215, 230–54.

33. Nolan and McGrath, *Tipperary,* pp. 241, 255; end-maps in Angus MacIntyre, *The Liberator: Daniel O'Connell and the Irish Party, 1830–1847* (London, 1965); K. T. Hoppen, "Landlords, Society, and Electoral Politics . . ." in C. H. E. Philpin (ed.), *Nationalism and Popular Protest in Ireland* (Cambridge, 1987), pp. 287–90; see further the articles by M. J. Bric, M. R. Beames, and L. P. Curtis Jr, in the same volume, with a dissenting essay by Tom Garvin, which locates Ribbonism in the least formally politicized outer Ulster regions: the balance of agrarian outrage incidents does not support him.

34. Hoppen, "Landlords, Society, and Electoral Politics"; T. W. Freeman, *Pre-Famine Ireland*

(Manchester, 1957), pp. 235–50, 264–8; Patrick Hickey, "Famine, Mortality, and Emigration: a Profile of Six Parishes . . ." in O'Flanagan and Buttimer, *Cork,* pp. 873–917.

35. W. H. Crawford, "The Evolution of the Ulster Town, 1750–1850" in Peter Roebuck (ed.), *Plantation to Partition* (Belfast, 1981), pp. 140–56.

36. S. J. Connolly, "Catholicism in Ulster, 1800–1850" in Roebuck, *Plantation to Partition,* pp. 157–66; Oliver P. Rafferty, *Catholicism in Ulster, 1603–1983* (Dublin, 1994), pp. 98–111, 145–55; Macaulay, *Patrick Dorrian*; Edward McCarron, *Life in Donegal, 1850–1900* (Cork, 1981), pp. 15–22, 52, 87–90.

37. Thus throughout the period 1837–1900 such categories rose from 65 percent (1837) to 87 percent (1855) to 91 percent (1900) of all U.S. migrants (P. J. Blessing, table 22.3, in Drudy, *Irish in America,* p. 20), although laborers fell from 56 percent of Ireland's agricultural workers (1841) to 38 percent (1881) to 23 percent (1926), with sons and relatives taking over much of the work, Samuel Clark in P. J. Drudy, ed., *Ireland: Land, People and Politics* (Cambridge, 1982), table 2.1, p. 22, and Damian Hannan, ibid., table 7.1, p. 145).

38. This was then noted (as novel) in the annual report of the American Protestant Society, 1849: "Many of the children and youth who now arrive from Ireland can read" (quoted in Ridge, "Hidden Gaeltacht in Old New York," p. 17); see data in John Logan, "Sufficient to Their Needs: Literacy and Elementary Schooling in the Nineteenth Century" in Mary Daly and David Dickson, *The Origins of Popular Literacy in Ireland* (Dublin, 1990), fig. 1, p. 116.

39. MacDonagh, "Irish Famine Emigration," p. 430.

40. See the articles by Proinsias Mac Aonghusa, Breandán Ó Buachalla, Liam Ó Dochartaigh, Breandán Ó Conaire, and Tomás de Bhaldraithe in Stiofán Ó hAnnracháin, ed., *Go Meiriceá Siar: na Gaeil agus Meiriceá* (Dublin, 1979); Dennis Clark, *The Irish Relations* (Rutherford, NJ, 1982), p. 222; Ridge, "Hidden Gaeltacht in Old New York," pp. 13–17.

41. Michael Buckley, *Diary of a Tour in America in 1870 and 1871* (Dublin, 1889), pp. 52, 151. Cf. the comments of a visiting English hatter and of a leading Yankee intellectual convert to Catholicism, both often thought anti-Irish: "Irishmen or the sons of Irishmen are often more American than the natives" (J. D. Burn, *Three Years among the Working Classes in the United States* [London, 1865]); "The Irish people, the laity, are far less unAmerican than their clergy" (Orestes Brownson to Isaac Hecker, undated [1 June 1855], in J. F. Gower and R. M. Lelinert [eds.] *The Brownson–Hecker Correspondence* [Notre Dame, IN, 1979], p. 183).

42. Buckley, *Diary of a Tour,* p. 152 (Boston, 25 Sept. 1870).

43. This is the realistic master theme of the five books (*Irish in Philadelphia; Irish Relations; Hibernia America; Erin's Heirs;* and *The Irish in Pennsylvania*) and thirty papers of Dennis Clark.

44. Harris and Jacobs, *Search for Missing Friends,* table 6, p. xxiv; Patrick J. Blessing, *The Irish in America: A Guide to the Literature and the Manuscript Collections* (Washington, DC, 1992), pp. 290–91. I have followed Harris, not Blessing, Winsberg, or the U.S. Census Bureau, by including Delaware, Maryland, and Washington, DC, in this region, as it was for both Irish and Scots-Irish before them.

45. W. V. Shannon, *The American Irish* (rev. ed., New York, 1966), p. 27; Carl Wittke, *We Who Built America* ([1939], rev. ed., Cleveland, 1964), p. 145; Wittke, *Irish in America,* pp. 23–31; Akenson, *Being Had,* pp. 37–107; D. H. Akenson, *Small Differences: Irish Catholics and Irish Protestants, 1815–1922* (Kingston and Montreal, 1988), p. 107. Earlier versions by Akenson follow his own Canadian studies by refusing to distinguish Scots-Irish migrants, and other early-nineteenth-century Protestant Irish settlers, from the post-1845 exodus, so that one may more charitably regard his assertion "there is no positive evidence available . . . for the existence of the

fundamental 'fact' of the history of the Irish as an ethnic group in America—that they were a city people" (D. H. Akenson, "Data: What Is Known about the Irish in North America?" in Oliver MacDonagh and W. F. Mandle, eds., *Ireland and Irish-Australia* [London and Sydney, 1986], p. 10).

46. David N. Doyle, "The Irish as Urban Pioneers in the United States, 1850–1870s," *Journal of American Ethnic History*, 10 (1990), pp. 36–59.

47. David Ward, *Cities and Immigrants* (New York, 1971), pp. 59–81; R. K. Vedder and L. E. Gallaway, "The Geographical Distribution of British and Irish Emigrants to the United States after 1800," *Scottish Journal of Political Economy*, 19 (1972), pp. 19–35; Vedder and Gallaway with V. Shukla, "The Distribution of the Immigrant Population in the United States: An Economic Analysis," *Explorations in Economic History*, 2 (1974), pp. 213–26.

48. Of earlier scholars alert to this urban reality, one did realize the pattern was well begun before the famine: George Potter, *To the Golden Door: The Story of the Irish in Ireland and America* (Boston and Toronto, 1960), pp. 170–75, dealing with 1820–40.

49. What follows summarizes Doyle, "Irish as Urban Pioneers."

50. U.S. *Seventh Census* [De Bow] (1850), p. 399; *Eighth Census* [Kennedy] (1860), xxxi–xxxii; *Ninth Census* (1870), Vol. 1, pp. 386–91; *Eleventh Census* (1890), pt 1, cxl; *Twelfth Census* (1900), Vol. 1, pp. 430–43, 796–800, 874–7.

51. Lawrence Gelfand, "The Problem of the Eastward Movement in America, 1850–1930" in Ciaran Brady (ed.), *The American City* (Dublin, 1988), pp. 39–44.

52. Stanley Lebergott, *Manpower in American Economic Growth: The American Record since 1800* (New York, 1964), figures at pp. 79–82, 86.

53. *Valedictory of the Hon. Thos Selby . . .* (San Francisco, 1871), p. 14, quoted in R. A. Burchell, *The San Francisco Irish, 1848–1880* (Manchester, 1979), p. 71; U.S. Dept of the Treasury, Bureau of Statistics [Edward Young, compiler], *Labor in Europe and the United States* (Philadelphia, 1875), pp. 739–47, 751, 753, 758–9, 785–8, 796–9, 804, 806.

54. Vinyard, *Irish on the Urban Frontier*, pp. 333, 346.

55. Brownson to Isaac Hecker, 29 Sept. 1857 (Gower and Lelinert, *Brownson-Hecker Correspondence*, p. 201); the problems of declining priest–people ratios in Ireland until 1847, and of servicing the diaspora thereafter, partly account for this frame of mind. Edmund M. Hogan, *The Irish Missionary Movement . . . 1830–1980* (Dublin, 1990), pp. 13–24, 62–8.

56. "Though the native stock were in a numerical minority, they had most firmly set their imprint on the form of San Francisco, and settled . . . what the major lines of development would be" (Burchell, *San Francisco Irish*, p. 180). Classic studies by Richard Wade on the urban frontier, Bayrd Still on Milwaukee, Bessie L. Pierce on Chicago, and Melvin Holli on Detroit show the same of those cities with demographically "foreign stock" majorities.

57. Burchell, *San Francisco Irish*, pp. 54–5; Michael R. Haines and Claudia Goldin in Theodore Hershberg, ed., *Philadelphia: Work, Space, Family, and Group Experience in the Nineteenth Century. Essays toward an Interdisciplinary History of the City* (New York and Oxford, 1981), ch. 7, pp. 256–79, and ch. 8, pp. 280–96; and Robert Ernst, *Immigrant Life in New York City, 1825–1863* (Syracuse, 1994), pp. 65–9, 214–17, recalculated.

58. In 1851, Welcome Sayles noted that many of these children, "chained to the wheel by poor or exacting parents," had had their only schooling in Ireland. Peter J. Coleman, *The Transformation of Rhode Island, 1790–1860* (Providence, RI, 1963), pp. 234–5, 238–41.

59. See later in this chapter.

60. Clark, *Irish in Philadelphia*, pp. 48–9, 200 n. 49; D. B. Cole, *Immigrant City: Lawrence, Massachusetts, 1845–1921* (Chapel Hill, NC, 1963), p. 29; Handlin, *Boston's Immigrants*, pp. 114–17; Jay P. Dolan, *The Immigrant Church: New York's Irish and German Catholics, 1815–1865* (Bal-

timore, 1975), pp. 33–40; Ernst, *Immigrant Life in New York City,* pp. 50–54; Brian C. Mitchell, *The Paddy Camps: The Irish of Lowell, 1821–61* (Champaign, IL, 1988), pp. 106–8, and table 4, p. 158. These death rates are the more startling when one notes that the age pyramid of the Irish-born disproportionately excluded those (under 15 and over 55) most subject to mortality (Deirdre Mageean, "Nineteenth-Century Emigration" in Drudy, *Irish in America,* fig. 3.1, p. 52).

61. Earl F. Niehaus, *The Irish in New Orleans, 1800–1860* (Baton Rouge, LA, 1965; New York, 1976), pp. 31–3, though his conclusion (that the Irish stayed put, and did not respond by out-migration and curbing in-migration) is in error: see later in this chapter.

62. Austin O'Malley, "Irish Vital Statistics in America," *Studies,* 7 (1918), pp. 623–32; L. I. Dublin and G. W. Baker, "Mortality of Race Stocks in Pennsylvania and New York," *Journal of the American Statistical Association,* 17 (1920), pp. 13–44; James J. Walsh, "Commentary Thereon," *Studies,* 10 (1920), pp. 628–32; Robert E. Kennedy, *The Irish: Emigration. Marriage and Fertility* (Berkeley, CA, 1973), pp. 45–65; U.S. Bureau of the Census, Dept of Commerce, *Immigrants and Their Children, 1920* (Washington, DC, 1927), pp. 198–9, 202–7. None of these figures is directly comparable to those of the 1850s because of standardization adopted to counteract the different age-pyramids of immigrants and native-born populations. It is striking that O'Malley attributed the causes to degeneracy caused by change of climate (in *Studies,* 5 (1916), p. 530) when so many of the conditions he saw, studied, and treated were stress-related, from cardiovascular deaths to mental disorders, or rooted in cultural poverty, as with high infant mortality; journalists better understood the pressures on the Irish; e.g., John Spargo, *The Bitter Cry of the Children* [1906], ed. W. Trattner (Chicago, 1968), pp. 25–7.

63. Patrick O'Flanagan, in O'Flanagan and Buttimer, *Cork,* pp. 410–67.

64. Kenneth Rexroth, "Afterword" in Frank Norris, *McTeague: A Story of San Francisco* (New York, 1964), p. 343; Sam Bass Warner Jr, *The Urban Wilderness* (New York, 1972), pp. 81–4.

65. Cahill in *Boston Pilot,* 28 Jan. 1860; Kennedy in *Tipperary Advocate,* 21 July 1860; Thomas Mooney, *Nine Years in America* (Dublin, 1850), pp. 37–41.

66. Miller, *Emigrants and Exiles,* p. 315.

67. Rising from 39 percent in 1831 to 85 percent in 1867 (above, v, tables 4 and 5, pp. 611, 612, and pp. 575–7). See also p. 739, n. 1.

68. See Ernst, *Immigrant Life in New York City,* pp. 61–72; Thernstrom, *Poverty and Progress,* pp. 15–32; Mark Wyman, *Immigrants in the Valley: Irish, Germans, and Americans in the Upper Mississippi Country, 1830–1860* (Chicago, 1983), pp. 75–105; Clark, *Hibernia America,* pp. 23–33; Wittke, *Irish in America,* pp. 37–9.

69. Given, or recalculated from data (East) in Handlin, *Boston's Immigrants,* tables 13 and 15, pp. 251, 253; Ernst, *Immigrant Life in New York City,* table 27, pp. 214–17; Clark, *Irish in Philadelphia,* p. 74 and table 1, p. 75; Theodore Hershberg and others, "Occupation and Ethnicity in Five Nineteenth-Century Cities: A Collaborative Inquiry," *Historical Methods Newsletter,* 7 (1974), pp. 174–216, graph 5; (West, Midwest) Walsh, "Big Wather," p. 10; Vinyard, *Irish on the Urban Frontier,* pp. 150, 390–91; Bessie Louise Pierce, *History of Chicago, 2: 1848–1871* (Chicago, 1940), p. 499; R. D. Weber, "Socioeconomic Change in Racine, 1850–1880," *Journal of the West,* 13 (1974), pp. 105–6; Burchell, *San Francisco Irish,* pp. 54–5; P. J. Blessing, "West among Strangers: Irish Migration to California, 1850–1880" (Ph.D. diss., University of California, Los Angeles, 1977), table 6.7, p. 289; Vinyard, *Irish on the Urban Frontier,* table A.48, p. 420; Lebergott, *Manpower … since 1800,* table A-25, p. 541.

70. Handlin, *Boston's Immigrants;* Ernst, *Immigrant Life in New York City;* B. Laurie, T. Hershberg, and G. Alter, "Immigrants and Industry: the Philadelphia Experience, 1850–1880," in Hershberg, *Philadelphia,* pp. 107, 110; L. A. Glasco, *Ethnicity and Social Structure: Irish, Germans and Native-Born of Buffalo, N.Y., 1850–1860* (New York, 1980), pp. 94–7. As the New York 1855

state census was conducted in summer, when male heads of family were often unlisted (being out of town as railroad, farm, or other laborers), the Buffalo and New York City figures are underenumerations.

71. Hershberg and others, "Occupation and Ethnicity," tables 9, 10, and 11; Thernstrom, *Poverty and Progress*, table 7, p. 119; Glasco, *Ethnicity and Social Structure*, pp. 132–40; Clark, *Irish in Philadelphia*, pp. 54–60; Burchell, *San Francisco Irish*, pp. 61–6; Clark, *Hibernia America*, p. 28.

72. Mooney, *Nine Years in America*, pp. 21–2; William Smith O'Brien, *Lectures on America* (Dublin, 1860), p. 15; Buckley, *Diary of a Tour*, pp. 144, 241; Peter O'Leary, *Travel and Experiences in Canada, the Red River Territory and the United States* (London, 1877), pp. 1, 6, 178–9, 220.

73. The widespread artificial linkage of "domestic service" with "general labouring" as a single occupational category, in tables both of outflowing emigrants and of the mid-century and later Irish American workforce, distorts this by consistently showing majorities of the Irish in the lowest bracket. But before c.1880 there was a familial migration with daughters, in service before marriage, supplementing incomes either at home or in America (Tom Mooney warned laborers they must so put their girls into service to avoid poverty); from 1880 onward, this pattern overlapped with an increasing differentiation of male and female experiences of America.

74. Ernst, *Immigrant Life in New York City*, p. 73.

75. Recalculated from ibid., pp. 214–17, and Sean Wilentz, *Chants Democratic* (New York, 1984), pp. 405–6.

76. E.g., Francis Wyse, *America* (London, 1846), vol. 3, pp. 10–26; Mooney, *Nine Years in America*, pp. 37, 84–93, 133–54.

77. Wilentz, *Chants Democratic*, table 15, p. 406.

78. David Doyle, "The Irish and American Labour, 1880–1920," *Saothar*, 1 (1975), p. 43.

79. Greagoir Ó Dughaill, ed., "Return of the Tradesmen of the Town of Galway, Their Rates of Wages . . . 15 Dec. 1845," *Saothar*, 1 (1975), pp. 66–7; cf. E. Almquist, "Pre-Famine Ireland and the Theory of European Proto-industrialisation: Evidence from the 1841 Census," *Journal of Economic History*, 39 (1979), pp. 699–718.

80. Ernst, *Immigrant Life*, pp. 214–17; Dale B. Light in Drudy, *Irish in America*, table 6.2, p. 118; Handlin, *Boston's Immigrants*, pp. 250–51; Vinyard, *Irish on the Urban Frontier*, pp. 62, 68; Glasco, *Ethnicity and Social Structure*, p. 97; Burchell, *San Francisco Irish*, p. 54. Recalculations are based on the classifications given by Vinyard, p. 363.

81. Lebergott, *Manpower . . . since 1800*, pp. 62–3.

82. Hershberg and others, "Occupation and Ethnicity," graph 5; Laurie, Hershberg, and Alter, in Hershberg, *Philadelphia*, p. 107; Clark, *Irish in Philadelphia*, pp. 76–87.

83. Handlin, *Boston's Immigrants*, pp. 94–100; Clark, *Irish in Philadelphia*, pp. 50, 52, 55–60; Alan Burstein and Stephanie Greenberg in Hershberg, *Philadelphia*, pp. 183–6, 194–9; and pp. 214–23; John T. Ridge, *The Flatbush Irish* (Brooklyn, 1983), pp. 6 ff.

84. Glasco, *Ethnicity and Social Structure*, pp. 15–21, 31–4, 42–3, 52–5, 60–61, 71, 80–139; Vinyard, *Irish on the Urban Frontier*, pp. 49–79, 87–8, 94–101, 193, 365–79; Kathleen N. Conzen, *Immigrant Milwaukee, 1836–1860* (Cambridge, MA, 1976), pp. 63–153; Burchell, *San Francisco Irish*, pp. 47–72.

85. Burchell, *San Francisco Irish*, p. 46.

86. Kerby Miller, David Doyle, and Patricia Kelleher, "'For Love and Liberty': Irish Women, Emigration, and Domesticity in Ireland and America, 1815–1920" in Patrick O'Sullivan (ed.), *The Irish World Wide*, vol. 4, *Irish Women and Irish Migration* (Leicester and London, 1995), pp. 41–65.

87. Generally for this paragraph Blessing, "West among Strangers," pp. 201, 284, 351–8;

Conzen, *Immigrant Milwaukee*, pp. 46–52; Glasco, *Ethnicity and Social Structure*, pp. 141–225; Vinyard, *Irish on the Urban Frontier*, pp. 106–13, 184–8, 192, 380–88, 409–19; Burchell, *San Francisco Irish*, pp. 78–87; Lynn H. Lees and John Modell, "The Irish Countryman Urbanized: A Comparative Perspective on the Famine Migration" in Hershberg, *Philadelphia*, pp. 352–5; Mokyr, *Why Ireland Starved*, pp. 32–7, 71–4.

88. For poverty in Irish America, see Dolan, *Immigrant Church*, pp. 32–7, 123–5; Dennis Clark, "Ramcat and Rittenhouse Square" in *Irish Relations*, pp. 158–69; Ernst, *Immigrant Life in New York City*, pp. 39–40, 48–60; Handlin, *Boston's Immigrants*, pp. 88–123; Neihaus, *Irish in New Orleans*, pp. 59–70, 135–46; Thernstrom, *Poverty and Progress*, pp. 20–32, 42–56; Carole Groneman, "The Bloody Ould Sixth: A Social Analysis . . ." (Ph.D. diss., University of Rochester, 1973). For poverty in Ireland, see Mokyr, *Why Ireland Starved*, pp. 6–29, 278–94; Timothy P. O'Neill, "The State, Poverty, and Distress in Ireland, 1815–1845" (Ph.D. diss., National University Ireland, University College Dublin, 1971).

89. Clark, *Erin's Heirs*, pp. 50–51, 54; James Roohan, *American Catholics and the Social Question, 1865–1900* (New York, 1976), pp. 40–71; Henry F. May, *The Protestant Churches and Industrial America* (New York, 1967) pp. 3–72; John R. Bodo, *The Protestant Clergy and Public Issues, 1812–1848* (Princeton, 1954; repr., 1980), *passim*; R. F. Hueston, *The Catholic Press and Nativism, 1840–1860* (New York, 1976), pp. 140–46, 185, 229, 249–74; H. J. Browne, *The Catholic Church and the Knights of Labor* (New York, 1976); Fergus McDonald, *The Catholic Church and the Secret Societies in the United States* (New York, 1946). Quoted phrases are from Dolan, *Immigrant Church*, pp. 33, 42.

90. Aaron Abell, *American Catholicism and Social Action: A Search for Social Justice, 1865–1950* (Notre Dame, IN, 1963; repr., Westport, CT, 1980), pp. 1–53; Florence D. Cohalan, *A Popular History of the Archdiocese of New York* (Estero, FL, 1983), pp. 78–9, 90–94; James F. Connelly, *The History of the Archdiocese of Philadelphia* (Philadelphia, 1976); Dolan, *Immigrant Church*, pp. 121–40; Charles Shanabruch, *Chicago's Catholics: An Evolution of an American Identity* (Notre Dame, IN, 1981), pp. 7, 22; Handlin, *Boston's Immigrants*, pp. 117, 161–3, 168–9.

91. *Boston Pilot*, 3 Jan. 1852, quoted in Hueston, *Catholic Press and Nativism*, p. 143.

92. Timothy P. O'Neill, "Poverty in Ireland," *Folklife*, 11 (1974), pp. 22–37; "Clare and Irish Poverty," *Studia Hibernia*, 14 (1974), pp. 7–27; O'Connell, quoted in Mokyr, *Why Ireland Starved*, p. 220; David Fitzpatrick, "Class, Family, and Rural Unrest in Nineteenth-Century Ireland" in P. J. Drudy (ed.), *Irish Studies II: Ireland: Land, Politics, and People* (Cambridge, 1982), pp. 37–75. But this contrast of mutual aid and mutual harshness must be qualified by the comment of John Stanley in 1845: "Irish farmers, from want of capital, could not . . . carry out production, with a high rate of wages. . . . Again money wages does [*sic*] not enter into the calculation of Irish farmers, commonly operating" (cited in Ó Gráda, *Ireland before and after Famine*, pp. 59–60).

93. In sequence (with those of Irish Episcopal succession, in italics): *Pittsburgh, Chicago, Hartford (CT), Little Rock (AR)*, and Milwaukee all in 1843; *Albany, Buffalo*, Cleveland, and Galveston in 1847; *Wheeling, St Paul*, and Savannah in 1850; *Brooklyn, Erie*, Newark, Burlington (VT), *Portland (ME)*, Quincy (IL), Covington, and San Francisco in 1853; Fort Wayne (IN), and Sault St.-Marie (WI) in 1857; Wilmington (DE.), *Scranton, Harrisburg, Rochester*, Columbus, Green Bay, and LaCrosse (both WI), *St. Joseph (MO), Grass Valley* (now *Sacramento*), all in 1868; *Springfield (MA)* in 1870; Ogdensburg (NY) and Providence, both in 1872; and Peoria, 1875, Leavenworth (KS.), 1877, and Allegheny (PA) in 1876. Data from Theodore Roemer, *The Catholic Church in the United States* (St. Louis, 1950), maps and appendices, pp. 202, 318 ff, 384 ff, 401–14, and J. B. Code, *Dictionary of the American Hierarchy* (New York, 1940). Additionally in these years Portland (OR.), Walla-Walla, and Nesqually were created as missionary dioceses

in the far northwest, and Santa Fe, San Antonio, and St. Augustine in once Spanish or Mexican lands.

94. D. W. Miller, "Irish Catholicism and the Great Famine," *Journal of Social History,* 9 (1975), pp. 81–98; Sean Connolly, *Religion and Society in Nineteenth-Century Ireland* (Dundalk, 1985), pp. 7–17, 41–60, which does not cite P. J. Corish, *The Catholic Community in the Seventeenth and Eighteenth Centuries* (Dublin, 1981), pp. 82–115; see also Corish, *Irish Catholic Experience,* pp. 166–215.

95. "The Roman Propaganda in Ireland," *New York Times,* 24 Oct. 1855; Emmet Larkin, "The Devotional Revolution in Ireland, 1850–75" in *American Historical Review,* 77 (1972), pp. 623–52.

96. Jay P. Dolan, *The American Catholic Experience: A History from Colonial Times to the Present* (Notre Dame, IN, 1992), p. 207.

97. See further David N. Doyle, "The Irish in Australia and the United States: Some Comparisons, 1800–1939," *Irish Economic and Social History,* 16 (1989), pp. 86–92 and citations; M. Doorley, "The Irish and the Catholic Church in New Orleans, 1835–1918" (M.A. thesis, University of New Orleans, 1987), tables 3 to 17, pp. 66–77.

98. R. A. Wells, *Ulster Migrants to America: Letters from Three Families* (New York, 1991); *Fifth Annual Report of the American Protestant Society* (New York, 1848), p. 3.

99. Dolan, *American Catholic Experience,* pp. 165–8, 195–8; and his *Immigrant Church,* pp. 13–14, 21–2, 45–67, 121–58.

100. Thomas Brady to Bishop John McCloskey, 1 Jan. 1861, in Mary C. Taylor, *History of the Foundation of Catholicism in Northern New York* (Yonkers, 1976), p. 187; J. Gilmary Shea to James F. Edwards, 16 Aug. 1890, in Richard Shaw, *John Dubois: Founding Father* (Yonkers, 1976), p. x; Patrick O'Kelly, *Advice and Guide to Emigrants Going to the United States of America* (Dublin, 1834), p. 19. O'Kelly had spent five years in America.

SUGGESTED READING

Patrick J. Blessing, "The Irish in America," in *The Encyclopedia of the Irish in America,* ed. Michael Glazier (Notre Dame, IN: University of Notre Dame Press, 1999), pp. 453–470.

P. J. Drudy, ed., *The Irish in America: Emigration, Assimilation, and Impact* (Cambridge: Cambridge University Press, 1985).

Lawrence J. McCaffrey, *The Irish Catholic Diaspora in America* (Washington, DC: Catholic University of America Press, 1997).

Kerby A. Miller, *Emigrants and Exiles: Ireland and the Irish Exodus to North America* (New York: Oxford University Press, 1985).

Kerby A. Miller with David N. Doyle and Patricia Kelleher, "'For Love and Liberty': Irish Women, Emigration, and Domesticity in Ireland and America, 1815–1920," in *Irish Women and Irish Migration,* Vol. 4 of *The Irish World Wide,* ed. Patrick O'Sullivan (London and New York: Leicester University Press, 1995), pp. 41–65.

William V. Shannon, *The American Irish: A Political and Social Portrait* (New York: Macmillan, 1963; Amherst: University of Massachusetts Press, 1989).

Conflicts of Identity

Chapter 6

Ulster Presbyterians and the "Two Traditions" in Ireland and America

Kerby A. Miller

In recent decades, the "Two Traditions" has become a hallowed concept both in professional Irish historiography and in Irish political and journalistic discourse. The term suggests or specifically connotes the permanent existence in Ireland of two separate ethno-religious groups with distinct historical experiences and sharply conflicting interests, outlooks, and political cultures. One is Gaelic, Catholic, nationalist, and "Irish"; the other is English and Scottish, Protestant, unionist or loyalist, and "British." Very recently, there has been a tendency in Northern Ireland to simplify this model even further, by distinguishing solely between the "Irish" and the "Ulster Scots" inhabitants of Ireland's northern province. Ironically, the latter trend has long precedence in the United States, where at least since the mid–nineteenth century the term "Irish" has almost invariably been applied only to Irish Catholic immigrants and their descendants, whereas all non-Catholics of Irish birth or ancestry generally have been designated as "Scotch-Irish." In America as in Ireland, the boundaries between the histories and even the "character" of the two groups have been sharply drawn.

However, there are several problems with the Two Traditions model—some conceptual, others practical. One conceptual problem lies in the presumed inclusiveness of each tradition, as by definition each encompasses ethnic, religious, cultural, and political criteria that may not all be shared by many members of each group. Another problem is that the concept is fundamentally ahistorical: it implies eternal differences, if not antagonism, between the Two Traditions' respective adherents, and therefore the model's exponents need to ignore or deemphasize contradictory evidence of cooperation, collaboration, and the blurring of boundaries. Hence, one practical or methodological problem for historians is that strict fidelity to the Two Traditions thesis inhibits their appreciation of the ambiguities and complexities of the histories of both Protestants and Catholics in Ireland and in America.

A final problem for historians stems from the fact that the Two Traditions thesis had its origins, at least in part, in the reaction of "revisionist" scholars against a "traditional" or "nationalist" model of Irish history that allegedly had marginalized or ignored Irish—especially Ulster—Protestants and their distinct historical experiences. Rhetorically, at least, the revisionists' emphasis on Ireland's Two Traditions aimed to persuade academics, students, and general readers to recognize and value equally

Ireland's and particularly Northern Ireland's Protestant/unionist/British tradition. In practice, however, revisionist scholars generally devoted their attention to analyses of the Gaelic/Catholic/nationalist/Irish tradition, perhaps in the belief that only through its deconstruction could the Protestant/unionist/British tradition emerge from its shade and attain at least equal visibility and validity.

Yet the ironic consequence is that revisionist historians have paid comparatively little attention to the historical development of Ulster's Protestant/unionist/British tradition, particularly during the half-century following the Act of Union, perhaps because they assumed that by the early or mid-1800s the emergence in Protestant Ulster of an apparently monolithic unionism was a natural, inevitable consequence of earlier religious and political conflicts.[1] It is equally ironic that recent critics of revisionist scholarship, in their concern to refute the latter's critiques of Irish nationalism, have also largely neglected the "other" tradition. In the United States, similar problems have been compounded by long-standing historiographical and institutional divisions between historians who have focused on the urbanized Irish Catholic immigrants of the nineteenth century, and the smaller numbers of scholars who have concentrated on eighteenth-century Ulster Presbyterian immigrants who settled in rural and frontier America. The overall consequence is that the history of Irish, and especially Ulster, Protestants has been comparatively understudied on both sides of the Atlantic.

At the end of this essay, I will return to the broad historiographical issues posed by the Two Traditions model. More specifically, however, my own recent research suggests the inadequacy of that model to explain the ambiguities and complexities of the history of Irish Protestants and of their relationships with each other (as well as with Irish Catholics) in Ireland and in North America.

This research has focused largely on the historical experiences and identities of Ulster Presbyterians, in Ireland and America, during the eighteenth and early nineteenth centuries.[2] Early on, a practical problem with important implications had to be faced: what to call—how to name or label—these people? "Ulster Presbyterians" is wonderfully specific, but it is too cumbersome for continual repetition. A synonym was needed, and both early and contemporary writers offered me a number of choices. These included "Ulster Scots," "Scotch-Irish," "Scots-Irish," or simply "Irish" (with or without a religious qualifier). Indeed, there was even a non-choice, suggested by the title Patrick Griffin chose for his recent book on early Ulster Presbyterian immigrants, *The People with No Name*.[3]

I decided to reject the term "Ulster Scots" as a viable synonym for Ulster Presbyterians. This decision was made hesitantly, for the "Ulster Scots" label has some historical antecedents (although it was not common in Ireland or America during the 1600s and 1700s) and much contemporary cultural, financial, and political recognition, especially among Northern Ireland's unionists. In addition, "Ulster Scots" is the term accepted by many linguistic scholars to identify one of the languages or dialects (*which* one is disputed) in the north of Ireland. As an ethnic or ethno-religious marker, however, "Ulster Scots" is problematic, particularly when it is used (as was the term "Scotch-Irish" in the United States) to encompass *all* Ulster Protestants or to imply the permanence of irreconcilable differences between their historical and political traditions and those of Ireland's Catholics.

Indeed, one of the "Ulster Scots" label's greatest appeals for some people may be its erasure of all references to "Ireland" and "Irish."[4] Moreover, in its generic usage the term also erases from Ulster's historical record the large and important body of northern Anglicans of primarily English descent. They are subsumed (as are smaller ethnic and denominational groups) in an "Ulster Scots" hegemony, which, in turn, logically implies Presbyterian primacy in the North's social, cultural, and political history. That implication, however, is very questionable. During the last three centuries, for example, Ulster's Protestant population has steadily become *less* Presbyterian, from a high mark of perhaps 60 percent in the early 1700s to less than half (46 percent) by 1926, and to less than two-fifths (39 percent) in 1971.[5] Equally important, it was the Ulster Presbyterians whose disputatious political culture—once the bane of Anglican bishops, landlords, and officials—was subsumed in the zealous monarchism and Tory conservatism that traditionally characterized Ulster's Anglicans, as well as in the latter's most distinctive institution, the Loyal Orange Order. In short, although the "Ulster Scots" label may reveal much about contemporary unionist thinking, for a student of eighteenth- and nineteenth-century Ulster history it seemed to obscure at least as much as it illuminated.

Eventually, I also decided to reject "Scotch-Irish" nomenclature, and only in part because I had always understood that "Scotch" should refer to whiskey, not to people. To be sure, "Scotch-Irish" has a long precedence in American popular and scholarly discourse. And as historian James Leyburn argued, "Scotch-Irish" can be "a useful term . . . express[ing] a historical reality."[6] If employed carefully and neutrally, the "Scotch-Irish" label can reflect broad distinctions among Ulster Presbyterian immigrants of Scottish origin; Irish Anglicans and other Protestant immigrants of mostly English descent; and Irish Catholic immigrants of Gaelic, Norman, and other backgrounds. Even the term's most specific and careful usage, however, homogenizes complex realities in both Ulster and America. For example, it obscures the fact that eighteenth-century Ulster Presbyterian society was differentiated internally both by local circumstances and by the diverse regional, social, and cultural origins of a migration from Scotland that consisted of distinct waves from different Scottish regions and social strata over a period of at least one hundred years.

Ulster Presbyterians whose parents had departed southwestern Scotland in the 1690s or early 1700s and who emigrated to the New World in the 1720s may have differed in significant ways from those whose ancestors had left the Scottish borderlands in the early 1600s and who themselves migrated to the American colonies in the late 1700s. If one also considers the regional, socioeconomic, cultural, and doctrinal differences that prevailed in eighteenth-century Presbyterian Ulster itself, then the possible variations and permutations among the migrants to America are practically endless. The varying backgrounds, outlooks, and proximity of migration from Scotland among Ulster Presbyterian emigrants who adhered to the orthodox Synod of Ulster, the liberal Antrim Presbytery, the evangelical Associated or Seceding synods, or the prophetic traditions of the Reformed or Covenanting congregations—or who were entirely "un-churched," as contemporary clergymen often complained—have scarcely been examined in terms of their socioeconomic, cultural, or political implications in the New World.[7]

Moreover, the very origins of the term "Scotch-Irish" are highly problematic, both in the British Isles and in America. In the late 1500s and 1600s, among Protestants in both Ireland and the Scottish Lowlands, the term "Scotch-Irish" usually had adverse Catholic and Gaelic connotations, specifically with reference to the Irish-speaking MacDonnells and other Scots Highlanders who migrated back and forth between Argyll, the Western Isles, and the glens of Antrim, causing military and political problems for officials in Dublin and Edinburgh alike.[8] Perhaps its early, negative associations help explain why in 1720 the Ulster-born Presbyterian minister, James McGregor of Londonderry, New Hampshire, when writing the famous petition that scholars would later cite as the "charter document" of "Scotch-Irish" history in America, did *not* employ the term to describe the settlers whom he had led from the Bann Valley to New England. Indeed, McGregor could identify the members of his congregation only in *negative* terms—as neither "Irish" nor "papists"—but he did not attempt to name them himself. This was ironic, because even the sympathetic New Hampshire officials who incorporated McGregor's settlement referred to it as "a company of Irish."[9] Likewise, Rev. James MacSparran, an Ulster Presbyterian clergyman of Scottish parentage (who subsequently converted to the Church of Ireland), identified the inhabitants of Londonderry, New Hampshire, as "Irish" when he wrote the first Irish emigrants' guidebook, *America Dissected*, published in 1753.[10]

Indeed, it appears that the term "Scotch-Irish" was not very common in eighteenth-century Ireland or America. In the latter country Leyburn himself found only a handful of recorded instances prior to the American Revolution, and virtually none for several decades afterward. Although subsequent scholars have discovered additional examples, Leyburn's conclusion still appears valid—namely, that in eighteenth-century America, "Irish" (with or without regional-origin or religious qualifiers) was the term most frequently employed both by contemporary observers and the generality of Ulster Presbyterian immigrants themselves.[11] Moreover, when the "Scotch-Irish" label *was* applied by "outsiders," as by Anglo-American colonists and officials, it often had negative implications, perhaps because of its initial application to Gaelic/Catholic Highlanders but more likely because of the alleged sociocultural and moral deficiencies of the "Scotch-Irish" themselves. Indeed, some of the latter's most savage critics, such as the Anglican clergyman Charles Woodmason, apparently thought that, of all the available names for a people they despised, "Scotch-Irish" had the most defamatory connotations.[12]

Unfortunately, scholars have not investigated the processes by which "Scotch-Irish" eventually lost its early Gaelic/Catholic associations and came to designate Ulster Presbyterian immigrants of Lowland Scottish origins. Nor have historians fully understood how the American label, in its application to Ulster Presbyterian immigrants and their descendants, assumed entirely "positive" sociocultural traits which were deemed antithetical to those of Irish Catholics. Certainly, however, those developments were complete by the mid–nineteenth century. And in the process, "Scotch-Irish" lost its specific and exclusive reference to Ulster Presbyterians. Like the term "Ulster Scots" in contemporary Northern Ireland, the term expanded to designate all Irish immigrants and their descendants who were *currently* Protestant, even if their

Henry Eaton (1808–1885), a native of County Tyrone, was recorded in the 1880 Census with his wife Sarah and son Robert (born 1858) living in Lewistown, about a dozen miles south of Emmitsburg, in western Maryland. Although his religious affiliation is not known, Eaton is an English name; thus his birthplace in Ulster indicates that he most likely was the descendant of Protestant settlers in the province. However, the clasped hands motif depicted on his gravestone appears, with some variations, as the earliest iconography of Irish America and no doubt is what caught the eye of photographer Marjory Collins in 1943. (Library of Congress, Prints and Photographs Division, LC-USW3-017684-D)

ancestors had been Anglicans of English descent or Catholics of Gaelic or Hiberno-Norman backgrounds. Thus, in the late nineteenth and early twentieth centuries, the authors of county histories as far afield as South Carolina and South Dakota happily re-baptized as "Scotch-Irish" the ancestors of Methodist merchants and Baptist farmers bearing names such as O'Hara and O'Brien![13]

The consequent inclusivity and vagueness of the "Scotch-Irish" label provided yet another reason to search for an alternative. A final reason was to avoid implication in the bitter late-nineteenth- and early-twentieth-century controversy over what Michael

O'Brien (the pioneering Irish-American Catholic historian) called the "Scotch-Irish myth."[14] O'Brien challenged early versions of the Two Traditions model of Irish-American history in two crude and somewhat contradictory ways: first by contending that Ulster Presbyterian immigrants to eighteenth-century America had been "Irish" in all but religion, merely because of their long residence in Ireland; and second by searching for native-Irish or Catholic antecedents for every Irish Protestant listed in early American records. However, O'Brien's "Scotch-Irish" adversaries were equally industrious and inventive. For example, one late-nineteenth-century author ethnically cleansed ("Scotch-Guarded") the early history of the Upper Shenandoah Valley in western Virginia by altering—by "Scotch-Irishizing"—all the native or "Catholic" Irish names that appeared in Elizabeth McDowell Greenlee's memoir of the Valley's first settlement. Thus, Cullen was changed to Coulter, Quinn to Green, and so forth.[15] In short, early scholars and publicists in neither camp were genuine pluralists or tolerant of ambiguity.

To embrace such complexities, I employed the term "Scots-Irish" as the most appropriate synonym for Ulster Presbyterians in both Ireland and America. In part, what appealed was the term's relative modernity and specificity: it is largely a scholars' invention, found much less commonly than "Scotch-Irish" or "Ulster Scots" in both the historical record and subsequent polemics. The most important consideration, however, was the hyphen, because it serves as a graphic symbol of the ambiguity and the fluidity of these people's—as of other people's—ethnic or "national" identities. Ultimately, the question of ethnicity is not one of ancestral birthplace or religious affiliation but one of individual and collective identification. This, in turn, is subjective and variable, conditioned by a multitude of shifting social, cultural, political, and psychological circumstances. Thus, the hyphen in "Scots-Irish" does not suggest linear movement or "progress" from one identity to another but, rather, the possibility of continual movement back and forth, contingent on ever-changing situations, including especially the social and political interests of those elites who attempt to speak for and define "their community."

With this in mind, a reevaluation of "Irish" identities in late-eighteenth- and early-nineteenth-century Ireland and the United States may be possible. For although "Irish" may then have been the most common name applied to Protestants as well as Catholics, the question remains of what it *meant* to be "Irish" in that era. Ethnic identification among those born in Ireland may have had both more and less significance than it does today. More because, prior to the American Revolution and the repeal of the Irish penal laws, a person's religious affiliation determined the extent of his civil rights and economic opportunities, to the benefit of Protestants (especially Anglicans) and to the detriment of Catholics. Yet also of less significance because the boundaries of "Irish" ethno-religious communities were more permeable at local and familial levels than they later became, and a remarkable degree of ethnic and religious fluidity prevailed in eighteenth-century Ireland and especially among its early migrants to America. In Ireland, for example, religious conversions, particularly from Catholicism to Protestantism, were much more common at all social levels than was later acknowledged.[16] On the other side of the Atlantic, especially among poor migrants, the relative frequence of intermarriage and conversion reflected a pragmatic understanding that ethnic and religious affiliations were not absolute but contingent on local circumstances. In short, early Irish emigrants appear to have been relatively nonchalant about what subsequent generations would regard as religious apostasy or ethnic treason. One result, as David Doyle has argued, was the absorption of nearly all early Irish Catholic (and poor Irish Anglican) emigrants into the Presbyterian faith that characterized the great majority of Ireland's eighteenth-century migrants to America.[17]

Moreover, the formal political or ideological boundaries of eighteenth-century Irish "nationality" were similarly fluid and expansive on both sides of the ocean. Especially after mid-century new secular and inclusive definitions of "Irishness" temporarily promised to subsume Ireland's different religious and ethnic strains. Simultaneously, in America there appears to have been an increasing tendency for Ulster Presbyterians to define themselves as "Irish," perhaps because of the "Scotch-Irish" label's negative connotations, but more likely in response to new tolerant and "enlightened" intellectual and political currents affecting their homeland and their adopted country alike. These currents—as well as shared business interests—were operative in the colonial seaport merchants' interdenominational St. Patrick's and Hibernian Societies, which flourished shortly before and after the American Revolution.[18] More important and revealingly, they were also evident in many Presbyterian immigrants' personal letters to relatives back in Ulster, where from the 1770s through the 1790s the Patriot, Volunteer, and, later, the United Irish movements were popularizing vague but equally inclusive notions of "Irish" nationality.

In 1774, for instance, James Caldwell, a young merchant in Philadelphia, informed his brother in north Antrim that, although the local "Scotch" immigrants were characterized invidiously by their "unbounded loyalty" to the British crown, "nine-tenths" of the "Irish . . . espouse[d] the American cause." Significantly, Caldwell was proud to include himself and his Presbyterian, Anglican, and Catholic business and political associates in an "Irish" community that was culturally pluralistic yet politically united, for in their common zeal for both American and Irish self-government, they happily combined what Caldwell called "the sagacity and calmness" of the northern Dissenters with "the enthusiastic chivalry" of the "native[s]" of southern Ireland. Likewise, shortly after the Revolution John Joyce, another Ulster Presbyterian in America, encouraged his kinsman in County Down to emigrate by assuring him that Virginia's inhabitants were "very fond of Irish emigration"—"it is given as a toast often at their fairs," he reported—and that the Virginians "much applaud the Irish for their . . . spirit of independence." And in 1802 a third Ulster Presbyterian, Robert MacArthur, this time in northwestern Pennsylvania, rejoiced that Thomas Jefferson's recent election had relieved him and the other "poor Irish" of the discriminatory legislation that Federalist anglophiles had imposed on them in the 1790s.[19]

This and other evidence suggests several conclusions. First, for a brief historical moment, in the era of the American and French revolutions, the "Irish" ethnic or "national" label had both broad and positive connotations among many (but, as we shall see, by no means all) native Americans: broad in the sense that the term encompassed all those of Irish birth or descent; and positive in that the "Irish" were viewed as imbibing the "spirit of independence" and republicanism to an exceptionally laudable degree. Second, during this moment it appears that many, perhaps most, Ulster

Presbyterians—both in America and in Ireland—were willing to embrace an "Irish" identity, the connotations of which were primarily political, not ethno-religious, and which was intimately associated with the "spirit of independence" hailed by reformers and radicals on both sides of the Atlantic.

Let us now first consider when and why that moment passed in the United States. Why did Ulster Presbyterians in America learn to reject the "Irish" label and to describe themselves as "Scotch-Irish"? Conversely, why and how did the meaning of "Irish" (among native and Irish Protestant Americans alike) resume its old connotations of "Catholic" and "inferior"?

There are a number of likely explanations for these developments. First, during the early nineteenth century, new Ulster Presbyterian immigrants were increasingly "Protestant," with mentalities shaped in Ireland not by the liberal or radical religious and political currents of the late 1700s but by fervent evangelicalism; by loyalism and Orangeism; and by cultural, material, and political conflicts with Irish Catholics who were, themselves, allegedly or actually becoming increasingly militant and "aggressive." Second, in America as in Ireland, religious revivalism created a heightened pan-Protestant religious consciousness that accentuated Protestant–Catholic differences (over education, for example), which, in turn, could escalate into political conflicts and even violent confrontations, as in the Philadelphia riots of 1844. Finally, the most common explanation is that Americans of Ulster Presbyterian (and other Irish Protestant) birth or descent formulated a "Scotch-Irish" identity to distinguish themselves from the embarrassing hordes of impoverished Catholic peasant immigrants of the Great Famine, and so to avoid the opprobrium heaped on the latter by native American Protestants.

Without rejecting those interpretations, I propose another which is located earlier in American history, in the 1780s and 1790s. I contend that the *modern* (and invidious) distinctions between the Protestant "Scotch-Irish" and the Catholic "Irish" first emerged as the result of a rhetorical strategy developed by Federalist Party politicians and conservative clergymen (often of Ulster Presbyterian descent) who were opposed to the "spirit of independence" associated with "Irishness" and with its perceived political, social, and cultural expressions in postrevolutionary American society. These "Irish" expressions included strong opposition in most states to the ratification of the U.S. Constitution, the so-called Whiskey Insurrections on the Pennsylvania and other frontiers, and, especially, radical Jeffersonian politics and journalism. They also included the intemperate drinking and boisterous fairs and other customs that scandalized middle-class Presbyterian lay people and clergymen—in long-settled Londonderry, New Hampshire, for example, as well as in the new backcountry regions. In short, I propose that the modern meanings and applications of "Scotch-Irish" were born out of the negative reactions, among conservative upper- and middle-class native and Ulster-stock Americans, to what they regarded as the dangerously democratic and licentious "excesses" of the American and the French revolutions, and to the prominent association of the "Irish" with those "excesses."[20]

It was neither accident nor ignorance that prompted Yankee Federalists to label their Irish-born political adversaries as "Wild Irish," employing a term that not only had obviously Gaelic and Catholic connotations but also specific associations with the alleged treachery and barbarism of those who perpetrated the (much-exaggerated) massacres of Ulster's Protestants in 1641. To be sure, that was a seminal event in northern Presbyterians' communal folklore, rivaled only by "memories" of the defense of Derry's walls in 1690, also against Irish "papists."[21] Nevertheless, canny Federalist politicians must have realized that the overwhelming majority of those in America whom they stigmatized as "Wild Irish" were Presbyterians, not Catholics (relatively few of whom had yet immigrated). By playing upon their old tribal prejudices, the Federalists were trying to revive Ulster Presbyterians' traditional sectarian loyalties. In effect they were also warning them that, unless they wished to share the "Wild Irish" stigma (thereby forfeiting their inherited claims to superiority as Protestants), they must espouse the Federalist (i.e., non-"Irish") virtues of order, deference, and temperance and forswear any political and social behaviors that were proverbially associated only with the "naturally" rebellious, violent, and intemperate "Irish" (Catholics).

One can recognize this strategy at work on scholarly and literary, as well as overtly political and polemical, levels—for example, in Jeremy Belknap's late-eighteenth-century *History of New Hampshire* (1784–92). It was surely no coincidence that this Congregational clergyman, Federalist Party pamphleteer, and future Harvard president was the first to discover and publish Rev. McGregor's famous Londonderry petition of 1720 as a signpost for New England's Ulster Presbyterians who wanted to follow the road from "Wild Irishness" back to non-"Irish"—that is, to Protestant "Scotch-Irish" —respectability. Likewise, it was scarcely fortuitous that when Hugh Henry Brackenridge, a Scottish immigrant and conservative judge in Pennsylvania, satirized his radical political opponents, William Findley and William Duane, in his serialized novel *Modern Chivalry* (1792–1815), he transformed them into the blundering, inebriated, violent, and politically unstable "stage Irish" character of Teague O'Regan, although, in fact, Findley was an Ulster Presbyterian of Covenanter stock and Duane was an American-born convert to the Episcopalian faith! For Brackenridge and his intended readers, it was Findley's and Duane's political opinions and style, not their religion or birthplace, that made them stereotypically "wild Irish" Catholic and Gaelic peasants.

Finally, this transition may be seen clearly in the popular poetry of Robert Dinsmoor, a grandson of an early settler in Londonderry, New Hampshire, and of David Bruce, an Ulster (according to some accounts, Scottish) Presbyterian immigrant in southwestern Pennsylvania. Bruce wrote and published his poetry in the 1790s, Dinsmoor between that decade and his death in 1836. Both men were arch-Federalists and conscious propagandists. Bruce may have been the first writer to employ the term "Scotch [or Scots]-Irish" in positive and modern ways (he signed his poems, "A Scots-Irishman"), while Dinsmoor was a fervent Calvinist and a nativist who proudly proclaimed that "The highest pedigree I plead" is a "Yankee born" of "true Scottish breed." Both men appropriated the dialectic form and poetic conventions employed by Ulster's contemporary "Rhyming Weavers," which was bitterly ironic because—like their mentor, Robert Burns—most of the latter, notably James Orr of Ballycary, had strong democratic and Irish nationalist sentiments. Nevertheless, Dinsmoor's and Bruce's themes and efforts would be conventional within a few decades. For instance, in his *History of Londonderry* [New Hampshire], published in 1850, Edward L. Parker, an Ulster-stock Presbyterian clergyman, blamed every embarrassing episode or trait in his people's past on their Scottish ancestors' brief but temporarily contaminating exposure to Ulster's Catholics.[22]

Thus, Parker and his predecessors were engaged simultaneously in two cultural and political projects: to draw sharp ethno-religious boundaries between "their people" and Irish Catholics; and to impose on the former conservative or bourgeois standards of opinion and behavior. The projects were interdependent and indeed inextricable, for those who formulated what O'Brien later called the "Scotch-Irish myth" were projecting onto Irish Catholic immigrants the "negative" attributes of any Ulster Presbyterians who deviated from those standards. The ultimate implication was that the "true Scotch-Irish" could be neither economic failures nor disloyal to conservatively defined "American values" because, by definition, the virtues inherent in their religion and British origins guaranteed their moral, cultural, and hence their economic and political superiority to Irish Catholics.

The means by which a dominant class (in this instance, the rising Ulster-American bourgeoisie) achieves cultural and political hegemony over its adherents (in this case, in order to prove the group's collective "worth" to Protestant America's governing classes) can be both coercive and subtle. The methods range from political punishments (as in the Federalists' Alien and Sedition Acts of 1798), to exclusion from religious community, to everyday signals that "loyal" or "respectable" behavior is a prerequisite for favorable leases, decent wages, steady employment, easy credit, or rapid promotion. Rather surprisingly, although Irish revisionist historians have exposed the coercive mechanisms and sociocultural pressures that helped ensure the success of bourgeois-led Catholic nationalist movements in Ireland, they have rarely investigated whether similar processes might have been at work in Ulster, from the late eighteenth century onward, to ensure the conversion of politically disaffected "Irish" Presbyterians into loyal "Ulster Scots" unionists. Was there in the north of Ireland a political and "ethnic" transformation being carried out, similar or even parallel to that taking place in contemporary America?

Even if they do not dismiss the radical "Irish" phases of Ulster Presbyterians' history as ephemeral or aberrational, historians usually argue that the latter's transition to loyalism in the decades following 1798 was natural and even inevitable. This is attributed to several interlocking factors. First, there was the Ulster Presbyterians' revulsion against Catholic massacres of Wexford Protestants in 1798, which confirmed traditional fears and prejudices. Second, the spread of Protestant evangelicalism heightened sectarian tensions, particularly when it complemented the Loyal Orange Order's growing popularity in response to the rise of Daniel O'Connell's "Catholic" nationalism. Last, and most important, the increasing prosperity of Ulster linen manufacturing (centered on Belfast and largely owned by Presbyterian merchants and manufacturers) was widely viewed as consequent to and guaranteed by the union with Britain.[23]

These explanations may seem convincing, but are they sufficient to explain such a rapid and total transformation in the Ulster Presbyterians' political culture? For example, Catholic atrocities perpetrated in 1798 against loyalists—some of whom were also Catholics—in distant Wexford paled by comparison with British and loyalist butcheries of Presbyterian and Catholic rebels and alleged rebels in Ulster itself.

Likewise, neither evangelicalism nor Orangeism became ubiquitous among Ulster Presbyterians until after the Great Famine of 1845–52. And although parts of east Ulster were relatively prosperous in the pre-famine decades—thanks to linen manufacturing—ordinary Protestants in mid-, south, and west Ulster suffered intensely from the demise of cottage spinning, which was now concentrated in Belfast's new mills, and from the contraction of most handloom weaving to Belfast's immediate vicinity.[24]

Students of the origins and development of nineteenth-century Ulster Unionism should take into account not only the factors mentioned above, but also the denominational, social, cultural, and political tensions and conflicts within Ulster Protestant society itself. These conflicts are often obscured by the fact that those who were most instrumental in constructing unionist hegemony also controlled most of the printed records on which historians traditionally rely. Nevertheless, scholars will discover that many of the tensions that prevailed in Ulster during the late eighteenth century— between Anglicans and Dissenters; among conservative, liberal, and radical Presbyterians; and among the social classes in both denominations—continued well into the mid–nineteenth century. They may discover as well that the creation of unionist hegemony in Ulster, like the development of "Scotch-Irish" hegemony in America, was at least as much a consequence of such tensions and conflicts as it was the product of "natural" or "inevitable" ethno-religious rivalries between Protestants and Catholics.

For example, there is suggestive evidence of intracommunal conflict hidden in the north of Ireland's population history, especially in the region known variously as mid-Ulster or as the "linen triangle," which is centered in County Armagh (in 1795 the birthplace of the Orange Order) but includes portions of west Down and east Tyrone as well. Specifically, the populations of mid-Ulster parishes in 1766 and in 1831 (there are no religious censuses between those dates, and not again until 1861) can be compared. This period spans the American and French Revolutions, the "Armagh Outrages," the strife between local Orangemen and the United Irishmen and the latter's Catholic Defender allies, the outbreak and suppression of the 1798 Rebellion, the Act of Union, and the years of severe economic depression and competition that followed the end of the Napoleonic Wars in 1815.

The results of this research are rather striking. In most mid-Ulster parishes (particularly in those with rich soils), between 1766 and 1831 the loyal members of the legally privileged Church of Ireland substantially increased their proportions of the local populations—and they did so at the expense of the region's Presbyterian as well as its Catholic inhabitants. For instance, in 1766 the parish of Moira (in northwest Down) was 34 percent Anglican, 34 percent Presbyterian, and 32 percent Catholic. By 1831 the Anglican share had risen to nearly 54 percent, whereas the proportion of Catholics had declined to 27 percent, and the Presbyterian share had fallen dramatically to 19 percent. Likewise, in the combined Armagh parishes of Loughgilly and Killevy, between 1766 and 1831 the annual growth rate among Anglicans was an unusually high 4.03, whereas among Catholics it was only 1.91, and among Presbyterians it was merely 1.17; as a result, the Anglican share of the local Protestant population rose from 5 to 26 percent, with the Presbyterian share declining in proportion. In other mid-Ulster parishes, Presbyterians actually experienced negative growth rates.[25]

To be sure, these changes in religious demography partly reflect the slight dispari-ties between Anglican and Presbyterian annual growth rates that prevailed in much of the north during this period. The radical alterations in mid-Ulster, however, may also demonstrate the effects of official and unofficial, overt and subtle, pressures imposed by Anglican landlords and magistrates and by ordinary Orangemen against local Pres-byterians (as well as local Catholics) who could or would not conform to the emerg-ing unionist order. Barring wholesale conversions to the established church, discrim-inatory post-1798 changes in local landlords' leasing policies may account for such dramatic changes in the region's ethno-religious and, hence, political composition.

In 1815–19 John Gamble noted the fiercely democratic sentiments expressed by Ulster Presbyterian emigrants to America; this may shed light on their reaction to the processes that impelled their departures.[26] Also revealing is the unexpected occur-rence of liberal, radical, and even Irish nationalist opinions in many letters written by such emigrants in the early and mid–nineteenth century, in a period when, accord-ing to accepted wisdom, such notions had been all but eradicated from Presbyterian political culture in Ulster itself.[27] Indeed, the combined evidence of demographic data and many emigrants' letters suggests that Presbyterian radicalism was not so much diluted in Ulster as exported overseas.

Finally, another example of demographic evidence can be offered, this time from the period of the Great Famine, the cataclysm that purportedly confirmed both the Ulster Protestants and the American "Scotch-Irish" in their sense of "natural" sepa-rateness from (and divinely ordained superiority to) "Irish" Catholics. Between 1841 and 1851 the population of the overwhelmingly Protestant and Presbyterian parish of Kilwaughter, in mid-Antrim, fell 36 percent—a decline comparable to those experi-enced in some of the most impoverished Catholic districts of Munster and Connacht. In the nearby parishes of Glenwhirry, Raloo, and Killyglen Grange, all with similarly large Protestant and Presbyterian majorities—the populations fell by one-fourth to one-fifth during the same decade. Moreover, between 1831 and 1861—the three dec-ades spanning the Famine crisis—the Presbyterian population of nine-county Ulster declined by 18 percent. This was almost precisely the same proportional decrease that Ulster's Catholics experienced, whereas by contrast the north's Anglican population fell only 13 percent.

In every Ulster county except Fermanagh, proportional losses in 1831–61 among Presbyterians were greater (often substantially greater) than among Anglicans; only in Antrim and Down were Presbyterian attrition rates less (only slightly) than among Catholics. Looking again at mid-Ulster, between 1831 and 1861 the Anglican popu-lation of County Armagh fell merely 8 percent and the Catholic population fell by 16 percent, while the county's Presbyterian population declined by a remarkable 31 percent! Lastly, between 1831 and 1861 the Presbyterian share of nine-county Ulster's entire Protestant population declined from 57 to 53 percent. Thus, while the Famine certainly helped make Ulster more "Protestant," it also made its Protestants more Anglican. As noted at the beginning of this essay, that trend, originating in the eigh-teenth century, would continue at least through the mid–twentieth century.[28]

What are the implications of these demographic patterns? Did Presbyterian attri-tion—the result of disproportionately heavy emigration to America and elsewhere—

promote the consolidation of Ulster Protestant loyalism and conservatism, both traditionally Anglican (and landlord) projects? Did mass departures by lower-class or politically disaffected Presbyterians help ensure among their remaining coreligionists the hegemony of Rev. Henry Cooke and others who led their people into the unionist alliance with Anglican proprietors, evangelicalism, and the Orange Order? Loyalty to that alliance increasingly became the poor Presbyterian's most reliable protection against famine, eviction, or unemployment. Was the consolidation of unionist hegemony in Ulster (and of its "Scotch-Irish" analogue in America) encouraged—indeed, even mandated, by elite needs to control or to ignore the existence of poor Presbyterians on both sides of the ocean. And did this ignore the intracommunal class conflicts that their very existence implied by ratcheting up a sectarian and supremacist rhetoric, which, in turn, sharply and simplistically divided Ireland's inhabitants and immigrants into merely Two Traditions: Protestants and Catholics, unionists and nationalists, the loyal and the disloyal, even the "worthy" and the "unworthy"?

More broadly, this essay has indicated the fluid and contingent nature of ethnic or "national" identities. Any model, such as the Two Traditions, which attempts to freeze ethnic identity in one single, historically conditioned definition, and claims for that definition a timeless quality or an eternal validity, is inherently flawed. Ironically, Irish revisionist historians know this well, for they have subjected the Irish nationalist tradition to intensive, deconstructive analysis, fully exposing its contingencies, paradoxes, and inadequacies. However, although they have denigrated the importance and belittled the success of the United Irishmen's attempt to forge a unifying alternative, revisionist scholars generally have not subjected Ulster's Protestant/unionist tradition (or its "Scotch-Irish" counterpart in the United States) to the same close scrutiny.

Also ironically, in their skillful efforts to deconstruct—and to destabilize the popular understanding of—the history of only one of the Two Traditions, revisionist scholars inadvertently undermined the logic of their Manichean model. Revisionists have demonstrated, at least to their own satisfaction, that the Catholic/nationalist tradition was not really historically representative but merely an aberrantly successful concoction of hare-brained schemes by a handful of "fanatics" and "ideologues," whose goals and methods most Irish people regarded with indifference or repugnance. Not surprisingly, however, as a result we find ourselves left with only one tradition still standing: the Protestant/unionist/British tradition, which, in the absence of equally corrosive analysis, apparently becomes by default not merely the equal of its historical antagonist, but unchallengeably superior and singularly valid in the past, present, and future.

Yet we must assume that revisionist historians, like their scholarly adversaries, strive for objectivity and fairness. Thus, we should conclude that their relative inattention to the foibles and contradictions of the Protestant/unionist/British tradition is not a result of personal or political bias but, perhaps, instead a consequence of their enormous condescension toward that very tradition. Logically, the revisionist project must be based on the profoundly optimistic assumption that some or most of Ireland's Catholic nationalists are sufficiently reasonable to be open to revisionists' arguments concerning the ambiguous origins, unsavory methods, and unintended consequences of Irish nationalism. By contrast, the revisionists' comparative neglect of the

Protestant/unionist/British tradition suggests that they perceive its adherents to be so thoroughly *un*reasonable and intransigent as to be impervious to the results of equally objective scholarly research.

However, that surmise derives from, and exposes the fallacies of, a purely theoretical analysis. For surely, there are no pragmatic or ideological reasons why more historians and other scholars should not train their critical eyes on Ireland's Protestant/unionist tradition—as well as on the "Scotch-Irish" in America. Perhaps such research will uncover many different and often conflicting "traditions," and perhaps one or more of them may offer better signposts to a brighter future than the perpetual polarization to which the Two Traditions model threatens to consign us.

NOTES

1. Of course, there are significant exceptions to this rule; for example, studies by Peter Brooke, Sean Farrell, Peter Gibbon, David Hempton and Myrtle Hill, Ian McBride, David W. Miller, and the late Frank Wright discuss the 1800–1850 period. Nevertheless, the number of recent, critical analyses of the origins and early development of nineteenth-century Ulster unionism is far exceeded by the avalanche of similar works focusing on Irish nationalism.

2. For this research in a fuller form, see Kerby A. Miller, Arnold Schrier, Bruce D. Boling, and David Noel Doyle, *Irish Immigrants in the Land of Canaan: Letters and Memoirs from Colonial and Revolutionary America, 1675–1815* (New York: Oxford University Press, 2003). See also Miller, "'Scotch-Irish,' 'Black Irish,' and 'Real Irish': Emigrants and Identities in the Old South," in *The Irish Diaspora*, ed. Andy Bielenberg (Harlow, England: Longman, 2000); and Miller, "'Scotch-Irish Myths' and 'Irish' Identities in Eighteenth- and Nineteenth-Century America," in *New Perspectives on the Irish Diaspora*, ed. Charles Fanning (Carbondale: Southern Illinois University Press, 2000).

3. Patrick Griffin, *The People with No Name: Ireland's Ulster Scots, America's Scots Irish, and the Creation of a British Atlantic World, 1689–1764* (Princeton, NJ: Princeton University Press, 2001).

4. To be sure, Ulster Scots Agency spokespersons contend that Ulster Scots culture is a cross-community, even cross-border phenomenon, and they deny that its promotion is linked to a unionist political agenda. However, see C. McCall, "Political Transformation and the Reinvention of the Ulster Scots Identity and Culture," *Identities: Global Studies in Power and Culture* 9, no. 2 (January 2002): 197–218.

5. W. E. Vaughn and A. J. Fitzpatrick, eds., *Irish Historical Statistics: Population, 1821–1971* (Dublin: Royal Irish Academy, 1978).

6. James G. Leyburn, *The Scotch-Irish: A Social History* (Chapel Hill: University of North Carolina Press, 1962), 327–34.

7. Two scholarly works that *have* begun to address these questions are William L. Fisk, *The Scottish High Church Tradition in America: An Essay in Scotch-Irish Ethno-Religious History* (Lanham, MD: University Press of America, 1995); and Ian McBride, *Scripture Politics: Ulster Presbyterians and Irish Radicalism in the Late Eighteenth Century* (Oxford: Clarendon Press, 1998).

8. Leyburn, *Scotch-Irish*; see also David Stevenson, *Scottish Covenanters and Irish Confederates: Scottish-Irish Relations in the Mid–Seventeenth Century* (Belfast: Institute of Irish Studies, 1981). Ironically, although in the early eighteenth century Ulster-born Presbyterian students at

Glasgow and Edinburgh Universities were formally registered as "Scottus Hibernicus," in the frequent and occasionally violent conflicts between them and Scottish-born students and academic officials, they were denominated as "Irish" by both their critics and supporters—and often as "stupid Teagues" by the former.

9. See Miller et al., *Irish Immigrants in the Land of Canaan*, chapter 49.

10. See ibid., chapter 8; and Miller, "Revd James MacSparran's *America dissected* (1753): Eighteenth-Century Emigration and Constructions of 'Irishness,'" *History Ireland* 11, no. 4 (Winter 2003): 17–22.

11. Leyburn, *Scotch Irish*.

12. Richard J. Hooker, ed., *The Carolina Backcountry on the Eve of the Revolution: The Journal and Other Writings of Charles Woodmason, Anglican Itinerant* (Chapel Hill: University of North Carolina Press, 1953).

13. For example, *Memorial and Biographical Record of Turner, Lincoln, Union and Clay Counties* [South Dakota] (Chicago: George A. Ogle, 1897).

14. For example, Michael J. O'Brien, "The 'Scotch-Irish' Myth," *Journal of the American Irish Historical Society* 24 (1925): 142–53.

15. Miller et al., *Irish Immigrants in the Land of Canaan*, chapter 20.

16. David N. Doyle, *Ireland, Irishmen, and Revolutionary America, 1760–1820* (Dublin and Cork: Mercier Press, 1981), chapters 1–2; Thomas P. Power, "Converts," in *Endurance and Emergence: Catholics in Ireland in the Eighteenth Century*, ed. Thomas P. Power and Kevin Whelan (Blackrock, Co. Dublin: Irish Academic Press, 1990), 108–28. See also Desmond Bowen, *History and the Shaping of Irish Protestantism* (New York: Peter Lang, 1995), and Roger Blaney, *Presbyterianism and the Irish Language* (Belfast: Ulster Historical Foundation, 1996).

17. Doyle, *Ireland, Irishmen, and Revolutionary America*. Furthermore, from the 1730s the first and second Great Awakenings in America began the process whereby many Ulster Presbyterian immigrants, Irish migrant converts to Presbyterianism, and their American-born descendants were absorbed in the Baptist, Methodist, and other evangelical churches, thereby promoting the creation of the pan-Protestant "Scotch-Irish" identity discussed earlier.

18. John H. Campbell, *A History of the Friendly Sons of St. Patrick and of the Hibernian Society* (Philadelphia: Hibernian Society, 1982), and Richard C. Murphy and Lawrence J. Mannion, *History of the Society of the Friendly Sons of St. Patrick in the City of New York* (New York: The Society, 1962).

19. Miller et al., *Irish Immigrants in the Land of Canaan*, chapters 58 (Caldwell) and 64 (MacArthur). John Joyce's 1785 letter is reprinted in "Virginia in 1785," *Virginia Magazine of History and Biography* 23 (1915): 407–14.

20. The arguments in this and the following paragraphs are expanded in Miller et al., *Irish Immigrants in the Land of Canaan*, especially chapters 49 and 67.

21. Ironically, of course, the ancestors of most eighteenth-century Ulster Presbyterian emigrants to America had not resided in Northern Ireland in 1641; they were still in Scotland. Likewise, given the huge Scottish migration to Ulster in the 1690s and early 1700s, it is questionable how many later emigrants were descended from Derry's defenders in 1690, although virtually all claimed to be so.

22. Miller et al., *Irish Immigrants in the Land of Canaan*, chapters 49 (on Belknap, Dinsmoor, and Parker) and 67 (on Breckenridge and Bruce).

23. For example, I make these arguments in Kerby A. Miller, *Emigrants and Exiles: Ireland and the Irish Exodus to North America* (New York: Oxford University Press, 1985), chapters 2, 5, and 6.

24. Indeed, in the early 1800s, lower-class poverty and social conflict were endemic among

Protestants in east Ulster and Belfast itself. See Kerby A. Miller, "Belfast's First Bomb, 28 February 1816: Class Conflict and the Origins of Ulster Unionist Hegemony," *Éire-Ireland* 39, no. 1–2 (Spring/Summer 2004): 262–80.

25. For fuller data and their explication, see Miller et al., *Irish Immigrants in the Land of Canaan*, appendix 2 (with Liam Kennedy).

26. John Gamble, *Views of Society and Manners in the North of Ireland*. Reprint ed. (New York: AMS Press, 1981).

27. For example, see the letters of the Kerr and the McElderry brothers, in MIC 144/1 and in T. 2414 and MIC 26, respectively, in the Public Record Office of Northern Ireland, Belfast.

28. Kerby A. Miller and Bruce D. Boling, with Liam Kennedy, "The Famine's Scars: The Ulster and American Odyssey of William Murphy," *Éire-Ireland* 36, no. 1–2 (Spring/Summer 2001): 98–123.

SUGGESTED READING

William L. Fisk, *The Scottish High Church Tradition in America: An Essay in Scotch-Irish Ethno-Religious History* (Lanham, MD: University Press of America, 1995).

Patrick Griffin, *The People with No Name: Ireland's Ulster Scots, America's Scots Irish, and the Creation of a British Atlantic World, 1689–1764* (Princeton, NJ: Princeton University Press, 2001).

Maldwyn A. Jones, "The Scotch-Irish in British America," in *Strangers within the Realm*, ed. B. Bailyn and P. D. Morgan (Chapel Hill: University of North Carolina Press, 1991).

Kerby A. Miller, "'Scotch-Irish' Myths and 'Irish' Identities in Eighteenth- and Nineteenth-Century America," in *New Perspectives on the Irish Diaspora*, ed. Charles Fanning, 75–92 (Carbondale: Southern Illinois University Press, 2000).

Kerby A. Miller, "'Scotch-Irish,' 'Black Irish' and 'Real Irish': Emigrants and Identities in the Old South," in *The Irish Diaspora*, ed. Andy Bielenberg, 139–57 (Harlow, England: Longman, 2000).

Kerby A. Miller, Arnold Schrier, Bruce D. Boling, and David Noel Doyle, *Irish Immigrants in the Land of Canaan: Letters and Memoirs from Colonial and Revolutionary America, 1675–1815* (New York: Oxford University Press, 2003).

Chapter 7

Religious Rivalry and the Making of Irish-American Identity

Irene Whelan

The relationship between Irish ethnicity and religious affiliation in the United States has had a mixed history. Since the nineteenth century the popular assumption has been that the terms "Irish" and "Catholic" are virtually synonymous, if not organic. Yet the character of the "Irish" imprint in eighteenth-century North America was very largely a Protestant one, to the extent, in fact, that the pioneers of three of the country's great religious traditions—Presbyterians, Methodists, and Quakers—could all claim Ireland as their mother country.[1] In a recent U.S. census, over forty million citizens claimed Irish ancestry, but a majority of this number claimed a Protestant rather than a Catholic heritage. Clearly, a major shift had occurred between the mid–eighteenth and mid-nineteenth centuries in which the Protestant Irish connection was lost sight of and the Catholic one came to dominate. How can we account for this?

The key to the intensity of the Irish Catholic identity in the New World is to be found in the world they left behind. In the period immediately preceding the arrival of the first wave of Catholic immigration from Ireland in the 1820s and 1830s, the countries of the English-speaking North Atlantic were swept by a counterrevolutionary tide that was expressed through a revival of Protestant fundamentalism, which refashioned the civic and political landscape according to the moral principles of evangelical Christianity. Societies as different from one another as industrial New England and the Canadian Maritimes, Upper New York State and the plantation south, industrial Britain and the highlands and islands of Gaelic Scotland were all consumed by revivalist flames. Fueling the spread was an almost apocalyptic belief that evangelical Christianity afforded the most effective and, for some, the only foundation for political stability and civic morality in a world destabilized by the secularism and infidelity unleashed by the American and French Revolutions.[2]

Within this world, Ireland was exceptional in that its population was overwhelmingly Catholic. Recently incorporated into the United Kingdom by the union of 1800, it was a country that was halfway between a colony and a kingdom, conquered but scarcely conciliated, with a colonial aristocracy divided and terrified by the shadow of the republican rebellion of 1798 and a native peasantry that was sullen, frightened, and directionless after the fearful carnage of the bloody year of insurrection. It is hardly surprising in this climate that the central message of evangelical Christianity with its emphasis on social hierarchy and loyalty to church and king should have been embraced with particular fervor. Neither is it surprising that the evangelical prescription for peace in Ireland—that is, the imposition of Protestant moral values on the native Irish and their eventual absorption into the Protestant faith—should have been embraced by so many elements within the Irish Protestant world, particularly the landed aristocracy.

As a result of the ascendancy of counterrevolutionary religious revivalism, the first two decades of the nineteenth century witnessed a phenomenal surge in the Protestant mission to win control of the minds and hearts of the rising Catholic population.[3] The promoters of this movement, popularly known as the "New" or "Second Reformation," had good reasons for believing it might succeed. The hunger of the Catholic poor for education and improvement, the willingness of the landed classes to provide moral and financial support, the money made available from public and private sources in Britain, and not least the readiness of missionaries to use vernacular Irish for textbooks and preaching were all serious elements in its favor. The great stumbling block in its path, it need hardly be said, was the Catholic Church, an institution only recently free from the trammels of the penal code, with its own claim to leadership of the nation-in-waiting that was Catholic Ireland. During the years of the Napoleonic threat when the Pope was beholden to the support of a conservative Britain, caution was observed in any Catholic response to the global ambitions of missionary-minded Protestants. Once Napoleon was safely fettered on St. Helena, however, the tide quickly changed, and the results were soon evident in Ireland. In 1819 at the instigation of a letter from Cardinal Fontana of the Propaganda Fidei, both Daniel O'Connell and Rev. John McHale came out in open opposition to the claims of the evangelical mission in Ireland, charging that it was subversive of the authority of the Church and the national interests of the majority population.[4]

Catholic indignation at the supremacist intentions implicit in the Second Reformation crusade was quickly harnessed to the emancipation movement and found institutional expression in the Catholic Association, founded by Daniel O'Connell in 1823. The phenomenal success of this organization was a consequence of its manipulation of the machinery of constitutional government, especially the use of the popular press and the mass organization of popular support at the local level. In both of these areas the Catholic hierarchy and clergy played a fundamental role. Bishops like James Warren Doyle of Kildare and Leighlin (the celebrated "J.K.L.") and John MacHale of Tuam provided ideological and inspirational leadership in newspapers and printed pamphlets, and priests throughout the country used their influence at the local level to mobilize support for O'Connell's emancipation campaign. After an intense five-year struggle, the consequence of this campaign was the passage of the Catholic Relief Act of 1829.[5] In its wake the country was left almost completely polarized, with Catholics and liberal Protestants on the one side and fundamentalist Christians and conservative landlords on the other. For hard-line Protestants it meant that "popery" had replaced atheistical Jacobinism as the great enemy of individual freedom and constitutional government. The agents of Rome were now seen to be aligned with the forces of popular democracy to present the Protestant establishment of church and state with an even more alarming scenario—that of a belligerent majority population steeped in the anti-Protestant tradition of the post-Tridentine papacy and under the political leadership of the priests.

As the conflict between fundamentalist Protestants and politicized Catholics worked itself out during the course of the 1820s, the public in both Ireland and Britain was deluged with religious polemics that revitalized all the old arguments between Roman "orthodoxy" and Lutheran "heresy." As old arguments and reminders of the terror of bygone days were revitalized, new forms of propaganda were developed to present them to a mass audience. Religious fundamentalists showed themselves to be masters of the newest methods of propaganda. Newspapers, journals, and pamphlet literature all carried accounts of the triumphs of the missionary campaign and the persecution of Protestants. Catholic clergy were publicly called upon to defend their office and their faith; mass open-air meetings were organized in which teams of Protestant theologians confronted priests on subjects like state payment of the clergy, Luther's break with Rome, and so on. Preaching tours and controversial sermons were organized to educate Protestants about the dangers with which they were threatened, and Bible society meetings were used to whip up popular frenzy about the threat from Rome. Individuals who emerged as leaders (the most famous were often converts from Catholicism) carried the news to Britain and repeated the procedure there.[6]

The polarizing impact of religious controversy was quickly exported from Ireland. The ease with which it spread was an indicator that the evangelical world was more than ever a united one, characterized by an intense interchange of personnel and correspondence. This had been true in the late eighteenth century and even more in the increasingly missionary-minded atmosphere of the first decades of the nineteenth. Religious division was also a natural part of the baggage, which accompanied emigrants of both denominations. Protestants who believed they saw the specter of Catholic supremacy in the successes of O'Connell and the emancipation movement were leaving Ireland in the late 1820s and early 1830s. Like their Catholic counterparts driven by economic necessity, most were headed for an English-speaking Protestant destination, either Britain, Canada, or the United States. Once resettled, they tended to reproduce the divisions they had carried with them from home.[7]

If the decade of the 1820s witnessed the revitalization of traditional anti-Catholicism, the 1830s saw its evolution into a full-blown political ideology, which served to strengthen and empower the hegemonistic ambitions of evangelical Protestantism. Catholicism was held up as the antithesis of the evangelical worldview, itself a religious/political phenomenon possessed of a unitary vision of a perfect world based on the principles of Christianity, free-market economics, and parliamentary government. Implicit in this concept of a divinely ordained world was the notion that the independent citizen should be free from slavery in all its forms—whether the chattel slavery of the American south which the African-American race labored under, or the spiritual and psychological slavery imposed on the Irish by Rome. Catholicism, therefore, served as an opposition against which Protestants could define themselves: Catholics were everything Protestants were not—disloyal, slovenly, untrustworthy, sexually licentious, ignorant, ultimately slaves to Rome, and unworthy of participation in the public sphere.

The presence of the Catholic antithesis not only made Protestants more secure in their sense of identity, it also provided them with a mission and a sense of purpose: in the first instance to effect the destruction of Catholic influence in the Protestant world and in the second to liberate those in bondage to Rome. In Britain and Ireland this dual objective found concrete expression in organizations like the Protestant Association and the Brunswick Clubs (dedicated to the political and often the physical defense of the Protestant interests) and in an array of voluntary philanthropic societies. These societies were designed to provide both material and spiritual relief and ultimately to effect the conversion of Catholics. The two tended to be intimately linked. Anti-Catholic networks were organized around evangelical organizations in Ireland and Britain, and the pattern was repeated in the United States. They were all in close contact with what was happening in Ireland, and with one another.[8]

This form of politicized anti-Catholicism in close affiliation with philanthropy made its appearance in the United States in the 1820s and early 1830s. It coalesced with an almost revolutionary sweep of revivalism, which originated in the burned-over district of western New York State, an area then undergoing an especially intense burst of social and economic change driven by the commercialization of agriculture that followed the opening of the Erie Canal. The most visible expression of this new religiosity was the emphasis on the "New Measures" spearheaded by the Rev. Charles Grandison Finney of Rochester who promoted a return to the more severe and exacting practices of seventeenth-century Puritanism over and against the deism that had become dominant in the eighteenth century. The intensity of this phase of revivalism may be illustrated by the Rev. Finney's faith in the motto that the entire globe could be "saved" as a result of the flame lit in western New York State.[9]

The forceful leadership of dynamic evangelical preachers and their ability to reach a huge audience through the media of print and pulpit made this phase of the revival a mass movement of extraordinary proportions and influence. In the highly charged atmosphere generated by intense religious fervor, Catholicism was an ideal and opportune scapegoat to whip up and sustain popular emotion. The anti-Catholic theme was not new, but it was given new impetus in light of the contemporary political situation in Europe and especially in the British Isles. It was one thing to see the power of Rome expand in the counterrevolutionary atmosphere of post-Napoleonic Europe, the traditional Catholic heartland. But the triumph of Catholic claims in Ireland, with what looked to many like the support of the British government, appeared to hardline fundamentalists as a sign that the Antichrist was abroad and poised to infiltrate the citadel of Protestantism that was the United States. Conspiracy theories abounded and were promoted by the most respected and influential of revivalist leaders, including Samuel B. Morse (the founder of the telegraph) and Boston's most famous preacher, the Rev. Lyman Beecher. Both these men subscribed to a highly sensational conspiracy theory that a plot was being hatched in Vienna to flood the United States with Catholic immigrants from Europe to populate the expanding frontier in the Mississippi and Ohio Valleys and thus act as a spearhead to win the entire country for the pope.[10]

Saving the West from Catholic colonization became one of the stock themes in the hysteria over the perceived increase in Catholic power in the United States. Other issues included the battle over trusteeship (or lay control of Church property) and the strictures concerning the reading of the Protestant Bible in schools funded by public money. Publicity and propaganda fueled the public appetite for controversy on these issues. Already by the early 1830s the pattern that had taken shape in Ireland during the 1820s was to be seen throughout the eastern seaboard: there were organized controversies involving public debates that often lasted for days, newspaper exchanges, and sensationalist propaganda that depicted the Catholic threat in language deliberately designed to arouse hostility and even violence. The consequences were predictable. Cities that were point-of-entry and settlement locations for immigrants from Ireland—New York, Baltimore, Boston, and Philadelphia, in particular—became flashpoints of sectarian controversy that frequently broke into open violence. As the most popular port for immigrants from Ulster, both Catholic and Protestant, Philadelphia was marked by particularly intense sectarian discord, a situation that was exacerbated by the presence of the belligerently defensive Rev. John Hughes, perhaps the most able and dynamic advocate of Irish Catholic claims in the entire country. Boston was not far behind, especially after the notorious burning of the Ursuline convent in Charlestown in 1834, an event widely believed to have been instigated by the inflammatory sermons of Rev. Beecher.[11]

The convent-burning incident revealed the level of danger attendant upon the combination of mob passion inflamed by sensationalist propaganda and conspiracy theories and backed by the most powerful voices of the evangelical world. The prelude to the Charlestown incident was the dissemination of lurid sensationalist propaganda regarding the horrors of convent life, especially the sexual exploitation of young women. As the preacher at the center of the Boston revival and the progenitor of a remarkable family that practically defined American Protestantism in the Victorian period, it might have been expected that the Rev. Beecher would have appreciated the dangers of arousing popular passion over such a subject; far from taking up a position of detachment, he made the anti-Catholic platform a central plank of his reforming crusade, and his influence was such that his sermons were widely believed to have been responsible for fomenting the discord that led to the convent-burning incident. The revulsion that followed this attack on defenseless women and their wards did little to dampen his commitment to the anti-Catholic cause, and his subsequent career was characterized by active involvement in efforts to curtail the spread of Catholic power, especially with regard to immigration and public education.

At the center of the furor over the alleged immorality of nuns and priests was the commercial interest of popular journalism. Nothing sold pamphlets and newspapers as successfully as the salacious and lurid accounts of the imagined goings-on behind convent walls. In 1836, the public furor reached it apogee with the publication of Maria Monk's bestselling *Awful Disclosures of the Hotel Dieu Nunnery in Montreal*, an infamous calumny against the convent in question. No evil was too great and no perversion too unimaginable to attribute to the priests and nuns protected by the walls of their enclosed orders and the evil incarnate that was Rome. The scurrilous story was based on the revelations of a young fugitive nun who had allegedly been exposed to macabre horrors, including the execution of nuns who would not comply with the carnal demands of male clergy and the murder of the babies born to such unions. Although an investigation revealed that the Montreal convent was innocent of the alleged charges, the belief in the immorality practiced behind the walls of convents and monasteries continued to be a prime source of popular anti-Catholic prejudice and necessarily a great stimulant for the reading public.[12]

The effect of the sustained anti-Catholic crusade of the 1830s was to strengthen the resolve of bishops and priests to counteract the assaults upon the integrity of their church by defensive protectiveness and exemplary conduct. The first line of defense was obviously to combat the designs of proselytizers on the Catholic poor by providing alternative institutions for the care and support they so desperately needed. The construction of orphanages, dispensaries, hospitals, shelters, relief organizations, and, above all, schools and colleges thus became a priority for church leaders. A less tangible but no less significant effect was the insistence on strict morality, particularly sexual morality. The taunts of evangelical propagandists that the morally inferior nature of Catholicism was most evident in the sexual licentiousness of its representatives in religious orders intensified what was an already strong emphasis on exemplary personal conduct and the need to supervise the morals of their flocks.

For the nuns and priests who were in the vanguard of Catholic defense, good behavior and a strict moral code was the most effective argument against Protestant allegations of sexual licentiousness. The challenge demanded that they never descend to the baseness attributed to them by their critics and, more important, that they set an example to their followers to do likewise. This raising of the morality stakes had the effect of providing the Irish with an incentive for the expression of self-respect on the one hand and a fierce resolve to rely on their own educational and charitable institutions on the other. Both trends solidified the already deep-seated contempt toward the condescending charity of their persecutors. It enabled them to successfully resist the stereotyping that reduced them to filth, immorality, and fecklessness and to aim for superior conduct in personal morality—in other words, to develop a competitive attitude in the cultivation of habits relating to morality, personal living habits, and upward mobility. What was created was a mirror-image effect, whereby the Irish, largely through the instrument of the Catholic Church, took control of the agencies, and this allowed them to develop the skills and attitudes necessary to assimilate into mainstream society.

The most vulnerable elements in Irish America were newly arrived immigrants, and the protection of this sector became a prime consideration of Church leaders. The use of Irish religious orders such as the Christian Brothers and the Sisters of Mercy and Charity were the most likely agencies employed for this purpose. In most cases these new orders were products of the resurgence of Catholic power in Ireland and arrived in the United States with their mission already well defined. The Sisters of Mercy, in particular, were a sign of the times. Born in the sectarian maelstrom of the 1820s, the Mercy Order affords the most clear-cut example of the mirror-image effect at work.

At the time of the Mercy Order's founding in Dublin in 1829, many thought that it was a Protestant enterprise because of foundress Catherine McAuley's upper-class accent and manners and her insistence on "lack of ceremony" among her followers. In fact, McAuley was a product of a tradition that was by then going out of fashion. As the child of a mixed marriage, she was raised in the Catholic tradition of her mother's

In this 1844 satirical lithograph, James Gordon Bennett, the editor of the *New York Herald,* confronts John Hughes, the Roman Catholic bishop of New York. The nativist climate of the 1830s–1840s included a war of words in American newspapers and periodicals, as Protestants attacked "papist" theology and practice in print with a rabidness only matched by the burning of Catholic property around the country. Hughes didn't shy away from defending his faith; here he swings his crozier and tells Bennett, "With all the power of Holy Church will I assail thee, most reprobate and contemptible viper," as one of his Irish parishioners rejoins, "Let me have a shlap at him wid the shillaly!" (Library of Congress, Prints and Photographs Division, LC-USZ62-28015)

family while her brothers were brought up in the Church of Ireland tradition of their father. Orphaned at a young age, she grew up in the home of her Protestant uncle, where she experienced immediate contact with the bitter prejudice against Catholics that had become commonplace in the 1820s. Her exemplary personal conduct and the care she took of the uncle caused him not only to convert to Catholicism but also to bequeath his entire estate to her. This legacy gave her the means to found the Sisters of Mercy. Initially, she had in mind for her organization a deliberately Catholic imitation of a Protestant ladies' charitable organization. Her sisterhood was several years in existence before it coalesced into the Mercy Order, with a formal system of rules and official sanction from Rome.[13]

The mission of the Mercy sisters was to educate Catholic girls and to care for and nurse the poor. Almost from the beginning, the order enjoyed phenomenal success in Ireland, not least because of the strong support of well-to-do Catholics who were anxious to combat the effects of evangelical missions among the poor. Concurrent with its phenomenal growth in Ireland was its expansion into the world of the Irish Catholic diaspora in Britain, Canada, and especially the United States. The order appealed to high-minded, usually well-to-do young women, who wished to dedicate their lives to useful labor among the most needy and neglected—an attractive and self-validating prospect for those in search of a worthy vocation in life. Like the Presentation and Charity sisters, the Mercy Order attracted women with money and property who dedicated their spiritual and material resources to the spread of their institution and opened exciting new avenues for the most energetic and ambitious of Irish women to serve their community at home and abroad.[14]

The open and energetic campaign by the Irish Catholic clergy to counter the assault on the integrity of their church and the inroads of evangelical missionaries on their congregations meant that denominational relations became more polarized as the century advanced. In the early 1840s the standoff was exacerbated by the prospect that the Westminster government was poised to bow to the political pressure of the Irish Catholic lobby in parliament and by granting an increase in its endowment to the Catholic seminary at Maynooth. The effect on the American Protestant world was immediate and extreme: violent rioting broke out in Philadelphia in 1844 and threatened to spread to New York.[15] Bishop John Hughes (who had earned his reputation in strife-torn Philadelphia) warned that if a Catholic church building in New York was touched the city could become a "Second Moscow," and he was not making an idle threat. Like Catherine McAuley, Hughes was a product of the particular circumstances of his Irish background. The combativeness and assertiveness he displayed on behalf of Catholic defense was a product of the sectarian cockpit that was Ulster in the early nineteenth century; the traits that went into the making of the famous "Dagger John" were not exclusively products of the New World environment.

No figure in the history of Irish-America in the nineteenth century illustrated the relationship between religion and the group survival of the Catholic Irish quite so effectively as John Hughes. With his transfer to New York in 1838, the full-blown element of Catholic defense was set in place in the most important diocese in the country. In this position of strength, Hughes more than fulfilled the promise he had shown as a stalwart of Catholic claims in Philadelphia. Under his watch, in a pattern that would be repeated in cities across the country, a proliferation of churches, schools, and colleges spread across Manhattan and the rapidly expanding surrounding cities of Brooklyn and Yonkers. Based on the parish system and centered on the church and parochial house, Catholic communities sprouted convents and monasteries; elementary and secondary schools; and orphanages, hospitals, community halls, and voluntary welfare agencies run by organizations like the Society of St. Vincent de Paul. The backbone of the system was the range of colleges and universities founded to train the legions of teachers, nurses, and administrators needed to keep the system in operation. Among the institutions that were part of the legacy of Hughes's tenure in New York were Fordham University, Manhattan College, the College of Mount St. Vincent, and Manhattanville College of the Sacred Heart.[16]

Within a decade of Hughes's transfer to New York in 1838, Ireland was hit with the devastating Great Famine, which was to have a cataclysmic effect on the Irish presence in the United States. Apart from turning the flood of Irish immigration to the United States into a torrent, the famine catastrophe and the record of denominational relations in Ireland during the period had enormous consequence for the tone of Catholicism across the Atlantic. With the advent of mass starvation consequent upon the failure of the potato crop and the inadequacy of relief measures in 1846, the crusade to convert the Catholic poor took an especially vicious turn. Driven by the millennial belief that the Famine was the hand of providence, the most extreme wing of the Irish evangelical world, backed by supporters in England, undertook a campaign to turn conditions in Ireland to their advantage by exploiting the vulnerability of the starving poor in the drive to make converts. "Souperism" as it was known (after the soup dispensed by missionaries in return, allegedly, for apostasy but most likely to children who attended proselytizing schools in the hopes of being fed) became widespread during the Famine years, especially in the hardest-hit western counties where Catholic manpower was scarce.

At the height of the Famine, mass conversions were being reported in Galway and Mayo, and the evangelical press was broadcasting the rout of popery in the west and the imminent collapse of the entire forces of the papacy in Ireland. For the Catholic hierarchy and clergy long accustomed to defending their Church and congregation against the encroachments of evangelical missionaries, the blatancy of what had been attempted during the Famine years laid bare the ambitions of the evangelical mission in a manner that could not be ignored.[17]

The Church emerged from the crisis years of famine with an attitude of hardened resolution toward the control of the religious affairs of its followers, particularly those that pertained to devotional practices, education, and morality. The post-Famine period saw an immense increase in the new religiosity spawned by revitalized Catholicism. The use of parish missions to introduce new devotional practices became widespread. Missions organized by the Jesuits, Redemptorists and Vincentians swept through the country in the 1850s and 1860s, particularly in the counties west of the Shannon River where proselytism had been most intense during the famine years. This was also the area of highest emigration to the United States, which continued into the 1920s.[18]

The effects of what has been called the "devotional revolution" meant that those emigrants who left Ireland in the post-Famine period were increasingly locked into the priest–people relationship, and often the only institutional structure they could look to for support and cohesion was the Catholic Church. The support and maintenance of their parish communities therefore became a prime objective of Irish immigrants as they moved up the social ladder. The system was self-contained and self-perpetuating since resources were channeled back to Ireland to fund further emigration, and new arrivals were more likely to succeed in an environment where the ground had been prepared for them to some extent. The system was particularly advantageous for women, who generally equaled and at times outnumbered men, and the majority of whom were obliged to emigrate alone. This was especially the case for those destined for careers in religious orders. For ambitious Irish girls educated by the Mercy and Charity Orders with little hope for successful careers at home, nursing and teaching careers as nuns in the United States was just about the highest career goal they could realistically aspire to.

By the 1860s the Irish had made an institution of the Catholic Church in the United States, and this perfectly suited their needs as an immigrant group facing discrimination in everything from housing to education and employment. The Irish controlled the Catholic hierarchy at the expense of other immigrant groups like the

Germans and later the Italians. By the last third of the century the Irish Catholic world in America was sufficiently entrenched to consider itself entitled to its own piece of the establishment pie. This proclivity was nowhere more forcefully expressed than in the mirroring of the "manifest destiny" syndrome of the Protestant establishment.[19]

According to this line of thought, the Irish were endowed by God with their own particular version of a providential mission. Because of their loyalty to the faith sustained through centuries of persecution they were now an elect, especially chosen to spread the Word of God. The place they occupied in the contemporary world—that of an English-speaking Catholic people forcibly dispersed from their traditional homeland into a world that was rapidly being globalized under the aegis of the British political and American mercantile empires—appeared to suggest that a divine plan was under way. The timing could only have been providential. As the oldest, largest, and most universal of the Christian churches, the Roman Catholic was now the claimant of the only acceptable answer to the problems of modernity: the materialism of the industrial capitalist order had failed people spiritually, and the godlessness of the socialist left was equally bankrupt.

It remained for the world to discover the ancient truths of the Catholic faith, and it was the designated mission of the Irish to lead them to this discovery. This was the "spiritual empire" thesis whereby the Irish were to carve for themselves an empire of the spirit to rival the political and mercantile empire of the British. It served to provide a unique group identity: that the Irish were a people with a special mission in the world whose role was designated by God.

The "spiritual empire" theory conferred an ideological coherence on the identity of Catholic Irish America that is difficult to overestimate. Backed by the institutional framework of the Church, it enabled Irish Catholics to transcend the social and racial inferiority attributed to them by the nativist establishment and to make a truly impressive contribution to national life. By maintaining their own independent educational structure, they were inspired to make of their schools and colleges the equivalent of the Protestant institutions. The exclusiveness of the system was maintained by funneling graduates from elementary through preparatory schools and into colleges and universities; this provided for an independent and alternative educational structure that was at once in opposition to the establishment and collusive with it.

What it meant in real terms was that when the Irish reached the point where they were in a position to breach the walls of the white-collar professional world, they were equal to the task. As the products of the Catholic educational system they were disciplined, obedient, and conservative—and eager to put their skills and ambitions to good account. And, it need hardly be said, they were literate, numerate, and able to hold their own when it came to the skills so beloved of the traditional American intellectual establishment, such as the knowledge of Greek and Latin. The protection and support afforded by the institutional might of the Catholic Church meant that they did not combat discrimination as much as sidestep or leap over it, all the while preserving a strong sense of cultural and ethnic identity. A vital element in maintaining continuity was the constant stream of new immigrants from Ireland, particularly abundant in the teaching orders, who instilled values acquired in Ireland into their second- and third-generation pupils.

The subject of how the Irish assimilated so successfully into the American main-stream, how they "became white," has been a topical question in recent years.[20] But the question, as Peter Quinn has so rightly posited, is not how they "became white" but how they stayed "Irish" for so long.[21] This can only be understood within the context of the religion-based ideological cold war, which spanned the nineteenth century. With the mass influx of Catholic Irish into the United States, this ideological standoff born out of the particular colonial condition in Ireland merely shifted gear to work itself out on a much larger canvas in the Unites States.

The preservation of the Catholic and Irish identity did not come without a price. The self-protective machinery of embattled Catholicism made Irish-Americans at one and the same time deeply conservative and uncomfortable with either self-criticism or self-expression. Dirty linen was kept in house because of the abiding fear that criticism of either social or religious affairs would be used against them; grievances with internal matters were not aired in the face of one's enemies and detractors, so they were covered over, denied, or drowned in alcohol.[22] In one of the more tragic legacies of Irish America, "silence" became one of the hallmarks of a people famed for vivac-ity, loquaciousness, and good humor. Some twentieth-century critics would go so far as to suggest that silence is *the* dominating characteristic of Irish-Americans, a people who, with the towering exception of Eugene O'Neill, have rarely found their voice in either literature or history.[23] Whether this is a uniquely Irish condition is open to de-bate; silence has ever and always been the hallmark of the oppressed and dispersed.

What is undeniable is that Irish-American phobia about evaluating or confronting their experiences as a particular ethnic group is characterized by certain easily iden-tifiable and deep-seated sensitivities: one is an abhorrence of confronting the truth about the poverty and ignorance from which they had arisen, and the other is an almost visceral intolerance of ridicule or criticism directed at the Catholic faith. The depth of this sensitivity was well illustrated by the widespread discomfort of many Irish-Americans over Frank McCourt's stripping the mask of poverty and clerical hypocrisy in his famous book about his childhood in Limerick. Among the most common negative responses of Irish-Americans to the revelations of McCourt was the opinion that he was exaggerating the poverty and misery of those at the lower end of the social scale. Even if things had been this bad, the author's candid revelations were unseemly; obscene poverty of this kind was best forgotten. Implicit in the opin-ion of those who reacted negatively to McCourt was the sense that to complain or question was to let down the side, to let the eyes of a hostile world look in on matters that were shameful and best kept out of sight because ultimately they would serve to vindicate all that the enemies of the Catholic Irish had been saying for generations.

Similarly, the highlighting of the more unsavory aspects of clerical control risked jeopardizing all the good related to the system. It betrayed the solidarity between priest and people and gave the lie to the genuine sense of indebtedness to the nuns and priests and brothers who had given so freely of their time and energy to educate and minister to their people, and without whom, at worst, the Irish might not have survived as a distinct community or, at best, would have remained as a permanent underclass.

The success with which the Church "processed" the Irish as solid citizens and members of the business and the professions made the Irish Catholic world an integral part of American society by the end of the nineteenth century. The growing power and respectability of the Church went hand in hand with the rise of the Irish in politics and the professions. In spite of this glowing record, the old anti-Catholic syndrome nevertheless took a long time to die and could always be reliably dredged up as a weapon of ideological consequence if the circumstances were favorable. The political prospects of New York governor, Al Smith, for example, were destroyed by an adept playing of the anti-Catholic card in the presidential race of 1928. Even the presidential campaign of John F. Kennedy was marked by a similar threat.[24]

But the irony was that the nuns and priests who were the backbone of the Catholic system came to be seen almost as moral arbiters and exemplars, an element that was looked to as the very enshrinement of peace, order, sound morals, and good government. This may have reflected the ease with which the political fallout from the cold war allowed Catholics to close ranks with the patriotic defenders of traditional American freedoms. But equally, it may be seen as a testimony to the good account given, in business, government, and the professions, by the millions of Irish Americans that were products of Catholic schools and colleges.

In the face of the upward march of the Catholic Irish that spanned the nineteenth and twentieth centuries, what was the fate of the Protestant Irish connection? Protestant immigration did not cease in the eighteenth century, but we know little or nothing about those who left after 1800. What was their role in the sustained anti-Catholic crusade of the nineteenth century? What, if any, was the connection between Protestant fundamentalism in the United States and its growth in Ulster, a region said to boast more saved Christians to the square mile than anywhere else on earth? Was there a connection between the great revival of 1857–8 in the United States and the Year of Grace in Ulster in 1859 when the province was swept by one of the most intense revivalist experiences in the modern world? These are questions we simply do not have answers for. Links have always existed between the American Bible belt and Northern Ireland, but except for incidents like the Rev. Ian Paisley's acquisition of a doctoral degree from Bob Jones University, they are rarely mentioned in the media coverage of that troubled province.

Equally submerged are the links with the liberal Protestants who fled Ireland after 1798 and made such enormous contributions to the development of the republic in the early years of the new century.[25] The bicentenary commemorations of the 1798 rebellion went some distance along the road of resurrecting the memory of men like Thomas Addis Emmet and William Sampson. But their place in the pantheon of Irish heroes is most likely to be that of "honorary Catholics"—that is, Protestants who perceived the rightness of the Catholic cause and joined ranks in patriotic sympathy —rather than enlightenment-inspired devotees of Thomas Jefferson's ideas on the separation of church and state or the idea of a virtuous republic as in Rousseau and Robespierre.

Irish republicanism, while it always found fertile soil for sympathy and support in the United States, never enjoyed an easy or harmonious relationship with the high command of the Irish Catholic clerical world. Republicanism tended to be the preserve of immigrants born in Ireland or their first-generation offspring, as opposed to the third- or fourth-generation assimilated and college-educated Irish-Americans. It was unlikely that the intellectual cream of Irish-America found much sympathy for the enlightenment philosophy at the great Catholic institutions where they received their higher education. When it came to the training they received in moral philosophy and politics, Thomas Aquinas and St. Augustine were much more likely to have been the models held up for emulation, as opposed to Rousseau and Jefferson or Theobold Wolfe Tone and Robert Emmet.

The Protestant Irish also had the additional problem of nomenclature when it came to identity and ethnic origins. The stereotyping and demonizing of the Catholic Irish by the exponents of the anti-Catholic crusade meant that "Irish" was an ethnic appellation not desirable to Protestants. Hence the emergence of the hyphenated Protestant, a process whereby a people who were proud (sometimes exaggeratedly so) to be known as "Irish" in the eighteenth century (when their Catholic countrymen were "natives" or "papists") became the Anglo-Irish in Ireland and the Scots-Irish in America in the nineteenth.[26] On the surface of American culture, the equation of Irish and Catholic is a standing testimony to the success of religious division in effecting the destruction of the inclusive ideal of subsuming denominational differences under the common name of Irishman.

NOTES

1. Francis Makemie (1658–1708), popularly known as the Father of American Presbyterianism, was a native of Rathmelton in County Donegal, Ireland; William Penn (1644–1718), who established the Quaker movement in the American colonies, had strong Irish connections. His mother was a native of County Clare, and his father held substantial property in Ireland, which William had managed as a young man. Barbara Heck (1734–1804) and Philip Embury (1728–75), known as the founders of American Methodism, were members of the Palatine colony of West Limerick who emigrated from the village of Ballingrane to New York in 1760.

2. Mark A. Noll, "Revolution and the Rise of Evangelical Social Influence in North Atlantic Societies," in *Evangelicalism: Comparative Studies of Popular Protestantism in North America, the British Isles, and Beyond, 1700–1900*, ed. Mark A. Noll, David W. Bebbington, and George Rawlyk (Oxford: Oxford University Press, 1994), 113–36.

3. Stewart J. Brown, "The New Reformation Movement in the Church of Ireland, 1801–29," in *Piety and Power in Ireland: Essays in Honour of Emmet Larkin*, ed. S. J. Brown and D. W. Miller (Belfast: Institute of Irish Studies, Queen's University of Belfast, 2000), 180–208.

4. The particular object of O'Connell's and MacHale's criticisms was the Kildare Place Society, an organization originally founded for the express purpose of providing an education acceptable to Catholics. Beginning in 1816, it was the recipient of government funds to expand its system. The decision of the board to deploy those funds among more overtly proselytizing organizations (particularly the London Hibernian Society) was a reflection of the ascendancy of evangelical opinion among its members. O'Connell resigned from the society over this issue, and the debate was given a national forum in the famous *Hierophilus Letters* (1821–3) of Rev. John MacHale, which drew national attention to the ambitions of the evangelical movement in Ireland.

5. Fergus O'Ferrall, *Catholic Emancipation: Daniel O'Connell and the Birth of Irish Democracy, 1820–30* (Dublin: Gill and Macmillan, 1985), 114–257.

6. See Stewart J. Brown, "Second Reformation: The Struggle for the Religion of Ireland, 1822–33" in *The National Churches of England, Ireland and Scotland, 1801–1846* (Oxford: Oxford University Press, 2002), 94–167.

7. For an account of emigration from Ireland in the decades immediately preceding the potato famine, see Kerby A. Miller, *Emigrants and Exiles: Ireland and the Irish Exodus to North America* (Oxford: Oxford University Press, 1985), 193–279.

8. John Wolffe, "Anti-Catholicism in Britain and the United States, 1820–60" in *Evangelicalism: Comparative Studies of Popular Protestantism in North America, the British Isles, and Beyond, 1700–1900*, ed. Mark A. Noll, David W. Bebbington, and George Rawlyk (Oxford: Oxford University Press, 1994), 113–36.

9. The social context in which the movement led by the Rev. Finney developed is described in Paul Johnson, *A Shopkeeper's Millennium: Society and Revivals in Rochester, New York, 1815–37* (New York: Hill and Wang, 1978).

10. Jenny Franchot, *Roads to Rome: The Antebellum Protestant Encounter with Catholicism* (Berkeley: University of California Press, 1994), 99–100.

11. Nancy Lusignan Schultz, *Fire and Roses: The Burning of the Charlestown Convent, 1834* (New York: Free Press, 2000).

12. For an account of the Maria Monk story, particularly its role as a stimulant of tabloid journalism in the mid–nineteenth century, see Rebecca Sullivan, "A Wayward from the Wilderness: Maria Monk's *Awful Disclosures* and the Feminization of Lower Canada in the Nineteenth Century," *Essays on Canadian Writing* 62 (Fall 1997): 201–22.

13. The career of Catherine McAuley and the early years of the Mercy Order are considered in Mary C. Sullivan, *Catherine McAuley and the Tradition of Mercy* (Dublin: Four Courts, 1995).

14. Mary Peckham Magray, *The Transforming Power of the Nuns: Women, Religion, and Cultural Change in Ireland, 1750–1900* (Oxford: Oxford University Press, 1998).

15. Michael Feldberg, *The Philadelphia Riots of 1844: A Study of Ethnic Conflict* (Westport, CT: Greenwood Press, 1975).

16. The career of Archbishop Hughes is covered in Richard Shaw, *Dagger John: The Unquiet Life and Times of Archbishop John Hughes of New York* (New York: Paulist Press, 1977).

17. Irene Whelan, "The Stigma of Souperism," in *The Great Irish Famine*, ed. Cathal Poirteir (Cork: Mercier Press, 1995), 135–54.

18. Emmet Larkin, "The Devotional Revolution in Ireland, 1850–75," *American Historical Review* 77 (1972): 625–52. Larkin's famous thesis on the "devotional revolution" of the post-famine period, while it has produced much discussion and some revision over the years, has maintained its usefulness as a key to understanding Irish society in the latter half of the nineteenth century. For a critique of the Larkin thesis, see Thomas G. McGrath, "The Tridentine Evolution of Modern Irish Catholicism, 1563–1962: A Re-Examination of the 'Devotional Revolution,'" *Recusant History* 20, no. 4 (October 1991): 512–23.

19. Among the most forceful exponents of this doctrine was Bishop John Lancaster Spalding (1840–1916) of Peoria, Illinois, whose *Religious Mission of the Irish People and Catholic Colonization* (1880) was one of the most influential and widely read tracts among the Irish-American community.

20. Noel Ignatiev, *How the Irish Became White* (New York: Routledge, 1995).

21. Peter Quinn, "How the Irish Stayed Irish," *America* 174, no. 9 (March 16, 1996): 14–19.

22. Miller, *Emigrants and Exiles*, 498–9.

23. For a valuable commentary on the "silence" syndrome in Irish-American history, see Peter Quinn's contribution, "Introduction: An Interpretation of Silences," *Eire-Ireland* 32 (Spring 1997): 7–19.

24. Kevin Kenny, *The American Irish* (New York: Longman, 2000), 218–9, 244–5.

25. Exceptions to this are David N. Doyle, *Ireland, Irishmen and Revolutionary America, 1780–1980* (Dublin: Mercier Press, 1981), and, more recently, David Wilson, *United Irishmen, United States: Immigrant Radicals in the Early Republic* (Ithaca, NY: Cornell University Press, 1998). Both examine the contribution of Protestant leaders who fled Ireland in the aftermath of the 1798 insurrection.

26. The historiography of the Scots-Irish has fared better in recent years, particularly with the publication of a magisterial collection of primary documents by Kerby Miller et al., *Irish Immigrants in the Land of Canaan: Letters and Memoirs from Colonial and Revolutionary America, 1675–1815* (Oxford: Oxford University Press, 2003). Conferences such as those organized by the Ulster-American Heritage Symposium also testify to the growing interest in the transatlantic connections of the Scots-Irish.

SUGGESTED READING

S. J. Brown and D. W. Miller, *Piety and Power in Ireland: Essays in Honour of Emmet Larkin* (Belfast: Institute of Irish Studies: Queen's University of Belfast, 2000).

Michael Feldberg, *The Philadelphia Riots of 1844: A Study of Ethnic Conflict* (Westport, CT: Greenwood Press, 1975).

Jenny Franchot, *Roads to Rome: The Antebellum Protestant Encounter with Catholicism* (Berkeley: University of California Press, 1994).

David Montgomery, "The Shuttle and the Cross: Weavers and Artisans in the Kensington Riots of 1844," *Journal of Social History* 5 (1972): 411–46.

Mark A. Noll, David W. Bebbington, and George Rawlyk, *Evangelicalism: Comparative Studies of Popular Protestantism in North America, the British Isles, and Beyond, 1700–1900* (Oxford: Oxford University Press, 1994).

Chapter 8

Address to the Ulster-Irish Society of New York, 1939

Henry Noble MacCracken

Mr. Goudy, President Stitt and member of the Ulster-Irish Society, and friends:

Forty-three years ago, in Harrisburg, Pa., my father, then Chancellor of New York University, made an address before the Scotch-Irish Society of America, on the subject "The Scotch-Irish American, what manner of man is he?" To him I owe my interest and love for the Irish of Ulster, and my pride in their leadership in American life. To his memory I raise my glass, and in his name accept with gratitude your medal.

The Scotch Irish, or as you call him, the Ulster Irish, has identified himself with his new country, America, more deeply than any but the first immigrant group. To begin with, he spoke the English language in its greatest purity, as it should be spoken, with strong, pure vowels, with an *r* that trilled and rolled on the tip of the tongue. His voice, clarified and fortified by a gargle of his own manufacture and of great potency in the stimulation of speech, rang full and true, not strangled at its roots by London fog.

He brought with him not only his gargle, but his songs and dances, his lilts and reels, his myths and legends, riddles and kissing games, weather wisdom and proverbs, his witches and charms; these are now the folklore of America, changed like his speech into the truest American quality. Though driven by oppression from his home in Ulster, he carried their memory with him, and planted them in the new soil. So we have Londonderry in New Hampshire and Antrim in Ohio, and Donegal and Armagh in Pennsylvania. In my own county, we have Hibernia, and I live on the old Livingston patent, while across the river are the twin counties of Ulster and Orange—no mistaking those names—flanked as they are by Sullivan and Montgomery counties.

The planting of the Ulster Irish is an oft-told tale familiar to this audience. I will not repeat it, except to point out that the Ulstermen sought the hills from Belfast, Maine, to Scottsboro, Alabama; that they bore the brunt of the Colonial frontier wars; that they fiercely resented the neglect of their needs by tidewater governments; and that they took part in the Revolution with a great determination to paddle their own canoe. Their chief line of migration to the west was down the Susquehanna, up the valley of the Shenandoah, through Cumberland Gap, and down the Tennessee. I do not know how my own great-grandfather went from Sunbury in Pennsylvania, but I know you will find MacCrackens scattered all along this trail—in Pennsylvania, Virginia, the Carolinas, Tennessee, and Kentucky—until at last the Tennessee River fronts the Ohio in McCracken County, at Paducah. I know, too, that there were McCrackens in the first shipload that landed in Maine, in 1735.

There is nothing more remarkable in all history than this vast swarming from a few little counties in a tiny corner of a small island, unless it be the Greeks spreading over Persia and the Orient. But the Greeks were an army of conquest, the Irish of Ulster poor farmers. No wonder people ask and ask again: what manner of men were these that so multiplied and spread over a million of miles, to stamp their culture in succeeding generations of settlers?

I will take a comparison from Ulster itself. On its north coast, a coast that is really wild and rockbound as Cape Cod is not, you come to the northern edge of County Antrim, and there you will find that wonder of the world, the Giants' Causeway. By some vast pressure of subterranean forces, ages ago, streams of lava were forced in jets to the light of day, and there under tremendous and regular pressure they hardened into marvelous columns. They are all six-sided piers, except for a few deviants of three, or seven, or nine; and there for ages they have stood, defying the waves and winds.

Now the Ulster Irish are like those columns of the Giants' Causeway. Their character was formed under the fire of suffering and starvation. Their resistance to tyranny created a terrible pressure, and the streams of families that survived lived in that pressure. When the light of day came, and passions cooled, the Ulster Presbyterians cooled off in hexagonal formation that has resisted every effort to change them. It is these six sides of their nature that have stood fast and made them the men they are.

These six sides or facets, or planes of power, are these: religion, education, government, industry, invention, philanthropy.

Of religion I have no need to say but a word. The Ulster-Irish sent ministers to America in every family. In the very heart of the wilderness they planted their congregations. If their religion was a little stern and without art, let you remember the privations in Ulster from which these folks had come. Yet it was a real religion. My father in his speech quotes three epitaphs of a father and two sons: "God, thou art my God; Jehovah first; I will go unto God, my exceeding joy. God shall save me." There was pith and substance in such a personal religion.

And with religion went education. Children learned Webster's spelling book, but they read McGuffey's Readers. The Irish schoolmaster licked the learning into the youth of the land. Even as late as my father's time, I recall his telling how, in what was then practically frontier in southern Ohio, he was confronted with rebellion in a village school. So he and the other teacher, a schoolmarm, divided up the whole school, and while he thrashed the boys she thrashed the girls, until the whole school had been disciplined and order restored. My grandfather had been a teacher, too, and taught school in a shed in his own backyard. My grandmother is credited with founding one of the earliest western women's colleges.

At every stage along the Ulster-Irish trail, a college has sprung up, like the orchards of Johnny Appleseed as he journeyed the same way. The American college is of Scots and Irish origin, with its trustees, its chapels, its loyal alumni, and its emphasis on life and character.

But the Irish Presbyterians were argufiers, tough-minded men. They wrestled over their sermons and liked exhausting argument. They sat long over church government. And so dominie and minister and session governed the frontier with as strong hands as they could. Minister, elders, and sessions easily became president, senators, and representatives, while the learned domines sat as Supreme Court. Presbytery and Synod were synonymous with county and state, while the General Assembly was a very good model for the Electoral College. So, at least, some students of our Constitution have contended; though it is only a part of the truth. What is true is this: that the Ulster Irish have furnished to the American government, in every office, groups of men of distinction out of all proportion to their numerical share of the people. Andrew Jackson and Stonewall Jackson, U.S. Grant and Woodrow Wilson, John C. Calhoun and Andrew Johnson—every state of opinion, but many strong men.

Religion, education, and government: on all these the Ulster Irish laid strong hands and wrought mightily. But even more significant were the contributions to industry and to invention. No wonder that in his westward trek he stopped to invent the harvester that made the great western farms realities. No wonder that the heavy industries fell into his hands. His energy was really prodigious. The forests fell, the stumps were pulled, the rivers stemmed. For this his life at sea in herring fishing, his weaving, and his hard work in stony fields had prepared him. But only the continuation of stern discipline, trained intelligence, and an outward pressure of opportunity equal to the repressive tyranny of eighteenth-century Ulster could have brought it about.

And lastly, philanthropy, that amazing trait of the American. The restless Ulster Irish, whose energy and training had brought rich rewards in the early harvest from American soil, had nothing left of the close thrift of his forebears in Ireland, that made them count every penny. He scattered millions with lavish hand, for churches, hospitals, colleges, libraries, sided powerfully by his brother Scots.

For two hundred years great waves of migration have beat against this six-planed column of basalt. Teuton and Slav, Latin and Jew have come. They have not essentially changed the nature of the American, as he crystallized from the Ulster Irish mold under the pressure of the great settlement. He still believes that religion and education form the bases of government. Forced in Ireland to choose between state and Church, he chose the Church but reserved his claim in government until he could assert it strongly in his new land. Inured to privation in Ulster, he did not shrink from the hardships of the frontier. Coming from a people not primitive, but on the contrary of standards of living high for the time, well-read in at least one book, the Bible, these frontiersmen demanded ministers of a metaphysical disposition, interested in debate and discussion. To keep up the supply in the next generation, log cabin schools were founded that soon became colleges.

Now, in all modesty, it is necessary to admit that the Ulster Irish did not discover America; that the English settlers outnumbered them about eight to one; that others came from Ireland's center and west, from Scotland, Germany, Sweden, and Holland, to make up our population. The Ulster Irish have no monopoly of any of the characteristics I have described. All honor to them. But, modesty aside, we celebrate tonight the Ulster-Irish Americans, and we are proud of the manner of man that history records him to be. To the Ulster Irish!

Chapter 9

American-Irish Nationalism

Kevin Kenny

Since at least the seventeenth century, all or part of Ireland has been under British rule. In the 1780s, Ireland achieved its own autonomous parliament, though still under ultimate British control. From 1801 to 1921, the country was ruled directly from London, with Irish representatives sitting in the British Parliament. Twenty-six Irish counties achieved their independence in 1921, but six counties remained under British control as the new state of Northern Ireland, which continues to exist today. Over the last two centuries, from the United Irishmen's insurrection of 1798 to the Belfast peace agreement of 1998, Irish men and women on both sides of the Atlantic have formed nationalist movements to win freedom for Ireland. These movements favored two principal approaches: constitutional nationalism, which sought greater autonomy for Ireland within the British Empire through gradual, peaceful, change; and physical force republicanism, which insisted on outright independence by whatever means necessary. These two separate if sometimes overlapping ideologies provide the key to understanding the history of nationalism, not only in Ireland but also in Irish America. The American Irish founded organizations dedicated to the liberation of their homeland wherever they settled in America, thereby giving Irish nationalism a critical American dimension.

From the United Irishmen to Young Ireland

The origins of Irish nationalism, on both sides of the Atlantic, can be traced to the republican movements of the 1790s. Ireland at this time had its own parliament, with autonomy over local affairs. But the United Irishmen, led by Theobald Wolfe Tone (1763–1798), wanted a fully independent republic. Irish republican clubs, including the American Society of United Irishmen, were formed in the United States in the 1790s, supporting Thomas Jefferson against his Federalist opponents. When the United Irishmen's insurrection of 1798 was crushed, many prominent Irish republicans came to the United States as political exiles, among them Thomas Addis Emmet (1764–1827), William MacNeven (1763–1841), and William Sampson (1764–1836). The insurrection was followed by the Act of Union of 1800, which abolished the Irish parliament and imposed direct rule from London.

During the first half of the nineteenth century, the primary aim of the Irish nationalist movement was to abolish the Act of Union. The movement was led by Daniel

O'Connell (1775–1847), one of the chief architects of Irish constitutional nationalism. O'Connell's goal was autonomy within the union of Great Britain and Ireland rather than full independence. His methods were always peaceful, never violent; moral persuasion through mass political agitation, he believed, could be used to force the British to give Ireland greater autonomy. The repeal movement attracted considerable support in the United States in the early 1840s, giving rise to the first major Irish nationalist movement on American soil. But American repealers turned against O'Connell when he urged them to support the abolition of slavery and condemned those who would not. The American repeal movement quickly dissolved, first in the South and then in the North. Meanwhile in Ireland, a group of O'Connell's younger supporters, impatient with his cautious strategy and moderate goals, broke away to found the Young Ireland movement, which launched an abortive rebellion in 1848. Many of its leaders made their way to America as exiles, the most influential being Thomas Francis Meagher and John Mitchel.

From the American Civil War to the New Departure

The chief importance of the Young Irelanders lay not so much in their influence on Irish-American history in the late 1840s as in their legacy to the later Fenian movement. The Fenian Brotherhood was founded in 1858 in New York City by John O'Mahony (1816–1877), another veteran of 1848, as a sister organization to the Irish Republican Brotherhood (IRB), which was organized in Dublin by James Stephens (1825–1901) in the same year. The aim of the Fenians and the IRB was to rid Ireland of English rule by providing American money and manpower to encourage insurrection. By 1865 the American Fenians had attracted an estimated 250,000 followers, many of them Civil War veterans, and an Irish republican government on the American model had been set up in Philadelphia. Rival Fenian factions also invaded Canada twice in 1866 and again in 1870, trying without success to provoke a war between England and the United States that might somehow work to Ireland's advantage. In Ireland, meanwhile, the long-anticipated Fenian uprising, betrayed by police informants, resulted only in sporadic rural skirmishes in March 1867. The Fenians survived in the United States under the erratic leadership of Jeremiah O'Donovan Rossa (1831–1915), but they were superseded in the 1870s by a new organization, Clan na Gael. Under the leadership of John Devoy, Clan na Gael became the most formidable exponent of Irish physical-force nationalism on either side of the Atlantic.

Throughout the late nineteenth century, however, constitutional nationalism remained much more popular than hard-line republicanism in both the United States and Ireland. Its preeminent leader was Charles Stewart Parnell (1846–1891), who led a mass movement for Home Rule in the 1880s. Parnell's primary goal was constitutional autonomy for Ireland rather than republican independence or reform of social conditions. He wanted a restoration of the Irish parliament that had been abolished in 1800, but within the framework of the British monarchical constitution. Although Parnell was prepared to enter into temporary alliances with the Fenians and Clan na Gael, he was never a man of violence, believing instead in peaceful change through parliamen-

Advertisement for Fenian brand shirt collars, circa 1866, the year Irish-American veterans of the Union Army invaded Canada in an attempt to liberate Ireland from British rule. (Library of Congress, Prints and Photographs Division, LC-USZ62-91448)

tary democracy. Nor was he especially interested in social reform, though he was prepared to enter into strategic alliances with land reformers when it suited his purpose.

Michael Davitt (1846–1906), in contrast, combined fervent nationalism with an equally sincere commitment to improving the position of the Irish peasantry. Jailed for his work on behalf of the Fenians in 1870, he was released in 1877 and traveled to the United States, where he met the social reformer and economist, Henry George (1839–1897), whose most influential work *Progress and Poverty* (1879) called for a single redistributive tax on unproductive landed wealth. With Devoy, Davitt discussed ways of combining nationalist agitation with the land question. In the radical journalist Patrick Ford he found his chief American supporter.

Irish-American support for the different types of nationalism varied widely according to social position and recentness of arrival in the United States. It is fair to say that, in general, the "lace curtain" or middle-class Irish, many of them second generation, were the least likely to support radicalism or extremism. They had nothing to gain by social reform in either Ireland or the United States, and they denounced the use of violence as providing grist to the nativist mill. Clinging to their hard-earned respectability, they favored Home Rule and moderate land reform in place of any form of revolution. They were Parnell's chief supporters in the 1880s. The case of recent immigrants is less clear-cut; some supported republicanism and even violence, while others (especially Irish-speakers from the west of Ireland) had little apparent interest in any form of nationalism. Finally, there was substantial support among the urban working class for tying the cause of nationalism to radical social reform in both Ireland and America. Few Irish-American women participated in the nationalist movement, except in the short-lived Ladies' Land League, established in 1881.

The various strands in Irish and Irish-American nationalism came together in the New Departure, a brief-lived but potentially very powerful political alliance formed in the early 1880s. An alliance between Irish land reformers, hard-line republicans, and constitutional nationalists in both Ireland and the United States would be almost unstoppable, but it was no easy task to bring it about. The IRB and Clan na Gael regarded Home Rule as at best a halfway house on the road to their goal of national independence, and they were interested in land reform only to the extent that it might mobilize the peasantry on behalf of the greater goal of independence. For their part, Parnell and the Home Rulers found the physical-force republicans too extreme and the reformers too radical. Reformers on both sides of the Atlantic, meanwhile, wanted an overhaul of the Irish tenant system and perhaps even outright ownership of the land by the people, with social and labor reform as a concomitant in the United States. Middle-class Irish nationalists on both sides of the Atlantic were determined to resist them.

In its origins, the New Departure appears to have been primarily political rather than social in orientation. That is, its principal goal was Irish national independence rather than a social revolution. The three main parties to the agreement were Devoy, Parnell, and Davitt. Devoy evidently believed, or allowed himself to believe, that Parnell's ultimate goal was an independent Ireland. Parnell certainly allowed Devoy and Davitt to believe that he was seeking both independence and land reform, not just constitutional change. In reality, however, he was probably using these causes to exert sufficient pressure on the British government so that it would have to concede Home Rule. Davitt, as an ex-Fenian, hoped the New Departure might secure some form of Irish independence, though from 1880 onward he devoted most of his attention to improving the lot of Irish tenants. In New York City, Ford supported Davitt in the hope of reforming Irish America as well, while Devoy was interested in Home Rule and land reform only to the extent that they might be mobilized in support of his uncompromising goal of full republican independence. It is scarcely surprising that so volatile an alliance could not last for long; but during the period of agitation that followed its formation, the alliance represented a very powerful new political force in Irish history. The period of agitation in question is known in Irish history as the Land War (1879–1882). The principal political organization involved was the Land League, which had branches in both Ireland and the United States.

In 1882 the New Departure began to split asunder. The result in both Ireland and the United States was a showdown between three different conceptions of nationalism: constitutional, physical force, and social reform. Devoy broke with Ford and Davitt in April 1881 while continuing to denounce Home Rule as inadequate. At the same time, as it became clear that the New Departure was no longer politically useful or necessary, Parnell and his supporters in both Ireland and the United States began to distance themselves from both radical reform and republican nationalism, con-

John Devoy, Charles Underwood O'Connell, Harry Mulleda, Jeremiah O'Donovan Rossa, and John McClure were among the Fenians given long-term prison sentences in the aftermath of the 1867 uprising in Ireland. Banished from the British Isles, they arrived in the United States on the S.S. *Cuba* on 5 January 1871. Devoy (1842–1928) went on to lead the Clan na Gael and became the senior Irish nationalist in the United States. (Library of Congress, Prints and Photographs Division, LC-USZ62-72818)

centrating instead on the single goal of Home Rule. On both sides of the Atlantic, socially and politically conservative constitutionalists had won control of the nationalist movements by the mid-1880s. But the Home Rule movement, in turn, fell apart in 1891 with the disgrace and early death of Parnell, and nationalism of all sorts went into a temporary decline.

Toward Independence

Constitutionalist nationalists on both sides of the Atlantic reorganized themselves at the turn of the century. In Ireland, John Redmond (1856–1918), who reunited the various factions within the Irish Parliamentary Party (IPP), visited the United States in

1901, where he helped found the United Irish League of America (UILA) to raise funds and generate public support for the cause of Home Rule. Like his predecessor Parnell, Redmond deliberately blurred the distinction between his own moderate constitutionalist position and full-fledged republicanism, thereby generating further support in America. The UILA was supported by the *Irish World* and its editor Patrick Ford, who had by now abandoned his earlier radicalism. The UILA, composed mostly of Irish Americans of high social standing and often considerable wealth, outspokenly opposed socialism and other radical movements.

Like the constitutionalists, the physical-force republicans were reunited at the turn of the century, after splitting into various factions following the unraveling of the New Departure. One important center of Irish-American republicanism in the early twentieth century was the Ancient Order of Hibernians (AOH), but the most influential was a rejuvenated Clan na Gael. In 1900 the Clan's factions were brought together again under the leadership of John Devoy and Daniel Cohalan in New York City and Joseph McGarrity in Philadelphia. Using Devoy's newspaper, the *Gaelic American*, the Clan attacked the IPP and UILA and their objective of Home Rule, calling instead for a fully independent republic in Ireland, to be achieved through force if necessary. The Clan retained the largely working-class support that had been its basis in the late nineteenth century, yet it was no more interested in advancing the cause of social reform than the UILA was. For Devoy, social reform could only represent a dilution of the cause to which he dedicated his long political life: an independent Irish republic.

The great turning point in the nationalist history of the Irish on both sides of the Atlantic came in 1916. Taking advantage of England's involvement in World War I, a small but committed group of hard-line Irish republicans decided to launch a rebellion, knowing that they would almost certainly sacrifice their own lives but hoping that in so doing they might galvanize the Irish people in support of the republican cause. Much of the impetus for the 1916 rebellion came from the United States. Some of the leading proponents of Irish physical force nationalism anywhere in the world were to be found in New York City in the late nineteenth and early twentieth centuries. Clan na Gael maintained close links with the Irish Republican Brotherhood in Dublin, was involved in the planning of the 1916 uprising, and acted as the main link between the rebels and the German government, whom it successfully asked for arms and ammunition in 1916. Leaders of the Clan and the AOH had fostered close relations with German Americans over the previous decade, in anticipation of conflict with Great Britain, and during the war Devoy published pro-German material in his newspaper, the *Gaelic American*. The Clan also funded the visit by the Irish nationalist Sir Roger Casement to Germany in order to liaise with the German leadership and to try to raise an Irish brigade from Irish prisoners who had been captured while serving in the British Army.

The insurrection of 1916 was a desperate gamble. Remarkably, it paid off, largely because the British execution of the rebels outraged a previously indifferent population. Before 1916, the majority of the Irish population in both Ireland and America had supported John Redmond and his crusade for Home Rule rather than the more militant demands of the hard-line republicans. Home Rule had even gone on the statute books in 1914, only to be postponed for the duration of World War I. But by the time of Redmond's death in 1918, his political party was in shambles and the cause of constitutional nationalism had been reduced to the margins of Irish political life. In a remarkable transformation, it was replaced by a vibrant republican tradition that now had the support of the majority of the Irish people on both sides of the Atlantic.

In the wake of the insurrection, Irish-American nationalism became a mass movement for the first time since the 1880s. News of the Easter Rebellion all but destroyed what remained of the UILA, as Irish Americans united almost unanimously behind the physical-force tradition. Clan na Gael sponsored an Irish Race Convention, which met in New York City in 1916, and out of it emerged the Friends of Irish Freedom (FOIF), which claimed more than 275,000 members at its peak in 1919. Between 1916 and 1921, Irish Americans raised an estimated $10 million in support of Irish independence. With the massive victory of the republican political party, Sinn Féin, in the Irish general election of 1918, the hard-line nationalist position of Clan na Gael and FOIF reigned triumphant in America by the end of World War I. When the war in Europe ended late in 1918, FOIF pressed the case for Irish independence as part of the postwar settlement. Mass meetings and demonstrations were held throughout the United States in support of Irish freedom. Another Irish Race Convention met in Philadelphia on February 22 and 23, 1919, demanding recognition of the right of Ireland to form a government of its own. When a treaty eventually emerged from the negotiations in Versailles and made no mention of Ireland, Irish Americans lobbied actively against it in Senate hearings and in meetings and demonstrations nationwide, contributing to its eventual defeat in November 1919.

In the wake of Versailles, serious differences emerged between republicans based in Ireland and their Irish-American counterparts. The preeminent Irish republican leader, Éamon de Valera, president of Dáil Eireann (the parliament of the de facto republic), toured the United States in 1919–1920 in search of support and funding for Ireland. During his eighteen-month stay, de Valera raised over $5 million in bond certificates to fund the new Irish republic (though only about half that figure ever reached Ireland). After meeting with Devoy, Cohalan, and other hard-liners, he issued a press statement declaring the Irish republican government to be the only lawful government of Ireland. In de Valera's opinion, Ireland did not need to be granted the right of self-determination by any council of international powers; it already possessed that right and had exercised it in the insurrection of 1916 and again in the election of 1918. Devoy and especially Cohalan, in contrast, insisted that Ireland's right to self-determination needed formal international recognition to be meaningful, and both were quite angry at President Woodrow Wilson for ignoring this demand.

De Valera increasingly came to regard Cohalan's obsession with American and international politics as a digression from the path necessary for the attainment of Irish independence. Irish Americans, he believed, should stop devoting their time and money to opposing the Versailles treaty and concentrate instead on directly helping Ireland in its war of independence against the British. To secure control over American funds, and to redirect the impetus of Irish-American nationalism, de Valera decided in the summer of 1920 to bypass the FOIF and, with the help of dissident

In 1919 Éamon de Valera toured the United States to drum up Irish-American support for an Irish Republic, a fledgling nation then engaged in a war for independence from Great Britain. Flyers, such as this one issued by the Southern California headquarters of the American Commission for Irish Independence in Los Angeles, asked Americans to buy bond certificates to finance a "constructive economic program" in Ireland. Nearly $10 million was ultimately raised. (Archives of Irish America, New York University, Gift of Sean Prendiville)

Irish-American republican Joseph McGarrity, set up his own organization, the American Association for the Recognition of the Irish Republic (AARIR). This organization rapidly eclipsed the FOIF, claiming some 800,000 members at its height in 1921. Only against this background of conflict between de Valera and Irish-American republicans is it possible to understand why, when civil war broke out in the newly created Irish Free State in 1922, Cohalan and Devoy, ostensibly arch-republicans, threw their support to Michael Collins and the pro-treaty forces and against de Valera and his hardline republican allies.

From the Irish Civil War to the 1998 Belfast Agreement

Very few Irish Americans opposed the Anglo-Irish treaty, but many embittered republican exiles made their way from Ireland to America, keeping the militant tradition of republicanism alive. Joseph McGarrity, who had sided with de Valera in the internecine quarrels with Devoy and Cohalan, continued to support the hard-line republican side in the 1920s and 1930s, even as de Valera reentered the mainstream of Irish constitutional politics and assumed control of the Irish government. During the Anglo-Irish War and the Irish Civil War, McGarrity supplied money and munitions to the Irish Republican Army (IRA), and in the 1930s he joined Irish militants in supporting a bombing campaign in English cities to demand a united, thirty-two county Irish republic. In Ireland de Valera (once a hard-liner himself) responded to this campaign by outlawing the IRA and imprisoning many of its leaders. The bombing campaign proved even more unpopular with the American Irish and had very few supporters outside McGarrity's circle. Not until the 1960s would the physical-force tradition reemerge as a major force in Irish and Irish-American nationalism.

In the mid-1960s, student activists in Northern Ireland had launched a civil rights movement for Catholics, modeled to some extent on the civil rights movement in the American South. They demanded an end to discrimination in employment and housing, along with recognition of full civil and political rights for Ulster's Catholic minority. The main organizations involved in this phase of the conflict were the Northern Ireland Civil Rights Association (NICRA, founded 1967) and the People's Democracy (PD), a revolutionary organization dedicated to the formation of an Irish socialist republic, founded by Bernadette Devlin. Singing American protest songs like "We Shall Overcome," and marching from Belfast to Derry in the manner pioneered by Dr. Martin Luther King, the protestors were met with baton charges and high-powered water cannons. Whereas the civil rights movement in the United States had used its tactic of nonviolent response to police brutality to capture the moral high ground and topple the old Jim Crow system of segregation and disenfranchisement, in Ireland the result was a long-term intensification of violence rather than a peaceful resolution. With the British Army called in to impose order, what began as a civil rights movement gave way to an armed struggle for a thirty-two county republic. Single-minded physical-force nationalism, in other words, had reemerged as a major political force.

The reaction among Catholic Irish Americans to the events in Northern Ireland was to rebuild both of the primary nationalist traditions, constitutionalist and republican. Already by 1967, a lawyer from Buffalo named James Heaney had founded the American Congress for Irish Freedom (ACIF), which had twenty-five chapters and three thousand members nationwide by 1969. The ACIF sponsored speaking tours by Irish civil rights activists but was generally conservative on American political matters, its members often supporting the war in Vietnam and opposing civil rights for African Americans even as they endorsed the cause of civil rights for Ulster Catholics. Much more radical, but considerably less powerful, than the ACIF was a second Irish-American nationalist organization, the National Association for Irish Justice (NAIJ), founded in 1969 by Brian Heron, a grandson of the revolutionary socialist of 1916, James Connolly. Tensions between activists in Ireland and Irish America were starkly revealed when the Ulster republican Bernadette Devlin toured the United States, alienating most Irish-American nationalists with her support for socialism and Black Power.

Developments in Irish-American nationalism over the subsequent violent generation closely paralleled developments in Ireland. In 1969, the IRA and its political wing, Sinn Féin, split into "Official" and "Provisional" camps, the former dedicated to the pursuit of a socialist Irish republic through mainly political means, and the latter sanctioning the use of armed struggle. Devlin and the more militant NICRA activists supported the new "Provos," while moderate constitutionalist nationalists organized a new political party, the Social Democratic Labour Party (SDLP) in 1970 to pursue the cause of civil rights for Catholics through peaceful means. In the United States, an Official IRA network composed mainly of old, left-leaning IRA veterans and the remnants of the radical NAIJ (which collapsed in 1970) coalesced in the James Connolly Clubs of New York and Massachusetts, which reorganized under Official Sinn Féin supervision into the Irish Republican Clubs (IRC) of the United States in 1971. The IRC endorsed the foundation of a socialist republic in Ireland, strongly supported the cause of civil rights in America, condemned the Vietnam War, and expressed its solidarity with the liberation movements of the Third World. Once again, however, this leftist orientation repelled all but a minority of Irish Americans, who were much more likely to support the moderate SDLP or, increasingly, the hard-line physical-force tradition based on the exclusive aim of Irish unification by whatever means necessary.

The dominant figure in the physical-force tradition in the United States was an Irish immigrant and veteran of the Irish Civil War, Michael Flannery. Flannery arrived in New York City in 1927 and became a leading figure in what remained of Clan na Gael. For the next forty years, he pursued a relatively peaceful career, but when the Troubles erupted in Ulster, he organized the Irish Action Committee, composed of militant nationalists. In 1969, Flannery traveled to Belfast to meet leaders of the newly emerging Provisional IRA and was asked to lead a new fund-raising organization to support a renewed military campaign aimed at uniting Ireland. In April 1970 Flannery announced the formation of the Northern Ireland Aid Committee. Better known by its acronym, NORAID, the new organization insisted that the funds it raised were used only for "humanitarian relief," but it is generally believed that they were employed mainly for the purchase of arms and ammunition, or at least freed other IRA funds to be spent in this manner. By 1972, NORAID claimed one hundred chapters and eighty thousand members and had established itself as the dominant Irish-American nationalist organization.

Concerned by the growing appeal of physical-force nationalism in the 1970s, some of the most prominent and powerful Irish Americans responded by reviving the peaceful, constitutionalist tradition. Irish diplomats in the United States joined with Irish-American business and civic leaders to create the Ireland Fund in 1976. Designed to undercut the appeal of NORAID, the Ireland Fund was founded to raise money for use in peaceful projects in Northern Ireland. The driving force behind this plan was the former international rugby star Tony O'Reilly, a national hero in Ireland and president of the H. J. Heinz Company. At the same time, Ulster's preeminent constitutional nationalist, John Hume of the Social Democratic Labor Party (SDLP) used his friendship with Senator Edward Kennedy to make contact with other influential Irish-American politicians, including Representative Tip O'Neill, Senator Daniel Patrick Moynihan, and Governor Hugh Carey of New York. Kennedy, O'Neill, Moynihan, and Carey came to be known as the Four Horsemen of Irish-American politics, working closely with John Hume to formulate a coherent position on Ulster and to issue a joint condemnation of the IRA in 1977. With the influence of NORAID beginning to decline by the late 1970s, the more moderate position of the "Four Horseman" looked as though it was about to provide a palatable alternative to violence.

Physical-force republicanism underwent a major revival, however, with the hunger strikes launched by IRA prisoners in Northern Ireland in 1981. Ten men eventually starved to death in protest at being denied the status of political prisoners. As the hunger strikes progressed throughout the first half of the year, Irish Americans united as rarely before in defense of Irish republicanism. Under the direction of NORAID, a newly militant AOH, and long-dormant chapters of Clan na Gael, physical-force nationalism flourished in the United States in the early 1980s in a manner not seen since the era of 1916. The high point of the physical-force tradition came, perhaps, when the martyred hunger striker Bobby Sands was elected grand marshal of the New York City St. Patrick's Day parade in 1982, followed by Michael Flannery of NORAID the following year.

Even as support for physical-force nationalism reached one of its historical peaks among the American Irish in the early 1980s, however, major changes were already under way within the republican movement in Ireland that would contribute in the following decade to a transformation of the political structure of Northern Ireland. Gerry Adams, the leader of Provisional Sinn Féin (the political wing of the Provisional IRA) had become convinced by the early 1980s that a military campaign by the IRA would never on its own be sufficient to bring about the withdrawal of the British from Northern Ireland. He embarked on a campaign to add a dynamic political component to the republican agenda, hoping thereby to displace the SDLP as the main representative of northern nationalists and to attract wider support in the Irish Republic. Sinn Féin therefore endorsed a new policy of achieving republican independence with "a ballot box in one hand and an armalite [rifle] in the other," as IRA spokesperson Danny Morrison famously put it in 1985. Sinn Féin politicians, including Adams, were elected to seats in the British Parliament (which they declined to occupy), and in the general election of 1983 Sinn Féin won 43 percent of the Catholic vote in Northern Ireland. While these electoral victories greatly encouraged Irish-American republicans, they also heralded a move away from pure violence toward mainstream politics, which would result in the declaration of cease-fires by the IRA in the 1990s and the eventual arrival at a peace settlement in 1998.

In the United States, the tide began to turn against the hard-liners from about the mid-1980s onward. In 1986 a second-generation Irish American, William Quinn, who had joined the IRA after a spell in NORAID and who had conducted bombing campaigns in Britain, was handed over by the American authorities to the British on charges of murdering a policeman. Great Britain and the United States had by this time agreed on a more restrictive extradition treaty, denying immunity for a range of crimes that had once qualified as grounds for asylum. Similarly, escaped IRA man Joseph Patrick Doherty was sent back to a British prison in Ulster in 1993, after a protracted, eleven-year legal struggle involving the Immigration and Naturalization Service, as well as the U.S. attorney general's office. Moreover, a variety of IRA gunrunners were convicted and sentenced to long terms in prison in Massachusetts and Florida between 1986 and 1991.

More important than these individual reverses to the republican cause were the shifting permutations of politics in Ireland and Great Britain. For the first time, the Anglo-Irish Agreement of 1985 recognized some role for the government of the Irish republic in the affairs of Northern Ireland. This agreement gave new life to the embattled cause of constitutional nationalism, led by John Hume of the SDLP, who continued to reach out to European and American politicians with his message of peaceful, gradual change. At the same time, Gerry Adams led a faction within the republican movement that was increasingly interested in restoring questions of civil rights and social justice to the agenda, without reneging on the ultimate goal of a thirty-two-county republic. This was no easy strategy to pursue. It led to splits within Sinn Féin, with some republicans (especially the breakaway body, Republican Sinn Féin) refusing to compromise on their single goal of a united Ireland. These divisions were mirrored in the United States, where hard-liner Michael Flannery withdrew from NORAID to protest its endorsement of Adams's position. Flannery formed a new organization, Cumann na Saoirse, to support Republican Sinn Féin, while Martin Galvin retained the leadership of NORAID. The process set in motion by Adams culminated in the declaration of a cease-fire by the IRA in August 1994, which was approved by NORAID, though not without additional divisions and defections. Once the cease-fire had taken effect, Adams was granted a visa to enter the United States (having been excluded as a terrorist up to that point), following in the footsteps of Parnell, Davitt, de Valera, and so many of his Irish nationalist predecessors.

The American government, especially President Bill Clinton and his unofficial emissary George Mitchell, played a critical role in bringing about the Belfast peace agreement that was ratified by the electorate in both parts of Ireland in May 1998. The agreement guaranteed that the province would not change its current status unless a majority of its population votes to do so, created a series of new constitutional and political bodies to govern Northern Ireland, and it promised to reform the police and judicial systems. The agreement was certainly a major triumph for constitutional nationalism (its chief architect, John Hume, received the Nobel Peace Prize in 1998, along with his Unionist counterpart, David Trimble). But it was by no means a defeat for the republican movement, except perhaps for its most extreme elements. This explains why most of the opposition to the agreement came not from Catholics but from extremist Protestants. Apart from some ominous splinter groups, support for the agreement among Catholics in both the north and the republic was overwhelming. Support in the United States was strong. Two hundred years after the great insurrection of 1798, as the twentieth century drew to its close, the dominant tone among Irish nationalists on both sides of the Atlantic was one of cautious optimism.

SUGGESTED READING

Thomas Brown, *Irish American Nationalism, 1870–1890* (Philadelphia: Lippincott, 1966).

Francis M. Carroll, *American Opinion and the Irish Question, 1910–1923: A Study in Opinion and Policy* (New York: St. Martin's Press, 1978).

Eric Foner, "Class, Ethnicity, and Radicalism in the Gilded Age: The Land League in Irish America," in *Politics and Ideology in the Age of the Civil War,* 150–200 (New York: Oxford University Press, 1980).

Terry Golway, *Irish Rebel: John Devoy and America's Fight for Ireland's Freedom* (New York: St. Martin's Press, 1998).

Victor A. Walsh, "Irish Nationalism and Land Reform: The Role of the Irish in America," in *The Irish in America: Emigration, Assimilation, Impact,* ed. P. J. Drudy, 253–270 (New York: Cambridge University Press, 1985).

Andrew J. Wilson, *Irish America and the Ulster Conflict, 1968–1995* (Belfast: Blackstaff Press, 1995).

David A. Wilson, *United Irishmen, United States: Immigrant Radicals in the Early Republic* (Ithaca, NY: Cornell University Press, 1998).

The 1981 Hunger Strikes: America Reacts (Archives of Irish America, New York University, 2001) on the web at http://www.nyu.edu/library/bobst/research/aia/exhibits/0501_hunger/index.html.

Chapter 10

Refractive History
Memory and the Founders of the Emigrant Savings Bank

Marion R. Casey

> Time can never efface the recollection of them.
> —Minutes, Emigrant Industrial Savings Bank,
> 13 January 1870

At the headquarters of the Emigrant Savings Bank on East 42nd Street in New York City, a long corridor leads to the executive dining room on the third floor. The portraits of dozens and dozens of men line that well-trod route to lunch or dinner, looking out at the visitor from behind black frames. Those uniform squares have little brass plates attached that bear the names of the men who have served as trustees since Emigrant's foundation in 1850.[1]

This portrait gallery is at once a visual representation of Emigrant Savings Bank's historical consciousness and at the same time a powerful statement about the contributions of individuals, alone and in concert. And yet these men, particularly those at its helm between 1850 and 1890, all respected and influential citizens in their own day, are virtually unknown outside the bank. They constitute an elite that is invisible to the modern eye even though their legacy survives, with thirty-six branches in the metropolitan area and $10.1 billion in assets.[2] The perseverance of Emigrant Savings Bank into the twenty-first century—given the demise of thrift giants in the industry, like the Bowery Savings Bank—is a remarkable story in itself.[3] So, too, is the quirk of municipal real estate that allowed its main building at 51 Chambers Street to escape demolition and gain historic landmark status.[4] No less astonishing is the hunger for memory that ensued when the discovery of Emigrant's Test Books was announced. These ledgers were opened for research during the winter of 1995–1996 and quickly became the most heavily used of all the New York Public Library's 3,300 collections.[5] A savings bank—an unusual source for genealogy or social history, yet an institution traditionally in the business of husbanding resources—suddenly became the means of resurrecting ordinary men and women from historical obscurity.[6] But those who were its facilitators remain elusive. What happens to erase such men from history?

How might the Irish founders of Emigrant Savings Bank have specifically shaped the way in which it has been remembered?

The answer lies in a dynamic between power and society, economics and politics, memory and history. The Irish in New York in the middle of the nineteenth century were particularly well placed to take advantage of shifts in elite formation as the city moved from the merchant culture of an Atlantic world port to the entrepreneurial milieu of an American industrial capital and immigrant metropolis.[7] In that process, some Irish had unprecedented opportunities for mobility; however, the official record of this period was constructed by non-ethnic powerbrokers and the complete absence of men like Emigrant's founders from histories of American business, philanthropy, and New York City reflects their marginalization from such key areas of historical inquiry. This is also a byproduct of the fact that the study of elites has not been a concern of historians of Irish America for the past thirty years.[8] Those at the opposite end of the social spectrum—the immigrant on the bottom, the laborer and the domestic servant, the powerless and the voiceless—have quite rightly been the subjects of research. But in our haste to conform to the accepted paradigms of what constitutes ethnic studies in the United States (and that is often presumed to be a variation on working-class history), we have compounded the vagaries of memory, forgetting that there were ethnic elites making critical decisions.

"More than memory shapes the past, and history is more than a collection of memories," wrote Richard White in his 1998 meditation on family history, *Remembering Ahanagran*. He suggests that Irish people prefer memory over history because it is malleable. Memories are tied to place, so that even as years pass, the same place serves as the backdrop for old stories that are subtly reworked "to meet the times."[9] They are made relevant to the present without necessarily being unfaithful to the spirit of the past. In the case of the founding of Emigrant Savings Bank, the facts are at odds with memory. Despite the portrait gallery of its trustees, the story that actually survives is that "New York's great Bishop, John Hughes" founded the bank.[10] This statement is equally as difficult to prove as disprove because it represents a refraction of reality and memory triggered by contemporary events during the late nineteenth century. An institution like Emigrant Savings Bank embodies all of the types of memory—individual, collective, popular, and historical—that scholars have analyzed separately in recent literature.[11] But what happens when these kinds of memories combine? What vanishes and what survives? The Hughes connection, in particular, has lingered in the bank down to the present and for that reason bears further examination.

History's "Elite" Medium

As David Doyle observed, "it is impossible to take the measure of the human patterns even of one's own time" while "short-takes and shorter memory must winnow even scholarly consensus by generation."[12] Nevertheless attempts are routinely made, most notably in the "official" record represented by national biographical dictionaries, the epitome of old-fashioned, elite history. Such works mediate the relationship of the past with the present and future in very political ways. At the turn of the twentieth century, France, Britain, and Germany were far ahead of the United States in draw-ing their national portraits through biographies. New York publishers responded by producing three variations on this kind of reflective history for the home market. *The National Cyclopaedia of American Biography* (1893) aimed to "exemplify and per-petuate, in the broadest sense, American civilization through its chief personalities," among which it was careful to include those responsible for the country's industrial and commercial progress since 1850. The twenty thousand entries in *Appleton's Cyclo-paedia of American Biography* (1898–1900), under the editorial direction of James Grant Wilson and John Fiske, built on the ten thousand entries in Francis S. Drake's *Dictionary of American Biography* (1872)—the rights to which were bought for that purpose—as well as "the latest result of historical research." *The Dictionary of Amer-ican Biography* (1927) was directly modeled on the British *Dictionary of National Biography* (1885–1901) and was produced, under the auspices of the American Coun-cil of Learned Societies, by a committee that included J. Franklin Jameson, John Er-skine, Frederic L. Paxson, and Frederick J. Turner. With Allen Johnson as editor, it was underwritten by ten annual payments of $500,000 from the New York Times Company.[13]

All of the key personalities involved in these enterprises belonged to a particular type of elite themselves. Fiske (Harvard), Jameson (Brown), Johnson (Yale), and Pax-son and Turner (both University of Wisconsin) were professional historians writing at the turn of the century. Erskine was professor of English at Columbia University, Wilson the biographer of Ulysses S. Grant and other military men, and Drake a Bos-ton antiquarian. These Anglo-American intellectuals were committing to paper the collective memory of their era, which in turn would inform the historical conscious-ness of the twentieth century. Their decisions about who to include as important con-tributors to the story of America simultaneously constructed memory and winnowed historical reality.

There were other ramifications. For example, in 1896 Henry Cabot Lodge—a histo-rian whom Irish-Americans considered biased—determined that fewer than 1 percent of all eminent Americans were of Irish origin based on his analysis of entries in *Apple-ton's Cyclopedia of American Biography*.[14] Lodge's Ph.D. in history from Harvard Uni-versity was one of the first granted in the United States.[15] Not only did he represent the beginning of a shift from remembered history to history taught by professors, but later as a politician he supported the idea of national origins when it was introduced in the Senate.[16] This restrictive legislation in the early 1920s was based on ancestral contributions to the United States that were determined by a surname analysis of the 1790 census. In this instance of Clio serving contemporary politics, the Irish were said to have constituted only 1.9 percent of the early national white population—it is a fig-ure that eerily echoes their portion of the first biographical dictionaries. Perhaps not coincidentally, the American Council of Learned Societies revised the highly con-tested Irish quota for the Johnson-Reed Immigration Act of 1927, thereby affecting the number of Irish emigrants who could legally enter the United States, the very same year its committee published the *Dictionary of American Biography*.[17] Even David Doyle's more reliable dataset of Irish entries from the *Dictionary of American Biogra-phy* (and its modern online equivalent, the *American National Biography*) still represents only 2 percent of all entries.[18] The problem with such sources for the study of Irish diaspora history is readily apparent.

There is no mention of the Emigrant Savings Bank in Archbishop John Hughes's entry in the *Dictionary of American Biography* or in the *American National Biography*.[19] Thus it comes as no surprise that the bank trustees I will focus on in this essay do not appear there either. But this absence cannot solely be attributed to the blinkered perspective of their compilers. The history of the Irish in America at the turn of the century was itself being constructed by two parallel forces: the American Irish His-torical Society (est. 1897)[20] and the *Catholic Encyclopedia* (begun 1905).[21] The former's emphasis on colonial and revolutionary era contributions, and the latter's focus on America's clerical and religious institutional past, virtually obliterated the memory of the founders of the bank in the history of record as effectively as the biographical dictionaries. When such evidence—that is, constructed history—contradicts popular memory, how is our understanding of the past affected? Is silence, in fact, deliberate obfuscation? Or are some things inevitably lost to history in the mundane reality of origins?

Could the popular story that Hughes founded the Emigrant Savings Bank be a mistake? There is no mention of a bank in John Hassard's biography published just two years after John Hughes's death, nor in Richard Shaw's published more than one hundred years later.[22] Apparently the archbishop had no financial expertise:

> [He] lacked all idea of order or system . . . he had a far-reaching, comprehensive mind but no head for details. . . . His books and papers were always in disorder. . . . He kept a bank account, but did not know how to manage it. If he wanted money, he asked his secretary for it, and he was almost always in debt to the diocesan fund. He made no minute of his deposits in [the] bank, . . . [and] he never knew how much money he had.[23]

Nevertheless, from the late 1880s Emigrant Savings Bank began to acknowledge that "it was to his wise counsels that the Bank owed its existence, and under his personal direction that it was Established."[24] Popular memory has translated that as "Hughes founded the bank." But much depends on how contemporaries understood those phrases "wise counsels" and "personal direction." The original trustees who knew Archbishop Hughes combine individual and collective memory with an institutional history, at the boundary of which lies a truth that perhaps can never be fully known.

Emigrant's Origins

On Emigrant Savings Bank's very first day of business, 30 September 1850, John Hughes opened Account No. 9 with $25. No doubt he was setting a positive example of thrift that he fully expected to be emulated. Like many of its depositors, Hughes was an immigrant himself, born in Annaloughan, County Tyrone, in 1797, the son of a small farmer and linen weaver. He followed his father and brother to America in 1817, settling in the Pennsylvania countryside, eventually attending the seminary at Emmitsburg, Maryland. After ordination in October 1826, Hughes was sent to Philadelphia and in 1837 to New York to assist its ailing Bishop John Dubois with his flock of about sixty thousand Catholics. In December 1842, when there were thirteen parishes in the city, Hughes became the fourth Roman Catholic bishop of New York.[25]

There were two things about New York City that could not have escaped Hughes's notice: immigrant arrivals—mainly Irish—at the port were approaching twenty-five thousand per annum, and it already had four savings banks. An entry in Philip Hone's diary written the day after the great fire that destroyed much of lower Manhattan in 1835 indicates an early acceptance of the savings bank ethos by the New York Irish. The fire caused a run on the Bank for Savings, and Hone witnessed a group of Irish men demanding withdrawals. Hone was disparaging in his comments about these "ignorant, and consequently the most obstinate white men in the world" because he felt their actions—just two weeks shy of the usual January 1st dividend payment—indicated their stupidity and rashness: "All the sums now drawn lose nearly six months interest, which the bank gains. These Irishmen, however, insisted upon having their money, and when they received it were evidently disappointed and would fain have put it back again." [26]

Such nativist (anti-immigrant and anti-Catholic) sentiment was on the rise in New York City in the late 1840s and very shortly would emerge as a full-blown political party, the Know-Nothings. Hughes responded by building a parallel set of institutions to serve New York's Catholic immigrants, including hospitals, colleges, and parochial schools.[27] Why not a savings bank? But a financial institution could not be staffed by religious orders as those others could. If the impetus for the Emigrant Savings Bank did indeed originate with Hughes, he would have had to turn to the only people in the community who knew anything about handling large sums of money—the Irish Emigrant Society, established in 1841. Through its agency, remittances (usually in the form of money orders and prepaid passage tickets) were being sent back across the Atlantic to Ireland.[28] In this way, what little discretionary income there was among Hughes's parishioners was being saved through sheer will power and self-sacrifice in order to bring out parents and siblings. In the fiscal year that overlaps with the founding of Emigrant Savings Bank (1 January 1850 to 1 January 1851), the Irish Emigrant Society remitted the modern equivalent of $4.6 million to Ireland.[29]

There is a visible line of descent in the Irish Emigrant Society's origins that is indicative of the overlapping social, political, and religious networks that sustained the pre-famine New York Irish community. As the volume of immigration began to increase in the late 1830s, the Friendly Sons of St. Patrick—a fraternal and benevolent society in the city since 1784—appointed a committee to investigate the need for a charitable society devoted solely to the welfare of these new Irish arrivals. At a meeting in March of 1838 Dr. Robert Hogan pointed out, for example, how often immigrants were the victims of fraud "by persons advertising themselves as Bankers [but] whose drafts proved worthless."[30] From this committee the Irish Emigrant Society was organized on 22 March 1841 to advise immigrants about routes to the interior, as well as employment on public works projects, to warn them about "improper lodging houses," to save them "from toilsome journeys inspired by elusive advertisements," and to preserve them "from crooked contractors, dishonest prospectuses, and remittance-sharpers."[31] The eminent physician, chemist, and professor of midwifery Dr. William James MacNeven was the society's first president.

Gregory Dillon (1782–1854), who left Jamestown, County Roscommon, after the 1798 rebellion, was the first president of the New York City–based Emigrant Industrial Savings Bank (1850–1854), as well as president of the Irish Emigrant Society (1841–1854). (Archives of Irish America, New York University, Gift of Donald A. Kelly)

For thirty years, political exiles from the failed 1798 United Irish rebellion had formed the leadership core of the Irish community in New York. By the 1840s, its surviving patriarch was MacNeven, who had been actively involved with the immigrant aid movement since his 1805 arrival in the city. His election as president of the Irish Emigrant Society no doubt gave immediate validity to the organization, but he was seventy-eight years old in 1841 and died within four months of its first meeting. Much of the credit for the valiant work of the Irish Emigrant Society during the era of the Irish famine belongs to Gregory Dillon, who succeeded to its presidency at the next election.[32]

In this capacity, Dillon automatically became an ex-officio state Commissioner of Emigration. Members of the society had worked with Bishop Hughes and other likeminded citizens in 1847 to lobby the New York State legislature to create this oversight board.[33] The Commissioners of Emigration were an elite group "composed of *men of the highest standing in the community*, who served without compensation, and to whom was entrusted the general care and supervision of the immigrants as they arrived."[34] It was in the City Hall offices of the Commissioners of Emigration that a new savings bank was conceived in the spring of 1850.[35]

Dillon and at least nine other members of the society—as well as Robert Minturn, the first head of the emigration commission—were among the men who petitioned the New York State legislature for a bank charter, which was granted in the name "Emigrant Industrial Savings Bank" on 10 April 1850.[36] "Industrial" was meant to convey the nineteenth-century connection between personal industry and thrift rather than any manufacturing or commercial association. Articles of incorporation were unanimously accepted at a meeting on 24 May, and Dillon assumed full-time duties as the bank's first president. In that capacity he was also to supervise the society's "increasing Bill Business." Dillon saw in this confluence of interests:

> the prospect of extending the benefit and usefulness of two Benevolent Institutions, first in furnishing the means of safe remittances to the distressed people of Ireland and of distributing in charities whatever of profits may arise therefrom and secondly, affording our people a safe deposit for their hard earnings, thereby establishing in perpetuity two *Irish-Americanized* institutions, the success of which, I do not doubt, will form one of the highest pleasures of our lives.[37]

Through the end of the century the bank's connection to the Irish Emigrant Society and to the Commissioners of Emigration would remain intimate. The founders of the Emigrant Savings Bank recognized this unique relationship: genealogical research in its Test Books reveals the depth of interest the bank took in the origins of its depositors.[38] Likewise, Emigrant's seal—under billowy clouds, a three-masted ship rests at anchor as passengers make their way ashore—is not only a straightforward reference to the great migration of people across the ocean but also an implicit acknowledgment of the bank's place in the Atlantic economy. Most of the eighteen original incorporators of the Emigrant Savings Bank were merchants whose livelihoods, in one way or another, were related to transatlantic commerce. John Nicholson and William Redmond, for example, both had importing houses on Pine Street; John McMenomy's business was linens at 156 Bowery; John P. Nesmith of Nesmith and Co. on Pine Street and Peter A. Hargous of Hargous Brothers on South Street were commercial merchants; Joseph Stuart, John Manning, Terence Donnelly, and Hugh Kelly all had dry goods firms; Felix Ingoldsby's hardware firm Ingoldsby and Boisseau was at 119 Maiden Lane; and Andrew Carrigan was a retired provisions dealer with some real estate interests.[39] Within its first fiscal year, to meet the growing administrative needs of the bank, its Board of Trustees was expanded from the original eighteen to twenty-seven men. Again, many were in business.

Among these twenty-seven Emigrant trustees, one-third were members of the Friendly Sons of St. Patrick. In fact, the same year the bank was founded, the Friendly Sons faced a crisis. It had had no meetings and no annual dinner on St. Patrick's Day. Because 1850 was still a famine year in Ireland, the most active Friendly Sons were more than occupied with the work of the Irish Emigrant Society and with organizing the

Emigrant Savings Bank. At a pivotal meeting on 6 March 1851, less than six months after the bank's opening, thirty Friendly Sons met to consider a proposed resolution that would transfer its $3,900 in assets and entire membership to the Irish Emigrant Society. In essence, the vote was on whether to dissolve the sixty-seven-year-old organization. The vote was ultimately lost for lack of a quorum; however, it is interesting to note that among those who urged the merger were Gregory Dillon, Felix Ingoldsby, William Watson, John Nicholson, and Joseph Stuart—all trustees of the bank.[40]

This incident indicates that the power dynamics within the Irish community in New York City were in flux as a new group of ethnic elites was emerging. The reins of leadership, forged by MacNeven and his compatriots, were being passed to younger men, among whom were those in Bishop John Hughes's inner circle—those whom, so the story goes, he is said to have encouraged to create the Emigrant Savings Bank. Who were these men and how did their contemporaries remember them?

Emigrant's Founders

Gregory Dillon, born in Jamestown, County Roscommon, on 18 April 1782, crossed the Atlantic following the 1798 Rebellion, in which his older brother had also been implicated, and took up employment as a clerk in a New York City countinghouse in 1800. During the War of 1812 he served as captain of New York's First Regiment of Riflemen,[41] a volunteer unit, on the Canadian frontier, then spent fourteen years in business in Augusta, Georgia, before returning to New York City, where he undertook philanthropic work in 1836. After more than a decade as president of the Irish Emigrant Society (to which he bequeathed $6,000) and four years as president of the Emigrant Savings Bank, Dillon died on 5 March 1854 at his home on Park Place. Obituaries accorded him much respect, cognizant of his role in the pioneering Commissioners of Emigration, the state body that had implemented many reforms at the port of New York since its inception in 1847.[42] "He was in the strictest sense of the word a self-made man in America," wrote the *New York Times*:

> By his constant devotion to business, and unwearied industry, he worked his way up from the condition of a poor and friendless emigrant in America to that of a wealthy and honored citizen. In manner he was remarkably retiring and modest, he shrank from all notoriety, rather choosing to act silently in his practical efforts in behalf of the friendless. His name is graven on the hearts of thousands through all parts of this land, who, when they were strangers and in a strange land, received from him that advice and assistance to which they are indebted for their present prosperity. By his demise the emigrant has lost a sincere friend and skilled counselor.[43]

Likewise, the city's Irish immigrants read a eulogy for Dillon in the *Irish-American*: "For a long time, he maintained in this his adopted city, a reputation for integrity and honor in every relation of life; and his last moments must have been consoled and sanctified by the reflection that he performed his duties, sincerely and truthfully, to society and his immortal interests."[44] The irony, of course, is that Dillon has been completely forgotten except within the bank itself, where his oil portrait graces the executive dining room on East 42nd Street. Of Dillon the bank minutes record "we lose in him, besides an enlightened, earnest and devoted cooperator in the councils of this Board, a worthy and most amiable Gentleman—a long tried, and valued friend who by his many excellent qualities had endeared himself to all."[45]

Gregory Dillon's successor, Emigrant's vice president Joseph Stuart, was president of the bank from 1854 to 1865. At the time Stuart was a partner with his brother James in the private banking house of J. and J. Stuart and Co., No. 33 Nassau Street. A Presbyterian from County Armagh born on 25 November 1803, Stuart immigrated to Philadelphia in 1827 where he established a dry-goods firm with his brothers John and David. The company's New York branch opened in 1835 and prospered enough to warrant yet another branch in Manchester, England. With capital from their profits, Stuart and his brother and partner in the New York office, James, got out of dry goods and became bankers in the 1850s.[46] Both men were active with the Irish Emigrant Society: James Stuart was its treasurer, and Joseph Stuart was a trustee. Together they oversaw the growth of the society's bill business. Their "promptness and sound judgement" in handling remittances to the Bank of Ireland translated into quite a large volume of business (over 46,000 drafts) by the end of the society's first decade, contributing in no small way to the establishment of the Emigrant Savings Bank.[47]

Stuart resigned from Emigrant in 1865 after eleven years at its helm. Officially, the reason given to the local press was compliance with a new law prohibiting an individual from holding positions in multiple financial institutions (Stuart had connections in both the United States and Europe); privately, the bank minutes record a disagreement with the trustees about how to handle an internal breach of trust by Emigrant's accountant.[48] Nonetheless, at his death on 18 November 1874 at his home on East 36th Street, the minutes of the bank paid handsome tribute to his services:

> [He was] one of the original associates who, taking for the field of their benevolence [the stranger landing on these shores] labored zealously in the establishment of [the Irish Emigrant Society, the Emigration Commission, and the Emigrant Savings Bank]. . . . His wide experience and sagacity as a banker contributed very materially to [Emigrant's] good management and financial success. . . . In his private acts of benevolence which, of necessity became known to us in consequence of our association with him, we can truly testify that not only was he always willing to aid the needy but that he did so without inquiry as to creed, country or political predilection.[49]

Stuart, much like Dillon, was also known outside the ethnic community. His *New York Times* obituary observed that "he occupied the highest position, and his opinion was frequently sought for in matters of moment in connection with banking and finance. His loss will undoubtedly be widely felt in business circles on both sides of the Atlantic."[50]

Stuart was succeeded by Henry Louis Hoguet who had become an Emigrant trustee in March of 1859. Hoguet was born in Dublin on 5 November 1816, the son of a French immigrant who had a furrier business on Grafton Street. In 1834 he emigrated to New York to act as a representative for his father's firm. His career there took him from fur to dry goods to auctioneering, then finally to the presidency of Emigrant in

Henry Hoguet (1816–1890), a Dublin native of French parentage, took over
the presidency of the Emigrant Industrial Savings Bank in 1865. (Archives of
Irish America, New York University, Gift of Donald A. Kelly)

1865.[51] For the next twenty-five years, far longer than either Dillon or Stuart, Hoguet
managed the bank. When he died on 9 May 1890 at his home on West 28th Street,
Emigrant remembered Henry Hoguet:

> [He was] of original and logical mind, of clear perception, great force of character, genial
> and sympathetic temperament, he commanded, in the highest degree, the confidence
> and regard of all connected with this institution. The interest of each depositor seemed
> his especial care. His wise and conservative direction of affairs was felt and valued, at all
> times, and is best attested by the uninterrupted growth of the Bank, in resources and in
> public confidence, during the long period of his Presidency.[52]

The *Evening Post* and *New York Times* covered his funeral from St. Patrick's Cathedral,
the latter newspaper noting Hoguet's reputation as a philanthropist whose "purse and
energies were at the command of many institutions in this city." The *Times* and the
Sun printed a memorial from the New York Catholic Protectory, the large reformatory

of which Hoguet was also president, which mourned his loss as a "public calamity": "A good citizen, an able and upright business man, a generous philanthropist, and a sincere Christian has fallen in our midst."[53]

Hoguet died unexpectedly in 1890, and eighty-three-year-old James Olwell succeeded him as president. Olwell had been on the board for forty years and served as first vice president from 1875 to 1890. His voice was the one remaining link to those of the first generation of trustees, but age could not long be denied. He tendered his resignation eighteen months later in 1892 and was replaced by an Irish American, James McMahon, in the first significant break in corporate continuity since 1850. The board insisted that Olwell, as its senior trustee, resume his old position as first vice president so "that we may continue to enjoy the benefit of his genial presence and wise counsels at the meetings of this Board for many years."[54] In their opinion Olwell had "most worthily merited and enjoyed the esteem and confidence of those distinguished men whose genius fashioned with skillful symmetry this noble institution—who have passed over to the vast and silent majority—but whose memories are treasured and venerated in the Catholic history of this splendid Commonwealth."[55]

Like those men, Olwell was an immigrant, too—born in County Cavan in 1807— and one of New York City's old merchants. In 1828 with his brother Matthew, he formed the wholesale grocery firm of J. and M. Olwell, No. 181 West Street, and remained in business for forty-seven years.[56] At his death on 12 August 1896, the bank minutes observed:

> Not only this Bank, but the mercantile community generally, sustains a great loss. When he gave his word nobody wanted his bond. . . . Of a most benevolent disposition, he never turned a deaf ear to the plea of the unfortunate; his charities were manifold but known only to God and a few of his most intimate friends, for he never alluded to them; a modest, good and faithful man has gone to his rest, and the world is poorer.[57]

James Olwell was a long-time member of Emigrant's finance committee, which was composed of five trustees elected annually. These men decided how the deposits should be invested in order to generate semiannual dividends for the depositors. Much of Emigrant's success before the Civil War can be credited to the shrewd investment policy of finance committee chairmen Felix Ingoldsby (1852–1859), Andrew Carrigan (1860–1862), and Daniel Devlin (1863–1864).[58]

Felix Ingoldsby was born in 1794 in County Leitrim. Apprenticed with his uncle in Dublin to learn the hardware business, Ingoldsby immigrated to Charleston, South Carolina, in 1818 to work in the same field. He relocated to New York in 1828 where he gained a reputation as "a most perfect and thorough hardware man." According to *The Old Merchants of New York City* (circa 1863):

> [His] pure, upright and modest character has prevented his having probably an enemy in the wide world. . . . In all his intercourse with mankind, and in his large control of funds, he was never known to take over seven percent in his life. More creditable and more Christian-like still, he was never known to refuse a worthy application made to him for benevolence, without regard to religion, politics or social position. We have few such men in the city.[59]

He remained active on Emigrant's board until his death on 20 January 1870 at age seventy-six. The bank minutes record the highest praise for him, resolving

> that the many noble qualities of our late Colleague have so endeared his memory to us, that time can never efface the recollection of them and they will serve as a beacon of light for those who are left behind. . . . We feel as though the Society has lost one of its brightest ornaments, his associates a wise Counsellor, the Emigrant a true friend and his family a loving and kind heart.[60]

Ingoldsby's successor as chairman of the finance committee was Andrew Carrigan, another native of Ireland who was a "widely known and greatly-respected citizen."[61] Although his county of birth in 1804 remains uncertain (Carrigans are associated with the Leitrim/Sligo area), he left Ireland circa 1821 and began his career in New York as a provisions dealer. Diversifying into real estate, Carrigan became successful enough to retire in his fifties, thereafter devoting himself to charity. Credited with doing the most work on the ground in Albany to push through the 1847 legislation that put immigration through the Port of New York under state control, he succeeded Dillon as president of the Irish Emigrant Society and as a Commissioner of Emigration in 1854. By the time of Carrigan's death in 1872, on 5 September, the work of the New York State Emigration Commission was nationally recognized. The Irish Emigrant Society believed that the state code for emigrants was the "best monument of [Carrigan's] wisdom and benevolence."[62] Of him the *New York Times* remarked:

> During the whole period of the late Archbishop Hughes' residence in this City no man enjoyed more of his affectionate regard and confidence than Andrew Carrigan, nor was any man more worthy of such distinction. Mr. Carrigan's life was one of quiet, unostentatious usefulness.[63]

Daniel Devlin, born in County Donegal in 1814, succeeded Carrigan as chairman of the finance committee. Before emigrating in 1834, he learned the tailoring trade. After a brief period in Lexington, Kentucky, he married the daughter of a wealthy New York Irish fruit importer who backed him in the ready-made clothing business there. He brought his brother Jeremiah over from Ireland in 1849 and established the firm of Devlin and Co. in a five-story building at the corner of Broadway and Grand Street. In 1851 when he joined Emigrant Savings Bank's board, Devlin's business was taking in about $160,000 annually, the equivalent of $3.7 million today.[64] In 1855 he was one of the few manufacturers in the city already to be using the sewing machine, with 150 cutters and clerks on the payroll and 2,000 others who took outwork.[65] The bank elected his brother Jeremiah to fill the vacancy on the board caused by Daniel's premature death at the age of fifty-three on 23 February 1867, recording in the minutes that Daniel Devlin was one of the board's "most efficient members, one, who during years of intimate association, we have found to be a courteous, honorable, high-toned gentleman, whose sympathies were large and whose purse was always open to the call of Charity."[66] The *New York Times* printed a letter from Mayor John T. Hoffman to members of the New York City Common Council that described Devlin as "an honest and just man, active in all public movements, extremely liberal in all public and private charities, a sincere and devout worshipper in the Church of which he was a member, and greatly honored and respected in all relations of life."[67]

Behind the common denominator of the Emigrant Savings Bank, these men were part of a network of overlapping associations that went beyond the mercantile and fraternal links discussed earlier. These can broadly be called philanthropic, and as such they take these men beyond the realm of elites within the Irish community and into the arena of municipal economics and politics where their efforts affected the dynamics of elite power in New York City.

Emigrant and the City

Between the Emigrant Savings Bank's date of incorporation in April 1850 and its opening day of business five months later, John Hughes was elevated from bishop to New York City's first archbishop. To the public, Hughes was a formidable presence, someone who had fearlessly championed the rights of Catholics in the city, earning his nickname "Dagger John" in battles over state funding for education and in doctrinal debates. Privately, he had few intimates, but they saw another side of his personality:

> In the company of his chosen friends he was one of the most genial of men. Wit and philosophy, fun and good sense, flowed together from his lips. . . . His conversation had none of the caustic tone which was so characteristic of his writings. . . . He joked; he told stories; and, by a rare combination of social gifts, he was a good listener.[68]

This was the John Hughes that the guiding brains behind Emigrant Savings Bank knew, and they had specific things in common with him (see table 1). They had all been through the emigration experience themselves, leaving Ireland as young adults. They were almost all from a handful of neighboring counties that formed the border between southern Ulster and east Connaught. With the exception of Gregory Dillon, they left Ireland after the end of the Napoleonic Wars, between 1817 and 1834, and with the exception of Joseph Stuart, they were all Catholics. They fit the pre-famine pattern of migration in which the number of Catholic departures from the northern part of Ireland was steadily increasing, as mechanization eliminated cottage weaving and spinning in the farms of the border counties. Kerby Miller recounts that in Protestant opinion those emigrating at this time were "the most industrious and virtuous part" of the Catholic population, "largely of Old English rather than Gaelic background" including noninheriting sons, small holders, and middle-class urban dwellers.[69] Finally, their maturity was spent in New York City during the mid-century years when it was becoming the new American metropolis. These were distinct elements in the bond between the Emigrant Savings Bank founders that, while difficult to historicize, are surely more than coincidence.

Archbishop Hughes could rely on these men precisely because their formative life experiences in many ways mirrored his own. Dillon, about fifteen years older than Hughes, and Carrigan were particularly close to the archbishop, and both were buried in St. Patrick's Cathedral with him as a mark of honor.

TABLE 1
Emigrant Industrial Savings Bank Founders in Archbishop John Hughes's Immediate Social Circle, by Date of Emigration from Ireland

Name	Date of Emigration	County of Origin	Age at Emigration	Occupation circa 1850	Age in 1850
Gregory Dillon	1800	Roscommon	18	Merchant	68
John Hughes	1817	Tyrone	20	Clergyman	53
Felix Ingoldsby	1818	Leitrim	24	Hardware	56
Andrew Carrigan	ca. 1822	Associated with Leitrim/Sligo	18	Merchant/real estate	46
James Olwell	1825	Cavan	18	Grocer	43
Joseph Stuart	1827	Armagh	24	Private banker	47
Daniel Devlin	1834	Donegal	20	Clothing	36
Henry Hoguet	1834	Dublin	18	Fur/auctioneering	34

Through the agency of Emigrant Savings Bank, Hughes was able to finance a brick-and-mortar infrastructure to serve the ever-increasing Catholic population in the archdiocese of New York, which by 1865 would number as many as 400,000.[70] Eleven new parishes were created in Manhattan in the bank's first decade, and older churches were renovated.[71] Emigrant's minutes and bond and mortgage records are replete with entries related to Catholic property in the metropolitan area. As early as April 1852, Emigrant loaned $20,000 at 7 percent interest to the trustees of St. Patrick's Cathedral against the old cathedral building on Mott Street.[72] The following year it received and approved an application for $10,000 against the property of the Church of the Annunciation, a brand new parish in northern Manhattan.[73] Hughes's colleague Bishop John Loughlin received a loan of $4,000 against ten lots in South Brooklyn in December 1853.[74] These were significant lump sums, only made possible by aggregating the small deposits of ordinary men and women saving with Emigrant. While the bank's trustees were happy to facilitate the expansion plans of their dear friend the archbishop of New York, Emigrant was no mere secular front for Hughes. In turning down Hughes's request for $18,000 shortly after a financial panic in 1856, Emigrant's trustees firmly expressed their opinion that "the statements of Clergymen, on business matters should always be received with some degree of caution, from the well known fact that their inexperience of the laws and usages which govern business transactions render them liable to misunderstand what, to laymen generally is of easy comprehension."[75]

Based as it was on real property ownership in a rapidly expanding metropolis, this practical relationship between the archdiocese of New York and Emigrant Savings Bank was a new dynamic that the city's patrician elites could not ignore. So, too, was the legitimate power that came from the bank's close ties with the Irish Emigrant Society and with the Commissioners of Emigration. Emigrant's trustees—clearly drawn from old mercantile and ethnic networks—became economic elites whose resources could be employed for specific ends, be it real estate development, public affairs, or Catholic charities.[76] Thus Emigrant Savings Bank was at the nexus of urban expansion on the one hand and urban reform on the other.[77]

The Commissioners of Emigration, in particular, demonstrate how the balance of power in New York City was shifting in the middle of the nineteenth century. The exploitation of immigrants at the port of New York was out of control during the

1840s; "finally, in 1845 and 1846, [it] assumed such fearful proportions, and became the object of such general abhorrence."[78] Unscrupulous individuals and shipping companies made profits from the naive immigrant, as well as by defrauding the city of bond money that was intended to support new arrivals who became indigent. There were two opposing ideas on how to accomplish reform: city authorities wanted to amend the extant bond laws to protect New York from the growing financial burden of Irish famine immigrants; "public-spirited citizens" wanted to do that plus offer humanitarian aid to vulnerable refugees. Among this latter group advocating more radical, liberal change were John Hughes, Andrew Carrigan, and John E. Develin, the son of an immigrant from County Tyrone, who had already worked closely with Bishop Hughes to incorporate St. John's College (est. 1841, now Fordham University).[79] Working assiduously behind the scenes in both Albany and New York City, in the face of intense political opposition, these men convinced the state legislature to pass a bill that created an independent Board of Commissioners of Emigration in May 1847.[80]

Suddenly into the vortex of confusion and extortion appeared a new entity with sweeping powers over immigrant lives and related finances in New York City. There were ten commissioners: six of them were appointed by law, and four others served ex officio (the mayors of New York and Brooklyn, and the presidents of the Irish Emigrant Society and the Deutsche Gesellschaft). Gregory Dillon, as president of the Irish Emigrant Society, and Andrew Carrigan, appointed by the governor, were both early commissioners associated with the formidable task of immigration reform.[81] More than a quarter of a million immigrants were landed on New York's docks the year the commissioners began their work. The need was great; still they encountered many obstacles that were politically motivated or faced lurid reports—rumors about dissecting the dead, for example—that tainted public opinion about their efforts.[82]

By 1855 the commissioners had, out of necessity, acquired and were managing significant property including Castle Garden (for a new immigrant landing depot) at the tip of Manhattan, the quarantine facilities on Staten Island, and the two-hundred-acre Ward's Island in the East River, where it operated "the largest hospital complex in the world."[83] Authorized to collect a head tax (ranging from $1 to $2.50) for every immigrant, the commissioners managed a fund that would be worth millions today, from which it reimbursed the city and state for anyone who became a burden on the public purse in their first five years in the country.[84] The Commissioners of Emigration created this new domain out of social and political chaos; it would last until 1875 when the United States Supreme Court in the decision *Henderson v. Mayor of New York* "ruled that the federal government, not the states, had primary responsibility for immigration." Over the next twenty-five years, the Board of Commissioners of Emigration was "phased out."[85]

The men who served on this commission represented a considerable new power combination. They were all drawn from a class of citizens that Amy Bridges calls "men of wealth" who were politically active in civic affairs but not professional politicians. They were loyal to party politics on the state and national levels but not necessarily to local machine politics. Indeed, their relationship to the various factions of the city's Democrats (including Mozart Hall and Tammany Hall) was fluid during the 1850s.[86] The membership list of the Commissioners of Emigration reveals a social

The first meeting of the trustees of the Emigrant Industrial Savings Bank took place in the offices of the Commissioners of Emigration in New York City, indicating a significant confluence of social and political interests. (Archives of Irish America, New York University, Gift of Donald A. Kelly)

network in which wealth and politics appears to have leavened religious and ethnic differences. Its Irish Catholic members with connections to Emigrant Savings Bank moved in the same elite power circles as William F. Havemeyer, a sugar refiner who was the first Commissioner of Emigration and three-term mayor of the city; Gulian Verplanck, the writer–politician who was head of the commissioners from 1848 to 1870;[87] and Robert Minturn, a principal of Grinnell, Minturn and Co., the old clipper shipping firm, who became one of the incorporators of Emigrant Savings Bank.[88]

In this critical period of the bank's early history and of the history of the Irish in New York, the possible reciprocal benefits of political connections for Emigrant Savings Bank are profoundly unclear but intriguing. John E. Develin, a lawyer and key member in the state assembly at the time the commission was created, served as an emigration commissioner during 1849–1851, as well as the commission's counsel during 1847–1878, overlapping with the start of his term as counsel to Emigrant Savings Bank in 1860.[89] Moreover, a third of Emigrant's assets were invested in the bonds of the city and county of New York. Daniel Devlin was the city chamberlain (i.e., treasurer), an appointed position, from 1860 to 1867, a period during which he was also chairman of Emigrant's finance committee, making decisions on the bank's municipal bond investments. Mayor Hoffman was a pallbearer at his funeral in 1867, ordering flags on all city buildings flown at half-staff in Devlin's honor even though it was

Washington's birthday.[90] Likewise, Gregory Dillon's son, Robert James Dillon (1811–1872), a vice president of Emigrant Savings Bank from 1860 to 1865, was elected corporation counsel (meant "to defend the legal interests of New York City") for two terms between 1852 and 1856. [91] According to contemporary reports, Robert Dillon was "a very active democratic politician . . . noted for his honesty of purpose" and was one of the original commissioners of Central Park.[92]

Richard O'Gorman, a political exile from the Irish rebellion of 1848, was also elected corporation counsel for the city in 1865, the same year he became a trustee of the bank.[93] From 1866 to 1869 O'Gorman was president of the Irish Emigrant Society, making him an ex-officio member of the Commissioners of Emigration. During the Tweed scandals that rocked the New York City Democratic Party shortly afterward, O'Gorman was in a political hot seat, only barely escaping blame for being remiss in his legal oversight duties.[94] His colleagues at Emigrant Savings Bank, John E. Develin and Charles O'Conor—both Democrats—strenuously opposed Tweed's rule at Tammany Hall.[95] O'Conor, another early advocate of the Board of Commissioners of Emigration, had been a bank trustee since 1851. The son of Thomas O'Connor, a 1798 political exile connected with New York's first Irish newspaper, the *Shamrock* (est. 1810), as well as with the founding of the Irish Emigrant Society, Charles O'Conor was "always a member of Tammany, but would accept nothing at its hands." Indeed, as special deputy attorney general for New York State, O'Conor brought suit against the Tweed Ring in 1871.[96]

It is in this blaze of financial scandals surrounding Boss Tweed that historians have firmly located the standard trope of "Tammany Hall equals Irish Democrat." But this has, in significant ways, obscured the political diversity and activism of the antebellum Irish elite. The official demise of the Commissioners of Emigration[97] came shortly after the restructuring of the local Democratic machine and coincided with another shift in the New York City power dynamic. John Kelly, elected a trustee of Emigrant Savings Bank in 1859, succeeded Tweed as the head of Tammany Hall in 1871, the first Irish and Catholic man to head the eighty-three-year-old Democratic organization. Then, in the national election of 1872, Charles O'Conor ran, as the first Catholic, for president of the United States (with John Quincy Adams as vice president). And in 1880 William R. Grace, an Emigrant trustee since 1877, became (with the help of John Kelly) the first Irish-born Catholic to be elected as mayor of New York. The timing of their ascendancy seems to have ensured entries for Kelly, O'Conor, and Grace in the *Dictionary of American Biography* and the *American National Biography.*

Emigrant Savings Bank and Memory Politics

During this period (1865–1890), Henry L. Hoguet was president of Emigrant Savings Bank. His tenure is significant for three reasons. It marked a shift to professionalism within the bank, as deposits increased tenfold from $4 million. In 1876, when Emigrant's surplus fund (excess of assets less liabilities) reached a comfortable margin of nearly 10 percent, the trustees voted that the office of president should be a paid position. Hoguet was the first to draw the salary: $8,000 annually (approximately 15 percent of the total payroll).[98] In addition, the completion in 1879 of St. Patrick's Cathedral on Fifth Avenue at 50th Street—Hoguet donated a stained-glass window dedicated to Saint Louis—was a visible sign of the maturity of the archdiocese of New York. John Hughes had signed the architectural contract for the cathedral in Emigrant's offices in 1859, and the bank held a mortgage on the property that would be worth $8.6 million today.[99] Finally, during 1885–1886 Hoguet supervised the construction of a new bank building for Emigrant on its original Chambers Street site, which he not only considered "an ornament to the City" but for which he donated a portrait of Hughes to be hung in the boardroom.[100]

This painting of John Hughes may, in fact, be evidence that Emigrant itself had a hand in obscuring its founders in the collective memory of both the Irish and New York City. Hoguet's gift appears to be the origin of the story that Hughes founded the bank. According to Emigrant's 1887 minutes, Hoguet "felt it was eminently proper that the Trustees of the Bank should revere the memory of this great and good man, for it was to his wise counsels that the Bank owed its existence, and under his personal direction that it was Established."[101] It is, of course, possible that this statement was exaggerated rhetoric on a ceremonial occasion. Moreover, the incident reveals opposing forces at work: on the one hand, Hughes's portrait has long since been lost, yet those of the bank's secular trustees survive; on the other hand, the Hughes story lives on, while the trustees themselves have been forgotten. By using the Hughes connection as shorthand for the bank's origins, those very heirs to Emigrant's founding trustees have fostered a "useful myth" in order to ensure its historical relevancy.[102] They bent the truth just enough to refract history.

There is only one exception to the historical amnesia blanketing the origins of Emigrant Savings Bank, and it is fruitful to ponder why Eugene Kelly is different because in many ways he shouldn't be. Kelly joined the bank's board in 1859, served on its finance committee from 1860 to 1865, and held the position of second vice president from 1875 to 1887. His first job in 1830—as a newly arrived twenty-four-year-old from Ireland—was with Terence Donnelly, a dry-goods importer on South William Street and one of the bank's original founders, whose sister he married. He might well have been a founder of Emigrant, too, except that in 1850 Eugene Kelly was in San Francisco not New York City. But like Archbishop Hughes, he was born in County Tyrone on 25 November 1806 at Trillick, no more than twenty miles from Hughes's birthplace in Annaloughan,[103] and in 1857 Hughes's niece Margaret became his second wife. He moved his west coast private banking operations to New York City in 1861.[104] After a decade on Emigrant's Board of Trustees, he used its model in 1870 to found a similar Irish institution, the Southern Bank of Georgia, in Savannah.[105] Emigrant's minutes record his death on 19 December 1894 in no less fulsome terms than any of his predecessors:

> Our State has lost an adopted citizen of exalted character, a patriot who was as loyal to his adopted country as he was true to that native land which he loved so well, and was ever ready to contribute princely of his large means to ameliorate the privations of her suffering children or promote their relief from political proscription; the business community has lost an eminent merchant and banker, whose long business life was illuminated by a most honorable career, free from spot or blemish.[106]

The *New York Times* added that Kelly "was not a demonstrative man. He shunned notoriety and sought comfort in private life."[107] Yet Kelly, unlike the other men who also made critical decisions during the early years of the Emigrant Industrial Savings Bank, was deemed to merit an entry in both the *Dictionary of American Biography* and the *American National Biography*.[108] Why? According to the latter, "Kelly's most enduring legacy occurred with his church-related philanthropy," including roles in the foundation of the Catholic University of America and Seton Hall College.[109] Indeed, Catholicism eclipsed Kelly's secular achievements almost immediately; in his eulogy at St. Patrick's Cathedral, Rev. Henry A. Brann—who had penned a biography of John Hughes two years earlier—said, "If you ask me what a merchant and banker may be when he practices the Catholic religion, I will point to the example which Eugene Kelly gave."[110]

Times had certainly changed, and not just in the local political arena, where Tammany held sway. The federal government had taken over immigration. By 1894 the archdiocese of New York was a powerbroker of its own. Earlier in the century, John E. Develin recalled in 1875, "to be a Catholic was certainly a business deprivation and almost a social horror."[111] Now, there was an acknowledged Catholic elite in the city whose fortunes had been made in business and who were ethnically first- or second-generation Irish. Just as the fraternal links of the Friendly Sons of St. Patrick had led to the creation of the Irish Emigrant Society and the Emigrant Savings Bank, so, too, did business ties with Emigrant Savings Bank lead to the creation, in 1871, of the Catholic Club, which became an elite social circle in its own right.[112] From this period, its members began to move from the margins to the center of New York life.[113] Many were well known to John McCloskey, John Hughes's assistant from 1844 and his successor in 1864, who became the first American cardinal in 1875.[114] In a reciprocal conferring of status by association, several prominent members were given papal honors, including Henry Hoguet, who was made a Knight of St. Gregory in 1877.[115] While this appears to have merited Hoguet, a contemporary of Eugene Kelly, an entry in *Appleton's Cyclopedia of American Biography*, he was not among those chosen for profile in the more prestigious *Dictionary of American Biography* (or the *American National Biography*) published thirty years later.

Nevertheless, Hoguet was prescient about the memorialization process. The Catholic Church was ascendant, and riding its coattails must have seemed the best means of ensuring that the institution that so many had given their lives to would not be forgotten. He may even have looked back with a sense of awe at how far Emigrant had come—by 1890, it had seventy thousand account holders and approximately $40 million in deposits[116]—as well as with genuine hero worship because of what Hughes had done for the Irish and for New York City. Hoguet's own intimacy with the Catholic hierarchy may have been a sentimental blind spot when he reflected on the very practical origins of the bank. Emigrant's relationship with John Hughes was real and significant, but it appears to have been far more complex than was implied in Hoguet's tribute on the occasion of the portrait unveiling. Whatever his actual motivation, the consequences of tightly associating John Hughes with the Emigrant Savings Bank at this precise moment refracted history, veering it off the careful memorial trajectory the trustees had invoked with every death of a founder so that time could "never efface the recollection of them."[117]

In 1906 bank president James McMahon told the board: "It is known that that well beloved and patriotic prelate, John Hughes, Bishop of New York, and subsequently first Archbishop of the diocese, took a prominent part in the organization of the bank, giving it his powerful influence and encouragement."[118] By 1936 Emigrant's creation story had evolved; now "Bishop Hughes conceived the idea of a Savings Bank to take care of the protégées of the [Irish Emigrant] Society, and thus, our great Institution was brought into being."[119] When the Franciscan publication *Padre* did a story on the bank in 1958, it used that phrase—"conceived the idea"—verbatim when referring to Hughes's role,[120] which becomes increasingly more proactive with the passage of time. In an advertisement for Emigrant circa 1969, the archbishop had "invited eighteen prominent businessmen of the city to meet with him and talk about his idea of founding an institution to protect the savings [of working people]."[121] The story became part of the bank's official image, projected within as well as without the institution, so much so that Hughes's name takes precedence, while the founders are otherwise anonymous men. Accounts of Hughes routinely omit any mention of the Emigrant Savings Bank, yet the bank points directly to Hughes. What slippage between history and memory triggered such faultlines? The role of trust in personal relationships—the reliance on a man's word or handshake, the lack of need for documentation among close friends—may have ramifications for the historical record. Likewise, the fickleness of professional historical interests, including an easy reliance on what has become the standard interpretation of the Irish in America, may lead to assumptions about sources and personalities that, in fact, require more rigorous scrutiny.

"This is not a Catholic bank and never was one," declared Henry Hoguet in 1889. "Our trustees have always included Protestants as well as Catholics, in about equal proportions. We do business without the slightest regard to religious sect."[122] Why then would a strong financial institution continue to identify itself with a nineteenth-century religious figure? Despite Hoguet's protest to the contrary, Emigrant Savings Bank was perceived as the city's "Catholic" bank, attracting the business of the archdiocese, as well as board members who were active in Catholic philanthropy for much of the first half of the twentieth century. Nevertheless, in the aggressive, secular world of banking such a label could be as much a liability as an asset. But as such institutions departmentalized, especially after World War II, public relations offices were added and agencies were hired to handle advertising.

Once Emigrant passed its centenary in 1950, its "history" became a promotional asset, but those writing it could only rely on reference works like the *Dictionary of American Biography* and the *Catholic Encyclopedia*. There it was easy to find John Hughes, but biographical information on Gregory Dillon, Joseph Stuart, and their colleagues remained buried in primary texts like the bank's own books of meeting minutes or in newspaper obituaries, both of which are labor-intensive to extricate. Even today, it is far easier to research John Hughes than his friends who oversaw the Emigrant Savings Bank. Hughes retains a vital presence in the twenty-first-century equivalent of the biographical dictionary, the internet, while his closest associates discussed in this essay have faded from general historical consciousness. He is a figure with his own "historic" momentum, be it as the Manhattan Institute's 1997 poster boy for solving the problems of the modern underclass or as a formidable cameo in Martin Scorsese's film *Gangs of New York* (2002).[123]

Such presence, in fact, makes Hughes an "elite" in the sense of surviving within the documentary record. By not questioning the criteria of relevancy that enable this, we have overlooked an important dimension of the Irish during what is arguably the most critical period in their connection with the American economic juggernaut. According to Edward Pessen, "about seventy-five percent of the New York City families constituting the plutocracy of the so-called industrial era of the mid-1850s were families that comprised the elite of the merchant-capitalist era of a generation earlier." The remaining 25 percent were newcomers, including German and Irish immigrants like the men profiled in this essay, who have not received adequate scholarly attention.[124] In 1855, the Irish-born accounted for 20 percent of "merchants" (including financiers, agents, traders, and speculators), even though that was only one-half of 1 percent of all gainfully employed Irish. In other words, they were a tiny elite within the ethnic community but a statistically significant proportion of the city's commercial elite; in both cases, historians have neglected them.[125] Although Robert Ernst concluded that such men were "an aristocracy aloof from the daily life of the great masses of immigrants,"[126] the public and private memorials to the founding trustees of Emigrant Savings Bank indicate extensive interactions with new arrivals, suggesting that a serious reappraisal of their role is necessary.

Gregory Dillon envisioned the Emigrant Savings Bank as a perpetual "Irish-Americanized" institution, and so it became. He and his colleagues in that endeavor—largely forgotten by posterity and its medium, the biographical dictionary—are indeed elites, although perhaps not in the way that term has been understood in the historiography. They were self-made men within the ethnic community but not exclusively confined by it; they mediated between the first generation and the host society, straddling the middle ground in American society and serving as the conduit—in both directions—for the tangible benefits of democracy.[127] Writing in the bank's eightieth year, William H. Bennett reflected:

> While there is little of public interest in the tranquil, internal workings of a financial institution, there is the deepest interest in the personality of the generations of Irishmen, their sons and a few of other races, whose unselfish labors to assist the immigrant, built up this eminently successful institution.[128]

Ultimately, Archbishop ("Dagger John") Hughes was the better story on which to hang history, the larger-than-life personality whom the public could and would remember, even as Emigrant Savings Bank quietly paid tribute to its founders in its little-known portrait gallery. The sobering consideration is that, without the survival of either—the assurance of which was never guaranteed—a significant dimension of Irish-American, New York, and American history could elude scholars indefinitely.

NOTES

1. This essay is an expanded version of the response given to David N. Doyle's paper, "Irish Elites in North America and Liberal Democracy, 1820–1920," in *Radharc* 3 (2002): 29–53 [hereafter cited as Doyle, "Irish Elites"], which was delivered as the fourth annual O'Malley Lecture at Glucksman Ireland House, New York University, on 14 November 2002. Doyle's work on the Irish American experience is seminal, and I am grateful to Glucksman Ireland House for the opportunity to appear on the same platform with such an eminent scholar, as well as generous mentor.

2. Available at http://www.emigrant.com/aboutus.shtml (accessed 16 September 2003).

3. See Marion R. Casey and Patrick J. Mullins, *Emigrant Savings Bank, since 1850: The Spirit of Thrift* (VHS, 28 mins., Time Lapse Media, 2000) [hereafter cited as Casey and Mullins, *Spirit of Thrift*]. For a synopsis of savings bank mergers or acquisitions by commercial banks, see the alphabetical "Institutional History of Banks" list on the website of the State of New York Banking Department, available at http://www.banking.state.ny.us/history.htm (accessed 12 February 2003).

4. Landmarks Preservation Commission, *1984 Designation List (LP-1438)* (New York: City of New York, 1984).

5. While in volume they accounted for only one-twentieth of 1 percent of the substantial holdings of the Manuscript Division, 14 percent of all its users in 1995–1996 were asking for the Emigrant Savings Bank records; *Newsletter of the Archivists Round Table of Metropolitan New York, Inc.* 3, no. 1 (Winter 1998): 6. For background, see Richard E. Mooney, "An Unexpected Treasure: Bank Books Shed Light on Irish Refugees," *New York Times*, 21 September 1995, A22; Harry Keaney, "Immigrant Treasure Trove Found," *Irish Echo*, 20 September 1995, 1. For genealogists' opinions, see "New York Emigrant Savings Bank Project," available at the GenExchange website, http://www.genexchange.org/esb/index.php.

6. See, for example, Tyler Anbinder, "From Famine to Five Points: Lord Lansdowne's Irish Tenants Encounter North America's Most Notorious Slum," *American Historical Review* 107, no. 2 (2002): 350–387.

7. For context, see David C. Hammack, *Power and Society: Greater New York at the Turn of the Century* (New York: Russell Sage Foundation, 1982) [hereafter cited as Hammack, *Power and Society*]; Richard C. Murphy and Lawrence J. Mannion, *The History of the Society of the Friendly Sons of St. Patrick in the City of New York* (New York: Society of the Friendly Sons of St. Patrick, 1962) [hereafter cited as Murphy and Mannion, *Friendly Sons of St. Patrick*]. See also Edward Pessen, *Riches, Class and Power before the Civil War* (Lexington, MA: D.C. Heath, 1973), and Douglas T. Miller, *Jacksonian Aristocracy: Class and Democracy in New York, 1830–1860* (New York: Oxford University Press, 1967).

8. A welcome exception is the monumental book by Kerby A. Miller, Arnold Schrier, Bruce D. Boling, and David N. Doyle, *Irish Immigrants in the Land of Canaan: Letters and Memoirs from Colonial and Revolutionary America, 1675–1815* (New York: Oxford University Press, 2003). The main studies of turn-of-the-twentieth-century Irish-American elites—namely, Stephen Birmingham's *Real Lace: America's Irish Rich* (New York: Harper and Row, 1973), and John Corry's *Golden Clan: The Murrays, McDonnells and the Irish American Aristocracy* (Boston: Houghton Mifflin, 1977)—have overlooked nineteenth-century elites such as the founders of the Emigrant Savings Bank.

9. Richard White, *Remembering Ahanagran: Storytelling in a Family's Past* (New York: Hill and Wang, 1998), 49, 66.

10. William H. Bennett, "A Chronological History of the Emigrant Industrial Savings Bank," typescript document, unpublished circa 1931, 1 [copy in possession of the author; here-

after cited as Bennett, "Emigrant History"]. For a more recent account, see Casey and Mullins, *The Spirit of Thrift*. I am currently engaged in writing a business history of Emigrant Savings Bank.

11. The classic theoretical work on memory is Maurice Halbwachs, *Les cadres sociaux de la mémoire* (Paris: F. Alcan, 1925), which has been edited and translated into English by Lewis A. Coser as *On Collective Memory* (Chicago: University of Chicago Press, 1992). The recent literature on the subject includes David Thelen, "Memory and American History," *Journal of American History* 75, no. 4 (March 1989): 1117–1129; Susan A. Crane, "Writing the Individual back into Collective Memory," *American Historical Review* 102, no. 5 (December 1997): 1372–1385; Alon Confino, "Collective Memory and Cultural History: Problems of Method," *American Historical Review* 102, no. 5 (December 1997): 1386–1403; Michael Kammen, *Mystic Chords of Memory: The Transformation of Tradition in American Culture* (New York: Knopf, 1991); Roy Rosenzweig and David Thelen, *The Presence of the Past: Popular Uses of History in American Life* (New York: Columbia University Press, 1998); Stephen Bertman, *Cultural Amnesia: America's Future and the Crisis of Memory* (Westport, CT: Praeger, 2000); "Cinqué and the Historians: How a Story Takes Hold—A Round Table," *Journal of American History* 87, no. 3 (December 2000): 923–950; David Glassberg, *Sense of History: The Place of the Past in American Life* (Amherst: University of Massachusetts Press, 2001); Gary R. Edgerton and Peter C. Rollins, eds., *Television Histories: Shaping Collective Memory in the Media Age* (Lexington: University of Kentucky Press, 2001). For studies of memory in the Irish diaspora see, for example, James S. Donnelly Jr., "The Construction of the Memory of the Famine in Ireland and the Irish Diaspora, 1850–1900," *Eire-Ireland* 31, no. 1–2 (Spring/Summer 1996): 26–61.

12. Doyle, "Irish Elites" (lecture, New York University, New York, NY, 14 November 2002); not included in *Radhare* 3 essay (previously cited).

13. Introduction to *The National Cyclopaedia of American Biography* (New York: James T. White, 1893), vii–x; Preface to *Appleton's Cyclopaedia of American Biography*, ed. James Grant Wilson and John Fiske (New York: Appleton, 1898), v–vi; Introduction to *The Dictionary of American Biography*, ed. Allen Johnson (New York: Scribner's, 1927), v–vi.

14. Marion R. Casey, "Ireland, New York and the Irish Image in American Popular Culture, 1890–1960" (Ph.D. diss., New York University, 1998), 147 [hereafter cited as Casey, "Irish Image in American Popular Culture"]; John R. Commons, *Races and Immigrants in America* (New York: Chautauqua Press, 1907), 22–23.

15. *American National Biography*, "Henry Cabot Lodge," available at http://www.anb.org (accessed 11 April 2003).

16. John Higham, *Strangers in the Land: Patterns of American Nativism, 1860–1925*, 2nd ed. (New Brunswick, NJ: Rutgers University Press, 1988), 323.

17. Casey, "Irish Image in American Popular Culture," 135–140.

18. Doyle, "Irish Elites."

19. Nor for that matter in *The Catholic Encyclopedia: An International Work of Reference on the Constitution, Doctrine, Discipline, and History of the Catholic Church*, ed. Charles G. Herbermann, Edward A. Pace, Condé B. Pallen, Thomas J. Shahan, and John J. Wynne (New York: Appleton, c. 1907–1914) vol. 7, 516–518 [hereafter cited as *Catholic Encyclopedia*]; Michael Glazier, ed., *The Encyclopedia of the Irish in America* (Notre Dame, IN: University of Notre Dame Press, 1999), 395 [hereafter cited as Glazier, *Encyclopedia of the Irish in America*]; or in Kenneth T. Jackson, ed., *The Encyclopedia of New York City* (New Haven: Yale University Press, 1995), 573 [hereafter cited as Jackson, *Encyclopedia of NYC*]. Ditto for Hughes's obituary in the *New York Times*, 4 January 1864, 8:1.

20. Edmund S. Leamy, *The Story of the American Irish Historical Society* (New York: By the

Society, 1951), and Kenneth J. Moynihan, "History as a Weapon for Social Advancement: Group History as Told by the American Irish Historical Society," *New York Irish History* 8 (1993–1994): 34–40.

21. *The Catholic Encyclopedia* is available online at http://www.newadvent.org/cathen/. See also *The Catholic Encyclopedia and Its Makers* (New York: The Encyclopedia Press, 1917), which is also available online at http://www.newadvent.org/cathen/00001a.htm (accessed 5 April 2003).

22. John R. G. Hassard, *Life of the Most Reverend John Hughes, D.D., First Archbishop of New York: With Extracts from His Private Correspondence* (New York: Appleton, 1866) [hereafter cited as Hassard, *Life of John Hughes*]; Richard Shaw, *Dagger John: The Unquiet Life and Times of Archbishop John Hughes of New York* (New York: Paulist Press, 1977).

23. Hassard, *Life of John Hughes,* 333–336.

24. Minutes of the Emigrant Industrial Savings Bank, 13 October 1887, still held by the bank [hereafter cited as EISB Minutes].

25. Leo Hershkowitz, "The Irish and the Emerging City: Settlement to 1844," in *The New York Irish*, ed. Ronald H. Bayor and Timothy J. Meagher (Baltimore, MD: Johns Hopkins University Press, 1996), 30 [hereafter cited as Bayor and Meagher, *New York Irish*]; Jay P. Dolan, *The Immigrant Church: New York's Irish and German Catholics, 1815–1865* (Notre Dame, IN: University of Notre Dame Press, 1983), 13 [hereafter cited as Dolan, *Immigrant Church*].

26. Allan Nevins, *The Diary of Philip Hone, 1828–1851* (New York: Dodd, Mead, 1936), 189–190 (entry for 17 December 1835).

27. Mary Elizabeth Brown, "John Joseph Hughes," in Glazier, *Encyclopedia of the Irish in America,* 395.

28. Marion R. Casey, "Friends in Need: Financing Emigration from Ireland," *Seaport* (New York's History Magazine) (May 1996): 30–33 [hereafter cited as Casey, "Friends in Need"].

29. Annual Report for the period 1 April 1850 to 1 April 1851 entered in the Minutes of the Irish Emigrant Society, 7 July 1851, New York Public Library [hereafter cited as IES Minutes]. The remittances for 1850–1851 were £40,700 ($198,209 with £1 = $4.87). The "purchasing power" of that dollar amount today would be $4,635,513.88, according to the Economic History Services calculator based on John J. McCusker, "Comparing the Purchasing Power of Money in the United States (or Colonies) from 1665 to Any Other Year Including the Present," Economic History Services, 2001, available on the web at http://eh.net/hmit/ (accessed 3 February 2003) [hereafter cited as McCusker, "Purchasing Power of Money"].

30. Quoted in Murphy and Mannion, *Friendly Sons of St. Patrick,* 275.

31. Richard J. Purcell, "The Irish Emigrant Society of New York," *Studies* (Dublin) 27 (1938): 588; see also Casey, "Friends in Need."

32. Murphy and Mannion, *Friendly Sons of St. Patrick,* 277. Robert Hogan, first vice president of the society, temporarily succeeded MacNeven at his death. IES Minutes, 30 August 1841.

33. See Annual Report for the period 1 March 1851 to 1 March 1852, IES Minutes, 5 April 1852; see also Friedrich Kapp, *Immigration and the Commissioners of Emigration* (New York: Nation Press, 1870; reprint, New York: Arno Press, 1969), 86 [hereafter cited as Kapp, *Commissioners of Emigration*].

34. Peter Condon, "The Irish (in countries other than Ireland), Part I: In the United States," in *The Catholic Encyclopedia* (New York: Appleton [1907–1912]), available at http://www.newadvent.org/cathen/08132b.htm (accessed 9 February 2003); emphasis added.

35. Bennett, "Emigrant History," 1.

36. Although its depositors always called it "Emigrant Savings Bank," its official name was "Emigrant Industrial Savings Bank" until 1967.

37. Letter from Gregory Dillon to the Executive Committee of the Irish Emigrant Society, 19 August 1850, IES Minutes, 22 August 1850; emphasis in the original.

38. For a glimpse at the level of detail in the bank's records, see Kevin J. Rich's transcriptions from Test Book No. 1 in *Irish Immigrants of the Emigrant Industrial Savings Bank, 1850–1853* (New York: Broadway-Manhattan Company, 2001).

39. Unless otherwise noted, all such information on occupation or business address was found in either Doggett's or Rode's *New York City Directory* for 1850–1851. The officers of the Emigrant Industrial Savings Bank at the end of its first year were Gregory Dillon, president; Joseph Stuart, vice president; Peter A. Hargous, vice president; Fanning C. Tucker, treasurer. Its trustees were Louis B. Binsse, Andrew Carrigan, Charles M. Connolly, Daniel Devlin, Terence Donnelly, Hugh Kelly, James Kelly, James Kerrigan, Felix Ingoldsby, John Manning, James Mathews, John McMenomy, John Milhau, Robert B. Minturn, John P. Nesmith, John Nicholson, Charles O'Conor, James Olwell, William Redmond, Cornelius H. Sheehan, Edward W. Tiers, Martin Waters, and William Watson.

40. Murphy and Mannion, *Friendly Sons of St. Patrick*, 281–282.

41. John D. Crimmins, *Irish-American Historical Miscellany. Relating Largely to New York City and Vicinity, Together with Much Interesting Material Relative to Other Parts of the Country* (New York: By the author, 1905), 164 [hereafter cited as Crimmins, *Irish-American Historical Miscellany*].

42. For background, see Kapp, *Commissioners of Emigration,* and Richard J. Purcell, "The New York Commissioners of Emigration and Irish Immigrants, 1847–1860," *Studies* (Dublin) 37 (1948): 29–42 [hereafter cited as Purcell, *Commissioners of Emigration*].

43. "Death of Gregory Dillon," *New York Times*, 8 March 1854, p. 3.

44. "Death of Gregory Dillon, Esq.," *Irish-American*, 11 March 1854.

45. EISB Minutes, 6 March 1854.

46. Bennett, "Emigrant History," 6; *New York Times* obituary for James Stuart, 27 March 1879, 2.

47. Letter from Gregory Dillon to the Executive Committee of the Irish Emigrant Society, 19 August 1850, in IES Minutes, 22 August 1850; for the number of drafts, see IES Minutes, 25 April 1854.

48. Letter from Joseph Stuart to the Board of Trustees of the Emigrant Industrial Savings Bank, 12 April 1865, EISB Minutes, 12 April 1865. His obituary gives the reason as the "passage of a law prohibiting one person from holding official positions in more than one institution, he being at the time a Director and Vice President of the National Mercantile Bank, besides being connected with various insurance companies in this country and in Europe." *New York Times,* 19 November 1874, 4.

49. EISB minutes, 20 November 1874.

50. "Obituary: Joseph Stuart," *New York Times*, 19 November 1874, 4.

51. Crimmins, *Irish-American Historical Miscellany*, 412; "Obituary: Henry L. Hoguet," *New York Times*, 10 May 1890, 4.

52. EISB Minutes, 10 May 1890.

53. *New York Times*, 10 May 1890, 4; 12 May 1890, 5; 13 May 1890, 8; *New York Evening Post,* 12 May 1890, 5; *New York Sun,* 11 May 1890, 7.

54. EISB Minutes, 10 December 1891.

55. EISB Minutes, 21 January 1892.

56. Bennett, "Emigrant History," 8; "Obituary: James Olwell," *New York Times*, 13 August 1896, 5.

57. EISB Minutes, 13 August 1896; reprinted in *New York Times*, 16 August 1896, 5.

58. Emigrant's finance committee chairman during its first year of operation was James Kerrigan, but I have been unable to locate any biographical information about him.

59. Walter Barrett [pseud. for Joseph A. Scoville], *The Old Merchants of New York City* (New York: Carleton, 1863–1869), 53; also quoted in Bennett, "Emigrant History," 4.

60. EISB Minutes, 13 January 1870.

61. "Obituary: Andrew Carrigan," *New York Times*, 6 September 1872, 5.

62. *New York Times*, 8 September 1872, 5; see also Kapp, *Commissioners of Emigration*, 85–104.

63. *New York Times* obituary, 6 September 1872, 5:4.

64. For conversion, see McCusker, "Purchasing Power of Money."

65. "Obituary: City Chamberlain Daniel Devlin," *New York Times*, 23 February 1867, 3; see also William E. Devlin, "Shrewd Irishmen: Irish Entrepreneurs and Artisans in New York's Clothing Industry, 1830–1880," in Bayor and Meagher, *New York Irish*, 184–186.

66. EISB Minutes, 23 February 1867.

67. "The Death of Mr. Devlin: Action of the Common Council," *New York Times*, 24 February 1867, 8.

68. *The Catholic Encyclopedia*, s.v. "John Hughes"; available at http://www.newadvent.org/cathen/ (accessed 5 April 2003); *American National Biography*, s.v. "John Joseph Hughes" available at http://www.anb.org (accessed 5 April 2003); quote from Hassard, *Life of John Hughes*, 330–331.

69. Kerby A. Miller, *Emigrants and Exiles: Ireland and the Irish Exodus to North America* (New York: Oxford University Press, 1985), 193–199, 240.

70. Dolan, *Immigrant Church*, 15.

71. Ibid., 13–15, 59.

72. See Bond and Mortgage Record Books, 1 (1851–1881), entry for 5 April 1852, Emigrant Savings Bank Records, New York Public Library.

73. See Finance Committee Minutes, Emigrant Savings Bank, 5 East 42nd Street, New York City, entries for 8 and 26 August 1854.

74. EISB Minutes, 14 December 1853.

75. Emigrant Savings Bank Trustees to Archbishop John Hughes, 8 December 1856, entered in EISB Minutes, 10 December 1856. The only scholarship on this period of the bank's history is Cormac Ó Gráda and Eugene N. White, "The Panics of 1854 and 1857: A View from the Emigrant Industrial Savings Bank," *Journal of Economic History* 63, no. 1 (March 2003): 213–240.

76. Several of Emigrant's trustees had oversight responsibilities for Catholic charitable operations that had a direct impact on welfare conditions in the city. Among the incorporators in 1863 of the new Roman Catholic Orphan Asylum (constructed next to the new St. Patrick's Cathedral) were Felix Ingoldsby, Daniel Devlin, Andrew Carrigan, and Henry Hoguet. That same year Henry Hoguet helped Archbishop Hughes found the New York Catholic Protectory, a large institution for juvenile delinquents. He served as its president for sixteen years alongside James Olwell, who was one of its original trustees. "The New Protectory for Destitute Catholic Children," *New York Times*, 24 July 1865, 5. See also George P. Jacoby, *Catholic Child Care in Nineteenth Century New York* (New York: Arno Press, 1974), and John O'Grady, *Catholic Charities in the United States* (New York: Arno Press, 1971).

77. For a discussion of elite categories and their relationship to urban power, see Hammack, *Power and Society*, 4–59.

78. Purcell, *Commissioners of Emigration*, 29–30; quote from Kapp, *Commissioners of Emigration*, 86.

79. "Death of Jacob Harvey," *Brooklyn Eagle*, 12 May 1848, 2; "John E. Develin's Death," *New York Times*, 24 February 1888, 8. Develin served as chief secretary of the Irish Famine Relief Fund Association.

80. Kapp, *Commissioners of Emigration*, 85–94.

81. Indeed, "the maintenance of German and Irish interests was left largely with the German and Irish members." Robert Ernst, *Immigrant Life in New York City, 1825–1863* (New York: King's Crown Press, 1949; reprint, Syracuse, NY: Syracuse University Press, 1994), 30 [hereafter cited as Ernst, *Immigrant Life in NYC*].

82. Kapp, *Commissioners of Emigration*, 227; Ernst, *Immigrant Life in NYC*, 29–32; Purcell, *Commissioners of Emigration*, 34.

83. Kapp, *Commissioners of Emigration*, 125–135; Edwin G. Burrows and Mike Wallace, *Gotham: A History of New York City to 1898* (New York: Oxford University Press, 1999), 738.

84. Kapp, *Commissioners of Emigration*, 98, 153, 158, 237. In 1853, for example, the commissioners reimbursed the City of New York, the counties of New York State, and several charitable hospitals and institutions in the amount of $151,872.17, which is the equivalent of $3,536,778.20 today. McCusker, "Purchasing Power of Money." Its deposit accounts with Emigrant Savings Bank are numbers 5461–5476.

85. Mary Elizabeth Brown, "Emigrant Relief Services (New York)," in *Encyclopedia of the Irish in America*, ed. Michael Glazier, 250; remarks of James McMahon, EISB Minutes, 18 January 1906.

86. Amy Bridges, *A City in the Republic: Antebellum New York and the Origins of Machine Politics* (Ithaca, NY: Cornell University Press, 1984), 126–131.

87. "Obituary: Hon. Gulian C. Verplanck," *New York Times*, 19 March 1870, p. 5. Verplanck's dozen years at the helm of the Commissioners of Emigration deserves more detailed treatment than it has received in recent literature.

88. Bennett, *Emigrant History*, 2; "Obituary: Andrew Carrigan," *New York Times,* 6 September 1872, 5.

89. "John E. Develin's Death," *New York Times*, 24 February 1888, 8; Bennett, *Emigrant History*, 3.

90. "An Aldermanic Coup d'Etat," *New York Times*, 25 December 1860, 4; "City Chamberlain Daniel Devlin," *New York Times*, 23 February 1867, 3; and "The Death of Mr. Devlin, Action of the Common Council," *New York Times*, 24 February 1867, 8.

91. See Dillon's obituary in the *New York Times*, 27 November 1872, 2; Jackson, *Encyclopedia of NYC*, s.v. "corporation counsel," 285.

92. "Obituary: Robert J. Dillon," unidentified newspaper clipping, circa 27 November 1872 [copy in possession of the author].

93. Bennett, *Emigrant History*, 4, 6.

94. Kerby Miller, "Richard O'Gorman," in *Encyclopedia of the Irish in America*, ed. Glazier, 727; Leo Hershkowitz, *Tweed's New York: Another Look* (Garden City, NY: Anchor Press, Doubleday, 1977), 196.

95. "John E. Develin's Death," *New York Times*, 24 February 1888, 8; Jackson, *Encyclopedia of NYC*, s.v. "Charles O'Conor," 860.

96. Bennett, "Emigrant History," 3; "Death of Charles O'Conor," *New York Times*, 14 May 1884, 5; *American National Biography*, s.v. "Charles O'Conor," available at http://www.anb.org (accessed 8 February 2003); Jackson, *Encyclopedia of NYC*, s.v. "Charles O'Conor," 860. On Thomas O'Connor, see Murphy and Mannion, *Friendly Sons of St. Patrick*, 277, and John P. O'Connor, "*The Shamrock* of New York: The First Irish-American Newspaper," *New York Irish History* 4 (1989): 4–5.

97. Castle Garden continued to operate under state control for another fifteen years until it was superseded by the federal facilities on Ellis Island.

98. EISB Minutes, 8 June 1876. The percentage was based on the 1881 payroll total of $50,450 when Hoguet's salary was still $8,000 per year ($139,942 today; see McCusker, "Purchasing Power of Money"). For perspective, the comptroller earned $7,000, the accountant $5,000, tellers $3,500, bookkeepers $1,800, porters $1,200, janitors $300, and messenger boys $250. See EISB Minutes, 21 July 1881.

99. John M. Farley, *History of St. Patrick's Cathedral* (New York: Society for the Propagation of the Faith, 1908), 115, 195–196. The $400,000 mortgage for "St. Patrick's (New Cathedral)" was paid in full by the 1870s. See Bond and Mortgage Record Books 1, no. 760 (1851–1881), Emigrant Savings Bank Records, New York Public Library.

100. EISB Minutes, 13 October 1887, and "President's Report," 16 January 1890.

101. EISB Minutes, 13 October 1887.

102. On "useful myths," see the seminal essay by Carl Becker, "Everyman His Own Historian," *American Historical Review* 37, no. 2 (January 1932): 221–236; see also Robert E. McGlone, "Deciphering Memory: John Adams and the Authorship of the Declaration of Independence," *Journal of American History* 85, no. 2 (September 1998): 411–438.

103. Annaloughan is a townland in the Barony and Parish of Clogher, one mile from Augher, County Tyrone. See Hassard, *Life of John Hughes*, 13.

104. Crimmins, *Irish-American Historical Miscellany*, 417–418.

105. "In Memoriam" [Southern Bank of Georgia for Eugene Kelly], *New York Times*, 30 December 1894, 5.

106. EISB Minutes, 20 December 1894.

107. "Death of Eugene Kelly," *New York Times*, 20 December 1894, 13.

108. John Hughes, as noted, has an entry, but he was not a trustee of the bank. The only other original trustee besides Eugene Kelly to have an entry in the *American National Biography* is the attorney Charles O'Conor. His entry appears to be for reasons related to his national political ambitions. He was not involved in the daily operation of Emigrant as were its presidents and finance committee chairmen.

109. *American National Biography*, s.v. "Eugene Kelly," available at http://www.anb.org (accessed 9 February 2003).

110. "Eugene Kelly Laid at Rest," *New York Times*, 23 December 1894, 4. The biography is Henry A. Brann, *Most Reverend John Hughes: First Archbishop of New York* (New York: Dodd, Mead, 1892). It does not mention Emigrant Savings Bank either.

111. Quoted in "Honor to the Cardinal," *New York Times*, 18 May 1875, 10.

112. Marion R. Casey, "Catholic Club of the City of New York," in Jackson, *Encyclopedia of NYC*, p. 190. Originally known as the Xavier Union, it was a membership organization centered around St. Francis Xavier Church on West 16th Street and was spun off from the Xavier Alumni Sodality established in 1863 for graduates of the College of St. Francis Xavier [now Xavier High School]. Among those Emigrant trustees with ties to St. Francis were Andrew Carrigan, James Olwell, and the Devlin brothers, Daniel and Jeremiah. See "Carrigan," *New York Times*, 7 September 1872, 7; "James Olwell," *New York Times*, 13 August 1896, 7; and "St. Francis Xavier College, Sixteenth Annual Commencement," *New York Times*, 6 July 1866, 8.

113. The Catholic Club was listed in New York's *Social Register* by the end of the century; see Hammack, *Power and Society*, 69.

114. *American National Biography*, s.v. "John McCloskey," available at http://www.anb.org (accessed 9 February 2003).

115. *Appleton's Cyclopedia of American Biography*, Vol. 3, s.v. "Henry Louis Hoguet" (New

York: Appleton, 1898), 230. Given Emigrant's relationship to the real estate of the archdiocese of New York, it is worth noting that the Order of St. Gregory was a nineteenth-century award conferred on laymen who "defended the temporal territory of the Church." James-Charles Noonan Jr., *The Church Visible: The Ceremonial Life and Protocol of the Roman Catholic Church* (New York: Viking, 1996), 112.

116. Annual Report of the Emigrant Industrial Savings Bank, 1916.

117. EISB Minutes, 13 January 1870.

118. EISB Minutes, 18 January 1906.

119. Patrick F. Walsh and Francis X. Meehan, "Historical Outline of the Emigrant Industrial Savings Bank and the Irish Emigrant Society," *Annals* 1, no. 4 (25 June 1936): 3 [internal bank typescript document, copy in the possession of the author].

120. Frank Hanifin, "The Bank the Irish Built," *Padre* 9, no. 3 (March 1958), published by the Franciscan Fathers of the Province of the Immaculate Conception.

121. "Eighteen Men with a Good Idea: How Emigrant Savings Bank Was Founded 120 Years Ago," advertisement from an unidentified newspaper reproduced in the *Emigrant Eagle*, 125th Anniversary Souvenir Issue, 1975 [copy in possession of the author]. The *Emigrant Eagle* was an in-house publication of the bank.

122. Quoted in "Denials Met on All Sides," *New York Times*, 8 December 1889, 6.

123. Hughes is described as "the catalyst for cultural change that liberated" the New York Irish, someone who did it with "no job-training program or welfare system" to aid him. William J. Stern, "Urbanities: How Dagger John Saved New York's Irish," *City Journal* 7, no. 2 (Spring 1997): 84, 105; available at http://www.city-journal.org/html/7_2_a2.html. See also Stern's op-ed in the *Wall Street Journal*, 17 March 1997, Eastern edition, A18, and "What *Gangs of New York* Misses," *City Journal*, 14 January 2003; available at http://www.city_journal.org/html/eon_1_14_03ws.html.

124. Edward Pessen, "The Egalitarian Myth and the American Social Reality: Wealth, Mobility and Equality in the 'Era of the Common Man,'" *American Historical Review* 76, no. 4 (October 1971): 1017. On German elites, see Stanley Nadel, *Little Germany: Ethnicity, Religion, and Class in New York City, 1845–1880* (Urbana and Chicago: University of Illinois Press, 1990), 83–87.

125. Ernst, *Immigrant Life in NYC*, 95.

126. Ibid., 98.

127. Irish Catholic laymen played a similar role in Savannah where, according to Paul Thigpen, "they became local leaders who interpreted the larger world for their followers." Quoted in Audrey D. McCombs, "Aristocracy of the Heart," *Savannah Morning News*, 20 February 1999; available at http://www.savannahnow.com/stories/022099/ACCirishcatholics.html (accessed 10 February 2003).

128. Bennett, "Emigrant History," i.

SUGGESTED READING

Marion R. Casey and Patrick J. Mullins, *Emigrant Savings Bank, since 1850: The Spirit of Thrift* (VHS, 28 mins., Time Lapse Media, 2000).

Friedrich Kapp, *Immigration and the Commissioners of Emigration* (New York: Nation Press, 1870; reprint, New York: Arno Press, 1969).

Richard C. Murphy and Lawrence J. Mannion, *The History of the Society of the Friendly Sons of St. Patrick in the City of New York* (New York: Society of the Friendly Sons of St. Patrick, 1962).

Cormac Ó Gráda and Eugene N. White, "The Panics of 1854 and 1857: A View from the Emigrant Industrial Savings Bank," *Journal of Economic History* 63, no. 1 (March 2003): 213–240.

Richard J. Purcell, "The Irish Emigrant Society of New York," *Studies* (Dublin) 27 (1938): 583–599.

Richard J. Purcell, "The New York Commissioners of Emigration and Irish Immigrants, 1847–1860," *Studies* (Dublin) 37 (1948): 29–42.

Chapter 11

Ubiquitous Bridget

Irish Immigrant Women in Domestic Service in America, 1840–1930

Margaret Lynch-Brennan

Is cuma leis an óige cá leagann sí a cos.
Youth does not mind where it sets its foot.

—Irish Proverb

Even if most of Ireland missed the Industrial Revolution in the mid–nineteenth century, it did not fail to affect the Irish people. The million and a half Irish men and women who fled to America from the Great Famine and its immediate aftermath during the decade from 1845 to 1855 discovered that the Industrial Revolution and its consequences created opportunities for them that were unimaginable at home. Irish women in particular benefited from the changes to American society in their search for means of support for themselves and their impoverished families in Ireland; the increasing demand for domestic servants created an opportune occupational niche for them. As American families reaped the benefits of the Industrial Revolution, the Anglo-American middle class adopted Victorian ideals, placing the home as moral center and forming what has since been termed a cult of domesticity.

In this way, the matriarch of the Anglo-American family, representing the center of the domestic sphere, and the female Irish immigrant, as a willing English-speaking domestic servant for hire, formed a symbiotic relationship wherein the one was able to pursue education, reform, and other Victorian ideals, while the other was able to provide for herself, and perhaps even her family in Ireland, by working as a maid, chambermaid, child nurse, cook, waitress, or laundress. Through this working relationship, the female Irish domestic became the face of the Irish for many Americans across a gulf of class, cultural, ethnic, and religious differences. The intimate sphere of the home allowed the kind of constant contact and interaction that is so rare in hired employment of men, as indicated by the term "domestic" servant itself. This contact helped pave the way for the Irish, as a group, to become acceptable to Americans and gave Irish women an opportunity to learn and internalize American middle-class values and social conduct, which they could in turn apply as a means of propelling their families up the social scale.[1]

The reputation of the Irish domestic took on such a strong emblematic value throughout the United States that, according to Blaine McKinley, "after 1850 domestic servants and the Irish became virtually synonymous." While the Irish were certainly not the only group employed as such, African-American, German, and Scandinavian immigrant women, who also worked as domestics, failed to gain the sort of prominence that the Irish did, particularly in the urban Northeast, Mid-Atlantic, and parts of the Midwest. This repute was so extensive that the American public came to use the name Bridget, or Biddy, as a generic soubriquet for Irish servants, along with the names Kate, Katy, Maggie, and Peggy, though these to a much lesser extent. So strong was the association between the name Biddy or Bridget and Irish domestics that when Bridget McGeoghegan came to America from Donegal in 1923, her aunts insisted on calling her Bertha instead of Bridget because of the American Biddy jokes about Irish servant girls. (McGeoghegan regretted the name change, saying, "I wish I never did have it changed, because I like Bridget.") From the mid–nineteenth century on, the Irish Biddy or Bridget became ubiquitous in American popular literature, where she was decried and derided in cartoons as well as text.[2]

Despite the stereotypes associated with being a "Bridget" or a "Biddy," Irish immigrant women flocked to the United States, where the demand for servants exceeded the supply. As the emigration rates for Irish women began to increase from the 1830s, females comprised about one-half of all Irish immigrants to the United States over the next century, a much higher female proportion than the European average. Most of them, ranging in age from late-teens to late-twenties, were the daughters of tenants of limited means from rural Ireland, rather than the children of either "strong" (that is, wealthy) farmers or poorer agricultural laborers. Many came in a chain migration in which male and female relatives brought over other family members over time. Family, not gender, was key to this type of migration. As Margaret Convery Horan, who came from Ireland in 1914 to become a domestic servant, explained, it was her brother Dan who "sent me my ticket to come" because "he got lonely so he wanted somebody [of the family] out so he sent for me." Many living in rural Ireland became familiar with the United States through the American letters written home by relatives and friends, which made emigration seem both attractive and possible. To Irish girls, American letters provided tangible evidence of the domestic service jobs available in the United States.[3]

If encouragement in American letters alone were not enough to spur Irish women to emigrate, they also found the necessity of a dowry to marry in Ireland a motivating factor. Needing a "fortune," as a dowry was called in Ireland, was a new predicament for many of these women, as before the Famine usually only daughters of the strong farmers needed one. After the Famine, however, marriages between the families of "small" farmers also came to be affairs arranged by parents, and a fortune became necessary for a girl to make a match. Most Irish parents of limited means could afford to provide a fortune for only one daughter. That left few options except emigration for the remaining daughters, for whom no fortune could be provided. In 1850, an Irish girl in Buffalo, New York, wrote to her mother in Ireland that "I would advise all the handsome girls in Gourtbane to come here, as it makes no matter with girls here whether they have money or not; the boys' here do not look for a fortune; but every boy a handsome wife." Marriage was important to women like her for various personal reasons; underlying many of these was the fact that it was through marriage that they would acquire adult status. In both pre- and post-Famine Irish society, this was the case, and those who were single endured the lower social standing associated with their marital status.[4]

American women hiring domestics during the century before 1930, when the Great Depression diverted Irish emigration to Great Britain and by which time African Americans had overtaken the Irish as the predominant group in service, naturally sought servants who could speak English. Not only did most Irish girls speak the language, they were also increasingly literate in it. In fact, by the end of the nineteenth century, almost all were literate, compared with approximately 29 percent in the 1850s, the increase due in no small part to the 1831 establishment of a system of national schools that facilitated the spread of English-language literacy in Ireland.[5]

While Irish women fit the bill for an employable servant in the United States, American women were eager to hire servants as they strived to meet the rising standards of cleanliness and gentility associated with the expansion of the middle class through industrialization and urbanization. Engaging servants brought status to the employing families, marking positively their class station. Even people of limited means were known to hire servants in order to enhance their social status. The matriarch of the domestic sphere was nothing if she could not keep up appearances; no matter how little resources a woman had to work with, the cult of domesticity dictated she maximize any means to maintain the exacting standards of at least a façade of gentility. Part of this social role was using any leisure time obtained through the employment of servants for pursuits such as reading, writing letters, taking morning naps, and making formal social calls. Servants also allowed many women to procure the spare time to do good works through activity in "the voluntary organizations known as the 'benevolent empire,'" working on "temperance, moral reform, Sabbatarianism, domestic and foreign missions, and aid to the poor."[6]

Ironically, the developing rich material culture inherent in the American, middle-class culture that bred the demand for the multitudes of domestics employed in the nineteenth and early twentieth centuries also meant there was a gulf between the mistress of the household and most Irish immigrant girls. Irish material culture was primitive by comparison, and even the small minority of women who had worked in service in Ireland before immigrating were unprepared for American domestic service. Rather than employ green girls from rural Ireland, American homemakers preferred experienced servants, not only because they found training servants to be hard work but also because training took time away from what was supposed to be their leisure. Their desire for trained servants was exacerbated by the fact that many middle-class American women did not themselves know much about proper methods of executing housework and were insecure in their relations with servants because few of them came from families that had employed servants.[7]

As might be expected, the result of such an awkward pairing was an abundance of complaints about Irish servants. To their critics, they were guilty of "ignorance, rawness . . . stupidity." "Bridget's ignorance and awkwardness" were said to be such that employers complained that "these Irish servants are the plague of our lives." She was

With her Irish Free State passport issued in 1932, Mary Anne (Molly) Ryan emigrated to the United States and found domestic service work in Albany, New York. (Courtesy of Donald F. Arnold Jr.)

"ignorant of the names of utensils, even of the use of scrubbing brushes, since her floor at home was the hard earth," as well as "ignorant of the manners of the country." She did not know how to light a fire in a stove and was unfamiliar with the concept of drinking glasses. Employers lamented that Bridget was also wont to take her duties less than seriously—one mistress complained she was likely to "find cuffs and collars tucked way in odd holes and corners, instead of being washed and ironed." The mistress might also find other mementos of Bridget's questionable work habits, such as "precious glass and china broken, and no word told of it till the moment of its imperative need for use," prompting some to call for making maids pay for any china that, through carelessness, they might break. Irish girls in the employ of the famous feminist Elizabeth Cady Stanton apparently exasperated her, for she revealed in her correspondence that "she feared being hung for 'breaking the pate of some stupid Hibernian for burning my meat or pudding on some company occasion.'" To what extent various domestics deserved this censure, we can only speculate.[8]

Differences in social codes, in addition to differences in material culture, separated Bridget from her American employer. In contrast to the ideal of the submissive woman expected of urban, middle-class American women in the cult of domesticity, culture in peasant Ireland permitted women to be verbally assertive, as indicated in the Irish proverb "a woman's tongue is a thing that doesn't rust." Since it was generally spirited and ambitious Irish women who came to the United States, popular American literature was rife with stories of the assertive Bridget. According to employers, Bridget was "insolent," "defiant," had a "temper," and "made it a point to be cross whenever there was company." She was known for being "impudent," for her "impertinence," and for her "self-assertion." She demanded "all her evenings out," and, when told to be in by 10 P.M., instead, remained out until midnight. As late as 1934, complaints were still being made about the assertiveness of Irish domestics. According to an employer, when she attempted to fire a waitress with "Hibernian temper," she was dismayed that the waitress' response to her dismissal was to argue that "she will not leave and that, what is more, she will call in a policeman. (Her brother is on the police force.)"[9]

Disparity between employer expectations and Irish domestic conduct also became a topic of complaint for mistresses. Problems sometimes arose from the fact that some Protestant employers did not consider Catholics to be Christians and thus tried to convert their Irish domestics to Protestantism. This problem seems to have been rather pronounced in Irish domestic–employer relations; there is little record of equivalent cases of religious discrimination of other ethnic groups during this period, though German Catholic domestics have yet to be adequately studied. Mistresses were often nonplussed by the refusal of Catholic servants to join in family prayers in the Protestant home and responded by firing them.[10]

In contrast, Irish Catholic servant girls' devotion to their own religion annoyed some employers. Catholic servants demanded time off to attend mass every Sunday (not just on occasion, as would have better suited employers) and every holy day of obligation (the number of which, to the employer's way of thinking, was excessive). As one author put it, the Irish Bridget demanded "the privileges of all the funerals, and every fast and festival of her Church." Servants' religious devotion had an adverse impact on household arrangements and mealtimes. It caused employers to face the problem of who would do the work when the servant was out of the house. The inconvenience of these kinds of scheduling conflicts drove one author to declare: "Many families have positively refused to employ Irish servants at all, and especially those who are Roman Catholic." Instead, American homemakers wanted to employ white, native-born American girls for servants. Consequently, some employers did phrase their advertisements for domestics in such a manner as to directly or obliquely indicate that no Catholics or no Irish need apply, Irish and Catholic being deemed equivalent terms.[11]

In 1868, for instance, one such ad seeking a woman "to take the care of a boy two years old, in a small family in Brookline," stipulated that "positively no Irish need apply." Nevertheless, it was Irish girls who ended up meeting the middle-class demand for servants because native-born Americans eschewed this low-status occupation in which servants were stigmatized by their work.[12]

The Catholic Church, toward which so much Protestant and nativist hostility was directed, played an important role in the emotional life of Irish domestics. Harriet Spofford commented in 1881 that Irish servants were "at home once more" in a Catholic church: "It is the atmosphere of the sweet old land that breathes about them; they have there the shadow of home . . . strangers in a strange land, the church is father and mother, home and country, too!" Through Catholic devotions, such as saying the rosary, their religion provided them solace. For those who feared (most of them, rightly so) that they might never again see their family in Ireland, the belief that all family and friends would be rejoined in heaven in the next life must have provided powerful consolation for their separation in this life. Irish immigrant Ellie Driscoll Enright offered Irish domestic Nora McCarthy just this type of consolation upon learning of Nora's sister Katie's untimely death in Ireland, writing, "poor Katie I hope she is in heaven . . . I hope we will meet [again] in heaven."[13]

The type of comfort provided by the Catholic Church was particularly important to domestics as they faced long workdays and long workweeks. The workday of live-in domestic servants was longer than that of other women working in more traditional out-of-home work, stretching to eleven to twelve hours per day. Service work "involved the hiring of a person rather than just the obtaining of her labor"—that is, servants were hired for their time rather than for specific tasks. Therefore, the employer expectation dictated that the servant should work constantly. Even during their few off hours, servants were often still on call to employers. For the most part, the workweek was a full seven days, with time off limited to one afternoon and one night per week, usually Sunday and Thursday, respectively. If a servant wanted additional time off, she was required to obtain the special consent of the employer, leading one Irish-American woman to complain that employers wanted "girls on tap from six in the morning till ten and eleven at night. 'Tis n't fair."[14]

Expectations associated with positions varied by employer, but it was those domestics in posts where they were the only servant employed in the household, thus known as the maid-of-all-work, who generally bore the heaviest workload. The ratio of staff to family was a key determinant in how taxing a servant's job would be, because more people meant more work. Domestics hoped to find employment in households that employed multiple servants because a given number of chores split among two or more people meant less work and the possibility of more free time for each. Specialized servants not only had less work than maids-of-all-work, but they earned more money, too.[15]

The majority of American households only hired one domestic servant, making the maid-of-all-work the easiest position to find. This was a daunting situation for some as they faced a typical morning such as the one described below by Blaine McKinley of an 1857 post:

> She was to rise early, about 5:30 A.M., in order to complete the dirtier work in the morning so she would be neat and presentable for the mistress's afternoon callers. "Before the family come down" to breakfast, the girl was to clean and polish the stove,

sweep the first-floor carpets, dust the furniture, sweep the front steps, shake the mats, prepare the breakfast, and set the table. While the family ate, the domestic was to make the beds and dust the bedrooms. Each family chamber was to be thoroughly cleaned once a week, "the carpets taken up and shaken, the floor scrubbed, the curtains shaken, and the furniture cleaned."[16]

In addition, the maid-of-all-work also was required to set the table, cook and serve the main meal of the day, answer the front door, respond to her employer when called, and run general errands. She was also expected to take care of the myriad chores involved in cleaning and dusting the dining room, parlor, and kitchen. Employer expectations for the maid-of-all-work continued to be remarkably similar over time. The tasks of a maid-of-all-work employed in 1904 provide a list of essentially the same responsibilities.[17]

Irish servants indicated that they found domestic service, especially as a maid-of-all-work, to be a hard grind that involved unpleasantness. Catherine Ann McFarland wrote from Philadelphia in 1855 to her mother: "If you new what i have to put upe with in ane ones kitchen . . ." In an undated letter of about 1871, Mary O'Hanlon complained that because all her chores had to be completed before she went to church, there was but one mass that she could attend on Sundays; she also lamented that she had so much work to do that it was difficult to finish a letter. She wrote to her mother that "I had to quit this letter 5 times & begin to make tea biscuit & set the teatable there was 12 for tea & what a lot of dishes & glasses its halfpast 8 now & I am just through dear mother . . ."[18]

Hannah Collins's correspondence in America with her friend and fellow Irish immigrant domestic Nora McCarthy indicates she, too, found housework to be hard work. In 1898, she wrote, "I am working every day and feels tired I don t have them Idle times like I used to in old Ballinlough." The following year she wrote to Nora that "I hope someday will come when I wont have to work so hard. . . . I do hate to get up every morning I am so tired." Unsurprisingly, Hannah sought to limit the amount of work required of her. She quit one job where the employer left her "tired out" and obtained for herself "another place."[19]

Hannah was not alone—letters written to Nora McCarthy by other friends who were also immigrant domestics provide further testimony to the hard work they faced and to the fact that the work increased in proportion to the number of people living in the employer's house. In 1897, for example, Mary Holland wrote from Boston: "I got to work hard enough." Mary Anne Donovan commented: "I got plenty to do I dont be Iddle." And Noney Hayes remarked: "I have eight in our family to work for so you Can Just Imagine what a snap I have." These women's comments explain why domestics tried to improve their lot by changing jobs in a continual search for an improved employment situation. As Noney Hayes wrote to Nora: "Intend leaving my Place pretty Soon If you should hear of a nice plase would you Please Let me know."[20]

The Irish found work in America to be much more demanding than in Ireland. Mary Malone wrote home from Chicago in the 1870s that her daughter Kate, who was working in service, was "living out with a Nice American family these 2 weeks" but she observed, "Kate was not used to work enough home [i.e., Ireland] to suit this country." In later correspondence to the Doyle family, Mary wished them to make

Hannah Collins, a domestic servant in Elmira, New York, 1898. (Courtesy of Patricia Trainor O'Malley)

note of "how hard people work in this country" and declared that while America was a good place for a girl who was "willing to work," she cautioned "still I dont advise any one that Can live home to Come altho there is ten chances here for the one there is in Ireland." Domestic service in America continued to be a taxing occupation for Irish girls as time went on. In 1906, Katie O'Sullivan wrote from San Jose, California, to her brother in Ireland that "tis work work all the time Nine in family." Margaret Convery Horan said of her first job in housework: "I worked for a lady that had . . . two children. . . . I had to do everything. . . . I had to learn to cook . . . and you done the wash, clean the house." Mary Catherine Theresa Boyle Kelly (hereinafter referred to as Mary Kelly), who came to America in 1929, said her work as a domestic in America always involved child care, as well as housework. Of one of the domestic jobs that she held she said: "There was three children and housework and you did . . . from ceiling to floors, everything."[21]

A key to appreciating the situation of Irish domestics is to remember that many of them began as teenagers—they were young, and in the nineteenth century, before the advent of compulsory education laws and child protective labor laws, some were extremely young. In October 1848, Helen Chapman wrote to her mother from Texas to tell her about her Irish servant, Ann Mitchell, who was "not yet thirteen." For young

Irish girls, domestic service could provide a lonely entree to American life. Letters to family describe this, as Irish domestic Anastasia Dowling wrote home from Buffalo, New York, in 1870: "I feel very lonesome here," noting that "the ways of this place is so diferent from home." Mary O'Hanlon wrote in 1871: "my dear mother after I came here at time I thought my heart would have broken thinking of you." Hannah Collins, too, confessed to Nora McCarthy in 1898: "I get homesick and lonesome often." While time probably diminished her lonesomeness, it did not completely eradicate it, for in 1900 she wrote "Well dear Nora I got so lonesome when I read your dear letter that I had to cry thinking of you and all our good old times." Mary Kelly said that once the realization set in that she could not easily return to Ireland "many times, many nights I went to bed and cried myself sick."[22]

In addition to loneliness and homesickness, domestic workers faced a difficulty usually thought of in terms of industrial workers—on-the-job injuries for which no compensation was provided and which might preclude them from continuing to support themselves. In 1897, Kate Monohan wrote to Nora McCarthy, excusing herself for taking so long in replying to Nora's last letter "was owing to a Sore hand which I had for a week or two past. . . . I burned my fore fingers & could not handle my pen for Some time but they are all better now with the exception of one which is quite Sore yet." Illness of any kind could cause a domestic to lose or at least fear to lose her employment, so some just ignored their ailments. Mary Cleer, for example, wrote to her uncle from Utica, New York, in 1899, saying that even though she had an abscess on her neck, "I worked through it all . . . done my work with my head on one shoulder. . . . I was afraid my head would never straighten." On-the-job injuries could also be suffered in the particularly awful form of employer-inflicted beatings. In 1857, a Hartford newspaper reported that an Irish servant named Bridget Kennedy was kicked and beaten by her male employer, who also tossed a manic cat at her.[23]

Given the long hours and hard work, why then did Irish girls flock to domestic service? Mary Feely Harren, who came to New York in 1927, responded to this question by saying, "What else could I do? . . . There was nothing else that I could do except housework." Ellen Brady, who came to New York in the 1920s, made the same point when she declared that "we [Irish immigrant girls] weren't equipped for any other job but housework." In addition, despite its low status, the wages for domestic work compared quite favorably with wages for other female occupations, when one factors in the receipt of room and board. In 1910, for example, Rheta Childe Dorr found the wages paid to domestics to be generally higher than those paid to teachers or to shop and factory girls. Also, there were plenty of job openings throughout this period during which servant turnover was high. Irish girls used various means to obtain positions as domestics, including the assistance of the Catholic Church and the Irish community, the use of employment agencies called "intelligence offices," the assistance of relatives, word of mouth, the perusal of newspaper advertisements, and the placement of "situation wanted" advertisements in newspapers.[24]

It was the provision of room and board—a roof over one's head and food to eat—that probably represented the most advantageous aspect of domestic service. In the absence of housing and food expenses, the domestics could save their wages and remit their "American money" to their relatives in Ireland where it greatly improved Irish material life. By 1880, female Irish domestic servants in Boston remitted more than $180,000 annually through a single Boston money exchange organization. This is not to claim that it was easy for them to save the money they remitted to Ireland; Irish girls sacrificed to send money home.[25]

While free room was appreciated, it was not necessarily comfortable. During this period American employers increased their physical separation from servants by expanding the practice begun earlier of isolating servant quarters from family living quarters within the private home. Separate servant entrances, separate staircases for servants, and separating kitchens from the principal rooms of a house represented planned designs to demarcate servant from employer. Servant quarters usually provided a marked contrast to the living space of the employer. Servant rooms were often located in attics, which frequently lacked heat and running water and were known to be cold in winter and hot in summer, or over kitchens. In some cases separate servant rooms were not provided at all; instead, servants were expected to sleep in the kitchen. Nannies like Helen Flatley Cleary often did not have their own bedrooms either, but, instead, "slept with the children."

In actuality, board or food was not always such a great benefit for domestics, either. Sometimes the food provided to servants contrasted unfavorably with that eaten by the family; it might have been of lesser quality or quantity. As a result, lack of adequate nutrition to perform the physically taxing job of domestic service was a problem for some servants. In addition, while she was supplied with room and board, the house in which a servant worked was not a home or refuge—instead, it was her work site. Thus Hannah Collins mourned, "I aint got any home here." This point was emphasized by an employer who told one servant: "If you take a servant's place, you can't expect to be one of the family."[26]

Contact with each other, and therefore a social life, was maintained through visiting back and forth with their American-based friends and family. In a letter he wrote in the 1880s from Philadelphia to his mother in Ireland, Owen O'Callaghan, for example, mentioned that his sister Bridget, who was a domestic, "enjoys herself with the other Waterford girls." A servant's ability to have company in to visit in the house in which she was employed depended, however, on the acquiescence of her employer, and considerable numbers of employers were not partial to the idea. Many employers opposed servants having visitors, in general, and were particularly opposed to servant girls having male visitors—that is, boyfriends, who were called "followers." And, even if a servant could obtain employer permission to entertain friends, she had no place in which to entertain. If permitted visitors, domestics usually received them in the kitchen.[27]

Religion factored into the social and the emotional life of Irish domestics, for the Catholic Church served as a contact point for servants to keep in touch with the Irish community. Hannah Collins alluded to this when she wrote to Nora McCarthy in 1898 that "you has a great old time mashing the fellows when you go to Church I wish I was there." That is, before and after mass, young people could chat and laugh while they socialized together in gatherings outside the church. During mass they could eye each other and admire the figures they cut while dressed up for church, for Sunday church-going provided Irish domestics with the opportunity to display the fashions of

Nora McCarthy, who worked as a domestic servant in Haverhill and Bradford, Massachusetts, with Mary Hayes, circa 1900. (Courtesy of Patricia Trainor O'Malley)

the day. Attending dances also necessitated appropriate apparel, for as domestic Mary Cox Harney, who immigrated in 1925, recalled, she "bought a flock of dresses and fancy clothes and everything. Then . . . went off to a[n Irish] dance." Fashionable dress brought them not only pleasure but criticism, for it offended middle-class Americans that their servants could dress so well that they could be mistaken for middle-class women.[28]

The social life of Irish domestics also included going to weddings, playing cards, enjoying sleigh riding, walking in parks, and joining in the 1890s American craze for bicycle riding. In the twentieth century, public amusements and going to the movies factored into the social lives of Irish servants. In New York City, Helen Flatley Cleary mentioned that she loved going with her fellow Irish Americans on picnics or on boat cruises that went up the East River or the Hudson River. Cleary also "learned how to have dinner out" in restaurants as a form of entertainment. If there were no parties on offering, other Irish domestics like Molly Ryan Fitzgerald of Albany, New York, spent their free time at the Ancient Order of Hibernians Hall. The social lives of those who worked for the very wealthy in multiservant households sometimes included taking part in so-called Servants' Balls provided for them by their employers. According to Ellen Brady, at such affairs, held in hired halls, "you'd dance, and eat, and you'd sing. It's just like a party for young people or old people."[29]

Some domestics were also lucky enough to live near married relatives who maintained a "home" where their Irish friends and relatives, male and female, could get together to socialize on their days off. Hannah Collins's correspondence with Nora McCarthy indicates that in the late 1890s, Hannah's cousin, Mrs. Dempsey, provided her with just such a "home" away from where she lived in service. Writing to Nora, Hannah said that Mrs. Dempsey "is kind to us we make our home with her and they do be a big crowd there Sundays." Likewise, Nora's sister Mary Donovan provided a "home" for Nora. As Hannah wrote to Nora, "its so nice for you to have your sisters home to go to Sundays and when you are tired or out of work."[30]

Thursday nights were big nights in the weekly social calendar of Irish immigrants, as it was usually maids' evening off. Dances were held that night because, as Owen O'Callaghan reported from Philadelphia in 1883, "thursday night [was] when all the girls are out." Accordingly, as historian John T. Ridge has pointed out, the ladies' Irish county organizations in New York City tended to hold their meetings on Thursdays to accommodate the large contingency of members who worked as domestics. Furthermore, because these members often had no place in which to entertain male friends, county organizations sponsored dances where the girls could meet suitable Irish men.[31]

Such Irish dances played a prominent role in the social life of Irish immigrant domestics in the United States. Mary King Conroy, who left County Galway for Boston in 1912, told stories about going to "dances in Lynn and Swampscott" while working as a domestic. Mary Cox Harney, who immigrated in 1925, commented that dances were such an important part of her social life that she left one service job "because I thought I was too far away from the dances." Irish servants' love of the Irish dances points to the fact that they wanted to meet men; they valued having beaux and were looking for husbands. In her letters to Nora McCarthy, Hannah Collins made frequent mention of her boyfriend (and later husband), Tom Cloke. In May 1898, for example, she wrote: "I got a fellow and he is this country born too Aint I smart he has got light hair and blue eyes his name is Tom Cloke so I will have a cloake to keep me warm in the winter nights dont you think I'm a great girl you must tell me about your fellow because I know you got one for they were always crazy about you."[32]

Irish domestics' interest in marriage shows the mismatch in employer and servant expectations regarding household service. American employers expected the Irish girls to constitute a servant class, to see service in America as a lifelong career. But Irish girls viewed their situation differently; they saw service as a taxing but temporary job. According to one author writing in 1909, there were three main reasons why girls left service: "To be married, or to go home to old Ireland, or to take care of a sick relative." Since Irish girls thought of service as a stop on the way to accomplishment of their real goal of marrying and having a family, it was for the first of these reasons that most Irish girls hoped to leave housework. Marriage not only represented the achievement of adult status, but it offered Irish girls an escape from the hard work that was domestic service. It often meant the end of sending money home to Ireland, too, because typically remittances were not expected from married people.[33]

While it was possible through time and job changes for a servant to acquire the skills necessary to work her way up to the typically higher-paying domestic job of cook, service offered little other occupational opportunity. Nor did it provide occupational security. Employers could not be relied on to care for domestics as they got

Sarah Byrne Green's employee record from Hall Farm notes that she "came to family immediately on landing" in 1888. (Park-McCullough House Association, Inc., North Bennington, VT)

older. Servants who, as they aged, became unable to perform the physically demanding work of housework faced dim prospects. They could be discharged without any sort of pension and possibly could end up in an almshouse. Such was the fate of Margrett Baggs, a domestic from County Tipperary who, after thirty-three years in America, in September 1880, at age sixty-six, entered the Rensselaer County Poor House in upstate New York. The notation on her record states the reason as "old age and no home."[34]

The fact that Irish domestics did not expect to spend their lives in service also affected their attitude toward the occupation. They were aware of and resented its low status, as Mary Feely Harren indicated when she discussed being required to use the servant staircase in one house in which she worked. Harren said: "I didn't like . . . the idea of going down the stairs, the back stairs that went in the house and all that. Kind of annoyed me in the beginning." Nonetheless, Irish girls usually did not lose their self-esteem doing housework. In fact, to the contrary, some employers complained of the "uppishness" or "pretentiousness" of the Irish servant girl who was said to scrutinize potential employment situations to see if they met with her notions of "gentility" and the exacting standards of her sense of "her own respectability," before agreeing to accept such employment. While it was clear to employers that "the ordinary mistress . . . occupies a higher sphere than the one where her servant dwells," to the annoyance of employers, the Irish domestic, known for her "hatred of superiority of all kinds," seemingly ignored the distinction in class between mistress and maid. Instead, as one employer declared, "servant-girls understand themselves to be politically and theoretically our equals."[35]

Scholars of Irish immigration agree that in domestic service, Irish girls were acculturated—as servants they learned the "manners and mores" of the American middle class. Hasia Diner, for example, contends that "domestic service provided perhaps the most intimate glimpse of what middle-class America was really like." Contemporary observers like Owen O'Callaghan agreed. In a letter to his brother in the 1880s, he wrote that his sister Maggie, a domestic, "is a regular Yank now Youd think by seeing her she was a native." Helen Flatley Cleary confirmed that in service she "learned a lot of the ropes." Through their experience in domestic service, then, Irish girls learned to bridge the gulf of class, cultural, ethnic, and religious differences that separated them from their American employers.[36]

The fact that in America most Irish domestic servants would in due course marry Irish men suggests that they did not perceive them as drunken louts, brutes, and wife beaters, as they have not infrequently been portrayed. While these, of course, existed, Irish women married Irish men because they came from the same religious and cultural background—they were familiar to each other—and because they were likely to meet each other at Irish affairs like the Irish dances. They also married Irish men because their ranks included good, kind men, who made good husbands and fathers, as well as the drunken oafs of contemporary stereotype. As Hannah Collins succinctly put it: "A sweet little Irishman he is the best of all." Irish domestic Bertha Devlin certainly remembered her Irish-born husband with great fondness, saying of him that "I'd marry the same man all over again. I had him for fifty-two years so, he's gone for ten, died ten years ago." And Irish domestic Rose Kelly Loughlin said of her Irish-born husband Owen that he "was a very good man" who she thought was the most "honest man in the wide world. He was so honest."[37]

Because they tended to marry their fellow Irish, the acculturating effects of domestic service provided a source of American influence in the families that Irish domestics began in America. Colleen McDannell, for example, maintains that, to the extent possible, in their own homes former domestics tried to reproduce the conditions of the middle-class homes in which they once worked. Contemporary observers agreed that the families of former domestics benefited from the women's experience, for they contended that the care former domestic servants took "of their children's diet and health" showed "the superiority of domestic service over factory training for developing intelligent home-makers." The recollections of relatives of former domestics support historian Janet Nolan's claim that, through their acculturation in domestic service, "Irish mothers were able to speed the assimilation of their American-born children." Patricia Trainor O'Malley remembers that her relatives who had worked in domestic service (her grandmother, Nora McCarthy, who came to the United States in 1895, and her grandmother's sister) insisted that the family "had to have a good dining room set and good china and good silverware. . . . You had to set that fine table. And it had to be done just right." In addition, they insisted that O'Malley's family distinguish themselves from the local Irish who used slang in their speech. As Dr. O'Malley put it, her family was "bound and determined we were going to sound like Yankees. You had to have the right accent. . . . We'd be drilled in how to pronounce things. . . . Go up listen to John McCormack records. Get the culture."[38]

As wives and mothers, Irish women dominated the Irish home in America, as they had in rural Ireland. They handled family financial matters and were ambitious for their children. Because they retained the traditional Irish value for education, Irish women fostered the group occupational and social mobility of the Irish—they were key to the movement of the Irish into the American middle class. Indicative of this rise and the female role in it is the fact that few daughters of Irish domestics followed their mothers into service. Instead, teaching school became the occupation of choice for second-generation Irish females. Janet Nolan asserts that by 1900–1910, Irish-American females became "one of the largest ethnic groups among public school elementary teachers, constituting one quarter of the teachers in Providence and Boston and fully a third of the teachers in New York and Chicago."[39]

Andrew Greeley's sociological work supports the idea that Irish women were successful in ensuring that their children were educated. Using data from the National Opinion Research Center's General Social Survey, he contends that, by the 1910–1920 era, "Irish Catholics had already exceeded the national average in college attendance and graduation and professional and white collar careers." As early as 1900, H. J. Desmond claimed that there "are more lawyers, doctors and authors among the second generation of Irish-Americans than there are saloon-keepers, and more teachers than policeman." Greeley contends that the Irish "continued to move into modest affluence in the nineteen twenties," only to have their rise temporarily halted by the onset of the Great Depression. Following World War II, however, Irish Catholics began to rise anew until reaching the point where Irish Catholics now comprise "the most affluent gentile ethnic group in America."[40]

Irish mothers pushed their children to Americanize, but not at the expense of their Catholic religion or by wholly abandoning their Irishness. The Irish acculturated themselves but generally retained their religion, as well as certain Irish attitudes. Irish mothers in America raised their children to be proud of being Irish, although they apparently failed to provide them with much information on the immigration experience or on Ireland. Instead, consciously or not, Irish women passed down their own particular Irish cultural notions. In pushing their families upward into the middle class while retaining their religion and certain Irish cultural attitudes, Irish women pioneered a new way to be American: they showed that one could be at the same time both ethnic Irish and American. As Marjorie Fallows put it: "What the Irish have demonstrated is that American life can encompass difference without insisting on eradicating it, and that an ethnic group can adopt an American identity without completely renouncing its historical sense of peoplehood." This was the legacy of Bridget, the Irish immigrant domestic.[41]

NOTES

1. For the purposes of this essay, the terms "domestic servant," "domestic," "servant," and "servant girl" will be deemed synonymous. Domestic service in American hotels and public institutions and Irish men in domestic service are topics beyond the scope of this essay.

2. Blaine Edward McKinley, "'The Stranger in the Gates': Employer Reactions toward Domestic Servants in America 1825–1875" (Ph.D. diss., Michigan State University, 1969), 152, quote from 282; Daniel E. Sutherland, *Americans and Their Servants: Domestic Service in the United States from 1800 to 1920* (Baton Rouge: Louisiana State University Press, 1981), 50, 56, 57; David M. Katzman, *Seven Days a Week: Women and Domestic Service in Industrializing America* (New York: Oxford University Press, 1978), 49, 51, 66, 67, 68, 69, 272; Faye E. Dudden, *Serving Women: Household Service in Nineteenth-Century America* (Middletown, CT: Wesleyan University Press, 1983), 60–64; Susan Strasser, *Never Done: A History of American Housework* (New York: Pantheon Books, 1982), 164; Stephen Steinberg, *The Ethnic Myth: Race, Ethnicity and Class in America* (New York: Atheneum, 1981), 153, 154, 156–157, 160–161, 166; H. J. Desmond, "A Century of Irish Immigration," *American Catholic Quarterly Review* (1900): 522; Morton D. Winsberg, "Irish Settlement in the United States, 1850–1980," *Eire-Ireland* 20 (1985): 7, 10, 12, 13; Mary Catherine Mattis, "The Irish Family in Buffalo, New York, 1855–1875: A Socio-Historical Analysis" (Ph.D. diss., Washington University, 1975), 138; Bertha (Bridget) McGaffighan (McGeoghegan) Devlin, interview by Dana Gumb, 19 September 1985, Interview AKRF-43, transcript, Ellis Island Oral History Collection, Ellis Island Immigration Museum, New York, New York, (hereinafter referred to as Ellis Island Collection), 32–34.

For reference to Biddy/Bridget in popular literature, see, for example, Virginia De Forest, "Biddy's Blunders," *Godey's Lady's Book and Magazine*, April 1855, 329–330; Kate Harrington, "Irish Blunders," *Godey's Lady's Book and Magazine*, April 1855, 247–248; Catharine E. Beecher and Harriet Beecher Stowe, *The American Woman's Home* (New York: J. B. Ford, 1869; Hartford, CT: Stowe-Day Foundation, 1994), 182, 311, 312.

3. Quotation from Margaret Convery Horan, interview by Paul E. Sigrist Jr., 24 April 1991, Interview EI-39, transcript, Ellis Island Collection, 26, 27. To preserve the authenticity of their written language, throughout this paper, I reproduce the language of Irish domestics as they wrote it, without either correcting it or writing [*sic*] after misspellings. Katzman, *Seven Days a Week*, 177; William Forbes Adams, *Ireland and Irish Emigration to the New World from 1815 to the Famine* (New Haven: Yale University Press, 1932; reprint, Baltimore: Genealogical Publishing, 1980), 223; David Fitzpatrick, "'A Share of the Honeycomb': Education, Emigration and Irishwomen," in *The Origins of Popular Literacy in Ireland*: *Language Change and Educational Development 1700–1920*, ed. Mary Daly and David Dickson (Dublin: Department of Modern History, Trinity College, Dublin, and Department of Modern Irish History, University College Dublin, 1990), 173; Rita Rhodes, *Women and Family in Post-Famine Ireland: Status and Opportunity in a Patriarchal Society* (New York: Garland Publishing, 1992), 252, 254; Kerby A. Miller with David N. Doyle and Patricia Kelleher, "'For Love and Liberty': Irish Women, Migration and Domesticity in Ireland and America, 1815–1920," in *The Irish World Wide: History, Heritage, Identity*, Vol. 4: *Irish Women and Irish Migration*, ed. Patrick O'Sullivan (London: Leicester University Press, 1995), 43; Pauric Travers, "Emigration and Gender: The Case of Ireland, 1922–60," in *Chattel, Servant or Citizen*: *Women's Status in Church, State and Society*, ed. Mary O'Dowd and Sabine Wichert (Belfast: Institute of Irish Studies, Queen's University of Belfast, 1995), 188; Arnold Schrier, *Ireland and the American Emigration, 1850–1900* (Minneapolis: University of Minnesota Press, 1958), 4; David Fitzpatrick, *Irish Emigration 1801–1921* (Dublin: Dundalgan Press, 1984), 8, 11, 13, 24, 25, 32, 602, 603; David Fitzpatrick, "Emigration, 1801–70," in *Ireland under the Union, Part 1: 1801–1870*, Vol. 5: *A New History of Ireland*, ed. W. E. Vaughan (Oxford:

Clarendon Press, 1989), 577; Robert E. Kennedy Jr., *The Irish: Emigration, Marriage and Fertility* (Berkeley: University of California Press, 1973), 66–67; Schrier, *Ireland*, 40–42.

4. Quotation from the *Boston Pilot*, 9 February 1850, 7, citing a letter printed in the *Newry* (Ireland) *Examiner*. See also Pauline Jackson, "Women in Nineteenth-Century Irish Emigration," *International Migration Review* 18, no. 4 (1984): 1009, 1010, 1014, 1017, 1018; David Fitzpatrick, "The Modernisation of the Irish Female," in *Rural Ireland 1600–1900: Modernisation and Change*, ed. Patrick O'Flanagan, Paul Ferguson, and Kevin Whelan (Cork: Cork University Press, 1987), 163, 164, 168, 169, 174–175; David Fitzpatrick, "A Share of the Honeycomb," 167, 175; Timothy W. Guinnane, *The Vanishing Irish: Households, Migration, and the Rural Economy in Ireland, 1850–1914* (Princeton: Princeton University Press, 1997), 158–160; Janet Nolan, *Ourselves Alone: Women's Emigration from Ireland, 1885–1920* (Lexington: University Press of Kentucky,1989), 73; S. J. Connolly, "Marriage in Pre-Famine Ireland," in *Marriage in Ireland*, ed. Art Cosgrove (Dublin: College Press, 1985), 92; Caoimhin O'Danachair, "Marriage in Irish Folk Tradition," in *Marriage in Ireland*, 99–100, 101.

5. Travers, "Emigration and Gender," 190; Joy Rudd, "Invisible Exports: The Emigration of Irish Women This Century," *Women's Studies International Forum* 2, no. 4 (1998): 309; Katzman, *Seven Days a Week*, 272–273; Strasser, *Never Done*, 176, 178; Fitzpatrick, "Modernisation of the Irish Female," 164; Miller et al., "For Love and Liberty," 63, note 41, citing correspondence Miller received from David Fitzpatrick; Fitzpatrick, "A Share of the Honeycomb," 168–170, 175–176, 178, 181, 183.

6. Both quotations from Dudden, *Serving Women*, 241; see also 115, 126–127, 137–145, 148, 155–192. See Suellen Hoy, *Chasing Dirt: The American Pursuit of Cleanliness* (New York: Oxford University Press, 1995), xiv, 5, 7; Strasser, *Never Done*, 163–164; Katzman, *Seven Days a Week*, 46, 59, 269; Judith Rollins, *Between Women: Domestics and Their Employer* (Philadelphia: Temple University Press, 1985), 52–53; *Boston Pilot*, 6 March 1852, 6; Alice B. Neal, "The Crisis," *Godey's Lady's Book and Magazine*, May 1857, 519, 520; John F. Kasson, *Rudeness and Civility: Manners in Nineteenth-Century Urban America*(New York: Hill and Wang, 1990), 173–174, 210.

7. Rose Kelly Loughlin said she worked as a domestic in Ireland before her 1925 emigration to work in service in America; see Rose Kelly Loughlin, interview by Janet Levine, 30 April 1995, Interview EI-607, transcript, Ellis Island Collection, 52. Nora Joyce also indicated that she worked in service before coming to America in 1928; see Ide O'Carroll, *Models for Movers* (Dublin: Attic Press, 1990), 35–37; Harriet Spofford, *The Servant Girl Question* (Boston: Houghton, Mifflin, 1881; reprint, New York: Arno Press, 1977), 20, 31–32, 64; C. Hélène Barker, *Wanted: A Young Woman to Do Housework* (New York: Moffat, Yard, 1915), 5.

8. Quotes listed in order of appearance in the text: "Bridget," *Harper's Bazaar*, 11 November 1871, first quote from 706; "Your Humble Servant," *Harper's New Monthly Magazine*, June 1864, second quote from 53 and third quote from 54; "Bridget," *Harper's Bazaar*, fourth, fifth, sixth, and seventh quotes from 706; Kate Harrington, "Irish Blunders," *Godey's Lady's Book and Magazine*, April 1855, 247; Anne Frances Springsteed, *The Expert Waitress* (New York: Harper and Brothers, 1894), 126; Christine Terhune Herrick, *The Expert Maid-Servant* (New York: Harper and Brothers, 1904), 18; Dudden, *Serving Women*, final quote from 121.

9. Quotes listed in order of appearance in the text: Kate Sutherland, "Cooks," *Godey's Lady's Book and Magazine*, May 1852, first four quotes from 393–394; "Our Domestic Service," *Scribner's Monthly Illustrated Magazine*, November 1875, fifth quote from 273; "Bridget," *Harper's Bazaar*, 11 November 1871, sixth quote from 706; Charles Dickens, "Servants in America," *All the Year Round*, 3 October 1874, 585, seventh quote from 586; "Bridget," *Harper's Bazaar*, 11 November 1871, eighth quote from 706; R. R. Bowker, "In Re: Bridget—The Defence," *Old and New* 4

(1871): 497; "A Dowager's Advice on How to Catch and Keep the Cook," *Arts and Decoration*, June 1934, last quote from 24. See also Peig Sayers, *An Old Woman's Reflections*, trans. Seamus Ennis (Oxford: Oxford University Press, 1962), 81; William Carleton, "Shane Fadh's Wedding," *Traits and Stories of the Irish Peasantry* (1853; reprint, Freeport, NY: Books for Libraries Press, 1971), 1:120; William Carleton, "Phelim O'Toole's Courtship," *Traits and Stories of the Irish Peasantry*, 2:206, 329.

10. "Morals and Manners of the Kitchen," *Nation*, 2 January 1873, 7; Sutherland, *Americans and Their Servants*, 40; Hartley, *The Ladies' Book of Etiquette*, 239.

11. Nothing in the literature I reviewed indicates that Catholic German servants faced the same sort of conflict with their mistresses over religion that Irish Catholics faced. Silke Wehner-Franco, *Deutsche Dienstmädchen in Amerika 1850–1914* (New York: Waxmann, 1994), 112, is the sole major work on German immigrant servant girls in America to date. Wehner-Franco, however, does not really deal with the issue of whether Catholic German servants were discriminated against. One could infer some possible religious discrimination, however, in the fact that, especially after the 1880s, a large number of ads specifically sought Protestant German domestics. The literature to date, however, focuses on the conflict between employers and Irish Catholic, as opposed to other Catholic, domestics. See Katzman, *Seven Days a Week*, 164; Mrs. J Sadlier (Mary Anne Sadlier), *Bessy Conway; or, the Irish Girl in America* (New York: D. and J. Sadlier, 1861; reprint, New York: D. and J. Sadlier, 1863), 205–207; "Bridget," *Harper's Bazaar*, 11 November 1871, first quote from 706; Veritas, "Trouble in Families: Servants as They Are Nowadays, No. IV," *Boston Daily Evening Transcript*, 7 February 1852, second quote from 1; Spofford, *The Servant Girl Question*, 32–33; Veritas, "Trouble in Families," *Boston Daily Evening Transcript*, 2 February 1852, 2; "Your Humble Servant," *Harper's Monthly Magazine*, June 1864, 57; Veritas, "Trouble in Families," *Boston Daily Evening Transcript*, 9 February 1852, 4.

12. Richard J. Jensen, "'No Irish Need Apply': A Myth of Victimization," *Journal of Social History* 36, no. 2 (2002): 405–439; *Boston Evening Transcript*, 3 August 1868, final quotes from 3; Lucy Maynard Salmon, *Domestic Service*, 2nd ed. (New York: Macmillan, 1901), 65, 163; Katzman, *Seven Days a Week*, 14, 44, 241–242; Sutherland, *Americans and Their Servants*, 4, 5.

13. Quotations from Spofford, *The Servant Girl Question*, 60. Robert C. Broderick, ed., *The New Catholic Encyclopedia* (Nashville, TN: Thomas Nelson, 1987), 529, says the rosary "is the name of both a devotion and the chain of beads used for counting the prayers"; Ellie Driscoll Enright, Washington, DC, to Nora McCarthy, 14 March 1900, transcript in the author's hand, original in the possession of Dr. Patricia Trainor O'Malley, O'Malley Collection.

14. Katzman, *Seven Days a Week*, first quote from 107, 110–113; Dudden, *Serving Women*, 178–179; Gail Laughlin, *Domestic Service: A Report Prepared under the Direction of the Industrial Commission* (Washington, DC: General Printing Office, 1901), 759; McKinley, "The Stranger in the Gates," 32; Helen Campbell, *Prisoners of Poverty: Women Wage-Workers, Their Trades and Their Lives* (Boston: Roberts Brothers, 1887; reprint, 1889), final quote from 227.

15. McKinley, "Stranger in the Gates," 12–16; Herrick, *Expert Maid-Servant*, 70–87.

16. Sutherland, *Americans and Their Servants*, 94; Massachusetts Labor Bulletin, *Social Conditions of Domestic Service*, No. 13 (February 1900), 2; McKinley, "Stranger in the Gates," 13, citing Mrs. Elizabeth Ellet's 1857 book, *The Practical Housekeeper*, 42–44.

17. McKinley, "Stranger in the Gates," 13, 14, 15. For a full list, see Herrick, *Expert Maid-Servant*, 56–69.

18. Catherine Ann McFarland, Philadelphia, to her mother, in Belfast, n.d., ca. 5 March 1855, transcript in the hand of Professor Kerby A. Miller, University of Missouri–Columbia, hereinafter referred to as Miller Collection; Mary O'Hanlon, New York City, to her mother, n.d., ca.

fall 1871, Miller Collection. Professor Miller's annotated list of documents suggests that O'Hanlon was a seamstress or factory worker. My review of the letter, however, particularly the quote I use, convinces me that she was a domestic servant at least at the time she wrote this letter.

19. Hannah Collins, Elmira, New York, to Nora McCarthy, Haverhill, Massachusetts, 9 June 1898, O'Malley Collection, first quote; Collins to McCarthy, 24 May 1899, O'Malley Collection, second quote; Collins to McCarthy, 5 April 1900, O'Malley Collection, third and fourth quotes.

20. Mary Holland, Boston, Massachusetts, to Nora McCarthy, envelope postmarked 11 April 1897, O'Malley Collection, first quote; Mary Anne Donovan, Lowell, Massachusetts, to Nora McCarthy, 17 March 1897, O'Malley Collection, second quote; Noney Hayes, Boston, Massachusetts, to Nora McCarthy, envelope postmarked 21 January 1897, O'Malley Collection, third and fourth quotes.

21. Mary Malone, Chicago, Illinois, n.d., ca. 1874, to Anne and John Doyle, County Carlow, Ireland, Miller Collection, first two quotes; Mary Malone to the Doyles, 5 September 1879, Miller Collection, third quote; Mary Malone to Anne Doyle, n.d., ca. 10 May 188?, Miller Collection, fourth and fifth quotes; Katie O'Sullivan, San Jose, California, to her brother, thought to be in County Kerry, Ireland, 5 December 1906, transcript in the hand of Arnold Schrier, Professor Emeritus, University of Cincinnati, hereinafter referred to as Schrier Collection; Margaret Convery Horan, Interview EI-39, Ellis Island Collection, 47, 48; Mary Catherine Theresa Boyle Kelly, Interview by Paul E. Sigrist Jr., 2 May 1995, EI-613, Ellis Island Collection, 30, 31.

22. Katzman, *Seven Days a Week*, 53; Caleb Coker, ed., *The News from Brownsville: Helen Chapman's Letters from the Texas Military Frontier, 1848–1852* (Austin: Texas Historical Association, 1992), first quote from 82; Anastasia Dowling, Buffalo, New York, to Mr. and Mrs. Dunny, 20 January 1870, Schrier Collection; Mary O'Hanlon, New York City, to her mother, n.d., ca. fall 1871, Miller Collection; Hannah Collins, Elmira, New York, to Nora McCarthy, envelope postmarked 21 June 1900, O'Malley Collection; Mary Catherine Theresa Boyle Kelly, Interview EI-613, Ellis Island Collection, 21.

23. Kate Monohan to Nora McCarthy, 13 February 1897, O'Malley Collection; Mary Cleer, Utica, New York, to her uncle, 14 May 1899, Miller Collection; Bruce Alan Clouette, "'Getting Their Share': Irish and Italian Immigrants in Hartford, Connecticut, 1850–1940" (Ph.D. diss., University of Connecticut, 1992), 68, citing the *Hartford Daily Courant*, 31 December 1857.

24. Mary Feely Harren, interview by author, 4 August 1996, tape recording; Ellen Brady [pseud.], Interview by Joan Morrison and Charlotte Zabusky, 7 March 1977, MZ 30, Ellis Island Collection, 36; Salmon, *Domestic Service*, 93, 98–99, comments on the favorableness of the wages paid to domestics; Rheta Childe Dorr, *What Eight Million Women Want* (Boston: Small, Maynard, 1910), 252–253; McKinley, "Stranger in the Gates," 19, on wages; Katzman, *Seven Days a Week*, 177, 270; "Bridget," *Harper's Bazaar*, 11 November 1871, 706; I. M. Rubinow, "The Problem of Domestic Service," *Journal of Political Economy* 14 (October 1906): 504. Regarding the Catholic Church assisting Irish girls in obtaining domestic jobs, see Maureen Murphy, "Charlotte Grace O'Brien and the Mission of Our Lady of the Rosary for the Protection of Irish Immigrant Girls," *Mid-America: An Historical Review* 74, no. 3 (October 1992): 269, and the *New York Daily Tribune*, 18 September 1905, 5. Regarding the Irish-Catholic community's assistance, see the *Boston Pilot*, 2 September 1865, 8. The Ellis Island Collection of interviews with Irish domestics indicates that some used employment agencies: see, for example, Theresa Gavin Duffy, interview by Paul E. Sigrist Jr., 24 September 1991, Interview EI-95, Ellis Island Collection, 30; the collection indicates that others got jobs through relatives: see, for example, Sarah Mackey Gillespie, interview by Harvey Dixon, 16 October 1979, Interview NPS-119, Ellis Island Collection, 11. Other Irish girls got jobs through word of mouth via acquaintances: see, for example, Sarah Brady, interview by Charlotte Zabusky, 11 October 1975, Interview MZ-9,

Ellis Island Collection, 4. Still others got jobs through perusal of newspaper advertisements: see, for example, Bertha McGaffighan Devlin, interview by Dana Gumb, 19 September 1985, Interview AKRF-43, Ellis Island Collection, 36. Irish girls also placed advertisements for their services in "situation wanted" advertisements in newspapers: see, for example, *New York Times,* 19 March 1928, 21. For detailed information on intelligence agencies from a contemporary source, see Frances A. Kellor, *Out of Work: A Study of Unemployment* (1904; rev. ed., New York: G. P. Putnam's Sons, 1915), chapter 7 on "Domestic Service and Intelligence Offices," 194–235.

25. Schrier, *Ireland,* 107, 112–122; Katie McCarthy to Nora McCarthy, 30 December 1895, O'Malley Collection; George Potter, *To the Golden Door* (Boston: Little, Brown, 1960), 121.

26. Helen Flatley Cleary, interview by author via telephone, 31 July 1996, tape recording, first quote; Dudden, *Serving Women,* 196; Katzman, *Seven Days a Week,* 110, 161; Hannah Collins to Nora McCarthy, envelope postmarked 22 July 1899, O'Malley Collection, second quote; Campbell, *Prisoners of Poverty,* third quote from 225, 230. See also McKinley, "Stranger in the Gates," 215–216, 236–277; A. J. Downing, *The Architecture of Country Houses* (Appleton, 1850; reprint, New York: Dover Publications, 1969), 278, 309, 326, 350, 360; Rollins, *Between Women,* 52.

27. Owen O'Callaghan to his mother in Ireland, n.d., Miller Collection; Dorr, *What Eight Million Women Want,* 266–267; "The Servant Question," *Nation,* 26 October 1865, 528; Robert Tomes, *The Bazaar Book of Decorum* (New York: Harper and Brothers, 1871), 231.

28. Spofford, *Servant Girl Question,* 59; Hannah Collins to Nora McCarthy, envelope postmarked 30 October 1898, O'Malley Collection, first quote; Mary Cox Harney, Interview EI-107, Ellis Island Collection, 35, second quote; "Your Humble Servant," *Harper's New Monthly Magazine,* June 1864, 55.

29. The O'Malley Collection letters provide details on the social life of immigrant Irish domestics. See Hannah Collins to Nora McCarthy 20 May 1898 and 30 June 1898 on going to weddings; Collins to McCarthy, 24 August 1899, on playing cards; Collins to McCarthy, 21 June 1899, on bicycles; Collins to McCarthy, 7 March 1900, on sleigh riding. See also Ellen Brady [pseud.], Interview MZ 30, Ellis Island Collection, 36, on going to the park; 25, on Coney Island; and 35, on going to the movies. See also Helen Cleary, 7 August 1996, on boat rides and Bear Mountain; Helen Cleary, 31 July 1996, on eating out; Betty Fitzgerald Arnold, interview by author, 26 March 1996, Albany, New York, tape recording, on her mother, Molly Ryan, going to the AOH; Ellen Brady [pseud.], Interview MZ 30, Ellis Island Collection, quote on what transpired at the balls from 31, location of Servants' Balls from 32.

30. Hannah Collins, to Nora McCarthy, 21 September 1898, O'Malley Collection.

31. Owen O'Callaghan, Philadelphia, to his sister, Maggie, Kilmacthomas, County Waterford, Ireland, n.d., ca. 17 September 1883, Miller Collection; John T. Ridge, "Irish County Societies in New York, 1880–1914," in *The New York Irish,* ed. Ronald H. Bayor and Timothy J. Meagher (Baltimore: Johns Hopkins University Press, 1996), 294, 296.

32. Aine Greany, "Oldest Irish Woman Dies in Boston," *Irish Voice* (New York), 29 July–11 August 1998, first quote from 36; Mary Cox Harney, Interview EI-107, Ellis Island Collection, second quote from 36; Hannah Collins to Nora McCarthy, envelope postmarked 27 May 1898, O'Malley Collection, for Collins's quotes.

33. Katzman, *Seven Days a Week,* 159–160. I concur with Nolan, *Ourselves Alone,* 68, 79, on the idea that Irish servants did not expect to spend their entire lives in domestic service. A Thankful Husband, "How My Wife Keeps Her Maids," *Harper's Bazaar,* 4 December 1909, first quote from 1231.

34. Quotation from New York State, Executive Department, State Board of Charities, "Record of Inmates, Rensselaer County Poor House, under Act Chapter 140, Laws of 1875," A1978,

Roll 171, New York State Archives, Albany. See also Salmon, *Domestic Service*, 89, 90; Dudden, *Serving Women*, 208–209.

35. Mary Harren, 14 August 1996, first quote; "Your Humble Servant," *Harper's Monthly Magazine*, June 1864, quotes two, three, four, and five from 54; "Mistress and Maid," *Donahoe's Magazine*, May 1885, sixth quote from 442; "Morals and Manners of the Kitchen," *Nation*, 2 January 1873, seventh quote from 7; Harriet Spofford, *Servant Girl Question*, eighth quote from 89.

36. I use "acculturate" to mean "adapt to or adopt a different culture," as defined in *The Oxford American Dictionary and Language Guide* (New York: Oxford University Press, 1999), 8. See Nolan, *Ourselves Alone*, 94; Dennis J. Clark, "The Irish Catholics: A Postponed Perspective," in *Immigrants and Religion in Urban America*, ed. Randall M. Miller and Thomas D. Marzik (Philadelphia: Temple University Press, 1977), 59; Miller et al., "For Love and Liberty," 55; Hasia Diner, *Erin's Daughters: Irish Immigrant Women in the Nineteenth Century* (Baltimore: Johns Hopkins University Press, 1983), 94; Owen O'Callaghan, Philadelphia, to his brother, Thomas O'Callaghan, County Waterford, Ireland, 12 December 1884 or 1888, Miller Collection, second quote; Helen Flatley Cleary, 31 July 1996, third quote.

37. Dennis Clark, *The Irish in Philadelphia* (Philadelphia: Temple University Press, 1973), 103; Diner, *Erin's Daughters*, 54–55, 57, 67; Colleen McDannell, *The Christian Home in Victorian America, 1840–1900* (Bloomington: Indiana University Press, 1986), 59; Carl Wittke, *The Irish in America* (Baton Rouge: Louisiana University Press, 1956), 41. Domestics who met their husbands at Irish dances include Mary Convery Horan, Interview EI-39, Ellis Island Collection, 58–59; Mary Feely Harren, 4 August 1996; Helen Flatley Cleary, 7 August 1996; and Kathleen Mannion McDonagh—Maryellen McDonagh (Kathleen's daughter), interview by author, 29 May 2002, tape recording. See also Hannah Collins to Nora McCarthy, 16 December 1898, O'Malley Collection; Bertha McGaffighan Devlin, Interview GPI-23, Ellis Island Collection, 33; Rose Kelly Loughlin, Interview EI-607, transcript, Ellis Island Collection, 47.

38. McDannell, *The Christian Home in Victorian America*, 73; Louise Bolard More, *Wage-Earner's Budgets: A Study of Standards and Cost of Living in New York City* (New York: Henry Holt, 1907), first two quotes from 137; Nolan, *Ourselves Alone*, quote from 94; Dr. Patricia Trainor O'Malley, interview by author via telephone, 16 October 1997, tape recording.

39. Rhodes, *Women and the Family in Post-famine Ireland*, 188–190; Catriona Clear, *Women of the House* (Dublin: Irish Academic Press, 2000), 183–193; Diner, *Erin's Daughters*, 17, 65–66, 94–95, 97–98; James J. Kenneally, *The History of American Catholic Women* (New York: Crossroad Publishing, 1990), 67; More, *Wage-Earners' Budgets*, 166, 167, 186; Patricia Trainor O'Malley, 16 October 1997; author conversation with Maureen Varley, 8 November 2001, regarding her Irish immigrant domestic grandmother; Philip L. White, "An Irish Immigrant Housewife on the New York Frontier," *New York History* 48 (1967): 188; Katzman, *Seven Days a Week*, 70; Desmond, "A Century of Irish Immigration," 522, 523; Janet Nolan, "Education and Women's Mobility in Ireland and Irish America, 1880–1920: A Preliminary Look," *New Hibernia Review* 2, no. 3 (Autumn 1998): quote from 78.

40. Andrew M. Greeley, "The Success and Assimilation of Irish Protestants and Irish Catholics in the United States," *Sociology and Social Research* 72 (1988): first quote from 231; ibid., 229: Greeley indicates that "there are 15, 238 respondents in the General Social Survey of whom the ethnic question was asked; 771 are Irish Catholics, who are 16 percent of the Catholic population. The surveys have been taken every year since 1972 with the exception of 1979 and 1981"; Desmond, "A Century of Irish Immigration," second quote from 523; Greeley, "Success and Assimilation of Irish Protestants and Irish Catholics in the United States," third quote from 231–232; fourth quote from 231.

41. Charlotte Ikels, "Parental Perspectives on the Significance of Marriage," *Journal of Mar-*

riage and the Family 47 (May 1985): 253–264; Michael Hout and Joshua R. Goldstein, "How 4.5 Million Immigrants Became 40 Million Irish Americans: Demographic and Subjective Aspects of the Ethnic Composition of White Americans," *American Sociological Review* 59 (February 1994): 64–82; Patricia Kelleher, "Gender Shapes Ethnicity" (Ph.D. diss., University of Wisconsin–Madison, 1995), 56, 444; Ann Rossiter, "Bringing the Margins into the Centre: A Review of Aspects of Irish Women's Emigration from a British Perspective," in *Irish Women's Studies Reader*, ed. Ailbhe Smyth (Dublin: Attic Press, 1993), 193; Ellen Somers Horgan, "The American Catholic Irish Family," in *Ethnic Families in America: Patterns and Variations*, 3rd ed., ed. Charles H. Mindel, Robert W. Habenstein, and Roosevelt Wright Jr. (New York: Elsevier Science Publishing, 1988), 46, 72; Kerby A. Miller, "Assimilation and Alienation: Irish Emigrants' Responses to Industrial America 1871–1921," in *The Irish in America: Emigration, Assimilation and Impact*, ed. P. J. Drudy (London: Cambridge University Press, 1985), 100; Marjorie R. Fallows, *Irish Americans: Identity and Assimilation* (Englewood Cliffs, NJ: Prentice Hall, 1979), 150.

SUGGESTED READING

Hasia R. Diner, *Erin's Daughter's in America: Irish Immigrant Women in the Nineteenth Century* (Baltimore: Johns Hopkins University Press, 1983).

Faye E. Dudden, *Serving Women: Household Service in Nineteenth-Century America* (Middletown, CT: Wesleyan University Press, 1983).

David M. Katzman, *Seven Days a Week: Women and Domestic Service in Industrializing America* (New York: Oxford University Press, 1978).

Maureen Murphy, "Bridget and Biddy: Images of the Irish Servant Girl in *Puck* Cartoons, 1880–1890," in Charles Fanning, ed., *New Perspectives on the Irish Diaspora* (Carbondale: Southern Illinois University Press, 2000).

Daniel E. Sutherland, *Americans and Their Servants: Domestic Service in the United States from 1800 to 1920* (Baton Rouge: Louisiana State University Press, 1981).

Chapter 12

Labor and Labor Organizations

Kevin Kenny

The Irish had a decisive impact on the history of labor in the United States, especially in the nineteenth and early twentieth centuries. The history of Irish-American labor is best understood in terms of the types of work the Irish did for a living, the traditions of protest they brought with them from Ireland, and the contributions they made to American trade unionism.

Before the Famine

The history of the American Irish in the first half of the nineteenth century can be summed up in two words: unskilled labor. Not every Irish immigrant was consigned to manual work, of course, but the majority (both men and women) were. The Irish worked as common laborers and as washerwomen, needle-workers, and domestic servants. The more skilled among them, known as artisans, included carpenters, masons, plasterers, and bricklayers, but most Irish were concentrated in crafts that were declining under the pressure of mechanization and factory labor, such as tailoring, shoemaking, and weaving. They were often employed as temporary out-workers and piece-workers rather than in factories or craftsmen's shops. Those who did work under craftsmen as apprentices often found their own paths to independence as full-fledged artisans blocked by the erosion of their craft in the face of industrialization.

Of the various forms of unskilled work that became the typical occupation of Irish-American men in this period, that of "common laborer" was definitive. Common laborers performed a wide variety of tasks. They worked as longshoremen on the docks; as cartmen and teamsters hauling goods throughout the cities; as coal heavers, lumberyard men, quarrymen, pipe layers, street pavers, ditch diggers, and boatmen. The Irish erected buildings, paved streets, quarried stones, and laid out parks in cities from New York to New Orleans and San Francisco. Half of the teamsters in Buffalo in 1855 were Irish-born, as were four-fifths of the teamsters and carters in New York City. Employment for casual laborers was sporadic, with payment often on a daily rather than a weekly basis. They were often laid off for the winter, especially from construction projects. They followed work to wherever it was available, leaving their families to fend for themselves until they returned (if indeed they ever did). Underpaid and miserably housed, they were not only despised by native-born workers but exploited by contractors and foremen who were more often than not Irish themselves.

From Canada to the Old Northwest and from the Northeast to the deep South, the Irish provided a cheap, expendable labor force for the construction of North America's emerging industrial and urban infrastructure. Chief among the types of work they did was canal construction. The more skilled work on these projects was typically done by English or Welsh miners and masons, but the Irish provided most of the muscle and brawn, living in shantytowns and tents along the banks of the Erie Canal and countless others they constructed across the Northeast. In the South, too, the Irish played a dominant role in canal construction, often working on the same projects as slave laborers. All over the South, Irishmen were used as substitutes for slaves in more dangerous tasks like draining plantations, building levees, and digging ditches and canals in malaria-infested land. Compared to the valuable investment of a slave, an Irish laborer was cheap and expendable. The New Basin Canal from New Orleans to Lake Ponchatrain was manned by Irish laborers specially recruited from Philadelphia and imported direct from Ireland. The thousands who died in the course of building the canal were commemorated in a popular song, which perhaps exaggerated the scale of the casualties: "Ten thousand Micks, they swung their picks, / To dig the New Canal / But the cholera was stronger 'n thay, / An' twice it killed them awl."

On the canals, public works, and railroads of early industrial America, the Irish fought back against their exploitation with violence. At first, workers from one part of Ireland did battle with those from another. The most commonly reported antagonists were the "Corkonians" (evidently from County Cork), the "Fardowners" (apparently from County Longford), and the "Connachtmen" (from Ireland's westernmost province) who clashed frequently on canal and railroad construction projects from Canada to New Orleans. These groups fought each other not for the sake of it but for access to employment, each side attempting to drive the other off the works. They also retaliated against bosses who were late in paying them by destroying the work they had done, in much the same way as fences were destroyed and pastureland dug up to render it fit for tillage (i.e., potato cultivation) in contemporary Ireland. Even more reminiscent of the Irish context was the presence of secret societies in Irish-American canal communities. Organizations of the "Whiteboy" and "Ribbonmen" type—complete with handgrips, passwords, recognition signs, oaths of secrecy, and coffin notices—were widely reported as being active among canallers in the Northeast and mid-Atlantic states.

If faction fighting and secret society violence represented a form of labor activism with its roots in the preindustrial Irish countryside, the form of organizing most suited to the prevailing conditions in industrial America was the trade union, with its standard weapons of collective bargaining and strikes. Already by the 1840s, the canal workers of North America were substituting strikes for violence and more formal labor organizations for secret societies. But it was in industry and the urban trades, rather than on the canals, that the antebellum Irish made their significant contribution to trade unionism.

Irish coal heavers, shoemakers, carpenters, construction workers, and boatmen played a central role in the massive strike that began in Philadelphia in 1835 and spread up the Schuylkill River to the anthracite region of northeastern Pennsylvania, making common cause with the leaders of the city's labor movement, the Philadelphia General Trades Union. While the leaders of this organization were largely British and native-born, two of the more prominent, John Ferrall and John Ryan, were born in Ireland. Inspired by this spirit of interethnic and interreligious solidarity pervading many labor movements in the Northeast in the mid-1830s, Irish Catholic and Protestant handloom weavers in the suburb of Kensington banded together to win better wages from their employers. This short-lived unity, however, quickly crumbled with the onset of economic depression between 1837 and 1844, and the labor movement of Philadelphia disintegrated into anti-Catholic violence. Similarly in New York City, the interethnic cooperation of the 1830s did not survive the downturn in the economy and consequent upsurge in nativism.

Just as nativists tended to regard the Irish as a source of cheap, scab labor, the Irish regarded African Americans in strikingly similar terms. African Americans and Irish immigrants vied with each other for jobs as personal and domestic servants, as laborers and waiters, and on the waterfront. Black workers were often used as strikebreakers to end strikes by Irish laborers. The Irish typically succeeded in displacing black labor quickly, with violence or through sheer force of numbers. Fears of a mass influx of black labor to the north in the event of slavery being abolished were central to Irish racism in the antebellum era, though the events of the Civil War and Reconstruction eventually demonstrated that these fears were unjustified.

The Famine Generation

Just as in the pre-famine period, common labor and domestic service were the dominant forms of work reserved for the Irish in the period from 1845 to 1870. Arriving without marketable skills, the majority of the Irish had to take whatever positions were available; they could not afford to be too choosy, given that most of them were virtually penniless and many were hungry, diseased, or dying. In New York City in 1855, 46 percent of the Irish-born worked as unskilled laborers or service workers (53 percent in the heavily Irish Sixth Ward). In Jersey City, 56 percent of Irish-born men worked in unskilled jobs in 1860. As late as 1870, four out of every ten Irish-born men gainfully employed in the United States worked as unskilled laborers, compared to only 16 percent of the total labor force. Three-quarters of New York City's laborers and half its domestics in that year were Irish-born. Those who avoided menial labor typically worked in skilled or semiskilled jobs rather than in the professions or as self-employed businessmen. Although the Irish tended to fare better the further west they moved, it is clear that the immigrants of the Famine generation were close to the bottom of the American social scale. There were many individual exceptions, of course, but the American Irish in the period 1845 to 1870 were clearly the least successful and the most exploited of all European Americans.

As well as in laboring and hauling, Irishmen were employed in a variety of other jobs in the mid–nineteenth century, most of them menial. They worked, for example, as stablemen, waiters, bartenders, innkeepers, and tailors. In 1855, 27 percent of New

York City's police force was Irish (slightly more than the Irish proportion of the city's population). Practically all the shoemakers in New York City in 1855 in the same year were foreign-born, and one-third of them were Irish. The Irish also worked in semi-skilled trades, notably as tavern keepers and grocers. They worked, too, in the emerging factories of the United States, especially in the textile industry and metal production. Furthermore, they were employed throughout the country in railroad construction and mining, typically filling manual rather than skilled positions, just as they had on the canals.

Irish women were also concentrated in menial, unskilled jobs. Domestic service was the single biggest form of employment for Irish women in America between 1850 and 1900. In New York City as early in 1855, 74 percent of all domestics were Irish and 45 percent of all Irish-born women aged under fifty were employed in this line of work. Servants worked extremely long hours, typically from four or five in the morning until nine or ten at night. They did the cooking, cleaning, washing, housekeeping, sewing and mending, and a host of other household tasks. Within the ranks of female servants there were important gradations from cooks and waitresses to personal servants, chambermaids, and menial kitchen help. Although domestic service was clearly onerous, many young Irish women found it preferable to the alternatives. Room and board were free, and employment was relatively secure; domestics could be fired at will, but they did not face the same pattern of sporadic, uncertain employment endured by women who took work into their home and by many factory workers. Domestic servants were usually able to save money for use as dowries or to finance the emigration of family members from Ireland.

Irish women who did not work as domestic servants found a variety of other jobs. Many took textile work into their homes or did temporary housework for others. Older Irish women (and many younger ones) took in washing or boarders to supplement their income. Those who worked outside the home were employed as bookbinders, peddlers, storekeepers, makers of umbrellas and paper boxes, and in the needle trades, which became their second major source of employment after domestic service. While needlework was often done at home on a piecework basis in the early nineteenth century, it was increasingly concentrated in factories and sweatshops thereafter, under conditions resembling the modern "sweatshop." One-third of Irish women under the age of thirty worked in the needle trades in New York City in 1855. Many of those who could not get work in service or sewing often had little choice but to make a living as prostitutes.

Given the extent of the Irish laboring population in the United States by the mid–nineteenth century, it is not surprising that Irish workers quickly emerged as leaders of American labor. The tradition of gangs and secret societies survived into the late nineteenth century but gradually gave way to involvement in the American trade union movement. The largest unions in New York City in the 1850s were those of the laborers, with the Irish making up the highest proportion of members. In 1855 nearly all the officers of New York's Tailor's Trade Association were Irish. The textile spinner's union in Fall River, Massachusetts, was also under Irish leadership at this time. In 1859 Irish immigrant spinners in Lowell, Massachusetts, who had replaced a largely female textile workforce over the previous decade, launched their first strike. The Irish also dominated longshoremen's work on the waterfront of New York City by this time, having driven out black labor and formed a powerful but racially exclusive trade union, the Longshoremen's and Laborers United Benevolent Society. Among its leaders were two recent Irish immigrants—Thomas Masterson, a Fenian shoemaker, and Robert Blissert (born in England of Irish parents), a tailor and organizer for the International Workingmen's Association who came to the United States in 1868.

Irish immigrants played a prominent role in the foundation and leadership of the American Miners' Union in 1861, and Irish-born miner John Siney was a founder and the first leader of the largest union in the country in this period, the Workingmen's Benevolent Association, which mobilized some 35,000 anthracite mine workers in Pennsylvania after its founding in 1868. The second largest union at this time, the Knights of St. Crispin, had its home among the largely Irish shoemakers; out of it would emerge the most powerful American union of the 1870s and 1880s, the Knights of Labor.

1870–1900

While Irish-American society by the late nineteenth century included a growing middle- and lower-middle class stratum employed as clerks, teachers, and sales personnel, unskilled labor remained the predominant source of employment for Irish immigrants to the United States, with domestic service as its female form. Study after study by historians of the American Irish in the Northeast and Midwest has shown that the Irish-born were disproportionately concentrated in menial labor until at least 1890. From Boston and Newburyport, Massachusetts, to Poughkeepsie, New York, to Philadelphia and Detroit, Irish immigrants worked much more often in unskilled jobs and much less often in skilled and professional work than both native-born Americans and Germans, the other principal immigrant group in the United States before the 1880s.

Women accounted for half of all Irish immigrants to the United States in the second half of the nineteenth century. Most of them were young and single. Domestic service remained the defining activity of Irish women in America, generating the pervasive stereotype of "Bridget." In sharp contrast, most native-born females (including Irish Americans) and most other immigrants (with the significant exception of Swedes, who entered service jobs at about the same high rate as the Irish), avoided domestic service almost entirely. To be a servant, male or female, in a republic was considered stigmatic. Jewish women, for example, preferred the garment factory and sweatshop to domestic service, no matter how bad wages and conditions might be. Italian women were even more resistant to domestic service. For an Italian girl to have gone to live alone in a stranger's house and work as his servant would have violated a series of taboos and threatened the traditional structure of family life. At the same time, most Jewish and Italian women married young, so that there were fewer single females available to become servants, even if their culture had condoned that decision. About as many Irish women worked in the garment industry and needle trades as in domestic service in the late nineteenth century, but wages and conditions were less favorable.

Given the large number of Irish-American women who worked in industry, it is not surprising that they quickly established themselves in the American labor movement. Kate Mullaney successfully organized the Irish collar laundresses in Troy, New York, in 1868. Winifred O'Reilly (née Rooney), who came to the United States with her parents as a child in the 1840s, became an active member of the Knights of Labor and introduced her teenage daughter, Leonora O'Reilly, to the world of trade unionism. Leonora eventually became an organizer for the United Garment Workers of America and helped found the Women's Trade Union League.

Another Irish-born organizer for the Knights was Leonora Barry, an immigrant from County Cork who was elected to the Knights' committee on women's work in 1885. Kate Kennedy led one of the first trade unions of public schoolteachers, demanding equal pay for equal work. Other Irish leaders of the movement to unionize schoolteachers included Margaret Healy and Catherine Goggins in Chicago. American-born Mary Kenny O'Sullivan, the daughter of immigrants from Ireland, became the first female organizer for the American Federation of Labor in 1892 and established the New York chapter of the Women's Trade Union League in 1904. Also active in radical circles was the Irish-born Populist leader Mary Elizabeth Lease, famous for her advice to America's farmers, "Raise less corn and more hell."

Irish men were even more prominent in the late-nineteenth-century American labor movement. John Siney and John Welsh, both Irish-born, led the Workingmen's Benevolent Association in the Pennsylvania anthracite region in the 1870s. An estimated one-third of the employees who went on strike in the great railroad strike of 1877 were Irish. Robert Blissert helped found New York City's powerful Central Labor Union in 1882. Terence V. Powderly (1849–1924), born in the anthracite region of Pennsylvania to Irish immigrant parents, was the leader of the Knights of Labor, the largest labor organization in the United States in the late 1870s and 1880s. Denis Kearney and Frank Roney, both immigrants from Ireland, dominated the San Francisco labor scene in the late 1870s and 1880s. Socialist Peter J. McGuire, the son of Irish immigrants in New York City, organized the Brotherhood of Carpenters and Joiners and helped form the American Federation of Labor in 1886; he is remembered as the "Father of Labor Day" (established by Congress in 1894). The Irish also dominated the workforce and trade unions in metal work, longshore work, and freight-handling in the 1880s and 1890s. The support of Irish-American shoemakers in Massachusetts was crucial in providing the American socialist movement some of its first electoral victories.

Yet, just as earlier in the nineteenth century, perhaps the most interesting aspect of Irish involvement in the American labor movement in the post-Famine era is not so much formal participation in trade unionism as the interaction between trade unionism and older forms of protest rooted in the Irish countryside. Irish branches of the Knights of Labor in the 1880s, for example, sometimes retained practices of secrecy, oath-taking, and ostracism that had originated in rural Ireland. The largely Irish District Assembly 49 of the Knights, organized in New York City in 1882, came into direct conflict with the organization's national leadership which, in an attempt to placate the Catholic Church, ordered an end to secrecy the same year. Another tactic imported from Ireland was the distinctive type of boycotting engaged in by Irish workers in New York City in the 1880s. Drawn from the Land War in contemporary Ireland, boycotting was adapted in the industrial United States for use against manufacturers, newspapers, shipping companies, and Chinese-made goods. The most famous and tragic example of Irish rural strategies being deployed in American industrial conditions was the case of the Molly Maguires, twenty of whom were hanged in Pennsylvania in the late 1870s for a string of assassinations stretching back to the Civil War.

Throughout the late nineteenth century, Irish trade unionists and labor activists continued to espouse racial exclusion even as they fought for other forms of social justice. While struggles between Irish and black workers persisted in the post-Famine era, the most intense form of Irish racial animosity in this period was directed against the Chinese. Organized labor in general, and indeed American society as a whole in the 1870s, shared in this animosity to a remarkable extent, but the hostility of Irish workers to the Chinese was arguably the most intense of all. This was especially seen in California where Irish immigrant workers, led by Denis Kearney and Frank Roney (both Irish-born), were at the vanguard not only of California labor politics but also of the successful movement to curtail Chinese immigration in the late 1870s and early 1880s.

The Twentieth Century

Toward the end of the nineteenth century, the number of American Irish confined to manual, unskilled jobs began to fall significantly. While the Irish-American occupational structure as late as 1880 closely resembled that of the 1850s and 1860s, significant progress was made in the last two decades of the century. By 1900 the Irish had achieved rough occupational parity with the native-born and greatly surpassed the "new immigrants" from southern and eastern Europe. As a predominantly urban people, the American Irish were concentrated much more heavily than the national workforce as a whole in skilled and unskilled labor rather than in agriculture. But, allowing for this urban–rural divide, their occupational structure closely resembled the national average: while 65 percent of American Irish males worked in industry and transportation, only 15 percent were unskilled manual laborers, most of them recent immigrants. About 6 percent belonged to the middle class, and 14 percent to the lower middle class, while 15 percent worked in agriculture.

Instead of being concentrated in menial labor, as they had been for much of the nineteenth century, the American Irish now worked disproportionately in the highly skilled, heavily unionized, and better paid trades. Irish Americans in 1900 greatly exceeded their proportion of the population in most of the skilled trades. In heavy industries like iron, steel, and mining, Irish Americans dominated blue-collar managerial posts, while the lowest-paid, manual labor was done by newly arrived Slavs, Hungarians, and Italians. Irish-born men (as distinct from American-born Irish males) still worked disproportionately in unskilled jobs (especially in the more socially strat-

Despite major advances in social mobility and unionization by 1900, sections of Irish America were still solidly blue collar, and the labor of children remained critical to the family budget. When Lewis Hine photographed Michael Keefe (13), Robert Magee (12), and Cornelius Hurley (13) in 1911, the boys worked in the #1 Mule [spinning] Room of the Merrimac [textile] Mill in Lowell, Massachusetts. (Library of Congress, Prints and Photographs Division, LC-DIG-nclc-02393)

ified Northeast), but to a much lesser extent than the "new" immigrants from eastern and southern Europe.

As for Irish-American women, those who were American-born tended to avoid domestic service for work as secretaries, stenographers, nurses, or—especially—as schoolteachers. Irish immigrant women did less well than the native-born, with a substantial majority of Irish-born females still working either as servants or in textile factories and sweatshops in the early twentieth century. In 1900, 54 percent of Irish-born women in America were house servants (compared to only 19 percent of the second-generation Irish), 6.5 percent were laundresses, and most of the remainder worked in industry.

The dominant trend in Irish-American trade unionism at this time was away from radicalism and toward conservatism and social respectability. While some Irish-Americans trade unionists, such as James Larkin, James Connolly, and John J. Murphy of Philadelphia continued to pursue a radical course, most Irish labor leaders in the early twentieth century emphatically did not. In 1900, Irish immigrants or their descendants held the presidencies of over 50 of the 110 unions in the American Federation of Labor (AFL), the most powerful but also one of the most conservative labor organizations in the country. Even in trades where they accounted for only a small minority of the workforce, Irish Americans often dominated the union leadership —for example in the Carpenters and Joiners, Brewery Workers, and Meat Cutters unions.

The typical Irish-American labor activist at this time was not an immigrant from the Irish countryside but a second- or third-generation American who had usually been raised in an industrial town or city. The AFL concentrated on winning better wages and conditions for its members, most of them highly skilled workers. These workers were mainly white, male, and of northwest European descent; blacks, women, and the "new immigrants" from southern and eastern Europe were largely excluded from this narrow and restrictive labor movement. Concerned with "bread and butter issues," and confined to a skilled elite, the AFL deliberately avoided programs for systematic social reform, let alone revolutionary change.

Irish Americans headed some of the most influential unions within the AFL. Among the most prominent were James O'Connell of the Machinists; Timothy Healy, leader of the International Brotherhood of Stationary Firemen; Frank Duffy of the Carpenters; and Peter McGuire and James Lynch of the Typographers. McGuire, an erstwhile socialist who had been instrumental in the creation of America's Labor Day (conveniently switched from May to September to undermine the socialists), abandoned his earlier radicalism to become Samuel Gompers's closest associate in creating a socially conservative, job-conscious AFL. Irish-American labor leaders played an active role in assisting Gompers in his campaign against socialism within the AFL. John Mitchell, the leader of the powerful United Mine Workers of America formed a special group, the Militia of Christ for Social Service, to coordinate antisocialist policies in the labor movement and to gain the support of the Catholic Church. In 1919 Irish-American unionists like John Hynes of the Sheet Metal Workers and Daniel Tobin of the Teamsters also joined Gompers in withdrawing the AFL from the new International Federation of Trade Unions, on the grounds that involvement in international solidarity could only distract the AFL from its purpose of safeguarding its members' material interests.

By the early twentieth century, Irish-American women were also playing a prominent role in the American labor movement. Leonora O'Reilly (1870–1926), the daughter of the Irish-born labor activist Winifred O'Reilly, was appointed to the board of the national Women's Trade Union League (WTUL) when it was founded in 1903. Mary Kenny O'Sullivan, who had been the first female organizer of the AFL in the 1890s, established the New York chapter of the WTUL. Agnes Nestor was elected president of the International Glove Workers Union, while Julia O'Connor was chosen to head the telephone operators' department of the International Brotherhood of Electrical Workers in 1912. Cork-born Mary Harris Jones (1837–1930), known as "Mother Jones," was one of the foremost labor activists in the United States. Jailed frequently, she devoted most of her life to helping impoverished and exploited workers and was particularly active among coal miners. In 1905 she helped found the radical labor organization, the Industrial Workers of the World (IWW), where she was joined by Irish-American activist Elizabeth Gurley Flynn (1890–1964).

That the IWW was headed by a labor activist of Irish descent, William "Big Bill" Haywood (1869–1928), indicates that the spirit of Irish-American radicalism, while clearly muted by the 1910s and 1920s, was far from dead. Other radicals from this period included William Z. Foster, the son of immigrants from County Carlow, who launched his career in 1919 when he and fellow Irish-American John Fitzpatrick helped organize a great national steel strike. Foster later became involved in the recently formed American Communist Party. Mike Quill (1905–1966), a former member of the Irish Republican Army (IRA) in Ireland, helped establish the powerful Transport Workers Union of America in 1934 and became its first president. Joe Curran, born in 1906 to an impoverished Irish family on New York's East Side, organized the sailors of the East Coast in the 1930s and became the first president of the National Maritime Union in 1937. When the Congress of Industrial Organizations (CIO) broke away from the conservative AFL in 1936 to organize all workers, not just the skilled elite, its leaders included Irish-Americans John Brophy, James B. Carey, and Mike Quill.

Irish-American influence in the U.S. labor movement reached its height in the mid–twentieth century, just as that movement as a whole was reaching its own peak of historical power. The two most powerful Irish-American labor organizers in this era were Philip Murray (1886–1952), the son of an Irish-born laborer, and William George Meany (1894–1979), the grandson of a famine refugee. As president of the CIO, Murray helped pave the way for its merger with the AFL in 1955. Meany was appointed president of the combined AFL-CIO and exercised an important influence on American politics. Since the 1950s, however, Irish-American identity has become much more diffuse, and the U.S. trade union movement has declined precipitously. Whereas 39 percent of nonagricultural employees in the United States belonged to unions in 1951, that figure had dropped to about 12 percent by the late 1990s. Americans of Irish descent, including Ron Carey of the Teamsters and John Sweeney of the AFL, have been elected to head important unions in recent years. But these leaders regarded themselves more as "American" than "Irish American," and they presided over a trade union movement that was considerably weakened compared with the century after the Great Famine, the heyday of both American and Irish-American labor.

SUGGESTED READING

David Brundage, *The Making of Western Labor Radicalism: Denver's Organized Workers, 1878–1905* (Urbana: University of Illinois Press, 1994).

David M. Emmons, *The Butte Irish: Class and Ethnicity in an American Mining Town, 1875–1925* (Urbana: University of Illinois Press, 1989).

Joshua Freeman, *In Transit: The Transport Workers Union in New York City, 1933–1966* (New York: Oxford University Press, 1988; 2nd ed., Philadelphia: Temple University Press, 2001).

Michael Gordon, "Irish Immigrant Culture and the Labor Boycott in New York City, 1880–1886," in *Immigrants in Industrial America, 1850–1920,* ed. Richard L. Ehrlich (Charlottesville: University of Virginia, 1977), 111–122.

Kevin Kenny, *Making Sense of the Molly Maguires* (New York: Oxford University Press, 1998).

David Montgomery, "Labor Movement," in *The Encyclopedia of the Irish in America,* ed. Michael Glazier (Notre Dame, IN: University of Notre Dame Press, 1999), 525–531.

Chapter 13

Race, Violence, and Anti-Irish Sentiment in the Nineteenth Century

Kevin Kenny

For most of the nineteenth century, the Irish were the dominant immigrant presence in the cities and towns of both the United States and England. They were also among the poorest and most disadvantaged people that either country had ever hosted, especially during the traumatic generation from 1845 through the 1870s. Historians have recently begun to tell the history of the Irish in America and in Britain as part of the same larger Atlantic story of migration and settlement, labor and race, politics and culture.[1] There were, of course, major differences as well as similarities between the national contexts in which Irish migration history unfolded. Proximity and politics dictated that Ireland and the Irish posed a direct threat to British political sovereignty in a way the American Irish never did to the United States, and this obviously had a significant influence on how the Irish were perceived. Still, insofar as Irish migration is concerned, the United States and Britain represent nationally specific variations on common themes. This essay examines one of the most controversial of these themes—the emergence of a distinctive form of anti-Irish racial sentiment on both sides of the Atlantic in the nineteenth century. In the American case, it is argued, the key to understanding this sentiment lies in the history of Irish collective violence, enacted in the context of a racial hierarchy defined by the existence of chattel slavery.

This essay takes a new look at a familiar image: that of the Irish savage, or ape-man. Descriptions of the Irish as inherently savage stood at one extreme of a wide spectrum of representation, much of it relatively mild and some of it richly comic. There were many images of the Irish in currency in the nineteenth century. These included the tall, respectable, northern Protestant farmer; the dull-witted but comic and harmless "Pat" or "Mick" with his Irish bulls and illogical banter; the somewhat menacing "Pat" or "Paddy" with his projecting mouth and jaw; and the full-blown simianized "Paddy," who in Perry Curtis's words "looked like a cross between monstrous ape and primitive man, owing to his high and hairy upper lip or muzzle, concave nose, low facial angle, and sharp teeth," and whose "destructive instincts were engraved on every line of his body." This version of "Paddy," Curtis argued, starkly portrayed the Irish as racially inferior to Anglo-Saxons—an inferiority inscribed in their phenotype and manifested in acts of savagery. By concentrating almost exclusively on this extreme image, to the exclusion of more benign varieties, Curtis may have given the impression that this was the *only* way that Englishmen saw Irishmen, or at least that they saw them this way most of the time. In the revised edition of *Apes and Angels*, he acknowledged as much by mapping out the wider spectrum of representation just alluded to. But not before his work had ignited a firestorm of controversy among historians.[2]

Citing images of the sort Curtis presented, some historians detected a racism that was apparently no different from that inflicted in the Americas on people of African descent. Others, however, insisted that the satirical distortions of political cartoons should not blind us to the fact that anti-Irish sentiment was really about economics, or religion, or politics—or anything but race. Today this seems like a false opposition, an unnecessary choice. There were many reasons why people disliked the Irish: their poverty and manners, their physical appearance, their perceived indolence, their relation to alcohol, their religion, their capacity for criminality or collective violence. But what these different forms had in common was that they could be, and were, expressed both verbally and visually in the language of race. Race is a powerful way of interpreting the world and explaining how it works. Victorian Englishmen and Gilded Age Americans presumably did not believe that the Irish actually *were* gorillas, but they found it effective to describe the Irish and their actions in ape-like terms. In other words, the language of race—whether verbal or visual—tells us less about why some people hated other people than about *how* they hated them. The detractors of the Irish did not hate the Irish because they were apes; they described them as apes because doing so could be a devastatingly effective mode of explanation and condemnation.

The term "race" carried no single meaning in the nineteenth century, and its valences changed over time. Americans and Englishmen often used the term loosely, to denote peoplehood. They sometimes used it in a specific scientific sense, whether environmental, phrenological, physiognomic, or hereditary. In this essay, one quite specific and readily identifiable meaning is at stake: race as a particular mode of social perception and representation that casts the world and its peoples in terms of fixed, hereditary group characteristics, discernible in physical appearance, which can explain and predict behavior. The closest equivalent in nineteenth-century terms was the science, or pseudo-science, of physiognomy: the belief that physical, and especially facial, features expressed the true character of men and women.

Race in this sense was an undeniable feature of the stark, and still shocking, forms of anti-Irish sentiment in the nineteenth-century Atlantic world. Several historians of the Irish in Britain have examined this question, as have several historians of the Irish in the United States, but these two schools of scholarship have rarely engaged each other. They deal with the same types of people, during the same period—people who originated in the same country and dispersed across the same Atlantic world—yet the artificial barriers of national history have produced quite separate, and barely related, stories. Bringing the American and British stories together, while also allowing for their differences, helps clarify what is useful and what is not about race as a category of analysis in Irish migration history.

"THE CHAMPION OF THE FENIANS."
The Democratic Nominee of Massachusetts.

When *Harper's Weekly* ran this cartoon on 21 October 1876, Fenians had been replaced by the Clan na Gael as the power behind Irish nationalism in America. But even without the moniker "Champion of the Fenians," little more than his facial features were needed to indicate this gentleman's ethnicity. From the 1830s the Irish had regularly been dehumanized—first in verbal descriptions, then in illustrations such as this one—depicted with ape-like faces and characterized as racially inferior to Americans of Anglo-Saxon origin. (Mick Moloney Irish American Collection)

I

The forms of racial representation under consideration had a relatively brief heyday, stretching at most from the 1840s through the 1880s, with some prefiguration before that and some faint echoes thereafter. They reached a peak in the 1850s, 1860s, and 1870s. That these three decades should coincide with the worldwide dispersal of some three million Irish migrants is hardly a coincidence. The expression of racial sentiment against the Irish in Britain and the United States was in large part an adjustment to the shock of their presence, and the particular form this sentiment took was determined by developments in the otherwise unrelated fields of natural history and Irish political history: the controversy ignited in the 1860s by Darwin's *On the Origin of Species* and the rise of militant physical force nationalism with the Fenians. The simianization of "Paddy" had begun before then, as had the natural scientists' debate over the ancestry of man. But both crystallized in the 1860s. If gorillas were now to be man's closest relative, then some breeds of men might at least be closer to them than others.[3]

The Irish immigrants of the mid–nineteenth century were certainly the poorest and most disadvantaged the United States had seen. While prejudice has a way of producing its own statistics, the Irish of the famine era topped the charts in figures for arrest, imprisonment, and confinement in poorhouses and mental hospitals in both the United States and Britain.[4]

Immigrants accounted for a higher proportion of the U.S. population in the 1840s and 1850s than ever before or since, and the Irish made up between one-third and one-half of the total flow. Because they settled in towns and cities, the American Irish —and not the slightly more numerous but more rural Germans—came to symbolize immigration and its attendant problems. They, and not the Germans, became the primary target of nativist, or anti-immigrant, sentiment. Many native-born Americans came to believe that this vast pool of impoverished unskilled labor threatened the welfare of the republic. Unable or unwilling to move upward through the social scale, the Irish poor heralded the arrival of forms of class stratification and social conflict that were considered typical of Europe, not America. Were such people, the nativists asked, really fit candidates for American citizenship and assimilation?

At the heart of the antipathy toward the new arrivals was their religion. In the generation before the Civil War, the Roman Catholic Church was transformed from an insignificant, genteel, largely southern and French-dominated institution into the largest single Christian denomination in the United States. Would these new Americans be loyal to the United States or to Rome? asked the American nativists. Were they capable of thinking independently on matters of religion and politics, or were they beholden to their priests? (This question conveniently ignored that Protestant immigrants tended to vote in a bloc for the Whig or Republican Party to the same extent as Catholics voted Democrat.) Was the hierarchical and authoritarian structure of the Roman Catholic Church compatible with basic republican values? Surely, the nativists argued, the self-governing structure of Protestant denominations was inherently more American. Furthermore, why did Irish Catholics want to organize their own schools instead of sending their children through the new public system that stood as one of the crowning glories of America's experiment in republican democracy? The presence of the Irish in America raised big questions, then, just as their presence in Britain raised a similar but distinctive set of questions in the United Kingdom. Because these questions had to do with labor, social conditions, politics, and religion, some historians have argued that race is irrelevant or at best peripheral in explaining anti-Irish sentiment. But does one really have to choose in so stark a manner, and does this choice do justice to the historical evidence?

In developing an answer to this question, Americanists might benefit from reviewing the strengths and weaknesses of an earlier debate about the Irish and race in British historiography. In *Apes and Angels*, Perry Curtis took as his subject "the gradual but unmistakable transformation of Paddy, the stereotypical Irish Celt of the mid-nineteenth century, from a drunken and relatively harmless peasant into a dangerous ape-man or simianized agitator." "In cartoons and caricatures, as well as in prose," Curtis argued, this fearsome figure of Paddy, came to resemble "the chimpanzee, the orangutan, and, finally, the gorilla."[5]

Sheridan Gilley's forceful critique of the Curtis thesis, published in 1978, was apparently quite influential at the time, but it does not stand up very well today. Gilley began by drawing a fundamental distinction between contemporary anti-black racism and nineteenth-century anti-Irish attitudes—something that Curtis, an "American liberal" blinded by the contemporary history of race in his own country, had allegedly been unable to do. For Gilley the matter was straightforward: equating what he called "anti-Negro racism" with "English dislike of the Victorian Irish" simply ignored "objective differences of race." "A Negro," he insisted "is identifiable at once: a 'Celt' does not have this separate racial character so visibly stamped upon him." The Irish, in other words, were not a race, because their skin color or physical appearance did not differ significantly from that of their putative Anglo-Saxon oppressors, who were themselves a motley crew. And, because they were not a race, they could not have suffered racism.[6]

Whatever about its plausibility a quarter-century ago, this formulation ignores what most historians today take as their starting point: *all* racial types are human inventions, and skin color in itself signifies nothing until, historically, it is made to do so. That this process may be stretched over centuries or millennia rather than decades should not place it beyond the grasp of a nineteenth-century historian. Unless, that is, race is held to stand outside history altogether and the inferiority of dark skin or physical difference asserts itself the moment it is perceived. Gilley was correct, in an obvious sense, to point out that the absence of what he called "an objective criterion of race like skin colour" made discussions of anti-Irish or anti-Celtic racial prejudice ambiguous and difficult.[7] But his response to this difficulty was to jettison the concept of race altogether, whereas Curtis had responded by trying hard to determine the racial content of the rich store of images he had unearthed in his research. If, as Gilley charged, Curtis's scheme was sometimes too rigid and all-encompassing, Curtis did at least directly confront the challenge his sources presented. Gilley, by contrast, sought to explain that challenge away.

If race was not the issue, then why did the British dislike the Irish so much? Gilley acknowledged a "fleeting," "euphoric" moment of Anglo-Saxon hereditarian racism in the 1860s, but he insisted that anti-Irish sentiment was at bottom political, social, cultural, or religious—again, anything but racial. To the extent that the Victorian English disliked the Irish, he concluded, the main reason was "the Irish rejection of English values," specifically religious and political ones. The Irish, after all, were Catholics, and they kept going on about constitutional autonomy, or even in some cases political independence. "Romanism and the revolutionary temper," as Gilley put it, were the true cause of English antipathy toward the Irish, and these were manifestly "non-racial factors."[8]

In retrospect at least, the weakness in this argument is clear: regardless of its origins, the antipathy in question could, and plainly did, assume a racial form. Even so restrained a contemporary critic as Gearóid O'Tuathaigh, who shared some of Gilley's discomfort with Curtis's intrusion into British historiography, found Gilley's rebuttal unpersuasive. "There was," O'Tuathaigh wrote, "an almost universal tendency from the 1840s onwards to describe the immigrant Irish and their problems in distinctly racial terms. . . . While the ineluctable fact of colour is missing here, it is still difficult to describe this kind of language as other than racial."[9]

Without conceding this minimal threshold of racial sentiment, how is one to explain the extent and character of anti-Irish prejudice? Given that all stereotypes about national character contain truth as well as falsity, Gilley asked, "can a prejudice be so called when what it alleges is true?" Not only did the Irish have deplorably bad taste in religion and politics, they lived in squalor, dressed in rags, and actually "looked like savages," as everyone from Froude to Engels attested. The English stereotype of the Irishman, in short, "rested on a body of social fact, however misinterpreted": rural squalor in Ireland, slums and criminal statistics abroad, a predilection for violence and drink everywhere. It is no wonder, Gilley concluded, that "so unlikeable a body was actively disliked." And one hardly needed to invoke "racial prejudice" to explain why this was so.[10] Unless, that is, the prejudice happened to be expressed in racial form—which is why Curtis wrote his book in the first place.

While Curtis's conception of race surely emerged strengthened rather than diminished in light of criticisms of this sort, he did acknowledge some of its flaws in the revised edition of 1997. The original book had been concerned primarily with the extreme form of anti-Irish racism, and to the extent that it had implied that this was the only image deployed against the Irish, *Apes and Angels* was partial and misleading. Moreover, as Roy Foster argued in his analysis of Irish imagery in *Punch* magazine, much of the material Curtis had drawn upon was plainly satirical and needed to be read as such. It was a matter of caricature, not sociology, and hence it ought not to be treated as though it were a literal account of English Victorian attitudes toward the Irish. Nor was it surprising, Foster suggested, that some Victorian Englishmen thought of the Irish in brutish terms, for portraying the plebeian and the foreign in dark or brutish terms was standard practice on both sides of the Atlantic in the nineteenth century.[11]

Yet a significant distinction is needed here. French simians, as Curtis pointed out in his response to Foster's criticism, may well have been commonplace; but they appeared as dandified monkeys, not as savage gorillas. The British poor and working classes may have been brutalized by their detractors, but they were not dehumanized nearly to the extent of the "Celtic Calibans." The extreme, full-blown simian Paddy was a uniquely bestialized and racialized figure. Why, then, was this particular form applied to the Irish, and apparently to them alone? And why was it applied in America as well as in Britain?[12]

II

That the Irish, alone among European immigrant groups in the mid–nineteenth century, were subject to forms of racial caricature is a proposition generally accepted by historians of the United States. To the extent that this proposition has won grudging acceptance among British historians as well, the most convincing explanations point to the effect of Irish nationalism in Britain, especially its extreme and violent forms. Gilley and Curtis agreed that anti-Irish sentiment in Britain peaked at times of Irish political agitation, whether Fenianism or the Phoenix Park murders—the only difference being that Gilley saw this correlation as proof of the priority of politics over race, whereas Curtis, more convincingly, detected a racial response to political agitation. While this response often came in the form of caricature, political cartoons nonetheless surely served a serious political purpose, as Peter Gray has demonstrated in his analysis of *Punch* and the Great Famine.[13]

The problem is that Irish nationalism cannot provide an explanation for the emergence of a similar type of anti-Irish racialism in the United States. Irish nationalism directly threatened the sovereignty of the United Kingdom, but it had no such influence on American life.[14] Another tradition of Irish violence—collective and social, and transplanted to America from the Irish countryside—did pose a direct threat to American social order, in a way that never applied in Britain to nearly the same extent. The United States also presented a distinctive racial and political context, one where chattel slavery survived until 1865 and where race, consequently, shaped the meaning of freedom and democracy in a direct and pervasive manner. These two considerations—the nature of violence and of race in the United States—call for a particular form of historical explanation that significantly distinguishes the American from the British case.

While nationalism was central to the emergence of anti-Irish racial sentiment in Britain, it was peripheral in the United States. Irish nationalism certainly had a prominent American dimension, as is well known. All of the major Irish nationalist movements since the 1790s have had American branches or offshoots, some of them peaceful and gradual in the constitutionalist tradition, others sanctioning violence in pursuit of a full-fledged republic.[15] The American Irish are generally better known for the latter tradition, even if the former has always been dominant. New York City, the home of John Devoy, was the principal center of Irish physical-force nationalism in the late nineteenth and early twentieth centuries. Furthermore, America was the launching ground for dynamite campaigns in Britain in the 1880s, for collaboration with the Germans during World War I, for significant gunrunning in the 1970s and 1980s, and for massive financial contributions throughout the nineteenth and twentieth centuries. But while Irish Americans gained the reputation, partly deserved, of supporting extremism with reckless detachment, Irish nationalism—even in its violent forms—never posed a threat to the sovereignty of the United States the way it did to the United Kingdom and the British Empire. The Irish never exploded bombs in American cities, even if they sometimes planned their British bombing campaigns from Boston, Chicago, or New York.

Ethnic nationalism did raise troubling questions of divided loyalty in the United States. On which side of the hyphen, Irish or American, would the immigrants come down? And when that nationalism involved support for physical force, as with the Fenians or the dynamiters of the 1880s, it reinforced a prevailing racialist sentiment that the Irish were by nature an inherently violent people. But retaining—or acquiring—an ethnic identity, far from hindering assimilation, was actually a precondition to becoming American. Many such ethnic identities—whether Irish-American,

Italian-American, Lithuanian-American, or Cuban-American—contained a national-ist component. Furthermore, the moderate forms of ethnic nationalism that predom-inated often served American ends, as Thomas N. Brown argued in the Irish case, enhancing the immigrants' respectability and demonstrating their political skills and their capacity for citizenship.[16] Moreover, even if the support of a vocal minority of immigrants for physical force nationalism enflamed anti-Irish sentiment in America, the critical point is that this sentiment was already firmly entrenched. How, then, had it originated?

Its origins in nineteenth-century America lay partly in the broad social, economic, and religious determinants of the famine era. But there was another, quite specific cause: the Irish tradition of collective violence. In the United States, the real grounds for concern were not so much the Fenians or the followers of O'Donovan Rossa as the numerous gangs, riots, secret societies, and general social turbulence with which the immigrant Irish were associated. The American Irish, for a generation on either side of the Famine, suffered from an alarming variety of social pathologies. Nativists may have exaggerated some of the problems, but the poverty and deprivation—and the social problems they gave rise to—were real enough. Among other things, the Ameri-can Irish became notorious for their rough and boisterous culture. But there was much more going on than drinking, carousing, and urban gang life. Only the most blinkered historian could deny that the American Irish engaged in sustained and sometimes spectacular episodes of collective social and political violence throughout the nineteenth century. This side of Irish life in America had nothing at all to do with nationalist politics, but in the eyes of nativists it posed a serious threat to the stability of the United States and cast grave doubts on the suitability of the Irish as citizens in a democratic republic. This threat called forth an explanation of the violence cast in terms of fixed attributes of Irish character that were ostensibly discernible in physical appearance—in other words, a racial explanation.

To the extent that collective violence determined racial perceptions of the Ameri-can Irish, it should be noted that this violence was by definition largely and often exclusively male. A full account of anti-Irish racial perception would require exten-sive consideration of how Irish-American women were perceived as well, especially in the already racialized form of labor for which they were best known and which they shared with African Americans: domestic service. There is some evidence that the racial response to the rough culture of Irish-American men was extended to cover women as well, with one famous image comparing Florence Nightingale with her Irish counterpart, "Bridget McBruiser."[17]

In both men's and women's history, labor is the best starting point. The story of Irish-American labor is bound up with the story of race, but with a significant twist: it involves not just racial sentiment directed against the Irish but also the forms of racism deployed against Americans of African and Asian origin. As labor history is the key, it will be useful first to clarify what it was like to be a working-class Irish Ameri-can in the mid-nineteenth century, and what forms of discrimination and prejudice working-class Irish immigrants did and did not endure.

Richard Jensen has recently argued that "No Irish Need Apply" signs may actually be one of the great myths of Irish-American history. No historian, at any rate, has ever held one of these signs, even if they have encountered some newspaper advertisements. Jensen implausibly infers from this absence of evidence that the American Irish therefore encountered no real prejudice at all, a conclusion that no historian of the field endorses. But his basic point about labor is a good one: demand for unskilled male heavy labor and unskilled female domestic labor in the nineteenth century was simply too great for the Irish to have suffered much by way of anti-hiring discrimination, racial or otherwise. As for skilled jobs: Irish immigrants lacked the qualifications for them rather than being excluded from work they might otherwise have done. To the theory of discrimination, then, must be added the fact that, more than any other immigrant group in the mid–nineteenth century, the Irish arrived in America and Britain without marketable skills. The tendency of the Irish to work at low wages in unskilled labor, along with their use as strikebreakers, led to considerable hostility from native-born American workers. But Irish Americans were not generally consigned to those positions by discrimination, whether legal or informal.[18]

Irish Americans quickly came to harbor strikingly similar sentiments against African Americans and Chinese Americans, lashing out at their use as strikebreakers and their apparent willingness to work for low wages. In the period up through the Civil War, Catholic Irish immigrants steadfastly opposed the abolition of slavery, convinced that it would lead to an influx of cheap black labor into northern cities, undermining their hard-won but still precarious niche in the economy. To build and protect that niche, they tried to drive African Americans out of work on the docks and in other forms of manual labor, replaced them in domestic service, and forced them out of neighborhoods like the Five Points section of New York City. Deep-rooted tensions between Irish and black workers, aggravated by the Emancipation Proclamation and the Conscription Act of 1863, exploded in violence in July of that year on the streets of New York. Irish workers lashed out against symbols of power and privilege in the city, especially those connected with the federal government, conscription, and the anti-slavery Republican Party. They harassed, beat, and lynched African Americans and burned the Colored Orphan Asylum to the ground.

Contemporary nativists, who had good reason to exaggerate, estimated the number killed in the riots at between twelve hundred and fifteen hundred. The official police figure of 119 dead is probably too low, but that would still make it, until recent reckoning, the worst riot in American history.[19] Only seven years later, massive Irish violence once again rocked New York City, this time involving internecine ethnic conflict rather than an anti-black uprising.

Irish Protestants had been holding parades in American cities on July 12 since the early nineteenth century, and there had been limited violence between these "Orangemen" and their Catholic opponents during several such celebrations. When the two sides clashed in 1870, at least nine men were killed and as many as 150 were injured. A year later, when Irish Catholics attacked the parade with stones, missiles, and gunfire, troops opened fire on the mob killing at least sixty and injuring about one hundred more.[20] Elite native-born Protestant northerners responded to the Irish racial violence of 1863 and 1870 with a racism of their own, producing some of the most sustained and virulent anti-Irish sentiment in American history. In this way, the racist Irish were themselves reduced to the level of the animal kingdom. In the wake of the draft riots, the patrician nativist George Templeton Strong described the Irish in America as "brutal, base, cruel, cowards, and as insolent as base"; they came from a land populated by "creatures that crawl and eat dirt and poison every community they infest."[21]

Irish anti-black riots in the generation leading up to the Civil War had their counterpart in the violent and often secretive labor organizations that arose on the public works, canals, railroads, and mining communities where Irish laborers found employment. As a predominantly rural country, Ireland did not have a significant trade union movement in the nineteenth century. Instead, its modes of organization and protest were marked by covert activity and violence: the faction fight and the secret society, rather than negotiation and arbitration, were the classic forms of protest. On the canals, public works, and railroads of early industrial America, the Irish adapted their traditions of rural violent protest to the new conditions they faced.

At first, the patterns of affiliation were local and regional, with workers from one part of Ireland banding together against those from another. In the generation before the Civil War, American canal and railroad construction projects saw frequent clashes between gangs of workers bound together by county of origin. Reports of their activities were heard all the way from Canada to New Orleans. They fought each other not for the fun of it, as the prevailing anti-Irish stereotype suggested, but in a desperate struggle for access to employment, with each side attempting to drive the other off the job. They also retaliated against bosses who were late in paying them by destroying the work they had done, a tactic strikingly reminiscent of the pattern of violence in contemporary Ireland whereby the rural poor tore down fences or dug up pastureland overnight to restore it for potato cultivation. Just as in Ireland, tightly organized secret societies soon emerged in Irish immigrant communities on the canal and railroad works—bearing names like "Whiteboys" and "Ribbonmen"; deploying the familiar paraphernalia of handgrips, passwords, recognition signs, oaths of secrecy, and coffin notices; and using direct and brutal violence as their favored strategy in labor disputes. This adaptation of Irish rural protest strategies to early American industrial conditions reached its tragic finale in the case of the "Molly Maguires," twenty of whom were hanged in the Pennsylvania anthracite region in the 1870s after having been convicted of sixteen murders.[22]

Episodes of this kind greatly reinforced the notion that the Irish were a uniquely violent people. To make sense of this violence, the historian needs to move beyond two poles of interpretation. On the one hand, hostile contemporaries tended to reduce groups like the "Whiteboys," "Ribbonmen," and "Molly Maguires" to the level of depraved killers who engaged in violence largely for the sake of it, that being the sort of people the Irish were. On the other hand, the American Irish undeniably did engage in collective social and political violence on a significant scale in the nineteenth century; they were not merely the innocent victims of oppression, whether economic, religious, or ethnic. The historian's task is to acknowledge and try to explain the violence that did take place, while at the same time treating contemporary explanations by nativists, corporate capitalists, and trial lawyers with the skepticism they deserve.[23]

The first part of this twofold task, explaining the nature of the violence, is not at issue here; the second, analyzing anti-Irish sentiment, is the main theme under

By the turn of the twentieth century, Irish Americans had generally succeeded in improving their public image—indeed the "Stage Irishman" had all but met his demise in the theatre—when new forms of popular culture provided a vehicle for old stereotypes. In silent cinema and penny postcards, such as this 1905 example by the New York printer Arthur Livingston, the simianized Irishman breathed anew, accompanied by iconography that was becoming increasingly hackneyed in non-Irish hands. (Mick Moloney Irish American Collection)

discussion. In Pennsylvania, hostile contemporaries responded to the violence of the Molly Maguires by detaching it from any rational or causal context. As a result, the violence was deprived not simply of a legitimating cause (whether social, economic, or political) but of social or historical explanation of any kind. Instead, it was presented as a fixed attribute of the Irish people, an unchanging essence that stood outside historical time altogether. Thus originated the myth of the Molly Maguires.

But where does race fit into this explanatory scheme? A discourse that posits innate, timeless savagery as a national attribute sounds awfully like a racial discourse. But is race really useful or necessary in this case? To answer that question, the historian needs to stake out a position on the recent, highly influential debate on "whiteness."[24]

III

Historians in the last decade have embarked on an intensive study of Irish racism and racial identity in the nineteenth-century United States. The thesis on "how the Irish became white" was put forth first (and best) by David Roediger in his study of the antebellum era, *The Wages of Whiteness*, and it has since been applied to American history and culture at large. The Irish, it is argued, arrived in the United States without a sense of being "white" and were depicted and treated as racial inferiors before eventually embracing "whiteness" as the central ingredient of their new American identity. In this way, race became a primary means of assimilation for Irish immigrants. Historians such as Eric Arnesen and Peter Kolchin have recently pointed to some of the shortcomings in this conception of American history. Here it will be sufficient to address two points: the nature of Irish self-perception, and the distinction between the Irish and other "racialized" groups in the United States.[25]

Although the existing literature makes large claims about Irish racial consciousness and motivation, it tells us surprisingly little about how the Irish saw themselves. We have no real sense of how most ordinary Irish immigrants in the United States thought about race, even if they often engaged in actions that can fairly be called racist. When historians examine the racial images in satirical and literary magazines, they often appear to be seeking a measure of the influence of British or American racism on the Irish. But Irish immigrants were not generally in the habit of reading the type of publication that Perry Curtis analyzed: they may have been unaware that they were being portrayed as beasts rather than men. These magazines really do not tell us much about the Irish or their feelings; they do tell us something about the publishers and their native-born, urban, middle-class readership. The Irish may well have seen and responded to the pejorative images under consideration here, but one cannot write about their perceptions and responses without citing some tangible evidence.[26]

Moreover, even if we concede that some Americans did not regard the Irish as "fully white"—the meaning of which is always elusive in the literature—the position of the Irish in American society seems to have suffered relatively little as a result. If we grant that the Irish in America were not initially regarded as "fully white," this does not mean that they were regarded or treated as "black" or "yellow." The Irish were never denied entry into the United States or the right to acquire citizenship; unlike Americans of African or Asian descent, they could vote, serve on juries, and move freely from place to place; and they were more likely to deliver violence than to receive it. On both sides of the Atlantic, to be sure, the Irish were subject to vicious racial caricatures and stereotypes. But in neither Britain nor America did prejudice translate into a system of racial discrimination or subordination enshrined in law. Invoking the ambiguities of Irish "whiteness" tends to obscure this distinction between prejudice and discrimination, with sometimes unfortunate results in the classroom, where Irish-American students, newly empowered with a sense of past victimhood, too often embrace a single lesson: "If we pulled ourselves up through hard work, then why can't they?"

The American debate on "whiteness" does contain several useful insights, however, and it has opened up a critical line of inquiry that will and should continue. The debate is based on the simple but neglected realization, made by W. E. B. Du Bois in the 1930s but not taken up again by historians for more than half a century, that "white" people, and not just "minorities," have a racial identity, and that this identity, like any other, developed historically and can be studied accordingly.[27] The debate has demonstrated conclusively that, in the American context, race and class have never been separate historically but have always constituted and reinforced each other. In nineteenth-century American history at least, one can rarely talk coherently about labor and class without talking about race. Certainly, one does not need to choose starkly between them, along the lines favored by Sheridan Gilley. From the beginning, the very meaning of American freedom has been construed in racial terms: slavery, as historians from Edmund Morgan to Eric Foner have demonstrated, was the bedrock of freedom, the standard against which it was defined and measured. But this is an American story. One needs to be wary of the over-ready application of the concept of whiteness to British history. At the very least, the absence in Britain of racial slavery (if one can ignore colonialism and the role of Britain's ports in the global slave trade) means that the process of becoming "white" (to the extent that it operated at all) would have been correspondingly different.[28]

How will future historical investigations of the Irish and race in the nineteenth-century Atlantic world proceed? One of the most promising grounds for research, ironically enough, lies not in the history of Irish racism but in the transnational history of Irish opposition to racism. Long overdue in this respect is a renewed interest in the central figure of Daniel O'Connell, and through him the subject of Irish abolitionism. As for anti-Irish sentiment, historians need to distinguish carefully between analyzing racial language and imagery deployed against the Irish and making claims about the effect of this language and imagery on the Irish themselves. Only by drawing this distinction can one begin to clarify what is useful and what is not about race as a category of analysis in nineteenth-century Irish Atlantic history. As far as the first of these approaches is concerned, Americanists can learn much from Perry Curtis, who was concerned not with the Irish per se but with their British detractors. By confining his analysis to those who thought of the Irish in racially derogatory terms, he tackled some important questions about British politics and culture. It is in this sense that race as a category of analysis seems most useful. The second and altogether different task—examining the racial consciousness of the Irish themselves—can be accomplished only to the extent that the surviving historical record permits. In this respect, the historical literature makes large claims resting on thin and shaky evidence.

In this essay I have been concerned only with the first task, discerning why some Americans disliked the Irish and expressed their contempt racially. In formulating an answer to this question, I have concentrated on Irish-American violence. In doing this, has my argument run the risk of duplicating Gilley's contention that the reason the Irish were disliked so much is that they were so dislikeable? Surely not. The argument presented here is not that that the Irish were portrayed as violent savages because they were violent savages. Instead, their violence—which had complex social, economic, and political origins that lie beyond the scope of this essay—caused grave concern to their American hosts in the mid–nineteenth century. This violence called forth a response that can best be described as racial, but the response in question must be distinguished clearly from other, much more severe expressions of racism in the United States.

As for the Irish themselves, the attempt to categorize them in racially inferior terms evidently did not do them much harm over the long run. From the historian's point of view, they ended up doing very well, very quickly in America; a little less quickly in Britain; and even more quickly in Australia and Canada. In the end, the success of the Irish and other European immigrants in the United States cannot be explained other than in racial terms. Assimilation, which lies at the heart of American immigration history, has always rested on its opposite: exclusion. The terms on which Europeans became Americans were set by slavery and Jim Crow, by Chinese exclusion, and by a whites-only naturalization policy adopted in the 1790s that was expanded to include Asians only in the 1950s. In this insight concerning the centrality of race to all of American history lies the enduring legacy of the recent debate on whiteness. To the limited extent that historians can apprehend what this process meant to the immigrants themselves, they have made a significant breakthrough.

NOTES

Thanks to Marjorie Howes, Jim Smith, and Peter Gray for reading earlier drafts of this essay.

1. Kevin Kenny, "Diaspora and Comparison: The Global Irish as a Case Study," *Journal of American History* 90, no. 1 (June 2003): 134–62.

2. L. Perry Curtis Jr., *Apes and Angels: The Irishman in Victorian Caricature*, rev. ed. (1971; repr., Washington: Smithsonian Institution Press, 1997), xxii.

3. Curtis, *Apes and Angels*, xxxi, 98–103.

4. See, for example, Kevin Kenny, *The American Irish: A History* (New York: Longman, 2000), 60–1, 104–9.

5. Curtis, *Apes and Angels*, xxxi.

6. Sheridan Gilley, "English Attitudes to the Irish in England, 1780–1900," in *Immigrants and Minorities in British Society*, ed. Colin Holmes, 91, 94 (London: George Allen and Unwin, 1978).

7. Ibid., 91.

8. Ibid., 94.

9. M. A. G. O'Tuathaigh, "The Irish in Nineteenth-Century Britain: Problems of Integration," *Transactions of the Royal Historical Society* Fifth series, 31 (1981): 149–73 (quotation at 160–1).

10. Gilley, "English Attitudes to the Irish in England," 99, 100.

11. R. F. Foster, "Paddy and Mr. Punch," in *Paddy and Mr. Punch: Connections in Irish and English History* (London: Allen Lane, 1993): 171–94.

12. Curtis, *Apes and Angels*, 116–47.

13. Peter Gray, "*Punch* and the Great Famine," *History Ireland* 1, no. 2 (Summer 1993): 26–33.

14. This is not to deny that Irish-American political power, especially at the municipal level, was perceived as a real threat.

15. See, for example, Kenny, *American Irish*, 40–1, 86, 126–9, 171–9, 192–9, 246–57.

16. Thomas N. Brown, *Irish-American Nationalism, 1870–1890* (Philadelphia: Lippincott, 1966); Eric Foner, "Class, Ethnicity, and Radicalism in the Gilded Age: The Land League in Irish-America," in *Politics and Ideology in the Age of the Civil War*, ed. Eric Foner (New York: Oxford University Press, 1980).

17. Samuel R. Wells, *New Physiognomy; or, Signs of Character as Manifested through Temperament and External Forms, and Especially in "The Human Face Divine"* (New York: Fowler and Wells, 1866).

18. Richard Jensen, "'No Irish Need Apply': A Myth of Victimization?" *Journal of Social History* 36 (Winter 2002): 405–9.

19. Iver Bernstein, *The New York City Draft Riots: Their Significance for American Society and Politics in the Age of the Civil War* (New York: Oxford University Press, 1990). Most of the dead

were Irish rioters shot by the police and military. Over three hundred African Americans died in Tulsa, Oklahoma, during a racially based slaughter in 1921, the details of which are only now fully emerging.

20. Michael Gordon, *The Orange Riots: Irish Political Violence in New York City in 1870–1871* (Ithaca, NY: Cornell University Press, 1993).

21. George Templeton Strong, *Diary of George Templeton Strong*, ed. Allan Nevins and Milton Haley Thomas, abridged by Thomas J. Pressly (Seattle: University of Washington Press, 1988), 244, 245; entry for July 19, 1863.

22. Peter Way, *Common Labour: Workers and the Digging of the North American Canals, 1780–1860* (Cambridge, England: Cambridge University Press, 1993); Kevin Kenny, *Making Sense of the Molly Maguires* (New York: Oxford University Press, 1998).

23. Kenny, *Making Sense of the Molly Maguires,* addresses this dual task.

24. When publishing the book on the Molly Maguires, I chose not to try to graft a layer of "whiteness" onto what I had already written. In doing the research, I had not been looking explicitly for signs of race or whiteness, and adding this dimension at the end would not have improved an already adequate argument on why certain Irish people, under particular historical circumstances, were portrayed as savage by nature. Nor would I add "whiteness" to a revised edition of the book, though an approach based on race in this sense would be quite compatible with my own.

25. David R. Roediger, *The Wages of Whiteness: Race and the Making of the American Working Class* (New York: Verso, 1991); Noel Ignatiev, *How the Irish Became White* (New York: Routledge, 1995); Matthew Frye Jacobson, *Whiteness of a Different Color: European Immigrants and the Alchemy of Race* (Cambridge, MA: Harvard University Press, 1998); Eric Arnesen, "Whiteness and the Historians' Imagination," *International Labor and Working-Class History* 60 (Fall 2001): 3–32; Peter Kolchin, "Whiteness Studies: The New History of Race in America," *Journal of American History* 89 (June 2002): 154–73. For an elaboration on these and other questions, see Kenny, "Diaspora and Comparison," 155–7.

26. Peter Gray, for example, has assembled some Irish political cartoons that responded to British caricatures, which he hopes to use in a future article.

27. W. E. B. Du Bois, *Black Reconstruction in America, 1860–1880* (1962; New York: Atheneum, 1935), 30, 700–1.

28. Edmund Morgan, *American Slavery, American Freedom: The Ordeal of Colonial Virginia* (New York: Norton, 1975); Eric Foner, *The Story of American Freedom* (New York: Norton, 1998).

SUGGESTED READING

L. Perry Curtis Jr., *Apes and Angels: The Irishman in Victorian Caricature* (rev. ed. 1971; repr., Washington, DC: Smithsonian Institution Press, 1997).

Roy Foster, *Paddy and Mr. Punch: Connections in Irish and English History* (London: Allen Lane, 1993).

Matthew Frye Jacobson, *Whiteness of a Different Color: European Immigrants and the Alchemy of Race* (Cambridge, MA: Harvard University Press, 1998).

Dale T. Knobel, *Paddy and the Republic: Ethnicity and Nationality in Antebellum America* (Middletown, CT: Wesleyan University Press, 1986).

David R. Roediger, *The Wages of Whiteness: Race and the Making of the American Working Class* (New York: Verso, 1991).

Popular Expressions of Identity

Chapter 14

Irish-American Popular Music

Mick Moloney

For as long as the Irish have been coming to America they have brought with them songs and tunes from a culture in which music has always played a central role. In their new home the musical creativity continued with new compositions being continually added to the great store of immigrant tunes and songs.

In America many different kinds of music have been called "Irish" over the centuries. Those responsible for academic scholarship have often separated these various musical expressions into different categories—classical, elite, folk, traditional, and popular. There are some compelling reasons to continue using these terms, albeit with considerable qualification, but in this article I concentrate on those unique forms of Irish music that have been created in America rather than the music that immigrants have brought with them. Most of these Irish-American forms or genres would fall within the compass of what is generally known as popular music.

Russell Nye stresses that the essential defining element of popular culture is the production and commodification of art for a mass audience:

> The appearance of a *popular* artistic tradition . . . derives from a shift initiated in the eighteenth century and completed during the nineteenth—from the patronage of the arts by the restricted upper classes to the support offered by a huge, virtually unlimited, middle-class audience, within the context of great technological, social and political change. . . . Popular art must be adaptable to mass production and to diffusion through the mass media. It is irretrievably tied to the technology of duplication.[1]

All through the nineteenth century in America the proliferation of print sources essentially blurred the lines that scholars traditionally have used to distinguish between elite, folk, and popular culture. By the mid–nineteenth century—particularly in urban America where new Irish immigrants formed communities alongside Irish Americans and people from other ethnic and racial groups—these demarcations had all but collapsed, as folk and traditional music was becoming more and more marketable to mass audiences, often in entirely unexpected ways. Irish songs and instrumental pieces of music brought to America by immigrants were to take their place in an emerging Irish-American popular repertory alongside songs and tunes composed in America.

Setting the Stage

Some of the oldest Irish strains in American music date back well over two hundred years. Irish immigrants, many from the northern part of the country, brought Irish songs and instrumental music with them to America in the eighteenth century. Many of these emigrants migrated into the southern states, and there their music and song blended with English, Scottish, African American, and possibly Cherokee traditions, creating the genre that is now called old time, old timey, hillbilly, or Appalachian music. In the mid–twentieth century this hybrid music went on to play a major role in the emergence of bluegrass and country music.

The elegant lyrical compositions of Thomas Moore (1779–1852) were big commercial successes in Ireland and England before they ever got to America. Moore used airs composed by seventeenth- and eighteenth-century Irish harpers as melodies for many of his most exquisite and most popular songs. Moore's compositions—such as "The Minstrel Boy," "Believe Me if All These Endearing Young Charms," and "The Last Rose of Summer"—sold in huge numbers in North America. A diverse audience purchased thousands of his compositions in songsters, songbooks, broadsides, and sheet music throughout the Victorian era, making Moore one of the most renowned songwriters of the nineteenth century. These songs helped establish genteel images of Ireland as an oppressed nation always looking backward wistfully at a Gaelic culture that had been lost and oppressed through centuries of colonial domination. Moore helped popularize symbols of Ireland, such as the harp and shamrock and the color green, as well as a sort of romantic fatalism permeated with a sense of victimhood.

The songs of another well-known Irish novelist and songwriter, Samuel Lover (1797–1868), also enjoyed considerable popularity in America; the "Low Back'd Car" and "Rory O'More" being particular favorites among stage performers.

Minstrelsy

Up to the 1830s mainstream American music was essentially an imported tradition, with a small body of natively composed material. That all changed with the advent of minstrelsy. Minstrelsy was America's first truly popular culture. The prevailing origin story of minstrelsy is that it began with Thomas Rice's introduction of a Negro dance component into his production of a popular play, *The Rifle*, in 1829. Rice, a journeyman and multitalented entertainer who put on one-man shows in the east and south, invented and popularized a dance called "Jim Crow," which represented a blacked-up white man dancing comically. This was introduced to Broadway in a so-called Ethiopian opera he produced at the Bowery Theater in 1830. It was a huge commercial success. Within months, blackface performers became known as Ethiopian delineators or minstrels, and minstrelsy became the new American rage. Irish-American Dan Emmett produced *The Essence of Old Virginny* also at the Bowery Theater in 1833 with a group that called itself "The Virginia Minstrels." By the next appearance of the show in Boston, the performers were sitting on stage in the familiar semicircle that was to become the hallmark of minstrelsy. Comic sketches in blackface were being performed along with instrumental music, songs, and dances, and full-fledged minstrelsy was born. The instant popularity of the Virginia Minstrels set in motion a spate of thousands of minstrel groups that performed and toured across America relentlessly from the mid-1830s onward.

The staple repertoire of the minstrel shows was a multicultural mix. The music and dances were taken from Scottish and Irish sources. There were jigs, reels, and songs old and new. There were sentimental ballads, Negro sermons, plantation sketches and steamboat sketches, and parodies and satires. There were thousands of Irish and Irish-American performers. In most companies there were Irish singers, comics, and dancers. The most prominent writer of minstrel songs, Stephen Foster, was an Irish American whose grandparents came from Derry. Joel Walker Sweeney, whose father was from Mayo, popularized the five-string banjo in minstrel music. Dan Emmet, who is often known as the father of minstrelsy, was the grandson of an Irish immigrant from County Mayo. The list of Irish Americans on the minstrel stage goes on and on. In America, the performing arts have always yielded accommodating occupations to marginalized populations, and even the most wretchedly poor and unwelcome of the arriving Irish in the years before and after the Great Famine were welcomed into minstrelsy if they had the performing skills.

At its core, of course, minstrelsy was a caricature of African-American plantation culture and, by implication, a rationalization of slavery. It was racist to the core. But as Eric Lott points out, one could not infer with certainty the motives or attitudes of individual minstrel performers or, for that matter, of audience members. Certainly, at the time it was one of the very few outlets for professional performers, and many just went along with the convention of blacking up without much reflection. Lott draws attention to the multiple social contradictions involved in minstrel representation of African-American life and in particular the paradox of Irish nationalists such as Daniel O'Connell and the American Catholic Church opposing slavery while their supporters both participated in and supported minstrelsy.[2]

By the 1860s there were over one hundred full-time national minstrel companies and thousands of small regional and local companies. Many toured abroad, and Dan Emmett and the Virginia Minstrels were to introduce minstrelsy formally to England and Ireland, where it was instantly successful. A steady stream of American minstrel touring performers visited Ireland for decades, introducing new songs and novel instrumentation, including the banjo, which went on to become a staple instrument in Irish traditional music.[3]

Eugene Waters and Matthew Murtagh in their book on Dan Lowry's Music Hall in Dublin described the music of minstrelsy in colorful fashion:

> "Pure" music at Dan's hardly existed. It had to be linked to the visible, the breath-taking, the comic, the ravishing, the pathetic, the cleverality. Such music was provided by American Christy Minstrels. A large Troupe of Twenty-five arrived in the Spring with a non-stop fund of song, dance and instrumentation. Quick pop-up gags, crass crosstalk, elastic legantics punctuated the incessant twanka-panka-panks of the banjo.[4]

The glory days of minstrelsy lasted over four decades until its decline in the 1880s. The post–civil war social and political climate made blackface comedy and minstrelsy's caricaturized depiction of southern plantation life socially less acceptable. In addition, there was increasing competition from other forms of popular entertainment, including variety theater and, later, vaudeville.

Variety Theater

Variety theater productions presented sequences of single acts, many of which had been developed for centuries in Europe and elsewhere. The format included a program of acrobats, magicians, jugglers and other novelty acts, singers, dancers, comic and dramatic sketches, and animal acts. These elements were combined into a single format by the 1840s in the United States. Much of the material was of a risqué nature. More often than not, variety theater took place in establishments not considered suitable for genteel female company. Alcohol was frequently served at these establishments, particularly in the milieu that became known as the concert saloon. Irish entertainers played a major role in variety theater, particularly as singers, dancers, and comedians. By mid-century, as historian Earl Niehaus put it, "Paddy was King of the boards" in American theater, occupying a position remarkably similar to that occupied by African Americans in contemporary American sports.[5]

In all of these forms there was a restricted set of images of the Irish that dominated the American stage. Some of these images presented the Irish as loyal, servile, and docile; others presented the Irishman as dim-witted and pugnacious. The latter images were represented by one of the most familiar figures in the nineteenth century —the stage Irishman. This character was basically a crystallized image of the Irish that had already been transmitted for over three centuries on the English stage. The American historian Carl Wittke described the stage Irishman as a "bizarre individual, preposterously dressed in a red-flannel fireman's shirt affecting a swagger, and with a shillelagh in hand ready to knock out all others in the cast at the proper moment."[6]

In his *Apes and Angels*, a study of stereotypical images of the Irish in nineteenth-century popular American culture, L. P. Curtis Jr. traces the history of this imagery, concentrating in particular on mid-nineteenth-century Victorian political cartoons and caricature. He concludes:

> The gradual but unmistakable transformation of Paddy, the stereotypical Irish Celt of the mid–nineteenth century, from a drunken and relatively harmless peasant into a dangerous ape-man or simianized agitator reflected a significant shift in the attitudes of some Victorians about the differences between not only Englishmen and Irishmen, but also between human beings and apes.[7]

Dale T. Knobel, in his study of the image of the Irish in antebellum America wrote "Ignorant, illiterate, credulous, and superstitious: servile, debased, degraded—these were the favorite descriptives for the Irish in nativist literature. The emphasis upon flawed character and its consequences was pronounced, as it was upon sources of character in environment."[8]

The paradigm of the stage Irishman had emerged in the seventeenth century when it became an established convention in English drama. It adapted well to America where the stage Irishman began to fill the slot of comic buffoon in the burgeoning American popular stage in the early years of the nineteenth century. Earl Niehaus wrote that "the years 1830 to 1860 were . . . the heyday of the stage Irishman. The caricature grew into such a giant that others including the Negro and the Yankee, were dwarfed."[9]

Oppressed peoples often adopt some of the negative characteristics imputed to them by their oppressors. Often this is done as a defense mechanism where the oppressed fulfill role expectations as a social strategy to avoid further oppression. Fake obsequiousness and deference have been used by the Irish in dealing with their ruling classes for centuries—a phenomenon well documented in the novels of Lover and Lever. This behavioral style became incorporated into those dramatizations of the Irish on the English and American stage that involved Irish performers.

This theatrical characterization found a ready home in nineteenth-century America where the establishment was British and Protestant and the immigrant Irish were the first major urban underclass of unskilled, uneducated wage-earners. There were many disapproving Irish-American reactions to the negative stereotyping of the Irish, and they were to gather momentum as the Irish achieved upward social and economic mobility.

The kind of song that most commonly presented the Irish as simple-minded drunken pugilists was the "Irish fight" song. All the songs in this vein basically had the same structure. A party or an "affair" was arranged. The occasion might be a wedding, wake, birthday, anniversary, or christening. The guests arriving would be introduced with a litany of Irish names. Festivities would begin with an abundance of food and drink. Then a verbal altercation would take place, usually as a consequence of some perceived insult. Verbal repartee would escalate into a fight, which would begin with fisticuffs; then shillelaghs and other weapons would be produced, which might include chair legs or other objects rescued from the debris. Murder and mayhem would ensue, with broken heads and sometimes corpses all around. The police would arrive, and sometimes they too became involved in the melee. The police would arrest the participants, and frequently the song would conclude with a description of the ensuing court case and the sentencing of the pugilists.

"Tim Finegan's Wake," written in New York in the early 1860s by Dublin songwriter John Poole, is a good example of the genre. Finegan, a bricklayer, has an apparently fatal work accident caused by the effects of a hangover. He is waked in true stage-Irish style, and all the friends and neighbors are invited. A fight breaks out when the guests start drinking, and the inevitable ruckus ensues:

> His friends assembled at his wake,
> Missus Finigan called out for the lunch,
> First they laid in tay and cake,
> Then pipes and tobaccy and whiskey-punch.
> Miss Biddy O'Brien began to cry:
> "Sich a purty corpse did you ever see?
> Arrah! Tim avourneen, an' why did ye die?"—
> "och noe o' yer gab!" says Judy Magee.
> Then Peggy O'Connor took up the job:

"Arrah, Biddy" says she, "you're wrong, I'm sure"
But Judy then gave her a belt on the gob,
Which left her sprawling on the flure,
Each side in the war did soon engage,
'Twas woman to woman and man to man;
Shillelagh-law was all the rage,
And a bloody ruction soon began

The images of the Irish in American popular culture were to soften in direct proportion to the rate of upward social mobility achieved by the group. The first major change in the image of the Irish on the stage in America can without doubt be traced to the emergence of Dublin-born playwright, actor, director, producer, and impresario Dion Boucicault (1820–1890), the most prominent figure in American theater in the middle decades of the nineteenth century. Traditional Irish songs were an integral part of several of his dramas, such as *The Shaughran*, Boucicault's best-known work, which achieved enormous commercial success all over America in the 1870s. The central figure, Conn the Shaughran, was depicted as "the soul of every fair, the life of every funeral, the first fiddle at all weddings and patterns." Songs were also featured prominently in another of Boucicault's Irish classics *The Colleen Bawn,* including "The Wearing of the Green," "Limerick Is Beautiful," "Cruiskeen Lawn," "Pretty Girl Milking Her Cow," and "Brian O'Linn."

The shape of American variety theater was to change dramatically in the 1870s. Tony Pastor, an Italian-American Catholic impresario and singer with a prodigious repertoire of Irish songs, was a familiar figure in variety theater in the New York area. He was a deeply moral man, concerned about the negative public image of variety theater and concert saloons. He opened his first establishment in New York City in 1861, to be followed by another in 1881. He presented variety entertainment aimed at a general family audience—with no alcohol, no profanity, and no off-color material of any kind. Pastor's theater was to be the forerunner of vaudeville, which dominated American popular culture between the early 1890s and the late 1920s. Vaudeville, in essence, was a cleaned-up version of variety theater. It took place in nice clean alcohol-free theaters and was a sanitized form of popular family entertainment for the lower and middle class multiethnic masses of both sexes.

Under the leadership of entrepreneurs Ben Keith and Ed Albee, a national vaudeville circuit was created. Agents for vaudevillians appeared on the scene, and a system of standardized wages and conditions for artists was introduced for the first time. The national circuit was mirrored in myriad smaller vaudevillian enterprises that mushroomed all over the country in the latter decades of the nineteenth century and the early decades of the twentieth.

Almost all the elements of variety theater appeared in vaudeville, particularly animal acts, magicians and jugglers, song and dance teams, comic duos, tenors, and lots of ethnic humor. The level of the stage acts was aimed at the lowest common denominator, with every attempt made to please a general audience. There was no pretension whatever toward high art. The vaudeville milieu was the urban environment, and during vaudeville's heyday America's cities were teeming with newly arrived ethnic populations from all over Europe. Elements of city life furnished the primary source of material for vaudevillian routines. Racial, occupational, sexual, and regional, national, and ethnic stereotypes abounded. In such an environment the images of the Irish were direct and unsophisticated.

During the halcyon days of minstrelsy and vaudeville, so-called legitimate theater flourished all over the United States. The line between legitimate and variety theater was often blurred. In fact, throughout the whole nineteenth century, there was a plethora of related popular theatrical performance contexts where Irish music was played, Irish songs were sung, and Irish dramatic sketches and routines were enacted. Many of these elements were present in the melodramatic creations that dominated the popular stage in the latter decades of the nineteenth century. It was in these milieus that the stage Irishman became part of American popular culture. T. Alston Brown, in his history of theater in New York, cites hundreds of Irish performances on the stage in various theaters in New York between 1732 and 1901.[10] G. C. O'Dell's monumental *Annals of the New York Stage* cites thousands, as do the issues of the variety magazine the *New York Clipper*.[11]

The following playbill describing an 1871 evening at the Bowery Theater is a good example of how the Irish material was incorporated into theatrical performance:

> The entertainment consisted of N. B. Clarke's Irish Drama, *The Irishman's Home or the Dark Days of the Green Isle*. Then followed an olio: Peter Cannon in Irish songs, Tommy Sully's Ethiopian sketch, Hughie Dougherty with a stump speech, Frank Kerns and Johnny Queen with song and dance, Sam Devere, banjo solo, James Clarke, Irish song and dance, and Larry Tooley with Dutch songs. The performance concluded with Cavaliers and Roundheads.[12]

Harrigan and Hart

Preceding and then side by side with the emerging national vaudeville scene were the creations of the remarkable duo Ed Harrigan and Tony Hart. Their theatrical and musical careers are well documented by E. J. Kahn and Richard Moody.[13]

Ed Harrigan was the nineteenth century's foremost dramatist of the life of the Irish in America. He was often described by critics as the Dickens of America. Like Boucicault, he combined writing with acting, production, and impeccable stage craft. He was intimately familiar with Irish-American life and concerns and with the interactions of the Irish with members of other ethnic communities in American cities, particularly in late-nineteenth-century New York City, one of the greatest interethnic social, political, and economic crucibles in the modern world.

Harrigan was born in 1844, on the Lower East Side of Manhattan. His father was the son of Irish immigrants in Newfoundland, and his mother was from New England. A Protestant himself, he grew up in a neighborhood that was overwhelmingly Irish and Catholic. As a child he was interested in minstrelsy and began his theatrical career on the variety stage in San Francisco by singing, playing the banjo, and acting in a variety of different ethnic roles.

Tony Hart's real name was Anthony J. Cannon. Both his parents were Irish immigrants from Mayo who immigrated to Worcester, Massachusetts, after the Famine.

Young Tony was constantly in trouble with the law, and his parents sent him to reform school at the age of twelve. He escaped after a month, joined a circus as a cook, and played the concert saloons as a song and dance performer until he joined up with the Arlington Minstrels in Providence, Rhode Island. He left them for a minstrel show of female impersonators known as Madame Rentz's Female Minstrels. While touring the Midwest he met up in 1871 with Ed Harrigan in Chicago who was there on tour with the minstrels, and the partnership was born.

Ed Harrigan's primary musical collaborator, violinist David Braham, was born in London in 1838 and emigrated to America in 1854. He joined a minstrel show orchestra in New York City and conducted the pit orchestra until he met and started a musical collaboration with Harrigan. The team of Harrigan and Braham has been compared by many commentators to Gilbert and Sullivan.

Harrigan and Hart began their career together with short variety sketches, which they later blended into larger, more loosely constructed productions. Their favorite productions were a series of plays and songs that featured as central characters the members of the Mulligan Guards, a mythical Irish-American company of the 1870s. Harrigan and Braham wrote the theme song for the series:

THE MULLIGAN GUARD

We crave your condescension, we'll tell you what we know,
Of marching in the Mulligan Guard from the Sligo Ward below,
Our Captain's name was Hussey, a Tipperary man,
He carried his sword like a Russian Duke, whenever he took command.

Chorus
We shouldered guns and marched and marched away,
From Baxter Street we marched to Avenue A,
With fifes and drums how sweetly they did play,
As we marched, marched, marched in the Mulligan Guards!

When the band played Garryowen, or the Connemara Pet,
With a rub a dub dub we'd march in the mud to the Military step,
With the green above the red boys, to show where we'd come from,
Our guns we'd lift with the right shoulder shift,
As we'd march to the bate of the drum.

Chorus

Whin we got home at night boys, the divil a bit we'd ate,
We'd all sit up and drink a sup of whiskey strong and nate,
Thin we'd all march home together as slippery as lard,
The solid min would all fall in and march with the Mulligan Guard.

The plays were satirically directed at target companies that were ethnically and socially biased. Target companies were the local forerunners to the National Guard. Some of them were fraternal and occupational and were often exclusionary in membership. They organized weekend shooting expeditions on a regular basis. They also got together for picnics, which were a major New York City summer institution in the latter decades of the nineteenth century. The picnics ranged from fancy to proletarian. Picnic groves abounded all over the city. There was a lot of drinking, particularly at the ethnic picnics. Raiding of the well-to-do picnics was common, and fighting often took place. The members of the target clubs characteristically wore elaborate and sometimes incongruous and ludicrous uniforms and regalia. All this was commented upon and satirized in the Mulligan Guard series, most of which were written between 1878 and 1881 with a rapidly expanding cast of characters.

Ethnic and class conflicts of various kinds were a primary part of Harrigan's plays. His primary biographer, Edward Kahn, describes a scene in one of the Mulligan Guard plays where an Irish bandleader, Paddy Brannigan, has his job taken from him by August Bimble, a German-American bandleader. The Irish-American exacts fitting revenge when the German asks for his advice on what music to play for an Irish picnic. Brannigan advises him to play "The Boyne Water," telling him that all Irishmen love the song and that the British considered it treasonable. When the German plays the song, a riot ensues over the unwelcome reminder of their historical loss to the English at the Battle of the Boyne and a mob attacks the musicians who had to flee for their lives. In a Harrigan and Hart play, *The Major*, an Irish couple made the crossing from Ireland to America to prevent the wedding of their son to a Dutch sausage maker. In another play, *The Doyle Brothers*, an Irish appleseller picks a fight with an Italian appleseller. An Irish policeman pulls them apart and immediately arrests the Italian even though he is clearly the innocent party. Interethnic conflicts of this nature abounded in the works of Harrigan and Hart.

Harrigan was concerned primarily with lower-class life in the slums. Most of his characters were first- or second-generation Irish, Italian, and German Americans. Also included were Chinese and African Americans. There were brawls known as "knockabout" or "slapbang" in practically every play, as well as lots of spectacle where scenic designers and stage set carpenters competed with one another for maximum visual effect. The tumult in Harrigan's plays reflected the social reality of the day in New York City. He drew on rogues, criminals, thugs, members of gangs, pickpockets, and the police for his characters. He bought his costumes directly from immigrants, vagrants, bums—in short, from anybody who looked colorful or exotic.

The themes of Harrigan's plays reflected the social issues of the day and they were heavily oriented toward Irish Americans. They dealt with social occupations, recruiting, ward politics and voting, confidence men and other types of criminals, language problems of immigrants, tenement housing, landlord tenant disputes, and on and on. He wrote hundreds of songs dramatizing these issues, which were woven into his plays. Many were written in frank language that would nowadays be totally unacceptable.

For example, "McNally's Rows of Flats" from the play *McSorley's Inflation* contains the following verse:

> It's Ireland and Italy, Jerusalem and Germany,
> Oh, Chinamen and nagers, and a paradise for rats,
> All jumbled up togayther in the snow or rainy weather,
> They represent the tenants in McNally's rows of flats.

One of Ed Harrigan's most popular songs was "Muldoon the Solid Man," which depicted a successful Irish immigrant making his way in American politics. The music

Songsters such as this one for *Squatter's Sovereignty* (1882), which featured the popular Harrigan and Hart song "Paddy Duffy's Cart," were inexpensive and thus widely circulated. Edward Harrigan (1844–1911), whose grandfather came from County Cork, documented the urban world of the nineteenth-century immigrant through dozens of plays which he wrote, produced, and acted in with partner Tony Hart (1857–1891). (Mick Moloney Irish American Collection)

of this song was published by E. H. Harding in 1874 and was written and sung by Ed Harrigan in his popular sketch of *Who Owns the Clothes Line!*

> I am a man of great influence,
> And educated to a high degree,
> I came when small from Donegal,
> In the *Daniel Webster* across the sea,
> On the city road I was situated,
> In a tenement house with me brother Dan,

'Til by perseverance I elevated,
And I went to the front like a solid man.

Chorus
So come with me and I will treat you dacint,
I'll sit you down and I will fill your can,
And along the street all the friends I meet,
Say there goes Muldoon he's a solid man.

At any party or at a raffle,
I always go as an invited guest,
As conspicuous as the great Lord Mayor boys,
I wear a nosegay upon me chest,
And when called upon for to address the meeting,
With no regard for clique or clan,
I show the constitution with great elocution,
Because you see I am a solid man.

Chorus
I control the tombs I control the island,
My constituents they all go there,
To enjoy their summer's recreation,
And to take the enchanting East River air,
I am known in Harlem I'm known in Jersey,
I'm welcomed hearty at every hand,
With my regalay on St. Patrick's Day,
I march away like a solid man.

Ed Harrigan, despite his liberal use of the stage Irish patois, generally depicts the Irish in a favorable light in the songs he wrote with David Braham and published in their best-selling songsters. Attention was drawn to the positive achievements and character of the Irish in America and to Irish ethnic pride.

Twenty-three of Ed Harrigan's plays ran for over one hundred performances on Broadway, an unprecedented phenomenon in the world of American urban theater. Songbooks from the plays sold extensively, extending his popularity throughout the nation.

In Good Company

Irish-American songwriters and Irish themes were widespread in the vaudeville era. William J. Scanlon, a native of Springfield, Massachusetts, was one of the most prolific writers of hit songs with Irish-American themes in the 1880s. These included "Moonlight in Killarney" (1883), "My Nellie's Blue Eyes" (1882), "Peggy O'Moore" (1885), "Remember Boy You're Irish" (1885), and "Why Paddy's Always Poor" (1885). Irish popular songs proliferated in vaudeville in the 1890s.

Several of the most popular songs of the decade were written by John Walter Kelly, a native of Pittsburgh. Kelly was brought up in the western Pennsylvania outskirts of the city and showed an early talent for the stage, though he began his working life as a steelworker. He ended up running his own variety theater in Chicago and became a colorful entertainer, popularizing many of his own songs, including "The Milwaukee Fire," "Slide Kelly Slide," "When Hogan Paid His Rent," "Come Down Mrs. Flynn," "Maloney the Rolling Mill Man," and his most popular hit of all, "Throw Him Down McCloskey" (1890). The latter was made famous by the formidable vaudevillian Maggie Cline, who would enlist the aid of the whole theater backstage crew to make appropriate banging noises as she roared out the song title line each time the chorus came around. The song, about a fight between two Irishmen, shows the stage Irishman in full cry. The last verse goes:

> They fought like two hyenas till the forty-seventh round,
> They scattered blood enough around by gosh to paint the town,
> McCloskey got a mouthful of poor McCracken's Jowl,
> McCracken hollered murther and his seconds shouted foul,
> The friends of both the fighters that instant did begin,
> To fight and ate each other the whole party started in,
> You couldn't tell the difference in the fighters if you'd try,
> McCracken lost his upper lip, McCloskey lost an eye.

Another hugely popular American songwriter of the 1890s was Joseph Flynn, who penned "Down Went McGinty" (1899), "The Night Maloney Landed in New York" (1888), "Casey's Wife" (1899), and "The O'Brannigan Fusiliers" (1899). Flynn and another vaudevillian, Frank B. Sheridan, were members of William Muldoon's Variety Players and specialized in classic stage Irish comedy skits, which made Flynn's songs famous. Sigmund Spaeth describes the 1890s:

> [They were] naive . . . because we had by no means outgrown the unsophisticated simplicities of behavior and thought that marked the Seventies and Eighties. Love still expressed itself in a kiss with marriage as the almost inevitable consequence though it was now generally admitted that true happiness could exist only in waltz time. Right was still right and wrong was wrong with special approval of mothers, sweethearts, courage and uniforms, a corresponding antagonism toward infidelity, dishonesty . . .[14]

The late nineteenth century was an era of unprecedented urban expansion in America, with a concomitant loss of rural populations and rural ways of life. The city was an exciting place but also could be cruel and heartless. It was not surprising that the rural life left behind should be sentimentalized and romanticized; this was often accomplished through the figures of mother and homestead. According to Spaeth: "Hard drinking songwriters . . . seem to turn automatically to sentimental thoughts of their mother's grave, girls' names and tender associations with mills, lanes, gates and other possible rendezvous."[15] In this vein were Joseph J. Murphy's "A Handful of Earth from My Mother's Grave" (1883) and Harry Kennedy's "A Flower From My Angel Mother's Grave," both of which became popular hits in the 1880s.

Another chapter in Irish-American contribution to American musical culture began with the arrival in New York in 1886 of Dublin-born Victor Herbert (1859–1924). In a glittering career spanning the next three decades, Herbert, who was a grandson of Samuel Lover, achieved fame as a musician, bandleader, and composer. In the process, he helped to create a whole new genre of American light opera. He was also one of the founding fathers of a new society that would protect the rights of composers. The principle was simple: the members would assign to the society the performing rights in their own works, and the society, in turn, would license the use of such works in return for royalties, which would be disbursed to the members. This performing rights society in time would become known as ASCAP, and it protects the rights of composers and performing artists to this day. It was one of Victor Herbert's most enduring legacies to American music.

Tin Pan Alley

Songwriters had flourished throughout the nineteenth century all over America in cities such as Cincinnati, New Orleans, Philadelphia, Chicago, and Boston. But toward the end of the century the center of the whole entertainment industry shifted to New York where most of the writers were based. Many of the publishing houses were located near all the theaters, clubs, and concert saloons where a never-ending stream of performers were looking for new material. Edward B. Marks (1935) describes in detail the colorful world of interaction between songwriters, publishers, song pluggers, and singers. Peter Gammond cites composer Monroe H. Rosenfeld (who wrote "I'll Paralyze the Man Who Says McGinty," 1890) as the likely source of the name "Tin Pan Alley."[16] Most of the publishing houses were situated on 28th Street near Broadway. In his newspaper columns Rosenfeld likened the din of all the piano players on the street to the clashing of tin pans, and the name caught on.

The publishing companies hired writers by the thousand who poured out song aimed at stage and recording artists that might make them famous. Songwriters often worked in teams, sometimes with exclusive contracts with performers and their agents. Tin Pan Alley churned out thousands of songs with Irish and Irish-American themes.

A great number of these songs extolled the virtues of young Irish-American women. They were published in sheet music with lavishly illustrated covers and established the image of the Irish-American girl next door as the idealized American female companion and ultimately wife. In real, lower-middle-class urban-American life, these Irish-American girls would have been the daughters or granddaughters of immigrant Irish women who had worked as domestics or in textile mills. Their offspring had graduated to respectable jobs as nurses, schoolteachers, and secretaries. As presented in the songs the Irish-American girls were beautiful, gracious, well-mannered, and of good character. Songs such as "Little Annie Rooney" (Nolan, 1890), "Sweet Rosie O'Grady" (Nugent, 1896), "The Daughter of Rosie O'Grady" (Donaldson, 1918), and "Kitty O'Brien, My Irish Molly O" (Jerome-Schwartz, 1905) were all big commercial successes and sold prodigiously in sheet music, which in the burgeoning years of Tin Pan Alley was marketed to huge mass audiences on an unprecedented scale.

This general climate set the scene for a proliferation of nostalgic songs about Ireland, with songwriters penning verses that looked back at a lost homeland, a place of beauty and innocence where everything was good and wholesome. Particular places in Ireland—the Lakes of Killarney, Galway Bay, Tipperary—became metaphors for this idealized corner of paradise.

The lyrics to "If They'd Only Move Old Ireland over Here" (1913) were penned by James Kelly, who also wrote "When Scanlon Sang Mavourneen" and "The Birth of the Shamrock." A native of County Longford, Kelly (1885–1971) emigrated from Ireland when he was seven and grew up in Brooklyn, New York. His career included stints as a newspaper pressroom helper, subway construction foreman, singer, songwriter, and vaudeville performer. After World War II, he became active in Brooklyn Democratic Party politics and retired in 1971 after twenty-seven years as deputy county clerk of Kings County. Simultaneously, he held the unpaid post of Brooklyn Borough historian, acquiring four million documents, which eventually became the James A. Kelly Institute for Historical Studies at St. Francis College. In 1988 the Kelly Collection was transferred to the New York City Municipal Archives. (Mick Moloney Irish American Collection)

Why did Irish Americans so readily buy into the idealized romantic vision of Ireland that was produced and marketed by the Tin Pan Alley songsmiths? By the turn of the century, many were the aging children or middle-aged grandchildren of survivors of the Great Famine; their economic comfort was at odds with the grim reality of the Ireland that had been left behind in the 1840s. Skilled Tin Pan Alley songsmiths with ready-made images of an invented homeland that were harmless and positive tapped into an Irish-American need for affirmation, as evinced in songs such as "Ireland

Must Be Heaven Cause My Mother Came from There" (Howard-Fisher, 1916), "If They'd Only Move Old Ireland over Here" (Gillen, 1916), and "All That I Want Is in Ireland" (Lloyd-Evan, 1917).

Scores of Tin Pan Alley songwriters were adept at writing songs with Irish themes that became popular American favorites. One of the most prominent was Chauncey Olcott (1858–1932). His mother was born in Ireland and came to America with her family when she was eight years old. They lived in what Olcott would later call "an Irish shanty" on the banks of the Erie Canal. In 1879, at the age of nineteen, he began what was to become a glittering career as an actor, playwright, and composer. Like Ed Harrigan he was a minstrel for several years. Olcott was very successful in the minstrel shows, but because of the special quality of his light lyric tenor voice, theater managers encouraged him to sing. He left minstrelsy and specialized as an actor, starring in Irish melodramas. An accomplished composer, Olcott wrote musical scores for a number of plays, including *Minstrel of Clare* (1896), *A Romance in Athlone* (1899), and *Old Limerick Town* (1902). In 1900 he appeared in *Eileen Astore*, in 1903 in *Sterrance,* in 1907 in *Old Limerick Town*, and in 1912 in *Machusla*. Olcott's most famous compositions were "My Wild Irish Rose" (1909), "Mother Machree" (Olcott and Ball, 1910), "A Little Bit of Heaven," "Sure They Call It Ireland" (1914), and "When Irish Eyes Are Smiling" (Olcott, Ball, and Johnson, 1912). The latter, especially, continues to be considered quintessentially "Irish," even though it was written in New York City for an Irish-American audience, raising interesting questions about the circulation of such popular songs by market forces on both sides of the Atlantic.

Other mainstream American Tin Pan Alley songwriters jumped on the Irish bandwagon. Theodore Morse (1873–1924), one of the most important composers of the period before and up to World War I, is a good example. Morse composed "It Takes the Irish to Beat the Dutch" (1903); "Santiago Flynn" (1908), about an Irish-Mexican tryst; and "Arrah Wanna" (1906), one of strangest Irish-American songs of the early twentieth century. "Arrah Wanna" tells the tale of an Indian maid courted by an Irishman. The sheet music cover brings together an Irishman playing a strange form of bagpipes and a Native American woman at the entrance to her teepee. The song is described as "An Irish Indian Matrimonial Venture."

> Arrah Wanna, on my honor, I'll take care of you,
> I'll be kind and true we can bill and coo,
> In a wigwam built of shamrocks green,
> We'll make these red men smile,
> When you're Mrs. Barney, heap much Carney,
> Of Killarney's Isle.

This was one of many humorous Tin Pan Alley songs that placed the Irish in incongruous situations with exotic "others." This indicates, as Bill Williams astutely points out, that as mainstream as the Irish in America had become, they were still not members of the establishment.[17]

There were many other Tin Pan Alley songwriters who jumped on the Irish bandwagon, such as Albert Von Tilzer and his brother Harry. Albert wrote "It's the Irish in Your Eye, It's the Irish in Your Smile" (1916), "Just Sing a Song for Ireland" (Von Tilzer

"Arrah Wanna" (1906) and "Santiago Flynn" (1908), both from the pen of composer Theodore F. Morse (1873–1924), represent a genre of comic parlor songs that focused on Irish amalgamation with non-white races, in this case American Indians and Mexicans. (Mick Moloney Irish American Collection)

—Sterling, 1898), and "On the Hoko Moko Isle" (1916). Harry wrote "A Little Bunch of Shamrocks" (1913), "Dear Old Fashioned Irish Songs My Mother Sang to Me" (1915), and "Says I to Myself" (1917). Both brothers wrote numerous other songs with Irish themes. In much the same vein were Percy Wenrich (1887–1952), John T. McKenna, and George M. Cohan, as well as songwriting teams like Jerome (actually William Flannery) and Schwartz, who wrote "If It Wasn't for the Irish and the Jews" (1912), "My Irish Molly O" (1905), and "When John McCormack Sings a Song" (1917).

Generally, the images of the Irish in American popular culture at this time were positive. Certainly, the Irish were still presented as brawling drunks and often as corrupt politicians, but they were also represented as hard-working, patriotic, loyal, compassionate, friendly, entertaining, and dedicated to family life and community. In a groundbreaking work, Williams traced the evolution and changes in the images of the Irish presented in sheet music through the second half of the nineteenth century and found the image of the Irish constantly evolving in a positive direction as the social and economic circumstances of the Irish in America improved.

The Irish Tenor, Pioneering Female Vocalists, and the Recording Industry

Not only was the Irish Tenor a prominent figure in American musical life all through the nineteenth century, but he also became the ultimate positive representation of

"Irishness," especially with the arrival of John McCormack (1883–1945) on the American concert stage in the early decades of the twentieth century. With a series of recordings he made for the Victor company beginning in 1906, McCormack became one of the biggest stars in the world of American popular music. His extraordinary success in America is still fondly remembered in Irish-American communities.

John McCormack was born in Athlone in County Westmeath and began singing in his teens. He won first prize at the Feis Cheoil in Dublin in 1903, and the reward for his success was to represent Ireland at the World's Fair in St. Louis in 1904. He left in high dudgeon before his contract was up, allegedly in part because of the overabundance of stage Irish representations at the fair. He went to Italy to study bel canto formally and returned to the United States in 1909 as one of the most accomplished operatic tenors in the world. Conscious of the wear and tear that singing in front of a full orchestra was likely to have on his relatively light voice, he elected to leave the operatic stage and become a solo performer. He had a remarkable career performing to sold-out concert halls for the next twenty years in the United States, England, Ireland, and Australia. His concert repertoire typically combined classical operatic selections with Irish and Irish-American songs like "Believe Me if All These Endearing Young Charms," "My Wild Irish Rose," and "When Irish Eyes Are Smiling." His Victor Red Seal recordings sold in the millions, and his success imparted a new legitimacy to Irish song, which could never have been achieved by vaudevillian Irish singers. Technology aided his meteoric rise in public popularity. As wonderfully accomplished a performer as McCormack was, he could not possibly have achieved his nationwide reputation so rapidly had he not been the beneficiary of the burgeoning popularity of the phonograph in the Western world. The recording industry changed forever the way in which people could "consume" musical performances. By the 1920s, countless Irish-American households possessed a stock of McCormack's Victor Red Seal recordings, thus placing his songs at the center of an evolving Irish-American middle-class sensibility.

McCormack's popularity also had major implications within the recording industry. Tenor Charles Harrison (1878–1965) was one of the most successful recording artists for Columbia and Edison, though he also enjoyed success with the Victor label, thanks in some part to John McCormack. He told historian Jim Walsh:

> When I began recording for Victor, they wanted a tenor who could make [John] McCormack records on a cheaper disc . . . so I was told to do some . . . McCormack songs. . . . A few months after these were released I was switched to other ballads and songs, and when I inquired about this was told by the recording manager that McCormack had raised hell because Harrison records were cutting into his royalties.[18]

Harrison's popular Victor records with an Irish theme include "I Hear You Calling Me" (1913), "Peg O' My Heart" (Fisher, 1913), and "Ireland Must Be Heaven, For My Mother Came from There" (Howard-Fisher, 1916).

Among others like Harrison who made a name for themselves singing Irish-American material, many written by the songsmiths of Tin Pan Alley, were Billy Murray, Ada Jones, and Nora Bayes.

Billy Murray (1877–1954), born of Irish immigrant parents in Philadelphia in 1877, grew up in Denver. In his teens he was drawn to the stage and spent ten years performing in vaudeville and minstrel shows. In the early twentieth century Murray joined Al G. Fields Minstrels, and his touring schedule brought him to the east coast, where he ended up staying. He started recording with Edison in 1903. Murray had the right kind of voice for acoustic recordings, and his enunciation was perfect. He sang flat out in full voice into the recording horns, and his delivery was perfect for making imprints on the wax recording surface. He recorded with both Victor and Edison, and later with many other companies, becoming a great commercial success. He recorded solo and with singing groups such as the Haydn Quartet, the Peerless Quartet, and the Premier Quartet (later to become the American Quartet); he also teamed up with a variety of other well-known singers like Len Spencer and Bob Roberts. But his greatest collaborations were with Ada Jones, and their duets, many of them of Irish-American songs, were among the most popular of the day.

Ada Jones (1873–1922) emigrated to Philadelphia in 1879, then to Newark, New Jersey, in the mid-1880s. From there, her stepmother took a job mending drapes for the Edison company, and Jones made her first cylinder recordings at that time. But it wasn't until 1904 that Ada Jones achieved national recognition when she was "discovered" by Billy Murray singing in Huber's Museum on West 10th Street in Greenwich Village. She went on to become the most prolific female artist in early American recording history, including many Irish and Irish-American songs.

Nora Bayes (1880–1928), born Leonora Goldberg in Joliet, Illinois, moved east as a teenager and had her Broadway debut in 1901. Her first big national success came in 1910 with the song "Has Anybody Here Seen Kelly?" Among her popular Irish-American recordings were "The AOHs of the USA," "Pull the Cork Out of Erin (Let the River Shannon Flow)," and "When John McCormack Sings a Song." She was a colorful, tempestuous figure, one of the biggest names in vaudeville and one of the first women to become a star on the American popular stage.

The popularity of these figures, among others, caused a variety of labels including Gennet, Vocalion, Victor, Columbia, and later Decca to target an ethnic rather than a mainstream American market. In the 1920s, there were also several solo performers and hybrid-style bands that recorded Irish-American songs, including Patrolman Frank Quinn, John Griffin, Dinny Doyle, James Mullen, the Four Provinces Orchestra, Dan Sullivan's Shamrock Band, Paddy Killoran's Irish Serenaders, James Morrison and His Orchestra, and the Flanagan Brothers.[19]

At the Microphone

But no one popularized the Irish-American song more than Bing Crosby (1903–1977), who broadcast on CBS weekly to a national radio audience for over twenty years. Crosby was by far the most famous Irish-American performing artist of the twentieth century. The fourth child of second- and first-generation Irish-American parents, Bing Crosby was born Harry Lillis Crosby in Tacoma, Washington; his well-known moniker came from his childhood nickname, "Bingo."

Crosby arrived in Los Angeles at the beginning of the major radio and film era and also at the onset of electronic recording. He quickly excelled in all three media forms, with technological advances allowing for his perfection of crooning. In his lifetime he sold over five hundred million recordings and starred in one hundred films, including *Duffy's Tavern, The Bells of St. Mary's,* and *Going My Way,* where he brought Irish-American songs such as "Too-Ra-Loo-Ra-Loo-Ra" (Shannon, 1913) to a worldwide audience. His national weekly radio show on CBS introduced scores of Irish-American songs into the general American repertoire, including such standards as "Galway Bay" (Colohan, 1947), "I'll Take You Home Again Kathleen" (Westendorf, 1874), "Danny Boy" (Weatherly, 1896), and, of course, the ubiquitous "Who Threw the Overalls in Mrs. Murphy's Chowder" (Geifer, 1937). An analysis of his discography up to 1940 shows that his Irish songs constituted just a tiny fraction of Crosby's prodigious recording output.[20] But, with over thirty years of radio performances, recordings, and film appearances, he extended the life of such Tin Pan Alley songs as "When Irish Eyes Are Smiling," "Too-ra-loo-ra-loo-ra," "My Wild Irish Rose," and "Mother Machree," making them the bedrock of Irish Americana in popular culture.

Mid-Century Performance

By the early 1930s, radio and movies superseded vaudeville in American popular culture, but the McNulty Family kept the art of Irish-American vaudeville alive in the eastern United States well into the 1950s. They played instrumental music, performed skits and sketches, and entertained audiences with song and dance routines grounded in an Irish-American social and cultural reality. Their repertoire was a mixture of Irish and Irish-American songs, some written or adapted by Pete McNulty. In a February 1978 interview in Hoboken, New Jersey, Eileen McNulty recalled their early years as stage performers in New York:

> At that time, I was singing all John McCormack's numbers, and that type—classic, semi-classic; "The Rosary," "Somewhere Voices Calling"—all those type of standard numbers, you know. But we were also performing songs like "Leaving Tipperary," "The Rocky Road to Dublin" . . . and we began doing these appearances in different functions like churches, meetings and gatherings and dances. . . . I think it was in 1926 or 1927, we put on "Danny Boy" for the first time at Holy Name School. . . . You know, the professor at the school wasn't really able to quite get the beat we wanted . . . so Mother began to play backstage, on these kinds of presentations while the two of us [Eileen and Pete] would go out [to sing and dance]. So somebody would say, "Why do you play back here?" So she says, "That's right. Why do I play back here?" . . . So it was somewhere in around 1927 that we appeared as the three on stage as the McNulty Family.[21]

"The Ballads" in the Bars

After a quarter century, the McNulty Family was dramatically eclipsed by the Clancy Brothers and Tommy Makem, who brought the ballad tradition and entwined it with

"ALL ASHORE THAT'S GOING ASHORE," FOR THE NEXT STOP IS
THE BROOKLYN ACADEMY OF MUSIC WITH McNULTY'S IRISH SHOW BOAT
"The Anchor's Weighed and the Gangway's Up, and the Program's On Board at Eight-Thirty Sharp"

MC NULTY FAMILY
IRISH SHOW BOAT

The brilliant craft steams away with a whole load of ENTERTAINMENT, carrying a treasure chest full up of
IRISH SONGS, DANCES, MUSIC AND COMEDY
BROOKLYN ACADEMY OF MUSIC   SUNDAY, MAY 2nd, 1937
Ashland & Lafayette Places—Admission 50c and 75c, plus tax

Billed as the "Royal Family of Irish Entertainers," Ann, Pete, and Eileen McNulty were a mother, son, and daughter team who enjoyed more than two decades of popularity on the Irish-American concert circuit. "Ma" McNulty was an accomplished accordion player in the mostly male Irish music world, but her family act specialized in a hybrid form that drew from both the traditional and popular. The McNulty Family Irish Showboat repertoire included songs like "A Mother's Love Is a Blessing," "The Darling Girl from Clare," "McNamara from Mayo," and "Mother Malone." (Archives of Irish America, New York University)

the thriving folk music scene of the 1960s. Tom, Paddy, and Liam Clancy, brothers from Carrick-on-Suir in County Tipperary, and Tommy Makem, from Keady in County Armagh, had grown up in very musical environments. Tommy Makem was the son of the great northern singer, Sarah Makem, whose local singing reputation and prodigious repertoire had attracted the attention of folklorists from England and America. The Clancys also came from a very musical household and had several relations, including their mother, who were fine singers. The Clancys were in New York City, however, not to sing but to make their reputation as actors; the idea of singing in public was something that arose quite casually. Here Liam Clancy tells his own story of the Clancy Brothers and Tommy Makem:

> We used to have midnight concerts to raise money for the rent. Since we were the only fellows around [among the folk singers] who were of Irish extraction, . . . we had become very popular. . . . None of us played an instrument—Tommy played, but his hand had been broken in an accident. The four of us would stand up and we'd sing, I think, "Kelly the Boy from Killane" was one of our big ones, and another was one of my mother's songs, "Whiskey You're the Divil, You're Leading Me Astray"; these were a few of the songs we knew together. . . .
> Kenny Goldstein [of Tradition Records] . . . thought it would be a great idea if we

recorded an album of Irish rebel songs. . . . Out of this emerged this album called *The Rising of the Moon*. Shortly afterwards we began to get communications from various clubs that were specializing in folk music to know if we would go and sing as a group, which seemed outlandish to us because we were all in the acting business, so we were in the field of communication in that sense, but we had never thought of ourselves as singers or musicians of any kind.

Shortly afterwards we recorded another album of drinking songs. This time we were getting a bit sophisticated. We got a guitar player by the name of Jack Kinnane to play with us, and Tommy's hand was better and he started to play a tin whistle, and this thing began to take a bit of shape. . . . To our amazement, when we were acting we were earning $40 a week each, singing we were making $150 to $160 each, some outlandish sum. So by God we took to it like ducks to water. . . . But we could not agree on a name. So when we arrived in Chicago to [play the Gate of Horn club] . . . the name was already up over the club, "The Clancy Brothers and Tommy Makem," and that stuck. We had about twelve people in the audience the first night, and they didn't know what to make of us, and we didn't know what to make of them. We bought four suits, collars, and ties and sat up on four high stools, and I played my three basic chords and Tommy played the tin whistle and Paddy the harmonica, and just by dint of performing and seeing how ludicrous our attempts at professionalism were in the field of music, we abandoned them right away. Got rid of the collars and ties. We resorted to the old thing we used to do in the pub, you know, late at night in the theater, and it just evolved from that. . . .

[At the Blue Angel in New York City] . . . we were seen . . . by the Ed Sullivan people. We did the *Ed Sullivan Show* wearing those sweaters our mother had given us for Christmas, and she knit one for Tommy as well. When the manager saw those things he said, "that's it, we've got to have those sweaters, it really looks good." So we did the show, and I heard later from the Irish Export Board that the sale of sweaters jumped 700 percent in America after the one television show. It really had become a business at this point. Then there was no hope of getting back to the acting. . . .

So from this emerged a couple of albums for Columbia Records with Pete Seeger playing the banjo on the first one and Bruce Langhorne on the other. At this point the Irish people didn't want to know about us. As a matter of fact, after we recorded an album with Pete Seeger, the Irish people sent us letters and calls and gave us terrible abuse saying that we were a bunch of Communists recording with a man like Pete Seeger.

So we didn't have any Irish following at all to begin with, and, of course, the music that we were singing was foreign to the Irish Americans. So it was a couple of years later that we began to get through to the Irish elements, and from there, I don't know what to tell you, we stayed in the entertainment field ever since.[22]

When Irish Americans started to get interested in the Clancy Brothers, according to Liam, there was an implicit repudiation of the invented Ireland of Tin Pan Alley:

It started with the younger people, and it started after the television exposure, the *Ed Sullivan Show,* and so on. The first couple of albums were out, and the younger people particularly who had gotten a bit bored, I think, of . . . the out and out sentimentalism. The younger kids were looking for something different, yet they still wanted to find something from their own heritage or background, and the songs we were singing seemed to be more authentic. I mean they knew for one thing that an awful lot of the songs were from Ireland. . . .

And then, of course, it is a kind of infectious music. . . . And we had a great time singing them, and I think the very fact that we were not professionals, that we never set out to be a scene group, we had no preconceived ideas of what this music should be about or we were never theorizing about it. . . . And I think it was the sense of fun, the sense of devil-may-care, no preciousness or anything like that about it, that communicates itself to the people. . . . we tried to avoid schmaltz as much as possible. We tried to give some sort of quality and integrity to what we were doing down the line in keeping with the background that we had in theater.[23]

By the early 1960s, the Clancy Brothers and Tommy Makem craze had very definitely caught on in folk music circles in America and was starting to be a major cultural force within the Irish-American community, particularly in the eastern United States. It wasn't too long before the effects were to spread back to Ireland through Columbia's distribution of their LPs there and subsequent airplay over Radio Eireann, the Irish national radio station. The Clancys and Tommy Makem went back in 1962 to do their first concert tour in Ireland, not knowing quite what to expect. Liam remembered their reception was "almost like Beatlemania."[24]

The songs they performed had something in them that would establish emotional communication with a diverse group of people, including many love songs, drinking songs, humorous songs, and rebel songs. The Clancys relied on lusty, full-throated, energetic delivery of their chosen songs with simple harmonies and straightforward musical accompaniment on combinations of guitar, harmonica, tin whistle, and five-string banjo—an instrument that Tommy Makem picked up in the 1960s in New York. The group's performance style and musical arrangements constituted a perfect example of a musical hybrid, a unique synthesis of elements from the rural Irish song tradition and the urban American folk revival tradition. The use of the guitar and the five-string banjo is particularly illustrative of the culture contact involved. Though both the guitar and the five-string banjo had appeared in the Irish music scene previously, neither had ever been used in a style remotely close to the way in which Tommy Makem and Liam Clancy used those instruments in their arrangements of the old country songs.

Tommy Makem emerged as a composer in the 1960s. By far the most popular of his compositions in both Ireland and America is "Four Green Fields," an allegorical song in the *Aisling* tradition eulogizing Ireland, extolling her fight for nationhood, and lamenting the continued enslavement of her fourth green field—the six counties of Ulster still under British rule. This song has become one of the most sung and recorded Irish songs in Ireland and America in the past three decades. It is so popular that it is generally thought of by Irish Americans as an old rebel song. Tommy wrote it during one of his many trips back to Ireland:

I was driving from Dundalk to Newry to buy something or do something in Newry, and I was passing between the Republic Customs hut and the Northern customs hut. And in between there's maybe a half a mile which I figured was no man's land and I saw a woman on the road, she was driving three or four cows probably taking them in to milk them or whatever. It [was] . . . 1967. . . . There were rumblings of something going to happen. And I began to think [how] . . . in bad times, Ireland was always referred to as a poor old woman. Like "The Old Hag of Beare," things like that. And in good times she was referred to as a queen, like *Caitlin ni hUalachain.* Here was this woman taking her cows in, and she probably had a couple of acres or whatever in this no man's land between the two customs huts. So I began thinking about it, and by the time I got to Newry I had the guts of a verse and did what I had to do in Newry, and then I was driving back to Dundalk and maybe got another verse and then when I got back I got the third verse to it. . . .

When I wrote "Four Green Fields" it was a plea that we should be left alone. For three hundred years we had people telling us how we should run our country, and it was time for people to just leave us alone. We had suffered enough. There were people perfectly capable of running the country. It wasn't meant as a rebel song.[25]

In a sense, the commercial success of the Clancy Brothers and Tommy Makem brought the Irish-American musical experience full circle. Once more it was songs from the homeland rather than songs composed in America that were primary. Indeed, since the 1960s there has been a greater interest among Irish Americans and American audiences in general in the music from Ireland rather than in the old Tin Pan Alley material. The traditional and traditionally inspired music from Ireland is perceived as more artistically advanced and more "authentic" than the Irish-American music of the past.

Recent Innovation

Recent developments in songwriting in Irish-American music are taking place in the world of urban rock. Examples would be the music of Larry Kirwan and Black 47 in New York, Flogging Molly in Los Angeles, and the Dropkick Murphys in Boston. In particular, the songs of Larry Kirwan and Black '47 address a variety of themes in modern American and Irish-American urban life, including racism, gender, sexual preferences, and alternative lifestyles. There is much more gritty realism than sentimentality in these new genres.

Over the past four decades—inspired in part by a sense of cultural heritage and connections with the homeland, as well as by new recording technology dating back to the invention of the cassette recorder—popular music has even affected ways in which traditional Irish music is played and disseminated by musicians born and raised in the United States.[26] Through a plethora of web sites on the internet, professional and semiprofessional Irish-American traditional musicians are now able to reach a worldwide audience that is exponentially greater than at any other time in the history of popular music. Indeed, the rules for commodification of all kinds of Irish and Irish-American music are being rewritten almost daily with infusions of new technology. There seems to be no way of knowing what will come next.

NOTES

1. Russell Nye, *The Unembarrassed Muse: The Popular Arts in America* (New York: Dial Press, 1970), 3–7.

2. Eric Lott, "Blackface and Blackness: The Minstrel Show in American Culture," in *Behind the Minstrel Mask: Readings in Nineteenth-Century Blackface Minstrelsy*, ed. A. M Bean, James V. Hatch, and Brooks McNamara (Middletown, CT: Wesleyan University Press. 1996), 3–34.

3. Michael Moloney, "The Banjo in Irish Traditional Music," in *The Companion to Irish Traditional Music*, ed. Fintan Vallely (Cork City, Ireland: Cork University Press, 1999), 22–24.

4. Eugene Waters and Matthew Murtagh, *Infinite Variety: Dan Lowry's Music Hall, 1879–97* (Dublin: Gill and Macmillan, 1975), 89.

5. Earl F. Niehaus, "Paddy on the Local Stage and in Humor: The Image of the Irish in New Orleans 1830–1862," *Louisiana History* 5 (Spring 1964): 117–134.

6. Carl Wittke, "The Immigrant Theme on the American Stage," *Mississippi Valley Historical Review* 39 (September 1952): 214.

7. Lewis P. Curtis Jr., *Apes and Angels: The Irishman in Victorian Caricature* (Washington, DC: Smithsonian Institution Press, 1971), vii.

8. Dale T. Knobel, *Paddy and the Republic: Ethnicity and Nationality in Antebellum America* (Middletown, CT: Wesleyan University Press, 1986), 141.

9. Niehaus, "Paddy on the Local Stage," 117.

10. T. Alston Brown, *A History of the New York Stage*, Vol. 1. (New York: Dodd, Mead, 1903).

11. G. C. O'Dell, *Annals of the New York Stage* (1927–49; repr., New York: AMS Press, 1970).

12. Brown, *History of the New York Stage*, 150.

13. E. J. Kahn, *The Merry Partners. The Age and Stage of Harrigan and Hart* (New York: Random House, 1955); Richard Moody, *Ned Harrigan: From Corlear's Hook to Herald Square* (Chicago: Nelson Hall, 1980).

14. Sigmund Spaeth, *The History of Popular Music in America* (New York: Random House, 1948), 252.

15. Ibid., 219.

16. Peter Gammond, *The Oxford Companion to Popular Music* (New York: Oxford University Press, 1991), 573.

17. William H. A. Williams, *'Twas Only an Irishman's Dream* (Bloomington: Indiana University Press, 1996).

18. As quoted in Jim Walsh, "Favorite Pioneer Recording Artists: Charles W. Harrison and Beulah Gaylord Young," *Hobbies* 57 (March–August 1952): 21.

19. Michael Moloney, "Irish Ethnic Recordings and the Irish American Imagination," in *Ethnic Recordings in America* (Washington, DC: American Folklife Center, Library of Congress, 1978), 85–103.

20. Gary Giddens, *Bing Crosby: A Pocketful of Dreams: The Early Years, 1903–1940* (Boston: Little, Brown, 2001), 593–606.

21. Eileen McNulty, taped interview with the author in Hoboken, New Jersey, February 1978.

22. Liam Clancy, taped interview with the author in Philadelphia, June 24, 1978.

23. Ibid.

24. Ibid.

25. Tommy Makem, taped interview with the author in San Francisco, November 10, 1991.

26. Michael Moloney, "Medicine for Life: A Study of a Folk Composer and His Music," *Keystone Quarterly* 20 (Winter/Spring 1977); Moloney, "Acculturation, Assimilation and Revitalization: Irish Music in Urban America, 1960–1996," in *Crosbealach an Cheoil—The Cross Roads Conference 1996*, ed. Fintan Vallely et al. (Cork: Ossian Publications, 1999), 125–134; Nuala O'Connor, *Bringing It All Back Home: The Influence of Irish Music* (London: British Broadcasting Company Books, 1991).

SUGGESTED READING

Tim Gracyk with Frank Hoffman, *Popular American Recording Pioneers, 1895–1925* (New York: Haworth Press, 2000).

E. J. Kahn, *The Merry Partners: The Age and Stage of Harrigan and Hart* (New York: Random House, 1955).

Eric Lott, *Love and Theft: Blackface Minstrelsy and the American Working Class* (New York: Oxford University Press, 1993).

Mick Moloney, *Far from the Shamrock Shore: The Story of Irish-American Immigration through Song* (New York: Crown, 2002).

William H. A. Williams, *'Twas Only an Irishman's Dream* (Bloomington: Indiana University Press, 1996).

Chapter 15

The Irish and Vaudeville

Robert W. Snyder

In vaudeville, during the late nineteenth and early twentieth centuries, the songs, dances, and jokes of polyglot cities were incorporated into a national theater industry that set the foundation for modern American show business. Irish performers, entrepreneurs, and audience members all played vital roles in this process, transforming both American and Irish-American culture. Irish contributions to vaudeville established a Celtic presence in the entertainment industry and invigorated the mainstream of American popular entertainment. The jokes, dances, and songs of vaudeville and related forms of popular theater were so widely enjoyed that a significant part of Irish-American identity would be expressed not in the ballads and fiddle tunes of immigrant generations but in products of American show business such as the songs "Muldoon, the Solid Man," "My Wild Irish Rose," and "H-A-R-R-I-G-A-N."

Vaudeville was, in every sense, the most popular form of theater in late-nineteenth- and early-twentieth-century America. Its form—separate acts strung together to make a complete bill—was the direct descendant of mid-nineteenth-century variety theater, which had catered to carousing men in concert saloons and music halls and to more mixed audiences of men and women in dime museums and theaters. Vaudeville also owed much to blackface minstrelsy, from which it took the convention of blacking up, ethnically and racially charged humor, and the sequential acts that were the hallmark of the olio segment of the minstrel show.

But vaudeville was variety in a new context. Beginning in the 1880s, showmen seeking to attract the wives and families of male variety fans, and thus create a wider and more lucrative audience, banned liquor from their houses and censored some of the bawdiness in their acts. They jettisoned the older name, "variety," with its stigma of vice and alcohol, and adopted the more refined–sounding "vaudeville." The result was a significantly broader audience—in many respects, the first mass audience—which included both men and women, working class and middle class, native-born and immigrant. Reciprocal cultural exchanges flowed in all directions as native-born, middle-class Americans encountered, through performers and audience members, immigrant and working-class cultures.

Irish performers with strong roots in the performance traditions of Ireland—the jig dancer Kitty O'Neill and the piper Patrick Touhey, for example—were prominent on the bills of early vaudeville houses. Such artists marked early vaudeville as a hybrid of both Irish immigrant and commercial American cultural forms. Surveying the dance scene in late-nineteenth-century vaudeville, William H. A. Williams writes: "Irish and Lancashire steps, mixed with African-American dance styles, created the intricate footwork upon which theatrical clogging and later tap was based."[1]

With acts such as "The Bards of Tara" and "The Boys from Limerick," the Irish were a prominent presence. Yet the portrayal of the Irish in vaudeville and the creative latitude afforded Irish performers were profoundly shaped, even limited, by the stereotyping that pervaded American theater from the nineteenth to the mid–twentieth century. According to this convention, every ethnic or racial group could be reduced to a distinct set of characteristics, usually one favorable and one unfavorable, which had enough reality to be plausible and too little breadth to provide a full portrait. (Indeed, a performer did not have to belong to a group to portray it, only to master the stereotype, as countless white performers did, for example, when they put on blackface.) While African Americans suffered the worst under this system, the Irish, like other immigrant groups, received their own rough treatment. The Irish were typically depicted as bellicose yet fun-loving, drunken yet brave, rowdy yet patriotic. In early vaudeville the typical Irishman's costume was a take-off on an immigrant workingman's clothing: plaid suit, green stockings, corduroy breeches, a square-tailed coat, a battered stovepipe hat with a pipe stuck in the band, a hod-carrier's rig, and chin whiskers. The image of the Irishman as bellicose lent itself naturally to wildly physical slapstick comedy, in which Irish comics pummeled each other with shillelaghs onstage.

Despite stereotyping, Irish performers were fully capable of presenting songs and comedy that fostered a vigorous sense of Irish identity. No performer was better at this in the early days of vaudeville than Maggie Cline. Cline, a Massachusetts-born daughter of a shoe factory foreman, worked her way up the rungs of variety and early vaudeville. By the 1890s, she was known as the "Irish Queen" and was the darling of the Tammany Hall chieftains and newsboys who cheered her at Tony Pastor's, a prominent early vaudeville house located in the Union Square theater district in New York City. Cline's songs about Hogan being behind on his rent and McClosky's epic boxing match were both rousing and rooted in the realities of Irish working-class life. If her songs had an element of stereotyping, they were, like the creations of Harrigan and Hart, rendered with an intimate knowledge of the audience and an affection that made for an enthusiastic reception—not just from the Irish but for non-Irish who went to vaudeville shows for an enjoyable introduction to a show business version of ethnic culture.

In vaudeville, Irish performers created a style that was both urban and ethnic—a testimony to their passage from being rural immigrants to being at home in American cities. Maggie Cline made much of her Irishness, but Irishness was intimately bound up with an urban sensibility. Once, when she finished the song "Don't Let Me Die Till I See Ireland," a man in the audience shouted, "Well, why don't you go there?" "Nit," called back Cline. "It's too far from the Bowery." She left the stage to cheers.[2]

Singer, dancer, and comedian Pat Rooney, whose son and grandson followed him into show business, also presented a vision of Irish Americans grounded in working-class life. His song of the 1880s, "Is That Mr. Riley?" expressed a combination of class-consciousness and racism that reflected Irish workingmen's hostility to competing

Chinese laborers. In the song, an Irishman who aspires to "the White House and Capital" vows to free Ireland, abolish railroad fares, help the cause of the working man, put only Irishmen on the police force, make Saint Patrick's Day the Fourth of July, and "get me a thousand infernal machines / To teach the Chinese how to die."[3]

By the early twentieth century, vaudeville—and its Irish performers and audience members—were in a transition. Under the direction of robber baron showmen like B. F. Keith and E. F. Albee, who created booking offices and circuits of theaters, vaudeville became a mass entertainment industry of national proportions. Although vaudeville continued to draw vitality from urban street life—and especially from Jewish and African-American performers—vaudeville was beginning to acquire a polish that made the old roughhouse Irish comics seem dated.

The Irish in America were changing as well, and with it their stage image. A significant percentage of the children and grandchildren of mid-nineteenth-century immigrants were seeing a modest prosperity as they moved into skilled trades, the civil service, commerce, and organization politics. Reflecting reality, the stage Irishman evolved from a hod-carrying laborer to a politician or a contractor and eventually an urban man about town. (The passage was not always easy: one of the most popular vaudevillian characters at the turn of the last century was Mike Haggerty, who expressed the awkwardness of social climbing by appearing in formal frock coat and a laborer's hob-nailed boots.)

Not only did older representations of the Irish give way to new ones, but old forms of comedy came in for censure. Most notable in vaudeville was the case of the Russell Brothers, who for years had performed a broad comic routine in which they spoofed two Irish servant girls. A campaign organized by the Ancient Order of Hibernians registered disapproval with the act: they booed, hissed, and hurled vegetables. By 1910 the Russell Brothers were gone from vaudeville—a testament to how both vaudeville and the Irish in its audience had moved away from the raw roots of vaudeville and toward a more refined, though still vigorous, form of mass entertainment. If driving the Russell Brothers from the stage was a measure of the cultural clout of the Irish members of the vaudeville audience, it was also a measure of the social unease of some socially ascendant Irish Americans with the kind of rowdy, ethnic farce that had entertained their tenement-dwelling ancestors in the nineteenth century.

More and more, vaudeville was assuming the characteristics of a bureaucratic entertainment industry. Its most prominent stage was the Palace Theater at 47th Street and Broadway in the Times Square area; its most prominent circuit was run by the United Booking Office, set up by Keith and Albee and housed on the sixth floor of the Palace. Pat Casey, booking manager at the Palace, arbitrated metropolitan tastes in vaudeville: a booking at the Palace helped to certify a performer as a nationwide star, but a rejection by Casey could irreparably harm one's professional reputation. (To Casey's credit, he allowed pianist Eubie Blake to appear at the Palace without the stereotypical blackface and overalls suggested by agents.) During a strike of vaudevillians from 1916 to 1917, primarily over the right to establish a union shop, Casey organized efforts to spy on pro-union performers and blacklist them.

Yet as much as showmen referred to "refined vaudeville"—as much as they organized their industry on a bureaucratic basis and aspired to lucrative monopolies—it was impossible to sever vaudeville entirely from its origins in the urban world of tenements, street life, and cheap amusements where so many Irish Americans had their origins. Foremost proof of this was the career of Timothy D. "Big Tim" Sullivan.

Sullivan, a Tammany politician based in the tenements of lower Manhattan, had strong connections to gambling and was accused—probably inaccurately, according to Daniel Czitrom, who has analyzed his career—of being implicated in prostitution.[4] As early as the 1890s Sullivan grasped the benefits of combining organization politics with show business in the form of mammoth parades and chowders that brought his working poor constituents flashy pleasures and full stomachs. Involvement in the management of music halls and burlesque houses in the 1890s was followed less than a decade later by Sullivan investments that helped turn the small-time vaudeville houses of Seattle theater manager John W. Considine into the Sullivan–Considine Circuit, which embraced some forty midwestern vaudeville theaters and a lucrative booking agency. Sullivan later worked with early movie houses in New York City, which presented a combination of films and vaudeville and also campaigned for city ordinances to allow movie showings and vaudeville shows on Sundays.

Sullivan's segue from vaudeville to the movie business was a testament to the momentum of the American entertainment industry: vaudeville was gradually being pushed offstage by the movies. Well into the 1920s Irish performers would appear on the vaudeville stage. But as early as the 1910s, the Irish Americans who appeared in vaudeville were less identifiably Irish and more generically urban—but in an urban style that bore an Irish imprint. Gracie Allen's zany independence was an echo of the young Irish women who had sought the joys of a Saturday night out on the Bowery in 1880. Pat Rooney, the son of the man who sang "Is That Mr. Riley?" in the nineteenth century, achieved fame in his own right doing comedy and dancing with Marion Bent. "What's your favorite stone?" he would ask her. "Turquoise," she would reply. "Mine's a brick," Rooney would conclude. The joke could be enjoyed in many ways, not least of which as a reminder of how many Irishmen had callused their hands and risen in the world by laying bricks.[5]

By the 1920s it was clear that vaudeville was in a terminal decline. For performers, vaudeville bookings became less and less an end in themselves and more a staging ground for careers in musical reviews, then radio and talking films. Those who made the transition brought the cocky, urban dimension of vaudeville with them, none more than Broadway star George M. Cohan, who toured in vaudeville with his parents, and Jimmy Cagney, whose bouncy, cocky, street kid's style came directly from vaudeville.

If performers like Cagney and Cohan carried vaudeville performing styles into the future, it fell to the Irish-American businessman and political patriarch Joseph P. Kennedy to bring the remaining structures of the vaudeville business into the new world of motion pictures. In 1928 Kennedy, then head of a film company, bought a large amount of stock in the newly merged Keith and Orpheum circuits, which were all that remained of bigtime vaudeville. Kennedy wanted to acquire the circuit's theaters for his film interests, which he ran in cooperation with the Radio Corporation of America (RCA). The combination produced Radio-Keith Orpheum, or RKO, soon to be a major force in the American entertainment industry. Vaudeville, the first form of mass entertainment, had now been absorbed into the newest: motion pictures.

By the 1930s vaudeville was dead. But Irish-American artists and entrepreneurs who apprenticed in vaudeville or were touched by its aura—such as Cohan, Cagney, Fred Allen, Jackie Gleason, and Ed Sullivan—would carry the dynamic, urban, inclusive vaudeville style into twentieth-century show business. In the process, they maintained an Irish presence in the entertainment industry. And as heirs to the vaudevillians, they ensured that the songs and styles of vaudeville and the popular stage, which resonated so deeply with the Irish because they bore a Celtic imprint to begin with, would sustain an Irish-American identity.

NOTES

1. William H. A. Williams, 'Twas Only an Irishman's Dream: The Image of Ireland and the Irish in American Popular Song Lyrics, 1880–1920 (Urbana: University of Illinois Press, 1996), 122.

2. Robert W. Snyder, The Voice of the City: Vaudeville and Popular Culture in New York (New York: Oxford University Press, 1989), 117.

3. Pat Rooney, "Is That Mr. Riley?" (New York: Harding, 1883).

4. Daniel Czitrom, "Underworlds and Underdogs: Big Tim Sullivan and Metropolitan Politics in New York, 1889–1913," Journal of American History (September 1991): 536–558.

5. Snyder, Voice of the City, 114.

SUGGESTED READING

Don Meade, "Kitty O'Neil and Her 'Champion Jig': An Irish Dancer on the New York Stage," New Hibernia Review 6, no. 3 (2002): 9–22.

Kenneth R. Rossman, "The Irish in American Drama in the Mid-Nineteenth Century," New York History 21, no. 1 (1940): 39–53.

Maxine Schwartz Seller, ed., Ethnic Theatre in the United States (Westport, CT: Greenwood Press, 1983).

Robert W. Snyder, The Voice of the City: Vaudeville and Popular Culture in New York (New York: Oxford University Press, 1989).

William H. A. Williams, 'Twas Only an Irishman's Dream: The Image of Ireland and the Irish in American Popular Song Lyrics, 1880–1920 (Urbana: University of Illinois Press, 1996).

Irish Traditional Music in the United States

Rebecca S. Miller

Irish traditional instrumental dance music originated centuries ago, primarily as accompaniment for social and solo dancing. Like most traditional arts, the music is passed down from the elder to the younger generation as an oral tradition, and learning takes place through imitation and listening. In general, Irish dance music has historically been composed anonymously, although in the last two decades, many tunes by known composers have become popular. On the whole, the music is crafted through a communal process. In the United States, both Irish and Irish-American players, as well as an increasingly large number of non-Irish musicians, learn the music from each other at informal music *seisiúns* (sessions), at Irish music festivals, as well as from recordings and radio airplay. Possibly one of the most popular genres of "world music" today, live performances of Irish traditional music are frequent and regular throughout the United States. These include formal concerts, folk and Irish traditional music festivals, and *seisiúns* as well as *ceilis* (group folk dances). Venues range from small bars and medium-sized clubs to such major performance venues as Lincoln Center in New York City and the Kennedy Center in Washington, D.C.

Prior to the advent of modern technology, playing style was transmitted from player to player; this process of dissemination was dramatically altered in the early decades of the twentieth century, however, first by the recording industry and later by the mass production of handheld tape recorders. In the United States, playing styles are derived in large part from different regional styles that originated in Ireland. For example, the Sligo fiddle style is one of the most popular among Irish-American players today. This is due, in part, to the 78-rpm recordings made by such labels as Decca, Victor, and Columbia between 1910 and 1940 of outstanding Irish immigrant musicians such as Sligo fiddlers Michael Coleman, Paddy Killoran, and James Morrison. Produced in the United States and sent back to Ireland by relatives and friends, these recordings privileged specific playing styles and repertoire to the neglect of others. In addition, these early recordings served to immortalize and perpetuate the playing styles of individual musicians, such as button accordionist John Kimmel, uilleann piper Patsy Tuohy, flutist John McKenna, concertina player William Mullaly, and, later in the 1960s, button accordionist Paddy O'Brien.

Among the most commonly heard instruments in traditional Irish music today are the fiddle, wooden flute, button accordion, tin whistle, and uilleann pipes (small, bellows-driven bagpipes), as well as the tenor banjo, concertina, mandolin, and harp.

Played with a subtle but propulsive rhythmic drive, traditional Irish music places an emphasis on melody. Because of this reliance on an often intricate melody line, harmonic accompaniment is a relatively new development. Accompaniment is most commonly provided by piano, guitar, *bodhrán* (a handheld frame drum), and, since the late 1970s, the bouzouki or cittern. Countermelodies and harmonies are uncommon in what practitioners consider strictly "traditional" music, although many younger Irish and Irish-American bands today increasingly incorporate such arrangements in performance.

Irish traditional dance tunes span a range of rhythmic meters and tempi: tunes in duple time include reels (4/4) and polkas (2/4), as well as stately marches and slower, syncopated hornpipes; those in triple time include jigs (6/8) and slipjigs (9/8). Other tunes commonly played by traditional Irish musicians include waltzes, slow airs (laments), and longer form set pieces. Regionalism plays a role in repertoire: Irish traditional musicians from the north of Ireland, for example, play highlands (also known as "flings"), mazurkas, schottishes, and barndances; players from the southwestern counties of Cork and Kerry are known for their preference for upbeat polkas and "slides."

Irish Song

Like Irish instrumental dance music, Irish traditional singing (*sean-nós* or "old style") has been passed down orally, also from older to younger generation. Sung unaccompanied, *sean-nós* songs are a solo endeavor and feature intricate ornamentation that requires concentration on the part of an audience, for the tale told (often in Irish) is usually long and complicated. Traditionally, *sean-nós* songs once served the local Irish communities as a source of public news and as an oral record of local lore and history. Today, *sean-nós* songs are sung strictly for entertainment, and contemporary *sean-nós* singers performing to American audiences tend to select repertoire in both Irish and English, and they shorten the songs to fit modern attention spans. Many *sean-nós* singers today were influenced by the virtuosic singing of the late Joe Heaney of Connemara, County Galway, who lived for many years in Brooklyn, New York, and later in Seattle, Washington.

Since *sean-nós* singing generally requires a command of the Irish language, as well as excellent vocal control, there remain far fewer practitioners than there are Irish instrumentalists and dancers. Historically, *sean-nós* singing has remained largely inaccessible to the general public due to the language barrier and so was by-passed in the revival of Irish music in the 1960s and 1970s. Instead, Irish songs in English, backed with rhythmic accompaniment (most typically the guitar) gained popularity among folk music fans. This new style of folk singing was best exemplified by the Clancy Brothers and Tommy Makem.

The Clancy Brothers and Tommy Makem spawned a new folk style from the old and captured the attention of an international audience. Eliminating most of the ornamentation found in *sean-nós* singing, they added instrumental accompaniment and performed their songs faster, with a driving beat. They sang mostly in unison, which not only gave them their particular trademark as a group but also allowed for audience participation, thus increasing their appeal. Their early appearances on television (then a relatively new medium) brought them immediate, widespread recognition. Moreover, their interest in political Irish songs at the time appealed to the sociopolitical sensibilities of large numbers of Irish immigrants and Irish-Americans and was congruent in spirit with the antiwar sentiment current in the 1960s in the United States.

Inspired in part by the Clancy Brothers and Tommy Makem, a folk-based singing style emerged in the late 1970s. This style typically features a solo lead singer (sometimes with harmony vocals) and back-up instrumentation, ranging from a single guitar to a complicated arrangement of various instruments. This style of singing often incorporates some of the simpler *sean-nós* vocal ornamentation into the delivery, a departure in style from that of the Clancy Brothers. The repertoire is typically in English (occasionally in Irish) and consists of historic ballads and songs, as well as recently composed pieces.

History

Massive numbers of Irish immigrants came to America beginning in the mid-1800s to escape the devastating effects of the Irish Famine. Unlike the earlier Scots-Irish who settled in rural areas throughout the eastern United States, the newly arrived Irish moved to America's big cities: New York, Chicago, Boston, Philadelphia, and New Orleans, among others. Irish traditional music survived the transition from rural Ireland to largely urban America and proved surprisingly resilient in the face of such social change. Master fiddlers, pipers, accordionists, flutists, and other instrumentalists and vocalists often found work in the vaudeville circuits, dance halls, pubs, and other venues.

By the early 1900s, New York City had become a focal point for Irish music when record companies reacted to the market potential of the "Golden Age of Irish Music" and began producing hundreds of 78-rpm recordings. During the first three decades of the twentieth century, the "Golden Age" was fueled by the arrival of hundreds of thousands of immigrants who hailed from the northern and western regions of Ireland. By the early 1930s, Irish immigration dramatically decreased due to the depression and, later, World War II. These considerations, along with a production-stopping wartime ban on shellac, curtailed the recording industry's interest in ethnic music in general.

Shortages of consumer goods and rising unemployment marked the years just after World War II in Ireland. Small farms and large families forced the young Irish to seek work elsewhere, but with little industry in Ireland, jobs were scarce, leaving many with little choice but to emigrate. Immigration to the United States picked up when Congress passed the Immigration and Nationality Act of 1952 (McCarran-Walter Act) allowing, among other things, unrestricted immigration from the Western Hemisphere and a stated preference for those with relatives who were American citizens. By favoring Irish immigrants, this bill opened the door to new arrivals.

By the 1950s, the traditional Irish music scene in the United States had waned to

The Avoca record label brought out an album of Irish dance music by the Traditional Irish Musicians Association, a New York City–based group founded in April 1965, at about the same time showband music was eclipsing it in Irish-American dancehalls. (Archives of Irish America, New York University, Gift of Dorothy Hayden Cudahy)

the point where there was little, if any, opportunity for public performance. (The exceptions were monthly *ceilis* sponsored in some East Coast cities by the Gaelic League and an annual *feis*, an Irish music festival and competition, in New York City, sponsored by the United Irish Counties Association.) In general, the new Irish immigrants were eager to assimilate into American society and leave behind the vestiges of folk culture. Many Irish traditional musicians who came to the United States during this era were thus forced to set aside their instruments as a professional endeavor or to learn a more contemporary style of music, such as Irish showband music or country-western music. The rare opportunity to play traditional music was at the occasional house *seisiún*.

A resurgence of interest in Irish traditional music had its beginnings in the mid-1960s as a result of a number of cultural and social developments both in the United States and in Ireland. Most influential was the international attention brought to Irish music by the Clancy Brothers and Tommy Makem with their gutsy renditions of folk Irish songs. Simultaneously, the revival of interest in traditional music in Ireland was sparked under the aegis of Comhaltas Ceoltóirí Éireann (Irish Musicians Association) and soon extended to America. As a result, music *seisiúns* began anew in pubs and

Irish social halls in New York, Boston, Philadelphia, Chicago, and elsewhere, and concerts of traditional bands from Ireland—Planxty, the Bothy Band, the Boys of the Lough, and the Chieftains, for example—were presented in both general and Irish-American venues. Eventually, many of the older traditional players who had immigrated in the 1940s and 1950s were invited to perform in similar venues.

The 1960s also saw the physical dissolution of many Irish neighborhoods in major American cities. As the demographics of these neighborhoods changed, Irish families increasingly moved to the suburbs, and, for a number of Irish and Irish Americans, the loss of immediate physical community, combined with the outside recognition of Irish traditional culture, encouraged a reevaluation of heritage and community. Unlike earlier generations, Irish immigrants from the 1940s and 1950s were able to retain closer ties with Ireland via affordable transatlantic flights. Irish-born parents could renew an interest in their heritage and inspire the same in their children.

The sense of importance of ethnicity thus rekindled, the 1970s and 1980s saw an unprecedented number of Irish-American youngsters flocking to schools for Irish traditional music and step dance in major American cities. Two of New York's most popular Irish music schools—John Glynn's in Brooklyn (taken over after his death in 1971 by his daughter, the late Maureen Glynn Connolly) and the late County Limerick fiddler Martin Mulvihill's in the Bronx—taught music on a variety of instruments to literally thousands of students.

By the late 1970s and early 1980s, several annual Irish traditional music festivals became well established, due, in part, to the availability of state and federal folk arts funding, as well as to the gradually increasing size of both Irish-American and non-Irish audiences. These festivals include the Philadelphia Ceili Group's Irish Music Festival; the Irish Arts Center's Irish Traditional Music Festival at Snug Harbor, Staten Island, New York; the Milwaukee Irish Music Festival; and the annual Washington Irish Folk Festival at Wolf Trap, Virginia.

The Irish traditional music community in the early twenty-first century in the United States is thriving. Musicians of all ages—immigrants, Irish-American, and non-Irish—can attend weeklong camps held throughout the country that focus on Irish music and song. Additionally, myriad weekly music sessions are held in large and small cities and music festivals are devoted either totally or in part to Irish traditional music. Both folk recording labels and major record labels are producing recordings by Irish and Irish-American musicians at an unprecedented rate. Irish radio programming on both public and commercial radio gives extensive air time to Irish traditional music, as well as to Celtic rock and other popular styles. With the recent phenomenon of the Irish dance extravaganza *Riverdance*, an interest in Irish cultural expression is clearly growing among Irish Americans and non-Irish alike.

Over the years, Irish traditional music has waxed and waned in popularity. That traditional Irish music has survived throughout the United States despite periods of unpopularity points to its inherent vitality as both an art form and an important symbolic component of Irish immigrant culture. And it continues to serve as an extremely visible vehicle for changing group identity. This enduring sense of ethnicity and the fact that increasing numbers of non-Irish are attracted to Irish traditional music bode well for its survival and creative adaptation into the future.

SUGGESTED READING

Lawrence E. McCullough, "An Historical Sketch of Traditional Irish Music in the U.S." *Folklore Forum* 7, no. 3 (July 1974): 177–191.

Rebecca S. Miller, "Irish Traditional and Popular Music in New York City: Identity and Social Change, 1930–1975." In *The New York Irish*, edited by Ronald H. Bayor and Timothy J. Meagher, 481–507. Baltimore: Johns Hopkins University Press, 1996.

Michael Moloney, "Irish Ethnic Recordings and the Irish-American Imagination." In *Ethnic Recordings in America: A Neglected Heritage,* American Folklife Center, 84–101. Washington, DC: Library of Congress, 1982.

Mick Moloney, "Irish Music in America: Continuity and Change." Ph.D. diss., University of Pennsylvania. Ann Arbor, MI: University Microfilms International, 1992.

Francis J. O'Neill, *Irish Folk Music: A Fascinating Hobby* and *Irish Minstrels and Musicians.* Both originally published in Chicago: Regan Printing House, 1910 and 1913, respectively; both reprinted, Darby, PA: Norwood Editions, 1973.

Graeme Smith, "My Love Is in America: Migration and Irish Music," in *The Creative Migrant,* Vol. 3 of *The Irish World Wide,* ed. Patrick O'Sullivan, 221–236 (London and New York: Leicester University Press, 1994).

William H. A. Williams, *'Twas Only an Irishman's Dream: The Image of Ireland and the Irish in American Popular Song Lyrics, 1800–1920* (Urbana: University of Illinois Press, 1996).

DISCOGRAPHY/FILMOGRAPHY

From Shore to Shore: Irish Traditional Music in New York City. 1993. VHS Videotape. Produced/Directed by Patrick Mullins; Co-produced/written by Rebecca Miller. Historian/Associate Producer: Marion Casey. New York City: Cherry Lane Productions. Distributed by the Cinema Guild, Inc., 1697 Broadway, Suite 506, New York, New York 10019-5904, (800) 723-5522.

The Clancy Brothers with Tommy Makem: Luck of the Irish. 1992. Reissue of classic recording on CD. New York: Columbia/Legacy CK47900.

Tom Doherty: Take the Bull by the Horns. 1993. CD/cassette recording. Produced by Rebecca Miller. Danbury, CT: Green Linnet Records, Inc. GLCD 1131

Wheels of the World, Vol. 1 and 2. Yazoo, 7008 and 7009. CD recordings. Reissues of archival recordings of legendary musicians from the early twentieth century, including Michael Coleman, Patsy Tuohy, James Morrison, and others. Newtown, NJ: Shanachie Records.

Chapter 17

Before *Riverdance*

A Brief History of Irish Step Dancing in America

Marion R. Casey

Any tradition is in the hands of the people who live with
it now. It is where they choose to take it.
—Colin Dunne, 1999

Since the Americans Jean Butler and Michael Flatley danced a modernized duet on
Irish television in April 1994, step dancing has emerged from its ethnic subculture in
the United States. Indeed, more people saw Irish step dancing in the subsequent
decade than ever saw it in the history of mankind. This has been primarily driven by
the commercial success of two stage shows that quickly spun off from Butler's and
Flatley's original five-minute piece. *Riverdance* (with five touring companies by 2003)
and *Lord of the Dance* (with three troupes) used the traditional precision of Irish step
dancing to create large choreographed works that emphasized heavy, synchronized
battering in line dancing and dance drama. Despite global tours claiming live audiences in the millions and television audiences in the billions, the United States is in
fact the primary source of profit for both shows.[1] If this success can be attributed to
American yearning for "tradition" as embodied in "folk" culture, then perhaps some
examination of step dancing's history on this side of the Atlantic is necessary to
understanding its twenty-first-century transformation into iconic phenomenon.[2]

While *Riverdance* and *Lord of the Dance* both emanated from Ireland, the innovations reflected in them were actually honed in the United States by American-born
dancers fluent in traditional step dancing methods. There has been Irish step dancing
in the United States for more than two hundred years. It originated in Ireland in the
late eighteenth century, coinciding with the first significant emigration of Irish people
to cross the Atlantic. From the beginning, the locus of Irish step dancing in America has been in urban centers. The earliest known reference occurs in Philadelphia in
1789 when the dancing master John Durang demonstrated a reel, jig, and hornpipe.
The entertainer Barney Williams, a native of Cork, performed jigs on and off stages
across America in the 1840s. And Dan O'Mahony and Francis X. Hennessy taught step

dancing in San Francisco and New York City, respectively, before the turn of the twentieth century.[3]

But the roots of Irish step dancing in the United States today date back to the late 1890s when Irish immigrants began to be influenced by the tenets of the Gaelic Revival. Important dancing schools were established in Boston by Tim Harrington, in New York by James McKenna and Tommy Hill, in Chicago by John McNamara and James Coleman, and in San Francisco by William Healy. Healy's school, founded in 1902, is said to be the oldest in continuous operation in the United States. These men were all immigrants from Ireland's southwestern province, Munster, which was renowned for its traveling dancing masters in the nineteenth century.[4]

There are five distinct types of traditional Irish step (or solo) dances: jigs, reels, hornpipes, slip jigs, and set pieces.[5] Jigs are danced in 6/8 time, slip jigs in 9/8 time, hornpipes and reels in common (4/4) time.[6] The step dancer's carriage is upright, with arms held parallel to the body; the legs and feet provide the only movement. The purpose of this carriage—which is a particular regional style associated with Ireland's southwestern counties[7]—is to convey athletic discipline, as opposed to restraint. Control of the torso was a prized skill as the dancer traditionally performed intricate steps in a very confined space, such as on a half door removed from its hinges or on the top of a table. It was said, according to Breandán Breathnach, that a good dancer "could dance on eggs without breaking them and hold a pan of water on his head without spilling a drop."[8]

Historically, dancers and musicians performed together because Irish traditional music *is* dance music. When Francis O'Neill, a captain on the Chicago police force, published *The Dance Music of Ireland* in 1907, it quickly became the standard work on the subject. Containing the musical notations for more than a thousand dance tunes in the traditional music repertoire, the majority of which were acquired from Irish Americans, it underscored the symbiotic relationship between the rhythmic percussion of the feet in step dancing and the tunes played live on instruments like the fiddle, flute, and concertina.[9] The earliest American commentary, the Kinneys' *The Dance: Its Place in Art and Life* (1914), noted:

> [Ireland's dances were] exclusively her own, unique in structure, and developed to the utmost limit of their line of excellence. Their distinguishing property is complicated rhythmic music of the feet. The Jig, Reel and Hornpipe of Ireland are at once the most difficult and the most highly elaborated dances of the clog and shuffle type that can be found. In them are passages in which the feet tap the floor seventy-five times in a quarter minute."[10]

By 1914, four American cities hosted annual Irish cultural festivals, called "feiseanna" or simply a "feis," at which step dancers could compete against each other. These were open to the public and usually under the auspices of the Gaelic League. New York City held a feis as early as 1911, followed by Chicago in 1912. At the Great 1919 Feis held at Hunt's Point in New York City, there were competitions for the hornpipe, double jig, slip jig, set piece, and three-, four-, six-, and eight-hand reels.

During this period the undefeated champion in all the American men's competitions was Tommy Hill (born 1890) who had emigrated from Cork in 1911.[11] New

York hosted a United States Championship as early as 1927; there was a Pacific Coast Championship in San Francisco from 1936. The United Irish Counties Association of New York (UICA) held the first of more than fifty annual feiseanna at Wingate Field in Brooklyn in 1933 (from 1941 it was held on the grounds of Fordham University in the Bronx).[12] The UICA created a standard for feis competition that eventually became the model in many American cities. Pat Roche, Mae Butler, and Kevin Shannahan encouraged Irish step dancing west of New York by creating feiseanna in Chicago, Toronto, and Cleveland, respectively.[13] The 1946 Feis in Chicago, only the second one sponsored by the Harp and Shamrock Club, attracted 750 contestants in eighty-four events.[14]

The North American Feis Commission (founded in 1968) is the umbrella organization for all step dancing competitions. As the twenty-first century opened, there were at least 190 feiseanna held annually in thirty states plus five Canadian provinces, ranging from the Feis in the Desert (Mesa, Arizona) to the Peach State Feis (Atlanta, Georgia) to the Christmas Feis (Nepean, Ontario). For those committed to this traditional art form, the Irish step dancing circuit is a year-round pursuit summed up by the expression "Gone Feiseann."

Outside the Irish-American community, the art's profile was also raised by exhibitions of step dancing at the 1904 World's Fair in St. Louis by Hugh O'Neill; at the Irish Village in Chicago (1934's Century of Progress) by the students of Pat Roche and John McNamara;[15] by the Healy School at the 1938 San Francisco Exposition; and by James McKenna's students at the 1939–1940 World's Fair in New York. In 1939 Tomas O'Faircheallaigh demonstrated Irish step dancing on the CBS radio network's "Major Bowe's" program.[16] CBS also broadcast the first television appearance of Irish step dancers in 1945. Some step dancers made concessions to the needs of the new media, as well as to the preconceived expectations of American popular culture, such as the taps used by Dorothy Hayden's Irish Memories troupe in its seven appearances on the *Ed Sullivan Show* during the 1950s.[17]

An unadulterated style of step dancing from Munster dominated North America especially between 1890 and the 1950s. In Ireland during this period, there was a gradual shift toward a new style of step dancing that originated in the northern province of Ulster. Whereas the Cork–Kerry style was known for its fast, strong battering that was danced low to the ground, the northern dancers used a slower pace that allowed for more complicated steps and more graceful—even balletic—movement of the legs and feet. When the Belfast–Derry style was introduced into the United States and Canada after World War II, it caused a sudden and dramatic change.[18] Irish-American step dancers saw the new style demonstrated on television (by the Anna McCoy School from Belfast) and live at the annual Toronto feis (by Mae Butler's students). The McCoy and Butler schools quickly created a demand in the United States to learn the new style. In New York City it became synonymous with the teachers Peter and Cyril McNiff (who had emigrated as teenagers in 1948) and in time replaced the old Cork–Kerry style. Many popular national television programs regularly showcased the McNiff dancers, in what has been called "the first recognition" of "Irish dancing as a viable entertainment commodity."[19] As more new-style teachers emigrated from Ireland in the 1950s, young American dancers like Peter Smith and Patsy Early changed schools. By the 1960s and 1970s they themselves were teaching *only* the Belfast–Derry style to a new generation of Irish Americans.[20] Thereafter, step dancing was regularly showcased as part of the U.S. concert tours of the Green Fields of America (organized by Mick Moloney in 1978) and the Chieftains.

Step dancing costumes and shoes, worn for either competition or formal performance, have also evolved since 1900. Men's costumes began as white shirt and black knee breeches, with a cummerbund and sometimes a tie. The northern style of dancing brought with it the kilt, about twenty years after it had been introduced into step dancing in Ireland. The McNiff dancers are said to have borrowed saffron kilts from one of the local bagpipe bands in New York in 1954, thereby initiating the change in the United States.[21] Men wore kilts with buttoned jackets, shirts and ties, and a short shawl secured at the shoulder by a Tara brooch or Celtic pin. Women's costumes originally included hooded cloaks or shawls nearly to the ground, pinned at hip and shoulder. During the 1930s these were abandoned for simple dresses with a small amount of Celtic embroidery, or skirts and blouses, both with a shorter shawl. Throughout the 1950s, 1960s, and 1970s, women's dresses became more elaborate, incorporating Irish crocheted lace collars and cuffs with embroidered belts and motifs such as the Ardagh Chalice and Celtic interlacing. Hemlines rose higher and higher. While men wore socks to the knees with their kilts, women opted at various stages for stockings, black tights, or knee or ankle socks.

Two kinds of shoes are worn. Soft-soled black leather slippers—"gillies" with laces that cross the arch of the foot and tie around the ankle—are worn for the reel and slip jig. Hard shoes originally had built-up heels and toes studded with round-headed nails to produce better sound when dancing the jig and hornpipe. These have been replaced since the 1980s with fiberglass tips that have made the shoes lighter and enable many more toe and heel clicks per bar of music. *Riverdance* and *Lord of the Dance* have revolutionized traditional costumes by incorporating the dance wear of the American entertainment stage, especially leotards, t-shirts, and lots of bare skin, as well as banishing the kilt for men.

Irish step dancing is an art learned orally and by demonstration. It is passed on in almost genealogical fashion from teacher to student, thus enabling some nineteenth-century settings for traditional dances like "The Blackbird" to survive in the diaspora for more than a century.[22] The famous Kerry traveling dance master Jerry Molyneaux, for example, taught James T. McKenna (1885–1977), who emigrated in 1903 and set up a legendary dancing school in New York in 1910. McKenna's assistant Jerry Mulvihill (b. 1921) opened his own school in 1951, where Donny Golden (b. 1953) learned his first steps. Golden later changed teachers, learning the northern style from Jimmy Erwin, a former pupil of Cyril McNiff. In 1970 Donny Golden became the first North American dancer to ever place in the top three at the World Irish Dancing Championships. Golden inherited Irwin's school later in the 1970s, and in the 1980s Jean Butler was his student. Her *Riverdance* partner, Michael Flatley, has a similar pedigree, descending over one hundred years from the Clare traveling dancing master Michael Hennessy through the Chicago schools of Pat Roche, Mary Campbell-Fahey, Marge Bartishell, and Dennis Dennehy.[23] Flatley was the first North American to win the

Professor James T. McKenna (1885-1977), from Castleisland, County Kerry, taught Irish step dancing to hundreds of students in New York City from 1910 until his death in 1977. (Archives of Irish America, New York University)

senior men's title (over age twenty-one) at the World Irish Dancing Championships in 1976.

The Irish Dancing Teachers Commission of America (IDTCA) was founded in 1953. In a landmark 1959 meeting, the IDTCA met with musicians to discuss the difficulties of accommodating the old and new styles of Irish step dancing. One required fast music, the other slow. The result was an agreement to permit two tempi each for the jig, reel, and hornpipe, regulated for all dancers by a metronome.[24] The introduction of the metronome was one of the most important changes to affect Irish step dancing during the twentieth century. A decade later, the Irish Dancing Teachers Association of North America (IDTANA) was established in 1964 at a meeting in the Irish Institute building in New York City. The IDTANA also emphasized the need for cooperation, focusing on developing a standardized syllabus, fair age categories, and

The Green Fields of America, featuring step dancers Eileen and Donny Golden, performed in Washington, D.C., on 29 September 1999, when Mick Moloney was presented with the National Heritage Award from the National Endowment for the Arts. The musicians, from left to right, are Eliot Grasso (hidden behind dancers), Fr. Charlie Coen, Jack Coen, Robbie O'Connell, Mick Moloney, Liz Carroll, and Zan McLeod. (Official White House Photo, RA P076059-019)

separate boy and girl championships at all feiseanna. It encouraged American teachers and feis judges to be certified, as required by Ireland's An Coimisiún le Rinci Gael-acha (the Irish Dance Commission established in 1929). In 1967 it sponsored the first TCRG (teacher) and ADCRG (adjudicator) certification examinations ever held outside of Ireland. Fifty candidates sat the exam in New York City. At Thanksgiving 1969 the IDTANA sponsored the first American National Championship (or Oireachtas) in the Tower View Ballroom in Woodside, New York. It received permission from An Coimisiún to make this a qualifying round for the world championships in Ireland, which had begun that same year; a west coast Oireachtas was established in 1974.[25]

Approximately five hundred Irish dancing teachers are registered in North America, nearly all of whom have been trained outside Ireland but pay dues to the Irish Dance Commission in Dublin.[26] Many teach step dancing full-time, some, like the dancing masters of old, traveling between states to classes. Annually they send about four hundred qualified students to compete for a coveted world title, demonstrating again and again that in all its aspects Irish step dancing in North America is equal to that found in Ireland.

As "to Riverdance" entered the American lexicon in the 1990s, enrollments in step dancing schools across the United States and Canada soared. In New York City, an area historically saturated with step dancing teachers, the Petri School of Irish Dancing opened its doors in 1991 with four students and had 250 just seven years later. "The kids we have now are not just Irish," Lisa Petri said in the premier issue of *Irish Dancer*, a magazine published in Mequon, Wisconsin. "We have Asian, Hispanic, and Italian kids. Even the kids who have Irish names do not have Irish-born parents and the majority of their parents never danced. Most of these kids saw *Riverdance* and *Lord of the Dance* and this piqued their interest. We have a lot of teenagers. Enough so that we can have a separate beginner class for teens."[27]

Yet long before *Riverdance*, in 1979 Mark Howard (one of Flatley's fellow students at the Dennehy School in Chicago) founded the Trinity Academy of Irish Dance. Howard pioneered dance drama for Irish step dancing, and his students introduced it into the world championships in the late 1980s, capturing choreography titles with artistic interpretations of Irish history like "The Mist" and "Granuaille."[28] In 1990 Howard created the Trinity Irish Dance Company for his older students to provide professional career opportunities outside of competition and beyond teaching; this ability to earn a salary for performance is arguably the most significant departure in Irish step dancing history. Calling itself the birthplace of "progressive Irish dance," the company's vision is indicative of the art's direction at the beginning of the twenty-first century: "By using Irish dance as an instrument and a metaphor, Trinity . . . [is] transcending craft to art and creating a new vocabulary for Irish step dancing."[29] This is distinct from older attempts that sprang from step dancing but little resembled it in the end, the best example of which is the stage dancing of George M. Cohan (1878–1942). Jerry Cohan taught his son the Cork-style of step dancing he had learned from his own father (a Famine-era emigrant) overlaid with "new world variations" like stop-time, clog, and buck or tap dancing.[30] But such innovations broke from the tradition rather than reinvigorating it, as Howard, Flatley, and Butler have done.

Putting aside its enormous influence in contemporary popular culture, Irish step dancing on this side of the Atlantic is interesting from a historiographical point of view. It offers a social and cultural example of Irish diaspora history that is not bound by the usual political borders. Not only are dancers from Canada and the United States seen as North Americans at the world championships, but the organizations that govern the instruction and demonstration of their art form are pan-American as well. If shows like *Riverdance* force us to ponder the global appeal of Irishness, perhaps step dancing can help us transcend the arbitrariness of some of the conventional boundaries in the study of the Irish abroad.

NOTES

1. See the websites for both shows: http://www.riverdance.com/ and http://www.lordofthe dance.com/.

2. Natasha Casey, "*Riverdance*: The Importance of Being Irish American," *New Hibernia Review* 6, no. 4 (2002): 23–24.

3. John P. Cullinane, *Aspects of the History of Irish Dancing in North America* (Cork: By the Author, 1997), 10, 15, 25 [hereafter cited as Cullinane, *Aspects*]. See also Marion R. Casey, "Keeping the Tradition Alive: A History of Irish Music and Dance in New York City," *New York Irish History* 6 (1991–1992): 28.

4. Cullinane, *Aspects,* 38, 25, 46.

5. There are two related Irish traditional dances: the set dance (derived from the quadrille) and the ceili (country or crossroads) dancing. Both incorporate the most basic movements in Irish step dancing (particularly the reel) but are executed by couples or in groups in formations similar to those in other kinds of ethnic folk dances. Set and ceili dancing are social rather than competitive. The most common ceili dances still performed by Irish Americans in the United States are the "Stack of Barley" (a round dance), the "Humours of Bandon" (a square dance), and "The Siege of Ennis" (a long dance). The American folklorist Elizabeth Burchenal visited Ireland before World War I where she recorded in detail the footwork of such Irish social dancing, complete with diagrams. In 1925 she published this research as *National Dances of Ireland.*

6. Breandán Breathnach, *Folk Music and Dances of Ireland* (Cork and Dublin: Mercier Press, 1971), 59–60.

7. See Terry Moylan's review of Helen Brennan, *The Story of Irish Dance* (Dingle, Ireland: Brandon Books, 1999) in *History Ireland* 8, no. 2 (Summer 2000): 51.

8. Breathnach, *Folk Music and Dances,* 53.

9. Ibid., 116–117.

10. Troy and Margaret West Kinney, *The Dance: Its Place in Art and Life* (New York: F. A. Stokes, 1914), quoted in Cullinane, *Aspects,* 17.

11. George Daly, "Life Story of Prof. Thomas P. Hill," in *Souvenir Journal for the Twenty-First Annual Ball of the Tommy Hill Association* (New York: By the Association, 1937), 1; photocopy in possession of the author.

12. Cullinane, *Aspects,* 33. Dates confirmed from the second and ninth programs of the United Irish Counties Association Feis; photocopies in possession of the author.

13. John P. Cullinane, *Further Aspects of the History of Irish Dancing (Ireland, Scotland, Canada, America, New Zealand and Australia)* (Cork: By the Author, 1990), 123 [hereafter cited as Cullinane, *Further Aspects*]. Also Kathleen M. Flanagan, "'Dance and Song of the Gael': Pat Roche and Irish Dance in Chicago, 1933–1953," *New Hibernia Review* 4, no. 4 (Winter 2000): 22–23.

14. Flanagan, "Dance and Song," 24.

15. Ibid., 12.

16. Cullinane, *Further Aspects,* 77, 139.

17. Casey, "Keeping the Tradition," 29, 26.

18. Cullinane, *Aspects,* 25–26.

19. Obituary, "Cyril McNiff, seminal dance teacher," *Irish Echo,* 5 March 1997.

20. Cullinane, *Aspects,* 26–28.

21. Ibid., 36.

22. Ibid., 29.

23. Ibid., 65.

24. Ibid., 80.

25. Ibid., 42.

26. See the website for the Irish Dancing Teachers Association of North America, http://www.idtana.net/.

27. "Irish Step Dancing, The Once and Future Dance," *Irish Dancer* 1, no. 1 (February/March 1998): 4.

28. *Green Fire and Ice* (VHS, Nextgen Video, 1994).

29. Available at http://www.trinitydancers.com/; also "Irish Step Dancing," 4.

30. Cullinane, *Aspects,* 15–16.

SUGGESTED READING

Breandán Breathnach, *Folk Music and Dances of Ireland* (Cork and Dublin: Mercier Press, 1971).

Marion R. Casey, "Keeping the Tradition Alive: A History of Irish Music and Dance in New York City," *New York Irish History* 6 (1991–1992): 24–30.

Natasha Casey, "*Riverdance*: The Importance of Being Irish American," *New Hibernia Review* 6, no. 4 (2002): 9–25.

John P. Cullinane, "Irish Dance World-Wide: Irish Migrants and the Shaping of Traditional Irish Dance," in *The Creative Migrant*, Vol. 3 of *The Irish World Wide*, ed. Patrick O'Sullivan (London and New York: Leicester University Press, 1994), 192–220.

Chapter 18

Irish-American Festivals

Mick Moloney

In late February every year the Irish-American festival season begins, a greening of America that extends across the nation for the following seven months. A survey of listings in Irish-American newspapers such as the *Irish Voice* and the *Irish Echo* in New York, the *Irish American* in Chicago, the *Irish Emigrant* in Boston, and the *Irish Herald* in California reveal a steady stream of advertisements for Irish festivals all spring, summer, and fall. One Irish music society did a national survey of Irish festivals in the United States in 2004 and reported that over sixty Irish festivals of various kinds took place throughout the year, spanning just about half the states in the union.[1] This does not take into account the scores of "Celtic" festivals in the United States and Canada, which also feature a strong Irish component.

During the first seven decades of the twentieth century, occasional small Irish festivals of various kinds were held sporadically in urban America. However, the current phenomenon of Irish-American festivals had its beginnings in the mid-1970s in the wake of Alex Haley's *Roots*, the best-selling book on African-American cultural heritage. In 1975, the book was produced as a television mini-series, which gripped the imagination of the nation and set in motion a search for cultural roots and heritage among Americans of all ethnic backgrounds. *Roots* helped to change American feelings about ethnicity very profoundly, giving rise to a movement that intensified in the nationwide bicentennial celebration of American Independence in 1976. For Philadelphia native Frank Brittingham, who had opened a marginally profitable Irish bar on the outskirts of Philadelphia a few years before, this was the turning point in his business:

> As soon as *Roots* was done—I don't know if it was the next hour or the next week—they were lined up out front. I'll never forget a girl with freckles, white skin, and red hair and her name was Martha Goldberg. She says, "but my great grandmother was Irish"! She was Jewish one hundred percent. I met black people who claimed they had Irish heritage. I met Lithuanians [who said they had Irish ancestry]. I'm telling you, there's hardly too many nationalities I didn't meet through the next six- to nine-month influx of people that were identifying their roots.[2]

The bicentennial became an occasion for a massive celebration of ethnic heritage all across the United States, legitimizing ethnicity in a way that contrasted sharply with the notion of Anglo-American conformity that had been instilled into American official ideology since the Declaration of Independence. This attitude had been promoted at all levels in school curricula all through the twentieth century from coast to coast. Nativists seemed fearful that the fragile unity of the republic could be threatened by too much diversity. Ethnic affiliations with old world cultures were to be kept safely to a manifestation of surface symbols; shamrocks, shillelaghs, parades, fiddle music, singalongs, and green beer were fine as long as it didn't go too much further than that.

But in 1976 there was a definite change. At an official level, the notion of America as a multicultural society received sanction for the first time. Now it became increasingly acceptable to display and celebrate ethnic affiliations without the danger of being labeled unpatriotic. By this time Irish Americans formed a large, diverse, and nationwide population most emphatically entrenched in all aspects of American life. They were also effectively mobilized through a profusion of social and fraternal societies and organizations, which were eager to act as potential sponsors for cultural initiatives. It was in this context that Irish-American festivals began to flourish, along with Irish-related courses in colleges and universities. Shades of green were increasing and deepening.

The late Victor Turner described communal festive occasions as "high tides, peak expressions in social life which mark an occasion or event with ceremony, ritual or festivals. People in all cultures recognize the need to set apart certain times and space for celebration."[3] R. J. Smith and Roger Abrahams also note with rich ethnographic detail the omnipresent urge toward festive celebration in world cultures, particularly at key points in the yearly cycle.[4]

Back in the predominantly agricultural home country that the Irish emigrants left behind, many of the oldest festivals marked the seasonal cycles with such ritual celebration. There were festivals associated with the onset of all the Celtic seasons: *Imbolc* (February 1), *Bealtaine* (May 1), *Lughnasa* (August 1), and *Samhain* (November 1). Added to those were important feast days in the Christian calendar, such as Christmas and Easter, both of which coincided with much older pre-Christian festivals. These seasonal festive occasions were times of both celebration and great social catharsis, when normal social conventions were temporarily set aside and behavior was tolerated that would be considered unacceptable at other times of the year.[5]

By contrast Irish-American festivals emerged as largely secular occasions where Irishness in a multicultural society would be celebrated through the public display of visual symbols of ethnic identity and the presentation of the performing arts, particularly music and dance. One could argue that the biggest Irish-American festivals are held on the move in a sea of green and marching pipe bands in cities and towns across the land in the week up to and including St. Patrick's' Day on March 17th. For over 150 years, this day has been the most visible public celebration of ethnicity in America and had taken its present shape in New York City by 1874 when Ed Harrigan and David Braham wrote their hugely popular song, "The Day We Celebrate," the lyrics of which follow:

> Saint Patrick was a gentleman, sure his name we celebrate
> And on the seventeenth of March the Irish congregate
> A brand new hat on each man's head and a green necktie that's newly made
> The left foot first then lightly tread on the Patrick's Day Parade

And it's two by two away we go up Broadway through rain or snow
We'd face the divil, friend or foe in the Patrick's Day parade.

We shout hurrah for *Erin go Bragh* and all the Yankee nation
Stars and stripes and shamrock bright arrayed
The Irish shout the girls turn out to see the celebration
We march stiff and starch in the Patrick's Day parade.

The parade, despite the rich and meaningful experience it may constitute for attendees, offers a restricted format for the performing arts, arts and crafts displays, foodways, and general interactions that are central to most festive experiences. But when one considers all the associated Irish performing arts activities that take place in bars, restaurants, clubs, and concerts halls in mid-March, it is clear that St. Patrick's Day is in a category unto itself when it comes to the public presentation of ethnic symbols in the Irish diaspora.

The Irish Tradition

There are various words in the Irish language for festival, including *feis* and *fleadh*. Their use is generally specific to the context, each with their own history and meaning. Here, we look at their denotation in the Irish-American context.

The *Feis*

The *Feis* was instituted in the early twentieth century by the Gaelic League. The League developed the idea from an ancient Gaelic festival of the same name that denotes a celebration of the Gaelic arts and the Irish language. The *feis* is now an event in which the focus is primarily on competitive dance. In occasional *fesiseanna* (the plural form of *feis*), there are music, language, literary, and even elocution competitions, each infused with a neo-Victorian concern for correctness, mirroring the original Gaelic League *feis* format. However, the overwhelming majority of *feiseanna* in the United States today are focused entirely on competitive dance.

The *feiseanna* are held year-round all over the United States, wherever there is an Irish-American population of any size within range of a dancing school.[6] The number of *feiseanna*, and also of Irish step dance schools nationwide, has mushroomed since the huge commercial success of *Riverdance* in 1994. In fact, many dance schools run their own *feiseanna* largely to promote the schools. There are local and regional *feiseanna*, and then there are the big regional and national *feiseanna*, where successful dancers can qualify to compete in the biggest and most prestigious *feis* of all: the world dance championships held in Ireland every Easter.

The *Fleadh*

As the ancient festivals which marked significant times in the agricultural calendar in Irish community life gradually disappeared, new festivals were organized in their stead. Founded in Dublin in 1951, Comhaltas Ceoltóirí Éireann (the Irish Musicians Association) revived an older form of music festival known as the *fleadh.* It became a great success, catching on in a big way in Ireland in the 1960s. Nowadays, county and provincial *fleadhanna* take place on selected weekends throughout the summer, culminating in the national *fleadh* held in late August.

The *fleadh* in Ireland has now become a major occasion for traditional musicians, singers, and general audiences to gather and enjoy themselves in informal sessions. The official centerpieces of the *fleadhanna* are the formal competitions for instrumentalists and singers, though in Ireland the competitions are largely ignored by the majority of musicians who attend the *fleadh.* The primary attractions are music sessions and the *craic.*[7]

In America, the *fleadh* is considerably less of a social event. Two regional *fleadhanna* are held each year in Chicago and New York, and sometimes over the years the organizers have had difficulty getting enough competitors to enter. This phenomenon goes in cycles. At the time that the Martin Mulvihill School of Irish Music was in its heyday in the late 1970s, there were upward of several hundred competitors who entered in the New York *fleadh* alone. The main purpose for musicians and singers in entering the competitions in the American *fleadhanna* is to qualify for the All-Ireland competitions back in Ireland. Doing well in these competitions represents a major validation of the diasporic musical culture, and American-born Irish have enjoyed great success in them over the past thirty years. First- and second-place winners qualify to compete in Ireland, and it was not unknown in past years for competitors who had failed to qualify in one competition to fly to the other and give themselves a second chance by entering again. An occasional session might take place at a nearby pub after a *fleadh,* but nothing remotely approaching the magnitude of the music making that attends the *fleadh* in Ireland. In the United States, playing in competition for adjudicators is the main and sometimes the only performing situation one finds in the *fleadh.*

After a low period in the early 1990s when numbers fell off, the American *fleadhanna* have made something of a comeback, and in 2004 there were once again over two hundred competitors in the New York *fleadh.*

The Irish-American Tradition

Basically two kinds of festivals present Irish music and dance in the United States:

1. Folk festivals of a multicultural nature that feature Irish music and dance.
2. Irish festivals organized by Irish-American organizations or individual promoters.

Irish Music in Multiethnic Festivals

Federal, state, and local nonprofit organizations have played an important role in the revitalization of traditional Irish music and dance since the mid-1970s. Over the past thirty years, Irish and Irish-American traditional musicians and dancers have appeared at numerous festivals devoted primarily to the presentation of the folk and traditional arts. These include the Smithsonian Institution's Festival of American Folk-life in Washington, D.C.; the National Folk Festival (the venue rotates all over the nation); the Border Folk Festival in El Paso, Texas; the Frontier Folk Festival in St. Louis, Missouri; the Lowell Folk Festival near Boston, Massachusetts; the Western Folk Festival in Marin County near San Francisco, California; the Cuyahoga Valley Folk Festival near Cleveland, Ohio; and numerous other local folk and traditional arts festivals across America.

Irish musicians resident in America and professional groups on tour from Ireland have appeared at many large multiethnic folk festivals, such as the Philadelphia Folk Festival in Pennsylvania—at the time of writing in its forty-fourth year. My first ever U.S. festival appearance in 1971 with a group called the Johnstons was at this festival, and I marveled at the sight of over ten thousand people gathered for fourteen hours a day in the steamy, hot August weather, completely absorbed with acoustic music in an outdoor setting.

Professional and semiprofessional Irish (often on tour from Ireland) and Irish-American performers with commercial recordings and agents or managerial representation have found a niche at the Wheatland Folk Festival in Michigan; the Winfield Folk Festival in Kansas; the Black Mountain Festival in North Carolina; the Clearwater Festival in New York; the Northwest Folklife Festival in Seattle; the California Traditional Music Festival north of Los Angeles; the Florida Folk Festival in White Springs; and the Celtic Festival in Sebastopol, California. Major folk festivals in Canada include the Vancouver Folk Festival; the Winnipeg Folk Festival; the Edmonton Folk Festival; the Mariposa Folk Festival in Toronto; and, most recently, Celtic Colors on Cape Breton Island in Nova Scotia. Beginning in the mid-1990s, bluegrass and country music festivals started to present Irish performers on a regular basis as well.

Irish-American Community Festivals

The Irish community festival season begins in March with festivals in Texas and Florida. In late spring and throughout the summer, there are festivals in the New York City area, in cities and towns all over New Jersey and Pennsylvania, and in Los Angeles, San Francisco, Chicago, Cleveland, Rochester, Indianapolis, Anchorage, Danbury, Carbondale, and Philadelphia. There are also Irish music festivals throughout the summer in the Catskill Mountains. This was long a vacation spot favored by the New York and Boston Irish, and it now enjoys a new popularity, after a low period between the 1960s and 1990s when Irish Americans took trips back to Ireland in preference to the traditional vacation spots in the Catskills or in Rockaway Beach. The list of festivals is quite extensive; there is even an Irish festival in Clare, Montana!

Some festivals sponsored by Irish organizations have a restricted focus. Over the last three decades a small number of festivals have sprung up which are dedicated almost exclusively to the presentation of strictly traditional Irish music, song, and dance. These are typically produced by small nonprofit Irish-American community organizations staffed by volunteers. The first of these festivals was produced by the Philadelphia Ceili Group in 1975, and it has run annually since that time in various

Music was the main draw at the 2000 Memorial Day Weekend Irish Festival in Chicago's Gaelic Park, as this advertisement from the *Irish American News* indicates. Ranging from traditional and folk to rock, music was performed in a carnival-like atmosphere amid various contests, including story telling, reddest hair, and most freckles. (Mick Moloney Irish American Collection)

sites in the Philadelphia area. Other Irish traditional music and dance festivals run over the past twenty years have included the Snug Harbor Irish Traditional Music and Dance Festival produced annually by the Irish Arts Center of New York City for over a decade in Staten Island, New York, and later in the Bronx before its demise in 1994. There was the Providence Irish Festival sponsored by the Providence Ceili Club in Rhode Island and the Glen Echo Irish Festival produced annually by the Greater Washington Ceili Club in Glen Echo Park, Maryland. This was later cosponsored by the National Council on the Traditional Arts, increased vastly in scale, and moved to Wolf Trap, Virginia. Its final home was in the county fairgrounds in Gaithersburg, Maryland, before it ended in 2000.

In addition, Gaelic Roots was run semiannually and then annually between 1994 and 2003 by the music and Irish studies departments at Boston College. This was more of a teaching week than an actual festival, though there were concerts held throughout the event. The primary focus was on learning. Pupils enrolled in specialized classes in Irish music and dance tailored to their levels of competence. The oldest such educational experience in Irish traditional arts is the Irish Week at the Augusta Heritage Festival at Davis and Elkins College in Elkins, West Virginia. This was started in 1982 and is still running now in its twenty-third year.

Other summer festivals where the emphasis is on teaching and learning are the Swannanoa gathering at Warren Wilson College in Asheville, North Carolina; Irish week sponsored by the Irish Sports and Cultural Heritage Institute in East Durham, New York; and the summer school run at the University of Wisconsin in Milwaukee by Irish Fest. Over the past two decades, Irish traditional artists have been featured with regularity at other summer camps and festivals all over the nation, including Ashoken, New York; the Puget Sound Guitar Workshop in Bellingham, Washington; Fiddle Tunes in Port Townsend, Washington; and the California Traditional Music Society at Soka College in Calabasas, California.

All the organizations running these festivals and summer schools chose to restrict their content to the traditional arts as an affirmative action move on behalf of high-quality, strictly traditional music and dance—cultural elements that their membership considered a neglected and endangered part of the Irish-American cultural heritage. With the exception of the Philadelphia Ceili Group (which chose not to submit grant applications), all have received support from various funding sources, including the Folk Arts Division of the National Endowment of the Arts and their respective state arts agencies. Artists are presented at these festivals in concerts, dances, and thematic workshops. Instructional workshops in step, set, and ceili dancing abound, typically with lots of audience participation.

These Irish music and dance festivals have created new contexts for the performance of Irish music in America. It has been a novel experience for many of the older Irish traditional musicians, for example, to play for the kind of attentive listening audiences that attend these events. In almost all cases, this has reinforced the musicians' own sense of self-esteem and their confidence in their art.

However, the overwhelming majority of the Irish-American festivals are not as restricted in content, format, or artistic merit. They typically offer many types and genres of popular entertainment, and the most successful attract huge crowds. In 2004, the North Texas Irish Festival in Dallas drew over 25,000 people, the Dublin Ohio Irish Festival drew over 70,000, and the granddaddy of them all, Irish Fest in Milwaukee, Wisconsin, attracted an audience of over 125,000.

Many kinds of Irish performing artists are employed to perform at these festivals. In some of the festivals, many of the artists hired fall into the category of commercial performers who specialize in general entertainment. The Leeds Irish Festival, which took place in the Catskill Mountains on Labor Day Weekend 1991, presented eight major Irish and Irish-American acts: Glen Curtin, Jerry Finlay and the Cara band, Johnny Murphy and the Clubmen, Gus Hayes Band, Pat Roper, Celtic Cross, Rutherford's Showband, the Sean O'Neill Band, and, direct from Ireland, the Dixies Showband. All of these are commercial entertainers who perform an eclectic mixture of Irish folk and modern and American popular songs, mostly up-tempo with heavy and loud instrumental accompaniment, emphasizing electric guitar and bass with a heavy dose of electronic keyboards.

The Rockaway Irish Festival, held on Rockaway Beach Boulevard in Queens, New York, on the weekend of July 28th and 29th, 1990, advertised twenty-one major head-lining Irish acts in their full-page ads in the New York Irish newspapers. The acts booked fell into the category of bar-type bands performing more or less in the Clancy Brothers style; Irish pop singers who performed in the showband or "commercial" style with an eclectic repertoire ranging from Irish rebel songs to popular American songs; and "wedding style" bands who played a mixture of every kind of Irish material possible, ranging from country ballads to Irish-American Tin Pan Alley songs. Most of the instruments used were electronically amplified. The emphasis, in short, was on professional and semiprofessional performers who were capable of putting on a show that would please a general, mostly Irish-American audience in an outdoor setting with a lot of ambient noise.

In these kinds of festivals, audience attention is sporadic at best, and quieter as-pects of Irish music such as unaccompanied songs or slow evocative pieces of instru-mental music are generally indifferently received. Hence performers of this kind of material are rarely booked for the majority of commercial Irish music festivals.

Terry George, who attended Irish festivals in the course of his work at the time as a writer at the *Irish Voice*, had this to say in his review of the Hunter Mountain Celtic Festival in his column, dated August 25, 1990:

> The music served up there is a fair representation of what goes on across the country from Florida to Chicago. . . . Pat Roper, a major attraction at many of the Festivals, appeared several times over the weekend at Hunter. . . . The audience were up and down like yo-yo's as the "Wild Colonial Boy" gave way to "Ireland Divided" and led us into a super patriotic finale with the "Halls of Montezuma," "America the Beautiful" and "It's a Long Way to Tipperary." . . . The American and Irish flags were paraded up and down the center of the huge tent, with many of the audience parading behind. As Pat pointed out, it was all for "our lads over in the Middle East." . . . In other tents lesser acts were regur-gitating Clancy Brothers, Wolfe Tones, and Dubliners standards with occasional waltz numbers thrown in.[8]

Based on his experience at Hunter Mountain's Celtic Festival and other Irish festivals like it, George concluded that Irish-American music today is "an uncomfortable mis-leading marriage of American patriotism, Irish Republicanism and schmaltz."[9]

The biggest and most successful Irish-American festivals go beyond the scenario described so compellingly by George.

Brian O'Donovan was the director for the 2004 Irish Connections festival, which was sponsored by the New England Irish Cultural Center in Canton, Massachusetts, drawing an audience of over 27,000. Born in 1957, Brian is an immigrant from County Cork who first came to the United States as a student in 1976. He returned to stay in 1980, married, and began to raise a family. He gained a graduate degree in media stud-ies at Emerson College, and that launched him into event management as the college radio station where he worked had to conduct its own fund-raising. He started out producing acoustic music festivals at the college in the early 1980s. In 1985 Ed Ward and other organizers of the Milwaukee Irish Fest were commissioned by Sullivan Stadium, home of the New England Patriots football team, to organize an Irish festival at the stadium. Ed hired Brian as the local co-coordinator, primarily because of his experience. Sullivan Stadium afterward offered Brian a full-time job as event coordinator.

Brian is intimately familiar with all the work that goes into managing a large festival:

> On the sheer logistics end of it, you've got to consider all things . . . that manage the experience for the festival goer—which is everything from publicity of the event, how they are hearing about it, how they access tickets for it, whether they buy in advance or buy at the gate, what the parking experience is like, what the walking experience to the gate is like—in other words, the sheer physical logistics of somebody accessing the festival. And then afterward when you've taken care of food and beverage and bathrooms and baby care and first aid and security and all that kind of stuff, the content is what really sets it apart. And in both Irish festivals and Celtic festivals or folk festivals for that matter, that's where the differential lies; it's what the content is and how it's presented.[10]

When it came to festival programming, Brian's philosophy is inclusive:

> In the case of Irish festivals . . . I have always operated on the principle [of inclusiveness]. My sensibilities gravitate toward almost the arcane traditional music that I would listen to myself, but in designing festivals I always looked at where we were, what were we doing, what was the market we were trying to develop. And I always had a very commercial sense of what needed to be included in the festival for it to be successful. So the simple principle I always adopted . . . is that everybody that comes to a festival like that should leave happy, and that means you are dealing with an extraordinarily diverse audience.
>
> First of all you're dealing with the diaspora, and in Irish music you're dealing beyond the diaspora because you're dealing with people who are not Irish at all but are attracted for a variety of reasons. They are interested in folk music; they are interested in ethnic music; they are interested because they went to Ireland one time. Especially in areas like the Northeast you've got to account for that, and yet you've to account for the graying demographic of the old Irish American—2nd, 3rd, or 4th generation—whose access to Ireland is through the old-style Irish radio shows . . . people who've been listening to Bing Crosby or the Wolfe Tones. If you can satisfy all those types, and it's not an easy thing to do, that's when you're creating a festival in America that's a truly successful Irish festival.[11]

Under Brian's artistic direction all of these elements are present, and there is also an educational component with a literary and crafts area.

Organizing a festival with high artistic content does require an artistic vision, and this is not something that is generally possessed in Irish fraternal or cultural societies in the United States. Even if the expertise exists, it is more often than not likely to be stifled by the process of decision by committee.

Putting on a festival can be a dauntingly risky venture for any nonprofit, largely volunteer-run, cultural organization. There are many variables, including most crucially the weather, which may affect attendance. There are now new concerns such as national security alerts, which can keep people away. Brian says that John Ashcroft's upgrading of a security code warning may have lowered attendance significantly at a number of New England cultural events in 2004. But if managed properly, a well-organized festival should be the biggest fund-raising event of the year and can make a very public statement about an Irish-American cultural organization's goals and mission.

Over 27,000 people attended the 2004 Irish Connections festival in Massachusetts. The total festival budget was close to $250,000, which included an artistic budget of $90,000. Admission fees mostly generated the revenues; the ticket price was $12 for each of the three days of the festival. The fee charged to vendors (an $800 flat fee) also provided a large revenue. The festival audience was cleverly drawn through the vendors' area before they could get into the performing events. On sale was the typical wide range of products found in Irish import stores: St. Brigid's crosses, Irish postcards and greeting cards, replicas of Celtic high crosses, calendars, and buttons. There were scores of Kelly green tee shirts, shillelaghs, and shamrocks, along with high-end tasteful modern Irish pottery, china, crystal, glassware, music and dance CDs, videos and DVDs, and a variety of books on Irish history and culture. The whole environment was permeated by a curious combination of expensive and cheap, arty and kitsch, real and fake. The range of products was vast. According to Brian, "people can buy leprechauns or they can buy the Book of Kells."[12]

Whether the organization structure is nonprofit or strictly entrepreneurial, typically there is a pivotal person or small group of people who do the booking of artists for the festival. Some organizers will be governed by primarily commercial motives and others less so. Yet, in order to ensure the continuity of the event, both may ideally want to show a profit, as well as realize some kind of artistic vision.

Gertrude Byrne has been organizing Irish-American music festivals since the 1970s. She and her husband owned a bar in the Bronx in the early 1970s, and in 1972 they started to bring out bands from Ireland. First, they performed just at the bar; later, she organized national tours for the performers. According to Gertrude, there were no Irish festivals going on at that time. In 1976 she and her husband moved from the Bronx and bought a business in the town of Leeds in the Catskills. She attended a country music festival in the area at the time, and that gave her the idea of starting an Irish festival. She organized her first festival in 1978 and has been running them since. She says her most successful venture artistically was the Day in the Bog Festival, which she ran for four years in the Bronx until the production costs grew too great. She also organizes fall and winter weekends in the Catskill Jewish resorts like the Neville House and a cruise in the Caribbean every January that attracts over two thousand customers. The greatest difference between running strictly bar events and festivals is the scale involved. Gertrude comments:

> The difference is that . . . you've got to use a variety of different bands. What I try to do with the cruises and with the festivals and with anything I do of any kind of magnitude at all is I try to give the people a choice, because not everybody is into the same kind of music, so that—depending on whether they are into showbands, or into set dancing, or they are into folk, or whatever—it is to give then an across the board spread. . . .

The Pines, a five-hundred-room resort in New York's Catskill Mountains, was the venue for an annual Irish Weekend during the last quarter of the twentieth century. In advertisements such as this one from the *Irish Echo*, promoter Gertrude Byrne likened the experience to a "cruise on land," no doubt in response to the popularity of Irish-themed Caribbean cruises that began in 1990. (Mick Moloney Irish American Collection)

A showband to me is one that has the whole lot: brass, the whole works, upbeat Irish country, or upbeat Irish tempo, the combination of different sounds. . . . It seems to be the bands from Ireland that have that—Dominic Kirwin, Declan Nearny, Patrick Feeney. Some American bands do as well—Celtic Cross, the New York Irish Showband.[13]

To promote her productions, Gertrude relies on heavy print advertising, word of mouth, and her own personal mailing list of over 100,000. Although her audience is varied, it is predominantly older Irish Americans with their spouses or partners who may or may not have Irish ancestry.[14]

There are Irish festivals now held indoors at resorts in the Catskills Mountains in the winter and early spring months, and the first of the festivals held on cruise ships on the high seas was the Irish Festival Cruise sponsored by the Clancy Brothers and Robbie O'Connell in 1990. It has continued annually ever since, spawning dozens of copycats in the process.

Milwaukee Irish Fest

Irish Fest in Milwaukee, held in August every year since 1980 on the banks of Lake Michigan, is by far the biggest Irish Festival in the world. I have performed in fifteen of the twenty-four fests and have had ample firsthand opportunity to observe its growth. The fest is a remarkable celebration of almost every conceivable aspect of Irish and Irish-American culture. Over the years, artists such as Denis Day, John Feeney, Carmel Quinn, and John Gary have performed on adjacent stages with Tommy Makem and Liam Clancy, the Clancy Brothers and Robbie O'Connell, Schooner Fare, Barley Bree, or the Wolfe Tones. These were followed by the likes of major traditional Irish or Irish-American bands such as the Chieftains, Altan, De Danann, Cherish the Ladies, Danu, Dervish, Nomos, the Green Fields of America, or hybrid groups such as Seven Nations and La Bouttine Souriante from Canada and Nightnoise from Portland, Oregon. All this might be interspersed with commercial or traditional musicians and dancers from cities all over the United States.

Milwaukee native Ed Ward has been the major force behind Irish Fest from the beginning:

I had been playing in an Irish band which I started when I was in law school called Blarney, and I was also attracted to the festivals which were currently down on the lakefront. One was a ten-day music festival called Summer Fest for which the grounds were originally built and then improved over the last twenty-four years, and then the Italian group in town put together a festival called Festa Italiana which was based on the old Italian festival [in] the parish of Our Lady of Pompei downtown near the festival ground. I had been a volunteer in . . . Summer Fest. I had enjoyed the festival at the time I volunteered there. . . .

At that time they did not have a very large staff so they relied on a lot of volunteers. So I sat in the administrative offices and was able to learn a lot of the do's and don'ts about operating a festival. . . . I went to Festa because a number of my friends were volunteers. We went down and helped them celebrate and I recall that Saturday in 1980 . . . telling my friends that we needed to start an Irish Fest. Bernie McCartan was in law school with me, and we went to the local Shamrock Club, which I had been a former president of, and told them we wanted their moral support. We also got the local Irish American Legion Post behind us just to make sure we had some support from local organizations. That was it at the time in Milwaukee in terms of Irish organizations. I put together a small board of five people and . . . we started to promote and contact people, and I handpicked the board of directors who were all people I had worked with in various projects in the Irish community—and we were off and running.[15]

Ed had also gained experience in working with Irish music and Irish-American politically connected friends and colleagues, all of which fed into the experience he brought to the early organization and production of Irish Fest:

> I had been promoting Irish concerts and events in Milwaukee, playing in an Irish band and also serving as a distributor of Irish records. I started a business called Irish Music Ltd., and Chuck [Ed's brother] joined me after a while. And I did have important political and community contacts. Interestingly enough, many of the key Irish Fest volunteers who helped get us off the ground had political campaign experience—they were activists, doers—and were also used to working with volunteers. This was a critical factor in our early success.[16]

From his experience at Summer Fest Ed figured that the first-ever Irish Fest could be run on a budget of $250,000. He was working for the county executive at the time and knew a lot of "movers and shakers in the Irish community." With their help, he was able to get support from corporate sponsors who supported their fund-raising efforts. He got modest sponsorships from Irish bars and small businesses. He describes the first event as a "shoestring operation" but a successful one because they ended up making $12,000 profit the first year with an attendance of over fifty thousand.

Irish Festivals Incorporated, which runs Irish Fest, is a nonmembership, nonprofit corporation. According to Ed, "it was never envisaged as a project to make anybody any money, and the original purpose as stated in our articles of incorporation was to promote and preserve the Irish and American-Irish culture."[17]

Irish Fest is governed by a seventeen-member board of directors, all of whom have had extensive experience working at the festival. Everyone on the board is assigned specific areas of responsibilities. A subcommittee of five makes all the artistic and booking decisions on the major stage acts. Irish Fest has over fifteen stages, over one hundred major area coordinators, and over four thousand volunteers. All these are supervised by Executive Director Jane Anderson, one other staff person, and a part-time bookkeeper. Ed feels that this, by any standards, is a remarkable story.

Many contexts exist within the festival for music presentation. They include full-scale concert performances on main stages in front of huge audiences; smaller concerts in more intimate venues, such as the areas the festival organizers have designated as the Pub, the Cultural Area, and the Hedge School; live music for step and ceili dancers in a special dancing area; and numerous groups of acoustic musicians stationed all through the Fest grounds or strolling at large. Beginning in 1991, a separate stage was designated solely for Irish rock or folk rock groups such as the Drovers from Chicago, Black '47 from New York, Bad Haggis from Los Angeles, and the Sawdoctors from Ireland.

Meanwhile, on other parts of the grounds, the tug of war, the Leprechaun, and the

"freckles" contests might be in full swing. On Lake Michigan, *currach* (Irish traditional boat) races take place. There is a schedule of the Irish national games of hurling
and Gaelic football. There are big daily parades and a colorful dog show with lots of
Irish dogs such as setters, terriers, and wolfhounds. There are shows specially designed
for children, theater performances, a folklore tent, and a genealogy area. A local and
national Irish-American history exhibit adds an educational component to the festival
that makes it especially appealing to family audiences:

> People like the quality and the diversity, the ambience, the atmosphere. There's a real
> focus on youth—people like the whole family nature of the festival, the kids' shows, the
> dogs, the parades. It's a total cultural experience instead of just a music festival. . . . It's
> a festival for all ages, the price is reasonable ($12 a day), children twelve and under are
> free. We've tried to make it affordable for families. There are a lot of kids involved in the
> festival. . . . The dance schools are a good example of that. There are over fifteen hun-
> dred kids dancing, and they bring in not only their families but also their grandparents,
> their friends.[18]

Irish Fest is by far the most colorful Irish cultural event in the United States or possibly anywhere in the world. Certainly, color was enhanced immeasurably in the early
years by a policy that gave free admission to anyone dressed as a leprechaun!

The Milwaukee Irish Fest is remarkable in the wide, eclectic range of different
types of Irish performers that it presents. Its scope remains unparalleled, but its production approach has been followed by the people who run the Dublin [Ohio] Irish
Festival[19] and also the organizers of the North Texas Irish Festival, first run in 1986
and since then an annual event.[20] The Irish Fair, held in various locations in Los Angeles, California, each year since 1985, adds "Gaelic Games" to its commercial and traditional music and dance performances. The Cleveland Irish Cultural Festival, held
annually, is a much smaller scale event, but it follows the same eclectic programming
approach, with a strong emphasis on more commercial entertainers.[21]

In 2004, Milwaukee Irish Fest incurred expenses of over $1.7 million. Included in
that figure were the rental fee for using the grounds, public relations costs, tent rentals
and ground setup, insurance, security and performers' fees, hotel, travel and hospitality, union stage hands, and a number of smaller items. Of the profits, 75 percent went
into the festival reserve after paying staff expenses. With this kind of budget, there is a
need for good management and a good business sense:

> [We have] good solid business people on board who bring checks and balances on how
> much we spend and how fast we grow, but our goal is to have at least one year's budget
> in reserve. We have a very good reserve to protect us against a bad year. We want to build
> that up to protect us against two consecutive bad years. The other option is to cut
> expenses. It's becoming very difficult the larger we get to be profitable, and that's going
> to be problematic going forward without major funding.[22]

Of the net surplus, 25 percent goes into the Irish Fest Foundation, which widens
the impact of the festival through a variety of cultural activities:

> In 1993 we put together a foundation to share some of our financial success with the
> local community, the state of Wisconsin and the United States and then Ireland itself.

Three primary areas which we set up the foundation to assist with: one was the civic community, one was cultural, and one was educational. One of our original goals was that we wanted to operate an Irish cultural or community center at some point in time. We delayed on that until 1998. The building finally became reality in 1998 when we purchased an 18,000 sq. ft. Masonic temple built in 1918 in the Milwaukee suburb of Wauwatosa.[23]

Like Brian O'Donovan, Ed sees new challenges emerging all the time, making it increasingly difficult to keep running large festivals at their current level:

We live in a much more complicated world. Issues of immigration, liability, licensing, taxes, and competition for the entertainment dollar present a much greater challenge than in the past. Growth and success present challenges as well. Throwing a party for 130,000 one must always be conscious of how the customer is treated. Major stage assignments affect traffic flow and density on the festival grounds, which affect the ease at which people can get access to food, drinks, restrooms, and good seats at one of our venues. A visit to our festival must be fun, entertaining, and comfortable, but also educational.

We have to try to stay on the cutting edge as well. Our experience with the Ward Irish Music archives has led to the introduction in 2005—our 25th year—of a "roots" tent which [will] entertain and teach people about the tremendous impact Irish music has had on a variety of forms of American music: popular, bluegrass, country, Tin Pan Alley, marching bands, etc. Even though a large percentage of people who visit Irish Fest are not of Irish ancestry, we must continue to grow and broaden our base to be successful. Expenses keep going up, and there are limits on what you can charge for food, beverages, and gate.[24]

According to Ed Ward, Irish Fest represents a commitment to cultural continuity and growth that now goes beyond the actual festival itself:

We've made a commitment that the whole purpose of the festivals is to leave a legacy for younger generations. If we don't accomplish that, then all the money we've made and all the notoriety we've gained doesn't mean much. Our focus became: let's put something aside here. Fifty percent of people who come to Irish Fest are from outside Wisconsin. We were taking these resources and promoting Irish culture and trying to promote it in a way that would benefit people locally but also people outside Wisconsin. We've put into place a lot of things we want to do to continue to promote our mission: the summer school, the archives, the foundation, a full-time Irish center with activities and concerts, and a music school. All these would succeed Irish Fest if it should stop.[25]

The Milwaukee Irish Fest presents in one extraordinarily rich format the full spectrum of possibilities of celebrating Irishness in America. A multigeneric, monoculturally focused event of the magnitude of Irish Fest could not have evolved in Ireland. Its success has not been simply due to good production and marketing and the festival's ability to draw for support on a larger population base but to the fact that the symbols of ethnic cultural identity are much more potent and highly charged in a multicultural environment than in the homeland. Irish Fest could only have happened in the global Irish diaspora.

NOTES

1. Web site: www.azirishmusic.com/fest_irish.htm.

2. Frank Brittingham, taped interview by Mick Moloney, 6 November 1991, Lafayette Hill, PA.

3. Victor Turner, ed., *Celebration: Studies in Festivity and Ritual* (Washington, DC: Smithsonian Institution Press, 1982), 11.

4. Roger Abrahams, "The Language of Festivals: Celebrating the Economy," in *Celebration: Studies in Festivity and Ritual,* ed. Victor Turner, 161–177 (Washington, DC: Smithsonian Institution Press, 1982); R. J. Smith. "Festivals and Celebrations," in *Folklore and Folklife,* ed. R. Dorson, 159–172 (Chicago: University of Chicago Press, 1972).

5. Rambunctious and often drunken cavorting by strawboys and guisers at Biddy Boy (February 1st) and St. Stephen's Day (December 26th) house visiting would be examples of occasions where social norms would be gleefully contravened without the kind of censure that would normally follow such antics. The roots of Halloween trick or treating where children are allowed to misbehave for one day can be found in similar early winter customs.

6. In fact, there does not even need to be the physical presence of a dancing school. Some renowned dancing teachers such as Mrs. Hall in Fresno, California, fly into remote communities in the far west of the United States a few times every month to conduct classes.

7. *Craic* is Irish for "fun"; it is pronounced "krak."

8. Terry George, "Hunter Mountain's Celtic Festival," *Irish Voice,* August 25, 1990.

9. Ibid.

10. Brian O'Donovan, taped interview by Mick Moloney, 20 September 2004, Newton, MA.

11. Ibid.

12. Ibid.

13. Gertrude Byrne, taped phone interview by Mick Moloney, 26 November 2004.

14. Ibid.

15. Ed Ward, taped phone interview by Mick Moloney, 27 October 2004.

16. Ed Ward, personal written communication with Mick Moloney, 19 December 2004.

17. Ward, interview by Moloney.

18. Ibid.

19. The Dublin Irish Festival is unique among Irish-American festivals in being produced by a municipality. It is run by the City of Dublin, Division of Community Relations, with the assistance of all city departments, the Dublin Irish Festival Committee, community volunteers, and the support of the Dublin City Council. A portion of the festival budget is generated from the City of Dublin hotel/motel tax fund, with additional funds coming from corporate sponsorships.

20. This Texas event has achieved the distinction of being the only Irish Festival ever to be "snowed out." I was one of the many victims of a calamitous snowstorm that struck the Dallas area in early March 1988 and spent a weekend holed up in the Quality Hotel, entertained enormously by the window view of Texas drivers trying valiantly to circumnavigate the unfamiliar icy highways.

21. John O'Brien, a native of Athlone and the prime mover in the organization of the Cleveland Irish Festival in the mid-1980s, saw the aim of the festival as more than simple entertainment and fund raising. (The profits from the 1991 event were donated to Project Children, which brings children from Northern Ireland to the United States.) O'Brien stated:

> We wanted to have a weekend with many aspects of our rich Irish culture that we could get. . . . We've grown in every aspect since then [the beginning]. Last year we embarked on a summer school that was very successful in bringing more of our historical culture

to people who wanted to learn more of their heritage, their roots and their history. (Quoted by J. C. Sullivan in an article on the festival in the *Irish Echo*, August 28–September 3, 1991)

22. Ward, interview by Moloney.

23. Ward, written communication with Moloney.

24. Ibid.

25. Ward, interview by Moloney.

SUGGESTED READING

R. J. Smith, "Festivals and Celebrations" in *Folklore and Folklife*, ed. R. Dorson, 159–172 (Chicago: University of Chicago Press, 1972).

Victor Turner, ed. *Celebration: Studies in Festivity and Ritual* (Washington, DC: Smithsonian Institution Press, 1982).

Chapter 19

Irish Americans in Sports
The Nineteenth Century

Ralph Wilcox

As the names "Fighting Irish," "Celtics," and other symbolic remnants of Gaelic influence have become deeply embedded in the popular consciousness of American athletic culture, it must be recognized that sport represents a significant yet complex chapter in the story of Irish America. It is a tale that spans the rude and all too frequently brutal world of the nineteenth-century prize ring, the continuing practice of traditional sports within the urban remnants of Gaelic ethnic enclaves, and the stunning accomplishments by Irish Americans at the pinnacles of sporting endeavor: the Olympic Games, the professional sports arena, and intercollegiate athletics.

As Irish men, women, and children departed from their homeland for America during the nineteenth century, they left behind a system of sport patterned on that found in England. While field sports such as fishing, shooting, and hunting were popular among Ireland's landed gentry, the great majority of the Irish devoted what little recreational time they had to the pursuit of simple athletic traditions practiced in the fields, on rural lanes, and at county fairs. For the most part, organized sport was controlled by the Amateur Athletic Association of England. It was not until 1884 that the Gaelic Athletic Association was founded, primarily as a response to this absentee control. In the years that followed, Ireland witnessed a resurgence in popularity of the traditional and ancient Tailtean Games, which, evidence suggests, predated the ancient Greek Olympic festivals. Above all, this late-nineteenth-century Gaelic athletic revival brought increased structure and codification to the traditional team sports of hurling and Gaelic football.

Searching for identity and status in their new home, Irish immigrants soon discovered that their participation in fishing, billiards, cockfighting, pugilism, pedestrianism (the predecessor of track and field), swimming, rowing, cricket, and, eventually, baseball pleased America's leaders who saw their fundamental responsibility as forging a new and unified nation out of the thousands of culturally diverse immigrants who were landing on their shores daily. Beyond the search for acceptance, experience showed Irish Americans that these sports could become a ladder for socioeconomic advancement—an important motivation for many immigrants.

Kings of the Ring: Irish-American Prizefighters

It is quite likely that more has been written about Irish-American success in the prize ring over the past 150 years than about any other ethnic group in sport. Indeed, a veritable library of biographies, novels, films, manuals, and newspaper and magazine accounts has, over time, built a reputation of mythical proportions for the Irish-American prizefighter. It is regrettable that so many commentators have found it necessary to dwell on Irish Americans' pugilistic endeavors at the expense of his other athletic pursuits and cultural contributions. It has long been argued by scholarly proponents of "ethnic succession" that throughout history boxing has witnessed its greatest appeal among oppressed minorities, promising them a rapid escape from poverty and discrimination. The Irish immigrant has surely done his best to reaffirm this belief. Such colorful characters as Sam O'Rourke, Cornelius Horrigan, John C. "Benecia Boy" Heenan, James "Yankee" Sullivan, and John Morrissey graced the antebellum American prize ring. James Ambrose "Yankee" Sullivan was born in Ireland in 1807. He earned his nickname from the American flag that he proudly wore around his waist in the ring. In 1853, Sullivan lost his American heavyweight title to fellow Irishman John Morrissey, who had earlier settled in New York City. Morrissey went on to be elected to the U.S. Congress in 1866, and again in 1868, lending support to the notion that Irish Americans treated boxing and politics with comparable passion.

Nor would the story change in the years following the Civil War, as the nation's foremost heavyweight fighters remained of Irish-American stock. Paddy Ryan, Jake Kilrain, John L. Sullivan, and "Gentleman Jim" Corbett each attested to the Gaels' affinity for the sport. The most prominent of America's golden age athletes was John L. Sullivan, better known as the "Boston Strong Boy." Born in 1858, the son of Irish immigrants, Sullivan was the link between the London Prize Ring and the Marquis of Queensbury Rules, pioneering the transition from bareknuckle boxing to the gloved era. World heavyweight champion from 1882 to 1892, Sullivan has been credited with anywhere between seventy-five and two hundred victories in the ring. The subject of at least nine autobiographical and biographical works, "John L." became the first modern sporting superstar. His career purse exceeded one million dollars, an enormous amount of money at the time.

Rough hewn and fond of the bachelor subculture of the saloon, Sullivan pioneered sporting celebrity status as his name recognition reached outside the prize ring and extended far beyond America's shores. Among his personal, entrepreneurial ventures that he used to supplement the purses from prizefights was a token appointment as sports editor of the New York–based *Illustrated News*, his endorsement of a Lipton Beef Company product, his numerous and varied stage roles, and even an attempt to establish his own "John L. Sullivan Motion Picture Company." Having met with royalty, Pope Leo, and every president since James A. Garfield, Sullivan's decision to pursue the favorite Irish career path of politics might have been expected. Failing in his bid to win a seat in the Massachusetts House of Representatives in 1895, and losing on the New York City ballot for alderman four years later, he eventually withdrew from a second congressional race in the Bay state.

The West Coast Irish in San Francisco sent James J. Corbett (1866–1933) to claim the heavyweight title from John L. Sullivan in 1892 under the newly adopted Marquis of Queensbury Rules. Corbett used the transition to gloves to his advantage, and it turned out to be a major shift in the sport that former bareknuckle champion Sullivan could only withstand until the twenty-first round. (Library of Congress, Prints and Photographs Division, LC-USZ62-104972)

Professionals at Play: Irish-American Pedestrians and Rowers

Pedestrian meets also offered poor Irish immigrants the opportunity to fill their pockets with prize money. While Edward Payson Weston is most often remembered as America's nineteenth-century "Champion Pedestrian of the World," the comparable achievements of Daniel O'Leary have frequently gone unnoticed. Born in County Cork, Ireland, in 1846, O'Leary immigrated to New York City at the age of twenty. Moving on to Chicago, his career as a professional pedestrian began with the defeat of Weston in a two-hundred-mile race in October 1874. One year later O'Leary won the $1,000 stake by beating Weston in a six-day walking match held in Chicago.

Weston's complaints of foul play were largely responsible for a long-awaited rematch at the Agricultural Hall in London, England, beginning on Easter Monday of 1877. Billed as "the greatest athletic feat on record," the $5,000 stake generated enormous interest, and the spectacle attracted upward of twenty thousand spectators. Once again, the Irish American was victorious covering a record 520 miles in six days. The London match might be considered to be the most important event in the relatively short-lived history of pedestrianism because it prompted Sir John Astley, eager to promote the sport further, to establish the Astley Belt Championship. The year 1878 saw the first Astley Belt race held in London before thirty thousand spectators. The *Irish World* described the significance attached to the contest thus:

> Being an international match, the honor of old England was at stake and a score of the very best legs in Britain were put on the track to keep the belt from getting into the hands of a Yankee and an Irishman. Parliament had officially adjourned to derive pleasure from the spectacle and give cheer to the noble Britons.

O'Leary beat his English challengers handily, winning the Astley Belt and $3,750 in prize money and gate receipts.

In October 1878, O'Leary returned to New York City to defeat John Hughes, a fellow Irish American, at Gilmore's Garden in the second running for the Astley Belt. Promised the opportunity to win the belt outright, the world champion took on all comers in New York the following year. Among his challengers were John Ennis, who had arrived in Chicago from Ireland in 1869, and Patrick Fitzgerald, another Irish-American resident of New York. O'Leary was expected to win, but an Englishman, Charles Rowell, took the belt and $20,398 in prize money. Accused of having thrown the race, O'Leary went on to establish the O'Leary Belt Race for the championship of America. The first running took place in Madison Square Garden in 1879.

In addition to the prize ring and the pedestrian arena, rowing presented early Irish immigrants the opportunity to earn fame and fortune in a familiar sporting milieu. Although the professional rowing community of northeastern stevedores was a world apart from the fraternal life of America's most prestigious colleges, it appears that professional boat races were afforded some legitimacy by mainstream American society. Fully entrenched in the labor traditions of northeastern ports, Irish Americans took to rowing with great vigor, forming such prominent boat clubs as Boston's Maid of Erin, Young Men's Catholic Lyceum, St. Mary's Temperance Society, and St. James Young Men's Catholic Total Abstinence; Albany's Celtic Boat Club; New York City's Young Irish-Americans and Emerald; Buffalo's Celtic, Hibernian, and Robert Emmet clubs; as well as the Hibernian Rowing Club of Newport, Rhode Island; and Portland, Maine's Emerald Boat Club. Challenges frequently appeared in the Irish-American press of the day as stakes, set between $250 and $1,000 a side, regularly attracted crowds of thirty thousand spectators.

The fact that Irish Americans dominated the professional rowing scene throughout the last three decades of the nineteenth century cannot be challenged. Among the leading scullers of the 1870s were Irishmen by the name of Thomas C. Butler, George Faulkner, Patsy Regan, J. J. O'Leary, and James O'Donnel. From 1885 through the turn of the century, the list of national amateur champions included such names as Daniel

J. Murphy, Martin F. Monahan, D. Donoghue, John J. Ryan, William Caffrey, and Joseph Maguire.

Emerald Diamonds: Irish Americans and the National Pastime

By 1870, baseball emerged as America's uncontested "national pastime," and Irishmen flocked in droves to the diamond. Some of them claimed that baseball had its origin in the ancient Gaelic game of *Iomain*, so feeding a need for ethnic identity and pride. Irish teams sprang up across the country in the years following the Civil War. The Shamrock (Holyoke, Woburn, and Boston, Massachusetts; Concord, New Hampshire; and Galt, Ontario), Fenian (Augusta, Georgia; and New Orleans), Celtic (Montreal), Emerald (Savannah, Georgia), Hibernian Green (San Francisco and Boston), and Plaid Stocking (Geddes, New York) baseball clubs suggest widespread Gaelic affiliation. Still other teams popularized the names of Irish national heroes, such as the Emmet (Woburn, Massachusetts, and Savannah, Georgia) and Owen Garvey (Pittsburgh) teams.

While the national pastime found broad appeal among immigrants, it was the professional players who won baseball laurels for Irish America. The reputation of Irish ballplayers soon became so great that others began to take Irish names to help them in their baseball careers. In 1872, a correspondent to the *Sporting News* claimed that one-third of major league players were of Irish extraction. By the turn of the century, another observer noted that "all the prominent clubs of last year were captained by Irish Americans," including Kelly (Brooklyn), Delehanty (Philadelphia), Collins (Boston), Donovan (St. Louis), Doyle (Chicago), Gleason (Detroit), McGraw (Baltimore), and Duffy (Milwaukee). Indeed, a stroll through the Baseball Hall of Fame, in Cooperstown, New York, reminds the contemporary visitor of the deep presence of professional Irish baseball players in the nineteenth century. It is no stretch to say that Roger Patrick Bresnahan (the "Duke of Tralee"), Tom Connolly, Joe Cronin, the Delehanty brothers, Hugh Duffy, Tim Keefe, "Wee Willie" Keeler, Joe Kelley, George Kelly, Cornelius McGillicuddy (better known as Connie Mack), "Iron Man" McGinnity, Tim Murnane, Jim O'Rouke, "Big Ed" Walsh, "Smiling Mickey" Welsh, and the incomparable Mike "King" Kelly could just as easily have constituted the passenger manifest of a steam packet arriving at Boston in the 1840s.

The "king" of baseball, Michael Joseph Kelly, was the son of an Irish immigrant papermaker, born in Troy, New York, in 1857. Making his debut with the Olympic Club of Patterson, New Jersey, in 1877, he went on to record a superlative professional career as a catcher, outfielder, and shortstop with the Buckeye Club of Columbus, Ohio; the Cincinnati Red Stockings; and the Chicago White Stockings. His subsequent "sale" to the Boston Red Stockings in 1887 was unprecedented in the sport and, while causing a furor in baseball circles, brought the "Ten Thousand Dollar Beauty" immediate renown. Best remembered for his base running and sliding abilities, his name was immortalized in the popular song, "Slide, Kelly, Slide," celebrating his eighty-four stolen bases during his first season in Boston. Later, in a stage adaptation of Ernest L. Thayer's *Casey at the Bat*, Kelly was cast in the title role alongside the

Boston Beaneaters center fielder Hugh Duffy (1866–1954) led the major leagues in home runs when this studio portrait was taken in 1895. According to press opinion at the time, baseball "teams need an infusion of Irish blood to make it [*sic*] win and that crafty Irishmen provided the sport with its generals and diplomats." Duffy was apparently intelligent, aggressive, and intimidating on the field. (Library of Congress, Prints and Photographs Division, LC-USZ62-123524)

London Gaiety Girls. Appearing in 1888, Thayer's musical featured lyrics about mythical baseball players, all with typical Gaelic names such as Blake, Cooney, Flynn, and, of course, Casey.

Of Gaelic Games and the Olympics: Irish Americans in Track and Field

Although Irish-American interest in track and field athletics might be viewed as a logical extension of their affinity for pedestrianism, the two sports possessed separate and unique pedigrees. Footraces, hurdling, jumping, and throwing events, which had long been part of native celebrations in rural Ireland, were soon included in Gaelic events in America. Many Irish immigrants used their athletic prowess for monetary gain as North American clubs sponsored an annual professional circuit of traditional Caledonian and Hibernian games. Yet the most significant contribution of Irish Americans to the sport was reserved for the highly respected, organized, and socially prestigious amateur track and field competitions of the 1890s.

Modeled after its London counterpart, the New York Athletic Club had opened its doors in 1868. Frequented by Astors, Belmonts, Roosevelts, Vanderbilts, and others of New York Knickerbocker Society, it was to be the best part of three decades before the first Irish-American athletes were found competing for the "Winged Footers." Due in large part to the exclusionary policies and practices of the New York Athletic Club, the Boston Athletic Association, and similar elitist organizations, Irish athletic clubs were formed in New York City and Boston during 1879. Later changing their names to Irish-American athletic clubs, they became powerful forces in international track and field by the turn of the century.

At its inaugural international track and field meet with the London Athletic Club in September 1895, the New York Athletic Club was represented by at least three Irish-American athletes; among them was J. T. Coneff who was born in County Kildaire in 1866. Running for the New York club, he won both the mile and three-mile events, while Thomas E. Burke, "the Lowell Mercury," won the 440-yard race. The following year, while representing the Boston Athletic Association, Burke ran to victory in the hundred-meter and four-hundred-meter events at the first modern Olympiad in Athens. Increasing Irish-American representation in Greece was Tom Curtis, who won the 110-meter hurdles race. At the Paris Olympics in 1900, Irish-born Mike F. Sweeney (high jump champion of the world from 1892 to 1895) took home 750 francs for winning the hundred-meter race, the high jump and long jump events for professional athletes. John F. Flanagan, a New York City policeman who was born in Limerick in 1868, won the Olympic hammer event for the New York Athletic Club. After winning the Metropolitan and Junior National Championships of the Amateur Athletic Union in 1904, the Greater New York Irish-American Athletic Association was represented at the St. Louis Olympics by Flanagan, who retained his Olympic title in hammer throwing; Martin Sheridan, who won the discus event; and, Jim Mitchell, who had come to America with the Gaelic Athletic Association's "invasion" of 1888.

The story of Irish-American Olympic success continued in 1908 when Flanagan became the first modern Olympic athlete to win three successive titles in a standard event. Once again, Flanagan found ample Celtic company in Sheridan who won his second gold medal, and another New York City policeman, Matt McGrath, who finished in second place in the hammer throw. Later joined by Pat McDonald and Pat Ryan, these athletic behemoths became known collectively as the "Irish Whales," each one a son or grandson of Ireland. Most of the "Whales" were members of the New York City police department.

Perhaps the most accomplished Irish-American athlete at the turn of the century was James Brendan Connolly. Born in South Boston in 1868, the son of Irish immigrants, Connolly became the first modern Olympic victor with the revival of the games in 1896, when he won the first event, the triple jump. He is now much better known as the author of twenty-five best-selling maritime novels and two hundred

short stories than as the exceptional athlete he was. After passing its entrance examination, in October 1895, Connolly enrolled at the Lawrence Scientific School of Harvard University to study engineering. His hopes of playing football for the "Crimson"
were dashed when he broke a collarbone in the first scrimmage. Joining the university
track team, Connolly won the amateur hop, step, and jump championship of the
United States at his first attempt. After his request for an eight-week leave of absence
was turned down by the Harvard University administration, Connolly chose to for-
sake a collegiate education in favor of paying his own way to the Olympic Games in
Athens. Representing the South Boston Athletic Club, Connolly recorded a first place
in the triple jump, second place in the high jump, and third place in the broad (long)
jump. Traveling to Paris in 1900 to defend his Olympic triple jump title, Connolly
placed second. Soon after, he left athletics to become a sportswriter for the *Boston
Globe* and went on to serve as a correspondent for *Colliers Magazine* during World
War I.

By the turn of the century, Irish-American athletes had begun to wrest the track
and field laurels from Scottish pioneers and members of the exclusive athletic clubs
for New York's Irish-American Athletic Club (IAAC). The emblem of the IAAC—a
green fist set against a background of green shamrock inserts, and traversed by a diag-
onal band of red, white and blue—was displayed victorious on the winner's podium
in stadiums the world over.

Sport and the Preservation of Irish Identity in America

It is important to note that the Irish immigrants' ready acceptance of, and participation in, the popular American sports of the day rarely constituted total assimilation.
The Irish-American athlete's insistence on Gaelic names for his rowing, baseball, track
and field, and lacrosse teams, while taking every opportunity to "parade the green" in
the sporting arena, helped satisfy the group's need to maintain a strong sense of cultural identity. Yet Irish-American sport also provided an abundance of evidence to
support the existence of intra- and intercultural conflict. While it is generally believed
that the unparalleled success of nineteenth-century Irish prizefighters did much to
change the self-esteem of their fellow countrymen, others saw it differently. As early as
1871, the *Irish World* cautioned:

> The Irish, from their connection with the English, have unfortunately acquired some of
> the barbarous habits and customs of the Saxons, as they did their language. But Irish-
> men even in the prize ring are not wholly lost to honor. The genuine Celt fights, not for
> money, but for fame—such poor fame as it is—and he could never forget his manhood
> so far as to make himself, like the Saxon villain, a bull-terrier gladiator for the sport of a
> blackleg nobility.

To set the blame on English soil was not unexpected, but still questions surrounding the moral virtue and worthwhile qualities of prizefighting could not be denied. As
one observer pointed out, "the rugged young men who survived [bare knuckle fights]

did their share to give the Irish a bad name by being usually either Irish or of second generation Irish stock." Moreover, at the same time as the "Boston Strong Boy" was being honored as a civic hero upon ascending the throne of world heavyweight champion, one local newspaper reported that "blue-blooded Boston is disgusted with the notoriety the Hub has gained through the brutal victory of its hard hitting son, Sullivan." Soon the middle-class, literary, lace-curtain Irish joined the fray, denouncing the Gaelic domination of the American prize ring as "human butchery," promoted by a "worthless, gambling class of lodgers" who frequented saloons, poolrooms, and other "gilded haunts." Such perceptions did much to fuel the common stereotype of the ignorant, drunken, belligerent, and pugnacious Irish buffoon so actively ridiculed by "polite" American society.

Indeed, while the Gaelic immigrant's physical proficiency often confirmed the Anglo-American Protestant stereotype that painted the Irish as having strong backs but weak minds, it also furnished an opportunity to advance the process of assimilation. As the nineteenth century wore on, the playing field increasingly became the pit in which cultural and political squabbles between immigrants and the Yankee establishment were settled. The annual encounter between the Maid of Erin and Harvard crews on the Charles River reflected a fundamental cleavage between Boston's Irish Catholic neighborhoods and New England's Puritan families. The words of a ballad written by the Reverend William R. Huntingdon, of the Harvard class of 1859, suggest a disguised satisfaction at his boat's triumph over the Irish-crewed Fort Hill Boy. Mocking all that is Irish, the accent, the dialect and open self-confidence, the author questions the trustworthiness of the losing crew whose payment of bets was dependent upon victory, an indication of their poverty and professional status. Reversing Irish ridicule of the Harvard "lady pets," "fops," and "Beacon Street swells," Huntingdon paints the social and athletic superiority of the university shell over the flat-bottomed ferry scow as beyond all doubt. Yet, perhaps such contests served as a cathartic outlet, replacing outright conflict with regularly scheduled and socially sanctioned clashes.

If Irish-American athletes found increased pleasure in waging war with other ethnic groups in the sports arena, the English became their favored adversary and John L. Sullivan their leading warrior. The "Boston Strong Boy" made a point of wearing green breeches in the ring and readily exhibited the contempt for Englishmen so common among his oppressed forbears. On one occasion, in Canada, he publicly declined to toast "Her Majesty" adding that, "A true Irishman never drinks the health of a British ruler, King or Queen." If such ethnocentric taunting angered anglophiles in the New World, he would commonly follow up with a calm and diplomatic appeal to their patriotism. Later, at the 1908 Olympic Games in London, the Irish-American disdain for the English resurfaced. That year, the American team included at least ten members of the Irish Athletic Club. Indeed, so prominent was Irish-American representation on the national team that a *Times* editorial went so far as to suggest that "owing to the number of Irish-Americans among their members, it might almost be said that the British athletes . . . competed with Irishmen, not Americans." The most memorable event at these Games was Ralph Rose's refusal, at the urging of his "Irish

Whale" teammates, to lower the Stars and Stripes before King Edward VII. His team-mate Martin Sheridan later famously explained that the American flag "dips to no earthly king."

Viewed as an instrument of assimilation, sport could also strengthen the search for ethnic independence and resistance to American nationalist attempts at cultural homogenization. Following the 1873 Irish National Games in Philadelphia, the *Irish World* posited: "Few, if any, who either participated in, or were spectators of, those manly games, were not forcibly reminded of home and fatherland. . . . The Germans, Scotch, English, and others have their national games, and why not We?" Eventually an increasing number of Irish-American militia, religious, political, benevolent, and cultural organizations included "Irish Games" on the program at their annual picnics and excursions. From the Fenian Brotherhood to the Ancient Order of Hibernians, St. Patrick's Mutual Alliance Association, Catholic Total Abstinence and Benevolent Society, and Young Men's Catholic Abstinence Society, members thronged to sites across the country to compete in footraces, hurdling, jumping events, throwing the light and heavy stone, boat races, and target shoots. By 1871, members of the Clan Na Gael Association of New York were joined at their second annual picnic by representatives from Troy, New York; Wilmington, Delaware; and Philadelphia, Pennsylvania. Including Gaelic football and hurling matches on the program, a reporter explained that "the object of these associations is not dissimilar to that of the German Turnverein. It aims at the physical, social, and intellectual elevation of the Irish in America. It promotes a love of literature and social life in its clubrooms and in its gymnastic exercises it helps develop the Irish muscle."

Advertisements appeared in the local press urging Irish Americans to join native excursions to Spy Pond, outside of Boston, and Jones' Wood in New York. By 1878, the Clan Na Gael picnic in New York attracted thirteen thousand participants. As purses grew, the festivals began to attract professional athletes. At the Emerald and Hamilton Rowan Clubs' picnic at Jones' Wood in 1878, "a leading feature of the occasion was the Irish national games and an athletic match between Duncan O. Ross, the Scottish champion, and James Lynch, the Irish athlete for $500 a side and the championship of the world."

Irish-American militia groups had appeared in New York City by mid-century and soon spread across the country. The Irish Dragoons (New York), Hibernian Rifles (San Francisco), League of St. Patrick (San Francisco), Green Isle (New York), Shamrock (New York), Celtic (New York), Irish Jasper Greens (Savannah, Georgia), and Irish Rifles (Cincinnati, Greenwich, Charleston, New Orleans, and New York) rifle clubs and companies left little doubt as to their Gaelic affiliation. Other associations such as the McMahon (San Francisco), Montgomery (San Francisco and New York), Meagher (San Francisco and New York), and John Mitchel Guards (New York and New Orleans), together with the Wolfe Tone (San Francisco and New York), Sarsfield (New York and San Francisco), Emmet (New York, San Francisco, Savannah, Albany and St. Louis), and O'Connell Rifles (New York) were named after Irish nationalist heroes.

While some might argue that the establishment of these organizations was a response to the exclusionary policies of "native" companies, the Fenian agitation of 1866 and the deeply held belief that one day they would return to liberate Ireland from the grip of England's "John Bull" suggested an alternate motive. Moreover, an article in the *Irish World* suggested that newfound democracy might have played a part in the rapid growth of Irish-American militia groups. As the author explained: "In Ireland the people are denied by law the right to bear arms; [whereas] in the United States it is deemed a patriotic duty in citizens to enroll themselves in military organizations." Nevertheless, many Americans continued to condemn foreign-born militia for fostering divided loyalties and standing in the way of assimilation. By the turn of the century, most groups had undergone a metamorphosis with the once active militia becoming competitive rifle clubs.

In 1881, a reporter for the *Boston Pilot* noted that "a large number of the Irish people in Boston are becoming interested in the exhibition of the games and pastimes of their ancestors." Traditional Irish sports were not new to America. In New York, Irish Americans practiced handball throughout the city's neighborhoods from their earliest arrival, while organized hurling teams first began to appear in the 1850s. Considered to be the most ancient of Irish sports, the earliest reference to organized hurling (*Caman* in Celtic, and *Iomain* in Gaelic) in the United States was the formation of a club in San Francisco in 1853. It was to be another four years before the Irish Hurling and Football Club was established in New York to revive that "truly Irish national sport." In the following thirty years, the New York, Emmet, Wolfe Tone, Brooklyn, Geraldine, and Men of Ireland teams promoted the game in New York while, following its earliest introduction to New England by the Irish Athletic Club of Boston in 1879, the *Boston* and *Shamrock* hurling clubs promoted the sport further afield. However, it could never be said that the sport flourished during these years. As one observer explained:

> When men are selected who understand the scientific way to play the national game. When men will play for the sake of the sport and not for the winning of a certain amount of money. When men will endeavor to strike the ball and not the man. When suitable grounds are secured and when the players will endeavor to imitate the game as played in ancient times . . . then indeed Ireland's national game, hurling, will become popular in every state in this great country.

The Gaelic Athletic Association's tour of North America in 1888 had a noticeable influence on the growth of hurling by the turn of the century. One correspondent optimistically reported:

> Since the Gaelic Invasion of America . . . hurling has taken a firm root on American soil, and the present series of games at the magnificent grounds at Celtic Park for the James R. Keane Cup are certain to arouse an amount of interest and enthusiasm, and to make the Irish national pastime extremely popular with the exiled Gaels of Greater New York.

The Greater New York Irish-American Athletic Association awarded the Keane Gaelic Hurling Trophy to the City's champion team, while in New England clubs competed for the John Boyle O'Reilly Hurling Cup.

Gaelic football does not appear to have shared the widespread following that hurling claimed. The earliest account of an organized team occurred in New Orleans, in 1859, where the game was first promoted by Irish fire companies and later by clubs

This team fielded by the Gaelic Society of New York (pictured on the grounds of Hicks Estate in Wood-side, New York, circa 1892) played football and hurling matches against teams in Philadelphia (Pennsylvania), Troy (New York), and Stamford (Connecticut). (Archives of Irish America, New York University)

bearing such nationalistic appellations as Erin Go Bragh and Faugh a Ballagh. In Philadelphia the leading teams were the Red Branch Knights and the Irish Nationalists, while San Francisco could boast the Emmets, Parnells, and Geraldines. In New York, the names of Irish national heroes were also favored, as the Sarsfield and Geraldines became the city's leading clubs. By 1899, the Dunn Trophy was donated to the Greater New York Irish-American Athletic Association, "intended for the encouragement of the Gaelic football game and amateur sports for which Ireland was noted." That season the association's twenty affiliated clubs competed for the trophy.

The ancient sports of Ireland received an impetus in 1884, with the establishment of the Gaelic Athletic Association (GAA) in Ireland. Intended to return the control of sport to Irishmen, it might be better perceived as a manifestation of the ongoing struggle for independence by the impoverished Irish Catholic majority. In 1888, the "American Invasion" saw more than fifty Irish athletes travel to the United States to compete at hurling and track and field in New York, Boston, Philadelphia, Newark, Patterson, Providence, and Lowell. Due in large part to the bad weather and popular preoccupation with the presidential campaign of that year, attendance was low and the tour was a financial disaster. The failures of the 1888 tour did not deter the Gaelic Athletic Association, which returned to the United States in 1926, 1927, and finally 1947 for the All-Ireland Football Final played before thirty-five thousand spectators at the Polo Grounds in New York.

The first Gaelic Athletic Association in America was organized in Chicago in 1890. Three years later the association had fifteen affiliated clubs (ten Gaelic football teams and five hurling teams), with a membership of two thousand. In Boston, a group of Irish Americans actively sought to organize a Gaelic Athletic Union in 1895 for "those interested in the revival of Irish sports." In New York City, control of Gaelic football and hurling shifted from the Irish-American Athletic Association to the Irish Counties Athletic Union, which was formed in 1904. Ten years later, the Gaelic Athletic Association of New York was established, taking over the role of athletic administration among the city's Irish-American sports teams and providing a foundation upon which the continuing practice of Irish sport would flourish throughout the twentieth century.

While the story of Irish Americans in sports has been less frequently recounted, it must, nevertheless, be considered as important as their influence on this nations' labor, political, public service, and religious institutions. Whether due to the trivial connotations of sport or, perhaps, to the cultural embarrassment that Irish-American prizefighters and other sometimes disreputable professionals brought to their fellow countrymen, the story of Irish Americans in sports has been frequently disregarded by its own culture's middle-class leaders who instead searched for an increased sense of respectability.

Yet one cannot deny the seemingly endless stream of cultural leaders, heroes, successes, and tragedies spawned by the Irish-American sporting tradition. Sports were clearly promoted as an adjunct to the political process. Furnishing an environment essential to the promotion of group identity, sport presented immigrants and their descendants a ready opportunity to unfurl the flag of their former homeland and to celebrate clannish identity through such cultural icons as the shamrock and the harp. The popular names of Irish-American athletes, teams, and arenas soon extended beyond immigrant enclaves, sometimes leading to tensions and conflict with other groups. Yet, more often than not, those names promoted a greater sense of cultural assimilation so critical to America's unity, as well as its ascendancy on the twentieth-century sporting stage.

BIBLIOGRAPHY

Connolly, James Brendan. *Seaborne: Thirty Years Avoyaging*. Garden City, NY: Doubleday, Doran, 1944.

Daley, Arthur. "The American Irish in Sports." *Recorder* 34 (1973): 43–100.

de Burca, Marcus. *The G.A.A.: A History of the Gaelic Athletic Association*. Dublin: Cumann Luthchleas Gael, 1980.

Isenberg, Michael T. *John L. Sullivan and His America*. Urbana: University of Illinois Press, 1988.

Marriner, Ernest Cummings. *Jim Connolly and the Fishermen of Gloucester*. Waterville, ME: Colby College Press, 1949.

O'Reilly, John Boyle. *The Ethics of Boxing and Manly Sports*. Boston: Ticknor, 1888.

Tansey, John R. *Life of Daniel O'Leary*. Chicago: n.p., 1878.

Wilcox, Ralph C. "The Shamrock and the Eagle: Irish-Americans and Sport in the Nineteenth Century." In *Ethnicity and Sport in North American History and Culture*, edited by George Eisen and David Wiggins, 55–74. Westport, CT: Greenwood Press, 1994.

SUGGESTED READING

Martin Appel, *Slide, Kelly, Slide: The Wild Life and Times of Mike "King" Kelly, Baseball's First Superstar* (Lanham, MD: Scarecrow, 1996).

Jerrold Casway, *Ed Delahanty in the Emerald Age of Baseball* (Notre Dame, IN: Notre Dame University Press, 2004).

Michael T. Isenberg, *John L. Sullivan and His America* (Urbana: University of Illinois Press, 1988).

Jeffery T. Sammons, *Beyond the Ring: The Role of Boxing in American Society* (Urbana: University of Illinois Press, 1988).

Ralph C. Wilcox, "The Shamrock and the Eagle: Irish-Americans and Sport in the Nineteenth Century," in *Ethnicity and Sport in North American History and Culture*, ed. George Eisen and David Wiggins, 55–74 (Westport, CT: Greenwood Press, 1994).

Chapter 20

Irish Americans in Sports
The Twentieth Century

Larry McCarthy

Often overlooked as merely amusement, sport represents a significant chapter in Irish-American history as it symbolizes both the transfer of native culture to sites of immigration and the adoption of a new nation's culture. Further, participation in American sport was more than a sign of acculturation; it was also one of a multitude of ways the Irish transcended marginalization to influence American culture. Public athletic performance made a name for the Irish as a group, as well, affecting their public reputation and contributing to the formation of stereotypes. In the eyes of the public, the images of Irish immigrants as drunken brawlers and champion boxers coalesced and seemed to validate the common epithet—"Fighting Irish."[1] Individual Irish Americans also influenced the way American professional sports operate today, from revolutionizing the way baseball franchises function as entrepreneurial enterprises to fostering more equal distribution of revenue in the National Football League.

Still Wearing the Heavyweight Crown: Irish Americans in the Ring until World War II

By the turn of the twentieth century, the reputation of the Irish or Irish-American boxer had virtually eclipsed that of the Irish in any other sport. The nineteenth-century traditions established by such Irishmen as Paddy Ryan, John L. Sullivan, "Gentleman Jim" Corbett, James "Yankee" Sullivan, and Jack McAuliffe set the stage for the entrance of additional Irish-American heavyweights to dominate the American boxing world until the 1930s. In particular, Jack Dempsey and Gene Tunney continued the tradition in the 1920s, contributing their own style and accomplishment to the already well-established lore.

In the 1920s, America had its sport heroes; though perhaps Babe Ruth cast his long shadow over the rest, Ruth was in the company of Red Grange, Bobby Jones, and certainly Jack Dempsey. In many ways Dempsey's public persona fulfilled expectations held for an Irish-American boxer at the time. Previous generations of boxers bequeathed the stereotype of the wild-eyed fighting Irish, and Dempsey combined that image with his own ability to fit "the American rags-to-riches prototype": a down-to-earth glad-hand with an irresistible assault and a Hollywood smile for the crowd when a fight was over. His ruthless fighting style, favoring relentless pursuit and two-fisted attacks, earned him the nickname "the Manassa Mauler," as he hailed from Manassa, Colorado. His humble beginnings in Manassa also contributed to his acclaim, as he fit the American rags to riches prototype. Dempsey came from a lower-class background and literally fought his way to the top after coming to prominence as a club fighter in Colorado, Utah, and Nevada. Under the influence of Jack "Doc" Kearns, he challenged heavyweight champion Jess Willard in 1919 and administered such a beating that Willard was unable to come out for the fourth round. Dempsey went on to defend his title against such renowned boxers as George Carpentier of France and Luis the "Wild Bull of Pampas" Firpo. Jack Dempsey gained celebrity by combining success in the ring with a sensationally masculine public image.[2]

Another Irish-American heavyweight champion, Gene Tunney, established himself as a champion boxer in stark contrast to the route of Jack Dempsey. Indeed, while Tunney was equally successful as Dempsey in the ring, his relative lack of popularity demonstrated how skill was superseded by persona when it came to the hearts of the American sports fan. Born in 1897 in New York City to parents from County Mayo, Ireland, Gene Tunney was an abstemious individual, less attracted by many of the social activities and vices that enhanced the reputation of his boxing predecessors. After a stint in the U.S. Marine Corps during World War I, Tunney fought his way through the middle and light heavyweight classes in the early 1920s. Viewed as a scientific boxer who carefully studied his opponents, Tunney preferred to outbox his opponents rather than attempt to knock them out. His relative intellectualism and general public reticence prevented him from ever being acknowledged as a people's champion, even though he retired as the undefeated heavyweight champion of the world. Neither the press nor the public took a liking to the prizefighter who was an avid reader, particularly one who read poetry. In 1928 a *Daily Mail* writer wrote of American antipathy toward Tunney: "he is not the most popular champion America ever had—it is felt, in a land of mass production, a pugilist should adhere to type."[3] With his scientific approach, love of literary pursuits, and public reserve, Tunney could never be accused of adhering to type.

Promoter Tex Richard signed Gene Tunney, who had been successful as both a middleweight and light heavyweight, to fight then–world heavyweight champion Jack Dempsey in September 1926. The fight took place at Sesquicentennial Stadium in Philadelphia and attracted a record crowd of more than 120,000 people who paid a total of $1.8 million to see Dempsey defend his title for the first time in three years. As with all his opponents, Tunney studied Dempsey's fighting style closely and, being well aware of his wild rushing style, easily defeated an opponent who had been somewhat softened by a playboy lifestyle. Wide interest in this first Dempsey–Tunney match led to an even greater audience for the Dempsey–Tunney rematch a year later, a fight that stands among the most famous boxing matches ever. The second bout drew another enormous crowd of 102,000 people to Soldier Field in Chicago, and the enormous attendance paid a record $2.6 million. The second Dempsey–Tunney fight is particularly known for the "long count," in which Dempsey, after knocking Tunney down, failed to go to a neutral corner before the count began and, as a result, was defeated by Tunney, who retained the world heavyweight crown.

Of wider significance than the long count was the way the media covered the rematch. The popular interest in the Dempsey–Tunney fight fostered what has grown to become a well-established, (usually) mutually beneficial relationship between sport and broadcast media in which the media uses the allure of sport to attract audiences and earn revenue through advertising. The *Boston Globe* reported that this fight was the greatest boon the radio business ever had, with a record number of radios being sold prior to the fight and nearly fifty million people listening to the commentary of Graham McNamee. Similarly, in the 1950s, sport contributed significantly to the sale of televisions, and the trend continues in recent years with sport being used as marketing strategy in the sale of digital television in a number of markets around the world.

With its record attendance and a huge radio audience, Tunney's long count victory marked the apex of the Irish in boxing; after his retirement as world champion in 1928, the role of the underdog battling with his fists for material reward and social recognition was mostly abandoned by the Irish. Newer immigrant groups such as the Italians, and later African Americans and Latinos, took the place of the Irish in the struggle through the ring for fame and fortune.[4] Interestingly, some members of these other ethnic groups chose to exploit the prominence of the Irish in boxing by using Irish-sounding ring names. Such was the case for Jack Sharkey, world heavyweight champion from 1932 to 1933, who was born Josef Paul Zukauskas in Binghamton, New York, and adopted the ring pseudonym of the retired boxer "Sailor" Tom Sharkey. Born in Ontario, Canada, Noah Brusso was the world heavyweight champion from 1906 to 1908; he fought under the name of Tommy Burns. Such a trend was not confined to boxers, as a social tendency for those immigrants in the public spotlight during the early twentieth century was to adopt Irish-American sounding names.

On the Field and Behind the Scenes of America's Game: The Irish in Baseball

Professional baseball has seen an endless pattern of ethnic succession from the time Irish and German players entered the game in large numbers during the late nineteenth century. Italian and Slavic players joined the game in the 1920s and 1930s, African Americans in the 1950s and 1960s, Latinos during the 1980s and 1990s, and Asian Americans in the 1990s. Baseball is singularly fascinated with ethnicity because, once baseball emerged as America's game in the 1870s, it became associated with what are termed "American values." Early in the twentieth century it was hailed as a metaphor of the American melting pot, displaying teamwork among its array of ethnicities as the nation continued to adjust to its own heterogeneity.[5] Even when celebrating the glory of the game, some historians have tended to see baseball through the lens of ethnic and racial stereotypes—perhaps none more so than for the Irish. Lawrence McCaffrey notes that while "Irish players came to represent American adaptability, and their skills in the arena gave them a more acceptable persona, that athleticism also

Born to Irish immigrants in Connecticut and christened Cornelius McGilli-
cuddy, Connie Mack (1862–1956) played baseball for clubs in Buffalo and
Pittsburgh in the 1890s before beginning a legendary career as a manager.
From his Philadelphia base, Mack was part of an early-twentieth-century
Irish-American front office triumvirate with John McGraw in New York and
Charlie Comiskey in Chicago. (Library of Congress, Prints and Photographs
Division, LC-USZ62-077890)

reinforced nativist opinion that the Irish were strong of back and weak of mind."[6]
Baseball histories such as Bill James's *Historical Baseball Abstract* and Benjamin
Rader's *Baseball: A History of America's Game* allude to the wild Irish players noted for
their rowdiness and drinking, none more so than Mike "King" Kelly. While Kelly stole
an amazing eighty-four bases in 116 games in a single season and led the Chicago
Cubs to a total of five National League pennants, his portrayal consistently draws
more attention to his off-field behavior than to his on-field accomplishments.[7]

Despite these negative stereotypes, many Irish-American players, managers, and
administrators managed to gain significant repute for their contributions to baseball.
Among these were Joe Cronin, Jimmy Collins, Ned Hanlon, Tim Keefe, Ted Lyons,
Connie Mack, Joe McGinnity, John McGraw, and Joe McCarthy, all of whom were

recognized by the Baseball Hall of Fame. Joe Cronin, who played with Pittsburgh, Washington, and Boston was the most valuable player of the American League in 1930, was a seven time All-Star, won a pennant as a rookie manager with the Washington Senators in 1937, and served two terms as president of the American League. Joe McGinnity was nicknamed the "Iron Man," though initially not because of his play but because he worked in a foundry during the off-season (as was common at the time). The name did come to personify his style of pitching, as he became famous for starting both ends of doubleheaders and was an important part of the pennant-winning teams in Brooklyn in 1900 and in New York in 1905.

While Cronin, Collins, Keefe, and Lyons were all elected to the Hall of Fame as players, Connie Mack, Joe McCarthy, Ned Hanlon, and John McGraw were elected for their contribution to the game as highly successful managers. Mack and McCarthy managed their clubs for a total of eighty-one years. Mack, who was born Cornelius Alexander McGillicuddy and abbreviated his name so it would fit on the scoreboard while playing, began managing the Philadelphia Athletics in 1901 and spent fifty years at the helm of the club as manager and team owner, until he retired in 1951 at the age of eighty-eight, a record unlikely to be broken. While he always regarded baseball as a business and was an exceptional field manager, his lack of financial acumen led to the breakup of two of the baseball dynasties he created. He was forced to disband his pennant-winning teams of 1910–14 due to competition in the Philadelphia market, and in the early 1930s he was forced to sell Mickey Cochrane, Jimmie Foxx, Al Simmons, and Lefty Grove—stars of his pennant-winning teams of 1929, 1930, and 1931—in part, because of the financial stress of the Great Depression. Known as the "tall tactician," he always wore a business suit while managing, and he directed his players by waving the scorecard from the dugout.

Joe McCarthy managed the New York Yankees through the 1930s and early 1940s. With one of the greatest baseball teams of all time, he won four consecutive World Series from 1936 to 1939 and a total of seven titles in all, a record unsurpassed in baseball. Among the Hall of Fame players he managed were Babe Ruth, Lou Gehrig, Bill Dickey, and Joe DiMaggio. Very few of the players were excited about his appointment as manager, least of all Ruth who had openly campaigned for the position. McCarthy was recognized as a great teacher of the skills of baseball, but he was not one to suffer the whims and fancies of his players. There was a strict dress code: every player had to show up in jacket and tie for breakfast at 8:30 AM, and he eliminated any distractions and diversions from the dugout so the players would focus on the game in the belief that any player who "could not attend to business with the high pay and the working hours so pleasant" had something wrong with him and he ought to move on.[8] McCarthy's no nonsense approach was highly successful, as he retired from baseball in 1950 with the highest ever career winning mark as a manager.

While Connie Mack and Joe McCarthy were the epitome of gentlemen as managers, very well respected by their players, John McGraw, the autocratic manager of the New York Giants from 1902 to 1932, was in total contrast. Nicknamed "Little Napoleon," the arrogant, abrasive, and pugnacious McGraw treated many of his players with utter disdain. Having played with the raucous Baltimore Orioles during the 1890s under the direction of Ned Hanlon, a team renowned for their abrasive tactics, dirty play, and browbeating of umpires, he brought the same abrasiveness to his management style. He had a knack for inciting crowds, and under his leadership the Giants became the most despised team in baseball. While he was very successful as a manager, winning a total of ten pennants and three World Series, he was also notorious as the central figure in many gambling incidents that never received much publicity or were ignored due to his prominence.

In turn, as McCarthy, Mack, and McGraw represent the Irish-American interest in managing baseball during the first half of the twentieth century, Walter O'Malley represents the ownership interest. Born in the Bronx, the only child of a father whose family originally came from County Mayo, O'Malley's career in law led him to become general counsel to the Brooklyn Dodgers in the early 1940s, which transitioned into complex ownership arrangements by which he and the club general manager Branch Rickey, along with a third partner, owned 75 percent of the club. The arrangement led to many disputes on how the club should best be managed; however, the Dodgers ownership was able to make some significant decisions, as is evinced by their move to introduce Jackie Robinson into the major leagues in 1946, thereby breaking the color barrier.

In time, Walter O'Malley defined himself as an ambitious entrepreneur, redefining the larger character of professional baseball in the process. Whereas most owners of that time tended to be conservative, in 1958 O'Malley made the controversial decision to move the Dodgers from Brooklyn to Los Angeles. O'Malley's willingness to move his team not only provoked hatred from fans but also sent shock waves through major league baseball. Those involved in baseball organizations were stunned by O'Malley's departure from the nation's largest market, but it underscored O'Malley's understanding of baseball as a business enterprise that required risk for profit.

Baseball more easily accepted and emulated O'Malley and co-owner Bill Veeck's emphasis on customer service, promotions, and relentless marketing. Their innovations changed the business of baseball by providing a model for other sports franchises. The Dodgers worked on their sales efforts all year round; they exploited the location of their stadium as a promotional tool, and they were willing to spend on the quality of the on-field product. O'Malley was also the first owner to recognize the potential of the Latino market, broadcasting Dodger games in Spanish from the team's first year in Los Angeles. While Veeck may have been the first baseball owner to understand that baseball should be treated as a product that had to be marketed extensively, it was O'Malley who successfully turned the idea into a business practice.

Dynasties Working for the Good of the League: The Irish in the NFL

If the Irish and Irish Americans made a significant contribution to baseball during the early twentieth century, their contribution to American football, while not as large, was nonetheless noteworthy. People such as John "Paddy" Driscoll,[9] Mike McCormack, Tommy McDonald, John "Blood" McNally, Ray Flaherty, Jim Kelly, Art Donovan, Hugh McElhenny, and Ed Healey are all distinguished by induction into the Professional Football Hall of Fame. Moreover, two Irish-American families have had their contribution to professional football recognized by having both a father and son enshrined in the Hall of Fame; the Mara family, owners of the New York Giants, and the Rooney family, owners of the Pittsburgh Steelers, are the only father and son combinations to be so honored. In their way, each family has made significant contributions to the creation and development of America's football league.

The elder Tim Mara came to the National Football League (NFL) just as the burgeoning league was adding to its already established franchises in Canton and Akron, Ohio; Chicago and Decatur, Illinois; Green Bay, Wisconsin; Frankford, Pennsylvania; and Kansas City, Missouri. The league recognized the press and publicity benefits of a showcase franchise in New York City, and in 1925 it granted one of five new franchises to the city. Born and raised in New York's Lower East Side, Tim Mara worked his way up from a bookie's runner to a full-fledged, successful bookie after leaving school at the age of thirteen to support his widowed mother. With bookmaking being legal at the time, by 1925 Mara had earned enough to buy the New York City franchise for the princely sum of $500, on the rationale that "a New York franchise to operate anything ought to be worth $500."[10]

Approaching his team with a mix of his own business sense and a willing dependence on the expertise of those with a stronger football background than himself, Mara cultivated what he saw as a ready professional football market in New York, already well developed by local college football teams. He attempted to establish his professional team by building it around a big-name player, the superstar Red Grange. However, he was unable to sign Grange, so he contracted for Grange's team, the Chicago Bears, to play his New York Giants. The estimated attendance at the Bears–Giants game—seventy thousand—confirmed Mara's belief that professional football had a future in New York.

Of course, his success did not go unnoticed and, though he was the only NFL franchise owner in the city, the league did not give exclusive territorial rights to any owner; as the largest market in the country, sport entrepreneurs and fledgling leagues viewed New York as potentially highly lucrative. Mara fought off an application for a rival NFL franchise at Yankee Stadium, as well as a number of attempts by the American Football League (AFL) and the All American Football Conference (AAFC) to establish franchises in the city. He directed the Giants for over forty years, building several successful teams that won numerous league championships, but his resilience and fortitude in creating, and maintaining, a successful professional football team in New York are his major contributions to the National Football League.

The Mara dynasty was established when Tim Mara handed down the leadership to his eldest son, Jack, in 1959, who was duly replaced by his younger brother, Wellington, upon Jack's death in 1965. Before becoming the Giants' president, Wellington Mara had already spent thirty years at various levels of Giants management, experience that contributed to his ability to remain highly involved in both the Giants organization and broader league business. Wellington Mara has long been noted for putting the collective interests of the National Football League ahead of the interest of individual franchise owners. He has consistently defended the strategy within the NFL of dividing revenues equally among each of the thirty-two franchises, so that each has a realistic opportunity of competing and winning. This strategy has helped transform the league from a collection of family run enterprises owned by the Maras (New York Giants), the Rooneys (Pittsburgh Steelers), the Modells (Cleveland Browns and Baltimore Ravens), and the Halas-McCaskeys (Chicago Bears) to a highly successful multi-billion-dollar, multinational sports enterprise. Mara remained stalwart in his work to maintain the league philosophy of the 1960s that the strength and attraction of the league does not depend on any one team or group of teams but, rather, depends on the total league. While new owners such as Jerry Jones (Dallas Cowboys), Daniel Snyder (Washington Redskins), and Steve Biscotti (Baltimore Ravens) have pushed for much greater autonomy in their business dealings, it is the continued influence of leaders such as Mara that has kept the NFL in its early model, enabling equal team development across the league and thus offering itself as a model for sports associations around the world.

Like the Maras, the other Irish-American father–son members of the Professional Football Hall of Fame, the Rooneys, have also been involved in the NFL for over seventy years and have had a tremendous influence on the direction of both their individual team and the league as a whole. Also like Tim Mara, Art Rooney was a gambling man, and it has been suggested that he bought the Pittsburgh Steelers franchise with the proceeds from a very good win on the horses. Art Rooney had to pay $2,500 for Pittsburgh in 1933, which highlights the bargain Mara received only eight years earlier with the New York franchise price tag of only $500. The son of Irish immigrants from Newry, County Down, Rooney grew up on the north side of Pittsburgh. He involved himself in sports at an early age and had such success in boxing that he was selected to represent the United States in the Olympic Games of 1920.

The Steelers took a very long time to repay the faith Art Rooney showed when he purchased the team. They struggled badly for many years, winning only twenty-four games in their first eight years. Rooney lost money on the team every year. To make ends meet, and to avoid the competition from more popular sports in the city of Pittsburgh, he was often forced to take the Steelers on the road—to Johnstown and Latrobe, Pennsylvania; Youngstown, Ohio; Louisville, Kentucky; and New Orleans, Louisiana. A tie for the Eastern Division title was the nearest the team got to a championship in the first forty years of its existence. However, the 1970s was a highly successful decade for the Steelers, and Rooney was amply rewarded for his faith in professional football in the Pittsburgh market. The Steelers dominated football, winning seven Central division titles, four AFC championships, and four Super Bowls, becoming the only team to win back-to-back Super Bowls twice, in the 1974–1975 and 1978–1979 seasons.

During these years of success, Art Rooney was still the owner of the Steelers, but by the mid-1960s he handed over much of the control of the team to his eldest son, Dan, as Tim Mara had done with his sons, Jack and Wellington. The dynastic succession meant that Dan Rooney already had a firm sense of his duties when he was named president of the Steelers organization in 1975, perhaps contributing to his ability to emerge as one of the NFL's most active and influential figures. Dan Rooney's achievement was in no small part due to his strong management philosophy, which emphasized open, practical, and efficient management, in combination with a supportive attitude toward his players. These practices resulted in Rooney both gaining the confidence and trust of the players' union and also being regarded as a voice of moderation among NFL owners.

With all this in mind, Dan Rooney seemed the apt choice as chairman of the NFL Negotiating Committee; indeed, he was instrumental in ending the players' strikes of 1982 and 1987, and he had a critical role in negotiating a labor agreement, signed originally between the players and the league in 1993 and extended until 2008.[11] At the heart of the agreement is a salary cap and a free agency system that allowed both the league and its players to flourish. Labor disputes, some culminating in player strikes, have been notable events in the history of American sport. Under the quiet and influential guidance of Rooney, the NFL was largely able to avoid such disruptions. Disruptions in leadership of the Steelers organization has also been avoided, as a July 2003 change in the Steelers's club directory was the only public indication that Dan Rooney had stepped down as president of the club in favor of his son, Art Rooney II, the third generation of Rooneys taking leadership in typical, quiet Rooney fashion.

Of Whales, Hammers, and Gold Medals: Irish Americans in Olympic Track and Field

While the focus of this chapter is on professional sport, a group of Irish and Irish-American amateur track and field athletes had a huge impact on American sport at the start of the twentieth century. This group (collectively known as the "Irish Whales") dominated the field events, particularly throwing events, at the American Athletic Union (AAU) national championships and at the Olympic Games between 1896 and 1924. So called because of their size and strength, many of the "Whales" were policemen attached to the New York City Police Department.

The Irish Whales' strength was evident in their event, the hammer throw—and it can be safely termed "their" event, judging by their dominance in the early decades of the twentieth century. The litany of names of Irish hammer medalists leaves little to distinguish one from another for the casual historian, but closer examination of these Whales reveals a rich culture of individuals entrenched in a battle for their own athletic achievement and also ensnared in their dual loyalties to both their Irish homeland and America. Among the most successful of the Whales was John Flanagan, who became the first modern Olympic athlete to win three successive titles in a standard event when he took the gold in the hammer at the Olympics in Paris in 1900, in St. Louis in 1904, and in London in 1908. Even upon his retirement from athletics and the New York City police force, Flanagan continued his involvement in Olympic track and field by moving back to Ireland and coaching Pat O'Callaghan to win the gold in the hammer at the 1928 and 1932 Olympic Games.

While Flanagan broke the record for the most consecutive medals, he also participated in the first instance of athletes born in a single country sweeping the medals of an event; in 1908 Flanagan shared the medal stand with Matt McGrath, a fellow Irish-American, and Con Walsh, an Irishman representing Canada. McGrath would go on to win his own gold in the following Olympics in Stockholm in 1912, as well as a second silver medal in Paris in 1924. McGrath also met fellow Irishmen Pat McDonald of

James P. Sullivan, known as "4.22 Jim," was a record-holding member of the Irish American Athletic Club, a New York–based track and field club. This card appeared as part of the Champion Athlete and Prize-fighter Series no. 2, produced by the Hassan cigarette company circa 1910. (Archives of Irish America, New York University, Gift of James T. Higgins, in memory of John P. Higgins [1915–1997])

County Limerick and Pat Ryan of County Clare at the 1912 and 1920 games, respectively, where each took the gold in the hammer event.

The hammer throw was not the only field event Irish Americans dominated, particularly with the participation of Martin Sheridan of Bohola, County Mayo, who took his own three golds in the discus event of 1904, 1906 (Intercalated Olympic Games), and 1908, as well as taking medals in the long and high jumps, pole vault, and shot putt. He is also the man credited with beginning the tradition of not dipping the American flag in the parade of nations at the opening ceremonies of each Olympic Games, after he and other athletes advised teammate Ralph Rose, the American flagbearer for the acrimonious games of 1908 in London, to refused to lower the flag as the team marched past the reviewing stand of King Edward VII. After the affront, Sheridan spoke out to the media with the curt response, "This flag dips to no earthly King."

Sheridan's patriotism surely helped curb some of the public criticism he and his fellow members of the Irish American Athletic Club (IAAC) received during the 1908 games, when the press questioned the loyalty of members of the IAAC to the United States over Ireland. The *New York Sun*, in particular, compared western and eastern athletes and questioned the easterners' focus on club or ethnic loyalties over their broader loyalty to the American team as a whole. The *Sun* wrote: "Among the New

York A.C. and the Irish A.A.C. there is bitter rivalry, the latter, except for John Flanagan, being out for the Irish club only."[12] Not wholly xenophobic, the *Sun's* comments were fueled by IAAC athletes' comments to the press, including those by Martin Sheridan himself, who told the *Irish American Advocate*, "I must have a good try, if only for the sake of the old country," the day before the *Sun* aired its concerns.[13]

This kind of public discourse contributed to an increased awareness of questions of assimilation and ethnic identity. Athletes offered a locus of dispute over representation; those hoping to locate Irish Americans outside hegemonic middle-class America relegated Sheridan and the other members of the IAAC to the position of transient Irishmen unconcerned with their adoptive country. Meanwhile, the impressive achievement of the Irish-American members of the Olympic team helped their position with the press; Americans took thirteen track and field events, eight thanks to members of the IAAC.[14]

The member of the Irish-American constituency on the 1908 Olympic team to receive the most attention by the press was a nineteen-year-old marathon runner named John Hayes. Hayes was not expected to even medal in the marathon, but the young IAAC member became the gold medalist after much dispute. The row started when English officials helped the Italian runner, Dorando Pietri, finish the race after his collapse just before the finish line; instead of disqualifying Pietri, the English officials declared him the winner, and it required a successful American protest to name John Hayes the rightful winner. After the race, Hayes became the favorite of the American press, with photographs and biographies flooding American papers with stories of Hayes training at night without a coach in order to maintain his job at Bloomingdale's six days per week. Hayes became the ideal representation of Irish-American pluck, as the *New York Sun* called him: "As Irish as you find them, with black hair, blue eyes, a good humored and freckled face and a ton of confidence in himself."[15] The victory by Hayes, excitement over the overall success of the Irish-American athletes, and the refusal of Rose to dip the Stars and Stripes for any "earthly king"—all these contented some suspicions against the team members. The *Gaelic American* portrayed the parade welcoming the athletes back to New York as a celebration of complementary loyalties:

> The buildings along the route of the parade were decorated with American flags, and American flags were carried by many of the paraders and spectators. The Irish flag was also in evidence, and the bands played "The Star-Spangled Banner," "Hail Columbia," and the "Wearing of the Green."[16]

The subsequent success of the Irish in assimilating into mainstream American society can obfuscate the past difficulties of Irish Americans, but the experiences of members of the IAAC during the 1908 Olympics offer a better understanding of these challenges. Furthermore, the sheer number of medals earned by Irish Americans in the hammer event imply a broader culture of sport than is often remembered through the football iconography of the "Fighting Irish" or in boxing and baseball. This alternate culture of sport has often been overshadowed by more mainstream participation. In the next section I provide a more in depth examination of Irish-American sport taken from the homeland and replicated, as much as possible, in its traditional form.

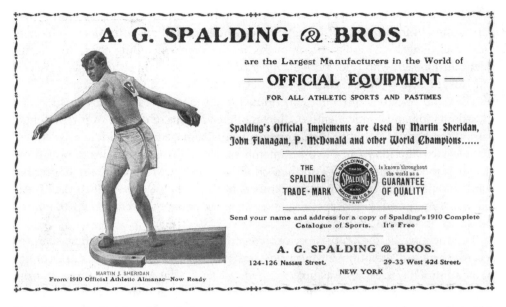

The Irish were the first American ethnic group whose sports heroes were used to endorse products. This February 1910 advertisement for the Spalding athletic equipment company prominently lists the names of members of the Irish American Athletic Club, as well as featuring an image of the track-and-field group's Olympic medal winner, Martin Sheridan (1881–1918). A native of Bohola, County Mayo, Sheridan was also a New York City policeman. The IAAC's motto was "Láimh láidir Abu!" or "Victory to the Strong Hand." (Archives of Irish America, New York University, Gift of James P. Higgins in memory of John P. Higgins [1915–1997])

Gaelic Sports on American Land: The Gaelic Athletic Association

While Irish and Irish-American athletes made a significant contribution to both American and international sport during the twentieth century, they also engaged actively in the two sports that are regarded as uniquely Irish: Gaelic football and hurling. At the turn of the twentieth century, organizations existed in Boston, Chicago, and New York for the promotion of Gaelic football and hurling principally under the aegis of the Gaelic Athletic Association (GAA). Founded in Ireland in 1884 with the intent of reviving native Irish sports and returning the control of Irish sport to Irishmen, the GAA was part of a much broader movement whose motivation was the creation of a politically independent Ireland.

The control of Gaelic games in the New York area, prior to the foundation of the Gaelic Athletic Association of Greater New York in 1914, rested initially with the Irish-American Athletic Association but transferred to the Irish Counties Athletic Union, formed in 1904 of the representatives of the county patriotic and benevolent associations (known as P and B Associations). The majority of Irish counties had such associations, and they were very powerful social organizations dedicated to advancing the cause of their particular county.[17] All the individuals elected as the first officers of the Gaelic Athletic Association of Greater New York represented a county, an organizational structure similar to that created by the GAA in Ireland. Twenty clubs took part in the initial New York championship in 1915 at Celtic Park in Queens, a privately owned facility that included a bar, dining hall, dance hall, and sports field. It was a very well supported center for hurling, football, and other sporting contests, including athletic competitions involving the aforementioned "Irish Whales." A Sunday at Celtic Park would involve a number of hurling and football games in the afternoon, dinner served in the dining hall, and a dance that would last long into the evening. It was very much a social occasion, an opportunity to meet fellow countymen and county-women, a chance to watch or participate in one's ethnic sports, and an opportunity to relax in the company of one's peers. The day's activity was very much modeled on the traditional picnics sponsored by associations such as the Ancient Order of Hiberni-ans, Clan na Gael, and St. Patrick's Mutual Alliance.

The popularity of Gaelic games in the United States ebbs and flows with the tide of emigration and, by extension, the state of the Irish economy. At the end of World War II, there was a wave of Irish emigration that was a signal for many of the county teams, which had disbanded during the war, to reorganize. The boom continued until the impact of the 1965 U.S. Immigration Act was felt in the 1970s, and there was a dra-matic drop in both participation and spectators. The 1970s saw the emergence of an Irish-American, as distinct from native Irish, participation in Gaelic games, and this helped keep many of the clubs active. The reduced number of immigrants contin-ued until the early 1980s, when many young Irish emigrated to the United States, and Gaelic games in the United States were reinvigorated. The economic conditions in Ireland in the early twenty-first century meant another dramatic decline in emigra-tion. The consequence is that GAA clubs have not been carried on by newcomers and are losing existing players, many of whom emigrated in the 1980s as young men but began to see themselves settling down in Ireland to take advantage of the economic boom of the 1990s, known as the Celtic Tiger.[18]

Those who played Gaelic games typically played with the teams representing their native counties. As a result, intercounty rivalries that existed between teams in Ire-land carried over to the United States. Playing with a particular county also affected one's career in New York. Because of their strong associations with various unions, trades, and crafts, whichever county one played with dictated, in many cases, what one started one's working life as in the United States, as the team offered a level of networking unachieved by otherwise unconnected immigrants. For many years those who played with Offaly were employed in the marble and stone cutting trades; those with Cork were employed in warehouses, particularly on the Brooklyn docks; those with Donegal received employment as mason tenders; and those with Longford re-ceived employment initially as doormen before advancing to being superintendents in luxury apartment buildings. As a result of the significant Irish participation in the construction boom of the early 1990s, close ties between the construction industry and the GAA developed.

While the GAA has traditional strongholds in cities such as Boston, Chicago, San Francisco, and New York, as of 2004, it had one hundred clubs in thirty other cities across the United States. One of the more interesting cases is the Milwaukee Hurling

Club, which was formed in 1996. Unlike clubs in other cities, Milwaukee has little affiliation with county organizations and selects its co-ed hurling teams on a draft basis so that there is a good balance of talent between all teams. It is the only club in the United States that offers co-ed hurling. While there is a sprinkling of Irish names among the team rosters, they are significantly outnumbered by names of other nationalities. Perhaps this organization offers an indication that the most ancient of Irish sports is spreading beyond its traditional narrow confines, or perhaps it provides an insight into the intermarriage of Irish Americans with members of other ethnic groups.

NOTES

1. Irish-American involvement in collegiate athletics is not considered in this review because the contribution of universities and colleges, including such institutions as Notre Dame, Boston College, Villanova, Providence, and Fordham Universities, among others, to American sport is so immense that it would be impossible to do justice to that contribution in a review such as this.

2. Harry Carpenter, *Masters of Boxing* (New York: Barnes, 1964), 190–200. John L. Sullivan, world heavyweight champion 1882–1892, provides the prime example of the rough, bachelor-boxer lifestyle; there are ample biographies of Sullivan that can provide more on this topic.

3. Ibid., 186.

4. William D. Giffin, *Book of Irish Americans* (New York: Times Books, 1990).

5. Lawrence Baldarasso, Foreword to *The American Game: Baseball and Ethnicity*, ed. Lawrence Baldarasso and R. A. Johnson (Carbondale: Southern Illinois University Press, 2002).

6. Lawrence J. McCaffrey, "Forging Forward and Looking Back," in *The New York Irish*, ed. Ronald Baylor and Timothy J. Meagher (Baltimore: Johns Hopkins University Press, 1996), 231.

7. Richard F. Peterson, "Slide Kelly Slide," in *The American Game: Baseball and Ethnicity*, ed. Lawrence Baldarasso and R. A. Johnson (Carbondale: Southern Illinois University Press, 2002).

8. Harvey Frommer, "Sport Profile of Joe McCarthy," BaseballLibrary.com, available at http://baseballlibrary.com/baseballlibrary/submit/Frommer_Harvey74.stm.

9. John "Paddy" Driscoll is particularly noteworthy because he not only played professional football for the Chicago Cardinals and the Chicago Bears in the 1920s but also he played professional baseball for the Chicago Cubs during the 1917 season.

10. Professional Football Researchers Association, "Mr. Mara," available at http://www.footballresearch.com/articles/frpage.cfm?topic=mara.

11. "Like Father . . . Dan Rooney Joining Father in Pro Football Hall of Fame," CNN/SI, available at http://sportsillustrated.cnn.com/football/nfl/2000/halloffame/news/2000/07/27/hof_rooney_ap/ (accessed 27 July 2000).

12. "Olympic Team Sidelights," *New York Sun*, 19 July 1908.

13. "Irishmen at Olympic Games," *Irish-American Advocate*, 18 July 1908; John Schaefer, "The Irish American Athletic Club: Redefining Americanism at the 1908 Olympic Games" (New York: Archives of Irish America, 2001), 10.

14. Schaefer, "Irish American Athletic Club," 8–9.

15. "Hayes a Real New York Boy," *New York Sun*, 25 July 1908.

16. "New York Welcome to Olympic Victors," *Gaelic American*, 5 September 1908.

17. John T. Ridge, "Irish County Societies in New York, 1880–1914," in *The New York Irish,*

ed. Ronald H. Bayor and Timothy J. Meagher (Baltimore: Johns Hopkins University Press, 1996), 290–292.

18. Sara Brady, "Irish Sport and Culture at New York's Gaelic Park" (Ph.D. diss., New York University, 2005).

SUGGESTED READING

Charles C. Alexander, *John McGraw* (New York: Viking, 1988).

Lawrence Baldarasso and R. A. Johnson, eds., *The American Game: Baseball and Ethnicity* (Carbondale: Southern Illinois University Press, 2002).

Sara Brady, "Irish Sport and Culture at New York's Gaelic Park" (Ph.D. diss., New York University, 2005).

Harry Carpenter, *Masters of Boxing* (New York: Barnes, 1964).

John K. Feyer and Mark Rucker, *Nineteenth-Century Baseball in Chicago* (Portsmouth, NH: Arcadia, 2003).

S. W. Pope, *Patriotic Games: Sporting Traditions in the American Imagination, 1876–1926* (New York: Oxford University Press, 1997).

Steven Reiss, *City Games: The Evolution of American Urban Society and the Rise of Sports* (Chicago: University of Illinois Press, 1991).

Reflections

Chapter 21

The Irish (1963, 1970)

Daniel Patrick Moynihan

New York used to be an Irish city. Or so it seemed. There were sixty or seventy years when the Irish were everywhere. *They* felt it was their town. It is no longer, and they know it. That is one of the things bothering them.

The Irish era began in the early 1870s, about the time Charles O'Conor, "the ablest member of the New York bar,"[1] began the prosecution of Honorable William Magear Tweed. It ended in the 1930s. A symbolic point might be the day ex-Mayor James J. Walker sailed for Europe and exile with his beloved, but unwed, Betty.

Boss Tweed was the last vulgar white Protestant to win a prominent place in the city's life. The Protestants who have since entered public life have represented the "better element." Tweed was a roughneck, a ward heeler, a man of the people at a time when the people still contained a large body of native-born Protestant workers of Scotch and English antecedents. By the time of his death in the Ludlow Street jail this had all but completely changed. The New York working class had become predominantly Catholic, as it has since remained. The Irish promptly assumed the leadership of this working class. "Honest John" Kelly succeeded Tweed as leader of Tammany Hall, formalizing a process that had been steadily advancing. In 1868 the New York diarist George Templeton Strong had recorded, "Our rulers are partly American scoundrels and partly Celtic scoundrels. The Celts are predominant, however, and we submit to the rod and the sceptre of Maguires and O'Tooles and O'Shanes."[2] But the American scoundrels disappeared, and soon Strong was writing only of the city's "blackguard Celtic tyrants."[3] A note of helplessness appears: "We are to Papistical Paddy as Cedric the Saxon to Front de Boeuf."[4]

In 1880 Tammany Hall elected the city's first Irish Catholic mayor, William R. Grace of the shipping line. This ascendancy persisted for another half century, reaching an apogee toward the end of the 1920s when Al Smith ran for president and Jimmy Walker "wore New York in his buttonhole."

The crash came suddenly. In June 1932 Smith was denied the Democratic renomination. The Tammany delegates left Chicago bitter and unreconciled. Two months later Mayor Walker resigned in the face of mounting scandal and decided to leave the country with his English mistress. A few days before his departure, Franklin Roosevelt had been elected president. The next man to be elected mayor of New York City would be Fiorello H. La Guardia. Next, a Jewish world heavyweight champion. DiMaggio became the new name in baseball; Sinatra the new crooner. So it went. The almost formal end came within a decade. In 1943 Tammany Hall itself, built while Walker was mayor at the cost of just under one million dollars, was sold to Local 91 of the International Ladies' Garment Workers' Union. Tammany and the New York County Democratic Committee went their separate ways. The oldest political organization on earth was finished. So was the Irish era.

This is not to say the Irish have disappeared. They are still a powerful group. St. Patrick's Day is still the largest public observance of the city's year. On March 17 a green line is painted up Fifth Avenue and a half-million people turn out to watch the parade. (In Albany the Legislative Calendar is printed in green ink.) The Irish have a position in the city now as they had before the 1870s, but now, as then, it is a lopsided position. "Slippery Dick" Connoly and "Brains" Sweeney shared power and office with Tweed, as did any number of their followers. But, with few exceptions, they represented the *canaille.* With the coming of the Gilded Age, middle-class and even upper-class Irish appeared. For a period they ranged across the social spectrum, and in this way seemed to dominate much of the city's life. The Tweed ring was heavily Irish, but so was the group that brought on its downfall. This pattern persisted. The Irish came to run the police force *and* the underworld; they were the reformers and the hoodlums; employers and employed. The city entered the era of Boss Croker of Tammany Hall and Judge Goff of the Lexow Committee which investigated him; of business leader Thomas Fortune Ryan and labor leader Peter J. McGuire; of Reform Mayor John Purroy Mitchel and Tammany Mayor John F. "Red Mike" Hylan. It was a stimulating miscellany.

All this is past. The mass of the Irish have left the working class, and in considerable measure the Democratic Party as well. But the pattern of egalitarian politics which they established on the whole persists, so that increasingly the Irish are left out. Their reaction to this is one of the principal elements of the Irish impact on the city today.

The Green Wave

The basis of Irish hegemony in the city was established by the famine emigration of 1846–1850. By mid-century there were 133,730 Irish-born inhabitants of the city, 26 percent of the total population. By 1855, 34 percent of the city voters were Irish.[5] By 1890, when 80 percent of the population of New York City was of foreign parentage, a third of these (409,924 persons of 1,215,463) were Irish, making more than a quarter of the total population.[6] With older stock included, over one-third of the population of New York and Brooklyn at the outset of the Gay Nineties was Irish American.

The older stock went far back in the city's history. Ireland provided a continuing portion of the emigration to North America during the seventeenth and eighteenth centuries. Much of it was made up of Protestants with English or Scottish antecedents, but there were always some Celtic Irish of Protestant or Catholic persuasion. The city received its first charter from Governor Thomas Dongan, afterward Earl of

Limerick. In 1683 Dongan summoned the first representative assembly in the history of the colony, at which he sponsored the Charter of Liberties and Privileges granting broad religious freedom, guaranteeing trial by jury, and establishing representative government. He was nonetheless suspected of plotting a Catholic establishment, and with the Glorious Revolution of 1688 the Catholics of New York were disfranchised.

This was a basic event. The Catholic Irish were kept out of the political life of the city for almost a century. It began a long tradition of denying rights to Irish Catholics on grounds that they wished to do the same to English Protestants. To this day the most fair-minded New York Protestants will caution that Irish Catholics have never experienced the great Anglo-Saxon tradition of the separation of church and state, although indeed they have known nothing but.

At the first New York Constitutional Convention in 1777, John Jay even proposed that Roman Catholics be deprived of their civil rights and the right to hold land until taking an oath that no Pope or priest could absolve them from sin or from allegiance to the state.[7] This proposal was rejected, but Jay did succeed in including a religious test for naturalization in the constitution which remained in force until superseded by a federal naturalization statute in 1790.[8] It was not until 1806 that a similar oath required for officeholders was repealed, permitting the first Irish Catholic to take his seat in the Assembly.

After the Revolution, Irish emigration began in earnest. Writing in 1835, de Tocqueville reported: "About fifty years ago Ireland began to pour a Catholic population into the United States." He estimated that with conversions the number of Catholics had reached a million (which was three times the actual amount.)[9]

In 1798 another of the native Irish revolts took place, and failed. In its aftermath came the first of a long trail of Irish revolutionaries, Catholic and Protestant, who disturbed the peace of the city for a century and a quarter. These were educated professional men who had risked their lives for much the same cause that had inspired the Sons of Liberty in New York a generation earlier. In general they were received as such. A few such as Dr. William J. MacNeven and Thomas Addis Emmet became prominent New Yorkers. Emmet served in 1812 as the state's attorney-general. Mr. Justice Story described him as "the favorite counsellor of New York."[10]

In the early nineteenth century a sizable Irish-Catholic community gathered in New York. By the time of the great migration it was well enough established. Charles O'Conor, John Kelly, and W. R. Grace were all native New Yorkers. For some time prior to the potato famine the basic patterns of Irish life in New York had been set. The hordes that arrived at mid-century strengthened some of these patterns more than others, but they did not change them nearly so much as they were changed by them. They got off the boat to find their identity waiting for them: they were to be Irish-Catholic Democrats.

There were times when this identity took on the mysteries of the Trinity itself; the three were one and the one three. Identity with the Democratic Party came last in point of time, but it could have been received from the hands of Finn MacCool for the way the Irish clung to it.

The Democratic Party

Tammany was organized in New York a few weeks after Washington was inaugurated at Federal Hall on April 30, 1789. The principal founder was one William Mooney, an upholsterer and apparently by birth an Irish Catholic. Originally a national organization, from the first its motif was egalitarian and nationalist: the Sons of St. Tammany, the American Indian chief, as against the foreign ties of the societies of St. George and St. David (as well, apparently, of the Sons of St. Patrick), or the aristocratic airs of the Sons of the Cincinnati. Its members promptly involved themselves in politics, establishing the New York Democratic party. (Until recently Tammany officially retained the Jeffersonian designation "Democratic-Republican" party. Far into the twentieth century the Phrygian cap of the French Revolution was an important prop in Tammany ceremonies; it will be seen atop the staff of Liberty in the New York State seal, contrasting with the crown at her feet.)

The original issues on which the New York political parties organized concerned the events of the French Revolution. Jefferson and his Democratic followers were instinctively sympathetic to France. Hamilton, Jay, and the Federalists looked just as fervently to England. This automatically aligned the Irish with the Democrats: the French Revolution had inspired the Irish revolt of 1798, and the French had sent three expeditions to aid it. The Federalists reacted with the Alien and Sedition Acts of 1798, designed in part to prevent the absorption of immigrants into the Jeffersonian party, but which only strengthened their attachment to it. In 1812 the Federalists bitterly, but unsuccessfully, opposed the establishment of more-or-less universal white suffrage, certain it would swell the immigrant Irish vote of New York City.[11]

So it did, and in no time the Irish developed a powerful voting bloc. In the 1827 city elections, a prelude to the contest between John Quincy Adams and Andrew Jackson, the Irish sided mightily with Jackson, himself the son of poor Irish immigrants, and thereupon entered wholeheartedly into the politics of the Jacksonian era. By 1832 the Whig candidate for president found himself assuring a St. Patrick's Day dinner that "some of my nearest and dearest friends (are) Irishmen."[12]

The contest for the "Irish vote" became an aspect of almost every New York election that followed. A week before the election of 1884 a delegation of Protestant clergymen waited on the Republican candidate James G. Blaine, at the Fifth Avenue Hotel, to assure him, in the words of Reverend Samuel D. Burchard, "We are Republicans and don't propose to leave our party, and identify ourselves with the party whose antecedents have been rum, Romanism, and rebellion."[13] Blaine, who had been making headway with the Irish, lost New York by 1,077 votes, and thereby the election, which ended the Republican rule of post–Civil War America.

By this time the New York City Irish were not only voting for the Democratic Party but thoroughly controlled its organization. Apart from building their church, this was the one singular achievement of the nineteenth-century Irish: "The Irish role in politics was creative, not imitative."[14]

New York became the first great city in history to be ruled by men of the people, not as an isolated phenomenon of the Gracchi or the Commune, but as a persisting, established pattern. Almost to this day the men who have run New York City have talked out of the side of their mouths. The intermittent discovery that New York did have representative government led to periodic reform movements. But the reformers came and went; the party remained. The secret lay in the structure of the party bureaucracy which ever replenished and perpetuated itself. It is only in the past decade, when the middle class at length discovered the secret and began themselves to move into the party bureaucracy that the character of the New York City government has begun to change. Even here, the party complexion persists: of the twenty-six members of the City Council, twenty-four were Democrats in 1963.

In politics, as in religion, the Irish brought many traits from the Old Country. The machine governments that they established in New York (as in many Northern cities) show a number of features characteristic of nineteenth-century Ireland. The exact nature of the relationship is not clear: much that follows is speculative. But the coincidence is clear enough to warrant the proposition that the machine governments resulted from a merger of rural Irish custom with urban American politics. "Politics," in Charles Frankel's words, "is a substitute for custom; it becomes conspicuous wherever custom recedes or breaks down."[15] But in nineteenth-century New York events did not permit one system gradually to recede as the other slowly emerged. The ancient world of folkways and the modern world of contracts came suddenly together. The collision is nicely evoked by the story of Congressman Timothy J. Campbell of New York, a native of Cavan, calling on President Grover Cleveland with a request the president refused on the ground that it was unconstitutional. "Ah, Mr. President," replied Tim, "what is the Constitution between friends?"[16]

There were four features of the machine government which are particularly noticeable in this context.

First, there was an indifference to Yankee proprieties. To the Irish, stealing an election was rascally, not to be approved, but neither quite to be abhorred. It may be they picked up some of this from the English. Eighteenth-century politics in Ireland were —in Yankee terms—thoroughly corrupt. George Potter has written:

> The great and the wealthy ran Ireland politically like Tammany Hall in its worst days. Had they not sold their own country for money and titles in the Act of Union with England and, as one rogue said, thanked God they had a country to sell? . . . A gentleman was thought no less a gentleman because he dealt, like merchandise, with the votes of his tenants or purchased his parliamentary seat as he would a horse or a new wing for his big house.[17]

But the Irish added to the practice, from their own social structure, a personal concept of government action. Describing the early period of Irish self-government, Conrad M. Arensberg relates:

> At first, geese and country produce besieged the new officers and magistrates; a favourable decision or a necessary public work performed was interpreted as a favour given. It demanded a direct and personal return. "Influence" to the countryman was and is a direct personal relationship, like the friendship of the countryside along which his own life moves.[18]

Second, the Irish brought to America a settled tradition of regarding the formal government as illegitimate and the informal one as bearing the true impress of popular sovereignty. The Penal Laws of eighteenth-century Ireland totally proscribed the Catholic religion and reduced the Catholic Irish to a condition of de facto slavery. Cecil Woodham-Smith holds with Burke that the lawlessness, dissimulation, and revenge which followed left the Irish character, above all the character of the peasantry, "degraded and debased":

> His religion made him an outlaw; in the Irish House of Commons he was described as "the common enemy," and whatever was inflicted on him he must bear, for where could he look for redress? To his landlord? Almost invariably an alien conqueror. To the law? Not when every person connected with the law, from the jailer to the judge, was a Protestant. . . .
>
> In these conditions suspicion of the law, of the ministers of the law and of all established authority "worked into the very nerves and blood of the Irish peasant," and since the law did not give him justice he set up his own law. The secret societies which have been the curse of Ireland became widespread during the Penal period . . . dissimulation became a moral necessity and evasion of the law the duty of every God-fearing Catholic.[19]

This habit of mind pervaded Tammany at its height. City Hall as such was no more to be trusted than Dublin Castle. Alone one could fight neither. If in trouble it was best to see the McManus. If the McMani were in power in City Hall as well as in the Tuscarora Regular Democratic Organization of the Second Assembly District Middle —so much the better.

Third, most of the Irish arrived in America fresh from the momentous experience of the Catholic Emancipation movement. The Catholic Association that the Irish leader Daniel O'Connell established in 1823 for the purpose of achieving emancipation is the "first fully-fledged democratic political party known to the world." Daniel O'Connell, Potter writes, "was the first modern man to use the mass of a people as a democratic instrument for revolutionary changes by peaceful constitutional methods. He anticipated the coming into power of the people as the decisive political element in modern democratic society."[20] The Irish peasants, who had taken little part in Gaelic Ireland's resistance to the English (that had been a matter for the warrior class of an aristocratic society) arrived in America with some feeling at least for the possibilities of politics, and they brought with them, as a fourth quality, a phenomenally effective capacity for political bureaucracy.

Politics is a risky business. Hence it has ever been the affair of speculators with the nerve to gamble and an impulse to boldness. These are anything but peasant qualities. Certainly they are not qualities of Irish peasants who, collectively, yielded to none in the rigidity of their social structure and their disinclination to adventure. Instead of letting politics transform them, the Irish transformed politics, establishing a political system in New York City that, from a distance, seems like the social system of an Irish village writ large.

The Irish village was a place of stable, predictable social relations in which almost everyone had a role to play, under the surveillance of a stern oligarchy of elders, and in which, on the whole, a person's position was likely to improve with time. Transferred to Manhattan, these were the essentials of Tammany Hall.

By 1817 the Irish were playing a significant role in Tammany.[21] Working from the original ward committees, they slowly established a vast hierarchy of party positions descending from the county leader at the top down to the block captain and beyond, even to building captains. Each position had rights and responsibilities that had to be observed. The result was a massive party bureaucracy. The county committees of the five boroughs came to number more than thirty-two thousand persons. It became necessary to hire Madison Square Garden for their meetings,—and to hope that not more than half would come. The system in its prime was remarkably stable. Kelly, Richard Croker, and Charlie Murphy in succession ran Tammany for half a century. Across the river Hugh McLaughlin ran the Brooklyn Democratic Party and fought off Tammany for better than forty years, from 1862 to 1903. He was followed shortly by John H. McCooey, who ruled from 1909 until his death a quarter century later in 1934. Ed Flynn ran the Bronx from 1922 until his death in 1953.

The stereotype of the Irish politician as a beer-guzzling back-slapper is nonsense. Croker, McLaughlin, and *Mister* Murphy were the least affable of men. Their task was not to charm but to administer with firmness and predictability a political bureaucracy in which the prerogatives of rank were carefully observed. The hierarchy had to be maintained. For the group as a whole this served to take the risks out of politics. Each would get his deserts—in time.

In the intraparty struggles of the 1950s and 1960s no one characteristic divides the "regular" Democratic Party men in New York City from the "reform" group more than the matter of taking pride in following the chain of command. The "reform" group was composed overwhelmingly of educated, middle-class career people hardened to the struggle for advancement in their professions. Waiting in line to see one's leader seemed to such persons slavish and undignified, the kind of conduct that could be imposed only by a Boss. By contrast, the "organization" regulars regarded such conduct as proper and well-behaved. The reformers, who tended to feel superior, would have been surprised, perhaps, to learn that among the regulars they were widely regarded as rude, unethical people. As Arensberg said of the Irish village, so of the political machine, "Public honour and self-satisfaction reward conformity."[22]

It would also seem that the term "Boss" and the persistent attacks on "Boss rule" have misrepresented the nature of power in the old machine system. Power was hierarchical in the party, diffused in the way it is diffused in an army. Because the commanding general was powerful, it did not follow that the division generals were powerless. Tammany district leaders were important men, and, right down to the block captain, all had rights.

The principle of Boss rule was not tyranny, but order. When Lincoln Steffens asked Croker, "Why must there be a boss, when we've got a mayor and—a council and—." "That's why," Croker broke in. "It's because there's a mayor *and* a council *and* judges —*and* a hundred other men to deal with."[23]

At the risk of exaggerating, it is possible to point to any number of further parallels between the political machine and rural Irish society. The incredible capacity of the rural Irish to remain celibate, awaiting their turn to inherit the farm, was matched by generations of assistant corporation counsels awaiting that opening on the City Court bench. Arensberg has described the great respect for rank in the Irish peasantry. Even after an Irish son had taken over direction of the farm, he would go each morning to his father to ask what to do that day. So was respect shown to the "Boss," whose essential demand often seemed only that he be consulted. The story goes that one day a fellow leader of Thomas J. Dunn, a Tammany Sachem, confided that he was about to be married. "Have you seen Croker?" Dunn asked. In 1913, when Governor William Sulzer refused to consult the organization on appointments, Murphy forthwith impeached and removed him. Rival leaders fought bitterly in the courts for the privilege of describing their club as the *"Regular"* Democratic Organization.

The narrow boundaries of the peasant world were ideally adaptable to precinct politics. "Irish familism is of the soil," wrote Arensberg. "It operates most strongly within allegiances to a definite small area."[24] Only men from such a background could make an Assembly district their life's work.

The parallel role of the saloonkeeper is striking. Arensberg writes of the saloonkeeper in Ireland:

> The shopkeeper-publican-politician was a very effective instrument, both for the countryside which used him and for himself. He might perhaps exact buying at his shop in return for the performance of his elective duties, as his enemies charge: but he also saw to it that those duties were performed for the very people who wished to see them done. Through him, as through no other possible channel, Ireland reached political maturity and effective national strength.[25]

Among the New York Irish, "the saloons were the nodal points of district organization."[26] It used to be said the only way to break up a meeting of the Tammany Executive Committee was to open the door and yell, "Your saloon's on fire!" At the same time a mark of the successful leaders was sobriety. George Washington Plunkitt, a Tammany district leader, related with glee the events of election night 1897 when Tammany had just elected—against considerable odds—the first mayor of the consolidated City of New York:

> Up to 10 P.M. Croker, John F. Carroll, Tim Sullivan, Charlie Murphy, and myself sat in the committee-room receivin' returns. When nearly all the city was heard from and we saw that Van Wyck was elected by a big majority, I invited the crowd to go across the street for a little celebration. A lot of small politicians followed us, expectin' to see magnums of champagne opened. The waiters in the restaurant expected it, too, and you never saw a more disgusted lot of waiters when they got our orders. Here's the orders: Croker, vichy and bicarbonate of soda; Carroll, seltzer lemonade; Sullivan, apollinaris; Murphy, vichy; Plunkitt, ditto. Before midnight we were all in bed, and next mornin' we were up bright and early attendin' to business while other men were nursin' swelled heads. Is there anything the matter with temperance as a pure business proposition?[27]

As a business proposition it all worked very well. But that is about as far as it went. The Irish were immensely successful in politics. They ran the city. But the very parochialism and bureaucracy that enabled them to succeed in politics prevented them from doing much with government. In all those sixty or seventy years in which they could have done almost anything they wanted in politics, they did very little. Of all those candidates and all those campaigns, what remains? The names of two or three men: Al Smith principally (who was a quarter English, apparently a quarter German, and possibly a quarter Italian), and his career went sour before it ever quite came to glory.

In a sense, the Irish did not know what to do with power once they got it. Steffens was surely exaggerating when he suggested the political bosses kept power only on the sufferance of the business community. The two groups worked in harmony, but it was a symbiotic, not an agency relationship. The Irish leaders did for the Protestant establishment what it could not do for itself, and could not do without. Croker "understood completely the worthlessness of the superior American in politics."[28] But the Irish just didn't know what to do with their opportunity. They never thought of politics as an instrument of social change—their kind of politics involved the processes of a society that was not changing. Croker alone solved the problem. Having become rich he did the thing rich people in Ireland did: he bought himself a manor house in England, bred horses, and won the Derby. The king did not ask him to the Derby Day dinner.

The Roman Catholic Church

The story goes that in the last days of one of his campaigns Al Smith was on a speaking tour of the northern counties of the state. Sunday morning he and all but one of his aides got up and trekked off to Mass, returning to find the remaining member of the party, Herbert Bayard Swope, resplendent in his de Pinna bathrobe and slippers, having a second cup of coffee, reading the Sunday papers. As the Catholics stamped the snow off their feet and climbed out of their overcoats, Smith looked at Swope and said, "You know, boys, it would be a hell of a thing if it turned out Swope was right and we were wrong."

That sums it up. The Irish of New York, as elsewhere, have made a tremendous sacrifice for their church. They have built it from a despised and proscribed sect of the eighteenth century to the largest religious organization of the nation, numbering some 43,851,000 members in 1963. This is incomparably the most important thing they have done in America. But they have done it at a price.

In secular terms, it has cost them dearly in men and money. A good part of the surplus that might have gone into family property has gone to building the church. This has almost certainly inhibited the development of the solid middle-class dynasties that produce so many of the important people in America. (Thomas F. O'Dea speculates that the relative absence of a Catholic *rentier* class has much inhibited the development of Catholic intellectuals.)[29] The celibacy of the Catholic clergy has also deprived the Irish of the class of ministers' sons which has contributed notably to the prosperity and distinction of the Protestant world. These disadvantages have been combined with a pervasive prejudice against Catholics on the part of Protestants that has not entirely disappeared.

The Catholic Church does not measure its success by the standards of secular society. Many of its finest men and women disappear from the great world altogether.

This is well understood and accepted by Catholics. What troubles a growing number of persons within the Church is the performance of the great bulk of Catholics who remain very much a part of the world in which they live. For a Church notably committed to the processes of intellect, the performance of Catholic scholars and writers is particularly galling. In the words of Professor O'Dea, formerly of Fordham:

> The American Catholic group has failed to produce . . . both qualitatively and quantitatively an appropriate intellectual life. It has failed to evolve in this country a vital intellectual tradition displaying vigor and creativity in proportion to the numerical strength of American Catholics. It has also failed to produce intellectual and other national leaders in numbers appropriate to its size and resources.[30]

It is notorious that Catholics have produced hardly a handful of important scientists. But this seems to be true of Catholics everywhere. The failure of the American Catholics seems deeper than that. Neither have they produced a great poet, a great painter, a great diplomatist. None of the arts, none of the achievements that most characterize the older Catholic societies seem to prosper here. "Is the honorable adjective 'Roman Catholic' truly merited by America's middle-class-Jansenist Catholicism, puritanized, Calvinized, and dehydrated?"[31] asked the Protestant Peter Viereck. What he perhaps really wanted to know is whether Irish Catholics are Roman Catholics.

It is impossible to pull the terms apart in the reality of American life. Thus *Time* magazine was apparently not conscious of having said anything odd when it referred, in 1960, to "the City's Irish-Catholic population, 1,000,000 strong and predominantly Roman Catholic." Since the early nineteenth century the American Catholic Church has been dominated by the Irish. This is nowhere more true than in New York, the preeminent Catholic city of the nation.

Obviously, the Irish Church in America was established in the nineteenth century in the sense that parishes were organized and the churches built at that time. But it is also apparent that certain essential qualities of the religion itself derive from the world that followed the French Revolution. The English in the seventeenth and eighteenth centuries practically destroyed the Irish Church. The *faith* remained, but the institution practically disappeared; Catholics had almost no churches, few clergy, hardly any organization. Mass was said in the mountains by priests who were practically fugitives. The Irish Church did not even have a seminary in Ireland until Pitt established Maynooth in 1794—to obviate the training of Irish priests in revolutionary France.

The Church that grew from this beginning was something different from the historical Roman Catholic Church,—not in theology, although there was a distinct Jansenist flavor, but in culture. It was a church with a decided aversion to the modern liberal state. This aversion began with the French Revolution (the Irish hierarchy had been trained in France and gave refuge to any number of émigré French clerics) and was confirmed by the events of Italian unification. It was a church that was decidedly separatist in its attitude toward the non-Catholic community, which for long, in America as in Ireland, was the ascendant community. It was a church with almost no intellectual tradition. Ireland was almost the only Christian nation of the middle ages that never founded a university. With all this, as Kevin Sullivan writes, "Irish Catholicism, in order to hold its own in a land dominated by an English Protestant culture, had developed many of the characteristics of English sectarianism: defensive, insular, parochial, puritanical."[32]

It emphatically did not, however, acquire the English fondness for royalty. In a passage which Father C. J. McNaspy has said "speaks volumes," de Tocqueville noted that Father Power, the pastor at the time of St. Peter's, the first Catholic Church in New York, "appears to have no prejudice against republican institutions."[33] This was surely because the Irish had no great fear of republican institutions, which far from disestablishing their church had had the effect of raising it to equality with Protestant churches. Moreover, republicanism had raised Irishmen to a kind of equality with Protestants: one man, one vote.

Beginning with Bishop John Hughes, who came to the city in 1838, the New York Catholic Church became anything but passive in asserting this equality. In 1844, when the good folk of Philadelphia took to burning Catholic churches, Hughes issued a statement that "if a single Catholic church were burned in New York, the city would become a second Moscow."[34] None was burned.

Accepting republicanism did not entail accepting liberalism. From the first the Irish Catholic clergy of New York have been conservative. The Revolutions of 1848, which involved European liberals in a direct physical attack on the papacy, produced a powerful effect on the American hierarchy. Bishop John Hughes of New York put his flock on guard against the "'Red Republicans' of Europe," as he called them. At this point the Church began to find itself in conflict not only with primitive, no-popery Protestants who burned convents, but also with liberal, educated, post-Calvinist Protestant leadership. An early episode involved the Hungarian revolutionary Kossuth. As Hughes reported to Rome in 1858, "the enthusiasm and admiration in which Kossuth was held by the American people were almost boundless." Dreading the influence such liberalism might have on Catholics, Hughes denounced Kossuth prior to his appearance in New York City, with the result, the bishop felt, that the visit was a failure.[35]

The divergence between liberal Protestant and Catholic views in New York grew when Catholics generally declined to support the movement for the abolition of Negro slavery. In July 1863, the New York Irish rioted against the newly enacted draft. For four bloody, smoke-filled days the mobs ranged the city. They attacked Negroes everywhere, lynched some, and burned a Negro orphanage. Strong's diary records absolute revulsion:

> The fury of the low Irish woman . . . was noteworthy. Stalwart young vixens and withered old hags were swarming everywhere, all cursing the "bloody draft" and egging on their men. . . . How is one to deal with women who assemble around the lamp post to which a Negro had been hanged and cut off certain parts of his body to keep as souvenirs? . . . For myself, personally, I would like to see war made on Irish scum as in 1688.[36]

In the post–Civil War period, when much Protestant energy turned to the issues of social reform, the Catholic Church continued to remain apart and, in the view of many, opposed. The New York diocese was notably alert to the perils of socialism.

One widely popular priest, Father Edward McGlynn, was temporarily excommuni-
cated in a controversy that followed his support of Henry George who ran for mayor
in 1897. (George had made headway by linking his single tax proposal to the problems of Irish land reform.) Bishop Corrigan even tried to get *Progress and Poverty*
placed on the Index of Prohibited Books, although without success other than to have
George's theories declared "false."[37]

These developments strengthened the separatist tendencies in the Church, although again, the basic decisions had been made prior to the great migration. Foremost of these was the decision to establish a separate school system.

In New York City, as elsewhere, education was largely a church function in the early
days of the republic. In 1805 a Free School Society was formed, "for the education of
such poor children as do not belong to, or are not provided for, by any religious society."[38] Its first address to the public proclaimed that "it will be a primary object, without observing the peculiar forms of any religious society, to inculcate the sublime
truths of religion and morality contained in the Holy Scriptures."[39] That year the state
legislature established a fund for the support of common schools which was distributed in New York City to the trustees of the Free School Society and "of such incorporated religious societies in said city as now support, or hereafter shall establish charity
schools."[40] Under this system Catholic schools, along with Baptist, Methodist, Episcopal, Reformed Dutch, German Lutheran, and Scotch Presbyterian ones, among others,
received state aid.

In 1823 it developed that the Baptist schools were padding their enrollment books
and requiring teachers to turn over part of their salaries. In the upshot, the distribution of state aid was turned over to the City Common Council, which thereafter channeled most of the public funds to the Free School Society, renamed the Public School
Society. By 1839 the society operated eighty-six schools, with an average total attendance of 11,789.[41]

As the society was strongly Protestant, most Protestants could accept this development, but Catholics did not. They persisted with their own schools. By 1839 there were
seven Roman Catholic Free Schools in the city "open to all children, without discrimination," with more than 5,000 pupils attending.[42] (Thus parochial school attendance
equaled almost half the average attendance of the "public" schools, a proportion not
far different from that of today.) Nonetheless, almost half the children of the city attended no school of any kind, at a time when some 94 percent of children of school
age in the rest of the state attended common schools established by school districts
under direction of elected officers.

This situation prompted the Whig Governor William H. Seward to make this proposal to the legislature in his message for 1840:

> The children of foreigners, found in great numbers in our populous cities and towns,
> and in the vicinity of our public works, are too often deprived of the advantages of our
> system of public education, in consequence of prejudices arising from difference of lan-
> guage or religion. It ought never to be forgotten that the public welfare is as deeply con-
> cerned in their education as in that of our own children. I do not hesitate, therefore, to
> recommend the establishment of schools in which they may be instructed by teachers
> speaking the same language with themselves and professing the same faith.[43]

Instead of waiting for the rural, upstate legislature to ponder and act upon this proposal of an upstate Whig governor, the Catholics in the city immediately began clamoring for a share of public education funds.[44] The Common Council declined on grounds that this would be unconstitutional. In October 1840, the bishop himself appeared before the council, even offering to place the parochial schools under the supervision of the Public School Society in return for public aid. When he was turned down, tempers began to rise.

In April 1841, Seward's Secretary of State John C. Spencer, ex officio superintendent of public schools, submitted a report on the issue to the State Senate. This was a state paper of the first quality, drafted by an authority on the laws of New York State (who was also de Tocqueville's American editor). Spencer began by assuming the essential justice of the Catholic request for aid to their schools:

> It can scarcely be necessary to say that the founders of these schools, and those who wish to establish others, have absolute rights to the benefits of a common burthen; and that any system which deprives them of their just share in the application of a common and public fund, must be justified, if at all, by a necessity which demands the sacrifice of individual rights, for the accomplishment of a social benefit of paramount importance. It is presumed no such necessity can be urged in the present instance.[45]

To those who feared use of public funds for sectarian purposes, Spencer replied that all instruction is in some ways sectarian: "No books can be found, no reading lessons can be selected, which do not contain more or less of some principles of religious faith, either directly avowed, or indirectly assumed." The activities of the Public School Society were no exception to this rule: "Even the moderate degree of religious instruction which the Public School Society imparts, must therefore be sectarian; that is, it must favor one set of opinions in opposition to another, or others; and it is believed that this always will be the result, in any course of education that the wit of man can devise." As for avoiding sectarianism by abolishing religious instruction altogether: "On the contrary, it would be in itself sectarian; because it would be consonant to the views of a peculiar class, and opposed to the opinions of other classes."

Spencer proposed to take advantage of the diversity of opinion by a form of local option. He suggested that the direction of the New York City school system be turned over to a board of elected school commissioners which would establish and maintain general standards, while leaving religious matters to the trustees of the individual schools, the assumption being that those sectarians who so wished would proceed to establish their own schools:

> A rivalry may, and probably will, be produced between them, to increase the number of pupils. As an essential means to such an object, there will be a constant effort to improve the schools, in the mode and degree of instruction, and in the qualification of the teachers. Thus, not only will the number of children brought into the schools be incalculably augmented, but the competition anticipated will produce its usual effect of providing the very best material to satisfy the public demand. These advantages will more than compensate for any possible evils that may be apprehended from having schools adapted to the feelings and views of the different denominations.[46]

The legislature put off immediate action on Spencer's report. But Catholics grew impatient. When neither party endorsed the proposal in the political campaign that fall, Bishop Hughes made the calamitous mistake—four days before the election—of entering a slate of his own candidates for the legislature. Protestants were horrified. James G. Bennett in the *New York Herald* declared the bishop was trying "to organize the Irish Catholics of New York as a district party, that could be given to the Whigs or Locofocos at the wave of his crozier." The Carroll Hall candidates, as they were known, polled just enough votes to put an end to further discussion of using public funds to help Catholics become more active citizens.

At the next session of the legislature the Public School Society was, in effect, disestablished. Spencer's proposal for an elected Board of Education in New York City was adopted. Each city ward was to have elected commissioners, inspectors, and trustees to run the common schools in its area. But the Protestants, foreseeing the numerical supremacy of the Catholics, blocked Spencer's proposal for local option on religious instruction: "In a word, the Protestants disliked secularism, but they disliked the Pope more."[47] The 1842 law provided that "no school . . . in which any religious sectarian doctrine or tenet shall be taught, inculcated, or practised [*sic*], shall receive any portion of the school moneys to be distributed by this act." Thus the sectarian position that the Spencerian analysis would describe as "non-sectarian" won out. New York became the first of the original thirteen states to prohibit the teaching of religion in public schools. The New York Catholic Church thereupon set about establishing its own school system. In 1850 Hughes declared, "the time has almost come when it will be necessary to build the schoolhouse first, and the church afterward."[48]

Along with the great effort of building and operating parish facilities and charitable institutions, the Church proceeded to establish a vast private school system. But it seems clear that the high intellectual tradition was slighted. In the New York dioceses today, for every fifteen students in Catholic schools, there is but one in a Catholic college.

Monsignor John Tracy Ellis has suggested that development of the parochial schools swamped an incipient Catholic intellectual movement which stemmed from the educated offspring of the Maryland gentry and was powerfully reinforced in the 1840s by the conversion of prominent Protestants, corresponding to the Oxford movement in England. A century later Richard Cardinal Cushing of Boston was to tell a CIO convention: "In all the American hierarchy, resident in the United States, there is not known to me one Bishop, Archbishop or Cardinal whose father or mother was a college graduate. Every one of our Bishops and Archbishops is the son of a working man and a working man's wife."[49]

It seems clear that the prestige of the Church declined as it became more Irish. In 1785 the dedication of St. Peter's, with hardly two hundred parishioners, could command the presence of the governor of New York and the president of the Continental Congress. Rome itself was not seen as the traditional threat to Anglo-Saxon liberties. But as the Irish question got in the way, some of this sympathy and esteem disappeared. The Irish were the one oppressed people on earth the American Protestants could never quite bring themselves wholeheartedly to sympathize with. They would consider including insurgent Greece within the protection of the Monroe Doctrine, they would send a warship to bring the rebel Kossuth safe to the shores of liberty, they would fight a war and kill half a million men to free the Negro slaves. But the Irish were different.

The Wild Irish

"The Irish," wrote Macaulay, "were distinguished by qualities which tend to make men interesting rather than prosperous. They were an ardent and impetuous race, easily moved to tears or laughter, to fury or to love."[50] His words evoke the stage Irishman, battered hat in hand, loquacious and sly, proclaiming, "Faith, yer Honor, if I'd of known it was Hogan's goat . . ."

There was little in Gaelic culture, "exclusive, despotic, aristocratic," as Sean O'Faolain described it,[51] to evoke the stage Irishman, but by the nineteenth century Gaelic culture had all but disappeared. The peasant Irish character that remained did have within it contrasting impulses to conformity and to fantasy, to the most plodding routine and the wildest adventure. This was overlaid with a kind of fecklessness with which the Celts survived the savagery of the English in eighteenth-century Ireland. Thus there was some truth in the caricature. The peasants who poured into America brought with them little by way of an Irish culture but a definite enough Irish character. It is not surprising then that in America they learned to act as they were expected to act. Within weeks of landing they were marching in the Mulligan Guards. Within a generation the half-starved people who had produced Blind Raftery were eating meat twice a day and singing about the "Overalls in Mrs. Murphy's Chowder."

Prior to the great immigration, the Irish community in New York was reasonably symmetrical. There was a base of laborers and artisans surmounted by levels of tradesmen, professional men, entrepreneurs, and even aristocrats. The top layers were a mixture of Celt and Saxon, Catholic and Protestant. The first president of the Friendly Sons of St. Patrick, organized in New York in 1784, was a Presbyterian. Speakers at today's session of the Friendly Sons can recount the mercantile triumphs of their first members. "As you undoubtedly know," a Fordham professor told a recent meeting, "most of the founders of your society were merchants, who formed the aristocracy of New York in olden days."

With each successive shipload of famine-stricken peasants, the Irish community became more unbalanced. The "wild Irish," as Henry II had called them, in just the sense Americans would describe the wild Indians, poured into the city to drink and dance and fight in the streets. These were not merchant adventurers. They were Paddies for whom the city had shortly to provide paddy wagons. They felt neither relation to nor respect for the business leaders of their colony. Rather than waiting until they might be asked to join the Friendly Sons of St. Patrick, in perhaps two or three generations, they founded the Ancient Order of Hibernians. St. Patrick was a Briton, a peer of St. David, St. Andrew, and St. George. Hibernians were plain Irish Catholics.

The result was the Protestants ceased being Irish. For a while they became "Ulster Irish" and took to celebrating the Battle of the Boyne. (Orange Day riots in New York began in the 1830s. That of 1871 killed fifty-two persons and wounded hundreds.) But before long the Protestant Irish blended into the composite native American stock that had already claimed the Scots.

These developments robbed the New York Irish of middle-class leadership at the very moment they most needed it. Just when it was important for the enterprising among them to start going into the counting houses, the signs went up that "No Irish need apply."

The detachment of the Protestants from the Irish community was unquestionably hastened by the rise of nativism. In 1834 Samuel F. B. Morse published in the New York *Observer* a dozen letters which subsequently appeared as a book entitled *Foreign Conspiracy Against the Liberties of the United States.* He propounded the existence of a conspiracy between the Holy Alliance and the papacy to gain control of the nation.

Morse ran for mayor of New York in 1841 on the Native American ticket, in the same election with Bishop Hughes's Catholic candidates. The Know-Nothing party, which emerged from this, almost won the 1854 state elections. It disappeared after 1856; most of its members went into the new Republican party—and helped confirm the allegiance of Irish Catholics to the Democrats.

Toward the end of the nineteenth century, the cultural and religious separation of the Irish Catholics from Protestant New York was intensified when the groups split on just that issue that had originally established a bond of sympathy between them: British rule in Ireland.

In the days of the American Revolution, the Irish and the American causes seemed very much the same. At Valley Forge, Washington ordered grog for the entire army on St. Patrick's Day. As much as 40 percent of his men appear to have been of Irish or Scotch-Irish stock. In the century and a quarter that followed, America came repeatedly to the brink of war with England. While Anglo-American hostility prevailed, Irish nationalism and American patriotism were easily reconcilable. But as the nineteenth century passed, each successive crisis with England was somehow resolved, and, as new empires emerged in Europe and Asia, England and America drew closer together. Irish nationalists in America, who in 1776 had been looked upon by George Washington as stalwart patriots, were looked upon by Woodrow Wilson in 1916, when the last Irish revolution began, as traitors. Wilson, to be sure, was Ulster Presbyterian.

The cruel part of this history is that by 1916 Irish nationalism in America had little to do with Ireland. It was a hodgepodge of fine feeling and bad history with which the immigrants filled a cultural void. Organized campaigns for Irish freedom, centered in New York, began early in the nineteenth century and grew more rather than less intense. "Indeed," Thomas N. Brown writes, "it was the ruling passion for many of the second and third generation who knew only of America."[52]

> Irish nationalism was the cement, not the purpose of Irish American organization. Essentially they were pressure groups designed to defend and advance the American interests of the immigrant. Nationalism gave dignity to this effort, it offered a system of apologetics that explained their lowly state, and its emotional appeal was powerful enough to hold together the divergent sectional and class interests of the American Irish. This nationalism was not an alternative to American nationalism, but a variety of it. Its function was not to alienate the Irish immigrant but to accommodate him to an often hostile environment.[53]

For the Irish, nationalism gave a structure to working-class resentments that in other groups produced political radicalism. A group of Irish managed to combine both. Elizabeth Gurley Flynn, whom Theodore Dreiser described as "an East Side Joan of Arc," was part of an Irish socialist movement that was active in New York at the turn of the century. Her autobiography begins with a chapter "Paddy the Rebel," which captures some of the atmosphere of the Irish-American home in the 1890s:

> The awareness of being Irish came to us as small children through plaintive song and heroic story. . . . We drew in a burning hatred of British rule with our mother's milk. Until my father died at over eighty, he never said *England* without adding, "God damn her!" Before I was ten I knew of the great heroes—Robert Emmet, Wolfe Tone, Michael Davitt, Parnell and O'Donovan Rossa, who was chained hand and foot, like a dog, and had to eat from a tin plate on the floor of a British prison.[54]

Flynn notes that her second-generation father felt much more strongly about Ireland than her mother, who was born there.

The nineteenth-century Irish discovered they were Celts, locked in ageless struggle with Saxons. The most bizarre notions evolved from this discovery: hardly credible, were it not a time when American cotton farmers were organizing tournaments and civilized Scotsmen were appearing in kilts. But somehow the contrast between Irish reality and pretense was more pitiful than ludicrous. The proceedings were, as George Templeton Strong declared, "full of gas and brag and bosh."[55] Referring to an exiled leader of the 1848 revolt, Thomas F. Meagher, Strong noted: "'Meagher of the Sword' they call that commonplace decent attorney-at-law. 'Tis he will sheathe that battle axe in Saxon gore.'"[56]

The speeches were grand; the rallies grander. One hundred thousand persons attended a Fenian gathering in Jones' Wood in New York in 1866—against the wishes of the archbishop! The Fenians hoped to free Ireland by capturing Canada. From their New York headquarters they raised an army and prepared for the invasion, with the full regalia of a modern government-in-exile.

They pledged their lives and honor and beseeched the intercession of the Saints:

> By the old rebel Pike
> By the waving sunburst
> By the immortal shamrock
> By the sprig of fern
> By the bayonet charge
> By the Irish hurrah
> We beseech thee to hear us, O'Toole[57]

Nothing came of it. A thousand men or so marched into Canada. And marched right out again. In the one battle of the whole fiasco, eight Irishmen were killed. With what contempt did Strong record: "Their raid into Canada is a most ridiculous failure. . . . Had there been an Old John Brown among them they would have failed less ignominiously, at least. But there are no Celtic John Browns, and there never will be, I think."[58]

Strong was mistaken. The Celtic John Browns did appear. The foremost of them, Eamon de Valera, like Old John Brown himself, was born in New York.

The Irish issue all but dominated English politics in the last third of the nineteenth century. Then, as earlier, many of the Irish leaders were Protestants. The principal Irish objectives were land reform and home rule. By 1914 it appeared these had all but been obtained, despite the obstinate stupidity of the Conservative Party. But in the meantime, a far more intransigent group had grown up, the Sinn Fein party, dedicated to the establishment of a Gaelic, Catholic republic. It received much of its inspiration and money from Irish Americans.

In 1869 the New York Irish established a secret society, Clan-na-Gael, dedicated to a radical, violent course in Ireland. This remained a vigorous, nationwide organization for half a century, led in the New York area by a Fenian exile, John Devoy, and a Tammany judge, Daniel Cohalan. During much of this time the Irish issue seemed to dominate New York as well. During the middle years of the century the arrival of Irish patriots in the port were occasions for great public celebrations. The exiles enhanced a tendency, apparent from the time of O'Connell, for Irish-Americans to be more extreme in their attitudes toward England than were the native Irish.

At the turn of the century, when an Anglo-American *entente* was becoming evident, a number of German- and Irish-Americans began to work together against it. When World War I came, this collaboration became an earnest, perilous affair. "A comparison of such Irish papers as *The Gaelic American* and *The Irish World* with the German-language press indicates how closely they followed a common propaganda line," writes Carl Wittke.[59] The fateful move was that of Clan-na-Gael, which actively participated with the Germans and Sir Roger Casement in plotting and financing the uprising in Dublin in Easter Week, 1916. It was at best a minority act, despite all the provocations to revolt. In the curious words of a recent Irish-American historian:

> The age-old hope of securing Irish Independence *through physical force* had been abandoned by most Irishmen and was cherished chiefly by some stout-hearted men of the I.R.B. [Irish Republican Brotherhood] who would stage the rising of 1916. The uncertain solution in the Irish national test tube could be precipitated only by the blood of heroes who were not afraid to die in order that a nation might live.[60]

The Easter Rebellion established the leaders of Irish-American nationalism as among those who wished to see Germany defeat England. This position was barely tolerated in America in 1916. In the election campaign that year such Irish were scorned by both sides as "hyphenated Americans." President Wilson came to regard Cohalan as little better than a traitor, refusing even to enter the same room with him.[61] The efforts of Irish-Americans, in which the Catholic hierarchy took part, to obtain Wilsonian self-determination for Ireland at the peace conference, received little sympathy and no real help from the Wilson administration.

After the war, in a sequence that was to become familiar, Irish affairs went from insurrection, to independence, to civil war, to neutrality. When Irish bases were refused even American forces during the Second World War, Ireland was off America's conscience for good, if indeed she had ever been on it.

The shame of it from the point of view of the New York Irish was that Irish nationalism went sour just when they themselves were becoming almost a symbol of American nationalism. Just when issues of Irish-American newspapers were being banned from the mails as seditious, "Wild Bill" Donovan was leading the Fighting Sixty-Ninth into the Argonne and George M. Cohan was proclaiming to all the world: "I'm a Yankee Doodle Dandy . . . Born on the Fourth of July."

> Red, White and Blue,
> I am for you,
> Honest you're a grand old flag.[62]

The Irish-American character had formed, and no longer needed Irish nationalism to sustain itself. This is not to say that most Irish-Americans had such a character, but the *image* had jelled and in the manner of such things began to verify itself.

The Irish-American character was not very different from that which Macaulay described, save in two respects: it was urban and it was egalitarian. Where the Irish had been wild, they now became tough. Where they had been rebellious, it now became more a matter of being defiantly democratic. In the words of Thomas Beer, "an infinitely pugnacious, utterly common and merry animal."[63]

Picture John Morrissey: heavyweight champion of the world, member of Congress, principal owner of the Saratoga race course, proprietor of gambling houses, husband of a famous beauty, and a leader of the "Young Democracy" that helped overthrow Tweed. In 1875 a respectable enough mayor named Wickham, who had been elected by the new Tammany group, posted a man in his anteroom at City Hall to receive the calling cards of visitors. Shortly thereafter, Morrissey, having no card, was refused admittance to the Mayor's office. As recounted by Morris R. Werner:

> A few days later, a friend met John Morrissey in City Hall Park. He was dressed in a swallowtail coat, patent leather boots, white kid gloves, and he carried a light coat over his arm. In his other hand was a thick book. His friend, John B. Haskin, said: "Hello, John, what's up now? Going to a wedding?" "No," answered Morrissey, "not so bad as that. I've just bought a French dictionary to help me talk to our dandy Mayor. I'm going in full dress to make a call, for that is now the style at the Hotel Wickham," pointing to the City Hall. "No Irish need apply now," Morrissey added.[64]

Fifteen thousand people followed him to his grave.

Let it be said that the Irish gave style to life in the slums:

> Boys and girls together, me and Mamie Rorke,
> Tripped the light fantastic on the sidewalks of New York.

They became the playboys of this new Western World. "None can Love Like an Irishman" was a favorite song of Lincoln's day. By the turn of the century it had become equally clear that none could run like them, nor fight like them, nor drink as much, nor sing as well. When it came to diving off the Brooklyn Bridge or winning pennants for the Giants, it took an Irishman. And who could write such bittersweet songs as Victor Herbert? Or enjoy life like "Diamond Jim" Brady? All was "bliss and blarney."

Much was forgiven them. Their failures, as they themselves said of their principal one, were "a good man's weakness." A certain compassion pervaded even their wrongdoing. Jimmy Walker was nothing so much as P. T. Barnum in a speakeasy: predatory, not evil. At their best such Irish had a genius for getting through to the people: no one in the history of New York has ever been able to explain state government to the voters in the way Al Smith did. Nor have they ever quite forgotten the compliment he paid their intelligence.

By degrees the Irish style of the gaslight era became less and less Irish, more and more the style of the American city. Al Smith came close to being for the people of the Lower East Side of America what Lincoln had been for the Frontier. Better still, what Jackson had been—two Irishmen, a century apart. When the comic strips began, the principal urban characters—Maggie and Jiggs, Moon Mullins, Dick Tracy— were Irish. When the movies began to fashion a composite picture of the American people, the New York Irishman was projected to the very center of the national image.

For whatever reason, perhaps because of the influence of New York Jews in the film industry, when Hollywood undertook to synthesize the Christian religion, they found it most easy to do in the person of an Irish priest: Pat O'Brien as Father Duffy in the trenches. When it came to portraying the tough American, up from the streets, the image was repeatedly that of an Irishman. James Cagney (a New Yorker) was the quintessential figure: fists cocked, chin out, back straight, bouncing along on his heels. But also doomed: at the end of the movie he was usually dead. The contrast with Chaplin tells worlds.

By the time the New York journalist, John O'Sullivan, coined the phrase "Manifest Destiny" as a compact apologetic for American expansionism, the Irish were seasoned nationalists. Their exploits, or their accounts thereof, in the Mexican and Civil Wars established the American institution of the "Fighting Irish." Thomas Beer recalled:

> This dummy figure of the Irishman had become deeply sacred with Americans; in 1898 a group of young journalists went hunting the first trooper to reach the blockhouse on San Juan Hill, assuring each other . . . that he would be a red-haired Irishman and warmly disappointed when he proved an ordinary American of German ancestry. . . . Nineteen years later, another group of journalists went hunting a red-haired Irishman who fired the first shot of the American Expeditionary Force in France.[65]

Success went to their heads; it also undermined the character of many. It is to be noted, as Beer does, that "the Irish were at once established as a tremendously funny, gay, charming people and concurrently were snubbed."[66] There was a touch of Sambo in the professional Irishman: he was willing to be welcomed on terms that he not forget his place. There was also more than a bit of mucker in the man-of-the-people pose. Derision of the hifalutin' all too easily shaded into contempt for intelligence and learning, particularly on the lace-curtain fringe. The Irish were flirting with the peril Whitehead pointed to in his remark that in the conditions of the modern world the nation that does not value trained intelligence is doomed.

This was painfully manifest in the Irish-American response to the extraordinary flowering of Irish literature in the late nineteenth century. The emigrant Irish may have brought with them a certain peasant respect for learning—"Isle of Saints and Scholars"—but two generations in the slums of New York killed it, if it ever existed. Instead of embracing and glorying in the new literature, the New York Irish either ignored it, or if they were respectable enough, turned on the Irish authors, accusing them of using bad language!

The Ancient Order of Hibernians raged and rioted when the Abbey Theatre brought the new playwrights to America. John Quinn, a New York lawyer, and an important patron of the Irish writers, showed an early copy of the *Playboy* to John Devoy, the Fenian journalist so dedicated to a dynamite-and-blood solution of the land question. Quinn later wrote Cohalan that for weeks and weeks in his paper "Devoy railed at the *language* of the *Playboy* as foul, un-Irish, indecent, blasphemous, and so on."[67] The Irish-Americans' reaction to the new literature was, of course, not very different from that of many or most of the native Irish.

Reilly and the 400 was fun, but it was not *Riders to the Sea.* When it emerged that the American Irish did not see this, their opportunity to attain a degree of cultural ascendancy quite vanished. After that began a steady emigration from the Irish "community" of many of the strongest and best of the young. This migration was as devitalizing in America as it was to the Irish nation overseas.

The image changed. At the turn of the century Ireland stood for brave things. The painter John Sloan was Scot by descent but preferred to think otherwise: "I'm an Irishman," he would say. "Therefore I'm agin' the government." But as time passed, the rebel receded, the policeman loomed larger. "We wur once the world's dramers af freedom," says the drunk old woman in Anthony West's *The Native Moment,* "—what are we now?"

There are, of course, no statistics or measures of this kind of movement, but the impression is overwhelming. Excepting those with a strong religious vocation, the sensitive, perceptive children of the American Irish born early in the twentieth century found little to commend itself in the culture to which they were born.

Of all the New York Irish to live with this and write about it, foremost was Eugene O'Neill. Only toward the end of his life was he able to do so. *Long Day's Journey into Night* recounts the agony of his family, "the four haunted Tyrones," headed by the actor father. (The O'Neills were the Earls of Tyrone.) Throughout one feels the rending insufficiency for the sons of the "gas and brag and bosh" of their father's Irishness.

EDMUND
Sits down opposite his Father—contemptuously
Yes, facts don't mean a thing, do they? What you want to believe, that's the only truth!
Derisively
Shakespeare was an Irish Catholic, for example.
TYRONE
Stubbornly
So he was. The proof is in his plays.
EDMUND
Well he wasn't, and there's no proof of it in his plays, except to you!
Jeeringly
The Duke of Wellington, there was another good Irish Catholic!
TYRONE
I never said he was a good one. He was a renegade but a Catholic just the same.
EDMUND
Well, he wasn't. You just want to believe no one but an Irish Catholic general could beat Napoleon.[68]

One of O'Neill's last plays, *A Touch of the Poet,* recounts the final defeat of Major Cornelius Melody, an Irish officer, late of Wellington's army. Descended to running a tavern near Boston, he is scorned by the Yankees and mocked by the Irish, neither of whom accept him as a gentleman. Melody returns from his crisis broken, a bog-trotter once more. He has killed his horse and dropped his English accent:

> Me brins, if I have any, is clear as a bell. And I'm not puttin' on brogue to tormint you, me darlint. Nor playactin', Sara. That was the Major's game. It's quare, surely, for the two av ye to object when I talk in me natural tongue, and yours, and don't put on airs loike the late lamented auld liar and lunatic, Major Cornelius Melody, av His Majesty's Seventh Dragoons, used to do. So let you be aisy, darlint. He'll nivir again hurt you with his sneers, and his pretendin' he's a gintleman, blatherin' about pride and honor, and his showin' off before the Yankees, and thim laughin' at him, prancing around drunk on his beautiful thoroughbred mare—For she's dead, too, poor baste.[69]

Melody rises and makes for the bar to drink with the Irish laborers he had scorned. From within he shouts a toast: "Here's to our next President, Andy Jackson! Hurroo for Auld Hickory, God bless him!" Melody was now, like the rest, an Irish Catholic Democrat—at peace with a world that would have it no other way.

"There Are Some of Us Left"

On the surface, the "Irish" in Irish-American is fast fading. "Sweet Rosie O'Grady" has become simply one of the old songs about the old-fashioned American girl. If any recognize the wild notes of "Garryowen," it is most likely as the charging call of the U.S. Seventh Cavalry, and the association is more with the battle of the Little Big Horn River than with the gay times of old on the banks of the Shannon.

Unquestionably, however, an Irish identity persists. It would seem that it now identifies someone as plain as against fancy American. In an urban culture, Irishness has come to represent some of the qualities the honest yeoman stood for in an earlier age, notably in the undertone of toughness and practicality. "Be more Irish than Harvard," Robert Frost told the young president in 1961.

Ethnic identity being mostly a matter of where one came from, it loses much of its content in the Middle and Far West where most persons came from the Eastern Seaboard in the character of Yankees, or Southerners, or whatever. New York being the first stop in America, however, most white New Yorkers continue to identify themselves as originating somewhere in Europe. Asked "What are you?" a New Yorker replies, "Italian," or "Greek," or "Jewish." Most Irish still answer, "Irish." For one thing, it is probably an advantage to do so. The more amiable qualities of the stage Irishman have persisted in tradition. The Irish are commonly thought to be a friendly, witty, generous people, physically courageous and fond of drink. There is a distinct tendency among many to try to live up to this image.

The problem with perpetuating this Irish type is that it is essentially proletarian and does not jibe with middle-class reality. Like Southern hospitality, the Irish temperament has become a tradition—valid enough, perhaps, but requiring constant reinforcement. Hence names acquire importance. The Maguires and O'Tooles and O'Shanes are continually reminded by others that they are Irish and are therefore less likely to forget (it normally being a pleasant thing to tell a man he is Irish). But the vast numbers of Irish Blacks and Whites, Longs and Shorts, Smiths and Joneses, not to mention the Comiskeys, Nagles, and Costellos, seem to lose their Irish identity more easily. In addition, there is a fairly strict rule of patrimonial descent: to be an Irish-American writer, an Irish last name is required. A kind of cultural rule also obtains: Henry James was pure New York Celt but is hardly regarded as an Irish-American author.

The three additional factors working toward a decline of Irish identity in America are the decline of immigration, the fading of Irish nationalism, and the relative absence of Irish cultural influence from abroad on the majority of American Irish.

The native Irish continue to emigrate (the population today is not half the pre-famine level), but most of the immigrants settle in England. A trickle of Irishmen arrives in New York, but it is barely sufficient to keep the county associations alive and to provide talent for and interest in the sporting events that are centered at Gaelic Park in the Bronx. A handful of declining Irish papers continues to be published, and the Ancient Order of Hibernians manages to keep an organization together, if only to arrange the St. Patrick's Day parade. But the first-generation immigrants are a declining, rather isolated group. A fair indication is the disparate course of development between the Jewish and Irish summer resorts in the Catskills. As the Jews have become more prosperous, their recreation centers in Sullivan County have developed into fabulous pleasure domes. By contrast, the Irish colonies in Greene County to the north seem to be dying out.

In truth, most of the recent immigrants are rather a disappointment to the American Irish, just as is Ireland itself to many Americans who go back. Neither the people nor the land fits the stereotype. Few sights are more revealing than that of a second- or third-generation Irish-American tourist sitting down to his first meal, boiled in one iron pot over the open peat fire, in his grandparents' cottage. Embarrassment hangs just as heavy over the Fifth Avenue reviewing stand of the St. Patrick's Day parade. The sleek, porcine judges and contractors, all uneasy bravado, simply don't know what to make of the smallish, dour Irish officials and emissaries gathered for the occasion. Neither do the guests from Eire seem to know quite what to make of the "O'Donnell Abu," Fighting 69th, "Top O'the Marnin" goings-on. In Dublin, March 17th is a holy day, the parade is like as not devoted to the theme of industrial progress; and until recently the bars were closed.

Modern-day Ireland has little to commend itself to the average Irish-American. Where the American granddaughters of Calabrian peasants are blossoming forth in Roman chic, there is no contemporary Irish manner to emulate. Even the most visible Irish contribution to the New York scene, the Irish saloon, is vanishing, decimated by prohibition and now unable to compete with the attractions of television and the fact that Italians can cook. A very considerable body of Irish traits and speech habits has become so thoroughly absorbed in New York culture as no longer to be regarded as

Irish. No one, for example, any longer thinks of Halloween as another of those curious days on which all the Irish in town get drunk. The result is fewer and fewer opportunities for Irish-Americans to associate themselves with their past.

Fewer and fewer need to do so in order to sustain their own identity. This is nowhere more evident than in the plight of the American Irish Historical Society. This
group was founded in New York in 1897 "to make better known the Irish chapter in
American history." There was certainly a case to be made that the Irish had been
slighted, and the society set out to right this imbalance with some vigor. But little
came of it. The membership was basically not interested in history; it was the imbalance of the present, not the past, that concerned them. When this was righted, the
purpose of the society vanished. Its *Journal,* which had inclined to articles by aspiring
judges beginning "While we know that an Irishman was in Columbus' crew on his
first voyage to the New World . . .," has long ceased publication. The society continues
to occupy a great tomb of a mansion on Fifth Avenue, with a fine library that few
seem interested in using and splendid meeting rooms where no one evidently wants
to meet.

The establishment of the Irish Free State and later the Republic of Eire, despite
the Ulster issue, has substantially put an end to the agitation for Irish independence
which contributed so much to the maintenance of Irish identity in America. As
Whitehead said of Protestantism, so of Irish-American nationalism: "Its dogmas no
longer dominate; its divisions no longer interest; its institutions no longer direct the
patterns of life."[70] On the contrary, the more militantly Irish circles in America have
become alarmed about the unorthodox behavior of the Irish government on issues
such as admission of Red China to the United Nations. The *American Mercury* has
published an article on the imminent possibility of a Communist takeover in Ireland.
The Brooklyn *Tablet* carries long pleas from Irish-Americans for ideological aid to "an
Ireland subject to the seductive siren call of the Left and the domination of an alien
and atheistic ideology."[71]

Ironically, it is precisely those persons who were most attached to the Irish cause
and the Irish culture of the nineteenth century who are having the most difficulty
maintaining such attachments in the present time. Ireland has not ceased to influence America. Contemporary American literature can hardly be understood save in
the context of Shaw, Wilde, Yeats, O'Casey, Joyce, and the like. Contemporary Irish
authors appear almost weekly in *The New Yorker.* But those who would most value
their Irishness seem least able to respond to such achievements. Irish writers have
been Irish indeed. Protestants, agnostics, atheists, socialists, communists, homosexu-
als, drunkards, and mockers, they have had but few traits that commend themselves
to the Catholic middle class. "A common drunk," Honorable James A. Comerford of
the Court of Special Sessions exclaimed in announcing that the playwright Brendan
Behan would not be marching in the 1961 St. Patrick's Day parade in New York.

In the coming generation it is likely that those persons who have the fewest conventional Irish attachments will become the most conscious of their Irish heritage.
This is already evident in writers such as Mary McCarthy and John O'Hara: things
Irish are to be found throughout their work. It would seem that any heightened self-
consciousness tends to raise the question of racial origin and to stir some form of

racial pride. Irish authors abound in the bookstores around Fordham. In Greenwich Village there is a distinct Irish strain, compounded of the literary and political traditions. Songs of the Irish Revolution have taken their place in the repertoire of the balladeers and are listened to rapturously by emancipated young Irish-Americans.

Irish consciousness would seem to be holding its own in the upper reaches of the business as well as the intellectual sphere. The Society of the Friendly Sons of Saint Patrick can hardly ever have been more prosperous than today, as it approaches the third century of its existence. The annual dinners, strictly adhering to a format that seems to have been fixed about the time Victor Herbert was president, are splendid affairs, moving in ponderous array from the Boned Diamondback Terrapin à la Travers with Bobadillia Amontillado, through the Chicken Forestière and Heidsieck Brut, to the demitasse, H. Upman Belvederes, and brandy. They leave no doubt that even if the Protestants have rather disappeared, the society remains, as it began, an organization of well-fed merchants. Perhaps the principal innovation of the past century is a middle course of boiled bacon, Irish potatoes, and kale, a wistful reminder of those far-off cabins in Roscommon. No one touches it.

Indications are that the Irish are now about the most evenly distributed group in New York in terms of economic and social position. They are perhaps a bit heavy on the extremes: rather more than their share of the men on the Bowery and on Wall Street, but generally about the right proportions. In this respect they are unique among the major ethnic groups in New York.

Their distribution within class strata is not nearly so even. O'Faolain has reminded us that the ancient Irish had a powerful distaste for commerce; through history the Irish were by preference lawyers and soldiers and priests, and the pattern rather persists in the New World. The Irish are well represented in Wall Street law firms. In one of the largest the Irish partners were recently considering whether a quota should be imposed. But they have shown relatively little talent as merchants, and most of those that did so have been quite overwhelmed by Jewish competition.

The principal Irish businesses in the city still tend to be family affairs, founded by working men and involving the organization of manual labor in forms that may begin small and grow larger. Thus in 1850, Michael Moran, just off the boat, began as a mule driver on the Erie Canal at 50¢ a day. Ten years later he put down $2,700 for half-interest in a towboat hauling barges from New York to Albany. Today his descendants operate the largest tugboat fleet in the world, with only two competitors left in New York Harbor. The *Sheila,* and *Moira,* and *Kevin,* and *Kathleen Moran*'s greet one and all as the great ships move in and out of the harbor.[72]

The Irish, in a sense, have never strayed far from the docks, where they established a singularly dispiriting regime of political, business, and trade-union corruption. They quickly enough got into the businesses of digging ditches and hauling freight, and Irish contractors have eviscerated, built up, knocked down, and again built up a good deal of New York City. Whether their firms will survive the rationalization process that appears to be going on in this industry remains to be seen. Considerable Irish fortunes were made in real estate speculation—a peasant attachment for land which O'Neill describes in his portrait of the elder Tyrone—but these seem not to have produced much in the way of continuing enterprise.

The Irish have done well in businesses such as banking, where there is stress on personal qualities and the accommodation of conflicting interests, and not a little involvement in politics. In 1850, at Bishop Hughes's suggestion, the directors of the Irish Emigrant Society, founded in 1841, established the Emigrant Industrial Savings Bank. As time passed, the bank became more active, and the charitable society less so until, in 1936, the society went out of existence. But the bank remains, on its original site behind City Hall, the fourth-largest savings bank in the nation and still very much an Irish affair. The Irish have also done well on Wall Street. James V. Forrestal, the son of an immigrant, was president of Dillon, Read and Co. before he entered the Roosevelt administration.

The Irish talent for political bureaucracy seems to have carried over into the world of business organization. The Irish have been content to get in the long lines of the giant corporations and for some time have been popping up in the front ranks as their turn came. In the long run, their patience may prove as important a commercial asset as Jewish daring or Yankee rigor.

For the moment, however, the relevant question is not how the Irish have succeeded, but why they have not succeeded more. The English and Dutch who preceded them in New York are now almost entirely middle- and upper-class. The Germans who accompanied them are predominantly middle-class. The Jews who followed them are already predominantly middle-class and soon will be exclusively so. If the majority of the Irish have climbed out of the working class, it has been only to settle on the next rung. Oscar Handlin has put it candidly that, just as the movement of Jews out of the ranks of unskilled labor was exceptionally rapid, that of the Irish was "exceptionally slow."[73]

A clue might be found in a cover story of *Life* magazine in 1947 on the "Peoples of New York." The Irish were not included among the major groups in the city but were relegated to a small block between the Romanians and the Arabs. The picture was that of a cop, and the caption read: "Once the victims of a violent prejudice, New York's many Irish are now thoroughly assimilated. Many of them become politicians or members of the city's police force."[74] Instead of profiting by their success in the all-but-despised roles of ward heeler and policeman, the Irish seem to have been trapped by it. As with the elder Tyrone, they seem almost to have ruined their talent by playing one role over and over until they could do little else.

For Tyrone, as for his sons, so also for the race: drink has been their curse. It is the principal fact of Irishness that they have not been able to shake. A good deal of competent enquiry has still not produced much understanding of the Irish tendency to alcohol addiction. It would seem, in the words of Charles R. Snyder, that

> Irish country culture appears to be an "ideal type" case of a deeply embedded tradition of utilitarian drinking. There is also a tradition of convivial social drinking in which drunkenness is common, but there is an extensive body of tradition which tends to orient individuals toward drinking for the effect of alcohol as a generalized means of individual adjustment.[75]

It seems to be agreed (but with less persuasiveness) that the Irish culture was "such as to create and maintain an immense amount of suppressed aggression and sexuality."[76]

The question may still be asked why drinking becomes addictive, and why the pattern persists in the New World. Aspects of the culture, particularly the suppressed sexuality, survive, of course. It may also be, as Roger J. Williams suggests, that the problem is at least in part heredity.[77]

Whatever the explanation, the fact itself is indisputable. In a study of a group on the Bowery, Straus and McCarthy found 44 percent of the whites to be Irish.[78] A dominant social fact of the Irish community is the number of good men who are destroyed by drink. In ways it is worse now than in the past: a stevedore could drink and do his work; a lawyer, a doctor, a legislator cannot.

In New York the Irish are competing with groups whose alcoholism rates are as phenomenally low as theirs is high. Studies almost invariably find the Irish at one end of the spectrum and the Jews at the very opposite. Meyer found "alcoholism is 74 times as important a cause of psychoses among men of Irish descent as it is among those of Jewish descent."[79] The Italians are well down on the scale. In 1947 Donald D. Glad reported the following incidence of inebriety in New York State based on first admission for alcohol psychoses per 100,000 population of each ethnic group:

Irish	25.6
Scandinavian	7.6
Italian	4.8
English	4.3
German	3.8
Jews	0.5[80]

It is evident enough that Irish drunkenness has given competitors a margin in business and the professions—it may even have tended to keep the Irish out of some of the professions. It is probably also true that it partially accounts for the disappearance of the Irish from organized crime. Gambling and related activities are among the largest business activities in New York and certainly among the most profitable. With their political power, even if declining, the Irish ought to have a share of control in them, but the Southern Italians, with Jewish connections, have completely taken over. Bookmaking, policy, and drugs are complex, serious, exacting trades. They are not jobs for heavy drinkers.

The relative failure of the Irish to rise socially seems on the surface to be part of a general Catholic failure. This hypothesis, with regard to Catholics, was put by a Notre Dame sociologist, John J. Kane:

> There may be some kind of lower middle or lower class orientation among them to education and occupation which tends to anchor Catholics in the lower socio-economic groups and which limits those who do achieve higher education to certain fields which appear to offer more security albeit less prestige and income. It may also be that leadership, even outside the purely religious field, is still considered a clerical prerogative, and the same seems equally true of scholarship. It seems that Catholics creep forward rather than stride forward in American society and the position of American Catholics in the mid-twentieth century is better, but not so much better than it was a century ago. Neither is it as high as one might expect from such a sizable minority with a large educational system and reputed equality of opportunity in a democracy.[81]

Such evidence as is available supports this hypothesis. In Detroit Gerhard Lenski found white Catholics to have the least positive attitude toward work of any of the major groups (Jews, white Protestants, Negro Protestants, and Catholics). Where Catholic attitudes were positive, it was, in contrast with Protestants, toward the less demanding, and hence less rewarding, positions. Positive attitudes toward work came close to being nonexistent (6 percent of the sample) among middle-class Catholics with Catholic education. In striking contrast, 28 percent of the middle-class Catholic males with a *public* education had a positive attitude.[82] The evidence also underlines the concentration of Catholics in certain activities. Kane found that in a sample of American Catholics in *Who's Who in America* 48.6 percent were lawyers or priests. Bosco D. Cestello found in a sample of Catholic businessmen in the same directory that 25 percent were in finance, two-thirds more than the national proportion, while only 7.7 percent, barely a quarter the national average, were in trade.[83]

The curious distribution of even successful Catholics—getting ahead as bankers before making much progress as merchants—raises the question whether the relative poor showing of Catholics in the business world is not primarily a poor Irish showing. The Italians and Poles and Puerto Ricans have not really been settled long enough to make it clear what their performance in normal circumstances will be. In time they may produce a Catholic business class that is quite up to average. But clearly, the Irish have not done so.

In New York this failure may well be related to the Irish success in politics. It is perilous to speculate in such matters, but a case can be made that contrary to the general impression politics is not a lucrative calling. This case is more confirmed than contradicted by the periodic scandals that reveal the large amounts of graft and benefactions passed between politicians and various legitimate and illegitimate businessmen: the politicians are often as not on their way to jail. The secret of the long tenure of many of the better known Irish politicians is that they were honest men by any standards, and certainly by the American standards of their time.

The equally relevant fact in a city like New York, with constantly changing neighborhoods, is the extreme difficulty of passing on political power from one generation to the next and in that way establishing prosperous family dynasties. The problem of Tammany leaders is not much different in this respect from that of champion prize fighters. A few Irish district leaders today are sons of old leaders, but they are rarely of the old breed. The *New York Times* recently ran a striking photograph of "The Clan Finn," the rulers of Greenwich Village from the 1870s to 1943. On the wall of the Huron Club, a three-story brick and stone edifice ("Pitched it up in an afternoon himself, he did.") hung a portrait of old "Battery Dan" Finn. Back stiff as a North River pile, and a head that must have been fashioned of cast iron. His eyes look straight ahead. Standing before the portrait is his son, "Sheriff Dan." Homburg and high collar, with the vast jowls of a prosperous official in an age when Luchow's and Tammany Hall shared Union Square. His eyes are glazed rather. Next to him is his son, "Bashful Dan." Gray flannels, hair and chin receding. Eyes downcast. "Bashful Dan" inherited his post in 1935. Eight years later Carmine G. DeSapio took it away from him.

The small potatoes of political success have become even less nourishing over the years. Swarms of Irish descended on the city government after the Civil War and began successions of low-grade civil servants. Here, as with the top-rank politicians, there was little cumulative improvement from one generation to the next. The economic rewards in America over the past century have gone to entrepreneurs, not to *fonctionnaires,* and hence, in that measure, not to the Irish of New York.

Even were the Irish rising faster socially and economically than seems to be the case, the first impression would be one of decline. People *disappear* into the lower-middle class, to emerge, if ever, only years or generations later, in the upper reaches of achievement. In the interval, they are outdistanced in the areas of popular achievement, which are particularly visible in an age of mass media. This has been painfully obvious for the Irish in New York, which is the center of the nation's entertainment industry and thereby the center of most of the popular arts. The past thirty years have been a time of steady decline for the Irish. The Irish fighters and ballplayers have gone down before Negroes and Italians. The Irish crooners have been driven out by Italians. Most of the popular comedians are Jewish. The best of the musicians are Negro.

A similar, if more complex, process is at work in the trade-union movement. The most important of the working-class leaders of the city, from Gompers to Dubinsky, have emerged from the Jewish Socialist tradition (Peter McGuire and George Meany excepted). This tradition, however, has about played out; the Jews have left the working class, and Jewish liberals have largely turned their interests elsewhere. During all this time the bulk of the trade-union leadership, notably in the craft unions, has been Irish. This leadership continues with a diminished, but by no means vanished, ethnic base. Of late the leadership has even been revived by the influence of Catholic ideological movements, symbolized in New York by the Association of Catholic Trade Unionists and the various church-related labor schools. It is likely that Irish influence in this area will continue for some time.

In their classic stronghold, the police force, the Irish have been forced to set up a society to protect their interests. For some time ethnic groups in the New York police, as in many of the city bureaucracies—as in the life of the city generally—have maintained fraternal organizations. The Italians were first to organize on an ethnic basis within the Police Department. In the 1930s they were followed by Jews, the white Protestants, the black Protestants, the Puerto Ricans, and the Poles. For a long while, the Irish were so dominant that it would have seemed ludicrous for them to organize. But by 1952 it was obvious that those days were passing; the Irish still had a majority of the force, but no longer a majority of the police academy, and so they set up the Emerald Society and took their place among the other minorities.

Turning lower-middle class is a painful process for a group such as the Irish who, as stevedores and truck drivers, made such a grand thing of Saturday night. Most prize fighters and a good many saloon fighters die in the gutter—but they have moments of glory unknown to accountants. Most Irish laborers died penniless, but they had been rich one night a week much of their lives, whereas their white-collar children never know a moment of financial peace, much less affluence. A good deal of color goes out of life when a group begins to rise. A good deal of resentment enters.

The cumulative effect of this process has been to produce among a great many Irish a powerful sense of displacement. It is summed up in a phrase they will use on hearing an Irish name or being introduced to another Irishman. "There are some of us left," they say. One could be in Connaught in the seventeenth century.

The Party of the People

The sense of displacement is nowhere more acute than in politics.

The basic cause of the decline of the political power of the Irish has been their decline as a proportion of the population. Where they accounted for a third of the population of the city in 1890, they are probably no more than one-tenth today. In 1960 there were 312,000 first- or second-generation Irish in the city, and a considerably larger number of older stock.[84] But like their English and Scotch predecessors, much of the old Irish stock has moved to the suburbs. Some, of course, have dispersed throughout the country. Many of the Irish who remain in the city have become Republicans, thus splitting the Irish vote, and of those who remain Democrats, a great many have been at odds with the prevailing ideology within their party. The result, inevitably, has been the rapid waning of Irish political power.

At first glance the Irish appear to be doing well enough, but only because they are passing out of political power. They have most of the very top jobs. But they have fewer and fewer of the bottom ones, a fact which means that in time they will lose the top ones. Seven of the last nine mayors of New York have been Irish, if one counts the latest, Robert F. Wagner, who is half Irish. Recently an Irish-Catholic Democrat from Brooklyn was chief judge of the Court of Appeals, the highest judicial post of the state. (He was succeeded by an Irish-Catholic Democrat from Buffalo.) A Manhattan Irish Democrat retired recently as chancellor of the State Board of Regents. A third of the New York delegation to the 1960 Democratic convention was Irish. In the city itself, as of 1961, the chief justice of the City Court and the chief city magistrate were Irish, but Italians and Jews predominated in the city courts. In 1959, of sixty-three state supreme court judges from New York, less than a quarter were Irish. During the Harriman administration in Albany, 1955–1958, New York City Jews received two jobs for every one given the Irish.

Nine of the nineteen Congressmen elected from New York City in 1962 were Irish, but only a fifth of the sixty-five Assemblymen were. Al Smith was the last Irish officeholder who could command a large vote in New York politics. Since he left office in 1928, only one Irish Catholic, James M. Mead of Buffalo, has been elected senator or governor. A series of Irish candidates were put up against Dewey with no success. It was not until 1954, when for the first time in memory the Democrats nominated a state ticket with no Irishman on it, that they won back the governorship. In 1962 James B. Donovan, the Democratic candidate for senator, managed even to lose his home borough of Brooklyn to the Republican Jacob K. Javits.

Within the Democratic Party the death of Edward J. Flynn of the Bronx in 1953 marked the end of Irish political leadership. Although the Irish continued with a majority of the county leaders, the initiative and leadership of the party passed almost

A young John Fitzgerald Kennedy (1917–1963) poses for an informal portrait in the 1940s with two powerful men—his father, Joseph P. Kennedy (center), and maternal grandfather, John F. Fitzgerald (left). After witnessing the crushing defeat of Al Smith in the 1928 presidential election, both Fitzgerald and the elder Kennedy worked assiduously to smooth out the rough edges of machine politics to groom an Irish-American candidate for the White House. (John Fitzgerald Kennedy Library, PX78-54:1)

entirely to the Italian leader Carmine DeSapio. In the great primary contest of 1961 over the mayoralty nomination, DeSapio was beaten, and with him most of the Irish that had survived. By 1963 the county leader in Manhattan was Armenian; Brooklyn and Queens had Jewish leaders, with only the Bronx and Staten Island lingering in Irish hands.

As stated, the principal cause of the decline of Irish political power in New York City is the decline of the Irish population. In the suburbs, to which many Irish have moved, they retain a good deal of power. Westchester, Nassau, and Suffolk all had Irish Democratic county leaders as of 1963. In the city, where the Irish established a system of popular rule, they no longer rule now that they account for only some 10 or 12 percent of the populace. But this is not the whole story. The ideological displacement of the Irish in the Democratic party has also been a major cause of their decline in New York.

The emergence of Irish political conservatism in recent years may seem to call for more explanation than is needed. The main thrust of Irish political activity has always been moderate or conservative in New York, but until recently it has not been articulately so. There is a well-known story about the Tammany Fourth of July fête at which a reporter asked why "Mister" Murphy had not joined in singing "The Star-Spangled Banner." "Maybe," came the reply, "he didn't want to commit himself." The functioning urban politician does not commit himself; he negotiates with the commitments of others. This came naturally to the Irish, who were the least encumbered with abstract notions about municipal ownership and trade-union rights.

Tammany conservatism has been greatly reinforced by the political developments which from the beginning of the Irish era to the present have kept the New York Democratic party isolated from that party in the rest of the country. Tammany stood for sin in a party wedded to virtue. This was never better expressed than by the Midwesterner speaking for Grover Cleveland at the Democratic convention in 1884. "They love Cleveland for his character," said the speaker, turning to the New York City delegation, "but they love him also for the enemies he has made." Tammany did not support the original nomination of a single successful Democratic presidential candidate between the Civil War and the Second World War. The ideas behind the programs of Cleveland and Wilson and Roosevelt largely passed them by.

Indifference began to turn to opposition about the time of the First World War. A great many New York Irish were bitter about Wilson's refusal to give American support to Irish independence, and the election returns showed it. Wilson's league became for them a symbol of American toadying to British imperialism. Cohalan organized five hours of testimony by the Friends of Irish Freedom before the Senate Foreign Relations Committee in the hearings on the Treaty of Versailles. The league was denounced as "an abomination," "a perversion of American ideals."[85] Many New York Irish Democrats entered the 1920s alienated from their party on what was then the fundamental issue of foreign policy.

The rejection of Al Smith, first by his country and then by his party, was the breaking point for many. The New York Irish gave their hearts to Smith, who was an Irish figure whatever his ancestry. He was in no sense a product of the slum, but rather a representative of a distinct New York urban culture that to this day asserts its own manner of speech and dress in a society otherwise overwhelmed by Brooks Brothers. Smith had not the slightest qualms about the adequacy of his education: it was hyperbole, and perhaps a sense of mockery, that led him to tell the New York State Assembly that he was a graduate not of Yale but of the Fulton Fish Market. He was the greatest state governor of his generation, perhaps of the century, but he was such without the pomposity of Good Government. He talked out of the side of his mouth, and mispronounced words. When he declared, "No matter how you slice it, it's still baloney," he seemed to strip the establishment of all the pretense and posture designed to keep the Irish and such in their places.

The bitter anti-Catholicism and the crushing defeat of the 1928 campaign came as a blow. The New York Irish had been running their city for a long time, or so it seemed. They did not think of themselves as immigrants and interlopers with an alien religion; it was a shock to find that so much of the country did. Worse yet, in 1932, when the chance came to redress this wrong, the Democrats, instead of renominating Smith, turned instead to a Hudson Valley aristocrat with a Harvard accent who had established his reputation by blocking Murphy's nomination of "Blue-eyed Billy" Sheehan for the U.S. Senate, and was soon to enhance it by getting rid of Jimmy Walker.

The main effect of the New Deal in the upper reaches of the Irish community in New York was to reveal to its members that while they had been rising socially and economically, the Democratic Party as a whole remained an organization of the masses. It rarely occurred to the Irish to stop being Democrats because they had become bankers, or whatever. The party was an ethnic and religious alliance, as much as an economic one. (In DeSapio's day, for example, the chairman of the board of the New York Stock exchange, a distinguished broker, son of an Irish policeman, regularly attended the Tammany Dinner.) Irish businessmen hated Roosevelt much as did other businessmen but with the special twist that they felt it was their own political party, overcome by alien influences, that was causing the trouble.

A distinctive quality of the anti–New Deal Irish during the 1930s is that they tended to identify the subversive influences in the nation with the old Protestant establishment. The well-to-do Irish felt it was Harvard, as much or more than Union Square, that was out to socialize America. The lower ranks of the New York Irish were powerfully attracted by Father Coughlin and his notions about social justice, Jews, and Wall Street bankers.

Al Smith openly endorsed the Republican candidate for the presidency in 1936. In a major address to an enthusiastic New York City audience he accused Roosevelt of preparing the way for a Communist-controlled America. The feeling of displacement is painfully evident. He told a Chicago audience that Jeffersonian Democrats were "out on a limb today, holding the bag, driven out of the party, because some new bunch that nobody ever heard of in their life before came in and took charge of things and started planning everything."[86]

When Jim Farley broke with Roosevelt in 1940, the Irish conservatives became even more united in opposition. Farley had hoped to succeed Roosevelt, only in the end to be pushed aside. For the Irish conservatives the Third Term became a racial insult as well as a constitutional affront. Farley's account of those years is bitter:

> What few people realize is that the relationship between Roosevelt and me had been basically political and seldom social. Strange as it may seem, the President never took me into the bosom of the family, although everyone agreed I was more responsible than any other single man for his being in the White House. Never was I invited to spend the night in the historic mansion. Only twice did I ever make a cruise on the presidential yacht. Both cruises were political. Never was I invited to join informal White House gatherings. My appearances there were for official social functions or for informal dinners followed by exploration of political and patronage problems. Mrs. Eleanor Roosevelt once said, "Franklin finds it hard to relax with people who aren't his social equals." I took this remark to explain my being out of the infield.[87]

Apart from his great talent, Farley was, after all, a man of honor and decorum in private life as in politics. He broke with Roosevelt on what he regarded as an issue of principle—only to find it interpreted as the inevitable incompatibility of landlord and tenant. He later wrote:

> What particularly irked me were the background articles emphasizing my quote humble unquote beginnings. I am an American of Irish descent. I have known many people of Irish descent. Fat, thin, tall, short—loquacious, taciturn, ebullient, and morose—but

never in my life have I met a "humble" one. It just doesn't run in the strain. The fact is that I have met few men of Irish descent who were not their own figurative secretaries of state. Whatever else they may lack, it isn't opinions or the willingness to fight for them. As to authenticity as Americans, while the Mayflower passenger list will be combed in vain for their names, sixteen Kelleys, seventeen Murphys, and hundreds of others of old sod ancestry have won the Congressional Medal of Honor—enough to assure even the unfairminded that the credentials of Americans of Irish descent are in order.[88]

The record would certainly support Farley's contention, but, if so, why bring it up? It was one thing to make a fuss over Irish performance in the Mexican War, when they were still new to the country and the nation for the first time faced a Catholic enemy. But a century later to carry on in the same way about, for example, the flyer Colin Kelly betrayed a curious defensiveness on the part of the Irish themselves.

Mixed with this defensiveness was a measure of aggression on the subject of Communism. The Irish revolutionary tradition contributed its portion of recruits to American radicalism. William Z. Foster, who organized the great steel strike of 1919, turned from the IWW to the Communist Party, ran as the Communist candidate for president in 1924, 1928, and 1932, and then became head of the Communist Party, was the son of Irish revolutionary exiles. The chairman of the Communist Party in America as of 1961 was Elizabeth Gurley Flynn. But none of these counted as Irish so far as the Irish were concerned because they had ceased to be Catholic. For the mass of the Irish who stayed within the Church, the reaction to the Russian revolution was as uniform as it was intense. In June 1919 the *Catholic World* declared:

> The excesses of the Bolshevik revolution are . . . not the exaggeration of otherwise worldly tendencies. They are the absolute subversion of all moral principles, the destruction of religion, and the overthrow of civilization.

The Catholic reaction was notably different from that of the New York Jews. In September 1920, *The American Hebrew* declared that the overthrow of Russian Czarism "was largely the outcome of Jewish thinking, of Jewish discontent, of Jewish effort to reconstruct." If there had been an initial "destructive" phase to Bolshevism, this had been supplanted by a "constructive phase" which was itself "a conspicuous expression of the constructive genius of Jewish discontent."[89] In the years that followed, the gulf, if anything, widened. On the issues of recognition of the Soviet Union, the Spanish Civil War, wartime collaboration with Russia, and postwar cooperation, the New York Catholics were profoundly at odds with a significant portion of the New York Jews. The Catholics kept seeming to get the worst of it. Russia was recognized, became our wartime ally, and seemed destined to be our postwar friend. The Communist influence in New York, in politics, in education, and in the trade-union movement, was abundantly evident.

This was not an easy period for the Catholic Irish. Disdained on the left as reactionaries, they were not really welcomed by the Protestant establishment, whose interests they sought to preserve. Even today if Catholics are admitted to have been profoundly right about Russian Communism, the suspicion is widely shared among non-Catholics that they were right for the wrong reasons. Two decades ago it was not even clear they were right.

The fact seems to be that non-Catholics did not pay very much attention to speeches of the kind in which Monsignor Fulton J. Sheen, in 1941, denounced "the colossal wastage of taxes to pay professors who would destroy America by teaching Russian Bolshevism," and went on to tell the Friendly Sons of St. Patrick:

> It is not to the point to say, as some newspapers do, that only 3 percent of the professors, and 20 percent of the students are disloyal to their country. Why is it you will not find a single Communist teaching in Manhattan College? Why none in Fordham? Why none in St. Patrick's Parochial School?

This climaxed with the announcement that "the professors in certain universities and colleges in New York City are the most learned professors in the world—because they are the 'best red.'"[90]

This kind of anti-Communism for a long period suffered from a characteristic Irish-Catholic failing. It was felt to be enough to know and to say that Communism was morally wrong. But nothing much was offered by way of specific advice to those who struggled in the world of day-to-day events.

The crisis came in the years immediately after the Second World War when evidence began to accumulate about the true nature of the Communist conspiracy— only to have the evidence, seemingly, ignored. Alger Hiss and William Remington and the Rosenbergs seemed proof enough for anybody—but not for a good number of persons in the Protestant-Jewish intellectual elite. To many Irish Catholics these innocents seemed to grow more arrogant as their failings proved more serious. The country seemed filled with persons who, in Irving Kristol's description, "prefer to regard Whittaker Chambers and Elizabeth Bentley as pathological liars, and who believe that to plead the privilege of the Fifth Amendment is the first refuge of a scholar and a gentleman."[91] This is the context in which the New York Irish turned overwhelmingly to the support of Senator McCarthy.

A clue to the nature of McCarthy's influence on the New York Irish is that he did not bring out the worst in them. New York Communism was primarily a Jewish affair, but Irish anti-Communism in the postwar period never became anti-Semitism. Even when it looked like anti-Semitism, and Jewish groups became disturbed—forty-two of the forty-seven employees suspended or refused clearance at Fort Monmouth after the McCarthy hearings, were Jewish—this was not the Irish-Catholic reaction. At best, the Irish position at this time rested on profoundly responsible religious convictions. At its worst, Irish anti-Communism was not directed at Communism at all. From start to finish, McCarthy got his largest response from the New York Irish when he attacked the institutions of the white Anglo-Saxon Protestant establishment. It was Harvard University and the State Department and the United States Army that seemed to be subverting the country. The faculty of Franklin Delano Roosevelt's college was riddled with Reds. Dean Gooderham Acheson would not turn his back on spies in the Foreign Service. George Catlett Marshall was a front man for traitors. Eventually McCarthy's aides began proposing that the biggest threat of Communism to the nation came from the Protestant clergy, and the senator himself intervened to put an end to the "real threat" to American security, the British blood trade with Red China. The Irish Catholics, and they had many supporters, could not believe the men running the country could be blind to the Communist threat that seemed so clear to them. There had to be a more sinister explanation. No action was too drastic to uncover it.

The Catholic hierarchy in New York left little doubt that it supported McCarthy. In 1954, despite the opposition of the Democratic city administration, the senator was invited to address the annual communion breakfast of the Police Department Holy Name Society of the New York Diocese. He received a tumultuous reception as he explained that an educator under Communist discipline with a "captive audience" was "ten times as dangerous" as even a traitor in an atomic plant.[92] Among some liberals there was a reaction almost of terror: the Fascists had won over the police! Preparations were actually discussed for an underground opposition in the event of a coup d'état.

McCarthy let the Irish down. He ended up a stumblebum lurching about the corridors of the Senate where it had been decided he was no gentleman. This left the Irish to defend a reputation that had become, in practical terms, indefensible. Yet the Irish achieved a strong temporary advantage from the McCarthy period that may or may not prove of permanent value. In the era of security clearances, to be an Irish Catholic became prima facie evidence of loyalty. Harvard men were to be checked; Fordham men would do the checking. The disadvantage of this is that it put the Irish back on the force. It encouraged their tendency to be regular rather than creative.

The agitation against Communists in government produced valuable results. But once the issue of Communist subversion at home was settled, the problem remained of what to do about Communist aggression abroad. Here the Irish had little to contribute. They had so committed themselves to the issue of internal conspiracy that they seemed to have no resources left for positive thinking. They remained with the FBI while Harvard men continued to run foreign policy—with an increasingly evident assist from the sons of Lower East Side radicals. When the "twenty years of treason" came to an end and Eisenhower installed his cabinet of "nine millionaires and a plumber," the plumber (appointed Secretary of Labor) was the Irish Catholic. Apart from a few persons such as Thomas B. Murray of the Atomic Energy Commission, the principal area of foreign affairs in which Irish Catholics have so far played a creative anti-Communist role has been in the international labor movement under the leadership of an Irish plumber from the Bronx, George Meany of the AFL-CIO, and even here the influence of the State Department and Jewish intellectuals has been much in evidence.

During the New Deal and, later, the McCarthy period, a great many New York Irish began voting Republican. Certainly a majority voted for Eisenhower. They were easily convinced that Stevenson was soft on Communism. It was Farley who said that "to send Governor Stevenson to negotiate with Mr. Khrushchev is to send the cabbage patch to the goat."[93]

The crisis for the conservative Irish came in 1960, when, for the second time, an Irish Catholic ran for president. It turned out that for many the estrangement from the Democratic Party had gone too deep to be overcome by more primitive appeals. Alfred E. Smith Jr. announced he was voting for Nixon. In fashionable Greenwich,

Connecticut, the grandson of John H. McCooey of Brooklyn turned up ringing doorbells for the straight Republican ticket. Kennedy probably got little more than a bare majority of the Irish vote in New York City. The students at Fordham gave him as much, but it appears it was the Jewish students in the College of Pharmacy who saved that ancient Jesuit institution from going on record as opposed to the election of the first Catholic president of the United States.

For some time a considerable number of New York Irish have been enrolling as well as voting Republican, but they have not made much progress in the Republican Party organization. Reversing earlier roles, the Jews and Italians are keeping the Irish out of things. Barely an eighth of the New York delegation to the 1960 Republican convention was Irish.

Contrary to appearances, within the New York Democratic Party, Irish fortunes probably took a turn for the better during the cataclysmic events of the 1961 mayoralty primary and election campaigns. The estrangement between the Irish organization leaders and the growing Jewish and Protestant liberal middle class, which intensified during the McCarthy period, became open warfare after Stevenson's defeat in 1952, which turned the attention of the latter group to local politics. Manhattan erupted in a series of Democratic primary fights in which the liberals set out to unseat the old guard Irish incumbents.

One by one the Irish district leaders were defeated. When this process had about run its course, the reformers turned on the leader of Tammany itself, Carmine De-Sapio, accusing him of being a boss, which was of course his proper function in the traditional system. The Tammany leader's position was, as always, ideologically indefensible. Unfortunately for DeSapio, it was also ecologically untenable: middle-class voters were pouring into his district and had begun to operate within the regular party system. Forced to choose between increasingly hostile forces, Mayor Robert F. Wagner came down on the side of the reformers, whereupon DeSapio in the classic manner set out to deny him renomination. As agreed by all involved, the essential power of the Democratic Party organization was not to elect its candidates but to choose them. Historically, no one could get the Democratic nomination without the support of the organization. The issue was of such central importance that the Irish county leaders of Brooklyn and the Bronx, along with the lesser figures in Queens and Richmond, joined DeSapio in a solid organization front.

Except for the Negro areas of the city, the primary contest that followed was bitter and pitiless in contrasting the appeals of the traditional, neighborhood-oriented party organization with the modern, mass-media-oriented, liberal establishment. "If Wagner wins," said one party leader, "you can close down every clubhouse in the city." Wagner won overwhelmingly.

It may be that the Wagner victory put an end to the Irish political system itself in New York, just as La Guardia in the 1930s had broken the hold of the Irish on the system. Wagner's victory was a triumph of middle- and upper-class political initiative, organization, and leadership over the traditional, conservative, working-class party. It was uniquely a victory of public opinion experts, communication specialists, and theoreticians allied with a haute bourgeoisie whose liberalism and genuine concern for the poor of the city were nonetheless combined with something very like old-fashioned Tory will-to-power. Tammany disciplined the masses and enabled them to rule. With that discipline broken, it is likely New York will revert to the normal municipal condition of rule by the centers of economic power in alliance with the communications media. Organized crime is likely to persist as one such center and may even grow more important. There are indications that the powerful political machines of the Tammany variety were the one social force capable of controlling organized crime —certainly the decline of Tammany was accompanied by the rise of Costello and the like—and it may well be that the future will see the liberal middle class and the criminal syndicates sharing power in a pattern that was already to be perceived during La Guardia's ascendancy.

If this should happen, the Irish have a role to play, for they have in significant numbers joined the middle and upper classes. A number of new Irish faces appeared in the ranks of the reformers, indistinguishable in most respects from their Jewish and Protestant counterparts, and helped perhaps by a tradition of being "politicians." Sharing the honors of primary day with Robert F. Wagner of Yale was James S. Lanigan of Harvard, who defeated DeSapio for district leader in Greenwich Village. The Irish liberals lack, for the moment at least, an ethnic constituency, but they are not less sensitive to the changed style of politics. "The old-line political club," said one reformer, "is concerned with individuals, getting a job for this one or doing a favor for that one. In our modern society, politicians have to deal with the problems of whole groups of people, and we reformers are concerned more with groups than with individuals." This was said by Peter P. Meagher, running for district leader on the West Side of Manhattan against the son of the McManus.

City of God and Man

The future of the Irish in New York politics will be profoundly affected by events within the Catholic Church, which is, and for a generation at the very least, will remain, essentially an Irish Catholic Church. If New York, like Washington or Paris, had no great cathedral on a main thoroughfare, it is not likely that 120,000 marchers and more would turn out on St. Patrick's Day. The great parade is no longer an *Irish* affair; it is even questionable whether a majority of the marchers are, in fact, Irish. The parade is rather an annual display of the size of the New York Catholic Church, whose priests and hierarchy on the whole are quite conscious of their Irish origins. The center of interest on the line of march is not the reviewing stand at 66th Street so much as the steps of St. Patrick's Cathedral, where Cardinal Spellman accepts the homage of his flock. This Catholic Church is now entering a new phase both for the clerics and the laity. Two items will evoke the period that is passing.

Some time prior to the 1928 campaign the *Atlantic Monthly* published a statement by an Episcopalian layman directed to Al Smith which, citing papal encyclicals and canon law, challenged the compatibility of Smith's religion with his loyalty to the United States Constitution. It was clear to Smith's advisers, who gathered to discuss it, that the governor would have to answer this challenge, but Smith himself was most reluctant. Hurt and dismayed, he said to Judge Joseph M. Proskauer (as reported by his daughter):

> Joe, . . . to tell you the truth . . . I don't know what the words mean. I've been a Catholic all my life—a devout Catholic, I believe—and I never heard of these encyclicals and papal bulls and books that he writes about. They have nothing to do with being a Catholic, and I just don't know how to answer such a thing.[94]

According to Reinhold Niebuhr's version of the meeting, which may be more accurate in spirit, Smith simply entered the room and asked all present, "Will someone tell me what the hell a Papal Encyclical is?"[95]

On the clerical side, a Catholic sociologist recently looked into Cardinal Cushing's remarks about the social origins of the parents of American Catholic hierarchy. He found the cardinal was substantially correct about the absence of college graduates, but not so much in his impression that the American bishops are the sons of working men and working men's wives. Only 5 percent of the fathers of some 133 prelates studied in 1957 had graduated from college, and 65 percent had not even gone to high school. But only 17 percent of these men remained unskilled laborers. The largest single group, 27 percent, became the owners of small businesses. Over half were either small businessmen, clerks, salesmen, foremen, or minor executives.[96]

All this is passing. It is hard to conceive an American Catholic of the future becoming a candidate for president of the United States without having acquired a fairly sophisticated understanding of Catholic dogma on the subject of relations of church to state. Nor is it likely that henceforth the prelates of the American Church will be drawn so preponderately from the lower-middle class. But the one social characteristic of the present New York Church which does not seem likely to change during the next generation is its Irishness. Of the eighteen bishops in the New York area, in 1961, one was Chinese, one was Italian, and the rest were Irish.[97] And in contrast to the police academy and the legislature, in the seminaries the Irish are holding their own.

The Catholic Church in New York during the remainder of this century will be characterized by an increasingly articulate and inquiring laity, ministered to by a steadily more sophisticated, predominantly Irish clergy. But the role of the Church in the life of the city is as yet uncertain. It will be determined by two sets of events: first, the course of Catholic education and intellectual life; second, the attitude of the Church toward social change.

There is nothing in the history of organized religion comparable with the effort of the American Catholic Church to maintain a complete, comprehensive educational system ranging from the most elementary tutelage to the most advanced disciplines. The effort absorbs so much of the energies and resources of the faithful as to prompt the remark of a New York Jesuit that a Catholic diocese is a school system here and there associated with a church. Lately, however, the strain on resources has become all but intolerable while serious misgivings have arisen as to the value of the end product.

Encouraged by the growing proportion of educated Catholics and much stimulated by the renaissance of Catholic thought in Europe, American Catholic intellectual life is going through, in the words of one nun, "an orgy of self-criticism."[98] (Fortunately, as Reverend Gustav Weigel, S.J., writes, "non-Catholics have politely and wisely kept out of the debate.")[99] The most widely discussed statement of the issue appeared in 1955 in the Fordham quarterly *Thought*. It was written by Monsignor John Tracy Ellis.[100] Msgr. Ellis began with Denis Brogan's statement that "in no Western society is the intellectual prestige of Catholicism lower than in the country where, in such respects as wealth, numbers, and strength of organization, it is so powerful."[101] "No well informed Catholic," said Monsignor Ellis, "will attempt to challenge that statement." He listed as causes: First, the deep anti-Catholic bias inherited from seventeenth-century England, which has discouraged Catholic intellectuals and fostered "an over-eagerness in Catholic circles for apologetics rather than pure scholarship." Second, the fierce problem of settling the immigrants which has preoccupied the Church until this generation. Third, the native American anti-intellectualism: "In that—as in so many other ways—the Catholics are, and have been thoroughly American." With no encouragement at home, and no well-established intellectual tradition to draw on from Ireland and Germany abroad, the American seminaries became unintellectual, and so also their products. Even the revival of scholastic philosophy was the work of non-Catholic institutions such as the University of Chicago.

Monsignor Ellis was particularly concerned with the studies that showed the abysmal performance of Catholics and Catholic institutions in scientific work. Two years earlier, Reverend Joseph P. Fitzpatrick, S.J., of Fordham, in the presidential address of the American Catholic Sociological Society, had said, on the same subject: "If this is true for the physical sciences, I would not hesitate to assert that it is more true of the social sciences." He suggested this was more than simply a matter of pedagogy; it had to do with the Catholic mind in a much wider sense:

> There is one state of mind, fairly common, that is confident in the possession of the ultimate answers to life's mysteries and does not see the need of seeking anxiously for the proximate answers also. There is another state of mind, also common enough, which is convinced that God saved the world without science; therefore prayer, sacrament and sacrifice are the things to be concerned about.[102]

Father Weigel has put the matter even more succinctly. In a paper presented to the Catholic Commission on Intellectual and Cultural Affairs, the group that has stimulated much of this discussion, he declared: "The postulate of all scholarly investigation is the nagging existence of mystery. The training of not a few young Catholics makes them believe that there is no mystery."[103] While at Fordham, Thomas F. O'Dea spoke out severely on the matter of the Catholic preoccupation with apologetics:

> The great Protestant and secular thinkers of America are not just men who made mistakes, like the "adversaries" of the scholastic manual. They have positive things to say to those American Catholics who have neglected the search itself. The partial segregation of Catholic life from that of the general community adds difficulties in that respect, but further defensiveness concealed under lethargic self-satisfaction is hardly an adequate response to the situation. We repeat: to be an intellectual means to be engaged in a quest, and if to be a Christian has come to mean to have the whole truth that matters—albeit in capsule form—in advance (to know, for example, that "Plato had an erroneous theory of human nature," that "Comte held God knows what, which is absurd") without ever having been introduced to a genuine philosophical experience, then we are hopelessly lost.[104]

To be sure, not every professor at Fordham holds this view, but the proposition fits the observed facts. Apart from a spate of half-apologetic articles on "Great Catholic Intellectuals" there has been surprisingly little dissent. On the other hand, this is an argument that disproves itself: the act of asserting the lack of Catholic intellectual standards is the first step of establishing them. The Catholic world is in fact astir with intellectual aspiration that carries with it the possibility of great achievement.

It is possible, even likely, that such a development will come quickly. Over the past half century there has been no lack of artists and intellectuals born and raised in Catholic, especially Irish-Catholic, environments, but the greater part of them have rejected this environment as one hostile to their aspirations to scholarly or aesthetic excellence. If this atmosphere were to change, as it is now changing, it is possible to envision an almost sudden emergence of a Catholic intellectual class, encouraged by the Church and sustained by the increasing relevance of religious doctrine to the intellectual concerns of the present age.

Whether this happens will depend largely on the quality of the education Catholics receive in the coming generation. The criticism of Catholic intellectual standards inevitably involved the quality of Catholic elementary and secondary schools as well as the colleges and universities. Despite evidence that parochial schools get a good quality student, the end results have simply not been good enough. Moreover, evidence exists that some of the better Catholic students have been avoiding competition in the tougher non-Catholic schools, with a resulting isolation that feeds on itself. In a study of New York City high school students who applied for state scholarships, it was found that while 34 percent of the Jews and 28 percent of the Protestants in the group were seeking admission to Ivy League schools, only 8 percent of the Catholics had submitted similar applications.[105] Without question, Catholic education came to a moment of crisis by the early 1960s.

There are three elements to this crisis. First, the Catholics have a large and rapidly growing population. Second, it is the teaching of the church and the wish of most of the laity that Catholic children should be educated in Catholic schools. Third, if this education is to meet their rising intellectual and social requirements, the already crushing cost will grow much greater; this leads to an increasingly adamant demand that in one form or another there be an end to the double taxation of the Catholic population for the cost of education.

The best available estimate of religious backgrounds in New York City identifies 48.6 percent of the total population in 1952 as Roman Catholic. Only 27.1 percent of the population was actually affiliated with a Catholic Church—but this figure, according to Leland Gartrell, the author of the study, would account for more than half the persons with religious affiliation in the city (some 50 percent having no affiliation).[106] It is unquestionably a growing group. Dr. Ronald A. Barrett, a Catholic sociologist, has recently shown that in the 1950–1959 decade American Catholic population increased twice as fast as the general population, accounting for 41.1 percent of the total United States population growth during that period.[107]

The cost of the Catholic school system in New York City is by any standards staggering. In 1960 in the dioceses of Brooklyn and New York (excluding those parts outside the city) there were some 360,000 students in Catholic elementary and secondary schools. This was 37 percent of the enrollment of the public schools, a proportion hardly changed from the days of Bishop Hughes. On top of this the dioceses maintain eighteen colleges and universities, with some thirty thousand students. The operating expenses of the city public schools came to $650 million in 1960, on top of which was the cost of the city colleges. The Catholic population of the city, barely a median income group, pay their share of the taxes that support the public schools in addition to the full cost of the Catholic education system.

The Catholics manage this by sacrifice and by what appears to be a high level of managerial efficiency. (The cost per pupil of Catholic elementary schools in New York is not one-third that of the public schools.) But there is a limit to such possibilities, and when that limit is reached, as it almost surely has been in some respects, the disparity in costs creates a difference in quality as well. In a period of rising intellectual expectations, this fact has led inevitably to active dissatisfaction with the existing arrangement under which Catholic schools are denied all but marginal public assistance.

Ironically, the crisis was precipitated by the election of President John F. Kennedy, which created a serious possibility that a program of federal aid to education would be enacted. For the president there was no apparent constitutional or political way to include aid to Catholic elementary or secondary schools in his program. But the New York Catholic Church, having been left out at the beginning of the era of state aid in the 1840s, was determined not to be excluded from the era of federal aid which seemed about to begin. Cardinal Spellman did not even wait for the new president to be inaugurated before denouncing in the strongest terms a proposal for federal aid prepared by advisers to the president-elect, and later adopted by him. "It is unthinkable," said His Eminence, "that any American child be denied the federal funds allotted to other children which are necessary for his mental development because his parents choose for him God-centered education."[108] Months later the vote of Democratic Congressman James J. Delaney of Queens killed the administration proposal in the House Rules Committee. Thereafter a stalemate ensued, with the cardinal becoming if anything more adamant. In 1962, at the eighteenth annual Archdiocesan Teachers Institute, he declared that it would be a "terrible crime" to exclude parents, children, and supporters of Catholic schools from the benefits of help from the national government. To do so, he said, would mean the "eventual end" of parochial schools: "We cannot compete with the federal government support and subsidy of the public schools alone."[109]

In the early 1960s elements of the New York Catholic Church seemed to be entering electoral politics for the second time in its history—but on the same issue. A series of Democratic congressional primary contests occurred in which the school aid issue was raised by militant Catholic groups. The New York State Federation of Citizens for Educational Freedom, a nonsectarian group but overwhelmingly Catholic, began endorsing candidates for office. In the 1962 elections this organization came out strongly for the Republican candidate for governor and the Democratic candidate for United States Senator.[110]

The prospects for the Church are at best doubtful. The basic problem is that Catholics have failed to persuade any significant number of non-Catholic opinion leaders of the justice of their case. The history of the 1840s has vanished for Catholic and non-Catholic alike. In New York, Catholic spokesmen have not yet been able to couch the issue in terms that have appeal, even perhaps meaning, for many Jewish or Protestant leaders, nor have they succeeded in providing Catholics in public and party office with any very coherent understanding of the problem. This is itself a measure of Catholic isolation from the liberal, secular tradition of the city that is epitomized by the *New York Times,* but this isolation is breaking down. At the same time, Catholics appear to be making some progress with their case among the public generally, and increasingly opinion leaders such as Walter Lippmann have been concluding that the national deadlock over federal aid to education can be broken only by including Catholic schools.

If an accommodation is reached on the school issue, there is likely to be some diminishment of Catholic defensiveness of the kind that led Heywood Broun to call the New York Irish "the cry babies of the Western world." This defensiveness takes the most painful and destructive forms, as in the continuing controversy over discrimination against Catholic scholars at Queens College.

Catholic defensiveness can be particularly destructive on the issue of Communist subversion and American loyalty. New York Catholics have been prone to think they have learned something when the leader of Tammany Hall informs a communion breakfast of the Sanitation Department Holy Name Society that "there is no Mother's Day behind the Iron Curtain."[111] When a number of the leading universities of the nation announced their opposition to the loyalty oath provisions of the National Defense Education Act of 1958 all over the country, as one disgusted Catholic scientist put it, "Catholic newspapers . . . proudly displayed front-page stories in which they told how Catholic students in Catholic colleges virtually demanded loyalty oaths."[112] This is at best a curious posture for members of a church whose principal effort in American society is to limit the role of the state in education.

The announcement in 1961 by the head of the John Birch Society that half his membership was Catholic—whether true or not—caused a stir in Catholic circles, as did in general the rise of the radical right in the post-Eisenhower period. Elements within the Church appeared to realize how uncritical and remote from reality large sections of lay opinion had become. There followed a series of lucid and eloquent statements denouncing extremist organizations and expounding the bases of effective anti-Communism, but whether the minds of those concerned had been conditioned beyond the reach of appeals to reason remained to be seen.

The excesses of Catholic militancy are producing a reaction among the laity as well. There is a suggestion of anticlericalism in the New York air. A student writer for the *Fordham Ram* recently devoted his column to ridiculing the Brooklyn *Tablet,* the official weekly of the Brooklyn Diocese, with this description of a typical issue:

> Well then you come to the editorial page and look at the cartoon. Usually you got some guy in a dark suit with "Outsider" written on him. Then there's a mountain with a building on it, and there's light coming out from behind it. This is generally a church or Truth or something. Then you got a rowboat between the man and the building, and it's marked "Penance" or "Hard Work" or something and the oars have "Guidance" written on them. Well all this is too deep for me. I like straight from the shoulder talk. None of this symbolism. . . .

I look at the letters section and see that people who write in are all against something. Generally it's Queens College. Once in a while a college kid complains about the "Tablet's" editorials or point of view. And they pull him apart like a broken accordion. Usually the poor sap says, "How can an adult newspaper be so stupid?" Well they never answer his question, but they knock him because he spelled a word wrong or mentioned Shakespeare or somebody.[113]

Although New York has for long been a center of clerical conservatism in the Catholic Church, it is also a center of Catholic intellecual activity that tends to "liberal" views in about the same proportion and along the same lines as intellectual opinion generally. The isolation of the Catholic community is rapidly breaking down as the great issues of the 1930s and 1940s recede. The passing of the Franco regime in Spain, already an object of strong criticism by the Spanish Catholic Church, will remove a time-honored source of misunderstanding, bitterness, and bona fide hostility. The expulsion of Communism from the power centers of American life has been acknowledged in most Catholic circles, while the appearance of Communism in Latin America must give Catholics pause in their assumptions about the process of Marxist subversion: no Protestant country has yet gone Communist. Increasingly, the prospect is that the various elements of Catholic opinion—liberal, conservative, radical—will merge with corresponding elements in non-Catholic groups, at one and the same time expanding the area of Catholic influence while diminishing the influence of the Catholic bloc.

The strong likelihood, therefore, is that the future will see Catholic opinion become increasingly variegated, reflecting the widely divergent views of a community that spans a broad social and ethnic spectrum. The development of Catholic social policy will almost certainly strengthen and hasten this process.

In 1962, some seven years after his widely read assessment of Catholic intellectual life, Monsignor John Tracy Ellis turned his attention to a potentially more dangerous situation: that the emergence of an intellectually trained and vigorous Catholic laity would bring with it "the curse of anti-clericalism." Already there was to be encountered "severe criticism of bishops and priests among the intellectuals and professional people."

This represented, of course, an almost entirely new situation for the American Catholic Church, reflecting the increased numbers of highly educated Catholics, but also the increasing intellectual stature of the Church itself. Whereas in the past a disgruntled Catholic intellectual, in Protestant-secular America, at a certain point would simply leave the Church, there now emerged the possibility of remaining Catholic but becoming an anticlerical!

Monsignor Ellis spoke with great feeling of the only solution he could envisage:

The laymen must be freed to speak and to act without hindrance on the vital problems that press for solution outside the realm of doctrine. If they are not given such freedom the superior training and education of which they are the recipients in rapidly mounting numbers will have been—insofar as the Church is concerned—largely wasted, and the Church itself will be exposed to the very real threat of having the laymen's repressed zeal and frustrated ambitions for the Mystical Body turned into a disillusionment and embitterment that will breed in our land the kind of spirit that has poisoned the relations of clergy and laity in so much of western Europe and in Latin America.[114]

The prospects for dissension within the Catholic community are strongest in the area of social policy, although here the structure most likely will be that of liberal clergy *and* laity alike combining in opposition to their conservative counterparts. Since the time of *Rerum Novarum* (1891) Catholic social doctrine has been opposed to many of the most cherished economic doctrines of American conservatism. However, this fact has, as it were, only gradually emerged. (It may be speculated that semantics is in part to blame: Catholic spokesmen have used the term "liberal" to refer to laissez-faire economics of the Manchester school, and have generously denounced same. However, Catholic and non-Catholic audiences alike would seem generally to have understood the term in its contemporary American reference to essentially non-laissez-faire views.) With the promulgation of the papal encyclical *Quadragesimo Anno* (1931), and more drastically, with *Mater et Magistra,* the American Catholic Church found itself committed to a systematic social doctrine that was almost certainly far to the left of the social thinking of most American Catholics, clergy and laity alike.

Mater et Magistra came as a distinct surprise to many. Reinhold Niebuhr, in a perhaps patronizing but authentic tone, noted in an editorial in *Christianity and Crisis* that the reaction of non-Catholics, secular and Protestant, had "been generally one of amazement that a church which they considered 'reactionary' should come out so clearly for such modern 'liberal' policies as social insurance, the whole philosophy of the 'welfare state' and aid to underdeveloped countries." The reaction of some conservative Catholics was disbelief bordering perilously (for a Catholic) on irreverence, as in the celebrated gibe "Mater sì, Magistra no" which appeared in the conservative *National Review.* The first reaction to the later encyclical of John XXIII, *Pacem in Terris,* was even more unusual. *The Commonweal* described the general attitude as follows:

> Of all of the responses that Pope John's encyclical, *Pacem in Terris,* could have been expected to arouse, perhaps none has been more startling than the general paralysis which has gripped American Catholics in the face of its implicit "opening to the left." For once it seems impossible to find any significant support for an important part of a major encyclical.

It is almost inevitable that American Catholicism will face a crisis of commitment as a result of the social doctrine set forth by Pope John XXIII. American Catholics, notably in areas such as New York, have not much thought of their religious obligations in terms of social action. A 1959 study of a Bronx parish, for example, found parishioners regarded the roles of civic leader, social leader, recreational leader, and reformer to be the least important functions of a priest. The role of administrator, for one, ranked well ahead.[115] More seriously, even were the Catholic community to commit itself fully to the social objectives of Catholic doctrine, the question remains as to how successful would be the outcome.

The function of Catholic education has been primarily pastoral (or has been widely regarded as such). Educators such as Professor John J. O'Brien have presented the thesis that

> the present *social* result of past American Catholic decisions in the field of education has been to establish a system of schools which have, . . . tended to encourage the development in their students of certain qualities which render them more or less ineffective in any effort to reconstruct American society along lines consonant with Catholic principles.

He described these qualities as "negativism, a faulty operational perception of the order of virtues, provincialism, and a certain moral-intellectual arrogance."[116] Strong meat, but hardly to be avoided in a conservative communion suddenly confronted with a radical and not particularly congenial mission. What is here reflected, of course, is not simply the difficulties which Catholics must face, but also the sense of urgency and purpose which such a mission can arouse. Clearly, such conflict can produce much good as well as much anguish.

Although the bulk of Catholic intellectuals will almost certainly associate themselves with the main body of American liberal opinion, Catholics are likely to have their most significant impact on conservative thought. American conservatism has for a century been notably inarticulate. Whatever Catholic doctrine might be, the generation of Irish Catholics now being educated has been steeped in conservative social feeling both at home and in their formal education. This sets them apart from any large group in America outside the South, save possibly the less numerous German Catholics. If the education of these Catholics is good enough, they will have the opportunity to create a sustained and comprehensive body of conservative opinion in the United States based on the Catholic doctrine of the rights and responsibilities of the individual, the limitations on the power of the state, and the transcendent purpose of the social order, combined with a scholastic respect for intellect.

Had John Fitzgerald Kennedy lived out his time he might profoundly have altered the course of the Irish-American world. Among his incomparable powers was an ability to bring together the sacred and profane streams of American public life that have somehow, for example, made foreign affairs genteel but domestic politics coarse. Out of such a consummation might have emerged a new American style, combining as did he himself the tribal vigor of ward politics with the deft perceptions of the chancelleries.

But he is gone, and there is none like him. Although he may yet emerge as the first of a new breed, all that is certain is that he was the last of an old one. The era of the Irish politician culminated in Kennedy. He was born to the work and was at every stage in his life a "pro." He rose on the willing backs of three generations of district leaders and county chairmen who, like the Good Thief, may in the end have been saved for their one moment of recognition that something special had appeared among them. That moment was in 1960 when the Irish party chieftains of the great Eastern and Midwestern cities, for reasons they could probably even now not fully explain, came together to nominate for president the grandson of Honey Fitz.

It was the last hurrah. He, the youngest and newest, served in a final moment of ascendancy. On the day he died, the president of the United States, the speaker of the House of Representatives, the majority leader of the United States Senate, the chairman of the National Committee were all Irish, all Catholic, all Democrats. It will not come again.

NOTES

1. *Dictionary of American Biography,* New York: Charles Scribner's Sons, 1934, p. 621.
2. Allan Nevins and Milton Halsey Thomas, eds., *The Diary of George Templeton Strong,* Vol. IV, New York: Macmillan, 1952, p. 236.

3. Ibid., p. 342.

4. Ibid., p. 368.

5. Florence E. Gibson, *The Attitudes of the New York Irish toward State and National Affairs, 1848–1892,* Studies in History, Economics, and Public Law, No. 563, New York: Columbia University Press, 1951, pp. 17–18.

6. Eleventh Census: 1890, Part I, pp. cixii, cixix. New York City did not then include Kings, Queens, or Richmond Counties. However, the proportion generally carried over. In 1890 three-quarters of the Brooklyn Assemblymen were Irish, as against slightly less than half those from Manhattan.

7. E. Wilder Spaulding, "The State Government under the First Constitution," Vol. 4: *History of the State of New York,* Alexander C. Flick, ed., New York: Columbia University Press, 1933, p. 158.

8. Frederick J. Zwierlein, "The Catholic Church in New York State," Vol. IX, ibid., p. 167.

9. John Tracy Ellis, *Documents of American Catholic History,* Milwaukee: Bruce, 1956, pp. 238–242.

10. *Dictionary of American Biography.*

11. Dixon Ryan Fox, "New York Becomes a Democracy," Vol. VI, *History of the State of New York,* Alexander C. Flick, Ed., New York: Columbia University Press, 1934, p. 28.

12. Quoted in George W. Potter, *To the Golden Door: The Story of the Irish in Ireland and America,* Boston: Little, Brown, 1960, p. 229.

13. Gibson, *Attitudes of New York Irish,* p. 390.

14. Thomas N. Brown, *Social Discrimination against the Irish in the United States,* The American Jewish Committee, November, 1958 (mimeographed), p. 30.

15. Charles Frankel, *The Democratic Prospect,* New York: Harper and Row, 1962, p. 11.

16. In his autobiography, George B. McClellan Jr. states that Cleveland told him the story was apocryphal. George B. McClellan Jr., *The Gentleman and the Tiger,* Harold C. Syrett, ed., Philadelphia: J. B. Lippincott, 1956, p. 311.

17. Potter, *To the Golden Door,* pp. 67–68.

18. Conrad M. Arensberg, *The Irish Countryman,* London: Macmillan, 1937, p. 178.

19. Cecil Woodham-Smith, *The Great Hunger,* New York: Harper and Row, 1962, pp. 27 ff.

20. Potter, *To the Golden Door,* p. 105.

21. Peel describes this as a predominant role, but he would appear to be at least two generations early in this respect. Roy V. Peel, *The Political Clubs of New York City,* New York: G. P. Putnam's Sons, 1935, p. 32.

22. Arensberg, *Irish Countryman,* p. 93.

23. Lincoln Steffens, *Autobiography,* New York: Harcourt, Brace, 1931, p. 236.

24. Arensberg, *Irish Countryman,* p. 107.

25. Ibid., p. 179.

26. Peel, *Political Clubs,* p. 38.

27. William L. Riordon, *Plunkitt of Tammany Hall,* New York: Knopf, 1948, pp. 107–108.

28. Thomas Beer, *The Mauve Decade,* New York: Knopf, 1926, p. 143.

29. Thomas F. O'Dea, *American Catholic Dilemma,* New York: Sheed and Ward, 1958, p. 152.

30. Ibid., pp. 35–36.

31. Quoted in John Tracy Ellis, "American Catholics and the Intellectual Life," *Thought,* Vol. XXX, No. 118, Autumn, 1955.

32. Kevin Sullivan, *Joyce among the Jesuits,* New York: Columbia University Press, 1958, p. 3.

33. C. J. McNaspy, S.J., "Patriarch of Parishes," *America,* Nov. 12, 1960.

34. John R. G. Hassard, *Life of The Most Reverend John Hughes, D.D.,* New York: D. Appleton, 1866, p. 276.

35. Ellis, *Documents of American Catholic History,* pp. 337–343.

36. Nevins and Thomas, *Diary of Strong,* Vol. III, pp. 334–342.

37. Robert D. Cross, *The Emergence of Liberal Catholicism in America,* Cambridge: Harvard University Press, 1958, pp. 119–124.

38. William Oland Bourne, A.M., *History of the Public School Society of the City of New York,* New York: 1870, p. 5.

39. Ibid., p. 7.

40. Quoted in "Report of the Secretary of State upon memorials from the city of New York, respecting the distribution of the common school monies in that city, . . ." *Documents of the Senate of the State of New York,* 64th Session, 1841, Document No. 86, Vol. III.

41. *New York Register,* 1840, pp. 337–338.

42. Ibid., p. 336.

43. *Documents of the Assembly of the State of New York,* 63rd Session, 1840, Document No. 2, pp. 5–6.

44. See Richard J. Purcell and Rev. John F. Poole, "Political Nativism in Brooklyn," *Journal of the American Irish Historical Society,* Vol. XXXII, 1941.

45. "Report of the Secretary of State," p. 6.

46. Ibid., p. 12.

47. Edwin R. Van Kleek, "The Development of Free Common Schools in New York State— The Campaigns to Eliminate the Rate Bill and to Divert Public Funds from Sectarian Schools," unpublished doctoral dissertation, Yale University, 1937, p. 162. Quoted in William Kailer Dunn, *What Happened to Religious Education? The Decline of Religious Teaching in the Public Elementary School, 1776–1861,* Baltimore: Johns Hopkins University Press, 1958, p. 255.

48. Quoted in Cross, *Emergence of Liberal Catholicism,* p. 137.

49. Quoted in John Tracy Ellis, "American Catholics and the Intellectual Life," *Thought,* Vol. XXX, No. 118, Autumn, 1955, p. 368.

50. Thomas B. Macaulay, *The History of England,* New York: 1866, Vol. I, p. 72.

51. *Irish Quarterly Review,* September, 1938.

52. Thomas N. Brown, "The Origins and Character of Irish-American Nationalism," *Review of Politics,* Vol. XVIII, No. 3, July, 1956, p. 331.

53. Brown, *Social Discrimination against the Irish,* p. 23.

54. Elizabeth Gurley Flynn, *I Speak My Own Piece,* New York: Masses and Mainstream, 1955, p. 13.

55. Nevins and Thomas, *Diary of Strong,* Vol. II, p. 276.

56. Ibid., Vol. II, p. 453.

57. From the litany of St. Lawrence O'Toole, quoted in Philip H. Bagenal, *The American Irish and Their Influence on Irish Politics,* Boston: Roberts Brothers, 1882, p. 137.

58. Nevins and Thomas, *Diary of Strong,* Vol. IV, pp. 90–91.

59. Carl Wittke, *The Irish in America,* Baton Rouge: Louisiana State University Press, 1956, p. 277.

60. Charles Callan Tansill, *America and the Fight for Irish Freedom, 1866–1922,* New York: Devin-Adair, 1957, pp. 134–135. Italics added.

61. Ibid., pp. 302–303.

62. George M. Cohan, *You're a Grand Old Flag* (New York: F. A. Mills, 1906).

63. Beer, *Mauve Decade,* p. 153.

64. Morris R. Werner, *Tammany Hall,* New York: Doubleday, Doran, 1928, p. 290.

65. Beer, *Mauve Decade,* p. 152.

66. Ibid., p. 152.

67. Quoted in Tansill, *America and the Fight for Irish Freedom,* pp. 126–127.

68. Eugene O'Neill, *Long Day's Journey into Night,* New Haven: Yale University Press, 1956, p. 127.

69. Eugene O'Neill, *A Touch of the Poet,* New Haven: Yale University Press, 1957, p. 168.

70. A. N. Whitehead, *Adventures of Ideas,* New York: Macmillan, 1935, p. 205.

71. *Tablet,* December 10, 1960.

72. Eugene F. Moran and Louis Reid, *Tugboat: The Moran Story,* New York: Charles Scribner's Sons, 1956.

73. Oscar Handlin, *The Newcomers: Negroes and Puerto Ricans in a Changing Metropolis,* Cambridge: Harvard University Press, 1959, p. 26.

74. *Life,* February 17, 1947.

75. Charles R. Snyder, "Culture and Sobriety: Signs of Alcoholism," *Quarterly Journal of Studies on Alcohol,* Vol. XVII, No. 1, March, 1956, p. 128.

76. Robert Freed Bales, "Cultural Differences in Rates of Alcoholism," *Quarterly Journal of Studies on Alcohol,* Vol. VI, No. 1, March, 1946, p. 485.

77. Roger J. Williams, "The Etiology of Alcoholism: A Working Hypothesis Involving the Interplay of Hereditary and Environmental Factors," *Quarterly Journal of Studies on Alcohol,* Vol. VII, No. 4, March, 1947, p. 583.

78. Robert Straus and Raymond G. McCarthy, "Non-addictive Pathological Drinking Patterns of Homeless Men," *Quarterly Journal of Studies on Alcohol,* Vol. XII, No. 4, December, 1951.

79. A. Meyer, "Alcohol as a Psychiatric Problem," in *Alcohol and Man,* H. Emerson, ed., New York: Macmillan, 1932, Chap. 11.

80. Donald Davison Glad, "Attitudes and Experience of American-Jewish and American-Irish Male Youth as related to Differences in Adult Rates of Inebriety," *Quarterly Journal of Studies on Alcohol,* Vol. VIII, No. 3, December, 1947, p. 408.

81. John J. Kane, "The Social Structure of American Catholics," *American Catholic Sociological Review,* Vol. XVI, No. 1, March, 1955, p. 30.

82. Gerhard Lenski, *The Religious Factor,* Garden City: Doubleday, 1961, pp. 85–87, 247–248.

83. Bosco D. Cestello, "Catholics in American Commerce and Industry, 1925–45," *American Catholic Sociological Review,* Vol. XVII, No. 3, October, 1956.

84.

TABLE 1

Country of Origin of the Foreign White Stock, New York City, 1960
(All figures are in thousands)

Country	Number	Country	Number
Total: Foreign Stock	3,785	Total: Foreign Stock	3,785
United Kingdom	175	U.S.S.R.	564
Ireland (Eire)	312	Lithuania	31
Norway	37	Finland	10
Sweden	28	Romania	62
Denmark	10	Greece	56
Netherlands	9	Italy	859
Switzerland	11	Portugal	5
France	35	Other Europe	59
Germany	324	Asia	103
Poland	389	Canada	66
Czechoslovakia	58	Mexico	7
Austria	220	Other America	204
Hungary	97	All other	10
Yugoslavia	20	Not reported	23

SOURCE: *United States Census of Population, 1960, New York,* Table 79.

85. *New York Times,* August 31, 1919.

86. *Syracuse Herald,* October 23, 1936. See also the brilliant essay by Richard Hofstadter, "The Pseudo-Conservative Revolt," *American Scholar,* Vol. XXIV, No. 1, Winter, 1954–1955.

87. James A. Farley, *Jim Farley's Story: The Roosevelt Years,* New York: Whittlesey House, 1948, p. 63.

88. James A. Farley, "What I Believe," *Atlantic Monthly,* June 1959.

89. Svetozar Tonjoroff, "Jews in World Reconstruction," *American Hebrew,* Vol. 107, No. 17, September 10, 1920, pp. 434, 507.

90. Friendly Sons of St. Patrick, 1941.

91. Irving Kristol "The Web of Realism," *Commentary,* Vol. 17, June, 1954, p. 610.

92. *New York Times,* April 26, 1954.

93. Address to the Rotary Club of Los Angeles, July 8, 1960.

94. Emily Smith Warner with Hawthorne Daniel, *The Happy Warrior,* Garden City: Doubleday, 1956, p. 183.

95. Reinhold Niebuhr, "Catholics and the State," *New Republic,* October 17, 1960, p. 15.

96. John D. Donovan, "The American Catholic Hierarchy: A Social Profile," *American Catholic Sociological Review,* Vol. XIV, No. 2, June, 1958.

97. That is, the names are Irish. Some could also be English, however. It should also be noted that Pope John has appointed a number of German-American cardinals.

98. Sister Joan Bland, Letter to the Editor, *New Republic,* October 10, 1960.

99. Gustave Weigel, S.J., Introduction to Thomas F. O'Dea, *American Catholic Dilemma,* p. xi.

100. *Thought,* Vol. XXX, No. 118, Autumn, 1955, p. 353.

101. Denis W. Brogan, *U.S.A., An Outline of the Country, Its People and Institutions,* London: Oxford University Press, 1941, p. 66.

102. Joseph P. Fitzpatrick, S. J., "Catholics and Scientific Knowledge of Society," *American Catholic Sociological Review,* Vol. XV, No. 1, March, 1954, p. 6.

103. Gustave Weigel, S.J., "American Catholic Intellectualism—A Theologian's Reflections," *Review of Politics,* Vol. XIX, No. 3, July, 1957, p. 305.

104. O'Dea, *American Catholic Dilemma,* pp. 112–113.

105. "A Survey of the Experience of 1235 New York State High School Graduates in Seeking Admission to College." American Jewish Congress, September, 1958 (mimeographed).

106. Leland Gartrell, "Religious Affiliation, New York City and Metropolitan Region," Department of Church Planning and Research, Protestant Council of the City of New York, November 1, 1958 (mimeographed).

107. *New York Times,* September 2, 1960.

108. *Catholic News,* January 21, 1961.

109. *Tablet,* February 17, 1962.

110. *New York Times,* October 18, 1962.

111. *New York Times,* May 11, 1959.

112. James B. Kelley, "Correspondence," *America,* October 1, 1960.

113. John R. Strack, "Between the Lines," *Fordham Ram,* November 17, 1960.

114. Right Reverend Monsignor John Tracy Ellis, "The American Catholic Laity—1962," Commencement address, Saint Mary's College of California, June 9, 1962 (mimeographed).

115. Joseph B. Schuyler, S.J., *Northern Parish,* Chicago: Loyola University Press, 1960, pp. 174–177.

116. John J. O'Brien, "Catholic Schools and American Society," *Social Order,* Vol. 12, No. 2, February, 1962.

SUGGESTED READING

Ronald H. Bayor and Timothy J. Meagher, eds., *The New York Irish* (Baltimore: Johns Hopkins University Press, 1996).

David N. Doyle, "Irish Elites in North America and Liberal Democracy, 1820–1920," *Radharc: Chronicles of Glucksman Ireland House* 3 (2002): 29–54.

Steven P. Erie, *Rainbow's End: Irish-Americans and the Dilemmas of Urban Machine Politics, 1840–1985* (Los Angeles: University of California Press, 1988).

Nathan Glazer and Daniel P. Moynihan, *Beyond the Melting Pot: The Negroes, Puerto Ricans, Jews, Italians, and Irish of New York City.* 2nd ed. (Cambridge, MA: MIT Press, 1970; originally published 1963).

Chapter 22

Once We Were Kings (1999)

Pete Hamill

That day I was in Ireland, in the dark, hard northern city of Belfast. I was there with my father, who had been away from the city where he was born for more than thirty years. He was an American now: citizen of Brooklyn, survivor of the Depression and poverty, one leg lost on an American playing field in the late 1920s, playing a game learned in Ireland, father of seven children, fanatic of baseball. But along the Falls Road in Belfast in November 1963, he was greeted as a returning Irishman by his brother Frank and his surviving Irish friends, and there were many Irish tears and much Irish laughter, waterfalls of beer, and all the old Irish songs of defiance and loss. Billy Hamill was home. And on the evening of November 22, I was in my cousin Frankie Bennett's house in a section called Andersonstown, dressing to go down to see the old man in a place called the Rock Bar. The television was on in the parlor. Frankie's youngest kids were playing on the floor. A frail rain was falling outside.

And then the program was interrupted and a BBC announcer came on, his face grave, to say that the president of the United States had been shot while riding in a motorcade in Dallas, Texas. Everything in the room stopped. In his clipped, abrupt voice, the announcer said that the details were sketchy. Everyone turned to me, the visiting American, a reporter on a New York newspaper, as if I would know if this could possibly be true. I mumbled, talked nonsense—maybe it was a mistake; sometimes breaking news is moved too fast—but my stomach was churning. The regular program resumed; the kids went back to playing. A few minutes later, the announcer returned, and this time his voice was unsteady. It was true. John F. Kennedy, the president of the United States, was dead.

I remember whirling in pain and fury, slamming the wall with my open hand, and reeling out into the night. All over the city, thousands of human beings were doing the same thing. Doors slammed and sudden wails went up. *Oh, sweet Jesus, they shot Jack!* And *They killed President Kennedy!* And *He's been shot dead!* At the foot of the Falls Road, I saw an enraged man punching a tree. Another man sat on the curb, sobbing into his hands. Trying to be a reporter, I wandered over to the Shankill Road, the main Protestant avenue in that city long ghettoized by religion and history. There was not yet a Peace Line; not yet any British troops hovering warily on the streets, no bombs or ambushes or bloody Sundays. The reaction was the same on the Shankill as it was on the Falls. *Holy God, they've killed President Kennedy:* with men weeping and children running aimlessly with the news and bawling women everywhere. It was a

Among the ceremonial gestures he made on his visit to Ireland in June 1963, President John F. Kennedy laid a wreath at the memorial to Commodore John Barry (1745–1803), often called the "Father of the American Navy," in Wexford town, County Wexford. Kennedy was a World War II Navy veteran. (John Fitzgerald Kennedy Library KN-C29399)

scale of grief I'd never seen before or since in any place on earth. That night, John Fitzgerald Kennedy wasn't "the Catholic president" to the people of the Shankill or the Falls; he was the young and shining prince of the Irish diaspora.

After an hour, I ended up at the Rock Bar, climbing a flight of stairs to the long, smoky upstairs room. The place was packed. At a corner table, my father was sitting with two old IRA men; one had only two fingers on his right hand. They were trying to console him when he was beyond consolation. His grief was real. No wonder. For the Catholic immigrants of his generation, men and women born in the first decade of the century, Jack Kennedy was forever and always someone special. His election in 1960 had redeemed everything: the bigotry that went all the way back to the Great Famine; the slurs and the sneers; *Help Wanted No Irish Need Apply*; the insulting acceptance of the stereotype of the drunken and impotent stage Irishman; the doors closed in law firms, and men's clubs, and brokerage houses because of religion and origin. After 1960, they knew that their children truly could be anything in their chosen country, including president of the United States.

"They got him, they got him," my father said that night, embracing me and sobbing into my shoulder. "The dirty sons of bitches, they got him."

And then "The Star-Spangled Banner" was playing on the television set, and everyone in the place, a hundred of them at least, rose at once and saluted. They weren't saluting the American flag, which was superimposed over Kennedy's face. They were saluting the fallen president who in some special way was their president too. The anthem ended. We sat down in a hushed way and drank a lot of whiskey together. We watched bulletins from Dallas. We cursed the darkness. And then there was a film of Kennedy in life. Visiting Ireland for three days the previous June.

There he was, smiling in that curious way, at once genuine and detached, capable of fondness and irony. The wind was tossing his hair. He was playing with the top button of his jacket. He was standing next to Eamon de Valera, the aged and gravely formal president of Ireland. Jack Kennedy was laughing with the mayor of New Ross in County Wexford. He was being engulfed by vast crowds in Dublin. He seemed to be having a very good time. And then he was at the airport to say his farewell, and in the Rock Bar, we heard him speak:

"Last night, somebody sang a song, the words of which I'm sure you know, of 'Come back to Erin, mavourneen, mavourneen, come back aroun' to the land of thy birth. Come with the shamrock in the springtime, mavourneen . . .'" He paused, but did not laugh at the sentimentality of the words; he seemed rather to be feeling the sentiment itself, the truth beneath the words, the ineradicable tearing that goes with exile. "This is not the land of my birth, but it is the land for which I hold the greatest affection." Another pause and then a smile. "And I certainly will come back in the springtime."

Thirty-six springtimes have come and gone, and for those of us who were young then, those days live on in vivid detail. We remember where we were and how we lived and who we were in love with. We remember the images on television screens, black-and-white and grainy: Lee Harvey Oswald dying over and over again as Jack Ruby steps out to blow him into eternity; Jacqueline Kennedy's extraordinary wounded grace; Caroline's baffled eyes and John-John saluting. We remember the drumrolls and the riderless horse.

Irish Americans of a certain age will carry those images to their graves. At the end of a century that began with much poverty and even more hope, the immigrants who are still alive and the children who are charged with remembering have much reason to rejoice. There are now few doors closed to Irish Americans. Irish Americans run vast corporations, control great wealth, and have triumphed in every field in American life—from the great universities to the halls of Congress, from movies and television to journalism and literature. We have our scientists, our doctors, our athletes, our scholars. Irish Americans can say with confidence: we have won all the late rounds.

The turning point, it seems to me, was the election of John F. Kennedy. Or, rather, the election and the assassination a thousand days later. The combination ended the last vestiges of the marginalizing of Irish-American society; the hyphen that so infuriated Kennedy's father was permanently removed (who refers to Mark McGwire as an Irish American?) or altered into an identity card that suggests admission, not exclusion; welcome, not rejection. The traumatic shock of the assassination itself created subtle shifts in the ways that other Americans perceived Irish Americans: there was a sense of dues paid, of finality. Many glib assumptions were shot away with that Mannlicher Carcano rifle. Among them were the assumptions of the larger society, expressed in the shorthand of stereotypes. But Kennedy's moment also ended the more timid assumptions of too many Irish men and women who believed that a desire for personal excellence or worldly success was a surrender to the sin of pride. They had created for themselves and their children what I've called elsewhere the Green Ceiling; Jack Kennedy smashed that ceiling forever. After he was buried, the men and women he had inspired did not go away.

To be sure, across those thirty-six springtimes, there have been alterations made— some of them drastic—to the reputation of John Fitzgerald Kennedy. Those who hated him on November 21, 1963, did not stop hating him on November 23rd; many carried their hatred to their own graves. Some who were once his partisans turned upon him with the icy retrospective contempt that is the specialty of the neoconservative faith. And time itself has altered his once-glittering presence in the national consciousness. An entire generation has come to maturity with no memory at all of the Kennedy years; for them, Kennedy is the name of an airport or a boulevard or a high school.

Certainly, the psychic wound of his sudden death triggered the Sixties, that era that did not end until Richard Nixon waved his awkward farewells and the North Vietnamese tanks rolled into the presidential palace in Saigon. Only a handful of addled right-wingers continue fighting over the Sixties. The revisionists have come forward; Kennedy's life and his presidency have been examined in detail, and for some, both have been found wanting. The Kennedy presidency, we have been told, was incomplete, a sad perhaps; the man himself was deeply flawed. Some of this analysis was a reaction to the overwrought mythologizing of the first few years after Dallas. The selling of "Camelot" was too insistent, too fevered, accompanied by too much sentimentality and too little rigorous thought. The Camelot metaphor was never used during Kennedy's one thousand days (Jack himself might have dismissed the notion with a wry or obscene remark); it first appeared in an interview Theodore H. White did with Jacqueline after the assassination. But it pervaded many of the first memoirs about the man and his time.

Some of the altered vision of Kennedy came from the coarsening of the collective memory by the endless stream of books about the assassination itself. The murder was submerged to a welter of conspiracy theories. In the end, nothing has been resolved. If there was a conspiracy, the plotters got away with it. In a peculiar way, the details of Kennedy's death obliterated both the accomplishments and the failures of his life.

Other tales have helped to debase the metal of the man: the smarmy memoirs of women who certainly slept with him and others who certainly didn't; the endless retailing of the gossip about his alleged affair with Marilyn Monroe, that other pole of American literary necrophilia; the detailed histories of the family and its sometimes arrogant ways. He was described in some gossip as a mere "wham, bam, thank you ma'am" character; other talk had him a hopeless romantic. By all accounts, he was attracted to beautiful and intelligent women, and many of them were attracted to him. And during the time he journeyed among us, this was hardly a secret. When I was a young reporter for the *New York Post* in late 1960, I was once assigned to cover Jack Kennedy during one of his stays at the Carlyle hotel. He had been elected but had not yet taken office. "We hear he brings the broads in two at a time," the editor said. "See what you can see."

There was nothing to see that night, perhaps because of my own naive incompetence as a reporter, or because I was joined in my vigil by another dozen reporters and about a hundred fans who wanted a glimpse of John F. Kennedy. Most likely, Kennedy was asleep in his suite while we camped outside the hotel's doors. But I remember thinking this was the best news I'd ever heard about a president of the United States. A man who loved women would not blow up the world. Ah, youth.

Two other events helped eclipse the memory of Jack Kennedy. One was the rise of Robert Kennedy and his assassination in 1968. The other was Ted Kennedy and Chappaquiddick. Some who had been drawn to politics by Jack Kennedy at last began to retreat from the glamour of the myth. A few turned away in revulsion, seeing after Chappaquiddick only the selfish arrogance of privilege. Others faded into indifference or exhaustion. At some undefined point in the late 1970s, the country seemed to decide it wanted to be free of the endless tragedy of the Kennedys. Even the most fervent Kennedy partisans needed release from doom and death. They left politics, worked in the media or the stock market or the academy. A few politicians continued to chase the surface of the myth: Gary Hart was one of them; in a different way, so was Bill Clinton. They helped cheapen Jack Kennedy's image the way imitators often undercut the work of an original artist.

Out in the country, beyond the narrow parish of professional politics, the people began to look for other myths and settled for a counterfeit. It was no accident that if once they had been entranced by a president who looked like a movie star, then the next step would be to find a movie star who looked like a president. The accidental charisma of Jack Kennedy gave way to the superb professional performance of Ronald Reagan.

The mistakes and flaws of the Kennedy presidency are now obvious. Domestically, he often moved too slowly, afraid of challenging Congress, somewhat late to recognize the urgency of the civil-rights movement, which had matured on his watch. He understood the fragility of the New Deal coalition of northern liberals and southern conservatives; he had been schooled in the traditional ways of compromise in the House and Senate and was always uneasy with the moral certainties of "professional liberals." When faced with escalating hatred and violence in the South, Kennedy did respond; he showed a moral toughness that surprised his detractors and helped change the region. But he was often bored with life at home.

Foreign policy more easily captured his passions. He was one of the few American presidents to have traveled widely, to have experienced other cultures. His style was urban and cosmopolitan, and he understood that developments in technology were swiftly creating what Marshall McLuhan was to call the "global village." But since Kennedy had come to political maturity in the 1950s, he at first accepted the premises of the Cold War and the system of alliances and priorities that had been shaped by John Foster Dulles.

Even today, revisionists of the left seem unable to forgive the role that Kennedy the Cold Warrior played in setting the stage for the catastrophe of Vietnam. He had inherited from Eisenhower a commitment to the Diem regime, and as he honored that commitment, the number of U.S. "advisers" grew from two hundred to sixteen thousand. By most accounts, Kennedy intended to end the American commitment to South Vietnam after the 1964 election. But since he'd won in 1960 by only 118,000 votes, he didn't feel he could risk charges by the American right that he had "lost" Vietnam. The quagmire beckoned, and at his death, Kennedy still hadn't moved to prevent the United States from trudging onward into the disaster.

For most of Kennedy's two years and ten months as president, Vietnam was a distant problem, simmering away at the back of the stove. Kennedy's obsession was Cuba. It remains unclear how much he knew about the various CIA plots to assassinate Fidel Castro. But the two major foreign-policy events of his presidency were the Bay of Pigs invasion of April 1961 and the missile crisis of October 1962. One was a dreadful defeat, the other a triumph.

According to Richard Goodwin and others (I remember discussing this with Robert Kennedy), Jack Kennedy had begun the quiet process of normalizing relations with Castro before his death. Although this, too, was to be postponed until after the 1964 elections, Kennedy had come to believe that Cuba was not worth the destruction of the planet. He waited, a prisoner of caution, and Fidel Castro—seven presidents later—is still the ruler of Cuba.

Today, it's hard to recall the intensity of the Cuban fever that so often rose in the Kennedy years. I remember being in Union Square when Brigade 2506 was going ashore. A week earlier, I'd actually applied for press credentials for the invasion from some anti-Castro agent in midtown; with great silken confidence, he told me I could go into Cuba after the provisional government was set up, a matter of a few days after the invasion. But from the moment it landed, the quixotic Brigade was doomed. And in Union Square on the second night, when it still seemed possible that the U.S. Marines would hurry to the rescue, there was a demonstration against Kennedy, sponsored by a group that called itself the Fair Play for Cuba Committee. Its members chanted slogans against the president. A year later, a much larger group demonstrated during the missile crisis. In a strange, muted way, these were the first tentative signals that the 1960s were coming. And later, after Dallas, when the world was trying to learn something about Lee Harvey Oswald, we all saw film of him on a New Orleans street corner, handing out leaflets. They were, of course, from the Fair Play for Cuba Committee.

During his years in power, as far as I can tell, John Fitzgerald Kennedy never uttered a word about Northern Ireland.

And yet . . .

And yet, across the years, learning all of these things from the memoirs and biographies and histories, understanding that Camelot did not exist and that Jack Kennedy was not a perfect man, why do I remain moved almost to tears when a glimpse of him appears on television or I hear his voice coming from a radio?

I can't explain in any rational way. I've tried. Hell, yes, I've tried. I've talked to my daughters about him, and to my wife Fukiko, after they've seen me turning away from some televised image of Jack. They've seen me swallow, or take a sudden breath of air, or flick away a half-formed tear. They know me as an aging skeptic about the perfectibility of man, a cynic about most politicians. I bore them with preachments about the need for reason and lucidity in all things. And then, suddenly, Jack Kennedy is speaking from the past about how the torch has passed to a new generation of Americans, born in this century, tempered by war, disciplined by a hard and bitter peace—and I'm gone.

There is more operating here for me (and for so many millions of others) than simple nostalgia for the years when I was young. Nothing similar happens when I see images of Harry Truman or Dwight Eisenhower. Jack Kennedy was different. He was at once a role model, a brilliant son or an older brother, someone who made us all feel better about being Americans. Not just those of us who are products of the Irish diaspora. All of us. Everywhere on the planet in those years, the great nations were led by old men, prisoners of history, slaves to orthodoxy. Not us (we thought, in our youthful arrogance). Not now.

"Ask not what your country can do for you," Kennedy said. "Ask what you can do for your country."

The line was immediately cherished by cartoonists and comedians, and Kennedy's political opponents often threw it back at him with heavy sarcasm. But the truth was that thousands of young people responded to the call. The best and the brightest streamed into Washington, looking for places in this shiny new administration. They came to Kennedy's Justice Department and began to transform it, using the power of law to accelerate social change, particularly in the South. They were all over the regulatory agencies. And after Kennedy started the Peace Corps, they signed up by the tens of thousands to go to the desperate places of the world to help strangers. It's hard to explain to today's young Americans that not so long ago, many people their age believed that the world could be transformed through politics. Yes, they were naive. Yes, they were idealists. But we watched all this, and many of us thought, "This is some goddamned country."

Out there in the wider world, people were responding to him as we were. It wasn't just Ireland or Europe. I remember seeing the reports of his 1962 trip to Mexico City, where a million people came out to greet him, the women weeping, the men applauding him as fellow men and not inferiors. I'd lived in Mexico and knew the depths of resentment so many Mexicans felt toward the Colossus of the North. In one day, Kennedy seemed to erase a century of dreadful history. The same thing happened in Bogotá and Caracas where four years earlier Richard Nixon had been spat upon and humiliated. This was after the Bay of Pigs. This was while the Alliance for Progress was still trying to get off the ground. I can't be certain today what there was about him that triggered so much emotion; surely it must have been some combination of his youth, naturalness, machismo, and grace. I do know this: In those years, when we went abroad, we were not often forced to defend the president of the United States.

We didn't have to defend him at home, either. He did a very good job of that himself. We hurried off to watch his televised press conferences because they were such splendid displays of intelligence, humor, and style. We might disagree with Kennedy's policies, and often did; but he expressed them on such a high level that disagreement was itself part of an intelligent process instead of the more conventional exchange of iron certitudes. He held sixty-four press conferences in his brief time in office (Reagan held fifty-three in two full terms) and obviously understood how important they were to the furthering of his policies. But he also enjoyed them as ritual and performance. He was a genuinely witty man, with a very Irish love of the English language, the play on words, the surprising twist. But there was an odd measure of shyness in the man, too, and that must have been at the heart of his sense of irony, along with his detachment, his fatalism, his understanding of the absurd. He was often more Harvard than Irish, but he was more Irish than even he ever thought.

I loved that part of him. Loved, too, the way he honored artists and writers and musicians, inviting them to the White House for splendid dinners, insisting that Robert Frost read a poem at the inauguration. He said he enjoyed Ian Fleming's books about James Bond; but he also brought André Malraux to the White House, and James Baldwin, Gore Vidal, and Saul Bellow, along with such musicians as Pablo Casals. Perhaps this was all a political ploy, a means of getting writers and artists on his side; if so, it worked. Not many writers have felt comfortable in the White House in all the years since, not even with Bill Clinton, who truly did make the effort.

Part of Jack Kennedy's appeal was based on another fact: he was that rare American politician, a genuine war hero. Not a general, not someone who had spent the war ordering other men to fight and die, but a man who had been out on the line himself. When he first surfaced as a national figure, at the 1956 Democratic Convention, reporters rushed to find copies of John Hersey's *New Yorker* account of the PT-109 incident in the South Pacific. They read: "Kennedy took McMahon in tow again. He cut loose one end in his teeth. He swam breaststroke, pulling the helpless McMahon along on his back. It took over five hours to reach the island."

Reading the story years after the event, some of us were stunned. Kennedy was the real article. There had been so many fakers, so many pols who were tough with their mouths and avoided the consequences of their belligerence. The type never vanishes. Over the past twenty years, the most fervent flagwavers, particularly among the Republicans, have been men who ducked service in Vietnam, their war. I think of them, and think of Kennedy, and they all seem to be frauds. Kennedy had been there, not simply as a victim but as a hero, a man who'd saved other men's lives. When he was president, that experience gave his words about war and peace a special authority. We also knew that his back had been terribly injured in the Solomon Islands and had tormented him ever since. He had almost died after a 1954 operation, and he wore a brace until the day he died. But he bore his pain well; he never used it as an excuse; he didn't retail it in exchange for votes. Hemingway, another hero of that time, had defined courage as grace under pressure. By that definition, Jack Kennedy certainly had courage.

Years later, long after the murder in Dallas and after Vietnam had first escalated into tragedy and then disintegrated into defeat; long after a generation had taken to the streets before retreating into the Big Chill; long after the ghettos of Watts and Newark and Detroit and so many other cities had exploded into nihilistic violence; after Robert Kennedy had been killed and Martin Luther King and Malcolm X; after Woodstock and Watergate; after the Beatles had arrived, triumphed, and broken up, and after John Lennon had been murdered; after Johnson, Nixon, Ford, and Carter had given way to Ronald Reagan; after passionate liberalism faded; after the horrors of Cambodia and the anarchy of Beirut; after cocaine and AIDS had become the new plagues—after all had changed from the world we knew in 1963, I was driving alone in a rented car late one afternoon through the state of Guerrero in Mexico.

I was moving through vast, empty stretches of parched mountainous land when the right rear tire went flat. I pulled over and quickly discovered that the rental car had neither a spare nor tools. I was alone in the emptiness of Mexico, on a road in its most dangerous state. Trucks roared by, and some cars, heading for Acapulco, but nobody stopped.

Off in the distance I saw a plume of smoke coming from a small house. I started walking to the house, feeling uneasy and vulnerable. A rutted dirt road led to the front of the house. A dusty car was parked to the side. It was almost dark, and for a tense moment, I considered turning back.

And then the door opened. A beefy man stood there, looking at me in a blank way. I came closer, and he squinted and then asked me in Spanish what I wanted. I told him I had a flat tire and needed help. He considered that for a moment and then asked me if I first needed something to drink.

I glanced past him into the house. On the wall there were two pictures. One was of the Virgin of Guadalupe. The other was of Jack Kennedy. Yes, I said. Some water would be fine.

Doris Kearns Goodwin, *The Fitzgeralds and the Kennedys: An American Saga* (New York: Simon and Schuster, 1987).
Thomas Maier, *The Kennedys: America's Emerald Kings* (New York: Basic Books, 2003).

Chapter 23

Democracy in Action (1988)

Calvin Trillin

Before there was democracy, there was Judge James J. Comerford. "He was a man of his generation," someone who knew the judge in his heyday said recently. "Self-assured. Strong-willed. He ruled with an iron hand." The Judge ruled the New York St. Patrick's Day parade, and, like a number of his predecessors, he ruled it well into his eighties. (According to Paul O'Dwyer, the former president of the City Council, "Parade-committee chairmen have had an arrangement with the Creator that established longevity.") During the Judge's reign, it is said, the man who was to have the honor of being grand marshal of the parade was not elected but anointed. An election was held, of course. Three delegates from every single organization that had a marching unit in the parade—whether the unit was as grand as the United Irish Counties Association or as simple as a high-school pipe band—had the right to vote for grand marshal, but as every single member of an old-fashioned Democratic clubhouse might have had the right to vote for precinct captain. In both cases, it was customary to present only one candidate. The Judge's choice would be nominated, sometimes by the monsignor who served as chaplain of the parade committee. The Judge would ask if anybody had any other nominations. Nobody would have any other nominations. The Judge's candidate would emerge victorious. Some of the grumblers among the delegates referred to the process as "democracy in action."

They didn't say that at a public meeting. James J. Comerford, judge of the Criminal Court of New York County, was a man who inspired widespread respect, and about as widespread fear. He was a stalwart of the Roman Catholic Church and the Regular Democratic Party and the Ancient Order of Hibernians—the fraternal organization that presides over the St. Patrick's Day parade. As a young man in Ireland, he had been wounded while fighting for the Irish Republican Army. He assumed the authority on the platform that he had on the bench of the Criminal Court, and, as he got older, he was capable of dealing with some trifling objection from the floor with a direct order: "Shut up and sit down. The people didn't come to hear you talk."

But Judge Comerford was not a dictator. He was a boss. In their chapter on the Irish in *Beyond the Melting Pot*, Nathan Glazer and Daniel Patrick Moynihan wrote, "the principal of Boss rule was not tyranny, but order." There was nothing arbitrary about the Judge's decision on who would be grand marshal. This, after all, was the greatest honor the Irish-American community had to offer. The grand marshal would lead the parade up Fifth Avenue. He would stop at St. Patrick's to pay his respects and to introduce his aides to the Cardinal. He would, after completing the route, join the mayor and the senators and the other dignitaries on the reviewing stand to take the salute of tens of thousands of his countrymen. The men chosen by the Judge to fulfill these duties were worthy men all. They were selected in a way that spread the honor around his various constituencies—a police commissioner one year, a labor leader the next year, a loyal soldier of the parade committee the year after that—and they were quietly confirmed in advance by a few men of influence. A worthy candidate need only wait his turn, and, in the view of Glazer and Moynihan, the Irish American's "phenomenally effective capacity for political bureaucracy" was based partly on a belief that waiting one's turn was somewhere between necessary and positively virtuous: "The incredible capacity of the rural Irish to remain celibate, awaiting their turn to inherit the farm, was matched by generations of assistant corporation counsels awaiting that opening on the City Court bench." When people who are active in the parade recall Judge Comerford's reign, the phrase of his they most savor is the one he often used when someone mentioned himself as just the sort of public-spirited benefactor of the Irish-American community who should be named grand marshal. The Judge would fix his eye on the supplicant and say, in a brogue still redolent of County Kilkenny, "It's not your year."

All in all, Judge James J. Comerford was not the kind of man one would expect to see bowled over by a tidal wave of democracy. That's what happened, though, in the early 1980s. The Judge was getting on in years by then, and he had also given evidence that he was not omnipotent. When Judge Comerford took over, as parade-committee chairman, in 1966, the time was passing when a great Irish institution like the St. Patrick's Day parade had so many "friends downtown" that it could simply brush aside the forces of darkness that constantly conspired against it—the forces that complained about its interfering with business or tying up midweek traffic. But the Judge, as he often reminded his troops, had continued to stave off the enemies of the parade. He had waved away the Protestant major who wanted the parade moved to Central Park ("We told him to go to hell") and fought the powerful Fifth Avenue Association to a standstill. Then, in December of 1981, he announced—suddenly and unilaterally—that the 1982 parade would be held not on March 17th but on the nearest Sunday. It was widely assumed that what the mayor and the merchants had failed to do had been managed by the Cardinal, who had publicly expressed horror at the "outrageous public behavior" seen on March 17th, mainly among suburban teenagers who had come to regard St. Patrick's Day in New York as a spring rite of falling-down drunkenness.

The response to the Judge's announcement was hardly the sort of ritualistic confirmation he was accustomed to receiving. He had apparently underestimated his people's allegiance to the Saint's Day itself. ("This is a subculture with its own gods," Paul O'Dwyer has said, "and the St. Patrick's day parade had become a symbol of that subculture.") The troops rebelled. Some organizations informed the Judge that they had no intention of marching past thin crowds on a Sunday, as if they were in some lesser ethnic event put on by the Germans or the Greeks or the Puerto Ricans. Only six days after the original announcement, the Judge was forced to reverse himself. He did so with his usual swagger. ("It's the only day for the New York Irish. Marching on a Sun-

Ed Koch, New York City's mayor, stopped by the reviewing stand for a photo-op with parade chairman Jim Comerford on every St. Patrick's Day during Koch's term in office (1978–1989). Under Comerford's direction from 1968 to 1984, the old-style politics behind the annual March 17th parade played out in microcosm the Irish America that Daniel Patrick Moynihan believed was already dying in 1960. (Archives of Irish America, New York University, Gift of John Concannon)

day is for the villages outside the city.") But, as they say in politics, he had begun to look vulnerable.

Naturally, the issue that actually led to the first democratic election of a grand marshal, a year later, was Northern Ireland. There had never been any doubt about where the parade stood on the question of a united Ireland. Some of the old-timers who served on the parade committee with the Judge dated from the era when many Irish immigrants to this country were diehards who had left Ireland after fighting on the anti-treaty side in the civil war that followed the Irish Rebellion—the war that broke out in 1922 after the new Irish government accepted a treaty that left the six northeastern counties under English control. For many years, the only placard allowed in the New York St. Patrick's Day parade has been "ENGLAND GET OUT OF IRELAND." Still, the

Judge and his colleagues had over the years become essentially conservative people. They regarded the parade as nonpolitical, and they didn't want it turned into a forum.

In 1983, a time when the IRA hunger strikes had brought emotional involvement in the latest Irish troubles to its peak among Irish Americans, the Judge's candidate for grand marshal was Al O'Hagan, a prominent Hibernian who worked in government liaison for the Brooklyn Union Gas Company. Just about everybody else's candidate, as it turned out, was Michael Flannery, one of the founders of the Irish Northern Aid Committee. In the words of the *Irish Echo*, the largest of New York's four Irish tabloids, Mike Flannery is "probably the most admired man in the Irish-American community." A contemporary of the Judge's, Flannery had fought as a lad against both the English and the pro-treaty government, and had found nothing in the events of the next sixty or seventy years to change his views on the issues involved. Just a couple of months before the voting for grand marshal, he had been among five members of the Irish Northern Aid Committee (NORAID) tried for running guns to the Provisional IRA. (Attorneys presented any number of persuasive arguments in defense, not including a denial that the defendants had been running guns to the IRA, and all five NORAID men were acquitted.) A soft-spoken, self-effacing man who was retired from an office job at Metropolitan Life, Flannery had devoted his life to Irish affairs— not just nationalism but the Tipperary Men's Association and the Irish Institute and the United Irish Counties Association and, particularly, the Gaelic Athletic Association. He was, of course, a member of the Ancient Order of Hibernians, and thus fulfilled the single official prerequisite for being elected grand marshal of the St. Patrick's Day parade. In fact, he had declined the Judge's offer of the grand marshalship a couple of times before. This time, he said he wanted it—for the Cause.

Al O'Hagan showed himself to be a man who can recognize an occasion for graceful withdrawal when he sees one, and by the night of the election one of Flannery's supporters was Judge James J. Comerford. One candidate, a construction man from Brooklyn, remained in the race against Flannery, and was defeated 299 to 5. The election of Flannery touched off a great furor. The government of Ireland, which has taken the position that the people Flannery seeks to arm are what the Irish prime minister at the time called a "band of murderers," withdrew its participation from the parade, and so did such prominent Irish-American political figures as Senator Daniel Patrick Moynihan and former Governor Hugh Carey. The Cardinal did not emerge from St. Patrick's Cathedral for the traditional greeting of the parade until Flannery had passed. NORAID supporters pointed to Flannery's victory as an indication that in the future nobody who was not an outspoken Irish nationalist could be elected grand marshal. What connoisseurs of parade politics saw in Mike Flannery's election, though, was that the days of anointing the grand marshal were over. Judge James J. Comerford, the last of the great bosses, retired from the chairmanship the following year.

In 1984 it was apparent that everything had changed. A number of candidates were nominated—none of them by the parade chaplain. The year after that, the grand marshalship was sought by a woman—Dorothy Hayden Cudahy, who was widely known in the community as the hostess of "Irish Memories," a radio show she had inherited from her father in the 1940s. There had certainly never been a woman grand marshal of the St. Patrick's Day parade; it had been only two years since women were first allowed on the dais at the grand marshal's installation ceremony, despite the fact that the honor of sitting on the dais was so broadly distributed that, in the words of one installation regular, "they had just about everyone up there but the waiters." Mrs. Cudahy's nomination was rejected by the new chairman, Frank Beirne, a man who had served many years under Judge Comerford. Beirne said that she was ineligible. Although she was a member of the ladies auxiliary of a Hibernian chapter in Queens, the rules clearly stated that the grand marshal must be a member of the Ancient Order of Hibernians. In other words, not quite everything had changed.

The reason that Mike Flannery had thought the Cause could be served by his leading the parade on St. Patrick's day was summed up by one of his supporters this way: "It's the only day of the year we can get the world to pay attention to the Irish." Before Flannery, the people in charge had treated the grand-marshal election not as a way to put forward someone who symbolized Irish-American priorities but as a way to reward someone who had served the Irish-American community through its duly constituted organizations. There has been a governor here and a police commissioner there, but for the most part the grand marshals of the St. Patrick's Day parade have been people whose distinction was absolutely clear only to someone who attended the same meetings they attended. That in itself is a symbol of Irish-American priorities, particularly when compared with the approach taken by the Italians, whose Columbus Day parade is the only other ethnic event that can command Fifth Avenue on a business day. In selecting their grand marshals, the Italians go straight for glory, no questions asked. In 1979, when the grand marshal of the St. Patrick's Day parade was John Sweeney, then the president of a union local that represented building cleaners, the grand marshal of the Columbus Day parade was Frank Sinatra. In 1980, the Irish had William Burke, a Transit Authority employee who had been executive secretary of the parade committee for many years; the Italians had Luciano Pavarotti. The Columbus Day parade is regularly led up Fifth Avenue by such celebrated Italian-Americans as Yogi Berra and Lee Iacocca. In 1983, the year Judge Comerford had planned to bestow the St. Patrick's Day honor on Al O'Hagan, of the Brooklyn Union Gas Company, the Italians selected Sophia Loren.

In a grand-marshal-nominating speech this year, Judge John Collins, of the Bronx Criminal Court, said that in the old days the message the Irish meant to send to the establishment on St. Patrick's Day was "Despite your religious and racial prejudice toward us this is what we Irish have accomplished: we are good citizens and proud of it." That was accompanied, of course, by a fear that people still afflicted with such prejudice would never think of the Irish as good citizens and would be looking for any excuse to label any St. Patrick's Day event an Irish brawl. Traditionally, the St. Patrick's Day parade committee went further than the sponsors of other ethnic parades in maintaining discipline among the marchers. When the Cardinal's criticism brought home the fact that St. Patrick's Day had come to be associated with, of all things, rowdy drunks, the Irish tightened whatever laxity had crept into the line of march and used the muscle they still had in the city to insist on a police crackdown. Teenagers who arrived in the city that March 17th with their usual St. Patrick's Day beer supply had it confiscated before they could get out of the train station.

But even a March 17th of unprecedented decorum wouldn't pass without some imprecations against the Irish. A lot of New Yorkers who think of themselves as people of unshakable tolerance take a sort of easement when it comes to the Irish, and their nastiest opinions tend to rise to the surface on St. Patrick's Day. "St. Patrick's Day in New York!" a character in William Styron's *Set This House on Fire* says. "Christ-almighty! A whole city at the mercy of a bunch of garbage collectors and bartenders." The New York St. Patrick's Day parade has been held in one form or another for two hundred years—it's an American invention; in Ireland, March 17th is observed as a nonfestive holy day of obligation—and in that time it has grown to a size that almost guarantees a certain amount of irritation. It's not unusual to have a million people on the street as spectators, and there often seem to be at least a million others in the bars. The marchers themselves can equal the population of a middle-sized city—so many of them that it can take six hours for the parade to pass a single point. "On a sunny day, we'll march as many as a hundred and twenty thousand people," someone long connected with the parade said recently. "We think it's the biggest parade in the world. Someone said that the May Day parade in Moscow might be bigger, but, of course, we don't march tanks."

Nobody blames the Italians or the Greeks for having a parade, but venom seems to rise at the sight of so many Irishmen marching up Fifth Avenue, wearing their County Association sashes and playing their pipes and carrying their banners about the English oppressors. In a country that has assimilated so many Irish for so long—a country where one out of five citizens has some Irish ancestry, a country where people with names like Robert McNamara and Ronald Reagan and Sandra Day O'Connor are thought of as mainstream Americans, a country where most people with Irish names think of a strong Republican as somebody like Robert Dole rather than somebody like Eamon de Valera—there are those who find it irritating that some people remain so willfully, maddeningly *Irish*.

The reason that a lot of them seem so Irish, as it happens, is that they're from Ireland. Although most Americans think of Irish immigration in connection with the potato famine of the 1850s, the last great wave of Irish migration to the United States was in the 1950s—from the end of the Second World War to the immigration-law changes in the 1960s that ended favored treatment for the countries of northern Europe and the British Isles. The marchers on Fifth Avenue every March 17th obviously include a lot of native-born Americans whose Irishness comes out once a year. Irish burghers join the Ancient Order of Hibernians—which until recently required its members to be "practicing Catholics"—the way their neighbors might join the Masons or the Odd Fellows. After the Second World War, Emerald Societies grew up in institutions like the Police Department, more or less as a way of looking after Irish interests—before the war, an organization of Irish policemen in New York might have resembled a committee of the whole—and an Irish policeman might join the Department's Emerald Society as routinely as an Italian policeman would join the Columbian Society.

But the people active in the County Kilkenny Association, the people who organize the Irish football league for the Gaelic Athletic Association, the people who stand for office in the Hibernian chapters, the people who run organizations like the St.

Patrick's Day parade committee—these people tend to be immigrants or sons and daughters of immigrants. It's axiomatic among Irish Americans that most of the third generation disappears into nonethnic America. The parade committee has simply passed from the hands of the immigrants of the 1920s to the immigrants of the 1950s. Frank Beirne, the retired bus dispatcher who now serves as chairman of the parade committee, is twenty-five years Judge Comerford's junior, but his brogue is slightly thicker.

"Just what is the Ladies Auxiliary part of—B'nai B'rith or the Daughters of Italy?" the *Irish Echo* wrote in 1985 in response to Beirne's ruling that Dorothy Hayden Cudahy was not a bona fide member of the Ancient Order of Hibernians (AOH). The issue was put to rest at the national convention of the Hibernians: the delegates voted to change the auxiliaries into AOH chapters for women. The nomination of Mrs. Cudahy for grand marshal was accepted in 1986. By that time, the election process would have been unrecognizable to someone accustomed to Judge Comerford's democracy in action. Without the Judge's guiding hand, it turned out, all sorts of people had ideas about who should be grand marshal of the St. Patrick's Day parade. In 1984, the year after the Flannery election swept away the boss system, some people from the longshoremen's union had realized that the grand marshalship was there for the taking by any group that could put together an effective campaign for a respected candidate, even a candidate who might not have attended enough officer installations and Gaelic festivals to impress Judge Comerford. The candidate they had in mind, not surprisingly, was their boss, Teddy Gleason, then the president of the International Longshoremen's Association.

Putting together a campaign to capture a purely honorary office has problems that might seem daunting even to people acknowledged to have a genius for politics. It's not that there's a problem figuring out where most of the votes are. The Hibernians, with marching units from chapters all over the metropolitan area, have more delegates than any other organization, and they are also considered more likely to show up on election night. Emerald Societies, which have now spread from institutions like the Police Department to institutions like the Transit Authority and the phone company and Consolidated Edison, have a lot of delegates, and so do the various county associations. Of course, a delegate might belong to two or three different organizations and also feel a strong association with something outside any organization at all —the Cause, for instance, or organized labor. Even assuming institutional loyalty, why should the delegates from, say, the Emerald Society of the United States Customs Service or a Hibernian chapter in Yonkers—not to speak of the marching band of Cardinal Hayes High School—cast their votes for one candidate rather than another? A candidate for grand marshal, after all, has no patronage to dispense; he doesn't even choose the aides who march with him at the head of the parade. He can hardly claim that on the strength of his record he is likely to do the job better than his opponents, since the job consists of walking up Fifth Avenue once.

As the longshoremen demonstrated, though, endorsements can be won. Pledges can be gathered. There are reminders of old loyalties and promises of future alliances. There are connections from counties like Nassau and counties like Tipperary. An Emerald Society may back a candidate because it has been asked by an influential

Emerald, or because the candidate came out in the snow for its installation of officers, or because the candidate's father was a cop. The people backing Teddy Gleason in 1984 began to round up delegates as they might for a Democratic National Convention. They ran full-page ads in the *Irish Echo* listing endorsements from Hibernian chapters and county associations and Emerald Societies and more labor organizations than anyone thought existed. They even leaked some endorsements to the *Daily News*. They won easily. The following year the hard-liners on Northern Ireland were determined to elect one of the people who had lost to Gleason: Peter King, a Queens politician with strong ties to the IRA. King's ads in 1984 had said his election would "send the right message." He had endorsements not just from Mike Flannery but from the family of the martyred hunger striker Bobby Sands. In 1985, he ran a high-powered campaign—it was said he used professional pollsters—and he won.

By 1986 even some of the people who had grumbled about Judge Comerford's ways were beginning to wonder whether democracy might have its limitations as a method of selecting a grand marshal. Was it really a good idea for candidates to launch advertising campaigns for what was supposed to be an honor bestowed by the community? Was it healthy for the parade to be used by people—the nationalist hard-liners, for instance—who had an agenda of their own? Should the delegates have to choose among half a dozen candidates? According to Flannery: "The present chairmen said to me, 'Well, Mike, you started something, all right. There's people now trying to get themselves nominated just to get their name in the paper.'"

And where did this sort of free-for-all leave someone like Al O'Hagan? The man who had withdrawn in the face of the Flannery tidal wave in 1983—the man known to some as Mr. Hibernian—had finished second to both Gleason and King. Jack Irwin, a former New York state president of the AOH, became the leader of a campaign to make 1986, the hundred-and-fiftieth anniversary of the Hibernians, Al O'Hagan's year. It was a quieter campaign in 1986—or, to put it another way, a more orderly campaign. No one objected when the chairman of the parade committee let it be known that advertisements supporting candidates for the office of grand marshal should cease. It had been assumed that O'Hagan's principal competition would come from William Burke, the senior vice president of the Bank of Ireland's New York office (and no relation to the 1980 grand marshal), who had entered the 1985 race late with an expensive flurry of ads. Burke agreed to step aside for O'Hagan. All sorts of influential people—nationalists, traditional parade-committee people, and particularly Hibernians—seemed to agree in advance that Al O'Hagan should be elected at last. He was. He got 181 votes—fifty-six more than his nearest rival, Dorothy Hayden Cudahy. To outsiders, 1986 was noted as the first year that women ran for grand marshal—Mary Holt Moore, a woman long active in both Irish cultural affairs and the Cause, was also nominated—but to people deeply involved in the politics of the Irish-American subculture it may have been more noteworthy as the year that the revisionists began to creep back into the temple.

"I do not want to be pushy, but there is no reason to wait," Dorothy Hayden Cudahy had said in 1985 when Frank Beirne suggested that she not attempt to be nominated while the old rules were in effect. No reason to wait! That was not the sort of talk the committee were accustomed to hearing. They were not reformers, after all;

they had served for years under Judge Comerford, waiting their turns to move up in the parade-committee hierarchy. From the beginning, they seemed unhappy with Mrs. Cudahy's candidacy. There were any number of theories to account for their unhappiness. It was said that they thought Mrs. Cudahy's son—Sean Cudahy, a federal Department of Labor employee, who campaigned relentlessly for his mother—was being too pushy. It was said that they blamed Mrs. Cudahy for forcing the issue upon them. It was said that some of them simply didn't want a woman to be grand marshal of the St. Patrick's Day parade. It was said that they resented being portrayed in the press as the sort of people who simply didn't want a woman to be grand marshal of the St. Patrick's Day parade. For whatever reason, the feeling lingered long after the 1985 nomination was rejected that the parade-committee officers were not on Mrs. Cudahy's side.

The press was very much on her side—not just the Irish press but the *New York Daily News*, which has always had a large Irish readership, and even the *New York Times*. Feature stories displayed distinctly unthreatening-looking pictures of her sitting in the living room of her bungalow in Queens—an ample, smiling grandmother in her sixties—and carried headlines like "Can a Woman Lead Them?" The *Echo*, which does not back specific candidates, took a strong editorial stand for electing a woman, and the *Times*, taking its first fling at advising its readership on the election for grand marshal of the St. Patrick's Day parade, more or less endorsed Dorothy Hayden Cudahy. The news stories seemed to show her making steady progress. In 1987, the year after she finished fifty-six votes behind Al O'Hagan, Mrs. Cudahy finished only twenty votes behind John Lawe, the leader of the Transport Workers Union. As this year's election approached, it seemed clear that if she made a similar improvement in her position she would be the first woman to lead the St. Patrick's Day parade.

That may have been how it looked in the news stories, but that's not how it looked to the people the *Echo* has referred to as "the boys in the know." To the boys in the know, Mrs. Cudahy's success in narrowing the margin of victory in the two previous elections may have seemed less significant than the fact that both winners—Al O'Hagan, a man who works for a utility, and John Lawe, a labor leader—had been nominated by the same person and had received almost precisely the same number of votes. The nominator with the magic touch was Jack Irwin, the Hibernian leader who had used the hundred-and-fiftieth anniversary of the AOH to gather the forces for O'Hagan. It appeared that Irwin and a few other people had, in effect, taken on the role of keeping order through an old device of the Judge's: passing around the grand marshalship to one constituency at a time. They had backed a strong Hibernian one year, a labor leader the next year, and, as it worked out for 1988, a businessman the year after that. Bill Burke, of the Bank of Ireland, had stepped aside for O'Hagan in 1986. When John Lawe, backed by the Irish American Labor Coalition, decided to run the next year, Burke had stepped aside again. To put it in terms that would be appreciated by Judge Comerford, who has now withdrawn from the fray to the St. Patrick's Home for the Aged and Infirm, in the Bronx, Bill Burke had waited his turn. In 1988, he would be the candidate of an alliance that included Al O'Hagan and Jim McNamara, who is in charge of public relations for both the parade committee and the

International Longshoremen's Association. The nominating speech would be delivered by Jack Irwin.

Publicly, the election campaign was not easy to discern. In the world of Irish-American organizations—the Emerald Society dinner dances and the Gaelic Athletic Association award ceremonies and the benefits for families down on their luck—both candidates had, in a way, been campaigning for decades simply by showing up. Like many people who vote in the election for grand marshal, Dorothy Hayden Cudahy has had a life divided between the routine of a city bureaucracy and the small glories of the Irish-American subculture. For twenty-two years, her days belonged to the New York City Department of Transportation—she began as a meter maid—and her evenings were devoted to the Irish Institute or the County Kilkenny Association or Division 14, Ladies AOH of Queens County. Bill Burke hasn't been to as many dinner dances and installations and board meetings and Irish festivals as Mrs. Cudahy, but that's only because he's nearly twenty years younger. She is president of the County Kilkenny Association, and he is president of the County Sligo Association. She has been the Grand Council of Emerald Societies Woman of the Year, and he has been the installing officer of the United Irish Counties. Both of them have strong connections to the mother country. She is the daughter of James Hayden, a County Kilkenny man who made a name for himself on the Irish dance-hall circuit around New York and eventually became the host of the "Irish Memories" show on WEVD, a radio station so receptive to New York's ethnic subcultures that it carries a weekly half hour in Albanian. Burke came here from Tubbercurry, County Sligo, twenty-seven years ago, and his accent is still so thick that when he refers to Mrs. Cudahy by her first name it's easy to get the impression that he's talking about some third candidate named Daugherty.

Issues didn't surface. Although there were undoubtedly delegates who would vote for or against Mrs. Cudahy on the basis of her sex, people were not publicly organized that way. Those delegates who believed that the only question in the grand-marshal election—or in just about any other election, for that matter—was its effect on "the English colonial rule in Ireland" were for Mrs. Cudahy, partly because she had participated in demonstrations for the Cause and partly because Burke's connection with the Bank of Ireland gave him some guilt by association with the government of the Republic of Ireland. ("The choice of a Grand Marshal for New York's St. Patrick's Day parade is always carefully monitored by the British and Dublin," the *Irish People*, a New York tabloid associated with NORAID, said in an editorial supporting Mrs. Cudahy. "Her election would be perceived as a defeat for the British and Free State, as well as a victory for the victims of British rule.") But Mrs. Cudahy has not really been identified strongly enough with the Cause to bring out its forces, and even among St. Patrick's Day paraders, the Northern Ireland issue no longer carries the emotional impact it had around the time of Flannery's election. Although a speaker can still draw applause with a line about a united Ireland, the current American immigration law's effect on Irish immigration may now be a bigger issue than the Cause.

Flannery favored Mrs. Cudahy partly because he believed that electing a woman grand marshal was a human-rights issue that should have the support of people concerned with human rights in Ireland, but he also thought Burke was young enough to wait for another year. "Dorothy probably wouldn't like me to say this," Flannery, who is himself eighty-seven, told a visitor a few weeks before the election. "But she's quite a good age." Burke had used the Bank of Ireland's promotion budget so lavishly in support of Irish-American activities—the Gaelic festival here, the Hibernian chapter's project there—that some people grumbled that he was trying to "buy the election" with the bank's money. But that didn't become an issue. It had never occurred to anyone, after all, that the political bosses who used to send around turkeys on Christmas paid for them out of their own pockets.

"It's one delegate at a time," Sean Cudahy said as the election grew near. "With us, it's more of a grass-roots campaign." Mrs. Cudahy was thought to have considerable strength in her home borough of Queens and in the county associations beyond just Kilkenny and Clare, where her husband is the president. Apparently, some of the older members of the county associations are particularly attached to the sort of music played on "Irish Memories"—songs like "My Lovely Rose of Clare" and "The Stone outside Dan Murphy's Door." On the Burke side, Irwin assigned supervisory responsibility for each of the largest voting blocks, reserving the Hibernians for himself. Burke worked at the county associations, and the Emeralds were approached by Tom Connaughton, an old friend of Burke's who is the president of the Grand Council of United Emerald Societies. A week before the election, Sean Cudahy seemed cautiously optimistic. It was close, he said, but "I think we've turned the corner." Around the same time, Jack Irwin and Bill Burke sat down at the Bank of Ireland to do a count. Going down the list unit by unit, they figured that, counting conservatively, they were a hundred votes ahead. Irwin said, "I honestly think that if we lose now it's because we didn't turn our people out."

The election for the grand marshal of the St. Patrick's Day parade is normally held at the Sheraton Centre Hotel, on the northern edge of the theater district, and a lot of the strategy sessions are held across the street at a restaurant called Rosie O'Grady's. This year, the votes were cast on a cold Tuesday night late in January. The delegates, crowded into one of the Sheraton's meeting rooms, were mostly middle-aged or older. The Hibernians presumably have the same problem other fraternal organizations have these days in attracting young men—problems that may be compounded by the close association with the Church. Most of the county associations, which were founded basically to assist immigrants, are now shrinking bands of older people. Because of some dismal economic times in Ireland, there have been a good number of immigrants in the past decade, but almost all of them are undocumented; their interest in joining Irish organizations is limited by, among other factors, their disinclination to put their names and addresses on a mailing list.

Before the nomination speeches, Frank Beirne asked Mary Holt Moore—a commanding-looking gray-haired woman who tends to give her speeches partly in Gaelic —to offer a tribute to Sean MacBride, a widely respected jurist and human-rights activist, who had died the previous week in Dublin. Then Jack Irwin placed the name of Bill Burke in nomination, emphasizing Burke's connection with the Hibernians and the Emerald Societies and the county associations and the Gaelic Athletic

Association. "Through Bill Burke's encouragement, the Bank of Ireland has offered financial support to scores of Irish-American organizations through the years," Irwin reminded the delegates. The nomination was seconded by, among other people, Al O'Hagan.

In a nominating speech for Dorothy Hayden Cudahy, Judge John Collins said, "Let this be the year for the first woman grand marshal." These days, Collins said, the grand marshal of the St. Patrick's Day parade had an opportunity to send a message beyond simply the traditional display of good citizenship. Through television and through the press, as well as on Fifth Avenue, the grand marshal could "lead a crusade for the minds and hearts of all New Yorkers and all Americans and some in Ireland as well. This parade must stand squarely for the principles of a free, united, thirty-two-country Ireland and a fair U.S. immigration law for the Irish." The chairman of the election committee explained the procedure by which delegates would be called, would mark their ballots, and would drop them into a pasteboard box that had been placed in front of the speakers' platform. It was announced that Frank Beirne would temporarily withhold the vote he had as a parade-committee officer, just in case a tie had to be broken. Then the balloting began.

It took an hour and a half. The delegates lined up in the aisles, waiting to cast their ballots. Two or three election-committee workers called off the names of the various parade units. Mrs. Cudahy bustled around trying to shore up her commitments. ("Don't change your mind.") Jack Irwin sat in the back of the room during much of the voting. Irwin is an affable, businesslike man with snow-white hair—a former child actor who now works for Merrill Lynch. He said he was confident of his count. After the couple of elections that he thinks of as "just chaos," the process is once again orderly enough to permit careful counting. It's true that the grand marshal is no longer anointed but elected—and by secret ballot. Promises can be broken. But Irwin couldn't see any developments that might have altered the picture since he and Burke had done their count a week or so before. There had been a startling development on the actual day of the voting: Sean Cudahy had twice suggested to Bill Burke that he withdraw in Mrs. Cudahy's favor, permitting the first woman grand marshal to be elected and assuring himself the job in 1989. But that had been dismissed by the Burke forces as another example of Sean Cudahy's being overaggressive on his mother's behalf. Irwin hadn't left the turnout of Burke's delegates totally to chance. Some of O'Hagan's loyalists from Brooklyn had been delivered in chartered buses.

While the ballots were being counted, reporters and television crews drifted into the room and collected in front of the platform. Then the chairmen of the election committee announced the results. Bill Burke had won by more than 130 votes. Mrs. Cudahy made a gracious little concession speech, which ended with her hopes for March 17th: "I hope the sun shines all day on Bill Burke." When Burke took the microphone, he said, "It was a tough race. We both campaigned hard for this. That's the democratic way." Later, the reporters who crowded around Burke asked him how he explained the results of the election, and he said, "I laid back for two years." Asked the same question, Frank Beirne said more or less the same thing. The reporters, apparently lacking a well-developed appreciation of the art of waiting your turn, seemed puzzled by the notion of lying back for two years as an effective campaign strategy.

Burke was asked a lot of questions about when there would be a woman grand marshal. He said that the next election would almost certainly be fought among three women, and that he had already committed himself to campaigning for one of them. Although he wouldn't say which one, he did mention Mary Holt Moore as someone who was expected to run. Burke's certainty about an all-female race was a way of saying that those who had restored some order to the process were planning to see to it that a woman—a representative of one more constituency—was elected in 1989. There are people who think that having all women candidates would smack of ladies' night at the lodge hall. There are people who think that some of the parade-committee officers will hold out against a woman as long as is possible. But the boys in the know seem to think that if the votes are lined up even the most conservative parade-committee officers will come around. They couldn't have served the Judge for all those years, after all, without absorbing one of the basic lessons of orderly rule: in the long run, the important question is not who the office-holder is but who appears to decide who the office-holder is. "Next year, without a shadow of a doubt, there'll be a woman grand marshal," Burke said to a radio interviewer. What he was telling reporters, in effect, was that women would have their turn. This just hadn't been their year.

SUGGESTED READING

Ronald H. Bayor and Timothy J. Meagher, eds., *The New York Irish* (Baltimore: Johns Hopkins University Press, 1996).

Nathan Glazer and Daniel P. Moynihan, eds., *Beyond the Melting Pot: The Negroes, Puerto Ricans, Jews, Italians, and Irish of New York City,* 2nd ed. (Cambridge, MA: MIT Press, 1970). First published 1963.

John T. Ridge, *The St. Patrick's Day Parade in New York* (New York: St. Patrick's Day Committee, 1988).

Chapter 24

Irish America, 1940–2000

Linda Dowling Almeida

Throughout the twentieth century, Irish America was well on its way to transitioning from an immigrant to an ethnic community. Located primarily in urban areas in the Northeast and Midwest as they had been since the mid–nineteenth century, the Irish were a well-established population in the United States, composed of immigrants, as well as second-, third-, and fourth-generation Americans. They had achieved conspicuous success in local Democratic Party politics and were assuming important positions of power nationally in the party. They also dominated the hierarchy of the Catholic Church and were well represented among religious men and women across the country. No longer the feared and despised Paddies and Bridgets of the Famine and post-Famine eras, they were gaining greater acceptance socially with each generation, although even the candidacy of John F. Kennedy for president of the United States in 1960 showed that many Americans still harbored prejudices against Catholics. The challenge for the Irish in the second half of the twentieth century was coming to terms with their social and economic success and the migration out of tight-knit urban communities to the anonymity and dispersion of the suburbs. Immigration and parish life in the city had long nurtured Irish Catholic identity. With money, education, and home ownership outside the neighborhood, the Irish had to work harder to be Irish.

Irish-American identity for about 150 years after the Famine was typically defined as urban, Catholic, and politically Democratic. Since the 1970s, however, Irish America has been less devoted to the Democratic Party and has dispersed beyond the ethnic neighborhoods of the country's largest cities. As for religion, since Vatican II in the early 1960s, socioeconomic affluence and life in the suburbs contributed to an Irish-American religious life that was less rigid and parish-based than it had been since the 1850s. It should also be noted that recent studies indicate that a large segment of the American Irish population is Protestant.[1] However, much less research has been devoted to the history of Irish-American Protestants than to Irish-American Catholics. Therefore, this essay focuses primarily on the much better–documented Irish-American Catholic population, which is arguably the community commonly perceived to be most representative of the Irish in America.[2]

In the 1930s, migration from Ireland to the United States had slowed to barely a trickle for a number of reasons. The primary cause was the Depression and the lack of economic opportunity in America for any newcomer. Life was so difficult in that

The tender to the ship—usually one of the large Cunard or White Star ocean liners—and the sight of the spires of St. Colman's Cathedral were the last things most Irish men and women experienced at Queenstown (now Cobh again since independence), County Cork, when emigrating to the United States, circa 1880s–1950s. (Mick Moloney Irish American Collection)

decade that one family in particular, the McCourts, left Brooklyn for Limerick when death and poverty became too much for them to bear away from family and familiar surroundings. The eldest son immortalized their experience sixty years later in *Angela's Ashes* (1996).[3] As a result, the total number of Irish arriving in the United States dropped from 211,000 in the 1920s to just about 11,000 in the 1930s.[4] As England moved closer to war, many Irish crossed the channel during the decade to find work in the factories that were supporting the buildup to armed conflict, to join the armed services, or to enter nursing programs. Transatlantic travel for civilians during World War II was virtually nonexistent, further inhibiting Irish entry into the United States. When the war ended, however, the Irish once more resumed their exodus out of Ireland. Emigration to Britain had become substantial during the war, and as Britain remained a full-employment economy after 1945, the bulk of the postwar Irish emigrants continued to go there. Nevertheless, between 1941 and 1961, sixty-eight thousand entered the United States.[5]

The postwar period in the United States was a time of growth and rejuvenation. Irish immigration, despite its resumption, paled in comparison with the numbers of foreigners, refugees, and war brides who traveled to America in hopes of starting a new life after the Depression and World War II. More than 3.5 million immigrants from around the world, more than the entire population of the Republic of Ireland, entered the United States between 1941 and 1960.[6] If the Irish no longer dominated the streams of immigrants as they had in the mid–nineteenth century, the postwar immigrants from Eire were welcomed by communities that were well established and far more secure than those found by their post-famine counterparts. By 1950, Irish

Americans were still concentrated in the Northeast and the Midwest, with about 60 percent of the population still living in Massachusetts, Illinois, New York, and New Jersey, but the prosperity of the postwar economy would propel the Irish and their children into the suburbs of metropolitan New York City, Philadelphia, Chicago, and Boston.[7]

That exodus was accelerated in part by the G.I. Bill and its college tuition and mortgage assistance. Congress provided sixteen million veterans of World War II, many of them hyphenated Americans, "an opportunity to navigate under their own power." Almost half of these veterans who took advantage of the opportunities presented by the bill went to college, received vocational training or found apprenticeships.[8] A historian of Iona College in New York City notes the juxtaposition of eighteen-year-olds and veterans in a 1946 classroom: "This student body was different: petty regulations designed for adolescents were out of place for those who had gone through the hell of Guadalcanal and Normandy."[9] By the 1970s, one study reported that the Irish were the most affluent and best-educated white ethnic group in the country behind the Jews.[10] And according to historian Kevin Kenny, they were overrepresented in law, medicine, and the sciences, elevating themselves in a generation from an occupational profile that was diverse but lodged in the lower rungs of the "occupational ladder."[11]

A more subtle benefit of the war and time served in the military for the Irish and other immigrant and ethnic groups was its influence in further integrating hyphenated Americans into the social and cultural fabric of the country. The Irish performed admirably in the war and did so in great numbers. They put to rest any lingering fears about the allegiance, patriotism, and commitment of the Irish to America. Conversely, life in the military introduced young men from neighborhoods in the Bronx, Dorchester, and the South Side of Chicago to their countrymen from Tennessee, Idaho, and Texas. The exposure could only benefit all involved and dispel or at least neutralize stereotypes about immigrants and ethnics.

The evolution of the Irish-American character is best reflected in some of the popular books and movies of the period. On the screen, Irish-American males had evolved from James Cagney's Tom Powers and Rocky Sullivan in *The Public Enemy* (1932) and *Angels with Dirty Faces* (1939) to his performance as the patriotic George M. Cohan in the Oscar-winning *Yankee Doodle Dandy* (1942). On the page, James Farrell's brutal portrayal of Chicago's Irish neighborhood life and emptiness in the *Studs Lonigan* trilogy [*Young Lonigan* (1932), *The Young Manhood of Studs Lonigan* (1934), and *Judgment Day* (1935)] was overshadowed ten years later by Betty Smith's nostalgic and extremely popular *A Tree Grows in Brooklyn* (1943), a coming-of-age novel about a young Irish-American girl in the early 1900s.

In the early 1940s, some of Hollywood's most popular films and actors were Irish American. *Going My Way* (1944) is a sweet, sentimental film about a crumbling New York City parish guided by a lovable old leprechaun of a pastor played by Barry Fitzgerald and his more modern, Irish-American assistant played by Bing Crosby. The film won four Oscars and is a much kinder view of city life and its citizens than *The Public Enemy* (1931), *Dead End* (1937), and *Angels with Dirty Faces* (1938), earlier films that dealt with many of the same issues and ethnic groups a decade earlier. Its success suggested that the American public was ready to accept the Irish, their priests, and communities as part of the larger culture and consider them lovable rather than dangerous. More honest and complex portrayals of Irish-American life appeared a decade or so later when Eugene O'Neill's *Long Day's Journey into Night* (written in 1941 and performed in 1956) and Frank D. Gilroy's *The Subject Was Roses* (1964) hit the stage and Edwin O'Connor published his Boston-based novels of politics, *The Last Hurrah* (1956), and the priesthood, *The Edge of Sadness* (1961). In the meantime, Cagney, Crosby, Pat O'Brien, Spencer Tracy, Tyrone Power, Errol Flynn, Helen Hayes, Laurette Taylor, Maureen O'Hara, Maureen O'Sullivan, John Ford, and John Huston were among the most popular, talented, and powerful actors and directors of the day. Their presence in the spotlight polished the image of the Irish in America.

Eugene O'Neill, the son of a Famine survivor, was probably the most decorated and respected of Irish-American theater artists in the twentieth century. A playwright who won four Pulitzer Prizes (1920, 1922, 1928, and 1957), was awarded a Nobel Prize for Literature (1936), and has had his work translated and performed all over the world, he once confessed to his son that his critics recognized him as a great American writer but often failed to acknowledge that he was Irish.[12] The posthumous production of *Long Day's Journey into Night* exemplifies the power of his observation. The show received critical acclaim and huge box office returns from the moment it opened on Broadway. It is often cited as one of the best American plays ever written. At its simplest, it is the story of a highly dysfunctional family named Tyrone at once torn apart and drawn together by their problems; at its most complex, it reflects the conflicts faced by all the immigrants who come to America with dreams and ambitions and faults, and the costs incurred pursuing and achieving their dreams. O'Neill, as a second-generation Irish American writing about his family's experiences in the new world, their struggle to find a place socially and culturally, and the fallout they suffered in their quest to succeed in America with all their Irish baggage, embodies at once the place the Irish earned in American society and the price they paid for their acceptance. Irish Americans find themselves in the play, but O'Neill also touches a more universal audience with his work, demonstrating in his art and in his own life how many families bridged the worlds of immigrant and ethnic life in the middle of the twentieth century.

The popularity of Irish-American writers and performers could also be observed on television and in newspapers. Ed Sullivan, a former journalist, hosted a popular television variety program on Sunday nights between 1948 and 1971 called *The Ed Sullivan Show* that was a viewing habit for millions of Americans. By welcoming rock and roll icons such as Elvis Presley and the Beatles on his stage, he made them acceptable to mainstream America. He also used the venue to introduce traditional Irish music and dance groups like the Little Gaelic Singers of Ireland (December 9, 1956) and the McNiff Dancers (March 16, 1958). The Clancy Brothers (March 12, 1961) debuted on his program, beginning decades of recording and concert success in the United States.[13] The Sullivan show also brought Irish culture to a national audience, acting as a platform that reinforced the celebrity and talents of well-known Irish-American entertainers such as Donald O'Connor, Rosemary Clooney, Gene Kelly, and Bing Crosby. Television in the 1950s also brought comics like Jackie Gleason and Art Carney to a national audience. The two starred in one of the medium's most famous and beloved comedies, *The Honeymooners* (1955–1956). The program was originally performed as a skit within Gleason's hour-long variety show called *The Jackie Gleason Show* (1952–1957). Gleason and Carney portrayed two blue-collar workers who live in a Brooklyn apartment house with their wives, go to work, and chase after the American dream. The program continues to have a huge following in reruns and on video.

The postwar period also saw the talents of Irish-American journalists surface nationally. Almost sixty years after Finley Peter Dunne (1867–1936) introduced the fictional Mr. Dooley to his *Chicago Evening Post* readers, New York City newspaper columnists Jimmy Breslin (1930–) and Pete Hamill (1935–) brought distinctively ethnic and urban voices to tabloid journalism. While they did not have a fictional mouthpiece, as did Dunne in Mr. Dooley, Breslin and Hamill opined regularly on the state of New York City, the nation, and the world, lending their perspective to everything from race to religion. Mr. Dooley made readers comfortable that a brogue did not equate with ignorance or unpatriotic behavior. Thanks in part to him, Breslin and Hamill had only to bring their wit and skill with words to a local and then a national audience. They were natural descendants of Dunne and went on to write fiction, some of which was translated to film. Breslin's commentary won him a Pulitzer Prize in 1986.

A third Irish-American writer achieved fame and a loyal following in print and on television in the same period, but he came at the craft from a different direction. Bishop Fulton J. Sheen (1895–1979) penned a regular column in the *Journal American* (New York City) newspaper and wrote prodigiously (sixty-six books) on religious and other topics. He opposed communism and was critical of the teachings of Sigmund Freud. But he was most famous for his thirty-minute televised "sermons" on his "Life is Worth Living" (1952–1957) television programs. His popularity and cross-over appeal was confirmed when he won an Emmy for Outstanding Television Personality in 1952, beating out Milton Berle, Jimmy Durante, and Lucille Ball. At its peak, the program reached 5.5 million households. Between 1952 and 1956 he was regularly listed among the Gallup Poll's ten most-admired men and appeared on the cover of *Time Magazine* (April 14, 1952).[14] Less notorious than his equally well known predecessor, Father Charles Coughlin, Sheen appealed to the masses with a straightforward oratory style that mixed humor, common sense, and topical issues. Dressed in his bishop's cape and cap, his message was not so much proselytizing as it was humanistic. He was telegenic and nonthreatening, allowing him to reach out beyond his Catholic viewers.[15] His elevation and acceptance on the national stage was a far cry from the threatening Thomas Nast caricatures of alligator-like clerics storming the shores of America in the 1860s.[16]

In the mid–twentieth century America was a popular and friendly destination for immigrants from Ireland. Postwar immigrants typically entered working-class communities in large industrial cities where other Irish immigrants had preceded them. They were primarily single and under the age of twenty-five. Most came from the western counties of the province of Connaught and the three Republican counties of Ulster, north of Dublin.[17] They lived with families and friends on couches or in basement apartments until they established themselves. The men found jobs in restau-

New York City's annual parade in honor of St. Patrick was able to draw eighty thousand marchers and one million people on its sidelines by the time Roger Higgins took this photograph in 1951 for the *New York World-Telegram and Sun*. Around the phenomenal growth and visibility of St. Patrick's Day parades across the country in the twentieth century was the transformation of March 17th from a civic and religious celebration of ethnicity into a secular and commercial holiday in the American calendar. (Library of Congress, Prints and Photographs Division, LC-GIG-ppmsca-01203)

rants, contracting, insurance companies, and civil service careers like law enforcement, firefighting, and transportation. The women entered office clerical pools in large companies, found jobs nursing in city hospitals, or worked in food service or as domestics in private homes. The typical immigrant had at least two years of high school.[18] They tended to marry, settle down in the communities to which they migrated, and send their children to Catholic school. They lived, worked, played, and socialized with other Irish Americans, forming Irish fraternal organizations, attending county association dances, and going to Mass every Sunday. They came to America seeking to become Irish American and to make a life for themselves that they could not make in Ireland.[19]

Ireland in the 1950s, particularly the western counties, faced a bleak future. As the rest of Europe and the United States were rebounding after World War II, Ireland stood still economically, socially, and culturally. Irish Prime Minister Éamon de Valera advocated a vision of an "Irish Ireland" that relied on self-sufficient farms and local industries to support the Irish market. But it never resonated with his constituents. The Irish looked around at the rest of the world and saw it moving forward and themselves left behind:

> Between 1949 and 1956 Ireland's income rose at only one-fifth the rate for the rest of Western Europe. From 1955 to 1957 Ireland was the only country in the Western World in which the total volume of goods and services consumed fell.[20]

Socially and culturally, Irish life was equally barren. Marriage rates hit a low of 5.1 per 1,000 in 1957, and by 1961 in Ireland the average age for new husbands was 30.6 and for first-time wives 26.9.[21] Because of the poor economy and prospects for the future, young Irish men and women were delaying the start of their own adult lives and families. One immigrant from the period who grew up on a farm, had an education, and a job in Galway with the civil service reported that even with what was considered "a good job" he could not pay his own rent. He relied on his parents for a subsidy, which they could not afford. He saw no other option but to leave. He obviously was not alone.[22]

Culturally, Irish life and some of its laws were dictated by the ideology and theology of the Roman Catholic Church. A political debate on the pros and cons of a national television network lasted for most of the 1950s and was influenced in no small part by the Church. The overwhelming majority of the country's population was Catholic, and it is not an exaggeration to observe that the sexual conduct of the country was dictated by the parish priest. Books and movies were monitored and censored. The national radio stations offered primarily traditional music. The political and religious leadership strove to keep the newly independent country free of outside influences.[23] But their vision was not shared by those living in the rural reaches of the country who had been isolated and desperately poor for decades. The leadership knew this, but in a government-commissioned study on emigration, the report mocked those who chose to leave, chiding their desire for greater disposable income as nothing more than the wish to purchase "conventional necessities [such] as cigarettes, cinemas and dances."[24] But it is probably safe to say that the emigrants' ambition extended beyond better access to Hershey bars. Young Irish living on farms in rural counties knew enough about the outside world from American cousins, newspapers, and foreign media like Armed Forces Radio to know that life in Boston or New York or Chicago was really about choices and opportunities, both of which they lacked in Ireland.[25]

The 1960s and 1970s were periods of transition for Irish living in the United States and Ireland. During the 1960s, the Irish government embarked on a program of internal investment and foreign outreach that brought Ireland into the twentieth century economically and culturally. The result of these changes was that marriage and fertility rates increased, educational opportunities for all Irish students expanded, employment rose and net out-migration dropped. In the 1970s, more people were entering Ireland than leaving it, including many of the migrants who had left Ireland after the war. At the same time that Ireland enjoyed this great turnaround, U.S. immigration law changed. In October 1965, Congress approved the Immigration and Nationality Act, which eliminated national origin as the basis for immigration and replaced it

In 1960, the second year of the Festival of Kerry held in Tralee, Co. Kerry, three American Roses, all recent immigrants, competed with six other women from Ireland and Britain for the title "Rose of Tralee." Left to right: Kathleen Nash representing Boston, Theresa Kenny representing Chicago (the winner that year), and Joan Dineen representing New York. (Courtesy of Marion R. Casey)

with a seven-preference schedule emphasizing family reunification and job skills as the primary standards for entrance into the United States.[26] The coincidence of both events would have repercussions for young Irish in the 1980s when that generation tried to immigrate into America. The immediate result of both events meant that immigration slowed again in the 1970s to about fifteen hundred persons per year for that decade.[27] Reduced immigration meant that the real numbers of Irish-born living in America declined. Kevin Kenny observes that by 1960 "the 'typical' Irish American belonged to the third generation" and later and that "by 1970 almost one in three Irish-born Americans was over seventy years old."[28] Without the influx of new Irish immigrants, the Irish communities of the nineteenth and early twentieth centuries were aging and shrinking.

Just as life was improving for the Irish in Ireland, the Irish continued to move up the social and economic ladder in America and out of the urban neighborhoods that had been their home for over one hundred years. By the 1970s Irish-American Catholics were among the best educated and best paid white ethnics in the country.[29] One of their own, John Fitzgerald Kennedy, had been elected president of the United States (1960–1963), and other Irish Catholics held major positions of power in government, business, and academia. The Irish had come a long way from the coffin boats of the 1840s, but their success had come at some cultural cost. Scholars and social observers criticized the community for Americanizing themselves out of an identity. The critics argued that in the quest to participate in the American dream, the Irish had erased all the Irishness off themselves. Others argued that the Irish were more Catholic in America than ethnic, and that in its effort to protect and civilize its flock, the leaders of the Church, many of whom were Irish, denied the immigrants and their children of their history.[30] Writer Edwin O'Connor offers the same lament in his novels about Irish-American life, the most famous being *The Last Hurrah* (1956) and *Edge of Sadness* (1961) for which he won the Pulitzer Prize in 1962. O'Connor's characters hail from immigrant and second-generation families that have succeeded in politics or the Church only to question their life decisions and the loss of the Irish spirit and community as each generation becomes more American and more successful.

The weakening of identity is not a straightforward change. It is unfair to point to the influence of the Catholic Church alone. The change was an evolution over time that was shaped by affluence, suburban life, public education, intermarriage with spouses of different faiths and ethnicities,[31] decline in immigration, and integration with the majority population. Living within the Irish neighborhoods of America's cities, the Irish were nurtured in their ethnicity. Immigrants, second generation ethnics, and their descendants lived together, went to school together, attended the same parish church, socialized, drank in local pubs, and joined the same fraternal organizations. It was easy for these Irish Americans to maintain their identity. The overlapping institutions of their lives reinforced who they were every day. The observation in a St. Patrick's Day essay by Pete Hamill, an Irish-American journalist born in Brooklyn in 1935 to Catholic parents from Belfast, says it all: "There were never major pronouncements, no manifestoes issued, no statements of purpose. You were born in America but you were Irish. You were Irish because your parents were Irish and all their friends were Irish."[32]

Traditionally Irish identity has been forged by three factors in Ireland and in America: nationalism, Catholicism, and either language (in Ireland) or Democratic Party politics (in the United States). Through the second half of the twentieth century, all of these factors were challenged in both countries. Removed from the urban parish, where residents identified their address by the name of their church, suburban Irish-American life was not so parish-centered. Among other factors, the loosened restrictions of Vatican II, the reduction in seminary and convent vocations, the greater number of students in public as opposed to parish-based schools, and the socioeconomic elevation of the population resulted in a congregation that was less reliant on its pastor, more selective regarding Church doctrine, and more demanding of its Sunday services.

At the end of the twentieth century both the Irish and the American churches were shaken by scandals involving the sexual and physical abuse of children in their care by clergy and religious teachers and the lax treatment of the abusers by Church hierarchy. The scandal has been arguably more damaging to the Church in Ireland because the role of the church and its clergy in the everyday lives of the Irish had been greater than it had been nationally in the United States. But the status of the Church on both sides of the Atlantic and its relationship with its believers is evolving from the paternalistic role it enjoyed in the nineteenth and twentieth centuries. That change will affect the way Catholics perceive themselves and how the outside world perceives them.

As for politics, the apex of the Irish-American moment was the election of John Fitzgerald Kennedy as president of the United States in 1960. In the nineteenth century through the early decades of the twentieth century, the Irish controlled the local politics of the country's largest cities, including New York, Chicago, San Francisco, and Boston.[33] At the very simplest level, the Irish were successful because they used patronage to secure votes—and since the Irish immigrants and their families were primarily city dwellers, the Democratic Party leaders recognized that the numbers and concentration of Irish assured them victory if they took care of their constituents. As more immigrant groups arrived in the early twentieth century, the Irish population no longer dominated voter rolls, but by then the Irish had moved on to office at the county and state levels. By 1928 Governor Alfred E. Smith of New York was the first Irish Catholic nominee for president running on the Democratic Party ticket. (Andrew Jackson was the first Irish president, but he was of the Protestant faith.) Smith lost for a variety of reasons, but his religion and association with the Tammany Hall politics of New York were severe strikes against him. Even though Smith lost the election, President Franklin D. Roosevelt appointed several Irish Catholics to prominent positions in his cabinet and inner advisory circle. With the New Deal, the Irish had arrived on the national stage, and thirty years later they placed one of their own in the White House.

President John Fitzgerald Kennedy (1961–1963) was a far cry from the starved, illiterate refugees of the Great Famine who stumbled into American cities 110 years earlier, or even from the cigar-chewing, Lower East Side–accented Al Smith. Kennedy had evolved from those earlier Irish, much as Edwin O'Connor's second- and third-generation characters had shed the remnants of their immigrant past. JFK was the son of a wealthy, powerful man who himself had served under FDR. The young man had been educated at Choate and Harvard, was a decorated officer of World War II, a Pulitzer Prize–winning author (*Profiles in Courage*, 1957), and a U.S. Senator from Massachusetts (1952–1960). At the time of his election, the speaker of the house (John McCormack, Democrat-Massachusetts, 1961–1971) and the senate majority leader (Mike Mansfield, Democrat-Montana, 1961–1977) were both Irish Americans. The Irish had indeed come a long way in a relatively short time. But two decades later, the Irish and the Democratic Party were no longer an automatic couple. Studies have shown that since at least the presidential election of Ronald Reagan in 1980, more Irish Americans and American Catholics voted Republican than in previous national elections for president and Congress.[34] Irish Catholics in America could no longer be stereotyped politically.

As for the varieties of nationalism, this essay will confine the discussion to the United States. It would be fair to state that since the 1970s the activity of militant Irish nationalists in America has waned. But by the end of the century the United States had become more directly involved diplomatically in the peace process in Northern Ireland than at any other time in the history of the conflict. In the 1950s and 1960s, Irish immigrants from the postwar years and from the 1920s had real memories of the troubles in Ireland and the separation of the state into twenty-six and six counties. In the late 1960s and early 1970s Irish nationalist groups in the United States became more engaged in the debate, as protests and violence increased in Ulster. Public unrest in Northern Ireland attracted attention on both sides of the Atlantic as activists interested in equal rights for Catholics and the end of religious-based discrimination in housing, employment, education, and political representation staged a series of civil rights actions based on the tactics of Martin Luther King and Mahatma Gandhi.

As the situation in Northern Ireland became more confrontational, the rejuvenated Irish Republican Army (IRA) received a lot of support from the United States, particularly after the Bloody Sunday incident of January 30, 1972. On that afternoon in Derry, British armed forces opened fire on a peaceful demonstration, killing thirteen of the participating marchers. The event prompted criticism and outrage in Ireland and the United States. According to one historian, Bloody Sunday brought the American Roman Catholic Church into the debate in a very public way. It became more engaged in relief efforts for Northern Ireland, and a number of clergy openly criticized the British government for the violent response to the demonstration and its policies regarding the North in general.[35] Among Irish Americans across the country, the accelerating crisis in Ulster increased activism and swelled membership in organizations formed to support nationalists.

While the more visible attention given to Ulster between 1970 and 1972 bolstered membership in several key nationalist organizations in the United States, the increased number still represented a minority of the Irish-American population. For example, at its peak, the Irish Northern Aid Committee (NORAID) had seventy to eighty chapters across the country with about seven thousand to ten thousand members. To put the numbers in context, the total population of just immigrants and second-generation American Irish of Irish-born or mixed parentage was about 1.5 million in 1970.[36] In addition to various levels of commitment to the issues in Ulster, Irish Americans were divided socially, culturally, politically, and economically. The differences were clearly drawn during the visit of Bernadette Devlin to the United States in August 1969. Her appearances around the country initially drew large audiences and major media attention because of her youth (aged twenty-two), her gender and attractiveness, and her charisma. However Ms. Devlin's socialist politics and her rhetoric comparing black militant activity in the United States, including the Black Panthers, to the Catholic cause in Ulster offended the very audiences she was soliciting for support. She alienated conservative groups like the American Congress for Irish Freedom (ACIF), the Ancient Order of Hibernians (AOH), and the county associations, as well as far-Left groups like Brian Heron's National Association for Irish Justice (NAIJ) over the themes of her speeches, her attacks on the Catholic Church and American politicians like Mayor Richard Daley, and how the money she raised should be spent in Ireland. The ACIF accused the NAIJ of corrupting the young Irish politician to promote its socialist agenda, while the AOH took back the money it raised for Devlin in Detroit and sent it directly to the Catholic Church in Ireland after she embarrassed the group over the admission of African Americans to her rally.[37]

While Devlin's visit highlights the differences between American Irish groups, it also points up the gap that existed between the Irish and Irish Americans and each group's understanding of partition and the concept of nationalism. Clearly, the Irish in America and the Irish in Ireland were not a monolithic group. The Irish in America had been shaped by their experiences in the United States and their memory of Ireland prior to immigration or from the stories told by immigrant ancestors. The Irish, like Devlin, lived in a country that had obviously evolved beyond the pre-1960 Ireland most Americans pictured. Each side's perception and subsequent position on the issue of Northern Ireland were based on different realities, so there were bound to be conflicts.

Northern Ireland continues to generate headlines in both mainstream and ethnic newspapers in the United States. In the twenty years after Bloody Sunday, many of the issues played themselves out in a public way in that traditional venue of Irish-American patriotism and pride, the St. Patrick's Day parade. The event in New York City, the largest in the country, has counterparts around the nation, but the march that heads north up Fifth Avenue past the archbishop on the steps of St. Patrick's Cathedral is the most visible. It is the venue for drawing attention to debates and groups within the Irish-American community. The theme of the 1972 parade was "Get England Out of Ireland." Marchers carried posters bearing photographs of the victims of Bloody Sunday, Mayor John Lindsay wore a black armband, and fraternal and nationalist organizations chanted militant slogans. One college marching group was barred from the parade when it was discovered it had performed in a program with a British Army unit.[38]

In 1978, Governor Hugh Carey was booed as he marched up Fifth Avenue because of a "series of unpopular speeches on Northern Ireland" he had given during the previous year.[39] In 1982, Bobby Sands, the IRA hunger striker who had died in an Ulster prison protesting the treatment of prisoners, was named Honorary Grand Marshall of the parade, and the following year he was succeeded by Michael Flannery.[40] Flannery, the leader of NORAID had been acquitted in November 1982 of conspiring to ship guns to the IRA in a trial that embarrassed the American intelligence agencies who wanted to make a connection between NORAID and the supply of arms to Northern Ireland.[41] His appointment as head of the parade met with criticism in America and England. Despite the controversy, several prominent New York politicians, including Mayor Ed Koch, Representative Geraldine Ferraro, Governor Mario Cuomo, and Senator Alphonse D'Amato, marched in the parade to avoid alienating their Irish-American constituents. Archbishop Terrence Cooke refused to bless the grand marshal and faced the wrath of parade-goers for his snub.[42] After more than a decade of escalating violence and publicity that included the extradition of IRA fugitive Joe Doherty in 1992, the United States became directly involved in diplomatic efforts to solve the conflict in Northern Ireland.[43]

Efforts to effect constitutional change in Ireland began in earnest during the Reagan administration and resulted in a resolution passed in the U.S. House of Repre-

President Bill Clinton welcomed Ireland's President Mary Robinson, the first woman to hold the office, to the White House on 14 May 1993. Robinson made the forging of closer links between Ireland and the Irish diaspora around the world a major theme of her presidency, at a time when Irish applications for U.S. green cards were on the rise. (Official White House Photo, P003634-07A)

sentatives in 1985 supporting the Anglo Irish Agreement, which, among other provisions, created an intergovernmental conference that allowed representatives of the British and Irish governments to meet on a regular basis and discuss issues related to Northern Ireland. President Reagan used his influence with Prime Minister Margaret Thatcher to urge her to sign the agreement and promised that the United States would financially support the International Fund for Ireland.[44]

Efforts to negotiate peace in Northern Ireland continued with active U.S. encouragement under President Bill Clinton. Sinn Fein representative and alleged IRA official, Gerry Adams, was granted a controversial visa after he engineered an IRA ceasefire in August 1994.[45] Prior to the ceasefire, Adams had been denied entry to the United States because he was identified as a terrorist. Clinton, the American president who became most involved in the Ulster conflict, was extremely supportive of the peace process in the North and sent his personal emissary, former Senator George Mitchell, to arbitrate between the two sides. His intervention was crucial to the signing of the Good Friday Agreement in May 1998.[46] The agreement established a complex arrangement of governmental bodies that incorporated the Irish Republic, Northern Ireland, and the United Kingdom and restored local governing power to Northern Ireland.[47] In the early years of the twenty-first century, the elements of the agreement continue to be worked out.

In terms of the significance of events in the North to the American Irish, the steps leading to the Good Friday Agreement and subsequent efforts to keep the peace alive demonstrate a concerted effort by the American government and prominent Irish Americans to use their power and influence to move away from "physical force" protest as the solution to partition and turn to political change to enforce a lasting and meaningful peace in the region. Clinton's efforts were encouraged and supported by Senator Edward Kennedy of Massachusetts, the younger brother of JFK. Their sister, Jean Kennedy Smith, was appointed ambassador to Ireland (1993–1998) by President Clinton, and she used her office and family name to push the proceedings along. In 1994, Irish-American publisher Niall O'Dowd led a contingent of Irish-American business leaders and politicians to Northern Ireland to encourage a peaceful resolution.[48]

The timing of these events coincided with several significant events within the American Irish community. First, the immigrants comprising the more militant members of the population were aging, while the newest generation of immigrants who arrived in the 1980s, the so-called New Irish, was not that interested in the issues related to the North. They had been born in the independent Republic of Ireland, in which the dominant issues of importance were the economy and finding work. They were not as involved in the troubles as their predecessors, and this created conflict between the two groups of immigrants in America.[49] Consider this exchange from the letters to the editor column of the *Irish Voice* following a 1989 visit to New York by Diana, Princess of Wales, and the absence of New Irish at a staged protest:

> Are [the New Irish] so selfish and uncaring as to not be concerned about British oppression and terror in the six counties? . . . The young Irish of today are complacent and apathetic, both in Ireland and when they emigrate here. Why should I, an American, be concerned about their plight and their status, when they will not take a few hours of their time to demonstrate in support of their brothers and sisters in the six counties? Why should I care about them and about Ireland, when they seem not to care themselves?[50]

> The majority of young immigrants came here to work, not to become political activists. We were forced to emigrate because the Irish government failed to provide jobs. Stone [the first letter writer] might think it some golden rule that once [in the United States] we are all obliged to turn into raving Provos.[51]

Many second- and third-generation Irish Americans were not involved in nationalist groups, either because they did not understand the politics of the North or could not endorse the violent tactics of the IRA. By the end of the century, the Irish population in the United States was quite diverse. The variety of opinions regarding what to do in the North was just one issue reflecting its complexity.

In terms of public perception of the situation in the North, several popular films about the troubles were released in the 1980s and 1990s, which projected a more ambiguous and less clear-cut vision of life in the North and the effect of the conflict on the Irish themselves. *Cal* (1984), *In the Name of the Father* (1993), *Some Mother's Son* (1996), and *The Boxer* (1997) all carried themes of injustice, confusion, and disruption, but since the perspective of events was from the inside out (because most of the writers, producers, and directors had lived through the events), viewers were forced to consider a more complex picture of the conflict. Resolutions were not simply reached by getting England out of Ireland or supplying guns to the Provos. The voice of the victims and survivors of more than twenty years of warfare was compelling. All these factors coalesced at some point in the mid-1990s to produce the conditions that facilitated the Good Friday Agreement and America's involvement in it.

The arrival of the New Irish in the United States marked a turning point in the history of the Irish in America. This generation of immigrants entered the country at a time when the Irish ethnic population in the United States was at its most comfortable and successful. By the end of the twentieth century, the Irish had distinguished themselves in several arenas, including politics, the Catholic Church, business, literature, education, entertainment, law, medicine, and sports. American Irish were in the best position they had ever been to receive and support a new generation of immigrants. However, the communities into which the Irish traditionally entered had disappeared as the population aged or dispersed to the suburbs or more affluent urban neighborhoods.

The New Irish themselves were a different kind of immigrant. The first generation to leave an independent and contemporary Ireland without colonial baggage, the Irish for the most part were not migrating to America to start a new life, as much as they were going to America for what they saw as an unfortunate interim exercise caused by economic failure in Ireland. These Irish had been raised to believe that they would not have to emigrate because of the prosperity and social progress the country had enjoyed through the 1960s and 1970s. So when the international recession of 1979–1980 forced the resumption of migration, the young Irish who were leaving were often resentful of their predicament. As a result, they did not consider their time in America to be a permanent situation as did most of their predecessors. Their experience in the United States was complicated by the fact that most entered as illegal aliens and never fully integrated themselves into the mainstream of American life.

The international oil crisis of 1979 caught Ireland unprepared and created an economic turmoil that strangled the country with double-digit inflation and unemployment. With more than half its population under the age of twenty-five and no jobs to offer them, Ireland lost thousands of young people to other countries. Between 1981 and 1990, about 360,000 Irish left the country, almost 10 percent of the population.[52] How many actually came to America was the subject of debate at the time. Irish advocates and support groups claimed the number to be about 100,000 to 150,000 and generated big headlines (and sympathy) with their rhetoric. The real number is probably about 50,000, about 10–15 percent of the migrant population, but the figure will always remain an estimate because so many of the immigrants were undocumented.[53]

The 1965 immigration laws emphasized family reunification rather than national origin as a condition for entry. Because of the 1970s immigration slow down, few New Irish had the U.S. relatives who could sponsor them. So most declared themselves to be tourists and overstayed their visas. Like previous generations, they were young, single men and women under the age of thirty. They originated from all over Ireland, not just the rural areas and by most accounts were better educated than previous generations of Irish.[54] A study of New Irish living in New York City in 1990 showed that they had at least the equivalent of a high school education, and many had one or two years of university training.[55] Often the New Irish had jobs when they left Ireland but were not satisfied with their jobs, either because of inferior pay or boredom. They had been promised more and been raised to believe they were the generation that would not have to emigrate.[56] It was not to be.

The prosperity of the 1980s made finding work in the United States easy. Most of the illegal aliens found jobs working "under the table" as domestics or in the building trades and in restaurants, just like their predecessors but for different reasons. The jobs did not advance the New Irish professionally, but the money was good and for many the new independence was quite liberating. While their status in the early part of the decade did not necessarily inhibit their employment, the Irish were vulnerable if they suffered serious illness or injury because they did not receive medical or health benefits through work and the cost of insurance was prohibitive, particularly to a population used to receiving free health care. As undocumented aliens they never quite entered the mainstream of American society or even Irish-American society. They tended to live in cities, the most popular being Boston and New York, but they traveled as far west as San Francisco. They entered existing Irish communities and often revitalized the neighborhoods by supporting the local Irish grocers, restaurants, and taverns. In New York City, many of the New Irish tended to ghettoize themselves in their neighborhoods.

But it was not just their legal status that encouraged their self-segregation. The New Irish often found it difficult to relate to, or identify with, the immigrants of the 1950s and their families. The New Irish carried with them the culture, style, and tradition of modern Ireland, and it was an Ireland that the traditional Irish American did not recognize. The New Irish did not identify with the Catholicism and nationalism of the past. They did not join the county organizations or fraternal clubs of the earlier generations. They were raised in the post-colonial era and grew up within the international pop culture that was transmitted via television into living rooms around the world. Advanced technology brought the world to Ireland. It was no longer the culturally, socially, or economically isolated island it had been in the immediate post-war decades. As a result, the New Irish did not feel that America was the intimidating power that the 1950s immigrants felt it was; they did not come seeking to become Irish American, and in many cases they were critical of American foreign policy, culture, and lifestyle. The older immigrants and established ethnic community thought the newcomers to be arrogant and ungrateful for the hospitality of their hosts. So the two groups often clashed.

Although the New Irish population was not composed completely of undocumented aliens or of immigrants who isolated themselves from mainstream American life, this group did receive the most media attention. In New York City, for example, a number of New Irish entered with the proper documentation and secured jobs as engineers, lawyers, or Wall Street executives. Another segment of the population, most of whom were probably illegal, chose to live in the more trendy, avant-garde neighborhoods of the Lower East Side, deliberately removing themselves from the more "ghettoized" immigrants of the outer boroughs of the Bronx and Queens. The latter group was seeking a more nonconformist or artistic lifestyle, while the professionals integrated themselves within the ranks of other young professionals in Manhattan. What they all had in common was their background in Ireland and their discomfort mixing with the established Irish-American community.

The most active of both communities came together, however, to effect the legislative change that helped rectify the problems arising from the 1965 immigration law. A small group of New Irish joined forces with some active members of the existing ethnic community to create the Irish Immigration Reform Movement (IIRM) soon after the passage of the 1986 Immigration Reform and Control Act. IRCA, as it was known, penalized employers who hired illegal aliens, set in motion restrictions that inhibited the formerly easy travel back and forth across the Atlantic for undocumented aliens, and contained an amendment that established a lottery for forty thousand unrestricted visas available to thirty-six countries, including Ireland, that were adversely affected by the 1965 law. The IIRM mobilized the Irish community to take advantage of the opportunity presented by the amendment, called the Donnelly Bill for the Massachusetts congressman who drafted it. Because of the coordinated grass-roots effort of the IIRM, the Irish won about 40 percent of the visas in the lottery.[57] The IIRM continued to move forward with its objective of legislative change and created a set of committees to draw attention to the plight of the New Irish to support its cause. A separate social outreach branch of the organization in New York was established, called the Emerald Isle Immigration Center (EIIC), which offered confidential advice for undocumented aliens with questions about employment, their legal status, housing, or any issue related to acclimating to life in a new country. Nationally the IIRM had at least seventeen branches by the end of the decade, and the EIIC had its counterparts in several cities around the country.[58]

The New Irish brought energy, a sense of entitlement drawn from the legacy of generations who preceded them, and the superior skills of an education earned in the new Ireland to their legislative agenda. The IIRM lobbied Congress successfully to create a diversity visa, which established a visa lottery as part of the Immigration Act of 1990 for immigrants meeting skill and education–based demands for entry, and who originated from countries excluded from the 1965 law.[59] In order to accomplish their achievement, which was remarkable both in its scope and the speed with which it was executed, they needed to tap into the resources of the established Irish-American leadership in the Catholic Church, business, and government to negotiate legislative change. In the process they awakened a sleeping giant. Take for example, in New York City alone, the leadership and power present in the members of the Irish Immigration Working Committee which met regularly in the late 1980s to discuss matters of significance regarding immigration with the New Immigrant Liaison of the Consul General of Ireland: Ancient Order of Hibernians (AOH), Catholic Charities, the Irish American Labor Coalition (IALC), and the Irish American Business Coalition (IABC). The leader of the IABC represents the latent forces touched by the New Irish.

> [He was an] attorney with the Securities Industry Association [who] founded the coalition and represented the group at the [Irish Immigration Working] committee meetings in the late 1980s. He lived in Woodside, Queens, and came into contact with the New Irish on a daily basis. He said his impetus for creating the coalition was a sense that some white-collar professionals were feeling removed from their ancestry, but were nonetheless interested in Irish-American causes. Immigration was an issue people like himself could embrace.[60]

For ethnic Americans like this business leader, immigration and the problems of immigrants were easier to relate to, and support, than the activities of the IRA or just trying to understand the issues separating nationalists and unionists in Ireland. In America everyone has an immigrant in their background, some more recently than others, so it is an issue that is simple to personalize.

The Catholic Church in the United States and Ireland responded to the presence of the New Irish in a very proactive way. In 1988, the Archdiocese of New York City established a program through Catholic Charities called Project Irish Outreach shepherded by Monsignor James Murray in cooperation with the Irish government of Prime Minister Charles Haughey and the Irish Bishops' Episcopal Commission. The objective of Project Irish Outreach and the institutions involved was that no young Irish person on his or her own, or living as an undocumented alien in New York, would fall through the cracks. The result was an agency with offices in the Catholic Charities headquarters on First Avenue that dealt directly with the New Irish by phone or in person. Primarily a counseling and referral service with a small staff, almost 60 percent of the questions fielded in the first year were related to legal problems, 18 percent to medical problems, and 13 percent to employment issues.[61] For many of the immigrants, fearful of revealing their status and feeling conspicuous in a new city, the confidentiality promised by the office and the fact that the director and the social service worker on staff were Irish were significant. Hearing a familiar accent could be comforting to a young person feeling vulnerable and confused.

Monsignor Murray built on the strategy of friendly voices in a foreign land by establishing a missionary program in cooperation with the Irish bishops in which Irish religious would be assigned to parishes in the archdiocese which were known to be popular with the New Irish. The first missionaries included three priests and a nun. Sending over religious women and clergy to minister to the faithful was not a new practice for the Irish Church. Irish missionaries have served in great numbers in America for more than one hundred years, establishing parishes, hospitals, orphanages, and schools. What was different in the 1980s and 1990s was the diminished stature of the Catholic Church among the New Irish. They were not as religious or at least as active in the Church as had been previous generations, so they were not going to Mass in great numbers. Therefore the missionaries had to reach out to the immigrants and find them where they lived and worked. Their mission was one of social relief and support, as well as spiritual solace. Recognizing the fragile nature of the relationship between the Church and the new immigrants, one of the missionaries had this to say:

> Their attitude toward the priest . . . varies. On the one hand, those who would put him on a pedestal think he has the cure for all ills—think he can cure cattle, can cure people, and solve almost any problem. On the other are those who see him as the root of all evils in Ireland.[62]

So significant was the impact of the outreach effort that Bishop Francis Mugavero of the Brooklyn diocese opened an apostolate office in Woodside, Queens, in 1988, and the issue of the New Irish plight was a topic of the 1989 conference sponsored by the National Conference of Catholic Bishops Committee on Migration and the U.S. Catholic Conference Office of Migration and Refugee Services held at Boston College in Massachusetts.[63] The bishops' program evolved, and "in 1997 a national director was appointed to assess and coordinate a response to the needs of recent Irish immigrants in the entire United States."[64] Called Irish Apostolate USA, the program has Irish chaplains in Boston, New York, San Francisco, Chicago, and Philadelphia, with an office in Atlanta, an outreach program in San Diego, and a summer outreach program in Ocean City, Maryland, to support the young immigrants who work in that seasonal resort community.[65] As the first chaplains learned, the ministry of the apostolate continues to be pragmatic social service outreach, as well as spiritual care, as the immigrants need "a sympathetic ear and a helping hand" for "the whole human person."[66]

In what may or may not be a coincidence, in the decade following the first visa legislation in 1986, the Irish experienced a renaissance in the United States. It was suddenly fashionable to be Irish. In the 1990 Census, forty-four million Americans, almost 17 percent of the population, claimed some Irish or Scotch-Irish ancestry. Ancestry was liberally defined by the U.S. Census so that "a response of 'Irish' might reflect total involvement in an 'Irish' community or only a memory of ancestors several generations removed from the individual."[67] Either way, the numbers of Americans who identified with the Irish was significant.

The popularity of Irish film, dancing, drama, music, and literature reached an all time high in the 1980s and 1990s. On Broadway, Martin McDonagh's *Beauty Queen of Leenane* (1998) won four Antoinette Perry (Tony) awards for Best Director (Garry Hynes), Best Featured Actress and Actor (Anna Manahan and Tom Murphy), and Best Actress (Marie Mullen). It was also nominated for Best Play. Films by Irish writers and directors were receiving the highest industry awards dealing with social issues and politics that were far removed from traditional fare like *The Quiet Man* (1952) from an earlier generation. *My Left Foot* (1989), a biography of disabled author Christy Brown and the first Irish film to win a Best Picture Oscar nomination, was directed by Jim Sheridan, who was nominated for Best Director and won Best Actor (Daniel Day-Lewis) and Best Supporting Actress (Brenda Fricker) Awards. An inspirational film about a young man who overcomes disability, it exposed American audiences to the urban poverty of twentieth-century Ireland. *The Crying Game* (1992), directed by Neil Jordan, won nominations for Best Picture, Best Actor (Stephen Rea), and Best Supporting Actor (Jaye Davidson). An unconventional story about an IRA operative who tries to leave the organization, the sexual ambiguity of the primary characters in the film was a provocative departure for Irish movies. *In the Name of the Father* (1993) won nominations for Best Picture, Best Director (Jim Sheridan), Best Actor (Daniel Day-Lewis), Best Supporting Actor (Pete Postlethwaite), and Best Supporting Actress (Emma Thompson). This powerful film explored a father/son relationship that is tested when the son is wrongfully accused of an IRA crime. Loosely based on the story of Gerald Conlon and the Guildford Four, whose trial was a cause célèbre in England, it is also testimony to the danger of unemployed idleness that was the lot of many young Catholic men in 1970s Belfast. These films and the artists involved introduced the world to Ireland's burgeoning film industry and the talent within, and they reflected the social change Ireland had undergone since the 1960s.

Irish-American culture thrived as well. *Riverdance* (1993) and *Lord of the Dance* (1997), two dance troupe productions choreographed and led by champion Irish-American dancer Michael Flatley of Chicago, were surprising international successes. Flatley drew attention for his flamboyance and was criticized by traditionalists who objected to the sensuality and theatricality he brought to Irish dance. The shows were compared variously to Las Vegas show girl productions and rock concerts. But he raised the visibility and popularity of the art form around the world and consistently drew sell-out crowds. Frank McCourt won the Pulitzer Prize for *Angela's Ashes* (1996), and Alice McDermott won the National Book Award for *Charming Billy* (1998). McDermott's work was the third in a series of novels she wrote about the post–World War II Irish experience in New York City and its suburbs. She brings warmth and sensitivity to her characters, often employing a narrative voice that represents the second and third generations observing the passing away of the immigrants who represent probably the last of the neighborhood, parish-based urban ethnics that have existed in New York since the middle of the nineteenth century. She deals with the typical topics of alcoholism, Catholicism, guilt, and family loyalty with humor and insight. Her writing often exposes a disregard for conventional chronology, opting instead to reveal her narrative the way the average person remembers the significant events in his or her life—out of order.

Edward Burns brought the Irish-American diaspora to film. His *Brothers McMullen* (1995), a small independent film that won the Grand Jury Prize (1995) at the Sundance Film Festival, was followed by *She's the One* (1996) and *No Looking Back* (1998), all films exploring the attitudes of working-class and middle-class ethnics who lead ordinary lives in and around New York City. His characters are the children of the diaspora who, with their parents, left Queens in the 1970s for Long Island, and head back to Manhattan as adults. He avoids the late-century film stereotypes of crazed Irish Republican fugitives and sympathizers that counted as Irish American types in the 1980s and 1990s and instead gives us characters whose decisions are determined by their upbringing and heritage but are struggling to come to terms with it. With *The Brothers McMullen*, the most self-consciously ethnic of the three, Burns confessed that he had exaggerated certain behaviors and opinions to make a point. But he is probably the first filmmaker to bring suburbia and middle-class Irish-American stories directly to film. The increased interest in things Irish, which persists into the twenty-first century, can also be found on college campuses. Across the country programs of Irish studies are offered to undergraduate and graduate students in history, literature, politics, film, language, and the performing arts, providing students exposure and context to the Irish experience in America.

In the last half of the 1990s, Ireland enjoyed a huge economic growth spurt, making it one of the richest economies in the European Union. As a result, the Irish enjoyed a net in-migration that included returning Irish as well as non-Irish immigrants who came in search of white-collar and blue-collar jobs. For the intercensal period, 1996–2002, estimated net in-migration for Ireland was 153,881 compared with an estimated net out-migration of 134,170 for the 1986–1991 period.[68] Legal migration to United States from Ireland fell through the 1990s. The average annual number of entrants from Ireland fell from 10,631 between 1991 and 1995, to 1,250 between 1996 and 2002.[69] Traditionally, emigrant-producing Ireland had become an immigrant destination and had some trouble adjusting to the change and to the influx of foreigners.

Despite the economic progress in Ireland, undocumented aliens continued to find their way into the United States. These young people were perhaps even more disadvantaged than the Irish of the 1980s because they were overlooked by both America and Ireland. Since the 1980s and the success of the IIRM, the assumption among most in the Irish-American community was that the problem of illegal aliens was over. According to advocates for the later group of undocumented Irish, they had neither the organizational skills nor the popular momentum that the community had had in the 1980s to be successful. Complicating their lives in America were stricter immigration regulations and employment rules for foreign labor. For example, "legislation passed in the 1990s also prevent[ed] immigrants who enter the United States after August 1996 from collecting welfare and Medicaid benefits until they have paid Social Security taxes for ten years or become U.S. citizens, except for emergency Medicaid."[70]

Travel restrictions were also tightened. The "three and ten"–year bans prevented undocumented aliens living in the United States for a period of time from departing and reentering the country freely. After April 1, 1997, if an alien who had been undocumented for more than six months left the country and attempted to reenter, he or she was barred from the United States for three years. If an alien was undocumented for more than one year, left and tried to reenter, he or she was barred for ten years.[71] The first visa lotteries that the Irish enjoyed in the 1980s were exhausted by 2000. Demand for the available diversity visa was very competitive, and eligibility required a specific set of skills or education.[72] By the end of the century making the decision to live and work in the United States was more complicated than boarding a plane.

In the wake of 9/11, American attitudes toward illegal immigration from any country were cautious at best. In short, legal entry to America and the acquisition of appropriate work documentation demanded advance planning and resources. Those unable to meet the challenges of living and working in the United States had problems. According to activists advising the immigrant community in New York City in 1999, where about one-quarter of the Irish entering the United States settled,[73] most of the Irish they met had neither work authorization, permanent resident status, or immigrant visas and little prospect of obtaining the appropriate documentation. They typically had the equivalent of a high school degree and were in their early twenties, and many more originated from Northern Ireland than in the first crop of New Irish.[74] In many significant ways, the undocumented aliens entering the United States at the beginning of the twenty-first century were at greater risk for failure than their predecessors from even a decade earlier. They appeared to be farther under the radar and without the peer support, popular enthusiasm, and opportunities to integrate into the mainstream of the U.S. economy or society.

Where does this leave Irish America at the beginning of the twenty-first century? The 2000 census reflects a drop in the number of people declaring their ancestry as Irish and Scots-Irish to 34.8 million Americans, about 12 percent of the population from forty-four million, or 17 percent of the population in 1990. Since the definition is so subjective, it is difficult to evaluate exactly what that might mean.[75] Nevertheless, despite the reduced census numbers, the slowdown in immigration, and the disappearance of the tight-knit urban communities of fifty years ago, the Irish-American community appears to be strong but evolving. In the second half of the twentieth century the American Irish were not only moving out of the old parish-based neighborhoods into the suburbs but were moving out of the Northeast and Midwest into sunbelt states like California, Arizona, and Florida.[76] American Irish participation in the peace process in Northern Ireland suggests active interest in the welfare of the old country, as does the intensified cultural awareness of Irish literature, film, and theater. Irish-American artists continue to explore the experience of second- and third-generation ethnics as they deal with either success or stagnation, as did Michael Patrick MacDonald in his memoir, *All Souls: A Family Story from Southie*, about living through the busing riots in Boston in the 1970s. New Irish writers like poet Eamonn Wall are interpreting the New Irish experience as they spread out from their original city bases into the suburbs and the country, and to raise families.

The technology and global economy of the twenty-first century make Ireland and America closer neighbors than they ever have been, so travel and communication between the two countries are relatively easy. That and Ireland's stronger economy have made permanent relocation out of Ireland an option rather than a necessity, except for the most disadvantaged and alienated of the Irish. So the ties between the countries appear to continue intact. But, what it means to be Irish American in the twenty-first century is not clear. The traditional standards for defining ethnic identity have altered considerably from the nineteenth and even the mid–twentieth century. How the community will define itself in the twenty-first century remains to be seen.

NOTES

1. Donald Harman Akenson, "The Irish in the United States," in *The Irish World Wide*, Vol. 2: *The Irish in the New Communities,* ed. Patrick O'Sullivan (Leicester: Leicester University Press, 1992), 100–101. Akenson notes a number of polls from the 1980s to the early 1990s that suggest the American-Irish population to be slightly more than one-half Protestant and about one-third Catholic.

2. More scholarship about the Irish Protestant experience in America is emerging. See, for example, Bruce Boling, David N. Doyle, Kerby Miller, and Arnold Shrier, eds., *Irish Immigrants in the Land of Canaan: Letters and Memoirs from Colonial and Revolutionary America, 1675–1815* (New York: Oxford University Press, 2003).

3. Frank McCourt, *Angela's Ashes* (New York: Scribner, 1996).

4. *1992 Statistical Yearbook,* Table 2: Immigration by Region and Selected Country of Last Residence, Fiscal Years 1820–1992, 27.

5. Ibid.

6. Ibid.; *Ireland Census 91,* Table 1, 24. Ireland's population in 1961 was 2.8 million.

7. Kevin Kenny, *The American Irish: A History* (Harlow, England: Pearson Education, 2000), 226.

8. Michael J. Bennett, "How the GI Bill 'Saved' America," *The World and I*, article 15348, October 1996.

9. Brother Charles B. Quinn, *Iona College: The First Fifty Years* (New Rochelle, NY: Iona College, 1990), 25.

10. Andrew M. Greeley, William C. McCready, and Kathleen McCourt, *Catholic Schools in a Declining Church* (Kansas City, MO: Sheed and Ward, 1976), 65–75; Andrew M. Greeley, *The American Catholic: A Social Portrait* (New York: Basic Books, 1977), 58–65.

11. Kenny, *American Irish*, 227–228. Kenny offers a very good profile of Irish American income, housing, and education in the postwar period in his chapter, "Irish America since the Second World War."

12. William V. Shannon, *The American Irish: A Political and Social Portrait* (New York: Collier Books, 1984).

13. Episode guests and dates can be found on "The Ed Sullivan Show Episode List" on the Web: at www.tvtome.com/tvtome/servlet/EpisodeGuideservlet/showed-1156/The_Ed_Sullivan_Show/.

14. Biographical details on Bishop Sheen can be found on the following Web sites: www.catholicleague.org/research/fultonsheen.htm and www.museum.tv/archives/lev/s/htmls/sheenfulton/sheenfulton.htm. The home page for Archbishop Fulton J. Sheen is www.elpaso.net/~bank/elpasohistory/sheen/encyc.htm.

15. *The Irish Wit and Wisdom of Bishop Sheen* (VHS) (Pittsford, NY: FJJ & Co., 1997).

16. Morton Keller, *The Art and Politics of Thomas Nast* (New York: Oxford University Press, 1968), 175, from Thomas Nast's cartoon: "The American River Ganges, the Priests and the Children," *Harper's Weekly*, September 30, 1871.

17. Central Statistics Office, *Ireland Census 91, Vol. 1: Population Classified by Area* (Dublin: Stationery Office, June 1993), Table 6, 30 and Table M, 17.

18. Immigration and Naturalization Service (INS), *1957 Annual Report*, Table 9. In 1956 the INS reported that 79 percent of the men and 77 percent of the women entering the United States from Ireland in that year were single. Linda Dowling Almeida, *Irish Immigrants in New York City: 1945–1995* (Bloomington: Indiana University Press, 2001), 32.

19. Almeida, *Irish Immigrants*, 23–44.

20. Ibid., 25. See also Fergal Tobin, *The Best of Decades: Ireland in the Nineteen Sixties* (Dublin: Gill and Macmillan, 1984), 4–5; J. J. Lee, *Ireland 1912–1985: Politics and Society*, 6th ed. (Cambridge: Cambridge University Press, 1993), 341–362; John A. Murphy, *Ireland in the Twentieth Century*, 2nd ed., in *The Gill History of Ireland*, ed. James Lydon and Margaret MacCurtain (Dublin: Gill and Macmillan, 1997), 142.

21. Lee, *Ireland 1912–1985*, 360.

22. Almeida, *Irish Immigrants*, 34.

23. See Almeida's discussion of Church influence on Irish media and leadership fears of cultural corruption; ibid., 29–30. See also Robert Joseph Savage Jr., "Irish Television: The Political and Social Genesis" (Ph.D. diss., Boston College, 1993).

24. Commission on Emigration and Other Population Problems, *Commission on Emigration and Other Population Problems 1948–1954 Reports*, Pr. 2541 (Dublin: Stationery Office, 1956), paragraph 295, 136.

25. Almeida, *Irish Immigrants*. See chapter 2 for a review of Irish life in the 1950s.

26. Ibid., 9–10. See also David Reimers, *Still the Golden Door* (New York: Columbia University Press, 1985), 17.

27. *1992 Statistical Yearbook*, Table 2, 28.

28. Kenny, *American Irish*, 228.

29. Andrew M. Greeley, "The Success and Assimilation of Irish Protestants and Irish Catholics in the United States," *Sociology and Social Research* 72 (July 1988): 229–236.

30. Nathaniel Glazer and Daniel Patrick Moynihan, *Beyond The Melting Pot: Negroes, Puerto Ricans, Jews, Italians and Irish of New York City* (Cambridge: MIT Press and Harvard University Press, 1963); Lawrence McCaffrey, *The Irish Catholic Diaspora in America* (Washington, DC: Catholic University of America Press, 1997), rev. ed. of *The Irish Diaspora in America* (Bloomington: Indiana University Press, 1976).

31. Kenny, *American Irish,* 228. Kenny notes that "by 1960 Irish Americans of the first and second generation were more likely to marry outside their ethnic group than within it, whereas three-quarters of all Irish immigrants in the United States in 1920 had married other Irish people (of either Irish or American birth)."

32. Pete Hamill, "Notes on the New Irish: A Guide for the Goyim," *New York,* March 15, 1972, 34.

33. Steven P. Erie, *Rainbow's End: Irish America and the Dilemmas of Urban Machine Politics, 1840–1985* (Berkeley: University of California Press, 1988), 27–28.

34. Kenny, *American Irish,* 246.

35. Andrew J. Wilson, *Irish America and the Ulster Conflict: 1968–1995* (Washington, DC: Catholic University of America Press, 1995), 65.

36. Ibid., 70, and Kenny, *American Irish,* 225.

37. See Wilson, *Irish America,* 31–40, and Kenny, *American Irish,* 246–251, for a full discussion of Devlin's visit to the United States and its repercussions.

38. Wilson, *Irish America,* 67.

39. Almeida, *Irish Immigrants,* 133. See also John T. Ridge, *The St. Patrick's Day Parade in New York* (New York: St. Patrick's Day Parade Committee, AOH Publications, 1988), 166, and *New York Times,* March 18, 1978.

40. Wilson, *Irish America,* 213.

41. Ibid., 208–211.

42. Ibid., 212–215.

43. Ibid., 26–262 and Kenny, *American Irish,* 255–256.

44. Wilson, *Irish America,* 246–250.

45. Kenny, *American Irish,* 256.

46. Ibid., 256–257.

47. Almeida, *Irish Immigrants,* 135.

48. Ibid.

49. For a discussion of relations and priorities between 1950s and 1980s immigrants in New York City, see ibid., 134–135.

50. Paul Stone, Floral Park, NY, letter to the *Irish Voice,* February 18, 1989, 9.

51. Rose Fitzgibbon, Brooklyn, NY, letter to the *Irish Voice,* March 11, 1989, 11.

52. Almeida, *Irish Immigrants,* 61. National Economic and Social Council (NESC), *The Economic and Social Implications of Emigration* (Dublin: National Economic and Social Council, March 1991), 59.

53. Almeida, *Irish Immigrants,* 62.

54. Ibid., 61–82.

55. Ibid., 65–67.

56. Ibid., 68.

57. See Linda Dowling Almeida, "'And They Still Haven't Found What They're Looking For': A Survey of the New Irish in New York City," in *The Irish World Wide: Patterns of Migration,* vol. 1, ed. Patrick O'Sullivan (Leicester, UK: Leicester University Press and New York: St. Martin's Press, 1992), 196–221.

58. Almeida, *Irish Immigrants,* 72–75.

59. *1992 Statistical Yearbook*, Appendix 1, 133, A.1–20.

60. Almeida, *Irish Immigrants*, 71. Quote taken from interview with the IABC leader on February 8, 1989.

61. Almeida, *Irish Immigrants*, 102–103.

62. Reverend Joseph Delaney, Project Irish Outreach, Archdiocese of New York, as quoted in *The New Irish Immigrant*, report on a conference sponsored by the National Conference of Catholic Bishops (NCCB) Committee on Migration and the United States Catholic Conference Office of Migration and Refugee Services, Boston College, February 25, 1989, 24.

63. Almeida, *Irish Immigrants*, 100–109.

64. Irish Apostolate USA: The Web site of the Irish Chaplaincies, their staffs and volunteers in the United States, http://www.usairish.org.

65. Almeida, *Irish Immigrants*, 146. Interview with Father Tim O'Sullivan, February 22, 2000.

66. Irish Apostolate Web site.

67. Almeida, *Irish Immigrants*, 64. Quotation from Department of Commerce, *1990 Census of Population and Housing, Population and Housing Characteristics for Census Tracts and Block Numbering Areas, New York, Northern New Jersey, Long Island, NY-NJ-CT CMSA (Part) New York, NY PMSA*, 1990 CPH-3-245H (Washington, DC: Government Printing Office, July 1993), section 6, B-2, for "Definitions of Subject Characteristics."

68. Central Statistics Office, *Ireland Census 2002, Vol. 4: Usual Residence, Migration, Birthplaces and Nationalities*, Table 1: Population of each Province at each census since 1926, distinguishing the components of population change in each intercensal period since 1911, 11. Taken from the Web: http://www.cso.ie/census/pdfs/vol.4_t1_17.pdf.

69. U.S. Department of Homeland Security, *Yearbook of Immigration Statistics, 2003* (Washington, DC: U.S. Government Printing Office, 2004); see Immigrants Admitted by Region and Country of Birth, Fiscal Years 1993–2003, Table 3, 16, at uscis.gov/graphics/shared/aboutus/statistics/2003Yearbook/pdf. U.S. Department of Justice, *1997 Statistical Yearbook of the Immigration and Naturalization Service* (Washington, DC: U.S. Government Printing Office, 1999); see Immigrants Admitted by Region and Country of Birth, Fiscal Years, 1987–1997, Table 3, 28, at uscis.gov/graphics/shared/aboutus/statistics/1997YB.pdf.

70. Almeida, *Irish Immigrants*, 144–145.

71. Ibid., 145.

72. The Schumer Program or Permanent Diversity Program (1994) requires that applicants have a high school education or the equivalent, or have two years' experience in an occupation within the five-year period prior to application. See Almeida, *Irish Immigrants*, 63, for more detail.

73. Harry Keaney and Patrick Markey, "The New Generation: Celtic Tiger Roars, but, for Many, Uncle Sam Still Beckons," *Irish Echo*, November 24–30, 1999. The authors cite an Immigration and Naturalization Service report that of Irish immigrants heading to the United States between 1981 and 1996 about 25 percent settled in the New York City area.

74. For more detail on the late-century situation in New York City, see Almeida, *Irish Immigrants*, 143–147.

75. Angela Brittingham and G. Patricia de la Cruz, "Ancestry 2000: Census 2000 Brief" (C2KBR-35), *United States Census 2000* (Washington, DC: U.S. Department of Commerce, Economics and Statistics Administration, U.S. Census Bureau, June 2004). See Web site http://www.census.gov/prod/2004pubs/c2kbr-35.pdf.

76. Kenny, *American Irish*, 226.

SUGGESTED READING

Linda Dowling Almeida, *Irish Immigrants in New York City: 1945–1995* (Bloomington: Indiana University Press, 2001).

Mary P. Corcoran, *Irish Illegals: Transients between Two Societies* (Westport, CT: Greenwood Press, 1993).

Steven P. Erie, *Rainbow's End: Irish America and the Dilemmas of Urban Machine Politics, 1840–1985* (Berkeley: University of California Press, 1988).

Andrew Greeley, "Achievement of the Irish in America," in *The Encyclopedia of the Irish in America*, ed. Michael Glazier, 1–4 (Notre Dame, IN: University of Notre Dame Press, 1999).

Kevin Kenny, *The American Irish: A History* (Harlow, UK: Pearson Education, 2000).

Lawrence McCaffrey, *The Irish Catholic Diaspora in America* (Washington, DC: Catholic University of America Press, 1997).

Andrew J. Wilson, *Irish America and the Ulster Conflict: 1968–1995* (Washington, DC: Catholic University of America Press, 1995).

Chapter 25

Twentieth-Century American Catholicism and Irish Americans

Thomas J. Shelley

In June 1908 the American Catholic Church formally came of age when the Holy See officially recognized that the United States was no longer a missionary country. An older generation of American Catholics used to regard this change as a milestone in the history of their Church. Today historians tend to minimize its significance and to emphasize instead the continuity of American Catholicism before and after the year 1908. They now locate the real turning point in twentieth-century American Catholicism later in the century, more precisely in the social and cultural changes that occurred in the Catholic community during the 1960s.

During the first two-thirds of the century, American Catholicism was characterized by a steady increase in the number of adherents, impressive institutional loyalty, and growing self-confidence as the immigrant Catholic Church of the nineteenth century sank deep roots in American soil and began to flex its muscles as an increasingly important influence in American society. In the words of one historian of twentieth-century American religion: "In terms of numbers the Roman Catholic Church was far more than a lusty infant," as the number of American Catholics more than doubled from 17,885,000 in 1920 to 42,104,900 in 1960.[1]

During the last third of the century, however, while the Catholic community continued to increase in size until it included one of every four Americans, it also experienced an erosion of unity and commitment among its members, as well as increasing signs of uncertainty about both the relationship of Catholicism to American society and the relationship of American Catholicism to the universal Church. There were many causes for the worldwide disarray in post–Vatican II Catholicism; it was by no means an exclusively American phenomenon. However, one reason the influence of the council proved particularly unsettling to American Catholics was that it coincided with the decline of the tight-knit ethnic Catholicism that for more than a century had provided a sense of security and self-identity for Catholics in America.

Concomitant with the decline of ethnic Catholicism after the 1960s was a muting of the Irish presence in American Catholicism and a shift in the leadership from Irish Americans to a broader-based representation of the descendants of the many ethnic groups who comprised the American Catholic community. The Hollywood movies of the 1930s and 1940s that stereotyped all American Catholic priests as Irish Americans were only reflecting the expectations of the general public at that time. Until well after World War II, the American hierarchy remained predominantly Irish American. Likewise, in the early twentieth century, most of the prominent American Catholics in fields as diverse as business, finance, labor, education, politics, sports, and entertainment were Irish Americans.

However, as early as 1900, two-thirds of all Irish Americans had been born in the United States, and their children and grandchildren had increasingly tenuous ties to Ireland. As these upwardly mobile second- and third-generation Irish Americans disappeared with increasing ease and frequency into the welcoming American mainstream, sociologists began to ask: "Where have all the Irish Catholics gone?" After the 1960s their absence was especially noticeable in the American Catholic Church.[2]

Ethnic Catholicism

At the beginning of the twentieth century, American Catholicism was more ethnically diverse than ever before, thanks to the large number of Catholic immigrants who had come to America during the pervious century. Among Protestant denominations, only the Lutherans came close to matching the Catholics in this respect. This was in contrast to immigration patterns consistent until the 1880s, when the American Catholic community was largely made up of Irish and lesser numbers of German immigrants and their descendants, with pockets of Chicanos in California, Texas, and the Southwest; French in Louisiana; French Canadians scattered across the Midwest; and remnants of the colonial Anglo-American communities in southern Maryland and central Kentucky.

The big transition came after 1880 with the massive immigration from Eastern and Southern Europe, peaking between 1900 and 1914, when thirteen million immigrants arrived in the United States. Among the newcomers during those three-and-a-half decades were some four million Italians, virtually all of them at least nominally Catholic. There was a comparable increase in the number of Slavic Catholics as Poles, Czechs, Slovaks, Slovenes, Croatians, Ukrainians, and Carpatho-Rusyns poured into the country, as well as non-Slavic peoples from Central and Eastern Europe, such as the Magyars and Lithuanians.

Not all of the immigrants came from across the Atlantic. French Canadians moved south from rural Quebec to work in the textile mills of New England, while landless Mexican and Central American peasants moved north in search of agricultural work, swelling many times over the size of the existing population in California, Texas, and the Southwest. By 1915, the American Catholic community consisted of twenty-eight different nationalities or language groups, with the Irish, Germans, Italians, Poles, French Canadians, and Mexican immigrants accounting for three-quarters of the Catholic population.[3]

During the first half of the twentieth century, the favored response of the U.S. bishops to this pastoral challenge continued to be the establishment of "national" parishes without territorial boundaries for all the members of a particular ethnic or language group. It was first tried in Philadelphia as far back as 1789 with the establishment of

Holy Trinity Church for the German Catholics of that city. The experiment proved to be so successful that it was repeated many times over during the nineteenth century. Unlike the territorial parishes, the initiative for establishing these national parishes typically came from the laity, who bought property for a church, raised the funds for its construction, and then petitioned the bishop to send them a priest of their nationality. Sometimes it was difficult to satisfy the expectations of both the clergy and the laity. In one Slovak parish in Haverstraw, New York, there were sixteen pastors in eight years.[4] Well into the twentieth century, the laity in many of these national parishes continued to exercise a degree of control, especially over financial matters, that would have been unthinkable in territorial parishes.

Although many of the national parishes were founded in the later nineteenth century, they reached the peak of their expansion and influence in the early twentieth century. By 1892, according to one estimate, there were 2,250 German national parishes and dependent missions. As the number of German parishes declined in the twentieth century, they were replaced by approximately 1,600 Slavic national parishes (about half of them Polish) and lesser numbers of national parishes for other ethnic groups.[5] The little coal-mining city of Hazleton, Pennsylvania, even had a national parish for the Tyrolese.

Some American Catholic bishops, notably John Ireland, the Kilkenny-born "Americanist" archbishop of St. Paul (1888–1918), questioned the wisdom of establishing such parishes for fear that they would retard the assimilation of the immigrants into the American mainstream and accentuate the foreign character of American Catholicism. "On the contrary," contended Father Joseph Fitzpatrick, a Jesuit sociologist at Fordham University:

> It was these very parishes at the heart of the immigrant community that gave the newcomers their sense of security in a strange land, that kept their sense of identity alive, that gave them the stability "to integrate from a position of strength" into American society.[6]

Although the ethnic diversity of the American Catholic community increased sharply in the thirty-five years before World War I, the Irish remained firmly in control of the levers of power through their domination of the hierarchy. In 1900, perhaps as many as two-thirds of the American bishops were either Irish-born or of Irish descent.[7] German dissatisfaction with this Irish domination of the hierarchy, or the "hibernarchy," as they sometimes called it, peaked in the late 1880s and 1890s with several appeals to Rome that met with only limited success. German restlessness remained strong until World War I, when an outburst of anti-German hysteria in the United States accelerated German assimilation and led to the rapid decline in the number of German national parishes, German-language newspapers, and German organizations like the Central Verein based in St. Louis.

As ethnic consciousness among German Americans waned in the early twentieth century, it remained strong among many of the newer Slavic immigrants. Polish priests were especially prone to complain of the alleged insensitivity of Irish-American bishops. A complicating factor among the Polish-American clergy was their own intense intramural rivalry. In 1904, dissident Polish priests from Chicago, Detroit,

An eleven-year-old famine emigrant from County Kilkenny, John Ireland (1838–1918) came of age in Minnesota. He was ordained for the Diocese of St. Paul in 1861 and named its first archbishop in 1888. Always outspoken in his beliefs, he was one of the members of the Catholic hierarchy who publicly advocated the "Americanization" of Catholic immigrants, which he believed would make them better church members as well as better citizens. (Library of Congress, Prints and Photographs Division, LC-USZ62-52059)

Buffalo, and other cities formed the Polish National Catholic Church, with its headquarters in Scranton, Pennsylvania, the one large-scale schism in the history of American Catholicism. At its peak, the Polish National Catholic Church had a membership of 130,000, only about 5 percent of the Polish-American population. Like the Germans before them, the Poles were also unhappy with their lack of representation in the hierarchy. Ironically, however, when Polish-American priests attempted to use the influence of the new Polish Republic to advance their cause in Rome after World War I, some of their severest critics proved to be the German-American archbishops of Chicago and Milwaukee, whose assimilationist views would have won plaudits from an earlier generation of Irish-American prelates.[8]

Perhaps the single biggest failure of the American Catholic Church in responding to the successive waves of Catholic immigrants involved the Ukrainian and Carpatho-Rusyn members. As Byzantine-rite Catholics (or Greek-rite Catholics, as they were commonly called), for centuries in Eastern Europe they had enjoyed their own hierarchy, liturgy, canon law, and the longstanding custom of a married clergy. In the United States, however, the latter practice aroused fierce hostility from the American bishops, who refused to permit it. "The possible loss of a few souls of the Greek rite," the U.S. archbishops declared in 1893, "bears no proportion to the blessings resulting from uniformity of discipline." As a result of this episcopal obtuseness, which deprived Byzantine-rite Catholics of the services of their own clergy, some 225,000 eventually left the Catholic Church and joined the hitherto numerically insignificant Russian Orthodox Church. The situation began to improve only after 1907 with the appointment of Stephen Ortynsky as the first Byzantine-rite bishop in the United States.[9]

The Irish Presence

The predominant role that the Irish assumed in the American Catholic Church in the early nineteenth century rested on more substantial foundations than their numerical superiority in the hierarchy. In the century after 1815, about three-quarters of the five million Irish who emigrated to the United States were Catholics, a larger number than any other Catholic ethnic group.[10] Moreover, as Philip Gleason, Lawrence McCaffrey, and others have pointed out, the Irish were uniquely qualified to lead the multiethnic American Catholic Church. First of all, they enjoyed the priceless advantage of familiarity with the English language, and they were accustomed to financially supporting the Church through their own contributions rather than through government backing. Furthermore, they were not particularly fazed by anti-Catholic bigotry because they had already experienced it in their homeland, and (thanks to Daniel O'Connell) they were adept at using liberal democratic political institutions to defend their religious interests.[11]

The sheer force of numbers also explains the privileged position that the Irish assumed in the nineteenth-century American Catholic Church and which continued well into the twentieth century. So many young Irish Americans entered the priesthood and religious life that religious communities like the Redemptorists and the Sisters of St. Joseph, originally German and French, respectively, quickly became Irish American. At St. John's College, Fordham, a French Jesuit faculty was transformed into an Irish Jesuit faculty within two decades. Irish communities like the Sisters of Mercy, the Presentation Sisters, and the Irish Christian Brothers thrived in America, as did religious communities of American origin like the various branches of the Sisters of Charity. In New York City the Sisters of Charity of Mount St. Vincent grew from 31 sisters in 1846, almost all of them Irish, to 420 sisters twenty-five years later.[12]

The abundance of vocations and the high level of religious practice among Irish immigrants in the late nineteenth and early twentieth centuries—in contrast to earlier Irish immigrants—reflected the influence of the Devotional Revolution in post-Famine Ireland. Another crucial element in the shaping of modern Irish and Irish-American Catholicism was the identification of Irish nationalism with Catholicism,

The Ninth Massachusetts Infantry, recruited in Boston and known as the "Irish 9th," heard Mass at Camp Cass in Virginia in 1861. While not part of the Irish Brigade, this unit is typical of the way in which most Irish volunteers served in the Union Army—as part of small ethnic companies within larger nonethnic regiments. Photograph taken by the Matthew Brady Studio. (Library of Congress, Prints and Photographs Division, LC-USZC4-4605)

promoted by Daniel O'Connell and encouraged in the later nineteenth century by such influential prelates as Archbishop William Walsh of Dublin and Archbishop Thomas Croke of Cashel. As a result, historian Kerby Miller notes, in "the United States, as in Ireland, Catholicism became the central institution of Irish life and the primary source and expression of Irish identity."[13]

Observers of American Catholic clerical life sometimes made invidious comparisons between the Irish-born priests and Irish-American priests. Alternately, Brother Paul Wattson, the convert Anglican founder of the Graymoor Franciscan friars, while a student at St. Joseph's Seminary, Dunwoodie, in the early twentieth century, praised the Irish-American seminarians because, he said, they "were so healthy, wholesome, contented, and devout in a natural way without being sanctimonious." One of the blessings that Brother Paul anticipated for the American Catholic Church from the Dunwoodie alumni was the end of "the old notion of the Catholic priest as a fat unruly Irishman," a sentiment that he was prudent enough to keep to himself.[14]

In the early twentieth century bishops in Florida, California, and other states with relatively few Catholics could not have staffed their parishes without the Irish priests whom they recruited directly from missionary seminaries like All Hallows College, Dublin. These Irish priests played an indispensable role in establishing the institutional foundations of the Catholic Church in much of the present-day Sunbelt, sometimes at great personal sacrifice. Michael Joseph Curley, the future archbishop of Baltimore, was the son of a Westmeath farmer, who as a young priest in Deland, Florida, in the early twentieth century had a parish of seventy-two hundred square miles, larger than the archdiocese of Baltimore. Curley lived in a rented room above a store and ate in a diner where he got twenty-one meals for $5.00 per week.[15] As late as the 1950s, three-quarters of the priests in the archdiocese of Los Angeles were the graduates of Irish seminaries, as were more than a third of the priests in the archdiocese of San Francisco a decade later.[16]

Sisters outnumbered priests by a margin of three or four to one, and they played an indispensable role as teachers, nurses, and administrators in Catholic schools and charitable institutions. Moreover, as often the only educated women in working-class neighborhoods, they also served as role models for many young Irish-American women who were attracted to the convent by their association with the sisters in their own parishes. Hasia Diner, who has documented the enormous services that sisters provided for Irish women in large American cities, has also called attention to the inchoate feminism of the Sisters of Mercy and the Sisters of the Good Shepherd. "No place in their statements of purpose," wrote Diner, "did they define the role of the order as that of helping poor young women enhance their prospects for successful matrimony. Instead, they sought to make these immigrant women and their daughters economically self-sufficient as part of the mission to heighten their spirituality."[17]

In the twentieth century, American sisters, many of them Irish, pioneered the expansion of higher education for Catholic women. Notre Dame Academy in Maryland received a college charter in 1896; thirty years later there were twenty-five Catholic women's colleges in the United States, one third of all the colleges accredited by the Catholic Educational Association. Some of them like Trinity College in Washington, D.C. (founded in 1900 by Sister Julia McGroarty, who was born on a farm in County Donegal) and the College of St. Catherine in St. Paul (founded in 1911 by Mother Seraphine Ireland, the sister of Archbishop Ireland) were far superior academically to many run-of-the-mill Catholic men's colleges.[18]

Irish influence in the American Catholic Church was not limited to the clergy and religious. For a half-century or more, Irish-Catholic Democratic machines dominated politics in New York City, Albany, Troy, Boston, Chicago, Omaha, Pittsburgh, St. Louis, Jersey City, Hoboken, San Francisco, New Orleans, and Kansas City. While the wall of separation between church and state remained theoretically intact, James Hennesey was only stating the obvious when he remarked that priests and religious came from the same families that produced the politicians. As a result he speculated, tongue in cheek, that "it could happen that surplus desks, destined for the bonfire, found their way into parochial school classrooms." He also noted that "the chaplaincy [sic], with salary, of the police or fire department made a nice perquisite for a deserving pastor." As a native of Jersey City, Hennesey was perhaps drawing upon personal knowledge when he mentioned that "the message was not lightly ignored when Boss [Frank] Hague took an interest in fund raising for a new diocesan seminary."[19]

The Irish-Catholic political machines have been faulted for their fiscal conservatism and their failure to use their political power to advance the cause of social reform. Daniel Patrick Moynihan claimed that "the Irish just didn't know what to do with their [political] opportunity. They never thought of politics as an instrument of social change." However, Steven P. Erie and others have shown that nineteenth-century Irish Americans were by no means "monolithically conservative." In New

York, Chicago, and San Francisco, working-class Irish Americans, influenced by Irish-American nationalism, had no qualms about voting for radical candidates when they felt that their own political leaders failed to represent their economic interests.[20]

Organized labor was another field where Irish Americans figured prominently. Well into the twentieth century as many as one quarter of all male Irish Americans earned less than a family wage, often in jobs that were very dangerous.[21] A crucial incident in the relationship between the Catholic Church and the American labor movement occurred in 1887, when Cardinal James Gibbons of Baltimore intervened in Rome to prevent a papal condemnation of the Knights of Labor. The Knights was the first large American labor union, and many of its members were Irish Catholics, as was the Grand Master Workman, Terence Powderly, who was also a leader of the Clan na Gael.

Sympathy for the plight of the workers led some radical Irish Americans like Elizabeth Gurley Flynn and William Z. Foster to leadership positions in the American Communist Party. At least two priests, Thomas McGrady and Thomas Haggerty, followed a similar path and abandoned the Church for socialism. More typical was Father Peter C. Yorke, the son of an Irish sea captain in turn-of-the-century San Francisco. Like Edward McGlynn in New York City two decades earlier, Yorke combined an intense interest in Irish nationalism with the defense of labor unions, especially during the great teamsters' strike of 1901. Father John J. Curran, a curate in the heart of the Pennsylvania anthracite coalfields and a former employee of a coal company himself, worked closely with the United Mine Workers for over thirty years, earning the respect of both labor and capital. "Labor priests" like Yorke and Curran were to have many successors in the twentieth century and help to explain why the Catholic Church in the United States, unlike the Catholic Church in many European countries, managed to retain the loyalty of the working class.

Though sometimes a tenuous one, another link between the Church and organized labor was provided by Irish-American women who were active as union organizers. The most famous was "Mother Jones" (Mary Harris Jones), "born in revolution" in Cork in 1830, who, after a lifetime of denouncing bourgeois Catholicism from the cutting edge of the radical labor movement, was buried at St. Gabriel's Church in Washington, D.C., allegedly at the age of one hundred. Other Irish-American women like Leonora Barry, another Corkonian, and Elizabeth Flynn Rogers, the mother of eight children, held important positions in the Knights of Labor. Mary Kenney O'Sullivan was the first woman organizer for the American Federation of Labor, and Leonora O'Reilly was active in both the United Garment Workers of America and the Women's Trade Union League. Still other Irish-American women were pioneers in efforts to unionize public school teachers—Kate Kennedy in San Francisco, and Margaret Haley and Catherine Goggins in Chicago.[22]

The Progressive Era and World War I

The first decade of the twentieth century witnessed a wide range of economic and social reforms on both the state and federal levels. For Catholics, however, the dark side of the Progressive Era was the reemergence of anti-Catholic bigotry, often fostered by sensationalist journalists and demagogic politicians. Anti-Catholicism had a long pedigree in American culture, stretching back to the colonial era. The Harvard historian Arthur Schlesinger Sr. once called it the oldest prejudice in American history. However, there was something new and different about the early-twentieth-century variety of anti-Catholicism. Its most vocal representatives were not the typical right-wing fundamentalist Protestant clergy, but left-wing populist politicians like former Congressman (and future Senator) Thomas E. Watson in Georgia, who pilloried the Catholic Church as the enemy of the social reforms of the Progressive Era. Also, unlike the nineteenth-century nativists, who were found mainly in cities like New York and Philadelphia that were teeming with Irish and German Catholic immigrants, their twentieth-century counterparts flourished in rural backwaters where Catholics were as scarce as hen's teeth. Both *Tom Watson's Magazine* and *The Menace*, the two most widely read anti-Catholic periodicals, were published in small towns of fewer than four thousand people.

Some of the most effective responses to this new wave of anti-Catholic bigotry came from the Catholic laity. In 1914 the Knights of Columbus, under the leadership of Patrick Henry Callahan, a wealthy Louisville industrialist, organized a Commission on Religious Prejudices to combat this latest wave of anti-Catholicism. In Tom Watson's Georgia, where Catholics numbered only fifteen thousand in 1916, they formed the highly effective Catholic Laymen's Association of Georgia to defend their interests after the state legislature passed an offensive Convent Inspection Act. The advent of World War I and growing American hostility to Germany led to a decline in this wave of anti-Catholicism, as the kaiser replaced the pope as Public Enemy Number One. However, the decline proved to be only temporary, and anti-Catholic prejudice was to resurface again, stronger than ever, during the xenophobic 1920s.

Although the Catholic Church had been the largest single religious denomination in the United States for the latter half of the nineteenth century, it could boast of little in the way of intellectual distinction, understandably so in view of the immigrant origins of most of its members. It is indicative of the intellectual poverty of the American Catholic community that when the Catholic University of America opened its doors in 1889, four of the original seven faculty members were foreign-born clerics and the other three were converts. Not one of them was Irish.[23] However, the very fact that the American bishops sponsored the establishment of the university at all was evidence that at least some of them realized the need for academic excellence in the Catholic community.

The leading proponent of the Catholic University was Bishop John Lancaster Spalding of Peoria, who was himself a graduate of the Catholic University of Louvain, Belgium. Pleading for a similar institution in the United States, he told his fellow bishops at the Third Plenary Council of Baltimore in 1884:

> When our zeal for intellectual excellence shall have raised up men who will take their place among the first writers and thinkers of their day, their very presence will become the most persuasive of arguments to teach the world that no best gift is at war with the spirit of the Catholic faith.[24]

Spalding was the descendant of persecuted English Catholics who came to Maryland in the 1650s, but his three principal supporters in the hierarchy were all natives of Ireland: Bishop John Keane, the first rector of the Catholic University of America; Archbishop John Ireland of St. Paul; and Denis O'Connell, the rector of the North American College in Rome. Another sympathizer was James Cardinal Gibbons, who was born in Baltimore but raised in Ireland. Together they came to be called the "Americanist" wing of the U.S. hierarchy. They found support for their views among the members of two small, but influential religious communities of men, the Sulpicians—who were the country's foremost seminary educators—and the Paulists, an American community founded by the convert priest Isaac Hecker to promote mutual understanding between Catholicism and America.

If the leading Americanists in the hierarchy were Irish (with the exception of Spalding), so were their conservative episcopal opponents, most notably Archbishop Michael Corrigan of New York and Bishop Bernard McQuaid of Rochester, New York, who looked with suspicion even on the Ancient Order of Hibernians. The promising effort of the Americanists to promote what a later age would call "acculturation" came to an abrupt halt in 1899 when Pope Leo XIII sent a public letter to Cardinal Gibbons warning the U.S. bishops of the dangers of "Americanism." Although the papal condemnation was couched in polite and veiled language, there was no mistaking the fear in Rome that American Catholics were succumbing to the lure of nationalism and entertaining dangerous dreams of a distinctively Americanized form of Catholicism.

Eight years later came another papal directive, the encyclical *Pascendi Dominici Gregis,* condemning the heresy of Modernism, which was defined in such broad and vague terms that it effectively quashed any critical or original work in theology, philosophy, or biblical studies. Moreover, when the Pope warned that the Modernists were to be found "not only among the Church's open enemies . . . but in her very bosom and heart," he unleashed a witch hunt against heretical "moles" that recalled the worst days of the Inquisition.[25] The campaign against Modernism was aimed primarily at Catholic scholars in Europe, but the impact was even more devastating in the United States where the scientific study of theology and related disciplines under Catholic auspices was still in its infancy.

Father James Driscoll, the rector of St. Joseph's Seminary, Dunwoodie, told a Protestant friend: "I can compare the crisis to nothing but a cyclone during which people must simply make for the cellar."[26] "Make for the cellar" is what Catholic scholars did indeed do, since virtually all of them were clerics and vulnerable to ecclesiastical sanctions. Two who left the Church were William Sullivan, a Paulist priest, and John Slattery, the superior of the Josephite Fathers. The combined effect of the papal condemnations of Americanism and Modernism was a tragedy that crippled Catholic intellectual life in the United States for the next forty years. "An intellectual coma" was how Peter Guilday, the future church historian, described his experience of seminary education during that period.[27]

The papal condemnations of Americanism and Modernism also put an end to the tentative efforts inspired by Isaac Hecker, John Ireland, and other Americanists to fashion a distinctively American Catholicism that would be both thoroughly Catholic in doctrine and thoroughly American in cultural expression. The new leaders of the American Church in the early twentieth century showed little interest in pursuing such initiatives. For the most part, they were American-born clerics who had received their seminary education in Rome and then used their Roman connections to advance their careers. They were much more eager to bring the blessings of *Romanità* to the American Catholic Church than to promote a dialogue between Catholicism and American culture.

Two of the three most influential newcomers to the American hierarchy in the early twentieth century were Irish Americans—William Henry O'Connell in Boston and Dennis Dougherty in Philadelphia. (The third, George Mundelein, appointed archbishop of Chicago in 1915, was to become the first German-American cardinal and the first "Cardinal of the West.") O'Connell, archbishop of Boston from 1907 to 1944, was one of eleven children of immigrant parents from County Cavan who settled in Lowell, Massachusetts, where his father worked in a textile mill. A born autocrat, he challenged the local Brahmins and delighted many members of his own flock when in 1908 he declared in typically triumphalistic style, "The Puritan has passed; the Catholic remains."[28]

O'Connell had a worthy soul mate in Dougherty, the archbishop of Philadelphia from 1918 to 1951, who was the son of immigrants from County Mayo during the Great Famine. "God's brick maker," Dougherty liked to call himself in self-recognition of the enormous number of churches and schools that he erected in his archdiocese. Philadelphia became a showcase of conservative East Coast Catholicism, reflecting what Charles Morris once called the "stodgy timelessness" of the city itself. As late as 1963 the archdiocese reported that 90 percent of the Catholics were married in church and 95 percent of them made their Easter duty. As in the case of O'Connell, Roman favor was the key to Dougherty's success, and he knew it. "After God," he admitted, "I owe what I am to the Holy See." Predictably O'Connell was made a cardinal in 1911 and Dougherty in 1923.[29]

Well into the twentieth century Irish-born priests continued to be appointed to major American sees. John Farley, a native of Armagh, was the last foreign-born archbishop of New York (1902–1918) and received the red hat in 1911. In the same year that Farley was appointed to New York, John Glennon, a graduate of All Hallows College, was made the coadjutor bishop of Kansas City, Missouri, at the age of thirty-four. Seven years later he became the archbishop of St. Louis, where he remained until his death as a newly created cardinal in 1946. John J. Cantwell, a native of Limerick, became bishop of Monterey–Los Angeles in 1917. When he died as the archbishop of Los Angeles thirty years later, the number of Catholics had tripled. Michael Curley became bishop of St. Augustine in 1914 at the age of thirty-four and succeeded Cardinal Gibbons as archbishop of Baltimore seven years later. A cantankerous individual whose reactionary political views irritated even many of his fellow bishops, Curley won the affection of the poor by his devotion to them. "There are no pockets in shrouds," he once observed about his propensity to give away his money.[30]

The outbreak of the war in Europe in August 1914 unleashed widespread sympathy in America for the British and the French, especially among Protestant churches with strong historical ties to Great Britain like the Episcopalians, Presbyterians, Congregationalists, and Methodists. Even before the entry of the United States into the war in 1917, many of their pulpits rang with bellicose denunciations of German militarism and appeals for America to join the crusade against the kaiser.

In contrast to the American Protestants, the sympathies of American Catholics were considerably more divided. Prior to 1917 both German-American and Irish-American Catholics were generally opposed to U.S. intervention in the war. In the case of Irish Americans, the failure of the British government to implement Home Rule in 1914 and the execution of the leaders of the Easter Rising of 1916 only intensi-fied anti-British feeling. Among a few Irish Americans like Judge Daniel F. Cohalan, anti-British sentiment ran so deep that it came close to being pro-German sentiment. In contrast, many Polish, Czech and, Slovak immigrants made no secret of their desire to see the defeat of the Central Powers in the hope that it would lead to the indepen-dence of their homelands. Working through their national parishes and fraternal organizations, often led by their clergy, Slavic Catholics raised funds and even re-cruited volunteers to assist the nationalist aspirations of their countrymen in Europe.

After the American entry into the war in April 1917, American Catholics closed ranks and offered virtually unanimous support for the war effort. Cardinal Gibbons visited President Woodrow Wilson in the White House to assure him of Catholic loyalty. Rumors circulated that Wilson, a descendant of Ulster Presbyterians and well known for his antipathy to Catholics, failed even to offer the octogenarian cardinal a chair. After the war, when asked to lend support to Irish independence at the Versailles Peace Conference, Wilson said: "My first impulse was to tell the Irish to go to hell, but feeling that this would not be the act of a statesman, I denied myself this personal satisfaction."[31]

However, not even Wilson could complain that Catholics failed to rally to the flag. Among the 3,989 conscientious objectors, only four were Catholics. The number of Catholic chaplains jumped from 28 to 1,525 as they struggled to care for the one mil-lion Catholics who served in the armed forces. The most famous chaplain of any de-nomination to emerge from the war was a New York diocesan priest, Father Francis P. Duffy, chaplain to New York's 69th National Guard Regiment, which had been the pride of New York's Irish Catholics ever since it refused to provide an honor guard for the Prince of Wales (the future Edward VII) on his visit to New York in 1860.[32]

Nonetheless, no matter how patriotic individual Catholics were, their Church was ill prepared institutionally for World War I because it had no national organization to act as a liaison with the federal government or to coordinate the activities of individ-ual dioceses and religious orders. The situation was rectified by Father John E. Burke, an amazingly versatile Paulist priest, who was the son of Irish immigrants in New York City. In 1917, Burke organized the National Catholic War Council (NCWC), which for the first time gave the American bishops a unified voice in Washington with a permanent staff headed by Burke himself as general secretary. The NCWC proved to be so valuable that the bishops decided to continue it after the war under the name of the National Catholic Welfare Council.[33]

Next to Burke, the most important official of the NCWC was Father John A. Ryan, a native of the small farming village of Vermillon, Minnesota, where his parents had settled after fleeing the Great Famine in Ireland. In 1919, as the director of the Social

Action Department of the NCWC, Ryan drew up a proposal for postwar social reforms that he intended to mention in a speech. However, the administrative board of the NCWC was so impressed with the contents that they published Ryan's text in the name of the American hierarchy as the Bishops' Program of Social Reconstruction. It was a fifteen-point proposal that called for such reforms as a federal minimum wage; equal pay for women; public housing; abolition of monopolies; government insurance for sickness, unemployment, and old age; federal regulation of public utilities; and the right of workers to collective bargaining.[34]

The Bishops' Program of Social Reconstruction contained in embryonic form much of the economic and social legislation that President Franklin D. Roosevelt was to enact fifteen years later as the New Deal. Neither liberals nor conservatives missed the novelty that such a progressive document should appear under official Catholic auspices. Upton Sinclair called it a "Catholic miracle." Stephen C. Mason, the president of the National Association of Manufacturers, wrote to Cardinal Gibbons, complaining that it was "partisan, pro-labor union, socialistic propaganda." However, Mason's secretary appended her own note to Mason's letter, assuring Gibbons that her boss had not even read the document.[35]

The Irish War of Independence (1919–1921) and the subsequent Irish Civil War (1922–1923) aroused deep and sometimes divisive emotions among Irish Americans. Thousands of American priests petitioned President Wilson to make self-determination for Ireland part of the agenda at the Versailles Peace Conference. In 1918, the Friends of Irish Freedom, a militant advocacy group, elected Father Peter E. Magennis its president and replaced him two years later with Bishop Michael J. Gallagher of Detroit. Cardinals Gibbons and O'Connell, Archbishop Patrick J. Hayes of New York, and many other American bishops gave strong endorsement to Sinn Féin's struggle for Irish independence. John Devoy, the veteran Fenian leader, could hardly believe the change of attitude on the part of the clergy since the days when, he said, "we were cursed from nearly every altar in Ireland."[36]

On November 3, 1920, six thousand people filled St. Patrick's Cathedral in New York City for a memorial Mass for Terence MacSwiney, the mayor of Cork who had died on a hunger strike in British custody. As the mourners emerged from the cathedral, they spotted the Union Jack flying from the Union Club, a bastion of the WASP establishment. Enraged at what they mistakenly considered a deliberate affront, they sent a volley of paving bricks crashing through the plate-glass windows of the club. In the St. Patrick's Day parade the following year, a group of women marched up Fifth Avenue with the banner, "As Much Religion as You Like from Rome, but No Politics," a reference to Vatican disapproval of the IRA. In the reviewing stand, an indignant Father Duffy jumped to his feet and demanded to know who was responsible for the banner. "I don't know who is responsible," replied Judge Cohalan, "but it is all right. Dan O'Connell said it."[37]

A major institutional crisis occurred in the American Church in 1922 when Pope Benedict XV died. William Cardinal O'Connell, the archbishop of Boston, who had ambitions to succeed the recently deceased Cardinal Gibbons as the unofficial leader of the American Catholic Church, used the opportunity to persuade the new Pope, Pius XI, to dissolve the NCWC on the grounds that it undermined the authority of individual bishops. O'Connell's subterfuge became apparent when the American bishops protested the papal decision so vigorously that the pope reversed himself and reinstated the NCWC. "I have been deceived," Pius XI told one of the American bishops.[38] The chief spokesman for the American bishops was Bishop Joseph Schrembs, a tenacious German-American prelate, who was ably assisted by Msgr. James Hugh Ryan, the director of the education department of the NCWC. Under the slightly altered name of the National Catholic Welfare Conference (the name was changed to "Conference" because "Council" frightened Rome), the NCWC made an invaluable contribution to American Catholicism and continued to do so after Vatican Council II as the National Conference of Catholic Bishops.

The formation of the NCWC was only one example of the professionalization that was taking place in the organization of the Catholic Church in early-twentieth-century America. The vast charitable work of the Church was in need of similar professionalism, as traditional poor relief by volunteers like the members of the St. Vincent de Paul Society yielded to the new profession of social work by trained and salaried employees. One of the first Catholics to address this need was Father William Kerby, professor of sociology at the Catholic University of America, who was instrumental in founding the National Conference of Catholic Charities in 1910. Kerby's successor as secretary of the NCCC was John O'Grady, a flamboyant Irish-born priest, who was especially committed to the concept of social service as a profession and cultivated ties with local diocesan directors of Catholic charities at his post from 1920 to 1940.[39]

A related development was the establishment of the National Catholic School of Social Service (NCSSS) in Washington, D.C., in 1921, due largely to John J. Burke, who persuaded the National Council of Catholic Women to sponsor it. Burke served as chaplain of the school until his death in 1936, while the real director was Agnes Regan of San Francisco, the secretary of the NCCW. Many of the social workers who emerged from the NCSSS and similar institutions were young Irish-American women like Rose McHugh in Chicago and Mary Gibbons in New York City, who began their careers in diocesan organizations and then moved on to private, state, and federal agencies where, wrote Elizabeth McKeon, "their outreach guaranteed a new degree of Catholic influence in public life."[40]

In New York City, Catholic charitable institutions had come under hostile scrutiny from city and state agencies. "Orphans and Pigs Fed from the Same Bowl," was one newspaper headline. In response, in 1920 Archbishop Hayes established the Catholic Charities of the Archdiocese of New York, an umbrella agency that coordinated and supervised the work of hundreds of Catholic charitable institutions and agencies. Under the leadership of Father Robert F. Keegan, the first director, Catholic Charities of New York became a model for similar diocesan agencies that bishops were establishing throughout the country during the first three decades of the twentieth century.[41]

The Tribal Twenties

American disillusionment with intervention in World War I gave way to a postwar retreat from world responsibilities, symbolized by the failure of the United States to join the League of Nations. At home, a wave of anarchist bombings, labor disputes, and racial strife immediately after the war fueled nativist nostalgia for a return to a mythical golden age when the United States was a virtuous, rural, self-reliant WASP nation. Warren G. Harding capitalized on the prevailing mood and rode it to the White House with the promise of a return to "normalcy."

The decade began on an upbeat note with what Professor Sydney Ahlstrom called "*the* great Protestant Crusade of the twentieth century," namely, national prohibition.[42] The ratification of the Eighteenth Amendment in October 1919 was the culmination of a half-century of effort on the part of evangelical Protestants, especially Baptists and Methodists, working through such organizations as the Women's Christian Temperance Union and the Anti-Saloon League. Like a wide range of other Protestants and many secular social reformers, the advocates of Prohibition believed that the suppression of the liquor trade would eradicate one of the principal sources of vice and degradation in American society.

Unfortunately, the cure proved to be worse than the disease and demonstrated the futility of trying to impose evangelical Protestant morality on the general public. Cardinal Gibbons had warned that Catholics did not regard the use of alcohol as evil. To the dismay of its promoters, Prohibition spawned a whole new industry of bootleggers and racketeers as Americans turned to illegal sources to slake their thirst. In heavily ethnic and Catholic Yonkers, New York, for example, enterprising entrepreneurs ran a fire hose for a mile through the city's sewers to deliver beer from a clandestine brewery to a garage that served as a distribution center. When the hose line was discovered, the city officials all expressed shock and disbelief. The local leader of the Anti-Saloon League was not amused when a professor of physics at New York University hailed the hose line as "the outstanding engineering feat" in the history of Prohibition.[43]

Prohibition contributed to the revival of nativism by identifying the gap between the "drys" and the "wets" with the division between rural Protestant America and the big cities with their large immigrant populations. Southern Methodist Bishop Joseph Cannon, the "Dry Messiah," shamelessly exploited small-town Protestant America's fear of corrupt big cities when he castigated the "wets" as "the kind of dirty people you find today on the sidewalks of New York . . . the Italians, the Sicilians, the Poles, and the Russian Jews."[44]

This xenophobia also manifested itself in the restrictive immigration laws of 1921 and 1924. For the first time in American history, Congress restricted European immigration through a quota system that effectively reduced to a trickle immigration from southern and eastern Europe. Although this legislation had less impact on immigration from Great Britain, Ireland, and northern Europe, it was the end, at least temporarily, of the era of the Immigrant Church for Catholics because of the devastating effect on Slavic and Italian immigration.

Still another example of the xenophobia of the 1920s was the reappearance of the Ku Klux Klan, which was re-founded at Stone Mountain, near Atlanta, Georgia, on October 16, 1915. The Klan was anti-black and anti-Jewish, as well as anti-Catholic, but, in the words of John Higham, the historian of twentieth-century American nativism, "anti-Catholicism actually grew to surpass every other nativistic attitude."[45] The

Klan reached its peak membership of approximately three million in 1923 and then declined, but it remained a political force throughout the decade in many rural areas of the South and Midwest. Photos of hooded Klansmen parading through the streets of the nation's capital added a sinister new element to American politics.

Another development with sinister implications for Catholics was the Oregon school law of 1922. Due to the work of the Masonic Lodges in that state, the new law required every child between the age of eight and sixteen to attend public school, reflecting a return to the nineteenth-century nativist mentality that only public schools could be trusted to inculcate an authentic sense of civic loyalty in America's children. When desperate Oregon Catholics turned to the NCWC for legal assistance, the leaders gladly took up their cause. Father John J. Burke and Father James Hugh Ryan welcomed the opportunity to demonstrate the value of the NCWC to some still-skeptical bishops.

The infringement of civil liberties in the Oregon school law was so glaring that the Episcopal Church, the Seventh-day Adventists, and the American Jewish Committee all joined the case as *amici curiae,* and the newly founded American Civil Liberties Union even offered its services, which were politely declined. On June 1, 1925, in a landmark decision, the U.S. Supreme Court unanimously overturned the Oregon school law, declaring that "the child is not the mere creature of the state." Leo Pfeiffer, a constitutional lawyer never known for his sympathy for church schools, called the Supreme Court decision "the magna carta of the parochial school system."[46]

The decade that began with a religiously inspired attempt to force all Americans to become teetotalers ended with a religiously inspired frenzy to keep a Catholic out of the White House. When Governor Alfred E. Smith of New York received the Democratic nomination for president in 1928, his religion was only one of several handicaps. A "wet" big-city Democrat with an irritating Lower East Side accent, Smith would have faced an uphill battle for the presidency in an era of Republican prosperity even if his ancestors had arrived in America on the *Mayflower.* Although closely identified with Irish New York, Smith was in fact a walking advertisement for the ethnic diversity of American Catholicism. He counted among his ancestors not just Irish but English, Germans, and Italians.

For American Catholics, Smith's candidacy revealed the extent to which they were still outsiders who were regarded with suspicion by many of their fellow citizens. In rural Georgia a photograph was circulated of Governor Smith at the dedication of the Holland Tunnel between New York and New Jersey. The caption claimed that it was a tunnel to Rome through which the Pope would travel to America to take over the country after Smith's election. Catholics at least retained a sense of humor. After Smith's defeat, they joked that he had sent the Pope a one-word telegram: "Unpack."

Not all of the anti-Catholic sentiment was so blatantly misguided. Many thoughtful Americans wondered how a conscientious Catholic president could balance loyalty to the teachings of his church with loyalty to the Constitution of the United States. In April 1927 Charles C. Marshall, a prominent Episcopalian layman and constitutional lawyer, gave expression to these fears in a widely read article in the *Atlantic Monthly.* Citing a number of papal encyclicals condemning religious freedom, Marshall questioned the suitability of Smith or any Catholic to hold the highest office in the land.

When Smith first read the article, he is said to have commented, "What the hell is an encyclical?" Although Smith was a highly intelligent man, he had little formal education and no training at all in theology. To compose a reply to Marshall, therefore, Smith turned for help to Father Francis P. Duffy. The result was a highly effective article that appeared in the following issue of the *Atlantic Monthly*. The words were Smith's, but the ideas were Duffy's, and between the two of them they routed Marshall by demonstrating convincingly that the Catholic Church had tacitly abandoned its previous opposition to religious freedom. The *pièce de résistance* was Smith's declaration of his personal creed as a Catholic in which he avowed his commitment to absolute freedom of conscience and separation of church and state.[47]

Although Smith did not win the presidential election, Duffy's argument that the development of doctrine had rendered obsolete previous Church teachings on church–state relations was to have an important sequel. It was to be taken up thirty years later and used successfully by the American Jesuit theologian John Courtney Murray, the son of an Irish father and a Scottish mother, who had the satisfaction of seeing it enshrined in the Declaration on Religious Freedom at Vatican Council II. Also, when the religious issue surfaced again in 1960 with the candidacy of John F. Kennedy, Kennedy sought to defuse the issue by effectively privatizing his religion, a tactic that would have had little appeal to Smith.

Depression and World War II

The Great Depression had an especially severe effect on American Catholics, since so many of them were blue-collar workers whose jobs were at risk. Their traditional loyalty to the Democratic Party was further strengthened by the New Deal legislation of President Franklin D. Roosevelt, who courted Catholic voters and appointed unprecedented numbers of Catholics to influential positions in his administration and the federal judiciary. The two most influential Catholic voices outside of government in Depression-era America were Irish-American clerics of very different temperament and opinions: Charles Coughlin and John A. Ryan. Coughlin was one of the most enthusiastic of Roosevelt's early Catholic supporters. By 1932, the famous Canadian-born "radio priest" of Irish ancestry and accent was attracting a national audience of thirty to forty million people for his weekly broadcasts from his parish church in Royal Oak, Michigan.

A spellbinding orator who had shifted the focus of his radio talks from religious to political and economic topics, in 1932 Coughlin declared with characteristic bravado that the choice before the country was "Roosevelt or Ruin," and he announced that "I will never change my philosophy that the New Deal is Christ's Deal." By 1936, however, Coughlin was so disenchanted with both Roosevelt and Governor Alfred M. Landon, the Republican candidate, that he called it a choice between "rat poison" and "carbolic acid." In protest, Coughlin founded a third party, the Union Party, which garnered fewer than one million votes in the presidential election of that year.[48]

Coughlin's popularity declined abruptly after 1936, but he continued to command the allegiance of a hard core of admirers, especially among working-class Irish Catholics in places like Boston and Brooklyn. David J. O'Brien, no admirer of Coughlin, perceptively identifies his success with his ability to communicate to his audience "the basic immorality of the old order's concentration of wealth, low wages, and social insecurity."[49] As Coughlin's popular base shrank, his rhetoric became more demagogic and contradictory, revealing his basic ignorance of economics. He also became openly anti-Semitic, going so far as to publish the notorious *Protocols of the Elders of Zion* in his magazine *Social Justice*. When his bishop finally silenced him in 1942 after the government threatened to prosecute him for wartime sedition, Coughlin was a spent force in American politics.

At the opposite pole to Coughlin was Father John A. Ryan, the author of the Bishops' Program of Social Reconstruction in 1919. A priest of the Archdiocese of St. Paul, Ryan was an admirer of his own progressive archbishop, John Ireland, as well as lay Catholic thinkers like Ignatius Donnelly, a populist politician, and Patrick Ford, the editor of the *Irish World*. Ryan lacked the charismatic personality of Father Coughlin, but he more than made up for it with a sounder grasp of economics and practical politics. Moreover, as both a professor at the Catholic University of America and the director of the Social Action Department of the NCWC, he was uniquely positioned to influence Catholic social thinking in the 1930s and 1940s.

Basing his social teaching primarily on the papal encyclicals *Rerum Novarum* and *Quadragesimo Anno,* Ryan formulated three bread-and-butter-principles: the right of every individual to a living wage (the subject of his 1906 doctoral dissertation at the Catholic University of America), the need for a more equitable distribution of wealth, and the legitimacy of state intervention in the economy in order to promote social justice. An enthusiastic, sometimes even uncritical, admirer of FDR, Ryan saw in the New Deal the practical application of papal social teaching and a vindication of his own theories. "Charity is a poison when taken as a substitute for justice," he once declared. A member of the American Civil Liberties Union and an outspoken critic of Father Coughlin, Ryan became, in the words of David O'Brien, "the link between American Catholics and liberal, progressive groups interpreting them to each other."[50]

A unique Catholic voice in Depression-era America was that of Dorothy Day.[51] A convert to the Catholic Church in 1927, Day had spent the previous twenty years of her life engaged in radical causes, and she did not cease to be a radical when she became a Catholic. Under the influence of Peter Maurin, an idiosyncratic French philosopher, she came to loathe the impersonality and secularism of modern society and the ruthlessness of capitalism. Together, Day and Maurin founded the Catholic Worker Movement, which published a newspaper of the same name (the first issue appeared on May Day, 1933), opened houses of hospitality (as she preferred to call shelters) for the homeless, established a few quixotic farming communes, and promoted the almost forgotten Catholic tradition of pacifism even during World War II.

The Catholic Worker Movement was an unprecedented phenomenon in American Catholic history—not only because of its radical social views, but also because it was a lay movement independent of the hierarchy. As to defining its radicalism, Jay Dolan once noted that it was "like trying to bottle a morning fog."[52] In fact, the Catholic Worker Movement was radical and reactionary at the same time: radical in its denunciation of laissez-faire capitalism, but reactionary in its nostalgia for a pre-industrial world of family farms and handicraft manufactures. The heart and soul of the movement was Dorothy Day herself, whose unselfish dedication to the poor and the disadvantaged earned the respect even of those who disagreed with her political opinions.

Organized labor continued to receive strong support from the Irish-American clergy during the Depression years. Among the archbishops who were firmly in labor's camp were Edward Mooney of Detroit, John T. McNicholas of Cincinnati, and Robert E. Lucey of San Antonio. John Maguire, C.S.V., a well-known "labor priest," delivered the eulogy at the funeral Mass for Mother Jones. Priests like John P. Boland in Buffalo, Dennis J. Comey, S.J., in Philadelphia, Charles Owen Rice in Pittsburgh, John T. Monaghan, Philip Carey, S.J., and John Corridan, S.J., in New York City were all instrumental in supporting union activities and in founding labor schools to train Catholic union leaders to combat both communism and corruption in the unions. At their peak there were over one hundred of these labor schools throughout the country.

By the turn of the twentieth century, almost half of the presidents of the unions in the American Federation of Labor were Irish. In a development that is hard to imagine happening anywhere else in the industrialized world, in 1938 three of the five original members of the executive committee of the newly founded CIO were committed Catholics—Philip Murray, James Carey, and John Brophy, all of them of Irish ancestry. They worked amicably with the Social Action Department of the NCWC under John A. Ryan and his successor, Father Raymond A. McGowan. Addressing the annual convention of the CIO in Boston in 1947, Archbishop Richard J. Cushing made the remarkably candid revelation that he was not aware of a single bishop in the United States whose father or mother was a college graduate. "Everyone of our bishops and archbishops," he announced proudly, "is the son of a working man and a workingman's wife."[53]

Although the American Catholic Church remained closely connected with its working-class roots, wealthy Catholics, especially those with Irish names, were an increasingly common phenomenon. Many of them were generous contributors to Catholic causes. Among the best known were William J. Onahan in Chicago; Patrick Cudahy in Milwaukee; Edward and John Creighton in Omaha; Frank J. Duffy in Natchez; James D. Phelan in San Francisco; Edward L. Doheny in Los Angeles; Martin Maloney in Philadelphia; James Joseph Phelan in Boston; and William R. Grace, Thomas M. Mulry, John D. Crimmins, Thomas Fortune Ryan, Thomas E. Murray Sr. and Jr., and Nicholas Brady and his wife Genevieve Garvan Brady in New York City. Mulry, president of the Emigrant Industrial Savings Bank, was instrumental in unifying the work of the St. Vincent de Paul Society throughout the United States and won national recognition for his efforts on behalf of disadvantaged children.

The Golden Age of Big-City Catholicism

For American Catholics the period between the two world wars was the golden age of the big-city parishes, which were an enormous source of strength to a Catholic community that had not quite shed its outsider status. Perhaps three-quarters of the Catholic population, almost exclusively working class and lower middle class, was concentrated in the industrial centers of the Northeast and the Midwest. Cities such as Boston, New York, Philadelphia, Cleveland, Chicago, and Milwaukee contained numerous ethnic neighborhoods where the Catholic parish church was the most important local institution.

In those cities it was a common practice for Catholics (and even for some non-Catholics) to identify their neighborhood by the name of the local Catholic parish. The parish church itself, often a large Romanesque or neo-Gothic edifice easily accommodating eight hundred or even one thousand worshipers, was regularly filled to capacity at several Masses every Sunday and remained open throughout the week for morning Masses, a variety of evening devotions, and private prayer by the faithful. A Philadelphia-born historian remarked that "an alien anthropologist landing in a working-class Philadelphia parish in the 1930s or 1940s would know instantly the centrality of religion to the lives of the inhabitants."[54]

For the diocesan clergy the opportunity to become the pastor of a big-city parish was the plumpest reward that their bishop could dangle in front of them. Once installed, big-city pastors enjoyed lifetime tenure and functioned like feudal barons within the diocese, with only minimum oversight from the bishop and even less accountability to the laity. When Paul Hallinan, a newly ordained priest of the Diocese of Cleveland, reported for his first assignment at St. Aloysius Church in 1937, he was greeted at the rectory by Monsignor James T. Malloy, a seventy-three-year-old native of County Mayo, who had been pastor for thirty-four years. There was no doubt who was the boss, and Malloy outlasted Hallinan at St. Aloysius.

Pastors of big-city parishes could rely on the services of three or four docile curates (like Paul Hallinan) to discharge the pastoral responsibilities, and they could leave the administration of the parochial school in the hands of a community of sisters who sometimes taught classes of sixty or more students. The pastor's own area of expertise was expected to be the financial management of the parish. As Garry Wills has pointed out in his evocative recollection of the pre–Vatican II American Catholic Church, the distinguishing mark of the successful pastor of that era was not personal sanctity or ability as a preacher but his acumen as a businessman and a fundraiser. Both bishops and laity often measured the ability of their pastors by those criteria.[55]

For the laity, big-city parishes were often the center of their social world as well as their religious life. A variety of parish-sponsored events such as plays, musicals, outings, and card parties provided the relief from the monotony of working-class life that was later to be supplied by the movies and television. An array of athletic programs and interparish sports competition, and later the diocesan-wide Catholic Youth Organization (founded by Bernard Sheil in Chicago in 1930), served a similar purpose by involving young people in the life of the parish. An integral feature of parish life was the proliferation of societies such as the Holy Name Society for men and the Rosary Altar Society for women, sometimes numbering hundreds of members, each with its own elected lay officers and a priest as spiritual director. At St. Stanislaus Kosta Church in Chicago, the largest Polish parish in the city, Andrew Greeley counted

This panoramic portrait by photographer Kenneth Spencer captured the lay and religious faculty of the University of Notre Dame in South Bend, Indiana, in 1914. Irish or Irish-Americans dominated its teaching and administrative positions, as well as its student body, from its establishment in 1842 until the early

sixty-seven parish societies.[56] There were also more select and specialized parish societies, such as the St. Vincent de Paul Society, which provided financial aid and other assistance to the poor in the privacy of their homes.

The sense of community engendered by the big-city parishes reached its apogee in the national parishes of the various Catholic ethnic groups. In the Archdiocese of Chicago in 1916, for example, in addition to the 93 territorial parishes (largely Irish in ethnic composition), there were also 122 national parishes caring for the pastoral needs of fifteen different ethnic groups. Nor were these national parishes confined to the big cities. In the small Pennsylvania city of Johnstown in 1926, there were no fewer than ten national parishes representing six different ethnic groups, as well as five territorial parishes.[57]

The big-city parishes of the early twentieth century, whether territorial or national, were remarkably effective instruments for preserving Catholic cohesiveness through several generations. Catholic immigrants, including the Irish, were eager to assimilate into American society, grateful to enjoy the liberty and economic opportunity often denied them in their homeland, but the protective canopy of the big-city parish community enabled them to assimilate to some degree on their own terms, without sacrificing either their religious faith or their ethnic heritage. Other factors also served to reinforce a sense of Catholic identity and separateness. Among the most powerful was the influence of the parochial schools, although they never enrolled a majority of Catholic children. In national parishes, parochial schools served an additional purpose by handing on knowledge of parents' language to the younger generation.

Rigid rules governing contacts between Catholics and non-Catholics were another factor in maintaining Catholic apartheid. Attendance at non-Catholic religious services was limited to weddings and funerals, with the stern reminder to avoid "active participation" in the ceremonies. When the pastor of Corpus Christi Church in Manhattan sent a basket of flowers to Riverside Church on the occasion of an anniversary celebration in 1940, he was rebuked for coming close to participating in non-Catholic worship by the chancellor of the archdiocese, Monsignor James Francis McIntyre, the future cardinal archbishop of Los Angeles.[58] If Catholics wished to marry outside the faith, they could obtain ecclesiastical permission to do so only if the non-Catholic spouse promised in writing to raise the children as Catholics. Even then, the couple

twentieth century. "The Fighting Irish" sobriquet replaced "The Irish" and "The Horrible Hibernians" for Notre Dame's athletic teams in 1927. (Library of Congress, Prints and Photographs Division, PAN SUBJECT —Groups no. 30 [F size])

had to forgo a church wedding and suffer the indignity of exchanging their vows at a private ceremony in the rectory. Catholic identity even persisted beyond death to the grave. Unless the deceased were to be buried in a Catholic cemetery, the family was denied a funeral Mass in their parish church. Few protested a rule that seemed to be the logical culmination of womb-to-tomb Catholicism.

The Catholic neighborhoods proved to be amazingly resilient to outside influences, such as movies, the most popular form of popular entertainment in the 1930s and 1940s. By that date, Hollywood had blanketed urban neighborhoods with theatres that posed a potential threat to the local clergy as the arbiters of moral standards. However, the hierarchy defused the looming crisis by opting for a mutually beneficial alliance with Hollywood. The movie studios avoided the threat of government censorship by adopting a production code that followed closely the standards of the Legion of Decency, an agency created by U.S. bishops in 1934.

The author of the code was Daniel A. Lord, S.J., but the key figures involved in working out the cozy arrangement between the Church and Hollywood were two Irish-American laymen: Chicago businessman Martin J. Quigley and Joseph Breen, an employee of the studios, who for many years was the enforcer of the code. Moreover, the Church had little reason to complain about the way that Hollywood depicted the Catholic priesthood. The image of the Catholic priest that movie-goers saw in their neighborhood theatres in films like *Going My Way* and *The Bells of St. Mary's* was that of the "superpadre," a spiritual leader who was "virile, athletic, compassionate, wise." As Garry Wills remarked about *Going My Way*: "The film celebrated all the Church's faults as if they were virtues—right down to Father O'Malley's practiced golf game."[59]

The growing number of affluent middle-class Catholics who sent their sons and daughters to Catholic colleges could also feel confident that the protective influence of the Catholic neighborhood would be duplicated on campus. Both the number of Catholic colleges and the percentage of Catholic college students attending Catholic institutions increased steadily throughout the 1920s. By 1928, they enrolled between one-half and two-thirds of all Catholic college students. At the all-male University of Notre Dame, Father John O'Hara, the prefect of religion (and future president of Notre Dame and cardinal archbishop of Philadelphia), knew almost every undergraduate by name. He periodically purged the library stacks of dangerous books like the novels of Ernest Hemingway and vigorously promoted his own Catholic version of muscular Victorian Christianity, which was an amalgam of sports and frequent confession and communion. In 1928, he calculated that the total number of communions "distributed" was 311,226.[60]

Six years later at Fordham University, the forty-three-year-old Irish-American Jesuit president dismissed out of hand the efforts of the academic accrediting agencies to raise the university's educational standards. "We refuse to be stampeded into following the pseudo-educational vagaries of experimentalists," he declared. At that same institution the head of the graduate philosophy department announced, "contemplation and not research is the activity we most cherish" and denied that the function of a graduate school "is to add to the sum of human knowledge."[61]

The philosophical basis of Catholic higher education was neo-scholasticism, a nineteenth-century European revival of the philosophy of St. Thomas Aquinas. It gave twentieth-century American Catholics the assurance that they possessed a coherent system of thought to supply them with the answers to all the problems of the modern world. As Philip Gleason explained, "Neo-scholastic philosophy formed the cognitive framework around which the whole intellectual edifice of Catholic higher education was built."[62] One admirer of the system recently described it as "the hardware that will run any software." In short, it was the intellectual equivalent of the protective canopy provided by the big-city parish. Nonetheless, there were indications that all was not well in this hothouse American Catholic subculture. The most talented Catholic writers of the 1920s—Theodore Dreiser, John O'Hara, James T. Farrell, F. Scott Fitzgerald, and Eugene O'Neill—all had an estranged relationship with the faith of their birth.

In the 1920s and 1930s few Catholics left their neighborhood to attend college, but many left every day for work. However, their Catholic identity followed them, if they happened to be policemen, firefighters, postal workers, telephone operators, department store clerks, or employees of other companies with a high percentage of Catholics. In such situations Catholics quickly organized their own religious associations, like the Police Department Holy Name Society. These societies flourished especially after World War II, when they typically sponsored an annual Mass and Communion Breakfast with a prominent speaker at a fancy downtown hotel. They attracted such large numbers of participants that local politicians vied with one another for a seat on the dais. In New York in May 1950, twenty-three hundred women employees of AT&T (they called themselves the "Telephone Ladies") turned out to hear former Postmaster General James A. Farley speak at their Communion Breakfast at the old Astor Hotel. That same month twelve hundred longshoremen attended Mass at the United States Line pier on the North River and then marched in military procession across midtown Manhattan to the Waldorf Astoria for their Communion Breakfast.[63]

Contrary to popular impression, the American Catholic community was never exclusively urban. A key figure in furnishing material assistance to scattered rural Catholics was Francis Clement Kelley, who traced his Irish heritage through Prince Edward Island where he spelled his name Kelly. He added the second "e" when he moved south of the border in search of greener pastures. In 1905, Kelley founded the Catholic Church Extension Society, which conducted highly successful fundraising drives to build churches, schools, rectories, and convents throughout rural America, where

Catholics were often a small and impoverished minority. An especially imaginative feature of the work of the Extension Society was the introduction of railroad cars, buses, and even boats fitted out as mobile chapels for itinerant missionaries.

After his appointment as bishop of Oklahoma City in 1924, Kelley continued his interest in rural Catholics by helping to establish the American Board of Catholic Missions. He also became nationally famous for his outspoken criticism of the Mexican government's persecution of the Catholic Church, especially through his controversial book, *Blood-Drenched Altars* (1935). Another significant figure in promoting the welfare of the Church in rural America was Edwin V. O'Hara, the son of Irish immigrants to Minnesota, who was instrumental in creating the Rural Life Bureau of the NCWC in 1920. He served as its first president, later became bishop of Great Falls, Montana, and died as bishop of Kansas City, Missouri, in 1956.[64]

World War II and After

During World War II an estimated 30–40 percent of the men and women who served in the armed forces were Catholics. Some three thousand chaplains cared for their spiritual welfare under the direction of the military vicar, Francis J. Spellman, archbishop of New York from 1939 to 1967. A native of Whitman, Massachusetts, Spellman parlayed a Roman education and a friendship with the future Pope Pius XII, and later with FDR, into the most spectacular clerical success story of the mid-twentieth-century American Catholic Church. During World War II as military vicar, Spellman became a reassuring symbol of Catholic patriotism to millions of Americans because of his well-publicized Christmas visits to the troops overseas. After the war, his militant opposition to communism at home and abroad made him an object of admiration to some and an object of scorn to others.

Although proud of his Irish ancestry, Cardinal Spellman (he got the red hat in 1946) preferred to emphasize his American nationality. When his authorized biographer, Father Robert I. Gannon, S.J., referred to him as Irish, Spellman asked testily how many generations his family needed to spend in the New World for him to qualify as an American. Fellow Bostonian Joseph P. Kennedy had a similar response for a newspaper reporter who called him an Irishman. "I was born here. My children were born here," Kennedy protested. "What the hell do I have to do to be called an American?"[65]

Despite his ambivalent relationship with his ancestors, Spellman contributed handsomely to the preservation of the "hibernarchy" by promoting Patrick J. O'Boyle to Washington, Edwin F. O'Hara to Philadelphia, and James Francis McIntyre to Los Angeles, all of whom subsequently became cardinals. Even at the height of his ecclesiastical influence, however, Spellman was effectively foiled from gaining control of the central administration of the NCWC by three resourceful Irish-American power brokers in the Midwest: Samuel Stritch in Chicago, Edward Mooney in Detroit, and John T. McNicholas (a native of Mayo) in Cincinnati. They were also successful (with the notable exception of the appointment of McIntyre to Los Angeles) in preventing Spellman from appointing bishops west of the Appalachians, "the Hindenburg Line," as they called it.[66]

In the aftermath of World War II, Catholicism flourished in America as part of the general religious revival experienced by the whole country. In many of the big cities of the Northeast and the Midwest, parish-pump Catholicism still exhibited the insular self-confidence of the 1920s and 1930s. As an illustration, Jay Dolan cites Alan Ehrenhalt's study of St. Nicholas of Tolentine parish in a working-class neighborhood in Southwest Side Chicago, "a solid, rock-ribbed Catholic area," in the words of one of the curates. Parishioners filled the eleven-hundred-seat church to capacity several times every Sunday morning, and the Irish-born pastor, Monsignor Michael J. Fennessy, was a carbon copy of the "ancient monsignor" that Paul Hallinan had met in Cleveland twenty years earlier. "The Church at the parish level in the Chicago of the 1950s was no dinosaur limping dejectedly toward its appointment with Vatican II," wrote Ehrenhalt; "it was a thriving, self-confidant institution at the peak of its influence."[67]

Vocations to the priesthood and religious life soared in postwar America, and bishops scrambled to keep pace with the demand for new churches, schools, rectories, and convents for the burgeoning Catholic population, especially in the rapidly growing suburbs. During the first fifteen years after his arrival in Los Angeles in 1948, Cardinal McIntyre opened a new church every sixty-six days and a new school every twenty-six days. In New York, the new diocese of Rockville Centre was established in 1957 for the suburbs of Long Island. "Nothing but euphoria was visible on the horizon," said one diocesan priest in 1958. Within a decade the Catholic population almost doubled to 926,397, and by 1994 this largely suburban diocese was the eighth largest in the United States.

The suburbanization of American Catholicism after World War II was facilitated by one of the most far-sighted acts of social legislation ever enacted by the U.S. Congress, the G.I. Bill of Rights of 1944, which provided veterans with the opportunity for a college education.[68] Together with low-cost government mortgages for veterans, the G.I. Bill had a profound influence on American Catholics, enabling many of them to be the first in their family to attend college and later to purchase their own home in the suburbs. According to Lawrence McCaffrey, "hundreds of thousands of Irish-Americans" benefited from the G.I. Bill, more than any other Catholic ethnic group, because Irish-Americans were more likely to be the graduates of Catholic high schools and thus better prepared academically for college. As a result, McCaffrey claims that Irish "ex-servicemen skipped one sometimes two generational rungs—peasant to Ph.D. or M.D.—on the mobility ladder."[69]

One unintended consequence of the suburbanization of American Catholicism was the decline of the big-city parishes in the neighborhoods that had once been the heartland of American Catholicism. With some exceptions, Catholics found it difficult to re-create in suburbia the tight-knit communities that their immigrant parents and grandparents had established in the inner city. Those declining neighborhoods in Chicago, Cleveland, Detroit, Philadelphia, and elsewhere now became a battleground between aging Catholic ethnics determined to defend their turf and blacks from the rural South and Latino immigrants seeking better housing opportunities for themselves.[70]

The G.I. Bill of Rights proved to be a mixed blessing for Catholic higher education. Although it led to a massive expansion in enrollment and facilities in Catholic colleges, it did little to improve academic standards. Complaints soon followed about the loss of Catholic identity, as well as a failure to meet the educational standards of the best public and private institutions. In 1955, Monsignor John Tracy Ellis, the country's most prominent Catholic Church historian, touched a raw nerve with his provocative lecture, "American Catholics and the Intellectual Life."[71] Ellis decried the mindless proliferation of academically weak Catholic colleges, as well as the general failure of American Catholic scholars to measure up to their own rich intellectual heritage. Ellis mentioned no names in his indictment of American Catholic higher education, but Lawrence McCaffrey observed that "for all practical purposes Ellis was indicting the Irish who dominated the educational and administrative structure of American Catholicism."[72]

In postwar America anti-Communism enlisted strong support from American Catholics, whether it was protesting the persecution of the Catholic Church in Eastern Europe or trying to eliminate Communist Party influence from labor unions at home. It was not surprising, therefore, that Senator Joseph R. McCarthy found a receptive audience among American Catholics when he launched his attack against Communist influence on the U.S. government in 1950. It is still a matter of dispute whether McCarthy received substantially stronger backing from Catholics than from other Americans. Donald F. Crosby, S.J., a close student of McCarthy and McCarthyism, concluded: "Catholics divided on McCarthy fully as much as the rest of the country though their support for him was broader than among other population groups." As for McCarthy's support among Irish Americans, Crosby noted that the leadership of the Irish-American community was as divided as other Americans, and he speculated that the same was true of the masses of Irish-American Catholics.[73]

The hierarchy kept a discreet distance from McCarthy, but Cardinal Spellman's presence at a New York City Police Department Communion Breakfast in April 1954, at which McCarthy was the guest speaker, was widely interpreted as a sign of Spellman's approval. Patrick Scanlan's *Brooklyn Tablet* and James Gillis's *Catholic World* attacked McCarthy's critics ("anti-anti-Communist" was the favorite phrase) when they were not defending the senator himself. On the other hand, both *America* and especially *Commonweal,* the two best known Catholic journals of opinion, voiced skepticism about McCarthy's methods and motives. Some of the senator's harshest critics were Irish Democrats like Maurice Tobin in Massachusetts and Congressman Eugene McCarthy in Minnesota. Five days after McCarthy's speech at the Communion Breakfast in New York, Auxiliary Bishop Bernard J. Sheil of Chicago pulled no punches before a friendly labor union audience in his hometown when he declared that McCarthy's anti-Communist crusade was "a monstrous perversion of morality."[74]

The Long Shadow of Vatican II

The 1960s was the decade when everything seemed to go wrong. It was a particularly difficult period for American Catholics who had to contend not only with the turmoil in American society but also with unprecedented changes in their Church. Disillusionment was all the greater because the decade began on an exceptionally optimistic

The St. Patrick's Missionary Society in Kiltegan, County Wicklow, had enthusiastic fundraisers in these young Irish men and women from the Germantown section of Philadelphia. The Kiltegan Fathers, as they were more commonly known, ordained and trained priests for service in Africa, particularly in Nigeria and Kenya. When this photograph was taken at the Irish Center on Emlen Street in Philadelphia in 1966, the funds successfully being raised for them in the United States were used primarily to expand the preparatory college facilities in Kiltegan and, thus, are a clear example of the strength of Catholic loyalties that contemporary Irish emigrants retained. Neither Evelyn Coyle (second row standing, seventh from right) nor Pat Reilly (first row standing, second from left), from Kilnaleck, County Cavan, and Dromhalry, County Longford, respectively, had any ties to the Kiltegan Fathers or to Wicklow. The social aspects of such religiously sanctioned socializing were no less important; Coyle and Reilly married in 1968. (Courtesy of Eileen Reilly)

note with the election of a new pope in 1958 and a new president in 1960. The pontificate of Pope John XXIII captured the imagination of the entire world, while the presence of John F. Kennedy in the White House gave American Catholics a new sense of acceptance in American society.

Tragedy struck early in the decade, however, with the assassinations of President Kennedy, his brother Robert F. Kennedy, and Dr. Martin Luther King Jr. The Vietnam War and the Civil Rights Movement precipitated widespread protests and demonstrations that left a whole generation of Americans bitterly polarized. For politically conservative American Catholics, it was a disorienting experience to see nuns in full habits participating in Civil Rights marches and to read about the antiwar activities of priests like the Berrigan brothers—Daniel, a Jesuit, and Philip, a Josephite—the descendants of Tipperary farmers.

Vatican Council II added to the sense of living in a strange new world where the old landmarks were fast disappearing. American Catholics generally welcomed changes like a vernacular liturgy and the Church's endorsement of religious liberty and ecumenism, but they were unprepared for other developments in the aftermath of the council such as the resignation of many priests and religious from the active ministry. For some American prelates like Paul Hallinan of Atlanta and John Dearden of Detroit, Vatican II was an eye-opening experience that transformed them into the leaders of the progressive wing of the U.S. hierarchy. Others, like Cardinal John Wright, once the hero of American Catholic liberals, moved sharply to the right, fearful of the disintegration of ecclesiastical authority. Even before the end of the council in 1965, Cardinal Spellman complained to an old Roman friend, "I am having a difficult time." He added, "I do not think things in Rome could be any more dizzy than they are here in the United States."[75] *Humanae Vitae,* Pope Paul VI's encyclical in 1968 reaffirming the prohibition against contraception, only added to the confusion when it encountered widespread opposition from both laity and clergy.

However one explains it, the period immediately after the council was a statistical watershed for American Catholicism. Although the number of Catholics continued to increase (from 46,246,175 in 1965 to 67,820,833 in 2005), virtually every other index of the vitality of organized Catholic life registered a decline that has yet to be reversed forty years later. The number of priests declined from 59,193 to 43,422, and the number of sisters declined from 181,421 to 69,963 over the same period. Even more ominous because of its implications for the future was the catastrophic decline in the number of teaching sisters from 103,832 to 7,085 and in the number of seminarians from 39,609 to 4,735.

The Catholic school system, once the wonder of the Catholic world, experienced serious difficulties. Enrollment in Catholic universities and colleges almost doubled from 413,261 to 772,767, but in many cases the Catholic identity of these institutions was considerably eroded.[76] On the high school and elementary school levels, more than one-third of the 13,350 schools closed, and enrollment dropped by half (from 5,582,354 to 2,556,370). On a brighter note, the number of permanent deacons, who did not exist in 1965, grew to 15,027, and their services became indispensable in many parishes. In 1965, only 550 of the 17,215 parishes lacked a resident pastor. While national statistics are not readily available about the number of parishes without a resident pastor in 2005, it was an increasingly common phenomenon in American Catholicism at the beginning of the twenty-first century. In some of the rural dioceses of the Midwest as many as one-third of all parishes lacked a resident pastor and were administered by priests, deacons, women religious, or lay people.[77]

Conservatives blamed the disconcerting statistics on Vatican II, or, more discreetly, on mistaken interpretations of the conciliar documents. Liberals traced the decline to underlying social and cultural changes, and they argued that the result of these changes on American Catholics would have been even more devastating without the council. While Dearden, Hallinan, and Archbishop John Quinn of San Francisco were among those who provided leadership for the progressive wing of the hierarchy, other Irish-Americans emerged as the leading conservatives. In Washington, Cardinal O'Boyle became embroiled in a bitter dispute with fifty-one priests who publicly dissented from *Humanae Vitae*; on the West Coast, Cardinal McIntyre was involved in an equally nasty conflict with the Immaculate Heart of Mary Sisters over their efforts to modernize their community. After tangling with O'Boyle and McIntyre over their resistance to a vernacular liturgy, Archbishop Hallinan complained to a friend: "There was very little support that an archbishop could call upon in the face of two cardinals, one of whom had simply repealed in his mind the documents of Vatican II."[78]

As American Catholics grappled with the new world of the post–Vatican II Church, one change was obvious to even the most superficial observers. Neither at the top of the American Catholic community nor at the bottom did the Irish play the dominant role that they once did. At the highest levels of the hierarchy there were still archbishops and bishops with names like Cody, Manning, Hickey, O'Connor, McCarrick, and Mahony, but they now had to share the leadership with an even larger number of Episcopal peers with names like Krol and Pilarczyk, Bevilacqua and Pilla, Medeiros and Flores, Weakland and Wuerl. It was difficult to resurrect the bugbear of the "hibernarchy" when there were twenty Latino bishops, ten African American bishops, and two bishops of Native American ancestry.

In the 1980s Joseph Bernardin, the son of Italian immigrants from Columbia, South Carolina, emerged as the unofficial leader of the American Church. A skilled consensus builder, Bernardin deftly secured the approval of the National Conference of Catholic Bishops for two controversial pastoral letters on matters of public policy, *The Challenge of Peace: God's Promise and Our Response* in 1983 and, three years later, *Economic Justice for All.* Both were noteworthy not only for the progressive tone of their contents but also for the extensive process of consultation involved in their formulation.

If the Irish no longer dominated the hierarchy in the post–Vatican II American Church, neither did they continue to set the tone for the laity. As Irish immigration to the United States slowed to a trickle, and as second- and third-generation Irish Americans became increasingly indistinguishable from other middle-class Americans, the "Greening of American Catholicism" had more of a socioeconomic than a cultural connotation. Young men and women of Irish ancestry had more career paths open to them than their parents and grandparents, and they were no more likely to choose the priesthood or religious life than the rest of their suburban Catholic neighbors. In striking contrast to the era when Irish-born clergy were to be found throughout the United States, the "international" priests who staffed many American parishes at the turn of the twenty-first century were likely to be natives of India, the Philippines, or several African countries.

Writing in 1997, Lawrence McCaffrey ventured the opinion that the Irish still constituted the single largest ethnic group in the American Catholic community at 18 percent of the total population.[79] That claim would be hotly contested less than a decade later because of the enormous growth in the size of the Latino-American Catholic population, who probably now constitute one-quarter of all American Catholics. In terms of sheer numbers, the Latino presence in contemporary American Catholicism resembles that of the Irish in the early nineteenth century. Likewise, the Latino resistance to assimilation and their desire to preserve their language and culture has striking parallels with the similar attitudes of German and Polish immigrants in the late nineteenth and early twentieth centuries. Whether in the long run Latinos will be any more successful than the Germans and Poles in resisting the allurements of the American melting pot remains a matter of conjecture.

The Catholic Church in the United States has always been the Immigrant Church. The only variable over the decades has been the place of origin of the immigrants. The Immigration and Nationality Act of 1965, which made possible the massive growth of the Latino population in the United States, also opened the door to increased immigration from Asia. As a result, for the first time in American Catholic history, there has been an influx of Asian Catholic immigrants, mainly Filipinos, but also Vietnamese, Koreans, Indians, Chinese, and others. The combined effect of the Latino and Asian immigration has been noticeable, especially in California. In the Archdiocese of San Francisco perhaps one-fourth of the Catholic population is Filipino, while in the Archdiocese of Los Angeles there are seventy-two ethnic groups, and Mass is celebrated on Sunday in forty-seven different languages.[80]

Sadly, Irish-American clerics were well represented in one of the worst crises ever to afflict the American Catholic Church—namely, the revelations of sexual abuse of minors by priests and bishops and the failure of American bishops to take corrective action to protect the most vulnerable members of their flock from clerical predators. The epicenter of the crisis in 2002 was Boston, the most Irish-American city in the nation, where the cardinal archbishop was forced to resign in disgrace for his mishandling of the situation in his own diocese.[81]

Conclusion

Those shameful revelations should not be allowed to distort the overall picture of the positive contribution that the Irish have made to American Catholicism over the course of three and a half centuries. John Henry Newman once remarked that English literature always will have been Protestant. Likewise, one can claim that American Catholicism always will have been Irish, with the heyday of the Irish influence occurring during the century and a half between the beginning of large-scale Irish Catholic immigration to America in 1815 and the end of Vatican Council II in 1965.

More than any other ethnic group, the Irish transformed the minuscule English, French, and Spanish Catholic communities of the colonial period into the single largest religious denomination in the country by the middle of the nineteenth century. As they laid the foundations of the institutional Church in the United States, the Irish demonstrated remarkable generosity despite their own poverty and, more than any other ethnic group, they contributed some of the best and the brightest of their sons and daughters to the priesthood and religious life. Throughout the nineteenth century the Irish also provided the bulk of the leaders for the American Church, with bishops as impressive and diverse as John England, John Hughes, John Ireland, James Gibbons, John Keane, and Bernard McQuaid, to name only a few.

As the American Catholic Church came of age in the twentieth century, the Irish-American contribution was especially noteworthy in the professionalization of the Church's institutional life. The establishment of the National Catholic Welfare Conference gave American Catholics a national Episcopal conference fifty years before Vatican II. Other more specialized organizations like the Catholic Church Extension Society and the National Conference of Catholic Charities did invaluable work in their respective fields. The expansion of Catholic higher education in the twentieth century owed much to the initiative of Irish-American educators, both men and women.

The cordial relationship between the Church and organized labor inaugurated by Cardinal Gibbons in the era of the Knights of Labor has endured to the present-day AFL-CIO, thanks to labor leaders like George Meany and John J. Sweeney and "labor priests" like Monsignor George G. Higgins. The tacit alliance between the Church and the Democratic Party, engineered by Irish-Catholic politicians in the nineteenth century, lasted through much of the twentieth century and reached something of a crescendo with the election of John F. Kennedy in 1960, only to come apart thereafter due to the changing economic interests of middle-class Catholics and the increasing secularism of the Democratic Party, especially over the issue of abortion.

For various reasons that have been mentioned above, as Irish Americans became more American and less Irish, so did the Catholic Church in the United States. Nevertheless, the role of the Irish in the shaping of American Catholicism has had an impact that continues into the twenty-first century, not only in the vast network of churches and institutions that the Irish built but also in their commitment to America's democratic political institutions, a commitment that cuts across the usual ideological division of conservative and liberal. The story of Irish Catholics in the United States is one of the most impressive chapters in the larger story of the role of the Irish Catholic diaspora in the English-speaking world, or what has been called with only slight exaggeration the story of the Irish Spiritual Empire.

NOTES

1. Winthop S. Hudson and John Corrigan, *Religion in America*, 6th ed. (Upper Saddle River, NJ: Prentice Hall, 1999), 371. James Hennesey, S.J., gives the figure of 19,828,000 American Catholics in 1920. James Hennesey, S.J., *American Catholics* (New York: Oxford University Press, 1981), 207.

2. Kerby A. Miller, *Emigrants and Exiles: Ireland and the Irish Exodus to North America* (New York: Oxford University Press, 1985), 511.

3. Jay P. Dolan, *In Search of an American Catholicism* (New York: Oxford University Press, 2002), 91.

4. Aloysius Blaznik to Joseph Dineen, October 9, 1922, Archives of the Archdiocese of New York (hereafter AANY), V-8.

5. *The Encyclopedia of American Catholic History,* ed. Michael Glazier and Thomas J. Shelley (Collegeville, MD: Liturgical Press, 1997), 575; *Harvard Encyclopedia of American Ethnic Groups,* ed. Stephan Thernstrom, Ann Orlov, and Oscar Handlin (Cambridge, MA: Harvard University Press, 1981), 395, 794, 932.

6. Joseph F. Fitzpatrick, S.J., "No Place to Grieve: A Honduran Tragedy," *America,* July 12, 1990, 37.

7. Dolan, *In Search of an American Catholicism,* 98.

8. Gerald P. Fogarty, S.J., *The Vatican and the American Hierarchy from 1870 to 1965* (Wilmington, DE: Michael Glazier, 1985), 211–213.

9. Hennesey, *American Catholics,* 193.

10. Lawrence J. McCaffrey, *The Irish Catholic Diaspora in America* (Washington, DC: Catholic University of America Press, 1997), 1.

11. Philip Gleason, "Thanks to the Irish," *America,* May 14, 1966.

12. *New York Freeman's Journal and Catholic Register,* February 18, 1871.

13. Miller, *Emigrants and Exiles*, 526.

14. Archives of the Franciscan Sisters of the Atonement, Brother Paul to Mother Lurana, November 17 and 30, 1909.

15. Thomas W. Spalding, *The Premier See: A History of the Archdiocese of Baltimore, 1789–1989* (Baltimore: Johns Hopkins University Press, 1989), 325.

16. Tim Unsworth, *The Last Priests in America* (New York: Crossroad, 1991), 35, cited in William L. Smith, "Priests from Ireland," *The Encyclopedia of the Irish in America*, ed. Michael Glazier (Notre Dame, IN: University of Notre Dame Press, 1999), 790. Smith calculated that, down to 1996, five Irish missionary seminaries trained 3,365 diocesan priests for service in the United States.

17. Hasia Diner, *Erin's Daughters in America: Irish Immigrant Women in the Nineteenth Century* (Baltimore: Johns Hopkins University Press, 1983), 136–137.

18. Philip Gleason, "Catholic Higher Education," in *The Encyclopedia of American Catholic History*, ed. Michael Glazier and Thomas J. Shelley (Collegeville, MD: Liturgical Press, 1997), 252.

19. Hennesey, *American Catholics*, 208.

20. Steven P. Erie, *Rainbow's End: Irish-Americans and the Dilemmas of Urban Machine Politics, 1840–1985* (Berkeley: University of California Press, 1988), 48–50.

21. Miller, *Emigrants and Exiles*, 504–505.

22. Diner, *Erin's Daughters in America*, 100–101.

23. C. Joseph Neusse, *The Catholic University of America: A Centennial History* (Washington, DC: Catholic University of America Press, 1990), 56–59.

24. John Lancaster Spalding, "The Higher Education," in *Means and Ends of Education* (Chicago: A. C. McClurg, 1909), 220.

25. Quoted from Pope Pius X, *Pascendi Dominici Gregis*, September 8, 1907, #2, in *The Papal Encyclicals, 1903–1939*, ed. Claudia Carlen, I.H.M. (n.p.: A Consortium Book: McGrath Publishing Company, 1981), 71.

26. Driscoll to Charles Augustus Briggs, December 8, 1907, in the Archives of Union Theological Seminary, Briggs Papers.

27. Cited in William M. Halsey, *The Survival of American Innocence: Catholicism in an Era of Disillusionment, 1920–1940* (Notre Dame, IN: University of Notre Dame Press, 1980), 44.

28. As quoted in James M. O'Toole, "William Cardinal O'Connell," in *The Encyclopedia of American Catholic History*, ed. Michael Glazier and Thomas J. Shelley (Collegeville: Liturgical Press, 1997), 1070.

29. Charles R. Morris, *American Catholic: The Saints and Sinners Who Built America's Most Powerful Church* (New York: Times Books/Random House, 1997), 169. On O'Connell, see the splendid biography by O'Toole, *Militant and Triumphant: William Henry O'Connell and the Catholic Church in Boston, 1859–1944* (Notre Dame, IN: University of Notre Dame Press, 1992). There is no biography of Dougherty, but see Hugh J. Nolan, "The Native Son," in *The History of the Archdiocese of Philadelphia*, ed. James F. Connelly (Wynnewood, PA: Archdiocese of Philadelphia, 1976), 339–418, and Charles R. Morris, *American Catholic* (New York: Times Books/Random House, 1997), 165–195.

30. Spalding, *Premier See*, 384.

31. Hennesey, *American Catholics*, 223.

32. Ibid., 225–226.

33. The best study of the origins and early years of the NCWC is Douglas J. Slawson, *The Foundation and First Decade of the National Catholic Welfare Council* (Washington, DC: Catholic University of America Press, 1992).

34. The text can be found in *Documents of American Catholic History,* ed. John Tracy Ellis (Wilmington, DE: Michael Glazier, 1987), 589–606.

35. For a perceptive analysis of the Bishops' Program, see Joseph M. McShane, S.J., *"Sufficiently Radical": Catholicism, Progressivism and the Bishops' Program of 1919* (Washington, DC: Catholic University of America Press, 1986).

36. Edward Cuddy, "The Irish Question and the Revival of Anti-Catholicism in the 1920s," *Catholic Historical Review* 47 (1981): 238–239.

37. Florence D. Cohalan, *A Popular History of the Archdiocese of New York* (Yonkers, NY: U.S. Catholic Historical Society, 1983), 244–245; *New York Times,* March 18, 1921.

38. "I affirm on my word as Pontiff that I have been deceived and I will do justice to the bishops of the United States." An account of the conversation between Schrembs and Pius XI given by Schrembs and taken down on December 21, 1939, Archives of the United States Catholic Conference, General Secretary Files, quoted in Douglas J. Slawson, *The Foundation and First Decade of the National Catholic Welfare Council* (Washington, DC: Catholic University of America Press, 1992), 158.

39. Dorothy M. Brown and Elizabeth McKeon, *The Poor Belong to Us: Catholic Charities and American Welfare* (Cambridge, MA: Harvard University Press, 1997), 70–71.

40. Jeffrey M. Burns, "William Kerby," in *Encyclopedia of American Catholic History,* 762; Elizabeth McKeon, "Catholic Charities," in *Encyclopedia of American Catholic History,* 244.

41. Neil A. Kelly, "'Orphans and Pigs Fed from the Same Bowl': Catholics and the New York Charities Controversy of 1916," M.A. thesis, St. Joseph's Seminary, Yonkers, New York, 1991.

42. Quoted from Sydney E. Ahlstrom, *A Religious History of the American People* (New Haven, CT: Yale University Press, 1972), 901.

43. *Yonkers Herald,* January 21, 1931.

44. Virginius Dabney, *Dry Messiah* (New York: Knopf, 1949), p. 188; quoted in Sydney Ahlstrom, *A Religious History of the American People* (New Haven, CT: Yale University Press, 1972), 905 n.16.

45. John Higham, *Strangers in the Land: Patterns of American Nativism, 1860–1925* (New York: Atheneum, 1981), 291.

46. Thomas J. Shelley, "The Oregon School Case and the National Catholic Welfare Conference," *Catholic Historical Review* 75, no. 3 (1989): 439–457.

47. Thomas J. Shelley, "'What the Hell Is an Encyclical?': Governor Alfred E. Smith, Charles C. Marshall, Esq., and Father Francis P. Duffy," *U.S. Catholic Historian* 15, no. 2 (1997): 87–107.

48. Quoted in David J. O'Brien, *American Catholics and Social Reform: The New Deal Years* (New York: Oxford University Press, 1968), 156.

49. O'Brien, *American Catholics and Social Reform,* 180.

50. The only biography of Ryan is Francis L. Broderick, *Rt. Rev. New Dealer: John A. Ryan* (New York: Macmillan, 1963). See also O'Brien, *American Catholics and Social Reform,* 120–149.

51. On Dorothy Day, see William D. Miller, *A Harsh and Dreadful Love: Dorothy Day and the Catholic Worker Movement* (New York: Liveright, 1973). The following discussion is from this volume.

52. Jay P. Dolan, *The American Catholic Experience: A History from Colonial Times to the Present* (Garden City, NY: Doubleday, 1985), 411.

53. Hennesey, *American Catholics,* 284.

54. Morris, *American Catholic,* 174.

55. Garry Wills, *Bare Ruined Choirs: Doubt, Prophecy and Radical Religion* (Garden City, NY: Doubleday, 1971), 24.

56. Andrew M. Greeley, "Catholicism in America: 200 Years and Counting," *Critic* 34, no. 4 (1976): 44.

57. Edward R. Kantowicz, *Corporation Sole* (Notre Dame, IN: University of Notre Dame Press, 1983), 66–67. See also *The Official Catholic Directory* (New York: P. J. Kenedy, 1926), 247.

58. The technical phrase was *communicatio in sacris*. George Barry Ford, *A Degree of Difference* (New York; Farrar, Straus Giroux, 1969), 107.

59. Morris, *American Catholic,* 196–209; Wills, *Bare Ruined Choirs,* 23.

60. *Official Bulletin of the University of Notre Dame* 34 (March 1928): frontispiece.

61. Quoted in Robert I. Gannon, S.J., *Up to the Present* (Garden City, NY: Doubleday, 1967), 187; George Bull, S.J., "The Function of the Catholic Graduate School," *Thought* 13 (1938): 378–379, 372.

62. Philip Gleason, "Catholic Higher Education," in *Encyclopedia of American Catholic History,* 252–253.

63. *New York Times,* May 8 and May 22, 1950.

64. There are excellent biographies of both Kelley and O'Hara. See James P. Gaffey, *Francis Clement Kelley and the American Catholic Dream,* 2 vols. (Bensenville, IL: Heritage Foundation, 1980), and Timothy M. Dolan, *Some Seed Fell on Good Ground* (Washington, DC: Catholic University of America Press, 1992).

65. Cited in William V. Shannon, *The American Irish* (Amherst: University of Massachusetts Press, 1966), xiii. I am indebted to the Rev. Thomas A. Lynch for Spellman's comment to his biographer.

66. Fogarty, *Vatican and the American Hierarchy,* 314.

67. Alan Ehrenhalt, *The Lost City: The Forgotten Virtues of Community in America* (New York: Basic Books, 1995), 112–120, cited in Dolan, *In Search of an American Catholicism,* 184.

68. Elizabeth A. Edmondson, "Without Comment or Controversy: The G.I. Bill and Catholic Colleges," *Church History* 71, no. 4 (2002): 820–847.

69. McCaffrey, *Irish Catholic Diaspora,* 176.

70. John T. McGreevy, *Parish Boundaries: The Catholic Encounter with Race in the Twentieth-Century Urban North* (Chicago: University of Chicago Press, 1996).

71. John Tracy Ellis, *American Catholics and the Intellectual Life* (Chicago: Heritage Foundation, 1956).

72. McCaffrey, *The Irish Catholic Diaspora,* 177.

73. Donald F. Crosby, S.J., *God, Church and Flag: Senator Joseph R. McCarthy and the Catholic Church, 1950–1957* (Chapel Hill: University of North Carolina Press, 1978), 242–243.

74. Hennesey, *American Catholics,* 292.

75. Spellman to Enrico Galeazzi, April 9, 1965. AANY, Spellman Papers.

76. For a critique of the secularization of many Catholic universities and colleges, see James Tunstead Burtchaell, *The Dying of the Light: The Disengagement of Colleges and Universities from Their Christian Churches* (Grand Rapids, MI: Eerdmans, 1998).

77. The statistics in this paragraph were taken from *The Official Catholic Directory* (New York and New Providence, NJ: P. J. Kenedy, 1966, 2005).

78. Archives of the United States Catholic Conference, Hallinan to Bishop William Connare, September 26, 1967, copy.

79. Lawrence J. McCaffrey, "Irish Catholics in America," in *Encyclopedia of American Catholic History,* 704.

80. Dolan, *In Search of an American Catholicism,* 221.

81. Two of the best books on the state of American Catholicism at the beginning of the twenty-first century are Peter Steinfels, *A People Adrift: The Crisis of the Roman Catholic Church*

in America (New York: Simon and Schuster, 2003), and David Gibson, *The Coming Catholic Church: How the Faithful Are Shaping a New American Catholicism* (San Francisco: HarperSan-Francisco, 2003).

SUGGESTED READING

Jay P. Dolan, *The American Catholic Experience: A History from Colonial Times to the Present* (Notre Dame, IN: University of Notre Dame Press, 1992).

Jay P. Dolan, *In Search of an American Catholicism: A History of Religion and Culture in Tension* (New York: Oxford University Press, 2002).

Gerald P. Fogarty, S.J., *The Vatican and the American Hierarchy from 1870 to 1965* (Wilmington: Michael Glazier, 1985).

James Hennesey, S.J., *American Catholics* (New York: Oxford University Press, 1981).

John T. McGreevy, *Parish Boundaries: The Catholic Encounter with Race in the Twentieth-Century Urban North* (Chicago: University of Chicago Press, 1996).

Peter Steinfels, *A People Adrift: The Crisis of the Roman Catholic Church in America* (New York: Simon and Schuster, 2003).

Chapter 26

The Fireman on the Stairs
Communal Loyalties in the Making of Irish America

Timothy J. Meagher

On September 11, 2001, some 343 firefighters died in the World Trade Center Towers attacks.[1] An entire nation watched them; an entire world, perhaps, and marveled at their heroism. In an America and indeed, dare we say it, a New York where only the rich, the famous, the notable, the notorious—in short the "successful"—had long seemed worthy of our attention, much less respect, "the grunts" as Peggy Noonan called them, "became the kings and queens of the city." The investment bankers, magazine editors and lawyers, the conservative Wall Street Journal columnist went on, had been rendered "useless," irrelevant.[2] For the first time in half a century, it seemed, "common" men and women, "average joes" or "janes," "regular guys" or "gals" were no longer the ultimate chumps or bums in the capitalist sweepstakes that many think is America, but heroes, the defenders of the nation, the very embodiments of its character and virtue.

Yet it was more than just a revived appreciation of the "grunt," the common man or woman, the regular guy, that caught my attention and the nation's. From the time of that disaster until the time I stood at its site—with a tape recording of the "Boys of Wexford" blaring in my ears—some eleven months later, I had been haunted by a recurring image, and I wondered about the broad meaning of the question that inevitably followed it. I was haunted by the vision of a fireman or firewoman on the stairs of one of the towers, about to begin his or her ascent: a fireman on the step. Why did he or she go up? Why march into that uncertainty, the real prospect of danger, the possibility—and as it turned out, the probability—of death?

Since that catastrophe many commentators have made much of the attacks on the World Trade Center as attacks on symbols of the American economy, indeed, on the principle of the free market that seems, for such observers at least, to be the definition of America.

But it was not self-interest—a quick and cold free market calculation of profit and loss, costs and benefits—that made those firemen or women climb those stairs. It was not for the sake of a fireman's salary (first-grade firemen made $60,000 a year): there were and are easier ways to make that kind of money.[3] If free-market principles ruled the firemen's actions, they never would have climbed those stairs. What became clear in interview after interview, talk after talk, story after story was that they went up those stairs from a sense of commitment, of duty. It was not so much an abstract ob-ligation, but a sense of commitment rooted in the concrete community of the fire department of their fellows—their brothers, sisters, uncles, cousins, and friends. They went up sometimes, quite literally, to rescue friends, even family members, but even when they went up to save strangers, their sense of duty was rooted in a community and its traditions and the need for the respect of their peers.

To many observers, these communal loyalties, these fierce bonds, are as strik-ing and intriguing as the heroism they produced. To many Americans, for whom the restless, wandering individualism of modern America is so much the norm that it seems commonplace, this communalism must have seemed foreign, almost exotic, if touching. To us as Irish Americans it may have been more familiar, but it still seemed strange—not because we did not know it or recognize it, but because we had not seen it for so long.

Men and women of many nationalities went up those stairs and it would be unjust —indeed, cheap, mean, and self-serving—not to recognize that fact. And yet, and yet (you will see that phrase written here a lot), a substantial proportion of the firefight-ers were Irish Americans. Of the 343 firefighters who died that day, 145 had been members of the fire department's Irish-American fraternal group, the Emerald Soci-ety. But we could have guessed that, listening to the litany of names—Brian Ahearn, John Bergin, Michael Brennan, Thomas Foley, John McAvoy, William McGovern, Thomas O'Hagan, and on and on like an Irish phonebook—or hearing of the neigh-borhoods they lived in (patches of Staten Island or Queens or Brooklyn), or even not-ing the songs they favored (the fire department football team's apparent anthem was "The Wild Rover").[4] Yet, it was not just the names, the neighborhoods, or even the songs that marked them as Irish American; it was also these tight bonds of communal loyalty that bound this community of working-class men and women, regular guys all, together.

If those Irish-American values of communalism and "regular guy egalitarianism" seem like an anachronism today, they have not always been so. For a long time noth-ing seemed to set Irish Americans apart more, nothing seemed more tellingly or in-delibly Irish American, than this kind of rough and ready communalism. Moreover, the conflict between such communal loyalties and the values and circumstances of the American environment—values of individualism and circumstances of economic abundance and racial and ethnic diversity—has been the central dynamic of the his-tory of the Irish in America.

Indeed, such a conflict may not just have been at the center of Irish-American his-tory but central to the nation's history as well. Over the last thirty or forty years, three issues have been the principal concerns of students of ethnicity and immigration: social mobility, or the nature of opportunity in America; the failure of the American left; and the making of "whiteness," white supremacy, in the United States.

In the 1960s and 1970s, eager to write the history of America from the bottom up and delighted by the apparent magical powers of computers, historians set out to find out if America really was a land of opportunity by tracing the working careers of thousands of ordinary people through city directories and census manuscript sched-ules. That interest seemed to fade out by the early 1970s—it was hard and dull work, and after a while it did not seem to matter much if the numbers you found in the town or city you studied were a few percentage points higher or lower than someone else found in a study of some other town or city.[5]

Even as scores of historians, myself included, were dutifully doing their counting, a second issue had emerged. This was the question of why there was no Socialist Party in America—why working-class people had never united to pursue their own interests through a sustained political movement. This was actually an old question, dating back to the beginning of the twentieth century, but the question was revived after the 1960s as a number of former student activists entered the history profession, searching for answers about why the left was so weak in America and seeking possible prescriptions for making it stronger in the future.[6]

By the 1980s, the interest in this question and the interest generally in what was called the new labor history began to fizzle. After Ronald Reagan's victories in that decade, labor and social historians were discouraged about the prospects of ever building a viable left in America. They were especially discouraged by the apparent strong support that blue-collar Democrats had given Reagan: the Reagan Democrats. Indeed, some became so discouraged that they began to wonder whether white American workers had ever had the potential to become a united and active force for radical change in America. Looking back into the beginnings of American industrialization and the birth of an American working class in the early nineteenth century, they detected a kind of "original sin" of racism, or belief in white supremacy that had seemed to infect the white working class from its origins and to doom white workers' ability to ally with non-white, class fellows ever after. These historians introduced a new term into American history, indeed, into many disciplines studying American culture: "whiteness." What they meant by this is that racial divisions are no so much biological as cultural, not so much physical differences as about what we make of physical attributes. They believed that the white race, like the black one, was not a biological given but made in history. They wanted to know, then, how people decided it was important to be white, and how people, particularly immigrants, learned to be or become white, and thus, tragically, learned how to turn their backs on African and Asian Americans.[7]

What does this have to do with Irish Americans, you are no doubt asking, while looking at your watch. Well, as it turns out, quite a bit, for the Irish in America figured prominently in the scholarship on all of these issues. Indeed, they have been at the center of all of these scholarly discussions, and it was not just them but their communalism—the stubborn power of their communal loyalties and its complementary populist egalitarianism more specifically—that seemed to figure in all of these scholarly controversies.

Such loyalties, many historians argued, for example, seemed to retard Irish Americans' upward mobility. Until recently Irish Americans have been the poster boys—not so much girls, as we will see—for economic failure in America. From historians like Stephan Thernstrom, to contemporary observers like Thomas Sowell and Daniel Patrick Moynihan, the "relevant question" has been, as Moynihan stated, "not how the Irish have succeeded, but why they have not succeeded more." And the answer, as often as not, has been Irish Americans' failure to act as individuals, to stand on their own, take responsibility for their lives, self-confidently assume risks, and make the improvements that would make them successful. Irish Americans failed to be individuals and move up, so this argument goes, not so much because of a lack of skills but a lack of will: individual mobility would break their ties to their community, Irish Americans allegedly feared, their bonds to their fellows, and this Irish Americans were reluctant to do.[8]

Without upward mobility—and thus not tainted by the corruption of capitalism's rewards—and also disdainful of American individualism, one would think Irish Americans would have been ready-made radicals, naturally fitted to embrace working-class solidarity and overthrow a capitalist system that did so little for them. Moreover, with political experience in the old country and facility in English, the language of their new home, Irish Americans quickly became politically savvy in America. They seemed, then, to be as well placed as any group in America to forge a working-class political movement. Irish Americans did use this savvy to work a "revolution" that made "common men" rulers of the great American cities, but it was a "revolution" that made Irish political bosses and machine men the new princes of the city, not a revolution that overthrew existing political and economic structures. Bound in tight networks of parochial loyalties, many historians have argued, bereft of ideas, and focused greedily and myopically on their own ambitions and needs, these bosses hardly represented much of a challenge to the existing system, nor, it seemed, were they even very responsive to the needs of their working-class constituencies.[9]

Yet some historians think the Irish failure was worse than that. The historians of whiteness think that the Irish failed to lead or even join a broad, radical, political movement because they "became white." These historians argue that the Irish deliberately rejected their fellows among the poor and oppressed, African and Asian Americans, for, in David Roediger's words, the "pleasures of white supremacy": the allurements of status deference and power on the street. Here again, the Irish are the poster boys—again largely boys—of American white supremacy.[10]

What are we to make of this: on the one hand, the communalism that bred the heroism of so many fire and police men and women on September 11th; on the other, a historical record, if these historians are to be believed, of a communalism that has led tragically to economic failure, narrow-minded and selfish politics, and even nasty racism?

Well, I am still not sure what to make of it. The only thing I am sure about is how much more I need to know. This is not false modesty—not Henry Glassie's shy Irish pub singer, who needs to be coaxed—I do offer my opinions. But I think it is worth taking this opportunity, afforded by the sudden visibility of the firefighters and their world, to explore and reflect on Irish-American communalism, even if no clear and easy conclusions seem evident. The question of Irish-American communal loyalties is *that* important to Irish-American history.

What I do here is explore the origins of communal loyalties in Ireland, why they seemed so important there, and then take up these issues of Irish-American performance in the American economy, roles in politics, and assumptions of whiteness. But I also take a look at how these issues have played out in Irish-American and American popular culture—that is, how Irish Americans, their communalism and their economic performance, political roles and racial poses, were represented by themselves and others in American culture. That, too, is part of the story, for it has shaped how Irish Americans understood their own communalism, as well as how others understood it.

To begin with where this communalism comes from, and why it has been so important to Irish Americans, we have to, of course, turn to Ireland. In *Emigrants and Exiles*, still the best book on Irish Americans ever written and maybe the best book ever written on any immigrant people in America, Kerby Miller contends that Irish Catholics' communal values sharply distinguished them from Protestants in Ireland and the Protestant nation that dominated the United States:

> In broadest terms, much evidence indicates that in contrast to the Protestants they encountered in Ireland and North America, the Catholic Irish were more communal than individualist, more dependent than independent, more fatalistic than optimistic, more prone to accept conditions passively than to take initiative for change and more sensitive to the weight of tradition than to innovative possibilities for the future.

Miller believes that this communalism was at the heart of "a distinctive Catholic worldview rooted deeply in Irish history and culture that long preceded the English conquest of Ireland and the mass migrations of modern times." Miller argues that, though born in the society and culture of ancient Ireland, such communal values became woven into the very vocabulary and syntax of the Irish language itself helping ensure the survival of an Irish Catholic communal worldview into the nineteenth and even twentieth centuries.[11]

As Miller would agree, however, we need not see Irish Catholic communalism as some mere survival—a throwback to a bygone ancient Gaelic age—a relic. John McGreevy reminds us in his new book, *Catholicism and American Freedom*, that the Catholic Church continued to take communalism very seriously in the nineteenth and twentieth centuries, and in Europe and America fulminated frequently against the evils of individualism. Reenergized by a Catholic Revival or Devotional Revolution that spread not only over all of Ireland but western Europe and America in the middle of the nineteenth century, and rearmed by a reconstruction of the philosophy of Thomas Aquinas, neo Thomism, the Church provided a living, breathing, powerful ideological influence for communalism. Irish immigrants and their children might have "heard" the communalism of their Gaelic past echoing in their brains, but they also heard communalism preached literally, loud and clear, in the Sunday sermons of their parish priests, saw it represented visually in statues or paintings of the communion of saints that crowded their churches, and participated actively in it in liturgies like the mass.[12]

But it is important not to see communalism, communal loyalty, as simply an idea, an abstract value, handed down and stubbornly maintained regardless of context or the concrete interests of those holding to it. Communalism—working together, depending on others—has also been a strategy, a tool. In scarce economies like Ireland's, as Bob Scally reminds us in his *End of Hidden Ireland*, where the rewards are so meager and the risks of reaching for them so great, it may not be very smart to go it alone. Individual ambition can be foolish; communal cooperation is the only means

Irish early Christian and nationalist symbolism combine with the iconography of Irish America—crossed flags, the eagle, and clasped hands—in this 1894 membership certificate for the Ancient Order of Hibernians. The AOH was founded in New York City in 1834 but by the end of the nineteenth century had branches (called Divisions) across the United States. It was a Catholic fraternal organization, similar in that respect to the Knights of Columbus. (Library of Congress, Prints and Photographs Division, LC-USZC4-6233)

for success or even survival. Kevin Whelan has argued this brilliantly in a little piece on the proliferation of *clachans* in the brutal grinding economy of nineteenth-century Ireland. Such scarce economies, as Scally has so eloquently argued, developed an ethos, a notion of a moral economy, based on the zero-sum game of a scarce economy. As Scally explains, in a scarce economy like Ireland's, peasants believed "the goods of the earth were finite and an unequal share could be had by one individual only at the expense of another." They thus developed a notion of a moral economy "that generally condemned private initiative and accumulation as something alien and inimical to the community." As Scally further elaborates and other social scientists like James Scott have argued, communal solidarity is also an essential weapon of the poor in their struggles with the rich. It is often the only hope for successful resistance to the powerful—the power of numbers against the power of money or supe-rior arms—by presenting a united front against oppressors. Like the rebels of Scally's study, from the townland of Ballykilcline, the poor can hide individual actions and, thus, foil the powerful's attempts to fix responsibility for resistance.[13]

Scarce economies abounded throughout the nineteenth century—and still do—so such communal strategies have not been unique to Ireland. Was there anything that made the Irish version of this communalism particularly powerful and potentially durable?

It appears that there may have been. Ireland, for example, was teeming with secret societies in the early nineteenth century, as the island's economy plunged into depres-sion and a bloated population made all economic resources, but particularly access to land, especially dear. In broad terms, the provocation for this secret society resistance was the relentless disruptive intrusion of the broader United Kingdom, European, or world markets into Ireland's local peasant economies. Secret society violence, there-fore, seemed most intense along the frontier of market integration as it inexorably moved throughout the society. Yet, though there were broad causes for their discon-tent, Irish peasants seemed to concentrate narrowly on their own local, concrete grievances; they seemed unaware of or simply indifferent to similar societies in other communities or regions. Their goals were also limited, and, in some ways, conserva-tive: preserve the status quo—our people renting our land, for without holding on to the land we would die. They were trying to defend the moral order of the older scarce economy. Secret societies were then as likely to assault a fellow peasant, who tried to take up one of his or her neighbors' farms, as a landlord or his agent.[14]

Still, this resistance took place in a colonial Ireland with an alien land-owning class and in a society laced with sectarianism. Scholars as diverse as Tom Garvin and Luke Gibbons have pointed to the rough, crude nationalist motives and organization of some of the societies, particularly the Ribbonmen, who operated in Ulster and along the Ulster borderlands. Even in the south, sectarian tensions often permeated secret society violence. James Donnelly points to the influence of a folk myth, "Pastorini's prophecy," which predicted the overthrow of the heretics, the Protestants, and the restoration of land and power to long-suffering Catholics, on the Rockites or "Cap-tain Rock" secret societies of Munster in the 1820s. So great was the Rockite conviction in Pastorini's prophecy that thousands of them rose in an abortive insurrection in northwest Cork in January of 1822, believing that they were helping to make the prophecy come to pass. Sectarian differences did not prevent intersectarian mixing, just as sectarian loyalties did not prevent intrasectarian conflict among classes, occu-pations, or even families. Catholic tenants, middlemen, landlords, and, indeed, Cath-olic priests were all often targets of Catholic secret society ire. Yet consciousness of sectarian divisions was profound throughout Ireland. This pervasiveness of sectarian-ism, and even the rough nationalism of people like the Ribbonmen, did seem to make Irish people perhaps more conscious of group boundaries and group loyalties than some other American immigrant groups.[15]

Communal loyalties might have made sense in Ireland, might even have been a logical, perhaps the only possible, strategy for survival, many historians might ac-knowledge, but the same historians doubt the usefulness of such tight loyalties in

America. Here, they argue, communalism was a hindrance. Mobility study after mobility study—those of Clyde Griffin and Stephan Thernstrom especially—carefully counted the numbers, and the numbers were not good for Irish Americans. In virtually all of those studies, the Irish were always the slowest to move up to better jobs and the first to fall from better jobs back to the bottom of the economic hierarchy. Long before Kerby Miller argued that Irish Americans seemed condemned to failure in America by the kind of communal values they held dear, that notion had become an article of faith among historians studying American social mobility.

And yet, and yet, as some Irish American historians were quick to point out, most of these studies were of cities or towns in the Northeast, most of cities or towns in New England. Long ago historians like Larry McCaffrey, David Doyle, and Jim Walsh pointed out that while Irish-American upward mobility was slow and grudging in New England and other parts of the Northeast, it was more rapid further west, particularly in California, and especially in San Francisco. More recently David Gleeson has suggested the same for Irish immigrants in the South (though his evidence is stronger for some parts of the South than others). Historians of Irish Canadians and Irish Australians have found the same pattern and made the same point, though with a sanctimonious sense of self congratulation and, indeed, a good bit of mean-spirited name calling that seems excessive. The simple point here is that if Irish culture matters, then the environment can matter, too. Obviously, Irish economic failures in America could not be caused by their communalism or other aspects of their culture alone. Otherwise, how could they succeed in one place and not another? The failure lay not in themselves but in the places where they settled.[16]

Yet the effects of Irish communalism on Irish immigrant economic performance remain unresolved, for as Joel Perlmann pointed out years ago, most Irish immigrants did not go to the West or to Australia or Canada; they came to the United States, and more particularly to New England, New York, and Pennsylvania (and if they did not come to the United States, more went to Britain—Scotland and England—than to the rest of the empire). More Irish-born men and women lived in New York City in 1890 than on the entire continent of Australia; and far more lived in Boston than in all of the Mountain States in America in the same year. The northeastern United States—New England and the Middle Atlantic states—was the core, the heart of the Irish diaspora, but here Irish Americans made slow economic progress, significantly slower than other ethnic groups here like the Germans, Scandinavians, British, and Jews. How do we account for these complications?[17]

Frankly, I don't know, but I think they have something to do with immigrant networks. Networks are those groups, clusters of friends and relatives, that made migration possible in the nineteenth century for people from countries like Ireland, Italy, and Hungary. They still do for poor people from Mexico, El Salvador, and Guatemala today. Most poorer immigrants, as Charles Tilly points out, migrate not as individuals but as parts of these networks, as "chains" of men and women following friends or relatives in long trails from home in the old country to home in the new. This helps the poor and ignorant—not stupid, just people without the education—to brave the fearful, unknown risks of going three thousand miles to a new country. Networks provide more than information. Friends who had already come to America often bought tickets for their relatives and friends at home. Irish Americans sent $260 million back to Ireland between 1848 and 1900: 40 percent or $104 million in prepaid tickets. In Worcester, where I come from, a steamship ticket agent named Richard O'Flynn sold sixty tickets on the White Star Line in December of 1884 and sent them to Ireland. Forty-three of the tickets were bought by people in Worcester for people with the same last name in Ireland: Sara Gleason for Maurice Gleason; Bridget McNamara for Andrew McNamara; John O'Connor for Jeremiah O'Connor.[18]

Networks not only help immigrants travel to a new country; they sustain newcomers when they get there. Networks help new immigrants find jobs and places to live. While most Irish immigrant women worked as domestic servants and lived in the homes of their employers, most immigrant men boarded out—not in big boardinghouses, but as groups of two or three with Irish immigrant families who had come to America before them. And when they went to get a job, Irish immigrants depended on friends to help them. In Worcester in 1901, there were twenty-one Irish-born policemen, but no fewer than five were from Killarney. Coincidence? I think not. Around the same time, a Worcester newspaper reported a woman from Ireland picked up by the police. She was crazed with fear, sobbing and crying. She had lost the addresses of her friends and relatives in Worcester and felt lost.[19]

Networks, friends, community could be essential here in America, an economy of abundance, as in Ireland, an economy of scarcity, because in nineteenth- and twentieth-century America, there may have been more opportunities for economic success than in Ireland, but there were also many risks, especially for poor people with few skills. The American industrial economy ran a roller coaster of boom and bust in the nineteenth century; job-related deaths or injuries were commonplace, and there was little backup or safety net—except for the poorhouse, and no one wanted to go there. Immigrants still needed help; they needed each other. This, then, was not just communalism as a new or old idea, but communalism embodied in the flesh and blood of friends and family.

Such networks seemed to take root early on here in the Northeast for the Irish and simply continued to draw them here. There were many reasons to come to New York or New England. The economies in this part of the country, particularly in New York, New Jersey, and Pennsylvania, were hardly moribund. New York City had some of the best wages in the country for laborers in the mid–nineteenth century and broad opportunities then and thereafter, if also stiff ethnic competition for positions up the occupational ladder. These regions had jobs then, if not the more spectacular opportunities further west. There were also practical reasons to settle in the eastern United States and not go west through America or to Canada or Australia. It cost money to go to the American West, much less to Australia. In the 1840s it cost an Irish immigrant as much to go inland to Chicago as it cost to cross the Atlantic Ocean. Before the transcontinental railroad, a ship ticket to San Francisco from New York ran a "cool" $100. Even after the railroad was completed in the late 1860s, tickets from East Coast cities to San Francisco cost $60 to $75. The price of passage to Australia, of course, was much higher, as much as five times the fare to North America in the 1850s.[20]

But I am not sure that such prices were the principal reason for Irish settlement patterns. They certainly were important, and may have been critical for the first wave of migrants, but once networks were set down in the Northeast, people continued to concentrate there. Joseph Ferrie did a huge study of Irish and other immigrants who came through New York City in the 1840s, tracing their movements around the country through the 1860s. He suggests that among all the migration currents he tracked, there was a noticeable flow *eastward* by immigrants, who had wandered west to lands of ample opportunities after their arrival in America in the 1840s, but now were coming "home" to the East in the 1850s. Ferrie estimates that as many as one-fifth of immigrants who had made it to the West by 1850 had moved back east by 1860. Ferrie does not identify these returning immigrants as Irish, or largely Irish, but other historians have pointed to the flows of Irish navies, construction workers, in and out of New York City throughout the mid–nineteenth century. Robert Ernst, for example, wrote of "the mass of Irish laborers—rootless, unmarried men and husbands, who returned in the off season to their families in New York City and other large cities." Consider this as well: the Irish-born population grew in only three of the nine regions of the United States in the 1880s—the Mountain States, Pacific States, and New England—but the growth in New England was over forty thousand people, or nearly three times the combined total for the two western regions. In New England, where economies were mature and growing slowly, social structures calcified, but it was where their friends lived.[21]

It is tempting to conclude from this that the people who went further west or to Australia were, in fact, very special people. It seems logical to conclude that maybe these were people who did not need "friends." Adventuresome, individualistic men and women—unlike us effete Easterners—these were people who could make it on their own. It seems logical, too, to assume that they may have been richer, better educated, better prepared somehow, to snap at opportunities, to seize the main chance. All of this is not only logical, it harmonizes neatly with American national myths and perhaps Australian and even Canadian myths as well: the hardy pioneer, loosed from European bonds, fears, servility, bravely making his or her way on an untamed frontier and reaping the riches his or her pluck deserved.

There were undoubtedly such Irish men and women: Marcus Daly, the Copper King of Montana; John Mackay, the Silver King of the Comstock Lode; Peter Donahue, who became owner of the San Francisco Gas Works; and James Phelan, banker and real estate speculator in San Francisco.[22]

And yet, and yet, these Irish Westerners, these Australian pioneers, may not have been richer or better educated, nor even more adventurous than their fellow Irish who settled in the diaspora's core, the eastern United States. David Fitzpatrick suggests that Irish immigrants to Australia were only "slightly more literate than their peer groups in the counties of origin," for example. Such immigrants may just have had different networks than Irish immigrants who went to New York, or Boston, or Providence, or Albany. Jon Gjerde and a host of American historians have pointed to the importance of migration chains and networks in the settling of the American West for groups as diverse as Norwegian fishermen, Dutch farmers, and Connecticut Yankees. Networks were, perhaps, even more crucial for Irish men and women going to Australia. Fitzpatrick reports that most Irish immigrants to Australia received some kind of support to get there—often, from provincial governments in Australia. These immigrants were usually nominated by people already living in Australia. Governments there, then, were, in effect, subsidizing Irish networks by bringing immigrants to the distant continent.[23]

Once they got there, to the American West or to Australia or parts of Canada, these Irish might not have need of "friends" anymore. More likely, however, they played upon their network connections to take advantage of opportunities on the land or in the fresh cities of their new homes. Even in western America—and David Emmons, author of *The Butte Irish*, would say *especially* in parts of the American West—communal links were critical to finding work. In his Butte, the most Irish city in America in 1900, there was no way to get and keep work in the mines unless you became part of an elaborate group of Irish fraternal and nationalist organizations.[24]

Nevertheless, networks in the eastern United States, where opportunities were more limited, were undoubtedly more important for the Irish immigrants who came here. They sustained; they nourished; they kept people alive. Tyler Anbinder, in his book about Five Points, reports that even in the foulest, most degraded Irish slum in America, immigrants from the most impoverished parts of Ireland—like Kenmare in southern Kerry—were opening bank accounts and saving money in the 1850s and 1860s. In the end Anbinder attributes this ability not so much to individual initiative as to "having so many of their kinsmen and former neighbors with them in New York. Virtually overnight, they created a large, intricate network that could be used to help find jobs, housing even spouses."[25]

Networks did not have to be inherited from Ireland, however. Irish immigrants and their descendants, like all immigrant and ethnic Americans, created new webs of friends and loyalties here in the United States. Irish immigrants might follow chains into city neighborhoods, but once settled, they and their children found new friends among their neighbors. Eventually, many Irish-American neighborhoods evolved into tight communities centered on churches, groceries, saloons, ethnic clubs, and gangs that constantly reinforced and strengthened communal ties. In cities from Boston to Chicago, neighborhoods sometimes took on the names of their Catholic parishes, such as St. Gregory's and St. Peter's in Boston's Dorchester district. Residents in such neighborhoods were not only often intensely loyal to one another, their shared "turf," and the hallmark institutions of church and club, but, like peasants from the old country, they nursed suspicions of those among them who threatened to rupture the bonds of community in pursuit of their own ambitions. As J. Anthony Lukas noted, "Up to me, up to me, but never above me" was the populist, communitarian, egalitarian, motto of the heavily Irish Boston neighborhood of Charlestown through the 1960s.[26]

Irish Americans, like other American ethnics, built occupational networks, too. Burrowing into specific trades or industries, they created "niches" for their own people. New York City's fire department, with its hive of Irish-American friends and relatives, is a classic example of this kind of niche, but there have been others. In New York, Irish Americans also established substantial niches among the longshoremen and transit workers at one time or another, and dominated the city's police department for decades. Irish-American occupational niches were common elsewhere as well. In David Emmon's Butte, Montana, Irish immigrants monopolized jobs in the city's copper mines, for example. Networks, then, were not merely bridges across the Atlantic, not merely means for the immigrants to get to the United States and weather their initial adaptations. They were essential parts of ethnic life for generations after the immigrants had passed away. As Charles Tilly has suggested, they were like vines that, once transplanted and stimulated by American necessity, flourished, grew, and transformed into ever expanding new webs in America.[27]

Networks, then, were and still are beneficial and sustaining for immigrants and their descendants. But they have another side. The more people depend on them, the thicker the links and bonds among such friends and relatives can become, and thus the harder it can be to even see outside the network, much less break out of them and grab new opportunities—to think, perhaps, not of being a fireman or a policeman, but, God forbid, a lawyer. That may have been part of the problem with upward mobility in the Northeast. Here, slower-growing economies and elites hostile and entrenched in their own networks made upward progress more difficult and helped push Irish Americans back into reliance on the help of their own people. As second-generation Irish John F. O'Connor told a St. Patrick's Day audience in Worcester, Massachusetts, in 1899:

> Where if I am a lawyer must I get my clientage? In the police court? One doesn't get rich there. . . . The young American steps out of college and is looked after. He has friends and connections to look after him and at the outset steps into a position of $3,000 a year while our Irish young men have to give themselves to menial work.

In the East, too, there were many competing ethnic groups—Italians, Jews, Poles, French Canadians, and others—all scrambling to establish their own niches in the economy and defend them against ethnic rivals. Such thick, fractious societies in northeastern cities thus seemed to inevitably reinforce Irish Americans living there to depend on friends and relatives.[28]

Irish-American upward mobility would eventually happen in the northeastern United States. If mid- or late-nineteenth-century immigrants or their children moved up painfully slowly, economic progress would accelerate swiftly for later Irish-American generations. They would pull even with or surpass Irish Americans in other regions, particularly the South, and match the achievements of most other ethnic groups in their own region. Joel Perlmann has found that Irish Americans pulled abreast of Native Stock American "Yankees" in Providence, Rhode Island, by the 1920s, and Andrew Greeley points to steady progress by Irish-American Catholics up the economic ladder after that decade. The reason their achievements began to match their Irish counterparts elsewhere in America appears to lie largely in the dynamism of the economies in the northeast United States: whether it was New York City's persistent renewals to maintain itself as the headquarters of the nation's economy or southern New England's dramatic transformation from textiles to computers. Why Irish Americans in those places were suddenly able to take advantage of those opportunities is less clear. Obviously they were more at home than their parents or grandparents with their environment and their environment with them. Yet was it because they were able to break from old networks and exploit opportunities as individuals, or was it because they cashed in on ever-expanding and ever-richer webs of connections?

This peek inside the Irish American home, called "St. Patrick's Day in America," was made by Philadelphia lithographers in 1872. It is striking for its portrayal of domestic material comforts that contrast with far more pervasive slum images, as well as for its attention to details of ethnic fidelity such as the framed print of St. Patrick, the green flag of Ireland over the Civil War portrait, and the little girl's "God Save Ireland" pennant. (Library of Congress, Prints and Photographs Division, LC-USZC4-12303)

It may be useful to point out, as Paula Fass reports, that through the middle of the twentieth century, ambitious and mobile Irish-American Catholics were *more* likely, not less to attend Catholic schools—that is, the success of most, certainly not all, of these ambitious Irish came by moving up, through the ethnic and religious community, not by escaping it.[29]

Yet the progress had been slow, at least through the early twentieth century, and the frustrations of slow progress echoed powerfully not just through Irish-American culture but through all of American popular culture as well. Oddly enough, perhaps the most interesting thing about Irish-American economic performance was not what actually happened (little success initially, galloping progress later) but how they and the broader American culture talked about it.

For no other group in America did the issues of upward mobility and status seem so important as for Irish Americans. No other group's members have seemed more obsessed with mobility's pain and costs; none have seemed so self-conscious about what changes in status meant. Even the Jews, I think, have not been so self-conscious about status and mobility—Woody Allen, Philip Roth, and Abraham Cahan notwithstanding. Think of John O'Hara, slavering over the WASP elite and nursing wounds of Irish exclusion over a lifetime of twelve novels, five novellas, and fifteen collections of short stories. Or F. Scott Fitzgerald, more genteel, but only slightly less fixated on the same issues. Irish-American status and mobility was also a theme in Eugene O' Neill's work, particularly in his *A Touch of the Poet*. Yet it was not so much in high culture as in popular culture that the Irish-American pursuit of mobility seemed so painfully, if farcically, examined and traced. What other group had a phrase, so rich in its connotation of middle-class pretensions and self-consciousness, and so publicly recognizable as "lace curtain." The Jewish "allrightnik" just did not have the same public resonance or lyricism. Irish-American mobility and its pains, as Bill Williams has pointed out, saturated American popular culture at the turn of the century. It became a staple of Harrigan and Hart and Finley Peter Dunne, for example, and it was the central conceit of the comic strip, "Maggie and Jiggs."[30]

There are undoubtedly many reasons for this obsession. The struggle that the Irish endured to make it in the new environments of the Northeast was certainly one, but there were others as well. One intriguing possibility may be traced back to Ireland and the distinctiveness of its colonialism there. It was not just that the Irish were poor peasants there; it was that once upon a time many of their families had not been poor, or so they thought, and this distinguished them from many of the poor peasant immigrants from other countries who flooded America. As Arthur Young reported from Ireland in the 1770s:

> The lineal descendants of the old families are now to be found all over the island working as cottiers on lands which were once their own. In such great revolutions of property, the ruined proprietors have usually been extirpated or banished. In Ireland the case was otherwise.

Young elaborated that the old Catholic gentry, now impoverished, did not forget their past status: "It is a fact that in most parts of the kingdom the descendants of the old landowners regularly transmit by testamentary deed memories of their right to those estates which belonged to their families." Such memories lingered into the nineteenth century. In August of 1835, Alexis de Tocqueville, for example, "found [himself] this morning on top of the coach beside an old Catholic [who] went on to tell me what had been the fate of a great many families and a multitude of estates, passing from the time of Cromwell to that of William III with terrifying exactitude." Playing upon such memories, nourishing them, sharpening their edge was an Irish language literature, largely poetry, which derided the English landholders as clumsy, nouveau riche oafs. Prophecies, too, like that of "Signor Pastorini's" were racing through Munster and other parts of Ireland in the 1820s, promising that these fortunes would soon be reversed—Protestants would be cast down and Catholics "restored" to their lands— could only have nourished such memories, too.[31]

We can make too much of this. Certainly we did in our family—"we're all descended from kings," in a kind of Shirley MacLaine channeling, reincarnation sort of way. Genealogists delight in this. No one has ever had ancestors who fed the pigs, could count only two teeth by the time they were fifteen, and died mercifully amid the muck of someone else's livestock.

Still, what is relevant here is not the truth of such memories (except when they pertain to the O'Meaghers) as their power and their ramifications in the culture of future Irish immigrants. As Kevin Whelan and others have pointed out, such memories helped fuel the fires of O'Connellite nationalism. Yet they must have had other effects as well. The memory of once being on top and then being pushed to the bottom—true or not—must have made Irish people and thus Irish immigrants, perhaps even their descendants, acutely aware or sensitive to the fragility of status and the vulnerability of wealth and position. The downturn in the Irish economy after 1815 that reduced so many families—my own mother's family, the McDermotts in Louth, for example, or the Narys and Hanlys from Bob Scally's Ballykilcline—could only have sharpened that sensitivity as well.[32]

What gave that lesson its sting—its poignancy and power—for the Irish, however, was the bitter and painful degradation that they had now fallen to: the unrelenting and hopeless poverty, the rags they wore, the hovels they lived in, the thousand and one bitter humiliations and gestures of deference that their new servility required.

This degradation was not just individual, but collective, and it was fixed, cast in powerful images by stereotypes of Irishmen on the stage. Paddy was not just poor and servile but ridiculous, and if his talk of pretensions to a genteel past might have made some landlords or colonial administrators squirm, it only made him seem all the more ridiculous to theater audiences in Britain and America.[33]

Whatever its sources, there are a couple of interesting patterns in this Irish-American obsession with mobility and status. The first is a very interesting distinction made in popular culture between Irish-American men and Irish-American women in their attitudes toward upward mobility. Women are almost always depicted as socially and economically ambitious. From Harrigan and Hart's Cordelia Mulligan to Finley Peter Dunne's Molly Donahue to Maggie of Maggie and Jiggs, it is women who aspire to a better life, women who dream of moving up, women who seize the chances to become "swells," and women who are intent on acting respectably. Men, in contrast, are laggards, indifferent—even opposed—to improving their status, and slyly poking fun at their wives' or daughters' pretensions. It is the men who are happy with the old life, and in particular, the community of old friends found in the old neighborhood and at the bar in the old tavern.

In a way, such depictions simply reflect a broader, longtime cultural stereotype that women are shallow, lightheaded, and easily bedazzled by the frivolous: parties, clothes, and the like. Yet there seems to be more than that going on here, and it is somewhat puzzling. It is true that Irish-American women were probably more familiar with middle-class life, its customs and values. As servants, Irish immigrant women had daily lessons in the proprieties of middle- or upper-class life, and their daughters, American-born women, were probably more successful than their second-generation Irish brothers. Daughters of Irish immigrants were particularly successful in finding teaching or other white-collar jobs, as Janet Nolan has recently pointed out.[34]

Yet should we take this popular culture representation at face value? Did Irish-American women have no communal ties, no friends, no relatives that they lamented leaving—no ties of loyalty? In fact, in the migration process, it was often women who bought those tickets for relatives, for sisters and brothers back in Ireland. It was domestic servants, too, who poured out their pennies, nickels, and dimes to build churches in America as a host of parish histories attest. It was those same serving girls

On 25 October 1920, the day Cork's Lord Mayor Terence MacSwiney died after seventy-three days on hunger strike in England, Irish-American protesters took to the streets to chastise the United States for its support of Great Britain, which continued to refuse to recognize the Irish Republic that had been declared at Easter in 1916. Although unidentified by the photographer, the women were probably members of the American Women Pickets for the Enforcement of America's War Aims, a loose national coalition that had been formed earlier that year. The Women Pickets orchestrated a boycott of British manufactured goods, as well as a strike on the New York City docks against loading cargo on British ships, all in support of MacSwiney. They telegrammed British Prime Minister Lloyd George in August: "The sound of death in the throat of Terence MacSwiney is the death knell of your adventure in Ireland." (Library of Congress, Prints and Photographs Division, LC-USZ62-6058)

who filled the seats of St. Patrick's Day concerts and speeches. In Worcester, in the late nineteenth century, some observers said the "live-in girls" made up half the audiences for the big St. Patrick's Day concerts. We are also only just beginning to investigate the roles of women in nationalist movements, from the Ladies Land League in the 1880s to the nationalist strike on the Chelsea Piers here in 1920. And, of course—until about twenty years ago—there was scarcely a boy or a girl in all of Irish-American history who did not have a maiden aunt, who took him or her Christmas shopping, or helped pay his or her tuition to St. Rose or St. Malachy or St. Somewhere Academy. Irish-American women often clearly seemed to align themselves on the side of respectability in the Irish-American community, but that did not make them enemies of community.[35]

That is not how the popular culture depicted it, however. It may have been not so much that men or women in the Irish-American community had different ideas about upward mobility; it may have been that Americans simply could not imagine an Irishman or an Irish-American man comfortable in white tie and tails, an easily graceful member of the upper class. Thomas Beer in his book about turn-of-the-century life, *The Mauve Decade*, tells a story of a rich, millionaire Irish American sitting down to dinner at a posh party and confronting a young woman, whom he had overheard talking about him. Exasperated, the rich Irish American says, "Did you expect me to bring a pig and shillelagh with me?" She replied, "Oh dear no! I don't suppose you even keep a pig? . . . Do you?" Yet Irish Americans themselves seemed to believe this. In a famous passage from John O'Hara's novel, *Butterfield 8*, the main character, Jimmy Molloy, confesses:

> I want to tell you something about myself that will help to explain a lot of things about me. You might as well hear it now. First of all, I am a Mick. I wear Brooks clothes and I don't eat salad with a spoon and I probably could play five-goal polo in two years, but I am a Mick. Still a Mick. Now it's taken me a little time to find this out, but I have at last discovered that there are not two kinds of Irishmen. There's only one kind. . . . What I want to say, what I started out to explain was why I said "you people, you members of the upper crust," and so on, implying that I am not a member of it. Well, I'm not a member of it.

Eugene O'Neill echoed such sentiments in his tragic play *A Touch of the Poet*. In that play the principal character, Major Con Melody, had flaunted a glorious Irish past, invoking an aristocratic lineage and boasting of martial heroism, before the Yankees of a New England Village in the 1820s. Yet he is eventually broken by their rejection of him and his daughter, and he descends into the depths of Paddy. He shoots the fine charger he had ridden through the town, sheds his Anglo-Irish accent for a thick brogue, and begins drinking with the peasant, immigrant navvies, for he recognizes that he is one of them now—was always one of them, but just did not know it: "He'll nivir again hurt you with sneers," he says referring to himself in the third person, "and his pretendin' he's a gentleman, blatherin pride and honor, showing off before the Yankees and them laughin at him." In Irish-American high culture, Irish Americans were often doomed to be Paddy or Mick forever.[36]

Yet Irish-American makers of popular culture like Ned Harrigan saw this differently. As Bill Williams pointed out in his book, *'Twas Only an Irishman's Dream*, Harrigan and others had been working for a generation in the late nineteenth century to transform the stereotype of Paddy. They did not do away with it, they only inverted the image: that is, they made Paddy's defects into virtues. The Irish-American Paddy's failure to move up, his resistance to leaving his fellows, was not a tragedy but a triumph—even if it was played out with some comic antics, and even if Irish-American women had to be made into ludicrous, ambitious, social climbing harpies in the process. In a merger of Irish-American communalism and American democratic celebrations of the common man, the Irish-American man would became the archetype of the "regular guy," the "average joe," who rejected aristocratic pretension, snobbery, and the blandishments of society and stood with his own, his boys.[37]

Irish Americans, however, had long before claimed that title. Since Andrew Jackson's day, their rhetoric had often rung with attacks on aristocrats and celebrations of "we the people." Men like Mike Walsh had made that rhetoric and that pose their specialty. Denouncing Yankee mill owners and lamenting the oppression of white workers in New Yorkese and a Cork brogue, and clad in workingmen's rough clothes, Walsh was a tough guy and a notorious drinker (he drank himself to death on St. Patrick's Day in 1859). He seemed to perfect the image early on of the Irish-American man of the people, even if he was born to the Church of Ireland in his native Youghal and his Spartan political club of roughnecks sometimes went toe to toe with Irish Catholics on the streets of New York's Five Points. By the 1830s, the new Irish Catholic majority in cities like New York had toppled their own inherited leaders, the Republican elite of the 1798 exiles, in favor of poorer men, born of less genteel station.[38]

Such common men, Daniel Patrick Moynihan has pointed out, worked a transformation in American politics. What Moynihan said of the Irish in New York City could be said of Boston, Chicago, and a host of other cities: "New York City became the first great city in history to be ruled by men of the people, not as an isolated phenomenon of the Gracchi or the Commune, but as a persisting established pattern."[39]

And yet, and yet, it was an odd revolution. It resulted not in a radical transformation—not a reworking of the economy and an overthrow of established society but the rise of the boss and his political machine. As Moynihan argued, the boss was a man of the people, or, at least more often, men of the people than his reformer antagonists. Bosses usually came from the poor, as observers as diverse as Moynihan, George Washington Plunkitt, and Thomas Merton have pointed out. "Honest John" Kelly might marry Cardinal McCloskey's niece, and Richard Croker might raise horses on an estate in Ireland, and even James Michael Curley might build a big house with shamrocks on the shutters in Jamaica Plain, but many of the machine men, the best of the bosses, never forgot their origins and had few pretensions to being gentleman. Indeed, even their title testified to their position of power without social distinction, for the word "boss," as David Roediger has brilliantly argued, was an invention of the new American republic to describe authority without invoking aristocracy.[40] The boss was not the master or lord; he may have been in charge, but he was of us—not "quality," not better.

More important, the ethos of the machine was communal, friendship, connections. The greatest ward boss of all time, Martin Lomasney of the West End in Boston, told Lincoln Steffens that in 1915. His words invoked frequently ever since, Lomasney told Steffens that day: "There's got to be in every ward somebody that any bloke can come to—no matter what he's done—and get help. Help, you understand, none of your law and justice, but help." The machine was a network on a ward or citywide scale, a political network of personal linkages. Like most networks, the machine was held together by communal values of reciprocity and the exchange of concrete benefits. The boss gave out jobs, peddler's licenses, contracts, even turkeys at Christmas or buckets of coal in winter; Irish immigrant voters and their children reciprocated with their votes. Steven Erie has said the jobs were few and not very good; he believed that the Irish were better off without them. But the Irish in the Northeast had few connections in industry and fewer skills that they could sell there. The spoils of office, the niche that they carved out in government, was, in many ways, the only employment niche that they had.[41]

Still would it not have been better if Irish Americans had worked a real revolution —not parceling out turkeys or jobs piecemeal, but forcing through legislation that changed the very structure of the economy and ensured that all poor people could eat or find work? Not divisible benefits for the few, but universal benefits for all?

But in the early twentieth century, Irish-American politicians did just that. Irish Americans in machines and outside them, fought for a whole bevy of reforms in legislatures across the Northeast and Midwest in the 1910s. The most notable example was here in New York, where Al Smith (partnered with German American ally Robert Wagner) capitalized on the outrage over the Triangle Shirtwaist Fire in 1911 to push through a whole host of reforms: factory safety, welfare, labor legislation, and limited working hours for women and children. Behind Smith and Wagner stood the power of the greatest city boss in history, Charles Francis Murphy. Murphy had stepped up from rule of the East Side's Gas House District to become the greatest boss in the history of the Wigwam, Tammany's headquarters. He is reputed to have said of Smith's and Wagner's reforms simply: "Give the people what they want."[42]

This "urban liberalism" was not confined to New York State. All across the Northeast and Midwest, as John Buenker detailed long ago, Irish Catholic–led Democrats had taken over state legislatures and state houses and pushed through legislation curbing the power of big business, laying the groundwork for the welfare state with widows' pensions and workmen's compensation. This took place, more or less, in Ohio, Rhode Island, Illinois, Connecticut, and Massachusetts. In Massachusetts, none other than Martin Lomasney, the Democratic leader in the Massachusetts House, was helped by the state's first Irish Catholic governor, David Ignatius (called David "Ignore us" by some of us from his homeland of Worcester County, Massachusetts) Walsh.[43]

This spate of reform took place during what historians call the Progressive Era, but it is not the model of progressivism that many historians then or since have found most comfortable. To those historians, reform came from elites, middle-class experts, armed with their expertise and their desire to rationalize society, or from women of conscience, intent on ameliorating the problems of the poor. But what Buenker was talking about came from below. It was rooted in the communalism of Irish and other Catholics and the social justice traditions of American Jews. The government should "help," as Lomasney said, and in the rough democratic charge Murphy enunciated, if the people want it, give the people what they want.[44]

Irish-American Democratic liberalism was not limited to the 1910s. Roots of this Irish-American government activism could be traced back to the working-class republicanism that flourished in the nineteenth century among the Irish Americans in the Knights of Labor in the 1880s or, as David Doyle pointed out years ago, more specifically among Irish-American editors of Catholic newspapers across the country who turned sharply left after the 1893 Depression.[45]

And it would continue on into the 1930s and 1940s. Some Irish-American politicians, in New York City and in Boston, would look upon Franklin Roosevelt with a jaundiced eye, but for others such as David Lawrence in Pittsburgh and Edward Kelly in Chicago, Roosevelt was, in Kelly's words, their "religion." Irish-American voters from Boston to Chicago would also vary in their enthusiasm for Roosevelt, but even in Boston, neither the spread of Father Coughlin's rancid racism nor the rising isolationist suspicions of intervention on behalf of the British Empire in 1940 would prevent Irish-American Democratic majorities.[46]

The New Deal and Harry Truman's Fair Deal made Irish Americans more powerful than ever before (the Fair Deal under Truman with its cabinet of Hannegan, Tobin, and McGrath was perhaps even more powerful than the New Deal). Irish Americans also steamrolled into power in state houses, through a "Bloodless Revolution" in Rhode Island in the 1930s led by Robert Emmet Quinn among others, for example, and a state house takeover in Massachusetts in the 1940s led by Paul Dever and Thomas P. "Tip" O'Neill.[47]

Their own brand of politics also came into its own. Rooted in the old communalism, it was populist or democratic in its rhetoric and masculine in its pose and bearing (even though Irish-American Catholic women like Mary Irene Atkinson and Jane Hoey would play important roles in the creation of the New Deal welfare state). They were regular-guy Democrats anchored in ethnic neighborhoods and spokesmen for common men and women.[48]

Yet it was not just in politics that this Irish, "regular guy," communal populism seemed to flourish. As Jim Fisher has pointed out, a whole host of Irish newspaper columnists and sportswriters had emerged by the 1950s, who were all pledged to celebration of the "regular guy," the street savvy, gritty "average joe." They included Ed Sullivan, Jack O'Brien, and Jimmy Kilgallen. Fisher tells of one Irish-American show biz columnist who derided a comic for being too intellectual: stop being so high falutin', was his advice; talk to a cab driver, someone real. This voice has a long history. Finley Peter Dunne, speaking through his Mr. Dooley a half century earlier, stood for the voice of common sense and the "average joe" against all pretension. Yet this voice seemed to become more powerful in the 1940s and 1950s, buoyed by the New Deal's celebration of the Common Man and World War II's heroes, the GI's.[49]

I should warn you, if you have not already guessed: I identify with this tradition. It is my grandfather's and father's tradition. My grandfather, the son of an Irish immigrant from Tipperary, was chairman of the Democratic City Committee in Worcester, Massachusetts, in the 1890s and an alderman in Worcester's city government in the early 1900s. Pictures of him and the Democrats of the city or county of Worcester on outings at lakes and ponds around central Massachusetts line my living room walls: rows of mustachioed men in boaters or derbies and wing collars staring happily into the camera. My father was an avid young New Dealer but rose to become treasurer of the Democratic Party in Massachusetts under Paul Dever in the late 1940s. Dever later appointed him to the state's Superior Court bench. I think of my father and his friends, men in fedoras and gray or blue suits with wide lapels, and their talk, sharp-witted and needling but also blunt and direct—straight-talking. They were staunch Democrats, resentful of the pretensions of Yankee elites, delighted to claim representation of common men and women, but men who were also tough and practical, who loved power and respected "heavyweights."

It is a nice story: how Irish egalitarian communalism merged with American democracy to make Irish Americans advocates for the common man and woman. And yet is it true? There are many questions.

For one thing, we are not exactly sure when Irish Americans became committed to the anti-aristocratic egalitarianism of republicanism, or, indeed, if they ever embraced it fully. Even after Irish Catholic Democrats rallied to Andrew Jackson and his successors in their attacks on privilege and aristocracy, plays by Dion Boucicault and others featuring clever peasant heroes but also virtuous Irish gentry flourished in the theaters of New York and other cities across the country. The invention of the clever peasant, a Boucicault transformation of the Irish fool, is easy to understand, but why the persistent deference to goodhearted gentle folk in such plays, and even more puzzling, why were those plays and thus that deference so popular among Irishmen glorying in the rough equality of New York streets? Eventually, Harrigan and Hart and others would create new characters in new settings—city toughs on the streets of New York or Philadelphia or Chicago, who would push Boucicault and his Irish gentry and peasants off the stage and put the bricklayer, the cop, the Tammany pol, all Irish-American regular guys, in their place.[50]

There was, however, another Irish-American cultural tradition, not so broadly popular but certainly powerful, which kept this deference to aristocrats alive. That was an emerging tradition of American Catholic novelists and short story writers like Mary Sadlier, Father John Boyce, and others. Here gentry of proper Catholic devotion and faithful Irish peasants were also celebrated and continued to be so until late in the nineteenth century. The villains here were upstarts, men on the make, greedy Methodists and Baptists, good capitalists, who destroyed community and tried to defy the natural rule of the well bred.[51]

And, of course, the Church itself remained committed to a hierarchically organized society throughout the nineteenth century. As John McGreevy points out, most Catholics did not oppose slavery because they did not necessarily see a republican world divided simply between slave and free; they saw a pre-republican, pre–American Revolution world of different statuses, different social roles—gentlefolk, clergy, commoners, servants, and slaves. Slave subordination should not be galling in a society of ranks where few were fortunate enough to be at the top and most were layered below, but where everyone knew and accepted his or her distinct place. American Catholic Church leaders adapted this view of society to the American republic, though they did so slowly and with some difficulty, as McGreevy makes clear. Still, the nature of the church itself, with a very clear hierarchy and lines of authority, contrasted sharply with this emerging populism—of the "regular-guy" Democrat. Indeed, it is one of the great paradoxes of Irish-American life that the princes of the church, such as William O'Connell of Boston and his rival Francis Spellman in New York, became more grand in their tastes, more insistent on their privileges, and more authoritarian in their demands for obedience in the twentieth century, even as Irish-American, regular-guy Democrats rose to the zenith of their power.[52]

That paradox, that juggling act, I cannot resolve here, but there are other questions about Irish-American regular-guy Democrats that are more pressing. If Lincoln Steffens, the great muckraker, lapped up Martin Lomasney's invocation of communalism that day, listening to the great ward boss wax philosophic in his office, it nonetheless should give us pause. James Connolly, who has written brilliantly about turn of the century politics in Boston, has pointed out that the communalism of the machine—

indeed, he has written specifically about Lomasney's machine—was often not so much the communalism of the neighborly as it was the greasy fellowship of the crony. Lomasney's "help" was not available to everyone, but only those willing to pay back and toe the line. And what good did the "help" of kickbacks, no-show jobs, and rake-offs do for the common good of poor communities? A whole generation of historians and scholars from the 1940s through the 1970s found much to admire in machine politics and bosses, but it is well to be wary of sentimentalizing Irish bosses, as Connolly and Steven Erie have pointed out more recently.[53]

Ultimately, bosses were interested in power. If they played upon traditions of communal loyalty in their constituencies, or if communal loyalties reflected some of their own values, they were, nonetheless, bottom-line men who wanted to rule. They included men like Frank "I Am the Law" Hague in Jersey City, who would resort to violence, suppression of civil liberties, and ballot-box tampering to hold on to power. Even Murphy's dictum, "give the people what they want," might be seen not so much as a rallying cry as the crafty maneuver of an astute politician who did what he had to do to win.[54]

Yet Murphy's command can also be read, I think, as both a clever political tactic and a kind of concession of failure. A number of historians and scholars have agreed that machine politicians might give into the people's wishes, but they could not articulate the people's needs and seemed unable to devise legislative solutions to meet them. As Daniel Patrick Moynihan has acidly asserted, "the Irish did not know what to do with power once they got it." Absent pressure from others, below or outside, they could not lead, because they had no ideas.[55]

Catholic social thought might have filled that gap. In the early twentieth century, Monsignor John A. Ryan wrote powerfully about the rights of workers to a living wage, national health insurance, and a variety of other reforms, while castigating excessive ambition and wealth in books, speeches, and articles like the one intriguingly entitled "The Fallacy of Bettering Oneself."[56]

But Catholic social thought came with its own burdens, such as its misty longing for the imagined communal harmonies of the medieval era. *The Thirteenth: The Greatest of All Centuries*, a popular book among American Catholics in the 1920s, would have been a hard sell for Irish Catholic politicians to make to their non-Catholic neighbors on the campaign trail. Al Smith's cry, "What the hell is an encyclical?" during the 1928 presidential campaign and his more formal, measured reply to his critic, Charles Marshall, "so little are these matters of the essence of my faith that I, a devout Catholic since childhood, never heard of them," may have been less a confession of ignorance of Catholic thought than a candid acknowledgement of an Irish-American politician's long-time calculated strategy of avoiding its potential encumbrances.[57]

Indeed, Irish-American politicians were not simply often bereft of ideas but appeared suspicious of them and the intellectuals who talked about them. The Church's dogmatism and its insistence on the perfect completeness of its neo-Thomist thought —and thus its refusal to countenance intellectual exploration or debate—encouraged such suspicion. So, in a way, did its militant opposition to communism and socialism.

Though most Catholic social thought would prove too complex and encumbered for Irish-American politicians to advocate, such politicians would find it too easy to pick out from the Church's thinking opposition to socialism and communism and mesh that opposition with American values and patriotism. This antiradicalism often became another reason to suspect ideas, visions, and programs and became a crippling diversion from reform, even for those who were committed to change and the interests of the poor.[58]

Irish-American communal, regular-guy politics in the early twentieth century was a complicated mix. It was more progressive than is usually credited, at least within the narrow ideological spectrum of American politics. Moreover, led by politicians who loved power and loved using it, and rooted in American urban, working-class neighborhoods, it boasted a technical virtuosity and grounding in the experiences of average, working people, which later generations of American Democrats could only hope for. (The technical virtuosity has not disappeared, amazingly, but is not limited to the Democrats now. Two Irish Americans, both graduates of Catholic University of America, chaired the two major parties in 2004: Ed Gillespie of the Republicans and Terry McAulliffe of the Democrats.) And yet it had trouble translating the experience of those people into broad positions and policies and could not be harnessed to a consistent progressivism.

Irish antisocialism and anticommunism had long roots. The first big wave came in the 1900s and 1910s, when the Church launched an antisocialist crusade that became so insistent that one reader wrote to his Irish-American newspaper, asking them to just stop talking about socialism all the time. The real surge, of course, took place in the 1940s and 1950s when Irish-American antiradicalism reached its climax, embodied in the dark and snarling presence of Joseph McCarthy. This was an important phase in Irish-American communal, regular-guy politics, for many strands came together. McCarthyism was not just another eruption of Irish Americans' long-time antiradicalism; it was also a new phase in Irish-American populist antielitism. Anticommunism became a weapon for a new, larger, and more demanding Irish-American and Catholic middle class to assail the Protestant establishment. It also wedged and widened the gap separating Irish and other regular-guy, Catholic Democrats from liberal intellectual Democrats. These trends, of course, often overlapped, as in Massachusetts, where Irish-American anticommunism became an anti-Harvard movement. Both these trends would come to fruition in the 1960s and 1970s, when the Protestant establishment would come tumbling down, and Ellis Island would come to rival and, perhaps, surpass Plymouth Rock as the nation's mythical birthplace.[59]

In those decades, too, many white ethnics, Irish and others, would begin to abandon the Democratic Party, first here in New York and then in many other states. By 1984, Ronald Reagan, of Irish ancestry himself, would roll up heavy majorities among Irish Catholics in states like New York and Illinois. Was this an escape from communalism by the upwardly mobile, flush with confidence in their individual abilities now untrammeled? Maybe, but the rhetoric was still often communal, and the pose populist. The new Irish-American Republicans—in language articulated by people such as Peggy Noonan—often talked of protecting the "average joe" from elites, this time liberal ones, and communities from intrusive government bureaucracies. It seems a long way from Charlie Murphy to Bill O'Reilly and Sean Hannity, but the path is there to trace.[60]

And yet, and yet, the death of regular-guy Democrats, to play upon the old Mark Twain cliché, may have been greatly exaggerated. It was, after all, Tip O'Neill, with all his weaknesses, including being a near stereotype of the Irish "pol," who emerged as Ronald Reagan's principal, if sometimes reluctant, shuffling opponent. Irish Catholics in Massachusetts did not vote for Nixon in 1972 or even Reagan in 1984 (though the state went for the president in the latter year). One might understand O'Neill and those votes as a last gasp of Irish-American Democrats. And yet today southern New England, with the heaviest concentration of Irish-American Catholics in the country, is also a Democratic Party bastion and contains some of the most liberal states in the union. Obviously, not all the Irish there are liberals or progressives or whatever terms we might use—there have been enough Louise Day Hickses, Albert Dapper O'Neills, and Eddie Kings—but many *are* liberals or progressives like current Massachusetts Congressman James McGovern, his mentor the late Congressman Joseph Moakley, or Rhode Island Representative Patrick Kennedy. Even the conservative Irish Americans have often remained Democrats. The result, at least in Rhode Island and Massachusetts, is a mixed-up political culture of cigar-smoking, back-slapping, sometimes corrupt Irish and Italian pols, who look like extras left over from John Ford's movie of Edwin O'Connor's *Last Hurrah*, and rafts of liberal legislation.

The reasons for this paradoxical combination are complex. Irish Americans hung on in the Democratic Party in Massachusetts and Rhode Island, at least in part, because it was still theirs; they still ran it, and it was still a useful vehicle for their ambitions (this had become less true in states like New York, for example, where the shift to the Republican Party was more decisive among Irish Americans.) Yet, the Irish commitment to the Democrats in New England might not have been entirely out of self-interest. The traces of communal antielitist regular-guy democracy cut a different way in the southern New England political culture for many Irish Americans in the region than for their fellow Celts elsewhere. Colleagues of Tip O'Neill on Capitol Hill —like the Republican Senator Howard Baker, for example—were astounded at the depth, power, and endurance of the Speaker's resentments of WASP privilege that O'Neill still felt from his youth. O'Neill preferred to think of it in other terms. After a tempestuous meeting with Ronald Reagan, O'Neill claimed: "He [Reagan] and I both came from the same side of the railroad tracks. I never forgot where I came from. He kind of forgot." It may not be such a long way from Martin Lomasney to a Boston Irish politician like the late Joe Moakley or even a Worcester one, Jim McGovern.[61]

Interestingly, though Irish-American politics has become more complicated in the last thirty years, that is not how Hollywood and television have seen it. In American popular culture, Irish-American men, in particular, have become the principal symbols of a corrupt and reactionary old order. From the movie *Joe* in 1970 to the most recent comedy, *It's All Relative* on ABC, Irish Catholics have seemed the quintessence of populist conservatism, embodied most recently in television's most popular conservative talk show hosts: O'Reilly and Hannity. Part of the explanation for the Irish-American image of reaction is rooted in perceptions of their regular-guy resentments of liberal elites, but perhaps an even more important cause has been the reputation Irish Americans have gained as racists. Through films from *Ragtime* and *True Confessions* to *L.A. Confidential* and in television shows as diverse as *Seinfeld* and *Homicide: Life on the Street*, Irish-American men have become consensus icons of reactionary racial attitudes in America.[62]

Sometime after this image began to develop in American popular culture, the Irish have become the focus of a new, powerful interpretation of the American past—a school of history—loosely a school called "whiteness studies." While whiteness historians have been interested in the broad problem of how the white race was made, how people learned that their white skin set them apart and established them as a privileged people, they have been particularly intrigued by the problem of how the Irish "became" white. As Eric Arnesen has pointed out, "the phrase 'how the Irish became white' has been repeated so often as to have become cliché. To numerous scholars the notion that the non white Irish became white has become axiomatic."[63]

The Irish are intriguing to whiteness scholars for several reasons: in part, because of the ferocity of their racism in such explosions of rage as the Draft Riots of 1863 and, in part, because they were such a substantial component of the white poor, white working class, who, if they had made common cause with American blacks or Chinese immigrants, might have revolutionized American life. Yet it is the poignancy of the Irish "choice" to become white that strikes whiteness historians, too, for here were people who came to America not only innocent of American notions of white and black—perfect examples of people who had to learn how to become white—but here were people who had been ruthlessly and systematically oppressed themselves in Ireland. As Theodore Allen, author of *Invention of the White Race* states: "No immigrants ever came to the United States better prepared by tradition and experience to empathize with the African Americans than the Irish, who were emerging directly from the historic struggle against racial oppression in their own country." Indeed, no less than Daniel O'Connell himself had seemed to understand the similarities and staunchly committed himself to the antislavery cause, as the whiteness historians have been quick to point out. There was a special tragedy, then, in Irish Catholic white racism, a kind of terrible irony: brutally oppressed in their own country and demeaned in this one, the Irish, nonetheless, "chose" to become oppressors themselves.[64]

Why did Irish Catholic immigrants choose not to stand with blacks? Why did they embrace white supremacy and thus became oppressors in their new home? There are many reasons, but most whiteness historians seem to believe that Irish Americans embraced whiteness and turned on blacks with a seemingly distinctive ferocity because they were afraid of being treated as blacks or nonwhites themselves. They were desperate not to be consigned to the American racial netherworld—desperate not to be black.[65]

Ironically, O'Neill's play *A Touch of the Poet* and O'Hara's novel *Butterfield 8* made this point years ago. In O'Neill's play, for example, when the Irish Major Con Melody tries to assert his status and thus his daughter's right to marry into a family of New England Yankees, servants, including a black servant prominently noted, bar his entry to the Yankees' house. And when O'Hara's Jimmy Molloy confesses to his girlfriend, Isabel, that he is a Mick, he points out that this self-revelation came to him after a descent into impoverished squalor. The only person who takes pity on him is a black servant woman, "the nigger woman," as he calls her, who brings him a sandwich and buys him some cigarettes. In America, then, O'Neill and O'Hara seem to say, if you fall far enough, you are in danger of falling below the depths of racial otherness, to depths where you look up to African Americans.[66]

Now there are lots of questions raised by historians about the whiteness school's interpretation of American working-class history in general and of Irish-American history in particular. Were any immigrants from Europe really in danger of becoming nonwhite, given the definition of naturalization laws from the 1790s? Wasn't the structure of racial boundaries in place long before Irish Catholics came to the United States in the early nineteenth century? Was it ever a given that poor people of all sorts of differences should come together naturally in class solidarity?[67]

But I would like to talk about aspects of this whiteness debate that pertain particularly to Irish Americans, and even more particularly pertain to the Irish communalism we are discussing here. Whiteness historians, I think, oversimplify how Irish history had prepared Irish immigrants to respond to America's racial divide. Even Irish peasants were aware, if dimly, of the racial hierarchies that ran through the western world in the early nineteenth century. William Carleton's peasants, for example, sprinkled their speech with epithets about blacks. So it is not clear that Ireland's peasants came here entirely ignorant—invincibly ignorant, as we Catholics used to say—of American racial attitudes. Still, whiteness historians are no doubt right to conclude that Irish immigrants come to America innocent of American racial practices. They may have heard about claims of black inferiority, even adopted it into their speech, but they were hardly familiar with it in all its foul realities. More important, the whiteness scholars seem to assume that Irish people came here with no idea of how groups related to each other, except for a simple sense of grievance against their own oppressors back in Ireland. Such scholars ignore Irish experience in group competition, conflict, boundaries, and loyalties in the homeland or assume that experience is irrelevant, when we know, as we have already discussed, that Ireland's history taught more lessons, bitter lessons than simply anticolonial nationalism or a potential sympathy for the underdog.[68]

It taught immigrants, as we have seen, the fragility, the vulnerability of status, for landowners could suddenly lose their land and be rudely forced down into the ranks of cottiers and laborers in a few generations. It taught them, too, as we noted before, that the means of prosperity—better, the means of survival (in Ireland this was only land)—were scarce, and that the only way to succeed or survive was to act together as members of a group. People needed to band together in secret societies to resist others, landlords, bailiffs, and other tenants, because their enemies' gains were inevitably their losses. And finally, it taught them about group boundaries, sharply and self-consciously drawn between Catholics and Protestants and sometimes violently defended or asserted. In the early nineteenth century, Irish immigration drew heavily from the Ulster borderlands where Protestants and Catholics had substantial populations and where sectarian violence was most common; consciousness of boundaries was thus most acute and defenses of them were most unyielding and desperate.[69]

So what did all this mean for the Irish in America? How did these lessons translate in the racially and ethnically diverse American environment? It meant, first, that if they had lost status before, it was easy enough to lose it again. It may have made Irish Americans especially sensitive to their vulnerability in the American racial hierarchy, that their few privileges of being white would be eliminated in the abolition of slavery, when African Americans and the ex-slaves' abolitionist, Republican allies would roll over them, the most impoverished and vulnerable of whites. There is a kind of satanic symmetry in the reversals of status predicted in popular Irish prophecies like Pastorini's at the beginning of the nineteenth century and dark hints of racial status reversal that filled the racist propaganda of the Democratic Party in America at the century's midpoint. It meant, too, that even in the abundance of America, Irish Americans would understand economic competition in group terms—that to succeed they must act together to fight competitors from other groups.

Whiteness historians ask why the Irish did not attack other groups or even other groups of Irishmen who competed for their jobs. The answer, of course—as we pointed out earlier—is that they did. Violence against blacks may have been more common because African and Asian Americans were so defenseless, abandoned by everyone, but Irishmen certainly attempted to exclude from jobs or streets or political power or church positions, Germans, Italians, Jews, or other Irishmen throughout the nineteenth and early twentieth centuries. In 1880 *New York Times* editors wrote with exasperation:

> The hospitable and generous Irishman has almost no friendship for any race but his own. As a laborer and politician he detests the Italian. Between him and the German American citizen there is great gulf fixed, but the most naturalized thing for the Americanized Irishman is to drive out all other foreigners, whatever may be their religious tenets.

Such sentiments were an exaggeration, as we shall see, but they do suggest that Irish Americans were not fixated on blacks in their prejudices but battled almost every group when they were moved to do so. Finally, it meant that Irish immigrants were simply used to the importance of group boundaries, of living with division—boundaries that might be crossed in the necessary interactions of day-to-day life but could suddenly crackle with hostility or erupt as violent battlegrounds with the least provocation.[70]

Whatever the weaknesses or strengths of the whiteness historians, they do call attention to a final question about Irish-American communalism. To use David Hollinger's phrasing: How wide was the circle of the Irish American's "we"?[71] Moreover, to whom did their communal loyalties extend? To whom did they not? Who was included and who excluded? Who was the "other"? Did Irish Americans' understanding of "we" change? Did their understanding of who was Irish American change, for example, or did they even define a "we" that stretched wider than Irish Americans? The *Times'* sour judgment depicts a people sunk in inevitable self-satisfied and pugnacious isolation. The unhappy story of Irish relations with racial minorities also suggests an Irish-American people holding fast to fixed boundaries and defending them ferociously. Yet, the very point that whiteness scholars make about Irish-American whiteness suggests not just a people ferociously defending an old boundary but learning to define a new one, of widening the circle of "we" (almost literally crowbar-ring it open) to plant themselves firmly among a "we" of whites. Irish-American conceptions of "we," the whiteness historians argue rightly, changed, but the suggestion by some of them, that this was just a change from Irish to white is much too simple. The story of how and why Irish Americans redefined "we," "our community," is more complicated than that.

The very meaning of being Irish American and the boundaries of an Irish-American group, for example, have changed over time in America—as they have for almost all immigrant groups confronting this new environment. Initially, for many, it was not clear that being Irish was as important as being from Cork or Kerry, Mayo or Longford. Sometimes Irish men fought other Irishmen, drawing the boundaries by county of origin in Ireland. In Lowell and Worcester, Massachusetts, and along the Chesapeake and Ohio Canal in Maryland, Irishmen from different counties battled each other in tenement allies, railroad cuts, and canal ditches.[72]

Religion was another significant, though not inevitable, division among Irishmen. In the early nineteenth century, Irishmen fleeing the 1798 rebellion, still flush with dreams of a nonsectarian republican Ireland, hoped to define an Irish America that would include both Protestants and Catholics from Ireland. By 1871, when over sixty dead or dying littered Eighth Avenue in Chelsea on July 12th, Orange Day, that was clearly no longer the case. In fact, long before then, Protestants and Catholics had been forming into two distinct peoples in America.[73]

Yet the shaping and reshaping of the circle of "we" for Irish Americans was not merely a sorting and resorting of Irish identity. In the American world of diverse ethnic and racial groups, to stand alone in ethnic isolation could be political suicide—at least if a group's members had any pretensions to power. The practical necessities of urban, church, and labor union politics required groups to find friends and define and isolate enemies. Few aspects of Irish life in America so clearly distinguish it from the rest of the Irish diaspora—the Irish in Britain, the Irish in Canada and in Australia—than the way in which Irish Americans wove their way through America's multiethnic, multiracial social and political terrain: including, excluding, gathering friends in coalitions, and isolating enemies. I say this because nowhere else was there the same degree of diversity so early, and nowhere else were the Irish so well situated to perform this negotiating, brokering role, or both. Irish Americans assumed this role at the end of the nineteenth century. At that point, William Shannon has argued, Irish Americans had come to straddle a boundary: "The Irish were the group closest to being 'in' while still being out. . . . Of necessity the Irishman finding himself the man on the scene became a kind of go between," with "the American inner group," WASPs, on one side, and a bevy of immigrants, Germans, Italians, Poles, Greeks, Jews, and racial minorities on the other. Assuming that role at the turn of the century, Irish Americans performed it, more or less, through the 1960s in urban and state and national politics, as well as in the Church and in labor unions. I think this brokering, negotiating role defined Irish America as much as anything else in that era.[74]

Recent historians have taken note of how the Irish excluded many groups but have been skeptical of how much "including" the Irish did. They point to the stubborn, bitter fights Irish union men waged to keep new immigrants and racial minorities out of their organizations or even out of the country. They have also, however, attacked Irish political bosses and machine men, once fabled for their easy cultural pluralism and solicitousness of newcomers: George Washington Plunkitt wearing yarmulkes at Jewish funerals and "Big Tim" Sullivan pinning dollars to statues of saints at Italian festivals. To Steven Erie and James Connolly, Irish-American machine men seem more indifferent, even hostile, to new groups than welcoming. Erie and Connolly argue that Irish-American politicians were so intent on preserving their precious caches of jobs and favors for other Irish Americans that they only dealt with new groups when they were pushed, and then grudgingly gave up only the cheapest of the political spoils they had to offer. These are two excellent historians, and their points are well taken. Erie and Connolly do well to dispel the nostalgic, sentimental haze that men like Plunkitt and even Lomasney conjured up to cover their coldly calculating politics.[75]

And yet, for all of Erie's and Connolly's well-justified criticism, it can still be argued, as Shannon did (and the great political scientist D. W. Brogan before him did) that Irish Americans did, indeed, make themselves leaders of the outs by the turn of the century and in the process widened the circle of their "we." The coalitions they created were often leaky, fractious, and temporary. Political coalitions that were reinforced by Church ones, and vice versa, were more durable than any others, however. Through most of the first half of the twentieth century, Irish-American efforts to forge Democratic political coalitions and a pan-ethnic American Catholic Church ran in an uncanny, but mutually reinforcing parallel. By the 1920s, and certainly by the 1950s, most American-born Irish—second, third, or fourth generation and later— were more likely to call themselves American Catholics, a definition that included other Catholic ethnics, than call themselves Irishmen or even Irish Americans. They had widened the circle of "we" to include others, even if those others were dragged in kicking and screaming, drafted to serve Irish aims, and still often treated as inferiors.

They were not selfless doing so, but soberly calculating in pursuit of their own interests. Brokering coalitions made them more powerful. They rarely "welcomed" other groups, especially the "newer races"—Italian, Polish, and Lithuanian Americans —on an equal basis. If they called themselves American Catholics, it was certainly American Catholics with a difference, distinctly different from those other Catholics, they deemed, less than themselves.

And yet, and yet, few ever believed that Irish Americans would widen the circle of "we" unless they had to do so. Power was a business, even in the Church—or maybe especially in the Church—and if people wanted in on the power Irish Americans held, they had to push their way in. Even Erie and Connolly, however, acknowledge that, if pressed, Irish Americans would make accommodations to new groups. Often, as Erie notes, "Irish bosses turned to collective benefits as a way both of securing the new immigrant vote and of maintaining the Irish monopoly over divisible benefits." That is—ironically—the cheapest rewards were progressive laws. In Charlie Murphy's terms, "give the people what they want" in mothers' pensions, factory legislation, the income tax, and utility regulation, or even civil rights laws outlawing discrimination, rather than give up some of the precious patronage jobs slated for Irish men to Italians, Poles, and Jews. If this suggests that the Irish bosses were hardly sentimental and that the machine's ability or willingness to incorporate new immigrants into the political system has been much overrated, it also suggests that Irish bosses' brokering had some exceptionally rich and useful outcomes, no matter their pragmatic—indeed, selfish—motives.[76]

Irish-American brokering, though rigorously self-interested and practical, could have broader positive consequences for community welfare than simply Progressive legislation, as important a benefit as that may have been. The best example of this Irish community building may come not from the Eastern cities but from the Midwest—the city of St. Paul, Minnesota. There, a relatively small number of Irish, Mary Wingerd reports, made St. Paul an "Irish town" by working their way to the center of a number of competing ethnic and interest groups and smartly maneuvering among them. The Irish in St. Paul played the same game of selective exclusion and inclusion, pushing Scandinavian Republicans to the margin, cultivating Germans, and making deals between capital and labor that ensured—for a while—both industrial peace and labor rights in St. Paul. If self-interestedness was always the principal goal of their maneuvers, Wingerd argues, the Irish in St. Paul nonetheless fostered a civic cohesion and sense of St. Paul community that contrasted sharply with the exploitative, big business, free marketeering of neighboring Minneapolis.[77]

But if Irish Americans seemed capable of widening the circle of "we" to include other whites, if grudgingly and on their own terms, what of the furthest out of the outs: African and Asian Americans? Did the Irish remain trapped forever in the whiteness they had seized so desperately upon arrival in the mid–nineteenth century? For many years throughout the nineteenth and twentieth centuries they did, though they often showed more regard for the fates of distant, nonwhite colonial peoples like the Filipinos in the early twentieth century—finding analogies in the Philippines insurrection to rebellions in Ireland—than for the interests of their African and Asian American neighbors.[78]

In 1974 and 1975, the old Irish working-class neighborhoods of Boston, Charlestown, and South Boston exploded in furious opposition to busing ordered by federal courts to integrate the city's schools. These protests, often ugly and violent, filled with assaults on African Americans and vile epithets, had been the climax of a long resistance to school integration in the city, stretching back to the mid-1960s and led by Irish-American politicians like Louise Day Hicks and John Kerrigan. Boston was not an isolated case. Irish resistance to racial integration of neighborhoods had also erupted in cities like Philadelphia and Chicago from the 1950s through the 1960s.

By the 1960s and 1970s, however, Irish-American Catholic views of race were becoming far more complicated. In the 1960s, for example, Irish-American congressmen from Northern cities voted almost unanimously for the Voting Rights Act of 1964—not a tough choice, since it passed overwhelmingly—but also almost unanimously for open housing legislation in 1966, a much tougher vote for a bill, that, in fact, failed to pass. Survey data from the 1960s and 1970s also suggests that Irish-American Catholics were more open to Civil Rights reforms than many, though by no means all, other white groups.[79]

When Boston erupted in the mid-1970s over busing, Irish Americans, as noted, were in the forefront of the opposition, but Irish Americans were prominent on all sides of the issue: Teddy Kennedy and Thomas P. "Tip" O'Neill became the targets of

The 2002 St. Patrick's Day parade in New York City, coming just six months after 9/11, brought unusual and often spontaneous displays of gratitude. Among the spectators on Fifth Avenue that March 17th was Bridget Cagney, an immigrant from Ireland's southwest, who held a simple "Thank You" sign for the police and fire contingents in the parade. (Courtesy of Scott Spencer)

busing opponents as they first temporized and then supported busing. J. Anthony Lukas notes:

> [The courtroom in the busing case] often resembled an Irish morality play, fought out between various conceptions of what it meant to be Irish in contemporary Boston. On the bench, of course, was Garritty [Judge Wendell Arthur Garritty] himself, the Clover Club Establishment Irishman. Representing the plaintiffs [seeking integration] was Nick Flannery, whose service in Washington, New York, Detroit and Mississippi qualified him as the cosmopolitan Irishman. Speaking for the State Board of Education [urging integration] was Sandra Lynch, the Emancipated Irishwoman. On the other side of the aisle [opposing busing], Kevin Maloney, faithfully representing Kevin White's ambivalence toward desegregation was the Political Irishman. And doing battle for the School Committee [opposing busing] . . . was the indomitable J. J. Sullivan, playing the role of True Irishman.[80]

And so what are we left with? When I began this project, I was in search of a "usable past" of Irish-American communalism for a present that—to me—often seems not to value communal obligations. Working back from the firemen, I hoped to pull a thread from Irish-American history of communal loyalty and self-sacrifice that might set a useful precedent for an alternative to a current, free-market individualism in America that seems to encourage indifference, even ridicule, of the poor and working people. But the past is more complicated than that, alas. Irish Americans' communalism often looked self defeating, parochial, sometimes even sordid and mean. It may have blinded Irish Americans to opportunities for their own self advancement, a more visionary politics, and the prospects of a rich fellowship with Asian and African neighbors.

And yet, and yet, the record *is* more complicated than *that* dismal catalogue as well, and if it scarcely fulfills my hopes, it does reflect a more complicated past than that shown in some historians' bleak assessments. Moreover, if the record of Irish-American communalism is mixed, wouldn't a catalogue of individualism's triumphs —the pursuit of knowledge and victories of character unchained by custom or communal approbation—and tragedies (the injuries inflicted, the disruptions caused by ambition and greed unguided by a vision of the needs of others) be just as mixed and complicated?

More than that, one wonders whether the problem is really communalism or communal values or the way those loyalties have been defined in the past. Can a people, can a nation, can a world, really, survive without some sense of our obligations, our loyalties to one another? Without firemen and women willing to go up those stairs? Can we, or any society, take care of our old, succor the poor, and nourish our children without some sense of community? John McGreevy has pointed out a poignant irony in his great book, *Parish Boundaries*: while on the one hand, Irish Americans' tight communalism often stoked their resistance to integration of their neighborhoods through most of the twentieth century, the same tight community values that suffuse Irish and other Catholic parochial schools in inner cities today have helped their current African and Latino-American students flourish.

Informed, soberly aware of Irish-American communalism's strengths and weaknesses, and nursing a good Irish sense of life's ironies, perhaps we can, indeed, draw upon that communalism for a usable past.

And in the end are such communal values so alien to America after all?

The poet laureate of America, Walt Whitman, was the great celebrator of the nation's anarchic individualism in "Song of Myself" and other poems. But Whitman also wrote "For You O Democracy":

> I will make the continent indissoluble
> I will make the most splendid race the sun ever shone upon
> I will make divine magnetic lands
> With the love of comrades
> With the life long love of comrades."[81]

NOTES

1. Terry Golway, *So Others Might Live: A History of New York's Bravest—The FDNY from 1700 to the Present* (New York: Basic Books, 2002), xiii.

2. Peggy Noonan, *A Heart, A Cross and a Flag: America Today* (New York: Free Press, 2004), 28–29.

3. Golway, *So Others Might Live*, 303.

4. Ibid., xiii; Richard Sandomir, "Sports Media; Giving New Meaning to 'Special Teams,'" *New York Times*, September 8, 2002, section 8, 8.

5. Some of the most important works done in this period include the following: Stephan Thernstrom, *The Other Bostonians: Poverty and Progress in an American Metropolis, 1880–1970* (Cambridge, MA: Harvard University Press, 1973); Howard Chudacoff, *Mobile Americans: Residential and Social Mobility in Omaha, 1880—1920* (New York: Oxford University Press, 1972); Stephan Thernstrom, *Poverty and Progress: Social Mobility in a Nineteenth Century City* (Cambridge, MA: Harvard University Press, 1964); Clyde Griffen, *Natives and Newcomers: The Ordering of Opportunity in Mid–Nineteenth Century Poughkeepsie* (Cambridge, MA: Harvard University Press, 1978). See also articles reviewing and critiquing the work: James Henretta, "The Study of Social Mobility: Ideological Assumptions and Conceptual Bias," *Labor History* 18, no. 2 (1977): 165–178; Howard Chudacoff, "Success and Security: The Meaning of Social Mobility in America," *Reviews in American History* 10, no. 4 (1982): 101–112; and Stanley Engerman, "Up or Out: Social and Geographical Mobility in the United States," *Journal of Interdisciplinary History* 5, no. 3 (1975): 469–489.

6. The number of books addressing this topic are too numerous to mention, but there are several reviews and reflections on the writing of labor history, class, and politics in America: David Brody, "The Old Labor History and the New: In Search of an American Working Class," *Labor History* 20 (1979): 111–126; Michael Kazin, "Struggling with Class Struggle: Marxism and the Search for a Synthesis of United States Labor History," *Labor History* 28, no. 4 (1987): 497–514; Michael H. Frisch and Daniel Walkowitz, Introduction to *Working Class America: Essays on Labor, Community and American Society*, ed. Michael H. Frisch and Daniel Walkowitz, ix–xvi (Urbana: University of Illinois Press, 1983); Lenard R. Berlanstein, "Introduction," in *Rethinking Labor History: Essays on Discourse and Class Analysis*, ed. Lenard R. Berlanstein, 1–14 (Urbana: University of Illinois Press, 1993).

7. David Roediger, *The Wages of Whiteness: Race and the Making of the American Working Class* (New York: Verso, 1991); Noel Ignatiev, *How the Irish Became White* (New York: Routledge, 1995); Theodore W. Allen, *Invention of the White Race: Racial Oppression and Social Control*, Vol. 1 (New York: Verso, 1994); Theodore W. Allen, *Invention of the White Race: The Origin of Racial Oppression in Anglo-America*, Vol. 2 (New York: Verso, 1997); Eric Arnesen, "Whiteness and the Historian's Imagination," *International Labor and Working Class History* 60 (2001): 3–32. See also the responses: James R. Barrett, "Whiteness Studies: Anything Here for Historians of the Working Class?" *International Labor and Working Class History* 60 (2001): 33–42; David Brody, "Charismatic History: Pros and Cons," *International Labor and Working Class History* 60 (2001): 43–47; Barbara Fields, "Whiteness, Racism and Identity," *International Labor and Working Class History* 60 (2001): 48–56; Eric Foner, "Response to Eric Arnesen," *International Labor and Working Class History* 60 (2001): 57–60; Victoria Hattam, "Whiteness: Theorizing Race, Eliding Ethnicity," *International Labor and Working Class History* 60 (2001): 61–68; Adolph Reed, "Response to Eric Arnesen," *International Labor and Working Class History* 60 (2001): 69–80; Mathew Frye Jacobson, *Whiteness of a Different Color: European Immigrants and the Alchemy of Race* (Cambridge, MA: Harvard University Press, 1998); Peter Kolchin, "Whiteness Studies: The New History of Race in America," *Journal of American History* 89, no. 1 (2002): 154–173.

8. Thomas Sowell, *Ethnic America: A History* (New York: Basic Books, 1981); Thomas Sowell, *Conquests and Cultures: An International History* (New York: Basic Books, 1998); Stephan Thernstrom, *The Other Bostonians: Poverty and Progress in the American Metropolis, 1880–1970* (Cambridge, MA: Harvard University Press, 1973), 111–174; Stephan Thernstrom, *Poverty and Progress: Social Mobility in a Nineteenth Century City* (New York: Scribner, 1969), 80–165. Quotation from Daniel P. Moynihan and Nathan Glazer, ed., *Beyond the Melting Pot: The Negroes, Puerto Ricans, Jews, Italians, and Irish of New York City* (Cambridge, MA: MIT Press, 1963), 256.

9. For comments about political machines or, more specifically, Irish Americans and their Democratic partisanship or machines' effects on working-class solidarity, see Steven Erie, *Rainbow's End: Irish Americans and the Dilemmas of Urban Machine Politics, 1840–1985* (Berkeley: University of California Press, 1988); Richard Jules Ostreicher, *Solidarity and Fragmentation: Working People and Class Consciousness in Detroit, 1875–1900* (Urbana: University of Illinois Press, 1986), 59–60; Martin Shefter, "Trade Unions and Political Machines: The Organization and Disorganization of the American Working Class in the Late Nineteenth Century," in *Working Class Formation: Nineteenth Century Patterns in Western Europe and the United States*, ed. Ira Katznelson and Aristide R. Zolberg, 267–276 (Princeton, NJ: Princeton University Press, 1986); Charles Leinenweber, "The Class and Ethnic Bases of New York City Socialism, 1904—1915," *Labor History* 22, no. 1 (1981): 31–56; John R. McKivigan and Thomas L. Robertson, "The Irish American Worker in Transition, 1877–1914: New York City as a Test Case," in *The New York Irish*, ed. Ronald H. Bayor and Timothy Meagher, 301–320 (Baltimore: Johns Hopkins University Press, 1996); and Eric L. Hirsch, *Urban Revolt: Ethnic Politics in the Nineteenth Century Chicago Labor Movement* (Berkeley: University of California Press, 1990). Erie had made the best case against Irish machines and labor politics: "Irish enthusiasm for labor politics dimmed as ever larger numbers were brought into the patronage system. The failure of labor parties in the big cities can thus partly be understood in terms of the threat they posed to the entrenched Irish machine and their ethnic beneficiaries" (Erie, *Rainbow's End*, 8). Hirsch says: "The Irish pulled together, believing that their future was tied to the success of their ethnic group and not necessarily to their class or trade" (Hirsch, *Urban Revolt,* 143).

10. Arnesson, "Whiteness and the Historian's Imagination," 13; Allen, *Invention of the White Race*; Ignatiev, *How the Irish Became White*, 1–3 and 149–166; Roediger, *Wages of Whiteness*, 136–137, 149–150, and 185–189. See also John Kuo Wei Tchen, "Quimbo Appo's Fear of Fenians: Chinese-Irish-Anglo Relations in New York City," in *The New York Irish*, ed. Bayor and Meagher, 125–152. Kevin Kenny critiques some of the whiteness assertions in his *The American Irish: A History* (New York: Longman, 2000): 38–39, 66–71.

11. Kerby Miller, *Emigrants and Exiles: Ireland and the Irish Exodus to North America* (New York: Oxford University Press, 1985), 6, 107.

12. John T. McGreevy, *Catholicism and American Freedom: A History* (New York: W. W. Norton, 2003), 7–42, 127–188.

13. Robert Scally, *The End of Hidden Ireland: Rebellion, Famine and Emigration* (New York: Oxford University Press, 1995), 14, 33, 71–104; Kevin Whelan, "The Modern Landscape: From Plantation to Present," in *Atlas of the Rural Irish Landscape*, ed. F. H. A. Allen, Kevin Whelan, and Matthew Stout, 79–89 (Cork: Cork University Press, 1997). James Scott, *Weapons of the Weak: Everyday Forms of Peasant Resistance* (New Haven: Yale University Press, 1985), 261–265.

14. James Donnelly and Samuel Clark, eds., *Irish Peasants: Violence and Political Unrest, 1780–1914* (Madison: University of Wisconsin, 1983); Gale Christensen, "Secret Society and Agrarian Violence in Ireland, 1790–1840," *Agricultural History* 46, no. 3 (1972): 369–384; Luke Gibbons, *Transformations in Irish Culture* (Notre Dame, IN: University of Notre Dame Press, 1996).

15. James Donnelly, "Pastorini and Captain Rock: Millenerianism and Sectarianism in the Rockite Movement of 1821–1824," in *Irish Peasants*, ed. James Donnelly and Samuel Clark, 125–142 (Madison: University of Wisconsin Press, 1983); Tom Garvin, "Defenders, Ribbonmen and Others: Underground Political Networks in Pre Famine Ireland," *Past and Present* 96 (1982): 133–155.

16. Lawrence John McCaffrey, *The Irish Diaspora in America* (Bloomington: Indiana University Press, 1976), 77–79; David N. Doyle, *Irish Americans: Native Rights and National Em-*

pires: The Structures, Divisions and Attitudes of the Catholic Minority in the Decade of Expansion, 1890–1901 (New York: Arno Press, 1976), 38–90; James Walsh, "The Irish in the New America: 'Way Out West,'" in *America and Ireland, 1776–1976: The American Identity and the Irish Connection*, ed. David N. Doyle and Owen Dudley Edwards, 165–176 (Westport, CT: Greenwood Press, 1980); David Gleeson, *The Irish in the South, 1815–1877* (Chapel Hill: University of North Carolina Press, 2001), 38–54. On Australia and Canada's differences, see Donald H. Akenson, *Irish Diaspora: A Primer* (Belfast: Queens University, 1993), and Donald H. Akenson, *Irish in Ontario: A Study in Rural History* (Kingston: McGill—Queens University, 1984). The best discussion is Bielenberg's own essay in Andy Bielenberg, ed., *The Irish Diaspora* (Harlow, England: Longman, 2000). (As an aside, one begins to wonder whether when looking at the Irish diaspora, we should think of zones and not nations. Malcolm Campbell has astutely called attention to the similarities between Irish experiences in Australia and San Francisco or California generally. One could think of other zones: New England and Britain; or the Canadian and American Great Lakes regions. See Malcolm Campbell, *The Kingdom of the Ryan: The Irish in Southwest New South Wales, 1816–1890* [Sydney, Australia: UNSW Press, 1997].)

17. Joel Perlmann, *Ethnic Differences: Schooling and Social Structure among the Irish, Italians, Jews and Blacks in an American City, 1880–1935* (New York: Cambridge University Press, 1989), 43; Michael Glazer, ed., *Encyclopedia of the Irish in America* (Notre Dame, IN: University of Notre Dame Press, 1999), 460, 461–462; Akenson, *Irish Diaspora*, 237.

18. Charles Tilly, "Transplanted Networks," in *Immigration Reconsidered: History, Sociology and Politics*, ed. Virginia Yans McLaughlin, 79–96 (New York: Oxford University Press, 1990); Jon Gjerde, "Following the Chains: New Insights into Migration," *Immigration and Ethnic History Newsletter* 33, no. 1 (May 2001): 1–2; Miller, *Emigrants and Exiles*, 357; Timothy Meagher, *Inventing Irish America: Generation, Class and Ethnic Identity in a New England City, 1880–1928* (Notre Dame, IN: University of Notre Dame Press, 2001), 39.

19. Meagher, *Inventing Irish America*, 40, 44.

20. Joseph Ferrie, *Yankeys Now: Immigrants in the Antebellum United States, 1840–1860* (New York: Oxford University Press, 1999), 56–57; R. A. Burchell, *The San Francisco Irish: 1848–1880* (Berkeley: University of California Press, 1980), 39; Patrick James O'Farrell, *The Irish in Australia: 1788 to the Present* (Notre Dame, IN: University of Notre Dame Press, 2000), 69.

21. Ferrie, *Yankeys Now*, 144; Robert Ernst, *Immigrant Life in New York City: 1825–1863* (New York: King's Crown Press, 1949), 63.

22. William Shannon, *The American Irish: A Political and Social Portrait* (New York: Collier Books, 1974), 87–92.

23. David Fitzpatrick, *Oceans of Consolation: Personal Accounts of Irish Migration to Australia* (Ithaca, NY: Cornell University Press, 1994), 11, 15; Jon Gjerde, *Minds of the West: Ethnocultural Evolution in the Rural Midwest, 1830–1917* (Chapel Hill: University of North Carolina Press, 1997), 79–102.

24. David M. Emmons, *The Butte Irish: Class and Ethnicity in an American Mining Town, 1875–1925* (Urbana: University of Illinois Press, 1990).

25. Tyler Anbinder, *Five Points: The Nineteenth Century New York City Neighborhood That Invented Tap Dance, Stole Elections, and Became the World's Most Notorious Slum* (New York: Free Press, 2001), 139.

26. John T. McGreevy, *Parish Boundaries: The Catholic Encounter with Race in the Twentieth Century Urban North* (Chicago: University of Chicago Press, 1996) 22, 13–28; Gerald Gamm, *Urban Exodus: Why the Jews Left Boston and the Catholics Stayed* (Cambridge, MA: Harvard University Press, 1999), 129–140; J. Anthony Lukas, *Common Ground: A Turbulent Decade in the Life of Three American Families* (New York: Knopf, 1985), 23.

27. Bruce Nelson, *Divided We Stand: American Workers and the Struggle for Black Equality* (Princeton: Princeton University Press, 2001), 4–45; Joshua Benjamin Freeman, *In Transit: The Transport Workers Union in New York City, 1933–1966* (New York: Oxford University Press, 1989), 30–34, 45–50; Emmons, *Butte Irish*; Tilly, "Transplanted Networks," 79–95.

28. Meagher, *Inventing Irish America*, 102.

29. Perlmann, *Ethnic Differences*, 55–64; Andrew Greeley, "The Success and Assimilation of Irish Protestants and Catholics in the United States," *Social Science Research* 72, no. 4 (1985): 229–235. Fass writes: "As Andrew Greeley and Peter Rossi (and others) have found, Catholic high school students of all social levels have gone on to college at higher rates than comparable non—Catholics and Catholics who did not attend Catholic high schools. Greeley and Rossi also found that 'Catholic school Catholics had increased their social class margin over other Catholics'" (p. 202). In a note, Fass addresses Irish Catholics who were more likely to go to Catholic high schools more directly: "According to Abramson, the possibility of graduating from college was very significantly higher for the Irish if they attended Catholic high schools rather than public high schools. . . . For them going to Catholic high schools or not literally meant the difference between succeeding and not succeeding educationally" (note 26, p. 293). Paula Fass, *Outsiders In: Minorities and the Transformation of American Education* (New York: Oxford University Press, 1989). See also Andrew Greeley, *That Most Distressful Nation: The Taming of the American Irish* (Chicago: Quadrangle Books, 1972), 194–202; Andrew Greeley, *The American Catholic: A Social Portrait* (New York: Basic Books, 1977), 112–125.

30. Shannon, *American Irish*, 142–150; William H. A. Williams, "Green Again: Irish-American Lace-Curtain Satire," *New Hibernia Review* 6, no. 2 (Summer 2002): 9–24.

31. Young quoted from Kevin Whelan, "An Underground Gentry: Catholic Middlemen in Eighteenth-Century Ireland," in *Irish Popular Culture, 1650–1850*, ed. James S. Donnelly Jr. and Kerby A. Miller (Dublin: Irish Academic Press, 1998), 149; Emmet Larkin, trans. and ed., *Alexis de Tocqueville's Journey in Ireland: July–August, 1835* (Washington, DC: Catholic University Press, 1990), 92; Donnelly, "Pastorini and Captain Rock," 102–154.

32. Scally, *End of Hidden Ireland*, 80.

33. Joseph Theodoor Leerssen, *Mere Irish and Fíor Ghael: Studies in the Idea of Irish Nationality, Its Development and Literary Expression Prior to the Nineteenth Century* (Notre Dame, IN: University of Notre Dame Press, 1997); William H. A. Williams, *'Twas Only an Irishman's Dream* (Urbana: University of Illinois, 1996), 58–88.

34. Hasia Diner, *Erin's Daughters in America: Irish Immigrant Women in the Nineteenth Century* (Baltimore: Johns Hopkins University Press, 1983), 30–42, 70–105; Janet Nolan, *Ourselves Alone: Women's Emigration from Ireland 1885–1920* (Lexington: University Press of Kentucky, 1989), 73–90.

35. Meagher, *Inventing Irish America*, 40–41, 184–193; Joe Doyle, "Striking for Ireland on the New York Docks," in *The New York Irish*, ed. Bayor and Meagher, 357–373; David Brundage, *The Making of Western Labor Radicalism: Denver's Organized Workers, 1878–1905* (Urbana: University of Illinois Press, 1994), 43–44.

36. Shannon, *American Irish*, 142; John O'Hara, *Here's O'Hara: Three Novels and Twenty Short Stories by John O'Hara* (Cleveland: World Publishing, 1946 reprint), 147–148; Eugene O'Neill, *A Touch of the Poet*, in *Complete Plays, 1932–1943* (New York: Library of America, 1988), 273; Thomas Beer, *The Mauve Decade: American Life at the End of the Nineteenth Century* (New York: Knopf, 1926).

37. Williams, *'Twas Only an Irishman's Dream*, 97–180.

38. Sean Wilentz, *Chants Democratic: New York City and the Rise of the American Working Class, 1788–1850* (New York: Oxford University Press, 1984), 326–335.

39. Moynihan, *Beyond the Melting Pot*, 323.

40. David Roediger, *Wages of Whiteness*, 43–64.

41. Erie, *Rainbow's End*, 65–91; quote from Howard P. Chudacoff, *The Evolution of American Urban Society* (Englewood Cliffs, NJ: Prentice Hall, 1975), 143.

42. Nancy Weiss, *Charles Francis Murphy: Respectability and Responsibility in Tammany Politics* (Northampton, MA: Smith College Press, 1968), 69–70, 78; Chris McNickle, *To Be Mayor of New York: Ethnic Politics in the City* (New York: Columbia University Press, 1993), 20–32, quote from Murphy on 26; Daniel Czitrom, "Underworlds and Underdogs: Big Tim Sullivan and Metropolitan Politics in New York, 1889–1913," *Journal of American History* 78, no. 2 (September 1991): 536–558; Christopher Finan, *Alfred E. Smith: The Happy Warrior* (New York: Hill and Wang, 2002), 73–104; Robert Slayton, *Empire Statesman: The Rise and Redemption of Al Smith* (New York: Free Press, 2001).

43. John D. Buenker, *Urban Liberalism and Progressive Reform* (New York: Scribner, 1973), 1–41.

44. For older notions of Progressivism as middle-class reform, see Richard Hofstadter, *Age of Reform: From Ryan to FDR* (New York: Knopf, 1955), and Robert Wiebe, *The Search for Order, 1877 to 1920* (New York: Hill and Wang, 1967). For a more recent discussion of Progressivism in middle-class terms, see Theda Skocpol, *Protecting Soldiers and Mothers: The Political Origins of Social Policy in the United States* (Cambridge, MA: Harvard University Press, 1992).

45. Leon Fink, *Workingmen's Democracy: The Knights of Labor and American Politics* (Urbana: University of Illinois Press, 1983); David Doyle, "Catholicism, Politics and Irish America since 1890: Some Critical Considerations," in *The Irish in America*, ed. P. J. Drudy (Cambridge: Cambridge University Press, 1985), 206.

46. Patrick D. Kennedy, "Chicago's Irish Americans and the Candidacies of Franklin D. Roosevelt, 1932–1944," *Illinois Historical Journal* 88 (Winter 1995): 263–278; Lyle Dorsett, *Franklin D. Roosevelt and the City Bosses* (Port Washington, NY: Kennikat Press, 1977), 21–34, 49–69, 70–111, Kelly quoted from 93; Gerald H. Gamm, *The Making of New Deal Democrats: Voting Behavior and Realignment in Boston, 1920–1940* (Chicago: University of Chicago Press, 1989); Charles H. Trout, *Boston: The Great Depression and the New Deal* (New York: Oxford University Press, 1977); McNickle, *To Be Mayor*, 41–51; Erie, *Rainbow's End*; George Flynn, *American Catholics and the Roosevelt Presidency, 1932–1936* (Lexington: University Press of Kentucky, 1968).

47. Alec A. Barbrook, *God Save the Commonwealth: An Electoral History of Massachusetts* (Amherst: University of Massachusetts Press, 1973); Edgar Litt, *The Political Cultures of Massachusetts* (Cambridge, MA: MIT Press, 1965), 39–47; Erwin L. Levine, *Theodore Francis Green: The Rhode Island Years, 1906–1936* (Providence: Brown University Press, 1963), 173–189.

48. Dorothy M. Brown and Elizabeth McKeown, *The Poor Belong to Us: Catholic Charities and American Welfare* (Cambridge, MA: Harvard University Press, 1997), 151–192.

49. James Fisher, "Alternative Sources of Catholic Intellectual Vitality," *U.S. Catholic Historian* 13, no. 1 (Winter 1995): 83–88.

50. Williams, *'Twas Only an Irish American's Dream*, 91–180.

51. Charles F. Fanning, *The Irish Voice in America: Irish American Fiction from the 1760s to the 1980s* (Lexington: University of Kentucky Press, 1990), 88–152; Paul Messbarger, *Fiction with Parochial Purpose: Social Uses of American Catholic Literature, 1884–1900* (Boston: Boston University Press, 1971), 102–113.

52. McGreevy, *Catholicism and American Freedom*, 43–67; Gerald Fogarty, ed., *Patterns of Episcopal Leadership* (New York: Macmillan, 1989), 171–182, 216–234; John Cooney, *The American Pope: The Life and Times of Cardinal Spellman* (New York: New York Times Press, 1984),

83–262; James M. O'Toole, *Militant and Triumphant: William Henry O'Connell and the Catholic Church in Boston, 1859–1944* (Notre Dame, IN: University of Notre Dame Press, 1992), 79–120, 227–250.

53. James J. Connolly, "Beyond the Machine: Martin Lomasney and Ethnic Politics," in *Faces of Community: Immigrant Massachusetts, 1860 to 2000*, ed. Reed Ueda and Conrad Edick Wright, 189–218 (Boston: Massachusetts Historical Society, 2003); James J. Connolly, "The Last Hurrah and the Pluralist Vision of American Politics," in *Boston's Histories: Essays in Honor of Thomas H. O'Connor*, ed. James M. O'Toole and David Quigley, 214–227 (Boston: Northeastern University, 2004); James J. Connolly, *The Triumph of Ethnic Progressivism: Urban Political Culture, 1900–1925* (Cambridge, MA: Harvard University Press, 1998); Erie, *Rainbow's End*.

54. Dayton McKean, *The Boss* (Boston: Houghton Mifflin, 1940).

55. Moynihan and Glazer, *Beyond the Melting Pot*, 229.

56. Charles Curran, *American Catholic Social Ethics: Twentieth Century Approaches* (Notre Dame, IN: University of Notre Dame Press, 1982), 25–90; Joseph McShane, *Sufficiently Radical: Catholicism, Progressivism and the Bishop's Program of 1919* (Washington, DC: Catholic University of America, 1986); Francis L. Broderick, *Right Reverend New Dealer, John A. Ryan* (New York: Macmillan, 1963); John A. Ryan, "Fallacy of Bettering Oneself," *Catholic World*, November 1907.

57. James J. Walsh, *The Thirteenth: The Greatest of All Centuries* (New York: Catholic Summer School Press, 1924); William Halsey, *The Survival of American Innocence: Catholicism in an Era of Disillusionment, 1920–1940* (Notre Dame, IN: University of Notre Dame Press, 1980); Thomas Shelley, "'What the Hell Is an Encyclical?': Governor Alfred E. Smith, Charles C. Marshall, Esq., and Father Francis P. Duffy," *U.S. Catholic Historian* 15, no. 2 (Spring 1997): 87–107.

58. Donald Crosby, *God, Church and Flag: Senator Joseph R. McCarthy and the Catholic Church* (Chapel Hill: University of North Carolina Press, 1978), 3–23.

59. Meagher, *Inventing Irish America*, 324; Crosby, *God, Church and Flag*, 230–243; Michael Kazin, *The Populist Persuasion: An American History* (New York: Basic Books, 1995), 165–193; M. J. Heale, *McCarthy's Americans: Red Scare Politics in State and Nation, 1935–1965* (Athens: University of Georgia Press, 1998), 149–212; Donald L. O'Connor, "'For God, Country and Home': The Origins and Growth of the Catholic War Veterans of the U.S.A., 1935–1957," *Long Island Historical Journal* 11, no. 1 (Fall 1998): 31–53; Mark Massa, *Catholics and American Culture: Fulton Sheen, Dorothy Day and the Notre Dame Football Team* (New York: Crossroads Press, 1999), 57–101.

60. William B. Prendergast, *The Catholic Voter in American Politics: The Passing of the Democratic Monolith* (Washington, DC: Georgetown University Press, 1999), 160–224; Mark P. Levy and Michael S. Kramer, *The Ethnic Factor: How America's Minorities Decide Elections* (New York: Simon and Schuster, 1972), 122–139; Carolyn Smith, ed., *The 88 Vote: ABC News* (New York: Capital Cities, 1989), 40, 127, 164; G. William Domhoff and Richard Zweigenhaft, *Diversity in the Power Elite: Have Women and Minorities Reached the Top?* (New Haven: Yale University Press, 1998); David Brooks, *Bobos in Paradise: The New Upper Class and How They Get There* (New York: Simon and Schuster, 2000); Kazin, *Populist Persuasion*, 222–266; Samuel Friedman, *The Inheritance: How Three Families and America Moved from Roosevelt to Reagan and Beyond* (New York: Simon and Schuster, 1996), 40–55, 69–84, 313–352; Richard Krickus, *Pursuing the American Dream: White Ethnics and the New Populism* (Garden City, NY: Doubleday, 1976), 202–306; Peggy Noonan, *What I Saw at the Revolution: A Political Life in the Reagan Era* (New York: Random House, 1990), 3–16.

61. Smith, *The 88 Vote: ABC News*, 141; Jerome Milieur, "Party Politics in the Bay State: The Dominance of Democracy," and Maureen Moakley, "Political Parties in Rhode Island: Back to

the Future," both in *Polity* (1997): 77–94, 94–112; Robert Erikson, Gerald C. Nugent, and John R. McIver, *Statehouse Democracy: Public Opinion and Policy in the American States* (New York: Cambridge University Press, 1993), 12–119; John Aloysius Farrell, *Tip O'Neill and the Democratic Century* (Boston: Little Brown, 2001), 16–18, 21–26, 539–672, quotation from 26.

62. Timothy Meagher "Irish Americans as Artifacts of Memory in Contemporary American Movies and Television," unpublished paper, presented at "Memory, Material and Meaning: Western Humanities Association Conference," Tanner Center, University of Utah, October 16, 2003.

63. Arnesen, "Whiteness and the Historian's Imagination," 13.

64. Allen, *Invention of the White Race*, 169; Noel Ignatiev, *How the Irish Became White* (New York: Routledge, 1995), v, 1–3; David R. Roediger, *The Wages of Whiteness: Race and the Making of the American Working Class* (New York: Verso, 1991), 137–138.

65. Roediger, *Wages of Whiteness*, 137–138; Ignatiev, *How the Irish Became White*, 2–3, 152–174.

66. O'Neill wrote: "'A flunky in Livery answered wid two others behind. A big nigger one was' . . . 'I'll have you know Mr. Harford don't allow drunken Micks to come here disturbing him,'" in *A Touch of the Poet*, 265; O'Hara, *Here's O'Hara*, 149.

67. Arnesen, "Whiteness and the Historian's Imagination," 3–32; Fields, "Whiteness, Racism and Identity," 48–56; Foner, "Response to Eric Arnesen," 57–60; Hattam, "Whiteness: Theorizing Race," 61–68; Reed, "Response to Eric Arnesen," 69–80; Kolchin, "Whiteness Studies," 154–173; Kenny, *American Irish*, 38–39, 66–71.

68. In William Carleton's story, "The Poor Scholar," published in 1844, for example, a peasant, who cared for the sick young scholar identified in the title, tells a Catholic bishop, "but sure my Lord, we couldn't be such nagers as to let him die." William Carleton, *Traits and Sketches of the Irish Peasantry* (Gerrard's Cross: Colin Smythe, 1990; facsimile of 1844 edition), 311, 310; see also 264.

69. David Fitzpatrick, *Irish Emigration: Studies in Irish Economic and Social History* (Dublin: Economic and Social History of Ireland, 1984), 12; Miller, *Emigrants and Exiles*, 198; Sean Duffy, ed., *Atlas of Irish History* (Dublin: Gill and McMillan, 2000), 91; David N. Doyle, "The Irish in North America, 1776–1845," in *A New History of Ireland*, ed. W. E Vaughn, Vol. 5: *Ireland under the Union*, 682–724 (Oxford: Clarendon Press, 1989).

70. Anbinder, *Five Points*, 405.

71. David Hollinger, "'How Wide the Circle of We': American Intellectuals and the Problem of Ethnos since World War II," *American Historical Review* 98, no. 2 (April 1993): 317–337.

72. Vincent Powers, "Invisible Immigrants: The Pioneer Irish of Worcester, Massachusetts, 1826 to 1860" (Ph.D. diss., Clark University, 1976), 247–363; Brian Mitchell, *Paddy Camps: The Irish in Lowell, Massachusetts, 1821–1861* (Urbana: University of Illinois Press, 1988), 109–111; Peter Way, "Shovel and Shamrock: Irish Workers and Labor Violence in the Digging of the Chesapeake and Ohio Canal," *Labor History* 30, no. 4 (1989): 489–517.

73. David A. Wilson, *United Irishmen, United States: Immigrant Radicals in the Early Republic* (Ithaca, NY: Cornell University Press, 1998), 56–95, 112–122; Michael Gordon, *The Orange Riots: Irish Political Violence in New York City, 1870–1871* (Ithaca, NY: Cornell University Press, 1993), 104–148.

74. As late as 1947, 90 percent of Australia's population was of British or Irish origin: Donald Akenson, *Small Differences: Irish Catholics and Irish Protestants—An International Perspective* (Montreal: McGill, 1988), 61. Canada's population was divided between French and British and Irish populations until the early twentieth century. In 1901, some 3,063,195 Canadians were of British and Irish origin and 1,649,371 of French origin out of a total population of 5,371,315:

F. H. Leacy, ed., *Historical Statistics of Canada*, web edition: http://www.statcan.ca/english. Irish Catholics and French Canadians vied for new Catholic immigrants, but Irish Catholics were never as well positioned to assemble big multiethnic political coalitions as they were in the United States or to overcome French opposition to create and rule a broadly inclusive Canadian Catholic Church: Terence J. Fay, *A History of Canadian Catholics: Gallicanism, Romanism, and Canadianism* (Montreal: McGill, 2002), 155–175. Quote from William Shannon, *The American Irish: A Political and Social Portrait* (New York: Macmillan, 1970), 132, 136.

75. Czitrom, "Underworld and Underdogs," 556; William Riordan, *Plunkitt of Tammany Hall* (New York: E. P. Dutton, 1963), 90–93; Erie, *Rainbow's End*, 93–111; Connolly, "Beyond the Machine," 197–205.

76. Erie, *Rainbow's End*, 103; McNickle, *To Be Mayor*, 23 (on the civil rights bill).

77. Mary Wingerd, *Claiming the City: Politics, Faith and the Power of Place in St. Paul* (Ithaca, NY: Cornell University Press, 2001).

78. David N. Doyle, *Irish Americans: Native Rights and National Empires—The Structure, Divisions and Attitudes of the Catholic Minority in the Decade of Expansion* (New York: Arno Press, 1976); Matthew Frye Jacobson, *Special Sorrows: The Diasporic Imagination of Irish, Polish and Jewish Immigrants in the United States* (Cambridge, MA: Harvard University Press, 1995).

79. From Chicago, Illinois: Finnegan, Murphy, and O'Hara; from Connecticut: Monagan; from Massachusetts: Boland, Burke, Donohue, O'Neill, Philbin; from New York City: Buckley, Carey, Delaney, Kelly, Keogh, Murphy, Rooney, Ryan; from Rhode Island: Fogarty—all voted for the Civil Rights Bill of 1964. *Congressional Quarterly, Almanac, 88th Congress Second Session 1964*, 20: 636–637. From Chicago: Murphy, O'Hara, and Ronan; from Connecticut: Monagan; from Massachusetts: Boland, Donohue, O'Neill, Philbin; from New York City: Carey, Kelly, Murphy, Rooney, Ryan—all voted for the Civil Rights Bill of 1966. *Congressional Quarterly: Almanac, 88th Congress Second Session 1966*, 22: 896–897. See also J. Anthony Lukas, *Common Ground: A Turbulent Decade in the Lives of Three American Families* (New York: Knopf, 1985); John McGreevy, *Parish Boundaries*, 29–110; Eileen McMahon, *What Parish Are You From? A Chicago Irish Community and Race Relations* (Lexington: University of Kentucky Press, 1995), 116–189.

80. Lukas, *Common Ground*, 246.

81. Walt Whitman, *Leaves of Grass* (New York: New American Library, 1964), 115.

SUGGESTED READING

David N. Doyle and Owen Dudley Edwards, eds., *America and Ireland, 1776–1976: The American Identity and the Irish Connection* (Westport, CT: Greenwood Press, 1980).

Steven Erie, *Rainbow's End: Irish Americans and the Dilemmas of Urban Machine Politics* (Berkeley: University of California Press, 1988).

Terry Golway, *So Others Might Live: A History of New York's Bravest—The FDNY from 1700 to the Present* (New York: Basic Books, 2002).

Lawrence J. McCaffrey, *Textures of Irish America* (Syracuse, NY: Syracuse University Press, 1992).

John T. McGreevy, *Parish Boundaries: The Catholic Encounter with Race in the Twentieth-Century Urban North* (Chicago: University of Chicago Press, 1996).

Timothy J. Meagher, *Inventing Irish America: Generation, Class and Ethnic Identity in a New England City, 1880–1928* (Notre Dame, IN: University of Notre Dame Press, 2001).

Chapter 27

The Tradition of Irish-American Writers
The Twentieth Century

Daniel J. Casey and Robert E. Rhodes

Defining a Hyphenate Literature

Since forty-four million Americans—nearly one in six of the population—trace their ancestry to Ireland, and the consensus is that the Irish are at heart inveterate poets, actors, and storytellers, it is not surprising that Irish Americans should be well represented in American letters. They have, in fact, produced major writers in all of the literary genres since the turn of the twentieth century, and they continue to contribute poetry, drama, and fiction to the commonwealth.

In attempting to define Irish-American writing, this essay concentrates on the critically significant writers who represent the best of a tradition that flourished from the 1920s to the 1970s. Eugene O'Neill, James T. Farrell, F. Scott Fitzgerald, John O'Hara, Mary McCarthy, and Flannery O'Connor are given center stage. Others are afforded supporting roles in the unfolding literary spectacle. Still others are omitted, for a number of reasons. It is not always clear who belongs to the Irish-American writing tradition and who does not. In a way, the Irish writers in America have defined themselves through their works. In spite of Mary Gordon's judgment, in a 1988 *New York Times Book Review* piece that bemoans "the faintness of the Irish-American voice in the world of letters," there have been more than a handful of world-class Irish-American writers, and there have been scores of writers who are crucial in defining the tradition. They are the focus of this essay.

The earliest writing in the tradition captures the experience of the Irish pilgrimage to the American "Land of Promise" and reflects the settling-in process, with all the accompanying miseries, aspirations, and triumphs. The literature into the 1970s is, then, a literature of transition that accents the values of the neighborhood and sets them against those of the Big World.

But a hyphenate literature is about identity and how identity plays itself out in a perhaps never-ending, complicated process of both assimilation and affirmation. Alice McDermott, for example, in her National Book Award–winning *Charming Billy* (1998) and in her earlier novels—*A Bigamist's Daughter* (1982), *That Night* (1987), and *At Weddings and Wakes* (1992)—carries the Irish-American tradition forward today. Her characters, including the lovable romantic Billy Lynch, whose tragic alcoholic life is celebrated at a Bronx wake, have a strong sense of family and neighborhood. The

Irish connection, through a cast of virtuous but guilt-haunted characters, becomes real and recognizable: the narrator describes the dissipated Billy Lynch at her father's kitchen table in East Hampton shakily maneuvering a spoonful of coffee to his mouth and losing himself as he recollects a pilgrimage home to Ireland:

> "Another thing about Ireland," he said. "We're all over there. All our faces." *To me*: "I saw your dad driving a Guinness truck in Dublin. And his dad was moving a herd of sheep across the road up in the northwest." . . . "I saw my mother," he went on. "Good Lord, I saw my mother in nearly every shop I went into, usually behind the counter. And my father's face was on one of the priests who said Mass at the retreat house."

It's all here: the grand Celtic vision and the annoying foibles that cross the cultural divide and make Irish Americans what they are. But there is, too, in *Charming Billy* the sober realization that the narrator of the novel has already married outside the clan and that, in all probability, the line ends with her.

Frank McCourt's *Angela's Ashes* (1997) is a brilliant memoir that moves from Depression-era Brooklyn to Depression-era Limerick and resurrects all of the horrors of his "miserable Irish Catholic childhood" on both sides of the wide Atlantic. The work also illustrates the dilemma of the literary (or cultural) cross-over. *Angela's Ashes* is, after all, an Irish-centered autobiography that recounts the awful poverty and hardships of a broken family of returned Irish immigrants.

The Early Writers in the Tradition

At mid–nineteenth century the newly arrived Famine immigrants in America were far more concerned with economic survival than with *belles lettres*. The earliest period writers, such as Mary Anne Madden Sadlier, who penned *Bessy Conway; or, The Irish Girl in America* (1861), *Con O'Regan; or, Emigrant Life in the New World* (1864), and *Willy Burke; or, The Irish Orphan in America* (1850), advanced a stereotype that exhorted immigrants to disavow the past and emulate the Yankee work ethic. As industrious laborers and steadfast domestics serving their "betters," the Irish would, they were told, earn high marks in this world and the next. Even the first serious challenge to the standard Irish stereotype in America, Thomas D'Arcy McGee's *History of the Irish Settlers in North America* (1855), extolled Ireland's ancient glories yet advanced the theory that the immigrant's failures were a consequence of his origin. Despite the length and strength of the Irish tradition, the nineteenth was, for the Irish, a century of upheaval and adjustment, not an age of leisure and high art.

There were Irish immigrants such as Fitz-James O'Brien, remembered for his dramas and tales of the supernatural, and John Boyle O'Reilly, editor of *The Boston Pilot*, who wrote popular fiction such as *Moondyne: A Story of the Underworld* (1879). But the first major writer in the Irish-American literary tradition as we are defining it is the Chicago journalist Finley Peter Dunne, who contributed hundreds of humorous dialect sketches to the national press between 1893 and 1919. Dunne's spokesman was Mr. Martin Dooley, a bartender-philosopher who provided a chronology of Bridgeport, an Irish neighborhood on Chicago's South Side.

The wit and wisdom of Bridgeport saloonkeeper Martin Dooley were the voice of journalist Finley Peter Dunne (1867–1936),
who successfully bridged the gap between the working-class
ethnic world of the South Side and mainstream America in
over three hundred columns for the *Chicago Evening Post* between 1893 and 1900. (Library of Congress, Prints and Photographs Division, LC-USZ62-14591)

The earliest sketches recall Dooley's desperation in his native Ireland—a land of
hunger, eviction, and emigration—and his disillusionment in America, a land of hard
labor, violent strikes, and long relief lines. In short, Dooley's life became a study of the
immigrant's lot and provided a graphic sense of the squalor that accompanied the
transition from Old World to New. But Dooley was no malcontent. He was sensitive,
generous, and honest, a classical humorist in an apron. He agonized over infant mortality, unjust wars, and political corruption, but he relished parish fairs and *ceilis* and
card playing. Dooley was described as "a fan of man."

Dunne's sketches offered political commentary and social history that added a new
dimension to Irish character. He was witty and well informed, and, for millions of
newspaper readers, his Mr. Dooley was the quintessential Irishman and the model for
all of the Irish characters in future literature.

Literary Giants: O'Neill to McCarthy

Dunne had opened the door, but there was a wealth of talent at the doorstep. There
was Eugene O'Neill, who was influenced by the Gaelic Revival playwrights, particularly

J. M. Synge and Sean O'Casey, and was arguably the most talented and inspired dramatist in American theater. O'Neill's early one-act plays—*The Long Voyage Home* (1917) and *The Moon of the Caribbees* (1918)—as well as *The Emperor Jones* (1920), *Anna Christie* (1921), and *The Hairy Ape* (1921), show the influence of the aforementioned masters.

When O'Neill moved from Provincetown, Massachusetts, to New York City's Greenwich Village and Broadway districts, he outdistanced his Irish mentors with a rush of major experimental dramas that established his preeminence as a world-class playwright. These visionary works included *Desire under the Elms* (1925) and *Mourning Becomes Electra* (1931). After his sole comedy, *Ah, Wilderness!* (1933), and another, failed play, he succumbed for a time to illness. He eventually broke his long stage silence with *The Iceman Cometh* (1946), but it was to be the last play produced before his death in 1953. His tour de force, *A Long Day's Journey into Night* (first performed in 1956), is an autobiographical drama about the disintegration of the Tyrone family. A damning indictment of family and culture, the play magnifies Irish-American dysfunction and failure.

After O'Neill's death, his wife allowed production of the works he had completed between 1933 and 1946, including *A Touch of the Poet*. Set in Boston in 1828, the play portrays the life of Con Melody, a hard-drinking Irish immigrant, who seeks to maintain the social status he enjoyed in the Ireland he has left behind. His determination not to be treated as just another Irish innkeeper is symbolized by his British army uniform and his refusal to speak or allow his daughter to speak in a brogue. At the end of the play, his uniform in tatters and his brogue as thick as clotted cream, he shares a drunken revelry with local Irish low-life. In spite of Marc Connelly's success in winning a Pulitzer Prize for *Green Pastures* in 1929, it was O'Neill's Nobel Prize for Literature in 1936 that marked the arrival of the American Irish writer on the world stage.

That era's next significant figure is James T. Farrell, a South Side Chicagoan who, in the 1930s, published an autobiographical trilogy that cataloged the short, sordid career of William "Studs" Lonigan. Farrell's fiction offered a comprehensive sociological study, albeit an uncomplimentary one, of the Chicago Irish from 1915 to the Great Depression. The Studs Lonigan trilogy (1932–35) traces the tribulations of the character's boyhood and adolescence. *Young Lonigan* (1932), *The Young Manhood of Studs Lonigan* (1934), and *Judgment Day* (1935) are the foundation of an edifice of fifty volumes providing a panorama of urban Irish America in the first three-quarters of the twentieth century.

Betty Smith's *A Tree Grows in Brooklyn* (1943), set in the Williamsburg section of Brooklyn in the same time period, captures the ambience of cold-water flats with empty larders and Tammany-sponsored children's excursions up the Hudson River. Her heroine, Francie Nolan, was not as scarred as Studs; but there was, in Smith's novels, a sense of desperation to "fly by those nets" of her ghetto neighborhood. Both Farrell and Smith—whose stepfather was Irish, although her mother was not—understood the ghetto mentality and the uncompromising code of the urban turf.

F. Scott Fitzgerald, Mary McCarthy, and John O'Hara were not graduates of street academies; they came from favored circumstances. Fitzgerald attended the Newman

School and Princeton; McCarthy graduated from Vassar; and O'Hara, a doctor's son, aspired to Yale, though his father's untimely death put Yale out of reach. Irish backgrounds are sublimated in the fiction of these three: "Irish" was, after all, a stigma among the *nouveau riches*. Yet, their fiction is also autobiographical. In *This Side of Paradise* (1920), Fitzgerald not only perfectly captures the burgeoning Jazz Age, he sheds his Irish identity; in *Memories of a Catholic Girlhood* (1957), McCarthy spurns her lace-curtain origins; and in *The Doctor's Son and Other Stories* (1935), O'Hara sounds a final salvo on his birthright. Jimmy Molloy, the young narrator of *The Doctor's Son*, experiences disillusionment. It is, coincidentally, the same Jimmy Molloy who, in *Butterfield 8* (1935), says:

> I want to tell you something about myself that will help to explain a lot of things about me. You might as well hear it now. First of all, I am a Mick. I wear Brooks Brothers clothes and I don't eat salad with a spoon and I probably could play five-goal polo in two years, but I am a Mick. Still a Mick.

Fitzgerald, McCarthy, and O'Hara spent their professional lives coming to terms with Molloy's dilemma.

Fitzgerald in 1933 explained his own version of the dilemma to John O'Hara, who shared Fitzgerald's uneasiness about his middle-class background. Fitzgerald writes:

> I am half black Irish and half old American stock with the usual ancestral pretensions. The black Irish half of the family had the money and looked down upon the Maryland side of the family who had, and really had, that certain series of reticences and obligations that go under the poor shattered word "breeding" (modern form "inhibitions"). So being born in that atmosphere of crack, wisecrack and countercrack, I developed a two-cylinder inferiority complex. If I were elected King of Scotland tomorrow after graduating from Eton, Magdalene to Guards, with an embryonic history which tied me to the Plantagenets, I would still be a *parvenu*. I spent my youth alternately crawling in front of the kitchen maids and insulting the great. I suppose this is just a confession of being a Gael though I have known many Irish who have not been inflicted by this intense social self-consciousness.

Fitzgerald's first novel was the semiautobiographical *This Side of Paradise* (1920), which traces its hero's defection from both his Irish-American roots and his Catholicism. Thereafter, Fitzgerald published four novels, *The Beautiful and the Damned* (1922), *The Great Gatsby* (1925), *Tender Is the Night* (1934), and the posthumously published *The Last Tycoon* (1941). Each work reveals the author's increasingly severe criticism of wealth and social privilege. The novels parallel Fitzgerald's own swing from a rejection of the Irish, to a moderate acceptance of them, to an Irish-American hero's victimization by wealth and power, to what may have been, in the last unfinished novel, a fuller examination of the Irish nature.

John O'Hara's first novel, *Appointment in Samarra* (1934) was an immediate critical and popular success. Arguably his best work, *Samarra* is set in Gibbsville and, like so much of O'Hara's other fiction, attempts to portray not just character but the society that produced the character. Returning again and again to a terrain he knew intimately and to his criticism of the spiritual poverty of the milieu from which he sprang, the sources of O'Hara's writing style resemble those of James T. Farrell.

Generally, O'Hara's feelings about social class are uncertain. He attacks the hypocrisy and vacuity of materialism in middle-class life, yet he seems genuinely awed by wealth. While his social and political sympathies may be described as "liberal," members of the lower orders often appear as bit players in O'Hara's work. Of the lower orders, none appear lower than the Irish American.

The 1980s might have modified O'Hara's view of the Irish in America, had he lived another decade. As it was, the Irish in America were always "Micks," gangsters, and outsiders to him. The Irish-American characters in his novels and short stories never make it socially—they are stereotyped as maids or social climbers or fat and complacent *nouveau riches*.

Mary McCarthy is a literary contrast to the previously mentioned writers. Despite her name and background, Irish-Americans do not figure prominently in McCarthy's fiction, and when they do, they are not portrayed sympathetically. For example, in *The Groves of Academe*, Henry Mulcahy, an untenured English instructor, a sometime "professional Irishman" and specialist in James Joyce, is clearly on the receiving end of McCarthy's mordantly witty satire. Her autobiographical *Memories of a Catholic Girlhood* (1957) bears the same relationship to her own life as *A Portrait of the Artist as a Young Man* does to Joyce's. Of the autobiographical work *How I Grew* (1987), McCarthy writes that it traces "the onset of intellectual interests" from her thirteenth year, when she was "born as a mind," to her first marriage at age twenty-one. On the whole, critics have found it less satisfying than her earlier memoir, and it is less revealing of the Irish dimension than her *Memories*.

In her works, McCarthy explains the loss of her Catholic faith and her less than intense interest in Irish Americana. Exposed to two strains of Catholicism—the simple faith of her gentle, convert mother, and that of Grandmother McCarthy, "a sour, baleful doctrine in which old hates and rancors had been stewing for generations, with ignorance proudly stirring the pot"—McCarthy, perhaps understandably, shed Catholicism. And, faced with two strains of "Irishness"—the too-brief influence of a recklessly extravagant and romantic father as opposed to the grim and tightfisted Irish Americanism of paternal grandparents—it may be equally understandable that she has chosen not to celebrate her Irish heritage.

Though Finley Peter Dunne imbued his Dooley with native intelligence and wit and Betty Smith added a dash of sentiment through Francie Nolan, these second-generation writers generally aspired to American respectability at the price of Irishness. What we find in the best fiction of the period—in the works of O'Neill, Farrell, Fitzgerald, O'Hara, and McCarthy—are frustration and bitterness with a transported Irishness that has restricted their social movements and shackled their imaginations. As a result, the Irish characters who populate their works too often come off as ignorant, materialistic, and corrupt. Obviously, the price of assimilation for the writer is high.

The Postwar Regionalists

By the middle of the twentieth century, the Irish in America had proven themselves. There was no longer a preoccupation with covering their "scars of immigration."

Along with the Germans, they had been this country's first white ethnics and most of them were already third- and fourth-generation American. The Celtic tide had crested at the eastern seaboard and washed across the northern half of continental America. About 60 percent of the immigrants had settled in New England and the Middle Atlantic states. Another 25 percent had pushed on with the westward migration into the north-central states. The rest had been scattered across the country with concentrations in the major rail centers and in the port cities of Louisiana, Texas, and California.

But, after World War II, the regional differences among the American Irish became more pronounced. The Bostonians, heirs to Old-World values, established the genteel tradition of the Yankee Irish. A majority of those in New York, Philadelphia, and Chicago, who had risen in the ranks of business and the civil service, melted into the wasteland of suburbia. In the Midwest and the South, where the Irish were often an indistinct minority, they sometimes sought a wider sense of community by emphasizing their Catholicism over their Irishness. From the 1940s onward, Irish Americans began to write in regional dialects, and, in the same period, more talented women writers came to the public eye.

Women are generally underrepresented in critical evaluations of ethnic literatures, and they are underrepresented in the Irish. Surely Mary McCarthy and Flannery O'Connor stand out as writers of genius, and Betty Smith is recognized for her social realism in *A Tree Grows in Brooklyn*, *Tomorrow Will Be Better* (1948), *Maggie-Now* (1958), and *Joy in the Morning* (1963). But other gifted women whose works have been published regionally, many in small editions, have been all but ignored by the critics. Others, such as Elizabeth Cullinan and Maureen Howard, and later Mary Gordon and Alice McDermott, have produced enduring prize-winning fiction. Still others have contributed drama and poetry.

Among the postwar regionalists, Ruth McKenny, Mary Doyle Curran, and Ellin Berlin have made their marks. McKenny, best known for the popular 1940s stage version of *My Sister Eileen* (1938), made an early contribution in *Industrial Valley* (1938), a little-known novel that exposed the grotesqueries of life among the impoverished rubber workers in Akron, Ohio, during the Depression. Mary Doyle Curran's only novel, *The Parish and the Hill* (1948), set in the red-brick tenements of a Yankee milltown, contrasts the squalor of the tenements with the poshness of life on the hill. Ellin Berlin, in *Lace Curtain* (1948), traces the social climb of the Irish from the shanties of the flats to Boston's Beacon Hill. Taken together, the fiction of these three women established a feminine voice in the literature that moved regional realism to a new level.

Edwin O'Connor's *The Last Hurrah* (1956), set "in a New England city" in 1948, is more than a political novel about the changing of the guard; it is an analysis of the passing of a tradition. O'Connor's Frank Skeffington calls himself "a tribal chieftain." Between wakes and dances, he liberally dispenses favors to petitioners. At the same time, he recognizes that he is the last of the line. In *The Last Hurrah*, O'Connor has fictionalized the final campaign of Mayor James Michael Curley of Boston and glossed over the corruption of his political machine, but he has also provided a memorable slice of New England Irish Americana. O'Connor's other major novels—*The Edge of Sadness* (1961), *I Was Dancing* (1964), and *All in the Family* (1966)—are overshadowed by *Hurrah*, though they complement O'Connor's notion that the Celtic world is in a "state o' chassis" and that the chieftain can no longer rise to the day's challenge.

O'Connor's Irish-American world is primarily a male world, and the leading males, as often as not, are elderly survivors of the immigrant years, with their battles against poverty and discrimination already won. Again and again, O'Connor's fiction emphasizes an end to the Irishness that kept immigrants closely knit in ward and parish. Their sons and grandsons have intermarried and been assimilated, and O'Connor has accepted the historical inevitability of the condition.

Maureen Howard, who was born in Bridgeport, Connecticut, and who also writes about New England, confessed in the April 25, 1982, *New York Times Book Review*:

> I find too many scenes and stories that instruct me on why I've become a writer—odd encounters with language in a mixed neighborhood, mostly working class, where by the mere inflection of "Hello" you could tell that the pert young widow had lost her beau, the Montours were coming up in the world this week, the Drews had not paid their grocery bill.

Here Howard shares a talent with the Irish in capturing telling moments, echoing nuances, and blending humor and pathos.

Howard has written six successful Irish-American novels—*Not a Word about Nightingales* (1961), *Bridgeport Bus* (1966), *Before My Time* (1975), *Grace Abounding* (1982), *Expensive Habits* (1986), and *A Lover's Almanac* (1999)—edited *Seven American Women Writers of the Twentieth Century* (1977); and introduced *Cabbage and Bones: An Anthology of Irish-American Women's Fiction* (1997). Maureen Howard is preeminent as a stylist in the tradition; she is wonderfully poetic and witty and satiric. She says that she writes fiction because she cannot sing or dance, though her work obviously benefits from a related lyricism. She is a remarkable writer who continues to illustrate the best in Irish-American fiction.

Elizabeth Cullinan perfectly catches the atmosphere of New York City, where she grew up in the security of pre–Vatican II Catholic Reformation. Her fiction, particularly her prize-winning novel *House of Gold* (1970) and the stories in *Yellow Roses* (1977), provides a chronicle of lower-middle-class Irish-American urban life and of the young women caught in the conflicts of tradition and modernism.

Though Cullinan's world is circumscribed—New York and, in *A Change of Scene* (1982), Dublin—she is more than a mere regionalist; she is always the conscious artist with an eye for detail and an infallible narrative sense. Her characters move in ordered worlds and confront moral dilemmas that matter. As often as not, they fail themselves because they espouse tribal virtues that no longer apply. They are typically intelligent women preyed upon by a world that conspires to control them. As a stylist and a storyteller, Cullinan ranks with the best of contemporary American writers.

Among the New Journalists, New Yorkers Jimmy Breslin, Joe Flaherty, and Pete Hamill have produced hard-hitting news copy and realistic fiction set in the city. In three autobiographical novels—Breslin's *World without End, Amen* (1973), Flaherty's *Fogarty and Co.* (1973), and Hamill's *The Gift* (1973)—these New York writers explore the tragic father-son generational chasm in Irish-American families. Later novels— Breslin's *Table Money* (1986), about a Medal of Honor–winning Vietnam vet named

Owney Morrison; Flaherty's *Tin Wife* (1983), about the New York police and the Brooklyn Irish; and Hamill's *Loving Women: A Novel of the Fifties* (1989) and *Snow in August* (1997)—delve deeper into common Irish life in the diocese of Brooklyn. Hamill's memoir, *A Drinking Life* (1994), makes that life even more real.

The Irish who turn up in the Midwest fiction of J. F. Powers are often clerics. In five story collections and two novels, Powers has annihilated scores of Irish. He takes on the collared golf pros, television personalities, trigger-happy exorcists, and bingo emperors, as well as the new liberals, the hippie priests promoting strobe-light masses, and drive-in confessionals. In his novels *Morte D'Urban* (1962) and *Wheat That Springeth Green* (1988), and in his story collections—*Prince of Darkness* (1947), *The Presence of Grace* (1956), *Lions, Harts, Leaping Does* (1963), and *Look How the Fish Live* (1975)—Powers is the comic-satirist who balances the sacred and the profane and makes Irish Americans laugh at their own excesses. He has won major literary awards, including a 1963 National Book Award for *Morte D'Urban*. One of the most talented writers in the tradition, Powers continues to contribute to the *New Yorker*, *Nation*, *Partisan Review*, and other literary journals.

Finally, among the regionalists, there is Flannery O'Connor, an important Southern writer of Irish background who was reared a Georgia Catholic. The Irish-American quality of O'Connor's work is sublimated; it is felt rather than stated, expressed as an intellectualized Catholicism rather than an Irish consciousness. Her God-haunted novels, *Wise Blood* (1952) and *The Violent Bear It Away* (1960), are fantastic in plot, grotesque in characterization, surreal in reverie, nightmarish in metaphor, and clotted in sentence structure. But their ultimate purpose may be to confirm orthodox religious belief through unorthodox content and form. O'Connor produced four major works in her brief career (she died in 1964 at the age of thirty-nine), and her literary reputation continues to grow.

The two novels (*Wise Blood* and *The Violent Bear It Away*) and the short story collection, *A Good Man Is Hard to Find and Other Stories* (1955), were published in her lifetime, as was a collection of the three entitled *Three: Wise Blood, A Good Man Is Hard to Find, The Violent Bear It Away* (1964). Posthumously published were the short story collection *Everything That Rises Must Converge* (1965) and *The Complete Short Stories* (1971). Her nonfiction prose was published in 1969 as *Mystery and Manners: Occasional Prose*, and her letters, *The Habit of Being*, appeared in 1979.

Despite a relatively slender output in fiction, O'Connor has achieved preeminence on the American literary scene. She received a National Book Award for *The Complete Short Stories* in 1972 and the National Book Critics Award for *The Habit of Being* in 1980, both posthumously. There have been more than a score of book-length studies and literally hundreds of critical essays that attest to her literary significance.

O'Connor does not concern herself with Irish Americana in ways that, for example, James T. Farrell and Edwin O'Connor do. But her lack of "Irishness" is not an evasion, as it was for Scott Fitzgerald; her interests lay elsewhere. O'Connor's intense preoccupation with religion—Catholicism and American Southern fundamentalist Christianity—brings the shock of recognition to Irish Catholics. Although, like Graham Greene and Francois Mauriac, O'Connor often appears to have worked out her own version of Christianity/Catholicism, she has written of herself: "I see from the standpoint of Christian orthodoxy. This means that for me the meaning of life is centered in our redemption by Christ and that what I see in the world I see in relation to that." Readers who seek a comfortable or sentimental Christianity in her works will find instead considerable violence in the macabre, the gothic, and the grotesque, as well as certain humor emanating from these qualities, a condition common enough in Irish writing.

Although O'Connor has staked out her claim as, in her words, "the action of grace in territory held largely by the devil," her work is firmly established in the American South, especially her native Georgia. That gives rise to the question of whether or not, pejoratively speaking, she is a "regionalist." The same question has, of course, been asked of James Joyce and his Dublin and might well be asked of James T. Farrell and his Chicago. Doubtless, the short answer is that O'Connor, like other such "regionalists," did not just aspire to the universal through the particular, she attained it.

The farther Irish-American literature has moved from Ireland and from the Irish ghettos, the less continuity it has had. Some authors, writing from the crumbling citadels of the culture, mourn its passing like the death of an old friend, while others regard it a nightmare from which they have never quite awakened. The echoes are becoming fainter, however. In regional fiction, Irish character is evolving and producing a new hybrid. That hybrid is now clearly rooted in the New World, and its idiom is now distinctly American.

The Contemporary Scene: New Wines

The preserve of more avant-garde writers is a territory that has been a feature of Irish writing from the start—the macabre, the grotesque, the blackly humorous. J. P. Donleavy and Tom McHale have given us two of the most outrageous comic novels in *The Ginger Man* (1955) and *Farragan's Retreat* (1971), respectively. Donleavy's dastardly anti-hero, Sebastian Dangerfield, romps through "dear, dirty Dublin," shattering the saints-and-scholars myths of the "oul' sod," while McHale's Farragan clan churns up the bigotry stewing in the hearts of the Irish-American superpatriots during the Vietnam travesty. Also, Mark Costello has offered a wonderfully crafted collection in *The Murphy Stories* (1973), case studies of the artist gone amok in a psychic tug-of-war. Like a number of Irish-American writers, Costello shows an Irish penchant for nonlinear thinking and language that, like much in Joyce and Beckett, border on, and sometimes cross into, the surreal, both in content and in shifting streams of consciousness.

Donleavy is the most important and prolific of the three. Born in Brooklyn in 1926, the son of Irish immigrants, Donleavy grew up in the Bronx. During World War II, he served in the U.S. Navy and, in 1945, attended the Naval Academy Preparatory School. There he first heard talk about good writing and James Joyce, and, through reading, learned about Ireland. Following his stint in the Navy, he applied to Trinity College, Dublin, and was accepted.

After considerable trouble with publishers over offensive passages, his first and most famous novel, *The Ginger Man*, was published in 1955. It was followed by *A*

Singular Man (1963) and by a series of comic misadventures in Dublin, New York, and other odd places. Donleavy's bizarre novels feature strange alliterative titles and curious protagonists running from reality. Among them are *The Saddest Summer of Samuel S.* (1966), *The Beastly Beatitudes of Balthazar B.* (1968), *The Onion Eaters* (1971), *The Destinies of Darcy Dancer, Gentleman* (1977), *Schultz* (1979), and *The Lady Who Liked Clean Restrooms: The Chronicle of One of the Strangest Stories Ever to Be Rumoured About around New York* (1997).

His plays, based largely on his fiction, have been published as *The Plays of J. P. Donleavy; with a Preface by the Author* (1972), and there is a volume of short fiction and sketches, called *Meet My Maker, the Mad Molecule* (1964). Many of Donleavy's essays have been collected and published in *The Unexpurgated Code: A Complete Manual of Survival and Manners* (1975).

Sebastian Dangerfield, the protagonist of *The Ginger Man*, has become a cult figure. He is Donleavy's most memorable character and one of contemporary literature's first anti-heroes: an amoral, anti-establishment outsider and rebel, a boozer, womanizer, wife-beater, liar, and thief. He has reappeared as a dimmer carbon copy in the subsequent works, but Donleavy is not a one-level author. He is a black humorist with an irrepressible urge to satirize modern life, and he has, as a satirist, won a large and faithful audience.

The last two decades have yielded a number of other promising titles, such as John Gregory Dunne's compelling murder mystery, *True Confessions* (1977), a savage and comical satire of Irish-American priests in the "cloudcuckooland of Los Angeles." Monsignor Timothy J. O'Fay, nutty as a fruitcake, owns a string of useless titles and has a penchant for breaking into "My Old Kentucky Home" at the wrong time. Monsignor Mickey Gagnon dies in bed in a whorehouse. Augustus O'Dea, vicar-general, has seen *The Song of Bernadette* eleven times, a fact readers are more apt to remember than that he was "a kind, holy man." Father Des Spellacy, an "Irish Medici," exploits his wartime role as "the Parachuting Padre," fixes a raffle, and plays golf—perhaps the most popular sport among priests in fiction. He is something of a fop.

James Carroll's *Mortal Friends* (1978) is the classic replay of the Irish-American saga, and his *Supply of Heroes* (1986) uses a bigger canvas for a historical thriller that portrays Irish Republican Army (IRA) men on the run and plays on two continents. Tom Clancy, who writes edge-of-your-seat, high-tech espionage-adventure novels such as *Patriot Games* (1987) and *Without Remorse* (1993), invents heroes Jack Ryan and John Kelly to move his action. Carroll and Clancy tell good stories and reach millions of readers.

Mary Gordon's escape to reality, *Final Payments* (1978), offers one of the most memorable of first novels. Her sensitive portrayal of Isabel Moore, who sacrifices herself to nurse an invalid father at home, rings true as tragedy in the Irish scheme of things. A later novel, *The Other Side* (1989), damns the Irish on both sides of the Atlantic. As four generations of MacNamaras gather in Queens for the matriarch's funeral, Dan MacNamara reflects: "They could never be happy, any of them, coming from people like the Irish. Unhappiness was bred into the bone, a message in the blood, a code of weakness. . . . You saw it everywhere in Irish history; they wouldn't allow themselves to prosper." In spite of its psychic bleakness, Gordon's novel often tells the hard truths and invites introspection. Her later fiction, such as *Spending: A Utopian Divertimento* (1998), does not measure up to *Final Payments*.

Thomas Flanagan stands above and apart from Carroll, Clancy, and company. His historical novels set in Ireland—*The Year of the French* (1979), *The Tenants of Time* (1988), and *The End of the Hunt* (1994)—are brilliantly conceived and executed. Grounded in nineteenth-century Irish history, they portray events that matter with an authenticity that leaves formula novels in the dust. Flanagan is a stylist of genius who introduces multiple narrators and creates a vivid and credible history in fiction. In effect, he has reinvented the genre, beautifully interpreting a century full of turmoil, betrayal, and deceit.

Yet another master writer in the tradition is William Kennedy, whose Albany trilogy—*Legs* (1975), *Billy Phelan's Greatest Game* (1978), and *Ironweed* (1983)—has won him international critical acclaim. In Kennedy's talent for re-creating the urban microcosm, where machine politics rule from rectory to poolroom, his vision goes beyond the reportorial. Set in the New York State capital, Albany, in the mid-1920s to mid-1930s, the trilogy teems with life: there are, in Kennedy's world, journalists, politicians, young toughs, gangsters, and decent working-class people. Kennedy not only captures the ambience of his city, he creates flesh-and-blood characters such as Francis and Billy Phelan. Like Joyce, Kennedy celebrates the virtues of common men and women. *Quinn's Book* (1988), set in the mid–nineteenth century, rehearses the plight of the immigrants. *Very Old Bones* (1992) and *The Flaming Corsage* (1996) continue the saga.

In an interview in 1985, Kennedy said: "I believe that I can't be anything other than Irish American. I know there's a division here, and a good many Irish Americans believe they are really American. They've lost touch with anything that smacks of Irishness as we used to know it." Kennedy came late to fiction, and his vision is historical. Though he emerges as its principal spokesman, he recognizes the certain loss of an Irish-American identity, "Irishness as we used to know it."

The emphasis in this essay has been fiction because most Irish-American writers have come from journalistic backgrounds and because the Irish love to tell a good story. Apart from Eugene O'Neill, most of the early playwrights produced period pieces, melodrama, and light comedy. But in the 1950s William Gibson made a sensation on Broadway with *The Miracle Worker* (1957); in the 1960s, William Alfred's *Hogan's Goat* (1966), far better than its title, won rave reviews; and, in the 1970s, John Guare's *House of Blue Leaves* (1971) proved that the Irish still had dramatic staying power. Guare's recent *Six Degrees of Separation* (1990) has made a convincing case for the strength of an Irish-American stage presence. It isn't a Celtic revival, but it is respectable drama from accomplished playwrights.

The poets are another matter. Though the best of them, like the best of the dramatists, have come to the fore since the mid–twentieth century, they show stronger and more direct Irish influences. Among first-line poets in the tradition are Frank O'Hara, John Logan, X. J. Kennedy, Galway Kinnell, Robert Creeley, and Tess Gallagher, who, in literally scores of collections, model themselves on Yeats and company. Phyllis McGinley, who won a Pulitzer, began as a serious poet but abandoned the quest in favor of the witty epigrams she contributed to the *New Yorker* over so many years.

The younger poets of promise are women of the 1990s whose works are in their own ways true to the tradition—poets such as Kathy Callaway, Ethna McKiernan, Renny Golden, and Mary Swander, to name but a few.

While established Irish-American writers emphasize the paralyzing grip of church and family and neighborhood on the psyche, others stress the need to break the soul-fetters of the past. They mock—sometimes savagely—the narrowness of traditional values and find little or no consolation in modernism. Like William Kennedy, they see that "their kind" has been assimilated, that they need no longer prove themselves. They have been admitted to the country club with unlimited credit lines.

What has happened in recent years is part of the grand evolutionary scheme. It's a kind of cultural trade-off written into the price of emigration. If Irish-American writers draw now from non-Irish and non-ghetto experiences, their fiction simply reflects those experiences. The current literature explores new ground; the conflicts that are played out emanate from an American subculture that is divorced from Ireland by generations. Apart, then, from an incidental reference or a "walk-on," by the 1990s Irish-American fiction had made the transition. As John Kelleher says in "Irishness in America," a 1964 essay in *Atlantic Monthly*, "Like it or not, we're on our own."

To what degree are the promising younger writers with Irish surnames Irish? Is there "something in a name," or has Irish-American literature simply run its course? What of Western writers such as Larry McMurtry, whose *Last Picture Show* (1966) and *Lonesome Dove* (1985) give us pause? What of Cormac McCarthy, whose *All the Pretty Horses* (1992) and *The Crossing* (1994), set in the badlands of Texas and Mexico, have recently attracted so much critical excitement? What of the daring of a T. Coraghessan Boyle in *World's End* (1987), *Budding Prospects* (1985), *East Is East* (1990), and *Without a Hero* (1994), his splendid story collection? It is becoming harder to measure the Irish-American dimension in the literature.

Irish Americans, like other ethnicities, have today gained access to the universities in unprecedented numbers. The writers among them have been introduced to literary traditions that deny old American and British stereotypes and foster a new pride. Thus, the younger generation of Irish Americans continues to explore American themes and give voice to the American imagination.

SUGGESTED READING

Daniel J. Casey and Robert E. Rhodes, eds., *Irish-American Fiction: Essays in Criticism* (New York: AMS, 1979).

———, *Modern Irish-American Fiction: A Reader* (Syracuse, NY: Syracuse University Press, 1989).

———, "Irish American Literature," in *New Immigrant Literatures in the United States: A Sourcebook to Our Multicultural Literary Heritage*, ed. Alpana Sharma Knippling (Westport, CT: Greenwood Press, 1996).

Charles Fanning, ed., *The Exiles of Erin: Nineteenth-Century Irish-American Fiction* (Notre Dame, IN: University of Notre Dame Press, 1987).

———. *The Irish Voice in America: 250 Years of Irish-American Fiction* (Lexington: University Press of Kentucky, 2000).

This 1932 photograph was taken during the construction of New York City's Rockefeller Center by Charles C. Ebbets who was working for publicist Hamilton Wright, Jr. It is known by two names, "Lunchtime atop a Skyscraper" and "New York Construction Workers Lunching on a Crossbeam," neither of which gives any hint of its ethnic significance. (Bettmann/CORBIS)

Chapter 28

Looking for Jimmy (1999)

Peter Quinn

The photograph of the eleven ironworkers perched nonchalantly on an I-beam suspended over midtown Manhattan may not enjoy the same celebrity as Dorothea Lange's *Dust Bowl* madonna, her handsome face plowed under by want and worry, or Alfred Eisenstadt's sailor kissing the nurse in Times Square on V-J Day, a serendipitous recapturing of Ulysses's return to Penelope, but it is famous enough. Several years ago, I purchased a copy outside the Time and Life Building from a street vendor, who told me it was his best-selling print.

I was drawn to the picture by what a cultural historian might call its "iconic significance." Like those photos by Lange and Eisenstadt, it seems to hold in frozen permanence not just a single moment but a whole era. It is one of those images that a historical novelist studies for long periods—scanning faces, clothes, gestures, searching foreground and background—in the hope of slipping away from the dead certainties of facts and dates to touch the kinetic intensity of a once living, now departed moment. The novelist's impossible dream isn't merely to distill the subtle particulars of a now-vanished instant but to unfreeze the entire scene and to melt into it, much like the main character in Jack Finney's novel *Time and Again*, who actually succeeds in transporting himself back to gaslight New York with the help of such visual aids.

I had the print of the ironworkers framed and hung it on the wall of my office. Although I have spent more working hours gazing at it than I care either to count or admit, I have never achieved the long-sought sensation of trans-temporal transport.

The discoveries I have made have been more prosaic, the result of a casual mix of research and reverie. According to Phil McCombs, a reporter for the *Washington Post* who investigated the photo's provenance several years ago, the image was taken as part of a shoot done in 1932 by Hamilton Wright Jr., a professional photographer and pioneer in the practice of public relations. Wright was involved in promoting the construction of Rockefeller Center and snapped this photo as part of that assignment.

McCombs tracked down Wright's son, who told him that either his father "'took it personally, or one of his guys.'" Whatever the case, the man behind the camera caught —or arranged—his subjects in a breathtaking tableau that juxtaposes the run-of-the-mill New York sight of construction workers enjoying a time out with a setting that would turn most inhabitants of terra firma into jelly. The ironworkers appear utterly oblivious to where they are. Aligned not unlike the figures in Da Vinci's *Last Supper*, they seem as at ease on their steel aerie as the disciples with Jesus in the cenacle.

On the left, a worker lights the cigarette of the man next to him. You can see the muscle in his biceps as he crooks his arm to offer the light. Three men in the middle are having a conversation. Several have in their hands what look like rolled-up newspapers. Four hold what appear to be cardboard lunch boxes. One is shirtless. The man at the extreme right provides the only exception to the subjects' unawareness of being photographed. He holds a flask and stares directly at the camera with a look of grumpy disdain, as though intent on puncturing the illusion of workers on an ordinary break who didn't know a photographer had them in his sights. To me, he has always seemed ready to lift his right hand with middle finger extended, a traditional New York gesture of disapprobation.

Several years ago, on a book-tour stop in Austin, Texas, I dropped into a soi-disant New York–style deli that had a poster-size version of the photo framed behind the counter. Usually, I concentrated my focus on the men. My routine was to start with the second figure on the left. He has his cap pulled down over his eyes, but his sharply chiseled profile reminded me of my mother's oldest brother, a World War I veteran and roustabout/bartender who died in 1933, fourteen years before I was born, and who I knew only from photographs. This time, however, perhaps because I was seeing it in an entirely new venue, my eyes didn't settle on my uncle's doppelganger but on the buildings beneath the men's dangling feet, especially the distant dome of Mecca Temple. (Described in the 1939 *WPA Guide* as "the largest Masonic Shrine in the city," the temple now operates as the city center.)

Judging by the position of the Mecca Temple, I suddenly realized that the building under construction was the RCA Building (now the GE Building), the main tower of the Rockefeller Center complex. I suppose this should have been obvious before, but obvious or not, it hadn't made an impression. Every working day for several years I had been looking out my office in the Time Warner Building at the very site where the photograph was taken without giving it a thought. This perception of missing the obvious drew me in even deeper. I wondered what else I had overlooked in my years of gazing at the faces mounted on my wall.

The year the picture was taken, 1932, the Dow-Jones Industrial Average, which had reached an all-time high of 381 in September 1929, bottomed out at 41. The American economic slump no longer had the feel of a cruel interlude but of a permanently altered reality in which the collapse or overthrow of capitalism was eminently possible. There is no hint of that crisis anywhere in the photograph. In fact, the combination contained in Wright's photo—the obvious brawn and casual daredevilry of the men on the beam, the soaring height of the edifice they are raising, the engineering and financial know-how that are implied, the sprawling city in the background, and the pall of auto exhaust and factory smoke that obscures Central Park and the Hudson River—all speak of a strength more elemental and enduring than the economic paralysis that was dragging the country to its knees.

The central show of confidence emanates from the men themselves. They are lean and wiry, their toughness of an old-fashioned kind, before Nautilus machines and steroids made the pretentious deltoids of Sylvester Stallone and Arnold Schwarzenegger an archetype of masculinity. These men didn't work at staying in shape. Life saw to it. They all look as though they could handle themselves in a fight, and probably had. They are union workers, men with steady jobs (as least as long as Rockefeller Center was under construction) in a period when millions were just scraping by or standing in breadlines. There is nothing sorrowful about them, no uncertainty or fear in their faces, least of all of heights. The talk going on among them seems natural and relaxed. Their everyday interaction is part of the magic of the scene, a surreal contrast of everyday behavior and extraordinary setting.

In all the years I have studied the faces in the photo, I have found in them a familiarity that goes beyond a single resemblance to an uncle of mine. These are faces I knew first-hand from my childhood in the Bronx—faces of relatives, teachers, priests, Christian Brothers, cops, firemen, fathers and brothers of friends, my own father's political associates—Irish faces that, in my mind, have no connection to the fields or boreens of Cork and Tipperary but are natural to the concrete precincts of New York, to its streets, bars, and parish halls. Looking at them, I have been struck by the thought that what they are sitting upon is more than merely a beam. It is the hyphen between Irish-American, and they are straddling it in perfect equipoise.

Six decades before Wright produced his photograph, the cartoonist Thomas Nast drew a scene with two figures sitting on metal pans, their feet dangling in space. The pans are suspended from the beam of a weighing scale. From the side of the beam labeled "South" hangs the pan holding Sambo, the barefoot, thick-lipped, bug-eyed stereotype of the ignorant Negro ex-slave whose recent elevation to citizenship supposedly threatened to subjugate defeated but chivalrous whites to the rule of "pickaninnies" and scalawags. From the other, labeled "North," hangs Paddy, a grotesquerie that Nast borrowed from contemporary English newspapers and journals and regularly employed as a pug-nosed, half-simian representation of Irish ignorance and savagery. The pans of Nast's scale are in balance: Sambo and Paddy embody the equal burdens of rural blacks and urban Irish, underclasses that weigh down the future of America's recently united Anglo-Saxon republic. (The sardonic solution to this dilemma was offered by the British historian Edward Freeman, who wrote that America might one day be a great nation "if only every Irishman would kill a Negro, and be hanged for it.")

The view of Irish-Catholics that reigned in Anglo-Saxon America through the later half of the nineteenth century is well described in Harold Frederic's 1896 novel, *The Damnation of Theron Ware*. Fredric's story of the loss of faith by Ware, a Methodist minister in the fictional town of Octavia, New York, is built upon his close encounter with the town's Irish Catholics—"this curiously alien race." Having served only rural congregations, Ware has no previous acquaintance with the Irish. This hasn't stopped him from acquiring a stark and disturbing impression:

> The Irish had been to him only a name. . . . But what a sinister and repellent name! His views on the general subject were merely those common to his communion and his environment. He took it for granted, for example, that in the large cities most of the poverty and all the drunkenness, crime, and political corruption were due to the perverse qualities of this foreign people. . . . The foundations upon which its dark bulk reared were ignorance, squalor, brutality, and vice. Pigs wallowed in the mire before its base. . . .

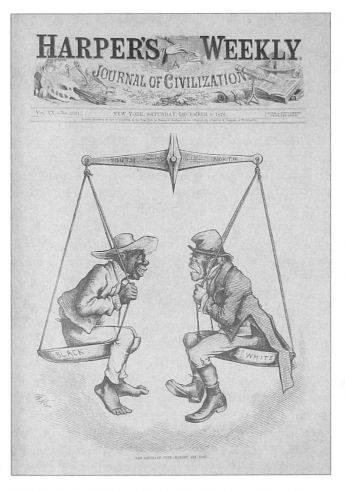

Paddy in the North balances Sambo in the South, according to Thomas Nast's cover for *Harper's Weekly,* 9 December 1876. The equation was racial as well as political. (Library of Congress, Prints and Photographs Division, LC-USZ62-57340)

Above were sculptured rows of lowering ape-like faces from Nast's and Keppler's cartoons, and out of these spring into the vague upper gloom—on the one side, lampposts from which Negroes hung by the neck, and on the other, gibbets for dynamiters and Molly Maguires, and between the two glowed a spectral picture of some black-robed tonsured men, with leering satanic masks, making a bonfire of the Bible in public schools.

The historian and musicologist William H. Williams has done an exhaustive study of the Paddy stereotype as it played out in popular music. In *'Twas Only an Irishman's Dream: The Image of Ireland and the Irish in American Popular Song Lyrics, 1800–1920,* he makes the case that the massive immigration of Famine-era Irish Catholics inundated the cities of the Northeast with Europe's poorest, most-unskilled peasantry, a population with no experience of English-style village life, never mind of rapidly industrializing urban centers. The utter unfamiliarity of the Irish with the routines and demands of city life, and the absence of any previous immigrant group to blaze a path or at least offer some hint of how to act or what to do, put the Irish at a distinct disadvantage. They would spend a long time climbing out of what Williams describes as "the worst slums in American history." Yet, Williams perceives that their unfamiliarity with cities also gave them an advantage:

> In spite of their peasant origins, they had none of the Jeffersonian suspicion of, or disdain for, the city. Having no place else to go, the Irish burrowed into American cities and came to understand them better than many Yankees, as they turned politics into a profession, instead of a nose-holding duty, a function of upper class noblesse oblige.

Williams makes clear that Thomas Nast wasn't alone in equating the Irish and blacks. (Indeed, one popular mid-century term for blacks was "smoked Irishmen.") On stage, Paddy and Sambo were both childlike buffoons—lazy, superstitious, and given to doubletalk, inflated rhetoric, and comic misuse of proper English. Unlike Sambo, Paddy was highly temperamental and always ready to fight, but this easy irascibility didn't diminish their shared status "as an endless source of fun." For both groups, the stereotype became so ingrained in popular attitudes and perceptions that it passed from being regarded as a theatrical parody to a predeterminate of group behavior. "An Irishman," writes Williams, "taking a drink, getting into a fight, or just generally having a high old time, was not like other men who might drink, fight, or celebrate. He was acting an elaborately scripted role. He was filling a grimly comic prophesy. He was playing the stereotype of himself."

The difference was that, although they lived on the periphery of American society, the Irish were not barred by law as well as custom from trades and professions, or routinely denied their civil rights. The mere fact that they could vote gave them a wedge, which they used forcefully. Starting far behind America's "old stock" Protestant whites, despised for their religion and clannishness, and burdened by poverty and social dislocation, they were at least allowed to compete. In terms of the theater, the rise of Irish Americans to prominent places as actors, performers, and songwriters allowed them not merely to suffer the Paddy stereotype but to change it to their own purposes. In the hands of a writer and producer like Ned Harrigan, whose "Mulligan Guard" plays were so popular that he had his own theater to house them, the stage Irishman was transformed from goonish Paddy to good-natured, hard-working, decent Pat.

Pat retained elements of the old Paddy caricature. He was volatile and a born brawler. But whereas Paddy had echoed Theron Ware's nightmare vision of Molly Maguires and their wild-eyed cousins who tried to incinerate New York City during the Draft Riots, Pat's combative instincts were tamed and Americanized. Instead of being a term of opprobrium, "Fighting Irish" became a moniker of the 69th Regiment and the University of Notre Dame football team. By the time of World War II, the association of Irish and fighting, once so basic to Paddy's disruptive image, had become a rallying cry for American patriotism. The 1944 movie *The Fighting Sullivans* portrayed a brood of five brawling Irish-American brothers, all lost on the same ship, as the apotheosis of loyalty and sacrifice. In the 1941 movie *Yankee Doodle Dandy*, which

After terms representing Massachusetts in both the U.S. Senate and House of Representatives, John Francis Fitzgerald (1863–1950), the son of immigrants from County Wexford, was elected mayor of Boston in 1906, when this portrait was taken. With his political base in the city's North End, his eldest daughter Rose's 1914 marriage to Joseph P. Kennedy, son of Fitzgerald's East End political rival, not only solidified the Irish hold on Boston but created a family dynasty that would affect American politics and society for the rest of the twentieth century. (Photograph by Theodore C. Marceau, Library of Congress, Prints and Photographs Division, LC-USZ62-96662)

celebrated the life and music of the Irish-American actor and songwriter George M. Cohan, the actor playing President Roosevelt says to Cohan (played by Jimmy Cagney), "I like the way you Irish Americans wear your patriotism on your sleeve." Gone were the days when Paddy was told not even to apply. Now Pat was assured that he was "in like Flynn."

Irish progress from Paddies to Pats was gradual and incremental. It both reflected and hastened the diminishment of anti-Irish prejudice. But it would be misleading to lump the ironworkers of Wright's photograph in either category: as the bog-trotting apemen of Thomas Nast's imagination, or as suburban-bound Pats about to spring-board on the G.I. Bill right into the middle of the American mainstream. These men are of another type. For them, rural Ireland is barely a memory, the never-never land of Tin Pan Alley productions such as "When Irish Eyes Are Smiling," or "A Little Bit of Heaven." Suburbia is still a white-collar, Protestant place. Their home is the city. It is the context that defines them, and which, in their hard-edged, streetwise style, in their slang and their gait, in the way they hang a cigarette out of their mouth or wear their cap or ogle a girl, they helped define. They are no longer a living part of urban America, but they remain a major ingredient in its DNA.

By the time the Depression struck, the urban Irish community that had been created willy-nilly in the aftermath of the Famine no longer ruled New York the way it once had. Along with making the Catholic Irish seem less threatening to America's Protestant majority, the waves of immigrants from Italy and Eastern Europe dwarfed the size and significance of Irish neighborhoods. The reflexive link between urban and Irish, which was forged in the 1840s and 1850s and which at one point was so strong in popular music that, as William Williams summarizes it, "an Irish name conjured up the American urban scene," was no longer as all-embracing or surefire as it had once been. Italians came to provide much of the city's crude, unskilled labor. Jews came to dominance in entertainment. The African-American migration from the South was adding a dynamic new element to the city's mix.

The relations of the Irish with these groups has mostly been framed in terms of conflict and struggle. Jews have frequently written about the pugnacious belligerency with which the Irish harassed and bullied them. Italians, though nominally sharing the same Catholic religion, found little welcome among the Irish. Black and Irish relations have long seemed synonymous with ethnic bitterness and strife. This was never the whole story, however. With the Jews, for instance, Tammany Hall had early on recognized the potency of their vote, and while many progressives were agonizing over the introduction of a Semitic strain to Christian America, Tammany was working hard to win and keep their loyalty.

Their shared religion might not have produced brotherly love between Italians and Irish but it did lead increasingly to intermarriage. *Coitus vincit omnia.* The parish school I attended in the east Bronx was made up of both Irish and Italians, so that by the 1940s, in addition to classmates named Caesar Di Pasquale and Dennis O'Shaughnessy, there was the Italo-Hibernian Salvatore Managhan.

The outcome of the Irish-black struggle, which began as a contest over which group would find itself relegated to permanent status as impoverished and oppressed outsiders (a position the Irish peasantry had centuries of experience in occupying), wasn't simply a case of Irish success in using their white skin as a trump card. Upper- and lower-class white Protestants continued to see Irish Catholics through much the same lens as Theron Ware. The revival of the Ku Klux Klan in the 1920s was more directed at up-and-coming immigrant Catholics than at segregated and disenfranchised blacks. The Irish presence in Ivy League schools and on corporate boards was tiny.

The gulf that separated urban Irish-Catholics from their white Protestant countrymen was portrayed in a revealing incident that occurred in Camp Mills on Long

Island, soon after the entry of the United States into World War I. The 69th New York, composed of mostly Irish Americans, was quartered near the 4th Alabama, a white Southern regiment. Relations were bad from the start. Albert Ettinger, a member of the 69th, remembered fistfights breaking out between the two regiments "at the taverns in Hempstead." Tensions mounted further when the 15th New York, "comprised of Negro troops," arrived in camp. In his memoir, *A Doughboy with the Fighting 69th*, Ettinger described what happened next:

> Our boys from the 69th received those of the 15th New York as buddies. Not so the Alabamians. They resented blacks coming into camp. Hell, they resented us! The first thing you know fights erupted all over the place, and the 69th guys actually stood up for the 15th men and fought alongside them against the Alabamians.

The camp commander required the men of the 15th New York—but not the Alabamians—to surrender their ammunition. Ettinger and others of the 69th "thought this was unfair" and slipped ammunition "to our fellow New Yorkers." The black New Yorkers, wrote Ettinger, "never forgot that, and once, when I visited a unit of the 15th in France, some of the fellows thanked me for it."

To the half-Irish, half-German Ettinger, the essential characteristic of the soldiers of the 69th New York was their identification as New Yorkers. Their "whiteness" created no instant camaraderie with "crackers" from the South. They were mightily impressed by the 15th New York in part "because their music was simply out of this world." Led by the famous black musician James Reece Europe, the 15th paraded into Camp Mills with a rhythmic swagger that made them "a sight to behold."

The Negro troops knew how to move. They had style, and what mattered most to profane, sarcastic New York Irish recruits like Joe Hennessy ("a con artist and wiseacre" whom Ettinger summarizes in three sentences: "'Fuck you. If you got any sisters, fuck them too.' That was Hennessy.") was the act of self-assertion, the distinctive way a man carried himself, the unmistakable impression he made. Perhaps because they were off their own turf, in unfamiliar circumstances, Hennessy and company could at least this once look past skin color and see in their black counterparts some reflection of themselves.

I suppose it would be possible to compare the roster of the 69th in 1917 with the payroll list (should it still exist) of ironworkers employed in building Rockefeller Center. Given the heavy presence of Irish Americans in both, it is feasible that a number of the same names would appear. In my free-form contemplation of Hamilton Wright's photo, I have come to imagine that Private Joe Hennessy is the man on the extreme right. Hennessy isn't about to allow himself to appear as if he is swinging over the void with no idea it's all part of a publicity stunt. Sorry, pal, that's something a cracker might do. But it's not my style. The sarcasm etched in his face says it: You know what you can go do, and if you got any sisters, they can go do it too.

The Irish working-class types like Hennessy were never of much interest to social scientists. By the 1920s, when urban studies were becoming a formal discipline, the Irish were largely regarded as part of a dying political order or subsumed into faceless categories. The intricate and far-flung parish infrastructure they had built, which created a unique network of schools, hospitals, and charities that paralleled those of secular society, went largely unexamined. Hennessy also lacked a literary chronicler. F. Scott Fitzgerald and John O'Hara, who shared Hennessy's ethnic background, were seeking to escape an Irish identity, not draw attention to it. James T. Farrell's *Studs Lonigan* captures some of the nuances of the Irish working class life in Chicago. (More often, it is flat and superficial, like bad journalism.)

Yet, if there was little sociological examination of the urban Irish and no poetic witness to do for their quotidian existence what James Joyce did for their Dublin counterparts—to evoke the dense complexity of lives that the privileged often saw as bereft of subtlety or depth—they are not so remote that it is impossible to venture any generalities about the way they were.

The smirk worn by that ironworker on the far right—the one I have identified as Hennessy—was widely applied. One on one, Hennessy would almost certainly be respectful of his parish priest. Together, in a bar, the urban Irish were derisive of everyone in authority, priests included. Sarcasm was embedded in their speech and attitudes. It was used for offense and defense. It was a weapon to cut down anyone in the community who might think or act like he was better than his peers, a pretension that both in Ireland and America was most often associated with those trying to gain entry to the realms of WASP culture. Such ambition was regarded as a form of treason. Sarcasm was equally a means for dismissing those realms as the preserve of frauds and pompous lightweights, whose philanthropic interest in the working class was forever motivated by the urge to control and remake them. Sarcasm was a form of subversion, a defense mechanism of colonized people like the Irish.

Boisterously patriotic, the urban Irish had at best a suspicious view of the country's political structure. They generally regarded the country's capitalist economy as a rigged game in which a workingman's best hope was sticking by his union and holding off any outside interference, whether from bosses interested in breaking the unions up or from radicals seeking to make them open to everyone, thus destroying what the Irish regarded as their own best guarantee against immiseration.

The genus Hennessy and his coworkers belonged to was best delineated by those two Jimmies—Walker and Cagney—who personified Paddy's transmogrification from mud-splattered, simpleminded, shillelagh-wielding spalpeen into skeptical, fast-talking urbanite who could never be mistaken for a greenhorn or rube. In his book *The City in Slang: New York Life and Popular Speech*, Irving Lewis Allen recounts how by the middle of the last century "Irishman's sidewalk" was used as slang for a city street. The implication was that, rather than the sidewalk, "the street was a more suitable place for the hated Irish to walk, or that perhaps they were too dumb to know the difference." Gradually, however, the Irish turned their association with the city streets from a slur into a strength.

In tandem, debonair Jimmy Walker, songwriter and politician, and Jimmy Cagney, the actor-hoofer with the looks of a handsome prizefighter lucky enough never to have had his face smashed in, expressed the style of the urban Irish in its definitive form. These Jimmies had the blend of musicality and menace, of nattiness and charm, of verbal agility and ironic sensibility, of what today is known as "street smarts," that the Irish, as New York's first immigrant outsiders, had developed. In their desire to belong, the Irish had created a behavior and bearing that was adapted to the pace and demands of the metropolis, a way of life totally different from what they had known in rural Ireland.

Jimmy had his own style of walking and talking that proclaimed his natural place on the sidewalks of New York. You can see it in the newsreels of Walker and in Cagney's films, in their gait, fast and loose, halfway between a stroll and a dance step, an evanescent strut, an electric edginess, as if they found it difficult to stand still, their ears permanently cocked to the syncopation of the streets. They move with the fluidity of tap dancers, a bastardized dance form that, in William Williams's analysis, mixes Irish, Lancashire, and African-American steps. When the African-American men of the 15th New York paraded into Camp Mills, they had a high-voltage version of that urban walk, which, as their cheering made clear, the Irish Americans of the 69th instantly recognized.

Fundamental to Jimmy's style was the presumption that the border between legal and illegal was a question of convenience rather than morality. The unforgivable offense was to be boring or colorless, to surrender to the tedious anonymity of the factory or the tenement. Long before Ronald Reagan obliterated the distinction, Tammany began erasing the line between entertainment and politics. Tammany was woven into the fabric of the city's wards, into the saloons and sporting clubs they were often home to, into the gangs and unions. Tammany was a regular provider of picnics, boat trips, and clambakes, as well as municipal jobs. Tammany's leaders usually made a name for themselves in the social orbit of the saloons before they began a career in politics. Richard Croker, the greediest of all Tammany bosses, began as the leader of a street gang; Charles Francis Murphy, the smartest, was an outstanding baseball player; Al Smith, Murphy's protégé, was an actor and singer.

Nowadays, a public recitation of Tammany sachem George Washington Plunkitt's attack on educated men in politics ("the dudes who part their names in the middle") would be greeted with laughter. But Plunkitt was serious. What did academics have to do with finding men jobs or bringing color and excitement into the monotony of gray streets? How did college equip a man to convey the style and strength that would cause, say, a gang of ironworkers to fall in and follow his lead? Didn't a good shortstop know more about teamwork and facing the opposition than a gaggle of sociology professors?

Jimmy never had time for the theories of educated men. Jimmy belonged to the concrete, to what won the respect of his peers and made him stand out. The urban Irish passion for nicknames—"Mugs," "Red," "Knocko"—evidenced their ceaseless pursuit of an identity that allowed them to stand out, to be a person who didn't sink under the mass sameness the industrial city constantly threatened to impose. From the days of the "Bowery b'hoys" in the 1840s—when a distinct urban street type first appeared—through the flashy, flip, fashionable mayoralty of Jimmy Walker, the Irish were makers and molders of the qualities that set city people apart. In the earliest phase, as immigrant Paddies, the very language used to describe the rough and tumble of the streets became replete with their presence: "hooligans," "shenanigans," "Micky Finns," and "paddy wagons."

Later on, as Jimmies, they pioneered the pose of cool detachment, of sangfroid, on which city dwellers, especially New Yorkers, pride themselves. Perhaps even today, after nearly seven decades, there is no better representation of that pose than the eleven ironworkers casually sitting on an I-beam suspended above midtown. High on their steel perch, their feet dangling in the air like a line of hoofers in mid jump, the Jimmies of Hamilton Wright's photo continue to embody some part of the bravado of city life, the determination to take everything in stride, never to be caught off balance, always to appear in control.

Speech or verbal agility was another important part of Jimmy's modus operandi. It is estimated that a third of the 1.5 million Irish who fled to America because of the potato famine were native-Irish speakers. English was, at best, a second tongue. Like their ancestors had done for centuries, the Irish in America maintained a cavalier attitude toward the English language. They never regarded it as a sacred inheritance, its rules incised in stone, but as a device with which to negotiate their way in an unfamiliar world, to soften their massive dislocation and assert their own identity. English was pliable and elastic, an instrument that could be adapted for purposes apart from grammatical purity.

In Jimmy's hands, one of the irradicable characteristics of urban speech became its glibness—a fast, smooth, nonstop flow that duplicated the pace of metropolitan life and was instantly recognizable as "city talk." The origin of the very word "glib" is uncertain, but one possible source is the forelock that the Irish wore in Elizabethan times and that they tugged on incessantly in their conversations with the English conquistadors. In English eyes, the pulling on the glib and the accompanying torrent of words were pieces of the same sly tactic, a stratagem to distract them from their work of conquest and settlement. The stereotype of Paddy preserved that perception. Paddy, writes Williams, was characterized by "volubility and loquaciousness."

In *Terrible Honesty*, a study of the intense and fecund mongrelization that took place in Manhattan in the 1920s, Ann Douglas traces the evolution of modern urban speech. Although she has little to say about the Irish, it is impossible to scan the pedigree she describes without perceiving the presence of Paddy and Jimmy: "Just as ragtime developed into the freer and more self-sufficient jazz form, comic Negro and ethnic dialect led to the use of Black English and white self-consciously modern urban slang. The two vernacular branches of the language, Negro and white, had much in common." Essential to that vernacular, beneath its playfulness, was a hard core of indignation, a pervasive resentment of the subtle and not-so-subtle barriers meant to keep the lower classes in their place. Slang was an implicitly subversive assault on proper grammar and usage, a bastion of social distinction. Irish, Jews, and African Americans, the three groups most responsible for the formation of urban slang, had long histories as outsiders. In each case, they cultivated a comic style designed to mock the pretensions of the well-to-do and cut the powerful down to size.

Sometimes the underlying resentment was too raw to be cloaked in humor. Ettinger recounts that during his service in France with the 69th he was unjustly thrown into the stockade. When he was finally released and returned to the regiment, he started "to blubber like a baby." The chaplain of the regiment, Fr. Francis Duffy (his statue stands in the middle of Times Square), put his arms around Ettinger and

helped him express "the irreverence toward secular authority in general" so characteristic of the Irish-American Doughboy:

> "All right Albert," Duffy told him, "forget about what has happened, just forget it. Repeat
> after me: 'TO HELL WITH THEM ALL!'"
>
> "To hell with them all!"
>
> "Fine! That's the spirit. Say it again louder: 'TO HELL WITH THEM ALL!'"

It was an old Irish imprecation. The Irish were a people who never "knew their place,"
or rather knew the place that others intended for them but refused to accept it. At
least since the sixteenth century, Irish Catholics had been resisting the laws and customs that assigned them to be "hewers of wood and drawers of water." Their chronic
resistance and restiveness led some English observers to detect a racial bent toward
querulous insubordination. In America, during his tour of the antebellum South,
Frederick Law Olmstead was told by a plantation owner that although Irish labor was
a less expensive alternative to the use of slaves, he didn't employ the Irish because they
were "dishonest, would not obey explicit directives about their work, and required
more personal supervision than negroes."

By the time Hamilton Wright trained his camera on an Irish-American construction
crew in 1932, the notion of ethnic and/or racial inferiority, of different groups having
a "natural place in the social order," had been clothed in the authoritative-sounding
pseudo-scientific gibberish of eugenics. Tom Buchanan's outburst in *The Great Gatsby*
about how "It's up to us who are the dominant race to watch out or these other races
will have control of things" echoed the widespread conviction that there was a moral
threat to America's Anglo-Saxon genetic stock, the source of the country's greatness,
from the growing numbers of immigrants and "colored." (The book cited by Buchanan as "*The Rise of the Coloured Empires* by this man Goddard" was in fact by
eugenicist Lothrop Stoddard and was prominently advertised in the debut issue of
Time in 1923.)

Eugenics had a pervasive influence on American medicine and underlay the widespread sterilization of the "feeble-minded." It also provided a scientific rationale for a
1923 revision of U.S. immigration laws, intended to end the influx of southern and
eastern Europeans in general, and Jews and Italians in particular. By the 1920s, some
eugenicists seemed ready to admit the Irish, or "Celts," to a racial status close to
Anglo-Saxons. But not all. In *The Passing of the Great Race* (1920), a widely read and
highly influential attack on "racial mongrelization," the eugenicist Madison Grant
waffled about where the Irish stood.

Grant observed that a physical change had occurred among the Irish in America.
The "Neanderthal physical characteristics of the native Irish—the great upper lip,
bridgeless nose, beetling brow with low growing hair, and wild and savage aspect"—
had largely disappeared. The Irish apemen of Nast's cartoons had evolved a more
human form. Yet, with the Irish, in Grant's view, looks could be deceiving. When it
came to intellectual and moral traits, "the mental and cultural traits of the aborigines
have proved to be exceedingly persistent and appear in the unstable temperament and
the lack of coordinating and reasoning power, so often found among the Irish."

Wearing his heavyweight championship belt, boxer Gene Tunney (1898–1978), the son of Irish immigrants from Bohola, County Mayo, and a U.S. Marine, epitomized the Irish male in the late 1920s. He went on to write *A Man Must Fight* (1932) and *Arms for Living* (1941), his autobiography, and served as director of the Boy Scouts of America. (Library of Congress, Prints and Photographs Division, LC-USZ62-17793)

For many, the irrefutable proof of this unstable and unreasonable temperament was the tie between Irish Americans and alcohol. The crime and corruption that besieged American cities in the wake of large-scale immigration were believed by many to grow out of the saloon, a putrescent institution joined at the hip with its Siamese twin, the Irish political machine. Prohibition was aimed at extinguishing the whole of saloon culture, which so offended the piety, propriety, and moral sensibility of mainline Anglo-Saxon Protestants.

Had it been attempted a generation or two earlier, Prohibition may have enjoyed a greater chance of success. At least there might have been more of a willingness to put Paddy once and forever in his place. But by the time Prohibition became law, on the eve of the "Roaring Twenties," Paddy had been replaced by Jimmy, and where Paddy had been a hairy, beetle-browed alien, with a "wild and savage aspect," Jimmy was slick, smooth, an evolutionary adaptation to the American scene who not only looked and acted like he belonged, but at some level seemed to incarnate what urban life was all about.

In the description Ann Douglas gives of Jimmy Walker, she makes clear his emblematic status as a rebel against the country's old code of behavior as well as the newer notion of a genetically predestined upper class:

> The debonair Walker came from working-class Irish stock; however dilatory and scant his reform impulses might be, his sympathies were with the people and they knew it. . . . He showed little prejudice against blacks or ethnic minorities; he lifted the restriction against the hiring of black doctors at Harlem Hospital, and he was among the few public officials who greeted Charles Lindbergh in 1927 after his transatlantic flight and found no need for references to Lindbergh's Nordic lineage.

There is a passage in John O'Hara's *From the Terrace* that describes the WASP resentment against the Jimmy-type, the Irish American who didn't know his place, who thought he could charm his way in, all the time wearing the subversive grin that said, 'TO HELL WITH THEM ALL." Though barely removed from his working-class origins, this Jimmy-type knows what to drink and how to dress. He seeks to insinuate himself among the privileged not because he admires their morals or envies their genes but because theirs is the power and the glory and the wealth and the beautiful, sophisticated women. In O'Hara's novel, the WASP protagonist is warned to watch out for a character named Duffy, who is assiduously trying to elbow his way into the smart set:

> There's a difference between a Catholic and a Mick, and Duffy is a Mick. Sharp, shrewd, brilliant, dresses well, good manners and all that. But when I meet an Irishman and I get that instinctive feeling that I can't trust him, I know he's a Mick. I've had it with grooms and I've had to fire them.

On the screen, the gangsters and hard men Jimmy Cagney played were powered by a mainspring of Mickness, a tightly wound inner coil of charm and resentment that could unwind into laughter, song, or a grapefruit in the face. It was rumored that Cagney's portrayal of Tom Powers, a street kid on the make, in *The Public Enemy* (1931) was modeled on Legs Diamond, a Mick from the slums of Philadelphia. Whether consciously derived from Diamond or not, Cagney caught the stylish surface and inner ferocity with which the tabloids made Legs synonymous. As William Kennedy described him in the novel *Legs*, Diamond was "one of the truly new American Irishmen of his day: Horatio Alger out of Finn McCool and Jesse James, shaping the dream that you could grow up in America and shoot your way to glory and riches."

Legs in the tabloids and Cagney in the movies raised the urban Irish hoodlum, a character of long standing in America's cities, to, in Kennedy's words, a "paradigm for modern urban political gangsters, upon whom his pioneering and his example were obviously not lost." Legs was an exaggerated version of Jimmy. Jimmy over the line. Legs was a vicious gangster, and yet many Americans saw in him something quintessential to life in the big city. In the case of Italian-American gangsters like Bugsy

Moran and Frank Costello, their adoption of Irish surnames was more than an attempt to take on less-foreign-sounding monikers. They wanted the aura the Jimmy mobster had, the wiry Mick in the expensive suit who knew how to handle himself wherever he went: the docks, the track, the streets, a hoity-toity nightclub, or a jail cell. Per Cagney and Hollywood, Jimmy became a celluloid role model for future generations of non-Irish gangsters.

Because he didn't "know his place," the Jimmy-type was invariably a Mick, and a Mick was naturally at home *in urbe* since this was the one space in which the very idea of knowing or having a place was forever in question. The odds are that when they took off their work clothes some of those eleven ironworkers (young, single, good looking, with a steady paycheck) slicked back their hair, put on a jacket and tie, and hit the clubs and speakeasies on 52nd Street, a stone's throw from where they worked. These watering holes were themselves well known for their casual mélange of clientele that blurred old lines of class and ethnicity, sometimes even of race.

Jimmy traveled around under the impression that he was as good as anyone else, that it all came down to the wad of bills in your pocket. Had he ever heard Fitzgerald's observation that the rich are different from the rest of us, Jimmy would tell you that if you gave him enough simoleons, he would be different too. Class rested on cash, not character, and Jimmy never regarded the pretensions of the upper class to higher morals or loftier values as anything but that. In many cases, this conviction had been passed down to him by aunts, uncles, grandparents, the maids and grooms who had lived behind the facades of the Big Houses, in America as well as Ireland, and washed and ironed wardrobes filled with the emperor's clothes.

The career of James Forrestal, the country's first secretary of defense, who committed suicide in 1949, provides a revealing look at the Jimmy-type. A descendant of Famine immigrants, Jimmy grew up in the Hudson River town of Beacon, New York. He left as fast as he could, a Mick who shook from his feet the dust of working-class Irish sandlots and headed off for the courtyards of Princeton, the executive suites of Wall Street, and the lush lawns of the North Shore. He knew where he wanted to go and was ready to do what it took to get there. He cut off his relatives, left the Catholic Church, married a WASP, and eventually pushed his way into the inner circles of the Anglo-Saxonry at the moment when the Old Boys were at the top of their game, not only running the country but, thanks to America's pivotal role in World War II, running the planet.

High as he went, however, at base James Forrestal stayed a Jimmy. First there was the face, a classic Irish mug, aptly punctuated by a broken nose. (Put a cap on Forrestal and a pair of work pants and he would make a perfect twelfth on that I-beam.) And then there was the attitude. Though he succeeded in becoming a player, Forrestal could never hide his belief that the game was rigged. He had Walker's cynicism about the eugenical delusion that society's distribution of wealth and privilege was rooted in biology. The most recent biography of Forrestal, *Driven Patriot* (1992), by Townsend Hooper and Douglas Brinkley, says he had "a detached and sardonic humor, as though commenting on the scene from outside it." One acquaintance wrote that his stance of ironic detachment made him seem "the non-Jewish equivalent of the wandering Jew." According to his son, Forrestal's financial success as a bond trader didn't deter his conviction that "the whole Wall Street apparatus was in major respects a discreet conspiracy to protect the already rich."

Forrestal threw himself out a window of the naval hospital in Bethesda in May 1949. He was a burnt-out case, exhausted from his years in Washington. Earlier on, his biographers tell us, Forrestal had perceived "it was better to be rich than poor, white than black, Protestant than Catholic," and aware of the degree to which his background reeked of the lesser essences, he expunged them. Yet, no matter how far he rose into the WASP empyrean, he couldn't rid himself of "the mental and cultural traits of the aborigines." A millionaire and powerbroker, he lived in a world that he never felt part of, a groom in Brooks Brothers clothing. He was left with a sense of being utterly alone. Perhaps in an attempt to reconnect himself to the world he had abandoned as a young man, Forrestal asked the chief psychiatrist at Bethesda to be allowed to see a Catholic priest. The psychiatrist turned him down because, Hopper and Brinkley speculate, "a Catholic confessional might risk disclosing sensitive national security information." (A wildly anti-Catholic conjecture that, if it truly describes the doctor's reasoning, couldn't have done much to lessen Forrestal's agonized feeling of isolation.)

Forrestal may have traveled too far, too fast, and suffered a case of the psychic bends, but he wasn't alone in his journey. Joe Kennedy was another Mick on the make. Raised in Irish Boston, married to the Irish-American mayor's daughter, Kennedy had no real hope of slinking unnoticed into the ranks of the social elite. He stormed the WASP citadels—Harvard, Wall Street, and the sanctum sanctorum, the Court of St. James—and though he often felt snubbed and out of place, he couldn't be deterred. Early on, he groomed his sons to shove through the breech he made and take hold of the very center of power, the White House itself.

Moving in tandem with the Kennedys was the bulk of Irish America. The social revolution brought about by the New Deal and the G.I. Bill, a revolution the urban Irish political machines endorsed and supported, paved the highways (real and metaphorical) that carried the Irish on the final leg of their journey, from immigrant spalpeens to urban insiders to suburban homeowners and whatever lies beyond. JFK's election was less a last hurrah than the political icing on a socio-economic cake that a great many Irish Americans were already consuming.

Like Paddy, Jimmy is history. The hard edges of the Irish-American urban experience —the struggle against prejudice, sickness, poverty, the conflicts with other races and ethnic groups—have been softened by the sepia tint of nostalgia and selective memory. There are still Irish construction workers, cops, and bartenders around, but most commute in and out of the city. The era that Jimmy was part of is dead and buried. Heroic capitalism has been replaced by digital-global-designer capitalism. Magazines no longer run pictures of the type Hamilton Wright took. If he were alive today, Wright would most likely be photographing cyber-geeks at computer terminals.

Jimmy's legacy is in the physical infrastructure he helped to build—tunnels, bridges, skyscrapers. This is the tangible part. The intangible part requires more searching. Jimmy never stepped foot in the intellectual and cultural inner circles of cosmopolitan New York. (A recent history of the city's intellectual life doesn't even have a reference to Irish or Irish American in its index.) Jimmy's influence was in the streets, in his understanding that a city is a theater and the street a stage. First off the boat, expelled from the most backward agricultural society in Western Europe, totally unfamiliar and unprepared for urban life, Jimmy's ancestors were bereft of a usable past. Yet, though instantly saddled with the Paddy stereotype, they came to see that they had the power to change their role. In the city, whoever the streets belong to gets to define what it takes to belong. Paddy learned that. Jimmy lived it.

Today, you won't find Jimmy where Hamilton Wright did, out on a steel limb. Don't bother looking in any of those phony Irish pubs that make a living selling $4 bottles of beer to tourists and money managers. Look instead in the places where attention is paid to all profound superficialities of the street/stage, how to walk, move, strut, dance. Look where there are no pretty illusions about what it takes to survive or succeed, where everybody knows the odds and appreciates how luck and connections can make the difference between a job and a jail cell, and where you never, no matter what, let on to being impressed or lost or afraid.

Yo, Jimmy.

Chapter 29

The Future of Irish America (2000)

Peter Quinn

The unique American subculture that the Irish created in the wake of the Famine—the culture I grew up in—a culture that cohered around the Catholic Church and the Democratic Party, with a working-class base and widespread aspirations to lace-curtain propriety, a culture deeply skeptical about WASP institutions and pretensions, and suspicious and resentful of the mainline tradition of Protestant moral reform and economic self-determination—is dead and gone. It's with Ed Flynn or Tom Prendergast—take your pick of big-city Democratic bosses of a generation or so ago—in the grave. It lingers in some pockets, for sure, and survives in the formative experiences of pre-Vatican II Irish Catholic fossils like myself. But it's as doomed as the dodo, and no amount of humpty-dumpty yearning for the way things were—or the way some like to imagine they were—will bring it back.

Today, it's almost impossible to recapture how distinct and apart that world was, how foreign Anglo-Protestant America seemed, how certain we were of our distinct identity and special destiny. We were a parochial people literally and figuratively. In the place I grew up, our basic compass was the parish we were from. That's how we identified ourselves: "I'm from St. Raymond's or St. Helena's or Sacred Heart or Tolentine or whatever." And we were parochial in the sense of being intellectually narrow-minded and constricted.

That narrow-mindedness has often been commented on, and often, I think, in a wrong-headed way. The adults I knew were avid devourers of books. They enjoyed the theater. They reveled in the pace and variety of urban life, a pace and variety the Irish had in fact helped create. They held high educational ambitions for their children. Almost everyone I knew was wildly addicted to movies, and many of us availed ourselves of the Legion of Decency's rating system, where the C or "condemned" list conveniently underlined what was *really* worth seeing.

The fundamental narrow-mindedness we suffered from wasn't so much in our attitude to the world as to ourselves. We wanted—we demanded—to be seen in one light and one light only. I remember seeing *The Bells of St. Mary's* on television around the same time that my aunt took me to one of those periodic theatrical re-releases of *The Wizard of Oz*. Although I sensed it at that moment, it would be some time later before I could articulate the feeling that the relationship between the parish presided over by Monsignor Barry Fitzgerald and his crooning curate Father Bing Crosby and the real-

The nineteenth-century stereotype of the Irish woman, typically a brutish domestic servant named Bridget, was considerably softened by the time Tin Pan Alley and the silent cinema got its hands on her. The "Colleen" became a handsome example of modern American beauty. Indeed her generically good looks were an advertisement for the assimilation potential of the Irish, with the only vestiges of ethnicity in lyrical names like Rosie, Kitty, and Peggy. The song "Pretty Kitty Kelly" was issued on 78 rpm and as sheet music in 1920. (Mick Moloney Irish American Collection)

life parish I lived in was the *reverse* of what existed between the Emerald City and Dorothy's Kansas.

The ecclesiastical Oz of the Reverends Fitzgerald and Crosby was populated with characters who bore some resemblance to people I knew first-hand. But on screen the ironic, tough-minded, combative, argumentative, believing, suspicious, hard-drinking, back-biting, funny, obnoxiously profane, relentlessly skeptical, gloriously complicated people I knew—people as contradictory as any Cowardly Lion and as manipulative as the Wizard himself—became as tame and predictable as Auntie Em's Kansas farmhands.

This, of course, was the nihil-obstat version that everyone in the parish applauded. All the adults I knew loved *The Bells of St. Mary's*, even the ones who never stopped badmouthing the clergy and couldn't say enough bad things about the licking they'd taken in parochial schools. This was how we wanted the world to see us, America's best-behaved ethnic group: a big-screen refutation of the lies once spread by nativists. The stage Irishman was okay as long as he looked and acted like Bing Crosby and, hell, if the stage Irishwoman wasn't only a nun but a nun played by Ingrid Bergman with a Swedish accent, well, *Hooray for Hollywood*.

The Irish in America—at least the Irish I grew up with—were still in the defensive crouch they'd arrived in during the Famine, still sensitive to the distrust and dislike of a *real* America, to the suspicions about our loyalty and supposed proclivity to raucous misbehavior. We were forever reminding ourselves—and the rest of America—of how many Irish fought with Washington, how many died at Antietam, and how many won the Congressional Medal of Honor, a litany of self-justification that implicitly accepted it wasn't enough we'd been here for over a century.

Even J.F.K.'s election as president didn't entirely settle the matter. Writing in 1965, in his one-volume *Oxford History of the American People*, Samuel Eliot Morison could dismiss the Famine Irish as having added, quote, "surprisingly little to American economic life, and almost nothing to American intellectual life." The good news, I suppose, is that Morison used the word "surprisingly"; the bad news: as far as he was concerned, this was pretty much the high point of the Irish Catholic role in America. From there, it was backward and downward to Tammany Hall and the corruption of American urban politics.

It's in this light that I'm particularly amused to read the currently popular bedtime tale *How the Irish Became White*. Here the old nativist canard that the Irish can never shed their essential foreignness, that they are a race of eternal strangers, that their attempt to become true Americans is intrinsically futile is turned on its head. Yes, the Irish still fail. In the eyes of some, the Irish will *always* fail. But now they fail upward. It's not that they weren't American enough, but *too* American, immigrant Esaus who traded their birthright of Irish resistance to oppression for the American pottage of material success.

If there's any central theme to the story of the Irish in America, it isn't, in my opinion, how they became white but how they stayed Irish: that is, how an immigrant group already under punishing cultural and economic pressures, reeling in the wake of the worst catastrophe to take place in Western Europe in the nineteenth century, a people not only devoid of urban experience but largely unacquainted with the town life prevalent throughout the British Isles, suddenly finding itself plunged into the fastest industrializing society in the world, regrouped as quickly as it did, built its own far-flung network of charitable and educational institutions, preserved its own identity, and had a profound influence on the future of both the country it left and the one it came to.

It was done imperfectly, for sure, and was marred by sins and stupidity, by mistakes and missed opportunities, but for me, the wonder is that it was done at all.

In general, I'm always suspicious about the search for single themes and unified theories that provide neatly apprehensible explanations for human behavior. As the historian Barbara Fields has written in an essay entitled "Ideology and Race in American History":

> Each new stage in the unfolding of the historical process offers a new vantage point from which to seek out those moments of decision in the past that have prepared the way for the latest (provisional) outcome. It is the circumstances under which men and women made those decisions that ought to concern historians, not the quest for a central theme that will permit us to deduce the decisions without troubling ourselves over the circumstances.

In the specific case of Irish Americans, the notion of definitively deciphering their history with the Rosetta stone of race at least provides the basis for a polar interpretation to the one enshrined in *The Bells of St. Mary's*. Next door to the idyllic never-never land of cinematic fantasy, there is now the mirror-image community of uniformly abusive nuns, ogre-like priests, parish after parish of solidly united bigots determined to get what they could for themselves by becoming active collaborators and supporters of the American system of racial exclusion and exploitation.

What's mostly lacking, I feel, is the saving grace that art can bring to the saga of any family or ethnic group or country, to unearthing the rich contradictions of Irish America, to delineating the bewildering, destructive, exhilarating journey between what were once not so much different cultures as different universes, to exposing the levels of struggle and failure, self-doubt and self-hatred, penetrating wit and indelible grievance, paralyzing depression and deep, resonant laughter.

I don't want to sound as though I'm entirely dismissing the role of history in this process of self-examination and reclamation. At its best, in books like Bob Scally's *The End of Hidden Ireland*, history can reach past the faceless, sexless sanitation of generalities and statistics to touch the lives of those now dead, to give us a sense of the density and intensity of every human life, and even to allow the poor and powerless a dignity that they were denied in their own lifetimes.

Recently, I stumbled across a small jewel of historical detective work that recounts the history of a case tried in the New York Surrogate's Court, in 1932. *The Recluse of Herald Square*, written thirty-five years ago by Joseph Cox, presents the story of Mrs. Ida Mayfield Wood who, along with her sister, spent a quarter of a century hiding in a hotel room. When her sister died and the police were called they discovered that amid the clutter and debris of her room, Mrs. Wood had nearly a million dollars in cash and bonds. This was at the bottom of the worst depression in American history. As well as her hidden treasure, Mrs. Wood had another secret, one that it would take dozens of lawyers, investigators, and would-be heirs to unravel. Without entirely ruining the mystery for those who might want to read the book, I'll simply point out that Mrs. Wood's secret casts a good deal of light on the status of the Irish in mid-nineteenth-century America and on a desire for "passing" that wasn't restricted to a racial disguise.

As a lapsed historian, however, I don't feel qualified to stand in public and pass judgment on the practices of a priesthood I'm no longer part of. I continue to pray that at the hour of my death, I'll be attended by a historian—preferably from a Catholic institution—who'll receive me back into the fold. Meantime, I continue to enjoy the happy, carefree life of the apostate, unburdened of a historian's scrupulosity, willingly giving in to every temptation to speculate and invent, to avoid the virtuous work of analysis and indulge in the pleasures of anecdote.

For instance, I remember my father—a remarkable, difficult, usually inaccessible man—on the triumphal night John Kennedy was elected president, the same night as my father was elected to the State Supreme Court, the fourteenth and last time he ran for office, this grandson of Famine emigrants, well-oiled and declaiming to the swaying crowd in our Bronx living room, "Well, now, Mr. Nixon, you can kiss our royal Irish ass!"

Beautiful, lofty things . . . a thing never known again.

In fiction Elizabeth Cullinan has captured that world, I think, and Alice McDermott and William Kennedy. Mostly, it remains enshrouded and unrevealed, pretty much entirely absent from the dominant form of American cultural self-examination —the movies. A story central to the making of the American identity, it has yet to be explicated and celebrated as fully as it should be. Perhaps it will never be.

Yes, then, Irish America is rich, successful, influential—fat and happy with its lists of successful entrepreneurs and zillionaires. We're headed somewhere, that's for sure. The momentum of the journey is increasingly weighted toward the American part of the Irish-American equation, which is why we came here in the first place. Anyone who has the courage to predict where it will end has more courage than I do—or less fear of being exposed as an idiot. But to paraphrase Captain Kirk, "as we boldly go where no Irishman or woman has ever gone before," I hope, as Sydney Carton hoped, "it is a far, far better place than we have ever gone before."

Let me suggest one possibility.

About a year ago, the *New York Times Sunday Magazine* ran a double page of photographs of American girls and boys whose multiethnic, multiracial background defied any easy characterization—a level of mongrelization that is continuing to gather steam, to the consternation of racial purists of various persuasions. The most common identity shared in this depiction of ethnic fusion—which may one day rise to the level of a racial meltdown—was Irish. Perhaps, then, the history of Irish Americans that will be written at the end of the twenty-first century will be entitled *How the Irish Became Brown*. What a wonderful prospect. What a welcomed fate. The Irish as the common denominator of a new American construct. The Irish as gravediggers for that last and most enduring of all nineteenth-century superstitions—scientific racism.

Whatever the future may hold, wherever it may take us, we can bring along only what we possess, and if we don't possess our past, if instead of a true history and a significant literature, we bring along only trivia, empty myths and a handful of stories, or—worst of all—the latest intellectually fashionable versions of ourselves, we will offer those to come after nothing of lasting consequence.

A long time ago, in a bar called the Bells of Hell, while I was in the embryonic phase of thinking about writing a novel about the Famine Irish in New York and was unsure whether there was a story worth telling—and where better to worry over an unborn novel than in a place named the Bells of Hell?—I heard the late Kevin Sullivan—ex-Jesuit, scholar of Irish literature and raconteur—recite Paddy Kavanaugh's poem "Epic."

It stayed with me across the years. It sustained me and still does. I've always found in it the antitoxin to the Irish-American original sin of self doubt. The poem goes like this:

> I have lived in important places, times
> when great events were decided, who owned
> that half a road of rock, a no-man's land
> surrounded by our pitchfork-armed claims.
> I heard the Duffys shouting "damn your soul"
> and old McCabe stripped to the waist, seen
> step the plot defying blue cast-steel—
> "here is the march along these iron stones"
> that was the year of the Munich bother. Which
> was more important? I inclined
> to lose my faith in Ballyrush and Gortin
> till Homer's ghost came home whispering to my mind
> he said: I made the Iliad from such
> a local row. Gods make their own importance.

Today, Irish America is powerful enough and wealthy enough to decide for itself where it's headed and what it will take on the journey. Wherever we may end up, suburbs or city, the south end of Jersey or the outer end of the galaxy, it is we the living who will choose what will be recorded, remembered, redeemed from silence and oblivion by scholarship and art.

Gods make their own importance.

Appendix

The Irish in U.S. Census: An Explanatory Note

A number—forty-four million Irish in the United States—has reverberated around the globe in recent years. It is blithely repeated without an understanding of how the U.S. Census Bureau defines "ancestry" and why it asks the question at all.

Prior to 1980, the decennial census of the United States determined its ethnic categories based on the responses to questions about place of birth (self and/or parental) and language. A question on "ancestry"—an altogether different concept—was first included in 1980. It was designed "to collect ethnic data on persons regardless of the number of generations removed from their country of origin" based on "self-identification."[1]

An ancestry question was repeated in 1990 and 2000, but in a manner that makes it difficult to compare the results systematically with those for 1980. The phrasing "What is this person's ancestry?" allowed for open-ended, highly subjective expression in a write-in format that resulted in more than a thousand ethnic categories for the 1980 Census. In 1990 and in 2000, the question was changed to "What is this person's ancestry or ethnic group?" to recognize the extent of ethnic intermarriage in the United States and of "ethnic options" beyond the second generation.[2] The respondent could understand "ancestry" as "ethnic origin or descent, 'roots,' heritage, or the place of birth of the person, the person's parents, or their ancestors before their arrival in the United States."[3] While multiple answers were allowed, as in 1980, in tabulations only the first and second answers were coded in 1990 and 2000. Thus, if one responded "English, German, and Irish," only English and German were counted. Once again, subjectivity lent a certain degree of arbitrariness to the conclusions. Among the eighty-six ancestry groups, "Scotch-Irish" was counted separate from either Irish or Scottish.

Most significantly for historians, the U.S. Census Bureau explicitly stated—even taking the Irish as an example—that "the intent of the ancestry question was *not* to measure the degree of attachment the respondent had to a particular ethnicity. For example, a response of 'Irish' might reflect total involvement in an 'Irish' community or only a memory of ancestors several generations removed from the individual."[4] Rather, "ancestry" was specifically designed to profile America's non-Hispanic, non-racial population,[5] while data on ethnicity "of broad population groups" was collected based "on social and political considerations—not anthropological or scientific ones."[6]

Therefore we present the following tables with the caveat that, as a measure of the number of Irish Americans and the meaning of Irish America, the U.S. Census—as rich a resource as it is for the study of American history—raises far more questions than it can immediately answer, challenging all of us to handle the results carefully.

NOTES

1. U.S. Bureau of the Census, *Ancestry of the Population by State, 1980 (Supplementary Report PC80-S1-10)* (Washington, DC: Bureau of the Census, 1983), 1.

2. Mary C. Waters, *Ethnic Options: Choosing Identities in America* (Berkeley: University of California Press, 1990); see also Stanley Lieberson and Mary C. Waters for the National Committee for Research on the 1980 Census, *From Many Strands: Ethnic and Racial Groups in Contemporary America* (New York : Russell Sage Foundation, 1988).

3. U.S. Bureau of the Census, Census 2000 Summary File 4, *Technical Documentation* (Washington, DC: U.S. Census Bureau, 2003).

4. U.S. Bureau of the Census, Census 2000 Summary File 4, *Technical Documentation* (Washington, DC: U.S. Census Bureau, 2003), and Census of Population and Housing, *1990: Summary Tape File 3, Technical Documentation on CD-ROM* (Washington, DC: Bureau of the Census, 1992); emphasis added.

5. "Explain Ancestry Groups," http://factfinder.census.gov/home/en/epss/ancestry.html.

6. "Explain Race or Ethnic Groups," http://factfinder.census.gov/home/en/epss/race_ethnic .html.

TABLE 1

First- and Second-Generation Irish in the United States, by Region and State,
according to the Census of 1890

States and Territories	Ireland[a] first generation (country of birth; i.e., immigrant)	Ireland[b] second generation (country of birth for both parents; i.e., American born)	Irish Americans (first and second generation only) as a perecentage of total Irish-American population in the United States
United States	1,871,509	2,164,397	4,035,906 (100%)
North Atlantic Division	1,241,116	1,358,707	64.4
Maine	11,444	13,340	0.61
New Hampshire	14,890	13,627	0.71
Vermont	9,810	13,749	0.58
Massachusetts	259,902	271,263	13.2
Rhode Island	38,920	39,663	1.95
Connecticut	77,880	89,008	4.1
New York	483,375	530,445	25.1
New Jersey	101,059	107,555	5.2
Pennsylvania	243,836	280,057	12.9
South Atlantic Division	48,003	57,108	2.6
Delaware	6,121	7,199	0.33
Maryland	18,735	23,562	1.05
District of Columbia	7,224	7,686	0.37
Virginia	4,578	4,492	0.22
West Virginia	4,799	7,383	0.3
North Carolina	451	377	0.02
South Carolina	1,665	1,878	0.09
Georgia	3,374	3,724	0.17
Florida	1,056	807	0.05
North Central Division	433,719	591,732	25.4
Ohio	70,127	95,329	4.1
Indiana	20,819	28,248	1.21
Illinois	124,498	154,231	6.9
Michigan	39,065	46,156	2.1
Wisconsin	33,306	55,481	2.2
Minnesota	28,011	43,583	1.8
Iowa	37,353	60,301	2.4
Missouri	40,966	53,155	2.3
North Dakota	2,967	2,938	0.15
South Dakota	4,774	8,007	0.32
Nebraska	15,963	23,092	0.97
Kansas	15,870	21,211	0.92
South Central Division	43,198	52,913	2.4
Kentucky	13,926	20,479	0.85
Tennessee	5,016	5,781	0.27
Alabama	2,604	2,879	0.14
Mississippi	1,865	2,012	0.09
Louisiana	9,236	12,822	0.55
Texas	8,201	6,719	0.37
Oklahoma	329	403	0.02
Arkansas	2,021	1,818	0.095
Western Division	105,473	103,937	5.2
Montana	6,648	6,049	0.31
Wyoming	1,900	2,246	0.10
Colorado	12,352	12,283	0.61
New Mexico	966	884	0.045
Arizona	1,171	908	0.05
Utah	2,045	1,769	0.095
Nevada	2,646	2,639	0.13
Idaho	1,917	1,607	0.09
Washington	7,799	6,942	0.36
Oregon	4,891	4,006	0.22
California	63,138	64,604	3.16

SOURCES: Department of the Interior, Census Office, *Report of the Population of the United States at the Eleventh Census: 1890* (Washington, DC: Government Printing Office, 1895).

[a] Table 32, p. 607.

[b] Table 38, p. 686.

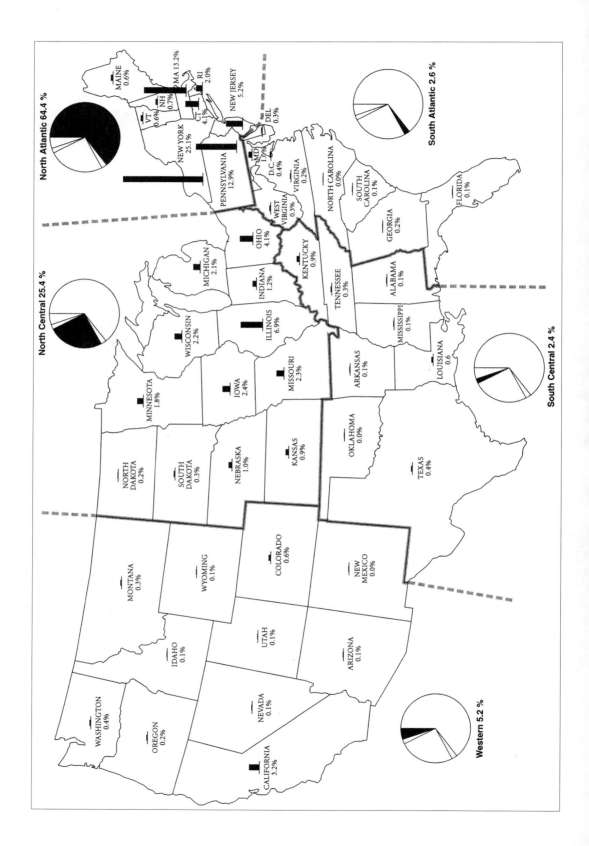

North Atlantic 64.4 %

MAINE
0.6%

MA 13.2%

RI
2.0%

NH
0.7%

VT
0.6%

CT
4.1%

NEW JERSEY
5.2%

DEL
0.3%

NEW YORK
25.1%

MD
1.0%

D.C.
0.4%

VIRGINIA
0.2%

PENNSYLVANIA
12.9%

WEST
VIRGINIA
0.3%

NORTH CAROLINA
0.0%

SOUTH
CAROLINA
0.1%

FLORIDA
0.1%

South Atlantic 2.6 %

GEORGIA
0.2%

OHIO
4.1%

KENTUCKY
0.9%

TENNESSEE
0.3%

ALABAMA
0.1%

MICHIGAN
2.1%

INDIANA
1.2%

North Central 25.4 %

WISCONSIN
2.2%

ILLINOIS
6.9%

MISSISSIPPI
0.1%

LOUISIANA
0.6

South Central 2.4 %

MINNESOTA
1.8%

IOWA
2.4%

MISSOURI
2.3%

ARKANSAS
0.1%

NORTH
DAKOTA
0.2%

SOUTH
DAKOTA
0.3%

NEBRASKA
1.0%

KANSAS
0.9%

OKLAHOMA
0.0%

TEXAS
0.4%

MONTANA
0.3%

WYOMING
0.1%

COLORADO
0.6%

NEW
MEXICO
0.0%

WASHINGTON
0.4%

OREGON
0.2%

IDAHO
0.1%

UTAH
0.1%

NEVADA
0.1%

ARIZONA
0.1%

CALIFORNIA
3.2%

Western 5.2 %

TABLE 2
Irish Ancestry in the United States, according to the Census of 1980

Ancestry response	Population no.
Irish (single ancestry)	29,828,349
Irish (multiple ancestry)	10,337,353
Total	40,165,702
Northern Irelander (single ancestry)	10,080
Northern Irelander (multiple ancestry)	6,338
Total	16,418
TOTAL	40,182,120

NOTE: The 1980 U.S. Census did not make a separate distinction for "Scotch-Irish" or "Celtic," as was done in subsequent decennial counts of the population.

SOURCE: *Ancestry of the Population by State: 1980 (Supplementary Report PC80-S1-10)* (Washington, DC: Bureau of the Census, 1983), online at http://www.census.gov/population/www/censusdata/pc80-s1-10.html.

TABLE 3
Irish Ancestry in the United States, according to the Censuses of 1990 and 2000

Ancestry response	Population no. 1990	Population no. 2000
Irish (first ancestry)	22,721,252	19,282,096
Irish (second ancestry)	16,047,948	11,246,396
Total	38,769,200	30,528,492
Scotch Irish (first ancestry)	4,334,197	3,283,065
Scotch Irish (second ancestry)	1,283,576	1,036,167
Total	5,617,773	4,319,232
TOTAL	44,386,973	34,847,724

NOTE: The 1990 U.S. Census counted the answer "Celtic" as part of the "Irish" ancestry category. It did *not* do this in the 2000 Census; in 2000, "Celtic" was a separate 65,638 persons.

"Irish" was an umbrella category that included "Irish" (code 050), "North Irish" (code 081), and "Celtic" (code 099). Under "Irish" the Census counted these answers: Black Irish, Clare, Cork, Donegal, Dubliner, Eire, Galway, Ireland, Irish Free State, Kerry, Kildare, Kilkenny, Laoighis, Leitrim, Leix, Limerick, Longford, Louth, Mayo, Meath, Monaghan, Offaly, Roscommon, Sligo, Tipperary, Waterford, Westmeath, Wexford, Wicklow. Under "North Irish" it counted these answers: Antrim, Armagh, Derry, Down, Fermanagh, Londonderry, Northern Ireland, Orangeman, Tyrone, Ulster. "Scotch-Irish" (code 087) also included Scot Irish. The source for this coding information is in the technical documentation for the 1990 Summary Tape File 3 online at http://factfinder.census.gov/metadoc/1990stf3td.pdf.

SOURCE: U.S. Census Bureau, American Factfinder, *1990 Summary Tape File 3 (STF 3)—Sample Data, Table PO33 (First Ancestry) and Table PO34 (Second Ancestry)* and *2000 Summary File 3 (SF3) —Sample Data, Table PCT16 (First Ancestry) and Table PCT17 (Second Ancestry)* online at http://factfinder.census.gov/.

Opposite: Distribution of the Irish in America, 1890, as a percentage of all those born in Ireland or native-born of Irish-born parents, by region and state, according to the U.S. Census of 1890. (Department of the Interior, Census Office, *Report of the Population of the United States at the Eleventh Census: 1890* [Washington, DC: Government Printing Office, 1895], table 32, p. 607, and table 38, p. 686)

NOTE: For the purposes of this map, we confine "Irish American" to the census categories "Foreign-born, Ireland" (i.e., first generation) and "Native White Persons Having Both Parents Born in Specified Countries, Ireland" (i.e., second generation). The U.S. Census of 1890 also recorded persons of mixed ancestry under foreign parentage; there were 760,000 who had one parent, either a father or mother, born in Ireland (for these numbers see table 41, p. 691, and table 44, p. 694, in *Report of the Population of the United States at the Eleventh Census: 1890*). We have not, however, included them in this map because of the variety of possible combinations, which requires detailed research.

Contributors

Linda Dowling Almeida is adjunct assistant professor of Irish studies at New York University. She is author of *Irish Immigrants in New York City, 1945–1995* (2001), as well as articles on twentieth-century Irish immigration to the United States, including "A Great Time to Be Irish in America: The Irish in Post–Second World War New York City" in *The Lost Decade: Ireland in the 1950s* (2004) and "And They Still Haven't Found What They're Looking For" in *The Irish World Wide: Patterns of Migration* (1992). She is book review editor for the annual journal *New York Irish History*.

Daniel J. Casey is the editor, with Robert E. Rhodes, of *Views of the Irish Peasantry, 1800–1916* (1977), *Irish-American Fiction: Essays in Criticism* (1979), and *Modern Irish-American Fiction: A Reader* (1989). With his wife, Linda, he edited *Stories by Contemporary Irish Women Writers* (1990); he has published more than 150 articles and reviews, as well as fiction and poetry. He is the author of *Benedict Kiely* (1974), which won a Choice Critics Award, and *Critical Essays on John Millington Synge* (1994). He is a four-time Fulbright recipient and has served as professor, dean, vice president of academic affairs, and president at universities in Great Britain, Finland, Ireland, Italy, Switzerland, and the United States. He is now a freelance writer and lecturer in Irish and Scottish studies.

Marion R. Casey is the author of the main entries on the Irish in *The Encyclopedia of New York City* (1995) and *The Encyclopedia of New York State* (2005), as well as assistant producer of the video documentary *From Shore to Shore: Irish Traditional Music in New York City* (1993). Her essay "'From the East Side to the Seaside': Irish Americans on the Move in New York City" was included in *The New York Irish* (1996), and "The Limits of Equality: Racial and Ethnic Tensions in the New Republic, 1789–1836" appeared in *Race and Ethnicity in America: A Concise History* (2003). She is adjunct assistant professor of Irish studies at New York University, where she is also responsible for the Archives of Irish America, a resource within NYU's Division of Libraries that focuses on the twentieth-century Irish experience.

David Noel Doyle is professor of modern history at University College Dublin. He is the author of *Irish Americans, Native Rights, National Empires, 1890–1901* (1976) and *Ireland, Irishmen and Revolutionary America, 1760–1820* (1981). With Kerby A. Miller, Arnold Schrier, and Bruce D. Boling, he co-authored *Irish Immigrants in the Land of Canaan: Letters and Memoirs from Colonial and Revolutionary America, 1675–1815* (2003). He edited (with Owen Dudley Edwards), *America and Ireland, 1776–1976* (1980) and (with Lawrence McCaffrey, James Walsh, and Margaret

Connors), the forty-two-volume series *The Irish Americans* (1976). In addition to many essays in *Irish Historical Studies, Irish Economic and Social History*, and the *Journal of American Ethnic History*, he recently published "Irish Catholicism in the Diaspora: The Case of the United States" in *Christianity in Ireland* (2002) and "The Irish Abroad (1860–2000)" in *The Encyclopedia of Ireland* (2003).

Pete Hamill is the author of numerous books, including the bestsellers *Downtown* (2004), *Forever* (2002), *Snow in August* (1997), and his memoir *A Drinking Life* (1994). He has been editor in chief of both the *New York Post* and the *New York Daily News*. In his writing for these publications, as well as for the *New York Times*, the *New Yorker*, and *Newsday*, he has captured life in his hometown, New York City. He is a member of New York University's Glucksman Ireland House Advisory Board, as well as Writer in Residence in NYU's Department of Journalism.

Kevin Kenny is professor of history at Boston College, author of *Making Sense of the Molly Maguires* (1998) and *The American Irish: A History* (2000), as well as editor of *New Directions in Irish-American History* (2003) and *Ireland and the British Empire* (2004). He has contributed articles to the *Journal of American Ethnic History* and *Labor History*, and his essay "Diaspora and Comparison: The Global Irish as a Case Study" appeared in the *Journal of American History* (2003).

J. J. Lee is director of Glucksman Ireland House at New York University. He chaired the history department at University College Cork for many years, also serving at various times as chair of the Irish Fulbright Commission and as an independent member of the Irish Senate. His *Ireland 1912–1985: Politics and Society* (1990) was awarded the Aer Lingus/Irish Times Prize for Literature (nonfiction), the Irish Independent/Irish Life Prize for History, and the James S. Donnelly, Sr. Prize of the American Conference for Irish Studies in Social Sciences.

Margaret Lynch-Brennan earned a Ph.D. in history from the State University of New York at Albany in 2002. Originally a classroom teacher, she has spent the last twenty-five years as an administrator with the New York State Department of Education.

Henry Noble MacCracken was president of Vassar College from 1915 to 1946. A graduate of New York University, he earned a doctorate from Harvard and served as a member of the English faculties of Yale and Smith. MacCracken was born into a distinguished educational family: his father was a chancellor of New York University from 1891 to 1910, and his grandmother was a pioneer of women's higher education in Ohio. MacCracken published extensively on English literature, education, and American culture.

Larry McCarthy is associate professor of management at the Stillman School of Business at Seton Hall University. His research includes marketing activities of professional sport organizations, Olympic marketing activities, and marketing sport to minority populations. He was appointed by the Atlanta Committee for the Olympic Games (ACOG) as an Olympic Envoy to the Olympic Council of Ireland for the 1996 Olympic Games.

Timothy J. Meagher is the author of *Inventing Irish America: Generation, Class, and Ethnic Identity in a New England City, 1880–1928* (2001), editor of *From Paddy to Studs: Irish-American Communities in the Turn of the Century Era, 1880–1920* (1986), and co-editor of *The New York Irish* (1996). His essays have appeared in the *Journal of American Ethnic History*, the *U.S. Catholic Historian*, the *New England Quarterly*, and the *Historical Journal of Massachusetts*. He is associate professor of history and university archivist at Catholic University of America in Washington, D.C.

Kerby A. Miller is professor of history at the University of Missouri, Columbia. He is the author of the award-winning *Emigrants and Exiles: Ireland and the Irish Exodus to North America* (1985) and co-author of *Journey of Hope: The Story of Irish Immigration to America* (2001). With David N. Doyle, Arnold Schrier, and Bruce D. Boling, he co-authored *Irish Immigrants in the Land of Canaan: Letters and Memoirs from Colonial and Revolutionary America, 1675–1815* (2003). He is a former senior research fellow, Institute of Irish Studies, Queen's University, Belfast.

Rebecca S. Miller is assistant professor of music of the Americas at Hampshire College. Formerly a public-sector folklorist, her work includes publications, recordings, festivals, radio, and video documentaries. She produced the award-winning public radio series "Old Traditions–New Sounds" and was the co-producer/writer of the documentary video *From Shore to Shore: Irish Traditional Music in New York City* (1993). Her essay "Irish Traditional and Popular Music in New York City: Identity and Social Change" appeared in *The New York Irish* (1996).

Mick Moloney is Global Distinguished Professor of Music at New York University, where he teaches traditional Irish music and Irish-American popular culture. He is also a renowned performer, having recorded and produced over fifty albums of traditional music and acted as advisor for scores of festivals and concerts all over America. He is the author of the essay "Irish Dance Bands in America" in *New Hibernia Review* (1998), *Far from the Shamrock Shore: The Story of Irish-American Immigration through Song* (2002) and *Irish Music in America: Continuity and Change* (forthcoming).

The late *Daniel Patrick Moynihan* was U.S. Senator from New York from 1977 to 2001 and member of the cabinet or subcabinet of Presidents Kennedy, Johnson, Nixon, and Ford. He served as U.S. ambassador to India and U.S. representative to the United Nations. He taught at many universities and is the author or editor of eighteen books, including *Beyond the Melting Pot: The Negroes, Puerto Ricans, Jews, Italians, and Irish of New York City*, edited with Nathan Glazer. In 2000 he received the Presidential Medal of Freedom.

Peter Quinn is a novelist, essayist, and member of the New York University Glucksman Ireland House Advisory Board; he was chief speechwriter for AOL Time Warner. His essays have appeared in magazines such as *World of Hibernia* and *Irish America*. He is the author of a best-selling Civil War–era novel, *Banished Children of Eve* (1994).

Eileen Reilly is associate director and adjunct assistant professor of Irish studies at New York University's Glucksman Ireland House. Focusing her research on the politics of popular culture, popular literature in particular, she is the author of "Irishwomen and the War" in *Ireland and the Great War: "A War to Unite Us All"?* (2002) and "J. A. Froude's Use of History and His Irish Prescription" in *Reading Irish Histories: Texts, Contexts, and Memory in Modern Ireland* (2003).

Robert E. Rhodes, now Professor Emeritus of Anglo-Irish literature at SUNY Cortland, where he taught Irish and Irish-American literature for over thirty years, has edited (with Daniel Casey) two books of Irish-American interest: *Irish-American Fiction: Essays in Criticism* (1979) and *Modern Irish-American Fiction: A Reader* (1989). The author of numerous articles and reviews on Irish and Irish-American literature, he is former president of the American Conference for Irish Studies and is a SUNY Faculty Exchange Scholar.

Thomas J. Shelley is associate professor of theology at Fordham University. He is the author of *Greenwich Village Catholics: St. Joseph's Church and the Evolution of an Urban Faith Community, 1829–2002* (2003), *The History of the Archdiocese of New York* (1997), and *Dunwoodie: The History of St. Joseph's Seminary* (1993), as well as co-editor of *The Encyclopedia of American Catholic History* (1997). His essay "Black and Catholic in Nineteenth-Century New York: The Case of Pierre Toussaint" appeared in the *Records of the American Catholic Historical Society of Philadelphia* (1991).

Robert W. Snyder is associate professor and director of journalism and media studies at Rutgers University. He is the author of *The Voice of the City: Vaudeville and Popular Culture in New York* (1989; 2nd ed. 2000) and *Transit Talk: New York Bus and Subway Workers Tell Their Stories* (1997); co-author of *Metropolitan Lives: The Ashcan Artists and Their New York* (1995); and co-editor of *Profiles in Journalistic Courage* (2001), *1968: Year of Media Decision* (2001), *Reporting the Post–Communist Revolution* (2001), and *The Problem of Equity in Journalism: What's Fair?* (2000). His essay "The Neighborhood Changed: The Irish of Washington Heights and Inwood since 1945" appeared in *The New York Irish* (1996).

Calvin Trillin has had an extensive career as a columnist for *Time*, the *New Yorker*, and the *Nation*. He is the author of over nineteen books, including comic novels, a travel book, family memoirs, an account of the desegregation of the University of Georgia, and a collection of short stories.

Irene Whelan is associate professor of history and director of the Irish studies program at Manhattanville College. She is the author of *The Bible War: The "Second Reformation" and the Polarization of Protestant-Catholic Relations in Ireland, 1800–40* (2005).

Ralph Wilcox is interim vice president and campus executive officer of the University of South Florida at St. Petersburg. He is the editor of *Sport in the Global Village* (1994) and co-editor of *Sporting Dystopias: The Making and Meanings of Urban Sport Cultures* (2003).

Permissions

Permission to reprint key essays has been generously granted by the following:

Glucksman Ireland House for Timothy J. Meagher, "The Fireman on the Stairs: Communal Loyalties in the Making of Irish America, 1880–1921," and Marion R. Casey, "Refractive History: Memory and the Founders of the Emigrant Savings Bank," which were originally published in *Radharc (New York University)* 3 (2002) and 4 (2003).

Hambleton Press, Glasgow, for Kerby A. Miller, "Ulster Presbyterians and the 'Two Traditions' in Ireland and America," which was originally published in *These Fissured Isles: Varieties of British and Irish Identities*, edited by Terry Brotherstone et al., 2003.

Pete Hamill for "Once We Were Kings," which was originally published in *Irish America*, November 1999.

Lescher & Lescher, Ltd./Calvin Trillin for Calvin Trillin's "Democracy in Action," which was originally published in the *New Yorker*, March 21, 1988.

MIT Press for Daniel Patrick Moynihan, "The Irish," which was originally published in *Beyond the Melting Pot: The Negroes, Puerto Ricans, Jews, Italians and Irish of New York City*, by Nathan Glazer and Daniel Patrick Moynihan, 1963.

The New York Irish History Roundtable for Henry Noble MacCracken, "Address to the Ulster Irish Society," which was originally published in *New York Irish History*, vol. 7 (1992–1993).

Oxford University Press for David Noel Doyle, "The Irish in North America, 1776–1845," and David Noel Doyle, "The Remaking of Irish-America, 1845–1880," which were originally published in *Ireland under the Union*, ed. W. E. Vaughan, vols. 5 and 6 in *A New History of Ireland* (1989, 1996).

Peter Quinn for "Looking for Jimmy: The Irish Face," which was originally published in *World of Hibernia*, spring 1999, and for "The Future of Irish America," which was originally published in *Irish America*, April/May 2000.

The University of Notre Dame Press for David Noel Doyle, "Scots Irish or Scotch-Irish" which was originally published in *The Encyclopedia of the Irish in America*, 1999.

Index

The names of fictional characters discussed in the text are in inverted order and include a qualifier indicating that the entry pertains to a character and not to a real person. For example: Buchanan, Tom (character), 674.

Page numbers in italics, such as *614*, refer to an illustration and/or caption on the page. Page numbers including an "n," such as 329n108, refer to an endnote on the page. Page numbers including a "t," such as 315t, refer to a table on the page.

4th Alabama, 670

15th New York, 670, 672

69th National Guard Regiment (Fighting 69th): African Americans, 670, 672; chaplain's advice, 673–674; Civil War, 29; Donovan ("Wild Bill") and, 493; leader, 493; members' ethnicity, 670; moniker, 667; New York Irish, 585; renown, 29; World War I, 493, 670

AARIR (American Association for the Recognition of the Irish Republic), 296

AAU (American Athletic Union), 465

Abbey Theatre, 107, 495

Abolitionism, 372, 376, 383, 485

Abrahams, Roger, 427

ACA (Army Comrades Association, the Blueshirts), 135–136

Academic markets, 47–48

Acheson, Dean, 509

ACIF (American Congress for Irish Freedom), 297, 558–559

Act of Union (1800): Catholic Emancipation, 82; Irish Catholics, 82, 88; Irish nationalism, 289–290; Irish parliament, 289; Irish Protestants, 81–82, 88; O'Connell (Daniel) and, 24; Orange Order, 82; Ulster, 265

Activism, 627–628

Adams, Gerry, 146, 299, 300, 560

Adams, John, 167, 183

Adams, John Quincy, 183, 202–203, 318, 478

Adams, W. B., 185, 193

Affluence, 550

AFL (American Federation of Labor), 359, 361–362, 381, 592

African Americans: 69th National Guard Regiment, 670, 672; Irish equated to blacks, 633, 665–667; Irish labor, 356, 358, 372–373; Irish rejection

of, 612; Irish relations with, 669; minstrelsy, 383; Sambo stereotype, 665–667, *666*; "smoked Irishmen," 667; as strikebreakers, 356; urban slang, 673; vaudeville, 407; whiteness, 638

Agricultural Party (Clann na Talmhan), 138

Agriculture: Americans engaged in, 192; crop failures in Ireland, 86, 90; farmers among emigrants, 223–224; Ireland's dependence on, 89; Irish Americans, 192, 193; Northern Ireland, 141

Ah! Wilderness (O'Neill), 652

Ahearn, Brian, 610

Ahlstrom, Sydney, 588

AIHS. *See* American Irish Historical Society

Aisling tradition, 402

Albee, E. F. (Ed), 386, 408

Alcohol addiction, 500–503, 675

Alfred, William, 660

Alien and Sedition Acts (1798), 264, 478

Alison, Francis, 168, 203

All Hallows College, Dublin, 579

All in the Family (O'Connor), 655

All Souls: A Family Story from Southie (MacDonald), 11, 569

All the Pretty Horses (McCarthy), 661

Allen, Fred, 410

Allen, Gracie, 409

Allen, Irving Lewis, 671

Allen, Theodore, 633

Allen, Woody, 621

Alliance for Progress, 532

Alliance Party, 145

Altan, 437

Amateur Athletic Association (England), 443

America (journal), 599

America and Ireland, 1776–1976 (Edwards and Doyle), 11

America Dissected (MacSparran), 258

"America the Beautiful" (song), 433

American Association for the Recognition of the Irish Republic (AARIR), 296

American Athletic Union (AAU), 465

American Catholics: G.I. Bill of Rights (1944), 598; intellectuals among, 520; Irish as a percentage of, 602; Kennedy (John F.) and, 600, 604; political power, 520; population growth, 515. *See also* Irish Catholics

American Civil Liberties Union, 589, 591

American Conference for Irish Studies, 44

American Congress for Irish Freedom (ACIF), 297, 558–559

American Council of Learned Societies, 304

American Dream, 2

American Federation of Labor (AFL), 359, 361–362, 381, 592

American Ireland Fund, 49. *See also* Ireland Fund

American Irish Historical Society (AIHS): establishment, 3; filiopietism, 3, 5, 15; historiography, 5, 305; journals, 5, 43, 498; Moynihan on, 43, 498; professionals and, 5

American Irish (Kenny), xv

American-Irish nationalism, 289–301

American Irish (Shannon), xv, 8, 15

American Irish Teachers Association, 22

American Jewish Committee, 589

American Mercury (journal), 498

American Miners' Union, 358

American National Biography, 304, 318, 320, 329n108

American nationalism, 492

American nativism. *See* Nativism

American Protective Association, 26

American Protestant Association, 25, 200

American Protestants: anti-Catholic sentiment, 16; conversion to Catholicism, 488; of Irish ancestry, 39, 40, 548; lack of sympathy for Irish, 488–489; ministers' sons, 483; xenophobia, 588–589. *See also* Irish Protestants; Nativism; Protestant evangelicalism

American Revolution (1775–1783): Federalists, 262–263; filiopietism, 3; FitzGerald (Edward) in, 80; Irish Catholics, 75, 490; "Irish" excesses, 262; Irish parliament, 75; Irish Protestants, 5, 74–75, 490; Scotch-Irish, 157, 165–169, 177–178; Ulster, 75; Ulster Presbyterians, 75, 261

American system (Henry Clay's), 191

Americanism, papal condemnation of, 583

Americanist wing (Catholic Church), 583–584

An Claidheamh Soluis (Sword of Light), 106, 116

An Coimisiún le Rincí Gaelacha (Irish Dance Commission), 422

An Gaodhail (journal), 224

An Gorta Mór (Great Hunger). *See* Great Famine

Anbinder, Tyler, 619

Ancient Order of Hibernians (AOH): Abbey Theatre, 495; Chair in Gaelic Studies, 6; Comerford and, 535; Devlin (Bernadette) and, 558; domestic servants, 342; establishment in America, 188, 489; establishment in Ireland, 95; Flannery (Michael) and, 538; German Americans, 294; Irish Immigration Working Committee, 564; Ladies Auxiliary, 541; membership certificate, *614*; Orange Order, 95; physical force nationalism, 294; picnics, 469; republicanism, 294; Russell Brothers act, 408; sports, 452; St. Patrick's Day parade, 538, 539; suspicion of, 583; tie to Catholic Church in America, 540, 545

Anderson, Jane, 438

Andrews, J. M., 141–142

Angela's Ashes (McCourt), *108*, 549, 567, 650

Angels with Dirty Faces (film), 550

Anglican Church of Ireland. *See* Church of Ireland

Anglo-Irish. *See* Old English

Anglo-Irish Agreement (1985), 146, 300, 560

Anglo-Irish literary revival, 107

Anglo-Irish Treaty (1921): Churchill's exhortation, 1; Collins (Michael) and,

126–127; Cosgrave and, 127; Cumann na mBan, 128; Dáil Éireann, 127; de Valera and, 127; dismantling of, 135–137; Griffith and, 126, 127; Irish Americans, 297; Lloyd George and, 126, 129; negotiation and acceptance, 126–128; Northern Ireland, 129

Anna Christie (O'Neill), 652

Anna McCoy School (Belfast), 419

Annals of the New York Stage (O'dell), 387

Anti-British sentiment: Cohalan and, 585; Great Famine, 22, 96; Irish in colonial America, 179; St. Patrick's Day parade (New York City), 537, 559; sports, 451–452

Anti-Catholic sentiment: alleged immorality of nuns and priests, 275–276; American Protestants, 16; Beecher and, 275; in Boston, 275; in Britain, 370; in cities, 198; Convent Inspection Act (Georgia), 582; English roots, 514; geography of, 582; Irish-American historiography, 217–218; Irish-American response, 578; Kennedy (John F.) and, 282, 548; Ku Klux Klan, 669; left-wing politics, 582; nativism, 213; New York Irish and, 506; pedigree, 582; in Philadelphia, 275; popular journalism, 275–276; Protestant evangelicalism, 273–276; scope, 197; Smith (Al) and, 16, 282, 506, 589–590; social mobility, 276, 320; Watson (Thomas) and, 582; World War I, 582

Anti-clericalism, 517–518

Anti-Communism, 508–510, 517, 631

Anti-egalitarianism, 168

Anti-Harvard movement, 631

Anti-hiring discrimination, 372

Anti-intellectualism, 514

Anti-Irish sentiment, 364–378; collective violence, 371, 373; dehumanization, *366* (*see also* Stereotypes); diminishment of, 668–669; discrimination *vs.*, 375; factional fighting among Irish laborers, 373; Irish-American historiography, 217–218, 365, 367; Irish anti-abolitionism, 372; Irish nationalism, 370; Irish racial violence, 372–373; loyalty of Catholics, 367, 550, 589–590; nativism, 200, 213, 372; "No Irish Need Apply," 371–372; Paddy stereotype, 364–365, 366–367; poverty, 197; racial perceptions, 365, 371; simianization, 366–367 (*see also* Stereotypes); statistical prejudice, 23, 367; in Victorian England, 368–369, 384

Anti–New Deal Irish, 507

Anti-Partition League, 142

Anti-radicalism, 631

Anti-Repeal Union, 104

Anti-Saloon League, 588

Anti-Semitism, 509

Anti-socialism, 631

AOH. *See* Ancient Order of Hibernians

"AOHs of the USA" (song), 398

Apemen stereotype: depiction of, *26, 366, 374*; evolution of, 367, 668–669, 674; *Puck* magazine (1894), 25, *26*; simianization, 366–367. *See also* Paddy stereotype

Apes and Angels (Curtis), 365, 367–370, 384

Apologetics, 514

Appalachian music, 382

Appleton's Cyclopaedia of American Biography, 304, 320

Appointment in Samarra (O'Hara), 653–654

Aquinas, Thomas, 283, 596, 613

Archdeacon, Tom, 48

Arensberg, Conrad M., 479, 481–482

Argument on Behalf of the Catholics of Ireland (Wolfe Tone), 77

Arms for Living (Tunney), 675

Armstrong, John, 167

Army Comrades Association (ACA, the Blueshirts), 135–136

Arnesen, Eric, 376, 633

"Arrah Wanna" (Morse), *395, 396*

Artisans, 235–236

Ashbourne Land Purchase Act (1885), 103

Ashcroft, John, 435

Ashe, Thomas, 121

Asian Americans, 603, 638

Asquith, Henry, 113–114, 115

Assimilation: acculturation of domestic servants, 345–346; American Catholic historiography, 240–241; Americanisation, 224, 346; British North America, 184; Catholic Church in America, 281–282, 604; counteracted by immigration, 214; eagerness for, 594; English immigrants, 175; ethnic identity, 370–371; German immigrants, 175; Great Famine, 184; Irish Americans, 175, 178, 179, 346, 528; Irish compared to other ethnic groups, 44, 175; Kennedy (William) and, 684; nativist attitude, 367; New York Irish, 500; predisposition towards, 24; race, 375; Scotch-Irish, 153, 169; sport and acculturation, 457; sports, 450, 452, 455, 466–467; transcending marginalization, 528. *See also* Social mobility

Association of Catholic Trade Unionists, 503

Astley, Sir John, 446

Astley Belt Championship, 446

At Weddings and Wakes (McDermott), 649

Atkinson, Mary Irene, 628

Atlantic Migration, 1607–1860 (Hansen), 7

Attlee, Clement, 142

Aud (ship), 117

Augusta Heritage Festival, 432

Augustine, Saint, 283

Australia, 172, 618–619

Awful Disclosures of the Hotel Dieu Nunnery in Montreal (Monk), 275–276

Aylen, Peter, 190

"B Specials," 145

Bad Haggis, 438

Baggs, Margrett, 344

Baker, Howard, 632

Baldwin, Connell, 189

Baldwin, James, 533

Baldwin, Robert, 189, 190

Baldwin, Stanley, 131

Balfour, Arthur James, 103, 104–105, 111

Ball, Lucille, 552

Bancroft, George, 201

Banished Children of Eve (Quinn), 35

Bards of Tara, 407

Barley Bree, 437

Barnum, P. T., 493

Barrett, Ronald A., 515

Barron, Edward, 199

Barry, John, *527*

Barry, Leonora, 359, 581

Bartishell, Marge, 420

Barton, Robert, 126–127

Baseball, 447–448, 459–462, 503

Baseball: A History of America's Game (Rader), 460

Baseball Hall of Fame, 447

Bayes, Nora (Leonora Goldberg), 397, 398

Bayor, Ronald, 36, 48

Bealtaine (season), 427

Beastly Beatitudes of Balthazar B. (Donleavy), 659

Beatles, 551

Beautiful and the Damned (Fitzgerald), 653

Beauty Queen of Leenane (McDonagh), 566

Beckett, J. C., 153

Beecher, Lyman, 274, 275

Beer, Thomas, 493, 494, 625

Before My Time (Howard), 656

Behan, Brendan, 498

Beirne, Frank, 539, 541, 542, 545, 546

"Believe Me if All These Endearing Young Charms" (Moore), 382, 397

Belknap, Jeremy, 263

Bellow, Saul, 533

Bells of St. Mary's (film), 399, 680–682, 684

Benburb, battle of (1646), 68

Benedict XV (Pope), 586

Bennett, James Gordon, *277*, 488

Bennett, William H., 322

Bent, Marion, 409

Bentley, Elizabeth, 509

Berean Order, 204

Bergin, John, 610

Bergman, Ingrid, 682

Berle, Milton, 552

Berlin, Ellin, 655

Bernardin, Joseph, 602

Bernstorff, Count Johann Heinrich von, 117

Berra, Yogi, 539

Berrigan, Daniel, 600

Berrigan, Philip, 600

Bessy Conway; or, The Irish Girl in America (Sadlier), 650

Beverley, William, 164

Beyond the Melting Pot (Glazer and Moynihan), 8–11, 535–536

Biddy (sobriquet), 333

Biddy Boy, 441n5

Bigamist's Daughter (McDermott), 649

Biggar, Joseph, 100

Bilingualism, 221

Billy Phelan's Greatest Game (Kennedy), 660

Binns, John, 178

Binsse, Louis B., 326n39

Birkenhead, Lord (Frederick Edwin Smith), 126

Birney, James G., 202

"Birth of the Shamrock" (Kelly), *394*

Biscotti, Steve, 464

Bishops' Program of Social Reconstruction, 591

"Black '47," 91–92. *See also* Great Famine

Black '47 (band), 403, 438

"Black and Tans" (Royal Irish Constabulary Auxiliary), 124, 125

Black Mountain Festival, 430

Blackface, 382

Blacks. *See* African Americans

Blaine, James G., 478

Blair, Tony, 145

Blake, Eubie, 408

Blenner-Hassett, Roland, 48

Blessing, Patrick, 2, 41, 46

Bliadhain an Air (Year of the Slaughter), 85

Blissert, Robert, 359

Blood-Drenched Altars (Kelley), 597

Bloody Sunday (1920), 125

Bloody Sunday (1972), 145, 558

Blueshirts (Army Comrades Association), 135–136

Bodnar, John, 11–12

Boer War (1899–1902), 109, 125

Boland, John P., 592

Boleyn, Anne, 64

Boling, Bruce, 39, 47

Bonnycastle, Sir Richard, 191

Book of Kells, 435

Bookishness, 222

Bookmaking, 501

Borden, Benjamin, 164

Border Folk Festival, 430

Boston Athletic Association, 449

Boston Globe (newspaper), 450

Boston hurling club, 453

Boston Irish: blue-collar jobs, 234; busing, 638–639; Catskill Mountains, 430; civic societies, 195–196; death rates, 231; Gaelic Athletic Association (GAA), 469; Handlin on, 7–8, 12, 14; male work force, 234; politics, 557, 580; population, 14, 616; poverty, 239; remittances, 341; sectarian discord, 275; social mobility, 12–13; songwriters, 393; Ursaline Convent (Charlestown), 275

Boston Red Stockings, 447

Boston's Immigrants (Handlin), 7–8, 11, 12–13

Bothy Band, 415

Boucicault, Dion, 386, 629

Boundary Commission, 129, 130–131

Boxer (film), 561

Boxing, 444, 450–451, 457–459, 464, 503

Boyce, John, 629

Boycott, Charles, 101

Boycotting, 101

Boyle, T. Coraghessan, 661

Boyne, Battle of the, 489

Boys from Limerick, 407

Boys of the Lough, 415

Brackenridge, Hugh Henry, 263

Brady, "Diamond Jim," 493

Brady, Ellen, 340, 342

Brady, Genevieve Garvan, 592

Brady, Nicholas, 592

Braham, David, 388, 391, 427–428

Branagan, Thomas, 184

Brann, Henry A., 320

Brannigan, Paddy, 389

Breathnach, Breandán, 418

Breen, Joseph, 595

Brennan, Michael, 610

Breslin, Jimmy, 552, 656–657

Bresnahan, Roger Patrick ("Duke of Tralee"), 447

"Brian O'Linn" (Boucicault), 386

Brick, Tom, 18–19, 21, 29

Bridgeport Bus (Howard), 656

Bridget (sobriquet), 333, 358, 548. *See also* Domestic service

Bridget (the name), 31

"Bridget McBruiser" (stereotype), 371
Brimble, August, 389
Brinkley, Douglas, 677–678
British Empire, 114
British North America: assimilation, 184; availability of capital, 187; emigration, 179, 184, 187; industrialization, 213–214; urbanization, 225
British Relief Association, 92
Brittingham, Frank, 426
Brogan, D. W., 637
Brooke, Sir Basil (later Viscount Brookeborough), 142
Brooklyn Tablet (newspaper), 498, 517–518, 599
Brophy, John, 363, 592
Brotherhood of Carpenters and Joiners (New York), 359
Brothers McMullen (film), 567
Broun, Heywood, 517
Brown, Christy, 566
Brown, John, 491
Brown, T. Alston, 387
Brown, Thomas N.: historiography and, 10; Irish American identity, 8; *Irish Layman*, 45; Irish nationalism, 10, 371, 490; "Nationalism and the Irish Peasant 1800–1848," 8
Browne, Noel, 138–139
Brownson, Orestes, 230, 242
Bruce, David, 263
Brugha, Cathal, 120–121, 122, 127
Brunswick Clubs, 274
Brusso, Noah, 459
Bryan, George, 151
Buchanan, Tom (character), 674
Buckeye Club, 447
Buckley, Michael, 220, 222, 235–236
Buenker, John D., 627
Buffalo (New York) Irish, 237, 354
Building Prospects (Boyle), 661
Burchard, Samuel D., 478
Burchell, R. A., 12–13
Burchenal, Elizabeth, 424n5
Burk, John D., 184
Burke, Edmund, 76, 77
Burke, John J., 585, 587, 589
Burke, Thomas E. ("the Lowell Mercury"), 449
Burke, William, 539
Burke, William (Bill), 542, 543–547
Burns, Brian, 48
Burns, Edward, 567
Burns, Robert, 263
Burns, Tommy, 459
Businessmen, 50, 51, 499–500, 507
Busing, 638–639
Butler, Jean, 417, 420, 423
Butler, Mae, 419
Butler, Mary, 107
Butler, Thomas C., 446

Butt, Isaac, 99
Butte Irish (Emmons), 619
Butterfield 8 (O'Hara), 625, 633–634, 653
Byrne, Gertrude, 435–437
Byron, Reginald, 37
Byzantine-rite Catholics, 578

Cabbage and Bones (Howard), 656
Caffrey, William, 447
Cagney, James (Jimmy): evolution of the Irish-American character, 550; fast-talking urbanite, 671; popularity, 551; in *Public Enemy*, 676; "street smarts," 671–672; style, 409, 410, 494
Cahan, Abraham, 621
Cahill, D. W., 233
Caitlin ni hUalachain (Cathleen ní Houlihan), 107, 403
Cal (film), 561
Caldwell, James, 261
Calhoun, John C., 288
California Irish, 225–226, 360. *See also* San Francisco Irish
California Traditional Music Festival, 430
California Traditional Music Society, 432
Callahan, Patrick Henry, 582
Callaway, Kathy, 661
Camelot metaphor, 529, 531
Campbell, Timothy J., 479
Campbell-Fahey, Mary, 420
Canadian Irish: emigration to British North America, 179; Famine immigration, 214–215; Fenians, 190–191; intermarriage, 191; intra-Irish differences, 189; Irish Americans, 213–214; Irish Catholics, 215; Irish Protestants, 215, 221; Maritime Provinces, 190–191; Orangeism, 171, 189–190; in politics, 189; Quebec Irish, 190; reemigration to U.S., 172; revivalism, 191; from Ulster, 187–188; unification of French Lower Canada and Upper Canada, 190
Canal-building, 186–187, 355, 373
Cannon, Joseph ("Dry Messiah"), 588
Cannon, Peter, 387
Canny, Nicholas, 47
Cantwell, John J., 584
Capitalism, 193
Cara Band, 432
Carey, Hugh, 49, 299, 538, 559
Carey, James, 592
Carey, James B., 363
Carey, Mathew: in America, 178; American system, 191; emigrant aid society, 181; Jackson (Andrew) and, 183; Philadelphia poor, 194
Carey, Philip, 592
Carey, Ron, 363

Carleton, William, 634
Carney, Art, 551–552
Carpentier, George, 458
Carrigan, Andrew: career, 313; Commissioner of Emigration, 313, 316; Emigrant Savings Bank, 308, 313, 314, 315t, 326n39; Hughes (Archbishop John) and, 313, 314, 315t; immigration reform, 316; Irish Emigrant Society, 313, 316; Roman Catholic Orphan Asylum, 327n76
Carroll, James, 659
Carroll, John F., 482
Carroll, Liz, 422
Carroll, William, 223
Carroll Club (New York), 195
Carroll Hall candidates, 488
Carson, Edward, 114, 116, 119
Carter, Jimmy, 14–15
Carton, Sidney (character), 684
Casals, Pablo, 533
Casement, Roger, 117, 294, 492
Casey, Charles, 193
Casey, Daniel J., 11
Casey, Marion R., 41, 46
Casey, Pat, 408
Casey at the Bat (Thayer), 447–448
"Casey's Wife" (Flynn), 392
Cass, Lewis, 201
Castro, Fidel, 531
Cathleen ní Houlihan (Caitlin ni hUalachain), 107, 403
Catholic Association: colonization, 186; founding, 272; O'Connell (Daniel) and, 83–84, 183, 272, 480; success of, 272
Catholic Charities, 564, 565
Catholic Charities of New York, 587
Catholic Church Extension Society, 596–597, 603
Catholic Church in America, 512–520, 574–608; 1920s, 587–590, 596; 1930s and 1940s, 590–597; abolitionism, 383; alleged immorality of nuns and priests, 275–276; American anti-intellectualism, 514; Americanist wing, 583–584; Ancient Order of Hibernians, 540, 545; anti-clericalism, 517–518; anti-Communism, 517, 631; anti-radicalism, 631; anti-socialism, 631; apologetics, 514; ascendency foretold, 197, 280; Asian Americans, 603; assimilation, 281–282, 604; attendance at non-Catholic religious services, 594; big-city Catholicism, 592–597, 598; big-city pastors, 593; Bishops' Program of Social Reconstruction, 586; Bloody Sunday (1972), 145; Byzantine-rite Catholics, 578; Catholic apartheid, 594–595; celibacy, 483; censorship, 595; charitable work, 587;

Church societies, 243; clerical conservatism, 518; clerical hypocrisy, 281; conversion of Protestants, 488; culture of, 484–485; deacons, 601; dioceses, 194, 240; dissension within, 519; domestic servants, 337, 341–342; education, 280, 513, 596, 603; emergence of, 24–25; English as the national language, 27; erosion of unity, 574; ethnic Catholicism, 575–578; Famine immigrants, 24; funeral masses, 595; German immigrants, 241, 576; G.I. Bill of Rights (1944), 598–599; Great Depression, 590–592; Great Famine, 279; group survival, 278; growth, 574; hierarchical organization, 629; Hollywood, 595; Immigrant Church, 602–603; individualism, 613; institutionalization of, 279–280, 603; intellectual life, 514–515, 518, 582–583, 599, 630–631; Irish American identity, 279–280; Irish Americans, 240–243, 278, 578–581, 602–603; Irish bishops, 27, 181, 195, 238, 240, 488, 513; as "Irish" institution, 214; Knights of Labor, 581; labor movement, 581, 592; laissez-faire economics, 519; Latinos, 602–603; lay opinion, 517; leadership, 194–195, 574–575, 578, 579, 602; "liberal" to, 519; liberalism, 485; marriage outside the faith, 594–595; McCarthy (Joseph) and, 599; movies, 595; national parishes, 575–578, 594; neo-scholasticism, 596; New Irish, 563, 565–566; nuns/sisters, 275–276, 580, 601; Oregon school law (1922), 589; other immigrant groups, 279–280; papal condemnation of Americanism, 583; papal condemnation of Modernism, 583; parish life, 27, 242–243, 548, 556, 593–594, 601, 680–682; parochial schools, 195, 199, 488, 515–517, 594, 601, 621; postwar years, 574, 598–599; power, 282; prestige of, 488; priests/priesthood, 275–276, 279, 519, 593, 598, 601, 602, 683; professionalization, 587; Progressive era, 581–584; Prohibition, 588; Protestant evangelicalism, 276–277, 279; "regular guy"communal populism, 629; republicanism, 485; respectability, 282; Roman Catholics, 484; rural Catholics, 596–597; schools question, 486–488; science, 484, 514; self-criticism, 513–514; seminarians, 601; settling immigrants, 514; sexual abuse, 557, 603; sister/priest ratio, 580; size, 367, 574, 582; slavery, 629; Smith (Al) on, 483; social policy, 518, 519; social sciences, 514; social thought, 630–631; "spiritual empire" thesis, 280; statisti-cal watershed, 601; strict morality, 276–277; suburbanization, 598; success debate, 281–282, 501–502; turning point, 574; Vatican II, 574, 590, 599–603; vernacular liturgy, 601; vitality, 601; womb-to-tomb Catholicism, 595; World War I, 584–587; World War II, 597; writing about, 45. *See also* American Catholics; Catholicism; Irish Catholics

Catholic Church in Ireland: continence, 95; Cullen and, 95; culture of, 484–485; de Valera and, 120; declaration of the Republic, 138; Fenians, 96; Gaelic Athletic Association (GAA), 106; Gaelic League, 106–107; Great Famine, 95; Home Government Association, 99; ITGWU strike (1913), 111; Land Act (1881), 101; nuns in convents, 94; postwar years, 554; Protestant evangelicalism, 272–273; puritanism, 95; repressiveness, 95; republicanism, 485; sexual abuse, 557; Sinn Fein, 120; Ulster lands, 155; ultramontane Catholicism, 95. *See also* Irish Catholics

Catholic Club, 320

Catholic Committee, 77, 78

Catholic Confederation, 68

Catholic Educational Association, 580

Catholic Emancipation, 82–84; Act of Union, 82; Catholic Relief Act (1829), 272; Emmet (Thomas) and, 183; Irish Americans, 171; New York Irish, 480; O'Connell (Daniel) and, 17, 24, 273; Sampson and, 183

Catholic Emigration Society, 186

Catholic Encyclopedia, 305, 321

"Catholic" equation with "Irish," 283

Catholic Herald (Philadelphia newspaper), 195

Catholic Laymen's Association of Georgia, 582

Catholic Relief Act (1778), 76–77

Catholic Relief Act (1829), 272

Catholic Revival. *See* Devotional Revolution

Catholic Telegraph (Cincinnati newspaper), 195, 197

Catholic Total Abstinence and Benevolent Society, 452

Catholic University of America, *123,* 320, 582, 583

Catholic Worker Movement, 591–592

Catholic World (journal), 508, 599

Catholic Youth Organization, 593

Catholicism: American culture, 197; coexistence with psychology/institutions of free men, 203–204; communalism, 613; conversion to, 488; Cromwell (Oliver) and, 68–69; domestic servants, 336–337; insularity, 598; Irish American identity, 35, 184, 195, 197, 221, 241–243, 247n41, 271; Irish life, 579; Irish nationalism, 578–579; Old English (Anglo-Irish), 72, 154; papal condemnation of Americanism, 583; papal condemnation of Modernism, 583; papal decrees/ encyclicals, 134, 512–513, 519, 583, 591, 601, 630; Penal Laws (18th c.), 71; Plantation of Ireland, 65; proscription of, 179; Scotland, 156; settlement patterns, 230; suspicions of, 6; ultramontane Catholicism, 95; womb-to-tomb Catholicism, 595. *See also* Anti-Catholic sentiment; Catholic Church in America; Catholic Church in Ireland

Catholicism and American Freedom (McGreevy), 613

Catholics. *See* American Catholics; Byzantine-rite Catholics; Irish Catholics; Roman Catholics; Ulster Catholics

Catskill Mountains, 430, *436,* 497

Ceannt, Éamonn, 116, 119

Ceilis, 414

Celibacy, 238, 481–482, 483

"Celtic," 6

Celtic baseball teams, 447

Celtic Boat Club (Albany), 446

Celtic Boat Club (Buffalo), 446

Celtic Colors, 430

Celtic Cross, 432, 437

Celtic Festival (Hunter Mountain), 433

Celtic Festival (Sebastopol), 430

Celtic festivals, 426

Celtic seasons, 427

Celtic Studies, 6–7, 48

Celtic Tiger, 141

"Celtics," 443

Censorship, 595

Census returns on ancestry, 37–38, 175, 687–691, *690*

Central Labor Union, 359

Cestello, Bosco D., 502

Challenge of Peace: God's Promise and Our Response (Bernardin), 602

Chamberlain, Austen, 126

Chamberlain, Neville, 135

Chambers, Whittaker, 509

"Champion of the Fenians" (Nast), *366*

Chanche, John, 242

Chaplin, Charlie, 494

Chapman, Helen, 339

Chappaquiddick, 530

Charitable Irish Society (Boston), 175

Charles I (King of Great Britain and Ireland), 67, 68

Charles II (King of Great Britain and Ireland), 69, 156, 157

Charless, Joseph, 184

Charming Billy (McDermott), 567, 649

Chastellux, Marquis de (François Jean de Beauvoir), 167

Cherish the Ladies, 437

Cheverus, Jean de, 242

Chicago Evening Post (newspaper), 552, 651

Chicago Irish: busing, 638–639; death rates, 232; Gaelic Athletic Association (GAA), 469; Irish Festival, *431*; politics, 557, 580; population, 14; radical candidates, 581; songwriters, 393

Chicago White Stockings, 447

Chichester-Clark, James, 144–145

Chieftains, 415, 437

Childers, Erskine, 129

Chinese immigration, 360

Christian Brothers, 276, 578, 665

Church of England, 64

Church of Ireland (Anglican): government subsidies, 98–99; Great Famine, 266; tithe paid to, 73, 85; Tithe War (1820s, 1830s), 74; Ulster parishes, 265; Ulster Presbyterians, 265–268. *See also* Irish Protestants

Churchill, Winston, 1, 126, 128, 137

Cincinnati Irish, 393

Cincinnati Red Stockings, 447

CIO (Congress of Industrial Organizations), 363

City in Slang: New York Life and Popular Speech (Allen), 671

Civil Authorities (Special Powers) Act (1922), 130, 144

Civil rights (Northern Ireland), 144, 297, 298, 300

Civil rights (United States), 600, 638

Civil War (Ireland, 1922–1923), 128–132, 586

Civil War (United States, 1861–1865): 69th National Guard Regiment, 29; Conscription Act (1863), 372; Fenians, 97; Irish 9th (Ninth Massachusetts Infantry), *579*; Irish American identity, 25, 29, 214; Irish racism, 356, 372; Paddy and Sambo stereotypes, 665–667, *666*; recruitment poster, *227*; small ethnic companies, *579*

Clan na Gael (Family of the Gael): Cohalan and, 492; Devoy and, 100, 109, 290, 294, 492; Easter Rising, 117, 120, 295; establishment, 492; Fenians, 290; Flannery (Michael) and, 298; Irish Americans, 200; Irish nationalism, *366*; Irish Parliamentary Party, 294; Irish Race Convention (1916), 295; Irish Republican Brotherhood, 294; McGarrity and, 294; Parnell and, 290; physical force nationalism, 294; picnics, 452, 469; political effective-

ness, 125; pro-German activities, 125, 294, 492; republicanism, 294; social reform, 294; sports, 452; United Irish League of America, 294; Wilson (Woodrow) and, 125; working-class support, 294

Clancy, Tom, 659

Clancy Brothers and Tommy Makem, 399–403, 412–413, 414, 437, 551

Clann na Poblachta (Republican Party), 138

Clann na Talmhan (Agricultural Party), 138

Clark, Dennis, 11, 12, 13, 44

Clarke, James, 387

Clarke, N. B., 387

Clarke, Thomas, 109–110, 116, 119

Clay, Henry, 191, 201, 240

Clearwater Festival, 430

Cleary, Helen Flatley, 341, 342, 345

Cleer, Mary, 340

Cleveland, Grover, 479, 506

Cline, Maggie, 392, 407

Clinton, Bill (William Jefferson): Kennedy (John F.) and, 530; Northern Ireland conflict, 146, 300, 560; Robinson (Mary) and, *560*; Smith (Jean Kennedy) and, 561; writers and artists, 533

Clinton, George, 175, 178

Cloke, Tom, 343

Clooney, Rosemary, 551

Clubmen, 432

Cochran, Alice, 12

Cochrane, Mickey, 461

Coen, Charlie, *422*

Coen, Jack, *422*

Coercion Act (1881), 101, 104

Cohalan, Daniel: anti-British sentiment, 585; Clan na Gael, 492; Collins (Michael) and, 296; de Valera and, 295, 296–297; Devoy and, 125, 294; Friends of Irish Freedom, 506; on O'Connell (Daniel), 586; Quinn (John) and, 495; self-determination for Ireland, 295; Versailles Treaty, 506; Wilson (Woodrow) and, 295, 492

Cohan, George M.: Irish themed songs, 396; stage dancing of, 423; style, 409, 410; in *Yankee Doodle Dandy*, 493, 667–668

Cohan, Jerry, 423

Coleman, James, 418

Coleman, Michael, 411

"Colleen," *681*

Colleen Bawn (Boucicault), 386

College of St. Catherine, 580

Colles, Christopher, 186

Colliers Magazine, 450

Collins, Hannah: boyfriend, 343; churchgoing, 341; correspondence

with Nora McCarthy, 338, 340, 341, 342, 343; on a home, 341, 343; homesickness, 340; on housework, 338; on Irish men, 345; photo of, *339*

Collins, Jimmy, 460–461

Collins, John, 539, 546

Collins, Marjory, *259*

Collins, Michael: Anglo-Irish Treaty, 126–127; Childers and, 129; Cohalan and, 296; de Valera and, 122; Devoy and, 296; Irish constitution, 128; Irish Republican Army, 127, 128; Irish Republican Brotherhood, 121; Irish Volunteers, 121; minister of finance, 122, 127; Pearse and, 121; popularity, 126; release from prison, 121; the "squad" ("G-men"), 125

"Color-bearers St. Patrick's Day" (Livingston), *374*

"Come Down Mrs. Flynn" (Kelly), 392

Comerford, James A.: Ancient Order of Hibernians, 535; on Behan, 498; Koch and, *537*; parade grand marshal and, 535–536; St. Patrick's Day parade (1961), 498; St. Patrick's Day parade (1983), 535–538, 541, 543

Comey, Dennis, J., 592

Comhaltas Ceoltóirí Éireann (Irish Musicians' Association), 414, 428

Comiskey, Charlie, *460*

Commercial Appeal (New York newspaper), 197

Commerford, John, 194

Commissioners of Emigration (New York State): Carrigan and, 313, 316; demise, 316, 318; Dillon (Gregory) and, 307, 309, 316; Emigrant Savings Bank, 27, 308, 316, *317*; Hughes (Archbishop John) and, 316; Irish Emigrant Society, 307–308, 315, 316; members, 308, 316–317; national recognition, 313; O'Gorman and, 318; operations, 316; origins, 307–308, 315–316; power and, 315–317; Stuart and, 310

Committee of Unionist Associations, 114

Commonweal (journal), 519, 599

Communalism, 609–648; African Americans, 612; anachronisms, 610; anti-Harvard movement, 631; Asian Americans, 612; assailing the Protestant establishment, 631; Boss Rule, 612; brokering coalitions, 636–638; busing, 638–639; Catholic social thought, 630–631; Catholicism, 613; civil rights movement, 638; concentration in Eastern U.S., 617–618, 632; county loyalty, 636; deference to aristocrats, 629; definition, 613; economics, 614–615; extent of communal loyalties, 635–640; government

activism, 627–628; hierarchical organization of Church and society, 629; immigrant historiography, 612; in Ireland, 613–615; Irish-American history, 612; Irish Catholics, 613; Irish Protestants, 613; Irish racism, 633–635; liberalism, 627–628; machine politics, 626–627, 629–630, 637–638; men on the make, 629; mixed record, 640; neighborhood loyalty, 619; networking, 616–621, 682; obsession with social mobility, 621–624; occupational networks, 619–620; opportunity for working-class solidarity, 612; "Pastorini's prophesy," 615, 622, 635; "regular guy" communal populism, 628–633; rule by men of the people, 626–628; secret societies, 615; self-help/self-reliance/voluntary cooperation, 203, 238–240, 276, 280; settlement patterns, 616; social mobility, 611–612, 616, 623–624, 634–635; whiteness, 611–612, 633–635
Communism, 508
Communist Party USA, 111, 362, 508, 581
Community festivals, 430–440
Complete Stories (O'Connor), 657
Con O'Regan; or, Emigrant Life in the New World (Sadlier), 650
Condon, Edward O'Meagher, 3
Coneff, J. T., 449
Congested Districts Board, 105
Congress of Industrial Organizations (CIO), 363
Conlon, Gerald, 566
Conn the Shaughran (character), 386
Connelly, Marc, 652
Connolly, Charles M., 326n39
Connolly, James: grandson of, 297; Irish Citizen Army, 116; Irish Socialist Republican Party, 110; nationalism, 110; Proclamation of the Republic, 119; socialism, 110; trade unionism, 361
Connolly, James Brendan, 449–450
Connolly, James J., 629–630, 637
Connolly, Maureen Glynn, 415
Connolly, Richard ("Slippery Dick"), 476
Connolly, Tom, 447
Connors, Margaret, 11
Conradh na Gaelige. See Gaelic League
Conroy, Mary King, 343
Conscription Act (1863), 372
Conservatism, 505–506, 520
Conservative Party (Great Britain): elections (1909), 113; Great Famine, 91; Home Rule, 103, 114; loans to tenants, 104–105; Local Government Act, 112; Moynihan on, 492; neglect of Irish issues, 100; successes

(1895–1905), 111; Unionist Party, 104, 114
Considine, John W., 409
Constitutional nationalism: Easter Rising, 294–295; goal, 289, 290; Good Friday Agreement (1998), 300; Irish Parliamentary Party, 108, 121; O'Connell (Daniel) and, 289–290; popularity, 290
Constructive unionism, 111–113
Convent Inspection Act (Georgia), 582
Cooke, Henry, 188, 267
Cooke, Terrance, 559
Cooper, Ivan, 144
Corbett, James J. ("Gentleman Jim"), 444, 445, 457
Cordelia's Aspirations (Harrigan), 31, 623
Corish, Paddy, 45
Cork Volunteer Journal, 189
Corn laws, 90
Cornwallis, Charles, 167
Corridan, John, 592
Corrigan, Michael, 583
Cosgrave, W. T.: Anglo-Irish Treaty, 127; Boundary Commission's recommendations, 131; Cumann na nGaedheal, 132; Fianna Fáil, 134; Fine Gael, 136; Griffith and, 132; opposition to, 134–135; prime minister, 129; transfer of land ownership to farmers, 133
Costello, Frank, 677
Costello, John A., 138, 139, 142
Costello, Mark, 658
Coughlin, Charles Edward (Father Coughlin), 507, 552, 590–591, 627–628
Council of Ireland, 127, 131
County Kilkenny Association, 540, 544
County loyalty, 24, 469, 636
County patriotic and benevolent associations (P and B associations), 468
County Sligo Association, 544
Courcy, John de, 63
Courtney, John, 590
Cox, Joseph, 683
Coyle, Evelyn, *600*
Craig, James (later Lord Craigavon), 115, 124, 131, 141
Creeley, Robert, 660
Creighton, Edward, 592
Creighton, John, 592
Crimmins, John D., 592
Crockett, James, 226
Croke, Thomas William, 106, 107, 579
Croker, Richard: election night (1897), 482; greed, 672; investigation of, 476; Irish estate, 483, 626; Tammany Hall leadership, 481
Cromwell, Oliver, 68–69, 622
Cromwell, Thomas, 64
Cronin, Joe, 447, 460–461

Crosby, Bing ("Bingo"), 398–399, 550, 551, 680–681
Crosby, Donald F., 599
Crossing (McCarthy), 661
"Cruiskeen Lawn" (Boucicault), 386
Crying Game (film), 566
"Cuba Five," 293
Cudahy, Dorothy Hayden, 538–539, 541, 542–547. *See also* Hayden, Dorothy
Cudahy, Patrick, 592
Cudahy, Sean, 543, 545, 546
Cullen, Paul, 95, 96, 99, 199
Cullinan, Elizabeth, 655, 656, 684
Culture, 195–197
Cumann Merriman conference (1976), 11, 14–15
Cumann na mBan (Women's League): Anglo-Irish Treaty, 128; anti-conscription campaign, 122; Easter Rising, 118; Irish National Volunteers, 115; members interned, 129; Sinn Fein, 122–123
Cumann na nGaedheal (Irish Party), 132–135, 136
Cumann na Poblachta (Republican Party), 128, 540
Cumann na Saoirse (Freedom Party), 300
Cuming, George, 178
Cuomo, Mario, 559
Curley, James Michael, 30, 626, 655
Curley, Michael Joseph, 579–580, 584
Curran, Joe, 363
Curran, John J., 581
Curran, Mary Doyle, 655
Curtin, Glen, 432
Curtis, L. Perry, Jr., 364–365, 367–370, 376, 384
Curtis, Tom, 449
Cusack, Michael, 106
Cushing, Richard J., 488, 513, 592
Cushwa Center at the University of Notre Dame, 46–47
Cuyahoga Valley Folk Festival, 430
Cztirom, Daniel, 409

Da Vinci, Leonardo, 663
Dáil Éireann (parliament of Ireland): Anglo-Irish Treaty, 127; constitutional changes (1937), 136; Cumann na nGaedheal, 132; de Valera and, 295; deputies (TDs) *(Teachtaí Dála),* 128, 129, 132, 136; first, 124; Irish Republican Army, 125; Lloyd George and, 122; meetings, 122; ministers, 122, 127, 129; second, 125; Senate of Ireland, 128; Sinn Fein, 122, 125; third, 132. *See also* Irish parliament
Daley, Richard, 14, 558
Dallas, George, 201
Daly, Marcus, 618
D'Amato, Alphonse, 559

Damnation of Theron Ware (Frederic), 665, 669

Dan Lowry's Music Hall (Dublin), 383

Dan Sullivan's Shamrock Band, 398

Dance, 417–425; An Coimisiún le Rinci Gaelacha (Irish Dance Commission), 422; evolution of, 407; *Feis (feiseanna)*, 418–419; Gaelic Revival, 418; hornpipes, 418; Irish dances (occasions), 343; jigs, 418; *Lord of the Dance* (show), 417, 420, 423, 567; McNiff Dancers, 551; reels, 418; *Riverdance* (show), 415, 417, 420, 423, 567; set dance, 424n5; set pieces, 418; step dancing, 417–425; tap dance, 672; traditional music, 418

Dance: Its Place in Art and Life (Kinney and Kinney), 418

Dance Music of Ireland (O'Neill), 418

Dangerfield, Sebastian (character), 659

"Danny Boy" (Weatherly), 399

Danu, 437

"Darling Girl from Clare" (song), *400*

Darwin, Charles, 366

"Daughter of Rosie O'Grady" (Donaldson), 393

Daughters of Ireland *(Inghinidhe na hÉireann)*, 109

Davidson, Jaye, 566

Davin, Maurice, 106

Davin, Nicholas, 189

Davis, Graham, 46

Davis, Thomas, 89

Davitt, Michael: Devoy and, 100, 291; Fenians, 291, 292; Ford (Patrick) and, 291, 292; George and, 291; hagiography, 491; Irish Americans, 177; Irish nationalism, 291; New Departure, 100, 292; Parnell and, 101

Day, Denis, 437

Day, Dorothy, 591

Day in the Bog Festival, 435

Day-Lewis, Daniel, 566

De Danann, 437

De Valera, Éamon: abdication crisis in Britain, 136; agenda following World War I, 120; American Association for the Recognition of the Irish Republic, 296; Anglo-Irish relations, *123*; Anglo-Irish Treaty, 127; birth, 119, 120, *123*, 491; Brugha and, 121, 122; Catholic Church in Ireland, 120; Catholic University of America, *123*; Churchill and, 137; Cohalan and, 295, 296–297; Collins (Michael) and, 122; Cumann na Poblachta (Republican Party), 128, 540; death, 139; Devoy and, 295, 296–297; Easter Rising, 119, 120; elections (1933), 135; elections (1948), 138; Executive Council presidency, 135, 136; Fianna Fáil (Warriors of Ireland), 132,

136, 139; Friends of Irish Freedom, 295–296; Griffith and, 122; honorary degree, *123*; imprisonment, 122; Irish Americans, 177; "Irish Ireland," 553–554; Irish Republican Army, 136, 297; Irish Volunteers, 120, 121; Kennedy (John F.) and, 528; League of Nations, 137; Lloyd George and, 121, 126; in London, 126; McGarrity and, 297; mother, 119, 120, *123*; neutrality, 137; Northern Ireland's constitutional status, 126; oath of allegiance, 134; ouster from power, 138; patriotism, 120; presidency of Dáil, 295; presidency of Irish Republic, *123*, 139; prime minister *(Príomh Aire)*, 126; release from prison (1917), 121; religion, 120; Republic of Ireland, *123*, 139; Republican Party (Cumann na Poblachta), 128, 540; republicanism, 121, 128–129; Roosevelt (Franklin) and, 137; self-determination for Ireland, 295; Sinn Fein, 22, 120–121, 132; Statute of Westminster, 134; as Taoiseach, *123*, 136, 137; in United States, *123*, 125, 295, *296*; Warriors of Ireland (Fianna Fáil), 132, 136, 139; Wilson (Woodrow) and, 125

Dead End (film), 550

"Dear Old Fashioned Irish Songs My Mother Sang to Me" (Von Tilzer), 396

Dearden, John, 600–601, 601

Death rates, 231–232

Declaration of Independence (Irish, 1782), 75

Declaration on Religious Freedom, 590

Declaratory Act ("Sixth of George I," 1720), 72–73, 75

Defenders, the, 74, 78, 81, 188

Defensiveness, 508

Deforestation, 193

Dehumanization, *366*

Delaney, James L., 516

Demme, Ted, 11

Democratic Party: anti-New Deal Irish, 507; Irish Americans, 174, 183, 215, 218–219, 557, 580, 631–632; Irish Catholics, 174, 198, 490; New York Irish, 318, 477–483, 504–512; patronage, 557; political power, 520; regulars vs. reformers, 481; southern New England, 632; virtue, 506; working class, 476. *See also* Tammany Hall

Democratic Republicans, 183, 478

Democratic Unionist Party, 146

Dempsey, Jack ("Manassa Mauler"), 457–459

Dennehy, Dennis, 420

Dennehy School (Chicago), 423

Dervish, 437

DeSapio, Carmine G., 502, 507, 511

Desire under the Elms (O'Neill), 652

Desmond, H. J., 346

Destinies of Darcy Dancer, Gentleman (Donleavy), 659

Develin, John E., 316, 317, 318, 320

Dever, Paul, 628

Devere, Sam, 387

Devlin, Bernadette, 144, 297, 298, 558–559

Devlin, Bertha, 345

Devlin, Daniel: career, 313–314, 317; Emigrant Savings Bank, 313, 315t, 317, 326n39; New York City treasurer, 317; Roman Catholic Orphan Asylum, 327n76

Devotional Revolution (Catholic Revival): influence in post-Famine Ireland, 578; Larkin (Emmet) and, 33, 284n18; people-priest relationship, 279; scope of, 613

Devoy, John: Bernstorff and, 117; Catholic clergy's attitudes, 586; Clan na Gael, 100, 109, 290, 294, 492; Clarke and, 109; Cohalan and, 125, 294; Collins (Michael) and, 296; "Cuba Five," 293; Davitt and, 100, 291; de Valera and, 296–297; Easter Rising, 117; *Gaelic American*, 294; Home Rule, 100, 292; land reform, 292; McGarrity and, 125; New Departure, 100, 292; New York City, 370; Parnell and, 100, 101; *Playboy of the Western World*, 495; pro-German material, 294; self-determination for Ireland, 295; social reform, 294; Wilson (Woodrow) and, 295

Dewey, Thomas, 504

Di Pasquale, Caesar, 669

Diamond, Legs, 676

Diana, Princess of Wales, 561

Dickey, Bill, 461

Dickson, R. J., 3–4, 161

Dictionary of American Biography, 304, 318, 320, 321

Dictionary of National Biography, 304

Dillon, Gregory: career, 309; Commissioners of Emigration, 307, 309, 316; Emigrant Savings Bank, 307–311, 315t, 322, 326n39; Friendly Sons of St. Patrick (New York), 308–309; Hughes (Archbishop John) and, 314, 315, 321; immigration reform, 316; Irish Emigrant Society, *307*, 307–308, 309, 316; non-Catholic, 314; portrait, *307*; son, 318

Dillon, James, 135

Dillon, Robert James, 318

DiMaggio, Joe, 461, 475

Dineen, Joan, *555*

Diner, Hasia, 30, 48, 345, 580

Dinsmoor, Robert, 263

Discrimination, 131–132, 372, 375
Disestablishment Act (1869), 99
Diversity visa (Immigration Act, U.S., 1990), 564
Dixies Showband, 432
Dobbs, Arthur, 164
Doctor's Son and Other Stories (O'Hara), 653
Doheny, Edward L, 592
Doheny, Michael, 224
Doherty, Joseph Patrick (Joe), 300, 559
Dolan, Jay P.: Catholic Worker Movement, 591; Cushwa Center at the University of Notre Dame, 46; immigration history, 45; insularity of postwar Catholicism, 598; Irish parish life, 242; relations between Irish and German Catholics, 36; study of Irish America, 11
Dole, Robert, 540
Domestic service, 332–353; abandonment of the name Bridget, 31; acculturation, 345–346; American-born Irish, 361; Ancient Order of Hibernians, 342; assertiveness, 336; Catholic Church in America, 337, 341–342; Catholicism, 336–337; employer expectations, 336, 343; employer-inflicted beatings, 340; "followers," 341; "home," 343; homesickness, 340; housework, 334–336, 338; immigrant women, 30–32, 33–35; Irish dances (occasions), 343; job security, 343–344, 357; laboring, 250n73; loneliness, 340; maids-of-all-work, 337–338; marriage, 343, 345; native-born girls, 336—337; in New York, 356; nutrition, 341; other immigrant groups, 358; physical separation from employers, 341; relations with different ethnicities, 36; remittances, 341, 343; self-esteem, 344–345; sobriquets for Irish servant, 333; social life, 341–343; as a source of employment, 357; status, 344–345; stigma, 358; time off, 337
Donahoe, Patrick, 195, 201
Donahue, Peter, 618
Dongan, Thomas, 476
Donleavy, J. P., 658–659
Donnelly, Ignatius, 591
Donnelly, James, 615
Donnelly, Terence, 308, 319, 326n39
Donoghue, D., 447
Donohue, Molly (character), 31, 623
Donovan, Art, 462
Donovan, James B., 504
Donovan, Mary Ann, 338
Donovan, Mary (née McCarthy), 343
Donovan, William J. ("Wild Bill"), 493
Dooley, Mr. (character): brogue, 5; *Chicago Evening Post*, 552; Chicago

neighborhood, 650–651; contemporary relevance, 40; Dunne (Finley Peter) and, *651*; intelligence/wit, 654; Molly Donohue (character), 31; philosopher of the people, 14, 628; undermining stereotypes, 43
Dorr, Rheta Childe, 340
Doughboy with the Fighting 69th (Ettinger), 670
Dougherty, Dennis, 584
Dougherty, Hughie, 387
Douglas, Ann, 673, 676
Dowling, Anastasia, 340
"Down Went McGinty" (Flynn), 392
Doyle, David N.: *America and Ireland, 1776–1976*, 11; Catholics becoming Presbyterians, 261; *Dictionary of American Biography* dataset, 304–305; East Coast Irish, 13; gender ratio in migration, 30; on human patterns, 303; importance, xvi; Irish-American governmental activism, 627; *Irish Immigrants in the Land of Canaan* (with others), 39, 47; leadership of trade unions, 35; *New History of Ireland* (Doyle), xvi, 16; Purcell (Richard) and, viii; social mobility of the Irish, 616
Doyle, Dinny, 398
Doyle, James Warren ("J.K.L."), 272
Doyle, Lawrence O'Connor, 190
Doyle Brothers (Harrigan and Hart), 389
Draft Riots (1863), 35, 372–373, 485, 633
Drake, Francis S., 304
Dreamers of Dreams (O'Donovan), 32
Dreiser, Theodore, 491, 596
Drinking Life (Hamill), 657
Driscoll, James, 583
Driscoll, John "Paddy," 462
Driven Patriot (Hooper and Brinkley), 677–678
Dropkick Murphys, 403
Drovers, 438
Du Bois, W. E. B., 376
Duane, William, 184, 263
Dublin Irish Festival (Ohio), 439, 441n19
Dublin Metropolitan Police, 111
Dublin Tramway Company, 110
Dubois, John, 305
Duffy, Charles Gavan, 89, 126
Duffy, Francis P., 494, 585, 586, 590, 673–674
Duffy, Frank, 362
Duffy, Frank J., 592
Duffy, Hugh, 447, *448*
Duffy's Tavern (film), 399
Duggan, Danny (character), 31
Duggan, Eamon, 126

Duggan, Mrs. Malachi (character), 31
Dulles, John Foster, 530
Dungannon Clubs, 109
Dunn, Thomas J., 482
Dunn Trophy, 454
Dunne, Colin, 417
Dunne, Finley Peter: Chicago, 14, 29; *Chicago Evening Post*, 552, *651*; Danny Duggan (character), 31; depiction of marital relations, 31; Fanning and, 14; Honoriah Nolan (character), 31; Molly Donohue (character), 31, 623; Mr. Dooley (character) (*see* Dooley, Mr.); Mrs. Malachi Duggan (character), 31; photo of, *651*; social mobility of the Irish, 622
Dunne, John Gregory, 659
Dunne, Robert, 46
Durang, John, 417
Durham, Lord (John George Lambton), 190
Dust Bowl (photograph), 663
Dynamism, 232

E. H. Harding (publisher), 390
Early, Patsy, 419
East-cost model of Irish-American history, 11–13
East is East (Boyle), 661
Easter Rising (1916), 116–119; American newspaper coverage, *118*; Clan na Gael, 117, 120, 295; constitutional nationalism, 294–295; Cumann na mBan, 118; de Valera and, 119, 120; Devoy and, 117; Irish-American nationalism, 295; Irish Republican Brotherhood, 117–118, 492; Irish Volunteers, 22, 117; MacNeill and, 117; Pearse and, 116–117, 118; physical force nationalism, 492; Redmond (John) and, 118; Sinn Fein, 119–120; United Irish League of America, 295; United Irishmen, 295
Eaton, Henry, 259
Ebbets, Charles C., 662
Economic Justice for All (Bernardin), 602
Economics: affluence, 550; anti-hiring discrimination, 372; capitalism, 193; communalism, 614–615; emigration and source country economic development, 159; emigration and U.S. business cycles, 185; "family economy," 230, 240; immigration, 36; Irish-American elites and mid-nineteenth century economy, 322; laissez-faire economics, 88, 90–91, 92–93, 94, 216, 273, 519; savings accounts, 26, 305, 306; scarce economies, 614–615; secret societies, 615; Ulster economic development, 157–160, 162

Ed Sullivan Show (TV show), 401, 419, 551

Edge of Sadness (O'Connor), 655

Edmonton Folk Festival, 430

Education: Catholic Church in America, 280, 513, 596, 603; college attendance/graduation, 346; early America, 486; G.I. Bill of Rights, 50; Irish Americans, 50–51, 550, 556; Irish Catholics, 39–40; Irish Protestants, 39–40, 203; loyalty oaths, 517; neoscholasticism, 596; secularism, 199; training in housework, 334–335; University of Notre Dame faculty, 594–595. *See also* Schools

Edward VI (King of England and Ireland), 65

Edward VII (King of Great Britain and Ireland), 108, 113, 452, 466, 585

Edward VIII (King of Great Britain and Ireland), 136

Edwards, Owen Dudley, 11

Edwards, Robin Dudley, 44

EEC (European Economic Community), 139, 140–141

Egalitarianism, 493, 610, 629

Egan, Maurice Francis, 175

Egremont, Lord (Charles Wyndham), 186

Ehrenhalt, Alan, 598

Eighteenth Amendment, 588

Eileen Astore (play), 395

Éire (Ireland; 1937–1949), 136–138

Eire-Ireland (journal), 44

Eisenhower, Dwight David, 510, 531, 532

Electioneering, 198

Electoral Amendment Bill (1927), 134

Eliot, Charles William, 6

Elites, 32, 303–305, 320, 322

Elizabeth I (Queen of England), 65–66, 154

Ellis, John Tracy, 45, 488, 514, 518, 599

Ellis Island, 631

Embury, Philip, 283n1

Emerald Club, 452

Emerald Isle Immigration Center (New York City), 564

Emerald Society, 503, 540, 541–542, 610

Emigrant Industrial Savings Bank, *307*, 500. *See also* Emigrant Savings Bank

Emigrant Savings Bank, 302–331; archdiocese of New York, 315; Carrigan and, 308, 313, 314, 315t, 326n39; Commissioners of Emigration, 27, 308, 316, *317*; deposit and remittance trade, 26, 318; Develin and, *317*, 318; Devlin (Daniel) and, 313, 315t, *317*, 326n39; Dillon (Gregory) and, 307–311, 315t, 322, 326n39; finance committee, 312, *317*, 319; founders, 309–314, 315t;

founding, 25–26; Friendly Sons of St. Patrick (New York), 306, 307–308; Hoguet and, 310–312, 315t, 318–319, 320; Hughes (Archbishop John) and, 303, 304, 305, 314–315, 315t, 320–321, 329n108, 500; Ingoldsby and, 308, 309, 312–313, 315t, 326n39; Irish Emigrant Society, 306–309; Kelly ("Honest John") and, 318; memory politics, 318–322; O'Conor and, 318, 326n39; officers, 326n39; Olwell and, 312, 315t, 326n39; origins, 305–309, 319; philanthropy, 25–26; professionalization, 318–319; real estate, 315, 330n115; St. Patrick's Cathedral, 315; Stuart and, 308, 310, 315t, 329n39; Test Books, 302; trustees, 303, 308, 309, *317*, 318, 326n39, 327n76, 329n108. *See also* Emigrant Industrial Savings Bank

Emigrants and Exiles (Miller), xv, 39, 46, 613

Emigration: ambitions, 554; assisted-emigration schemes, 86; bilingualism, 221; British government policy, 179–180, 185–186; business cycle in U.S., 185; Catholic Emigration Society, 186; country emigration rates, 220–221; crises in Ireland, 185; economic development (source country), 158; embarkation, 185; emigration aid societies, 181; epicenter, 221, 232; fares, 179; farmers, 223–224; from England, 174–175; from Germany, 174–175; from Ireland, 171–172, 173, 179–180, 184–185, 186, 213, 413, 469, 554, 562; from the Irish "community," 495; from Ulster, 151, 158, 187–188, 223; gender ratio in, 30, 279; Great Famine, 92, 215–217, 219–220; Irish Catholics, 74, 191; Irish fertility, 172; Irish Protestants, 221; literacy level, 180, 188, 223, 224; mechanics of, 185; overpopulation, 245n17; post-Famine (1860–1881), 216; post-Famine era, 94; postwar, 549; pre-Famine years, 173, 215; prepaid passages, 204; regional variation in, 219; reliability of figures, 161–162; remittances, 318; reported destinations, 216; Scotch-Irish, 157, 159–163; survival, 224; terminus for Liverpool sailings, 185; to Britain, 186, 549; to British North America, 179, 184, 187; Ulster Catholics, 191; Ulster Presbyterians, 73, 74, 86; unemployment, 173; women, 333; youthfulness, 172–173, 224. *See also* Commissioners of Emigration; Immigration

Emmet, Robert, 84–85, 201, 283, 491

Emmet, Thomas Addis: in America, 178; brother, 84; Catholic Emancipa-

tion, 183; memory of, 282; in New York City, 477; nonsectarianism, 17; refugee status, 17, 289; son, 201; United Irishmen, 84

Emmet baseball teams, 447

Emmet militia, 452

Emmets (Gaelic football team), 454

Emmet's revolution (1803), 85

Emmett, Dan, 382, 383

Emmons, David, 46, 619

Emperor Jones (O'Neill), 652

Employment. *See* Work

Encyclopedia of the Irish in America (Glazier), xv, 39

End of Hidden Ireland (Scally), 613–615, 683

End of the Hunt (Flanagan), 660

Enfranchisement, 198

Engels, Friedrich, 369

England, John, 195, 197, 603

English as the national language, 27

English Pale, 63–64, 72

Ennis, John, 446

Enright, Ellie Driscoll, 337

"Epic" (Kavanaugh), 685

Episcopal Church, 589

Erie, Steven P., 580, 626, 630, 637

Erie Canal, 186–187, 355

Erin Society (St. Louis), 175

Erin's Heirs (Clark), 13

Ernst, Robert, 7–8, 12, 322, 618

Erskine, John, 304

Erwin, Jimmy, 420

Essence of Old Virginny (Emmett), 382

Ethiopian opera, 382

Ethnic elites, 32, 303–305, 322

Ethnic identity: among Irish-born, 260–261, 267; assimilation, 370–371; ethnic Catholicism, 575–578; German Americans, 576; Middle and Far West, 496; New Yorkers, 496; suburbanization, 41, 548, 556

Ethnicity: being ethnic Irish and American, 346; diversity within Catholic Church in America, 575–578; diversity within New York City Police Department, 503; ethnic fusion, picture of, 684; ethnic mini-segregation, 159; interethnic cooperation, 356; legitimizing, 426–427; multiethnic festivals, 429–430; nativism, 426–427; public celebrations of, 427; relations between ethnicities, 36; sense of importance of, 415

Ettinger, Albert, 670, 673–674

Eugenics, 674

Europe, James Reece, 670

European Economic Community (EEC), 139, 140–141

Evangelicalism. *See* Protestant evangelicalism

Everything That Rises Must Converge (O'Connor), 657
Evictions in Ireland: agrarian violence, 85, 101; Great Famine, 21–22, 96; "Ulster Custom," 99
Expensive Habits (Howard), 656
External Relations Act (1936), 138

Factory work, 218, 226, 230
Fagan, James B., 79
Fair Play for Cuba Committee, 531
"Fallacy of Bettering Oneself" (Ryan), 630
Fallows, Marjorie, 346
Families, Anglo-American, 332
"Family economy," 230, 240
Family formation, 237–238
Family of the Gael. *See* Clan na Gael
Family reunification, 306, 562
Famine: Ulster, 158. *See also* Great Famine
Fanning, Charles: Dunne (Finley Peter) and, 14; Irish Studies program, 48; Mr. Dooley pieces, 40; social ambition, 31; study of Irish America, 11
Fantasy, 489
Farley, James A. (Jim), 507–508, 510, 596
Farley, John, 584
Farmers, 133, 135, 223–224, 251n92
Farmers' Party, 134, 135
Farrel, John, 194
Farrell, Elizabeth, 118
Farrell, James T.: Catholicism, 596; Chicago, 658, 671; Danny O'Neill (character), 40; literary tradition, 649; *Lonigan* trilogy, 550, 652; O'Hara (John) and, 653; Studs Lonigan (character), 40; working-class life, 671
Fass, Paula, 621
"Father of Labor Day," 359
Faulkner, Brian, 143, 144, 145
Faulkner, George, 446
Fay, Frank, 107
Fay, William, 107
FBI, 510
Fecklessness, 489
Federalists, 182, 262–263, 478
Feeney, John, 437
Feeney, Patrick, 437
Feetham, Richard, 130
Feis (feiseanna), 414, 418–419, 428
"Fenian Banner" (poem), 97
Fenian baseball teams, 447
Fenian brand shirt collars, *291*
Fenians (Fenian Brotherhood), 96–100; aim, 290; Canadian Irish, 190–191; Catholic Church in Ireland, 96; "Champion of the Fenians" (Nast), *366*; Civil War (United States), 97; Clan na Gael, 290; Davitt and, 291, 292; "Fenian Banner," 97; founding,

22, 290; Gladstone and, 98–99; insurrection (1867), 98; invasion of Canada, 491; Irish-American militia groups, 452–453; Irish Americans, 22, 171, 200, 223; Irish Games, 452; Irish nationalism, *366*; Land Act (1881), 102; leaders, 290; O'Donovan Rossa and, 290; Parnell and, 290; split into factions, 98; uprising (1867), *293*
Fennessy, Michael J., 598
Ferguson, Samuel, 107
Ferrall, John, 356
Ferraro, Geraldine, 559
Ferrie, Joseph, 618
Fertility patterns, 172–173, 219, 238
Festival of American Folklife, 430
Festivals, 426–442; Celtic festivals, 426; *Feis (feiseanna)*, 428; *Fleadh (fleadhanna)*, 428–429; in Ireland, 427; Irish-American community festivals, 430–440; multiethnic festivals, 429–430; music festivals, 411; secularism, 427; traditional music festivals, 415
Fianna Fáil (Warriors of Ireland): Clann na Poblachta, 138; Cosgrave and, 134; Cumann na nGaedheal, 134–135; de Valera and, 132, 136, 139; elections (1927), 134; elections (1932), 134; elections (1933), 135; elections (1937), 137; elections (1943), 138; elections (1948), 138; founding, 132; Lemass and, 139; Northern Ireland conflict, 140; oath of allegiance, 134; O'Kelly and, 139; time in power, 139
Fiddle Tunes, 432
Fields, Barbara, 683
Fighting 69th. *See* 69th National Guard Regiment
"Fighting Irish," 443, 457, 494, 595, 667
Fighting Sullivans (film), 667
Filiopietism: American Irish Historical Society, 3, 15; American Revolution, 3; break between Catholics and Protestants, 5; example, 286–288; negative stereotypes, 25; Scotch-Irish, 165; Scotch-Irish Society, 3, 15
Fillmore, Millard, 217
Final Payments (Gordon), 659, 660
Findley, William, 182, 263
Fine Gael (Irish Tribe), 136, 138, 140
Finlay, Jerry, 432
Finn, "Bashful Dan," 502
Finn, "Battery Dan," 502
Finn, "Sheriff Dan," 502
Finney, Charles Grandison, 274
Finney, Jack, 663
Firpo, Luis ("Wild Bull of Pampas"), 458
Fisher, Jim, 628
Fisher, Joseph R., 130

Fiske, John, 304
Fitzgerald, Barry, 550, 680–681
FitzGerald, Desmond, 134
FitzGerald, Edward, 80
Fitzgerald, F. Scott: *Beautiful and the Damned*, 653; Catholicism, 596; *Great Gatsby*, 653, 674; Irishness, 657, 671; *Last Tycoon*, 653; literary tradition, 649; O'Hara (John) and, 653; the rich, 677; social mobility of the Irish, 622; *Tender is the Night*, 653; *This Side of Paradise*, 653, 654
FitzGerald, Garret, 140, 146
FitzGerald, Garrett Mór, 64
FitzGerald, Garrett Óg, 64
Fitzgerald, John F., *505*, 668
Fitzgerald, Lord Edward, 80
Fitzgerald, Maureen, 33
Fitzgerald, Molly Ryan, 342
Fitzgerald, Patrick, 446
FitzGerald, Vesey, 83–84
Fitzgeralds (Earls of Kildare), 63–65, 66
Fitzpatrick, David, 618–619
Fitzpatrick, John, 192, 362
Fitzpatrick, Joseph P., 514, 576
FitzSimmons, Thomas, 183
Flaherty, Joe, 656–657
Flaherty, Ray, 462
Flaming Corsage (Kennedy), 660
Flanagan, John, 465
Flanagan, John F., 449
Flanagan, Thomas, 660
Flanagan Brothers, 398
Flannery, Michael: Clan na Gael, 298; NORAID, 298, 300, 538; St. Patrick's Day parade (1983), 538, 542, 544–545, 559
Flannery, Nick, 639
Flatley, Michael, 417, 420–421, 423, 567
Fleadh (fleadhanna), 428–429
Fleming, Ian, 533
Fleming, Michael, 191
Flogging Molly, 403
Flood, Henry, 177
Florida Folk Festival, 430
"Flower From My Angel Mother's Grave" (Kennedy), 392
Flynn, Bill, 50
Flynn, Ed, 481, 504, 680
Flynn, Elizabeth Gurley, 362, 491, 508, 581
Flynn, Errol, 551
Flynn, Joseph, 392
Fogarty, Gerald, 45
Fogarty and Co. (Fogarty), 656
FOIF (Friends of Irish Freedom), 125, 295–296, 506
Foley, Marc, 33
Foley, Thomas, 610
Folk music, 381, 402, 413
"Followers," 341

Fondness for drink, 496
Foner, Eric, 377
Fontana, Francesco, 272
Football (American), 462–465
Football (Gaelic), 452, 453–454, 468
Football Hall of Fame, 462
For Faith and Fortune: The Education of Catholic Immigrants in Detroit (Vinyard), 12
"For You O Democracy" (Whitman), 640
Ford, John, 551, 632
Ford, Patrick, 291, 292, 294, 591
Fordham Ram (newspaper), 517–518
Fordham University, 578, 596
Foreign Conspiracy Against the Liberties of the United States (Morse), 490
Forrestal, James, 677–678
Foster, Roy, 369
Foster, Stephen, 218
Foster, William Z., 362, 508, 581
"Four Green Fields" (song), 402–403
Four Horsemen of Irish-American politics, 49, 299
Four Provinces Orchestra, 398
Foxx, Jimmie, 461
Frank Leslie's Illustrated Newspaper, 222
Frankel, Charles, 479
Franklin, Benjamin, 166
Frederic, Harold, 665
Free immigration, 182
Free Presbyterian Church, 143
Free School Society (New York City), 486
Free speech, 182
Freedom of the press, 182
Freeman, Edward, 665
Freeman, T. W., 223
Freeman's Journal (New York newspaper), 175, 195
French Revolutionary Wars (1792–1801), 77, 478
Freud, Sigmund, 552
Fricker, Brenda, 566
Friendliness, 496
Friendly Brothers of St. Patrick (New York), 25
Friendly Sons of St. Patrick (New York): Catholics in leading positions, 198; Dillon (Gregory) and, 308–309; Emigrant Savings Bank, 306, 307–308; first president, 489; Irish Emigrant Society, 308, 320; prosperity of, 499; Sheen address to, 509
Friendly Sons of St. Patrick (Philadelphia), 25, 175
Friends, U.S. Constitution among, 479
Friends of Ireland, 183
Friends of Irish Freedom (FOIF), 125, 295–296, 506

From Paddy to Studs, 1880–1920 (Meagher), 12
From the Terrace (O'Hara), 676
Frost, Robert, 496
Froude, James Anthony, 369
Fundamentalism. *See* Protestant evangelicalism

"G-men," 125
GAA. *See* Gaelic Athletic Association
Gaelic American (newspaper), 294, 467, 492
Gaelic Athletic Association (GAA), 468–470; active members, 540–541; American tour (1884), 454; Boston Irish, 469; Catholic Church in Ireland, 106; Chicago Irish, 469; county loyalty, 469; establishment in America, 455, 468; establishment in Ireland, 443, 454; Flannery (Michael) and, 538; hurling, 453, 468; Irish Republican Brotherhood, 106, 110; leaders, 110; networking, 469; New York Irish, 469–470; popularity, 107; San Francisco Irish, 469–470
Gaelic Athletic Union, 455
Gaelic clans, 65
Gaelic football, 452, 453–454
Gaelic games, 448–449, 468–469
Gaelic Irish: Cromwell (Oliver) and, 69; end of, 66, 154; Irish parliament, 72; Ulster, 67, 154; Ulster risings (1640s), 67–68
Gaelic League *(Conradh na Gaelige):* Catholic Church in Ireland, 106–107; *ceilis,* 414; *Feis (feiseanna),* 428; founding, 106; influence, 107; Irish Americans, 171; Irish language, 133; Irish Republican Brotherhood, 110; leaders, 110; suppression of, 122
Gaelic Revival, 105–109, 418
Gaelic Roots, 432
Gaeltacht, 133
Gallagher, Michael J., 586
Gallagher, Tess, 660
Galvin, Martin, 300
"Galway Bay" (Colohan), 399
Gamble, John, 266
Gandhi, Mahatma, 558
Gangs of New York (film), 35, 322
Gannon, Joe, 49
Gannon, Robert I., 597
Garda Siochána (Guardians of the Peace), 133, 135
Garfield, James A., 444
Garritty, Wendell Arthur, 639
Gartrell, Leland, 515
Garvin, Tom, 615
Gary, John, 437
Gehrig, Lou, 461

General Irish Relief Committee of the City of New York, 20
Generosity, 496
George, Henry, 291, 486
George, Terry, 433
George III (King of Great Britain, Ireland, and Hanover), 82–83
George V (King of Great Britain and Northern Ireland), 113, 125–126
Geraldines (Gaelic football team), 454
German immigrants: assimilation, 175; Catholic Church in America, 241, 576; descendants of, 37; ethnic consciousness, 576; Irish Americans, 214; in Pennsylvania, 162; Scotch-Irish, 165; unskilled labor, 358
G.I. Bill of Rights (1944), 50, 550, 598–599
Gibbons, James: birthplace, 583; Knights of Labor, 581, 604; leadership of American Catholic Church, 603; Mason to, about FDR, 586; O'Connell (William) and, 586; Wilson (Woodrow) and, 585
Gibbons, Luke, 615
Gibbons, Mary, 587
Gibson, Florence, 7
Gibson, William, 660
Gideonite Society (Philadelphia), 188
Gift (Hamill), 656
Gillespie, Ed, 631
Gilley, Sheridan, 368–370, 377
Gilroy, Frank D., 551
Ginger Man (Donleavy), 658–659
Gjerde, Jon, 618–619
Glad, Donald D., 501
Gladstone, William Ewart: Fenians, 98–99; Home Rule, 103, 105, 111; Irish Protestants, 99; Parnell and, 102, 104, 105; retirement, 106; self-determination in Ireland, 103
Glassie, Henry, 612
Glazer, Nathan, 8–9, 535
Glazier, Michael, xv
Gleason, Jackie, 410, 551–552
Gleason, Maurice, 617
Gleason, Philip, 45, 578, 596
Gleason, Sara, 617
Gleason, Teddy, 541–542
Gleeson, David, 46
Glennon, John, 584
Glorious Revolution (1688–1689), 69–70, 477
Glucksman, Lewis, 48
Glucksman, Loretta Brennan, 48
Glucksman Ireland House (New York University), 51
Glynn, John, 415
Goff, John W., 476
Goggins, Catherine, 359, 581
Going My Way (film), 399, 550

Goldberg, Leonora, 398
Goldberg, Martha, 426
Golden, Donny, 420, *422*
Golden, Eileen, *422*
Golden, Renny, 661
Goldstein, Kenny, 400–401
Gompers, Samuel, 362
Gonne, Maud, 109, 138
Gooch, William, 164
Good Friday Agreement (1998), 49, 146, 300, 560–562
Good Man Is Hard to Find and Other Stories (O'Connor), 657
Goodwin, Doris Kearns, 1–2
Goodwin, Richard, 531
Gordon, Mary, 649, 655, 659–660
Government of Ireland Act (1920): Council of Ireland provision, 127; Northern Irish view, 129; passage, 123–124; proportional representation, 131; repeal, 146; two parliaments, 123–124
Government of Ireland Bill (1912), 114
Gowan, Ogle, 189–190
Grace, William R., 318, 475, 477, 592
Grace Abounding (Howard), 656
Gráda, Cormac Ó, 161
Grange, Red, 457, 463
Grant, Madison, 674
Grant, Ulysses S., 288
Grasso, Eliot, *422*
Grattan, Henry, 75–76, 81–82, 86
Grattan, James, 186
Grattan, Thomas Colley, 153, 197, 200, 203
Grattan's parliament, 74–76
Gray, Peter, 369
Graymoor (Franciscan Friars of the Atonement), 579
Great Depression, 36, 548–549, 590–592
Great Famine, 90–96, 219–224; American government aid, 21, 217; anti-British sentiment, 22, 96; assimilation, 184; "Black '47," 91–92; British response, 90; as a Catholic affliction, 22–23; Catholic Church in America, 279; Catholic Church in Ireland, 95; causation debate, 20; cholera, 93; Church of Ireland, 266; Conservative Party, 91; crime, 91–92; crop failures, 86, 90; deaths from, 93–94; emigration, 92, 215–217, 219–220; evictions in Ireland, 21–22, 96; family formation, 237–238; foreign aid, 92, 217, 239; grain exports, 90–91; grain imports, 91; humanitarianism, 216; immigration from, 7–8, 16, 18, 23, 24, 93, 213, 214–215, 219, 230, 262–264, 316, 367, 476, 489; Irish-American relief, *239*; Irish language, 95; Irish nationalism, 20; Irish Protestants, 217,

266; as a killer, 21; laissez-faire economics, 90–91, 92–93, 94, 216; landlords in Ireland, 22, 90–91, 93–94; legacy, 15–23; marriage, 333; memories of, 17–20, 21, 216, 218; nativism, 217; Peel and, 90–91, 94; physical landscape, 94–95; *phytophthora infestans*, 90; political implications, 95–96, 216–217; post-famine era, 94–96; religious devotion, 33, 95; soup kitchens, 93, 94; "souperism," 92; trauma, 218; type of country America became, 22; wages, 91; Young Ireland, 89, 218
Great Gatsby (Fitzgerald), 654, 674
Great Hunger *(An Gorta Mór). See* Great Famine
Great Lakes–Mississippi basin, 192–193
Greater New York Irish-American Athletic Association (NYIAAA), 453, 454, 468
Greeley, Andrew: on *Beyond the Melting Pot*, 9; ethnic identity in suburbs, 41; *Irish Americans*, 42; Irish women, 346; National Opinion Research Center, 38; parish societies, 593–594; Protestants of Irish ancestry, 39, 40; social mobility, 620; stereotypes of Irish, 42; study of Irish America, 10–11
Greeley, Horace, 32
Green, Rodney, 15–16
Green, Sarah Byrne, *344*
Green Fields of America, 420, *422*, 437
Green Isle, 452
Green Pastures (Connelly), 652
Greene, Graham, 657
Greenlee, Elizabeth McDowell, 260
Gregory, Lady Augusta, 107
Griffin, Clyde, 616
Griffin, John, 398
Griffin, Patrick, 39, 47, 256, 398
Griffin, William D., 49
Griffith, Arthur: Anglo-Irish Treaty, 126, 127; British Army recruitment, 117; Cosgrave and, 132; de Valera and, 122; death, 129; Free State government, 128; imprisonment, 122; minister of home affairs, 122; as prime minister *(Príomh Aire)*, 127; Sinn Fein, 107–108, 117, 119, 120
Grove, Lefty, 461
Groves of Academe (McCarthy), 654
Guadalupe Hidalgo, Treaty of (1848), 218
Guardians of the Peace (Garda Siochána), 133, 135
Guardianship of Infants Act (1957), 140
Guare, John, 660
Guilday, Peter, 240, 583
Guildford Four, 566
Guinnane, Timothy, 33
Gus Hayes Band, 432

"H-A-R-R-I-G-A-N" (song), 406
Habit of Being (O'Connor), 657
Haggarty, Mike, 408
Haggerty, Thomas, 581
Hague, Frank, 580, 630
Hairy Ape (O'Neill), 652
Hales, Sean, 129
Haley, Alex, 426
Haley, Margaret, 581
Hallinan, Paul, 593, 598, 600–601, 601
Halloween, 497–498
"Halls of Montezuma" (song), 433
Hamill, Pete, 552, 556, 656–657
Hamilton, Alexander, 478
Hamilton Rowan Club, 452
Hammer throw, 465–466
Handball, 453
"Handful of Earth from My Mother's Grave" (Murphy), 392
Handlin, Oscar: Boston Irish, 7–8, 12, 14; *Boston's Immigrants*, 7–8, 11, 12–13; famine migrants, 242; *Harvard Encyclopedia of American Ethnic Groups*, 7; *Irish in Chicago*, 10; Schlesinger, Sr. and, 11; social mobility of the Irish, 11, 500; *Uprooted*, 11, 219, 223; urban history, 225
Hanley, Brian, 50
Hanlon, Ned, 460–461
Hanna, Charles, 3–4
Hannan, Damian, 30
Hannegan, Robert E., 628
Hannity, Sean, 632
Hansen, Marcus Lee, vii, 7, 225
Harding, Warren G., 588
Hargous, Peter A., 308, 326n39
Harkness, D. A. E., 30
Harney, Mary Cox, 342, 343
Harp and Shamrock Club, 419
Harper's Weekly (magazine), *239*, 366, 666
Harren, Mary Feely, 340, *344*
Harrigan, Edward, 387–391; minstrel past, 395; primary musical collaborator, 388; social ambition, 31; St. Patrick's Day, 427–428; transformation of the Paddy stereotype, 625. *See also* Harrigan and Hart
Harrigan and Hart (songwriters), 387–391; ethnic and class conflicts, 389; Irish-American characters, 629; Irish women, 623; knowledge of the audience, 407; Mulligan Guards, 388–389, 667; social mobility of the Irish, 622; stereotypes, 391
Harrington, Tim, 418
Harrison, Charles, 397
Harrison, William, 201
Hart, Gary, 530
Hart, Tony (Anthony J. Cannon), 387–391. *See also* Harrigan and Hart

Harty, Patricia, 50, 51

Harvard Encyclopedia of American Ethnic Groups (Thernstrom), 2, 7

Harvey, Beauchamp Bagenal, 80

"Has Anybody Here Seen Kelly" (song), 398

Haskin, John B., 493

Hassard, John, 305

Haughey, Charles, 140, 565

Havemeyer, William F., 317

Hayden, Dorothy, 419. *See also* Cudahy, Dorothy Hayden

Hayden, James, 544

Hayden, Tom, 37

Hayes, Helen, 551

Hayes, John, 467

Hayes, Noney, 338

Hayes, Patrick J., 586

Healey, Ed, 462

Healy, Margaret, 359

Healy, Timothy, 362

Healy, William, 418

Healy School (San Francisco), 418, 419

Heaney, James, 297

Heaney, Joe, 412

Hearts of Oak (Oakboys), 74

Hearts of Steel (Steelboys), 74

Heath, Edward, 145

Heck, Barbara, 283n1

Hecker, Isaac, 242, 583

Heenan, John C. ("Benecia Boy"), 444

Hemingway, Ernest, 133, 533, 596

Henderson v. Mayor of New York, 316

Hennesey, James, 580

Hennessy, Francis X., 417

Hennessy, Joe, 670–671

Hennessy, Michael, 420

Henry II (King of England), 63, 489

Henry VII (King of England), 63–64

Henry VIII (King of England), 63–64, 65, 72

Herbert, Victor, 392–393, 493, 499

Heron, Brian, 297, 558

Hersey, John, 533

Hewetson, James, 192

Hibernia America (Clark), 12

Hibernian Benevolent Association (Troy, New York), *196*

Hibernian Boat Club (Buffalo), 446

Hibernian Green baseball teams, 447

Hibernian Institute (Hartford), 195

Hibernian Lyceum (Boston), 195

Hibernian Rifles, 452

Hibernian societies, 261

Hibernian Society (Baltimore), 175

Hibernian Society (Charleston), 175, *181*

Hibernian Society (New Orleans), 175

Hicks, Louise Day, 632, 638

Hierophilus Letters (MacHale), 283n4

Higgins, George G., 604

Higgins, Roger, *553*

Higham, John, 17, 588

Hill, Tommy, 418

Hillbilly music, 382

Hincks, Francis, 190

"Hindenburg Line," 597

Hine, Lewis, *361*

Hiss, Alger, 509

Historical Baseball Abstract (James), 460

History of Londonderry (Parker) [New Hampshire], 263–264

History of New Hampshire (Belknap), 263

History of the Irish Settlers in North America (McGee), 2, 650

Hobson, Bulmer, 109

Hoche, Lazar, 78

Hodges, Graham, 35

Hoey, Jane, 628

Hoffman, John T., 313, 317

Hogan, Patrick, 133

Hogan, Robert, 181, 306

Hogan, Thomas, 194

Hogan's Goat (Alfred), 660

Hoguet, Henry Louis: Emigrant Savings Bank, 310–312, 315t, 318–319, 320; Hughes (Archbishop John) and, 315t, 319, 320, 321; New York Catholic Protectory, 327n76; portrait, *311*; Roman Catholic Orphan Asylum, 327n76

Holland, Mary, 338

Hollinger, David, 635

Holmes, Thomas, 190

Holy Name Society, 593

Holy Name Society (New York City Police Department), 510, 596

Holy Name Society (New York City Sanitation Department), 517

Home Government Association, 99

Home Rule: anti-Home Rule campaign, 115; conscription by the British, 122; Conservative Party, 103, 114; constructive unionism, 111–113; Devoy and, 100, 292; Gladstone and, 103, 105, 111; Home Government Association, 99–100; Home Rule Act (1914), 122; Home Rule Bill (1886), 104; Home Rule Bill (1893), 106; Home Rule Bill (1913; aka Government of Ireland Bill), 114–116; "Home Rulers," 99; Irish National Volunteers, 115; Irish nationalism, 115, 492; Irish Parliamentary Party, 114, 115, 119; Irish Republican Brotherhood, 115; Irish Unionists, 103; Liberal Party, 103, 105; Liberal Unionists, 103; Lloyd George and, 119; Local Government Act, 112; Orange Order, 115; Parnell and, *102*, 104, 105; Redmond (John) and, 114, 294–295; reform of British House of Lords, 113–114; revision of local government, 112; social amelioration, 111; Ulster

unionism, 114–115, 121; Ulster's exclusion from, 119

Homicide: Life on the Street (TV show), 633

Hone, Philip, 306

Honeymooners (TV show), 552

Hoodlums, 676–677

Hooper, Townsend, 677–678

Hooray for Hollywood (film), 682

Hoover, Herbert, 16

Horan, Margaret Convery, 333, 339

Hornpipes, 418

"Horrible Hibernians," 595

Horrigan, Cornelius, 444

Horton, Robert Wilmot, 185, 186

House of Blue Leaves (Guare), 660

House of Commons, British, 82, 109

House of Commons, Irish, 480

House of Gold (Cullinan), 656

House of Kildare, 63–65

House of Lords, British, 72, 82, 113–114

House of Lords, Irish, 72

How I Grew (McCarthy), 654

How the Irish Became Brown (proposed title), 684

How the Irish Became White (Ignatiev), 35, 682

Howard, Mark, 423

Howard, Maureen, 655, 656

Hoy, Suellen, 33

Hughes, John (Archbishop; "Dagger John"): as an elite, 322; attacks on churches, 200, 278; birthplace, 319; Broadway Tabernacle lecture (1847), 20; career, 305–306, 314; Carrigan and, 313, 314, 315t; Carroll Hall candidates, 488; cartoon attacking, *277*; Catholic candidates (1841), 488, 490; Commissioners of Emigration, 275, *277*; *Dictionary of American Biography* entry, 305; Dillon (Gregory) and, 314, 315, 321; Dubois and, 305; Emigrant Savings Bank, 303, 304, 305, 314–315, 315t, 320–321, 329n108, 500; famine immigrants, 316; in *Gangs of New York,* 322; Great Famine's cause, 20–21; Hoguet and, 315t, 319, 320, 321; Internet, 321; Irish Emigrant Society, 196, 204, 207, 500; Kossuth and, 485; leadership of American Catholic Church, 603; leadership of Irish in New York, 309, 316; legacy, 278; liberalism, 485; Manhattan Institute, 322; in New York, 195, 305, 314–315, 316, 485; New York Catholic Protectory, 327n76; nickname, 322; niece Margaret, 319; ordination, 305; *Padre* article, 321; painting of, 319; parochial schools, 199, 516; personality, 322; in Philadelphia, 305; presence in the 21st century,

321–322; private property, 20–21; quoted, 15; religion and group survival, 278; St. Patrick's Cathedral, 319; stereotypes, *277*; Stuart and, 315t

Hughes, John (boxer), 446

Hughes, William, 224

Humanae Vitae (encyclical), 601

Humbert, Jean Joseph, 80–81

Hume, John: constitutional nationalism, 300; contact with American politicians, 299; election to parliament, 144; Nobel Peace Prize, 300; Northern Ireland conflict, 146; Social Democratic Labour Party and, 299, 300

Huntingdon, William R., 451

Hurley, Cornelius, *361*

Hurling, 452, 453, 468

Huston, John, 551

Hyde, Douglas, 106–107, 128, 137

Hylan, John F. "Red Mike," 476

Hynes, Garry, 566

Hynes, John, 362

Hyphenation, 283, 528, 550, 649

"I Hear You Calling Me" (song), 397

I Was Dancing (O'Connor), 655

IAAC (Irish American Athletic Club), 450, 451, 466–467, *468*

IABC (Irish American Business Coalition), 564

Iacocca, Lee, 539

IALC (Irish American Labor Coalition), 543, 564

Iceman Cometh (O'Neill), 652

Ickringill, Steve, 15

Identity. *See* Irish American identity

IDTANA (Irish Dancing Teachers Association of North America), 421–422

IDTCA (Irish Dancing Teachers Commission of America), 421

"If It Wasn't for the Irish and the Jews" (Flannery), 396

"If They'd Only Move Old Ireland over Here" (Kelly), *394*

Ignatiev, Noel, 35

"The Ignorant Vote – Honors are Easy" (Nast), *666*

IIRM (Irish Immigration Reform Movement), 564, 568

"I'll Paralyze the Man Who Says McGinty" (Rosenfeld), *393*

"I'll Take You Home Again Kathleen" (Westendorf), 399

Illegal immigration, 36, 562–563, 568

Illustrated News (newspaper), 444

Imagination, 51

Imbolc (season), 427

Immaculate Heart of Mary Sisters, 601

Immigrant historiography: 1960s and 1970s, 610–611; advances, 43–49; communalism, 612; national biographical dictionaries, 303–305; pioneers of, 2–15; race, 365, 367; relations between ethnicities, 36; role of anti-Irish and anti-Catholic sentiments, 217–218; whiteness, 611–612; whiteness interpretation of working-class history, 634. *See also* Irish-American history

Immigrant Life in New York City, 1825–1863 (Ernst), 7–8, 12

Immigration: alienation, 40–41; American-born Irish Americans (1900 census), 41; Americans claiming Irish ancestry, 37–38, 39, 40, 426, 566, 568–569, 687, 691t; Australia, 172, 618–619; census returns on ancestry, 37–38, 175, 687–691; Chinese, 360; circumstances in Ireland, 30; colonial America, 74; competitiveness of mid-19th-century-America, 40; conspiracy theory of, 274; continuous arrivals, 214; counties with biggest number of ancestral representatives, 50–51; diversity visa, 564; early nineteenth century, 86; economics, 36; Emerald Isle Immigration Center (New York City), 564; eugenics, 674; Famine immigration (1846–1855), 7–8, 16, 18, 23, 24, 93, 213, 214–215, 219, 230, 262–264, 316, 367, 476, 489; female settlement patterns, 32; first-generation immigrants, 40, 689t, 690; first great wave, 21; free immigration, 182; from Canada, 172; from Ireland, 162, 171, 172, 178; gender ratio, 30, 279; Great Depression, 36, 548–549; historiography, 30–31; host society, 13, 24; illegal immigration, 36, 562–563, 568; immigration history, 45; in-migration to Ireland, 567–568; industrialization, 213; Irish-born Americans (1890 census), 689t, 690; Irish-born Americans (1900 census), 41; Irish Catholics, 74; Irish Protestants, 151; knowledge of English, 27–29; location of Irish immigrants, 32; loneliness, 40–41; post-Famine immigration, 16, 21, 29–30, 94, 176, 279; postwar immigration, 36, 413, 469, 549–550, 552–553, 555 (*see also* New Irish); pre-Famine immigration, 16, 17–18, 193, 476, 477, 489; quotas, 36; reform, 316; relations between ethnicities, 36; Scotch-Irish, 151, 178–179; second-generation immigrants, 689t, 690; seventeenth century, 153; transport revolution, 186–187; Ulster Presbyterians, 73, 74, 86; Ulster Protestants, 151; unclosed America, 226; visa lottery, 564, 568; women's role, 30, 33. *See also* Emigration

Immigration Act (U.S., 1965), 469, 562, 564, 602–603

Immigration Act (U.S., 1990), 564

Immigration and Nationality Act (1952, McCarran-Walter Act), 413

Immigration legislation, 304

Immigration Reform and Control Act (1986, IRCA), 564

Imperial Conference (1926), 134

In the Name of the Father (film), 561, 566

Incorporated Hibernian Society (South Carolina), *181*

Indentured servitude, 179, 181

Individualism, 612, 613, 639

Industrial Revolution, 332

Industrial Valley (McKenny), 655

Industrial Workers of the World (IWW), 110, 362

Industrialization, 213–214, 226

Inghinidhe na hÉireann (Daughters of Ireland), 109

Ingoldsby, Felix: Emigrant Savings Bank, 308, 309, 312–313, 315t, 326n39; Roman Catholic Orphan Asylum, 327n76

Insubordination, 674

Insurrection Act (1796), 78

Intermarriage, 38, 152, 191

International Brotherhood of Electrical Workers, 362

International Federation of Trade Unions, 362

International Glove Workers Union, 362

International Ladies' Garment Workers' Union, 476

International Longshoremen's Association, 541

Invention of the White Race (Allen), 633

Iomain, 447, 453

IPP. *See* Irish Parliamentary Party

IRA. *See* Irish Republican Army

IRB. *See* Irish Republican Brotherhood

IRC (Irish Republican Clubs), 298

IRCA (Immigration Reform and Control Act, 1986), 564

Ireland: advanced technology, 563; bookishness, 222; communalism in, 613–615; emigration from, 171–172, 173, 179–180, 184–185, 186, 213, 413, 469, 554, 562; English language literacy, 334; ethnic identification of Irish-born, 260–261, 267; farmers, 251n92; fertility patterns, 172, 219; festivals in, 427; history (*see* Ireland, history of); immigration from, 162, 171, 172, 178; in-migration, 567–568; Irish Americans' influence, 176–177; Irish identity in, 556; map, 62; marriage rates, 554; as a parent nation, 1; population (18th c.), 77; population (19th c.), 85;

Ireland *(continued)*
  population (1846–1860), 215–216; population (post-Famine), 94; religious conversions, 260; sectarian divisions, 615; sports in, 443; trade unionism, 373; unionism (*see* Irish unionism); urbanization, 232–233; wages, 235, 236, 251n92
Ireland, history of, 63–147; 13th century, 63; 15th century, 63; 16th century, 63–64, 66, 72; 17th century, 66–70; 18th century, 70–81; 19th century, 81–109; 1990s, 567–568; Act of Union (1800) (*see* Act of Union); agrarian violence, 85; Anglo-Irish Treaty (1921) (*see* Anglo-Irish Treaty); British rule, 22, 289; Catholic Emancipation (*see* Catholic Emancipation); Catholic Relief Act (1778), 76–77; Catholic Relief Act (1829), 272; crop failures, 86, 90; dependence on agriculture, 89; Easter Rising (1916) (*see* Easter Rising); *Éire* (Ireland; 1937–1949), 136–138; Emmet's revolution (1803), 85; English Pale, 63–64, 72; evictions (*see* Evictions in Ireland); Fenians (*see* Fenians); Gaelic Revival, 105–109; Grattan's parliament, 74–76; Great Hunger (*see* Great Famine); Home Rule movement (*see* Home Rule); Industrial Revolution, 332; industrialization, 110; Irish Civil War (1922–1923), 128–132, 586; Irish Free State (*see* Irish Free State); Irish nationalism (*see* Irish nationalism); labor movement, 110; land reform (*see* Land reform in Ireland); landlords (*See* Landlords in Ireland); mortality in, 110; Moynihan on modern-day, 497–498; Northern Ireland (*see* Northern Ireland); oil crisis (1979), 562; partition (1920), 122–124; Penal Laws, 70–71, 72, 84, 480; Plantation of Ireland, 65–69, 154–155, 159; postwar period, 553–556; potatoes, 85–86; rebellion (1798) (*see* Rebellion of 1798); repeal of union movement, 24, 86–89, 200–203; Republic of Ireland (1938–present), *123*, 138–141, 143; secret societies, 73–74, 85, 88, 101; self-determination, 15, 103, 125, 295; "surrender and regrant" policy, 65; Tithe War (1820s, 1830s), 74; War of Independence (1919–1921), 124–126, 129, 586; World War I (1914–1918), 116, 119–122; World War II (1939–1945), 137–138, 141–142
Ireland, John: leadership of American Catholic Church, 603; national parishes, 576; photo of, *577*; progressiveness, 591; Ryan (John A.) and, 591; support for Spalding, 583
Ireland, Seraphine, 580
Ireland Act (1949), 142
Ireland and the Emigration (Schrier), 47–48
"Ireland Divided" (song), 433
Ireland Fund, 298–299. *See also* American Ireland Fund
"Ireland Must Be Heaven, For My Mother Came from There" (Howard-Fisher), 397
"Irish": in eighteenth century America, 258, 261–262; equation with "Catholic," 283; Protestant imprint, 271; Ulster Presbyterians as, 261; "Wild Irish," 262–263
Irish 9th (Ninth Massachusetts Infantry), *579*
Irish Action Committee, 298
Irish Agricultural Organization Society, 111, 116
Irish America: double dislike of, 6; Ernie O'Malley lecture, 51; historiography, 8–11; identity of, xvi; as object of systematic scholarly inquiry, 47; perception of, 213; proletarian corollary to North American capitalism, 193
Irish America (magazine), 50
Irish-American Athletic Association, 455
Irish American Athletic Club (IAAC), 450, 451, 466–467, *468*
Irish American Business Coalition (IABC), 564
Irish American (Chicago newspaper), 426
Irish American Cultural Institute, 44
Irish-American festivals. *See* Festivals
Irish-American history, 6, 7, 11–13, 612
Irish American identity: agitation for Irish independence, 498; alcohol addiction, 500–503, 575; awareness of, 491; Brown (Thomas) and, 8; Catholic Church in America, 279–280; Catholicism, 35, 184, 195, 197, 221, 241–243, 247n41, 271; census returns on ancestry, 37–38, 175, 687, *690*; Civil War (United States), 25, 29, 214; communalism (*see* Communalism); conformity, 481, 489; decline of, 497–504, 556; defensiveness, 508; egalitarianism, 493, 610, 629; emergence of an Irish-American community, 177; eternal stranger, 682; factors forging, 556; Famine memories, 17–20; fantasy, 489; fecklessness, 489; figurative secretaries of state, 508; fondness for drink, 496; friendliness, 496; generosity, 496; group consciousness, 175, 178, 183, 214; imagination, 51; influences on, 25; insubordination, 674; interdenominational informality, 184; Irish-American nationalism, 198; Irish bishops, 195; Irish nationalism, 8; Irish traditions, 175–178, 183–184, 224, 241, 281, 346, 359–360, 371, 373, 479–480, 682; Irishness, 178; memories of the Great Famine, 21; middle-class reality, 496–497; narrow-mindedness, 680–681; O'Neill (Thomas P.) on, 632; people skills, 51; physical courage, 496; pluck, 467; the policeman, 495, 500; political skills, 16, 51, 218–219, 636; practicality, 496; professional Irishman, 494; querulousness, 674; the rebel, 495; respect for learning, 494; sarcasm, 671; security, 501; self-criticism, 281; self-expression, 281; silence as a hallmark, 281; "spiritual empire" thesis, 280; sports, 450–452, 455; suburbanization, 41, 548, 556, 598; suppressed sexuality, 501; temperament, 496–497; toughness, 493–494, 496, 530; turning lower-middle class, 503; urbanization, 493, 548, 556, 669, 671–673; whiteness, 374–376, 611–612, 633–635; winning late rounds, 528; wit, 496; wrongdoing, 493. *See also* Stereotypes
Irish American Labor Coalition (IALC), 543, 564
Irish-American nationalism, 168, 198, 295
Irish-American Nationalism 1870–1890 (Brown), 10
Irish American (New York newspaper), 235
Irish-American pluck, 467
Irish Americans: agriculture, 192, 193; American attitudes toward, 193, 203–204, 217–218, 233, 242, 261–262, 332, 375; American-born (1900 census), 41; Americans claiming Irish ancestry, 37–38, 39, 40, 426, 566, 568–569, 687, 691f; Anglo-Irish Treaty (1921), 297; assimilation, 175, 178, 179, 346, 528; in big business, 50; bishops/clergy, 181; as brokers, 636; Canadian Irish, 213–214; Catholic Church in America, 240–243, 278, 578–581, 602–603; Catholic Emancipation, 171; civic rights for foreign-born, 198; civil society, 195–197; Clan na Gael, 200; Davitt and, 177; de Valera and, 177; death rates, 231–232; dehumanization, *366*; Democratic Party, 174, 183, 215, 218–219, 557, 580, 631–632; dispersal of, 173, 176, 181–182, 192–193, 203, 213, 214, 228, 548, 562, *690*; dynamism, 232; education, 50–51;

electioneering, 198; emergence of an Irish-American community, 177; enfranchisement, 198; family formation, 237–238; Federalists, 182; Fenians, 22, 171, 200, 223; fertility patterns, 172–173; Gaelic League, 171; German immigrants, 214; grievances, 182; influence on Ireland, 176–177; intracounty marriage, 24; Irish-born (1890 census), 689t, *690*; Irish-born (1900 census), 41; Irish Civil War (1922–1923), 586; Irish language, 221–222, 224; Irish nationalism, 213, 215, 291, 490 (*see also* Irish-American nationalism); Irish Republican Army, 561; Irish Volunteers, 22, 171; Irish War of Independence (1919–1921), 586; Jackson (Andrew) and, 174; Jefferson and, 178, 182–183, 261; Land League, 22; left-wing politics, 298, 558; life expectancy, 232, 249n62; in management, 51; music as a bonding mechanism, 29; *New York Times* on, 241; obsession about, 219; O'Connell (Daniel) and, 177, 202; other immigrant groups, 9, 50, 174, 198, 482–483, 502–503, 504–512, 520, 548, 580, 630; poverty, 193–194, 219, 230, 231, 281; prejudice against (*see* Anti-Irish sentiment); reforms advocated by, 198; regions associated with, 180–181; religious practices, 33; remittances, 617; repeal of union movement, 200–203; Republican Party (United States), 557, 631–632; savings, 26; schools, 199–200; self-help/self-reliance/voluntary cooperation, 203, 238–240, 276, 280; Sinn Fein, 171; success debate, 39–43; survival, 224, 230, 240, 278; Union Army, 29; urban living, 23; urban population, 215; urban slang, 673; urbanization, 13–14, 23, 181, 185, 203, 215, 224–240; working-class, 581. *See also* Irish Catholics; Irish Protestants

Irish Americans (Greeley), 42
Irish Arts Center (New York), 415, 431
Irish Athletic clubs, 449
Irish Bishops' Episcopal Commission, 565
Irish Catholic Diaspora in America (McCaffrey), xv, 11, 12
Irish Catholics (in Ireland and/or America): Act of Union, 82, 88; American Revolution, 75, 490; American system (Henry Clay's), 191; anti-British sentiment, 179; in Canada, 215; Canadian Irish, 215; Catholic Relief Act (1778), 76; Catholic Relief Act

(1829), 272; communalism, 613; conservatism, 520; Cromwell (Oliver) and, 68–69; Democratic Party, 174, 198, 490; disenfranchisement in New York, 477; earnings, 39–40; educational level, 39–40; emigration, 74, 191; exclusion from landowning classes, 157; exclusion from politics, 71, 73, 76, 82–83; first Irish Catholic mayor of New York, 13, 23, 475; Gaelic groups, 66; G.I. Bill of Rights, 50; Great Famine as an affliction, 22–23; group consciousness, 184; historiography of, 4; indentured servitude, 179; Irish Protestants, break with, 5, 15, 17–18, 22–23, 69–71, 82, 88, 156–157, 225, 262–264, 272–275, 485–486; Irish Protestants, commonalities with, 32, 191, 490; Jackson (Andrew) and, 174; Kennedy (John F.) and, 9; knowledge of English, 27; number of, 38; Oath of Allegiance, 76; Old English (Anglo-Irish), 66, 67; parish life, 27, 242–243, 548, 556; Penal Laws, 71; politicization of, 84; Protestant evangelical attempts to convert, 274, 278–279; Protestant nation of Ireland, 73; repeal of union movement, 88; Republican Party (United States), 511; role of females, 32; Scotch-Irish, 4; social barriers, 174; social mobility, 28–29, 501; success, 39–40; Treaty of Limerick, 70; in Ulster, 4; World War I, 116. *See also* American Catholics; Ulster Catholics
Irish Citizen Army, 111, 116, 117–118
Irish Civil War (1922–1923), 128–132, 586
Irish Clergyman (McAvoy), 45
Irish Connections Festival (Canton, Mass.), 433–435
Irish Counties Athletic Union, 455, 468
Irish Cultural Festival (Cleveland), 439, 441n21
Irish Dance Commission (An Coimisiún le Rincí Gaelacha), 422
Irish Dancer (magazine), 423
Irish dances (occasions), 343
Irish Dancing Teachers Association of North America (IDTANA), 421–422
Irish Dancing Teachers Commission of America (IDTCA), 421
Irish Department of Agriculture and Technical Instruction, 111
Irish diaspora: epicenter, 616, 618; Irish Spiritual Empire, 604; national biographical dictionaries, 305; St. Patrick's Day parade (New York City), 428; scope, 47; Scotch-Irish, 153; Ulster Presbyterians, 153
Irish Dragoons, 452
Irish Echo (New York newspaper), 426, *436, 538, 541, 543*

Irish Emigrant (Boston newspaper), 426
Irish Emigrant Society: Carrigan and, 313, 316; Commissioners of Emigration, 307–308, 315, 316; Dillon (Gregory) and, *307*, 307–308, 309, 316; Emigrant Savings Bank, 306–309; founding, 306–308; Friendly Sons of St. Patrick (New York), 308, 320; Hughes (Archbishop John) and, 196, 204, 207, 500; MacNeven and, 307; president, *307*, 316
Irish Export Board, 401
Irish Fair (various locations), 439
Irish Fest Foundation, 439
Irish Fest (Milwaukee), 432, 434, 437–440
Irish Festival (Chicago), *431*
Irish Festivals Incorporated, 438
Irish fight songs, 385–386
Irish film, 566–567
Irish Free State (Saorstát Éireann, 1922–1937), 126–137, 586; boundary with Northern Ireland, 127, 130–131; British national debt, 131; conservatism, 133; constitutional reforms, 136–137; Cumann na nGaedheal, 133–135; dismantling Anglo-Irish Treaty, 135–137; Executive Council, 128, 135, 136; farmers, 135; Imperial Conference (1926), 134; Irish Civil War (1922–1923), 128–129, 586; Irish language, 133; Irish Protestants, 133; League of Nations, 134; Lloyd George and, 126–127; neutrality, 135; Statute of Westminster (1930), 134; Taoiseach (chief), 136, 137. *See also* Ireland
Irish Herald (California newspaper), 426
Irish historiography, Two Traditions of, 255–256, 267–268
Irish Hurling and Football Club (New York), 453
Irish identity in Ireland, 556. *See also* Irish American identity
Irish Immigrants in the Land of Canaan (Miller et al.), 39, 47
Irish Immigration Reform Movement (IIRM), 564, 568
Irish Immigration Working Committee, 564
Irish in America (Maguire), 2–3
Irish in America (Wittke), 2
Irish in Chicago (McCaffrey), 10
Irish in San Francisco (Burchell), 12–13
Irish Independent (newspaper), 110
"Irish Ireland," 553–554
Irish Jasper Greens, 452
Irish language: Gaelic League, 133; Great Famine, 95; Irish Americans, 221–222, 224; Irish Free State, 133; Irish song

Irish language *(continued)*
  (sean-nós songs), 412–413; urban
  slang, 673
Irish Layman (Brown), 45
Irish Loyal and Patriotic Union, 104
"Irish Memories" (radio program), 545
Irish Memories troupe, 419
Irish Music Festival (Irish Arts Center),
  415
Irish Music Festival (Philadelphia), 415
Irish Music Ltd., 438
Irish Musicians' Association (Comhal-
  tas Ceoltóirí Éireann), 414, 428
Irish National Land League (the Land
  League), 22, 100–103, 104, 292
Irish National Volunteers, 115
Irish nationalism (in Ireland and/or
  America): Act of Union, 289–290;
  anti-Irish sentiment, 370; approaches,
  289, 292; Brown (Thomas) and, 10,
  371, 490; Casement and, 117; Catholi-
  cism, 578–579; Clan na Gael, *366;*
  constitutional nationalism *(see*
  Constitutional nationalism); county
  loyalty, 24; Davitt and, 291; discrimination against nationalists, 131–132;
  feelings of alienation in America, 8;
  Fenians, *366;* Gaelic Revival, 106;
  Home Rule, 115, 492; Irish American
  identity, 8; Irish Americans, 213, 215,
  291, 490; Irish Volunteers, 121; land
  reform, 492; Moynihan on, 490; New
  Departure, 292; New Irish, 563; New
  York Irish, 490–493; objectives, 492;
  O'Connell (Daniel) and, 223, 264,
  289–290, 578; origins, 289; Parnell
  and, 290–291; physical force nationalism *(see* Physical force nationalism);
  radicalism and, 109–111; revisionist
  historians, 256; Scotch-Irish, 153;
  Social Democratic Labour Party, 147;
  social reform nationalism, 292, 294;
  sovereignty of the United Kingdom,
  370; support for Boers, 109; threat to
  American social order, 370; Ulster
  Catholics, 223; Ulster Presbyterians,
  266; Wilson (Woodrow) and, 490;
  Wolfe Tone and, 289; women, 292;
  Young Ireland, 89
Irish Northern Aid. *See* NORAID
Irish parliament: Act of Union, 289;
  American Revolution, 75; English
  parliament, 72; evolution of, 71–72;
  Gaelic Irish, 72; Grattan's parliament,
  74–76; independence from British
  parliament, 86–89; Irish Protestants,
  70, 72; O'Connell (Daniel) and,
  86–89; patronage, 75; Protestant Volunteer movement, 77; undertaker system, 75; United Irishmen, 77. *See also*
  Dáil Éireann

Irish Parliamentary Party (IPP): anti-
  conscription campaign, 122; balance
  of power, 104, 113; Clan na Gael, 294;
  constitutional nationalism, 108, 121;
  eclipse of, 105–106; elections (1918),
  122; Home Rule, 114, 115, 119; Irish
  National Volunteers, 115; leaders, 111;
  Parnell and, 100, 105; Redmond
  (John) and, 111, 293–294; Sinn Fein,
  119
Irish Party (Cumann na nGaedheal),
  132–135, 136
Irish People (tabloid), 544
Irish Presbyterians, 152, 288. *See also*
  Ulster Presbyterians
Irish Press (newspaper), 30
Irish Protestant Association (Boston),
  188
Irish Protestants (in Ireland and/or
  America): Act of Union, 81–82, 88;
  American Revolution, 5, 74–75, 490;
  American system (Henry Clay's), 191;
  British parliament, 72; in Canada, 215;
  Canadian Irish, 215, 221; communal-
  ism, 613; conversions in Ireland, 260;
  Cromwell (Oliver) and, 68–69; earn-
  ings, 39–40; education, 39–40, 203;
  emigration, 221; evangelicalism,
  271–275; Gladstone and, 99; Great
  Britain, 72; Great Famine, 217, 266;
  historiography of, 4; hyphenated
  Protestants, 283; immigration, 151; as
  "Irish," 5; Irish Catholics, break with,
  5, 15, 17–18, 22–23, 69–71, 82, 88,
  156–157, 225, 262–264, 272–275,
  485–486; Irish Catholics, commonalities with, 32, 191, 490; Irish Free State,
  133; Irish parliament, 70, 72; knowledge of English, 27; nation, 73, 130;
  "New" or "Second" Reformation, 272;
  Norman ancestry, 72; number of, 38;
  Old English (Anglo-Irish), 72; Patriotism, 72–73, 74–75, 100, 108; Penal
  Laws, 70–71, 72; political evolution in
  U.S., 174; political independence for
  Ireland, 72; post-1800, 282; repeal of
  union movement, 88; repudiation of
  Irishness, 38, 152, 213, 262, 283,
  489–490; role of females, 32; secular-
  ism, 488; social barriers, 174; southern
  unionism, 104; success, 39–40; termi-
  nology, 4; "Ulstermen" and, 4; Volun-
  teer movement, 77; World War I, 116.
  See also Church of Ireland; Ulster
  Presbyterians; Ulster Protestants
Irish Race Convention (1916), 295
Irish Race Convention (1919), 295
Irish Race in America (Condon), 3
Irish racism: ante-bellum influx of
  black labor, 356; busing, 638–639;
  communalism, 633–635; Coughlin

and, 627–628; Draft Riots (1863), 35,
  372–373, 485, 633; gravediggers of scientific racism, 64; minstrelsy, 383; as a
  stereotype, 683; trade unionism, 360;
  whiteness, 611–612, 670
Irish Republican Army (IRA): American support, 558; assassinations by,
  134; banning of, 136; Boer tactics, 125;
  ceasefire (1994), 560; Clann na
  Poblachta, 138; Collins (Michael) and,
  127, 128; Cumann na nGaedheal, 135;
  Dáil Éireann, 125; de Valera and, 136,
  297; escalation of violence, 145; Four
  Horsemen of Irish-American politics,
  299; growth, 145; guerrilla warfare,
  125, 129–130; internment without trial,
  145; Irish Americans, 22, 561; Irish
  Civil War (1922–1923), 128–129; martial law, 125; McGarrity and, 297;
  membership, 136; Northern Ireland,
  129–130, 142–143, 145–146, 298–300;
  Provisional Irish Republican Army
  ("Provos"), 145, 298, 299, 561; Quill
  and, 362; ratification of the republic,
  124; split into official and provisional
  wings, 145, 298; struggles to reorganize, 142; *Supply of Heroes,* 659; suppression of, 130, 134; the Troubles,
  298–300; Vatican disapproval, 586;
  War of Independence (1919–1921),
  124–125, 129
Irish Republican Brotherhood (IRB):
  aim, 290; Biggar and, 100; Clan na
  Gael, 294; Collins (Michael) and, 121;
  Easter Rising, 117–118, 492; establishment, 96; Fenian Brotherhood, 290;
  founding, 290; Gaelic Athletic Association (GAA), 106, 110; Gaelic League,
  110; Home Rule, 115; Irish National
  Volunteers, 115; Irish Volunteers, 121;
  leadership of other organizations, 110,
  121; Pearse and, 121; president of the
  supreme council, 121; revival of, 109;
  Sinn Fein, 110, 121; Stephens and, 290;
  World War I, 116
Irish Republican Clubs (IRC), 298
Irish Rifles, 452
Irish Socialist Federation, 110
Irish Socialist Republican Party, 110
Irish Society, 67
Irish Society of Boston, 25
Irish song *(sean-nós* songs), 412–413
Irish Spiritual Empire, 604
Irish Sports and Cultural Heritage
  Institute, 432
Irish Studies, 6, 43–44, 48
Irish Temperance Society, 195
Irish tenors, 396–397
Irish Times (newspaper), 30
Irish Transport and General Worker's
  Union (ITGWU), 110–111

Irish unionism, 104, 111–113. *See also* Ulster unionism

Irish Unionist Alliance, 114

Irish Unionists, 103

Irish University Act (1908), 113

Irish Victory Fund, 125

Irish Voice (New York newspaper), 426, 433, 561

Irish Volunteers: anti-conscription campaign, 122; British Army recruitment, 117; Childers and, 129; Collins (Michael) and, 121; de Valera and, 120, 121; Easter Rising, 22, 117; guerrilla warfare, 124; gun smuggling, 129; Irish Americans, 22, 171; Irish nationalism, 121; Irish Republican Brotherhood, 121; Irish War of Independence, 124; president, 121; Sinn Fein, 117, 120–121. *See also* Irish Republican Army

Irish War of Independence (1919–1921), 124–126, 129, 586

Irish Weekend (So. Fallsburg, New York), *436*

"Irish Whales," 449, 465

Irish World (newspaper): Astley Belt Championship, 446; editor, 591; Irish-American militias, 453; Irish prizefighters, 450; national games, 452; United Irish League of America, 294; World War I and, 492

Irishman's Home or the Dark Days of the Green Isle (Clarke), 387

"Irishman's sidewalk," 671

Ironweed (Kennedy), 660

Ironworkers, photograph of, *662, 663, 665, 673, 674, 679*

Irwin, Jack, 543, 545, 546

"It Takes the Irish to Beat the Dutch" (Morse), 395

Italian immigrants, 501, 503, 669

ITGWU (Irish Transport and General Worker's Union), 110–111

"It's a Long Way to Tipperary" (song), 433

It's All Relative (TV show), 632

"It's the Irish in Your Eye, It's the Irish in Your Smile" (Von Tilzer), 395

IWW (Industrial Workers of the World), 110, 362

Jackie Gleason Show (TV show), 552

Jackson, Andrew: among Irish-American presidents, 557; Carey (Mathew) and, 183; election (1844), 201; Irish America after, 214; Irish Americans, 174, 183, 198, 478; Irish Catholics, 174; MacNeven and, 183; O'Connell (Daniel), 198; parents, 177; presidential accession (1829), 184; repeal of union movement, 202–203; Scotch-

Irish, 168; Suffern and, 183; Taney and, 197; Ulster Irish, 288

Jackson, Stonewall, 288

Jacobsen, Matthew Frye, 48

James, Bill, 460

James, Henry, 497

James A. Kelly Institute for Historical Studies, *394*

James Connolly Clubs, 298

James I (King of England; also James IV of Scotland), 67, 154

James II (King of England, Scotland, and Ireland), 69–70, 78, 156

James IV (King of Scotland; also James I of England), 67, 154

James Morrison and His Orchestra, 398

James R. Keane Cup, 453

Jameson, J. Franklin, 304

Javits, Jacob K., 504

Jay, John, 182, 477, 478

Jefferson, Thomas: Democratic Republicans, 478; Irish Americans, 178, 182–183, 261; as a model for emulation, 283; Protestant supporters, 184; Scotch-Irish, 168; separation of church and state, 282; United Irishmen (American Society of), 289; U.S. Constitution, 182

Jensen, Richard, 371–372

Jerome and Schwartz (song writing team), 393, 396

Jewish immigrants: alcoholism rate, 501; American Jewish history, 44; Catskill mountains, 497; communism, 508; organized crime, 501; relations with Irish, 669; social mobility, 503; success, 550; Tammany Hall, 669; urban slang, 673

Jigs, 418

Jimmy stereotype, 671–673, 675–679

Jobs. *See* Work

Joe (film), 632

John Birch Society, 517

John Boyle O'Reilly Hurling Cup, 453

John Mitchel Guards, 452

John XXIII (Pope), 519, 600

Johnson, Allen, 304

Johnson, Andrew, 288

Johnson, R. M., 201

Johnson-Reed Immigration Act (1927), 304

Jones, Ada, 397, 398

Jones, Bobby, 457

Jones, Jerry, 464

Jones, Maldwyn, 15, 41, 48, 179

Jones, Mary Harris ("Mother Jones"), 362, 581

Jordan, Neil, 566

Josephite Fathers, 583

Journal (American Irish Historical Society), 43, 498

Joy in the Morning (Smith), 655

Joyce, James, 498, 654, 658, 671

Joyce, John, 261

Judgement Day (Farrell), 550, 652

"Just Sing a Song for Ireland" (Von Tilzer, Sterling), 395

Kahn, Edward, 389

Kane, John J., 501–502

Kate (sobriquet), 333

Katy (sobriquet), 333

Kavanaugh, Paddy, 685

Keane, John, 583, 603

Keane Gaelic Hurling Trophy, 453

Kearney, Denis, 359, 360

Kearney, Hugh, 47

Kearns, Jack ("Doc"), 458

Keefe, Michael, *361*

Keefe, Tim, 447, 460–461

Keegan, Robert F., 587

Keeler, William Henry ("Wee Willie"), 447

Keith, B. F. (Ben), 386, 408

Kelleher, John, 6, 49, 661

Kelleher, Patricia, 30

Kelley, Francis Clement, 596–597

Kelley, Joe, 447

Kelly, Colin, 508

Kelly, Dennis, 191

Kelly, Edward, 627

Kelly, Eugene, 319–320

Kelly, Gene, 551

Kelly, George, 447

Kelly, Hugh, 308, 326n39

Kelly, James, 326n39

Kelly, James A., *394*

Kelly, Jim, 462

Kelly, John (character), 659

Kelly, John ("Honest John"): Emigrant Savings Bank, 318; marriage, 626; McCloskey and, 626; native-born, 477; Tammany Hall, 318, 475, 481; Tweed and, 318, 475

Kelly, John Walter, 391–392

Kelly, Mary Catherine Theresa Boyle, 339, 340

Kelly, Mike ("King"), 447–448, 460

"Kelly the Boy from Killane" (song), 400

Kennedy, Bridget, 340

Kennedy, Caroline, 528

Kennedy, Edward (Ted): busing in Boston, 638–639; Chappaquiddick, 530; Four Horsemen of Irish-American politics, 49, 299; movement away from physical force nationalism, 561

Kennedy, Harry, 392

Kennedy, Jacqueline, 528, 529

Kennedy, John F., 526–534; aid to parochial schools, 516; American Catholics, 600, 604; anti-Catholic

Kennedy, John F. *(continued)*
sentiment, 282, 548; appeal, 533; the
arts, 533; assassination, 49, 526–528;
Bay of Pigs, 531; Camelot metaphor,
529, 531; charisma, 530; Cuba obsession, 531; de Valera and, 528; domestic
policies, 530; foreign policy, 530–531;
health, 533; image of Catholic Irish, 9,
38; legacy, 520; Mexico, 532, 534; missile crisis, 531; Moynihan on, 9–10, 49,
520; New Deal coalition, 530; New
York Irish, 511; Northern Ireland, 531;
pain, 533; personality, 532–533; philan-
dering, 529–530; photo of, *505, 527*;
presidency of, 530–531; presidential
election (1960), 2, 10, 16–17, 516, 528,
556, 557, 682, 684; press conferences,
533; privatizing religion, 590; *Profiles
in Courage,* 557; PT-109, 533; reading
habits, 533; reputation, 529; toughness, 530; Vietnam War, 530–531; visit
to Ireland, 2, 10, *527,* 528
Kennedy, Joseph P.: on being called an
Irishman, 597; Fitzgerald (John F.)
and, *668*; a "Mick on the make," 678;
photo of, *505*; Radio-Keith Orpheum
(RKO), 409
Kennedy, Kate, 359, 581
Kennedy, Michael, 233
Kennedy, Patrick, 632
Kennedy, Robert F., 530, 531, 600
Kennedy, William: assimilated Irish
Americans, 661; *Billy Phelan's Greatest
Game,* 660; *Flaming Corsage,* 660;
Irish assimilation, 684; *Ironweed*
(Kennedy), 660; *Legs,* 660, 676;
Quinn's Book, 660; as a source of
inspiration, 40; *Very Old Bones,* 660
Kennedy, X. J., 660
Kenny, Kevin: *American Irish,* xv; on
Irish in professions, 550; Irish Studies,
36–37, 47; on relevance of the Irish
Diaspora, 47; on typical Irish Ameri-
can (1960), 555
Kenny, Theresa, *555*
Kenrick, Francis, 192, 195, 197, 199
Keough, Donald R., 48, 50
Kerby, William, 587
Kerns, Frank, 387
Kerrigan, James, 326n39
Kerrigan, John, 638
Keystone View Company, 19
Khruschev, Nikita, 510
Kildare Place Society, 283n4
Kilgallen, Jimmy, 628
Killoran, Paddy, 411
Kilrain, Jake, 444
Kiltegan Fathers, *600*
Kilwarden, Lord (Arthur Wolfe), 85
Kimmel, John, 411
King, Eddie, 632

King, Martin Luther, Jr.., 297, 533, 558,
600
King, Peter, 542
King, Rufus, 182
Kinnell, Galway, 660
Kinney, Troy and Margaret, 418
Kinsale, Battle of (1603), 66
Kirk, Captain (character), 684
Kirkham, G., 161
Kirwan, Larry, 403
Kirwin, Dominic, 437
"Kitty O'Brien, My Irish Molly O"
(Jerome-Schwartz), 393
Knights of Columbus, 582, *614*
Knights of Labor: Catholic Church in
America, 581; Gibbons (James) and,
581, 604; Irish traditions, 359–360; ori-
gins, 358; republicanism, 627
Knights of St. Crispin, 358
Knobel, Dale T., 384
Know-Nothing movement, 25, 306, 490
Knox, Samuel, 203
Koch, Ed, *537,* 559
Kolchin, Peter, 376
Kossuth, Lajos, 485, 489
Kristol, Irving, 509
Ku Klux Klan, 25, 588–589, 669

L.A. Confidential (film), 633
La Bouttine Souriante, 437
La Guardia, Fiorello H., 475, 511
Labor Day, 362
Labor history, 30, 611
Labor movement: ante-bellum influx of
black labor, 356; anti-hiring discrimi-
nation, 372; Catholic Church in
America, 581, 592; city-wide unions,
194; faction fighting, 355, 373; Famine
generation, 356–358; heydey, 363; in
Ireland, 110; Irish American influence,
50, 363; occupational structure, 360;
pre-Famine, 354–356; secret society
violence, 355, 373; strikebreakers, 356,
372; women, 362. *See also* Trade
unionism; Work
Labour in Irish History (Connolly), 110
Labour Party (Great Britain), 113, 132,
138, 140
Labourer's Act (1906), 113
Lace Curtain (Berlin), 655
Lacy, Hugh de, 63
Ladies Land League, 292, 624
Lady Who Liked Clean Restrooms (Don-
leavy), 659
Lafontaine, Louis, 190
Laissez-faire economics: Catholic
Church in America, 519; Great
Famine, 90–91, 92–93, 94, 216; O'Con-
nell (Daniel) and, 88; Protestant
evangelicalism, 273
Lalor, James Fintan, 89, 96, 100, 103

Lamy, Jean Baptiste, 242
Land League (Irish National Land
League), 22, 100–103, 104, 292
Land reform in Ireland, 100–105; Con-
gested Districts Board, 105; Devoy
and, 292; farmers, 133; Irish national-
ism, 492; Lalor and, 100, 103; Land Act
(1870), 99; Land Act (1881), 101; Land
Act (1887), 104, 111; Land Act (1891),
103, 111; Land Act (1903), 103, 113; Land
Act (1909), 113; Land Act (1923), 133;
middle-class Irish, 291; Parnell and,
100, 103
Land War (1879–1882), 292
Landlords in Ireland: boycotting of, 101;
Great Famine, 22, 90–91, 93–94; Land
League targets, 101; O'Connell
(Daniel) and, 88; in Ulster, 159–160
Landon, Alfred M., 590
Lange, Dorothea, 663
Langhorne, Bruce, 401
Langrishe, Hercules, 76
Language and social mobility, 27–29.
See also Irish language
Lanigan, James S., 512
Larkin, Emmet, 33, 284n18
Larkin, James, 110–111, 132, 177, 361
Last Hurrah (film), 632
Last Hurrah (O'Connor novel), 551, 556,
655–656
Last Picture Show (McMurtry), 661
"Last Rose of Summer" (Moore), 382
Last Supper (painting), 663
Last Tycoon (Fitzgerald), 654
Lawe, John, 543
Lawrence, David, 627
Leader, The (Moran), 107
League of Nations, 125, 134, 137, 587–588
League of St. Patrick, 452
Lease, Mary Elizabeth, 359
"Leaving Tipperary" (song), 399
Left-wing politics, 298, 558, 582, 611
Legion of Decency, 595, 680
Legitimate theater, 387
Legs (Kennedy), 660, 676
Lemass, Sean, 139, 140, 142, 143
Lenski, Gerhard, 503
Leo XIII (Pope), 583
Lever, Charles, 385
Levine, Edward, 10
Leyburn, James, 15, 257, 258
Liberal Party (Great Britain): Disestab-
lishment Act (1869), 99; elections
(1909), 113; Great Famine, 91, 94;
Home Rule, 103, 105; Parnell and, 104
Liberal Unionist Party, 103, 104, 111
Liberalism, 485, 627–628
Life expectancy, 232, 249n62
Life (magazine), 500
"Limerick is Beautiful" (Boucicault),
386

Lincoln, Abraham, 2, 493
Lindbergh, Charles, 676
Lindsay, John, 559
"Line of Ireland," 167
Lions, Harts, Leaping Does (Power), 657
Lippmann, Walter, 517
Literacy: emigrants', 180, 188, 223, 224;
   women's English language literacy,
   334
"Little Annie Rooney" (Nolan), 393
"Little Bit of Heaven" (Olcott), 395
"Little Bunch of Shamrocks" (Von
   Tilzer), 396
Little Gaelic Singers of Ireland, 551
Livingston, Arthur, *375*
Lloyd George, David: Anglo-Irish
   Treaty, 126, 129; Dáil Éireann, 122; de
   Valera and, 121, 126; Home Rule, 119;
   House of Commons veto power, 113;
   Irish Free State, 126–127; Northern
   Ireland's constitutional status, 126;
   Sinn Fein, 125–126
Local Government Act (1898), 112
Lodge, Henry Cabot, 304
Logan, James, 164
Logan, John, 660
Logan, Michael, 224
Lomasney, Martin: among ward bosses,
   626; communalism, 629–630; Irish
   politicians, 632; in Massachusetts
   House, 627; politics of, 637
London Athletic Club, 449
London Hibernian Society, 283n4
Lonesome Dove (McMurtry), 661
Long, Walter, 122
Long Day's Journey into Night (O'Neill),
   495, 551, 652
Long Voyage Home (O'Neill), 652
Longshoremen's and Laborers United
   Benevolent Society, 358
Lonigan, Studs (character), 40
Look How the Fish Live (Power), 657
Lord, Daniel A., 595
Lord of the Dance (show), 417, 420, 423,
   567
Loren, Sophia, 539
Lott, Eric, 383
Loughlin, John, 315
Loughlin, Rose Kelly, 345
Louis XIV (King of France), 70
Louisiana Irish, 225–226. *See also* New
   Orleans Irish
Lover, Samuel, 382, 385, 392
Lover's Almanac (Howard), 656
Loving Women (Hamill), 657
"Low Back'd Car" (Lover), 382
Lowell Folk Festival, 430
Loyalty oaths, 517
Lucas, Charles, 73
Lucey, Robert E., 592
Lughnasa (season), 427

Lukas, J. Anthony, 619
"Lunchtime atop a Skyscraper"
   (Ebbets), *662*
Lynch, Billy (character), 649–650
Lynch, James, 362, 452
Lynch, Sandra, 639
Lyon, Matthew, 179, 182
Lyons, Ted, 460–461

MacArthur, Robert, 261
Macauley, Thomas Babington, 489, 493
MacBride, John, 138
MacBride, Sean, 138, 139, 545
MacCool, Finn, 477
MacCracken, Henry Noble, 5
MacCurtain, Margaret, 33
MacDiarmada, Seán, 109–110, 116, 119
MacDonagh, Oliver, 219, 244n13, 245n17
MacDonagh, Thomas, 116, 119
MacDonald, John, 190
MacDonald, Michael Patrick, 11, 569
MacDonnell, Randall, 155
MacHale, John, 283n4
Machine politics: Boston, 580; changing
   circumstances, 512; Chicago, 580;
   communalism, 626–627, 629–630,
   637–638; merger of Irish traditions
   and American politics, 479; New
   Orleans, 580; New York, 479, 512, 580;
   San Francisco, 580
Machusla (play), 395
Mack, Andrew, *79*
Mack, Connie (Cornelius
   McGillicuddy), 447, 460, 460–462
Mackenzie, William Lyon, 190
MacLaine, Shirley, 622
MacNeill, Eoin: Boundary Commis-
   sion, 130, 131; Easter Rising, 117; Gaelic
   League, 106; Irish National Volun-
   teers, 115; Irish Volunteers, 117; minis-
   ter of industry, 122
MacNeven, William James: in America,
   178; Irish Emigrant Society, 307; Jack-
   son (Andrew) and, 183; leadership of
   Irish in New York, 309; in New York
   City, 477; nonsectarianism, 17;
   O'Connell (Daniel) and, 183; refugee
   status, 17, 177, 289
MacSparran, James, 258
MacStiofáin, Seán, 145
MacSwiney, Terence, 586, 624
Madame Rentz's Female Minstrels, 388
Madison, James, 182
Magee, Robert, *361*
Mageean, Deirdre, 33
Magennis, Peter E., 586
Maggie (sobriquet), 333
Maggie and Jiggs (comic strip charac-
   ters), 494, 622, 623
Maggie-Now (Smith), 655
Maguire, John, 592

Maguire, John Francis, 2–3, 173, 220
Maguire, Joseph, 447
Maid of Erin (club), 446, 451
Maids-of-all-work, 337–338
Major, John, 146
Major (Harrigan and Hart), 389
Makem, Sarah, 400
Makem, Tommy, 399–403, 412–413, 414,
   437
Makemie, Francis, 160, 283n1
Malcolm X, 533
Mallon, Seamus, 147
Malloy, James T., 593
Malloy, Jimmy (character), 633–634
Malone, Kate, 338
Malone, Mary, 338–339
Maloney, Kevin, 639
Maloney, Martin, 592
"Maloney the Rolling Mill Man"
   (Kelly), 392
Malthus, Thomas, 185
Man Must Fight (Tunney), *675*
Management, Irish Americans in, 51
Managhan, Salvatore, 669
Manahan, Anna, 566
Mangan, James Clarence, 89
Manhattan Institute, 322
Mann, Horace, 199
Manning, John, 308, 326n39
Mansfield, Mike, 557
Mara, Jack, 463–464
Mara, Tim, 463
Mara, Wellington, 463–464
Mariposa Folk Festival, 430
Markievicz, Constance, 109, 119, 120
Marks, Edward B., 393
Marriage: adult status for women, 334;
   domestic service, 343, 345; Dunne's
   (Finley Peter) depiction of, 31; inter-
   marriage, 38, 152, 191; intracounty
   marriage, 24; Irish American women,
   24, 33; marriage outside the Catholic
   faith, 594–595; rate in Ireland, 554;
   remittances, 343; strategic marriages,
   95, 333; Ulster, 152
Married Women's Status Act (1957), 140
Marshall, Charles C., 589–590, 630
Marshall, George Catlett, 509
Martin Mulvihill School of Irish Music,
   429
Martyn, Edward, 107
Mary I (Queen of England), 65, 69, 70
Mason, Stephen C., 586
Masterson, Thomas, 358
Mater et Magistra (encyclical), 519
Matthews, James, 326n39
Mauriac, Francois, 657
Maurin, Peter, 591
Mauve Decade (Beer), 625
Maxwell, Sir John, 118–119
McAteer, Eddie, 143

McAuley, Catherine, 276–277, 278
McAuliffe, Jack, 457
McAulliffe, Terry, 631
McAvoy, John, 610
McAvoy, Thomas, 45
McCaffrey, Lawrence J.: contributions to Irish-American history, 44; G.I. Bill of Rights, 598; Irish as a percentage of American Catholics, 602; on Irish baseball players, 459–460; *Irish Catholic Diaspora in America*, xv, 11, 12; *Irish in Chicago*, 10; Irish use of political power, 9; leadership of the American Catholic Church, 578, 599; obstacles faced by immigrants, 13; social mobility of the Irish, 616; success debate, 41
McCaine, Alexander, 203
McCarran-Walter Act (1952, Immigration and Nationality Act), 413
McCartan, Bernie, 437–440
McCarthy, Cormac, 661
McCarthy, Eugene, 599
McCarthy, Joe, 460–462
McCarthy, Joseph R., 509–510, 599, 631
McCarthy, Mary, 498–499, 649, 652–653
McCarthy, Nora: correspondence with Hannah Collins, 338, 340, 341, 342, 343; home for, 343; photo of, *342*; sister's death, 337; year came to United States, 346
McClellan, George B., *26*
McClenahan, John, 223
McCloskey, John, 320, 626
McClure, John, *293*
McCombs, Phil, 663
McCooey, John H., 481, 511
McCormack, John (Massachusetts Democrat), 557
McCormack, John (singer), 346, 397, 398, 399
McCormack, Mike, 462
McCourt, Frank: *Angela's Ashes, 108*, 549, 567, 650; clerical hypocrisy, 281; depiction of poverty, 281
McCracken, Henry Joy, 80
McCready, Bernard, 191
McCullough, Denis, 109
McDannell, Colleen, 345
McDermott, Alice: Irish-American generational relations, 40; novels by, 567, 649; prize-winning fiction, 655; world captured by, 684
McDonagh, Martin, 566
McDonald, Pat, 449, 465
McDonald, Tommy, 462
McElhenny, Hugh, 462
McFarland, Catherine Ann, 338
McGarrity, Joseph, 125, 177, 294, 297
McGee, Thomas D'Arcy: Catholic organizations, 196; flight from New York,

215; *History of the Irish Settlers in North America*, 2, 650; injustices in America, 219; relocation to Canada, 190; repeal of union movement, 201–202
McGeoghegan, Bridget, 333
McGillicuddy, Cornelius (Connie Mack), 447, *460*, 460–462
McGinley, Phyllis, 660
McGinnity, "Iron Man" Joe, 447, 460–461
McGloin, John, 192
McGlynn, Edward, 486, 581
McGovern, James (Jim), 632
McGovern, William, 610
McGowan, Raymond A., 592
McGrady, Thomas, 581
McGrath, J. Howard, 628
McGrath, Matt, 449, 465
McGraw, John ("Little Napoleon"), *460*, 460–462
McGready, James, 168
McGreevy, John, 613, 629, 640
McGregor, Rev. James, 258, 263
McGroarty, Julia, 580
McGuffey, William, 203, 287
McGuinness, Frank, 116
McGuire, Peter J., 359, 362, 476, 503
McGwire, Mark, 528
McHale, John, 272, 283n4
McHale, Tom, 658
McHenry, James, 167, 183
McHugh, Rose, 587
McIntyre, James Francis, 594, 597, 601
McKay, John, 618
McKean, Thomas, 166–167, 178, 182
McKeehan, David, 184
McKenna, James, 418, 419, 420, *421*
McKenna, John, 411
McKenna, John T., 396
McKenny, Ruth, 655
McKeon, Elizabeth, 587
McKiernan, Ethna, 661
McKinley, Blaine, 333, 337–338
McKinly, John, 167
McLaughlin, Hugh, 481
McLeod, Zan, 422
McLuhan, Marshall, 530
McMahon, James, 312, 321
McMahon Guards (militia), 452
McMenomy, John, 308, 326n39
McMullen, James, 192
McMurtry, Larry, 661
McNally, John ("Blood"), 462
"McNally's Rows of Flats" (Harrigan and Hart), 389
McNamara, Andrew, 617
McNamara, Bridget, 617
McNamara, John, 418, 419
McNamara, Robert, 540
"McNamara from Mayo" (song), *400*

McNamee, Graham, 459
McNaspy, C. J., 485
McNicholas, John T., 592, 597
McNiff, Cyril, 419–420
McNiff, Peter, 419–420
McNiff Dancers, 551
McNulty, Ann, *400*
McNulty, Eileen, 399, *400*
McNulty, Pete, 399, *400*
McNulty Family, 399, *400*
McQuaid, Bernard, 583, 603
McSorley's Inflation (Harrigan and Hart), 389
Mead, James M., 504
Meagher, Peter P., 512
Meagher, Thomas Francis, 290, 491
Meagher, Timothy J., 13
Meagher militia, 452
Meagher's Brigade, 29
Meany, George, 363, 503, 510, 604
Mechanics, 235–236
Meenan, James, 30
Meet My Maker, the Mad Molecule (Donleavy), 659
Mellows, Liam, 129
Melody, Cornelius (character), 496, 625, 652
Memories of a Catholic Girlhood (McCarthy), 653, 654
Memory politics, 318–322
Men: archetype of the "regular guy," 625; attitude towards social mobility, 623–624; career options in Ireland, 94; celibacy, 238, 481–482; death rates, 231; "followers," 341; laborers, 234, 354–355; relations with different ethnicities, 36; rough culture of, 371; stereotypes of, 345; on television, 632–633; work in postwar America, 552–553. *See also* Marriage
Menace, The (magazine), 582
Merchants, 322
Merton, Thomas, 626
Metress, Seamus, 46
Mexican Irish, 191–192
Meyer, A., 501
Michigan Catholic (Detroit newspaper), 224
Mick stereotype, 364, 676–678
Middle-class culture, 334
Midwestern Irish, 228, 230
Migration. *See* Emigration; Immigration
Milhau, John, 326n39
Militia groups, 452–453
Militia of Christ for Social Service, 362
Mill work, 240
Miller, Kerby: on Brick, 18–19; Catholicism in Irish life, 579; *Emigrants and Exiles*, xv, 39, 46, 613; gender ratio in migration, 30; industrialism, 219; *Irish*

Immigrants in the Land of Canaan (with others), 39, 47; Protestant view of Catholic emigrants, 314; studies of mid-century Irish in North America, 233–234; success debate, 40–41

Miller, Randall, 45

Milwaukee Hurling Club, 469–470

Ministers' sons, 483

"Minstrel Boy" (Moore), 382

Minstrel of Clare (play), 395

Minstrelsy, 382–384, 395

Minturn, Robert, 308, 317, 326n39

Miracle Worker (Gibson), 660

Mr. Dooley. *See* Dooley, Mr.

Mitchel, John: assessment of the Famine, 96; on Famine's cause, 20; nationalism, 214, 223; refugee status, 290; Young Ireland, 89, 290

Mitchel, John Purroy, 476

Mitchell, Ann, 339

Mitchell, Art, 2

Mitchell, George, 49, 146, 300, 560

Mitchell, Jim, 449

Mitchell, John, 362

Mitchell scholarships, 49

Moakley, Joe, 632

Modernism, 583, 661

Molloy, Jimmy (character), 625, 653

Molly Maguires, 360, 373–374, 666, 667

Moloney, Mick, 420, *422*

Molyneaux, Jerry, 420

Molyneaux, William, 72

Monaghan, John T., 592

Monahan, Martin F., 447

Monk, Maria, 197, 275

Monohan, Kate, 340

Monroe, James, 183

Monroe, Marilyn, 529

Monroe Doctrine, 203

Montana Irish, 46

Montgomery, David, 35, 42

Montgomery Guards (militia), 195, 452

Monument Avenue (film), 11

Moon of the Caribbees (O'Neill), 652

Moondyne: A Story of the Underworld (O'Reilly), 650

Mooney, Edward, 592, 597

Mooney, Thomas: agriculture to Irish Americans, 193; dispersal of Irish Americans, 203; Irish in New York, 193–194; laboring, 233, 235; O'Connell (Daniel) and, 201

Moonlighters, 103

Moore, Mary Holt, 542, 545, 546

Moore, Thomas, 218, 382

Moran, Bugsy, 676–677

Moran, D. P., 107, 112

Moran, Michael, 499

Morgan, Edmund, 377

Morison, Samuel Eliot, 682

Morpeth, Lord (George William Frederick Howard), 202

Morris, Charles, 584

Morrison, Danny, 299

Morrison, James, 411

Morrissey, John, 444, 493

Morrissey, Kevin, xvii, 49

Morse, Samuel F. B., 274, 490

Morse, Theodore, 395, *396*

Mortal Friends (Carroll), 659

Morte D'Urban (Power), 657

Mother and Child Scheme, 138

"Mother Machree" (Olcott and Ball), 395, 399

"Mother Malone" (song), *400*

Mourning Becomes Electra (O'Neill), 652

Movies, 595, 680–681, 684

Moynihan, Daniel Patrick: American Irish Historical Society, 43, 498; *Beyond the Melting Pot* (with Glazer), 8–11, 535–536; on Comerford, 535–536; on the Conservative Party, 492; foundational work by, 10; Four Horsemen of Irish-American politics, 299; Hume and, 299; Irish identity in America, xvi; on Irish nationalism, 490; Irish successes in New York, 28, 500–503; Kennedy (John F.) and, 9–10, 49, 520; on modern-day Ireland, 497–498; political power of Irish Americans, 9, 580, 630; rule by the less genteel, 626; social mobility of the Irish, 501, 611; St. Patrick's Day parade (1983), 538; success debate, 500–503

Mugavero, Francis, 565–566

Mulcahy, Richard, 127, 129

"Muldoon the Solid Man" (Harrigan and Hart), 389–390, 406

Mullaly, William, 411

Mullaney, Kate, 359

Mullanphy, John, 192, 204

Mulleda, Harry, *293*

Mullen, James, 398

Mullen, Marie, 566

Mulligan, Cordelia (character), 623

Mulligan, Dan (character), 31

Mulligan Guards (characters), 388–389, 667

Mullins, Moon (character), 494

Mulroney, Brian, 215

Mulrooney, Margaret, 33

Mulry, Thomas M., 592

Multiculturalism, 426–427

Mulvey, Elizabeth, *34*

Mulvihill, Jerry, 420

Mulvihill, Martin, 415

Mundelein, George, 584

Munro, Robert, 68

Murnane, Tim, 447

Murphy, Charles Francis (Charlie): among Tammany Hall bosses, 481, 672; election night (1897), 482; path to Irish-American Republicans, 632; patronage jobs, 637; place among city bosses, 627; Roosevelt (Franklin) and, 506

Murphy, James J., 446–447

Murphy, John, 80

Murphy, John J., 361

Murphy, Johnny, 432

Murphy, Joseph J., 392

Murphy, Maureen, 22

Murphy, Tom, 566

Murphy, William Martin, 110

Murphy Stories (Costello), 659

Murray, Billy, 397–398

Murray, James, 565

Murray, Philip, 363, 592

Murray, Thomas B., 510

Murray, Thomas E., Jr., 592

Murray, Thomas E., Sr., 592

Murtagh, Matthew, 383

Music, 381–416; Appalachian music, 382; blackface, 382; bonding mechanism, 29; *ceilis*, 414; dance music, 418; Ethiopian opera, 382; family entertainment, 386; *Feis (feiseanna)*, 414; female vocalists, 398; folk music, 381, 402, 413; Harrigan and Hart (*see* Harrigan and Hart); hillbilly music, 382; images of Ireland, 382; images of the Irish, 386; Irish-American girls, 393, *681*; Irish fight songs, 385–386; Irish Musicians' Association (Comhaltas Ceoltóirí Éireann), 414, 428; Irish song (*sean-nós* songs), 412–413; Irish sources, 381–382, 383; Irish tenors, 396–397; Irish themes, 391, 395, 396; legitimate theater, 387; minstrelsy, 382–384, 395; music festivals, 411; nostalgia for Ireland, 393–394; old time/old timey music, 382; popular culture, 381, 386; recording industry, 397–398, 411, 413; Scotch sources, 383; *seisiúns*, 414–415; sheet music, *394*, *396*, *396*, *681*; songs of the Irish Revolution, 499; stage Irishman (*see* Stage Irishman); Tin Pan Alley, 393–396, 401–402; Traditional Irish Musicians Association, *414*; traditional music, 381, 411–416, 418, 429; traditional music festivals, 415; urban rock, 403; urbanization, 413; variety theater, 384–387; vaudeville, 386–387, 391–393, 399, 406–410; Ward Irish Music archives, 440

Mussolini, Benito, 135

"My Irish Molly O" (Jerome and Schwartz), 396

My Left Foot (Brown), 566

"My Nellie's Blue Eyes" (Scanlon), 391
My Sister Eileen (McKenny), 655
"My Wild Irish Rose" (Olcott), 395, 397, 399, 406
Myler, Walter, 197
Mystery and Manners (O'Connor), 657

Na Fianna Éireann (Warriors of Ireland), 109
NAIJ (National Association for Irish Justice), 297, 558–559
Napoleonic Wars (1803–1815), 86
Narrow-mindedness, 680–681
Nash, Kathleen, *555*
Nast, Thomas: apemen, 669, 674; caricatures of clerics, 552; "Champion of the Fenians," *366*; equating Irish with blacks, 665, 667; *Harper's Weekly, 239, 366,* 665, 666; Irish-American relief, *239*; stereotypes, *366, 666,* 669, 674; "The Ignorant Vote – Honors are Easy," *666*
Nation (newspaper), 89
National Association, 96
National Association for Irish Justice (NAIJ), 297, 558–559
National biographical dictionaries, 303–305
National Bureau of Economic Research, 30
National Catholic School Social Service (NCSSS), 587
National Catholic War Council (NCWC): bishops' authority, 586–587; Burke (John J.) and, 585; founding, 585; O'Connell (William) and, 586–587; Oregon school law (1922), 589; purpose, 585; Rural Life Bureau, 597; Ryan (John A.) and, 585–586, 592; Social Action Department, 586, 591, 592; Spellman and, 597; successor, 585; Vatican II, 603
National Catholic Welfare Council, 585, 587
National Centre Party, 135, 136
National Conference of Catholic Bishops, 602
National Conference of Catholic Bishops Committee on Migration, 566
National Conference of Catholic Charities (NCCC), 587, 603
National Council of Catholic Women (NCCW), 587
National Council on the Traditional Arts, 431
National Cyclopaedia of American Biography, 304
National Endowment of the Arts, 432
National Folk Festival, 430
National Gazette (newspaper), 183
National identity, 267

National League, 104
National Maritime Union, 363
National Opinion Research Center, 38
National Repeal Convention (1842), 201
National University of Ireland, 113
National Volunteers, 116
"Nationalism and the Irish Peasant, 1800–1848" (Brown), 8
Nationalist Party (Northern Ireland), 143, 144
Native Moment (West), 495
Nativism: anti-Catholic sentiment, 213; anti-Irish sentiment, 200, 213, 372; attitude towards assimilation, 367; defined, 243n2; discrediting of, 200; ethnicity, 426–427; Great Famine, 217; Irish as cheap labor, 356, 372; Irish as eternal strangers, 682; Irish as strikebreakers, 356, 372; Irish poor, 367; Know-Nothings, 306; legitimizing ethnicity, 426–427; New York, 200, 306; Philadelphia, 200; Prohibition, 588; repeal of union movement, 202; repudiation of Irishness by Irish Protestants, 390; urbanization, 582; violence, 200
Naturalization, 182, 477
NCCC (National Conference of Catholic Charities), 587, 603
NCSSS (National Catholic School Social Service), 587
NCWC. *See* National Catholic War Council
Ne Temere (encyclical), 134
Nearny, Declan, 437
Neo-scholasticism, 596
Nesmith, John P., 308, 326n39
Nestor, Agnes, 362
Networking, 469, 616–621, 682. *See also* Self-help/self-reliance/voluntary cooperation
Neumann, John, 242
Nevins, Allan, 7
New Catholic Association, 83
New Departure, 100–103, 292
New England Irish Cultural Center, 433
New History of Ireland (Doyle), xvi, 16
New Irish, 561–569; Catholic Church in America, 563, 565–566; dispersal of Irish Americans, 562; diversity visa, 564; family reunification, 562; illegal status, 562–563, 568; Immigration Act (U.S., 1965), 562, 564; Immigration Act (U.S., 1990), 564; Irish arts, 566–567; Irish nationalism, 563; nonconformists, 563; Northern Ireland, conflict in, 561; professionals, 563; reasons for emigrating, 561; relations with established Irish-American community, 563–564; self-segregation, 563; travel restrictions, 568; visa lottery,

564, 568; welfare and Medicaid benefits, 568
New Journalists, 656–657
"New Measures," 274
"New" or "Second" Reformation: Irish Protestants, 272
New Orleans Irish: civic societies, 195; early settlement, 191–192; Hibernian Society, 175; politics, 580; public works, 354; songwriters, 393
New Side Presbyterianism, 166
New York Athletic Club, 449, 466–467
New York Catholic Protectory, 311–312, 327n76
New York City Police Department (NYPD): Emerald Society, 503, 540, 610; ethnic diversity, 503; Holy Name Society, 510, 596; Irish Americans, 347, 476, 503; "Irish Whales," 465; Spellman's Communion Breakfast speech, 599
New York Clipper (magazine), 387
"New York Construction Workers Lunching on a Crossbeam" (Ebbets), 662
New York Daily News (newspaper), 543
New York Herald (newspaper), *277,* 488
New York Irish, 475–525; 69th National Guard Regiment, 585; American nationalism, 492; anti-black uprising, 372–373; anti-Catholic sentiment and, 506; anti-clericalism, 517–518; anti-Communism, 508–510; anti-New Deal Irish, 507; arrival of Irish revolutionaries, 477; assimilation, 500; blue-collar jobs, 234; Boss Rule, 481–482; boycotting, 360; Broun on, 517; Carroll Hall candidates, 488; Catholic Emancipation, 480; Catholic parishes, 194; Catskill Mountains, 430, 497; civic societies, 195–196; Clan na Gael picnic, 452; clerical conservatism, 518; conformity, 481, 489; conservatism, 505–506; Coughlin and, 507; culture of, 494–496; death rates, 231; decline of Irish American identity, 497–504; Democratic Party, 318, 477–483, 504–512; disenfranchisement of Catholics, 477; distribution within class strata, 499; docks, 499; domestic servants, 356; Draft Riots (1863), 35, 372–373, 485, 633; elites, 309; ethnic conflict, 372; exiles from the 1798 rebellion, 307; exploitation of, 315–316; Famine immigration, 476, 489; fantasy, 489; *Feis (feiseanna),* 418; first Irish Catholic mayor, 475; *Fleadh (fleadhanna),* 429; Gaelic Athletic Association (GAA), 469–470; Gaelic games, 468–469; Great Famine relief aid, 217; informal government, 480;

Irish city, 475; Irish nationalism, 490–493; Irish traditions, 479–480; Irish village writ large, 480–481; job prospects, 230; Kennedy (John F.) and, 511; laborers, 356; male work force, 234; mayoral election (1952), 511–512; merchants, 322, 499; mid-nineteenth century, 303; middle-class Irish, 476, 490, 512; Montgomery Guards, 195; nativist violence, 200, 306; Orange Day riots, 372, 489, 636; Orange-Green Riots (1824), 17; over-crowding, 203; papal honors, 320; parochial schools, 195, 515–517; physical force nationalism, 370; police (*see* New York City Police Department); political accomplishment, 483; political power, 482–483, 502–503, 504–512; politics, 479, 512, 557, 580; population, 616; position in the city, 476; post-Great Depression, 669; poverty, 193–194; pre-Famine immigration, 476, 477, 489; precinct politics, 482; public works, 354; radical candidates, 581; replacement of Protestants, 475; Republican Party (United States), 504, 507, 510–511; rights for, 184; role of priests, 519; rule by men of the people, 478–479; St. Patrick's Cathedral, 319, 497; saloonkeepers, 482; saloons, 482, 497; Saturday night, 503; savings bank ethos, 306; schools question, 199–200, 486–488; sectarian violence, 278; social change, 483, 580–581; social mobility, 12–14, 23, 303, 501; stealing elections, 479; success of, 500–503; support for Senator McCarthy, 509–510; tensions among, 181; traditional music, 413; underworld, 476; Union Club incident, 586; upper-class Irish, 476, 512; voting bloc, 478; wages, 236; working class leadership, 475. *See also* Emigrant Savings Bank; Friendly Sons of St. Patrick; Irish Emigrant Society; New Irish; Tammany Hall
New York Irish (Bayor and Meagher), 14, 41, 48
New York Irish History Roundtable, 49
New York Irish Showband, 437
New York State Federation of Citizens for Educational Freedom, 516
New York Tailor's Trade Association, 357
New York Times (newspaper), 241, 543, 635
New York World-Telegram and Sun, 118
New Yorker (magazine), 498, 533
New Yorkers, 496
Newenham, Edward, 177
Newman, John Henry, 603
Nicholls, George, 186

Nicholson, Asenath, 22
Nicholson, John, 308, 309, 326n39
Nicknames (sobriquets), 333. *See also* Stereotypes
NICRA (Northern Ireland Civil Rights Association), 144, 297, 298
Niebuhr, Reinhold, 513, 519
Niehaus, Earl, 10, 384, 385
"Night Maloney Landed in New York" (Flynn), 392
Nightingale, Florence, 371
Nightnoise, 437
Niles, John, 21
Nixon, Richard, 510, 529, 532
"No Irish Need Apply," 371–372
No Looking Back (film), 567
"No Rent Manifesto," 103
Nobel Peace Prize, 300
Nolan, Francie (character), 652, 654
Nolan, Honoriah (character), 31
Nolan, Janet: Irish-American women, 346; Irish mothers, 345; Irish women, 36; social mobility of the Irish, 623; women's role in immigration, 30, 33
Nomos, 437
Nondenominational schools, 199
"None can Love Like an Irishman" (song), 493
Nonsectarianism, 17
Noonan, Peggy, 609, 631–632
NORAID (Irish Northern Aid): Flannery (Michael) and, 298, 300, 538; formation, 298; influence, 299; Ireland Fund, 298–299; *Irish People*, 544; membership in, 558; republican movement in Northern Ireland, 50
Normans, 63, 72
North American College in Rome, 583
North American Feis Commission, 419
North Texas Irish Festival, 432, 439
Northern Ireland, 141–147; agriculture, 141; Anglo-Irish Treaty (1921), 129; boundary with Irish Free State, 127, 130–131; constitutional status, 126; decommissioning arms, 147; discrimination against nationalists, 131–132; dual citizenship, 146; dual identity, 152; economy, 142; gerrymandering in favor of Unionists, 131; Irish Civil War period (1922–1923), 129–132; Irish Republican Army in, 142–143, 145–146, 298–300; NORAID, 50; paramilitary terrorism, 145–146; parliament of, 124; partition of Ireland (1920), 122–124; Protestant state for a Protestant people, 130; Republic of Ireland, 143; republican movement, 50; sectarian violence, 132; shipbuilding, 141; Sunningdale Agreement (1943), 145; the Troubles (*see* Northern Ireland, con-

flict in); "Ulster Scots" in, 258; welfare state, 142; World War II, 137, 141–142
Northern Ireland, conflict in (the Troubles): American involvement, 558–561, 569; Anglo-Irish Agreement (1985), 146, 300, 560; cease fires, 299, 300; Four Horsemen of Irish-American politics, 49; Good Friday Agreement (1998), 49, 146, 300, 560–562; hunger strikers, 299; Irish Republican Army, 298–300; New Irish, 561; physical force nationalism, 297–298
Northern Ireland Civil Rights Association (NICRA), 144, 297, 298
Northern Ireland Labour Party, 142
Northwest Folklife Festival, 430
Not a Word about Nightingales (Howard), 656
Notre Dame, University of, 594–595, 595–596
Notre Dame Academy (Maryland), 580
Nuns/sisters: alleged immorality, 275–276; civil rights, 600; in Ireland, 94; number of, 580, 601; role, 580
Nye, Russell, 381
NYIAAA (Greater New York Irish-American Athletic Association), 453, 454, 468
NYPD. *See* New York City Police Department

Oakboys (Hearts of Oak), 74
O'Boyle, Patrick J., 597, 601
O'Brien, David J., 591
O'Brien, Fitz-James, 650
O'Brien, Jack, 628
O'Brien, John, 441n21
O'Brien, John J., 519–520
O'Brien, Michael J., 3, 179, 259–260, 263
O'Brien, Paddy, 411
O'Brien, Pat, 494, 551
O'Brien, William Smith, 220
Observe the Sons of Ulster Marching towards the Somme (McGuinness), 116
Observer (newspaper), 490
O'Callaghan, Bridget, 341, 345
O'Callaghan, Edmund Bailey, 202
O'Callaghan, Owen, 341, 343, 345
O'Callaghan, Pat, 465
O'Casey, Sean, 110, 133, 498
O'Connell, Charles Underwood, 293
O'Connell, Daniel: Act of Union, 24; Anglo-Irish relations, 183; attitudes toward England, 492; Baldwin (Connell) and, 189; Catholic Association, 83–84, 183, 272, 480; Catholic Emancipation, 17, 24, 273; Catholic Emigration Society, 186; Catholicism, 578; Cohalan on, 586; conciliation of Britain, 202; constitutional nationalism, 289–290; defense of religious

O'Connell, Daniel *(continued)*
interests, 578; Democratic Republicans, 183; election to British parliament (1828), 84; Fleming and, 191; Friends of Ireland, 183; identification of Irish nationalism with Catholicism, 578–579; independence of Irish parliament, 86–89; influence on Irish immigrants, 24–25; Irish abolitionism, 376, 383; Irish American support, 202; Irish Americans, 177, 191; on Irish lower classes, 240; Irish nationalism, 223, 264, 289–290, 578; Jackson (Andrew) and, 198; Kildare Place Society, 283n4; laissez-faire economics, 88; MacNeven and, 183; Mooney (Thomas) and, 201; opposition to Protestant evangelicalism, 272, 283n4; physical force nationalism, 202; print depicting, *87*; property owners, 88; Repeal Association, *87*, 88; repeal of union movement, 24, 86–89, 201; secret societies, 88; slavery, 201–202, 290, 633; Stanley (Lord) and, 191; successes of, 273; trade unionism, 88; Young Ireland, 290
O'Connell, Denis, 583
O'Connell, J. J., 128
O'Connell, James, 362
O'Connell, Robbie, *422*, *437*
O'Connell, William Henry, 584, 586, 629
O'Connell Rifles, 452
O'Connor, Donald, 551
O'Connor, Edwin: *Last Hurrah* (film), 632; *Last Hurrah* (novel), 551, 556, 655–656; second- and third-generation characters, 557
O'Connor, Flannery, 649, 657–658
O'Connor, Jeremiah, 617
O'Connor, John, 617
O'Connor, Julia, 362
O'Connor, Michael, 195
O'Connor, Rory, 128, 129
O'Connor, Sandra Day, 540
O'Connor, Thomas, 184, 318
O'Connor, Thomas H., 14
O'Conor, Charles: *American National Biography*, 329n108; Emigrant Savings Bank, 318, 326n39; as a lawyer, 329n108, 475; native-born, 477; Tweed and, 318, 475
O'Dea, Thomas F., 483, 484, 514
O'Dell, G. C., 387
O'Donnel, James, 446
O'Donnell, Hugh, 67
O'Donovan, Brian, 433–435, 440
O'Donovan, Jeremiah, 220
O'Donovan Rossa, Jeremiah: "Cuba Five," 293; Fenians, 290; followers, 371; funeral, 116; knowledge of, 491; photo, *293*

O'Dowd, Niall, 50, 561
O'Duffy, Eoin, 135–136
O'Dwyer, Paul, 48–49, 535
O'Faircheallaigh, Tomas, 419
O'Faolain, Sean, 489, 499
Offenses Against the State Act (1939), 137
Official Unionist Party, 145, 146
O'Flynn, Richard, 617
O'Gorman, Richard, 318
O'Grady, John, 587
O'Grady, Standish, 107
O'Growney, Eugene, 106
O'Hagan, Al, 538, 539, 542–544, 546
O'Hagan, Thomas, 610
O'Hanlon, John, 173, 193
O'Hanlon, Mary, 338, 340
O'Hara, Edwin V., 597
O'Hara, John (prefect of religion), 595
O'Hara, John (writer): *Appointment in Samarra*, 653–654; background, 652–654; *Butterfield 8*, 625, 633–634, 653; Catholicism, 596; *Doctor's Son and Other Stories*, 653; Farrell (James T.) and, 653; Fitzgerald (F. Scott) and, 653; Irishness, 498–499, 671; literary tradition, 649; social mobility of the Irish, 621–622; *From the Terrace*, 676
O'Hara, Maureen, 551
O'Higgins, Kevin, 129, 134, 135
O'Higgins, T. F., 135
O'Kelly, Sean, 139
Olcott, Chauncey, 395
Old Age Pensions Act (1908), 113
Old English (Anglo-Irish): Catholicism, 72, 154; Cromwell (Oliver) and, 69; Earls of Kildare (Fitzgeralds), 63, 66; Irish Catholics, 66, 67; Irish Protestants, 72; power, 66; Ulster risings (1640s), 67–69
"Old Hag of Beare" (song), 402
Old Limerick Town (play), 395
Old School Presbyterianism, 188
Old Side Presbyterianism, 166
Old time/old timey music, 382
O'Leary, Daniel, 445–446
O'Leary, J. J., 446
O'Leary, Peter, 235
O'Leary Belt Race, 446
Oliver, John, 203
Olmstead, Frederick Law, 674
Olwell, James, 312, 315t, 326n39, 327n76
Olympic Club (baseball team), 447
Olympics, 449–450, 451–452, 465–467
O'Mahony, Dan, 417
O'Mahony, John, 96, 98, 224, 290
O'Malley, Cormac, 51
O'Malley, Donogh, 139
O'Malley, Father (character), 595
O'Malley, Patricia Trainor, 345–346

O'Malley, Walter, 462
"On the Koko Moko Isle" (Von Tilzer), 396
On the Origin of the Species (Darwin), 366
Onahan, William J., 592
O'Neill, Albert Dapper, 632
O'Neill, Danny (character), 40
O'Neill, Eugene: *Ah! Wilderness*, 652; *Anna Christie*, 652; Catholicism, 596; *Desire under the Elms*, 652; *Emperor Jones*, 652; *Hairy Ape*, 652; *Iceman Cometh*, 652; influences on, 651–652; Irish voice, 281; literary tradition, 649; *Long Day's Journey into Night*, 495, 551, 652; *Long Voyage Home*, 652; *Moon of the Caribbees*, 652; *Mourning Becomes Electra*, 652; Nobel Prize, 652; playing one role, 28; *Touch of the Poet*, 496, 625, 633, 652
O'Neill, Francis, 29, 418
O'Neill, Hugh, 419
O'Neill, Hugh (Earl of Tyrone), 67, 154
O'Neill, Kitty, 406
O'Neill, Owen Roe, 68
O'Neill, Terence, 143–144
O'Neill, Thomas P. ("Tip"): busing in Boston, 638–639; Four Horsemen of Irish-American politics, 49, 299; Massachusetts state house takeover, 628; on Reagan, 632
Onion Eaters (Donleavy), 659
Opper, Frederick, 25, *26*
Orange Association (Philadelphia), 188
Orange Day riots, 372, 489, 636
Orange-Green Riots (1824), 17
Orange Order: Act of Union, 82; Ancient Order of Hibernians, 95; establishment in New York, 188; formation, 77–78; Home Rule, 115; marches, 132; Paisley and, 143; poor Presbyterians, 267; popularity, 264; strength, 80; Unionist Party, 115; United Irishmen, 265; in United States, 183, 188
Orangeism, 171, 189–190
O'Regan, Teague (character), 263
Oregon school law (1922), 589
O'Reilly, Alexander, 191–192
O'Reilly, Bill, 632
O'Reilly, John Boyle, 650
O'Reilly, Leonora, 359, 362, 381
O'Reilly, Tony, 298–299
O'Reilly, Winifred (née Rooney), 359, 362
Organized crime, 501, 512
"Origins and Character of Irish-American Nationalism" (Brown), 8
O'Rourke, Jim, 447
O'Rourke, Sam, 444
Orr, James, 263

O'Shaughnessy, Dennis, 669
O'Shea, Katherine, 105
O'Shea, William, 105
O'Sullivan, John, 494
O'Sullivan, Katie, 339
O'Sullivan, Mary Kenny, 359, 362
O'Sullivan, Maureen, 551
Oswald, Lee Harvey, 528, 531
Other Bostonians (Thernstrom), 12
Other Side (Gordon), 659
O'Tuathaigh, Gearóid, 368–369
Owen Garvey baseball teams, 447
Oxford History of the American People (Morison), 682

P and B associations (county patriotic and benevolent associations), 468
Pacem in Terris (encyclical), 519
"Paddy Duffy's Cart" (Harrigan and Hart), 390
Paddy Killoran's Irish Serenaders, 398
Paddy stereotype: anti-Irish sentiment, 364–365, 366–367; archetype of the "regular guy," 625; disappearance of, 548; downward mobility, 623; Harrigan and, 625; history, 678; in Irish-American high culture, 625; loquaciousness, 673; origins, 665; paddy wagons for Paddy, 489; replacement by Jimmy, 675–676; Sambo and, 665–667, 666; transformation into Pat, 625, 667; Williams (William) on, 673
Padre (Franciscan publication), 321
Paisley, Ian, 143, 144, 146, 282
Papineau, Louis, 202
Parish and the Hill (Curran), 655
Parish Boundaries (McGreevy), 640
Parker, Edward L., 263–264
Parliament Act (1911), 114
Parnell, Charles Stewart: Clan na Gael, 290; Davitt and, 101; death, 105; Devoy and, 100, 101; fall of, 105; Fenians, 290; fundraising in America, 101, *102*; ghost's persona, 105; Gladstone and, *102*, 104, 105; Home Rule, *102*, 104, 105; Irish Americans, 177, 291; Irish nationalism, 290–291; Irish Parliamentary Party, 100, 105; knowledge of, 491; land reform, 100, 103; Liberal Party, 104; mother, *102*; New Departure, 100–103, 292; O'Shea (Katherine) and, 105; photo, *102*; physical force nationalism, 292
Parnells (Gaelic football team), 454
Parochial schools, 195, 199, 488, 515–517, 594, 601, 621
Pascendi Dominici Gregis (encyclical), 583
Passing of the Great Race (Grant), 674
Pastor, Tony, 386

"Pastorini's prophesy," 615, 622, 635
Pat stereotype, 371, 667–668
Paterson, William, 167
Patriot Games (Clancy), 659
Patriot movement, 261
Patronage, 75, 557, 637
Patton, James, 164
Paul VI (Pope), 601
Pavarotti, Luciano, 539
Paxson, Frederic L., 304
Paxton uprising (1763), 165, 166
PD (People's Democracy), 297
Peace Corps, 532
Pearse, Patrick, 116–117, 118, 119, 121
Pedestrianism, 445–446
Peel, Sir Robert, 84, 90–91, 94, 202
Peep O'Day Boys, 78
"Peg O' My Heart" (song), 397
Peggy (sobriquet), 333
"Peggy O'Moore" (Scanlon), 391
Penal Laws (Ireland), 70–71, 82, 84, 480
Penn, William, 283n1
People skills of Irish Americans, 51
People with No Name (Griffin), 39, 47, 256
People's Democracy (PD), 297
Pepper, George, 214
Perlmann, Joel, 616, 620
Pessen, Edward, 322
Petri, Lisa, 423
Petri School of Irish Dancing, 422–423
Pfeiffer, Leo, 589
Phelan, James D., 592, 618
Phelan, James Joseph, 592
Philadelphia Ceili Group, 415, 430–431, 432
Philadelphia Folk Festival, 430
Philadelphia Irish: artisans, 236; busing, 638–639; churches outside the city, 19; Great Famine relief aid, 217; male work force, 234; nativist violence, 200; overcrowding, 203; parochial schools, 195; poverty, 194; St. Tammany Society, 181; Scotch-Irish, 161; sectarian discord, 275; sectarian violence, 278; social mobility, 13; songwriters, 393; tensions among, 181
Physical courage, 496
Physical force nationalism: Ancient Order of Hibernians, 294; Clan na Gael, 294; Easter Rising, 492; goal, 289; Irish Americans, 297–300, 561; Kennedy (Edward) and, 561; New York, 370; Northern Ireland, conflict in, 297–298; O'Connell (Daniel) and, 202; Parnell and, 292; repeal of union movement, 201–202
Pieri, Dornando, 467
Pilot (Boston newspaper), 195, 201, 453, 650
Pitch-capping, 78

Pitt, William (the Younger Pitt), 81–83, 484
Pittsburgh Catholic (newspaper), 195
Pius IX (Pope), 222
Pius XI (Pope), 136, 586–587
Pius XII (Pope), 597
Plaid Stocking baseball teams, 447
Plantation of Ireland, 65–69, 154–155, 159
Planxty, 415
Playboy of the Western World (Synge), 107, 495
Plays of J. P. Donleavy (Donleavy), 659
Playwrights, 651–652, 660
Pluck, 467
Plunkett, Horace, 111–112, 119, 121
Plunkett, Joseph, 116
Plunkitt, George Washington, 482, 626, 637, 672
Plymouth Rock, 631
Poets, 660–661
Police. *See* Dublin Metropolitan Police; New York City Police Department
Policy (numbers running), 501
Polish National Catholic Church, 577
Politics: anti-Communism, 508–510, 517, 631; anti-Harvard movement, 631; anti-radicalism, 631; anti-socialism, 631; Boss Rule, 481–482, 612; Campbell on, 479; changing conditions, 512, 580, 626–627, 629–630, 637–638; civic rights for foreign-born, 198; conservatism, 505–506, 520; educated men in, 672; electioneering, 198; enfranchisement, 198; free immigration, 182; free speech, 182; freedom of the press, 182; Irish-American grievances, 182; Irish traditions, 479–480; left-wing politics, 298, 558, 582, 611; line between entertainment and politics, 672; machine politics (*see* Machine politics); naturalization, 182, 477; opportunity for working-class solidarity, 612; patronage, 75, 557, 637; peasant qualities, 480; political accomplishment, 483; political implications of the Great Famine, 95–96, 216–217; political power, 9, 50, 174, 198, 482–483, 502–503, 504–512, 520, 548, 580, 630; political skills, 16, 51, 218–219, 636; precinct politics, 482; reforms advocated by Irish Americans, 198; "regular guy"communal populism, 628–633; religious tests, 182, 477; restricted franchises, 182; rule by men of the people, 478–479, 626–628; social change, 483, 580–581; stealing elections, 479
Polk, James, 21, 201, 217
Pollock, Oliver, 192
Poole, John, 385–386

Poor Law Amendment Act (1834), 89
Popular culture, 386
Portrait of the Artist as a Young Man
    (Joyce), 654
Postlethwaite, Pete, 566
Potato famine. *See* Great Famine
Potter, George, 8, 479, 480
Potter, James, 167
Poverty: anti-Irish sentiment, 197;
    Boston Irish, 239; death rates, 231–232;
    "family economy," 230; Irish Ameri-
    cans, 193–219, 219, 230, 281; McCourt's
    depiction, 281; New York Irish,
    193–194; Philadelphia Irish, 194
Powderly, Terence V., 359
Power, James, 192
Power, Tyrone (1797–1841), 186, 192, 197
Power, Tyrone (1914–1958), 551
Powers, J. F., 657
Powers, Tom (character), 676
Poyning's Law (1494), 72, 75
Practicality, 496
Prendergast, Tom, 680
Presbyterianism: Catholics becoming
    Presbyterians, 261; Free Presbyterian
    Church, 143; Irish Presbyterians, 152,
    288; New Side Presbyterianism, 166;
    Old School Presbyterianism, 188; Old
    Side Presbyterianism, 166; Scots Pres-
    byterianism, 156. *See also* Ulster Pres-
    byterians
Presence of Grace (Power), 657
Presentation Sisters, 578
Presley, Elvis, 551
"Pretty Girl Milking Her Cow" (Bouci-
    cault), 386
"Pretty Kitty Kelly" (song), *681*
Prince of Darkness (Power), 657
Pro Deo, pro rege, pro patria, 68
Proclamation of the Republic, 119
Professional Football Hall of Fame,
    462
Profiles in Courage (Kennedy), 557
Progress and Poverty (George), 291, 486
Prohibition, 588, 675
Project Children, 441n21
Project Irish Outreach, 565
Proletarian corollary to North Ameri-
    can capitalism, 193
Proskauer, Joseph M., 513
Protestant Association, 274
Protestant evangelicalism: anti-Catholic
    sentiment, 273–276; attempts to con-
    vert Irish Catholics, 274, 278–279;
    Catholic Church in America, 276–277,
    279; Catholic Church in Ireland,
    272–273; Irish Protestants, 271–275;
    Irish self-reliance, 276; "New Mea-
    sures," 274; O'Connell (Daniel) and,
    272, 283n4; post-Famine Protestant
    evangelicalism, 95, 264–265; saved

Christians, 282; Ulster Presbyterians,
    264–265
Protestant extremists, 145
Protestant Public Schools Society (New
    York), 199
Protestant Reformation, 66, 154
Protestant Revival. *See* Protestant evan-
    gelicalism
"Protestant Ulster," 4
Protestant Unionist Party, 144
Protestantism. *See* American Protes-
    tants; Church of Ireland; Irish Protes-
    tants; Presbyterianism; Protestant
    evangelicalism; Scotch-Irish; Ulster
    Presbyterians; Ulster Protestants
Protocols of the Elders of Zion, 591
Providence Ceili Club, 431
Providence Irish Festival, 431
Public Enemy (film), 550, 676
Public Safety Act (1927), 134
Public School Society (New York City),
    486–488
Public works, 187, 234, 354
Puck (magazine), 25, 26
Puget Sound Guitar Workshop, 432
Pulitzer Prize, 552
"Pull the Cork Out of Erin (Let the
    River Shannon Flow)" (song), 398
Purcell, John, 195
Purcell, Richard J., vii, viii, 240

Quadragesimo Anno (encyclical), 519,
    591
Quakers (Religious Society of Friends),
    92, 93, 166
Quarter, William, 195
Quebec Irish, 190
Queen, Johnny, 387
Querulousness, 674
Quiet Man (film), 566
Quigley, Hugh, 220
Quigley, Martin J., 595
Quill, Mike, 362–363
Quinn, Carmel, 437
Quinn, David, 47
Quinn, Frank, 398
Quinn, John, 495, 601
Quinn, Peter, 1, 35, 281
Quinn, Robert Emmet, 628
Quinn, William, 299–300
Quinn's Book (Kennedy), 660

Race, 365, 367, 375
"Race" in nineteenth century, 365
Racism. *See* Irish racism
Rader, Benjamin, 460
Radio Corporation of America (RCA),
    409
Radio Eireann, 30
Radio-Keith Orpheum (RKO), 409
Radio Telefís Eireann (RTE), 30

Ragtime (film), 633
Railroad building, 187, 226, 234, 373
Rea, Matthew, 164
Rea, Stephen, 566
Read, George, 166–167
Read, Joseph, 166–167
Reagan, Ronald: Anglo-Irish Agree-
    ment, 560; Irish American Republi-
    cans, 557; Irish Catholics, 631; left in
    America, 611; line between entertain-
    ment and politics, 672; as main-
    stream, 540; O'Neill (Tip) and, 632;
    press conferences, 533
Rebel, A Drama of the Irish Rebellion
    (Fagan), 79
Rebellion of 1798 (Ireland): commemo-
    rations, 109, 282; fear of aftermath,
    271; French Revolutionary Wars, 478;
    Ireland's colonial aristocracy, 271;
    New York, 477; Penal Laws, 82; politi-
    cal exiles from, 289, 307; preparations,
    78–80; Ulster, 80, 265; Ulster Presby-
    terians, 264; United Irishmen, 78–80,
    84, 289, 307; Wexford rebellion, 80
Recluse of Herald Square (Cox), 683
Recorder (American Irish Historical
    Society), 43
Recording industry, 397–398, 411, 413
Redemptorists, 578
Redmond, John: death, 121, 295; disso-
    lution of Parliament (1909), 113;
    Easter Rising, 118; Home Rule, 114,
    294–295; Irish Parliamentary Party,
    111, 293–294; National Volunteers, 116
Redmond, William, 308, 326n39
Reels, 418
Reformation. *See* Protestant Reforma-
    tion
Regan, Agnes, 587
Regan, Patsy, 446
"Regular guy" communal populism,
    628–633
Regulator movements, 165
Reilly, Pat, *600*
Reilly and the 400 (play), 495
Relief Act (1793), 77
Religious practices (in Ireland and/or
    America): anti-clericalism, 517–518;
    comparative studies of, 46; conver-
    sions in Ireland, 260; demographic
    change in Ulster, 265–268; Devotional
    Revolution, 578; gender ratio, 33;
    Great Famine, 95; pluralism, 214; pro-
    hibition on teaching religion in pub-
    lic schools, 488; "souperism," 92;
    superstitiousness, 223; tithe paid to
    Church of Ireland, 73, 85. *See also*
    Catholic Church in America; Catholic
    Church in Ireland; Catholicism
Religious Society of Friends (Quakers),
    92, 93, 166

Religious tests, 182, 477

"Remember Boy You're Irish" (Scanlon), 391

Remembering Ahanagran (White), 303

Remittances: Boston Irish, 341; domestic service, 341, 343; Emigrant Savings Bank, 26, 318; emigration, 318; Irish Americans, 617; marriage, 343

Remmington, William, 509

Repeal Association, *87*, 88, 89, 188

Repeal of union movement, 24, 86–89, 200–203

Republic of Ireland (1938–present), *123*, 138–141, 143

Republican Party (Clann na Poblachta), 138

Republican Party (Cumann na Poblachta), 128, 540

Republican Party (United States): Irish Americans, 557, 631–632; Irish Catholics, 511; Irish Protestants, 490; New York Irish, 504, 507, 510–511; Ulster Americans, 183

Republicanism: Ancient Order of Hibernians, 294; Catholic Church, 485; Clan na Gael, 294; de Valera and, 121, 128–129; Knights of Labor, 627; United Irishmen, 485

Rerum Novarum (encyclical), 519, 591

Respect for learning, 494

Revisionist historians, 256, 264, 267

Reynolds, Albert, 146

Reynolds, James, 178

Rhode Island Irish, 240

Rhodes, Robert E., 11

Ribbonmen, 85, 355, 373, 615

Ricardo, David, 185

Rice, Charles Owen, 592

Rice, Thomas, 382

Rickey, Branch, 462

Riddle, Samuel, 191

Riders to the Sea (Synge), 495

Ridge, John T., 343

Rifle (Rice), 382

Rischin, Moses, 7, 8, 13, 44

Rise of the Coloured Empires (Stoddard), 674

Rising of the Moon (album), 401

Riverdance (show), 415, 417, 420, 423, 567

Robert Emmet boat clubs, 446

Roberts, William R., 98

Robespierre, Maximilien Marie Isidore de, 282

Robinson, Fred, 6

Robinson, Jackie, 462

Robinson, Mary, *560*

Robinson, Peter, 185

Roche, Pat, 419, 420

Rockaway Irish Festival, 433

Rockefeller Center (under construction), *662*

Rockites, 85, 615

"Rocky Road to Dublin" (song), 399

Roediger, David, 48, 375–376, 612, 626

Rogers, Elizabeth Flynn, 581

Roman Catholic Orphan Asylum (New York), 327n76

Roman Catholics, 484

Romance in Athlone (play), 395

Roney, Frank, 359, 360

Rooney, Art, 464

Rooney, Art, II, 465

Rooney, Dan, 464–465

Rooney, Pat, 407–408, 409

Roosevelt, Eleanor, 507

Roosevelt, Franklin Delano: anti-New Deal Irish, 507; appointments of Irish Catholics, 557; Catholic voters, 590–591; Coughlin and, 590; de Valera and, 137; economic/social legislation, 586; Farley (Jim) and, 507–508; Irish-American politicians, 627; Irish businessmen, 507; Murphy (Charles) and, 506; president, 475; Ryan (John A.) and, 591; Spellman and, 597; Walker (Jimmy) and, 506

Roosevelt, Theodore, 152, 506

Roots (Haley), 426

Roper, Pat, 432

"Rosary" (song), 399

Rosary Altar Society, 593

Rose, Ralph, 451–452, 466

Rosenberg, Ethel and Julius, 509

Rosenfeld, Monroe H., 393

Ross, Duncan O., 452

Roth, Philip, 621

Rousseau, Jean Jacques, 282, 283

Rowan, Archibald Hamilton, 177

Rowell, Charles, 446

Rowing, 446–447, 451

"Royal Family of Irish Entertainers," *400*

Royal Irish Constabulary Auxiliary ("Black and Tans"), 124, 125

Royal Ulster Constabulary (RUC), 130

RTE (Radio Telefís Eireann) Guide (periodical), 30

Ruby, Jack, 528

RUC (Royal Ulster Constabulary), 130

Russell, Lord John, 90–91

Russell Brothers, 408

Ruth, Babe, 457, 461

Rutherford's Showband, 432

Ryan, Dennis P., 14

Ryan, Jack (character), 659

Ryan, James Hugh, 589

Ryan, John, 356

Ryan, John A.: Bishops' Program of Social Reconstruction, 591; "Fallacy of Bettering Oneself" (article), 630;

influence, 590; Ireland (John) and, 591; National Catholic War Council, 585–586, 592; workers' rights, 630

Ryan, John J., 447

Ryan, Mary Anne (Molly), *335*

Ryan, Paddy, 444, 457

Ryan, Pat, 449, 466

Ryan, Thomas Fortune, 476, 592

Saddest Summer of Samuel S. (Donleavy), 659

Sadlier, Mary Anne, 629, 650

St. James Young Men's Catholic Total Abstinence, 446, 452

St. John's College, 578. *See also* Fordham University

St. Louis (ship), 42

St. Mary's Temperance Society, 446

St. Patrick's Cathedral, 315, 319, 497, 512

St. Patrick's Day: among public observances in New York City, 476; Irish-American festivals, 427; "St. Patrick's Day in America" (print), *621*; stereotypes, *374*; suburban teenagers, 536

St. Patrick's Day parade (New York City), 535–547; Ancient Order of Hibernians, 538, 539; anti-British sentiment, 537, 559; banner at 1921 parade, 586; Behan banned from 1961 parade, 498; Beirne and, 539, 541, 542, 545, 546; Bloody Sunday, 559; booing at 1978 parade, 559; Columbus Day parade, 539; Comerford and, 498, 535–538, 541, 543; date of, 536; "Day We Celebrate" (Harrigan-Braham), 427–428; Emerald Society, 541–542; Flannery (Michael) and, 538, 542, 544–545, 559; grand marshal, election of, 545; grand marshal 1982 parade, 299, 559; grand marshal 1983 parade, 535–547; illustration of 1894 parade, *25*, *26*; Irish diaspora, 428; marchers, 512; Moynihan and, 538; penny postcard, *374*; performing arts activities, 428; placards allowed, 537; reviewing stand, 497, 512; sidelines, *553*, *639*

St. Patrick's Home for the Aged and Infirm (Bronx, New York), 543

St. Patrick's Missionary Society, *600*

St. Patrick's Mutual Alliance Association, 452, 469

St. Patrick's societies, 261

St. Stephen's Day, 441n5

St. Tammany Society (Philadelphia), 181

St. Vincent de Paul Society: financial aid provided by, 594; in mid-1840s, 204; post-Famine philanthropy, 25; unification of its work, 592; welfare agency, 278, 587

St. Francis College, 394

Saloonkeepers, 482

Saloons, 482, 497, 675

Sambo stereotype, 665–667, *666*

Samhain (season), 427

Sampson, William: in America, 178; Catholic Emancipation, 183; memory of, 282; nonsectarianism, 17; refugee status, 17, 289

San Francisco Irish: from Australia, 172; Corbett and, *445*; Gaelic Athletic Association (GAA), 469–470; job prospects, 230; Kelly (Eugene), 319; politics, 557, 580; public works, 354; radical candidates, 581; social mobility, 12–13, 23

Sands, Bobby, 299, 542, 559

"Santiago Flynn" (Morse), 395, *396*

Saorstát Éireann. *See* Irish Free State

Sarcasm, 671

Sarsfield militia, 452

Saturday night, 503

Savings accounts, 26, 305, 306

Sawdoctors, 438

Scally, Robert J. (Bob), 613–615, 623, 683

Scanlon, William J., 391

Scarce economies, 614–615

Schlesinger, Arthur, Jr., 7

Schlesinger, Arthur, Sr., vii, 7, 225, 582

Schools: nondenominational schools, 199; Oregon school law (1922), 589; parochial schools, 195, 199, 488, 515–517, 594, 601, 621; prohibition on teaching religion in public schools, 488; public schools catering to minority convictions, 199; Roman Catholic Free Schools, 486–487; schools question, 486–488; sectarianism, 487. *See also* Education

Schooner Fare, 437

Schrembs, Joseph, 587

Schrier, Arnold, 39, 47–48

Schultz (Donleavy), 659

Schwarzenegger, Arnold, 664

Science, 484, 514

Scorsese, Martin, 35, 322

Scotch-Irish, 151–170; American Revolution, 157, 165–169, 177–178; Americans claiming ancestry, 687, 691; anti-egalitarianism, 168; assimilation, 153, 169; borrowings by, 162–163; British dimension, 152–154; change in attitude toward, 15; coherence as a group, 178; colonial America, 162; cultural diversity in U.S., 169; dependence on British-run Irish polity, 156; diaspora, 153; economic development, 157–160, 162; emigration, 157, 159–163; exclusion from landowning classes, 157; filiopietism, 165; frontiersmen, 158, 162–165, 168–169, 188, 286; German immigrants, 165; immigration, 151, 178–179; Irish-American nationalism,

168; Irish Catholics, 4; Irish nationalism, 153; Jackson (Andrew) and, 168; Jefferson and, 168; Leyburn on, 15; "Line of Ireland," 167; Philadelphia Irish, 161; pre-Famine immigration, 17–18; prejudice against, 167; Quakers, 166; settlements in America, 154, 159, 164–165, 168; slavery, 165; the South, 3; states rights, 167–168; states with strongest presence, 182; triple identity, 152; "Ulstermen" in Scotch-Irish discourse, 4; U.S. Constitution, 182; usage of the term, 151–154, 263; writings about themselves, 4. *See also* Ulster Presbyterians

"Scotch-Irish," 257–260, *261, 262–264*

Scotch-Irish: A Social History (Leyburn), 15

Scotch-Irish Society, 5, 15, 286

Scotland, Catholicism in, 156

"Scots-Irish," 260, 263

Scots Presbyterianism, 156

Scott, James, 614

SDLP. *See* Social Democratic Labour Party

Sean-nós (Irish song), 412–413

Sean O'Neill Band, 432

Seanad Éireann (Senate of Ireland), 128, 136

Seasons, 427

"Second" Reformation, 272

Secret societies: communalism, 615; eighteenth century, 73; labor violence, 355; market integration, 615; nineteenth century, 85; O'Connell (Daniel) and, 85; Penal Laws, 480; reemergence, 101

Secularism, 199, 427

Seeger, Pete, 401

Seinfeld (TV show), 633

Seisiúns, 414–415

Self-criticism, 281

Self-determination for Ireland, 15, 103, 125, 295

Self-expression, 281

Self-help/self-reliance/voluntary cooperation, 203, 238–240, 276, 280

Semiskilled artisans, 235–236, 357

Senate of Ireland (Seanad Éireann), 128, 136

Senior, Nassau William, 186

September 11 Terrorist Attacks (2001), 568, 609–610, 639, 640

Set dance, 424n5

Set pieces, 418

Set This House on Fire (Styron), 540

Seton, Elizabeth, 181

Seton Hall College, 320

Settlement patterns: Catholicism, 230; communalism, 616; Eastern U.S., 617–618; females, 32; Irish American

dispersal, 173, 176, 181–182, 192–193, 203, 213, 214, 228, 548, 562, *690*; Irish American urbanization, 13–14, 23, 181, 185, 203, 224–240; Scotch-Irish, 154, 159, 164–165, 168; success debate, 39–40; Ulster Presbyterians, 74; Ulster Protestants, 74

Seven American Women Writers of the Twentieth Century (Howard), 656

Seven Nations, 437

Seventh-day Adventists, 589

Seward, William H., 199, 486–487

Sexual abuse, 557, 603

Sexuality, suppressed, 501

Shamrock baseball teams, 447

Shamrock Club (Milwaukee), 437

Shamrock hurling club, 453

Shamrock militia, 452

Shamrock (newspaper), 184, 318

Shamrock Society (New York), 175

Shannahan, Kevin, 419

Shannon, William V.: *American Irish*, xv; Carter and, 14–15; foundational work by, 10; internal philanthropy, 49; on the Irish, 225; Irish American leaders of the outs, 637; Irish Americans as brokers, 636; Merriman conference proceedings, 14–15; Philadelphia compared to Boston and New York, 13; Rischin and, 8

Sharkey, Jack, 459

Sharkey, Tom ("Sailor"), 459

Shaughran (Boucicault), 386

Shaw, George Bernard, 133, 498

Shaw, Richard, 305

Shea, Ann M., 46

Shea, John Gilmary, 240, 243

Sheehan, "Blue-eyed Billy," 506

Sheehan, Cornelius, 326n39

Sheen, Fulton J., 509, 552

Sheet music, *394, 396, 396, 681*

Sheil, Bernard J., 593, 599

Shelley, Thomas J., 45

Sheridan, Jim, 566

Sheridan, Martin, 449, 466, 467, *468*

She's the One (film), 567

"Shiners war," 190

Silence as a hallmark of Irish Americans, 281

Simmons, Al, 461

Simpson, Wallis, 136

Sinatra, Frank, 475, 539

Sinclair, Upton, 586

Siney, John, 358, 359

Single European Act (1987), 140–141

Singular Man (Donleavy), 659

Sinn Fein: abstention from Westminster, 120; Adams (Gerry) and, 146, 560; anti-conscription campaign, 122; armed resistance, 142; British Army recruitment, 117; Butler (Mary) and,

107; Catholic Church in Ireland, 120; conscription crisis, 121–122; Cumann na mBan, 122–123; Cumann na nGaedheal, 132; Dáil Éireann, 122, 125; de Valera and, 22, 120–121, 132; Easter Rising, 119–120; elections (1921), 125; elections (1927), 134; elections (1955), 142; founders, 107–108; Government of Ireland Act, 124–125, 131; Griffith and, 107–108, 117, 119, 120; Irish Americans, 171; Irish Civil War (1922–1923), 128; Irish Parliamentary Party, 119; Irish Republican Brotherhood, 110, 121; Irish Volunteers, 117, 120–121; leaders, 110, 121; Lloyd George and, 125–126; name, 107; national convention (*Ard Fheis*), 120, 132; Northern Ireland's constitutional status, 131; Northern Irish parliament, 124; objectives, 120, 492; policy of political abstention, 146; president, 22, 121; pro-German activities, 120; pro-treaty elements, 132; program, 108–109; Provisional Sinn Fein, 299; Republican Sinn Fein, 300; rise of, 119–122; split into official and provisional wings, 145, 298; suppression of, 122
"Sinn Féiners," 118
Sisters/nuns. *See* Nuns/sisters
Sisters of Charity, 276–278, 279, 578
Sisters of Charity of Mount St. Vincent, 578
Sisters of Mercy, 276–278, 279, 578, 580
Sisters of St. Joseph, 578
Sisters of the Good Shepherd, 580
Six Degrees of Separation (Guare), 660
Skeffington, Frank (character), 655
Skerrett, Ellen, 33
Skilled artisans, 235–236
Slang, 673
Slattery, John, 583
Slavery: abolitionism, 372, 376, 383, 485; Catholic Church in America, 629; O'Connell (Daniel) and, 201–202, 290, 633; Scotch-Irish, 165
"Slide, Kelly, Slide" (song), 447
"Slide Kelly Slide" (Kelly), 392
Slip jigs, 418
Sloan, John, 495
Smith, Alfred E. (Al): accent, 557, 589; ancestors, 589; anti-Catholic sentiment, 16, 282, 506, 589–590; "baloney," 506; on Catholic Church, 483; cigars, 557; on encyclicals, 512–513, 630; endorsement of Republican presidential candidate (1936), 507; memories of, 483; Murphy (Charles Francis) and, 672; presidential election (1928), 475, *505*, 512–513, 557, 589–590; privatizing religion, 590; as reformer, 627;

vote-getting power, 504; voters' intelligence, 494
Smith, Alfred E., Jr., 510
Smith, Betty, 550, 652, 654, 655
Smith, Jean Kennedy, 561
Smith, Peter, 419
Smith, R. J., 427
Smith, Robert, 183
Smithsonian Institution, 430
"Smoked Irishmen," 667
Snow in August (Hamill), 657
Snug Harbor Irish Traditional Music and Dance Festival, 431
Snyder, Charles R., 500
Snyder, Daniel, 464
Snyder, Robert W., 41
Sobriquets (nicknames), 333. *See also* Stereotypes
Social change, 483, 580–581
Social Democratic Labour Party (SDLP): Anglo-Irish Agreement, 146; founding, 298; Hume and, 299, 300; Irish nationalism, 147; Mallon and, 147; Nationalist Party, 144; Sunningdale Agreement, 145
Social Justice (magazine), 591
Social mobility: anti-Catholic sentiment, 276, 320; attendance at Catholic school, 621; Boston Irish, 12–13; communalism, 611–612, 616, 623–624, 634–635; disdain for American individualism, 612; downward mobility, 622–623, 634–635; Doyle on, 616; Dunne (Finley Peter) and, 622; east coast model, 12–13; failure to rise socially, 501; Fitzgerald (F. Scott), 622; gender differences in attitudes towards, 623–624; German immigrants, 27–28; Handlin and, 11, 500; Harrigan and Hart, 622; horizontal *vs.* vertical, 41; images of the Irish in popular culture, 386; Irish Catholics, 28–29, 501; Jewish immigrants, 503; language, 27–29; McCaffrey and, 616; Moynihan and, 501, 611; networks, 620–621; New York Irish, 12–14, 23, 303, 501; Nolan (Janet) and, 623; northeastern United States, 620–621; obsession with, 621–624; O'Hara (John) and, 621–622; Philadelphia Irish, 13; political and bureaucratic rut, 28, 500; regional variation, 10–11, 12–13, 616; San Francisco Irish, 12–13, 23; sports, 443; Thernstrom and, 10, 611, 616; Walsh (James P.) and, 616; Williams (William) and, 622; women, 346. *See also* Assimilation
Social reform nationalism, 292, 294
Social sciences, 514
Socialist Party of Ireland, 110

Society of United Irishmen. *See* United Irishmen
Solemn League and Covenant, 115
Some Mother's Son (film), 561
"Somewhere Voices Calling" (song), 399
Sons of Tammany. *See* Tammany Hall
"Souperism," 92
South Boston Athletic Club, 450
Southern Irish, 46, 229
Southern unionism, 104
Sowell, Thomas, 611
Spalding, John Lancaster, 582–583
Spellman, Francis Joseph: aid to parochial schools, 516; Catholic patriotism, 597; homage to, 512; McCarthy (Joseph) and, 599; National Catholic War Council, 597; rival, 629; Vatican II, 601
Spencer, John C., 487–488
Spencer, Kenneth, *594*
"Spiritual empire" thesis, 280
Spofford, Harriet, 337
Sporting News (periodical), 447
Sports, 443–471; Ancient Order of Hibernians, 452; anti-British sentiment, 451–452; assimilation, 450, 452, 455, 466–467; baseball, 447–448, 459–462, 503; boxing, 444, 450–451, 457–459, 464, 503; Clan na Gael, 452; football (American), 462–465; football (Gaelic), 452, 453–454, 468; Gaelic Athletic Association (GAA) (*see* Gaelic Athletic Association); Gaelic games, 448–449, 468–469; hammer throw, 465–466; handball, 453; hurling, 452, 453, 468; in Ireland, 443; Irish American identity, 450, 452, 455; Olympics, 449–450, 451–452, 465–467; pedestrianism, 445–446; product endorsements, 468; rowing, 446–447, 451; social mobility, 443; track and field, 448–450, 465–467; traditional Irish sports, 453
Squatter Sovereignty (Harrigan and Hart), *390*
St. Paul (Minnesota) Irish, 638
Stack, Austin, 127
Stage Irishman stereotype: amiable qualities of, 496; Crosby (Bing) as, 682; evolution of, 408, 667; legitimate theater, 387; turn of the twentieth century, *374*; Variety Theater, 384–385; vaudeville, 408; Wittke on, 384
Stallone, Sylvester, 664
Stanley, John, 251n92
Stanley, Lord (Edward George Geoffrey Smith), 191
Stanton, Elizabeth Cady, 335–336
States rights, 167–168
Statute of Westminster (1930), 134
Steelboys (Hearts of Steel), 74

Steffens, Lincoln, 481, 626, 629

Step dancing, 417–425

Stephens, James, 96, 98, 177, 290

Stephenson, George M., vii

Stephenson, Robert, 179

Stereotypes, 663–679; apemen (*see* Apemen stereotype); Biddy, 333; boxing/fighting, 458, 667–668; Bridget, 333, 358; "Bridget McBruiser," 371; "Colleen," *681*; dehumanization, *366*; "Fighting Irish," 494, 667; filiopietism, 25; Greeley (Andrew) and, 42; Harrigan and, 625; Harrigan and Hart, 391; Hughes (Archbishop John) and, *277*; Irish-American pluck, 467; Irish-American reactions, 385; Irish men, 345, 623, 625; Irish peasants, 489; Irish politician, 481; Irish racism, 683; Irish tenors, 396–397; Irish women, 623–624; Jimmy, 671–673, 675–679; Kate, 333; Katy, 333; Maggie, 333; Mick, 364; Mr. Dooley (character) and, 43; Nast and, *366, 666*, 669, 674; Opper and, 25, *26*; Paddy stereotype (*see* Paddy stereotype); Pat, 667–668; Peggy, 333; priests in movies, 595; racial caricature of the Irish, 369–370; racial exclusion and exploitation, 683; St. Patrick's Day, *374*; Sambo, 665–667, *666*; servants, 333; sheet music, 396; stage Irishman (*see* Stage Irishman); success debate, 42–43, 376–377; Tin Pan Alley, 394–395; toughness, 494, 496, 530; uniquely violent people, 373–374; variety theater, 384; vaudeville, 407; Williams (William) and, 673; Yankee Doodle Dandy, 493

Sterrance (play), 395

Stevenson, Adlai, 510, 511

Stewart, Delia Tudor, *102*

Stoddard, Lothrop, 674

Stone, William, 197

Story, Justice, 477

Stritch, Samuel, 597

Strong, George Templeton, 373, 475, 491

Stuart, Joseph: career, 310, 326n48; Commissioners of Emigration, 310; Emigrant Savings Bank, 308, 310, 315t, 326n39; emigration, 314; Hughes (Archbishop John) and, 315t; National Mercantile Bank, 326n48

Studs Lonigan trilogy (Farrell), 550, 652

Styron, William, 540

Subject Was Roses (Gilroy), 551

Suburbanization: big-city Catholicism, 598; G.I. Bill of Rights (1944), 550, 598; Irish American identity, 41, 548, 556, 598; New Irish, 562; success debate, 41

Success debate, 39–43, 500–503; alcohol addiction, 500–501; American idea of

success, 42; Catholic Church's role, 281–282, 501–502; economic success, 39–40; educational accomplishment, 39–40; first-generation immigrants, 40–41; Irish Catholic *vs.* Irish Protestant, 39–40; Irish values, 40–41; letters home, 40–41; McCaffrey and, 41; mid-nineteenth century, 356; Miller (Kerby) and, 40–41; Moynihan on, 500–503; other ethnic groups compared to Irish, 356, 500–501, 503; political success, 502–503; return migration, 41; settlement patterns, 39–40; stereotypes, 42–43, 376–377; suburbanization, 41; writers, 40

Succession Act (1957), 140

Suffern, Thomas, 183

Sullivan, Ed, 401, 410, 551, 628

Sullivan, J. J., 639

Sullivan, James P. ("4.22 Jim"), *466*

Sullivan, James ("Yankee"), 444, 457

Sullivan, John, 179

Sullivan, John L. ("John L.," "Boston Strong Boy"), 24, *445*, 451, 457

Sullivan, John L. ("Young America" theorist), 203

Sullivan, Kevin, 485, 684–685

Sullivan, Robert Baldwin, 189

Sullivan, Timothy D. ("Big Tim"), 409, 482, 637

Sullivan, William, 583

Sullivan–Considine Circuit, 409

Sully, Tommy, 387

Sulzer, William, 482

Sunningdale Agreement (1973), 145

Supply of Heroes (Carroll), 659

"Sure They Call It Ireland" (Olcott), 395

"Surrender and regrant" policy, 65

Survival of Irish Americans, 224, 230, 240, 278

Swander, Mary, 661

Sweeney, "Brains," 476

Sweeney, Joel Walker, 383

Sweeney, John J., 363, 539, 604

Sweeney, Mike F., 449

"Sweet Rosie O'Grady" (song), 393

Swierenga, Robert, 161

Swift, Jonathan, 72

Swope, Herbert Bayard, 483

Synge, John Millington, 107

Synod of Ulster, 157

Table Money (Hamill), 656–657

Talbot, Richard, 69

Tammany Hall (Sons of Tammany): ceremonial Phrygian cap, 478; conservatism, 506; cost to build, 476; Croker and, 481; Democratic Party, 476, 478, 506; Dunn and, 482; Grace and, 475; headquarters, 627; Jewish immigrants,

669; Kelly ("Honest John") and, 318, 475, 481; line between entertainment and politics, 672; Murphy (Charles Francis) and, 481, 672; New York Irish, 318, 475, 481; organization, 478; sale of, 476; saloons, 482; sin, 506; Stevenson's defeat, 511; Sullivan (Timothy D.) and, 409; Tweed and, 318, 475; Walker (Jimmy) and, 475; the Wigwam, 627; Wilson (Woodrow) and, 506

Taney, Roger B., 197

Taylor, Laurette, 551

Tchen, John Kuo Wei, 35

Tenant League, 99

Tenants of Time (Flanagan), 660

Tender Is the Night (Fitzgerald), 653

Tenors, Irish, 396–397

Terrible Honesty (Douglas), 673

Test Act (1704), 162

Texas Irish, 46, 192

That Night (McDermott), 649

Thatcher, Margaret, 146, 560

Thayer, Ernest L., 447–448

Theater: legitimate theater, 387; stage Irishman (*see* Stage Irishman); variety theater, 384–387; vaudeville, 386–387, 391–393, 399, 406–410

Thébaud, Alphonse, 242, 244n9

Thernstrom, Stephen: *Harvard Encyclopedia of American Ethnic Groups*, 2, 7; inspiration, 14; *Other Bostonians*, 12; social mobility of the Irish, 10, 611, 616

Thirteenth: The Greatest of All Centuries (Walsh), 630

This Side of Paradise (Fitzgerald), 653, 654

Thomas, Lord Offaly ("Silken Thomas"), 64

Thompson, Charles, 167

Thompson, Emma, 566

Thornton, Mathew, 179

Thought (quarterly), 514

Three (O'Connor), 657

"Throw Him Down McCloskey" (Kelly), 392

Thurneysen, Rudolf, 6

Tiers, Edward W., 326n39

Tilly, Charles, 616, 620

"Tim Finegan's Wake" (Poole), 385–386

Time and Again (Finney), 663

Time Magazine, 552

Tin Pan Alley, 393–396, 401–402

Tin Wife (Flaherty), 657

Tipperary Men's Association (New York City), 538

Tithe War (1820s, 1830s), 74

To the Golden Door (Potter), 8

Tobin, Daniel, 362

Tobin, Maurice, 599, 628

Tocqueville, Alexis de, 197, 477, 485, 487, 622
Toleration Act (1719), 162–163
Tom Watson's Magazine, 582
Tomorrow Will Be Better (Smith), 655
"Too-Ra-Loo-Ra-Loo-Ra" (song), 399
Tooley, Larry, 387
Touch of the Poet (O'Neill), 496, 622, 625, 633, 652
Toughness, 493–494, 496, 530
Touhey, Patrick, 406
Toussaint, Pierre, 242
Track and field, 448–450, 465–467
Tracy, Dick (character), 494
Tracy, Spencer, 551
Trade unionism: boycotting, 360; Connolly (James) and, 361; conservatism/respectability, 361; interethnic cooperation, 356; in Ireland, 373; Larkin (James) and, 361; leadership, 35, 355–356, 357–358, 359, 361–362; O'Connell (Daniel) and, 88; protest rooted in Irish countryside, 359–360, 373; racial exclusion, 360; women, 359. *See also* Labor movement; Work
Traditional Irish Musicians Association, *414*
Traditional music, 381, 411–416, 418, 429
Transport revolution, 186–187
Transport Workers Union of America, 363
Treaty of Limerick (1691), 70
Treaty Stone, *108*
Tree Grows in Brooklyn (Smith), 550, 652, 655
Trevelyan, Charles, 91, 92
Trimble, David, 147, 300
Trinity Academy of Irish Dance, 423
Trinity College (Washington, D.C.), 580
Trinity Irish Dance Company, 423
Troubles, the. *See* Northern Ireland, conflict in
True Confessions (Dunne novel), 659
True Confessions (film), 633
Truman, Harry, 532, 628
Truth Teller (newspaper), 184
Tucker, Fanning C., 326n39
Tuke, James Hack, 193
Tunney, Gene, 457–459, *675*
Tuohy, Patsy, 411
Turner, Frederick Jackson, 165, 304
Turner, Victor, 427
'Twas Only an Irishman's Dream (Williams), 625, 666–667
Tweed, William Magear ("Boss"), 318, 475, 476, 493
Two Traditions, 255–256, 267–268
Tyler, John, 201
Tyler, Robert, 201, 202

UILA (United Irish League of America), 84, 294, 295
Ulster: Act of Union, 265; agrarian violence, 77–78; American Revolution, 75; animosity between Catholics and Protestants, 15, 68; British settlement of, 67; Canadian Irish, 187–188; change in religious demography, 265–268; church lands, 155; counties of, 151; economic development, 157–160, 162; emigration, 151, 158, 187–188, 223; ethnic mini-segregation, 159; exclusion from Home Rule, 119; famines, 158; Gaelic Irish, 67, 154; intermarriage, 152; landlord structure, 159–160; O'Neill (Hugh) in, 66; Plantation of Ireland, 67, 154–155, 159; population, 4, 151, 158, 161; post-Famine Protestant emigration, 95; Presbyterians (*see* Ulster Presbyterians); prosperity, 74, 265; "Protestant Ulster," 4; rebellion (1798), 80, 265; risings (1640s), 67–69, 156, 263; saved Christians, 282; Scots Presbyterianism, 156; secret societies, 74; Synod of Ulster, 157; tensions in eighteenth century, 265; Year of Grace (1859), 282. *See also* Northern Ireland; Northern Ireland, conflict in; Scotch-Irish
Ulster Americans, 183, 184
Ulster Catholics, 78, 191, 223
Ulster Constitution Defence Committee, 144
"Ulster Custom," 99
Ulster Defence Association, 145
Ulster Freedom Fighters, 145
Ulster-Irish Society of New York, address to, 286–288
Ulster Presbyterians (in Ireland and/or America), 255–270; American Revolution, 75, 261; in American South, 164; Church of Ireland, 265–268; democratic sentiments, 266; differences among, 257; emigration, 73, 74, 86; exclusion from landowning classes, 157; Federalists, 262–263; as "Irish," 261; Irish diaspora, 153; Irish nationalism, 266; Peep O'Day Boys, 78; Protestant evangelicalism, 264–265; radicalism of, 266; rebellion (1798), 264; revisionist historians, 264; settlements in America, 74; synonyms for "Ulster Presbyterian," 256–260; Union of Scotland and England (1707), 157. *See also* Irish Presbyterians; Scotch-Irish
Ulster Protestant Action, 143
Ulster Protestants, 151, 188
"Ulster Scots," 5, 256, 258
Ulster Society of New York, address to, 286–288
Ulster Special Constabulary, 130

Ulster unionism: Craig and, 115, 131; elections (1918), 104; Government of Ireland Act, 129; Home Rule, 114–115, 121; origins, 265; strength, 104. *See also* Irish unionism; Ulster Unionist Party
Ulster Unionist Council, 115
Ulster Unionist Party, 147
Ulster Volunteer Force (UVF): 36th (Ulster) Division, 116; class C constables, 130; establishment, 115; leadership, 115; Paisley and, 144
"Ulstermen," 4
Unexpurgated Code (Donleavy), 659
Union Army, 29
Union Club riot (1920), 586
Union of Scotland and England (1707), 157
Unionist Party, 104, 114, 115, 122
United Garment Workers of America, 359, 581
United Irish Counties Association, 414, 419, 538
United Irish League of America (UILA), 84, 294, 295
United Irishman (newspaper), 107–108
United Irishmen (Society of United Irishmen), 77–81; American dimension, 171; American Society of, 289; Defender movement, 74; Easter Rising, 295; Emmet (Thomas) and, 84; founding, 77; group consciousness, 184; Irish parliament, 77; Jefferson and, 289; national identity, 261; Orange Order, 265; rebellion (1798), 78–80, 84, 289, 307; republicanism, 78; Young Ireland, 89
United Mine Workers, 581
United Nations, 139
U.S. Catholic Conference Office of Migration and Refugee Services, 566
U.S. Constitution, 479, 589
University Bill (1873), 99
University of Notre Dame, 594–595, 595–596
Upper Canada: Orangeism, 189–190
Uprooted (Handlin), 11, 219, 223
Urban employment, 32
Urban history, 225
Urbanization: big-city Catholicism, 592–597, 598; British North America, 225; dissolution of Irish neighborhoods, 415; Ireland, 232–233; Irish American identity, 493, 548, 556, 669, 671–673; Irish Americans, 13–14, 23, 181, 185, 203, 215, 224–240; Jimmy stereotype, 671–673; nativism, 582; romanticizing of rural life, 392; sarcasm, 671; social scientists, 670; traditional music, 413; urban Irish hoodlum, 676–677; urban slang, 673; "wets," 588

Ursaline Convent (Charlestown, Mass.), 275

Van Buren, Martin, 197, 198
Van de Velde, James, 242
Van Wyck, Robert A., 482
Vancouver Folk Festival, 430
Varela, Felix, 242
Vargo, Trina, 49
Variety theater, 384–387
Vatican II, 574, 590, 599–603
Vaudeville, 386–387, 391–393, 399, 406–410
Vecoli, Rudolph J., 11
Veeck, Bill, 462
Vernacular liturgy, 601
Verplanck, Gulian, 317
Versailles, Treaty of (1919), 295, 506
Very Old Bones (Kennedy), 660
Vidal, Gore, 533
Viereck, Peter, 484
Vietnam War, 530–531, 600
Vincent, A. W. B. (Bill), 49
Vinyard, JoEllen, 12
Violent Bear It Away (O'Connor), 657
Virginia Minstrels, 382, 383
Visa lottery, 564, 568
Volunteer movement, 261
Von Tilzer, Albert, 395–396
Von Tilzer, Harry, 395–396
Voting Rights Act (1964), 638

Wages of Whiteness (Roediger), 375–376
Wagner, Robert F. (1877–1953), 627
Wagner, Robert F. (1910–1991), 504, 511, 512
Walker, James J. (Jimmy): Barnum in a speakeasy, 493; Douglas's description, 676; fast-talking urbanite, 671; mayoralty of, 672; Roosevelt (Franklin) and, 506; "street smarts," 671–672; Tammany Hall, 475; wrongdoing by, 493
Walsh, "Big Ed," 447
Walsh, Con, 465
Walsh, David Ignatius, 627
Walsh, James Joseph, 630
Walsh, James P. (Jim), 11, 12–13, 14, 616
Walsh, Mike, 626
Walsh, Robert, 183
Walsh, William, 579
Walter, Thomas U., 229
War of Independence (1919–1921, Ireland), 124–126, 129, 586
Ward, Chuck, 438
Ward, Ed, 437–440
Ward Irish Music Archives, 440
Ware, Theron (character), 669
Warriors of Ireland (Fianna Fáil). *See* Fianna Fáil

Warriors of Ireland *(Na Fianna Éireann),* 109
Washington, George, 3, 166, 490
Washington Ceili Club, 431
Washington Irish Folk Festival, 415
Waters, Eugene, 383
Waters, Martin, 326n39
Watson, Thomas E., 582
Watson, William, 309, 326n39
Wattson, Paul, 579
We Who Built America (Wittke), 2
"Wearing of the Green" (Boucicault), 386
Webster, Daniel, 240, 287
Weigel, Gustav, 513–514
Welfare organizations, 25
Wellington, Duke of (Arthur Wellesley), 84
Welsh, John, 359
Welsh, "Smiling Mickey," 447
Wenrich, Percy, 396
Werner, Morris R., 493
Western Folk Festival, 430
Westminster Confession, 160
Weston, Edward Payson, 445–446
"Wets," 588
Wheat That Springeth Green (Power), 657
Wheatland Folk Festival, 430
Whelan, Kevin, 614, 623
"When Hogan Paid His Rent" (Kelly), 392
"When Irish Eyes Are Smiling" (Olcott, Ball and Johnson), 397, 399
"When John McCormack Sings a Song" (Flannery), 396, 398
"When Scanlon Sang Mavourneen" (Kelly), 394, 528
Whig Party (United States), 199, 200
"Whiskey You're the Divil, You're Leading Me Astray" (song), 400
Whisky Insurrection (1794), 165, 262
Whitaker Report (1958), 139
White, Kevin, 639
White, Richard, 303
Whiteboys, 73–74, 85, 355, 373
Whitehead, Alfred North, 494
Whitelaw, William, 145
Whiteness, 374–376, 611–612, 633–635, 670
Whitfield, James, 194
Whitman, Walt, 640
Who Owns the Clothes Line! (Harrigan and Hart), 390–391
"Who Threw the Overalls in Mrs. Murphy's Chowder" (Geifer), 399
Who's Who in America, 502
"Why Paddy's Always Poor" (Scanlon), 391
Wickham, William H., 493
"Wild Colonial Boy" (song), 433

"Wild Irish," 262–263
Wilde, Oscar, 498
Willard, Jess, 458
Willcocks, Joseph, 189
Willcocks, William, 189
William of Orange (William III; King of England, Ireland and Scotland), 70, 71, 622
Williams, Barney, 417
Williams, Roger J., 501
Williams, William H. A. (Bill): evolution of dance, 407; Famine Irish, 16; Irish names, 669; mainstream Irish Americans, 395; social mobility of the Irish, 622; stereotype of Paddy, 673; tap dancers, 672; *'Twas Only an Irishman's Dream,* 625, 666–667
Wills, Garry, 593, 595
Willy Burke; or, The Irish Orphan in America (Sadlier), 650
Wilson, Grant, 304, 492
Wilson, Harold, 144
Wilson, Sir Henry, 128
Wilson, Woodrow: Clan na Gael, 125; Cohalan and, 295, 492; de Valera and, 125; Devoy and, 295; Gibbons (James) and, 585; Irish nationalism, 490; Irish Republic, 125; on Scots Irish, 152; self-determination for Ireland, 15, 125, 295, 506; Tammany Hall Democrats, 506; Ulster Irish, 288
Winfield Folk Festival, 430
Wingerd, Mary, 638
Winnipeg Folk Festival, 430
Wise Blood (O'Connor), 657
Wit, 496
Without a Hero (Boyle), 661
Without Remorse (Clancy), 659
Wittke, Carl: German propaganda in Irish papers, 492; history of Irish immigration, 8; *Irish in America,* 2; Irish in Ireland *vs.* Irish in U.S., 225; on stage Irishmen, 384; *We Who Built America,* 2
Wizard of Oz (film), 680–681
Wokeck, Marianne, 161
Wolfe Tone, Theobald, 78–81; *Argument on Behalf of the Catholics of Ireland,* 77; Irish nationalism, 289; Irish Republican Brotherhood, 96; knowledge of, 491; as a model for emulation, 283; views, 77
Wolfe Tone militia, 452
Wolfe Tones, 437
Womb-to-tomb Catholicism, 595
Women: adult status, 334; American attitudes toward Irish women, 332; Anglo-American families, 332; attitude towards social mobility, 623–624; celibacy, 238, 481–482; domestic service (*see* Domestic service); dowry-

less, 94; emigration, 333; English language literacy in Ireland, 334; female settlement patterns, 32; fertility, 172–173, 219, 238; gender ratio of migration, 279; Irish-American girls in song, 393; Irish Catholics, 32; Irish homes, 346; Irish nationalism, 292; Irish Protestants, 32; job prospects for females, 32; labor history, 30; labor movement, 362; needle trades, 357, 358–359; nuns (*see* Nuns/sisters); prostitution, 357; relations with different ethnicities, 36; Republic of Ireland, 139–140; social mobility, 346; strong-willed, 33; trade unionism, 359; traditional Irish values, 346; union organizers, 581; unskilled labor, 357; women writers, 655; women's history, 30–31; work in postwar America, 553. *See also* Marriage
Women's Christian Temperance Union, 588
Women's history, 30–31
Women's League. *See* Cumann na mBan
Women's Trade Union League (WTUL), 359, 362, 581
Wood, Ida Mayfield (character), 683
Wood, Sir Charles, 91
Woodham-Smith, Cecil, 480
Woodmason, Charles, 164, 258
Worcester (Massachusetts) Irish, 628–629
Work, 233–240; agriculture/farming, 192, 193; anti-hiring discrimination, 372; arts and skills of mid-Victorian modernity, 223; banking, 302–322; black labor, 358; blue-collar jobs, 234; businessmen, 50, 51, 309–314, 499–500, 507; canal-building, 186–187,

355, 373; deforestation, 193; dispersal, 228; domestic service (*see* Domestic service); factory work, 218, 226, 230, 354; housework, 31, 334–336, 338; housing, 354; indentured servitude, 179, 181; job availability, 230–231; job prospects for females, 32; marketable skills, 372; mechanics, 235–236; merchants, 309–314, 322, 499; mill work, 240; nativists, 356; needle trades, 357, 358–359; nonagricultural employment, 204; occupational networks, 619–620; occupational structure, 360; out-work, 313, 354; overwork, 238–239; piece-work, 354; plumbers, 510; postwar America, 552–553; prostitution, 357; public works, 187, 234, 354; railroad building, 187, 226, 234, 373; saloonkeepers, 482; semiskilled/skilled artisans, 235–236, 357; servants, 181; skilled work, 360; stevedores, 503; strikebreakers, 356, 372; truck drivers, 503; unskilled labor, 233–235, 250n73, 354–355, 356, 357, 358, 360, 503; urban employment, 32; wages, 91, 235, 236, 251n92, 354, 372, 556. *See also* Labor movement; Trade unionism
Working Men's Party, 198
Workingmen's Benevolent Association, 358, 359
World Trade Center attacks (2001), 568, 609–610, 639, 640
World War I (1914–1918), 116, 119–122, 492, 584–587
World War II (1939–1945), 137–138, 141–142, 550, 597
World with End, Amen (Breslin), 656
World's End (Boyle), 661
Wright, Frances, 171
Wright, Hamilton, Jr.: photo of ironworkers, 662, 663, 665, 673, 674, 679

Wright, John, 601
Writers, 649–661; 1920s to 1940s, 651–654; avant-garde, 658–659; Clinton and, 533; continuity, 658; emotional baggage, 652–653; hyphenate literature, 649; modernism, 661; New Journalists, 656–657; nineteenth century, 650–651; non-Irish/non-ghetto experiences, 661; playwrights, 651–652, 660; poets, 660–661; postwar regionalists, 654–658; success debate, 40; traditional values, 661; women writers, 655. *See also specific writers and works*
Wrongdoing, 493
WTUL (Women's Trade Union League), 359, 362, 581
Wyndham, George, 103
Wyse, Francis, 173, 197

Xenophobia, 588–589

Yankee Doodle Dandy (film), 493, 550, 667–668
Year of Grace (1859), 282
Year of the French (Flanagan), 660
Year of the Slaughter (*Bliadhain an Air*), 85
Yeats, William Butler, 105–106, 107, 128
Yellow Roses (Cullinan), 656
Yorke, Peter C., 581
"Young America" movement, 203
Young Ireland, 89, 96, 218, 290
Young Lonigan (Farrell), 550, 652
Young Manhood of Studs Lonigan (Farrell), 550, 652
Young Men's Catholic Abstinence Society, 452
Young Men's Catholic Lyceum, 446

Zukauskas, Josef Paul, 459